THE CAMBRIDGE HISTORY
OF EIGHTEENTH-CENTURY
POLITICAL THOUGHT

This major work of academic reference provides a comprehensive overview of the development of Western political thought during the European Enlightenment. Written by a distinguished team of international contributors, this Cambridge History is the latest in a sequence of volumes that is now firmly established as the principal reference source for the history of political thought. Every major theme in eighteenth-century political thought is covered in a series of essays at once scholarly and accessible, and the essays are complemented by extensive guides for further reading, and brief biographical notices of the major characters featured in the text, including Rousseau, Montesquieu, Kant, and Edmund Burke. Of interest and relevance to students and scholars of politics and history at all levels from beginning undergraduate upwards, this volume chronicles one of the most exciting and rewarding of all periods in the development of Western thinking about politics.

MARK GOLDIE is a Senior University Lecturer in History and a Fellow of Churchill College, Cambridge.

ROBERT WOKLER is Senior Lecturer in Political Science and in the Special Program in the Humanities, Yale University.

THE CAMBRIDGE
HISTORY OF
EIGHTEENTH-CENTURY
POLITICAL THOUGHT

EDITED BY
MARK GOLDIE
University of Cambridge

AND

ROBERT WOKLER
Yale University

CAMBRIDGE
UNIVERSITY PRESS

CAMBRIDGE UNIVERSITY PRESS
Cambridge, New York, Melbourne, Madrid, Cape Town, Singapore, São Paulo

Cambridge University Press
The Edinburgh Building, Cambridge CB2 2RU, UK

Published in the United States of America by Cambridge University Press, New York

www.cambridge.org
Information on this title: www.cambridge.org/9780521374224

© Cambridge University Press 2006

First published 2006

Printed in the United Kingdom at the University Press, Cambridge

A catalogue record for this publication is available from the British Library

ISBN-13 978-0-521-37422-4 hardback
ISBN-10 0-521-37422-7 hardback

Contents

Contributors   *page* xi
Acknowledgements   xiii
Citations and abbreviations   xv

Introduction   I

Part I: The *ancien régime* and its critics

I The spirit of nations   9
   SYLVANA TOMASELLI
   I   Lessons from the Franks and the Greeks   9
   2   The Roman legacy   15
   3   Voltaire and the English question   19
   4   The spirit of the laws: know thy country   26
   5   The spirit of the laws: the science of freedom   28
   6   The spirit of the laws: commerce and civility   31
   7   The spirit of the laws: the Gothic constitution   34

2 The English system of liberty   40
   MARK GOLDIE
   I   The Revolution debate   40
   2   The Allegiance Controversy and the Jacobites   43
   3   The reception of Locke   47
   4   The claims of the church   50
   5   The claims of Ireland and Scotland   54
   6   The claims of the people   60
   7   The claims of women   62
   8   The Country platform   64
   9   'Robinocracy' and its enemies   70
   10 The Court Whigs   75

v

Contents

3   Scepticism, priestcraft, and toleration   79

RICHARD H. POPKIN AND MARK GOLDIE

   1   Scepticism, Judaism, and the natural history of religion   79
   2   French scepticism and perfectibilism   88
   3   The limits of toleration   92
   4   Arguments for toleration   99

4   Piety and politics in the century of lights   110

DALE K. VAN KLEY

   1   Gallicanism and Jansenism in France   110
   2   The 'Jansenist International' in Italy, Iberia, and Austria   119
   3   Pietism in Lutheran Germany   132
   4   European Calvinism and English Dissent   139

Part II: The new light of reason

5   The comparative study of regimes and societies   147

MELVIN RICHTER

   1   The ambiguities and resources of comparative method   147
   2   Montesquieu   151
   3   Voltaire   159
   4   Hume   161
   5   Raynal, Diderot, the *Deux Indes*, and the *Supplément* to Bougainville   165
   6   Herder   169

6   Encyclopedias and the diffusion of knowledge   172

DANIEL ROCHE

   1   English philosophy, encyclopedism, and technical knowledge   173
   2   French encyclopedism, the academies, and the public sphere   175
   3   Censorship and the commercialisation of enlightenment   180
   4   The *Encyclopédistes* and their readers   186
   5   The political thought of the *Encyclopédie*   189

7   Optimism, progress, and philosophical history   195

HAYDN MASON

   1   Optimism   195
   2   Progress   199
   3   Philosophical history   204
   4   Voltaire   206
   5   Gibbon   210

Contents

8   Naturalism, anthropology, and culture   218
WOLFGANG PROSS

    1   A Counter-Enlightenment?   218
    2   Mankind and the dark abyss of time   223
    3   The history of the human mind   227
    4   The anthropological history of man   232
    5   The regularity and plurality of culture   238

Part III: Natural jurisprudence and the science of legislation

9   German natural law   251
KNUD HAAKONSSEN

    1   The reception of modern natural law   251
    2   The political context of German natural law   255
    3   Christian Thomasius   261
    4   Christian Wolff   268
    5   Immanuel Kant   279

10   Natural rights in the Scottish Enlightenment   291
JAMES MOORE

    1   The context of Scottish natural jurisprudence   291
    2   Academic reform and the law of nature   295
    3   Gershom Carmichael: reformed scholasticism and natural rights   297
    4   Francis Hutcheson: civic virtue and natural rights   299
    5   David Hume: natural rights and scepticism   302
    6   Lord Kames: disquieting opinions and the law of nature   304
    7   Adam Smith: the natural and sacred rights of mankind   307
    8   Natural rights and the four stages of society   310
    9   Dugald Stewart and the demise of the natural rights tradition   314

11   The mixed constitution and the common law   317
DAVID LIEBERMAN

    1   The mixed constitution   318
    2   Parliamentary sovereignty   321
    3   The balanced constitution   324
    4   The separation of powers   331
    5   Delolme versus Price   336
    6   The common law   340

12   Social contract theory and its critics   347
PATRICK RILEY

Contents

1	The historical background	347
2	The equilibrium between consent and natural law in Locke	350
3	Bossuet and the challenge of divine right to contract theory	354
4	The anti-contractarianism of Hume and Bentham	355
5	French contractarianism before Rousseau	358
6	Rousseau and the radicalisation of social contract theory	362
7	Kant and the social contract as an ideal of reason	369
8	The decline of social contract theory	373

Part IV: Commerce, luxury, and political economy

13	The early Enlightenment debate on commerce and luxury	379
	ISTVAN HONT	
1	The spectre of luxury	379
2	Fénelon	383
3	Mandeville	387
4	Shaftesbury	395
5	Hutcheson	399
6	Berkeley	401
7	The early Montesquieu	404
8	Melon	409
9	Voltaire	412

14	Physiocracy and the politics of *laissez-faire*	419
	T. J. HOCHSTRASSER	
1	Physiocracy in its historical, intellectual, and political setting	419
2	The development of physiocracy: from Quesnay to Turgot	425
3	From wealth creation to legal despotism	429
4	Critiques of physiocracy and later responses	434
5	Physiocracy outside France	438
6	Conclusions	441

15	Scottish political economy	443
	DONALD WINCH	
1	Adam Smith's pre-eminence	443
2	Legislators versus politicians in a mercantile state	449
3	The conditions of growth	452
4	The positive duties of the legislator in commercial society	457

16	Property, community, and citizenship	465
	MICHAEL SONENSCHER	

Contents

1	Prologue: Babeuf	465
2	Needs and society	471
3	Property and the progress of the arts and sciences	475
4	The Gracchi and their legacy	480
5	A modern agrarian	488
6	Conclusion	492

Part V: The promotion of public happiness

17	Philosophical kingship and enlightened despotism	497
	DEREK BEALES	
1	The idea of the philosopher king	497
2	Frederick II, Catherine II, Joseph II	504
3	The idea of despotism	511
4	The idea of the enlightened despot	514
5	Conclusion	522
18	Cameralism and the sciences of the state	525
	KEITH TRIBE	
1	The development of cameralism	525
2	'Oeconomy' and the *Hausvaterliteratur*	530
3	Justi	537
4	Sonnenfels	542
19	Utilitarianism and the reform of the criminal law	547
	FREDERICK ROSEN	
1	Liberty and the criminal law	548
2	Crime and punishment in Beccaria	551
3	Bentham's theory of proportion	557
4	The debate over the death penalty	563
5	Transportation and imprisonment	566
6	Enlightenment and reform	568
20	Republicanism and popular sovereignty	573
	IRING FETSCHER	
1	Rousseau	573
2	Mably	577
3	Diderot	579
4	Venice and Geneva	583
5	Kant	587
6	Fichte	592
7	Humboldt	596

Contents

Part VI: The Enlightenment and revolution

21 The American Revolution   601
GORDON S. WOOD
  1 The English constitution   601
  2 Virtual and actual representation   607
  3 Constitutionalism   610
  4 The extended republic   616
  5 The sovereignty of the people   620

22 Political languages of the French Revolution   626
KEITH MICHAEL BAKER
  1 Competing discourses of the Old Regime   626
  2 Revolutionary improvisation   628
  3 Two languages of liberty   639
  4 The people's two bodies   648
  5 Virtue, regeneration, and revolution   653

23 British radicalism and the anti-Jacobins   660
IAIN HAMPSHER-MONK
  1 Nostalgia and modernity   660
  2 The Wilkites and pro-American radicalism   663
  3 Rational Dissent   668
  4 Edmund Burke and the debate on the French Revolution   673
  5 Radical political economy   683

24 Ideology and the origins of social science   688
ROBERT WOKLER
  1 The invention of the modern nation-state   688
  2 The French revolutionary invention of social science   690
  3 The *idéologues* and their distrust of politics   695
  4 The origins of social science in Britain   702
  5 Saint-Simon and the legacy of Enlightenment political thought   704

Biographies   711
Bibliography   787
  General works   787
  Primary sources   789
  Secondary sources   830
Index   901

Contributors

KEITH MICHAEL BAKER
Professor of Humanities, France-Stanford Center for Interdisciplinary Studies, Stanford University

DEREK BEALES
Emeritus Professor of Modern History, and Fellow of Sidney Sussex College, University of Cambridge

IRING FETSCHER
Professor of Political Science, University of Frankfurt-am-Main

MARK GOLDIE
Senior Lecturer in History, and Fellow of Churchill College, University of Cambridge

KNUD HAAKONSSEN
Professor of Intellectual History, University of Sussex

IAIN HAMPSHER-MONK
Professor of Political Theory, University of Exeter

TIM HOCHSTRASSER
Senior Lecturer in International History, London School of Economics

ISTVAN HONT
Lecturer in History, and Fellow of King's College, University of Cambridge

DAVID LIEBERMAN
Professor of Law and History, University of California at Berkeley

HAYDN MASON
Emeritus Professor of French Language and Literature, University of Bristol

JAMES MOORE
Emeritus Professor of Political Science, Concordia University, Montreal

The late RICHARD H. POPKIN
Formerly Professor of Philosophy, Washington University, St Louis

WOLFGANG PROSS
Professor of German and Comparative Literature, University of Bern

MELVIN RICHTER
Emeritus Professor of Political Science, Graduate School and Hunter College, City University of New York

PATRICK RILEY
Professor of Political and Moral Philosophy, University of Wisconsin at Madison

DANIEL ROCHE
Professor of the French Enlightenment, Collège de France

FREDERICK ROSEN
Emeritus Professor of the History of Political Thought and Senior Research Fellow, Bentham Project, University College, London

MICHAEL SONENSCHER
Lecturer in History, and Fellow of King's College, University of Cambridge

SYLVANA TOMASELLI
Director of Studies in History and Social and Political Sciences, and Fellow of St John's College, University of Cambridge

KEITH TRIBE
Visiting Senior Research Fellow, University of Sussex

DALE K. VAN KLEY
Professor of History, Ohio State University, Columbus

DONALD WINCH
Emeritus Professor, School of Humanities, University of Sussex

ROBERT WOKLER
Senior Lecturer in Political Science and in the Special Program in the Humanities, Yale University

GORDON S. WOOD
Professor of History, Brown University

Acknowledgements

This is the fifth volume to appear in the Cambridge History of Political Thought series. The four earlier volumes are: *The Cambridge History of Medieval Political Thought, c. 350–c. 1450*, edited by J. H. Burns (1988); *The Cambridge History of Political Thought, 1450–1700*, edited by J. H. Burns and Mark Goldie (1991); *The Cambridge History of Greek and Roman Political Thought*, edited by Christopher Rowe and Malcolm Schofield in association with Simon Harrison and Melissa Lane (2000); and *The Cambridge History of Twentieth-Century Political Thought*, edited by Terence Ball and Richard Bellamy (2003). It will be followed by *The Cambridge History of Nineteenth-Century Political Thought*, edited by Gregory Claeys and Gareth Stedman Jones.

We owe a debt of gratitude to the advisers who, at an early stage, commented on our prospectus: James Burns, Knud Haakonssen, James Moore, John Pocock, Quentin Skinner, Donald Winch, Keith Baker, and Melvin Richter. The staff of Cambridge University Press have been forbearing and constantly supportive, most especially Richard Fisher and Jeremy Mynott. Alison Powell expedited production, and Linda Randall applied her impeccable copy-editing skills.

This volume has been too long in gestation. We are grateful for the patience of contributors who produced on time what was requested, as well to those who stepped into the breach when gaps appeared in the cast list. We are indebted to George St Andrews and Sylvana Tomaselli for translating chapter 8 from the French and to George St Andrews for translating chapter 20 from the German. To them and to Rachel Hammersley and Tim Hochstrasser we are grateful for help in preparing biographical data. For research and editorial assistance we owe much to David Adams, James Martin, Sara Pennell, Jacqueline Rose, Sami Savonius and Jane Spencer. Tom Broughton-Willett generously stepped in at short notice to prepare the index. Preparation of the index was assisted by grants from the John K.

Castle Fund (honouring one of the founders of Yale University) and the Department of Political Science, Yale University.

We remember the careers and writings of three distinguished scholars, two of whom, but for their untimely deaths, might have contributed to this volume, Maurice Cranston (1920–93) and Judith Shklar (1928–92), and one of whom, a contributor, died while this book was in production, Richard Popkin (1923–2005).

Citations and abbreviations

All quotations (except for poetry) have been modernised. Phrases and book titles in foreign languages are provided with English-language translations, except where the meaning will be readily understood by Anglophone readers. All citations of texts published in the series Cambridge Texts in the History of Political Thought are to the editions in that series. The following abbreviations are used throughout this volume.

IPML   Jeremy Bentham, *An Introduction to the Principles of Morals and Legislation*. Cited by page references to the edition by J. H. Burns and H. L. A. Hart, with a New Introduction by F. Rosen (Oxford, 1996). 1st pr. 1780 and publ. 1789.

LJA, LJB   Adam Smith, *Lectures on Jurisprudence*. Cited by page references to the Glasgow edition by R. L. Meek, D. D. Raphael, and P. G. Stein (Oxford, 1978). Report A, 1762–3; B, 1763–4. Repr. Liberty Classics, Indianapolis, 1982.

SC   Jean Jacques Rousseau, *The Social Contract (Du contrat social)*. Cited by book and chapter number, and page references to *The Social Contract and Other Later Political Writings*, ed. V. Gourevitch (Cambridge, 1997). 1st publ. 1762.

SL   Charles de Secondat, baron de Montesquieu, *The Spirit of the Laws (L'Esprit de lois)*. Cited by book and chapter number, and, where appropriate, page references to the edition by A. M. Cohler, B. C. Miller, and H. S. Stone (Cambridge, 1989). 1st publ. 1748.

THN   David Hume, *A Treatise on Human Nature*. Cited by book, part, and section. The standard modern edition is by D. F. Norton and M. J. Norton (Oxford, 2000). 1st publ. 1739–40.

TMS   Adam Smith, *The Theory of Moral Sentiments*. Cited by part, section, chapter, and paragraph number, from the Glasgow edition by D. D. Raphael and A. L. Macfie (Oxford, 1976). 1st publ.

1759; expanded and revised final (6th) edition, 1790. Repr. Liberty Classics, Indianapolis, 1982.

TTG   John Locke, *Two Treatises of Government*. Cited by treatise and section number, and page references to the edition by P. Laslett (Cambridge, 1988). 1st publ. 1689 (but bearing date 1690).

WN   Adam Smith, *An Inquiry into the Nature and Causes of the Wealth of Nations*. Cited by book, chapter, and section number, from the Glasgow edition by R. H. Campbell, A. S. Skinner, and W. B. Todd (2 vols., continuously paginated, Oxford, 1976). 1st publ. 1776. Repr. Liberty Classics, Indianapolis, 1981.

Introduction

In framing our original plan of this work, we adopted a number of guidelines which formed our prospectus for the contributors and which, by and large, still lend direction to and map the limits of this volume. We were determined in the space available to provide as comprehensive a treatment as possible of eighteenth-century political thought in the diverse historical contexts of the period, instead of a series of essays on our subject's acknowledged masters. We wished to give due weight to the polemical character of eighteenth-century disputations and to the circumstances surrounding the composition of the works at issue, rather than to subsume their differences of principle or perspective in separate chapters manifesting the internal logic of each author's career. We accordingly aimed for a largely thematic framework in preference to an interconnected collection of intellectual biographies. In addition to focusing on the seminal writings of the vanguard of the eighteenth-century's republic of letters, we also wished to address the texts of relatively minor figures who often couched their contributions to both national and international debates in locally specific contexts and idioms. We sought to survey not only the towering treatises of the age of Enlightenment but also a large number of its disparate *pièces fugitives*, in part because we thought it necessary to fill in the valleys from which the peaks arose, but more generally because, in our judgement, some of the most centrally recurrent topics of eighteenth-century political thought were pursued in works that were perhaps of greater historical than philosophical significance.

Our temporal limits were of course determined by the structure of the series as a whole, but the logic which required that we begin around 1700 and end around 1800 seemed internally compelling as well as appropriate to the broader narrative shaped by the volumes before and after this one. *The Cambridge History of Political Thought, 1450–1700* closes with Locke but does not address the great issues of toleration which his writings highlighted around the turn of the eighteenth century and thereby provided one of the principal mainsprings of the age of Enlightenment embraced by this work. If we have not sought here to retrace the first appearance of such terms as 'The Enlightenment', 'The Scottish Enlightenment', 'The Counter-Enlightenment', or 'The Enlightenment Project' (in English dating from the late nineteenth century, the early twentieth century, the late 1950s, and the early 1980s, respectively), our reasoning is that these terms need to be situated even more in the post-Enlightenment philosophical and political contexts which gave rise to them than with reference to the ideological currents they were introduced to define. The periodisation of the age of Enlightenment, particularly with respect to its initial phase, in so far as that epoch of European intellectual history can be regarded as marking the advent of modernity, has itself been a subject of much scholarly debate. Paul Hazard, for instance, in his *Crise de la conscience européenne* (The Crisis of the European Mind) of 1935, dated its origins from a thirty-year span around 1680, and Michel Foucault, in *Les mots et les choses* (The Order of Things) of 1966, on the other hand, concentrated instead upon an interval of similarly rapid epistemic change beginning 100 years later. Since this volume addresses themes in eighteenth-century political thought and not the period's later historiography, scholarly differences of interpretation that turn around or reflect different chronologies are beyond our scope.

It in fact suits our purpose well that in other quarters there should be disagreements about the origins, nature, and limits of the Enlightenment, since our perspective of eighteenth-century political doctrines lies comfortably within the orbits of such competing claims as those of Hazard and Foucault. It also accords with the perception of a number of Enlightenment thinkers themselves to the effect that their age was launched around the time between the Revocation of the Edict of Nantes in 1685 and the death of Louis XIV in 1715, drawing inspiration in that period above all from Newtonian science and Lockean epistemology, as well as ideas of toleration derived not only from Locke but also from Bayle. Ernst Cassirer adopted roughly the same chronological perspective in his *Philosophie der Aufklärung* (The Philosophy of the Enlightenment) of 1932, albeit on more philosophical foundations, in distinguishing the eighteenth century's 'systematic spirit' from the seventeenth century's 'spirit of system', a contrast he drew directly from d'Alembert, who first made this claim in his *Discours préliminaire* to the *Encyclopédie* of 1751.

Our closing this volume with the rise of Napoleon in the mid- to late 1790s rather than with the demise, by the early 1780s (at least in France), of most of the major *philosophes* is, we believe, justly warranted by the parallel chronologies of the eighteenth-century's intellectual and political histories.

The French Revolution of 1789, even more than the American Revolution of 1776, was perceived by both contemporary advocates and critics as a realisation or practical culmination of Enlightenment ideals, or, alternatively, as a descent into political chaos that the *philosophes* had foreseen and sought to avert. To have ignored the French Revolution would have been tantamount to our denying the immediate influence and proximate political impact of much late Enlightenment thought, as well to our disengaging from our subject those political thinkers of this period for whom the Terror seemed to have been generated by dangerous currents of eighteenth-century philosophy. A conception of the unity of theory and practice may be said to lie at the heart of many Enlightenment programmes of political or constitutional reform, but it is also with regard to that intellectual movement's bearing on the eighteenth century's two great revolutions that the realisation of this pragmatic principle has often been identified as the Enlightenment's chief philosophical objective.

The late 1790s was no doubt a period of pivotal significance in both closing a debate about the Enlightenment's influence on the Revolution and inaugurating fresh perspectives on political thought that would come to prevail not only in Restoration France but throughout Europe in the early nineteenth century. We seek in this work to address that closure but not to map the new paths that arose from it. We thus include Burke but not de Maistre, Smith but not Malthus, Kant but not Hegel. We consider concepts of both ancient and modern liberty in the philosophies of Montesquieu, Hume, Rousseau, Smith, and Ferguson, but exclude the foundations of liberalism in the doctrines of Constant and Mme de Staël. We address Bentham's seminal utilitarian works but not his subsequent constitutional theories. In concluding this volume with the concept of 'ideology' in the late 1790s we mean both to bring the history of eighteenth-century political thought to its chronological term and to lay a bridge to the series' next volume.

Framed by an English Revolution on the one side and a French Revolution on the other, with an American Revolution between them, the doctrinal battles that form the hundred years' war of the period's intellectuals, publicists, and even some of its heads of state, were waged around a great variety of issues. As presented here across several chapters we conceive one of this work's central themes to be the interpenetration of political and religious ideas in both theory and practice, as witnessed not only in the progressive disengagement of secular from sacred authority throughout the eighteenth century, but also in appraisals of the theological and political ambitions of both the papacy and different Protestant churches. These debates turned, for instance, around the claims of Jacobitism in England, ultramontanism and Gallicanism in France, Josephinism in Austria, and the tensions between priestcraft, deism, and scepticism that marked numerous controversies throughout much of Europe in this period.

The imputed conjunction of knowledge with power, or *savoir* with *pouvoir*, in the age of Enlightenment, often the subject of critiques of the period which trace its protagonists' political ambitions to their advocacy of science, comprises an equally major theme of this volume. It is examined here in a variety of contexts, including the promotion of ideas of progress or even eschatological optimism that inclined many progressive thinkers of the period to regard religious faith and orthodox beliefs as tantamount to barbarism, to the diffusion of dictionaries and newspapers that enabled readers in metropolitan centres to form themselves into new political classes, to the attempts of writers, kings, and queens to realise Plato's ancient ambition of promoting genuinely philosophical kingship, by the late eighteenth century already defined as 'enlightened despotism' by certain figures sympathetic to that doctrine's objectives.

A number of chapters address themes that turn around the political economy of the period, embracing both national and international debates on property, citizenship, commerce, and luxury, and the competing claims of virtue and wealth, as well as the development of physiocracy in France, cameralism in Germany and Austria, and the association of economics with moral philosophy that in Scotland was to form the nexus of the most advanced of all the human sciences of this period. Other chapters, including those that address a German tradition of natural jurisprudence, conceptions of the social contract and the common law of England, concentrate instead upon juristic themes, while still others are focused upon national arguments about political parties, notions of liberty, and ideals of patriotic rule, or on internationalist perspectives and philosophies of history which in the eighteenth century informed both doctrines of naturalism and the comparative study of societies. If we have not sought to engage with modern philosophers and contemporary social theorists about the central tenets and tendencies of the age of Enlightenment as a whole, we hope that attentive readers of this volume who have been drawn by other commentators to reflect on the eighteenth-century's putative public spheres, metanarratives, romantic reaction to rationalism, roots of totalitarian democracy, or passage from classicism to modernity, will here find such evidence as may enable them to navigate through such thickets of interpretation.

In so far as they inform so much of the political thought of the period as a whole, several of the themes addressed in this work, especially with regard to jurisprudence as well as to theology and economics when those subjects have manifest political ramifications, are traced across long spans and with reference to a wide range of thinkers, thereby necessitating brisker treatments of individual works than chapters which provide commentaries on national debates or traditions, or, as with respect to the American and French Revolutions, which deal with texts produced in highly concentrated periods of political ferment. In attempting to situate eighteenth-century political tracts and arguments within the specific contexts that occasioned them, we may be thought to have adopted a methodology appropriate to the *Cambridge History of Political Thought* as a whole, but that would be to exaggerate both the depth of our ambition and the extent of our control over the various chapters we commissioned. More strictly biographical formats for each chapter have been adopted by the editors of other volumes in this series, and, aside from introducing obvious chronological divisions, no attempt has been made to establish a consistent format throughout the collection. Not least because eighteenth-century thinkers often envisaged their political writings as contributions to wider subjects scarcely circumscribed by such disciplinary boundaries as were to arise after the age of Enlightenment, we have tried to be undogmatic about defining the meaning of political thought and therefore the range and boundaries of our work, even while acknowledging that the thematic divisions we have preferred cannot but exclude other perspectives.

The limitations of our approach have occasionally and even increasingly seemed to us just marginally less compelling than its merits. Particularly with reference to the pre-eminent thinkers of the eighteenth century, we recognise that in emphasising specificity and context we have been obliged to leave less scope for biographical continuity and philosophical coherence than some scholars might have wished, and we have attempted to meet such concerns as best we could by way of subdivisions of each chapter which often turn around the careers of separate authors and, even more, in our biographical appendix. If the length of our entries in that appendix appears to be inversely correlated with the historical significance of their subjects, that is just because we rely upon (and direct our readers' attention to) other sources that provide fuller biographical treatments of the most major figures than are appropriate or possible here.

Neither have we managed or even sought to impose our design of this work upon its separate authors, many of whom adopted an alternative view of their task and each of whom interpreted his or her assigned brief independently of the others. In the spirit of the eighteenth century's republic of letters we solicited contributions from experts of different generations with diverse backgrounds based in several countries in both Europe and North America. In a few instances we were confronted by the difficulty of integrating a contributor's style, choice of topics or interpretation of texts even within the loosely designed framework we provided, and in order to produce this work at all we accordingly came, reluctantly, to feel obliged to abandon our original hope that its separate compositions might appear to have been drafted seamlessly by an invisible hand. Much effort has nonetheless been devoted to achieving that effect, so far as it has been in our power, at least in order to maintain some consistency of style and balance, as well as to fill in gaps and strike out overlaps where they arose.

I
The *ancien régime* and its critics

I

The spirit of nations

SYLVANA TOMASELLI

I Lessons from the Franks and the Greeks

Montesquieu's *L'Esprit des lois*[1] (The Spirit of the Laws, 1748) stands among
the most intellectually challenging and inspired contributions to political
theory in the eighteenth century. The scope of the book, its sustained reflection, its impact on social and political debates throughout Europe, as well as
its enduring influence make it an exceptional work. As its subtitle indicates,
it purports to examine the relation laws must have to the specific constitution, civil society, and physical circumstances of the country in which they
are being made or enforced. To apprehend the spirit of a nation's laws is thus
to understand the relationship which pertains between a number of social,
political, and material factors peculiar to that nation. What the remainder
of the subtitle further suggests, and the body of the text makes explicit,
is that the knowledge which such an examination both requires and produces is historical in nature. In linking history and law and making both
central to political theory Montesquieu, together with the Scottish school
of political economy, which he profoundly influenced, set the tone and
form of modern social and political thought. He paved the way leading to
Hegel, who recognised the true nature of his genius better than most of his
admirers (Hegel 1991, pp. 29, 283, 310–11; 1999, p. 175; see also Carrithers
2001a).

The importance of history to the art of the legislator had long been recognised by the beginning of the eighteenth century (see especially Pocock
1999–2003). Unsurprisingly, the Historiographer Royal, Voltaire, whole-
heartedly endorsed it; but, as will be shown below, Voltaire's reading of

---

1 Its full title is *De l'esprit des lois ou du rapport que les lois doivent avoir avec la constitution de chaque
gouvernement, les moeurs, le climat, la religion, le commerce, etc. A quoi l'auteur a ajouté des recherches nouvelles
sur les lois romaines touchant les successions, sur les lois françaises et sur les lois féodales*, which translates as *On
the Spirit of Laws or on the Relation which Laws Ought to Bear to the Constitution of each Government, Mores,
Climate, Religion, Commerce, etc. to which the Author Has Added New Research on Roman Law relating to
Successions, French Laws, and Feudal Laws.*

history differed markedly from that of Montesquieu. Along with lesser-known political writers, however, both he and Montesquieu participated in an already established political debate about France's political identity in which history played a crucial role, not least since Bodin's *Methodus ad facilem historiarum cognitionem* (Method for Learning History Easily, 1566), a work which greatly affected the demarcation between secular and ecclesiastical history. It is this protracted political argument about France's true nature that provides the context for Montesquieu's political reflections as well as those of many of his contemporaries. The power struggles involving the crown and, at various times, all or parts of the clergy, the aristocracy, and the magistracy had engendered a large body of literature, ranging from political testaments, such as that of Richelieu, published in 1688, and memoirs from the leading protagonists of the Fronde, such as those of the Cardinal de Retz, which appeared in 1717, to substantive political treatises addressed to heirs to the throne. Amongst those who drew on history for the latter purpose was Bossuet in his *Politique tirée des propres paroles de l'écriture sainte* (Politics Drawn from the Words of Scripture, 1679) which, together with his *Discours sur l'histoire universelle* (1681), sought to present the then Dauphin, Louis XIV's heir apparent, with all that could be gleaned from history, sacred and profane, that was necessary 'to wise and perfect government' (see Riley 1990, pp. xiii–lxviii). Not all political works made systematic use of history, but they were all informed by it to some degree by the turn of the century, and no-one in the intellectual world could be unaware of its deployment.

An instance of a book which appealed to Greek mythology, rather than history sacred or profane, was the exceedingly widely read and highly influential *Les Aventures de Télémaque, fils d'Ulysse* (1699), which Fénelon wrote for the moral edification of Louis XIV's grandson, the duc de Bourgogne. Fénelon was far less accepting of the mores of his age than many of his contemporaries, and was highly critical of Louis XIV's conception of the aim of government and the nature of glory on earth. It was Fénelon's hope, therefore, that, once on the throne, his pupil, the young prince, would prove to be the antithesis of his grandfather, the Sun King Louis XIV; that is, that he would be a peaceful, frugal, and generally self-denying monarch, and that far from seeking to be involved at every level of the kingdom's administration, he would interfere as little as possible with, and hence delegate most of, France's governance (Fénelon 1994, p. 299) – a theme which echoed through some eighteenth-century political works in contrast to calls for a *dirigiste* approach to reform.[2] Through Mentor's teachings, Telemachus is prepared to surpass his father Ulysses, and the predominant lesson, one that is consonant with Fénelon's quietist belief that Christians must strive to love God for no other reason than that he is God, and hence must love God in a entirely disinterested manner, is that of selflessness (Keohane 1980, pp. 341–3; Riley 1994, pp. xxv–xxviii). Telemachus must learn to rule not for himself, but for the good of the people. He is encouraged in particular to forsake luxury and not to think of glory in terms of magnificence. He is not to build superb buildings, nor engage in wars of aggrandisement, but leave behind him a contented, industrious, and virtuous people who, whilst welcoming to merchants and engaged in trade, are primarily agrarian and live a simple life uncorrupted by luxury (Fénelon 1994, pp. 294–301). Fénelon's unequivocal disapproval of luxury, which he linked to women and their presence at court, which they corrupted, runs throughout his political writings.[3] In his *Examen de conscience pour un roi* (1734) Fénelon reminded his royal charge of the lack of ostentation of his ancestors' abodes before the reign of Francis I, at which time women began to appear at court, and praised St Louis in particular for the modesty of his house and the economy with which it was run (Fénelon 1747a, pp. 14–20). Next to luxury, it was war that concerned Fénelon most, and the *Examen* stresses the iniquity of wars and argues that it is best for the nation that its king seeks to maintain a position of equality with the rest of European countries so as to maintain a peaceful equilibrium. This was also the subject of his remonstrance to Louis XIV in a letter first published by d'Alembert in 1787, in the latter's *Histoire des membres de l'Académie française* (Fénelon 1964, pp. 299–309). For Fénelon all wars were civil wars. Humanity was a single society and all wars within it the greatest evil, for he argued that one's obligation to mankind as a whole was always greater than what was owed to one's particular country (Fénelon 1810, p. 62). Aside from the negative duty of desisting from the self-indulgence of opulence and warring, Fénelon mentioned also a positive one. He deemed it incumbent on princes to study the true form of the government of their kingdom. He thought it their God-given duty to study natural law, the laws of nations, as well as the fundamental laws and customs of their particular nations. This entailed knowing the way the kingdom had

2 For an account of Fénelon's influence and the plans which he, together with the dukes of Beauvillier and Chevreuse, hoped to put to the prince once he was king, the *Plans de gouvernement* or *Tables de chaulnes*, see Keohane 1980, pp. 343–6.
3 On luxury, see ch. 13 below.

been governed under the different waves of Germanic invasions; what *parlements* and Estates General were; the nature of fiefdoms; how things had come to be as they were. From this it followed further that 'the study of the history, mores and ancient form of government in all its detail should be regarded not as a matter of idle curiosity but as an essential duty of monarchs' (1747a, pp. 9–10).[4]

While *L'Esprit des lois* clearly shows Montesquieu's determination to contribute to the wisdom and virtue of princes and legislators, his aim was not only to press history – understood as a catalogue of examples to emulate or avoid – into the service of monarchs, but also to discover its dynamics through an analysis in which the character of rulers and the particular forms of government of their respective countries were only two, albeit crucial, of the several variables which, combined, made for the spirit of nations. This said, in devoting one third of his *magnum opus* to a discussion of the origins of the monarchy in France and its ancient laws, Montesquieu was following an old intellectual tradition. The question of the nature of France's monarchy was centuries old, and so was turning to the country's earliest history to endeavour to answer it (see, for instance, Kelley 1970, esp. pp. 283ff). No less than *L'Esprit des lois*, one of the most famous treatises of this kind, François Hotman's *Francogallia*, first published in 1573, looked back as far as the political culture of the Germanic peoples described by Tacitus, to support, in Hotman's case, a theory of resistance. Partly fuelled by partisan uses of France's past, several important works of historical compilation were available by the end of the seventeenth century, which, unlike Hotman's, were acknowledged by Montesquieu, including André Duchesne's *Les Antiquités et recherches de la grandeur des rois de France* (1609), Charles Ducange's *Glossarium mediae et infimae latinitatis* (1678), Etienne Baluze's *Regum francorum capitularia* (1677), and, later still, Leibniz's *De l'origine des Francs* (1720). The historical knowledge diffused by such annals informed competing conceptions of monarchy which were published from the beginning of the eighteenth century. Montesquieu took issue with (or rather dismissed out of hand) two of them in particular, the Abbé Jean Baptiste Dubos's *Histoire critique de l'établissement de la monarchie française dans les Gaules* (A Critical

---

4 One could think of the eighteenth century as being divided between those who, wittingly or not, followed Fénelon in seeking to imagine a fundamentally different moral order, one that placed restraints on material consumption and the inequalities that came with it; and those who sought to work within what they took to be human nature and the limitations placed on their society by historical and other contingencies. Rousseau was to follow Fénelon, whereas Montesquieu was not. Whatever the similarities and differences between their respective political perceptions, what divided them was their respective stance on the system of luxury, understood as a non-eradicable part of political reality.

History of the Origin of the French Monarchy in Gaul, 1735) and Henri comte de Boulainvilliers's *Histoire de l'ancien gouvernement de France et de l'Etat de la France* (A History of the Ancient Government of France and of the French State, 1727; see Carcassonne 1927).

Inspired in part by Hotman, Boulainvilliers claimed that the rise of monarchical government in France was in conflict with its ancient, Frankish, constitution. The Franks, he argued, had originally been free and equal. Their chiefs had exercised local authority in fiefdoms not subject to the rule of a remote king. Their nobility had been defined by a lineage of racial descent and by ties of reciprocity and mutual respect, whereas the French monarchy had managed progressively to displace them by filling its coffers with the proceeds of manufactured ennoblements which enabled it to employ mercenary troops. In describing feudal government as the greatest political masterpiece of the human mind, Boulainvilliers thus advanced what came to be termed the *thèse nobiliaire*, or Germanist theory, of the pre-history of the French state. Dubos, by contrast, put the case for Roman imperial rule, under which the tribes of ancient Gaul had not been enslaved by Rome but instead welcomed an authority that protected them from marauding tribes of Vandals and other barbarians while preserving their indigenous customs, laws, and language. The Capetian dynasty of the French monarchy had thus been prefigured by a beneficent imperial presence under which the Gauls had not been dispossessed of their lands and which had provided a model for stately order before the advent of fiefdoms and their attendant seigneurial rights claimed by the French nobility. Dubos's depiction of the conquest of Gaul as, in essence, a peaceful settlement which established a sovereign power in France that had preceded the rise of feudalism in the middle ages came to be termed the *thèse royale*, or Romanist theory, of the origins of the French state (see Ford 1953 and Keohane 1980, pp. 346–50).

What made Montesquieu's voice especially distinctive in this debate was the deployment of his thesis within the dual context of continuing admiration for republican forms of government and growing regard for modern commercial and powerful England. Momentous lessons could be drawn from both models, yet France had no cause to seek to imitate either; it could and indeed had to draw from its own well to meet its own unique circumstances. Such was the view which Montesquieu had developed into a philosophical position, namely that, to paraphrase Hegel's *Philosophy of Right* (1833), legislation both in general and in particular had to be treated not abstractly and in isolation, but as integral to the whole of the features which make up the character of the nation (Hegel 1991, para. 3, p. 29).

The background against which Montesquieu wrote was by no means a politically or intellectually complacent one (Keohane 1980). Contrary to a notion that remains prevalent, the *ancien régime* was not a static social and political entity against which its so-called 'critics' raged. The political reality of the regime was such that it had nearly always been in a state of contestation, scrutiny, and self-criticism. From the court down to obscure pamphleteers there were proposals for reform, criticisms of such proposals, and defences of counter-measures, plans, and visionary schemes – all of which involved definitions and redefinitions of the nation and the legitimate source of authority within it. As the eighteenth century unfolded so did the intricacy of the web of arguments about France's identity, its true institutional character, and the policies required to maintain it or restore it to its authentic form, for those who thought the nation had already departed, or was at risk of departing, from its true nature. The perennial question of the extent and limits of papal jurisdiction over France's religious institutions provided further occasions for analyses of its constitutional nature.[5] The controversies drew in many participants, although most of them focused on specific aspects of the debate, such as the fiscal, commercial, or demographic, whilst in his magisterial work Montesquieu brought them all together. Two comparisons were repeatedly deployed within this body of literature: one with ancient Rome, the causes of whose rise and fall continued to be an absorbing subject of analysis throughout Europe; the other with modern England, whose commercial success was likewise fascinating to political observers. A number of broad themes prevailed within the discussions of the character of France's and other European governments, namely, the way to administer public finances, the demarcation between ecclesiastical and secular powers, the question of population growth, toleration, and the importance of mores to political concerns. *L'Esprit des lois* dealt with all these issues and is famous for its accounts of both Rome and England. Montesquieu had, however, made notable interventions on these subjects before 1748. They will be the subjects of the next section; the object of the subsequent one is to provide a contrast with Montesquieu's reflections on the nature of France by drawing on some of Voltaire's writings on this topic; the final parts of the present chapter will be devoted to his *magnum opus*.

5 For which see ch. 4 below.

2   The Roman legacy

As d'Alembert remarked, Montesquieu's *Considérations sur les causes de la grandeur des Romains et de leur décadence* (Considerations on the Causes of the Greatness and Decadence of the Romans, 1734) could appropriately have been entitled 'Histoire romaine, à l'usage des hommes d'état' ('Roman History for Statesmen') (Montesquieu 1964, p. 25). True to the practice of the day, Montesquieu did indeed turn to Roman history to impart lessons to modernity and had already done so in his *Dissertation sur la politique des Romains dans la religion* (Dissertation on Roman Politics in Relation to Religion), presented to the Academy of Bordeaux in 1716. The principal use which Rome had for the president of the Bordeaux *parlement* (which Montesquieu became in that year) was to illustrate his views on the relationship between church and state.

Justly deemed one of the most interesting of his minor works (Shackleton 1961, p. 22), the *Dissertation* is notable partly because it makes clear that, while every society needs religion as a matter of psychological and moral necessity, the Romans required one solely for political purposes. In a period in which quasi-anthropological accounts of the origins of religion considered fear, in the main, as providing the primary explanation for the human disposition to believe in the supernatural, it is noteworthy that Montesquieu denied this to have been naturally the case with the Romans. Although not always consistently, he claimed the Romans feared absolutely nothing; in fact, it was because of their fearlessness that it had been a matter of political necessity to instil awe of deities into them. Montesquieu further contended that the Roman legislators had had no need to reform mores, nor to ground ethics and civil duties in religious faith. Morality and religion – and this was the most striking point in an age in which the issue of loss of faith was debated in terms of its consequences for morality – were thus presented as entirely distinct. The social utility of religious belief resided in the fact that it afforded control over the Roman population, and the entire priestly hierarchy was subordinate to the civil authorities. Religion was established in Rome as an instrument of political domination over an otherwise indomitable people. Perhaps surprisingly, Montesquieu believed the manipulation of the population by the political leadership did not imply that the elite was itself devoid of faith. Calling on the authority of Ralph Cudworth, one of the Cambridge Platonists and the author of a polemic against atheistic materialism, *The True Intellectual System of the Universe* (1678), Montesquieu argued that 'enlightened' Romans believed in a supreme deity.

15

They were theists. What is more, given that the ancient Romans regarded with indifference the form which worship assumed, they were a tolerant people, who considered all theologies, all religions, 'as equally good' (1964, p. 41).[6] They were intolerant only of inherently intolerant religions (Bianchi 1993; Rotta 1993; Tomaselli 2000; Kingston 2001).

That toleration was an unquestionable moral and political good was a crucial conviction of Montesquieu's (Linton 2000b). Describing intolerance in his *Lettres Persanes* (Persian Letters, 1721) as an epidemic illness that had spread from the Egyptians to the Christians, he traced it to the spirit of proselytising that the Jews had taken from their Egyptian captors. He believed intolerance violated the eternal laws of natural justice (which he regarded as emanating as a matter of necessity from God's nature, but which would exist even if God did not), and undermined sound politics, for it deprived a nation of the skills and knowledge that were often specific to a particular religious community. States benefited from a multiplicity of religions, as those in the minority, being excluded from the system of honour and dignity reserved for the dominant one, strove through industriousness to distinguish themselves by the acquisition of riches. Moreover, established religions themselves gained from the presence of other faiths within a nation as it encouraged them to keep corruption in check (Montesquieu 1964, pp. 106–8). Cataloguing the upheavals and demise of the Roman Empire in the East in the *Considérations*, Montesquieu made much of the Emperor Justinian's and his successors' religious intolerance and claimed that it was the inability to recognise the proper limits of ecclesiastical and secular powers which had been the most poisonous source of the Eastern empire's ills. 'This great distinction', he explained, 'which is the basis of the tranquillity of peoples, is founded not only in religion, but also in reason and nature, which dictate that entirely separate things, which can only subsist separate, never be confounded' (p. 483). Whilst the clergy did not constitute a separate estate amongst the ancient Romans, the distinction between secular and clerical was as clear to them as it was to his contemporaries.

Important though this subject and all matters relating to it were to Montesquieu, a clear demarcation was drawn around it. For if Rome's history had important lessons to impart to French legislators in terms of the relationship between church and state, religion and society, lessons which Montesquieu was at pains to draw repeatedly in his writings, it was emphatically not the proper mirror to hold to France when it came to understanding

---

6 All translations from this text are mine.

its true constitutional nature. Montesquieu was, of course, not ignorant of the legacy of Roman law. On the contrary, he went to some length to demonstrate its extent, as he sought to present it, not as a welcome inheritance but as an embarrassment and a burden on the nation. Thus, in Letter 100 of the *Lettres Persanes*, Rica, one of the imaginary Persians through whose epistles the author voiced his political and moral disquiet, mocked the French for the pride they took in dictating fashion and culinary tastes to the whole of Europe, despising all that was foreign, while remaining wholly unconcerned that they themselves followed alien political and civil practices. 'Who would believe the oldest and most powerful kingdom in Europe to be governed for the last ten centuries by laws which are not its own?', asked the Persian. This might have been credible had the French been a conquered, rather than a conquering, nation. As it was, this proud people 'had abandoned the ancient laws made by its first kings in the general assemblies of the nation. What is more, the Roman laws they had taken instead were partly made and partly codified by emperors contemporary to their own legislators' (Montesquieu 1964, p. 115).[7] The oddity of taking on freely and for no apparent reason another people's law could not have been made more explicit. Completing their self-imposed and wholly unwarranted servitude, the letter went on, the French showed unqualified obedience to every single papal decree. Nor did the 'bizarrerie of the French spirit' stop there, for as another protagonist, Usbek, remarked in a subsequent epistle, despite the infinite number of 'useless or worse' laws which the French had taken from the Romans, they had failed to take from them paternal authority, *patria potestas*, on which these laws were grounded (p. 131), a point made by Hotman and others in the preceding century (Kelley 1970, pp. 285–6).

While in his early writings Montesquieu already conceived of the Roman legacy as perverting France's true character, he did not believe, however, that Rome's constitution was devoid of interest even from a French political perspective. One of the first 'lessons' which Montesquieu drew in the *Grandeur des Romains* is central to the whole of his political thought. It bears on the mechanism inherent in some nations by which any deviation from their true political nature can be amended. What made Rome's government admirable, according to him – and here, as indeed throughout his study of the republic, he was closer to Bossuet's account than has been thought (*pace* Shackleton 1961, pp. 165, 176) – was its capacity to rectify abuses of power

---

7 This criticism was by no means novel. As Kelley (1970) has noted, Pasquier, Le Caron, and others bemoaned the intrusion of Roman law into French jurisprudence and its consolidation through the teaching of law in the universities as well as through canon law.

through the spirit of its people, the strength of its senate, or the authority of some of its magistrates. Only in this respect could the example of Rome be instructive politically to French legislators, for Rome owed its liberty to this self-correcting capacity, for which, contrary to the claims made by Italian republics about their own perpetuity, Montesquieu found no parallel in either ancient or modern history beside that of England, to which he compared Rome. 'The government of England is wiser', he wrote, 'because it has a body which constantly scrutinises it, and constantly scrutinises itself; whatever its mistakes, they do not last long and are often useful by the very attentiveness they give to the nation.' He held it to be of the utmost importance that 'a free government, that is one that is always agitated, was open to corrections through its own laws', for it could not otherwise maintain itself long (Montesquieu 1964, p. 452).

Montesquieu balanced this point with cautionary remarks on the prudence of leaving long-established forms of government alone, explaining in terms now more readily associated with Edmund Burke's *Reflections on the Revolution in France* (1790) that the reasons which had sustained such states over time were often complicated and unknown and would continue to operate in the future (1964, p. 470). In France's case, the complexities of its political structure as well as its essence were perceptible through a comprehension of its history following the Germanic invasions. This history was by no means simply an account of the *de facto* triumph of barbarism over civilisation, or of one set of political and social customs and practices replacing another. What was peculiar to France was that its vanquished past remained perversely and distortedly alive. The country had inherited two conflicting characters, one disciplined to the point of submission, the other independent to the point of unruliness, one southern, the other northern. This dichotomy Montesquieu strengthened in an essay *Sur les causes qui peuvent affecter les esprits et les caractères* (On the Causes which Can Affect the Mind and Character, first published in 1892, but believed to pre-date *L'Esprit des lois*), by juxtaposing Catholicism, associated with the spirit of submission, to Protestantism, identified with that of independence (1964, pp. 493–4). The barbarian spirit of independence was so infectious that it had contaminated even the Romans when they came into contact with the northern Germanic tribes. Thus the age in which the Romans sentenced their own children to death for a victory secured against orders was replaced by one during which, by all accounts, the wars against the Goths were replete with acts of insubordination (*Considérations*: Montesquieu 1964, p. 473).

Whether in narrating particular historical events or in broader claims about France's political identity or that of nations worldwide, Montesquieu was consistent in depicting the south in sharp contrast to the north, the Roman temperament as opposite to the barbarian one, and his native country as all but a happy integration of both. Moreover, much of what he said about the south, even when initially seemingly complimentary, led to claims about its inherent submissiveness, while what he said about the north, even when he seemed to be critical, led to its exaltation as the realm of freedom. Thus, having described southerners as timorous, Montesquieu went on to say that they showed a good deal more sense than the demented northerners who risked their lives in pursuit of vainglory. However, he was quick to point out that this very pursuit – which, it might be noted, had been the butt of renewed condemnation by moralists through Europe in the seventeenth century – had a vital effect: for while common sense and a balanced frame of mind in the southerners still gave rise to servitude as an eventual consequence, the derangement of the northerners produced liberty; similarly, the strength of the minds of the former lessened as that of the latter grew, since servitude destroyed the mind whereas freedom fortified it. It was but a small step in his argument that led Montesquieu to proceed to link Protestantism and the advancement of learning to the northern European predilection for individual liberty (*Sur les esprits et les caractères*: 1964, pp. 493–4).

3   Voltaire and the English question

Discussions of the aptness of the Roman model were obviously not confined to France. Montesquieu himself compared the Roman and the English constitutions and was not alone in so doing. Voltaire, whose views may be profitably juxtaposed to those of Montesquieu, opened his first letter on the subject of England's political institutions, '*Sur le Parlement*', by noting how very fond the English Members of Parliament were of comparing themselves to the ancient Romans. The rest of this, the eighth of his highly influential *Lettres philosophiques* (first published in an English translation, as *Letters concerning the English Nation*, in 1733, and burnt by order of the *parlement* of Paris when published in French in 1734), endeavours to demonstrate the total inappropriateness of the analogy. The Romans never fought one another over minor differences in religious practices, nor by the same token had their civil wars resulted in anything other than further enslavement. Those of England had led to increased liberty. Only the English had regulated the power of their kings by resisting them to such an extent that they were now graced by a wise government whose prince 'all powerful to do good, has his hands tied to do evil, where lords are great without insolence and without vassals, and where the people partakes of government without tumult', phrases he was not alone in borrowing from Fénelon (Voltaire 1964b, p. 55). The balance of power between the two Houses of Parliament, over which the king presided, could not place the English government in greater contrast to that of the Romans.[8] The Roman senate and the plebeians had been in perpetual conflict, as the one strove to distance the other from government and did so through imperial expansion. England, by contrast, had no need of such a remedy. The king held the balance between the two chambers; the country as a whole was not only jealous of its liberty, but also eager to contain the ambitions of expansionist neighbouring nations.

Voltaire's *Lettres philosophiques* were to have a great impact on both the French and English nations' self-perceptions. While the *Lettres* do not in themselves bear comparison in either breadth or analytical depth to *L'Esprit des lois*, when read in the light of Voltaire's other works – especially *Le siècle de Louis XIV* (1751), the *Essai sur les moeurs et l'esprit des nations* (Essay on the Mores and Spirits of Nations, 1756), the *Dictionnaire philosophique* (1764), and the *Histoire du parlement de Paris* (1769) – they nevertheless provide a useful counterpart to Montesquieu's views on both nations. The England depicted by Voltaire was the land which was quick to adopt Lady Mary Wortley Montagu's introduction of smallpox inoculation following her residence in Turkey; it was the birthplace of Bacon ('the greatest experimentalist'), Locke ('the wisest man'), and Newton ('the greatest of men'), in contrast to the country of Descartes ('who had spread greater errors than he had dispelled'), Malebranche ('whose illusions were nothing short of sublime'), the cynical La Rochefoucauld, and the sceptical Montaigne. The partisanship of Voltaire's idealisation of England did not lessen its impact, any more than did Montesquieu's. Both authors helped propagate the view that England exemplified in modern times the causal interconnection between commerce, science, military might, religious toleration, liberty, and a stable and prosperous government.

What Voltaire did not glorify were the barbarians and their reputed legacy. According to him, neither in England nor in France did the spirit of liberty owe anything to the invading hordes' insubordination and independence. He spoke of the legitimate power of the king in France and of that of the

---

8 Montesquieu and Voltaire constantly refer to 'England' and it is indeed to the ancient English constitution and its development that they refer; however, from the Union of England with Scotland in 1707, England was part of a new political entity, Britain.

king and the people in England as having eroded the lawless supremacy of the feudal barons, and he was keen to stress in the ninth letter that the happy balance between the Commons, the Lords, and the king was a recent phenomenon which owed very little to a so-called 'ancient constitution', deriding the idea that Magna Carta enshrined the freedom of Englishmen. Unlike the civil wars in France, which had had no purpose beyond factionalism and sedition for their own sakes, the English Civil War had had liberty as its object and parliament had had a clear conception of its own intentions and how to secure them (a subject Voltaire had already addressed in English in his *Essay on Civil Wars* of 1727). Prior to that conflict, England had not been essentially freer than any other European country. Over the centuries, however, successive kings had checked the power of the barons. This, combined with the slow acquisition of land by commoners and their gradual enrichment, had laid the ground for liberty in England.

Voltaire made much of the extent to which the Lords were constrained by the Commons and all subjected to a single tax on land. For this tax, being neither onerous nor unfair, encouraged the growing number of rich 'peasants' to remain on the land where they did not have cause to fear displaying their wealth. This said, England's wealth was owed above all to commerce, and it was commerce which, in his tenth letter, Voltaire claimed had contributed to freeing the English, while this same liberty had in turn benefited commerce, thereby building the greatness of the state and England's mastery of the seas. Hence merchants who, unlike their French or German counterparts, were highly esteemed by their compatriots at all levels, were rightly proud of their achievements and could, with some justice, compare themselves to Roman citizens.

Having praised nearly all things English and, more overtly than not, criticised almost all aspects of his native country, Voltaire left his readers in no doubt about the lessons which could be learned by anyone concerned to increase the power and wealth of a nation. Liberty, especially freedom of expression, and religious toleration went hand in hand with commerce, military might, and scientific advance. What is more, in dismissing the idea of the ancient provenance of the institutional guarantees of liberty in England, Voltaire simplified the issue of its establishment or fostering elsewhere.

He was to use similar argumentative strategies in his *Histoire du parlement de Paris* by stressing the vicissitudes of all European political systems, emphasising discontinuities in legislative practices, and undermining the notion that the French *parlements* in particular had a long history and enduring conventions and aims. Instead he portrayed them as having been haphazard in their composition, venal, often ignorant of, or uninterested in, the good of the nation as a whole, and subservient to factional or regal power, sometimes also to Rome. This purported history of the *parlement* of Paris was in fact a history of the tribulations of the monarchy until the reign of Henri IV and his minister Sully. The same is true of his account of the meetings of the Estates General. When Voltaire related the convoking at Rouen in 1596 of what he called 'a kind of estates general under the name of an assembly of notables', he spelled out a point made throughout the work, namely that 'it is quite easy to see from all these different convocations that there is nothing fixed in France'; for him, 'these were not the ancient *parlements* of the kingdom, which all the noble warriors attended by right' (Voltaire 2005, p. 354). Nor were they the diets of the empire, the estates of Sweden, the *cortes* of Spain, or the parliaments of England, for these, he stressed, had their membership fixed by the laws. By contrast, any man of substance who could undertake the trip to Rouen was admitted to the estates. In practice the Estates General could bear neither the constitutional nor symbolic weight placed on it by the advocates of limited monarchy. The lack of fixity and the absence of the rule of law were, for Voltaire, characteristic features of a nation marked by *privilèges*, that is, dispensations, generally granted to aristocrats, exempting them from legal obligations and constraints.

Unreserved praise and respect for the *parlement* of Paris is displayed in this work only in relation to its persistent refusal to ratify the decrees of the Council of Trent and its resistance to Rome's authority in secular matters (Voltaire 2005, pp. 361, 460–2). Here Voltaire echoed Montesquieu in deploring the papacy's persistent attempts to violate French sovereignty. To have signed those decrees would have brought on France the shame of a subjected nation, Voltaire argued, and the issue of national sovereignty is the background for much of his long harangue against the church. On the need to keep ultramontanism in check and thereby the separation of the state and church, as well as on the civil perils of religious superstition, the utility and happiness engendered by religious toleration, and the natural right to freedom of conscience, the two great anglophiles of the century were agreed.

To emulate England was unquestionably desirable for Voltaire. This was ultimately a question of administration from above; it was also a matter of luck, to which political reality set what at times were insurmountable limits. Not surprisingly, in a century that witnessed a resurgence of admiration for Henri IV, Voltaire, himself the author of an epic poem *La Henriade* (1723; 1728), thought much hung on the quality of any given ruler and his or her advisers. Anne of Austria's regency (1643–51), for instance, would have been tranquil and absolute, in his view, had there been a Sully or a Colbert to administer France's finances. Even so, he doubted whether either of these two administrative geniuses would have been able to attend to the current financial chaos, surmount the prejudices of the nation, establish a fair system of taxation, encourage both commerce and agriculture, '*and do finally what is done in England*' (Voltaire 2005, p. 434; my emphasis).

As things were, Voltaire stressed that France was very different from her neighbour across the Channel. Though he thought them regrettable for the most part, there were aspects of this difference that he clearly would not have eradicated. That the *parlement* of Paris bore no resemblance to the English parliament (Voltaire 2005, p. 442), and that it pursued only its often ridiculously narrow self-interest, were points on which he insisted; but while the latter fact was obviously deplorable, the former was not a cause for lament. Indeed, Voltaire used it, as he did the *parlement*'s history (as he presented it) to undermine the court's authority. Its tribulations, the precariousness of its standing, and the uncertainty surrounding some of its procedures were all invoked by him to belittle the *parlement* in the eyes of his readers. In particular, he made much of the continual arguments over orders of precedence in the *parlement* between, on the one hand, France's nobility of ancient lineage and, on the other, the nobility of the robe,[9] that is, those who had bought their offices; and while the ancient aristocracy in his portrayal tended to lose little of its dignity and that of the robe left to shoulder most of the ridicule, he used the conflicts to conclude 'that it is only in France that the rights of these bodies thus float in uncertainty' and that 'each step one takes in the history of France proves, as we have already seen, that almost nothing was settled in a uniform and stable manner, and that chance and the short-term interest of passing whims, were often the legislators' (Voltaire 2005, p. 467). According to Voltaire, the *parlement*, far from being like the Estates General and an integral part of government, as it seemed to see itself, was a precarious institution of questionable merit.

The status of France's *parlements* and, indeed, the source and extent of regal authority more generally, were subjects on which sixteenth- and seventeenth-century political writers throughout Europe had expressed views. What is more, the very idea of the reality of absolute power had itself not gone uncontested within these deliberations. Thus, Leibniz, disputing Hobbes's notion that sovereignty must be unitary or else anarchy

---

9 In French, the *noblesse d'épée* and *noblesse de robe*.

would ensue, argued in 1677 that such a unitary conception of state power had never existed in practice and all European states admitted of a degree of division of power. Nor was it the case that they were in constant political turmoil as a result. Leibniz further challenged the cognate idea that an empire such as the Holy Roman Empire was in any sense unnatural or 'monstrous', as Pufendorf had put it. Combining these several points, he argued that if the German assemblies were indeed monstrous then he 'would venture to say that the same monsters are being maintained by the Dutch, the Poles and the English, even by the Spanish and the French' (*Caesarinus Fürstenerius*: Leibniz 1988, p. 119). He also noted that 'half of France consists of provinces called *les pays des Etats*, like Lesser Brittany, Gallia Narbonensis, the county of Provence, the dukedom of Burgundy, where the king certainly cannot exact extraordinary tributes with any more right than can the king of England in his realm', adding, 'anything further, exceeding custom or law, can have force only if it succeeds in the king's councils'. Not even the emperor of Turkey, Leibniz went on, enjoyed absolute supremacy, concluding, 'therefore Hobbesian empires, I think, exist neither among civilised peoples nor among barbarians, and I consider them neither possible nor desirable, unless those who must have supreme power are gifted with angelic virtues' (Leibniz 1988, pp. 119–20).

Nowhere was the case for their unqualified undesirability more strongly presented than in *L'Esprit des lois*. That such empires could and did exist was, however, made abundantly clear. Indeed, Montesquieu, who was to treat despotism as a form of government in its own right, one driven by fear and characterised by the absence of fundamental laws and, consequently, of their repositories (*SL*, II.4, p. 19), saw its evil residing in more than its form; but just as Leibniz and other commentators had proved incredulous in the face of Hobbes's notion of unitary power, so many were to deny the reality of Montesquieu's description of despotism, arguing, as Voltaire did, that it was not a natural form of government, but rather, as the conventional view had it, an abuse or corruption of monarchical power. At stake, of course, was the status of France's monarchy past and present. In undermining the coherence and realism of his conception of despotism, Montesquieu's critics sought to lessen the power of the spectre the *président à mortier* was holding up in warning.

Like Leibniz, Voltaire contended, in his *Pensées sur l'administration publique* (Thoughts on Public Administration), that even 'le grand Turc' swore on the Koran to obey the laws (Voltaire 1994a, p. 221; see also Pocock 1999–2003, I, pp. 97–119). Given that Voltaire defined liberty as the rule of law, this rendered Turkey (the commonplace example of despotism in contemporary literature) no less a potential site for freedom than any other nation. That it did not qualify for admission to his list of free countries – Sweden, England, Holland, Switzerland, Geneva, Hamburg, Venice, and Genoa – was perhaps as circumstantial as France's absence. What was beyond doubt, according to Voltaire, was that, *pace* Montesquieu, who made much of environmental considerations, climate was not a factor, any more than religion, mores, or customs. The best form of government, Voltaire wrote, was one in which all ranks were equally protected by the laws (1994a, p. 217). That, however, was not the bone of contention. If, as Voltaire himself claimed, partisanship was decisive in shaping the views that political commentators proffered about France's true political nature – with ministers arguing in favour of absolute power, barons for a division of power, and so forth – the question was first and foremost one of establishing an authoritative vantage point from which a form of government could be said to be the best for contemporary France. For Voltaire, history did not deliver an unequivocal judgement on this issue; as we have already seen, he found little in France's past to warrant conceiving of a continuous political tradition of institutionalised representation. It would be wrong to suppose that Montesquieu's reflections on France's history provide a clear-cut contrast. His purpose in the final part of *L'Esprit des lois* is no more simplistic than in the parts that precede it. His account is complex and not entirely unambiguous. As we have seen, what can be gleaned of his interest in the political history of France from his earliest political writings is an image of France with a somewhat puzzling past in that, despite having been vanquished, the Romans remained a presence within it, through law. Reading his chapters on the laws of the different waves of conquering races shows Montesquieu at pains to stress that these invaders were not themselves bereft of laws. There was no legal vacuum for Roman law to fill, nor a simple process by which one code of law supplanted earlier ones. Indeed, his exposition used a substantial number of sources and derided what he saw as simplified versions of a multi-faceted legal past. The territory over which French monarchs ruled was one that had witnessed waves of invasions, each of which brought different ways of determining guilt and innocence, dealing with retribution, relations between men and women, fathers and children, property and inheritance, levies, privileges, and so forth, and of conceiving of the source of political sovereignty. Codification, the obliteration of legal particularism, rather than the devastation brought by conquests, emerged as the greatest threat to liberty in *L'Esprit des lois*.

4   The spirit of the laws: know thy country

'Laws, in the widest sense, are the necessary relations which derive from the nature of things' is the opening sentence of the first chapter of *L'Esprit des lois*; 'in this sense, every being and every thing has its laws', it continues. From God downwards, every entity is linked to the rest of creation and these connections are not random. Montesquieu's intricate map presented an overview of the various levels of law from divine to human, although he warned that he would not treat political and civil laws separately as his purpose was to not to examine laws themselves but their spirit, that is the various relations which laws can have with various things (*SL*, 1.3, p. 8). First to be studied was the relation which laws have (or ought to have if true to type) with what he defined as the three essential forms of government; namely republican, in which sovereign power resides with the people; monarchical, in which it is vested in one person but in accordance with established laws; and despotic, in which there are no fixed laws (see Carrithers 2001b; Paul 2001). Having, in the first ten chapters, examined the nature of republican government, both in its democratic and aristocratic forms, as well as of monarchical and despotic types of government, compared their respective principles and pedagogical, civil, criminal, and sumptuary laws, discussed how each comes to degenerate and how each provided for its defence, and raised the subject of conquest, Montesquieu devoted the next three chapters to political liberty. From this, he went on to consider the constraints climate might have on human agency and whether it and other physical factors might, partly or wholly, causally determine slavery and the condition of women (see Shklar 1987, pp. 93–110). Commerce, money, demography, and the relationship between religion and law provide the topics of another six chapters. The book's divisions are, however, anything but rigid. England features in several chapters, Rome in many, and so do women, war, luxury, wealth, marriage, and parental authority. The culture and trade of China and Japan as well as the impact of the discovery of America on Europe, not to mention numerous historical and anthropological vignettes, and the detailed account of France's legal history, all contribute to the making of this great didactic exercise, in which prescription and description are intertwined to convey the absolute necessity of as thorough an understanding as is humanly possible of the domain in which one proposes to act politically.

It is somewhat ironic that an author who so admired Caesar and Tacitus for their brevity and thought falsehoods required volumes of explanations, including the three 'deadening volumes' that made up Dubos's *Histoire critique de l'établissement de la monarchie française dans les Gaules*, should himself have written such a long book (*SL*, xxx.2, p. 620, xxx.23, p. 659). Although Montesquieu said he had left out the 'details', the sheer abundance of the various kinds of observations it contains, and the often arbitrary sequence in which they are reported, add to the challenge of seeing the whole through its parts. Yet, the whole, and not the parts, was very specifically what Montesquieu had begged the readers of his preface to judge *L'Esprit des lois* by. His intention could only be discerned, he had added, by 'discovering' the aim of the work in its entirety, and the full import of the truths it contained could only be truly gauged once their chain-like connection to each other was apprehended. Following his somewhat enigmatic opening, Montesquieu disclosed some of the hypotheses which he had tested in the writing of the work, namely, that the diversity of laws and mores did not entail that mankind was governed solely by whim and, by implication, that systems of law and patterns of social behaviour could be the object of understanding, not least because he believed each individual law to be linked to another or to depend on a more general one. He also presented some of his conclusions, namely, that only those who have the gift of seeing the entire constitution of a state are in a position to propose any changes to it; that it was important for the people to be 'enlightened' as the prejudices of the nation became those of the people in authority; and that the more informed one's judgement, the more one could assess the full ramifications of any potential change, the implication being that one would be likely to desist from making it. Just as he had asked the reader in relation to his book not to fasten on single pronouncements in isolation from the rest, so he thought the mark of enlightened statesmanship consisted in the capacity to perceive the whole network of potential consequences of any one political act. Montesquieu expressed furthermore some of his most heartfelt wishes. He hoped that the work might eradicate prejudices, lead to greater love of one's duties, prince, motherland, and laws, and induce rulers to increase their knowledge of what they legislated about. 'Know thy country' was effectively his injunction to them from the very beginning, and in contributing to increased national self-awareness Montesquieu claimed he was practising not a narrowly conceived virtue, but universal love.

The didactic purpose of this quintessential Enlightenment work could hardly have been made clearer. Nor did its preface leave any doubt that a true apprehension of the nature of things would usher in the realisation that the scope for improvement through political change was severely limited, as Montesquieu postulated that greater insight tended to heighten perception of the nefarious consequences of the seemingly most obvious or benign legislative remedies. This said, he did not seem to wish to induce a state of enlightened political paralysis in legislators. His book begins with the claim that every aspect of the universe is governed by law, and is replete with illustrations of the constraints on human political agency as well as of acts of folly, but it also contains many an example of decisiveness and indeed greatness. It is a guide to righteous legislation and within the mirror-for-princes genre; it is a mirror for legislators, addressing the question of who they ought to strive to be and how they ought to act in their legislative capacity. Their character was crucial and as Montesquieu asserts in book 29, 'On the Way to Compose the Laws', chapter 1, 'On the Spirit of the Legislator', 'I say it, and it seems to me that I have written this work only to prove it: the spirit of moderation should be that of the legislator' (1989, p. 602).

In arguing that moderation was an essential virtue in legislators, Montesquieu was aligning himself – at least in one respect – with the oldest school of political theory, which went as least as far back as Aristotle. By illustrating the point here through reference to judicial practice, he demonstrated that his evident love of law – which stirred or was stirred by an aesthetic response to some systems of laws, most notably feudal law (*SL*, xxx.1, p. 619) – came with a profound anxiety that law might ultimately destroy itself or what it made possible. Indeed, for all that he wrote about despotic government, with fear as its principle and therefore requiring very few laws (v.14, p. 59), he lavished more attention on the many ways in which law, rather than the want of it, might make for various forms of tyranny.

5 The spirit of the laws: the science of freedom

Law, Montesquieu argued, restored the equality that man initially enjoyed in the state of nature but had lost in the early stages of society, owing to his shedding a sense of his own weakness, a loss that led to the state of war (*SL*, viii.3, p. 114). More importantly, law engendered freedom. To study law, its history, and the spirit which emanated from it, was to study freedom – what ensured or threatened it – and placed one in the position of measuring its extent at any given time. Hence the study of the history of the world's legal systems was of the greatest possible interest to mankind, as nothing could have served it better than to place criminal law on the surest foundation; for in a state enjoying the best possible laws, that man who is tried, sentenced, and hanged is freer than any pasha in Turkey, a view which Rousseau, one of Montesquieu's earliest and most enthusiastic followers, made the kernel of his *Contrat social*. It is living under civil law which makes us free and explains why princes are not free amongst themselves, for they are not governed by law, but by violence (XXVI.20, pp. 514–15). They constrain, or are constrained by, each other. That is the brute reality of international relations. In what is probably the most Hobbesian passage of his work, Montesquieu further claimed that the duress under which agreements between nations emerged did not in any way lessen their signatories' obligation.

That freedom was the fruit of law, according to Montesquieu, and that it was uniquely enjoyed in civil society, wherein the rule of law prevailed, cannot be overstressed. What mankind knew in the state of nature was independence, not freedom – another point that was not lost on Rousseau:

> It is true that in democracies the people appears to do what it likes: but political liberty does not consist in doing what one wants. In a state, that is, a society in which there are laws, liberty can only consist in being able to do what one ought to want, and not to be constrained to do what one ought not to want. One must bear in mind what *independence* is, and what *liberty* is. Liberty is the right to do everything that the laws permit; and if a citizen were able to do what they prohibit, he would cease to be free, because all the others would have the same power. (*SL*, IX.3, p. 155; my emphasis)

As freedom was entirely dependent on the rule of law, the issue was very much the authorship *and* composition of laws. This is the subject and title of book XXIX, and in some sense the last book of *L'Esprit des lois*; for while much is to be gleaned from the final two books that follow it, these belong to, and expand, a legal history of what became France, which can be found in preceding books. In book XXIX, Montesquieu reiterated and brought together several of the tenets of his philosophy of law. Continuing from his opening comments about the moderation needed in legislators, he drew attention to the style in which laws are to be written, explaining that they must be models of precision as well as simplicity and thus leave little room for differing interpretations. He urged that they not be modified without sufficient reason and that any justification a law might proffer for its existence be given in an appropriate tone; it had to be honourable in every aspect. Montesquieu stressed throughout his text the importance of maintaining the dignity of law, its majesty. Indeed, one of the prime concerns exhibited in his writing was the desire to understand how laws come to lose their authority and the awe they ought to inspire (e.g. XI.11, pp. 545–6). Another was that laws ought not be taken out of the context in which they were written. Their aim could only be grasped by placing them firmly back within it (XXIX.14, p. 611). Nor should laws from different legal systems be compared. It was meaningless, for instance, to compare the respective penalty for bearing false witness in France and England (XXIX.11, p. 608). To judge whether laws were in conformity with reason, one had to evaluate entire legal systems and not proceed piecemeal. In legislating or in commenting on legal matters, it was necessary to seek to understand and to enter into the spirit of laws. How this was to be achieved was the overt purpose of the work as a whole.

Within it, however, Montesquieu expressed a number of other worries. This included his anxiety about *l'esprit de système*, about which he wrote on several occasions, and especially in book XXIX. Possibly because his emphasis on clarity and simplicity raised it, the question of uniformity was given its own chapter. Chapter 18 of book XXIX, 'On Ideas of Uniformity', is but one paragraph long. Characteristically (for while the book is long, the crucial passages are pithy) it contains one of Montesquieu's most significant pronouncements (see Courtney 1988). Ideas of uniformity, he noted, did on occasion strike great minds as they had Charlemagne, but, more often than not, they occurred to those with mediocre ones:

They find in it a kind of perfection they recognize because it is impossible not to discover it: in the police the same weights, in commerce the same measures, in the state the same laws and the same religion in every part of it. But is this always and without exception appropriate? Is the ill of changing always less than the ill of suffering? And does not the greatness of genius consist rather in knowing in which cases there must be uniformity and in which differences? In China, the Chinese are governed by Chinese ceremonies, and the Tartars by Tartar ceremonies; they are, however, the people in the world which most have tranquillity as their purpose. When the citizens observe the laws, does it matter if they observe the same ones? (p. 617)

Thus Montesquieu not only thought that one should desist from comparing laws outside the legal framework in which they existed, or indeed from evaluating them outside of the specific historical context in which they originated, but he also went to great lengths to describe a legal past in which a variety of legal codes co-existed under one political umbrella and noted, for instance, the benefit brought to commerce by a Visigoth law which, given that trade brought so many different people together, stipulated that individuals be tried according to the law and by a judge of their native country (XXI.18, p. 387). Montesquieu's dread of uniformity resonated in the writings of his nineteenth-century followers, especially Benjamin Constant, in response to the imposition of the Code Napoleon, and Alexis de Tocqueville, in the face of what he perceived to be increased political centralisation. *L'Esprit des lois* was nothing short of a celebration of the diversity between and complexity within legal systems. Several of the examples on which Montesquieu drew to laud or deplore various laws were regulations governing the freedom of religious communities within larger political units, especially Jewish ones within Muslim or Christian countries, leaving little doubt that his argument for legal diversity was part and parcel of his plea for religious toleration. His political vision was of a world in which various levels of customs, regional practices and differences, and above all common law, were left to co-exist as they had in the past. It made for a society in which peoples of different cultures brought together by commercial activity could live and be judged and tried by the laws under which they were born.

Despotism, conceived as the rule of one person in the absence or paucity of laws, was only one form of political terror; for there were at least two kinds of tyranny, according to Montesquieu, one he called 'real', which consisted in a violent government, the other, 'of opinion', 'which was felt when those who govern establish things that run counter to a nation's way of thinking' (XIX.3, p. 309). To understand how a nation thought, it was necessary to understand its character or *esprit général*, and that in turn required historical understanding and sensibility on a grand scale, as illustrated by *L'Esprit des lois*; it meant taking into account all the variables, physical as well as social, that the book argued were relevant, as well as their interrelations. Thus Montesquieu devoted book XXIX to explaining the necessity of ensuring that the laws of a nation be made in accordance with the mores and manners of its people or peoples; laws could, however, also contribute to shape these mores and manners provided they were very specifically tailored to them.

6   The spirit of the laws: commerce and civility

Nothing could have been further from Montesquieu's mind than the kind of general blanket modelling of France on England which Voltaire entertained. England, because it was comparable in principle to France was, if anything, one of Montesquieu's frequent sources of examples to be avoided (Courtney 2001b). While, for instance, he commended the English for prohibiting the confiscation of foreign ships in times of war, except in reprisal, he was quick to balance the compliment with a critical assessment when he claimed that it was against the spirit of both commerce and monarchy to allow the nobility to engage in commerce as they did across the Channel (XX.4, p. 346, XX.21, p. 350). Quite apart from his belief that liberty in

England was a very precarious thing because the power of its nobility – which together with the judiciary he thought so essential to moderate monarchy – had been undermined in a number of ways, Montesquieu was at pains to stress the importance of knowing the legal and historical peculiarities of each individual nation (II.4, pp. 18–19). This said, while his work to a large extent addressed his fears and aspirations for France, and while he urged readers to be attentive to particulars and seek to comprehend France's specific identity, that identity could not be grasped without a mastery of general principles – in this case, the general features of moderate monarchies and the dynamics of commerce and finance. Theoretical understanding and specific historical knowledge had to be conjoined to be of any purpose. Thus he gave vent to more than one of his apprehensions when he explained that it was through 'ignorance of both the republican and monarchical constitution' that the Scottish financier, John Law, 'had been one of the greatest promoters of despotism Europe had ever seen'. 'Besides the changes he had made', Montesquieu continued, 'which were so abrupt, so unusual, and so unheard of, he wanted to remove the intermediary ranks and abolish the political bodies; he was dissolving the monarchy by his chimerical repayments and seemed to want to buy back the constitution itself' (II.4, p. 19).

Montesquieu's recurring criticisms of Law's financial scheme, with which his writings are peppered, were part of a wider concern about the politically destabilising effects of paper credit, which in turn constituted one aspect of his interest in the movements and stability of currencies. He specifically praised France's ancient laws for treating men of business with the distrust reserved for enemies (XI.18, p. 182). In this instance again, his point was not that France should be handicapped in the quest for wealth and the competition for it within what was the clearly growing phenomenon of international trade. The issue here was that nothing be undertaken without the moderation that could only be the outcome of a profound understanding of the many levels of interconnected economic, social, and political mechanisms involved. To continue with the question of the desirability of a commercial nobility, he called upon, amongst other sciences, social psychology, and the understanding of the benefits that could accrue to commerce and the whole nation from ensuring that while those in business could not be nobles, they could acquire noble rank (XX.20–2, pp. 349–50). What was needed was an awareness of the vanity of the French people and how, as argued in Mandeville's *Fable of the Bees* (1714), which Montesquieu cited, this vanity could be socially beneficial (XIX.9, p. 312). It required an appreciation of the true nature of the principle of monarchy, honour, as also of the nature of false honour, measured in terms of appearances, privileges, and outward distinctions, not real moral worth or a patriotic desire for the common good; such a sense of honour as characterised the aristocracy with its ambition and its craving for distinction. This realisation had to be matched, however, with another, namely that *false* honour gave monarchical government vitality, and moved all the parts of the body politic, linking all as 'each person works for the common good, believing he works only for his individual interests' (III.7, p. 27). All this and more was needed to avoid calamitous policies such as those that had led to the introduction of Law's scheme. *L'Esprit des lois* held up a mirror to princes in which they could see what they needed to know to act responsibly. That knowledge would have been formidable had Montesquieu only presented them with a typology and analysis of governments together with a number of histories, such as of money, commerce, conquest, wars, empires, and laws of punishment and rewards, from which various lessons could be drawn.

He did more, however, in asking them to endeavour to comprehend the relation of cause and effect between a multiplicity of generically different factors. Amongst these was one not usually present in works on the art of governance, namely women. Political theorists had spoken of their nature and place in society since antiquity. Many had written about illustrious women. Others, most notably Machiavelli, whom Montesquieu greatly admired, had warned princes of the dangers of maltreating them and used ancient history in support of his claim that dynasties and empires had been brought down by a single act of rape. Montesquieu wrote of the close connection between domestic servitude and specific forms of government, between the liberty of women and the liberty enjoyed in a nation as a whole, between their status and the luxury and commercial status of their country, as well as on changes in the laws concerning divorce, dowries, regal, and other rights of succession and inheritance. Even his own statement that 'everything is closely linked together: the despotism of the prince is naturally united with the servitude of women; the liberty of women, with the spirit of monarchy' does not fully convey the complexity of politics as he saw it, although some of the many authors who drew inspiration from him in their histories of women understood him well enough (XIX.15, p. 316). Were one to know one thing alone about a state, the precise condition of women in it, one would be able to deduce everything else about it (Tomaselli 2001b).

33

7   The spirit of the laws: the Gothic constitution

In so far as Montesquieu appealed to history, he was fully aware that, while essential to political understanding, it could in and of itself be as dangerous as it was vital. In any event, it was not an unproblematic pursuit. 'When one examines the records of our history and our laws', he admitted, 'it seems that everything is a sea and that the sea lacks even shores.' Yet, these 'cold, dry, insipid, and harsh' legal and historical books had to be read, devoured even (*SL*, XXX.11, p. 629). They had, however, to be read critically. They had to be read with just that astuteness which their reading was alleged to generate. When Montesquieu discussed the code known as the Establishments of St Louis, he offered a glimpse of the manner in which he interpreted these arid texts. He questioned how it had been composed and by whom; what the *intention* behind the work was – which, incidentally, Montesquieu argued had never been intended for the entire kingdom, thus finding another occasion to undermine the idea that wide-scale legal codification was inherent to the spirit of French laws (XXVIII.37, p. 589). He looked to the origins of the different laws brought together in the Establishments, which in this case mixed Roman laws with ancient French jurisprudence, something which rarely, if ever, met with Montesquieu's approval; he also queried its authenticity at various levels. In writing or rewriting history himself, Montesquieu wanted to avoid what he thought of as the obvious partiality of historians whose respective political motivation was transparent: 'The count of Boulainvilliers and the Abbé Dubos have each made a *system*, the one seeming to be a conspiracy against the Third Estate, and the other a conspiracy against the nobility (XXX.10, p. 627; my emphasis).[10]

The Abbé Dubos was a favourite object of Montesquieu's derision as a historian, having based his system 'on the wrong sources', drawn 'from poets and orators', and misinterpreted and distorted others as well as invented facts when it suited him (*SL*, XXVIII. 4, p. 537, XXX.12, pp. 631–2, XXX.17, p. 643). Towards the end of his work, Montesquieu even thought it necessary to devote the three last chapters of book XXX, 'On the Theory of Feudal Laws among the Franks in their Relation with the Establishment of the Monarchy', to the errors committed by Dubos; for, as Montesquieu remarked, he and Dubos were so diametrically opposed that only one of them could possibly be right. The dispute between them was whether the Franks had

---

10 For a summary of the *thèse nobiliaire* and of the *thèse royale*, see Ford 1953 and Keohane 1980, pp. 346–50.

entered Gaul as conquerors or whether, as Dubos saw it, they had been 'summoned by the peoples', and had simply taken the place and donned the mantle of the Roman emperors (XXX.24, p. 659). For Montesquieu, Clovis had truly conquered Gaul and duly subjugated it. Contrary to Dubos's claim, he insisted further that the Franks had a system of ranks, as did the Burgundians. They had also a complex judicial order, and early France had not been like Turkey, the eighteenth-century shorthand for despotism, an amorphous people under the rule of one sole authority (XXX.25, p. 668). Montesquieu went through the evidence that Dubos used and found it wanting in every respect.

Along with political bias and prejudice of one form or another, Montesquieu was also wary of the danger of anachronism. 'To carry back to distant centuries the ideas of the century in which one lives is of all sources of error the most fertile', he wrote (XXX.14, p. 636). In short, Montesquieu sought to establish a vantage point from which he, and legislators reading him, could be freed from the imaginative restrictions imposed not just by human nature but also by modernity. He said in his preface that greater general enlightenment would lessen the risk of ignorance and misconceptions in rulers. He clearly thought, however, that only the gifted few could intuit the general spirit of the nation and hence legislate wisely. This required in the first instance that they know their country's history from its very beginning, but, as his critique of both Boulainvilliers and Dubos made clear, it was essential that princes and law-makers generally be informed by reliable historians.

In the case of French legislators, this meant that they had to go back to the old French laws, for those laws contained the spirit of monarchy (*SL*, VI.10, p. 83). They had to read Tacitus and learn the ways of the first races (see Momigliano 1990, pp. 109–31). This would spell out how monarchy originated and developed from the Germanic nations which spread through the Roman Empire. Whilst in Germany the whole nation assembled, it became too dispersed to do so following their conquest of the Empire. They therefore carried their deliberation as a nation through representatives:

Here is the origin of Gothic government among us. It was at first a mixture of aristocracy and monarchy. Its drawback was that the common people were slaves; it was a good government that had within itself the capacity to become better. Giving letters of emancipation became the custom, and soon the civil liberty of the people, the prerogatives of the nobility and of the clergy, and the power of the kings, were in such concert that there has never been, I believe, a government on earth as well tempered as that of each part of Europe during the time that this government continued to exist; and it is remarkable that the corruption of the government of a conquering people should have formed the best kind of government men have been able to devise. (*SL*, XI.9, pp. 167–8)

Montesquieu was wont to speak of 'our fathers, the ancient Germans' and wrote of them with more than a degree of fondness (*SL*, XV.14, p. 243). This sentiment was one that we have seen evinced in his early writings. He admired their vitality and spiritedness, and thought they enjoyed liberty of a kind and to a degree unknown by any of the other many peoples discussed in his works, not least because a people that did not cultivate land, as he insisted they did not, had greater freedom. Moreover, their kings or chiefs had very limited powers, and the Franks in Germany had no king at all (XVIII.30). The '*germe*' or essence of the history of the 'first race' was that while they had vassals, they did not have fiefdoms, as they did not have land, but had companions and earned their glory on the battlefields (XXX.2–4, pp. 620–2). Had the Franks in conquering Gaul established fiefdoms everywhere, the king would have had the power of a Turkish sultan (XXX.5, pp. 622–3), a claim he identified with Dubos's position. Montesquieu insisted throughout that the Germans did not cultivate land; they were a pastoral people (XXX.6, p. 623). Most importantly, he tried to show that the barbarians were by no means lawless. They were barbarians in the sense that they were spirited and psychologically unsubdued, not in the sense that they were ignorant and lacking in rules of conduct. Indeed, their codes were very precise and included fixed fines, despite the fact that there was little money amongst them; every crime had its fixed penalty in kind. Interestingly, Montesquieu also argued that the initial impetus for regulated justice amongst the Germans was the protection of the *defendant* against the vengeance of the victim. It was to oblige the victim to accept reparation as decreed by the law (XXX.20, p. 651). The culprit paid the judicial cost since he benefited from it. Montesquieu explained much of early jurisprudence through the medium of this primordial intent.

To return to the origins of a people and comprehend the nature, context, and purpose of its jurisprudence from its infancy was the crucial knowledge necessary to prescribe laws in accordance with the spirit of a nation. This was essential because despotism could assume two different forms, in Montesquieu's view. It could manifest itself through the usurpation of power and the arbitrary will of one individual, to be sure, but it could also take the form of unbefitting laws. The first one he called 'real' despotism, consisting in a violent government; the other he labelled despotism 'of opinion', and said, it 'was felt when those who govern establish things that run counter to a nation's way of thinking' (*SL*, XIX.3, p. 309). Had Montesquieu only feared the one, he might conceivably be placed within the debate dividing the advocates of the *thèse nobiliaire* from those of the *thèse royale* (although he seemed to reject both positions in any case), but he did not worry only about the legitimacy of those making and executing laws, perhaps the predominant preoccupation of some of those most indebted to him, such as Rousseau. Montesquieu was concerned at least as much with the nature and form of the laws' content; or, to quote again the title of one of the final books, book XXIX, he was as anxious about 'the way to compose the laws' as about their authorship. It is in his effort to attend to the much more difficult, because less tangible, question of how this should be done that he distinguished himself from his immediate contemporaries and most political theorists ever since.

History, on his account, was the handmaiden of the legislator, and within it pride of place had to be given to the history of laws and everything relevant to their individual conception. This included a genuine study of mores and the manner in which laws followed mores and mores laws (*SL*, XIX.26, p. 325). It required an understanding of climate and geography. Legislators, moreover, had to be in a position to understand axioms of the kind provided, for instance, in Montesquieu's summary of his discussion of luxury, namely, that 'republics end in luxury; monarchies in poverty' (VII.4, p. 100). Again they had to know that a 'monarchical state should be of a medium size' (VIII.17, p. 125). They had to understand the history and fluctuations of currencies. They had to be aware of the dynamics of population growth and decline, and of the role of education and religion. They had to be sensitive to the status of women and know the limits of legislation. All this had to be mastered, and much more besides. Montesquieu was committed to the view that the material and human world could in principle be comprehended and that it was incumbent on us to undertake its study.

History also had to be used in a more traditional way, namely, to come to grips with human nature, and as a source of models of good governance and hence good princes. It taught moderation and also the importance of good fortune. To create a moderate government was a delicate task:

In order to form a moderate government, one must combine powers, regulate them, temper them, make them act; one must give one power a ballast, so to speak, to put it in a position to resist another; this is a masterpiece of legislation that chance rarely produces and prudence is rarely allowed to produce. (*SL*, V.14, p. 63)

This difficulty explained why, despite mankind's love of liberty and hatred of violence, most peoples lived under despotic regimes. A despotic government, Montesquieu wrote by way of contrast, 'leaps to view, so to speak; it is *uniform* throughout; as only passions are needed to establish it, and everyone is good enough for that' (*SL*, v.14, p. 63; my emphasis). Awareness and recognition of the force of the passions was indispensable. For it was essential to work with the passions and ensure that self-interest resulted in the common good. Moreover, self-awareness was important, for like Voltaire, Montesquieu thought laws 'always meet the passions and prejudices of the legislator', but he added that 'sometimes they pass through and are coloured; sometimes they remain there and are incorporated' (xxix.19, p. 618). It was 'a misfortune attached to the human condition, [that] great men who are moderate are rare' and that 'it is easier to find extremely virtuous people than extremely wise men' (xxviii.41, p. 595). Nevertheless, he singled out some wise men, and for all his emphasis on law, he had much to say about individuals. Despite the weight he gave to causal relations between the multitude of factors which made up the spirit of nations, he recognised that some rare individuals could intuit what was required of them to shape their political world. Of the men and women he singled out in his account, he lavished most praise on Charlemagne, who had managed to keep the nobility in check and made his children models of obedience. He made and enforced admirable laws:

His genius spread over all the parts of the empire. One sees in the laws of this prince a spirit of foresight that includes everything and a certain force that carries everything along . . . Vast in his plans, simple in executing them, he, more than anyone, had to a high degree the art of doing the greatest things with ease and the difficult ones promptly . . . Never did a prince better know how to brave danger; never did a prince better know how to avoid it. He mocked all perils, and particularly those which great conquerors almost always undergo; I mean conspiracies. This prodigious prince was extremely moderate; his character gentle, his manners simple; he loved to live among the people of his court . . . He regulated his expenditures admirably; he developed his domains wisely, attentively, and economically; the father of a family could learn from his laws how to govern his household. (xxxi.18, pp. 697–8)

Much could be said here by way of comparison and contrast between Montesquieu and those who from the Renaissance onwards had written like him about the virtues of great princes and the true nature of glory. In his commendation of Charlemagne's simplicity and his parsimony, this passage brings Fénelon's comparable praise of St Louis, for instance, particularly to mind. However, notwithstanding the great trials he overcame,

Charlemagne did not have to contend with what Montesquieu saw as the unique challenge faced by eighteenth-century princes. They had to comprehend the unprecedented nature of modernity, socially, militarily, and commercially (*SL*, XXI.21, pp. 392–3). Montesquieu did not simplify their task. On the contrary, he warned them, and all who might advise them, of the terrifying complexity of it all.[11]

11 For their comments on a draft of this chapter I would like to express my gratitude to Istvan Hont, as well as to Mark Goldie, Robert Tombs, and Robert Wokler.

2

The English system of liberty

MARK GOLDIE

1   The Revolution debate

In the winter of 1688 King James II was deposed. Within months of the offer of the crown to William III commentators sensed that a decisive shift had occurred in what it was possible to say in public about the nature of kingship. Remarking on a speech by a judge to the effect that 'kings are made by the people', Robert Harley declared that this 'would have been high treason eighteen months ago'.[1] The enthusiasts for the Revolution were clear about what had been achieved. The earl of Stamford told a grand jury that Britain had been liberated from 'tyranny and slavery *à la mode de France*' (*RLP*, I, p. 54).[2] Grateful contemplation of the 'wonderful and happy Revolution' of 1688 quickly spawned complacent and repetitive clichés about Britannic liberty which reverberated down the succeeding decades. They were echoed in Montesquieu's celebrated eulogy on the 'beautiful' system of the English (*SL*, XI.6). All Europe, declared the American James Otis in 1764, was 'enraptured with the beauties of the civil constitution of Great Britain' (*RLP*, III, p. 8).

Commentators agreed that the Revolution had replaced absolute with limited monarchy. The king was 'only a sort of sheriff to execute [parliament's] orders', observed the bishop of Derry in 1700 (qu. Rubini 1967, p. 202). Daniel Defoe told the readers of his newspaper *The Review* that the Revolution had thrown off the 'absurdities' of the divine right of kings and erected monarchy 'upon the foundation of parliamentary limitation' (30 Aug. 1705). The Revolution, it was said, had rebalanced the constitution into its rightful harmony, embracing the three classical forms of government – monarchy, aristocracy, and democracy – incarnated in king, Lords, and Commons. This became a ubiquitous shibboleth, whereas in

1 Historical Manuscripts Commission, *Portland*, III, p. 439.
2 In this chapter, *RLP* stands for *The Reception of Locke's Politics*, ed. Mark Goldie, 6 vols. (London, 1999).

pre-Revolution England it had been a seditious doctrine, formally condemned by Oxford University in its book-burning of 1683.

The Revolution was said to have conferred many benefits. It made freedom of the press a 'palladium' of liberty. It drew the sting of religious violence, quelling both the repressiveness of church hierarchies and the fanaticism of apocalyptic puritanism. All of this laudation was accompanied by a new historical commonplace that the Stuart century had been a train of 'tyrannical proceedings' and 'popish bigotry'. Such a view, conspicuous for example in Paul Rapin's popular *History of England* (1723–5), was endorsed by Viscount Bolingbroke in his *Remarks on the History of England* (1730–1), and it was not seriously challenged until the publication of David Hume's *History of England* in 1754–62 (Forbes 1975).

The belief that the light of liberty shone in Britain was increasingly given a manichean sharpness and a Protestant evangelical fervour under the pressure of the second Hundred Years War which Britain fought against France after 1688. 'Protestant, free, virtuous, united, Christian England' would withstand 'the whole force of slavish, bigoted, unchristian popery, risen up against her', announced the *London Daily Post* (18 Apr. 1739). The European foreigners' world of 'Bastilles and inquisitions' – as Henry Fielding put it – was scarcely a whit removed from the slavish despotism identified as endemic among 'Asiaticks' (Acherley 1727, p. 14; Lamoine 1992, p. 336). The English system of liberty was given cosmic significance when it was discovered to be implied in the very structure of God's government of the whole of creation, a theme explored in John Desaguliers's *The Newtonian System of the World the Best Model of Government* (1728) (Force 1985).

Even so, amid all this celebration, countervailing voices were no less emphatic, and the era after 1688 was not short of jeremiads on the fragility of liberty. Much of this chapter will be devoted to examining the gamut of protests that arose against the post-Revolution state. 'The late happy Revolution . . . was not so highly beneficial to us, as was by some expected', complained William Stephens (1696, p. 10). At the heart of these protests lay the dismal consequences that were said to have arisen from the doctrine and practice of the sovereignty of crown-in-parliament. Many came to believe that the absolute power of kings had merely been replaced by the absolute power of parliaments. In 1742 *The Craftsman* argued that 'a parliamentary yoke is the worst of all yokes, and that yoke is the only one we have, in reality, to fear'.

The problem of the Revolution constitution may be illustrated by an analogy. The great offices of state in England, such as the treasury or the chancellorship, were sometimes 'put into commission'. They retained all their powers, but were managed by a committee instead of a single person. After the Revolution the monarchy itself was, so to speak, put into commission. The crown retained its formal potency, but its powers were increasingly managed by a cabinet of ministers who commanded a majority in parliament. In the sphere of political doctrine, this development had a peculiar effect. The theory of sovereignty, fashioned for the defence of monarchs by Jean Bodin, Sir Robert Filmer, and Thomas Hobbes, and vaunted by Civil War Royalists in the 1640s and by high Tories in the 1680s, was transmuted into the dogma of the supremacy of the Westminster parliament, which was then handed down by Revolution Whigs and Revolution Tories to the legal positivists of the nineteenth century, such as John Austin and Albert Dicey. Every state must have a power that is 'absolute, omnipotent, uncontrollable, arbitrary, despotic': this 'is called the sovereign', and in Britain the sovereign is parliament. Such was William Paley's summation of eighteenth-century verities in 1785 (Paley 1860, p. 136). According to a tract of 1696, 'nothing is impossible in England to a parliament' (Anon. 1696, p. 12). Thus the Revolution had proved Hobbes right, for he had been careful to say that absolute sovereignty might as readily lie in a corporate body as in a single person.

As a consequence of the speedy adoption after 1688 of the idea of absolute parliamentary supremacy, the anxieties of those who were sceptical of the powers exercised by the English state came to focus on the tendency for the crown-in-parliament to be managed by a 'junto' of ministers and courtiers, England's 'Venetian oligarchy', which was armed with immense powers of patronage and purse. Baron d'Holbach observed in 1765 that the English state achieved through patronage what the French state achieved through despotism. The crucial issue became the relationship between overweening executive power on the one hand, and the rights of the wider political community, both within parliament and outside it, on the other. Simultaneously, however, there also emerged a vigorous defence of the legitimacy of executive control in a parliamentary system of liberty. Accordingly, the central theme in post-Revolution political thought is the dialogue between a dominant doctrine of parliamentary sovereignty, coupled with a doctrine of the efficacy of executive power, and a broad-based culture of opposition which challenged those ideas. The political culture of opposition took many forms: a dynastic, Jacobite revanche on behalf of the hereditary right of the fallen House of Stuart; an ecclesiastical rejection of secular supremacy over the church; a repudiation of metropolitan empire by peripheral states and colonies, particularly Scotland and Ireland, and later North America; a theory of popular sovereignty that placed supremacy directly in the community instead of in parliament; and a quasi-republican demand for the wholesale devolution of central executive power. Each of these oppositional voices will be surveyed here.[3]

2   The Allegiance Controversy and the Jacobites

The problem of the 'parliamentary yoke' was not, however, immediately apparent in the aftermath of the Revolution. The first task of the friends and enemies of the Revolution was to vindicate or repudiate the new regime itself. The language of the Allegiance Controversy of 1689–91 belonged firmly to the political theory of resistance bred in the European Reformation and its wars of religion.[4] The Calvinists of late sixteenth-century France and Scotland had declared decisively in favour of a right of revolution against tyrants, and that claim had subsequently been reiterated by defenders of the English rebellion of the 1640s. This tradition was invoked once again in 1689, when Philippe du Plessis Mornay's *Vindication against Tyrants* (1579) and George Buchanan's *Rights of the Kingdom of Scotland* (1579), together with Philip Hunton's *Treatise of Monarchy* (1643), and John Milton's *Tenure of Kings and Magistrates* (1649), were all republished. John Locke's *Two Treatises of Government*, published in the autumn of 1689, recapitulated that tradition. Meanwhile, more historically minded Whigs elaborated on the depositions of the medieval kings Edward II and Richard II. This broad stream of ideas also inspired those few republicans, like the former Leveller, John Wildman, who believed that the moment of 'dissolution' that occurred when James II fled should be seized to deprive kingship of virtually all its powers. In *Some Remarks upon Government* (1689), Wildman envisaged a gentry commonwealth in which magistrates, army officers, clergy, and officials in town and parish would all be elected by particular constituencies rather than appointed from above by the crown (Goldie 1980a).

Yet the events of 1688–9 were not only justified in terms of the Calvinist theory of revolution. It was vital for the success of the new regime that the Revolution was portrayed in more moderate and ambiguous terms. This

---

3 For contrasting surveys of British political thought in this period see Clark 1994a; Dickinson 1970; Goldsmith 1994; Gunn 1983; Ihalainen 1999; Kenyon 1977; Phillipson 1993a; Pocock 1985, 1993a. See also ch. 11 below.

4 On the political thought of the Allegiance Controversy see Goldie 1977, 1980b, 1991a; Kenyon 1977; Nenner 1995; Straka 1962; Worden 1991. For Leibniz's role see Jolley 1975; Riley 1973.

was partly because the event resembled less a domestic rebellion than an invasion by a foreign prince, and crucially because of the need to placate the Tories who were inured to the doctrine of 'passive obedience and non-resistance' and to abhorrence of the 'king-killing doctrines' they associated with puritans and Jesuits. The need to assuage the troubled consciences of conservatives ensured that the Allegiance Controversy became chiefly an exercise in casuistry: the resolving of conscientious scruples by the application of general moral principles to equivocal practical contingencies. The matter was made pressing by the imposition of a new oath of allegiance to King William and Queen Mary, demanded of those who had previously solemnly sworn fealty to James II. Once again, an earlier debate was invoked, that surrounding the Engagement Controversy of 1649, when people had been required to swear allegiance to the English republic in the aftermath of the execution of Charles I. Anthony Ascham's *Of the Confusions and Revolutions of Government* (1649) was republished, advising stoical acquiescence to power and the dispositions of divine providence.

A theory of the right of revolution was unpalatable to many, perhaps most, who confronted the enormity of the Revolution, and a series of redescriptions of the events of 1688–9 avoided the necessity for such a doctrine. The claim that James II had abdicated by his flight to France circumvented the claim that the nation had a right to depose its monarch.[5] The description of the Revolution as a just war waged by one sovereign prince against another likewise bypassed the notion that subjects could overthrow their monarchs. The principle of hereditary right was protected by the fiction that the newborn son of James II, the prince of Wales, was an impostor, smuggled into the queen's bedchamber in a warming pan. Hence, the rightful heir of James was his elder daughter Mary who, in a judicious invention of a dual monarchy in 1689, was enthroned alongside her husband William of Orange. A yet further device for assuaging consciences was the drawing of a distinction between *de jure* and *de facto* rulers. This sidestepped the question of dynastic legitimacy and allowed for a provisional allegiance to be paid to the monarch 'in possession'. Such allegiance was sanctioned by the new oath of allegiance, which delicately omitted the traditional designation of the monarch as 'rightful and lawful'.

Various intellectual resources were required to sustain these positions. The account of the nature of allegiance offered by the distinguished jurist

5 However, Slaughter 1981 argues that 'abdicate' was often used to mean a thing *done to* the king. An example is Toland: 'James II was justly abdicated . . . because he was an enemy of the people' (Toland 1697, p. 14) Cf. Miller 1982.

Sir Edward Coke and the oath-taking casuistry of the theologian Robert Sanderson were called in aid. So also the laws of just war in Hugo Grotius's *On the Laws of War and Peace* (1625), which were skilfully deployed by Edmund Bohun in his *History of the Desertion* (1689) and by William King in his *State of the Protestants of Ireland* (1691), to show that William of Orange was a legitimate conqueror of James II, but not of the peoples of England and Ireland. No less valuable was the formula provided by Hobbes in *Leviathan* (1651) that allegiance is owed to whichever power has the capacity to protect us. Isaac Newton, MP for Cambridge University, was one of those who found the Hobbesian formula persuasive: 'Allegiance and protection are always mutual and therefore when King James ceased to protect us we ceased to owe him allegiance' (Newton 1959, p. 10). It was a thesis which was vulnerable to the charge that it opportunistically embraced power without right. Its most notorious exponent was the high Tory clergyman, William Sherlock, who wrote a series of tracts defending allegiance to a *de facto* regime and was rewarded with ecclesiastical promotion for his conversion to the Revolution. Despite protesting in one of his title pages that he was not 'asserting the principles of Mr Hobbes', he nevertheless attracted a tide of accusations that he had resorted to naked 'Hobbism' (Sherlock 1691).

All this equivocation saved England – though not Ireland or Scotland – from a new civil war, for it bonded Tories to the Revolution. To hardline Whigs it was evasive nonsense: for them only a crystalline theory of revolution would do. They – Locke among them – pressed for an enhanced oath of allegiance, with the 'rightful and lawful' clause reinstated. At the opposite end of the political spectrum, Jacobites and Nonjurors also judged that Tory casuistry amounted to hypocritical apostasy from old Royalist principles. They categorically repudiated the Revolution and upheld the dynastic claim of James II and his heirs. Such tracts as Abednego Seller's *History of Passive Obedience* (1689) were laments for an Anglican Royalist catechism now brutally betrayed by the Revolution Tories.

The Jacobites sustained a powerful ideological tradition until their decisive military defeat on the battlefield of Culloden in Scotland in 1746. In large measure, Jacobite political theory was a direct continuation of the absolutist doctrines that had been taught on behalf of the House of Stuart throughout the seventeenth century. It was a *mélange* of Bodin's idea of monarchical sovereignty, Sir Robert Filmer's account of the patriarchal origins of kingship, and scriptural defences of the subject's duty of Christ-like passive obedience. Its cardinal claims were that the authority conferred by God upon Adam, the first husband, father, and king, was the archetype of all legitimate human authority; that the hereditary right of royal succession was unimpeachable by any human institution; that every state must have a sovereign authority, which could not be mixed or divided or shared; and that St Paul in the Epistle to the Romans had insisted that 'the powers that be are ordained of God' and that 'he that resists shall receive damnation' (Romans 13:1). These were doctrines which were fulsomely expressed week after week in Charles Leslie's influential journal *The Rehearsal* during Queen Anne's reign in the early 1700s.[6]

Such ideas were, however, far from being unalterably fixed in an idiom established by King James I and Sir Robert Filmer early in the seventeenth century, for it was an ideology capable of reformulation for Enlightenment audiences. Revision might take the form of a use of Cartesian logic, in the elaborate 'lemma', 'propositions', and 'axioms' to be found in Matthias Earbery's *Elements of Policy, Civil and Ecclesiastical, in a Mathematical Method* (1716), or in the (almost Kantian) deductivism of George Berkeley's *Passive Obedience* (1712), in which non-resistance was demonstrated to be a logical entailment of the idea of sovereignty. Alternatively, it could take the form of fictional allegories depicting the education of a virtuous patriot prince. These took their inspiration from Fénelon's *Télémaque* (1699) and the most notable of them was Andrew Ramsay's *Voyages of Cyrus* (1727). Moreover, the Jacobites became adept at appropriating the language of liberty against oppression. A rich popular culture of Jacobitism arose, expressed in signs and symbols, in martyrology, and in riotous charivari against post-Revolution 'tyranny'. For decades the Jacobite cause became a vehicle for resentment against the Revolution regime, against 'Dutch' and Hanoverian taxes and soldiery, and the suppression of civil liberties. There was a persistent strain of what may be termed 'Whig Jacobitism', beginning with the Quaker William Penn, who remained loyal to James II because he had conferred religious toleration on Protestant Dissenters, and continuing through those factions at the Jacobite Court in exile which were willing to champion popular rights and civil liberties against the post-Revolution state. It was even possible for Jacobite newspapers in the 1710s and 1720s to make use of Locke, by turning Whig arguments against the Whig state. A cartoon of 1749 depicted the Jacobite claimant Prince Charles (the 'Young Pretender') studiously reading in a library, with 'Locke' among the books on the shelves. Jacobitism was, therefore, by no means merely a repository for the atavistic

---

6 Filmerian patriarchalism had several afterlives, for example in the reaction against Tom Paine and French revolutionary doctrines in the 1790s, and in the anti-capitalist defence of slave society in the Southern United States in the 1850s (Bowles 1798; Fitzhugh 1854).

or nostalgic defence of divine right monarchy – and, as this example shows, the reception of Locke proved a complex phenomenon.[7]

3   The reception of Locke

The pre-eminent influence of Locke's *Two Treatises of Government* (1689) in post-Revolution political thought was once a conventional textbook wisdom. His book was taken to be the classic apologia for the Revolution, the encapsulation of Whig doctrine. Locke was said to have filled the vacuum left by the collapse of the 'divine right of kings'. Modern scholarship has drastically revised this picture, such that Lockean political thought now seems a fugitive and elusive presence, at least before the 1760s. There are several reasons for this revision. First, the discovery in the 1950s that the *Two Treatises* was written around 1679–82 undermined the possibility that Locke could have written his book as an apology for a revolution that had yet to occur. Secondly, Locke kept his authorship a secret until his death in 1704, and his fame, which lay chiefly with his *Essay concerning Human Understanding* (1689), did not for some while attach to the *Two Treatises*. Thirdly, the radicalism of Locke's doctrine of the dissolution of government, his devolution of political power to the people, and the association of his book with the extreme Whigs, rendered the book an embarrassment amidst so cautious and compromising a Revolution. Fourthly, such attention as the *Two Treatises* began to receive was often profoundly hostile. Charles Leslie's assault in *The Rehearsal* signalled the resilience of patriarchalist Toryism, an outlook by no means confined to doctrinaire Jacobites. Even when Locke did acquire renown, he tended to be part of an imprecise litany of Whig political virtue, standing alongside John Milton, James Harrington, Algernon Sidney, Marchamont Nedham, John Somers, James Tyrrell, and Benjamin Hoadly. Lastly, large doubts have been raised about the supposition that theories of 'natural right' and 'social contract' constituted the only available languages of political understanding in the eighteenth century. The political arguments of that century, we have come to see, were conducted in languages of, *inter alia*, political economy, empire, ancient constitutionalism, natural sociability, and civic humanism; and none of these characterise Locke.

---

7 On Jacobite political thought see Berman 1986; Chapman 1984; Cherry 1950; Clark 1994a; Cruickshanks 1982; Erskine-Hill 1975, 1979, 1998; Henderson 1952; McLynn 1985; Monod 1989; Pittock 1991, 1994; Sack 1993; Szechi 1997.

This revisionism is salutary, but it is overstated. It is clear that in the first decade of the eighteenth century 'Locke on government' did in fact achieve distinctive status. In 1703 Leslie was provoked to his assault by the reputation of 'the great L—k' who, dangerously, 'makes the consent of every individual necessary' (*RLP*, II, p. 62). In 1709 a cartoon depicted the Whig polemicist Benjamin Hoadly at his writing desk with 'Locke on government' on his bookshelf. By 1716 the *Two Treatises* was quoted in parliament. Locke's influence was facilitated by informal means of transmission. The anonymous *Vox Populi, Vox Dei* (1709) was a bestselling anthology comprising extracts from Whig-approved texts, including the *Two Treatises*. Extracts from the *Two Treatises* also appeared in John Toland's *Anglia Libera* (1701) and elsewhere. Some early readers of the *Two Treatises* saw it as a handbook for political education, designed to wean the gentry elite from the dangerous (and largely clerical) absurdities of pre-Revolution doctrine. It represented a guide to 'polite' citizenship, free of the sycophantic dogmas of absolutist Court society. This role is explicit in William Atwood's *Fundamental Constitution of the English Government* (1690) which urged that people should 'take every morning some pages of the *Two Treatises of Government*, for an effectual catholicon against nonsense and absurdities' (*RLP*, I, p. 39). The *Two Treatises* continued to be an instrument of instruction against the follies of the 'divine right of kings' in Hoadly's works and in John Shute Barrington's *The Revolution and Anti-Revolution Principles Stated* (1714).

In the meantime, the *Two Treatises* entered a tradition of academic consideration. As early as 1702–3, Gershom Carmichael was using it as a counterpoint to Samuel Pufendorf in his lectures at the University of Glasgow (see ch. 10 below). On the Continent of Europe, the book became established in the canon of natural jurisprudence and was extensively used by Jean Barbeyrac in the annotations to his edition of Pufendorf's *On the Law of Nature and Nations* (1706; English trans., 1717). By 1725 Locke's book was being put to use in North America. Citing the fifth chapter of the Second Treatise, with its argument that labour creates property rights, John Bulkley argued against native American claims to property in American land, on the ground that, through the natives' lack of tillage – they were mere roaming hunter-gatherers – their lands remained common wastes until cultivated by European labour (*RLP*, VI, pp. 191–223).

Locke's influence as a political theorist, moreover, was not confined to the *Two Treatises*. Of perhaps unexpected importance was his *Some Considerations of the Consequences of the Lowering of Interest*, published in 1692, which was frequently cited on fiscal questions, and on the relationship between land and trade. Viscount Bolingbroke, in his anti-Walpolean newspaper *The Crafts-man*, quoted it in a discussion of the importance of maintaining the slave trade with America: 'the judicious Mr Locke' had warned that a trade once lost is hard to retrieve (*RLP*, VI, pp. 229–30). Locke's *Essay concerning Human Understanding* was seen by both its friends and critics to carry political implications embedded in its epistemology, its moral philosophy, and its implied ecclesiology. Locke's reputation was drawn thereby into a vortex of polemic about the claims of Christianity as well as claims to authority by churches and priesthoods. In 1707 Locke was denounced from a London pulpit, in a sermon to commemorate King Charles the Martyr, as an 'agent of darkness', his 'principles fit for nothing, but to ruin kingdoms and commonwealths, to overturn churches, to extirpate Christianity' (Milbourne 1707, p. 11). It was a reading probably provoked by Matthew Tindal's shocking (and, to its critics, inaptly titled) *Rights of the Christian Church* (1706) which invoked Locke in mounting a comprehensive assault on the powers of the clergy.

More generally, it is clear that Locke was read eclectically, so that he was not confined to a discourse of 'natural law' and 'social contract'. The distinctions drawn by modern scholars between supposedly discrete political discourses, for example between the natural rights, the civic humanist, and the ancient constitutionalist traditions, do not do justice to the syncretism constantly found in post-Revolution political writing. James Tyrrell, in his compendium of Whig attitudes, *Bibliotheca politica* (1692–4), married the *Two Treatises* to a Tacitean and legal-historical vision of Saxon liberties and the ancient constitution, although Locke had himself shown little interest in historically grounded theories of liberty. This helps to explain an apparent oddity about Hume's critique of social contract theory: he had in mind not simply Locke, but a composite Whig doctrine, which treated the idea of contract as a historical as well as an ahistorical phenomenon (Buckle and Castiglione 1991; Thompson 1977). Another type of eclecticism is found among authors whose primary intellectual resources lay among the Greeks and Romans. Walter Moyle, writing in the 1690s, applauded the *Two Treatises* in the midst of an account of the hero-lawgiver Lycurgus of Sparta, not an approach to political reflection that Locke himself had adopted (*RLP*, I, p. 291). Much the most complex mixture can be found in John Trenchard and Thomas Gordon's *Cato's Letters* (1720–3), which seamlessly drew upon Lockean natural rights as well as upon the canon of Roman republican virtue (Hamowy 1990). This kind of eclecticism was to be found throughout the eighteenth century, for example in James Burgh's *Political Disquisitions* of 1774–5, one of the most popular political textbooks of its era (Zebrowski 1991).

Among political theorists of the late twentieth century, particularly in North America, there has been a tendency to assume a radical incompatibility between the 'liberal individualist' tradition, preoccupied with private rights and personified by Locke, and the 'civic humanist' tradition, preoccupied with public virtue and personified by James Harrington, the republican theorist of the 1650s. The fate of modern rights theory is accordingly made to depend on establishing whether Locke was central or marginal in the eighteenth century and beyond. He was not, however, understood in so narrowly partisan a way in the eighteenth century; his influence was more protean and indeterminate.

It will be recalled that a central paradox of the post-Revolution English state was that the vaunted 'system of liberty' stood alongside extensive powers claimed for the authority of the crown-in-parliament and for the crown's ministers who managed parliament. For many, the claim of 'liberty' thereby came to seem hollow. Three distinct attempts to limit, in theory and in practice, the sovereign authority of the post-Revolution state can be identified: first, claims made on behalf of the autonomy of the church; secondly, claims made in defence of the autonomy of Ireland and Scotland; and thirdly, claims on behalf of the collective body of the people outside parliament. All were ideologically potent, but none of them was politically successful during this era. The same may be said of a fourth claim, on behalf of women against men.

4   The claims of the church

The Lutheran view that the government of the church belonged to the civil magistrate had long been challenged within the Church of England by a quasi-Catholic claim that the church possessed an authority independent of the secular state. The church, especially its bishops, claimed to derive authority by succession from the Apostles, to whom Christ had entrusted His church. In High Church Anglicanism this entailed the indefeasibility of episcopal authority, and the untrammelled right of the church to punish heretics and schismatics in order to preserve the truths and unity of the Christian church. All this amounted to a forceful set of limitations on what earthly rulers were permitted to do in governing Christ's church.

The Revolution was a terrible blow to orthodox churchmen.[8] Hitherto the church had had the means to achieve religious uniformity and to punish

---

8 On post-Revolution theories of church and state see Bennett 1975; Clark 1985; Cragg 1964; Every 1956; Goldie 1982; Stephen 1876; Taylor 1992; Young 1998.

'schismatics' through coercive laws, and it had in particular sought to crush puritan Nonconformity. The Toleration Act of 1689 liberated the Protestant Nonconformists, or 'Dissenters', who rapidly achieved a prominence in English society and politics. An unprecedented religious pluralism, for Protestants if not for Catholics, was now enshrined in statute. The Revolution entailed a whole series of further blows to the church. The spread of Arian, Socinian, deist, and 'atheist' heresies by means of a freer press, the legal establishment of a rival, Presbyterian church in Scotland, and the peremptory deposition by the secular state of the English 'Nonjuring' bishops – those who refused to swear allegiance to the Revolution – all served to provoke a militant High Church movement that aimed to recapture the lost authority of the church. Francis Atterbury's *Letter to a Convocation Man* (1697), a litany of the church's tribulations, demanded the summoning, and free conduct, of Convocation, the church's parliament. When Convocation was allowed to convene in 1701, it proceeded to vex the secular rulers by pronouncing episcopacy to be by 'divine right' and by condemning several authors for heresy.

High Churchmen and Nonjurors asserted the Catholicity of the church, said to be universal and not merely national. The 'Keys of the Kingdom' given by Christ (Matthew 16:18), which were the keys of doctrine and discipline, were entrusted to spiritual and not to secular governors. Episcopacy was ordained by Christ, so that modes of church government were not a matter of temporal utility. Deploying Aristotelian and Johannine terminology, High Church theologians described the church as a corporation with a distinct *telos*, a communion or *koinonia*, which had an inherent right of public assembly. The encroachments of the civil magistrate were seen to pose as great a threat to the church as the pope of Rome. Charles Leslie's *Case of the Regale* (1700) attacked secular power as fulsomely as he attacked papal power. 'The Western church', he pronounced, 'was (like her master) crucified betwixt the usurpations of the Pontificate on the one side, and the Regale on the other'.[9] Henry Dodwell likewise protested that the Revolution state would 'destroy the very being of the church as a society', and Matthias Earbery feared that the Christian creed might become 'as subject to a repeal as the Game Act' (Dodwell 1692, p. 3; Earbery 1716, p. 49). Similar fears were articulated in such works as George Hickes's *Constitution of the Catholick Church* (1716) and William Law's *Three Letters to the Bishop*

---

9 Leslie 1700, p. 161. Leslie was alluding to the fact that Jesus Christ was crucified between two thieves. 'Regale' meant kingly rights.

of Bangor (1717–19). All these authors detected the influence of Hobbesian Erastianism in the Revolution doctrine of the church, foreshadowing a ruthless subordination of religion to secular utility and parliamentary whim.

The contrasting Low Church view of the church's powers was put in William Wake's *Authority of Christian Princes over their Ecclesiastical Synods Asserted* (1697), which countered Atterbury's constitutional claims for Convocation. Wake's image of a godly prince summoning church councils over which he would preside and determine their agendas derived from the intellectual tradition of Marsilius of Padua, the late medieval conciliarists, and the 'caesaropapal' arguments advanced by the apologists for the Henrician Reformation. In the circumstances of the post-Revolution English state, the 'godly prince', Wake argued, was now parliament.

The final phase of the contest over Convocation is known as the Bangorian Controversy (1717–20), named after the Whig bishop of Bangor, Hoadly, whose *Nature of the Kingdom, or Church, of Christ* (1717) provoked 400 tracts in response. Hoadly went much further than Wake in his attack on the independent powers of the church, arguing that Christ 'left behind him no visible human authority', so that any claim to it was a dangerous denial of civil authority. Hoadly all but dissolved the church as a corporate body: it was no other than the secular commonwealth at prayer, and the clergy were, in effect, civil servants. Between the state and private conscience Hoadly found no role for an autonomous church. He was duly condemned by Convocation for tenets tending 'to destroy the being of those powers, without which the church, as a society, cannot subsist'. In order to rescue Hoadly, the Whig government abruptly closed down Convocation. It did not meet again for more than a century (*RLP*, v, pp. 143ff).

A similarly devastating dissolution of the church's claims occurred in Matthew Tindal's *Rights of the Christian Church* (1706). Both Hoadly and Tindal wavered between a Lockean doctrine of the separation of church from state, and an Erastian and Hobbesian insistence on the secular magistrate's supreme authority in ecclesiastical matters. Arguably they, along with the deist John Toland, envisaged not so much the reduction of the church to a private voluntary association – within civil society, having no part of the state – but rather inclined towards turning the church into a civil religion that would be national and public, yet open and tolerant. A civil religion would inculcate the social virtues and would be cleansed of clericalism and credal dogmatism.

In his *Alliance between Church and State* (1736), William Warburton made a signal attempt at a theoretical reconciliation between those (Catholics) who made 'the state a creature of the church' and those (Erastians) who made 'the church a creature of the state'. In an ingenious reworking of contract theory, he proposed that the original autonomy of the church, 'independent of civil government', was superseded by a contract or 'free convention' which the church entered into with the state. This contract was coterminous with the civil contract that established the state, and hence it could be found 'in the same archive with the famous original compact between magistrate and people'. It was a contract of mutual benefit by which the church 'shall apply its utmost influence in the service of the state; and the state shall support and protect the church'. Warburton stipulated that the contract dictated that there should be freedom of worship for all Protestants, but that the Test Acts, the laws which preserved to members of the Anglican state-church a monopoly of public office, should remain in place. With stunning bathos, he thus discovered eternal underpinnings for contemporary English arrangements, pronouncing that 'an established religion and a Test law [rest] upon the fundamental principles of the law of nature'. Warburton was singled out for comment by Rousseau in his chapter on civil religion in *The Social Contract* (1762), and Warburton's own revised edition of his book responded with a critique of Rousseau's deism and the Frenchman's taking of liberty to 'ridiculous excess' (*RLP*, v, pp. 194, 206, 215, 220–1, 224, 238, 274; *SC*, iv.8, p. 146, also ii.7, p. 72; see Taylor 1992).

Warburton's narrowly juridical approach to the supposed 'alliance' between church and state seemed to leave civil rulership devoid of god-liness, and the church, after the 'alliance' was made, at the mercy of the state. For many churchmen, a more satisfying thesis could be found in Edmund Gibson's *Codex Juris Ecclesiastici Anglicani* (1713), a painstakingly judicious account of the union of the two societies, ecclesiastical and secu-lar, but one that was more deliberately evangelical in the weight it gave to the state as a propagator of Christian truth and morality, and more insistent upon the authority of the clergy. The book made possible a rapprochement between Whig politics and Anglican churchmanship. Gibson and Warbur-ton set patterns for later eighteenth-century variations on the theme of the semi-detached alliance of church and state, which are to be found, for example, in Sir William Blackstone and William Paley.

A more determined critique of the idea of a state church is to be found among the Dissenters, exemplified by the introduction to the second part of Edmund Calamy's *Defence of Moderate Nonconformity* (1704) and John Shute Barrington's *The Rights of Protestant Dissenters* (1704–5). These treatises weaned Presbyterianism from its lingering aspiration to displace Anglicanism as the national church, and from the more intolerant traditions within Calvinism. They endorsed denominational pluralism, detaching religion from the state by dwelling on the Lockean conception of the church as a voluntary society. Their insistence that a church was no more than a free association within civil society ensured that 'Locke on toleration' increasingly came to be seen as a partisan defence of Protestant Dissent (Bradley 1990; Haakonssen 1996b; Lincoln 1938; Watts 1978).

Beyond the boundary of formal ecclesiology, the drive to make priests civil, to strip them of their pretensions to public authority, became a strong cultural imperative in what may legitimately be called the early English Enlightenment. In some circles, post-Revolution sensibility was deeply anticlerical and the new term 'priestcraft' entered the vocabulary with some suddenness during the 1690s. Exposing the historical and anthropological roots of the sham of priestly power became an objective even of popular newspapers, such as *The Independent Whig* (1720–1), as well as of deistic treatises and Whig sermons such as those collected in Richard Baron's *Pillars of Priestcraft and Orthodoxy Shaken* (1768). There was no more outrageous or persistent enemy of clerical authority than John Toland, whose *Christianity not Mysterious* (1696) left little room for a sacerdotal caste.[10]

5 The claims of Ireland and Scotland

There was no British state before the Anglo-Scottish Union of 1707 and no United Kingdom before the British–Irish Union of 1800. In the seventeenth century there was a union only of crowns, for there were three kingdoms, three parliaments, and three privy councils, under a single monarch. At the same time of course the theoretical equality of the Three Kingdoms was belied by the predominance of English power and the claims of the English parliament. For England, the overriding consideration after 1688 was the need to prevent the regal union from fracturing. Whereas the Revolution in England was bloodless, Ireland had to be reconquered at the Battle of the Boyne in 1690 in order to defeat James II, and Scotland likewise posed a dynastic threat through repeated Jacobite insurrections that were marked in blood from the Battle of Killiecrankie in 1689 to that of Culloden in 1746. Both kingdoms also offered opportunities for France to expand its theatres of warfare, during what were, in effect, the Wars of the British Succession,

10 On Toland and anticlericalism see Berman 1975; Champion 1992, 2003; Daniel 1984; Force 1985; Goldie 1993a; Harrison 1990; Jacob 1981; O'Higgins 1970; Redwood 1976; Sullivan 1982.

which began in 1689. Nor were the Catholics and Jacobites of Ireland and Scotland the only recalcitrants, for Protestant patriots in both kingdoms also resented English overlordship. In consequence, and despite the military crushing of insurrection, there were vigorous movements which sought to limit or dissolve the power of the metropole, of the English state. When such movements carried their nations to the verge of complete independence from England – in Scotland in the early 1700s and in Ireland in the 1790s – they were trumped by imperial incorporation into the English state, achieved in the Unions of 1707 and 1800. What had once been only a union of crowns became thereby a union of parliaments and states.

In protest against London's control of its legislative agenda, the Irish parliament of 1692 asserted its right to initiate bills for taxation. Anger was soon heightened by the English parliament's legislative assault on the Irish woollen industry, seen as a commercial threat to England's vital textile trade. This provoked William Molyneux's influential *Case of Ireland* (1698), which reached a tenth edition by 1782.[11] Molyneux's book was a protest against metropolitan policies, fashioned into a federal interpretation of the regal union. Ireland, he insisted, was equal in status to England, a 'separate and distinct kingdom' with its own supreme parliament, not subject to English jurisdiction. Although Molyneux's book has sometimes been interpreted as a textbook of 'colonial nationalism', he was no modern 'nationalist', having no interest in cultural identity or in breaking the regal connection. As a member of the Protestant settler 'Ascendancy', he ignored the Catholic majority of Ireland, who did not begin to find their own patriot voice until the 1750s, in Charles O'Connor's writings. Molyneux took for granted a common inheritance of ancestral English liberties 'enjoyed under the crown of England for above five hundred years'. In fact, he was not necessarily averse to an incorporating union as a solution to Ireland's unequal treatment, a union by which Irish members would be elected to an imperial parliament in London, provided that such a union would indeed bring full economic equality. This was a case more fully explored in Henry Maxwell's *Essay towards an Union of Ireland with England* (1703). Much later, when the Irish parliament did achieve considerably greater autonomy, Molyneux's remark in favour of full union was suppressed in the edition of his book published in 1782. Even so, *regal* union was still not questioned, and Molyneux's federal solution dominated Irish 'patriot' discourse throughout the century, until

11 On Molyneux and Irish political thought see Bartlett 1995; Boyce *et al.* 1993, 2001; Eccleshall 1993; Gargett and Sheridan 1999; J. Hill 1995; Kearney 1959; Kelly 1988, 1989a, 1989b; Ohlmeyer 2000; Simms 1982, 1986. For the broader pattern of English imperial ideology see Armitage 2000b.

Wolfe Tone, under the influence of French revolutionary principles, called for a fully independent and republican Ireland in 1798.

Molyneux argued that the Irish people had made a free contract with the English crown – not the English state – and that no laws could be introduced without their consent. His book made striking use of Locke's 'incomparable' *Two Treatises of Government*. Quoting Locke, he asserted that upon 'equality in nature is founded that right which all men claim, of being free from all subjection to positive laws, till by their own consent they give up their freedom, by entering into civil societies'. In particular, the 'patriots of liberty and property' will abhor 'taxing us without our consent' (*RLP*, I, pp. 222, 225, 272, 280). This invocation of Locke's remarks in paragraphs 140 and 142 of the Second Treatise provided a prototype of the use to which the *Two Treatises* would be put by colonial rebels in North America in the 1760s. Molyneux's book was cited in Boston newspapers, and there were copies in the libraries of Thomas Jefferson and James Madison.

In the late 1690s, John Cary and William Atwood, defenders of the English Whig ministry, responded to Molyneux with an aggressive assertion of England's imperial rights, often borrowing Tory arguments in so doing. Cary insisted that Ireland was 'a colony of England' by right of conquest, and that it had a parliament only by 'concession', not of right. The conquest of the Irish in the thirteenth century had aimed, in Roman manner, 'to civilise them into good manners and useful arts', out of 'barbarism and ignorance'. This rigorist approach to unitary statehood was buttressed by a remark that the contemporary German city-states were 'not exempt from . . . dependence' on the emperor, whatever measure of autonomy they were granted (Cary 1698, ep. ded.). Atwood was similarly unabashed in saying that Dublin was part of 'this empire' of England, in the same manner as any English provincial town. He offered a brutal reminder to Irish Protestants of the falsity of their position: 'if their consciences are squeamish let them renounce their right to the lands of the [Catholic] natives' (Atwood 1698, p. 44).

The English parliament formally condemned Molyneux's *Case of Ireland* as contrary to 'the subordination and dependence that Ireland hath . . . to the imperial crown of this kingdom'. It continued to legislate for Ireland and in 1720 passed a Declaratory Act describing Ireland as 'a dependent and subordinate kingdom'. Molyneux's tradition continued, notably in Jonathan Swift's *Drapier's Letters* (1724), which were a powerful assault on English overlordship. In his fifth letter, dedicated to Viscount Molesworth, Swift declared that, after 'long conversing with the writings of your lordship,

Mr Locke, Mr Molyneux, Col. Sidney, and other dangerous authors', he had derived the maxim 'that freedom consists in a people being governed by laws made with their own consent; and slavery in the contrary' (Swift 1939–68, x, pp. 85–7).

In the first decade of the eighteenth century, Scottish self-assertion took an even more dramatic turn. It was sponsored by a volatile combination of militant Presbyterians, republicans, and Jacobites. At the Revolution, in 1689, the Scottish parliament, more forthright than the English, resolved that James II had 'forfeited' his crown, for having 'invaded the fundamental constitution . . . and altered it from a legal limited monarchy, to an arbitrary and despotic power'. Rapidly thereafter, the parliament, previously carefully managed by the Stuart crown, seized the constitutional initiative, snubbed English ministers, and overthrew episcopacy, putting Presbyterianism in its place, thus formally establishing a different religion in the northern kingdom. During the 1690s, resentment against England was fuelled by famine, by the economic disruption of the French wars, and by the Darien disaster, in which a Scottish attempt to found a colony in Panama came to human and financial grief. The upshot was the remarkable parliament of 1703, which asserted a right to control Scotland's foreign policy and to settle the inheritance of the crown differently from England. The Scots, wrote Gilbert Burnet, exhibited 'a national humour of rendering themselves a free and independent kingdom' (qu. Ferguson 1964, p. 96).

Ideologically, the lead was taken by Scottish patriots who, if not literally republican, aimed to reduce the crown to a mere figurehead. They did not propose total separation of the kingdoms, but instead a loose federal relationship. Their ideas were expressed in purest form by Andrew Fletcher of Saltoun, hailed as the Cicero of the Scottish Country Party.[12] Fletcher was a powerful orator, a religious sceptic, and a professional rebel. Although today regarded as a key figure in the canon of Scottish nationalism, he was largely 'antique' in his commitments, preoccupied with the austere civic virtue of the Greek and Roman city-states. The Spartans, he noted, had maintained a free state for 800 years, and the Swiss cantons were the happiest and freest commonwealths in the world.

Fletcher pronounced Scotland to be 'more like a conquered province than a free independent people'. It must liberate itself from 'perpetual dependence upon another nation'. He inveighed against the 'horrid corruptions' of the

---

12 On Fletcher and Scottish political thought see Bowie 2003; Ferguson 1974; Goldie 1996; Hont 1983, 1990; Kidd 1993; Lenman 1992; Levack 1987; McPhail 1993; Phillipson 1993a; Robertson 1987b, 1993, 1994, 1995; Scott 1992.

English court, and its bleeding dry of the Scottish taxpayer. His own scheme of limitations on the crown was drastic in its wholesale transfer of powers to the Scottish parliament. There were to be annual parliaments, electing their own president; for every new peerage created there must be a new commoner member of parliament; all officers of state and judges were to be chosen by parliament; the royal veto on legislation was to be abolished; parliament would have a veto over foreign policy; there was to be no standing army without parliamentary consent; and a citizen militia was to be created. Fletcher proposed a final clause, the trump card: if the crown broke these rules, it was to be declared forfeit. Scotland's parliament would thereby become 'the most uncorrupted senate in Europe' (Fletcher 1997, pp. 133, 141, 162–3, 164–5).

For Fletcher, this reconstruction of civic institutions would be the prelude to a more general social and economic regeneration. He differed from other defenders of ancient virtue by refusing to resort to Arcadian sentimentalism, and he did not hold that commerce or market economics were harbingers of modern decadence and oppression. He roundly condemned Scotland's feudal institutions, and rackrenting by absentee noblemen. Despite advocating the promotion of commerce, he also rejected emulating England's commercial system. His *Account of a Conversation* (1704) is a profound analysis of the position of subordinate provinces in such a system. Poor countries suffer more than they gain from rich metropolises: they have the advantage of low wage costs, but the disadvantages of underdeveloped expertise, and the immobility of a rigid pre-modern social structure. A union, he said, would lead to England draining Scotland of its resources (Hont 1990).

In his utopian moments, Fletcher dreamed of a pan-European federation of small, free, and non-expansionary republics. Within the British Isles, London, Bristol, Exeter, York, Edinburgh, Stirling, Dublin, Cork, and Derry might become regional capitals. This was grounded on the Greek system of city-states with their agrarian hinterlands, autonomous but associated in a league. It was a riposte to two rival models of international relations: the Counter-Reformation aspirations of Spain and France for universal Catholic empire, and the theory of a balance between major superpowers who engrossed small states under their supposedly protective wings. Later, Rousseau would contemplate writing Fletcher's biography. His central claim would be that the Anglo-Scottish Union of 1707 was a classic instance of the corruption of modern civilisation in the servile sacrifice to a monstrous empire of a once vigorous small nation.

Other writers who shared Fletcher's opposition to an incorporating union explored the historical and constitutionalist case for Scotland's independence, in echoes of the Molyneux debate over the parallel status of Ireland. Scotland's Molyneux was George Ridpath, whose *An Historical Account of the Antient Rights and Powers of the Parliament of Scotland* (1703) endeavoured to manufacture a Scottish 'ancient constitution' grounded in a parliamentary tradition. Jacobites like Sir Robert Sibbald, Archibald Pitcairne, and Thomas Ruddiman endorsed 'Country' principles and likewise dwelt, in the words of Sibbald's title, on *The Liberty and Independency of the Kingdom and Church of Scotland* (1702).

From England, William Atwood riposted with a treatise called *The Superiority and Direct Dominion of the Imperial Crown of England over the Crown and Kingdom of Scotland* (1704), which argued that Scotland was merely a province of England. However, the English pro-Union case relied especially on economic arguments. Daniel Defoe, sent to Edinburgh on behalf of the English government, extolled the economic virtues of free trade, warned of the imminent collapse of the Scottish economy if union was rejected, and promised commercial and agrarian regeneration if it succeeded. The choice lay between 'peace and plenty' and 'slavery and poverty'. He insisted that the rhetoric of Scottish independence was an illusory fantasy: Scotland was a bankrupt backwater in need of a firm dose of English commercialisation. True patriotism, echoed Sir John Clerk of Penicuik, lay in the pursuit of economic improvement. William Seton of Pitmeddon agreed: 'this nation, being poor, and without force to protect its commerce, cannot reap great advantage from it, till it partake of the trade and protection of some powerful neighbour nation' (qu. Mitchison 1983, p. 135).

The case for union was not, however, only juridical and economic, and William Seton, the earl of Cromartie, and Viscount Tarbat also offered a political analysis. They held that imperfect federal unions did not flourish. In the partial unions of Denmark with Norway, Aragon with Castile, and Portugal with Spain, the weaker party always suffered. Only full integration with the metropolis dissolved the disadvantages suffered by unequal partners. Cromartie pointed to the exigencies of the European balance of power, to French aspirations to universal monarchy, and to the weakness of an independent Scotland amidst Great Power politics. His cry was 'May we be Britons, and down go the old ignominious names of Scotland, of England' (qu. Scott 1979, p. 27).

The threat of a Scottish Jacobite republic, albeit a political oxymoron, galvanised English political resources to engineer the Union of 1707. The

Scottish parliament was persuaded to abolish itself in return for free trade and guarantees of the autonomy of the Scottish legal system and the Presbyterian church establishment. For diehards like Lord Belhaven the Union was 'an entire surrender': 'we are slaves for ever' (qu. Daiches 1977, p. 148).

In European intellectual history thereafter, Scotland remained a test case for those who sought to understand the relationship between polities and economies. Over time, the comparison became less one between England and Scotland as such, and more one between British Scotland – the Protestant, commercial Lowlands – and the 'feudal', Jacobite, and largely Catholic Highlands. The Highlands continued to resist the process of incorporation until the British government deliberately dismembered Highland clan society after the crushing of the Jacobites in 1746. In Karl Marx's political sociology, the analysis of the transition from feudalism to capitalism, dependent as it was on the work of the Scottish economists of the late eighteenth century, contained a distinct echo of the relations between economy and polity in a nation where the boundary between Highland and Lowland, Jacobite and Hanoverian, agrarian and commercial, 'backward' and 'modern', seemed so palpable. Post-Union Edinburgh's anxious contemplation of the Highlands thus sponsored some of modernity's most fundamental conceptions.

6 The claims of the people

Within post-revolutionary England, a further challenge to the supremacy of the Westminster parliament lay in the populist claim that parliament was not the plenary and sovereign embodiment of the political community. Rather, the voice of the people was autonomous and ultimately supreme. This view remained subordinate: it would fare better in revolutionary America and France. The challenge it faced was to formulate a reply to the dominant English anti-populist position, which rested on two axioms. The first was the principle of 'virtual representation', by which the whole community was deemed to be fully and really present in parliament, so that 'the people' did not have a corporate existence independent of its representatives in parliament. The second was the principle that members of parliament were not delegates but representatives, who exercised personal judgement in parliament, without being bound by instructions or mandates from their constituents. Every edition of Edward Chamberlayne's *Angliae Notitia* from 1699 to 1755 spoke of a member of parliament as having a 'power absolute to consent or dissent without ever acquainting those that sent him'

(Chamberlayne 1700, p. 159). The two axioms were most famously articulated in Edmund Burke's *Speech to the Electors of Bristol* (1774). In defence of the second he was especially vehement. 'Authoritative instructions, mandates issued, which the member is bound blindly and implicitly to obey, to vote, and to argue for, though contrary to the clearest conviction of his judgement and conscience, these are things utterly unknown to the laws of the land, and which arise from a fundamental mistake of the whole order and tenor of our constitution' (Burke 1987, p. 110). Memories of the Civil War lent urgency to these positions, for when eighteenth-century politicians condemned 'tumultuous petitioning' they remembered how seventeenth-century mobs had intimidated parliament.

Although the dominant axioms remained largely impervious to serious populist counter-attack until the colonial revolt in America and the English franchise agitation during the 1760s, the issues at stake did become explicit early in the eighteenth century, in the affair of the Kentish petition. In 1701 several Whig gentlemen of the county of Kent petitioned parliament, listing a series of policy demands, and urging the House of Commons to 'have regard to the voice of the people'. The Tory Commons jailed them, accusing them of 'tending to destroy the constitution of parliaments'. Daniel Defoe responded with his stunningly forthright *Legion's Memorial*, a manifesto by the 'people of England', 'your masters'. If parliaments 'betray their trust, and abuse the people . . . it is the undoubted right of the people of England to call them to an account for the same, and by convention, assembly or force, may proceed against them as traitors and betrayers' (Defoe 1965, pp. 83–4). Defoe quickly reached a pinnacle of fame when he elaborated this theme in his poem *The True-Born Englishman* (1701) and in an essay called *The Original Power of the Collective Body of the People of England* (1702) (*RLP*, 1, pp. 325–54). The Kentish petitioners were also defended in *Jura populi Anglicani* (1701), probably written by Lord Somers, the Whig leader and friend of Locke. This tract described MPs as 'the delegates of the people', and construed the *Two Treatises* as authenticating a natural right of petitioning (Somers 1701, pp. 30, 53).[13]

The Whig defence of the Kentish petitioners provoked several sustained Tory ripostes. Charles Leslie published a tirade that initiated his career as the most influential Tory journalist of Queen Anne's reign. His *New Association* (1703) assailed, among others, Defoe, Swift, and 'the great Locke in his

---

13 The whole quarrel was allegorised by Jonathan Swift in his *Contests and Dissensions between the Nobles and the Commons in Athens and Rome* (1701; Swift 1967). There was a unique conjunction here of Locke, Defoe, and Swift.

Two Discourses of Government', as 'fanatic' revivers of the 'mob principles' of the Civil War era. Their claims enabled 'every party and faction to call themselves the people' and to declare those whom they hate to be 'the public enemy of the people'. They dangerously denied the principle that the House of Commons was 'virtually the people, and the whole power of the people [is] lodged in them' (*RLP*, II, pp. 62ff). While Leslie was a half-disguised Jacobite, other Tories turned to defend the unimpeachable authority of parliament with more conviction. Notable were Humphrey Mackworth in his *Vindication of the Rights of the Commons* (1701) and Offspring Blackall in *The Subject's Duty* (1705). Their endorsement of parliamentary sovereignty, and transference from personal monarchy to crown-in-parliament of the old Tory doctrine of the subject's duty of 'passive obedience and non-resistance', marked a decisive repudiation of the royal absolutism of pre-Revolution Toryism. It created a parliamentary Toryism which, on the one hand, was freed from the stigma of dynastic loyalty to the deposed House of Stuart, and, on the other, was armed against the coming century of democratic populism.

7   The claims of women

The final element in this survey of the aspects of civil society over which supremacy was asserted, or reasserted, in the wake of the Revolution is the relationship between the sexes. Any claim that revolutionary ideology entailed a reaffirmation of patriarchy must necessarily be speculative, since no tangible crisis occurred in gender relations to warrant extended theorising. Nonetheless, it is evident that an arresting epigram on behalf of the female sex penned by Mary Astell in 1706 was provoked by irritation at Revolution Whig doctrine. 'If all men are born free, how is it that all women are born slaves?' (Astell 1996, p. 18; *RLP*, II, p. 116). By exploring the homology between the public and private spheres, Astell sought to expose the contradictions in what was rapidly becoming a comfortable Whig intellectual buttress of the Revolution.[14]

Between 1694 and 1709 she published several tracts which not only explored the predicament of women, but also assaulted Whiggery, Dissent,

14 On Astell see Astell 1986, 1996, 1997; Gallagher 1988; Kinnaird 1979; McCrystal 1993; Perry 1986, 1990; Smith 2001; Springborg 1995. More generally, Smith 1998, Weil 1999. For the claim that the Revolution was construed negatively by female authors, see P. McDowell 1998, chs. 3–5, and Perry 1990. McDowell has in mind such writers as Jane Barker, Aphra Behn, Elinor James, and Mary Manley, all Jacobites or Tories. On Barker see King 2000.

philosophical materialism, and deism. Her reputation was made by her first book, *A Serious Proposal to the Ladies* (1694), which was a prospectus for a female academy (unwisely termed a 'monastery'), that would be devoted to learning, piety, and the cultivation of the 'female virtuoso'. In a vein similar to Mary Wollstonecraft a century later, she lambasted women's shallowness, their vanity and slavery to fashion, their reading of 'idle novels and romances', and their failure to pursue virtue and govern their passions (Astell 1997, pp. 13, 18).

Her next tract, *Reflections upon Marriage* (1700), achieved a third edition in 1706, to which she added the preface in which her epigram occurs. She neither challenged the institution of marriage nor the due subordination of women within it. She acknowledged that when a woman marries she 'elects a monarch for life . . . giv[ing] him an authority she cannot recall however he misapply it'. However, the tract attacked male brutishness and contempt for women, and beseeched men to 'treat women with a little more humanity'. It repeated the criticism of women's trivial pursuits, and called on women to be more circumspect and less deluded in their expectations of marriage and their choice of husbands (Astell 1996, pp. 1ff; *RLP*, II, pp. 109ff).

Astell was discovered by feminist scholars in the 1980s and granted the appellation 'first English feminist', despite her dogmatically Tory and High Church views. She upheld the Tory doctrine of passive obedience and believed that the godly response to tyranny, in politics and in marriage, was stoical suffering. She was ferociously hostile to religious Nonconformists, whom she thought of as rebels and responsible for the murder of King Charles the Martyr. She deplored the spread among the 'rabble' of pamphlets which found fault with 'their superiors' and called on the magistrate to discipline the 'vicious and immoral lives' of the people (Astell 1704, pp. xxxviii, xlii). She was no populist radical.

Her 'feminism' arises from her preferred critical tool of irony. She constantly made telling points against her Whig adversaries through sarcasm and inversions of their positions. Her epigram of 1706 was hypothetical: *if* the doctrine of natural equality were true, *then* women as well as men must naturally be free. But Astell held no such premise. Her language was not of rights. Instead, she adopted the standard Tory doctrines of the common fatherhood of the race in Adam and of the origins of society known from the book of Genesis, as a refutation of the 'meer figment' of 'that equality wherein the race of men were placed in the free state of nature' (Astell 1704, p. xxxv). We are born into subjection, and although men may select their kings and women their husbands, their assent does not authorise rulership, nor does it license rebellion when dissatisfied. Astell rejected the notion of a fundamental right of self-preservation, instead advocating Christian stoicism. The Christian, by embracing the cross of Jesus, can triumph over the rage and power of tyrants, and 'love is all the retaliation our religion allows'. She invited men and women to suffer. What she offered women was a guide to better education and conduct, and the possibility of choosing to remain unmarried. She invited women to transcend the sensual world and cultivate the virtues.

What Astell did most successfully was constantly to apply Whig doctrine to the private sphere, thereby hoping to expose its absurdity in the public sphere, anticipating that no-one would concede Whig principles in the relations between men and women. 'Why is slavery so much condemned and strove against in one case, and so highly applauded and held so necessary and so sacred in another?' 'If absolute sovereignty be not necessary in a state, how comes it to be so in a family?' Contrasting the political state and the state of marriage, Astell remarked that 'whatever may be said against passive obedience in [the one] case, I suppose there's no man but likes it very well in this; how much soever arbitrary power be disliked on a throne, not Milton himself would cry up liberty to poor female slaves, or plead for the lawfulness of resisting a private tyranny' (Astell 1996, pp. 17–19, 46–7; *RLP*, II, pp. 115–16).

8   The Country platform

As has already been remarked, in post-Revolution circumstances the doctrine of parliamentary sovereignty was quickly transposed into a doctrine of the supremacy of the executive. This was because in the English parliamentary system the king's ministers sat in, and had considerable influence over, the two Houses of Parliament. There was no separation of the executive and legislative arms of government. Consequently, the pre-Revolution fear of overt tyranny by a monarch ruling without parliament gave way to a new fear of covert tyranny by an oligarchy which controlled parliament. Alarms that parliament's independence would be undermined and corrupted replaced fears that parliament would be abolished. According to Viscount Bolingbroke, parliament was now 'induced by corruption' rather than 'awed by prerogative'. The chief instrument for such corruption was the use of 'placemen': members of parliament who held salaried offices of state, and whose votes could be influenced by the offer or withdrawal of such offices. Through the weight of 'placemen', and mechanisms of party discipline, the crown's ministers secured a biddable parliament.

To purists, this was the reverse of the proper ordering of the polity, in which the executive should be the servant and not the master of the legislature. Parliament, as the embodiment of the Country, should stand supreme over the Court. Hence arose the powerful critique of executive power which became known as the 'Country platform'. It emerged in the 1690s and flourished in diverse forms throughout the eighteenth century. As a result, the division between Whig and Tory was sometimes overlain, though never obliterated, by the conflict between Court and Country, in a complex political mosaic that might see Country Whigs and Country Tories united against their Court enemies. Contemporaries and historians have given the 'Country platform' many alternative names: Old Whig, True Whig, commonwealth, republican, civic humanist, and neo-Harringtonian. As these labels imply, the ideological core was broadly Whig, yet when Whigs were installed in power and worked the levers of executive influence, 'Old Whig' principles could be adopted by excluded Tories and used against those ministerial Whigs who, they claimed, had betrayed the cause.[15]

Within a decade of the Revolution, Court Whigs were seen as betrayers. Charles Davenant's *True Picture of a Modern Whig* (1701) indicted the 'Junto', the Whigs in office, for having 'departed from the principles they professed twenty years ago'. They now protected corrupt ministers, proliferated docile sinecurists, and advocated standing armies. The charges would mount. When invested with unprecedented power after the Hanoverian succession of 1714, the Whigs replaced triennial general elections with septennial elections (1716), undermined the autonomy of that great city-state, the City of London, in the City Election Act (1725), and attempted a Peerage Bill (1719) which would have rendered their control of the House of Lords invulnerable.

What most dramatically altered the terrain of post-Revolution political thought was the impact of the 'financial revolution', which vastly increased the executive's power of the purse.[16] The post-Revolution regime rebuilt the fiscal foundations of the state, fighting a phenomenally expensive war

15 On the 'commonwealth' tradition see Bailyn 1967; Goldie 1980a; Gunn 1983; Hayton, Introduction to Cocks 1996; Houston 1991; Pocock 1975, 1985; Robbins 1959; Wootton 1994c; Worden 1978, 2001.
16 On the financial revolution and its fiscal and military consequences see Brewer 1989; Carruthers 1996; Dickson 1967; Hellmuth 1990; D. W. Jones 1988; Stone 1994.

against France, funded not only by the burdensome land tax and the intrusive excise tax, but also by deficit finance, through the creation of the National Debt in 1694. The new fiscal instruments, combined with the fast-growing role of joint-stock enterprise, created a species of wealth, and a *rentier* class, not rooted in the land. The presumed grounding of autonomous citizenship, of political personality, of gentility, in real estate seemed suddenly vulnerable. The new world of financial wealth constantly provoked commentators to denounce ignoble greed and avarice. The fickleness, mobility, and intangibility of cash, commerce, and credit (enhanced by a phantasmagoria of lotteries, stock bubbles, 'projectors', and embezzling courtiers) seemed a sickness ultimately fatal to the body politic. A prolonged quarrel between 'land' and 'money' ensued, exemplified in the fictional coffee-house arguments between the landed squire Sir Roger de Coverly and the urban plutocrat Sir Andrew Freeport in the pages of Joseph Addison's *Spectator*. It was also there that 'Publick Credit' was personified as a virgin lady whose virtue it was the prime duty of the state to defend (3 Mar. 1711). It is tempting to presume a simple dichotomy in these arguments, the one side antique and fixated in nostalgic seigneurial distrust for the new commercial age, pitted against a modern Whig embrace of commerce and the market, the latter epitomised in the shamelessly bourgeois Defoe's investiture of trade as the carrier of modernity. The anti-commercial position could certainly produce near caricature: a fiercely Spartan hatred of the 'luxury' and 'effeminacy' of commercial society persisted as late as John Brown's popular jeremiads published in the 1750s (Canovan 1978). Yet the picture was more complex. Few landed gentlemen avoided commerce or investment in government debt. For all its invocation of ancient virtue, the anti-government paper, *Cato's Letters*, embraced commerce.[17] Applause and abuse of commerce and public debt produced no exact political alignments, as compared with more sharply defined issues like placemen and standing armies, but they provided rich rhetorical resources for the conduct of political argument and, by and large, it would be the 'Country platform' which would adopt a stance of hostility towards the institutions of the new 'fiscal-military' state.

The 'Country' vision came into focus in the mid-1690s, particularly in the Grecian Coffee House in London, among a circle of 'Commonwealthmen' that included Robert Molesworth, Anthony Ashley Cooper (later third earl of Shaftesbury), Trenchard, Moyle, and Toland. They were galvanised,

---

17 On the ideological impact of the financial revolution see Bloom and Bloom 1971; Brantlinger 1996; Goldsmith 1977; Nicholson 1994; Pocock 1975. For Bernard Mandeville's role see ch. 13 below.

after the Peace of Ryswick in 1697, by anger that the Court proposed to maintain a standing army, allegedly to withstand the continuing threats proposed by France and the Jacobites. The Country party expressed passionate hostility against 'mercenary armies', 'royal guards', and 'janissaries'. These sentiments gave rise to a reverence for the ideal of a citizen militia, which lent to the Country tradition its most recalcitrantly antique construal of the attributes of free citizenship, through its invocation of Spartan models of martial citizenship. They also made use of Machiavelli's condemnation of mercenaries in his *Discourses*, a text which acquired pride of place in the Country tradition. The theme was signally stated in Moyle and Trenchard's *An Argument Shewing, that a Standing Army is Inconsistent with a Free Government* (1697) and in Trenchard's *Short History of Standing Armies* (1698), and the Spartan vision was perfected in Fletcher's scheme for sending all male citizens to rural encampments for a period of training. Opposition to mercenary armies, alongside 'mercenary' parliaments, came to dominate the landscape of opposition in the first half of the eighteenth century. That professional ('standing') armies were nonetheless becoming a ubiquitous institution of modern states during this period marks out the militia ideal as an anachronism, but it was an extraordinarily tenacious ideal, and it had a significant afterlife in the American conception of the citizen's right to bear arms (Malcolm 1994; Robertson 1985; Schwoerer 1974).

Contemporaneous with the standing army controversy of the late 1690s was a remarkable campaign of republication of earlier texts, and of textual manipulation, which bequeathed 'commonwealth' handbooks to the coming century, and established what became a hackneyed canon of political high virtue. This was chiefly the work of the prolific Toland. The Whig martyr Algernon Sidney's *Discourses concerning Government*, for which he had been executed in 1683, appeared in 1698; the *Works* of John Milton came out in 1699; those of the republican James Harrington in 1700. In a shrewd piece of editorial revision, Toland transformed the tone of Colonel Edmund Ludlow's Civil War *Memoirs*, written in the 1660s, and published in 1698, softening Ludlow's militant godly zeal into a secular moralism more suited to Enlightenment sensibilities. To take just one instance of Toland's technique, a hero of the Civil Wars who in the original manuscript went to his execution like 'a lamb of Christ', in the printed edition 'died like a Roman' (Worden 1978, 2001).

What is striking about the Country frame of mind is that it often dwelt on the ethic of citizenship rather than on institutions or policies. At its heart was an analysis of civic personality, of the 'spirit', manners, or ethos of liberty, of the things that led to self-enslavement and those that were proof against it. The discussion revolved around several ubiquitous dichotomies, virtue against corruption, public good against private advantage, transparency of counsel against the secret cabals of juntos and cabinets. Such discussions readily moved into a domain of moral philosophy, dominated by ideals of sociability, civility, and 'politeness', encapsulated in Shaftesbury's *Characteristics* (1711) and Addison's *Spectator*. Country writers also endorsed a Stoicized Protestant moralism that was embodied in the 'reformation of manners' movement, which sought to improve moral discipline in order to create sober, industrious citizens.[18] Eclecticism is, again, manifest. Even the High Church Tory Astell slid easily between quoting the Gospel's 'contempt for riches' and quoting Machiavelli on behalf of the poverty that would serve the 'conservation of . . . liberties', and, likewise, juxtaposing the Biblical 'eye of the needle' with Lycurgus's banishment of riches from Sparta (Astell 1704, pp. vii, xxxii).

This was an idiom, more Ciceronian than Lockean, in which the 'character' of the citizen figured more prominently than claims of their 'rights'. It was an idiom that centred on the contrast between autonomy and dependence. A free citizen was one who had the economic means of self-sufficiency and who owed others none of the deference due from a wage-earner, servant, child, or woman. Likewise, the free citizen was untainted by the deference to government that was cynically purchased from citizens who depended on income from investment in government stock. The citizen was the Aristotelian head of an independent household, an *oikos*. A free citizen was not only one for whom economic independence bred moral independence of judgement, but also one enjoying sufficient freedom from toil to be able to participate in the commonwealth. Citizenship was marked by the constant habit of governing, in the holding of public office, as justice of the peace, grand juryman, sheriff, militia lieutenant, vestryman, or parish constable. Holding office arguably mattered more than the right of franchise, the power to vote in parliamentary elections, for, until the 1760s, extension of the parliamentary franchise and the 'fair' distribution of seats were practically absent from reform agendas, and officeholding was more widespread than the right to elect Members of Parliament (Goldie 2001). This way of speaking about political character could serve those both at the highest and most humble levels of householder-citizenship. The aristocrat

---

18 On 'politeness' see Bloom and Bloom 1971; Klein 1989, 1994; Langford 1989; Phillipson 1993a. Editions: Shaftesbury 1999; Addison 1979; Addison and Steele 1965; Steele 1987. On the 'reformation of manners' see Bahlman 1957; Burtt 1992; Claydon 1996.

was the citizen writ large, his economic independence so great that he could resist the blandishments of Court bribery and exercise senatorial restraint over Courtly excess. Yet equally the citizen might be a modest freeholder or urban shopkeeper or artisan, a holder of office and participant in decision-making in parish and ward. At least until the era of Thomas Paine late in the century, the axiom of householder-citizenship took precedence over individualist and universalist – in a word, democratic – ideas of citizenship and suffrage. Finally, in the Country idiom, a free citizen was also said to be intellectually independent, and not befuddled by superstition and 'priestcraft' into craven deference to pseudo-sanctified authority. As Robert Molesworth warned, 'jure divino' doctrines provide ideological props to despotism, and a wise statesman is one who keeps the clergy firmly within bounds (Molesworth 1694).

In Country eyes, post-Revolution England was threatened by a legal, parliamentary tyranny, which would come not by the sword, but by legislation and by corrupted parliamentary majorities. Modern tyranny was no melodrama of massacre, but the quiet suffocation of the public good by private greed and ambition. Citizens must therefore be alert to the underhand erosion of liberty. The treatment of this theme was saturated with classical allusion and conducted on terms of intimate familiarity with the history of ancient Rome. No historical moment became so allegorically powerful in the English political imagination as Rome's transition from republic to empire, under the guise and cloak of liberty and the constitution, and no historical figures became so ubiquitous as the republic's defenders, Cicero and Cato. The fullest encyclopedia of Country attitudes carried the title *Cato's Letters,* and Joseph Addison's play *Cato* (1713) was one of the century's theatrical triumphs. Citizens were enjoined to beware of 'Caesarian tyranny', brought in, like Julius Caesar's and Augustus's, under the 'show' of a senate and the 'appearance' of the people's choice of its tribunes and praetors. Classical learning was deeply embedded in political debate. The parliamentary speeches of the Country MP Sir Richard Cocks between 1698 and 1702 were peppered with references to Aristotle, Cicero, Seneca, Livy, Plutarch, and Sallust (Cocks 1996).[19] That classical heroes should not entirely sit on the opposition benches mattered considerably to the Court: Conyers Middleton's *Life of Cicero* (1741) was dedicated to Prime Minister Sir Robert Walpole.

19 For classicism in political culture see Ayres 1997; Bolgar 1979; Erskine-Hill 1983; Rawson 1989; Turner 1986; Weinbrot 1978.

The language of Rome did not, however, exclude another resource that also retained its efficacy, the idyll of the Ancient Constitution. This was a 'Gothic' rather than Roman idiom, and gentlemen were no less well read in the histories of the Saxon and medieval European polities. They believed those polities to have been balanced constitutions in which monarchs, noblemen, and commoners had their respective roles and held each other in check. In 1716 Addison wrote of a Buckinghamshire alderman who, when drunk, 'will talk [to] you from morning till night on the Gothic Balance' (Addison 1979, p. 264). It was held that many nations had, since the Renaissance, lost their 'Gothic balance', and become monarchical despotisms. Nations had lost their freedoms, for example, when kings had crushed feudal nobilities, leaving themselves unrestrained by an aristocratic counterweight. This was the message of Molesworth's *Account of Denmark* (1694), which told of the Danish constitutional revolution of 1660 that installed an absolute monarchy by stealth, and warned of a similar fate for England if it should cease to be vigilant. There was a vital textual link between the Roman and Gothic idioms, in Tacitus's *Germania*, which had reproached the corruptions of imperial Rome and held up for admiration the robust virtues of the Teutonic tribes in the forests of Germany. Tacitus provided the ur-text for the Gothic ideal, and it was this Tacitean tradition which Montesquieu invoked in his famous remark that the 'beautiful system' of the English found its origins 'in the forests' (*SL*, XI.6).[20]

9 'Robinocracy' and its enemies

The regime of Prime Minister Sir Robert Walpole (1722–42) provoked an opposition of stunning ferocity, intellectual ingenuity, and literary fecundity. In the eyes of Tories, Jacobites, and dissident Whigs, loosely amalgamated into a Country party, Walpole was the incarnation of parliamentary tyranny, a chief minister who held his monarch in captivity and who corruptly suborned parliament. The years of his rule were strewn with opposition bills and motions aimed chiefly at four targets: reversal of the Septennial Act, hatred of which served to entrench the ideal of 'annual parliaments' down to the era of the Chartists in the 1840s; banishment of servile 'placemen'

20 On Saxonism and the Ancient Constitution see Cairns 1985; Colbourn 1965; Francis and Morrow 1988; Gerrard 1994, pt 2; Kliger 1972; Lutz 1988; Pocock 1960, 1987; Smith 1987; Sullivan 1982. Montesquieu's phrase, 'beautiful system' ('beau système'), is rendered more flatly as 'fine system' in the recent Cambridge edition (p. 166).

and 'pensioners'; dissolution of the standing army; and curtailment of the instruments of fiscal despotism, notably the excise taxes.

These campaigns benefited from a lavish literary renaissance, which opened with Swift's *Gulliver's Travels* in 1726. Walpole was here caricatured as Flimnap in the Voyage to Lilliput, the impresario of the circus tricksters who win pretty ribbons from the Lilliputian king. A nobler monarch was the king of Brobdingnag, a patriot who transcended faction and outlawed mercenary armies and moneyed men. In John Gay's *Beggar's Opera* (1728), Walpole was represented as Captain Macheath, the highwayman. Or maybe he was Peachum, the receiver of stolen goods. The play prompted the government to impose censorship on the theatres. Gay's play was in part a reprise of St Augustine's story, in *The City of God*, of the encounter between the Emperor Alexander and a pirate: the moral is that a ruler is merely a pirate who has achieved larceny on a grand scale (IV.4). This trope was repeatedly refashioned, from Henry Fielding's *Jonathan Wild* (1743) to Bertolt Brecht's *Threepenny Opera* (1928). In Alexander Pope's poem *The Dunciad* (1728), Walpole was portrayed as the Great Dunce, the puppeteer of a band of knaves and fools. In David Mallet's play *Mustapha* (1739), Walpole becomes an evil bashaw. The intricate iconography of William Hogarth's paintings *The Harlot's Progress* (1732) also yields up anti-Walpolean satire. The allegorical canon of evil personae for Walpole was inexhaustible: he was equated with such royal favourites and grasping ministers down the ages as Sejanus, Tiberius, Clodius, Gaveston, Wolsey, and Buckingham.

In its later phase, the Country opposition attached itself to King George II's estranged heir, Frederick, prince of Wales, and prompted the literati to compose hymns to a patriot prince who would overcome corrupt faction, a chivalric, redemptive, and martial Protestant hero. Henry Brooke's play *Gustavus Vasa* (1739), which is this idiom at its most majestic, was banned by the censor. Belshazzar and Samson in Handel's operas belong to the same tradition. There were also literary reminiscences of several Prince Hals, and a new cult of the Saxon hero King Alfred. In Gilbert West's *Order of the Garter* (1742), the chivalry of the white plume sweeps away the mercenary politicians and crafty courtiers. James Thomson's poem *Liberty* (1735–6), in which the goddess Liberty embodies the spirit of public virtue, won for its author a pension from Frederick. A key opposition demand was for a forward foreign policy, Protestant and imperial, in place of Walpole's fiscal pacifism. This encouraged cults of Queen Elizabeth and Sir Walter Raleigh, and recollections of the defeat of the Spanish Armada. Thomson penned a masque, *Alfred* (1740), for which he wrote the lyrics of 'Rule Britannia'. The meaning of the word 'patriotism' became steadily transformed, retaining its implication of selfless public service and vigilance for liberty, while also acquiring a new sense of celebration of nation, seafaring, and military prowess abroad.

Orchestrating the opposition to Walpole's 'Robinocracy' was Lord Bolingbroke, whose dazzling early career as a Tory statesmen was wrecked after 1714 by the Hanoverian and Whig ascendancy. He briefly went over to the Jacobite court in France, and endured exclusion from the House of Lords as a condition of parole when he was allowed to return from exile.[21] His exclusion from parliament forced him to lead the Country movement with his prolific pen, and to do so literally from the country, a circumstance which reinforced the cult of bucolic retreat, the purity of the garden in contrast with the corruption of the city. In that classically educated age, such an ideal was underwritten by the reading of Horace, Virgil's *Georgics*, and Cicero's *Tusculan Disputations*. The ideal achieved architectural form in Alexander Pope's grotto at Twickenham, the home of frugal virtue, of the sage in the cave. Bolingbroke's chief literary vehicle was the newspaper, *The Craftsman*, which lambasted Walpole for ten years, surviving many prosecutions. From the hundred essays which Bolingbroke wrote for it there emerged in book form his *Remarks on the History of England* (1730–1) and his *Dissertation upon Parties* (1733–4), followed by *The Idea of a Patriot King*, written in 1739 and published in 1749.

Bolingbroke was an outlandish type of Tory, a deist and libertine, for whom the old Filmerian theory of the divine right of kings was an absurd superstition, and whose vision of English history can be reduced to what we now call 'the Whig interpretation of history'. Through the centuries the English had struggled to entrench their liberties in a series of valiant conflicts against oppressive rulers. To oppose Walpole was to defend Magna Carta and the Petition of Right. Bolingbroke had a pressing need to remove from his movement the taint of Jacobitism, so he zealously adhered to 'Revolution principles'. He also wished to fuse together a disparate opposition of Tories and dissident Whigs, so he announced the redundancy of the party

---

21 On the political thought (and the cultural and literary aspects) of the campaign of Bolingbroke and his circle, and the anti-Walpoleans see Armitage 1997; Atherton 1974; Burns 1962; Cleary 1984; Colley 1981; Cook 1967; Cottret 1995; Dabydeen 1987; Dickinson 1970; Downie 1984; Erskine-Hill 1998; Gerrard 1994; Goldgar 1977; Hart 1965; Kramnick 1968; Lock 1983; Loftis 1963; Mack 1969; Nicholson 1994; Pettit 1997; Pittock 1997, ch. 3; Rivers 1973; Rogers 1970; Skinner 1974; Smith 1995.

labels 'Whig' and 'Tory' and their replacement by 'Court' and 'Country'. It was also necessary to disarm the notion that 'opposition' was inherently seditious, and this he did by relentless appeals to patriotism, and by elevating loyalty to the constitution over loyalty to the ministry. Walpole's ministry was thus identified merely as a 'faction' masquerading as a government. Bolingbroke's surpassing intellectual eclecticism encompassed Lockean natural rights, a Harringtonian theory about the balance of property and power, Saxon ancient constitutionalism, and Machiavellian warnings about the need to preserve civic spirit as the guarantee of liberty.

Bolingbroke's ideal of the Patriot King who would rule without corrupt courtiers was an echo of the Renaissance mirror-for-princes genre. In Bolingbroke, old Tory divine right theory, which he called 'dressing up kings like so many burlesque Jupiters', gave way to moralising about the princely virtues and dignities. There was in fact a substantial eighteenth-century literary tradition that dwelt on the princely virtues. Diverse examples include Mary Manley's *New Atalantis* (1709), a programme of moral education for the future George II inspired by Fénelon's *Télémaque*, Defoe's *Royal Education* (1728), Charles Jennens's libretto for Handel's *Belshazzar* (1744), and Catherine Macaulay's quasi-republican celebration of King Alfred in the 1770s. Defoe tends in modern interpretations to be identified as the relentless voice of a new middle-class world, but this neglects his frequent applause for heroic warrior princes (Schonhorn 1991). This powerful tradition of princely perfectibilism was Britain's version of the *philosophes'* admiration for philosopher-kings. In the latter part of the eighteenth century, princely perfectibilism could co-exist with republicanism. In the 1760s James Burgh wrote his *Political Disquisitions* (1774–5), which became an admired textbook for Anglo-American republicans, and yet he also wrote 'Remarks Historical and Political', an address to George III inviting him to take on the mantle of a patriot prince (Hay 1979a, 1979b; Zebrowski 1991).

Bolingbroke's salience perhaps threatens a misreading of what Toryism had become. The crypto-Jacobitism of Thomas Carte's *History of England* (1747–55), which attributed the ancient healing power of the Royal Touch to the Stuart Young Pretender, was still grounded in the sanctity of patriarchal hereditary right. Yet undoubtedly even Jacobitism took on a Bolingbrokean hue. The Jacobite Pretender's declaration of 1750 was entirely Bolingbrokean: it offered annual or triennial parliaments, a militia in place of a standing army, and the retrenchment of placemen. This Tory and

Jacobite embrace of Country ideals created fertile ground which in some circumstances (such as Wolfe Tone's Irish rebellion of 1798, or the Scottish Catholic conspiracies of the 1790s) would make a transition from Jacobitism to Jacobinism easily achievable. Likewise the Tory populism of men like William Beckford, who advocated a wider franchise in the *Monitor* (1750s), carried over into the Wilksite parliamentary reform movements of the 1760s and beyond. Moreover, while it is tempting to regard the Country voice, quintessentially in Alexander Pope, as nostalgic, pessimistic, bucolic, and anti-commercial, that voice could equally be, as in James Thomson, expansive, commercial, and imperial.

One of Bolingbroke's most enduring influences lay in his impact upon Montesquieu, who was his guest in England between 1729 and 1731. The famous account of the English constitution in the *Spirit of the Laws* purports to be descriptive, but it is grounded in Bolingbrokean prescription (Mason 1990; Shackleton 1961). Its 'doctrine' of the separation of powers, of the need particularly to prevent the executive from trespassing upon the legislative power, was the ideal type of the Bolingbrokean assault on placemen. Capturing a moment of transition in British constitutional evolution, Montesquieu hesitated uncertainly between two typologies, one of harmony and balance between the three estates of the realm, king, Lords, and Commons, the other of harmony and balance between the three functions of government, executive, judicial, and legislative. It so happened that in early eighteenth-century Britain these two conceptions could be mapped one upon the other: the king headed the executive, the Lords supplied the supreme judiciary, and the Commons was the principal legislative body. The ancient doctrine of estates thereby gave way imperceptibly to the modern doctrine of functions.

There was, however, never in Britain a *separation* of powers or functions of the sort Bolingbroke and Montesquieu seemed to envisage. It is true that there were moments in early eighteenth-century Britain when the Country party's ambition to achieve the complete statutory exclusion of officers of state from membership of the legislature was within sight of achievement. Had it been achieved, then the executive and legislative arms of government would have become truly separate. But in Britain no such constitutional transformation has ever come about. Instead, the ideal became a commodity for export. In drawing up the constitution of the United States, Montesquieu's American readers succeeded where the British anti-Walpoleans failed.

10   The Court Whigs

In modern scholarship, Bolingbroke's luminaries have overshadowed the ideology of the Court Whigs.[22] Walpole did, however, command extensive intellectual support, notably from Lord Hervey and Bishop Hoadly as well as a team of sophisticated journalists, including William Arnall and James Pitt, who supplied him with a mouthpiece in the *London Journal*. Their urgent task was to absolve the ministry from the charge of 'corruption'. Trading in veneration for such Whig heroes as Locke and Sidney, they did obeisance to Whig pieties. James Pitt called himself a 'True Whig', an 'Old Whig', 'as thorough a Whig as any man now living' (*DG*, 29 Nov. 1735). Yet, despite the insistence on loyalty to 'Old' Whiggery, a distinctive doctrine of 'modern liberty' emerged, which owed more to an analysis of the post-Revolution polity than to the teachings of the Old Whigs. The Court Whig theorists aimed to show that the Bolingbrokean catalogue of complaint was historically obsolescent, and that Roman republican moralising was so much daydreaming.

The most forthright statement of the 'modern system' was Hervey's *Ancient and Modern Liberty Stated and Compar'd* (1734). For him, liberty dated only from 1688. Pitt likewise pronounced that the 'British monarchy is, since the late Revolution, better than the Roman commonwealth was in all its glory' (*LJ*, 4 Apr. 1730). This was because the Revolution 'fixed and settled' that liberty of person and property which had been impossible 'till the power of the barons was destroyed by Henry VII, and the power of the church by Henry VIII' (*LJ*, 1 Sept. 1733). The Court Whigs were impatient with Ancient Constitutionalist notions of Saxon liberties. There was no Ark of the Covenant of liberty handed down from Teutonic forebears. Medieval institutions were the product of feudalism, not reminiscences of, or deviations from, a Saxon constitutional idyll. Consequently 'the so much boasted and celebrated Magna Charta' was 'no contract with, nor grant to, the people. It was only some concessions to the churchmen and barons, which the power of their swords wrested out of the hands of the king' (*C*, 6 Apr. 1734; *LJ*, 23 Mar. 1734). Neither Roman maxims nor Saxon myths had any place in modern times. Nor, as Arnall's *Clodius and Cicero* (1727)

---

22 On the political thought of the Court Whigs see Browning 1982; Burtt 1992, ch. 6; Dickinson 1977, ch. 4; Downie 1984; Forbes 1975, ch. 6; Gunn 1983; Horne 1980; Targett 1991, 1994; Urstad 1999. The following passage is especially indebted to Targett 1991 and 1994. Abbreviations: *BJ* = *British Journal*; *C* = *Craftsman* (after its takeover by Walpole); *DG* = *Daily Gazetteer*; *FB* = *Free Briton*; *LJ* = *London Journal*.

made clear, was there a place for the mythology of Spartan simplicity and the deprecation of 'luxury'. Modern liberty marched hand in hand with modern commerce.

The Court Whigs offered an analysis of the modern constitution. They paid ritual homage to the doctrine of the balanced constitution, but they argued that, far from there being an imbalance in favour of the king's ministers, the tendency of modern history was for power to move towards the commoners and hence their representatives in the House of Commons. James Harrington provided the tools for analysis. It was argued that since the sixteenth century the balance of property and power had shifted decisively towards the Commons, who were by now masters over king, nobles, and church. The balance of the constitution was 'already strongly on the side of the Commons, because the wealth of the kingdom [was] with them', so that it was 'almost impossible that [parliamentarians] should lose their independence' (*LJ*, 23 Feb. and 16 Mar. 1734). Since the constitution was not self-equilibrating, it was now necessary to enhance the crown's executive authority deliberately, in order for government to be conducted at all. Accordingly, the use of 'influence' was imperative if the king was not to become a cipher like the doge of Venice. The power of patronage was thus an 'equivalent' to compensate for the fact that the king had no 'real power' and was in danger of becoming wholly dependent on the legislature. The king's business must be done, and it could not be done in some semblance of the anarchic Polish Diet where every member had a veto. A commonwealth of wholly independent gentry was only one step away from national ungovernability.

Complaints against a standing army were similarly judged to be inapposite. The army was 'not a standing royal army, but a national army, raised by the people, for the safety of the people' (*LJ*, 12 Feb. 1732). In so far as the army was an executive instrument for the public safety, it was one which restored to the crown 'real weight in the constitution' (*FB*, 21 Feb. 1734). In modern times 'all the world is armed; every nation has disciplined troops, managed horse, and trains of artillery' (*LJ*, 2 Jan. 1731). The ancient ideal of the citizen militia was therefore another dispensable myth.

These themes were accompanied by a stress upon the arts and skills of government. The Walpolean authors displayed an anti-utopian distrust for the intellectual luxuries of opposition. Prudence, experience, and pragmatism, not Platonic schemes for political perfection, were needed. The opposition was, wrote James Pitt, 'wild with the fancies of Plato's commonwealth, Sir Thomas More's utopia, and other visionary schemes of government, not reducible to practice' (*LJ*, 20 July 1734). Hoadly agreed: 'government is a matter of practice and not of speculation' (*LJ*, 26 Oct. 1723). In Augustinian mood, the Walpoleans showed how rulers must work with the grain of fallible human nature. Arnall's essays on Machiavelli, Hobbes, and La Rochefoucauld reveal a marked distance from the moral optimism of his contemporaries. 'Violence and rapine seem to be [man's] great characteristics'; 'we talk of social virtues . . . but in fact, there are very few (I believe none) who have not the same propension to oppress in more or less degree, and who do not devour, if they can, whatever may be a desirable prey' (*BJ*, 16 Nov. 1728). Government, therefore, provides the power needed to protect people from the tyranny of their marauding fellow citizens. The best that can be hoped for from government is 'to reform by degrees, to gain upon inconveniences, and regulate society with moderation' (*FB*, 9 Apr. 1730).

The argument for the necessity of placemen, together with this unheroic view of human nature, combined to produce the assertion that men may, indeed must, be tempted into office by material incentives. Pitt remarked that it was a 'romantic notion, and mere visionary virtue' to expect that 'men in power and office should pursue the good of the public, without any regard to their own particular interest' (*LJ*, 25 Sept. 1731). Arnall put it more bluntly: 'there would be few candidates for power, if nothing beneficial was annexed to it' (*BJ*, 3 Feb. 1728). Indeed, Bolingbrokean politics was regarded as no more than the politics of envy and disappointed ambition, forged into a corrupt alliance of sanctimonious Whigs, backwoods Tories, and treasonable Jacobites. The Court Whig case was, in sum, a 'hymn to political management' (Gunn 1983, p. 106).

The Court Whig essayists produced a systematic analysis of the claims of modern executive power. It remained for David Hume to synthesise that outlook in his essays on luxury and the independence of parliament (1741–2). For instance, his key contention, in 'Of the Independency of Parliament', is that 'the share of power, allotted by our constitution to the House of Commons, is so great, that it absolutely commands all the other parts of the government', particularly the power of the purse. Consequently, it was vital to rebalance the constitution by favouring the executive, so that the system of distributing crown offices, notwithstanding that it is invidiously called 'corruption' and 'dependence', is to 'some degree . . . inseparable from the very nature of the constitution, and necessary to the preservation of our mixed government' (Hume 1994a, pp. 25–6). Later, that other theorist of the modern system of liberty, Adam Smith, took up the parallel topic of armies, asserting 'the irresistible superiority which a well-regulated standing army has over a militia' and the irrelevance of militias after 'the great revolution in the art of war' that had occurred in modern times (*WN*, v.1.a). Hume's and Smith's position has been called 'sceptical' or 'scientific' Whiggism, for it pushed aside what they saw as the superannuated clichés and sentimentality of old Whiggery (Forbes 1975, 1976). The doctrines of the 'scientific' Whigs helped to entrench what Walter Bagehot proclaimed in 1867 to be 'the efficient secret of the English constitution', namely 'the close union, the nearly complete fusion, of the executive and legislative powers' (Bagehot 2001, pp. 8–9). In spite of all the voices of opposition that were heard in the decades after the Revolution of 1688, this was, as Bagehot saw, the enduring essence of the English system of liberty that was bequeathed by the Revolution.[23]

23 I am much indebted to Clare Jackson for comments on a draft of this chapter.

3

Scepticism, priestcraft, and toleration

RICHARD H. POPKIN AND MARK GOLDIE*

1   Scepticism, Judaism, and the natural history of religion

Philosophical scepticism, the questioning of the adequacy of evidence to justify any view or belief, and the questioning of the criteria for deciding intellectual issues in any domain whatsoever, reached its high point in modern philosophy during the eighteenth century. At the beginning of the century the complete edition of Pierre Bayle's *Dictionnaire historique et critique* (1702) appeared, raising sceptical problems about matters in philosophy, theology, science, and history, and providing what Voltaire called 'the arsenal of the Enlightenment'. Bishop Pierre Daniel Huet's *Traité philosophique de la faiblesse de l'esprit humain* (Treatise on the Weakness of the Human Mind), a forceful presentation of Pyrrhonism, written at the end of the seventeenth century but published posthumously in 1723, became a sensation (Popkin 1993, p. 139). The *Traité* appeared twice in English, and in Italian, Latin, and German in short order. In 1718 the most scholarly edition of the writing of Sextus Empiricus was published by J. A. Fabricius, with the Greek text and Latin translations. This was soon followed by two printings of a French translation of Sextus's *Hypotyposes* (Outlines of Pyrrhonism), and David Hume carried the sceptical analysis of human reasoning to its highest point in his *Treatise of Human Nature* (1739–40). A mitigated form of scepticism was developed by many French Enlightenment thinkers, culminating in the radical scepticism of Jean-Pierre Brissot and Condorcet in the last quarter of the century.

These sceptical developments concentrated chiefly on questions of evidence and reasoning, and on the dubiousness of human judgements in the sciences, philosophy, and theology. Another facet of scepticism emerged just before the century began, and dominated much of the discussion, namely the application of sceptical analysis to the question of the truth of the Christian religion, or principal parts thereof, sometimes even advocating disbelief in

---

* Sections 1 and 2 by Richard Popkin, 3 and 4 by Mark Goldie. Richard Popkin died on 14 April 2005.

Christianity or in religion in general. This became a principal meaning of 'scepticism' from then onward (Popkin 1979, chs. 1–2). The development of this scepticism against religion, and how it became one – if not the main – basis for religious toleration, will be traced here.

The Renaissance rediscovery of ancient Greek sceptical thought, and especially of its major texts, the writings of Sextus Empiricus, had an impact upon the religious controversies of the Reformation and Counter-Reformation. Ancient Greek scepticism, Pyrrhonism, provided ammunition to both Catholic and Protestant polemicists, as well as providing a fideistic 'defence' of religion: since nothing can be known, one should consequently accept religion on faith alone, a view offered around 1700 by both the Catholic Bishop Huet and the Protestant Bayle.

In the latter part of the seventeenth century sceptical arguments were turned against the special status of the Bible, and against the knowledge claims of the Judaeo-Christian religious tradition. Several developments played a role in bringing this about: the intellectual crisis caused by the re-evaluation of ancient polytheism; the work of the Bible critics, Isaac La Peyrère, Baruch Spinoza, and Richard Simon; the growing awareness of the criticisms of Christianity written by Jewish intellectuals in Amsterdam; and doubts about Judaism sponsored by the careers of such false Messiahs as Sabbatai Zevi (Popkin 1987a).

One of the most potent attacks on religious traditions was the notorious *Les Trois Imposteurs, Moses, Jesus, et Mahomet, ou l'esprit de M. Spinoza* (The Three Imposters . . .), probably written in its present form in the last decade of the seventeenth century, but only printed in 1719 (Anon. 1994). (A Latin work, *De Tribus Impostoribus*, with a quite different content, purporting to be from the end of the sixteenth century, was also part of the clandestine literature of the time.) *Les Trois Imposteurs* circulated widely in a great many manuscripts found all over Europe and North America. Introductory materials attached to it pretend that the work was written by the secretary of the Emperor Frederick II in the thirteenth century. However the work uses critical views about religion that appear in seventeenth-century theorists including Hobbes, Spinoza, Gabriel Naudé, and François La Mothe le Vayer, and quotes freely from them. It portrays the three great religious leaders as impostors, playing political roles for their own ends. It offers as an explanation of how and why religions develop the psychological evaluations provided by Hobbes and Spinoza. The possibility that such an attack on Judaism and Christianity (and Islam) could be available was mentioned quite often in the seventeenth century. There was discussion about whether such a work actually existed. Queen Christina of Sweden offered a huge sum for a copy. But manuscripts of the work only surfaced at the end of the seventeenth century and were quickly copied and dispersed. The same happened with the unpublished work of Jean Bodin, the *Colloquium Heptaplomeres* (Colloquium of the Seven about the Secrets of the Sublime, 1593), a fictional discussion between believers in various religions, in which the Jewish participant wins the argument. The work surfaced in the mid-seventeenth century, and manuscript copies were made. Leibniz and his associates prepared the text for publication, but it was not printed until the nineteenth century (Popkin 1988, pp. 157–60).

The question of whether religious belief could still be sustained in the light of modern knowledge appears in Bishop Edward Stillingfleet's attack on John Toland and John Locke. Stillingfleet feared that applying the empirical theory of knowledge to religious belief would simply lead to unbelief. A similar problem seems to have been involved when the French Reformed Church in the Netherlands declared it a heresy to seek clear and distinct evidence for religious belief (Carroll 1975; Popkin 1971, 1993).

The actual content of religious belief came into question in the controversies between Jews and Christians at this time. In the seventeenth century some Jewish scholars, who had been raised as forced converts to Christianity in Spain and Portugal, and who escaped to the Netherlands, presented forceful critiques of Christian beliefs using the dialectical techniques they had been taught at Iberian universities. In the tolerant atmosphere of seventeenth-century Holland, these Jewish theorists could set forth their case without fear of punishment so long as they did not print their work. Instead, their attacks on Christianity circulated widely in manuscript (Kaplan 1989, chs. 9–10). Various deistically inclined people tried to obtain manuscripts, and finally in 1715 a group of them were auctioned in The Hague. The arguments in these manuscripts were described without comment in the final edition of Jacques Basnage's *Histoire des juifs* (History of the Jews, 1716) – a book which, when it first appeared in 1706, was the first history of the Jews since Josephus. Considering the Jewish views, Basnage concluded that Christians should give up trying to convert Jews by arguments, since the Jews knew the materials better and usually won the debates. Instead one should leave the task of converting Jews to God alone.

The Jewish anti-Christian arguments became known to such figures as Anthony Collins, Voltaire, and Holbach, and they were used as powerful ammunition against the Christian establishment. These widely circulated manuscripts sought to show that there was no evidence that Christianity is the fulfilment of Judaism and that there was no good evidence that the Messiah had yet come. Holbach published some of the arguments of the Jewish philosopher, Isaac Orobio de Castro, under the title *Israel vengé* (Israel Avenged, 1770), thereby making them widely available. Some of the manuscripts found their way to Harvard University Library, and a New England preacher, George Bethune English, came across them. His Christian beliefs were thoroughly shaken. After consulting the rabbi of New York he converted to Islam (English 1813). These Jewish anti-Christian arguments could therefore undermine intellectual conviction in Christianity, and some of them were considered the strongest evidence against Christian belief (Popkin 1992, 1994). In one copy of *Israel vengé* an unidentified reader wrote that Orobio proves by Sacred History that the Messiah has not yet come. A letter pasted in this volume states that Christians cannot answer Orobio's claims.[1] Zalkind Hourwitz, the French royal librarian of the Oriental collection in Paris at the time of the Revolution, asserted that one either had to abandon Christian claims of superiority over Judaism, or risk turning people into complete sceptics about religion (Hourwitz 1789).

However, another kind of scepticism also developed against Judaism itself. One source was the intellectual debacle following the Jewish Messianic movement of 1666, and another was the growing treatment of the Old Testament as the secular history of a peculiar group of people of antiquity. Jews everywhere became excited when Sabbatai Zevi of Smyrna announced in late 1665 that he was the long-awaited Messiah, and that the Messianic age was beginning. He changed Jewish law and appointed his friends and relatives the new kings of the world. It is estimated that 90 per cent of the Jewish world at the time accepted him. A few months later the Turkish sultan had Sabbatei Zevi arrested and threatened with death. The 'Messiah' quickly converted to Islam, and lived the rest of his life as an Ottoman functionary. The Jewish world was swept by doubt and dismay. Many Jews began to question the nature of Messiahship, and how the sacred texts could be understood (Scholem 1973).

Christian opponents suggested that Jews lacked a trustworthy criterion for telling a true Messiah from a false one (Evelyn 1669; Leslie 1715). But freethinking people could equally suggest that Christians too lacked an adequate criterion for determining who was the Messiah. The historical knowledge upon which both religions depended began to be subjected to sceptical criticism, as in Voltaire's article, 'Méssie' (Messiah) in the *Dictionnaire*

---

[1] Bibliothèque Nationale, Paris, Rés. D2.5193.

philosophique. This involved the gradual transformation of 'revealed' truth into natural, secular facts, by treating the scriptures as ordinary human writings, best understood solely in the context of the human authors' milieux. Hobbes, Spinoza, and the early English deists did most to advance this view. In his *Tractatus theologico-politicus* (1670), Spinoza said that the science of interpreting the Bible should be like, or almost the same as, the science of nature. La Peyrère, Hobbes, and Spinoza all pointed out discrepancies, inconsistencies, and contradictions in the Biblical texts, and maintained that Moses could not be the author of the Pentateuch. They dwelt upon problems of canonicity and transmission. Readers could not be sure that the Bible they now possessed was the same as the ancient texts, given all of the redactions and transmutations that had taken place in the intervening centuries. The greatest seventeenth-century Bible scholar, Father Richard Simon, revealed the apparently endless historical and textual problems that lay between the present-day reader and the original authors and texts (Popkin 1979).

Over the next hundred years more and more problems were raised about whether one could be sure that Moses was the author of the first five books of the Bible, or whether they had one author, or whether the author or authors were divinely inspired. The sceptical side of the debate was summed up in Thomas Paine's comment in *The Age of Reason* (1794–5): 'Take away from Genesis the belief that Moses was the author, on which only the strange belief that it is the word of God has stood, and there remains nothing of Genesis, but an anonymous book of stories, fables and traditionary or invented absurdities or downright lies' (Paine 1795a, p. 14). The consequences of scepticism about Mosaic authorship were drawn even more sharply by the Jewish writer, David Levi, who said that 'if a Jew once calls in question the authenticity of *any part* of the Pentateuch, by observing that one part is authentic i.e., was delivered by God to Moses, and that another part is not authentic, he is no longer accounted a Jew, i.e., a true believer'. Levi then insisted that every Jew is obliged, according to Maimonides's principles, 'to believe that the whole law of five books . . . is from God' and was given by Him to Moses. Christians should be under the same constraints regarding the Old and New Testament, for 'if any part is by once proved spurious, a door will be opened for another and another without end' (Levi 1789, pp. 14–15).

Spinoza claimed that we could understand the Biblical narrative in terms of the secular history of the primitive peoples of Palestine. He developed a thoroughgoing scepticism about the possibility of mankind having any access to supernatural information. This then allowed him to see all historical claims, Biblical or other, as just statements about how human beings behaved at various times and places. The fact that some people said that they received messages from God, or had revelations, was interesting data about those people and their psychological states, rather than reports of genuine divine communications. Reading scripture in this manner resulted in the Bible becoming an object *in* human history rather than a framework for explaining it (*Tractatus*, chs.1–7; *Ethics*, bk 1, appx). David Hume, in the mid-eighteenth century, argued for a more modest sceptical claim, namely that it was extraordinarily improbable that any report of supernatural events was believable, and that it would always be more probable that the report was false. 'No testimony is sufficient to establish a miracle, unless the testimony be of such a kind, that its falsehood would be more miraculous, than the fact, which it endeavours to establish' (Hume 1951, pp. 115–16). At the end of the essay, 'Of Miracles' (1750), Hume suggested examining the Pentateuch as the production of a mere human writer and historian, rather than as the word of God. Then, we would see it as a book

presented to us by a barbarous and ignorant people, wrote in an age when they were still more barbarous, and in all probability long after the facts it relates; corroborated by no concurring testimony, and resembling those fabulous accounts, which every nation gives of its origin. Upon reading this book, we find it full of prodigies and miracles. It gives an account of a state of the world and of human nature entirely different from the present: Of our fall from that state: Of the age of man, extended to near a thousand years: Of the destruction of the world by a deluge: Of the arbitrary choice of one people, as the favourites of heaven; and that people the countrymen of the author: Of their deliverance from bondage by prodigies the most astonishing imaginable. (Hume 1750, pp. 205–6)

This historical contextualism, and psychological evaluation of Biblical religion, led at the end of the eighteenth century to the religion of reason, and to what Kant described as religion within the bounds of pure reason, both of which accepted this desacralization of the central documents of Judaism and Christianity.

Thus a radical scepticism developed about the significance of the Judaeo-Christian religious tradition seen as other than an allegorical or mythological presentation of a code of ethics. This interpretation began around 1700 with the German convert to Judaism, Moses Germanus, and was then adopted by Johann Edelman and Hermann Reimarus (Grossmann 1976; Popkin 1994; Schoeps 1952). Jesus was seen as an inspiring ethical teacher, following a long line of Jewish moral leaders going back to the prophets. He had been unjustifiably deified a couple of centuries after the actual events, thereby creating a Christianity which had no basis in historical fact.

The Christian story could be, as the *Traité des trois imposteurs* said, an imposition foisted upon the human race, a story perpetuated by manipulative priests and politicians in order to control people through fear and superstition. Churches and religious and political institutions were established to carry this on from generation to generation even though it was fundamentally a fraud or hoax generated to gain and keep political power. This charge was taken seriously enough by two leading English theologians, Ralph Cudworth and Edward Stillingfleet, for them to try to raise countervailing doubts about the possibility of such a conspiracy. They sought to show the implausibility of so many people in so many times and places keeping up the imposture for so many centuries, without anyone detecting the fraud (Cudworth 1678; Stillingfleet 1662).

English deists, starting with Charles Blount (who published the first English translation of any of Spinoza's writings), saw Spinoza's naturalistic reading of the Bible as supporting their own view that the Bible as we know it is only one of many human attempts to portray a natural religion in specific cultural terms, an attempt which is open to comparison with many differing ancient and modern pagan versions from various parts of the planet (Blount 1683; Champion 1992; Popkin 1991). This was coupled with Bayle's reading of the Old Testament narrative as comparable with any historical narrative, in which the characters, like the patriarchs and King David, can be judged in the same way as any other moral or immoral actors on the human stage. Bayle proceeded to show the immoral, dishonest activities of the heroes and heroines of ancient Israel to be as bad as those of pagan characters, of European kings and queens, and of religious leaders from post-Biblical times to the present. Bayle contended that there is no necessary relation between religion and morality, and that a society of atheists could be as moral as a society of Christians. He portrayed the 'atheist' Spinoza as an almost saintly figure, while painting contemporary Catholic and Protestant leaders as liars, hypocrites, and cheats.

The story of Spinoza's own religious career, centring on his excommunication from the Amsterdam synagogue, became a symbolic picture of the malign power of priests and priestcraft. The first biography of Spinoza, *La Vie de M. Spinosa*, by Jean-Maximilien Lucas (often found alongside *Les*

Trois Imposteurs) created a lasting picture of the saintly Spinoza, victim of the religious intolerance of the priests of Judaism, the chief rabbi the epitome of the priestly tyrant. The Amsterdam Jewish community was portrayed as one of rigid outmoded orthodoxy, unable to endure a brave truth-seeker. So a horrendous excommunication ritual took place, and Spinoza had to flee. Although this was a misrepresentation of the Amsterdam Jewish community and its leaders, the legend persisted, and became crucial in the mythology of the sainted progenitor of the Enlightenment (Israel 1985, 2001; Méchoulan 1991).

Added to this was the appearance of the autobiography of Uriel da Costa in the publication of the friendly debate between the tolerant Remonstrant scholar, Philip van Limborch (a close friend of John Locke) and Isaac Orobio de Castro (Limborch 1687). Da Costa, a Portuguese priest of Jewish origins, fled the Inquisition for Amsterdam. There he offered his own version of Judaism, and was excommunicated. He eventually recanted, was dreadfully punished, readmitted, and soon again was excommunicated. Finally he committed suicide. Until Limborch published it, his autobiography was unknown. It quickly was taken as more evidence of the hideous intolerance of religious establishments. Bayle, in the *Dictionnaire*, was not the only writer to wallow in the pathos of Da Costa's case, and he became the intellectual forefather of Spinoza, the two men the twin victims of priestcraft. Near the end of his autobiography Da Costa cried out, 'Don't be a Jew or a Christian. Be a man!'

The English deists, impressed by the discovery of so many different kinds of religion in the ancient and modern worlds, developed a comparative study of religion, partly to understand what it represented in different times, places, and cultures, and partly to try to find an inner core in all religions that might represent the 'ur-religion', the original and natural religion of mankind. John Toland's *Christianity not Mysterious* (1696), and Matthew Tindal's *Christianity as Old as the Creation* (1730), sought to find pre-Christian or original Christian sources that constituted this basic religion, as well as to account for contemporary Christianity as a disastrous deformation of natural religion that occurred when an institutional priestcraft took over and controlled religion, supported by, and allied with, arbitrary political powers. The deists sought to show that ancient religion, stripped of unwarranted accretions, was a civic and ethical code, rather than a priestly, credal, and ceremonial religion (Champion 1992; Goldie 1993a). They took some of their inspiration from attempts by such Cambridge Platonists as Ralph Cudworth, in his *True Intellectual System of the Universe* (1678), to discern fragments of universal religious truth shining dimly through the local and often perverse traditions that had grown up among actual historical religions. The deists' notion that, at bottom, much of Christian priestcraft was a design to wrest political and social power from the secular magistrate found expression in the penultimate chapter, 'Civil Religion', of Rousseau's *Social Contract* (1762). Here Rousseau remarks that Hobbes 'dared to propose reuniting the two heads of the eagle, and to return everything to political unity' (*SC*, IV.8, p. 146). Deist religious anthropology also culminated in seeing all religions as natural human developments. By the middle of the eighteenth century, Hume could write a work entitled *The Natural History of Religion* (1758) in which polytheism was seen as the natural religion, which through psychological developments ended up as the fractious splintered warring views of theologians in the present.

Oddly, however, scepticism could serve to bolster fideistic belief in Christianity as well as destructive doubt. Bayle contended, whether sincerely or not, that doubt must be put aside and Christianity accepted without or against reason, for faith is built upon the ruins of reason. Religious thinkers came to see the purported fideism of Bayle and even of Hume as a defence of religious orthodoxy. Bayle's contemporary and erstwhile colleague, Pierre Jurieu, insisted that Bayle was ridiculing religion and was actually an atheist. But Bayle, for over twenty-five years, defended his fideism before the tribunal of the French Reformed Church of Rotterdam, answering Jurieu's charges and those of other Calvinist ministers (Labrousse 1985, chs. 7–9). Later some theologians, especially in France, began to see Bayle as an ally in arguing that religion was built on faith and not reason (Kors 1990, ch. 7; Rétat 1971). Similarly, Hume ended his *Dialogues concerning Natural Religion* (*c.* 1750, publ. 1779), after destroying the cognitive value of arguments proving the existence of God, with an ironic 'fideist' observation: 'To be a philosophical sceptic is, in a man of letters, the first and most essential step towards being a sound, believing *Christian*' (Hume 1980, p. 89). Hume's contemporaries, who called him 'the great infidel', would not have seen him as a 'sound, believing Christian'. However, the German mystic J. G. Hamann read the passage in the *Dialogues* and proclaimed, 'This is orthodoxy and a testimony to the truth from the mouth of an enemy and persecutor' (Hamann 1821–43, I, p. 406; Merlan 1954). Bayle and Hume were transformed from heroes of the *avant garde* to allies of the *ancien régime*. Hume became a mentor of the Counter-Revolution in France, admired by Louis XVI and by Joseph de Maistre, the reviver of conservative Catholicism (Bongie 1965; Rétat 1971).

2   French scepticism and perfectibilism

In France, where Catholicism was the official religion and rigid control
was exercised to prevent the spread of heretical or unorthodox ideas, one
finds a covert spread of sceptical irreligious ideas from the Netherlands and
England. Spinoza's *Tractatus* appeared in French translation in 1678, Bayle's
Dictionnaire, and French translations of Locke and the English deists were
read by rebellious intellectuals like the young Voltaire (Betts 1984; Vernière
1954). From this, two main developments stemmed, one a 'rational' scientific
approach to natural and human knowledge within the bounds of a moderate
scepticism, and the other an almost rabid attack on religious institutions and
practices.

The first was a distillation of what French thinkers saw as the empirical
fruits of modern science in Isaac Newton's accomplishments, in the translation into French of Locke's *Essay concerning Human Understanding* (1700),
by a friend of Bayle's, Pierre Coste, who emphasised the sceptical themes
in Locke's philosophy, and in the moderate version of the total scepticism
of Bayle and Huet. The latter himself had said at the end of his *Traité* that
the sceptic should follow the attitude and practice of the Royal Society
of England, which combined an epistemological scepticism about ultimate
knowledge with a practical way of gaining useful scientific knowledge (Huet
1723, bk 2, ch. 10, p. 221). In the French version this practical scientific
knowledge would help explain natural phenomena, and also would help
promote understanding of mankind and its problems and provide ways of
solving them.

The traditional account of Enlightenment thought portrays it as a positive, even dogmatically positive, rejection both of tradition and sceptical
doubt, in favour of the power of truth through reason. Condillac said that
Bayle's doubts were justified as long as there were so many dark, blind outmoded philosophies. But once modern science had gained ascendancy, the
power of reason would lead people to new truths (Condillac 1947–9, III,
p. 22). However, a strong strain of scepticism persisted. Such leading figures as Diderot, d'Alembert, Condillac, and Maupertius accepted that our
knowledge was based on sense experience, was very limited, and could not
extend beyond experience to metaphysical reality. Within these sceptical
limitations the empirical sciences of nature and of man could be developed,
which the *philosophes* proceeded to do. These sciences within the bounds of
a limited scepticism extended to what Hume called 'the moral subjects', psychological, social, and political questions. Hume's *Treatise of Human Nature*

was significantly subtitled 'Being an Attempt to Introduce the Experimental Method of Reasoning into Moral Subjects', the 'experimental method of reasoning' being, of course, that which Newton had so successfully applied to the understanding of natural matters. Hume's essays on moral and political subjects, published from the 1740s, and quickly translated into French, provided a model for sceptically based social studies, examining man and society in terms of experience. Hume had called history the laboratory for examining human nature (Hume 1951, p. xxiii). The *philosophes* studied religion, political societies, variations in human nature, and human abilities in empirical terms.

Where the physical sciences could improve human life by providing new sources of power, labour-saving devices, means of transport, and so forth, so the human sciences could lead to the reform of human institutions, so that, in the view of Turgot, there could be an indefinite progressive improvement in human life in the future. Turgot, a leading mathematician, economist, and politician, was Hume's closest personal friend among the French *philosophes* in the 1760s.

Turgot gradually realised, as reform projects became more important, that the limited scepticism of the *philosophes* was not compatible with the total scepticism of Hume. Turgot finally saw that Hume's thoroughgoing scepticism actually completely opposed the *philosophes*' programme for the reform of human understanding and society, and that Hume was in fact an enemy of what the *philosophes* considered 'Enlightenment'. Hume had written to Turgot criticizing the view 'that human society is capable of perpetual progress towards perfection, that the increase of knowledge will still prove favourable to good government, and that since the discovery of printing we need no longer dread the usual returns of barbarism and ignorance' (Hume 1932, II, p. 180). To show this, Hume cited what he considered terrible things that were happening in England at the time. Turgot replied that Hume should not be blinded by local events, but should consider the larger picture and realise that human beings and their knowledge are perfectible and that progress is inevitable. Turgot then said farewell to Hume, saying 'Adieu, monsieur – car le temps me presse' ('Farewell, sir – time is pressing').

In 1777 the young Jacques Pierre Brissot de Warville, a journalist, and political commentator, one of the last *philosophes*, suggested to d'Alembert that they produce an encyclopedia of Pyrrhonism. The ageing editor of the *Encyclopédie* seemed uninterested, but Brissot, then in his early twenties, worked away at the project, apparently begun in an extant unpublished ninety-page manuscript on Pyrrhonism.[2] In 1782 Brissot published *De la vérité, ou méditations sur les moyens de parvenir à la vérité dans toutes les connaissances humaines* (Concerning the Truth, or Meditations on the Means of Approaching the Truth in all Human Studies, republished in 1792), exploring whether we can know anything with certainty in any of the sciences. Brissot's work is, perhaps, the most extended presentation of French Enlightenment scepticism. He concluded that the sciences can never reach the final degree of perfection, and that it is necessary always to doubt. Because of sceptical difficulties and human fallibility, there is extremely little that we know with any certainty. He wanted to avoid any positive metaphysical views. We should confine ourselves to probabilities and practicalities, discovering within each science the limited truths that they will yield. He thought it would take him several years to do this. But, then, in a footnote, he said that if his work on legislation and politics permitted, in two or three years he could present a 'tableau' of these truths. A reasonable scepticism could, he thought, still yield political and social reform (Brissot 1792, p. 361n). He was visiting America, where he was about to establish a utopian republican community in Kentucky, when he learned of the revolutionary events in France, to which he returned and there became a leader of the Girondins. He was guillotined before he could complete his intellectual work.

Turgot's leading disciple, Condorcet, was an ally of Brissot in trying to end slavery and in advocating liberal reforms during the Revolution. Condorcet pushed the sceptical and optimistic sides of French Enlightenment thought to their highest levels. One of the best mathematicians of the age, he developed Turgot's proposal to apply mathematics to human problems. Condorcet was also one of the few French readers of Hume's *Treatise of Human Nature*. In fact he got his clue for applying mathematics to the social sciences from a confusing section of Hume's text on chance and probability (Baker 1975, pp. 135–55). Condorcet developed an advanced sceptical epistemology and used this as support for his positive views and his belief in the unending progress of human knowledge. He criticised the sceptics for belabouring the obvious, 'that neither in the physical sciences nor in the moral sciences can we obtain the rigorous certainty of mathematical propositions', when, nonetheless, 'there are sure means of arriving at a very great probability in some cases and of evaluating the degree of this probability in a great number' (Baker 1975, p. 129). Condorcet held that we cannot arrive at a necessary science of nature due to human limitations. Empirically we can

2 Archives Nationale, Paris: 446/AP/21.

observe what happens but not why it happens. Newton's laws did not yield
a guarantee that nature will always behave in certain ways and cannot act
otherwise. We cannot attain logical demonstrative certainty in the study of
nature as we do in mathematics. However, our uncertainty does not lead to
complete scepticism. We can induce laws from empirical observations and
intuitively recognise relations of ideas. These laws are only probable because
we do not know if nature will be uniform, and therefore we do not know
if the future will resemble the past. The development of the mathematics of
probability allowed people to formulate a mathematics of reasonable expectation, provided that one presumed that nature would remain uniform. This
mathematics does not inform us what will happen, but rather tells us what
human beings can reasonably expect might happen. This conclusion is then
the basis for the expectation that the moral sciences can then have the same
sort of precision and exactitude as the natural sciences, and the same kind
of certainty. So, in spite of sceptical questions, we can know with certainty
about the empirical study of nature and of man and society, providing we
can accept that nature and man will act uniformly. Both physical and human
sciences can then be developed in terms of probabilities. Our knowledge
in these areas can grow indefinitely, and can be used to improve the human
scene. Hence, we can expect the indefinite progress of human knowledge,
and the perfectibility of mankind.

Hume's doubts about humankind's ability to improve the world led to
his dismissal of believers in progress, expressed in his essay on 'The Idea of
a Perfect Commonwealth' (1752): political projectors will do more harm
than good. Nonetheless Condorcet spent the years before the Revolution
offering solutions to problems such as eliminating slavery in the colonies.
During the revolutionary period he was most active, writing up proposals
for reforming education, law, hospitals, and prisons, and a liberal democratic
constitution, projecting the politics of a future age until he died while
imprisoned by the Jacobins.

Condorcet and Brissot (who were friends of Thomas Jefferson and admirers of Benjamin Franklin) believed that in the liberal world that was emerging in the United States and the one they were trying to create in France,
religion would no longer be a dominant and dominating force. They were
minimal deists rather than atheists, and saw a thoroughly secular world arising in which people would not have to believe anything in particular. Theirs
would be a completely tolerant world, in part because traditional religion
was a system of superstition that was being superseded. Now, with enlightenment, humankind no longer needed churches and priests. Their function

could be replaced by secular academies and scientific organisations which would lead people to the most probable truths, and to the knowledge that could improve the human condition.

3   The limits of toleration

Much eighteenth-century debate on the political and social implications of religion turned on the pressing and contingent problem of religious toleration. Minorities sought freedom to worship as they chose and sought equal rights as citizens; in this they continued to be opposed by dominant parties in church and state. The fulcrum upon which these debates turned was Louis XIV's Revocation of the Edict of Nantes in 1685, the effect of which was to drive the Huguenots from France. Two hundred thousand fled, and in so doing brought the word 'refugee' into the language. Many who remained were forcibly converted, killed, or sent to the galleys. Within the Huguenot diaspora, a vigorous defence of toleration emerged. A fleet of tracts was published, such as Henri Basnage's *Tolérance des religions* (1684), Aubert de Versé's *Traité de la liberté de conscience* (1687), and Jacques Basnage's *Traité de la consience* (1696). Two tracts achieved lasting influence. One was Pierre Bayle's *Commentaire philosophique* (Philosophical Commentary, 1686). It was written in the aftermath of the death of the author's brother in a French jail, after daily visits by a Jesuit priest who promised him release if he would recant. The other was John Locke's *Letter concerning Toleration*, composed in 1685–6 and published in 1689. Locke of course was not a Huguenot but, as an exile in Holland close to this circle of Huguenot publicists (so much so that his anonymous tract was at first attributed to one of them, Jacques Bernard), it is appropriate to set him in this context.[3]

Almost as provocative as Louis XIV's Revocation was the tragic paradox of Pierre Jurieu's position. A Huguenot, an exile, and therefore a victim too, Jurieu nonetheless upheld the duty of the Christian magistrate to enforce the true religion. For him, the Revocation was evil only because it served a false religion. What gave Jurieu hope was an apocalyptic belief in the imminent overthrow of French power, for he believed that the providence of God would manifest itself in the conquering sword of King William III. Jurieu brought to Holland the panoply of Calvinist synodical authority, rooting out heretical deviations towards Arminianism and Socinianism within the exile

---

3 The literature on Locke on toleration is extensive. Key items include Bracken 1984; Cranston 1991b; Dunn 1991; Harris 1994; Marshall 1994; Waldron 1991. The best recent general account of toleration in Enlightenment Europe is Grell and Porter 2000. For the Bernard attribution: Bayle 2000a, p. 236.

community. The synod in Amsterdam condemned the proposition that 'the magistrate has no right to employ his authority to crush idolatry and prevent the growth of heresy' (qu. Kamen 1967, p. 236). Bayle was sacked from his professorship for taking a different line. For Jurieu, toleration opened the door to unbelief, and the contents of Bayle's *Dictionnaire* (1697) did little to assuage such fears. The pamphlet duel between the two men lasted many years.[4]

Bayle's and Locke's tracts became widely dispersed in the new century. Locke's arguments were deployed in Brandenburg-Prussia by the Huguenot exile Jean Barbeyrac in the footnotes to his editions of Pufendorf. From Barbeyrac they passed to Louis de Jaucourt and Jean Romilly, whose articles in the *Encyclopédie*, especially 'Tolérance' and 'Liberté de conscience', brought about the suspension of the *Encyclopédie*'s publication in the face of condemnation by the *parlement* of Paris (Adams 1991; Zurbuchen 1995).

If the Revocation was the quintessence of intolerance for the early Enlightenment, the case of Jean Calas was so for the later. In Toulouse in 1762 Calas, a Protestant, was tortured and executed for the alleged murder of his son who had supposedly converted to Catholicism. Through Voltaire's *Traité sur la tolérance* (Treatise on Tolerance, 1763) all Europe came to know of it. For good measure, the following year Voltaire added a translation of Locke's *Letter* to his own tract. Calas was posthumously exonerated, and after the French Revolution a statue to him was ordered to be built at the place of his death (Adams 1991; Bien 1960; Gargett 1980).

An oddity about the brutality of the Calas trial is that within a decade it came to seem aberrant. Tolerationist sensibility in France, at least among intellectuals, seems to have made some headway by the 1770s. In the 1680s many French intellectuals had defended the Revocation. Bishop Bossuet had done so. Fénelon, whatever his later notions, thought it right to organise the abduction of Calvinist girls. By contrast, in the 1770s many French authors pressed for relaxation of the laws against Protestants: Turgot, Malesherbes, Morellet, Le Paige, and Lafayette among them. In Hamburg, the tolerationist resolutions of the Patriotic Society founded in 1765 found more support than had its timid predecessor of the 1720s.

This, however, is to begin to flatter the late Enlightenment's own self-regard as to the progress of humane sensibility. At the close of the eighteenth century public commentators were apt to applaud edicts and laws for

---

4 On Bayle, Jurieu, and the political thought of the Huguenot diaspora see Bracken 1984; Dodge 1947; Kilcullen 1988; Knetsch 1967; Labrousse 1963–4, 1982, 1983; Laursen 1995; Simonutti 1996; Yardeni 1985.

toleration as redolent of the spirit of the new enlightened age. Yet in practice the concessions made by European states were limited and grudging. In England the Act of Toleration of 1689 allowed public worship by Protestant Dissenters, yet excluded them from political offices; Catholics did not even gain freedom of worship. Accordingly, although Protestant worship was freed, Dissenters continued eloquently to demand civil liberty, notably in the campaigns of the 1770s.[5] Not until 1791, at a moment when Christianity of every denomination seemed threatened by revolutionary atheism, were English Catholics allowed openly to worship; and not until 1828–9 were Catholics and Dissenters admitted to public office. The French Edict of Toleration of 1787 did not even address the question of public worship, but only made provision for certain civil liberties, principally the authentication of Huguenot births, marriages, deaths, and wills. In Austria, the Emperor Joseph II's edict of 1781 allowed freedom of worship to Lutherans, Calvinists, and Orthodox, but not to others; it forbad non-Catholic churches to have spires or bells; and it left intact the Catholic clergy's fees for the rites of passage. The Hamburg decree of 1785 put similar restrictions on church buildings, did not tolerate Mennonites or Jews, and retained the Lutheran monopoly on public office. Perhaps only under Islam, in Ottoman Transylvania, did the Christian religions have real equality of treatment. In general, throughout Europe, the concessions were modest, late, and resisted. They were also, for the most part, granted by the gracious, and revocable, fiat of rulers who did not concede the general principle that the state had no *right* to make impositions in religion. Hence, in the *Rights of Man* (1791–2), Paine protested that 'Toleration is not the opposite of intoleration, but is the counterfeit of it. Both are despotisms. The one assumes to itself the right of withholding liberty of conscience, and the other of granting it' (Paine 1989, p. 102).

As these examples show, it is important to distinguish between different degrees of freedom granted to those who professed minority religions. Private worship, public worship, and admittance to the professions and political office were not the same things, and allowance of one did not necessarily entail allowance of others. In the German lands the presence or absence of spires and bells represented the contrast between *exercitium religionis publicum* and *exercitium religionis privatum*; in turn, there was the more restricted *exercitium religionis domesticum*. These were categories embodied in the religious

5 Fownes 1773; Kippis 1772. On the 'Rational Dissenters' see Barlow 1962; Clark 1985; Haakonssen 1996b; Kramnick 1990; and ch. 23 below. On toleration and the English Revolution see Grell *et al.* 1991; Walsh *et al.* 1993.

provisions of the Treaty of Westphalia (1648), which brought to an end the
Thirty Years War (1618–48). They were categories which entered the academic treatises of eighteenth-century jurists and were drawn upon in the
Emperor Joseph's edict of 1781. At an early stage, in some parts of Germany,
the Westphalian settlement produced remarkable and diverse arrangements,
exemplifying what might be called toleration by attrition, the result not of
principle but of stalemate. Such arrangements could include the installing
of rulers of alternating confessions, as at Osnabruck; the sharing of church
buildings; and even a tri-confessional convent, as at Schildesche near Biele-
feld (Grossmann 1979, 1982; Whaley 2000, pp. 179–81).

Toleration continued to be regarded with suspicion throughout Europe,
and it would be a mistake to suppose that by the age of Enlightenment the
tide had turned decisively towards acceptance of religious pluralism. This
was neither the case in practice nor in debate. Arguments for intolerance
continued to be upheld throughout the century. Not least among these was
the deployment of a phrase in St Luke's Gospel, 'Compel them to come in'
(Luke 14:23). A gloss upon this as providing divine sanction for pastoral coercion was first enunciated by St Augustine in his battle against the Donatist
heretics in the fifth century. The Catholic pulpits of Louis XIV's France
regularly resorted to this claim, as did the Anglican pulpits of England prior
to the Toleration Act (Goldie 1991c). Bayle's classic tolerationist treatise has
as its full title *Commentaire philosophique sur les paroles de Jésus Christ 'Contrains
les d'entrer'* (A Philosophical Commentary on the Words of Our Lord,
'Compel them to Come in'). He argued that the persecutor who invoked
Luke is a kind of antinomian, for to persecute is to allow the word of
God to overrule the laws of natural morality. Any literal interpretation of
scripture which promotes moral iniquity must be a false reading (Bayle
1987, I.I, p. 28). The argument from Luke remained persistent enough to
require constant addressing by the friends of tolerance. Edward Synge, a rare
Protestant voice in Ireland arguing for the relaxation of the penal laws against
Catholics, took the critique of the conventional reading of Luke to be his
task in a sermon called *The Case of Toleration* (1725). Later, Kant adverted
to the argument from Luke in his *Religion innerhalb der Grenzen der blossen
Vernunft* (Religion within the Boundary of Pure Reason, 1793) (Kant 1838,
p. 253).

During the century, the defence of intolerance turned increasingly
towards the claim that toleration was a licence for religious indifference
and heresy. Behind toleration, its critics claimed, there sheltered not so
much diversity of faiths, but rather scepticism and atheism. On this ground,

the French clergy powerfully resisted relaxation of the laws against the Huguenots right up to the eve of the Revolution. Orthodox Huguenots themselves continued to be fearful that toleration mishandled would unleash Socinianism and deism: some Huguenots were distinctly uncomfortable at having Voltaire's advocacy on their side in the Calas case, and Voltaire was in turn irritated at their ingratitude (Adams 1991). In Hamburg, and throughout Germany, Johann Melchior Goeze, 'Der Inquisitor', author of more than 100 tracts, kept up, until his death in 1786, a barrage of arguments on the perniciousness of toleration. 'To have been attacked by Goeze was almost in itself to be enlightened' (Whaley 1985, p. 151). In Italy, in the year of the French Revolution, Tommaso Vincenzo Pani, Dominican inquisitor in the Papal States, continued to argue for the necessity of the Inquisition for the preservation of religion in his *On the Punishment of Heretics* (Davidson 2000, p. 230).

Not all arguments for intolerance were strictly theological. Often they turned upon the alleged temporal dangers posed by minority groups. Even in the mid-eighteenth century French Catholics still denounced Calvinists as fanatics, republicans, and rebels. The canard that Calvin had authorised the murder of heretic children continued to be spread. The stain of the sixteenth-century wars of religion, and of successive waves of Calvinist rebellion, was impossible to cleanse. When the Huguenot pastor Antoine Court wrote his *Histoire des troubles des Cévennes* (1760) he was at pains to dissociate modern Huguenots from their forebears who had staged the Camisard rebellion of 1702, notwithstanding the fact that the Camisards had been courageously resisting state oppression of their religion. Antoine portrayed the rebellion as a primitive peasant *jacquerie*, with barbarisms committed on both sides (Haour 1995).

Another charge against the Calvinists was that they were not themselves believers in toleration. Calvin's burning of Servetus for heresy in 1553 was constantly mentioned. The Servetus case allowed Catholics to say that the demand for toleration was merely a Machiavellian plea by the weak, who would abandon the tenet if ever they gained power (see Bayle 1987, pt 2, ch. 5). Voltaire, no friend to persecution, used his *Siècle de Louis XIV* (The Age of Louis XIV, 1751) to congratulate Louis on presiding over a growth of manners which rendered Calvinistical dogmatism a superannuated idiom of a darker age. In his *Traité sur la tolérance* (Treatise on Tolerance) he wrote that in earlier times the Huguenots had been 'drunk with fanaticism and steeped in blood' (Voltaire 1994c, ch. 4, p. 22). The point for Voltaire was that toleration was possible in modern times now that barbarism was receding and all sections of society had advanced towards civility. Voltaire was vehement in his attacks on the madness of much of the Calvinist tradition. His defence of Calas was in part a retort to accusations that he was indifferent to the actual injustices suffered by contemporary Huguenots.

In Protestant states, the case against tolerating Catholics tended to turn less on the old claim that there was a godly duty to repress popish 'idolatry' and 'superstition' – in the age of Pope Benedict XIV and Muratori even Catholicism could seem enlightened in Protestant eyes – but rather on the question of whether Catholics could be good citizens. If Catholics owed their ultimate allegiance to a foreign temporal power, the papacy, and if the papacy still claimed a right to depose heretic princes, then Catholics were unsafe. Worse, if Catholics still held that 'faith need not be kept with heretics', then they were guilty of dissolving all the ties of mutual trust which held society together. The case of Jan Hus, the proto-Protestant who was given a safe conduct to attend the Council of Constance in 1415, and who was then arrested and executed, was endlessly charged against Catholicism. As for the papal deposing power, as late as the 1790s the British prime minister William Pitt sought the opinion of European universities as to whether it was the authentic doctrine of the Catholic Church: they pronounced that it was not. In 1791 the Irish radical Wolfe Tone averred that 'in these days of illumination' the doctrine of the pope's temporal supremacy was too absurd for anyone seriously to believe it. Accordingly, he concluded, Catholics had now transcended their self-incurred impediments to citizenship (Tone 1791, pp. 34–5). Locke's *Letter concerning Toleration* was a crucial text in the Anglophone world in shifting the basis of anti-Catholicism away from the older preoccupation with 'idolatry' and 'superstition'. For Locke, the fact that Catholics held absurd beliefs was of no political consequence, but the fact that they held dangerously uncivil opinions was. What mattered for him was the empirical question of whether Catholics still upheld the papal deposing power and the rightness of 'not keeping faith with heretics'. As an English Catholic priest remarked in 1791, 'since Locke published his letter on toleration the dispute has been less whether the Catholic tenets be true or false, than whether they are reconcilable with the principles of good government' (qu. Fitzpatrick 1977, p. 3).

If edicts and laws for toleration were limited in scope, if the case against toleration remained persuasive, the arguments in favour of toleration were, correspondingly, seldom expansive. Rarely did they defend a general entitlement to freedom of thought and expression, or advocate a diversity of ways of life as valuable in itself. They did not, in short, advocate secular pluralism.

Toleration was not often grounded in thoroughgoing religious scepticism, in the claim that because we cannot be certain of any religious belief we cannot plausibly enforce it. Bayle might seem a candidate, for his *Dictionnaire* was, and is, read as an encyclopedia of covert Pyrrhonism. But though he had a sturdy sense of human fallibility, he probably remained a Calvinist believer, and he did not base his tracts for toleration on radical doubt. The argument from radical doubt would not, in any case, help in dissuading persecutors from coercion, since persecutors tend to be wholly convinced of their possession of the truth. Bayle sought arguments that might appeal to the prudence of persecutors given their own standpoint. For example, he made much of the argument from reciprocity. If persecution is permissible to those who believe that they know the truth, then any group holding such a belief will consider themselves licensed thereby. Consequently, dominant groups in every nation, whatever their religion, will persecute their minorities, and the true religion will not thereby be served. To counter this argument by saying that persecution is only permitted to those who *do really* have the true religion, and not to those who falsely think they have the true religion, is fruitless, because every religion fervently believes itself to be the true one, and in different nations different religions hold power. If it is right for Catholics to oppress Protestants in France, it will be right for Protestants to oppress Catholics in England, and for Muslims to oppress Christians in Constantinople. Therefore, if we wish to protect the welfare of fellow believers everywhere, toleration is the prudent policy (Kilcullen 1988).

As has been noted, arguments from sceptical doubt played only a minor role in the case for toleration. Few people claimed that the state should not uphold Christianity because Christianity was not true. On the contrary, the premise of many arguments for toleration was that the question to be addressed was what it was proper for the state to do in the face of an 'erring conscience'. How should the state treat someone who holds a false belief or wishes to practise an heretical faith? Given that Christianity (Catholicism, Protestantism, or whatever) is true, what are the legitimate and appropriate ways of inculcating it? Perhaps only Spinoza, the lapsed Jew, stood beyond this confined framework (Israel 2001, pp. 265–70).

The framework of debate could be extraordinarily limited. In the 1770s in France the principal material issue was the authentication of Huguenot marriages, births, and testaments. A potent rebuke to the Catholic state was that its intolerance had the effect of spreading immorality among Huguenots, for by not licensing Huguenot marriages, Huguenot men could be rid of their inconvenient wives and unwanted children. Toleration of Huguenots would therefore stiffen public morality. This was Lafayette's theme when he wrote to George Washington in 1785: it shamed the Catholic state that Huguenot 'wills have no force of law, [and] their children are to be bastards' (Poland 1957, p. 71).

Another, quite different, example of the restricted and apparently arcane purlieu of debates about toleration was the claim, developed since the Reformation, that foreign embassies were entitled to keep chapels for the practice of otherwise disallowed religions. Modern international law on the extra-territoriality of embassies in fact owes much to quarrels over embassy chapels. The chapels mattered considerably, since attendance at their worship was rarely confined to diplomatic staff. The embassy chapels thereby became fortresses of religious diversity within important metropolises (Grossmann 1979).

A yet further special case of arguments for toleration was the millenarian defence of charity towards the Jews, readmitted to England by Oliver Cromwell in 1655. Here the ground for tolerance was an apocalyptic reading of scripture: the conversion of the Jews was a necessary prelude to the fulfilment of prophecy and the end of earthly time. In France in 1785 the Academy of Sciences of Metz posed the question, 'How to make the Jews happy and useful in France'. The Abbé Henri Grégoire, in his prize-winning *Essai sur la régéneration physique, morale et politique des Juifs* (Essay on the Physical, Moral, and Political Regeneration of the Jews, 1789), insisted on the necessity of the moral and political regeneration of the Jews in order to prepare them for the millennium. He advocated their personal freedom and political rights as a means to this end.

4   Arguments for toleration

If we turn to what might be called the mainstream of Enlightenment arguments for toleration, we notice, as was remarked above, the common premise that the question to be addressed was the state's treatment of the 'erring conscience'. Arguments for toleration were broadly evangelical in nature. They were confessional, not secular, and they debated toleration and the relationship of the church to the state within the context of the Christian duty to evangelise. They began from the belief that all people should be of the true religion and that all godly people should seek to put an end to heresy and schism by winning over the errant and godforsaken. The crucial question was whether, in bringing about this desired end, it was legitimate or feasible to use the powers of the state, either minimally, in the form of restrictions on freedom of action by minorities, or maximally, in the form of forced conversion. Locke, in his *Letter*, declared that 'I would not have this understood, as if I meant hereby to condemn all charitable admonitions and affectionate endeavours to reduce men from errors; which are indeed the greatest duty of a Christian.' The issue, rather, was whether 'force and compulsion are to be forborne' (Locke 1983, p. 47). Even for Locke, therefore, toleration was closely tied to pastoral issues for the evangelising Christian. A book like Pietro Tamburini's *On Ecclesiastical and Civil Tolerance* (1783) was as much a pastoral handbook on the handling of people lost in intellectual error as it was a sustained defence of toleration (Davidson 2000, pp. 239–40). The Emperor Joseph II wrote to his mother in 1777 that he wished that everyone in their realm was a Catholic: the issue was only one of *toleration*, not of *approval* of heresy (Chadwick 1981, p. 434). The question was what it was appropriate for the civil power to take in hand, notwithstanding a prince's or a subject's pastoral duties as Christians.

Evangelical tolerationists came to the view that it was neither right nor necessary to use the state as an instrument of conversion. Strictly speaking, the point was that it was not right that *any* agent should use coercion, although in practice this meant the state, as the state had the monopoly of authorised force. Several reasons were adduced for this conclusion. First, Christianity was a religion of meekness and charity. Persecution was therefore un-Christian. 'Blessed are the meek', Jesus had proclaimed in the Sermon on the Mount. Locke went so far as to say that toleration was 'the chief characteristical mark of the true church' (Locke 1983, p. 23). 'If you want to be like Jesus Christ, better to be a martyr than a hangman', wrote Voltaire (Voltaire 1994c, ch. 14, p. 98).

Second, it was said that most of the things that divided Christians from one another were not essential to Christian belief and practice. The errancy of Christian brethren was generally in minor matters, not necessary for salvation. In this argument, a strongly eirenic, or Erasmian, strain flowed from the Reformation through the Enlightenment and onwards. Christian faiths, it was said, had a common core, God had not prescribed this or that way of worship, and much of dogmatic theology was mired in tendentious earth-bound metaphysics rather than enlivened by simplicity of faith. The differences of the churches were so many Babels of scholastic jargon. Such eirenicism could even extend across the divide of Catholic and Protestant. Schemes for the reunification of Christendom regularly surfaced, often called Cassandrian or Grotian by their critics, after the attempts at reunion proffered by Georg Cassander in the 1560s and Hugo Grotius in the 1640s. Leibniz brought together the Catholic Cristobal de Spinola and the Lutheran Gerhard Molanus in the 1680s for discussions towards a common creed. Archbishop William Wake of England corresponded with the Genevan liberal Calvinist J. A. Turretini in the 1720s in search of an agreed minimal common doctrine, which would put aside speculative non-essentials and differences that were derived only from custom and tradition. The theme was pursued in Germany by such Pietists as Auguste Franke.

In other hands, the eirenic case for tolerance merged into a general indictment of priestly dogmatism, or priestcraft, *priestertum*, the persecutory spirit of clerics who were said to be always in search of temporal weapons to enhance their own authority and wealth. Pombal, chief minister in Portugal, devoted his *Brief Relation* (1758) and *Exposition of Facts and Motives* (1759) principally to assaults on Jesuit tyranny, and on their clerical empire, an empire of a literal kind, that over native Americans in Latin America. Pietro Giannone's *Istoria civile del regno di napoli* (Civil History of the Kingdom of Naples, 1723) was a plea for tolerance in so far as it was a chronicle of priestly and papal oppression.

Eirenical encyclopedias began to treat Christian denominations eclectically, finding spiritual heroes within diverse traditions. Often Platonist in inspiration, this Erasmian tradition revived in Ralph Cudworth's *True Intellectual System of the Universe* (1678), which sought out fragments of eternal truth amid the rubble of historically and culturally diverse religious traditions, non-Christian as well as Christian. A similar enterprise was Gottfried Arnold's *Unparteiische Kirchen- und Ketzerhistorie* (Impartial Ecclesiastical and Heretical History, 1699–1700), which Thomasius urged that his students must buy even if they had to starve or beg to get it (Grossmann 1982, pp. 131–5). J. L. von Mosheim's *Institutione's historiae Christianae* (Institutes of Ecclesiastical History, 1755) likewise sought to understand the different manifestations of Christian truth, free of confessional partisanship. Johann Jakob Brucker's great compendium of philosophical traditions, *Historia critica philosophiae* (1742–4), cited Grotius for the motto of his approach: 'as there never was any sect so enlightened as to see the whole truth, so there never was any sect so erroneous as to be entirely destitute of truth'.

The eirenic case moved imperceptibly into an ethic of sensibility, of pity, of simple horror at the human cruelty so often perpetrated in the name of religion. In the *Bibliothèque germanique* of Isaac de Beausobre there are scarcely arguments as such for toleration, rather a litany of affecting narratives of the senseless sufferings of myriad Christian sects over the centuries, whose members are shown to have been pious and virtuous, in spite of the variety and quirkiness of their Christian witness. Patiently he exposed the falsehoods in the black propaganda traditionally used against the sectaries, such as the suspicious frequency with which charges of sexual licence were levelled against them. The sheer ghastliness of the St Bartholomew's Day Massacre of 1572 was an obvious topic. Louis Mercier's play *Jean Henauyer* (1772) took as its hero a bishop who would not comply with the massacre of Protestants. A good deal of Voltaire's polemics consisted of gruesome narratives of Christian brutality through the ages, the Crusades, the Inquisition, St Bartholomew, the Irish Massacre of 1641. His epic poem *La Henriade* (1723) dwells at length on the hideous brutality of 1572. 'Intolerance has covered the earth with corpses.' This was indeed, he claimed, a peculiar legacy of Christianity, for pagan Greece and Rome had known no intolerance in religion (Voltaire 1994c, ch. 4, p. 29). Alongside the exhortation to pity went the genre of satire. Jonathan Swift, in *Gulliver's Travels* (1726), depicts a society viciously divided over whether the great founder of religion had intended that a boiled egg should be broken at the sharp or the blunt end, and whether high or low heels should be worn.

A third and crucial element in the evangelical case for tolerance was a rejection of the logic of Augustine's invitation to the Christian emperor to use force to bring the Donatists back into the fold of the church. The tolerationists argued that the idea of 'forced conversion' is based on a fundamental error. It is not actually possible to compel belief. Compulsion in religion cannot, in principle, achieve its stated end. The outward actions of the body can be compelled but not the inward convictions of the mind. Argument and persuasion are the necessary and only means of bringing about a change of belief, a change that ends with inner conviction. The use of force will not produce converts, but only martyrs or hypocrites. The case here was not a moral or theological one, but rather one that coercion in religion was, instrumentally speaking, simply irrational. It cannot be rational to use force, since it is impossible that force could be a means to its stated end, for between physical force and inner belief there is a radical disjuncture. 'Penalties in this case', wrote Locke, 'are absolutely impertinent; because they are not proper to convince the mind . . . Penalties are no ways capable to produce . . . belief . . . Light can in no manner proceed from corporal sufferings' (Locke 1983, p. 27). This point was constantly repeated. Pufendorf wrote that 'force and human punishment will not lead to illumination of the mind and to a truly inner assent to dogma, but can only yield hypocritical obedience' (qu. Grossmann 1982, p. 133). In Marmontel's bestselling novel *Bélisaire* (1767),

Belisarius defends tolerance against the Emperor Justinian: 'With edicts one will only create rebels or scoundrels. The heroic will become martyrs, the cowardly turn hypocrite, while fanatics from all parties will be transformed into tigers on the rampage' (ch. 15).

The avoidance of hypocrisy might almost be said to be the characteristic mark of eighteenth-century debate about the 'erring conscience'. It was a debate which saw a substantial shift of emphasis from the first to the second word in the phrase 'erring conscience'. Objectivism about errancy tended to give way to subjectivism about conscience. If a person's conscience remained stubbornly wrong-headed, what mattered was their sincerity, the authenticity of their search after truth. Faith, the holding of dogmas, gave way to being 'of good faith'. Sincerity became the cardinal virtue, and conscience inviolable. Good acts are those done according to conscience, and we may have to defer to error, because the right of conscience is paramount, and motives and dispositions matter more than being right. 'God is satisfied to exact no more . . . than a sincere and diligent search after truth', wrote Bayle, for 'it is enough if each one sincerely and honestly consults the lights which God has given him' (Bayle 1987, II.9, p. 182). The unmolested privacy of a person's conscience was not necessarily construed as a right, juridically conceived, but rather as the proper spiritual condition of a soul earnestly searching after truth. Arguably, and as many commentators on Kant and Hegel have suggested, later doctrines of personal autonomy, of what is owed to conscience, perhaps also Romantic conceptions of authenticity, owed as much, in their stress on the right of conscience, to the Pietist strain in Lutheranism and the evangelical legacies of puritanism, as to the jurisprudence of the natural law tradition or the metaphysics of the unconditioned will. The ethic of sincerity did, however, steadily detach itself from its evangelical roots. Rousseau declared, through the voice of the Savoyard vicar in *Emile* (1762), that 'True worship is of the heart. God rejects no homage, however offered, provided it is sincere' (bk 4).

The fourth claim of tolerationists, at least of the more radical among them, hung upon a functional distinction between the business of a state and the business of a church. It is not, they argued, the purpose of the state to save souls. The state exists for temporal benefits, to protect life and property. The church by contrast exists for eternal well-being and, though the church might excommunicate the errant, it has no physical power at its disposal. The prince is not a pastor; or, rather, he is not a pastor in his capacity as a prince; the prince is indeed a pastor just as other godly people are, but the fact of being a Christian gives no new powers or functions to the Christian ruler. Jesus Christ left temporal kingdoms exactly as he found them, for 'my kingdom is not of this world' (John 18:36). Because the function of the state is temporal, the only criterion by which the ruler could determine that a religious practice was inadmissible was if it injured the security of the state or its members. The 'original, end, business' of the state is 'perfectly distinct' from the church, wrote Locke. 'The business of the laws is not to provide for the truth of opinions, but for the safety and security of the commonwealth.' Thus, 'the salvation of men's souls cannot belong to the magistrate' (Locke 1983, pp. 27, 33, 46). Voltaire, citing Locke, concluded that every citizen must be permitted religious freedom 'provided always that he threatens no disturbance to public order' (Voltaire 1997, ch. 11, p. 71). In the *Social Contract* Rousseau laid down that all religions must be tolerated 'in so far as their dogmas contain nothing contrary to the duties of the citizen' (*SC*, IV.8, p. 151). Or, earlier, Bayle: 'In deciding which opinions the state should tolerate, the criterion should not be whether they are true or false, but whether they endanger public peace and security' (Bayle 1987, II.v).

Of course, ascertaining which beliefs and practices do in fact constitute a danger to civil society is not easy. Locke, as noted earlier, thought Catholics must be excluded. He also thought atheists were intolerable, because 'promises, covenants, and oaths, which are the bonds of human society, can have no hold upon an atheist' (Locke 1983, p. 51). Bayle, by contrast, shockingly did not exclude atheists. There are, he said, virtuous atheists and vicious Christians. Theistic belief by itself is no guide to how people will in practice behave (Schneewind 1997).

Four arguments for toleration have been surveyed: that Christianity is a religion of charity, that differences between religions are mostly unimportant, that compulsion is irrational, and that saving souls is no business of the state. These four arguments were all expressed in Locke's *Letter* and in many eighteenth-century writings, though the third and fourth were especially prominent in Locke, while the first and second tended to be emphasised elsewhere. These arguments could be framed evangelically, in terms of what the Christian can legitimately do to spread true religion. The third and fourth, however, most readily go beyond an evangelical framework, and we need for a moment to consider these arguments further, in order to point out some philosophical conundrums to which they gave rise.

The third, that it is impossible to force a change of belief, depends upon a more general epistemology of belief, upon a claim about the relationship between states of mind and external causes. As such, it is an argument open to epistemic objections, which were made both at the time and subsequently.

These claims run along the lines that compulsion, while not directly capable of achieving a change of belief, can shock and provoke an unreflective person into rethinking their ideas: force can be efficient in confronting an unwilling person with evidence and information, for example in the form of sermons or catechising or books. Force can 'awaken' and 'arouse from lethargy' those who refuse to examine the truth. A horse cannot be made to drink, but it can be led to water. After all, God himself induced trauma on the road to Damascus which led St Paul to rethink his beliefs, and Christians surely applaud the outcome. This is the argument – an Augustinianism grounded in analysis of states of mind – which was persuasively put in the 1690s by Locke's High Church critic Jonas Proast.[6]

The fourth argument moves from an evangelical frame to a juridical one, for the claim that religion is no business of the state is a close ally of an argument about what people rationally choose as the remit of political authority when they establish civil government. It is at this point that Locke's argument about the social contract in the *Two Treatises of Government* (1689) connects with his case for toleration in his *Letter concerning Toleration*. Religious coercion cannot be part of a contract entered into by people who have a rational consideration of their interests. To compel in religion cannot be a power 'vested in the magistrate by the consent of the people' (Locke 1983, p. 26). The tolerationist case here takes on a character that approximates to modern liberal political theory. Locke argued emphatically for a separation of church and state, for churches to be understood merely as 'voluntary societies', associations within civil society, and not bound up with the state. This was a marginal view in the eighteenth century, and it found almost no exemplars in practice. There were perhaps only two: revolutionary France and the United States. The Abbé Grégoire, who spoke passionately for religious freedom in the Assembly in 1793, succeeded in passing a law separating church and state in 1795; it was soon repealed (see Grégoire 1793). More durable was the constitution of the United States, which specifically precluded Congress from making any law to establish a religion. Thomas Jefferson drafted similar clauses in the Virginia Act for Establishing Religious Freedom (1786), though by no means all the states of the Union disestablished their churches.

Bayle was less emphatic than Locke on the score of the state's support for the church. He partially adhered to older notions of the godly prince as

---

6 The quotations are from Bayle 1987, pt 2, ch. 1, pp. 87–8, where he considers this objection. For Proast's objection, and its recent reiteration, see Goldie 1993b; Nicholson 1991; Vernon 1997; Waldron 1991.

the 'nursing mother' of the church. A Christian prince should 'send forth his doctors and preachers to confute heretics'; the church can expect that princes shall 'protect and cherish it', so long as they 'do no violence to anyone' (Bayle 1987, pp. 137–9). It should be reiterated that Locke himself, while giving no special place to the magistrate, did not exempt individuals, as Christians rather than as citizens, from a strenuous and mutual examination of their own and their brethren's beliefs. His case is on behalf of tolerance of, not privacy for, nor indifference to, the mental states of others (Dunn 1991).

That the minds of the devout will not succumb to coercion, and that the achievement of religious uniformity is no business of the state, were arguments that could be expressed in more *politique* forms. These forms amounted, on the one hand, to a 'reason of state' case which demonstrated that great damage was done to the economic prosperity of the state by the practice of intolerance, and, on the other, a psychological case about the perverse and destabilising effects upon minorities who are subjected to coercion. Tolerated minorities would become useful contributors to the nation's commercial vigour. It was argued that intolerance had, as a matter of historical experience, been tried and found ineffective. It exhausted the police powers of the state while rarely being thorough enough to achieve even outward conformity. Intolerance provoked sedition, turning religious eccentricity into dangerous fanaticism. Here the claim that religious dissenters must be suppressed because they were rebellious was turned on its head: it was persecution which turned minorities into rebels, as a result of their desperation. Persecution generated in a suffering minority a psychology of dogmatic righteousness, of desocialised seclusion from the world, even a pathological yearning for martyrdom. (The pathologies of marginalised and alienated minorities were explored, for example, by Malesherbes in his *Mémoire sur le marriage des protestants*, 1785–6). Admit all minorities into the ordinary business of the marketplace and of communal self-government in town, village, and trade guild, and they would be normalised, made civil, their religion rendered a private and peaceful avocation. Religious fanaticism could be cured by people rubbing along together in public spaces. This was a theme in the ethic of 'politeness', the virtues Joseph Addison inculcated in the *Spectator*, in the 1710s, and frequently taken up in philosophic journals across Europe in later decades. It is a theme central to Voltaire's *Lettres philosophiques* (translated as *Letters concerning England*, 1734). At the Stock Exchange in London, he observed, 'Jew, Mahometan, and Christian deal with each other as though they were all of the same faith, and only apply the word infidel to people who go bankrupt' (letter 6). In a world which was still close to an era when societies had been torn apart by wars of religion, commerce and sociability could seem a balm, instruments for the polishing of manners, and not least for polishing the barbarous manners of religious zealots (see Hirschman 1977).

A pragmatic, *politique* case for toleration found a footing in the developing discipline of political economy. It was increasingly said that toleration benefited the economy. This claim had special salience because religious minorities often congregated in particular trades, and because such groups often emigrated, taking their skills with them, thus damaging the well-being of the society they left behind, by reducing its wealth and population. A prolonged debate turned on estimates of the demographic impact of the Revocation of the Edict of Nantes, negative for the French economy, and positive for Britain, Holland, and Prussia. In the 1730s the Abbé Prévost, in his journal *Le Pour et Contre* (1733–40) underscored the economic damage done to France by the Revocation.

Parallel debates occurred in more local contexts. The city-state of Altona in north Germany deliberately sought to build its economic strength upon a religious pluralism denied in its rival and neighbouring city-state of Hamburg, a fact not lost on the advocates of toleration within Hamburg. Syndic Nicolaus Matsen protested against the folly of the commercial harm done by the orthodox churchmen through their insistence upon placing restrictions on those who differed only in 'a few dogmatic trivialities'. 'Happy is the city', wrote Johann Peter Willebrandt, 'where one need only worry about how much the peaceful inhabitants and foreigners contribute to the common good, and not about what they believe' (Whaley 1985, pp. 147, 158; cf. Méchoulan 1990). In the Austrian empire, when heresy broke out in Moravia in the 1770s, Prince Kaunitz counselled tolerance: persecution was contrary to the interests of the state and would depopulate the land. In Russia, Catherine the Great gave liberties to non-Orthodox Christians in her search for migrants to colonise the East. In many chancelleries, a preoccupation with demographic growth as the engine of economic development, and the phenomenon of the religious refugee with economically valuable skills, drove the case for toleration.

In Britain's case, the pragmatics were rather different. An economic case for tolerating Dissenters, who were concentrated in urban trading and artisanal communities, had indeed been persuasively made on behalf of Protestant minorities since the late seventeenth century. A century later, however, in the face of the growing turbulence of the American colonies, it was considerations of empire which drove forward emancipation for Catholics, particularly the necessity of guaranteeing the loyalty of Catholics in French Canada after their conquest by the British. The price of Canadian Catholic loyalty was the Quebec Act (1774) which guaranteed the freedom of Catholics. Many English Protestants were appalled that parliament should 'establish' Catholicism within the Empire. Yet the Quebec Act paved the way for a Catholic Relief Act for England (1778), which allowed Catholics to acquire and inherit property. In Ireland, with Edmund Burke's help, Catholic freeholders secured the franchise in 1793. Hitherto, the friends of toleration on the European Continent were often unimpressed by Britain's pretensions to toleration, given her treatment of non-Protestants in her imperial possessions, pointing especially to the brutality of the penal laws against Irish Catholics. An indigenous Irish claim for toleration found its first voice in Charles O'Connor's *Case of the Roman Catholics* in 1755. It got impassioned support from Burke in his *Letter to Sir Hercules Langrishe* (1792), which became a text vigorously promoted by the Catholic Committee, alongside Wolfe Tone's manifesto, *An Argument on Behalf of the Catholics of Ireland* (1791). Burke wrote that he could find nothing in the Thirty-Nine Articles, the official doctrine of the Anglican Church, that 'is worth making three million of people slaves' (qu. Henriques 1961, p. 102). But, in practical politics, it was in North America that the dam burst, for the path to Catholic emancipation in the British Isles began with the Quebec Act. Even so, government calculation and the voices of tolerationist intellectuals were sharply challenged by the Gordon Riots of 1780. It is salutary to note that these, the most savage and destructive riots of the eighteenth century in Britain, had popery as their target.

This has been a survey of the ways in which intellectuals, who were mostly believers, reflected on coercion in relation to their duty to assist the truth.[7] Sometimes criticism of religious intolerance by Christians became indistinguishable from an assault on Christianity as such. We noted earlier the pervasiveness of anticlerical polemic against 'priestcraft'. During the Enlightenment this polemic came to be shared by believers and unbelievers alike, the latter of whom held that all religion was merely a system of repressive falsehood. Churchmen, it was said, were not so much ignorant or foolish, but prejudiced, because they had a material interest in holding to their dogmas. Voltaire learned from Bayle above all other writers that the chief obstacle to rational judgement is not ignorance but prejudice,

---

7 This coda is chiefly owed to Wokler 2000b, pp. 75–6.

and many of the French *philosophes* who adopted his campaign to 'Ecrasez l'infâme' – 'Crush the infamy' – owed Bayle a similar debt. Bayle it was who fanned irreverence.

A number of writers came to identify the acceptance of theological dogmas not as belief but as superstition. Increasingly among the *philosophes* of the latter half of the century, religious conviction came to be denounced as blind faith, at once barbarous and irrational. Even when they acted dutifully in accord with their own Christian scruples, they often supposed, contrary not only to Hobbes and Mandeville but also scripture, that human nature was fundamentally sociable, or, when they succumbed to the Pelagian heresy, that it was made of a pliant clay which could be cast in perfectible ways. What they could no longer accept, because it was no longer philosophically appropriate to do so, was the theological doctrine of mankind's original sin, now regarded as a myth invented by clerics to regulate the salvation of gullible souls.

At the heart of the *philosophes'* commitment to the progressive education of mankind lay a crusade against all the dark forces of idolatry. 'Civilisation', a term which first acquired its current meaning around 1750, came progressively during the century to be identified with the abandonment of the trappings of religions, whose gospels, shrouded in mysteries and revelation, only obscured the truth. It was in reason's light that philosophers of every denomination now sought to dispel the shadows in which their adversaries lurked. Voltaire, Diderot, Turgot, d'Alembert, and Condorcet joined Helvétius, d'Holbach, and other materialists, in their perception of human history as one great struggle between the friends and enemies of enlightenment – between nefarious tyrants, priests, and barbarians, on the one hand, and civilised, educated, and liberated men of science and letters on the other. They held the arcane dogmas of Christian theology responsible for fanaticism and hypocrisy throughout history – for wars of religion, for the Inquisition, for bigotry everywhere. *Philosophes* who espoused ideas of toleration, grounded in conceptions of history and the progress of civilisation, sought to overcome mankind's enthralment to gospels which stood in the way of each person's attainment of worldly knowledge of the good and their desire to practise it.

4

Piety and politics in the century of lights

DALE K. VAN KLEY

An older historiography of the Enlightenment took the defence or rejection of Christian belief as its starting point and, dividing the world into 'believers' and 'unbelievers', regarded political thought as derivative of these groupings. Unbelief unleashed a 'liberal' assault on monarchy and social hierarchy, while belief came to the defence of these institutions, resulting in 'conservative' political thought (see, for example, Martin 1962). This model does justice to something that was incontestably new in the eighteenth century: namely, the emergence of emancipated, secular thought. Yet it is not without its limitations, chief among them being its underestimation of the 'enlightenment' of, and dissent within, 'believing' communities. Accordingly, this chapter explores the political ramifications of the divisions between 'orthodox' and 'heterodox' *within* eighteenth-century Europe's believing communities. It asks to what extent the religious and theological differences separating Jesuits from Jansenists, orthodox Lutherans or Calvinists from Pietists, and High Church Anglicans from English Dissenters took the form of differing political visions, not only about the church but also about state and society. In so doing, it broaches the relationship between divergent religious sensibilities and differing kinds of political thought. The heart of the most 'irreligious' of Europe's Enlightenments, France, should provide the acid test of any religiously oriented construal of eighteenth-century political thought. France, therefore, must be this European grand tour's first and longest stop.

1   Gallicanism and Jansenism in France

The history of religious controversy in Catholic France during the eighteenth century is in part the history of the undoing of the Declaration of the Liberties of the Gallican Church of 1682. Promulgated by an extraordinary meeting of the General Assembly of the Gallican Clergy at the behest of Louis XIV, who was then in conflict with Pope Innocent X, that declaration proclaimed the king of France to be independent of the papacy in temporal affairs and the Gallican Church to be independent of Rome in matters of canonical and liturgical 'usages'. It also subjected the papacy's doctrinal decisions to the approval of the Gallican clergy in France, while subjecting both in turn to the authority of ecumenical councils in accordance with the decrees of the Council of Constance of 1414–18. The types of national and ecumenical councils that the Declaration contemplated were, like the assembly that promulgated it, composed primarily of bishops. This conception of the Catholic polity as a papal monarchy tempered by an aristocracy of bishops stood in asymmetrical contrast to the Declaration's defence of an absolute French monarchy.

No sooner, however, had this ecclesiastical and political 'orthodoxy' been proclaimed, than it came into tension with theological 'orthodoxy' as defined in opposition to French Jansenism, against which both the king and his bishops sought papal help. As early as 1693 Louis XIV disavowed the Declaration of 1682, or at least its conciliar provisions, and in 1695 he issued an edict reinforcing the authority of his bishops over a priesthood already infiltrated by Jansenism. This edict also fortified the clergy's 'spiritual' jurisdiction over the sacraments and doctrine from challenges by the royal Courts already inclined to protect Jansenists in the name of the Gallican liberties as defined in 1682. But the monarch's strategic retreat from the Declaration was as nothing compared with the royal rout represented by the final condemnation of Jansenism. Solicited by an ageing Louis XIV and promulgated by Pope Clement XI in 1713, the bull *Unigenitus* condemned not only many Jansenist propositions taken from Pasquier Quesnel's *Réflexions morales* (1693), but also some Gallican ones, such as the proposition that the Catholic Church was the whole 'assembly of the children of God'. The controversy over this papal bull raged until 1770, making the French eighteenth century as much the century of *Unigenitus* as that of Enlightenment.

Yet Clement XI would have found it difficult to single out uniquely 'Jansenist' propositions for condemnation from Quesnel's treatise, for by the early eighteenth century 'Jansenism' had already coalesced with extraneous elements, Gallicanism among them, and the term now denoted more than the theological and moral legacy of the movement's seventeenth-century founders. To be sure, eighteenth-century Jansenists never renounced that legacy: namely Cornelius Jansen's (and St Augustine's) insistence on a 'fallen' and 'concupiscent' human nature's dependence on an 'efficacious' grace as opposed to a merely 'sufficient' grace that depended on the penitent's free will; as well as the Abbé de Saint-Cyran's rigorous penitential requirement of signs of a 'conversion', characterised by contrition or true love for God,

in advance of absolution and reception of the eucharist. But however preposterous Jean Filleau's denunciation in 1654 of a Jansenist plot to destroy
Catholicism by making the sacraments all but inaccessible to the faithful
(Filleau 1654), it is true that eighteenth-century Jansenists further accen-
tuated Saint-Cyran's and Antoine Arnauld's original strictures against frequent communion. And however absurd Filleau's charge that the Jansenists
plotted to disguise Calvinism as Catholicism, it is also true that Jansenism,
like Calvinism, accented the infinite distance between a uniquely majestic
God and concupiscent humanity below. Indeed, from the perspective of the
monarchy Jansenism's exaltation of God and demotion of everything else
was one of its original political sins, implicitly demoting sacral kingship. A
final salient characteristic of Jansenism relevant to its political theology was its
stark moral contrasts: natural innocence before the Fall and the degeneracy
of everything since, the righteousness of God alone and the unworthiness
of everything else, and the non-existence of morally indifferent acts.

To these doctrinal and penitential inheritances the eighteenth century
added its keen endorsement. Although Lemaistre de Sacy's vernacular Bible
dated from the seventeenth century, eighteenth-century Jansenist biblicism was more militant, adding several new translations and insisting on
their being read by the laity. This biblicism included the Old Testament,
inspiring Jansenism's penchant for the Psalms and some of its hymnody. It
also inspired another theological development, the hermeneutic called 'fig-
urism', whereby the Old Testament was read as prefiguring the New and
both in turn as prefiguring contemporary events, such as the bull *Unigenitus*,
as well as events to come, such as the return of the prophet Isaiah and the
conversion of the Jews. That hermeneutic, together with persecution, lay
not only behind the miracles produced around the tomb of the Deacon
Pâris in the Parisian cemetery of Saint-Médard in the late 1720s, but also
the 'convulsions' that succeeded them (Maire 1998, pp. 250–326, 378–440).

The most salient feature of eighteenth-century Jansenism, however, was
its rapid and dramatic politicisation. While the movement's perceived potential for subversion and characteristic appeal to the individual conscience may
have accounted for persecution in the first place, it took Louis XIV's destruction of the Jansenist centre at Port-Royal, Cardinal Fleury's shower of *lettres
de cachet*, the systematic purges of the priesthood, the religious orders, and the
Sorbonne, and the public denial of their sacraments, to bring that potential
to the point of active expression. The process culminated in its attacks against
Chancellor Maupeou's reform and purge of the French *parlements* in 1771.

Commenting at the height of that protest in 1772, the radical journalist Pidansat de Mairobert welcomed Jansenism's help against the 'hydra' of 'political despotism' and its transformation into 'the party of patriotism' (Mairobert 1774–6, II, p. 351).

Politicisation began in earnest when, invoking the conciliar features of Gallicanism, four Jansenist bishops appealed against *Unigenitus* to a general council in 1717. Opposed by the government, the appeal highlighted the growing distance between absolutism and those parts of the Gallican legacy which now functioned as elements in an oppositional Jansenist ideology. In the absence of much episcopal support, the appeal also dramatised Jansenism's support within the laity and lower ranks of the priesthood, to which Jansenist theologians responded by defining the church as the whole 'assembly of the faithful', including parish priests and the laity. This brand of Gallicanism or 'Richerism' hence defined itself against the Gallican bishops as well as the monarchy, holding that parish priests derived their sacerdotal mission directly from Christ rather than indirectly through the bishops and that, although jurisdictionally subordinate to bishops, they still had a right to attend both synodical and general councils as 'judges of the faith'. In order to legitimate that ecclesiology, Jansenist theologians hardly had to rely on Edmond Richer's condemned *Libellus de ecclesiastica et politica potesta* (Tract on Ecclesiastical and Political Power, 1611), and more typically appealed to unimpeachably 'orthodox' utterances by such fifteenth- and early sixteenth-century Gallican Sorbonnists as Jean Gerson, John Mair (Major), and Jacques Almain (Gerson 1706).

'Richerist' ecclesiology also made room for the laity, if not as 'judges of the faith', at least as 'witnesses to the truth', competent to raise a 'cry of conscience' amidst the silence of a derelict hierarchy. In practice this lay *témoignage* meant the judicial milieu, especially the order of barristers in the *parlement* of Paris, to which Jansenist priests began to appeal against the adverse sentences of anti-Jansenist bishops and their ecclesiastical courts. The barristers responded with published judicial memoirs which were exempt from royal censorship, and which vindicated the intervention of the secular courts in such spiritual affairs. In their reading, inspired by William of Ockham and Marsilius of Padua, Gallicanism meant that the Catholic Church was a purely spiritual institution, an entire stranger to coercion and the 'spirit of domination', and subject to the state in all matters impinging on public welfare, including churchmen in their capacity as citizens.

113

This line of argument received classic expression in Gabriel Nicolas Maultrot's and the Abbé Claude Mey's two-volume *Apologie de tous les jugemens rendus par les tribunaux séculiers en France contre le schisme* (1752) which, as its title implies, justified the *parlement* of Paris's attempt to prevent the public refusal of the sacraments of the viaticum and extreme unction to those who had earlier rejected *Unigenitus*, or who were otherwise suspected of Jansenism. This work drew some of its force from the authority of the Louvain canonist Zeghert Bernhard van Espen, whose much-cited *Jus ecclesiasticum universum* (1700) had laid down the patristic bases of anti-papal episcopalianism and regalism. In adapting van Espen's argument to the French situation, however, Maultrot and Mey stretched the Louvain canonist's episcopalianism almost to the point of parochial congregationalism, and applied his regalism to the *parlement* of Paris, holding not only that it was the unanimous consent of Catholic churches – not just the general council – that ultimately validated doctrine, but also that the question of whether such validation had occurred was an 'external' fact which the 'prince' – that is, the *parlement* – had the right to judge. This radical version of the argument in turn undergirded the victory of the *parlement* over the episcopacy in the refusal of sacraments controversy of 1757, as well as its dissolution of the Jesuits in the 1760s (Van Kley 1984, pp. 149–65).

It was also later to justify the Revolution's nationalisation and radical reorganisation of the Gallican Church – the famous Civil Constitution of the Clergy – in 1790 on the grounds that diocesan boundaries, the mode of episcopal election, and the relation of the Gallican clergy to the papacy, were all palpably 'external' matters under the jurisdiction of the state alone, as opposed to purely spiritual dogmas defined by the church. Whether actual Jansenists had a hand in making or defending the Civil Constitution (they did) is less important than that the 'Gallicanism' invoked to justify it had been drastically radicalised by Jansenists, and was no longer as it had been defined in 1682.

All these issues pitted the *parlement* of Paris against not only the episcopacy but also the crown. Herein lay the legacy of the sixteenth-century wars of religion, for behind the *parlement* stood a Protestant-seeming doctrine sponsored by an alliance of lawyers and Parisian priests, while with the monarchy stood the episcopal hierarchy. Although the *parlement* defended the king's regalian rights against a theocratic church, it less conspicuously but no less surely redefined the monarchy in exclusively judicial terms – that is, as the *parlement*.

114

One such attempt at redefinition was the Jansenist barrister Louis Adrien Le Paige's immensely influential *Lettres historiques sur les fonctions essentielles du parlement* (1753–4), which revived Henri de Boulainvilliers's argument that the whole Frankish nation had once met in general assemblies without whose consent the king might do nothing, that the medieval Estates General had succeeded the ancient assemblies, but that things had gone despotically downhill ever since (Boulainvilliers 1727). Following the apologists for the Fronde – the rebellion against the crown in 1648 – Le Paige substituted the *parlement* of Paris for the defunct Estates General, giving the French 'nation' a 'representative' institution which was alive and well in eighteenth-century Paris and in a position, if not to legislate on the nation's behalf, at least to refuse to 'register' royal legislation that violated historic constitutional or 'fundamental' law. What gave Le Paige's Estates General a Jansenist tonality despite its obvious indebtedness to earlier sources is that his *parlement* 'testified' or 'witnessed' to antique constitutional 'truth' amidst the defection of royal despotism, much as the appeal to *Unigenitus* had 'witnessed' to patristic 'truth' amidst the 'obscurity' of episcopal and papal apostasy.

The dominant justification for resistance to the monarchy within the judicial milieu until around 1770, Le Paige's constitutionalism tended to give way to what might be called a conciliar constitutionalism after that date, as Chancellor Maupeou's temporarily successful reform and purge of the *parlements* revealed the limitations of these venal courts as effective 'representatives' of the national will. While this kind of constitutionalism reserved a place for the *parlement* as a judicial guardian of the nation's constitutional laws, it held that the *parlement* resisted the king not by virtue of lineal descent from Frankish legislative assemblies, but by mandate from the temporarily inactive but more representative Estates General. What made this constitutionalism in some sense conciliar is that its chief architects, again drawing on the radical conciliarism of the fifteenth-century Sorbonnists, thought of the Estates General as the secular counterpart to the church's ecumenical council. What made conciliar constitutionalism a potentially greater threat to Bourbon absolutism was its admission that, whereas a council 'cannot make an aristocracy or democracy out of the monarchical government established by Jesus Christ himself', the nation assembled in Estates General 'has the right to change the form of its government, when it has good reasons for doing so' (Maultrot and Mey 1775, I, p. 269). Best expressed in Maultrot and Mey's monumental *Maximes du droit public françois* (Maxims of French Public Law), conciliar constitutionalism culminated in the *parlement* of Paris's appeal to the authority of the Estates General on 6 July 1787, resulting in the actual meeting of that body two years later.

Thus there is a direct line of political thought and action that leads from the appeal of the papal bull *Unigenitus* to a general council in 1717 to the *parlement's* appeal of the king's fiscal edicts, and to the Estates General in 1787. One of judicial Jansenism's most signal contributions to revolutionary ideology was therefore to help domesticate the thesis of national sovereignty in France by way of conciliar Gallicanism, as well as to warrant a certain version of French history.

A conciliar and parochialised Catholic Church subjected in all externals to the monarchy, which was in turn legislatively subjected to the *parlement* acting on behalf of the nation – this version of Gallicanism is hardly that defined by the General Assembly of 1682, and did not sit well with either the crown or the Gallican episcopate. It therefore fell to the crown and bishops, aided and abetted by the Jansenists' worst enemies, the Jesuits, to defend the political and ecclesiastical 'orthodoxy' of 1682 against the 'heretical' *parlements* aided by Jansenists. In contrast to the *parti janséniste*, this alliance of episcopal and Jesuitical defenders of monarchy and religion was known as the 'pious' or 'devout party' (*parti dévot*). Like the early seventeenth-century party of the same name, this *parti dévot's* politics had roots in a particular religious sensibility.

Natural in some ways, it is in other ways surprising that a *parti dévot* should have defended anything calling itself Gallicanism. The early seventeenth-century *parti dévot* had grown out of the Catholic League, and was therefore frankly pro-papal or ultramontane; as such it opposed assertions of the temporal independence of the French king when proposed by the Third Estate in 1614. Papal exemptions from episcopal jurisdiction in addition to their vow of obedience to the papacy had once made the Jesuits in particular anathema to most Gallican bishops, attached as were the latter to Gallican canonical usages, and to their own jurisdictional authority. Time had altered these associations, however. The Jesuit at the royal Court had become a symbol of absolutism and French Jesuits had loyally stood by Louis XIV in his conflict with the papacy that led to the Declaration in 1682. *Unigenitus* further reconciled the *parti dévot's* rival commitments to papacy and monarchy, since to defend that bull was to defend the monarchy which had solicited it and tried to enforce it. Transforming 'devout' sentiment into a 'party' to an equal if opposite degree to that of Jansenism, *Unigenitus* added the force of reconciled interests to that of an inherited defence of divine right monarchy.

Divine right absolutism's notion of the king's person as a palpable representation of divinity sat well enough with baroque piety's tendency to fasten upon human institutions and tangible objects as conduits of grace and symbols of sanctity. A residual Aristotelianism enabled Jesuits especially to adapt to the century's new emphases on experiential sense and sensibility, coming together as these did in the highly external affective cult of the Sacred Heart of Jesus, the 'devout' devotion *par excellence*, and a favourite at the French Court (Languet de Gergy 1729). Rather than simply add 'moral reflections' to the sacred text, as did Quesnel, 'devout' Catholicism would have gladly paraphrased the Bible as a proto-Romantic novel, as did the Jesuit Isaac Berruyer (Berruyer 1728–55). Even the 'devout' defence of human free will against Jansenist efficacious grace was politically apropos, since the Jesuits defended the legitimacy of the king's mere will against judicial Jansenism's tendency to reduce it to the *parlements* and to bind it by fundamental laws.

The obvious danger in such a defence, however, was to blur Bishop Bossuet's classic distinction between 'absolute' and 'arbitrary' government, and to be as unfaithful to the spirit of the Declaration of 1682 in one direction as Jansenists were in another. Already visible in the demand for submission to *Unigenitus* by such *dévot* bishops as Etienne de La Fare of Laon and Jean Joseph Languet de Gergy of Soissons in the 1720s and early 1730s, the tendency to be more royalist than the king (La Fare 1730) – or at least than his first minister Cardinal Fleury – grew more pronounced in the 1750s and 1760s when a real *parti dévot* took shape at Court while royal religious policy itself made concessions to the *parlement* in return for fiscal help in the Seven Years War. 'Absolute' monarchy became pretty 'arbitrary', at least in such definitions as that of the Abbé Bertrand Capmartin de Chaupy who, maintaining in 1754 that the king was the 'master' and not just the administrator of his realm, laid it down that 'the king is the state', and that 'the will of the king is the will of the state' (Chaupy 1756, 1, pp. 53–4). In the 1770s and again on the eve of the Revolution the same thesis was defended in secularized form by the incendiary journalist Simon Henri Linguet who had revolted against a Jansenist upbringing and published his first pamphlet in defence of the Jesuits (Linguet 1771, 1788).

Some of the same brittleness clung to the *dévot* defence of episcopal authority against Jansenist parochialism. Bishops alone 'possessed' the sacerdotal power given them by Christ, argued the Abbé Le Corgne de Launay in 1760; to them exclusively belonged the right to delegate that power to *curés* and other subordinates. The 'precious liberties' of 1682, Le Corgne made clear, consisted in the distribution of sacerdotal power among an 'aristocracy' of bishops, but not among a dependent presbytery of priests (Le Corgne 1760, pp. 154, 336–7). If episcopal possession needed to be protected from Jansenist priests, then how much more so from their lay allies. In defending temporal power against papal pretensions, the Gallican Declaration, maintained Bishop Lefranc de Pompignan, 'had not meant to confuse the true liberties of the Gallican Church with a shameful slavery which, against the institution of Jesus Christ, would enfief the ecclesiastical ministry to the secular power' (Pompignan 1769, p. 348). It was of course to protect that spiritual jurisdiction that bishops and Jesuits exalted the power of the monarchy and called upon it to discipline the *parlements*. Comparing the *parlement* of Paris to the English parliament, *dévot* defenders of the faith could claim to be upholding Gallican orthodoxy against judicial Jansenism's 'heretical' tendencies towards Erastianism, parochialism, and laicism. But if in fact the monarchy's religious policy did not much differ from the *parlements*' or was powerless to impose its own policy, nothing remained for these Gallican bishops except to disavow 'Gallicanism' altogether and distance themselves from absolute obedience to the crown. This occurred in the case of the most 'devout' bishops during the decades of the preponderance of the *parlements* from 1750 to 1770. If forced to choose between being ultramontane 'vicars of the pope' on the one hand and 'mandatories of the people' on the other, he and his colleagues would choose the former, confessed Lefranc de Pompignan in 1769. For all practical purposes, he thought, the 'ultramontane theologians' maintained the church as a 'mixture of aristocracy with monarchy', whereas Gallicanism as interpreted by the Jansenist lawyers reduced it to the 'tumults' and 'discords' of 'popular tribunals' (Pompignan 1769, pp. 203–5). The absolute throne was absolute only vis-à-vis lay subjects.

To be sure, bishops and the *parlements* tended towards reconciliation after Louis XVI's restoration of the old *parlements* in 1775, the two uniting in a common defence of 'property' against the monarchy's attack on venal offices in the early 1770s and ecclesiastical immunities in the 1780s. That eleventh-hour alliance in defence of privilege took the edge off episcopal absolutism and ultramontanism on the eve of the Revolution – so much so that the very last meeting of the General Assembly of the Gallican Clergy in 1788 actually remonstrated on behalf of the *parlements* and against the cardinal-minister Loménie de Brienne's offensive against them. The French bishops had become such 'Gallicans' and 'patriots' after 1775 that they meekly acquiesced in the nationalisation of ecclesiastical property by the Constituent

Assembly in 1789, and the suppression of contemplative monastic orders in February 1790. It took nothing less than the National Assembly's refusal to declare Catholicism to be France's national religion in April 1790, and then the passage of the Civil Constitution of the Clergy during May and June, to shake the French bishops out of their uncharacteristically undogmatic slumbers and into the formation of something like a clerical–royal Right. It was then that proto-conservative 'throne and altar' again raised their hydra heads against a Protestant–Jansenist–*philosophe* plot to 'destroy the Catholic religion in France', in the works of the Abbé Augustin Barruel (Barruel 1790) and the Comte Emmanuel d'Antraigues (d'Antraigues 1791), before becoming a watchword of full-blown conservatism in the works of Joseph de Maistre, the Vicomte Louis de Bonald, and the early works of Hughes-Félicité de Lamennais.

2 The 'Jansenist International' in Italy, Iberia, and Austria

Such was eighteenth-century France, in which competing Catholic pieties made a religious contribution to the formation of both liberalism and conservatism despite the existence of a 'third party' of self-consciously anti-Catholic *philosophes*. But a virulently anti-Catholic – and, in some of its moods, anti-Christian – Enlightenment fully cognisant of its distance from all parties to religious controversies was unique to France. To what extent, therefore, is the French case instructive elsewhere in eighteenth-century Catholic Europe, in particular for Spain, Austria, and the Italian states?

Obvious differences leap immediately to view on the other side of either the Alps or the Pyrenees. In none of these realms was there a 'Gallican' consensus liable to come undone, if by 'Gallicanism' is meant a tradition of conciliarist or episcopal, much less priestly, independence from the papacy. The only part of Gallicanism with a counterpart elsewhere in Catholic Europe was a tradition of royal independence from Rome and of control over the church – regalism or royal jurisdictionalism, or 'cameralism', as it was better known in the German lands. This meant that Gallican 'liberties' for bishops *à la française* had to be won rather than be defended, and that such bishops as wished to win them had to do so in alliance with the Catholic princes in a trajectory quite different from that of France. Such royal–episcopal alliances could be contemplated in Spain, Austria, and the Italian states because, in ironic contrast to the supposed French home of the Enlightenment, all of these Catholic realms boasted relatively 'enlightened' monarchs by the end of the century – most notably Carlos III in Spain, Maria Theresa and Joseph II in Austria, and Joseph's brother Peter Leopold in Tuscany (see ch. 17). An 'enlightened' yet Catholic monarchy was a possibility in these realms because in them the Enlightenment was far less anti-Catholic – so much less so, indeed, that the notion of a 'Catholic Enlightenment' works well there in a way that it does not in France. Although 'Jansenism', or something at least called that, was not unknown to any of these realms, it tended to be a latecomer and is less easy than in France to distinguish from things 'enlightened' or even regal. For, in the absence of sympathetic estates or anything like the French *parlements*, Jansenism also looked to monarchies for support (Cottret 1998).

The capital of the Catholic Enlightenment in Europe was Italy – indeed Rome itself – where it flourished under the long pontificate of Prospero Lambertini (Benedict XIV) from 1740 to 1758. Here there occurred an informal entente between 'Enlightenment' and papal infallibility that represented consensus, while 'Gallicanism', when it came, took on a radicalised form as a result of the *Unigenitus* controversies and hence represented the beginning of polarisation. As characterised by Bernard Plongeron, this Catholic Enlightenment elaborated a new 'religious anthropology' which insisted upon the rights of 'reason' within the bounds of a Christological religion, and was open to the possibility of secular amelioration within the bounds of a less rigidly hierarchical Christendom (Plongeron 1969, pp. 555–605). Catholic patrons of enlightenment hence tended to oppose Aristotelian scholasticism in favour of 'purer' patristic sources, notably St Augustine. They sympathised with textual criticism of the Bible, even translations in the vernacular, favoured less partisan ecclesiastical histories, even at the expense of the church's reputation, and aspired to purge Catholic devotion of 'superstitions', both the 'idolatrous' veneration of the saints and the 'external' cult of the Sacred Heart of Jesus. These tendencies made the enlightened Catholic the successor of the Christian humanism of Pietro Bembo and Lorenzo Valla that had been driven underground by the adversarial reformations of the sixteenth and seventeenth centuries. 'Reason' had, however, not stood still in the meantime, orienting the Catholic Enlightenment more towards the observation of nature and the future than the somewhat Platonic 'reason' of the Christian humanists.

That same 'reason' made enlightened Catholics critical of curialist claims to temporal authority and the clergy who defended them, notoriously the Jesuits. These traits, along with opposition to devotions, gave this Catholic Enlightenment common cause with what was called 'Jansenism'. Thus one of the most salient characteristics of the Catholic Enlightenment outside

France was its imperceptible shading into Jansenism. What also distinguished the Catholic Enlightenment, however, was its typically 'enlightened' distaste for 'enthusiasm' or 'fanaticism', shying away from the polemical vehemence typical of Jansenism. Hence advocates of Catholic Enlightenment tended to gravitate towards what Emile Appolis has called the Catholic 'third party' (Appolis 1960). Not to be confused with the 'third party' of anti-Catholic *philosophes* in France, this distinctively *Catholic* third party tried to remain equidistant from pro-*Unigenitus* and ardent curialist 'zealots' on the one side and anti-*Unigenitus* and radically Gallican Jansenists on the other. For although *Unigenitus* was nowhere as controversial and polarising as it was in France, it left its mark throughout Catholic Europe, forcing clergymen everywhere to define their own theological and ecclesial tendencies in relation to it.

The person who best exemplifies at once the notions of a Catholic Enlightenment and a third party is Lodovico Antonio Muratori who, though a priest, spent most of his productive life as a librarian in the service of the duke of Modena. An admirer and historian of the primitive purity of apostolic Christianity, he cultivated an encyclopedic interest in secular novelty, writing tracts on electricity and extolling the theatre as a possible school for virtue. An opponent of the Jesuits' 'fanatical' defence of the doctrine of the Immaculate Conception of Mary, Muratori admired the Jesuits as civilising missionaries in Paraguay and as enlightened hagiographers in the work of the Bollandists. A critic of popular 'superstitious' beliefs as author of *Della regolata divozione de' Cristiani*, he urged the people's material welfare as a reason for reducing the number of religious feast days (Muratori 1747) – the book was called *The Science of Rational Devotion* in its English edition of 1789. His espousal of 'public felicity' as opposed to the pursuit of glory and competitive *raison d'état* as the proper business of a paternal absolutism made Muratori an ally of most *philosophes* in political thought (Muratori 1749). Although as much opposed to philosophic unbelief as to sectarian heresy, truth was truth, he thought, even in the works of *philosophes* and heretics.

But it was not possible to agree with everyone in religion, even in the unenthusiastic eighteenth century, and so Muratori engaged in sustained polemics on most of the matters he cared about: with Jesuits about devotion to the Sacred Heart and the doctrine of the Immaculate Conception, with Franciscans about the validity of 'private' revelations, and so on. A good Italian, he also accepted the thesis of papal infallibility, and with it the authority of the bull *Unigenitus*, putting him at odds with French Jansenists on the

issues of grace and obedience, although sharing with them an interest in vernacular translations of scripture and liturgical reform. To be sure, Muratori
could also be critical of the papacy, censoring the morality of individual
popes in his histories and disputing its temporal claims to Comacchio in
Modena in his own time. But Muratori's concern was less doctrinal or
juridical than moral, in the tradition of Lorenzo Valla's critique of the
Donation of Constantine. On the one occasion when Benedict XIV's disapproval of some of his works became apparent, Muratori felt cut to the quick,
protesting his good intentions and offering to retract anything heretical (*Atti
del convegno internazionale di studi Muratoriani*, 1975).

He need not have worried too much, because Benedict XIV shared most
of his 'enlightened' and moderate instincts, as did many others in Italy in
the first half of the Italian *settecento*, such as Giovanni Lami, editor of the
Florentine periodical *Novelle Letterarie*. But the high noon of both an Italian
Catholic Enlightenment and a third party began to pass with the death of
Benedict in 1758. For it was then that the Abbé Augustin-Charles-Jean
Clément de Bizon, a French Jansenist, undertook a trip to Rome, first
to obtain a doctrinal statement from Benedict XIV favourable to French
appellants, and then, after Benedict died, to observe and perhaps influence
the papal election with the help of his Italian philo-Jansenist friends in
the curia such as Cardinal Neri Corsini, his host in Rome (Rosa 1992).
Influence the election, alas, they certainly did not. For the election of Carlo
Rezzonico as Clement XIII followed by the death of the secretary of state
Alberico Archinto and his replacement by the pro-Jesuitical Ludovico Maria
Torregiani were in every way the catastrophes for the Jansenist cause that
Clément and his Italian friends thought they were. But the results were to
be catastrophic for the Jesuits as well.

The first result was the reinforcement and formalisation of what had
been a desultory correspondence between Clément and some Italian
Augustinians – Giovanni Gaetano Bottari, first guardian of the Vatican
Library and confidant of Cardinal Corsini; Giuseppe Simioli, a professor
at the University of Naples and theological consultant to Cardinal Spinelli;
Cardinal Domenico Passionei, a passionate enemy of the Jesuits if not a
Jansenist; and eventually many others (Ambrasi 1979). Italian Augustinians
and anti-Jesuits, they now entered the French Jansenist International. The
second result was the suppression of the Jesuits in France.

The first of the Jesuit dominos to fall, it is true, was in peripheral Portugal,
where Sebastião Carvalho e Melho, the future marquês de Pombal and chief
minister to José I, alleged the complicity of the Jesuits in an attempt on the

king's life in order to expel them from both the metropolis and the American colonies (Miller 1978). This Portuguese precedent revealed that the deed could be done, and no doubt encouraged the French to do likewise. Yet even more crucial for France was the advice that Clément, Le Paige, and their cohorts received in late 1758 and early 1759 from their new Italian friends that, because the papacy would probably never disavow *Unigenitus*, their French co-belligerents should 'attack the Jesuits from whatever angle that does not concern the bull or that unites them with the court of Rome', that once the Jesuits were gone *Unigenitus* would no longer matter, and that France alone could rid Christendom of the Jesuits (Archives de la Bastille, MS 2883, fos. 152, 157). To be sure, neither Italian nor French Jansenists could have created the right circumstances – the bankruptcy of the French Jesuits' mission in Martinique in 1759, the favourable disposition of the duc de Choiseul and his spectacular rise to power at the same time – but their close connections to the *parlement* of Paris through Le Paige are enough by themselves to account for the *parti janséniste*'s determination to profit from such circumstances as arose, providentially or otherwise. By 1764 the Society of Jesus was no more in France (Van Kley 1975).

The fall of the Jesuits in France was also much more decisive than in Portugal – as decisive, indeed, as the Italian Jansenists had predicted it would be. Being, in effect, an international state within many states, the Jesuits suffered the adverse consequences of the alliance or third Bourbon 'family pact' negotiated by Choiseul between France and Spain in 1761, just as the *parlement* of Paris was striking the first decisive blow against the Jesuits in France. Alleging Jesuit complicity in a popular 'Hats and Capes' riot in Madrid in March 1766, Carlos III promulgated an edict expelling all Jesuits from metropolitan Spain and all the colonies a year later, whereupon he and Choiseul extended the terms of the family pact to include the aim of an eventual papal dissolution of the Society and put pressure on the Bourbon satrapies of Naples and Parma to follow the Spanish and Portuguese examples, which they respectively did in November 1767 and February 1768.

When, however, tiny Parma tried to emulate France by asserting control over all ecclesiastical appointments and banning all papal briefs and bulls that did not carry the duke's permission, an outraged Clement XIII struck back, issuing a brief annulling Duke Ferdinand's edict, and fulminating a bull of excommunication – actions recalling medieval papal claims to temporal power and the spectre of their most extreme expression in the papal bull *Unam sanctam* (1302). Whereupon it was the turn of the Bourbons and their sympathisers in Italy to be outraged, as French *parlements* condemned Clement's brief, French troops occupied Avignon and Naples and seized the papal enclaves of Benevento and Portecorvo – and raised the spectre of Philip the Fair (against whom *Unam sanctam* had been issued) if not the hated Hohenstaufens. Thus the initiative to expel the Jesuits returned to Italy like a boomerang, dividing Italian Catholics into latter-day Guelfs and Ghibellines. Thus too did France foist its polarised ecclesiastical situation on to Italy, ironically by Italian invitation, and thus the age of Benedict XIV ended in Italy. Nor did the pacific Lorenzo Ganganelli as Pope Clement XIV bring it back by formally dissolving the Company of Jesus by papal brief in 1773, as even many anti-Jesuitical Italian churchmen felt what they perceived to be the shame of papal capitulation in the face of what amounted to a Bourbon ultimatum.

A more polarised religious situation developed in the wake of the ecclesiastical and political one. Without common Jesuit – and, to some extent, Franciscan – theological enemies, Dominicans and Augustinians increasingly turned on each other, accentuating the theological differences between them and producing what Appolis has called 'the fragmentation of the third party' (Appolis 1960). The rift became wider in the 1760s and 1770s, as Clément in Auxerre and Dupac de Bellegarde in Utrecht engineered an avalanche of French Jansenist books that descended on their many Augustinian correspondents in northern Italy (Vaussard 1959). Unlike earlier eighteenth-century Augustinian rigorists, the new generation took their ecclesiology as well as their theology from France, allying a radical or Jansenised Gallicanism with indigenous traditions of regalism. In reaction, Dominicans like Tommaso Maria Mamachi rushed to the defence not only of orthodoxy but also of the prerogatives of the papacy.

It was above all in northern Italy – the republic of Genoa, the kingdom of Piedmont, Habsburg Lombardy, and the Grand Duchy of Tuscany – that a largely clerical 'Jansenist party' took shape towards the end of the century. Its ranks contained bishops like Scipione de' Ricci of Pistoia and Prato, university theologians like Pietro Tamburini at Pavia, and priests like the Abbate Bartolomeo Follini, one of the editors of the Tuscan *Annali ecclesiastici*, an Italian counterpart to the *Nouvelles ecclésiastiques*. Symptomatically, this periodical took the place of Lami's more irenic *Novelle Letterarie* in Florence as the main organ of ecclesiastical news around 1780 and took a far more engaged and embattled editorial stance than had its literary predecessor. This Jansenist journalistic offensive provoked a proto-conservative response in the form of the *Giornale ecclesiastico di Roma* which, edited in Rome by Mamachi and Luigi Cuccagni, ran from 1785 to 1798.

The high-water mark of anti-curial Jansenism in alliance with 'enlightened' absolutism came in the Tuscany of Grand Duke Peter Leopold in 1787. In that year Scipione de' Ricci convoked a diocesan synod of his bishopric of Pistoia and Prato with the encouragement of Leopold and the theological guidance of Tamburini. The synod's offensive against the excesses of baroque and popular piety maintained a certain contact with the Catholic Enlightenment of Lami and Muratori. But it also subscribed to a Jansenist doctrine of grace as well as endorsing the Gallican liberties as defined in 1682. To have embraced, as did this synod, a number of Quesnel's formulations and explicitly recommended his *Réflexions morales* to lay parishioners, gave an anti-papal flavour to a Jansenist conception of grace. By welcoming parish priests as 'co-operators' and 'judges of the faith', and by calling the papacy the merely 'ministerial head' of the church, the synod carried its anti-curialism well beyond the Gallicanism of 1682, and kept pace with the evolution of Gallicanism in France. What the Synod of Pistoia took from the papacy with one hand it was ready to give to the temporal 'prince', that is, Leopold, with the other, including the rights to set the diriment impediments to marriage, to reform or abolish religious orders, and to redraw parish boundaries (Bolton 1969; Lamioni 1991).

Whether the synod would have been just as willing to vest those rights in an elected temporal assembly is less clear, for Leopold left Florence to take his deceased brother's place in Vienna before implementing his plans to create such an assembly, and the reforms of the synod itself soon suffered shipwreck on the shoals of clerical and popular hostility. But the Jansenist veterans of the Synod of Pistoia were soon to be tested by the French National Assembly's Civil Constitution of the Clergy, which enacted on purely lay authority many of the reforms that the synod had urged on Peter Leopold as grand duke of Tuscany.

Some Italian Jansenists like Paolo Marcello del Mare of Siena predictably opposed the Civil Constitution on the grounds that the concurrent authority of the church in at least conciliar form was needed to implement it, but the editors of the *Annali* and Ricci himself took the lead in applauding it and entering into correspondence with the Abbé Henri Grégoire, informal leader of the French constitutional church. The reception of the Civil Constitution prefigured Italian Jansenist reception of the Revolution itself when it came to northern Italy in the train of French armies during 1796–9. While some like Pietro Tamburini in his *Lettere teologico-politiche*

(1794) remained attached to the ideal of enlightened absolutism as exempli-fied by Peter Leopold or Joseph II, and regretted the French Revolution's violent disruption of indigenous ecclesiastical reform, more accepted the Italian republics with varying degrees of enthusiasm, ranging from Eustachio Degola's distinctly Catholic Christian republicanism as editor of the *Annali politico-ecclesiastici* in Genoa to Giuseppi Poggi's virtual dissolution of his Jansenist past in the heady solvent of Jacobinism as editor of the *Repub-licano evangelico* in the Cisalpine Republic. Thus, in Ernesto Codignola's judgement, Jansenism provided a kind of bridge from Catholicism to the Risorgimento for many, perhaps indirectly even for Mazzini and Cavour, 'in the end winning for the cause of liberty and revolution large circles of believers and clerics who would have remained unmoved by the attraction of enlightened rationalism' (Codignola 1947, p. 312).

Jansenist republicans were prominent enough to have attracted the atten-tion of the editors of the *Giornale ecclesiastico*, and to have lent credence to the thesis that absolute thrones took leave of the infallible papal altar at their own peril. So long as it had been only absolute monarchies or royal duchies that had sponsored 'Jansenist' anti-papal ecclesiastical reforms, pro-papal polemi-cists in Italy had tended to pose as defenders of absolutism, putting monarchs on their guard against the political dangers of extreme ecclesiastical reform; while for its part the *Giornale* had been nothing if not nuanced, defending 'true' Augustinianism against Jansenism, and sometimes even the 'moderate' Gallicanism of 1682 against the Synod of Pistoia. But that stance changed after the events of 1789 in France sent a far sterner warning to monarchies than papal preachments had ever done, and the French National Assembly treated Europe to the spectacle of a radical Gallican reform of the church from 'below'. It then became possible for Roman apologists – and ex-Jesuits – like Rocco Bonola and Gianvincenzo Bolgeni to cut some of their losses with reformist absolutism and, with crucial theoretical help from Nicola Spedalieri's *De' diritti dell'uomo* (Rights of Man, 1791) to advance a neo-Thomist theory of the social contract that situated the obedience of lay subjects to their temporal sovereigns within a larger 'contract' obligating these same sovereigns to the spiritual authority of a hierarchical church. On this condition – an important one – the papal altar buttressed threatened thrones in the pages of the *Giornale* and other works by its editors, who also discovered Edmund Burke and the Abbé Barruel, and denounced Jansenist complicity in a plot which had culminated in Jacobinism. By then the papacy itself had mustered the courage to condemn the Synod of Pistoia in the brief *Auctorem fidei* (1794), thereby joining the *Giornale ecclesiastico* in an increasingly strident and international defence of throne and altar (Pignatelli 1974, pp. 107–13, 139, 145–7, 151–203).

That defence included the Spanish throne, which, however, took longer than the other Bourbon thrones to perceive its temporal salvation as standing or falling with papal infallibility. Indeed, Carlos IV refused to permit the publication of Pius VI's *Auctorem fidei* until a full six years after its publication. It was only in the waning months of the eighteenth century that he and his chief minister, José Antonio Caballero, authorized this publication while simultaneously rescinding their 'Gallican' permission to Spanish bishops to grant matrimonial dispensations ordinarily reserved for the pope. Thereby they symbolically distanced the crown from the alliance with the cause of Jansenist Enlightenment against papal curialism that had been one of the hallmarks of the reign of Carlos III.

The Spanish counterpart to the reign of Peter Leopold in Tuscany, that of Carlos III, had presided over an Enlightenment as fully Catholic as the earlier Italian one, personified in the encyclopedic Benedictine monk Benito Gerónimo Fejyóo y Montenegro. Like Muratori in Modena, Fejyóo busied himself with everything – theology and philosophy of course, but also literature, history, geography, natural science, and mathematics – everywhere opposing scholasticism, 'superstition', and belief in false miracles. As in Italy, unlike in France, the pejorative *filosofos* was uttered almost synonymously with 'Jansenists', a term that might designate ministerial advocates of greater royal control over the Catholic Church like Pedro Rodríguez de Campomanes, *fiscale* of the Council of Castile, as well as people of pronounced Augustinian theological tendencies like Francisco Saverio Vasquez, general of the Augustinian Order. In and out of the royal ministry in the 1780s and 1790s, Gaspar Melchor de Jovellanos figures importantly in accounts of both the Spanish Enlightenment and Jansenism, reconciling categories thought to be incompatible in Cartesian France.

It was with the applause of both 'enlightened' and Jansenist advisers that Carlos III undertook his characteristically 'enlightened' Catholic reforms – the shifting of resources from regular to secular clergy, requiring the royal permission or *exequatur* for the publication of papal pronouncements, drawing a tooth or two from the Spanish Inquisition – culminating with the expulsion of the Jesuits in 1767. Even that act enjoyed wide support from a monarchically appointed episcopate still immune from the *Unigenitus*-engendered polarisation across the Pyrenees.

As in Italy, however, the expulsion of the Jesuits saw the beginning of the end of consensus, as Augustinians quarrelled with Dominicans over the educational and confessional spoils, and the ubiquitous Abbé Clément journeyed to Spain in search of recruits. Although Clément did not find very many bona fide 'friends of the truth' in 1768, he found some in high places: Antonio Tavira y Almazan, Carlos III's court preacher; Maria Francisco de Sales de Portecarrero, Condesa de Montijo, who presided over an influential salon in Barcelona; as well as some influential 'friends on the outside', like Manuel de Roda y Arrieta, minister of grace and justice. But the trip served to establish a system of correspondence and a web of connections which, replenished by the fallout from the Augustinian–Dominican conflict, grew to the proportions of a Jansenist party by 1780 (Appolis 1966).

As in Italy, Spanish Jansenists looked to the crown to enhance the authority of bishops and priests vis-à-vis the papacy and regulars, to put pressure on the Inquisition to allow the publication of 'good' books, and to sponsor curricular reform in the universities. To a degree, the government of Carlos IV obliged, appointing sympathetic inquisitors, allowing Jansenist professors to use the work of Tamburini in theology and van Espen and Johann von Hontheim (Febronius) in canon law, and – when they became available – the acts of the Synod of Pistoia and the text of the Civil Constitution of the Clergy as cases in point. Jansenist influence under Carlos IV reached its high-water mark in 1797–9 when Jovellanos occupied the ministry of grace and justice and, with Mariano Luis de Urquijo, promulgated the decree allowing bishops to grant matrimonial dispensations.

That act, however, was to be Jansenism's last legislative achievement in Spain. For Jansenist reformers had of course produced a proto-conservative reaction by Dominicans, Franciscans, some bishops, and noble *Grandes de España*, setting off a contest for the soul of the monarchy and the ultimate 'duel', in Jean Sarrailh's words, 'between the partisans of Jansenism and those of Ignatius Loyola' (Sarrailh 1951, p. 19). On this growing division the French Revolution – and Counter-Revolution – exerted their powerfully polarising forces, providing conservatives with lessons in the dangers of a disunited absolute throne and papal altar. Among many exiled Spanish ex-Jesuits, who obtained permission to return to Spain after Napoleon's invasion of the papal states had dislodged them from there, was Lorenzo Hervás y Panduro, author of the *Historia de la vida del hombre* (1789–90), which argued that Filleau's original Jansenist plot to dismantle the Catholic altar had culminated in an alliance with *filosofos* to topple the French throne (Herr 1958, pp. 411–13, 420). This version of history would eventually triumph under Fernando VII with the publication of a Spanish translation of the ex-Jesuit Rocco Bonola's *La lega della teleogia moderna colla filosofia*

(1798), itself a prelude to the Capuchin Rafael de Vélez's *Apología del altar y del trono* (1818–25).

It was this curialist reaction that won the day in the person of Caballero in 1800, resulting in the 'disgrace' and exile of numbers of Jansenist ministers and former ministers, including Jovellanos and Urquijo. Although by French standards Spanish Jansenists scarcely sustained persecution, they lost all influence with the monarchy. Some of the older ones including Urquijo himself later served King Joseph Bonaparte when Napoleon imposed his brother on the Spanish throne in 1807, while younger Jansenists like Joachín Lorenzo Villanueva were able to think their way to the principle of national sovereignty and some kind of republic, albeit a Catholic one, with the help of a mythical version of a Visigothic constitutional past not unlike Le Paige's Frankish one. Enough Jansenists elbowed Jacobins in the revolutionary Cortes of 1808–10 and again in 1820–3 to amount to a case for a religious origin of liberal Spanish nationalism.

In sharp contrast to Spain, no Jansenists apparently surfaced in 1794 among the sixty or so 'Jacobin' conspirators uncovered in Vienna in 1794. So seamless and relentless was the reaction to everything that smacked of the Enlightenment or reformed Catholicism in Austria after the death of Emperor Leopold II (formerly Peter Leopold of Tuscany) in 1792 that, except for the far-flung provinces of Lombardy and the Austrian Netherlands, Jansenists under Habsburg rule found no opportunity to evolve from neo-Gallican regalism to anything else.

As it happens, Habsburg Italy and the Netherlands were where many of the Austrian Jansenists had originated, imported in the 1750s and 1760s by Empress Maria Theresa, daughter of a Protestant mother whose conversion to Catholicism had been facilitated by Jansenist books. It was not, however, for the purpose of converting Protestants – although she was concerned about that – but as part of an effort to modernise the whole Habsburg state in the wake of successive defeats by Protestant Prussia, that she used Jansenists in her administration. The first contingent came from Italy or from Austrians who had studied there: Giuseppi Bertieri, Pietro Maria Gazzaniga, but above all Simon Stock who discovered 'true doctrine' at, of all places, the Jesuit-run German College in Rome, and who took over the direction of theological education at the University of Vienna at the partial expense of the Jesuits. Quite moderate despite a common hostility to Jesuits and popular devotion, they remained under the influence of Muratori's brand of Catholic Enlightenment and *regolata divozione*. More radical reinforcements from the Austrian Netherlands came later in the train of Gerhard van

Swieten, personal physician to Maria Theresa, among them Jean de Terme, Stock's successor at the University of Vienna, and Anton de Haën, van Swieten's successor as the empress's physician and a native parishioner of the excommunicated Jansenist diocese of Utrecht. Unlike the Italian and Spanish cases, Austrian Jansenism can be blamed not on the Abbé Clément, who knew no German, but on his friend and correspondent Dupac de Bellegarde, ubiquitous spokesman for the diocese of Utrecht, who stopped off in Vienna on his way to Rome in 1774.

A reformed theological and canonical education at Vienna in combination with a relaxed censorship under van Swieten's direction eventually added to the stock of indigenous Jansenists: for example the abbot Stephan Rautenstrauch, one of the authors of the anti-papal *Was ist der Papst?* (What is the Pope?) published on the occasion of Pius VI's visit to Vienna in 1781; and Marc-Anton Wittola, editor of a Jansenist periodical called the *Wiener-ische Kirchenzeitung*. This Austrian equivalent of the *Nouvelles ecclésiastiques*, the translation and publication of Jansenist books, easy access to power by way of the empress's physician and personal confessor, some sympathetic bishops, and control over theological education in Vienna and at seminaries in Brünn and Leibach – all these factors 'forbid judging Austrian Jansenism as an ephemeral phenomenon' in the estimate of Peter Hersche, at least at the height of its influence around 1780 (Hersche 1990, p. 256).

Ephemeral or not, Austrian Jansenism would have little bearing on eighteenth-century political thought had it not served as a kind of Catholic theological justification for the awesome assault by Maria Theresa and her son and successor Joseph II on baroque piety and the Austrian Catholic Church's 'external' presence. By the time the dust from 'Josephism' had settled, the emperor had used his secular political authority to subject all papal correspondence to imperial inspection, to sever relations between Austrian monastic orders and their 'foreign' generals in Rome, to abolish all contemplative monastic orders and reduce the monastic population by more than half, to redraw both parish and diocesan boundaries, to abolish all diocesan seminaries in favour of a few general seminaries, to declare war on all forms of *Aberglaube* or popular baroque devotion, and – last but not least – to banish the bull *Unigenitus*. This Josephist variant of neo-Gallicanism went further than any other similar ecclesiastical reforms except the Civil Constitution of the Clergy, which Austrian Jansenists for the most part applauded.

To be sure, not all of the ideological underpinning for this programme of reform was specifically Jansenist. The Austria of Haydn and Mozart's Masonic *Die Zauberflöte* (The Magic Flute, 1791) did not remain immune to the influence of another Enlightenment in the latter half of the century. Nor was there anything specifically Jansenist about the vaguely 'enlightened' and cameralist political thought of publicists and professors like Heinrich Gottlieb von Justi, Karl Anton Martini, and Joseph von Sonnenfels, who tended to invoke natural law to justify the state's meliorist intervention in all manner of matters including the church (see ch. 18); or even the work of Johann Nikolaus von Hontheim (alias Justinus Febronius), suffragan bishop of Trier, whose *De statu ecclesiae* (1763) transmitted a radical neo-Gallican mixture of conciliarism and regalism to the German Catholic world and became a favourite textbook (Bernard 1971).

Yet here, as elsewhere in Tridentine Catholic Europe, the boundary between neo-Gallican or Jansenist and more enlightened forms of regalism was indistinct. Moreover, the whole Josephist programme would have produced a much earlier and even stronger reaction had it not borne a distinctly Catholic aspect, preached in the name of a purified and interiorised piety against what the emperor himself called a 'ridiculous externalisation' (*abgeschmackteste Veraüsserlichung*) of religion, for the benefit of a useful and pristine parish clergy as opposed to a useless monastic one, and on the neo-Gallican grounds of the Christian prince's rightful purview over the public and external aspects of even the most 'spiritual' of the church's functions.

Nonetheless 'orthodox' Catholicism eventually reacted and found its voice. In the Austrian Netherlands, where Jansenist priests and professors were outspoken in defence of Josephist reforms, the ex-Jesuit François-Xavier de Feller, editor of the conservative *Journal historique et littéraire*, in 1787 reprinted the Jesuit Louis Patouillet's updating of Filleau's original 1654 version of the Jansenist Bourgfontaine plot, explaining in his preface how this long conspiratorial fuse had now reached a Josephist phase (Sauvage 1787). In the non-Habsburg Catholic German lands, a number of ex-Jesuits collaborated on the publication of anti-Josephist tracts and treatises, among them the Mainz *Religionsjournal* and the Augsburg *Kritik über gewisser Kritiker*. In Vienna itself, Cardinal-Archbishop Christoph Anton Migazzi fought a rearguard action in defence of a threatened throne and papal altar until a more public counter-offensive took shape after the death of Joseph II in the form of Leopold Hoffman's periodical *Wiener Zeitschrift*, which proposed to prevent 'every throne [from being] buried in its own debris' by attacking 'irreligion' in all its manifestations (1792, pp. 2–6). The religion that Hoffman proposed to defend, however, seems to have been generically Christian, good for Catholicism but for Protestantism too, and thereby addressing Protestant Germany as well.

3   Pietism in Lutheran Germany

Corresponding to the Catholic Enlightenment in Tridentine Europe was an equally pious one in Lutheran Germany. If, by the end of the century, Lutheran Pietism discovered that it could not go the second mile with the German *Aufklärung* of, say, Friedrich Nicolai and his periodical *Allgemeine Deutsche Bibliothek* (1765–1806) – and also rediscovered in that *Aufklärung* the rationalism it had tried to leave behind in Lutheran orthodoxy – it had covered much common ground during the century's first mile. When for example he and his *collegium philobiblicum* had come under orthodox attack in Leipzig in the late 1680s, August Hermann Franke, one of the fathers of the Pietist movement, had found an eloquent defender in Christian Thomasius, father of the German Enlightenment. Together they virtually founded the University of Halle. This originally Pietist university also found a place for Christian Wolff, the disciple of Leibniz, who saw his rationalistic theology as forwarding the purification of Christianity begun by Luther and continued by the Pietists. The Pietist emphasis on a pure life as opposed to pure belief (*reine Lehre*) found enlightened echoes in the *Nathan der Weise* (Nathan the Wise, 1779) of the *Aufklärer* Gotthold Ephraim Lessing, who for his part found a positive if provisional place for Christianity in his dialectical *Die Entziehung der Menschengeschlechtes* (1780). Founder of the famous Moravian community called *Heernhut*, the Pietist Nicolaus Ludwig Graf von Zinzendorf distinguished between the innocent and common-sensical understanding (*Verstand*) and the dangerously and uselessly speculative reason (*Vernunft*) in a way that anticipates the critique of metaphysics and systematic theology in the philosophy of Immanuel Kant, himself the product of a Pietist upbringing and a professor at a heavily Pietist university (Herpel 1925, p. 16). Like Zinzendorf's and Pietism's generally, Kant's religion was decidedly an affair of practical rather than pure reason. Pietism and the German Enlightenment shared a hostility to scholastic Lutheran orthodoxy, a predilection for the practical and useful, a robust interest in philanthropy and education, and an espousal of religious toleration (see Lagny 2001; Melton 2001a).

The Pietist movement heralded by the publication of Philipp Jakob Spener's *Pia desideria* (Pious Desires, 1676) aspired to reform the Protestant Reformation, mainly from within the Lutheran and to a lesser degree Reformed churches. The kind of new reformation it had in mind was less doctrinal than moral, an attempt to act on Calvin's 'third' or sanctifying use of the Mosaic Law as well as on Luther's original insistence that the 'freedom of the Christian man' spontaneously yet necessarily expresses itself in some 'good works'. Pietism therefore stood for the practice of Christian piety (*praxis pietatis*) as against intellectual assent to objective truth, a biblicism in preference to confessional orthodoxy, and a priesthood of all lay believers in contrast to that of the clerical few, but above all an inward, experiential, and personal appropriation of the Gospel as opposed to either doctrinal or sacramental formalism (Stoeffler 1965, 1973; Wallman 1990).

Since Jansenism has served as the starting point for this survey, a brief comparison with Pietism serves to put the latter in sharper relief. Like Jansenism, Pietism insisted on evidence of 'conversion' and 'regeneration', or what Pietists called a *Widergeburt*, that found fulfilment in a life of charity, and dared not rest on the dubious laurels of any 'justification by faith alone'. The difference between people's condition before and after conversion, between the Pauline 'old man' and 'new man', struck Jansenists and Pietists alike as fundamental, making both groups hostile to the notion of some moral middle ground or *adiaphora* consisting in acts neither good nor bad in themselves. Pietist pastors, like Jansenist priests, frequently got themselves into trouble with the established church for denying communion to the still unconverted, for distinguishing too sharply between the regenerate and unregenerate. Although both movements mainly remained within their respective churches and tried to avoid the onus of schism, Pietists like Jansenists tended to separate into conventicles – what Spener called *ecclesiolae in ecclesia* – and to constitute themselves as churches within the church.

Conventicular piety found some of its best exemplars in the laity in Pietism as in Jansenism, for Pietism too held out for a less rigidly hierarchical, more participatory ecclesiology, and sought to diminish the distance between clergy and laity. That laicism took the form of vernacular translations of the Bible and an emphasis on lay Bible study, as well as an interest in psalmody, hymnody, and a more accessible liturgy. A more practical pastoral theology dear to both movements stood in sharp contrast to a detested scholastic orthodoxy. So did the theology of St Augustine and other fathers of the early church, which both groups venerated as superior to that of the middle ages. Viewing their own times, too, as a period of defection or apostasy, both groups looked not only backwards but also forwards toward the millennium. Among Pietists, Spener, Joachim Lange, and especially Johann Albrecht Bengel in Württemberg indulged an interest in eschatological exegesis and the future conversion of the Jews. Corresponding, then, to Jansenism's *témoignage de la vérité*, or minority 'witness to truth' in times of trouble and obscurity, was Pietism's *Zeugnisse der Wahrheit*, which figures so prominently in Gottfried Arnold's *Unparteiische Kirchen-und Ketzerhistorie* (1699–1700), published as the eighteenth century began (Roberts 1973, pp. 151–2).

However close these doctrinal and devotional similarities, the two religious phenomena diverged in precisely those areas most pregnant with political possibilities. To be sure, Pietists, like Jansenists, frequently appealed to the individual conscience or *Gewissen* and later evolved into 'patriots', but in Pietism's case neither of these translated into adversarial politics. Unlike eighteenth-century Jansenism, which persisted in arguing Augustinian grace against *Unigenitus*, Pietism's quarrel with Lutheran 'orthodoxy' was not really doctrinal. While Pietists may have wanted less emphasis on doctrine, they did not call for a different doctrine. Their de-emphasis of reason in favour of the heart gave Pietism the political consistency of pudding. That absence of polemical edge extended even to the domain of ecclesiology where, despite Spener's inaugural condemnation of caesaropapism and a marked impatience with rigid hierarchicalism, Pietism did not really call for structural reform. Nothing in Pietism corresponds to Richerism or conciliarism.

In contrast, then, to Jansenism's residual Cartesianism, Pietism more consistently eschewed reason in favour of emotion, making for an affective religious sensibility and a more sensual sense of the sacred. Taking its most extreme form in Zinzendorf's cult of Christ's blood and wounds in the 1740s, that affective and emotional sensibility had more in common with the Jesuits' devotion to the Sacred Heart – or, as Albert Ritschl argued in the nineteenth century, with elements in late medieval monastic piety – than with anything in Jansenism, and perhaps enabled Pietism to maintain a more reverential attitude towards secular and ecclesiastical *weltliche Obrigkeiten* (Ritschl 1880–6). Hand in hand, finally, with these baroque elements in Pietism went a chronic attraction to forms of mysticism and quietism, in particular to that of Jakob Boehme, to whose French counterparts – Madame Guyon and François Fénelon – Jansenists stood unalterably opposed (Angermann *et al.* 1972, pp. 27–95).

Since Pietism escaped wholesale persecution, it is not clear whether it was its political theology or concrete circumstances that accounts for its reluctance to challenge the powers that be. In the ducal and Lutheran Württemberg studied by Mary Fulbrook, where Pietists came closest to adversarial politics, they sustained sharp polemical fire from orthodox Tübingen theologians like Johann Wolfgang Jäger, lost a few of their more radical pastors to disciplinary action, and in 1710 endured the forcible closing of a noisy nocturnal conventicle in Stuttgart and the imprisonment of some its devotees. Orthodox opposition, concentrated in the church's governing Consistorium (*Kirchenrat*), stalled Pietist reforms such as the compulsory teaching of the catechism, the addition of adult confirmation to infant baptism, and the requirement of stricter penitential preparation for the eucharist. Yet Württemberg's Lutheran establishment adopted all these measures, culminating in the so-called *Pietistenreskript* of 1743 granting permission to hold extra-ecclesial conventicles everywhere in Württemberg so long as pastors presided, thereby successfully absorbing the Pietist presence (Fulbrook 1983, pp. 76–80, 130–52).

What worked in the Pietists' favour is that, in pressing for these reforms, they could take on the church without engaging the state. For, unlike the Gallican Church in France and the Lutheran Church in some other parts of the Empire, the Lutheran Church in Württemberg was not an adjunct of the princely court, its bishops being independently promoted and sitting with townsmen in the duchy's representative estates or *Stände*. That unique arrangement meant that Pietists were able to make common cause with other churchmen in defence of constitutional and ecclesiastical 'liberties' against the periodical attempts by the lilliputian Württemberg–Mömpelgard dynasty to free themselves from all fiscal and legislative control by the *Stände*, and to imitate the absolutist trend of its larger neighbours elsewhere in the Empire and in France. As it happened, the first such attempt by Duke Eberhard Ludwig took place just as the strength of Pietism was peaking towards the beginning of the century. Apeing the example of Louis XIV, he unconstitutionally raised revenues, footed a standing army, and built a baroque court at Ludwigsburg replete with mistress, music, and French wigs.

It was in the first of these constitutional confrontations between the *Stände* and the Württemberg dukes that Swabian Pietists most distinguished themselves as a group – with the *Oberrat* Johann Jakob Sturm spending three years in prison and the court pastor Johann Reinhard Hedinger preaching courageous sermons against immorality in high places. A second confrontation in the 1730s, between Duke Karl Alexander and the *Stände*, saw Pietists less conspicuously in the field, even though this Catholic duke added religious insult to constitutional injury by trying to legalise public Catholic worship. In the third attempt at what was now denounced as 'despotism', Duke Karl Eugen empowered himself with his French ally's subsidies during the Seven Years War but encountered the determined opposition of the well-known Pietist imperial constitutional jurist Johann Jakob Moser, then a legal consultant to the *Stände*. This constitutional crisis did not conclude until the Seven Years War had run its course, Moser had spent five years in prison, and the *Stände* had more or less prevailed, with the help of both Austria and Prussia.

Moser's personal involvement in this confrontation and his loquacity after his release provide a rare glimpse of the political reflection of a Pietist under pressure, at the same time that Chancellor Maupeou's absolutist assault against the constitutionalism of the French *parlements* was forcing Jansenists from a passive constitutionalism to a more active conciliar one. Passive to the point of inertia, Moser's earlier *Teutsches Staats-Recht* (1737–53) had been a sprawling, formless museum of the German Empire's surviving judicial artefacts. At once antiquarian and anti-historical, this compendium seems innocent of even the passive resistance and limited political purpose justified by Le Paige's thesis of historical continuity between Merovingian national assemblies and eighteenth-century *parlements* in his simultaneously published *Lettres historiques*. But five years in the Hohentwiel Fortress followed by a conflict with the *Stände's* Smaller Committee engendered more pamphlets and a *Neues Teutsches Staats-Recht* (1766–79) which displayed Moser's confessional colours more boldly as well as supplying greater conceptual coherence, balancing description with prescription and condemning 'despotism' in the name of 'patriotism'. Parallelling the transition in Jansenist political thought from judicial to conciliar constitutionalism was a clearer distinction in Moser's thought between justice and legislation as well as an indictment of the *Stände* as being less than representative of Württemberg's citizenry.

Yet Moser stopped short of according legislative sovereignty or even co-sovereignty to the Estates; his ducal 'master remained always a master', and that was all there was to it (qu. Walker 1981, p. 270). Where the Jansenist Catholics Mey and Maultrot were simultaneously having recourse to the authority of such Protestant political theorists as Samuel Pufendorf and Emmerich Vattel to effect a powerful if unstable synthesis of historic 'fundamental' laws with natural law in opposition to Bourbon absolutism, the Pietist Protestant Moser continued to wash his hands of Pufendorf's rationalism and to appeal, in good Pietist fashion, to raw 'experience' in explicit preference to 'reason' or *Vernunft*. While it was true, as Moser argued, that sycophantic physiocrats in France and Johann Adam von Ickstatt and his cousin Peter Josef in Bavaria were also appealing to 'reason' to justify the 'despotic' ways of rulers to subjects, it was also true that it would take more than an amorphous 'experience' to oppose absolutist reason of state (Krieger 1957).

It may at least be possible, then, that Pietism's experiential political theology stunted its prolongation as a contestatory political conscience. For, in contrast to Pietist political activity in the era of Duke Eberhard Ludwig, Moser spoke for few besides himself in the era of Duke Karl Eugen. Although such indubitable Pietists as Jakob Heinrich Dann agitated for Moser's reinstatement after his release from prison in 1764, they do not seem to have added up to a Pietist party in the *Stände*. Moser not only acted alone but suffered alone, Pietists having long ceased to be persecuted for Pietism's sake. So successfully had Pietists blended into Württemberg's ecclesiastical landscape since the *Pietistenreskript* of 1743 that they could leave it to the bishops and townsmen of the *Stände* to defend their interests.

A very different political trajectory, more comparable to Jansenism's or reformed Catholicism's in Peter Leopold's Tuscany or Joseph II's Austria, is evident in eighteenth-century Brandenburg-Prussia, where Spener and Franke themselves finished their reformist careers and where, so far from being persecuted, Pietism became something like a state religion in alliance with the monarchy *against* both the Lutheran Church and the Prussian *Stände* (Gawthrop 1993). There, a confessionally Reformed or Calvinistic Hohenzollern dynasty ruling over a conglomeration of mainly Lutheran territories welcomed Calvinist Huguenot refugees from Louis XIV's France at about the same time that it began to perceive in an irenic and tolerant Lutheran Pietism an antidote to its confessional isolation vis-à-vis Lutheran orthodoxy. Since, in Prussia, the Lutheran Church fell under the control of the various *Stände*, and since the Hohenzollern dynasty was just then completing its drive towards absolutism at the expense of the local political power of those same noble-dominated estates, Pietists tended to do double duty as allies on that front also. Finally, Friedrich I and Friedrich Wilhelm I did not fail to see in Hermann August Franke's fledgling but impressive educational, philanthropic, and economic enterprises in Halle the perfect means to maximise some human, material – even spiritual – resources in the service of their well-ordered paternal and military state. As Franke put it to Friedrich Wilhelm I in 1711, Pietism promised to produce 'honest subjects and faithful servants in all estates and professions' (Deppermann 1961, p. 166).

What Pietism obtained in return for this help, and for the halo with which it surrounded the transformation of the Prussian electorship into a monarchy, was protection from Lutheran orthodox hostility, which was nowhere more intense as the eighteenth century began. That protection translated into the founding of the University of Halle, initially a Pietist preserve, as well as privileges for Franke's other philanthropic and educational enterprises. A little later the same king imposed Pietist professors on the University of Königsberg, transforming it into another Pietist redoubt. This growing symbiosis between Pietism and *Preussentum* culminated in the 1720s and 1730s when the Prussian state began to impose Pietist graduates from Halle and Königsberg on all Lutheran parishes, even ones formally in the patronage of Junker nobles, as the Hohenzollerns consolidated their control over the ecclesiastical as well as other public aspects of Prussian life. Whatever reservations Spener may have had about the caesaropapism of Lutheran states when he published his *Pia desideria* in 1676 had clearly disappeared by the time he died in Berlin in 1705 (Spener 1676, p. 17).

Pietist political thought in eighteenth-century Prussia therefore took the form of a cameralist rationale for state interventionism to maximize material welfare which, in Marc Raeff's words, 'would redound to the benefit of the state and the ruler's power and provide for the proper framework for a Christian way of life' (Raeff 1975, p. 1225). Pietist cameralism, at which even Moser tried his hand before it got burnt by Karl Eugen in Württemberg, is thus comparable to Jansenist cameralism in Catholic Austria or Spain, except that the Lutheran Church in Prussia had even less autonomy than the Catholic Church in those realms.

The price paid by Pietism for its dependence on and contribution to Prussian absolutism became apparent during the reign of Frederick II 'The Great', who not only spoke French in preference to German and brought Voltaire to Potsdam, but favoured 'enlightened' pastors for Lutheran parishes in preference to Pietist and orthodox alike. Pietist reaction to this turn of events hence tended to blend into its reaction to the French Revolution, and therefore coalesced with other conservative voices. By the 1790s the Pietist challenge to Lutheran orthodoxy lay too far in the past for German conservatism to have taken an explicitly anti-Pietist cast. When for example Ludwig Adolf Christian von Grolman and Johann August Stark's conservative periodical *Eudämonia* (1795–8) directed its venom against 'every guttersnipe [who] feels free to throw dung at every monarch and every altar', it had enlightened *illuminati* mainly in mind, although Stark threw in Protestant dissenters and Catholic Jansenists for good measure in his own version of the basically *aufklärisch* conspiracy against thrones and altars culminating of course in the French Revolution (Epstein 1966, pp. 511, 514, 516, 540).

In the end, Pietism's most distinctive political legacy was its contribution to German nationalism by way of late eighteenth-century 'patriotism'. As argued by Koppel Pinson in 1934 and more recently by Gerhard Kaiser, that connection between Pietism and the literary stirrings of German nationalism seems most evident in the 'patriotism' of Moser's son Friedrich Karl and in the Pietist backgrounds of many of the major figures of the German *Sturm und Drang* (Storm and Stress) movement, like Goethe, Hamann, Novalis, and Friedrich Schleiermacher (Kaiser 1961; Pinson 1968). But it also seems evident in the revolt against French in favour of German, the rejection of 'reason' in preference to ardent feeling and emotion, in the rehabilitation of the common people or *Volk* as the true carriers of piety in advance of national character, and Zinzendorf's celebration of confessional diversity over national diversity. Indeed, Zinzendorf's use of the term *nationalismus* while in London in 1746 to designate something possessed by the English, French, and Spanish but not by the Germans must be one of the first such instances in any European language (Zinzendorf 1962, VI, p. 111). But unlike the Jansenist 'patriotism' of the early 1770s that was just as anti-'despotic' as it was anti-ultramontane, German 'patriotism' remained for the most part without that constitutional element, except perhaps for the cases of Johann Jakob Moser and his son Karl Friedrich. That German nationalism eventually took an authoritarian rather than constitutional turn may say something about the nature of the religious bridge between the German Old Regime and political modernity.

4 European Calvinism and English Dissent

If eighteenth-century Jansenists were more adversarial than Pietists at least in part because their theology and ecclesiology were a little like Calvinism's, what of Calvinists themselves? Did Calvinists live up to their reputation for political indocility so deservedly acquired in the sixteenth century? This survey will conclude with a brief glance at the European Reformed community.

It goes without saying that where Calvinism had triumphed and become an 'establishment', as in Geneva and the northern Netherlands, it acquired the same vested interest in its own perpetuation as any such establishment and hence every reason to minimise its potential for self-subversion. Such subversion depended on heterodox challenges from within those establishments. But the Pietist form that such challenges typically took in the eighteenth century packed no more political punch than they did in Lutheran establishments. At the other extreme were areas like southern France and the Upper Palatinate where Calvinism had been so thoroughly uprooted that little force for resistance remained. It is true, however, that the Huguenot diaspora in England and the Netherlands made no small contribution to anti-absolutist political thought in the eighteenth century, beginning with Pierre Jurieu's *Lettres pastorales* (1686–8) which tried to encourage the indigenous Huguenot community after the Revocation of the Edict of Nantes, and ending with French-language periodicals that provided political news for the whole literate French community on the eve of the French Revolution (Popkin 1989). When, meanwhile, Jansenists like Mey and Maultrot turned to the works of Grotius, Gerard De Noodt, and Pufendorf with such devastating effect in the 1770s, they read them in French translations by Jean Barbeyrac, another refugee from Louis XIV's France *toute catholique*.

It was in the pulpits of revolutionary New England that Calvinism made its greatest and still characteristic impact on political thought and action, but New England was not Europe. European enough, however, was England itself, where the work of James Bradley among others has focused renewed attention on the role of Nonconformity or Calvinist 'Old Dissent' in the politics of pro-Americanism and the transformation of Commonwealthman ideology into the political radicalism of the late eighteenth century (Bradley 1990, 2001). While the radicalism of Richard Price, Joseph Priestley, and the London Association may be too 'enlightened' to qualify as Calvinist, Bradley's examples of provincial pastors in some open parliamentary boroughs – Caleb Evans in Bristol, James Murray in Newcastle, David Rees in Norwich – would seem to be Calvinist enough. Their congregationalist separatism made these Dissenters subject to the Test and Corporation Acts which, though hardly tantamount to religious persecution, excluded them from public office and sustained a minority mentality. Led by such ministers or prominent laymen, Dissenters both voted and petitioned with ideological consistency for Whig candidates until the latter 1760s, then in opposition to the North administration's American policy in the 1770s and 1780s.

Throughout this period these pastors preached and published in defence of the American colonial rebellion and against the policies of George III and the North administration, sometimes treasonably so. Like Jansenist pamphleteers on behalf of the contemporaneous anti-Maupeou 'patriot' movement in France, they invoked an 'ancient constitution' and true 'patriotism' against despotic degeneration, and urged rejection in the name of God and the constitution of 'passive obedience' to tyranny. Behind these audacities there stood a conception of God so transcendent that it tended to demote all temporal hierarchies, ending in a kind of apologia for the temporal sovereignty of the Christian *vox populi* as the best echo of the *vox Dei*. Even more important, in Bradley's estimation, was the congregationalist polity that, more radically than the Jansenist one, effectively resisted the Anglican state's 'domination', while also acting as a model for temporal governance. Although, finally, these ministers argued mainly from the scriptures and in particular from the Old Testament – one Solomon being worth 'a thousand Rousseaus', in James Murray's opinion – they saw no inconsistency in also appealing to 'reason' and 'natural rights' as defined by the publicists of the Commonwealthman tradition, John Locke not least among them.

As it happened, Methodist 'New Dissenters' led by John Wesley also learned from Locke. The Wesleyan Locke was not, however, the Locke of 'reason' or the *Two Treatises of Government*, but rather the apologist of sensate 'experience' and the *Essay concerning Human Understanding*. Faith for Wesley, as for Pietists, was not an understanding but rather experiential; the final validation of one's regeneration was not 'reason' but 'feeling'. So strong was Wesley's distrust of discursive reason and so consistent was his empiricism that he followed Condillac in eliminating pure introspection as a source of ideas and experimented throughout his career with the hypothesis of a 'religious sense' comparable within its domain to Francis Hutcheson's moral sense (Dreyer 1983, pp. 12–30). Like Pietists, too, his was a 'reformation, not of opinions (feathers, trifles, not worth the naming), but of men's tempers and lives'. Nor was his quarrel with the Anglican Church doctrinal or even ecclesiological. On the contrary, Wesley's most chronic doctrinal quarrel was his 'Arminian' defence of the human will against 'speculative Antinomianism and barefaced Calvinism', against preachers like Caleb Evans.

But no more than in the case of Pietists or Jesuits did that espousal of free will translate into a free politics. Throughout the 1760s and 1770s Wesley and his cohorts resolutely defended the principles of the divine right of kings and the obligation of 'passive obedience', and parliament's policies of excluding John Wilkes and of taxing the American colonists, blaming Calvinist Dissenters in particular for both colonial rebellion and domestic unrest (Semmel 1973, pp. 56–80).

But no-one could preach the divine origin of political power and the duty of passive obedience as convincingly as Anglican divines, which they indeed did, apparently with renewed vigour. Tory authoritarianism was resurgent in reaction to the Wilkesite agitation and the American and French Revolutions, and comparable to the rise of ultramontane political theory on the Continent (Clark 1985, pp. 216–57). So lofty had the High Anglican view of the Hanoverian monarchy become that in 1776 it was possible anonymously to republish an extract from a late seventeenth-century Jacobite political treatise as a tract for new times, as if what had been said on behalf of the 'indefeasible right' of the deposed Stuart James II was equally applicable to the Hanoverian usurper George III. Like Lefranc de Pompignan arguing in 1769 against Rousseau and Jansenists, latter-day Laudians like William Jones, John Whitacker, and George Horne argued against Locke and the Dissenters that, since the right over one's life or anyone else's could not be derived from any putative state of nature, political authority had to have come from God and not the people. Although some of these theorists, like Samuel Horsley, left room for different forms of government, including even a 'balanced' constitution, the weight of the argument clearly favoured monarchy, and entailed a close union between crown and mitre.

It is altogether plausible that this context of Wesleyan and High Anglican political theology is important in the genesis of Edmund Burke's conservatism. When he wrote (apparently against French revolutionary rationalism) that 'we know, and what is better we *feel* inwardly that religion is the basis of civil society', Burke took Wesley's side against Dissenting 'reason' (my emphasis). When he maintained (apparently against the Civil Constitution of the Clergy) that for Englishmen the church was 'the foundation of . . . the constitution, with which, and with every part of which, it holds an indissoluble union', he also took Anglicanism's side against voluntaristic congregationalism (Burke 2001, pp. 254, 264).

England, it has been argued, avoided anything like a French Revolution because Methodism enrolled enough of the English working class into its ranks to have taken the edge off class consciousness and political radicalism (Thompson 1963). Be that argument as it may, the absence of an anti-Anglican revolution and the tremendous role reserved for Methodism and other forms of Nonconformity in the nineteenth century has made it easy to acknowledge the place of religion in the formation – or reformation – of political parties and political modernity in England. Traditionally, such a case has been harder to make for Continental, especially Catholic, Europe, where the 'Jansenist' or reformed Catholic alternative fell victim to the clash between an anti-Catholic Revolution and the Catholic reaction. However, that what was variously called Jansenism, Gallicanism, regalism, and Febronianism, might have made as large a contribution to liberal nationalism as *dévot* or *zelanti* Catholicism did to conservative nationalism is one of the principal hypotheses suggested by this survey.

The other conclusion, perforce more tentative, has to do with religious sensibility as a factor in the process of politicisation. It would seem that the circumstance of real or perceived persecution, while sometimes important in drawing out the political implications of given religious sensibilities, was not crucial in determining their basic direction. On the one hand, no religious group was as persecuted as were the Jesuits after 1765 or so; yet that persecution served only to accentuate the society's penchant in favour of ecclesiastical and political hierarchies, even if in defending them some ex-Jesuits defined themselves against some hierarchs. On the other hand, it is hard to imagine how any amount of persecution might have made German Pietists as politically pugnacious as French Jansenists, regardless of the many points of religious contact between them. Where they diverged in their respective emphases on affective emotion as opposed to discursive reason seems everywhere to have been a pivotal point in the direction of politicisation. For not the least of the paradoxes of eighteenth-century piety is that it was the ensemble of a God accessible to the human will via affective experience that tended towards conservatism, while it was the opposite ensemble, a transcendent God known to be such by discursive reason but unamenable to affective will, that produced the most wilful politics and ran in a liberal direction.

II

The new light of reason

5

The comparative study of regimes and societies

MELVIN RICHTER

1 The ambiguities and resources of comparative method

Comparison and contrast were used by eighteenth-century European thinkers to characterise their nations and continent, as well as their historical epoch. This was done by distinguishing the arrangements of each nation from its neighbours', by contrasting European regimes, societies, economies, cultures, and religions with those elsewhere in the world, and by juxtaposing their own time with periods preceding it. This comparative mode of analysis was deployed in conflicts between the champions and enemies of Enlightenment, in the sharp disagreements separating defenders of absolutism from those opposed to it, and in disputes about established churches and their theologies. Although political theory was often conducted through comparison and contrast between European regimes, the application of the method to the rest of the world was no less significant. Some modern interpreters hold that European thinkers assumed their continent's superiority, and thus that 'Enlightenment' went hand in hand with imperial subjugation of non-Europeans. Others, on the contrary, say that xenophilia, *étrangisme*, and the conviction of European inferiority, decline, and corruption prevailed among intellectuals (Baudet 1988, pp. 50–1).

This chapter addresses some of the numerous and complex ways in which European writers used comparative discourse. It examines the extent to which key concepts in this discourse were shaped by theorists' preferences and their positions on domestic controversies within their respective nations, as well as on issues during conflicts among European states within their own continent and in overseas competition for colonies. It asks whether there was any consensus about the superiority of Europeans over the rest of world, or about the legitimacy of European conquests, colonisation, and commerce, including the slave trade.

Comparison turned out to be a profoundly ambiguous and controversial operation, holding in suspension a number of disparate intentions and methods. When writers such as Voltaire, Gibbon, or Robertson contrasted eighteenth-century Europe with its medieval and sectarian past, they tended to be cautiously optimistic about its future. They saw Europe as a prospering commercial society, as having recovered from religious civil wars either by the triumph of toleration or by the imposition of peace by absolute monarchy, as having moderated international conflict by the invention of the balance of power, and as participating in an unprecedented advance of science, technology, and knowledge. Although some held this benign Europe already to be one progressive republic, others did not. Rousseau warned the Poles against losing their national identity by adopting the uniform way of life he attributed to commercial Europe. Herder emphasised the differences among European nations and ascribed their merits to their uniqueness. Comparison was condemned by Herder, who argued that its real function was to suppress the rich diversity of human cultures and languages within and beyond Europe. He also ridiculed as reductionist the four stages theory of the Scottish Enlightenment, as well as the tables, statistics, and systems theory of the Göttingen 'universal' or 'world historians', Johann Christoph Gatterer and August Ludwig von Schlözer. Adam Ferguson, and sometimes Adam Smith, stressed the moral costs inflicted by the advent of commercial society. Anquetil-Duperron asked why European ways of thought and worship should be thought superior to those of the great Asian civilisations. Attempts to seek 'parallels' between societies or periods were denounced by J. R. Forster; explanations derived from differences of national character by Thomas Paine (Paine 1945, II, p. 249). Arguments about the worth of alternatives to existing arrangements were habitually presented by comparing or contrasting them with non-European regimes called Oriental, or with 'savage' or 'barbarian' societies in the New World, the South Pacific, or with other historical periods where preferred or condemned models were said to have flourished. Thus contestation could extend to questioning the value of comparative analysis or the quality of the empirical evidence on which it was based.

The range of variation in subjects, categories of analysis, and comparative methods was great. Yet many writers built their theories on the distinction between moral and physical causes: Montesquieu and Hume stressed the first; Diderot the second; Herder, their interaction. Generalisations were increasingly tested by their applicability to all known peoples, continents, and practices. In his *Essai sur les moeurs et sur l'esprit des nations* (Essay on the Mores and Spirit of Nations, 1756), Voltaire derided Bossuet for treating the histories of only six peoples. By the end of the century, the belief that the entire world comprised a single system was shared not only by Smith and Robertson, but also by Gatterer and Schlözer.

From which sources did literate Europeans derive their information? How did they order it when they compared societies and regimes? Ever since the fifteenth century, the reading public had had a huge appetite for accounts of societies other than their own, written by commercial travellers, explorers, diplomats, missionaries, and colonial administrators. Governments, particularly those holding or seeking colonies, were no less interested in acquiring crucial details about their inhabitants' mode of life. Beginning with the sixteenth-century collections by Hakluyt and Purchas, such sources were often translated and published. Almost all the European authors discussed here prided themselves on their knowledge of travel literature since the first age of exploration. Many tried to acquire and assimilate the discoveries of their own time embodied in books by Bougainville, Cook, and the Forsters, father and son. Yet to collect all such works was difficult even for those who could afford them. Travel books were mostly read in the great eighteenth-century collections vigorously promoted by their publishers, and often pirated at home and abroad.

Principal among such works in English were *A Collection of Voyages and Travels* (1704), published by Locke's booksellers Awnsham and John Churchill, another travel library edited by John Harris (1705), Thomas Astley's *New General Collection of Voyages and Travels* (1745–7), and *The Universal History* of Smollett and Campbell (1765). Pre-eminent in French was the Abbé Prévost's *L'Histoire générale des voyages* (20 vols., Paris, 1746–89), although *The Universal History* was also translated, as had been an earlier work allegedly by Locke, *The History of Navigation* (1704). Although Prévost began by translating the first seven volumes of Astley, he then turned to a general history of discoveries and colonisation up to his own time, preceded by a general survey of his sources. His history resembles the *Encyclopédie* in its topics. Prévost's skills as novelist and journalist enabled him to write an engaging narrative capable of capturing a general audience, as well as providing otherwise unavailable sources for more demanding readers. Raynal was to enjoy a similar success.[1]

Virtually all sustained comparisons played large parts in ostensibly unrelated discourses prescribing political regimes and determinate forms of religious, social, and economic organisation for European states. Yet the vocabularies of comparison did not alter as much as might have been expected.

---

1 Convenient accounts of travel literature are given in Marshall and Williams 1982, ch. 2, and Duchet 1995, ch. 2.

Some concepts ('society' or 'civil society', 'the savage' and 'savagery', 'the barbarian' and 'barbarism'), took on new senses, acquired novel paired opposites, or were assigned positions in a patterned sequence of stages. Yet instead of coining neologisms to express conceptual novelties, theorists maintained a surprising continuity in their terms of comparison. These, however, authors felt free to redefine. Otherwise they assumed that their readers, without explicit discussion, would understand usages peculiar to an author. Seldom did theorists refer to either the discrepant senses of the same terms by their contemporaries, or to the understandings of earlier practitioners of comparison. One egregious example is Voltaire, who, despite citing Locke on the need to define the terms of discourse, never himself explicated the key concepts in the title of his *Essai sur les moeurs et l'esprit des nations*.

Other treatments of comparative analysis were more critical. The article 'Comparison' in the *Encyclopédie* suggested that making comparisons could produce errors, leading to the identification of relationships that did not exist. Typical in the eighteenth century was the attempt to compare modern 'primitives' with the inhabitants of the ancient world known from classical sources. In his *Moeurs des sauvages américains comparées aux moeurs des premiers temps* (Customs of the American Indians Compared with the Customs of Primitive Times, 1724), the Jesuit missionary Father Lafitau sought to demonstrate similarities between the religious beliefs of indigenous Canadians and those reported as prevalent in European classical antiquity. Nonetheless, the article in the *Encyclopédie* had concluded that it was to the credit of humans that they engaged in comparison more than any other species. A Humean version of this conclusion is found in the entry for 'Comparison' in the first edition of the *Encyclopedia Britannica* (1771):

Comparison, in a general sense, [is] the consideration of the relation between two persons or things, when opposed and set against each other, by which we judge of their agreement or difference . . . A person in prosperity becomes more sensible of his happiness by comparing his condition with that of a person in want of bread.

The eighteenth-century German work most nearly comparable to the *Encyclopédie* was edited by Johann Zedler (1733–64). Despite the many differences separating the greatest encyclopedic achievements of the century, their articles on terms of comparison were remarkably similar. Both referred to the original Latin terms from which these concepts were developed. The Zedler entry on *Sitten* begins by identifying the concept with *mores*, and hence *moeurs*; while *Gewohnheit*, the Latin equivalent for which was *consuetudo*, is synonymous with *coutume*. The enduring but unreflective effects of repetition are subsumed under the Aristotelian category of *habitus*. In the long discussion of *Sitten*, there are differentiations of custom from national character, the components of which are sketched and the causes of its formation explained. As sources for the concept, Zedler cites John Barclay's *Icon animorum* (1614) in the original Latin, as well as Bodin's *Methodus* (1565) and *De Republica* (1576). For the concept of character, Theophrastus is invoked as a source, as well as La Bruyère. Careful attention is given to the question of whether different regime types determine national character, or vice versa.

These examples illustrate that the eighteenth-century notion of distinctive national characters was a comparative concept designed to point up each people's singularity and difference from all others. Early in the century, the study of national character was put on the agenda of French historians in an influential manual by Lenglet-Dufresnoy. Later Montesquieu, Voltaire, Diderot, Herder, and Hume all made use of this integrating concept. But each did so in his own way and for his own purposes. As with other terms of comparative study, the ubiquity of 'national character' as a concept more often concealed differences than pointed to consensus. Some argued that political regimes determined the institutions and the 'manners', or *moeurs*, of a people. Others thought that *moeurs* overrode the effective capacity of regimes to legislate. Religion was frequently denoted the ultimate determinant of character. And there was disagreement about whether national character represented an organic singularity, or if it should be understood as the unstable result of internal contradictions.

2 Montesquieu

In the second half of the eighteenth century, political, social, and legal theory from Russia to America centred on the categories devised by Montesquieu for comparative study. Political theory was dominated by the regime types introduced in books II–VIII of his *Esprit des lois* (The Spirit of the Laws, 1748): *république, monarchie, despotisme*. What would today be called social theory centred on his novel classifications of peoples by their modes of subsistence in book XVIII: *sauvages*, or *chasseurs*; *barbares*, or *pasteurs*; *nations policées* (savages or hunters; barbarians or shepherds; civilised nations), which were either agricultural or commercial. Legal theorists discussed Montesquieu's classification of systems in terms of their reliance upon *lois, moeurs, manières* (laws, mores, manners), as well as by the presence or absence of institutionalised constitutional limits upon government. Finally, as a synthesis of all these subjects, in book XIX, Montesquieu provided an inventory of the range and foci of the overarching national character or general spirit (*esprit général*), which he claimed unified every people's life and distinguished it from all others. Almost every writer on politics, society, and law felt compelled to defend or attack Montesquieu's categories.[2] His numerous hostile critics included theorists as diverse as Voltaire, Linguet, Anquetil-Duperron, Herder, and Justi. How did Montesquieu reconceptualise the vocabulary of comparison he inherited?

Comparison, Montesquieu held, was indispensable for the analysis of human collectivities. People understood political and social phenomena only when they could cite some alternative arrangement in place elsewhere. Montesquieu's use of comparison was often intended to prove that deplorable practices and laws might be replaced by superior measures. He insisted that the comparative method could be put on a rigorous basis only through classifying nations and governments by ideal types such as he constructed. At his most ambitious – he was the first to include systematically within political theory an investigation of the 'laws, customs, and varied usages *of all peoples*' – he claimed to have discovered certain general laws applicable to all governments, societies, and legal systems. By such laws, every individual datum could be explained; every law linked to another, or derived from a more general law (*SL*, 1). In practice, he often subverted such purported regularities by citing exceptions to them.

Montesquieu's interests were almost equally divided between, on the one hand, establishing resemblances among polities and societies widely separated in time and space; and, on the other, understanding what distinguishes one from the other. He has been praised for his achievements in both types of analysis. Durkheim saw in him the authentic precursor of sociology, understood as establishing the uniformities shared by all societies. Yet Montesquieu was also fascinated by difference, by complexity, by organic and unplanned historical development. On occasion he discovered the hidden wisdom of custom, and could refer to the generally beneficent, if unintended, consequences of religious faith. Voltaire, by contrast, had scant use for either custom or organised religion. Hume, while sharing Voltaire's distaste for churches and sects, did not share his enthusiasm for applying reason as the standard by which to judge existing arrangements. It was to be Hume who argued that only custom makes judgement possible, and that habit is the foundation of political stability and civilised society.

2 The study of politics, society, and law were not as yet set off from one another. This was particularly true of comparative law. For the great significance of legal studies for what are now considered the social sciences see Kelley 1990.

Montesquieu assumed that comparison presupposes a 'distancing' on the part of the analyst. Only in this way can the capacity be acquired to treat the features of one's own society as problematic, rather than natural. In his *Lettres persanes* (Persian Letters, 1721) he had made relativism into a new technique for comparison. This was his first book, written in the form of letters by two Persians who had never before left their country. Although not the first to use the device of presenting his own society as it would appear to outside observers, Montesquieu here displayed a remarkable capacity to treat his own government, society, and religion as phenomena to be investigated objectively. What before, in the sixteenth-century writer Montaigne, had been a philosophical and religious scepticism, now became a means of analysing the newly revealed range of diversity in governments and societies. Combining wit, malice, and fable, the *Persian Letters* is among the few works of genuine philosophical consequence to treat serious matters irreverently. Hence its enormous popularity. Montesquieu presented a remarkably fresh and detached view of France, in which almost every aspect of its life was relativised and made problematic and amusing. Such a method might serve as a solvent of traditional values and modes of thought.

This applied especially to the political agenda of the *Persian Letters*, its attack on the absolute monarchy constructed by Louis XIV, later reconceptualised in *The Spirit of the Laws* as despotism. In the earlier work, Montesquieu treated this subject indirectly through the sustained sequence of letters between Usbek, the more philosophical of the two Persians visiting Paris, and his seraglio (as Montesquieu calls the harem) of wives, and the eunuchs who guarded them. In devoting so large a part of the book to depicting the inner life of the seraglio, Montesquieu created an image of despotism altogether novel in its detail, in its compelling account of the human passions that sustain it, and above all in its representation as a system of power.

In the seraglio letters, there are three parties to a relationship that is despotic: Usbek, the master of the seraglio, who is absent in Paris; his eunuchs, to whom he has delegated power; and his wives. This is a system of power that involves paradoxes and contradictions. Its ostensible purpose is to establish the conditions regarded by its master as requisite for maintaining the purity, obedience, and modesty proper to marriage, as practised by the Persians. Of course, there immediately arises the question of whether the seraglio is compatible with human nature and the law of nature. Relativism cuts two ways, and if customs and institutions are to be regarded as merely the products of a society's physical environment and historical experience, then what is regarded as natural by Westerners and Christians is as arbitrary as any Oriental practice.

Usbek believes the seraglio is connected to virtue and duty; he sees its maintenance as closely connected to that of authority and dependence. Usbek is a man who wishes to be loved by his wives as a husband rather than feared as a master. Yet he, and they, are part of a system which by its logic links love to fear, the distinguishing characteristic of despotic rule. Despotism cannot be enlightened; its principle is fear, and this cannot be moderated or checked, despite Usbek's efforts. The eunuchs reveal the implacable logic of despotic rule. But Montesquieu does not exaggerate the omnipotence or permanence of this system. Even with it, some sort of consent is necessary, as Roxana points out in her final letter. Absolute rule is not only more subject to corruption than any other, but also when sedition occurs, it produces more violent effects than in other systems. Here Montesquieu's treatment is largely psychological; later it will be political and legal.

In *The Spirit of the Laws* he classified governments in terms of three types, each of which is characterised by its nature and principle. By the 'nature' of a government he meant the structure, the framework within which the person or group holding power must function; by 'principle', that passion which must animate those involved in a form of government if it is to operate at its strongest and best, or survive at all (*SL*, III.1). When classified by their nature, governments fall into three categories. A republic is that form in which the people as a whole (democracy), or certain families (aristocracy), hold sovereign power. A monarchy is that in which a prince rules according to established laws that create intermediate groups as channels through which royal power flows. Montesquieu's examples of such channels include an aristocracy administering local justice, *parlements* with political functions, a clergy with recognised rights, and cities with historical privileges. Despotism is the unlimited rule of a single person, directed only by his will and caprice.

The principles of these governments differ: virtue is the principle of republics, honour of monarchies, and fear of despotism. Montesquieu subdivided republics into democracies and aristocracies. His image of the first was taken from classical Greece and Rome. When he assigned virtue to them as their distinctive principle, he meant those political qualities requisite to their maintenance: in the case of democracies, love of country (*patrie*), belief in equality, and the frugality and asceticism which lead men to sacrifice their personal pleasures to the general interest. His model for aristocracy was drawn from early modern Italian city-states ruled collegially, such as Venice. Hence he classified aristocracies, along with democracies, as republics in his special sense. Although such aristocratic republics required virtue on the part of their governing classes, the form it took in them was that of the moderation needed to mitigate their characteristic weaknesses.

Montesquieu thought that monarchy, as he defined it stipulatively, was the modern regime best suited to ruling free societies intermediate in scale and commercial in their economy. The principle of monarchy he defined as honour, based on *esprit de corps*, the sense of belonging to a social formation which demands and receives privileges. When such privileges are granted voluntarily by the monarch, the nobility of a monarchy is recognised as a semi-autonomous, intermediate group between the king and people. Although its claims are selfish and exclusive, the nobility helps maintain liberty through resistance to any attempts by the crown to exceed its constitutional prerogatives. Montesquieu summed up his conviction that such a nobility is essential to a monarchy (as opposed to a despotism) in the phrase: 'Without a monarch, no nobility; without a nobility, no monarchy. For then there is only a despot' (*SL*, II.4). But he also insisted that a monarchy must recognise other intermediate groups.

Montesquieu made the concept of despotism into a regime type which was so widely used in a pejorative sense during the second half of the eighteenth century that it helped undermine the legitimacy of the French monarchy. Despotism replaced tyranny as the term for a corrupted monarchy. The makers of the French Revolution described themselves as overthrowing a despotic system. Absolute European governments had often before been called tyrannies, but the implication remained that bad rulers could be replaced. In Montesquieu's conceptualisation, despotism was systemic, and alien to France, a system that might be extirpated, but never reformed.

Like the other two types of government, despotism was driven by an operative passion, in this case fear. Yet Montesquieu did not expect to find any of his types empirically embodied in all their aspects. Thus, although the king of Persia might be able to force a son to kill his father, the same king could not force his subjects to drink wine. Montesquieu avoided making categorical statements about religion; instead he carefully distinguished the effects of religion upon each type of regime. Under monarchy, there must be a constituted body that includes the clergy. This is as valuable to monarchy as it is pernicious in a republic. Since no other power can affect a despot, religion alone on occasion can moderate this regime (*SL*, II.4). Such an approach to the political effects of religion was in conspicuous contrast to Voltaire and Hume, neither of whom could see anything positive about organised religion. They perceived it as producing only superstition, fanaticism, and irrational enthusiasm. Voltaire was obsessed with the power of the Catholic Church; Hume with Protestant sects in the rebellions of the seventeenth century.

Several key concepts figure in the title of Montesquieu's crucial chapter: 'How a Nation's Laws may Contribute to its *moeurs, manières*, and Character' (*SL*, XIX.27). Here his political and legal sociology is applied to Britain, thus greatly amplifying the picture given earlier of its constitutional protections of citizens' liberties (*SL*, XI.6). Again, there is a carefully elaborated, if implicit, contrast with France. Montesquieu asked what social forces make for a free polity. Crucial to his account is his theory of the causes of national diversity. Why does a people have certain laws, institutions, and social structures, and not others? His broad answer was that every nation has its *esprit général*, which is determined not only by physical, but also by moral causes: laws, *moeurs, manières*, religion, upbringing, a shared style of thought, mode of subsistence, economy, and trade (*SL*, XIX.4). What results is a specific ordering of aspects. Some aspects may cut against others. Montesquieu did not assume that societies are always integrated; often he emphasised internal contradictions which might cause corruption or decline within a system.

Government, he asserts, should conform to the character (*naturel*) of the people for whom it was established. So great are the differences in the *naturels* of nations that the laws of one almost never suit another. Thus laws ought to be made relative to the nature and principle of a government, and the physical and social characteristics of a people (*SL*, I.3).

Montesquieu's starting point was also that of Hume, who wrote, in his essay 'Of the Origin of Government': 'such is the frailty . . . of our nature that it is impossible to keep men . . . in the paths of justice . . . This great weakness is incurable in human nature.' Therefore, 'a great sacrifice of liberty must necessarily be made in every government' (Hume 1994a, pp. 20, 22). To maintain order, Montesquieu thought, every political society requires at least some repression of men's wills and imaginations. However, and here he is more sociological than Hume, this repression may be accomplished by such means as religion or principled self-repression of impulse on the part of citizens brought up to put the common good above personal interest.

In book XIX, Montesquieu treated laws and constitutions as but one way of affecting human conduct. Such is the method used by governments. Civil society has others: *moeurs, manières*, religion. These may serve as surrogates for laws enforced by penal sanctions, and they can have compelling power comparable to that of laws. Such forces originating in civil society may also limit and check state action. *Moeurs* apply internalised restraints upon conduct; *manières* apply external, social restraints (*SL*, XIX.16). Though laws, *moeurs*, and *manières* are analytically distinct, they may operate together, or else a single component may dominate and set the tone of a nation. Japan was dominated by *lois*, Sparta by *moeurs*, and China by *manières*. The basic laws of the Chinese were designed primarily to establish internal tranquillity. All aspects of conduct were subject to ritual. When the rites were observed exactly, China was well governed. But whenever rulers sought to use physical punishments as sanctions, the state fell into anarchy, because the general spirit of Chinese government had been fatally violated (*SL*, XIX.17).

Religion is another moral cause independent of government which affects a nation's character. To the extent to which religion is an effective force, there is less need of state power. Religion can even save a government, which left to its own police power would be overturned. Religion may also determine a people's orientation towards economic activity and liberty. In a remark later cited by Max Weber, Montesquieu commented that the British had known best how to combine religion, commerce, and liberty.

Another set of concepts and theories were formulated in book XVIII. This registered Montesquieu's reaction to a further source of diversity: the societies discovered outside Europe were not all of the same type. Some, like China and the Ottoman Empire, were highly cultured with recorded laws, sciences, arts, and written archives, as well as bureaucratic, judicial, and military structures comparable to those of Europe. Other societies were made up of hunters and gatherers, or of nomadic shepherds, dependent on orally transmitted customs, and without a state apparatus. A third type was based on settlement and agriculture, where it was possible to divide up land and to develop laws of private property.

To deal with these diverse societies, Montesquieu developed additional categories based on modes of subsistence, climate, and characteristics of terrain. These he classified as physical causes. He argued that climate and other environmental influences may affect, sometimes crucially, a people's character and mode of life. In several notorious passages, Montesquieu exaggerated the effects of climate. However, he ultimately rejected deterministic versions of environmental causation. He argued that moral causes overrode physical causes. In response to the contention that in the Caribbean and in the North American colonies African slaves were necessary because Europeans could not work in the tropics, he held that anywhere in the world agriculture is best performed by free labour. Hume, in his essay 'Of National Characters' (1748) altogether denied the importance of physical causes, and was perhaps countering Montesquieu, though both agreed that national character is best explained by moral causes.

In book XVIII, Montesquieu focused on the different modes of subsistence and the types of law appropriate to each. Nations engaged in trade require legal codes broader and more detailed than those exclusively practising agriculture. Even the latter, however, need more legislation than nations subsisting by flocks and herds, and those living by hunting, which require fewest legal rules of all. Montesquieu drew a widely accepted distinction between 'savage' dispersed clans of hunters, and 'barbarian' small nations of herdsmen and shepherds. He then gave an account of how the laws and governments of savage (*sauvages*) and barbarous (*barbares*) nations differ from those which cultivate land and use money. Native Americans, Arabs, Tartars, and Africans were among the examples given, as were the Germans described by Caesar and Tacitus. All were contrasted with those *nations civilisées* or *policées* which cultivated the earth and/or engaged in commerce.

Although Montesquieu also attributed differences in *moeurs* and governments to the mode of subsistence, he showed no interest, by contrast with later Scottish theorists, in ranking nations as higher and lower on an ascending scale of development. His tone is remarkably equable. He notes that among peoples who do not use money there are fewer wants and greater equality. *Moeurs* rather than laws are predominant among those nations which have never divided up their lands. Among them, the old have greatest authority because they control the memory of past practices. Nor does Montesquieu perceive liberty to be determined by modes of subsistence. Among pastoral nations, Arabs are free, Tartars are not. Of such peoples, only the Natchez of Louisiana have a despotic political system (*SL*, v.13).

Montesquieu used comparison to show differences and to demonstrate similarities among peoples and their laws. What is remarkable is the way in which he ranged freely through space and time in search of evidence for his comparative analysis. He contrasted the polities of classical antiquity with those of modern Europe; he was among the first to treat the laws, government, and property of feudal Europe as a system distinctly contrasted with the altogether novel type of society subsequently created by developments in commerce, government, and society. At crucial points, he offered a sustained juxtaposition of British and Chinese society. To do so was unprecedented in a major treatise by a European political philosopher.

Montesquieu thought of himself as cosmopolitan and humanitarian, as condemning cruelty and intolerance. He held a pluralist view of human diversity. Denouncing European conquests, colonialism, and the slave trade, he attacked the arguments that supported these practices. He scorned arguments for slavery as based on contempt for those of different *moeurs*, or on the absurd pretension that a nation reduced to slavery could be converted to the true faith. How pleasant to act as bandits in the name of Christian zeal! Slavery, he argued, violated the law of nature. Nor was it justifiable on utilitarian grounds. Deleterious to master and slave alike, slavery in the long run was fatal to monarchies and republics. Holding that colonies would weaken rather than enrich metropolitan powers, he added economic to moral reasons for condemning colonialism (*Lettres persanes*, letter 121). Later Raynal and Diderot followed his lead.

3 Voltaire

Voltaire likewise regarded comparison as indispensable to philosophical history. He gave disparate reasons. Historical truth – philosophical enlightenment, as distinguished from Christian orthodoxy – he claimed, could be attained only by comparing the history of Europe with those of nations outside it. He also argued from utility: a modern commercial society needs knowledge which can be gained only from comparison, alerting statesmen and citizens to what they must emulate if they are to improve arts, agriculture, and commerce (Voltaire 1966, p. 323). By emulation, Voltaire meant learning from another nation so as to compete effectively against it, as when Louis XIV and Colbert purchased English stocking machines in order to make France self-sufficient in their manufacture: one of Louis XIV's main preoccupations was to inspire 'that spirit of emulation without which all enterprise languishes' (Voltaire 1966, p. 141). What unified Voltaire's analysis was the concept, familiar from Barclay and Bodin, that every nation had a distinctive character (*esprit, naturel, génie*). National characters, he claimed, rarely change. Everything worth knowing about history can be found in 'l'esprit, les moeurs, les usages des nations' (Voltaire 1963a, 1, p. 195). Readers of his *Essai* will find that the most sustained portrait of national character was his poisonous attack on the allegedly unchanging qualities of the Jews from the Old Testament to his own day.

Voltaire equivocated over the degree of similarity and difference in human nature, as variously interpreted by seventeenth-century theorists. Though he recognised, from Montaigne, the great diversity in ways of life outside Europe, or during other periods of history, he did not renounce the theory, to be found in Pascal and La Bruyère, of a single uniform human nature.

The equivocation is apparent in his contrast between nature and custom. 'Everything intimately linked to human nature is similar from one end of the world to the other: everything that can depend on custom is different . . . Custom spreads variety throughout the universe, nature, unity' (Voltaire 1963a, II, p. 810).

Custom often amounted to the debris of the past. Thus 'the power of custom' explained the peculiar privileges of the French clergy (Voltaire 1966, p. 200). Like superstition, ignorance, and fanaticism, custom works against reason and enlightenment. Because custom is irrational, diversity is random and not ultimately justifiable. Where for Montesquieu human diversity is explicable and desirable, for Voltaire uniformity was the aspiration. In 1764 Voltaire wrote that, despite having long been governed by the same principles, the governments of France and England now differed as much as those of Morocco and Venice. In guarded language, he explained that England was free and France was not (Voltaire 1994a, pp. 55–61). In the same year, he published an article on *lois*. Asserting again that Britain alone possessed good laws, he dismissed all legal and constitutional arrangements elsewhere. In a startling incendiary metaphor, he advocated discarding existing laws everywhere else, including France. 'London only became worth living in since it was reduced to ashes . . . If you want to have good laws, burn what you have, and create new ones' (Voltaire 1994a, p. 20).

The *Essai* ends with a chapter entitled 'Les moeurs asiatiques comparées aux nôtres'. This sustained comparison is crucial to determining the extent of Voltaire's Eurocentrism and 'Orientalism', as well as to evaluating the depth of his commitment to the greatness of high cultures outside Europe, which he had extolled. He vigorously defended Asian peoples over the ten centuries he discussed against Montesquieu's charge that their governments were despotic. This was because Voltaire rejected the concept of despotism. He also repudiated Montesquieu's evidence as inaccurate. The little that was valid in Montesquieu's theory was best described by distinguishing monarchy and its abuses. Voltaire thus dismissed what Montesquieu had made into the greatest single difference between Europe and Asia. The way seemed open for Voltaire to deny any essential differences and to encourage each to 'emulate' the other. Yet at the end, he inexplicably drew back from this conclusion, asserting that 'everything differs between them and us: religion, maintenance of order, government, *moeurs*, food, clothes, styles of writing, expression, and thought' (Voltaire 1963a, II, p. 808).

Voltaire commented on European conquest, colonisation, and slavery. His hatred of injustice and cruelty overcame any easy identification with, and defence of, European actions. He strongly criticised European explorers, missionaries, and traders. He defended indigenous peoples whom they 'discovered', invaded, and exploited. He could find no evidence that the allegedly barbaric practices of peoples of other continents had ever approached the atrocities of Europe's worst periods. This did not prevent Voltaire from prejudicial views of the supposedly innate qualities of Jews and Africans (Bitterli 1976, pp. 274–80). But he did share with Montaigne, Raynal, Diderot, and Montesquieu the contention that, when overseas, civilised Europeans acted as barbarians.

4 Hume

There was a long-standing relationship between the intellectual traditions and political allegiances of France and Scotland. David Hume and his Scottish contemporaries were well connected with the salons and *philosophes* of Paris. Hume and Smith rejected the 'vulgar Whiggism' which classified the French as living in political slavery, as contrasted with British freedom (Forbes 1975). In his essay 'Of Civil Liberty' (1741), Hume depicted France as a modern commercial society, governed by laws protecting the civil liberties and property of her subjects (Hume 1994a, pp. 54–5). In Hume's typology of regimes, 'Of National Characters', France is a 'civilized monarchy', characterized by 'civility, humanity, and knowledge' (Hume 1994a, p. 85).

'Of National Characters' is perhaps the most sophisticated specimen in English of a genre popularised throughout Europe by Barclay's *Icon animorum*. A second generation Gallicised Scot, Barclay added national character to the agenda of historians – Lenglet-Dufresnoy's influential manual on historical study recommended Barclay alongside Bodin as models on this topic. In refining the mode, Hume followed Voltaire and Montesquieu in making *l'esprit des nations*, their customs, and their 'manners' into characteristic topics of philosophical history. But Hume made distinctive contributions.

As to the balance which Hume struck between uniformity and diversity, his *Treatise of Human Nature* (1739–40) pointed to his lasting concern with what is common to all human beings. This underlay his epistemology, moral philosophy, and project for a science of politics. To a lesser extent, Hume was also concerned with diversity, with variations among regimes and societies, above all, with explaining his position on the quarrel between Ancients and Moderns, thus contrasting classical and modern Europe. In the 'Dialogue' published at the end of his *Enquiry concerning the Principles of Morals* (1751),

Hume replied to the contention that 'fashion, vogue, custom, and law were the chief foundations of all moral determinations', and that wide differences separated civilised from barbarian natures (§ 25: Hume 1998, p. 116). Hume argued that variant conclusions were derived from universal principles, a fact discovered 'by tracing matters . . . a little higher, and examining the first principles, which each nation establishes, of blame or censure' (§ 26: Hume 1998, p. 116).

For Hume, as an admirer of Newton, explaining the workings of the human mind meant the reduction of complexity to a few causes; and the discovery of the laws of mental operations by verifiable experience. Thus his treatment of human nature, and later politics, would be successful to the extent that it was simple, empirical, and not subject to indefinite variations. Hume believed that a science of politics was both possible and necessary. Like Voltaire, Hume regarded human nature as uniform, and believed that most diversities in behaviour, institutions, and beliefs were due to customs, manners, and national characters. But unlike Voltaire, he thought that most human differences could be accounted for by differences in regime types:

Men cannot live without society, and cannot be associated without government. Government makes a distinction of property, and establishes the different ranks of men. This produces industry, traffic, manufactures, law-suits, war, leagues, alliances . . . and all those other actions and objects, which cause such a diversity, and at the same time, maintain such an uniformity in human life. (*THN*, ii.iii.i, p. 402)

Critics have disagreed about whether Hume sustained a stable position about human nature in his later *Enquiry concerning Human Understanding* (1748). Some stress his failure to admit historical and cultural variability in statements such as: 'Mankind are so much the same in all times and places, that history informs us of nothing new or strange.' Others call attention to his qualifications: 'We must not, however, expect that . . . all men, in the same circumstances, will always act in precisely the same manner, without making allowances for the diversity of characters, prejudices, and opinions' (Hume 1975, pp. 83–4).

Unlike Voltaire, Hume attacked rationalism, and viewed human customs and habits positively. A mitigated sceptic, he set out to prove that reason alone cannot justify our judgements. These, he argued, are the work of our imagination. In his *History of England* (1754–62), he held: 'Habits more than reason, we find in everything to be the governing principle of mankind' (Hume 1884, v, p. 184). For Voltaire, custom was an impediment to rational politics; but Hume distrusted abstract principles, *a priori* reasoning about politics and morals.

Hume held that comparison is not merely an intellectual operation. It involves the passions of pain and pleasure, malice and envy. 'The misery of another gives us a more lively idea of our happiness, and his happiness of our misery.' Comparison is often 'a kind of pity reversed, or contrary sensations arising in the beholder, from those which are felt by the person, whom he considers' (*THN*, II.ii.viii, p. 375). Other nations are praised or criticised because of the psychological consequences for those comparing them. 'This is the reason why travellers are commonly so lavish in their praises to the Chinese and Persians, at the same time, that they depreciate those neighbouring nations, which may stand upon a foot of rivalship with their native country' (*THN*, II.ii.viii, p. 379). Hume here offers an analysis pointing not to a Eurocentrism deprecating 'the other', but rather to the assertion that neighbours are more apt to be hated than are more distant societies. Adam Ferguson also stressed that European societies were bitterly divided internally and externally.

From his *Treatise* to his final essay, 'Of the Origin of Government' (1777), Hume emphasized the crucial role of government. Comparison of regimes involved judgement of their relative merits rather than reference to any 'fixed unalterable standard in the nature of things'. Seeing himself as an impartial observer transcending local partisanship, as a citizen of Europe, Hume attempted a new set of political classifications. This was not done in treatise form, but in the course of essays and history writing. He distinguished between absolute monarchies and free governments, and between regular and arbitrary governments. Regimes which were both absolute and arbitrary he tended to call 'barbarous monarchies' or despotisms, and these he identified with both the Roman emperors and with 'Eastern', that is, Asian or Oriental, regimes, such as the Ottoman Empire. But such governments could arise in Europe. Hume called Oliver Cromwell's Protectorate 'military and despotic'; it 'parcelled out the people into so many subdivisions of slavery' (Hume 1983, VI, p. 74). But absolute monarchies may also be 'civilized', by which Hume meant that although their kings had sovereign authority, they chose to govern according to general laws. He argued that the French monarchy was of this kind. The king is limited by 'custom, example, and the sense of his own interest'. In the civilised monarchy of France, liberty, not arbitrary coercion, prevailed. Property was secure, 'industry encouraged; the arts flourish, and the prince lives secure among his subjects, like a father among his children' ('Of Civil Liberty', Hume 1994a, p. 56).

Free government 'admits of a partition of power among several members, whose united authority is no less, or is commonly greater than that of any monarch; but who . . . must act by general and equal laws, that are previously known to all the members and to all their subjects' (Hume 1994a, p. 23). The two varieties of free government are limited monarchies, such as Britain, and pure republics, the worst form of which was direct democracy. But if improved in a number of ways he detailed, even a republic could become a 'perfect commonwealth' (Hume 1994a, pp. 221–33).

Hume's comparison of absolute monarchy and free government narrowed the choice between them. He argued that both France and Britain regularly enforced the rules of justice, and protected the property of their subjects. Differences between them were marginal. Free governments encouraged commerce more than did civilised monarchies; while in civilised monarchies the arts flourished more. Thus Hume subverted the commonplace contrast between French slavery and British liberty dear to the 'vulgar Whigs'. He regarded this conclusion as a triumph over British self-congratulatory prejudice. His favourable judgement of French monarchy ignored the views of those in France who were critical of it. The Revolution that occurred after his death would have been inexplicable on his analysis.

As a comparative analyst, Hume's acuity was more evident in questions of method, as in his essay on national character. This contains no sustained empirical analysis of actual societies. (His most extended comparison in terms of group characteristics occurred in his 'Dialogue', where he playfully contrasted the ancient Athenians with the modern French.) In 'Of National Characters', Hume accepted, but qualified, the familiar notion that each nation has a peculiar set of 'manners'. The diversity of nations is due either to moral causes or to accidents; physical causes produce no discernible effects. Human history demonstrates that manners are spread through the laws made by governments. In this way a uniform national character can be stamped upon even a far-flung empire. Despite variations in their climate, the Chinese have the greatest similarity of manners. Here Hume attacks Montesquieu's apparent doctrine of climatic determination, but overlooks Montesquieu's argument that moral causes could override physical ones, and the fact that he had explained Chinese uniformity by close analysis of the use of ritual.

In his essay, 'Of Refinement in the Arts' (1752), Hume stated what he regarded as the distinctive traits of European civilisation in his time. When commerce and industry flourish, the spirit of the age affects all the arts and the minds of men. The more these refined arts advance, the more sociable men become. Flocking to cities, they learn to receive and communicate knowledge; to show their wit and breeding, their taste in conversation, and styles of living. As it becomes possible for men and women to meet in an easy and sociable manner, their behaviour becomes more refined. Thus 'industry, knowledge, and humanity are linked together by an indissoluble chain' (Hume 1994a, p. 107). For laws, order, police, discipline cannot be perfected before human reason has been refined by commerce and manufacture.

Hume was most interested in comparing the Europe of his time with that of classical antiquity, thus taking a firm stand in the quarrel of the Ancients and the Moderns, on the side of the latter. He regarded modern Britain and France as the most civilised and polished commercial societies yet known. He interrupted the narrative in his *History of England* to contrast the lowlier stages of manners and governments in earlier centuries with those of the present time. He rejected the attacks on modern arts and sciences by Rousseau and Ferguson. Hume displayed little interest in the world beyond Europe. Where Montesquieu and Diderot used comparison with the non-European world to distance the arrangements of their own society, as a means to insights for its reform, Hume showed no interest in such a procedure. His remarks about non-European peoples are categorical and haphazard. There was none of the careful qualification, weighing of evidence, and criticism of sources found in his impressive essay, 'Of the Populousness of Ancient Nations' (1752). Perhaps the comparison most important to Hume was that between Britain and France, with regard to which he established a distinction between what has been dubbed 'scientific Whiggism' and, by contrast, the 'vulgar Whig' complacency of his British contemporaries (Forbes 1976). Yet many in France accepted just the view rejected by Hume.

5   Raynal, Diderot, the *Deux Indes*, and the *Supplément* to Bougainville

Few comparative studies have been so widely read in their own time – and so neglected after it – as the ten volumes produced by the Abbé Raynal. Its baroque title states both its method and global concerns: *A Philosophical and Political History of the Settlements and Trade of the Europeans in the East and West Indies* (1770); more simply the *Deux Indes*. Alongside Voltaire, Montesquieu, and Rousseau, Raynal ranks among the eighteenth-century French authors most often translated and discussed abroad. Published in more than thirty editions and twenty-four abridged versions, his work was an international bestseller. It was read and interpreted in discrepant but seldom uncontroversial ways throughout the world (Lüsebrink and Tietz 1991). It is said to have inspired the Haitian revolutionary Toussaint L'Ouverture, and to have prompted Napoleon's invasion of Egypt.

A vast project which occupied Raynal for twenty years, the *Deux Indes* contained forty-eight maps, as well as the best available statistical information about European expansion and commerce worldwide. Although based in part on travel accounts, Raynal's data was gathered primarily from an unprecedented number of government documents, furnished by a network of officials and informants in all the colonial powers. This extensive coverage was combined with bold moral judgements stating an anti-colonial position, linked to radical criticism of European governments. The book popularised the condemnation of European conquests, the maltreatment of non-Europeans, and the slave trade. After the Paris *parlement* condemned the third edition in 1781 as 'a book apt to produce popular uprisings', it was burnt by the public hangman (Benot 1970, p. 163; Feugère 1922, p. 278). In a list of the bestselling illegal books in France between 1769 and 1789, the *Deux Indes* ranked fifth (Darnton 1995). Over 25,000 copies were sold in the American colonies alone (Wolpe 1957, p. 9).

Although initially accepted as the work of Raynal alone, in fact he enlisted or purchased the collaboration of figures associated with the *Encyclopédie*, above all Diderot. The *Deux Indes* thus continued the work of the *philosophes* (Wolpe 1957). Its collaborative nature shows through in the contradictions and ambiguities within it, and the divergences between the first three editions. It is a polyphonic text. But Raynal conceived its design, gathered its materials, and controlled its organisation, printing, and diffusion (Benot 1991; Duchet 1991).

In this immensely ambitious book virtually all known peoples appear and are successively the subjects of comparison. Colonisers and colonised are contrasted in terms of their laws, governments, religions, *moeurs*, customs, usages, practices, commerce, and general spirit. The book also reflects the political issues at stake in the intense contemporary disagreements about how to evaluate the Chinese and Russian empires.

The *Deux Indes* is among the most significant demonstrations that, by the end of the eighteenth century, many European thinkers had transcended the limits of their own continent. More than any other major work of the century, the book systematically reversed prior judgements about the old world's political and moral superiority. It did so by inverting the values of the polar oppositions long made in European thought between barbarism and civilisation, between *l'homme sauvage* and *l'homme policé*, savage man and civilised man. These familiar invidious dichotomies were reversed in Diderot's indictments of European conquests and colonisation. The conclusions drawn are summarised in the contrast between *peuples sauvages* and *peuples policés* or *civilisés* (Diderot 1992, pp. 193–7). Diderot engages in a spirited demonstration of the superiority of savage peoples, whose mode of life is contrasted with the corruption and injustice of 'polished' European societies. He condemned the practices of Europe as contradictory to its own self-proclaimed values.

Readers of the third edition were struck by the thundering apostrophes, at once denunciatory and sentimental. Commenting on the slave trade, Diderot addressed his audience: 'Reader, do you not share the indignation which fills my heart when I read this?' On the question of whether the European discovery of the Americas had been beneficial, the *Deux Indes* answered unequivocally that its effects had been catastrophic. Nor had Europeans behaved better elsewhere. Of the Portuguese in India, Diderot spoke of 'European barbarians . . . I protest solemnly . . . You are no better than birds of prey. You have no more morality, no more conscience' (Raynal 1780, bk I, ch. 24, pp. 225–6). Missionary proselytisation, the treatment of native Americans, the slave trade, are all condemned with a violence that called explicitly for revolt by subject populations abroad, and which have been interpreted as carrying an implicit appeal for revolution in Europe.[3] Condemning the rule of the East India Company, Diderot wrote: 'Sooner or later justice must be done. If not, then I shall address the people: "You, whose cries of rage have so often made your masters tremble, what are you waiting for? You have your torches and the stones which pave the streets. Tear them up"' (Raynal 1780, bk II, p. 398).

Although Diderot's contributions to the *Deux Indes* were not identified until the middle of the twentieth century, the same was not true of his *Supplement to the Voyage of Bougainville, Or Dialogue between A and B on the Inappropriateness of Attaching Moral Ideas to Certain Physical Actions that do not Accord with them* (1772; publ. 1796; Diderot 1992, pp. 35–75). Comparison in the *Supplément*, as in Montesquieu's *Lettres persanes*, is combined with wit to form a brilliant rhetoric designed to engage and persuade the

---

3 There are two competing interpretations of this passage. The first is that he was indeed calling for revolution in Europe (Benot 1970, p. 194; Strugnell 1973, p. 209). The second is that Diderot never abandoned his allegiance to limited monarchy. Even when praising tyrannicide, he had no vision of a new order alternative to the French monarchy (Mason 1982, pp. 345–6).

reader on controversial points too dangerous to make explicitly. Like much else by Diderot, it was written in dialogue form, and intended to provoke reflection on and stimulate criticism of French and European culture, particularly Christian sexual morality. The *Supplément*'s subtitle stated the central argument: to restrict human sexuality by moral and religious codes was unnatural and harmful. Comparing the sexual code of the Tahitians to that of Europe, Diderot rejected the European. He tells of a Tahitian, Aotourou, who was brought to France by Bougainville, the commander of a French mission exploring the South Pacific. This man, accustomed to natural liberty, perceived French *usages* and *lois* as chains. When he returned, the Tahitians could not comprehend his account of France, 'because in comparing their own ways with others, they'll prefer to regard Aotourou a liar than to think us so mad' (Diderot 1992, p. 40).

Although comparative, Diderot's argument was not relativist. Human nature was his standard. He condemned the sexual attitudes, legal codes, and social practices of Europe because of their arbitrary evaluations of natural actions. Through their civil codes, and through religion, Europeans had introduced an artificial man into natural man, and instigated a war between them. In Tahiti, religion, morality, and legislation did not repress natural sexual impulse, and the concept of property did not apply to women or to the relations between the sexes. Hence in Tahitian society there was polygamy, and the absence of concepts of adultery, promiscuity, sexual fidelity, and, above all, chastity. Of all European practices, the vow of chastity taken by the clergy was least comprehensible to the Tahitians, a point made in a conversation between the Tahitian Orou and the ship's Catholic chaplain. Tahitian hospitality led Orou to offer his wife and daughters to the clergyman; after initially refusing them, he eventually decides he could not offend them.

Diderot was of course indebted to a substantial tradition of male sexual utopianism; his Tahiti is based on male virility and female fecundity. Moreover, his playful radicalism is brought to a close with carefully modulated reformist conclusions. Summing up, A asks what conclusions should be drawn from the Tahitians' *moeurs* and *usages*. B answers that when laws contradict nature, they become impossible to enforce because they produce *moeurs* and individuals at war with themselves. Should Europeans try to overthrow their bad laws, or accept the practices of their nations? The *Supplément*'s conclusion applies equally to political and moral arrangements: 'We must speak out against senseless laws until they are reformed and, in the meanwhile, abide by them. Anyone who . . . violates a bad law thereby authorises everyone else to violate the good' (Diderot 1992, p. 74).

6   Herder

Herder's work is indispensable to any discussion of eighteenth-century comparative method. While most authors believed human beings everywhere fundamentally are the same, and hence capable of comparative treatment, Herder scorned all efforts to establish commensurability among human societies. Herder's first major work, *Yet Another Philosophy of History* (1774), derided comparison and all those who attempted to practise it. Comparisons of ways of life, literatures, and political systems were meaningless, as were all efforts to classify or rank them. To do so was to miss precisely what distinguishes them. Human nature and the image of happiness change with each condition and climate. Diversity is to be celebrated, and no single standard can be applied to the infinite variety of cultures. 'All comparison is unprofitable' (Herder 1969, p. 186).

Herder learned from Hamann to dismiss as superficial the qualities most esteemed by the major writers of his age (Berlin 1981, pp. 1–4). 'The general philosophical philanthropical tone of our century wishes to extend "our own ideal" of virtue and happiness to each distant nation, to even the remotest age in history' (Herder 1969, p. 325). In part, this critique was due to Herder's emphasis on difference; in part, to his distrust of abstract concepts. He came to hold an abiding hostility to Montesquieu. This is puzzling, for they shared many attitudes. Both were hostile to the absolute monarchies of their time, Herder regarding them as regimes fatal to civic virtue, as well as to moral obligations. He especially had in mind the threat posed by Russian despotism to the republican government of Riga. Both men attacked European colonialism and conquest, and the marriage of commerce and religious mission. Thus Herder remarks:

Soon there will be European colonies everywhere. Savages all over the world become ripe for conversion as they grow fonder of our brandy and our luxuries . . . Trade and popery, how much have you already contributed to this great undertaking! Spaniards, Jesuits, and Dutchmen: all you philanthropic, disinterested, nobler, and virtuous nations. (Herder 1969, p. 206)

Herder convicted Montesquieu of empty abstraction, overlooking his commitment to empirical investigation, and to the values found in tradition. He mistook an ideal-type analysis of political regimes for reductive crudity.

In our political economy and political science, philosophy has offered us a bird's eye view in place of an arduously acquired knowledge of the real needs and conditions of the country . . . The principles developed by Montesquieu allow a hundred different peoples and countries to be reckoned up extempore on a political multiplication table. (Herder 1969, pp. 198–9)

In no small measure, Herder's critique was part of a wider attack on the dominance of French cultural values, and resentment at the Francophilia of princes like Frederick II of Prussia. In fact, besides a few visits outside of Germany, Herder was far less cosmopolitan in outlook than many of the French writers he criticised. His own treatment of Africans and Chinese in his *Ideas for the Philosophy of the History of Mankind* (1784–91) derived from uncritical European standards of value.

Herder, a Lutheran pastor, had a further reason for his hostility. He condemned the heirs of Bayle – Montesquieu, Voltaire, Diderot, Hume – as thrusting Europe into a whirlpool of scepticism. Their abstractions were built upon their spiritual nullity. One remark against Montesquieu's alleged reductionism points to the shape of Herder's own philosophy of history: 'The history of all times and peoples, whose succession forms the great, living word of God, is reduced to ruins divided neatly into three heaps . . . O, Montesquieu!' (Herder 1969, p. 217). Herder's celebration of difference stemmed from a theology in which cultures were identified as revelations of the divine in history. There was a scheme of human development according to a divine plan, in which successive cultures implicitly carried their predecessors within themselves. 'The Egyptian could not have existed without the Oriental, nor the Greek without the Egyptian; the Roman carried on his back the whole world. This indeed is genuine progress, continuous development' (Herder 1969, p. 188). In his late work, he conceives of all peoples, arts, and sciences as developing towards a common *Humanität*.

It has become an orthodoxy to assume that the comparative analyses conducted in the Enlightenment were wholly dependent on binary distinctions between Europe and the 'Other', and were designed to reinforce European domination of non-Europeans. Of course, assertions of European cultural superiority were rife, as were defences of colonialism and conquest. Yet a significant minority turned the pretensions of Europeans against themselves, and their books found a readership. Structured analysis of experience elsewhere in the world became a source of polemical critique of European practices and values. Just as Adam Smith looked with ambiguous apprehension upon the effects of the modern commercial system, so others looked with similar misgiving upon the impact of the modern international state system. In 1791, William Robertson, pillar of the Church of Scotland and of the University of Edinburgh, wrote:

In whatever quarter of the globe the people of Europe have acquired dominion, they have found the inhabitants . . . different in . . . complexion and . . . habits of life. In Africa and America, the dissimilitude is so conspicuous, that . . . Europeans thought themselves entitled to reduce the natives of the former to slavery and to exterminate those of the latter. (Robertson 1791, I, p. 80)

6

Encyclopedias and the diffusion of knowledge

DANIEL ROCHE*

By way of its conception, production, and distribution, the *Encyclopédie* illustrates, more forcefully than any other publishing venture of the eighteenth century, how innovative philosophies of the period came to be disseminated, and how the market of ideas in the age of Enlightenment was organised.[1] Current research on the *Encyclopédistes*, and on their allies and enemies, makes plain that both the economic and social forces which underpinned their enterprise, as well as those which resisted it, were for technical and political reasons joined together in the same ideological world. Thanks to the growth of literacy and the economic, cultural, and scientific institutions which literacy served, books came throughout the eighteenth century to acquire an unprecedented significance. The advent of commercial society allowed for the wide circulation of the printed word through newspapers, magazines, and other publications. Authors could manage to earn a livelihood from their writings alone. Intellectuals could become a political class. A system of signs could be transformed into systems of thought, and by way of their diffusion to readers impressed by them, revolutionary ideas could come to have revolutionary implications.

This 'immortal work', as Voltaire once termed the *Encyclopédie*, has for virtually the whole of the period since its completion appeared the emblematic monument of eighteenth-century culture. While in principle conceived as a work of reference and a compendium of knowledge distilled from other sources, the vast collection of more than 70,000 articles assembled in 25,000 folio pages, comprising seventeen volumes of text, eleven tomes of plates

---

* Translated by George St Andrews and Sylvana Tomaselli and adapted by Robert Wokler.
1 In the past thirty years scholarship on the *Encyclopédie* has benefited from work by specialists studying the history of book production and the book trade as well as those working on the text itself. The starting points are Lough 1968, 1971; Proust 1962, 1965, 1972. There are indexes and inventories in Schwab *et al.* 1971–3. For the *Encyclopédie* as an enterprise see Bowen 1969; Kafker 1976; Venturi 1946; and especially Darnton 1979. For its early press reception: Birn 1967; Lough 1971, pp. 98–111. On the wider intellectual background: Chartier 1990; Furet 1965; Roche 1965–70, II.

and seven volumes of supplements and tables, in fact came to occupy a central place within Europe's republic of letters and even managed to help shape its political landscape. At once hounded and protected by Europe's prevailing regimes, the *Encyclopédie*, by way of the history of its publication and diffusion, attests to some of the most crucial features of the genesis of political modernity in the period from 1750 to 1800.

'Since the rebirth of letters amongst us', wrote Diderot in his 'Prospectus', 'it is in part to dictionaries that we owe the general enlightenment which has spread throughout society . . . How important, then, to have a work of this kind . . . to guide those with the courage to seek . . . to enlighten those who learn only for themselves' (Diderot 1875–7, XIII, p. 130). In announcing the imminent publication of the *Encyclopédie*, Diderot proceeded to acknowledge his debt to the vast intellectual effort made before him, since the Renaissance and the age of humanism, which had, through the multiplication of general and scientific dictionaries, established the pedagogy of Western civilisation by way of defining words and explaining the meaning of concepts. The enterprise which he and d'Alembert were about to launch could be justified as different in character from its numerous precursors and only now possible for the first time, even while preserving an inherited legacy of erudite learning and arcane curiosities, since it adopted a fresh perspective which presupposed a new kind of public comprised of lay readers, receptive to an orderly classification of known facts and received wisdom conveyed in a vernacular language. In their collective endeavour the *Encyclopédistes* ventured to supplant both the cosmic systems and canonical principles of medieval theologians, and the dialectic of ancient and modern traditions adopted by Renaissance humanists, with models inspired by the work of engineers, geometricians, and empirical scientists, an enterprise which accorded well with the preferences and capacities of a new generation of readers.

i   English philosophy, encyclopedism, and technical knowledge

At least three related features of the intellectual milieu of the eighteenth century made this transformation possible: first, the encounter between Cartesian modes of analysis and English empiricist perspectives; secondly, the rise of utilitarianism in the light of which inventories of knowledge could be perceived as indispensable to the progress of society; and, finally, new standards of cultural sociability in Europe which brought with them a perceived conjunction of institutions of knowledge and power.

Locke's *Essay concerning Human Understanding* (1689), often regarded as having launched the age of Enlightenment as a whole, was lavishly praised by French commentators throughout the eighteenth century, among them Voltaire in his *Lettres philosophiques* (1734) and d'Alembert in his 'Discours préliminaire' to the *Encyclopédie*, who each made plain, with central reference to Locke's work, the debt owed by contemporary French thinkers to British philosophy. In discussing the simple ideas perceived by persons who had undertaken research in physics, Locke had expressed the hope that the words they employed to signify the things they knew should be accompanied by small line engravings which would represent them. Even before Locke, Francis Bacon's *Novum organum* (New Organon, 1620) – whose system of classification of the sciences d'Alembert borrowed and placed at the head of the *Encyclopédie* – followed by Descartes's *Discours de la méthode* (1637) and Newton's *Principia mathematica* (1687), had articulated a growing demand among scientists and philosophers for a synthetic systematisation of knowledge made transparent by a precise use of language (see Furet 1965). Newton's description of words as irreducible sketches of reality and Locke's focus on the fundamental relation between thoughts and words together illustrated how the progress of the human mind was tied to the use of concrete terms expressing general ideas. Locke's and Newton's analyses of language thus showed how its careful use was indispensable to experimental science. They regarded language as an active means of knowing, no longer defining essences or pointing to innate ideas, but depicting the real.

The stress placed by Locke and his followers on sensation as the ultimate source of ideas, and on the use of language for an empirical understanding of reality, helped to shape intellectual currents favourable to the introduction of concrete data in dictionaries on both sides of the English Channel. The pursuit of scientific precision and mathematical exactitude thus contributed greatly to that spirit of secularisation which characterised the production of books in both Britain and France throughout the eighteenth century. A critical spirit of a kind equally necessary for this development had already been plainly manifest in Pierre Bayle's *Dictionnaire historique et critique* (1697), which had also shown the potential advantages a dictionary could afford by virtue of its very genre, introducing a simple arrangement in alphabetical order rather than any principles of deduction, hierarchical precedence, and subordination. Entries classified lexically rather than cardinally were thus each equally eligible, in principle, to independent scrutiny (Matoré 1953; Rétat 1971). This triumph of the fact, which came to revolutionise both metaphysics and history, marked a fundamental attitude of the *Encyclopédistes* in general, bringing a fresh outlook upon all the productions of the human mind together with an optimistic faith in the capacities of human reason to progress towards the triumph of truth. The *Encyclopédie* managed to apply to the whole of human knowledge a method which for Bayle had been restricted to theology and history alone. Yet its dedication to the classification of facts by way of a lexical ordering of information also implied new methods of controlling that information. In applying inductive methods drawn from their precursors to social institutions and political concepts, no less than to natural phenomena, Diderot and d'Alembert opened up the prospect of the organisation and analysis of the human sciences along lines mapped by the disciplines of English experimental science and physics.

While the prospectus of 1750 acknowledges a debt to earlier English dictionaries, including John Harris's *Lexicon Technicum* (1704–10) and Thomas Dyche's *New General English Dictionary* (1735), the *Encyclopédie* followed such precursors mainly in its lexical organisation and critical attitude, rather than by recapitulating specific entries. The influence credited to Ephraim Chambers's *Cyclopedia or an Universal Dictionary of Arts and Sciences*, which first appeared in 1728 and was itself inspired by earlier French, Italian, and English dictionaries, might have proved of a different order, if the initial aspiration of the *Encyclopédie*'s publisher, André François Le Breton, to produce nothing more than a translation of Chambers's text, had been pursued. Johann Jacob Brucker's *Historia critica philosophiae* (first published in Leipzig between 1742 and 1744, with a supplementary volume in 1766) was, however, to remain a constant model for Diderot in particular, many of whose articles on philosophical and political themes proved little more than French translations of the Latin text of this German pastor, whose own entries had been inspired by both Pufendorf and Bayle. Diderot also borrowed much material from other sources, including the Abbé Gabriel Girard's *Synonymes français* (1736), while d'Holbach, in his own philosophical contributions, drew heavily from, and frequently refers to, the *Grosse vollständiges Universallexicon aller Wißenschaften und Künste* (Universal Lexicon of Human Knowledge and Arts), published in Leipzig between 1732 and 1750 (Matoré 1968).

2   French encyclopedism, the academies, and the public sphere

All these and other dictionaries and encyclopedias of the late seventeenth and early eighteenth centuries were conceived as works of reference which could embrace both ancient and modern science and scholarship in a fresh idiom. But in France the conjunction of at least three exceptional advantages made it possible for them to assume major cultural significance in the public domain. First, the substantial resources of several Parisian publishing houses brought power to their format of the printed word as nowhere else in Europe. Secondly, the universalist pretensions of the French language, with its precise vocabulary, controlled grammar, and enriched lexicon, served to enhance the imperial status of a regime politically characterised as an absolutist monarchy. And, thirdly, the especially animating roles of d'Alembert and above all Diderot, in particular, whose zeal, competence, and network of chosen collaborators enabled them to edit their work as they saw fit, made it possible for them to assert their freedom and autonomy as intellectuals.

The editors' conscription of a society of men of letters to their cause would contribute to the drawing of new boundaries of politeness and cultivated discourse, excluding archaic terms, neologisms, obscenities, and base and trivial words, somewhat in the manner of the dictionaries of the language of classicism undertaken by Pierre Richelet in 1680, Antoine Furetière in 1690 and the first *Dictionnaire de l'Académie française* (1694). But the distinctions often consecrated in these earlier projects between the vocabularies of *l'honnête homme* (a gentleman), on the one. hand, and of artisan crafts and technical expertise, on the other, were of scant interest to them. Furetière himself sought to append inventories of everyday words to his dictionary, and the multitude of technical manuals and medical textbooks that appeared in the years preceding the publication of the *Encyclopédie* bears testimony to the growing appeal in that period of a new, more technical, conception of science and the Baconian conjunction of practical activity with speculative thought. By virtue of their extraordinary attention to the minute details of artisan manufactures and occupations, the *Encyclopédistes*, however, went much further in plumbing the depths of a commercial world deemed unfit for serious scrutiny in the age of classicism. They turned to and recovered an older tradition of practical treatises on arts and crafts, partly inspired by the sixteenth- and seventeenth-century *théâtre des machines*, and they capitalised upon a number of late seventeenth- and early eighteenth-century treatises and collections which drew upon that tradition, including Thomas Corneille's *Dictionnaire des arts et des sciences*, Chomel's *Dictionnaire économique*, and Jacques Savary Desbrulous's *Dictionnaire universel de commerce* (1723). By 1758, as recorded in Durey de Noinville's *Table alphabétique*, nearly five hundred dictionaries were available to the public (Matoré 1953; Proust 1962).

Such enthusiasm for dictionaries and manuals attests to the growth of a fresh market which publishers throughout Western and Central Europe were eager to harvest, with those based in Paris possessing the most ample means to cultivate it. The new fashion also had political significance, to which Diderot was especially attuned. It coincided with the emergence into print of French political economy (Perrot 1984). After the economic crises of the early eighteenth century, including the collapse of John Law's schemes of reform around 1720 which had greatly shaken the social fabric of France, fresh avenues of self-promotion and economic mobility came to be improvised whose steps could be lexicologically followed and plotted. In spite, or perhaps even because, of its indiscreet theological bias, the Abbé Noël Antoine Pluche's *Spectacle de la nature* (The Spectacle of Nature, 1732–50) symbolised the new state of mind, in uniting the practical utilitarian goal of cataloguing and disseminating knowledge of the natural world with a philosophical history of humanity's evolution and progress. In propounding a providential ethic of work which gave warrant to human enterprise and ambition, it helped undermine the holistic, static, and unadventurous principles of Christian political economy before the age of enterprise. While marvelling at the wonders of God's creation, Pluche was equally enraptured by the ingenuity of inventors and scientists, whom he invited to join with philosophers so as to publicise the practical experience accumulated by generations of artisans. He held the advance of human thought and science to be inseparable from material progress. In his eulogy of economically productive forces, reconciled with due respect for dogma, can be found one of the great fissures that separated eighteenth-century France from its classical heritage as well as the hidden hand and force which was to steer a new culture of sociability.

In his own article, 'Encyclopédie', published in 1755, Diderot criticises Europe's learned societies for their excessive specialisation and their neglect of organising plans and principles of research. But the reasoned dictionaries of the arts and sciences of the mid-eighteenth century were also the direct and indirect heirs of Europe's learned societies and the academic movement which in the seventeenth century gave rise to them. The *Encyclopédistes'* references to new terms drawn from the 1718 and 1740 editions of the *Dictionnaire de l'Académie française*, and to material drawn from the *Mémoires de l'Académie des inscriptions* and the *Histoire et mémoires de l'Académie des sciences*, bear ample testimony to such debts. Despite the French monarchy's control of both the membership and publications of its national academies, there was substantial collaboration and exchange between their diverse milieux and the world of Diderot and his contributors: 'An encyclopedia is not produced on command' (Diderot 1992, p. 22). Inspired by the Abbé Bignon, Réamur, and Fontenelle, academicians accumulated manuscripts and scientific documents in archives, thereby collecting descriptions and drawings of crafts and technical procedures in much the same manner as the *Encyclopédistes*. Through the pages of the *Journal des savants*, the *Dictionnaire* of Savary or the publications of the *Académie française* itself, the *Encyclopédistes* had direct access to this information and greatly contributed to its diffusion. In their own fashion they subscribed to the manner of thinking, the methods, and style of the *Académie's* centenarian permanent secretary, Fontenelle.

In seeking to imitate the Parisian establishment of the *Académie française* and *Académie des sciences* the provinces of France soon followed the example of their capital. Some twenty learned societies which brought together notable local amateurs and professional specialists to cultivate both the sciences and *belles lettres* obtained their letters patent in the early eighteenth century – among them the *Académie de Dijon* whose announcement of a prize competition on the moral effects of the progress of the arts and sciences in 1749 was to launch the career of Rousseau, at once the author of the principal articles on music and political economy for the *Encyclopédie* and chief critic in the age of Enlightenment of its central aspiration to promote virtue through knowledge. His first discourse on these themes was rebuffed by d'Alembert in his 'Discours préliminaire' to the *Encyclopédie*. Such provincial academies, in Besançon, Bordeaux, Lyons, Metz, and Toulouse, as well as Dijon – like their counterparts in Bristol, Edinburgh, Königsberg, Lausanne, and Naples – were modelled more in the image of the open-textured Royal Society of London than of the narrowly specialist academies of Paris, in so far as they embraced scholars and scientists of whom the amateurs among them in particular were often polymaths. But no less than their Parisian counterparts, they provided the *Encyclopédie's* contributors with a vast network of information and, through their national and cosmopolitan connections, brought high levels of integration to bear on the Enlightenment's chief collaborative publishing venture (Proust 1968; Roche 1978).

Of cultural significance above all else, such assemblages of intellectuals dedicated to the advancement of learning for utilitarian ends were also political organisations, both in the sense that their members were highly influential in their communities, and in so far as their meetings were facilitated by the prevalent authorities. By way, in effect, of authorising the academies of the late seventeenth century and their multiplication in the eighteenth, the French state implicitly participated in projects of reform, thereby depicting its own absolutist principles as progressive and enlightened. On more than one occasion when France's ecclesiastical powers sought to suppress the

Encyclopédie, Malesherbes, the official director of publications, intervened to save it, as when, on the evidence of his own *Mémoires sur la librairie* (1758), he ensured the protection of its plates following the orchestrated ban of Helvétius's *De l'esprit* (1758) which threatened Diderot's work in its wake. The standards of sociability promoted by Diderot's and d'Alembert's international republic of letters were, in many respects, more politically conservative and more legally conformist than were d'Alembert and especially Diderot themselves. But in their creation of what Jürgen Habermas has termed a *bürgerliche Öffentlichkeit* or bourgeois public sphere, in the interstices of their collaboration by virtue of which talent took precedence over noble birth, they helped grant to a new class of intellectuals a social standing and political influence never achieved before (Habermas 1989). Their endeavours gave a special flavour to older notions of autonomy and freedom, and their principal social and economic achievement was not so much to secure the triumph of the bourgeoisie as the emancipation of knowledge.

It is mainly in the light of such developments that the question of the relationship between freemasonry and the *Encyclopédie* may still be regarded as significant, even though there are scant grounds for supposing any causal connection (Venturi 1946, pp. 16–23). The *Discours* of the Chevalier Andrew Ramsay, undoubtedly known in masonic lodges from the late 1730s, differed on many counts from Diderot's and d'Alembert's principles, but it expressed much the same aspirations for the enlightenment of public opinion, and there can be little doubt that a number of the contributors enlisted to the camp of the *Encyclopédistes* were indeed freemasons of diverse affiliations. But the chief impact of freemasonry upon the eighteenth-century republic of letters perhaps lies elsewhere – in that the lodges, more even than the academies, put into practice on an unprecedented scale an ideal of a meritocracy that would also prove characteristic of the encyclopedic enterprise. All these institutions together thus proved to be agents of a new culture of sociability based upon talent or intellectual merit alone, thereby removing one of the most central, if informal, anchors of the *ancien régime* without directly attacking its political structures. In a spirit of free association, shorn of the trappings of rank, even secret societies which had little interest in publicising the achievements of the new sciences could, like the *Encyclopédistes*, contribute to revolutionary change. So too, with equal inadvertence, could the religious and political bureaucracies which – internally divided, in doubt of their own powers, and apprehensive of fomenting public protest – came to oppose Diderot's project. The *Encyclopédie*'s fortunate success in its publication and distribution owed much to the hesitation and irresolution of its enemies. As Diderot would later discover, to his horror, his principal censor had been his own publisher, who needlessly expunged many passages in anticipation of offence to both the state and the church which they never had occasion to cause.

3   Censorship and the commercialisation of enlightenment

The expanding mid-eighteenth-century market for books published in French, and the lucrative profits to be gained by those who catered for it, were perceived, by authors, publishers, and also the state, as too considerable to be kept in check. While requiring legal recognition by way of a royal copyright system of *privilèges*, the book trade in France comprised a growing, and ever more popular, feature of an economy whose main priorities and principles of taxation otherwise won it few friends among the more progressive arbiters of public opinion. The transformation of Le Breton's original aim of 1745 – to produce a French translation of Chambers – to his subsequent enlisting, first, of the Abbé Gua de Malves and later Diderot, to enlarge the work and bring in other contributors, all required the complicity of the authorities, not least because the work's chief editor was then unfortunately detained in prison. Where Rousseau's plaintive letters to the authorities failed to obtain his friend's early release, the commissioned efforts of several magistrates, the keeper of seals, the lieutenant-general of police, and Chancellor d'Aguesseau collectively succeeded. Malesherbes would even claim later that Diderot and d'Aguesseau had jointly concocted the plan of the work. This launch of Diderot's responsibility was to prove the first of several instances of an exemplary bond forged between certain milieux of the royal administration and the *Encyclopédistes* which, in return, required of the *philosophes*, and especially Diderot himself, a number of formal concessions in the light of which political protection could be afforded to the exercise of his creative liberty. After 1750 the scrutiny of Malesherbes would be constant and his interventions frequent, thus ensuring the completion of the enterprise (Gordon and Torrey 1947; Grosclaude 1961).

In 1752, following the Jesuit *Journal de Trévoux*'s denunciation of the Abbé de Prades's doctoral dissertation and his associated article 'Certitude' for the *Encyclopédie*, Malesherbes covertly counteracted the official ban and threatened judicial proceedings, thereafter turning a blind eye to the various subterfuges of the *philosophes* in their defiance of the church and the *parlements* which sought either to suppress their work or to censor it. In 1759, following a campaign of vilification through newspapers and satirical pamphlets provoked two years earlier in the wake of Damiens's attempt on the life of King Louis XV, Malesherbes once again brought legal proceedings against the *Encyclopédie* to a halt. In January of that year the *parlement* of Paris condemned the work, while in May the royal council revoked the king's *privilège*, but Malesherbes managed to save the enterprise by ensuring that the publication of subsequent volumes could proceed with tacit permission, the cancellation of full *privilège* actually serving the editors' interest by sparing them the rigours of preliminary censorship which could have accompanied advance scrutiny of the text.

The publishers' principal argument, accepted by Malesherbes, and through him the crown, was that if the *Encyclopédie* came to be published abroad, the French state and the persons gainfully employed in the work's production would incur a substantial financial loss. Paper manufacturers, typographers, binders, booksellers, and other journeymen engaged in trades associated with the burgeoning industry of the printed word would become unemployed, while pirated editions produced in Geneva, Liège, Lucca, and even St Petersburg, where other workshops were eagerly awaiting their chance, would proceed to flood the French market. 'The old institution of *privilège* . . . of its essence a manifestation of absolutism, was thus made to serve the cause of economic and ideological liberalism' (Proust 1962, p. 76). In point of fact, the *Encyclopédie*'s articles on theological themes were a good deal less incendiary than Bayle's and especially Voltaire's, while its philosophical and political essays were often remarkably tame if not downright insipid. Such threats to the established order which the work was perceived as posing only became visible in the light of criminal activities, like the attempted assassination of the king, which, according to its critics, irrupted when proselytes were stirred by its alleged irreverence for authority. The encyclopedic *machine de guerre* could then be portrayed as if it were a swirling tide of dissidence, gathering momentum on the horizon. But its ideological success, however that might be measured, was more prosaic. Not only were its philosophical advocates more resolute than its detractors; they also found an economy receptive to its charms because the authority of reason and public opinion which had already gained ascendancy in England and Holland in the previous century had now come, in the French-speaking world as well, to undermine the traditional hegemony of both church and crown.

By 1765, seventeen folio volumes of text had appeared, completing the alphabet, but as yet none of the volumes of plates, nor the supplements, nor the index were available. In the fourteen-year interval since its launch an Anglophile Parisian publisher, Le Breton, who had undertaken a modest project of releasing a translation of a text produced several decades earlier to cater for what he hoped might be a latent public interest in learned essays on curiosities, had become enviably rich, realising a profit of two and a half million livres on a turnover of four million, gained from several thousand subscribers. In spite of his obligation to share those profits with his lesser known associates – Claude Briasson, Antoine David, and Laurent Durand – he managed, by the time of his death in 1779, to pass on one and a half million livres in his will, having multiplied his capital thirty times since his marriage almost forty years earlier. He not only aroused in almost equal measure the contempt of the ecclesiastical and civil powers, but also of the *Encyclopédistes* themselves once they discovered that their trust had been abused. He not only gave impetus to the establishment of an intellectual class in Paris which has survived to the present day: he also unleashed the jealousy of his fellow publishers, who for a period of thirty years sought to emulate his success by bringing out their own editions of the *Encyclopédie*, in Geneva, Leghorn, Lucca, Neuchâtel, Lausanne, and Berne, so that by 1782 more than 25,000 sets of the work had been printed, those published outside Paris characteristically less costly because produced in a smaller format (Darnton 1979; Kafker 1976; Lough 1968, pp. 1–51; Merland and Reyniers 1979).

All these operations, located entirely in Switzerland and Italy, were steered essentially by one man – Charles Joseph Panckoucke – who, after coming to Paris from Lille, contrived to create an editorial empire on a European scale that would only be achieved again by a few overweening publishing magnates of the twentieth century. Virtually a recruiting officer of scribblers and polygraphs in the academies, salons, ministerial boudoirs, and bookshops, he assembled an effective journalistic network to secure control of a number of francophone newspapers, including the *Mercure*, the *Gazette*, the *Journal de Bruxelles*, and the *Journal de Genève*, and by bringing many second-rank Grub Street publicists together with luminaries like Voltaire and Buffon, he showed undiscriminating entrepreneurial talent of considerable aplomb. Under his direction, moreover, the imitations of Diderot's and d'Alembert's great endeavour were rendered in even more tranquil tones, fit for a still larger audience, for whom such daring as had marked at least the troubled publication of Le Breton's edition meant nothing. In spreading the word of the age of Enlightenment, Panckoucke thinned and tamed it. First by republishing the folio edition, then by adding tables of contents and supplements, then by negotiating a quarto edition, and finally by launching in 1781 the still more massive *Encyclopédie méthodique*, designed to encompass all that had come before and even surpassing it, Panckoucke managed to defuse the original script by diffusing it (Bowen 1969; Darnton 1979; Tucoo-Chala 1977).

The unscrupulous commercialisation of the Enlightenment achieved in Panckoucke's hands is amply demonstrated in the stratagems, false accounts, and projections adopted throughout all the contractual negotiations for the republication and improvement of the *Encyclopédie* in which he was engaged (Darnton 1973). In its manifestation of the entrepreneurial spirit of capitalism, Panckoucke's career was exemplary. By publishing his editions outside France he of course freed himself from such interference as the *parlements* and French clergy had sought to exercise over his Parisian precursor, while at the same time adding to the attractions of a work which could be portrayed as having barely escaped the clutches of aspiring censors. No less than Le Breton, moreover, Panckoucke had powerful official protectors in France as well, whose best endeavours helped bring his speculative ventures to fruition, smoothly oiling the path of volumes poised for prohibition by discreetly promoting them instead. If the crisis of 1759 had briefly obstructed the *Encyclopédie*'s first publication, in Italy the republic of Lucca's defiant refusal to register the papal denunciation endorsing the Paris *parlement*'s and French royal council's censure, exhibited both Tuscan independence from the Holy See as well as an indigenous receptivity to progressive currents further afield (Rosa 1972).

In England, with a more prevalent, if still restricted, tradition of freedom of the press, the public appeared to be more bemused than entranced by such Continental adventures, and no pirate edition of the text was contemplated after the 1750s. A notable letter to the *Edinburgh Review* by Adam Smith in 1756 made plain that, at least in enlightened Scotland, interest in the *Encyclopédistes*' daring and in the political and economic influence of their ideas could be readily mustered, but in England the 1772 translation of the *Esprit de l'Encyclopédie* proved unsuccessful. The republication in five volumes of Chambers's *Cyclopedia* between 1778 and 1786 occasioned no fresh references to the Parisian counterpart originally conceived in its image, while William Smellie, the editor of the first edition of the *Encyclopedia Britannica* (1768–71), judged the French *Encyclopédie* unremarkably similar to other works whose authority he invoked. The *Britannica*, commissioned by the master printer Colin Macfarquhar and the engraver Andrew Bell, both from Edinburgh, was conceived for a much more limited market than the *Encyclopédie*; in appointing Smellie, himself a journeyman printer with scholarly inclinations, they launched a three-volume work of reference, initially designed for publication in weekly instalments, on a scale whose modesty was beneath the horizons towards which Le Breton, Diderot, and Panckoucke sailed.

Unsigned and often the work of Smellie himself, the great majority of the *Britannica*'s articles were less than fifteen lines long, the most substantial devoted to the subject of politics – the article 'Parliament' – inoffensively providing descriptions of legislative procedure. While readers of the article 'Government' might detect editorial hostility to the abuse of princely powers by contemporary governments in Continental Europe, they were more likely to notice the sympathy shown to latitudinarian theology in articles devoted to scripture and church history and, above all, they could consult its (by and large authoritative) surveys of medical, mathematical, and natural-historical topics which Smellie himself found most engaging. Not until 1814, when James Mill undertook to address the subjects of 'Education', 'Government', 'Jurisprudence', and 'Liberty of the Press' for the supplements to the fourth, fifth, and sixth editions of the *Britannica* did an English-language encyclopedia come to be read as a crusading work of political propaganda. Not until 1819–20, with the publication of Abraham Rees's forty-five-volume *Cyclopedia*, could Anglophone subscribers purchase a work whose bulk rivalled that of the *Encyclopédie*. Not until the middle of the nineteenth century were the encyclopedic battles of the Enlightenment becalmed, as epic series lying heavily on the bookshelves. The *Encyclopédie méthodique* came by 1832 to embrace 158 volumes. Not to be outdone, the German *Œkonomische Encyklopädie*, launched in 1773, grew by 1858 to 242 volumes. In both countries, while the *Encyclopédie* might be consulted, its influence remained circumscribed within intellectual and political contexts that lacked virtually all trace of the explosive character which it assumed in France (Kafker 1994).

None of Panckoucke's new editions was particularly faithful to the text of the original, whose intended meaning had in any case been obscured by Le Breton's unauthorised and uncalled for expurgations of, as well as personal additions to, articles not only by Diderot himself, but also by Jaucourt, d'Holbach, Turgot, and Saint-Lambert. In a letter to the printers Le Breton justified his own cavalier editorial practices on the grounds that a catalogue of differing opinions should embrace both arguments supporting and arguments opposed to contentious propositions, thus, by way of introducing a freely selective appropriation of conflicting ideas, overruling Diderot's professed wish to offer his readers coherent expositions of a philosophy shared in broad outline by the select members of his society of men of letters. The cuts and emendations introduced by Le Breton were the outcome, on the one hand, of what he took to be the technical imperatives of a work whose scale and format were subject to a calculus of profitability, but at the same time, on the other, they embraced a publisher's assessment of fashionable taste, unencumbered, before the cult of the written word had come to be prevalent, by a need to respect his authors' pronouncements to the letter. In Lucca much the same principles were adopted for local contingencies of a different kind by an editorial team assembled by Lorenzo Diodati, whose alterations laid emphasis instead upon the achievements of Italian scientists and philosophers, while also underlining, especially after the crisis of 1759, the extent to which Italy's culture of enlightenment was politically moderate and theologically conservative, by contrast with that of France. The last tomes of the Lucca edition even embraced violent denunciations of Voltaire, Rousseau, atheism, materialism, and the radicalism of Parisian politics in the name of enlightened Catholicism and a spirit of reform, thereby purifying reprobate features of the original articles so as to refine their base metal and render it negotiable currency (Rosa 1972; Venturi 1971).

The Leghorn enterprise, modelled upon that of Lucca but launched after the condemnations of Rome, was similarly committed to textual modifications, in this instance partly inspired by a desire to bring up to date a work of reference that had been conceived more than twenty years earlier. In each case the original character of the *Encyclopédie* was filtered through a new lens, altered in the light of commercial interests which enabled the publishers to justify their employment of fresh crews of scholars with sufficient local knowledge to revise the text for new readers. With scientific and historical annotations in particular thus modified, but also incorporating numerous adaptations of cultural, legal, and political entries, the later transcriptions at once broadened the original text's learning while tempering its tone. As Panckoucke observed in 1770 to another publisher in connection with his negotiations for a new folio edition to be published in Geneva, 'We must not allow ourselves any impious boldness which might frighten the magistrates . . . The work will have to be written with . . . such wisdom and moderation as might even merit the endorsement of your government' (Lough 1968, p. 85). Articulating different priorities for different readers, and progressively refracted and diffused by its successive editorial adaptations, the *Encyclopédie* continued to be perceived as a useful instrument of change, but its thrust had been blunted.

4   The *Encyclopédistes* and their readers

What might be termed the generational sociology of the work's reception still requires detailed mapping, but if we assume that its authors were also its first readers, some rough impressions may be formed in the light of Diderot's own article 'Encyclopédie' (1755), expressing his ideal of a republic of letters, followed by his lament of 1768 to the effect that his contributors had changed their character and become trimmers. Initially the authors he and d'Alembert had assembled formed an open society bound by no ties of patronage, united instead by its members' 'sense of mutual good will' and their commitment to the 'general interest', he claimed (Diderot 1992, p. 22). Later, as the work fell prey to the vicissitudes of circumstance, second-rate men of letters, prompted by interest and ambition, were conscripted to join experts of greater intellect and nobler zeal. Its first authors had been recruited not only on account of their skills, but frequently also because they were personally well known to, and sometimes close friends of, the editors. D'Alembert, turning to his acquaintances among natural scientists and mathematicians, invited Antoine Louis, Pierre and Louis Daubenton, and Louis Le Monnier. Diderot, calling upon the circles he knew of writers on the arts and society, hired Antoine Eidous, François Toussaint, d'Holbach, Turgot, and Rousseau. Luminaries of the republic of letters were conscripted by bohemian sleuths of the literary underworld, no less significant for being less known, who could in turn, as, for instance, did Louis Goussier, introduce their employers to their own acquaintances among artisans, engravers, draughtsmen, and typographers. Through such contacts was formed a major avenue along which the cultivated classes of the *ancien régime* could make common cause with the active and industrious urban population. Other ways were opened by fresh contributors brought in for each volume, constantly renewing the authors' membership and, on account of their diversity, lending vitality to the enterprise as a whole.[2]

According to John Lough's tabulation, the first volume was produced by twenty-two collaborators, of whom only six survived to see the work completed; seven new authors joined the team that produced volume two, among them d'Holbach and the redoubtable Chevalier de Jaucourt (alone responsible for more than one quarter of the entire text), three of whom stayed on to the end (Lough 1973). While after 1752 several contributors

2 For the contributors to the *Encyclopédie* see: Kafker and Kafker 1988; Lough 1968, 1973, 1975; Proust 1962, pp. 9–43; 1965, pp. 78–105; Roche 1965–70, II. On individual contributors: Hankins 1970; Morris 1979; Naves 1938. Estimates of the number of contributors have varied from 139 to 179.

in holy orders thought it prudent to take cover, Diderot's efforts to foment greater publicity brought billings for some of the pre-eminent writers of the age, such as Buffon and Voltaire, whose other agendas and large egos, however, left the *Encyclopédie* graced by little more than their names. Punctuated by disagreements over editorial policy, which managed quickly to dispose of Voltaire but also came eventually to cost the services of d'Alembert, the work's relentless rhythm and schedule of publication kept it continually in the public eye, its crises, however costly to its editors and authors, in fact enhancing its attractions to its purchasers and readers. From the academicians, who volunteered for glory's sake, to the 'Tartars' who laboured for a wage, from Diderot's own indentured service on behalf of a great cause, to the freelance but also full-time efforts of Jaucourt, the diversity of the *Encyclopédie*'s contributors and their motives formed a prism of the cultural forces of their age. Contrary to claims once prevalent about their collective identity and ideology, they did not form a homogeneous vanguard of a rising bourgeoisie (Roche 1965–70, II; cf. Soboul 1962). Of the 150 or so contributors whose identities have been established, only around 4 per cent belonged to the bourgeoisie, with another 4 per cent being of noble birth and around 8 per cent clergy. The great majority belonged to the open-textured world of talents, scholarship, and the arts, which afforded the possibility of either a literary career or positions in public service and administration. Their influence was exercised less by class allegiance or social mobility than through the permeable channels that literacy in an incipient commercial age made possible.

For the political and religious forces of the *ancien régime* which did not welcome it, the most useful barrier against the work's circulation was not censorship but its price. Few townsmen and virtually no peasants – still forming the overwhelming bulk of the population of France – could afford to purchase a set, even if inclined to do so; their access to the work could only be indirect. Little by little, however, as each fresh edition appeared, new segments of French and European society came to be conquered. The first, luxury, edition, was destined for wealthy readers, the elite of the capitals and major centres, court circles, and lay or religious libraries, if sufficiently rich and independent; the *haute bourgeoisie* was greatly conspicuous among the work's subscribers if not its contributors. More than 2,000 copies were distributed in France and around the same number again throughout the rest of Europe, and it was these readers or institutions with deep pockets, whose faithfulness may have been due as much to their resolve to own a complete set as to their interest in its contents, that enabled the publishers to persevere despite their difficulties. The editions which appeared abroad multiplied this initial circulation nearly six times, with the Genevan folio edition winning French subscribers on much the same scale as the Paris text, thereby gaining access to a somewhat broader base of French society, while the Leghorn and Lucca folio editions penetrated wealthy and enlightened circles in southern Europe. The quarto and octavo editions, mainly intended for the urban middle classes, extended the *Encyclopédie*'s influence virtually everywhere.

From French subscription lists to the quarto edition, the extent of the work's diffusion, facilitated by clever advertising and aggressive salesmanship on the part of publishers' agents and booksellers who travelled throughout the kingdom, can be clearly traced. Subscribers proved more numerous in political and academic centres than in predominantly commercial or industrial towns, such as the Atlantic ports or textile centres of northern France. Wherever cultural sociability had long prevailed or had more recently taken root – within the administrative nobility, the intellectual clergy, and 'notables' such as officers, lawyers, physicians, and gentlemen of leisure among the *ancien régime*'s bourgeoisie – the *Encyclopédie* acquired readers drawn to its aims on account of their professions or their interests. For two generations, from 1750 to 1789, the work's audience thus widened, its readership reflecting and reinforcing the tastes and ambitions of classes already cutting new channels through the social landscape of France. In the same period those paths became progressively politicised. Just by virtue of its systematic classification of the arts in its prominently displayed chart of human knowledge, the *Encyclopédie* broke with a long tradition of technical secrecy which had characterised the legacy of guilds and corporations, its pedagogical aims thereby highlighting the public benefits of innovation and invention, and the attractions of a society open to talents by contrast with venerable institutions' stability and closure. Even the editors' use of cross-references could be seen as subversive, in mounting oblique assaults upon theological certitude beneath and between the lines across several volumes, which astute readers could recognise as necessary in order to circumvent censorship. As Robert Darnton has remarked, 'the widespread diffusion of the *Encyclopédies* symptomized a widespread disposition to question the ideological basis of the Old Regime' (1979, p. 540). But while the work's themes and language occasionally articulated both the ideals and rhetoric of the French Revolution of 1789, it was not by way of the reception of its various editions that the tributaries which would feed that great flood came to be formed.

5   The political thought of the *Encyclopédie*

Diderot's own articles, 'Art' in volume I and 'Encyclopédie' in volume V, illustrate not only his own but also his whole team's attachment to the mechanical arts as instruments of the moral improvement of mankind. They assess the revolutionary impact of technological innovations and call for greater co-operation between specialists of different disciplines – more interpenetration of the theory and practice of science, and of liberal with mechanical arts – so that knowledge may be invested in applications which promote public welfare. The dissemination of such useful knowledge formed the most central objective of the *Encyclopédie*. For to make intelligible the successive achievements of extraordinary individuals which constitute 'the march of the human spirit', as Diderot put it, is to enhance the quality of life of the general mass of mankind (Diderot 1992, p. 23). It shows the value of criticism and reveals how the authoritative precepts of one age become dead dogma to another, lifting the yoke of precedent and pointing the way towards reason (pp. 21–7).

These ideas, elaborated in the article 'Encyclopédie' in particular, recapitulate some of the themes of d'Alembert's 'Discours préliminaire' to the first volume, which complements Diderot's account of the transmission of knowledge through signs, etymology, and language in general with an assessment of the revolutionary impact upon human history of science and invention. To that argument d'Alembert appended lengthy tributes to Bacon, Newton, Locke, and other eminent philosophers and scientists of the seventeenth and early eighteenth centuries, whose achievement, he claimed, had laid the foundations of the *Encyclopédie* itself, launched at the highest point civilisation had yet attained. His distinction in this essay between the *esprit systématique* of his own enlightened age and the *esprit de système* prevalent in the metaphysical cosmologies of Descartes, Leibniz, Spinoza, and Malebranche encapsulates the preference of the *Encyclopédie*'s editors for British empiricist thinkers over their more abstract contemporaries in Continental Europe, and it was to become the leitmotif of Ernst Cassirer's *Die Philosophie der Aufklärung* (The Philosophy of the Enlightenment, 1932), still among the most influential modern interpretations of Enlightenment philosophy. The 'Discours préliminaire' and the article 'Encyclopédie' may together be regarded as comprising a manifesto of the age of Enlightenment as a whole, produced by the editors of perhaps its most seminal work. Each of these essays, moreover, draws attention to the philosophy of Rousseau, who, just prior to the publication of the first volume, had in his *Discourse on the Arts and Sciences* (1751) produced an account of the moral effects of civilisation which seemed to contradict the very purpose of the *Encyclopédie*. In 1755, when the fifth volume was published, Diderot was still Rousseau's closest friend, but he would soon have occasion to regret his encomium of a man whom he here asserts that 'he never had the strength to hold back from acclaiming' (Diderot 1992, p. 26).

If the article 'Encyclopédie' forms a part of his philosophy of history, Diderot's more specifically political contributions concentrate instead on principles such as justice, authority, and natural right, illustrated with examples drawn most often from antiquity. After the crisis of 1752 deprived him of the services of a number of liberal theologians who had been responsible for material on the history of political thought, Diderot took over this subject himself, borrowing copiously from Sully, Fontenelle, Bayle, Gabriel Girard, Claude Buffier, and other sources, and relying above all on the political thinker whose authority throughout the first half of the eighteenth century was unrivalled – that is, Pufendorf. In the article 'Cité' he adopts Pufendorf's formulation of the idea of the state as a corporate body entrusted with the collective will of its various members, and in the article 'Citoyen' he accepts Pufendorf's distinction between the duties of man and those of the citizen, while nevertheless objecting to his preference for native-born as opposed to naturalised citizenship on grounds prevalent in ancient Athens but superseded by the more permeable entitlements offered in Rome (Diderot 1992, pp. 12–17).

In the article 'Autorité politique' in volume I, Diderot subscribes to Pufendorf's conception of the true source of authority, which must lie in the consent of the people themselves, rather than in nature or force. In relinquishing their liberty to their princes, the inhabitants of civil society act in conformity with right reason and so establish a common power in the public interest. This is the doctrine of the social compact, which binds citizens to the prince, but also princes to their subjects, limiting their authority, as Diderot conceived it, under conditions stipulated by natural law (Diderot 1992, pp. 6–11). The moral foundations of the state might thus appear to be without need of any theological framework. Yet, together with Pufendorf, he contends that subjects retain no right of resistance against the authority they have established, however despotic they might judge it, since they are bound by religion, reason, and nature to abide by their undertakings. Men should remain free in matters of conscience, Diderot observes in his article 'Intolérance' in volume VIII, since conscience can only be enlightened, never constrained, and violence merely renders a man a hypocrite (pp. 29–30). But he does not follow the anabaptists or Locke, who held similar views, in their suggestions that conscience and good faith may justify a right of resistance. The argument of 'Autorité politique' gave rise to no such implications, though it excited fierce hostility, in the *Journal de Trévoux* and elsewhere, mainly on the part of advocates of the divine right of kings. To allay any misunderstanding, Diderot added an erratum to the article, which appeared in volume III, to the effect that subjects' consent to the rule of their princes does not contradict but rather confirms the proposition that real authority stems ultimately from God (pp. 11–12).

Pufendorf had put forward his account of the popular and contractual foundations of monarchy in conjunction with a theory of human nature and a speculative history of the origins of civil society. Much persuaded by the Hobbesian doctrine of man's fundamental insecurity and selfishness, he nevertheless maintained that Hobbes had been mistaken to suppose that man was by nature a solitary creature whose ambitions incline him towards war, since, on the contrary, the weakness of savages must have led them to seek survival through association with their neighbours, their selfish sociability prompting them to establish and accept the regulations of civil law. In his article 'Droit naturel' (Natural law), published in volume V, Diderot pursues much the same critique of the idea of natural conflict, reproaching Hobbes, whom he portrays as a 'violent interlocutor', for supposing that each person's passions must bring 'terror and confusion to the human race'. The Hobbesian thesis is either insane or evil, he observes, 'for man is not just an animal but an animal which thinks', capable of exercising his reason in accordance with justice (Diderot 1992, pp. 18–19). In his *Suite de l'Apologie de l'abbé de Prades* of 1752, forming his own defence of a maligned contributor to the *Encyclopédie*, Diderot had already remarked that the pure state of nature was an *état de troupeau* – a barbarous condition of men living in herds, each individual motivated by fear and his natural passions alone. But only a contemptible Hobbesian could suppose that the unlimited power of princes had been established as a remedy for man's original anarchy, since the passage of the human race from an *état de troupeau* to an *état de société policée* – from its natural state to the state of civil society – had come about just because of men's recognition of their need to subject themselves collectively to laws whose beneficial effect was manifest to them all.

In 'Droit naturel' Diderot considers how selfish individuals, motivated by private interest, can form such agreements. Before the institution of governments, he claims, justice can only be settled by what he describes as the tribunal of mankind as a whole. For although 'private wills are suspect . . .

the general will is always good', and each of us partakes of that general will by virtue of our being members of the human race, prescribing both our fundamental duties as well as our inalienable rights (Diderot 1992, pp. 19–20). It was in this way that Diderot introduced his idea of the *volonté générale*, a term which had achieved some currency in the theology of Malebranche in the late seventeenth century and had been taken up again from time to time in the eighteenth, but which had been of scant significance in the history of political thought before the publication of the *Encyclopédie*. In his own article 'Economie politique', published in the same volume, Rousseau employed the term himself for the first time, with a cross-reference to Diderot's article, already cited in the original manuscript, which has survived (Rousseau 1997b, p. 7; Wokler 1975, p. 71). Here, in his sole political contribution to the *Encyclopédie*, deeply inspired by Plato's *Laws*, Rousseau defines the *volonté générale* as the will of the body politic as a whole, serving as its source of laws and its standard of justice, although his ascription of that principle to the whole of humanity retains some resemblance to the argument of Diderot's 'Droit naturel'. Later, in *The Social Contract* (1762), he was to attribute a very different meaning to the concept, insisting that it could only be realised within, and never outside, the state.

Diderot conceived the law of nature to be a rational principle of common humanity, which restrained the selfishness of individuals and made the establishment of civil society both necessary and possible. Many philosophers of natural law had put forward similar notions before, but from his references and allusions to both the *De jure naturæ et gentium* (On the Laws of Nature and Nations, 1672) and the *De officio hominis et civilis* (On the Duty of Man and Citizen, 1673), it is clear that his account was principally indebted to Pufendorf alone. That debt, however, was by and large indirect, since Diderot drew most of his Pufendorfian principles not from their original source but from Brucker's *Historia critica philosophiae*, which he consulted time and again, many of his own contributions on subjects drawn from that work – which accordingly must be regarded as one of the mainsprings of the whole *Encyclopédie* – amounting to little more than plagiarism. Yet while the article 'Hobbisme' is an almost literal translation of Brucker's account of Hobbes, it includes a postscript of Diderot's own conception, comparing the system of Hobbes with that of Rousseau, to the detriment of both thinkers (Diderot 1992, pp. 27–9). According to Diderot, mankind is neither simply naturally good nor simply naturally wicked, since goodness and evil, together with happiness and misery, are finely balanced in human nature. If Hobbes had falsely supposed that men are by nature vicious, Rousseau had been equally wrong to believe that they always become so in society. For Diderot, virtue and vice were each natural and social, and man was thus at once impelled and enabled to form civil associations which brought both benefits and harm to the human race. A Pufendorfian perspective of a society of selfish agents could therefore be invoked as a corrective not only to Hobbes but to Rousseau as well. With the publication of his *Theory of Moral Sentiments* in 1759, Adam Smith made such sceptical principles central to his philosophy and later came, in his *Wealth of Nations* of 1776, to envisage the place they occupied among the necessary foundations of commercial society.

It was Rousseau, however, rather than Smith, who lent weight to Diderot's Pufendorfian political theory – and that by way of refutation. For just as Diderot had attempted to rebut both Hobbes and Rousseau in his article 'Hobbisme', so Rousseau, in the draft of *The Social Contract* known as the *Geneva Manuscript*, sought to challenge Hobbes and Diderot together (Rousseau 1997b, pp. 153–61; Wokler 1975, pp. 90–110). Arguing against 'Droit naturel', he also employed the dialectical approach of the article 'Hobbisme', since he judged Hobbes correct to surmise that outside civil society there could be no agreed principles of law constricting our natural rights, but wrong to imagine that the exercise of such rights unavoidably led to conflict. The idea of natural right was thus a chimerical concept, he claimed, because it ascribed a moral rule to a state of mere licence, though Diderot had rightly perceived that even in their natural state men could still live in peace. As an alternative to each doctrine Rousseau advanced a theory of benign but amoral human nature, transformed either for better or worse by the establishment of civil society. Both his philosophy of history and his theory of the social contract thus address themes brought to his attention by Diderot's contributions to the *Encyclopédie*.

Readers who sought information about the meaning of natural right and the foundations of political authority had access not only to Diderot's and Rousseau's pronouncements in these articles but also to the views of Boucher d'Argis in another article on 'Droit', published in volume v, as well as to those of Jaucourt on 'Gouvernement' in volume vii, or, within the broader context of moral philosophy, the definitions of 'Intérêt' supplied by the Marquis Jean-François de Saint-Lambert in volume viii. While justifiably aggrieved at the liberties taken by his publisher with the text he supplied, Diderot himself promoted the work's multiplicity of voices – of deism, materialism, and even orthodoxy in theological matters, for instance, or liberalism and mercantilism in political economy. His choice of diverse authors and his provision to them of a porous vessel designed to promote freedom of thought thus had the same effect of tempering any alleged dogmatic character of the whole enterprise as did its publishers' self-censorship. In his own article 'Ecletisme', itself recapitulated from Brucker, Diderot commends the heterodox perspective which imbues the character of his work as a whole. Fashionably radical points of view expressing ideals of civil liberty and free trade, and limiting the powers of a nation's representatives in the light of its people's imprescriptible rights, were incorporated in the long articles on national revenue, 'Vingtième', mainly by Etienne Damilaville, and on representation, 'Représentants', by d'Holbach, in volumes XVII and XIV, respectively. But the *Encyclopédie* was not throughout all of its entries imbued with the gospel of a new age, and ironing out the diverse perspectives it incorporated formed no part of its editors' endeavour.

For that reason above all, there would be little point in attempting to assemble even the broad outlines of the French Revolutionary Declaration of the Rights of Man out of its pages. Its contributors' occasional criticisms of monarchical institutions remained moderate, seldom more severe in tone than the article 'Oppresseur', from whose anonymous author no inference about any contemporary regime could be drawn. Subjected to their criticism were not so much the religious and political institutions then prevalent in France as the trappings of all ideological systems which obstructed the advancement of knowledge and the free exchange of ideas. Inspired by images of a harmonious society in which particular interests could be reconciled to the general interest, and intent upon providing philosophical, scientific, and technical solutions to social and political problems, the *Encyclopédistes* managed to command the attention of many of Europe's traditional elites, the tasks they set themselves facilitated by the commercialism of their publishers, whose ambitions enabled their enterprise to conquer a wider market than had been gained or even sought by the editors of any major works of reference before. Perhaps the most paradoxical feature of their triumph, rendering its cultural and political impact deeply ambiguous, turns around the fact that neither the intellectual speculation which informed the *Encyclopédie*, nor the financial speculation which saw it to press and ensured its diffusion, could have achieved its authors' or patrons' objectives without the ministrations of progressively minded civil powers at the very heart of the *ancien régime*.

7

Optimism, progress, and philosophical history

HAYDN MASON

1 Optimism

From the early seventeenth century a new age of rationalism sprang up, with Descartes as its main progenitor, and Spinoza and Leibniz as epigones. Since Descartes contributed so heavily to establishing confidence in reasoning as a reliable human instrument, it seemed useful to apply critical enquiry to the ancient mystery of evil and suffering. Did theodicy, that branch of philosophy concerned with the justification of God's goodness and the refutation of arguments based on the existence of evil, still remain a valid approach? The traditional Christian explanations – the Fall and the redemption, original sin, eternal reward and punishments – no longer appeared to suffice as answers to the conundrums posed by the new philosophies.

The basic problem was not new. Epicurus had stated it centuries earlier: if evil exists then God must be either malevolent or impotent. No-one reformulated this dilemma with greater trenchancy than Pierre Bayle who, in his voluminous *Oeuvres diverses* (1727–31) and even more so in his *Dictionnaire philosophique et critique* (1697), was constantly engaged in forcing rationalist thinkers into a corner. Why, in a God-given universe, is mankind exposed to disease, hunger, and pain? Why do men have any inclination to evil? God must have foreseen, and therefore wished to prevent, human sin. It cannot be any justification to argue that God permitted sin simply to demonstrate his own powers. Such a God would be odious. Free will can scarcely be deemed a desirable gift if it can lead to everlasting damnation. These powerful arguments, developed most notably in the *Dictionary* articles 'Manichéens' and 'Pauliciens', led Bayle to the conclusion that every attempt to explain evil by rational means must end in either deism or total scepticism. Blind faith independent of all ratiocination, he claimed, was the only viable answer.

Bayle's views quickly set him at odds with rationalist theologians like Jean Le Clerc and Isaac Jacquelot, and right up to his death he maintained a lively debate with them. But it was Leibniz's response to Bayle in his *Essais de théodicée* (1710) which especially affected the course of debate. These essays represented a far-reaching refutation of Bayle's arguments. Leibniz feared, contrary to Bayle, that scepticism would ensue not from rationalist explanations but rather from Bayle's corrosive attacks on the powers of human reason. In Leibniz's view, reason was essentially constructive, and he saw no basic conflict between reason and faith. He himself made no attempt to deny that evil existed, but he saw it as an absence, like cold and darkness, a negative, a privation of good. Evil is an unavoidable element in our universe, but we must accept that God could not have created a better one than he did, bound as he necessarily was by eternal truths and the principle of sufficient reason. This world is not designed uniquely for human happiness; that is only a part of God's plan. Nature necessarily contains and preserves the utmost order consonant with the utmost beauty and truth, and God cannot, simply to lessen evil, disturb the whole natural order. In Leibniz's view, everything follows from the basic premise of God's infinite goodness and wisdom. Hence this is the best of all possible worlds. 'One must believe that it is not permitted to do otherwise, since it is not possible to do better' (pt II, para. 124; Leibniz 1951, pp. 197–8).

Leibniz's perspectives on optimism were expounded and developed by his disciple Christian Wolff, who attracted the keen interest of, amongst others, Voltaire's fellow scholar and mistress Madame du Châtelet. In 1740 she brought out her *Institutions de physique*, where she expressly developed Leibniz's metaphysical opinions as she had discovered them in the works of Wolff. By this time Voltaire had himself been reading Wolff in the company of Madame du Châtelet, although his disaffection with metaphysical thinking in general was already clear. Metaphysics, he wrote to Frederick of Prussia in 1737, consisted of two things, the first what all men of common sense know, the second what they will never know. His reaction to Leibnizian optimism was ambivalent from the start, though he did not initially express outright hostility.

The term 'optimism' seems to have made its first appearance in French in 1737, in a review of Leibniz's *Theodicy* by the Jesuit periodical, the *Mémoires de Trévoux*, where the author defined it as a theory according to which 'the world is an optimum'. From 1750 we find *optimisme* in the dictionaries. But the optimist philosophy did not only derive from Germany. England too had made an important contribution through Alexander Pope's *Essay on Man* (1733–4). It seems likely that Pope owed some of his opinions to his acquaintance with Viscount Bolingbroke; certainly Pope acknowledged a debt.[1] Voltaire, a keen admirer of Pope's *Essay*, agreed that Bolingbroke played an important part, but reproached the poet for neglecting to mention the third earl of Shaftesbury as an inspiration (Voltaire 1964a, II, p. 139n). Bolingbroke's theist beliefs reveal his satisfaction with the Creation, the work of a God both good and wise, in such writings as his *Reflections upon Exile*, where he attacked those who criticised divine Providence; he himself approved of the Great Chain of Being, whereby everything in the cosmos is united in one great design (Fletcher 1985, pp. 9–12). Shaftesbury's own optimistic views had appeared in print even before Leibniz's *Theodicy*, as Leibniz himself acknowledged, while making clear that he had not read them until after the composition of his own work (Barber 1955, p. 118 n. 4). Shaftesbury had denied that the world was defective; on the contrary, its beauty was the result of contradictions, since universal harmony comes from a perpetual struggle between elements and creatures. When annotating his reflections on the Lisbon earthquake, *Poème sur le désastre de Lisbonne*, in 1756, Voltaire was in no doubt that Pope had derived his system from Shaftesbury (Voltaire, 1877–85, IX, p. 465n).

Whatever its inspiration, it was Pope's *Essay* which engaged public attention both in England and on the Continent, the first French translation appearing in 1736. More particularly, it aroused Voltaire's admiration, the *philosophe* describing it as the most beautiful, useful, and sublime didactic poem ever written in any language (Voltaire 1964a, II, p. 139). Pope's version of theodicy, situating man in the universal scheme of things, argued that happiness is 'our being's end and aim' (epistle IV). Man has his appointed place in the Great Chain of Being, which reaches 'from Infinite to thee, / From thee to Nothing' (ep. I). But it is not for man to comprehend the universe: 'know then thyself, presume not God to scan' (ep. III). The famous lines which close the first epistle trenchantly sum up Pope's opinion on the question of evil:

> All Nature is but Art, unknown to thee;
> All Chance, Direction, which thou canst not see;
> All Discord, Harmony not understood;
> All partial Evil, universal Good;
> And, spite of Pride, in erring Reason's spite,
> One truth is clear, WHATEVER IS, IS RIGHT.

In brief, evil was an illusion. Pope, like Leibniz, simply denied its existence. His aim was above all to console humanity and to celebrate what was good

---

1 *Observations, Anecdotes, and Characters of Books and Men*, cited in Fletcher 1985, p. 7. See Spence 1966.

in the world. Leibniz too had wished to reassure his readers, but he had felt that this could be done only by arguing from the logical necessity of evil. Both writers in the end advocated resignation to the human lot and trust in the divine order. Nonetheless, Pope's work was not influenced by Leibniz, of whose writings he was ignorant, just as the sources of his inspiration, Bolingbroke and Shaftesbury, were also independent of the German philosophy. That there were two separate strands indicates the extent to which the problem of evil was of topical concern in the early eighteenth century.

In Germany Wolff's exposition of Leibnizian optimism ensured its continuing success. Optimism fitted in well with the new advances in science, a point demonstrated by Leibniz himself, who was interested in physics and metaphysics alike. From 1733 onwards the appearance of the *Essay on Man* led to Pope's name being generally associated with that of Leibniz in the debate. In 1755 the Berlin Academy ran an essay competition whose topic was 'an examination of Pope's system, contained in the proposition "Whatever is, is right"'. The winning entry represented an attack upon Leibniz. In France, too, general interest remained high as the question attracted contributions (though usually hostile) from La Mettrie, Condillac, Maupertuis, and the Jesuit *Mémoires de Trévoux* (see Barber 1955).

By the 1760s, however, the doctrine of optimism had largely run its course. Such a change in *mentalité* inevitably had complex causes, but three were of some particular importance: the Lisbon earthquake (1755), the Seven Years War (1756–63), and Voltaire's *Candide* (1759). The Lisbon disaster proved a profound shock to European opinion, no great European city ever having hitherto suffered so cataclysmically. Probably 10,000–15,000 people perished, and the central part of the city was gutted by fire. The earthquake aroused a widespread response throughout Europe (França 1965). In Germany it was studied by Kant and commented upon later by von Humboldt and Goethe; Samuel Johnson, Oliver Goldsmith, and Thomas Gray wrote about it in England; while in France Voltaire was first upon the scene with his *Poème sur le désastre de Lisbonne*, composed within ten days of his hearing the news. Here at last Voltaire turned decisively against optimism, as a theory both chimerical and cruel when set against so much suffering. It was the passive fatalism inherent in the doctrine that particularly aroused the *philosophe*'s anger, and both Pope and Leibniz were subjected to criticism in his attached preface and notes. But, while Voltaire could still praise the high moral quality of the *Essay on Man*, there was no moderation in his treatment of Leibniz. If the stupid optimist Pangloss in *Candide* is a German, there can be little doubt that his very nationality helped to reinforce Voltaire's devastating attacks upon such Leibnizian concepts as the principle of sufficient reason.

Candide was the ultimate assault upon optimism. Voltaire had already agonised over the problem of evil in his poem on the earthquake, which essentially consisted of a prolonged question, Why? The poem represented a protest, couched in urgent terms, not only with regard to the earthquake itself, but even more so against the insulting justifications of it by the optimists. By the time of *Candide* its author had internalised that passion and transmuted it into irony and satire. The *conte* probes with remorseless clarity the unclarity of human behaviour and reasoning, nowhere more evident than in the ridiculous antics of Dr Pangloss. By its elaborate use of ordered antithesis and balance it shows up the disorder of a cosmos that, in Voltaire's words elsewhere, 'exists on contradictions'. *Candide* was immediately and hugely successful, running to seventeen editions published in four different countries and probably amounting to 20,000 copies, before the year of publication was out. Despite the rejoinders by orthodox apologists, the tale played an important part in reshaping mental attitudes to the doctrine that 'all is well'. But the reception of the *conte* must also be set in the context of the Seven Years War, which brought so much suffering to the heart of Europe. According to Frederick the Great, half a million Prussians died. France lost vast territories overseas and control of the high seas. Furthermore, the settlement of the War left an uneasy stalemate. If optimism can be seen as 'in essence an apologia for the status quo', its demise fitted in well with the darker mood, complementing the decline of sanguine hopes that science and reason might guarantee human progress (Willey 1965, p. 48). Kant's immediate response to the Lisbon earthquake took the form of papers reviewing the theories of earthquakes, while he noted somewhat complacently that, as part of the natural process, they are to be endured, and even in some respects welcomed. But later in life Kant would leave all such theodicy behind him as showing the limitations of theoretical reason in the field of speculative metaphysics.

2   Progress

Voltaire had seen clearly the ultimate paradox about optimism: it was inherently pessimistic, because it contained the seeds of fatalism. An 'apology for the status quo' cohered ill with an age that, for all its reservations, held to a general belief in the capacity of human beings to achieve progress.

John Locke's *Essay concerning Human Understanding* (1689) provided the basic philosophical groundwork. Locke maintained that our knowledge of the outside world was entirely acquired from sensory experience. At birth the human mind was a blank sheet, and morally neutral; Descartes's theory of innate ideas was firmly rejected. As we mature, our sense-impressions, combined with our capacity for reflection upon them, give us the necessary information for our ideas and consequently for our language. Locke sought to understand man as a natural object, explicable by the scientific methods of what we should now call psychological observation. The mind can be as much a source of empirical investigation as the stars or the theory of gravitation. Therefore, since we derive our knowledge of the world entirely through the senses, we should logically be able to go on continually enhancing our awareness by the addition of ever more such contacts, provided they are controlled by our reflective powers. The greater our experience, the more enlightened and the more moral we should be. Voltaire led the way in arguing that Locke was the first thinker to write a history (as opposed to a *roman* or novel) of the mind (Voltaire 1964a, letter 13, 1, p. 63). The English philosopher's approach opened up the possibility of improving the quality of human consciousness and its interaction with the environment. Since the environment was seen to play such a vital role, it became important to help the mind to profit from what the senses received; the fundamental value of education was a logical corollary.

No-one exploited this 'sensationalist' doctrine more fully for educative ends than Claude Helvétius. For the French *philosophe*, reflection was subordinated to the external impact on the senses. In *De l'esprit* (1758) and yet more so in *De l'homme*, published posthumously in 1772, Helvétius asserted that mankind was motivated at heart by the love of pleasure and fear of pain. Thus human nature, morally neutral in its essence, is disposed towards virtuous conduct only if the social milieu controls it by the use of agreeable incentives or disagreeable disincentives. This can be achieved by the establishment of laws that channel rather than contradict natural impulses and operate in conjunction with self-love, which is the only sure basis for human behaviour. It is in order to ensure that self-love is enlightened that education becomes of prime importance. Knowledge, for Helvétius, is necessarily related to happiness, just as self and society are naturally in harmony. The educational system which he envisaged stood in opposition to the traditional teaching of the Jesuit colleges, based on theological principles and the study of Latin. Instead he calls for a modern curriculum, taught in the vernacular and involving the study of physics, history, and mathematics: a secular system intended to raise up citizens free of religious ties, and adapted to modern techniques and professions. It was *De l'homme* which, following the general thrust of *De l'esprit*, concentrated more particularly on education. Helvétius boldly claimed that human talents and virtues are the product not of one's basic nature but of how one is educated. Man is born ignorant, but he becomes a fool through bad teaching. The reason for intellectual inequality is to be found not so much in our different physical endowments as in the kind of schooling that people have received. Nor does 'education' simply mean schooling; used by Helvétius in the classical sense, it starts at birth and with the impact of surrounding objects upon us. His philosophy of education in *De l'esprit* and *De l'homme* was to inspire much of James Mill's argument in the essay on the subject of 'Education' which he drafted early in the nineteenth century for the *Encyclopedia Britannica*, and through Mill it was to become a source of English utilitarianism.

Since Helvétius aimed to increase human happiness through a better knowledge of our true nature, morality became a science of great social utility if it was linked to legislative and political direction. Religious sanctions are replaced by a concern for communal welfare. But not all the *philosophes* took the implications of sensationalism as far as Helvétius. For him – as he put it in a passage of *De l'esprit* inspired by Locke, taken up by Quesnay in the article 'Evidence' for the *Encyclopédie* and challenged by Rousseau in *Emile* – 'to feel is to judge'; there is no qualitative difference between sensation and thought. Diderot, by contrast, himself quite as much a materialist as Helvétius and equally indebted to the Lockean heritage, believed that there was a gap between pure sense-impression and judgement. In his view, the mind is not wholly dependent on the senses; comprehension is more than just feeling. Diderot stressed rather the variable factor of individuality, thereby rendering more concrete the abstract concept of man adopted by Helvétius. In Diderot's view human beings were not so simply malleable; the enigmas of human aberration, energy, and genius remained. But like Helvétius he laid emphasis upon the need for, and the possibility of, greater enlightenment, as in his own article 'Encyclopédie' in the great work of that name, where Diderot makes clear that the whole aim of the *Encyclopédie* was to 'change the common way of thinking'.

Not all the *philosophes* were as sanguine as Helvétius. Even Diderot was all too conscious of how easily one could slip back to barbarism. The expansion of trade and the development of luxury might well lead to corruption. Like many contemporaries he saw world history as cyclical, the fact of growth inevitably entailing a future decline. Progress towards enlightenment could never be a straightforward linear matter. Diderot's exhortations to action, though based on a sincere hope for the future, were tempered with scepticism. This darker side to the general belief in progress by Enlightenment thinkers was conclusively demonstrated in Henry Vyverberg's classic study *Historical Pessimism in the French Enlightenment* (1958). Few *philosophes* were exempt from doubts about human betterment. Fontenelle saw how history provided ample evidence of passions and whims deflecting mankind from moral improvement. Montesquieu's *L'esprit des lois* (The Spirit of the Laws, 1748) is concerned with possible reforms but, like his earlier *Lettres persanes* (Persian Letters, 1721), reveals a fear of decadence. Book VIII of *L'esprit des lois* is entirely given over to a discussion of how corruption of government in all its various forms comes about. To call the Enlightenment period the 'age of progress', as was once common practice, would be dangerously simplistic.

Yet there is no denying the hope of progress that was felt virtually everywhere, albeit often cautiously and beset by apprehensions of danger on every side. For all his scepticism about human nature, Fontenelle believed firmly that experience was the sole source of human knowledge, and also that human error was useful because its elucidation led to truth. Helvétius's materialistic beliefs were similar to those of d'Holbach, who took the line that when religious tyranny had been crushed and society rebuilt on a firm system of morality informed by education a better world would dawn. The very system of determinism to which he held fast assured d'Holbach, as it did Helvétius, that progress was practically inevitable. Human reason, once freed from theological prejudice, must necessarily seek out the truth. No-one presented the case for systematic human improvement more comprehensively than Condorcet, whose *Esquisse d'un tableau historique des progrès de l'esprit humain* (Sketch of an Historical View of the Progress of the Human Mind, 1795) was written, ironically, during the French Revolution, at a time of mounting personal unpopularity and stress for its author, which was to end with his death as he tried to escape from capital punishment, to which he had been condemned by the Jacobins. In the *Esquisse* Condorcet traces the development of civilisation through nine ages, from earliest times to the present day, and ends on a confident prophecy that the tenth and future epoch will, through the spread of scientific progress, move ever forward to greater enlightenment, equality, peace, and justice. This evolution towards perfectibility was both certain and unlimited; progress for Condorcet had become virtually a religion. Indeed, he has been called one of the 'prophets of Paris' (Manuel 1962), and in his secular faith Condorcet can be aligned with nineteenth-century writers like Saint-Simon, Fourier, and Comte.

Somewhat earlier, Turgot had already expounded his own theory of progress in a famous discourse delivered at the Sorbonne in 1750 while he was still a young man. Turgot too conceived great hopes of the future; but the way he couched them at this time painted a more balanced picture:

> Empires rise and fall . . . Self-interest, ambition, and vainglory continually change the world scene and inundate the earth with blood; yet in the midst of their ravages manners are softened, the human mind becomes more enlightened . . . and the whole human race, through alternate periods of rest and unrest, of weal and woe, goes on advancing, although at a slow pace, towards greater perfection. (Meek 1976, p. 41)

This steady accumulation of knowledge, based on Lockean sensationalism, is the ultimate assurance of progress. Whereas perfectibility was denounced by Rousseau in his *Discourse on Inequality* (1755) as a tragic desire in mankind, it represented for Turgot the foundation for growth and diversification. Arts and sciences develop from human needs and experience. But though the sciences, dependent on a quantitative knowledge of nature, are infinitely expandable, the arts had already reached their pinnacle under the Emperor Augustus. Turgot thereby combined a modernist belief in progress and movement with an exemplary classical aesthetic, in a manner characteristic of many other thinkers of his age. Basically holding to a deist belief in a providential universe, he attempted in his own way to solve the problem of theodicy and to give a meaning to history independent of divine rewards and punishments (Manuel 1962, p. 46).

In this general picture of reformist attitudes one exceptional figure must not be overlooked: Vico, largely unread in his day but fully recognised in ours. Vico rejected the Baconian argument that the accumulation of knowledge led to progress. In his view this opinion sprang from a false analogy drawn between history, essentially based on subjective factors, and the objective methods of the sciences, whose laws operated without reference to human will and purpose. Historical change depended on language, myth, poetry, religion, and jurisprudence, all phenomena deriving from man's creative and often irrational drives. Hence social development is organic, not linear, each culture possessing structures valid within its own context. Though Vico stops short of the nineteenth-century concept of *le devenir* (becoming), his work is a clear anticipation of it, 'the whole doctrine of historicism in embryo' (Berlin 1976, p. 38).

3   Philosophical history

Generally speaking, the concept of progress was the basis of historical writing in the eighteenth century. If the past shows human development, it must be the historian's task to trace the stages. During the age of Enlightenment a philosophy of history began to emerge. In the preceding century the classic view of world history had been set forth in Bossuet's *Discours sur l'histoire universelle* (1681). This survey of the past, from man's origins to Charlemagne, was composed with the intention of demonstrating the providential hand of God in human affairs. Since, for Bossuet, God directs all hearts and all nations, the notion of chance or fortune in historical events is utterly fallacious. More specifically, this is a Christian universe. In that perspective, the history of the Jewish people acquired a special importance because it prepared for the coming of Christ. The philosophical historians of the eighteenth century found this kind of teleological view unacceptable. Instead, history now had to be seen in a purely secular way, determined by causes explicable in terms from which God has been removed. It took on the aspect of a physical science, from which one could hope to deduce significant laws and principles. Societies were seen to evolve not because of divine intervention but because of their own inherent structures.

No-one addressed himself more attentively to a study of such patterns than Montesquieu, both in the *Considérations sur les causes de la grandeur des Romains et de leur décadence* (Considerations on the Causes of the Greatness and Decadence of the Romans, 1734) and more comprehensively in *The Spirit of the Laws*. The former work shared Bossuet's belief that fortune does not rule the world, but the reasons advanced to explain that view are quite different. There are, Montesquieu claims, underlying causes which preside over the establishment, maintenance, or ruin of a particular form of government, and all seeming accidents are subject to them (ch. XVIII; Montesquieu 1965, p. 169). These causes, whether physical or moral in nature, become the subject of prolonged scrutiny in the *Spirit of the Laws* – so much so that, although not primarily a historical text, the work established itself as of crucial importance to Enlightenment historiography. The relationships elucidated by Montesquieu between political power under diverse forms of government, and such fundamental aspects as the religious life, manners, laws, and climate of a particular country, encouraged historians to banish metaphysical explanations from their work, along with the gratuitousness of chance occurrences. Henceforth it became feasible to seek out a general order underlying and accounting for change.

Montesquieu thereby helped to pave the way for the great historical works of the century, by Hume, William Robertson, and Edward Gibbon in Britain, and Voltaire in France. Hume's *History of England* (1754–62) was a six-volume work that began, paradoxically, with the Stuarts but eventually unfolded backwards to 55 BCE so as to set the more recent British monarchy in perspective. Chapter 1 made clear the author's view of history in general. Revolutions are so capricious and cruel that 'they disgust us by the uniformity of their appearance'. The only sure ways of research by nations into their past lie in considering 'the language, manners, and customs of their ancestors'. Hume's profound scepticism about metaphysical truths did not inhibit him from intellectual perseverance where a 'science of man' might be developed. In consequence his readers were offered 'the first genuinely political history of England', in which civilisation, in terms of law, customs, religion, and culture, is constantly interrelated with political behaviour, as Montesquieu had also described (Phillipson 1989, p. 139).

Robertson's *History of the Reign of Charles V* (1769) is somewhat overshadowed when set beside the work of Hume and Gibbon. Yet its preface, entitled 'A View of the Progress of Society in Europe', is an exemplary Enlightenment statement of how Europe had moved from the darkness of the middle ages into light through its adherence to reason. The first chapter, on 'Interior Government, Laws, and Manners', indicated once again that in this development cultural matters had their place alongside political. The progress of science, though circumscribed, 'may be mentioned, nevertheless, among the great causes which contributed to introduce a change of manners into Europe'. So too with commerce, which 'did not fail of producing great effects', improving men's manners, uniting them, and disposing them to peace; Montesquieu's influence with regard to these themes was explicitly acknowledged.

Along with this heightened sense of an internal dynamism in human affairs went an increased meticulousness by historians in their use of sources. The veracity of facts became an essential aim. This development owed much to sceptical historians of an earlier age, and in particular to Fontenelle and Bayle. Fontenelle's *Histoire des oracles* (1686) was a rationalist critique of the human propensity for error, summed up succinctly in the famous anecdote of the golden tooth. In Silesia in 1593 a seven-year-old boy's second teeth had included one such, inspiring scholars to a learned debate with many diverse theories on its significance – until a goldsmith thought to examine it and found that the gold had been skilfully applied. The lesson Fontenelle derived from this tale was simple and direct: 'Let us make quite sure of the fact, before concerning ourselves with the cause' (ch. 4).

Bayle, for his part, sought to free historical evidence from the tenacious hold of prejudice. People believed false stories because they were mentally lazy and simply followed fashion or long-established tradition; or were polemically inclined, or overwhelmed by deceit, or vanity, or passion. Few historians escaped the many pitfalls and consulted their sources with honesty and a proper devotion to learning. Bayle's own extraordinary breadth of erudition enabled him to expose the falsehoods of historical writing with considerable success, practising a Cartesian approach of methodical doubt which bears witness to his view of the discipline as a science. Not that his approach was entirely negative, for all his pessimism about human nature. Like any science, historical investigation could be undertaken with positive hopes of truth. Certain rules of evidence existed: if all the parties agreed on a fact or motive, if the party prejudiced by it nonetheless accepted it as true, if the opposing side did not contest it even though it brought glory to the enemy. So he argued in his *Critique générale* (1682) (II.1). Few, however, were capable of such high ideals; an historian had to be totally disinterested, and history must be 'touched only by pure hands', as he put it in his article 'Richard Hall', in the *Dictionnaire historique et critique* (1697). Bayle's delight in historical facts and dedicated pursuit of them because they were more closely connected with experience than the mathematical truths dear to Descartes made him a figure who significantly influenced the burgeoning discipline of history.

4   Voltaire

Pre-eminent among Bayle's heirs in this domain was Voltaire. Although Voltaire nowhere expressed praise of Bayle's capacities as an historian, it is clear that in his critical examination of sources he closely followed Bayle's criteria, citing the same rules of evidence as had Bayle for judging authenticity. Besides, he was anxious to have Bayle's *Dictionnaire* by him as a source-reference when working on the *Essai sur les moeurs et l'esprit des nations* (Essay on the Mores and Spirit of Nations, 1756), and a large number of details from the *Dictionary* were taken up in his work (Mason 1963, pp. 128ff). Like Bayle, Voltaire treated with reserve oral traditions and harangues, and made clear his wariness of historians motivated by party spirit. Bayle's wide-ranging criticism of the Old Testament not only provided Voltaire with abundant polemical material, but also helped to pave the way for his secular approach to history. Since Voltaire did not appear to have been closely acquainted with other leading sceptical historians, such as Jean Hardouin and Louis Jean Lévesque de Pouilly, his debt to Bayle in this regard would appear to have been much greater than he acknowledged (Brumfitt 1970, p. 33).

Voltaire did not, however, share Bayle's dedication to total impartiality. In his view history was a weapon in the struggle against ignorant superstition and for the furtherance of enlightenment; to cite a famous phrase from his pen in a letter to his friend Nicholas Thieriot on 31 October 1738, 'Il faut écrire l'histoire en *philosophe*' ('One must write history as a philosopher') (Voltaire 1964b, p. 431). Unlike other great figures of the period such as Rousseau and Diderot, Voltaire both cared deeply about history and devoted a large part of his life to the writing of it. He was invited to write the *Encyclopédie* article on the subject, a fitting recognition of his standing as an historian and former historiographer to Louis XV. His epic poem *La Henriade* (1723), one of his first major compositions, already departs from tradition in that genre by being based on a modern period (the age of Henri IV in the late sixteenth and early seventeenth centuries) rather than classical, Biblical, or mythical times. By 1727 he had already written, in English, his first historical work proper, the *Essay upon the Civil Wars of France*. In 1731 Voltaire's first important contribution to the discipline, the *Histoire de Charles XII*, appeared; at about this time he began work on *Le siècle de Louis XIV* (The Age of Louis XIV, publ. 1752), one of his two major historical works. The other, the *Essai sur les moeurs*, was launched in the 1740s. To this *Essai* Voltaire added, in 1765, a substantial and important preface, *La philosophie de l'histoire*.

Le siècle paid tribute to one of the few ages of mankind when, in the author's opinion, civilisation had flowered. The *Essai* had a much broader scope. It was nothing less than a history of the world, but one quite different in conception from Bossuet's *Discours sur l'histoire universelle*, which Voltaire referred to slightingly as a 'so-called world history, which deals with only four or five peoples, and especially the tiny Jewish nation' (Voltaire 1877–85, XXVII, p. 237). The *Essai sur les moeurs* was a global account of civilisation, with the emphasis primarily laid upon intellectual and social history. Voltaire saw the essential elements of civilisation as humane government and tolerant religion, permitting the development of trade, affluence, and leisure, and thereby providing the necessary conditions for enlightened living in which the arts and sciences can flourish. The *Essai* was essentially a history of peoples rather than of kings, who for Voltaire were of interest only in so far as they had improved the living conditions of their subjects. The title of the opening chapter revealed the perspective Voltaire wished to adopt: 'De la Chine, de son antiquité, de ses forces, de ses lois, de ses usages, et de ses sciences' (On China, its antiquity, its strengths, its laws, its customs, and its sciences). Voltaire was able to stress at once the cosmopolitan nature of his history by starting out in Asia, and, furthermore, with a nation of far greater antiquity than those in Europe or the Middle East. From China he progressed to India, Persia, Arabia, and Islamic culture before arriving, only in chapter 8, in Christian Rome, which was thereby put in Voltaire's view into appropriate perspective. The discussion of China was typical. Voltaire was particularly interested in its institutions and customs: the size and nature of the towns, the state of the finances, the manufacture of paper and silk, the sciences of chemistry and astronomy, and much else besides, including above all an account of Chinese religion. In beginning with the antiquity of China Voltaire also served notice that he was setting his history in a secular chronology that took no account of the conventional Biblical dating of the Creation. This point was underlined in the *Philosophie de l'histoire*, where Voltaire reminded his readers that the Chinese empire was founded more than 4,000 years ago (ch. 18). This did not of itself contradict the traditional Christian assumption, advanced by Archbishop Ussher in the seventeenth century, that the world had been created in 4004 BCE, but the ironic inference was unmistakable. Evident too was Voltaire's resolutely secular stance in treating the Jewish people. Not only did he deny them any special status; he judged them to be inferior in every way to their Arab neighbours (ch. 6). The rationale of this approach was made clear in the *Philosophie de l'histoire*: 'We shall speak of the Jews as we should of the Scythians and the Greeks, weighing up the probabilities and discussing the facts'. Indeed, the Jewish nation was even denied any claim to antiquity: 'this nation is amongst the most recent' (ch. 38).

As for the Christian church, heir to the Judaic tradition, it had exercised a baneful effect upon the world during practically its whole history. In particular, ever since the massacres of the Albigensian heretics in the thirteenth century, blood had never ceased to flow because of religious persecutions instigated by the church. Voltaire went on to say that the whole history of Christianity is a collection of crimes, follies, and misfortunes, in which only a few virtues and a few happy times were discernible, like dwellings distantly scattered in deserts (ch. 197). On occasion the author strung together a chain of senseless horrors in a manner reminiscent of *Candide*. One such example was an enumeration, some 300 words long, of murders and mutilations in eighth-century Constantinople (ch. 29). The details were horrifying – eyes gouged out, tongues and noses cut off, a murdered man's skull serving as a cup for his killer to drink from; but Voltaire also brought out the madness of these atrocities with a meaningless word-list, turning the protagonists into grotesque puppets. However, by contrast with *Candide*, it was a tone of regret rather than mordant irony which dominated the *Essai*. When, for instance, referring to the Catholic accusation that Luther had consulted the devil and also thanked him for his help, Voltaire rejected facile humour, observing that one should not joke about sad matters where the happiness and torments of so many were at issue (ch. 128). History was not to be mocked, for all the follies of its participants. Instead we should be inspired with pity and a sense of justice, the two basic elements of Voltaire's moral code.

Nor was history futile. Despite the quasi-universal lunacy of historical events, the main theme of the *Essai* was that mankind gradually made progress. This was especially the case in Europe, whose civilisations began later than those of China and India but had now overtaken them. From the twelfth century onwards culture steadily reaches out from Italy into the whole of Western Europe. As true enlightenment gained the ascendant, belief in myth decayed and human reasoning, encouraged by the new intellectual climate, came to prefer what was true to being seduced by the marvellous. Fortunate periods had existed, like Athens in the time of Pericles, or the age of Louis XIV. There had been great men, like King Alfred of England or Henri IV. The *Essai* was therefore able to conclude on an optimistic note: 'When a nation is acquainted with the arts, when it is not subjugated . . . it emerges with ease from its ruins and never fails to restore itself.' It was always possible for the cultured members of society to exploit the love of order and the gregariousness that were endemic in human nature and to triumph over barbarism.

Hence the possibility of writing history *en philosophe*. History could be an instructive indicator of social change, whether the field was economic, technological, artistic, or institutional. To that end, Voltaire amply sourced himself from documents. But the documentation was sometimes flawed by a disregard for precise detail; not for Voltaire the pedantic concern for exactness at all costs if the matter seemed to him only trivially significant. The essential criterion was utility: would the material help towards changing society for the better?[2] In the *Essai* Voltaire compiled what other historians had had

---

2 It has been argued that Voltaire was less unreliable than is sometimes supposed: Brumfitt 1970, pp. 134–5; Pomeau 1995; Brumfitt in Voltaire 1969, p. 49.

to say, rather than undertaking his own research. Furthermore, he relied on written sources; extra-literary sources were scarcely considered; and he showed scepticism towards evidence such as contemporary medals (Voltaire 1963a, I, pp. xxi–xxii, II, p. 802). In addition, his judgement was somewhat blinkered. Voltaire depended heavily on the notion of *vraisemblance*: was an event or motive a likely possibility, when one considered the persons and circumstances involved? Such an approach inevitably carried the risk of subjective miscalculation, especially given Voltaire's rationalist views when confronted with the apparently irrational and religious. He rejected, for instance, the idea that temple prostitution could have existed in Babylon, on the *a priori* grounds that no man would be involved in such a practice when those he respected were present (ch. 34).

Yet, despite these weaknesses, Voltaire was commendably assiduous in searching for evidence of what had to be excluded as erroneous. Even the respected Roman historian Tacitus was sharply called to task on occasion. It was not Voltaire's way to build up a system on purely hypothetical constructs, as Rousseau did in the *Discourse on Inequality*. Whilst he may thereby have shown the limits of his imagination, he also demonstrated a concern for the factual, at least when large issues were not involved. Despite his scant regard shown for the middle ages, despite his tendentious refusal to see any cultural values in the medieval church, the contribution made by the *Essai* to historical writing in general is substantial: Voltaire had shown the possibility of a history of civilisation, and of its progress.

5 Gibbon

In a broad sense, Gibbon was at one with Voltaire. He too showed an unswerving allegiance to secular history, even though the approach was less polemical. With ironic respectfulness, Gibbon distanced himself from religiously orientated historians when he came to discuss the 'progress of the Christian religion'. 'The theologian may indulge the pleasing task of describing religion as she descended from heaven, arrayed in her native purity. A more melancholy duty is imposed on the historian' (Gibbon 1994, I, p. 446). The latter's task was to analyse the combined error and corruption into which religions fell among 'weak and degenerate' human beings. Gibbon conceded that there was an obvious reason for the triumph of Christianity: 'the convincing evidence of the doctrine itself and . . . the ruling providence of its great author'. That said, the historian must be concerned with 'secondary causes' (1994, I, pp. 446–7). His subject of enquiry must be man, not God, whose purposes are unknowable and therefore outside the scope of rational investigation.

Gibbon had been much impressed by Montesquieu because the latter had sought to discover, beneath the flux of human events, basic interrelated structures and factors motivating historical change. In Gibbon's first published work, the *Essai sur l'étude de la littérature* (1761), he paid Montesquieu a great compliment: 'let us carefully preserve every historical fact. A Montesquieu may discover, in the most trivial, connections unknown to the vulgar' (Gibbon 1970, p. 110). These connections were allied, for Gibbon as for Montesquieu and Voltaire, to a belief in the universality of human nature. Gibbon saw man as a volatile mixture of constructive reasoning and destructive passions, as had always been the case since his most primitive state. But the presence of that rational faculty gave grounds for hope of human progress.

This optimism, however, Gibbon restrained. He adapted Voltaire's famous phrase in stating that history is 'little more than the register of the crimes, follies, and punishments of mankind' (Gibbon 1994, I, pp. 109–10). But, like Voltaire, he discerned the possibility of improvement for the human race, albeit this was problematical in view of human nature's unpredictability when faced with the complexity of events. Man's progress, he felt, had been 'irregular and various', composed of a series of vicissitudes, including on occasion a swift decadence after long periods of slow improvement. Even so, taking the long view, there was reason for hope. How far mankind might go in the attainment of perfection was impossible to guess. Some gains, however, appeared to be permanent: 'no people, unless the face of nature is changed, will relapse into their original barbarism' (1994, II, p. 515).

On what was this prognosis founded? Essentially, on the facts of social change. The human race had raised itself out of savagery because certain basic skills had been acquired: the use of fire, metallurgy, hunting, fishing, navigation, agriculture, simple technology, and the domestication of animals. These techniques had been definitively acquired, in Gibbon's opinion, because they required no special genius and were therefore distributed widely. Despite the fact that the barbarians overthrew Rome, the humble scythe, for instance, continued unchanged to reap the annual harvest in the Italian countryside (1994, II, pp. 515–16).

So what was assured in human progress turned out to be modest in its dimensions. On a more sophisticated plane matters became doubtful. Gibbon cited the developments in law, politics, commerce, manufactures, and the arts and sciences as having the appearance of solid permanence.

Likewise, 'many individuals may be qualified, by education and discipline, to promote in their respective stations the interest of the community'. But since all this is the result of 'skill and labour', it could easily be lost through the eruption of violence or time's decay (1994, II, pp. 515–16).

The overall balance-sheet, however, tended to be positive, as the conclusion to Gibbon's 'General Observations on the Fall of the Roman Empire in the West' demonstrated. The arts had been propagated everywhere through the effects of war, commerce, and religion (an equivocal observation typical of its author); they could not therefore be lost. Hence, in the final words of the 'General Observations', Gibbon arrived at 'the pleasing conclusion that every age of the world has increased and still increases the real wealth, the happiness, the knowledge, and perhaps the virtue of the human race' (1994, II, p. 516). Contemporary Europe was a safer place than imperial Rome. Unlike the incompetent oligarchy which ruled the Empire, Europe was now divided into no fewer than fifteen major states and many smaller ones, all of them constrained by motivations of fear and shame and therefore possessing, in varying degrees, a spirit of moderation. No new barbarian invasion could ever conquer them all. Indeed, the very success of any potential conqueror would spell their downfall, since their skills in military warfare would necessarily bring greater knowledge and with it greater enlightenment, destroying their barbarism from within.

It would, however, be unwise to ignore the temporising note of the very last words in the 'Observations': 'and *perhaps* the virtue of the human race' (my emphasis). For all the technical and material improvements it had enjoyed, had mankind become any wiser or more just? A certain scepticism was permissible. This stance of ironic detachment characterised the *Decline and Fall* throughout. Tongue in cheek, Gibbon contrived to keep his readers in doubt, refusing them any easy conclusions. History was an uncertain, approximate, record of events, often mysterious, drawn from unreliable witnesses. Very little in Gibbon's work was entirely black or white; heroes and villains alike were rarely totally so. Amongst the former must surely be placed Julian the Apostate, one of the most admirable figures in the *Decline and Fall*. The combination of courage, wit, and intense application in his character, said Gibbon, would have brought him eminence in any field he had cared to choose. As emperor, Julian did not distinguish between duty and pleasure, and constantly endeavoured to ensure that authority was meritorious, and that happiness went hand in hand with virtue. But these excellent qualities were offset by a belief in the pagan gods so total that it 'would almost degrade the emperor to the level of an Egyptian monk'. Had Julian not been prematurely killed in battle, his oppression of the Christians and efforts to re-establish paganism as the dominant religion would have led the Empire into civil war. As Gibbon put it, with a typically judicious element of iconoclasm: 'When we inspect with minute or perhaps malevolent attention the portrait of Julian, something seems wanting to the grace and perfection of the whole figure' (1994, I, p. 863). The phrase 'or perhaps malevolent', at first reading almost an afterthought, allows the reader the freedom, if desired, to believe that Gibbon was being uncharitable. Nonetheless, this even-handed refusal of all idolatry was trenchant.

If Julian ranked with the best of those who made an appearance in the *Decline and Fall*, Constantine quite clearly belonged with the less worthy. From Constantine's time dated the definitive decline of the Empire into corruption, as he committed the irreparable error of founding a rival city to Rome that would become one of the major causes of its fall. Whereas under the rule of the Antonine emperors Rome had been 'united by laws and adorned by arts', comprehending 'the most civilized portion of mankind', after the reign of Constantine it became, in 410 CE, subject to a barbarian conquest, 'delivered to the licentious fury of the tribes of Germany and Scythia' (1909–14, I.1, 1.28 and III.321–2). As Gibbon envisaged it, the collapse of Rome's grandeur initially under the Goths and then, in the east a thousand years later, ultimately under the Turks, virtually portrayed the sagas of Livy's *Rise of Rome* and Virgil's *Aeneid* in reverse. In each case it had been subject to waves of pressure from outside, the Gothic invasion largely inspired by the Goths' displacement at Rome's Danubian border by the Huns, the Turks by pressure emanating from Central Asia by the Tartars. But in each case Rome was above all weakened by internal decay, and Constantine's adoption of Christianity as the Empire's official religion was the most pivotal development of all, for it emasculated its military strength by progressively turning its population's attention inwards, away from its collective identity and instead merely to the salvation of individual souls. It also engendered an internal cancer, which through the Crusades would eventually lead to the sacking of the Eastern Empire by Western Christendom's marauding armies.

Gibbon observed with sardonic amusement the spectacle of this emperor, mad with arrogance, tracing out an ever-larger area for the future city before his incredulous assistants. Constantine uttered the fatuous reply of one who thought he was God's instrument on earth: 'I shall still advance . . . till he, the invisible guide who marches before me, thinks proper to stop.' The historian's comment, seemingly reserving judgement on divine matters, is crushing: 'Without presuming to investigate the nature or motives of this extraordinary conductor, we shall content ourselves with the more humble task of describing the extent and limits of Constantinople' (1994, I, p. 593). Yet even Constantine, also ignominious for instituting the persecution of heretics, was not wholly a force for evil. He had founded a great new capital city whose size and amenities fascinated Gibbon; and in the 'General Observations' the historian showed that events in some measure confirmed Constantine's judgement because Constantinople preserved order in the East against the barbarians while the West was in decay.

But, even if they resulted in ambiguity, the facts must always be respected. On this account Gibbon found Montesquieu wanting, and Voltaire even more so (Baridon 1977, p. 691; Porter 1988, p. 71). The latter was memorably rebuked in the opening chapter of the *Decline and Fall*: 'M. de Voltaire, unsupported by either fact or probability, has generously bestowed the Canary Islands on the Roman empire' (Gibbon 1994, I, p. 54 n. 87). Castigating both the ecclesiastical historian Louis Maimbourg and Voltaire for their excessive eagerness to take (different) sides, he slightingly adds: 'The prejudice of a philosopher is less excusable than that of a Jesuit' (1994, III, p. 583 n. 65). Gibbon was of the firm persuasion that a true historian must root out all prejudice. Narration of detail must be of the most exacting rigour. In fact, the range of Gibbon's reading was enormous.[3] He acquainted himself with all the printed editions of primary sources that he could find, as well as a wealth of supporting material like travel literature. After careful checking, fellow historian William Robertson paid him this compliment: 'I find that he refers to no passage but what he has seen with his own eyes' (Porter 1988, p. 73). To all this one must add the insights gained by a long experience of human nature, which may on occasion supply the want of historical material (Gibbon 1994, I, p. 253). For ultimately facts were only a means to the end of history, which helped us to enlarge our horizons: 'To the eyes of the philosopher events are the least interesting part of history. It is the knowledge of man, morality and politics he finds there that elevates it in his mind' (Gibbon 1814, p. 126).

Like Voltaire, Gibbon allowed an element of reasonable surmise when facts were absent. Writing of the years 248–68 CE, a particularly bloody period for emperors, he argued that the successive murders of so many of them must have loosened the ties of allegiance between sovereign and people. This conjecture appears probable. But the approach carried the same

3 Porter 1988, p. 72, counts 8,362 references in the *Decline and Fall*.

dangers as for Voltaire, since in the end it must come down to the chances of success that a reasonable guess by an eighteenth-century writer might have for uncovering the truth about other times and places. In addition, Gibbon's research stopped short at written sources, in this regard breaking no new ground with reference to other kinds of evidence (Momigliano 1966, p. 40). So his history was most reliable when strongly supported by printed material. But when, as in his confessed ignorance of 'Oriental tongues' (Gibbon 1994, III, p. 151 n. 1), he is unable to use sources in those languages for studies such as his account of Mohammed, his limitations are clear. However, these constraints must not be allowed to blind one to the formidable achievements of the *Decline and Fall* and its global, universalist, perspective.

History might be full of paradox and ambiguity; but it was not absurd. Nevertheless, civilisation was a fragile artefact. Gibbon felt that any investigation of the causes of the Roman collapse should not start from the premise that it required an exceptional explanation, as though it were an extraordinary event: 'instead of enquiring why the Roman empire was destroyed, we should rather be surprised that it had subsisted so long' (1994, II, p. 509). Even so, this fragility did not preclude the possibility of civilisation, thanks to enlightened human effort. Similarly the historian, by allying erudition to rational intelligence, stood a chance of understanding the past, and thereby (since human nature was universal), the present. The *Decline and Fall* stood as the practical proof of that theory.

Gibbon did not attempt a systematic causal account of the ruin of the Empire. But the 'General Observations' on the fall of Rome gave useful pointers to his thinking. He felt that the decline of Rome was above all the natural result of over-expansion: 'Prosperity ripened the principle of decay . . . the stupendous fabric yielded to the pressure of its own weight.' One had the sense of a phenomenon almost as physically fatal in its effects as metal fatigue. Hence it followed that for Gibbon the history of that decline was 'simple and obvious' (1994, II, p. 509). In practice, it was even possible to isolate certain fatal causes. The division of the Empire between Constantinople and Rome was important in encouraging dangerous jealousies between East and West, which themselves increased arbitrary and despotic government. Military power had grown stronger, at the expense of the civil authority. Not least, 'the introduction, or at least the abuse, of Christianity had some influence on the Decline and Fall of the Roman empire' (1994, II, p. 510).

As with all else in Gibbon, there were no simple lessons to be learned from the rise of the Christian religion. On the one hand it had undermined the spirit of religious toleration that had prevailed under the pagan rituals of the imperial *Pax Romana*, when its subjects' diverse 'modes of worship . . . were considered by the people as equally true; by the philosopher as equally false; and by the magistrate as equally useful' (1909–14, I.28). On the other hand, through its network of churches and bishops, Christianity had actually helped to support the unity of the Empire, which it had further assisted by preaching obedience to lawful authorities. Besides, its moral purity helped to tame the fierce barbarians of the North. On balance, however, the nefarious influence of the church had far outweighed these advantages. The new religion undermined the structures of society. Civic pride was discouraged, military valour despised. Much of the Empire's wealth was given away to 'the specious demands of charity and devotion'. Christian zeal fired religious strife, so that factionalism became widespread, creating a new kind of tyranny and turning devotees of the religion into 'the secret enemies of their country' (1994, II, pp. 510–11).

Gibbon's indictment was formidable, encapsulating the lengthy account to which he devoted chapters 15 and 16, where he analysed the 'secondary causes' of this success story. Christianity represented an entirely new phenomenon, because it set out to proselytise. Heir to the unattractive element of exclusiveness already existing in the Judaic religion, it had gone further in preaching to the faithful that they had a duty to convert others to their cause. Pagan idolatry had been regarded as the devil's work; so pagans had to be persecuted for the good of their souls. In addition, the Christian religion had preached an active belief in eternal rewards and punishments: bliss for all true followers, but eternal torture for the unbelievers, depicted with particularly horrific exultation by Tertullian. Furthermore, all this was imminent; for the Second Coming was at hand. In such a feverish state of waiting Christians had withdrawn from all active participation in the wider society, whether civil, administrative, or military. Above all else they held moral purity and asceticism in awe, whilst abjuring all earthly delights, rejecting all knowledge outside the scriptural, despising all cultural appurtenances (art, music, dress, furniture, food, housing). What Gibbon was describing here was an upsurge of fundamentalist enthusiasm, triumphant by virtue of the strict discipline it imposes on its members. The stage was set for the persecutions of the heretics that would begin in earnest after Constantine.

Thus Christianity came to be invested with much of the blame for the collapse of Rome. But one must not oversimplify Gibbon's story. The fall, as we have seen, was not in his view monocausal. Nor must we forget that his great history did not end with the pillage of Rome by the Goths in

410. Gibbon set himself the task of narrating the later course of the Eastern Empire right up to the fall of Constantinople in 1453: the rise of Islam, the Crusades, the conquests of Tamberlane. The canvas continued to be immense, its elements collectively producing what Gibbon in the conclusion – in a passage that may have inspired, in his *Reflections*, Burke's strikingly similar assessment of the world-historical significance of the French Revolution – as 'the greatest, perhaps, and most awful scene in the history of mankind' (Gibbon 1994, III, p. 1084). No greater challenge could have been set the eighteenth-century historian. Through Rome Gibbon approached the history of civilised society in general, that finest product of human effort, incorporating despite its delicacy all the values by which enlightened people should live. For Gibbon, history was more than scientific enquiry; it was evidence of a passionate concern with promoting human development through the 'knowledge of man, morality, and politics' which for him was to be drawn from a study of the past.

8

Naturalism, anthropology, and culture

WOLFGANG PROSS[*]

1 A Counter-Enlightenment?

When the roots of Romanticism are traced to the age of Enlightenment, they are often located in the hinterland of Europe, where, at the margins of civilisation, solitary thinkers like Vico in Naples, Rousseau in Neuchâtel, or Herder in Lithuania are portrayed as having cast themselves adrift from the prevailing intellectual currents of their day. In opposing the idea of progress such proponents of what in the late nineteenth century came to be termed the Counter-Enlightenment are alleged to have subscribed to diverse notions of primitivism, preferring ancient mythology over modern science, popular intuitions over abstract ideas, and uncouth human nature over the refinements of culture. In confronting Enlightenment philosophy they are taken to have undermined its most central premises and subverted its aims in the manner of prophets harking back to a world we have lost, betrothed to fictitious ideals of uncultivated simplicity which, while derided by their contemporaries, have made their doctrines seem peculiarly post-modern and thereby apposite to a post-Enlightenment world.

Such perspectives, however, do grave injustice to the careers of Vico, Rousseau, Herder, and their disciples. When he put forward his now-celebrated notion of 'ricorso' – that is, of 'repetition' or 'return' – in just the last of his three formulations of a *New Science* of the laws of development of human society (*Scienza nuova*, 1725, 1730, and 1744), Vico was not advocating mankind's reversion to a state of barbarism. As the Italian scholar Giuseppe Giarrizzo remarked, Vico's political science was actually conceived 'to save mankind from the return of barbarism' (Giarrizzo 1981, p. 21). For his part, Rousseau insisted, against the critics of his first *Discourse on the Arts and Sciences* (1751), that the return of humanity to its primeval state was neither possible nor desirable, adding in his second *Discourse on the*

* In dedicating this essay to Oskar Bätschmann, the author also wishes to express his gratitude to Simone De Angelis, Martin Immenhauser, and Robert Wokler for their helpful comments and assistance.

Origin of Inequality (1755) that he deemed it necessary to make his way in this world as a loyal citizen bound by his state's laws. Much of his own political science was inspired by the teachings of the great masters of natural law, in many instances mediated by the commentaries upon their works provided by Jean Barbeyrac, as Robert Derathé has shown (Derathé 1950). Herder, moreover, while criticising the state as a soulless machine which deprives the individual of his rights and autonomy, set out in *Another Philosophy of History for the Benefit of the Education of Mankind* (1774) a critique of the merely formal principles of contractual obligation deemed to establish the foundations of government, such as those portrayed in Cesare Beccaria's *On Crimes and Punishments* (*Dei delitti e delle pene*, 1764) or Adam Ferguson's *Essay on the History of Civil Society* (1767). Each of these authors, together with many others throughout the eighteenth century, drew upon the same sources of natural jurisprudence, including, most particularly, an argument employed by Pufendorf in his *On the Laws of Nature and Nations* (*De jure naturae et gentium*, 1672), where he remarks that 'hidden within the individuals who comprise the state are, metaphorically speaking, the seeds of power, stirred and made to flourish by contracts, which combine these individuals into a body' (VII.iii, § 4). One of Herder's chief concerns was to make this point about the state's foundations by way of confining the state's power, so that its omnipotence could not irretrievably supersede the natural qualities of its members, whose total subjection would stifle the vital force of not only the individual but also the whole nation.

The erroneous identification of Vico, Rousseau, and Herder as Counter-Enlightenment thinkers has been largely based upon decontextualised interpretations of their meaning proffered by commentators inattentive to their sources or with only isolated interests in particular themes they addressed. In the case of Vico, Hegelian readings of his philosophy of history advanced by Francesco de Sanctis, Benedetto Croce, Giovanni Gentile, and their followers have for the most part ignored not only its roots in natural law but also its debts to philosophical and scientific speculation prevalent in Naples around 1700. Vico owed much to Lionardo da Capua's mythological model of the history of medicine and to Giuseppe Valletta's constructions of a history of science, but the influence upon his writings of these naturalists, and of Gian Vincenzo Gravina's theory of evidence directed against Descartes's 'cogito ergo sum', has seldom been addressed, despite the pioneering scholarship in these areas of Nicola Badaloni, Enrico De Mas, Paolo Rossi, Leon Pompa, Giorgio Tagliacozzo, and Harold Stone (Stone 1997). The study of myth, certainly one of the keys to Vico's theory of history, was already for Gravina before him (*Delle antiche favole* (On Ancient Fables), 1696) a wholly adequate and legitimate form of cognition as well as of poetry, enabling soaring flights of fancy to reign supreme, as had been recognised in mankind's antiquity. But it is within the framework of the concepts of natural law, in the wake of Grotius, Pufendorf, and Gravina (a jurist of distinction in his own right) that Vico shaped his outlook on the state of nature and the establishment of laws among nations, transforming the crucial juridical problem of a 'natural law of nations' into the cornerstone of a philosophy of history.

Rousseau, for his part, was not only well versed in the natural jurisprudence of Grotius, Pufendorf, Barbeyrac, Burlamaqui, and other thinkers; he also read both Hobbes and Locke meticulously in absorbing their respective scientific and theological notions of politics within his own philosophy. The third book of his *Social Contract* (1762) comprises one of the most elaborate treatments of Montesquieu's *Spirit of the Laws* (1748) in the whole of the eighteenth century. No major writer on political themes in the period was better acquainted with Condillac's philosophy of language, whose implications for the study of politics itself he pursued in works such as his *Letter to d'Alembert on the Theatre* (1758) and his posthumously published *Essay on the Origin of Languages* (1781). No work exercised a greater impact upon his conception of mankind's civil history in his second *Discourse* than the first three volumes of the *Natural History* (1749–51) of the Enlightenment's pre-eminent historian of the natural sciences, Buffon.

Herder, no less than Vico and Rousseau, has come to be regarded as a prophet of Counter-Enlightenment, by virtue of his imputed intellectual isolation, on account of his alleged adherence to Johann Georg Hamann's theological mode of reasoning, and because of his seemingly 'irrational' opposition to his former teacher, Kant. Such erroneous descriptions of his marginality underpin the legend of his paternity of German nationalism, if not of the pan-Germanism of the Third Reich, with its dreadful consequences in the twentieth century. Max Rouché's interpretation, published just before the German invasion of France, greatly helped to perpetuate that reading, despite the endeavours of F. M. Barnard (Barnard 1965a; Rouché 1940). When Herder, together with the young Goethe whom he had met in Strasbourg in 1770, presented the 'flying leaves' *Of German Style and Art* (*Von deutscher Art und Kunst*, 1773), they appeared not only to have launched a manifesto for the literary *Sturm und Drang* movement but also to have voiced the battle cry of the Germans demanding to take their place as a young, ruthless nation in the community of age-stricken civilisations. And the 'pamphlet', as Herder called it himself, of the following year – *Another Philosophy of History* – seemed to summon the dark middle ages to snuff out the pervasive light of reason and to discard all achievements of the modern world and its advocates, Voltaire and the *Encyclopédistes* foremost among them. Although there is scarcely a grain of truth in such perspectives, legends ascribing to Herder doctrines of medievalism, nationalism, and irrationalism are ineradicable, because they engender a mysterious aura of darkness, so well suited to the prophets of post-rationalism and post-modernity. Thus has 'darkness' once again become a favourite subject of research with respect to Herder today. Yet Herder was profoundly acquainted with the political, philosophical, and historical writings of contemporary European thinkers – with French authors, such as Montesquieu, Antoine-Yves Goguet, Guillaume-Thomas Raynal, and, of course, Voltaire, Diderot, and the authors of the *Encyclopédie* (to whom he owes a debt that can scarcely be exaggerated); with the English-language discourses of Hume, Ferguson, Monboddo, Robertson, and Gibbon; with Italians such as Denina, Giannone, or Muratori, not forgetting the whole tradition of Italian anti-curialism from Machiavelli to Paolo Sarpi. Above all, perhaps, historical perspectives drawn from the Scottish Enlightenment, combined with the idea of a 'history of the human mind' such as had been developed by Locke, Condillac, and Diderot, helped him to frame an interpretation of man as a social being with reference to different stages of human culture. It was not nationalism but what he termed the 'obliteration of national characters' which he expected would prove the destiny of modern Europe, as he explained in the last volume of his *Ideas towards a Philosophy of History of Mankind* in 1791 (bk XVI, vi: HW, III/1, p. 650).[1] There is no difference between the central theme of that work and the philosophy of history he had put forward in his *Journal of my Voyage in the Year 1769*: 'We run riot', he had already remarked there,

if we praise, like Rousseau, times that have vanished, or a time that did not exist . . . You must become a preacher of the virtues of *your own age*! What a great theme, to show that – in order to be what you should be – you have to turn neither into a Jew, nor an Arab, a Greek, a savage, a martyr, or a crusader; but simply be the man God demands you to be, according to the stage of our culture: enlightened, instructed, refined, reasonable, educated, virtuous, and capable of pleasure. (*Journal meiner Reise im Jahr 1769*: HW, I, p. 375)

---

1 Throughout this chapter HW stands for Herder 1984–2002.

Interpretations of Herder have also suffered from a fundamental misunderstanding of Enlightenment philosophy of history, in so far as it has been deemed to be devoid of the genuine historical comprehension achieved in the historical writing of the nineteenth century. The 'genetic' and 'organic' methods attributed to German historiography by commentators who seek to distinguish them from their allegedly 'rationalist' counterparts in other Western European traditions could hardly constitute less specifically historical explanations for the development and metamorphoses of human cultures. Herder's conceptions of organic forces, despite their antecedents in Leibniz, were in fact borrowed wholesale from the writings of French naturalists like Buffon, Charles Bonnet, and Jean Baptiste René Robinet, or from philosophers, including Diderot or d'Holbach, themselves inspired by such ideas (cf. Roger 1963). The German scientist and writer Georg Christoph Lichtenberg spoke in his *Waste Books* of 'the term "organisation" that has become now so fashionable among the French' (Lichtenberg 1967–92, I, p. 704). The concept of history to which Herder subscribed embraced the 'naturalisation' of history and the formulation of 'laws' that governed it (cf. Pross in HW, III/2, pp. 589–603).

From the beginning of his career Herder emphasised the need for Newtonian laws of human history, such as he believed had been overlooked by Montesquieu in the *Spirit of the Laws* (*Gedanken bei Lesung Montesquieus*, 1769: HW, I, pp. 468–73). In his *Dialogues* on Spinoza (*Gott. Einige Gespräche*), published in 1787, together with the theoretical fifteenth book of his *Ideas*, he spoke of a 'mathematical-physical and metaphysical formula', which might equally explain the laws of nature and of history (HW, II, p. 775). The history of humanity was to be understood in its association with the processes of nature, whose evolution had only been apparently arrested with the appearance of the most perfect animal on earth – that is, with man. The key to Herder's theory of culture is to be found in notions of this kind, linking him not only to the philosophical works of Bacon, Campanella, Gassendi, and Spinoza in the previous century but also to Vico, who, in his first *New Science*, had remarked that none of the sciences

has yet contained a meditation upon . . . the humanity of nations . . . with which to measure the stages through which the humanity of nations must proceed . . . [nor] gained scientific apprehension of the practices through which the humanity of a nation, as it rises, can reach this perfect state, and those through which, when it declines from this state, it can return to it anew. (*New Science*, 1725, bk I, ch. 2: Vico 2002, p. 11; cf. Vico 1971, p. 173)

2 Mankind and the dark abyss of time

Despite their different intellectual backgrounds, and most particularly the domination of jurisprudence and rhetoric in Vico's education and that of philosophy and natural history – especially geography and physiology – in Herder's, a common point of departure marks each of their ways of conceiving a 'new science' and their respective philosophies of history that stem from it: the questioning of chronology entailing a radical change in the concept of history. Vico's and Herder's 'new sciences' of history challenged Christian chronocentrism as much as Copernicus and Galileo had shaken Christian geocentrism, albeit with different results. According to the Aristotelian division in the *Poetics*, 'historia' spoke only of particular events, quite differently from poetry, the repository of what concerns mankind in general. Universal history had therefore been conceived exclusively in terms of sacred history, through which providence had governed the course of one chosen nation. The history of the gentiles, therefore, had been considered only as a series of events that accompanied the elected Jewish people on their path towards the epiphany of the Messiah. This history of the sons of Cham and Japheth had been curtailed to fit Biblical chronology as established by Archbishop James Ussher in his *Annals of the Ancient and New Testament* (1650–4), who had determined that the creation of the world had occurred in the year 4004 BC. Bossuet's endeavour to sustain this scheme in his *Universal History* (1681) had already been undermined, without his being aware of it. For in 1658, in the *First Decade of the Annals of the Chinese Empire* (*Sinicae historiae decas prima, Res à gentis origine . . .*), the Jesuit missionary Martin Martini had published an account of the reign of the first Chinese emperors, which apparently conflicted with Ussher's chronological frame of universal history. The Chinese annals purportedly made plain a sequence of unbroken continuity from 2952 BC, 604 years before the Flood had swept away all human life on earth in the year 2348 BC or the year 1656 of the world after its Creation, according to the scheme of Genesis as dated by Ussher. If the Chinese annals were right, the Flood of the Bible was not an event of universal impact, and the Bible would have been proved to be wrong.

The Bible itself contained mysterious references to 'Giants', whose existence within the annalistic framework proved to be a crucial question: was there a possibility of 'Pre-Adamites', human life before Adam and outside God's creation? Isaac de La Peyrère's *Men before Adam* (*Systema theologicum ex Praeadamitarum hypothesi*, 1655) had raised this impious doubt, only one year after Ussher's seemingly conclusive annalistic work (cf. Rossi 1984). Ethnographers and antiquarians with their reports on the chronology, myths, and antiquities of Mexico, Peru, Tibet, India, Egypt, Phoenicia, or Chaldaea widened the gulf between sacred history on the one hand, and the outlines of a new chronology on the other, making the descriptions of antiquity offered by Lucretius and Diodorus Siculus appear to approximate the truth more closely than the story of Paradise and its loss. Chronology, therefore, played an important part in Vico's conception of history; already in the *Universal Right* (*Diritto universale*, 1720) the principles of the 'new science' were based on reflection on sacred chronology in comparison with data on the history of the gentiles (*Universal Right*, bk II, pt II, ch. 1: *De constantia philologiae*: Vico 1974, pp. 386–401). In his definitive redaction of the *New Science* (1744) Vico begins, after an exposition of the idea of his work, with a Chronological Table which faithfully reproduces Ussher's framework of dates for the sacred history, trying to fit in the history of the gentiles divided into the three ages of the gods, heroes, and men (*New Science*, 1744, bk I, *Annotazioni alla tavola cronologica*: Vico 1971, pp. 399–431). It is precisely this acknowledgement of the Christian tradition that aroused serious doubts about the orthodoxy of Vico's method. Was there enough time – within the traditional chronology after the Flood when the sons of Noah, according to Vico, dispersed in order to turn into those 'bestioni', animal-men in the sense of Lucretius – for re-creating or re-inventing all the cultural techniques which mankind had possessed before its extinction through God's wrath? This was the question raised by the Dominican Germano Federigo Finetti in his *On the Principles of Natural Law and the Law of Nations* (*De principiis juris naturae et gentium*, 1764), using the name of his brother Gian Francesco to conceal his identity (Finetti 1764, II, bk XII, ch. 6, pp. 307–17). The state of nature, conceived as 'ferinitas' ('ferocity') was fundamentally incompatible with sacred history, so Finetti argued against Vico and Rousseau. Genesis teaches us that God created man, endowed him with language and notions of the world appropriate to his capacities, and finally placed him, by creating Eve, into a 'domestic society' that allowed the transmission of Adam's knowledge to his posterity (I, bk V, ch. 4, p. 292). This form of society, entailing man's peaceful sociability, is what Finetti opposes to the 'absurd propositions' of Hobbes, Pufendorf, Vico, and Rousseau concerning the solitude, weakness, and uneasiness of mankind in the natural state. When Rousseau tried to avoid the problem in his *Discourse on the Origin of Inequality* by presenting his views as mere hypotheses ('Let us set aside all the facts!'), the same Finetti, placing the citizen of Geneva alongside the philosopher of Naples, remarked shrewdly:

But he [Rousseau] addresses his readers in that way: *O man, whatever are your origins and opinions, listen: here is your history which I believe I did not read in the books of your equals who are liars* – and who cannot see that he [Rousseau] classifies among those liars Moses, the first and even the only true author of the history of mankind? – *but in nature which never lies.*

Finetti continues by asking what sort of 'nature' this could be, if not a substance estranged from God, or – worse – Spinoza's substance which incorporates God into nature? (I, bk v, ch. 4, p. 281). Mankind would have to be regarded as abandoned by universal providence to its own resources, and despite all professions of adherence to Catholic doctrine on Vico's part, the formula of the blasphemous eleventh Prolegomenon of Hugo Grotius's *On the Law of War and Peace* (*De jure belli ac pacis*, 1625) would become the programme of this 'new science'. There must be a law which governs human behaviour even if God's existence were not susceptible to incontrovertible proof ('etsi non daretur Deus').

When Finetti pointed to the consequences of abandoning the book of Genesis as the unique and genuine source of history, he merely proffered the same argument against Rousseau, and implicitly Vico, that had already been used in Naples at the end of the seventeenth century against Thomas Burnet, in the wake of Cartesian mechanics and Spinozist monism. To question sacred chronology was to eliminate the 'architect from his creation'. The world would therefore come to be lost not only in the infinity of space and matter but also in the abyss of unfathomable time (Rossi 1979, p. 98). But by 1764, the cause of sacred history was lost. It is true that, fourteen years after Vico's last *New Science*, Antoine-Yves Goguet could still present afresh Ussher's scheme in his *On the Origins of Laws and the Arts and Sciences* (*De l'origine des loix, des arts, et des sciences*, 1758) as a chronological framework for his, otherwise revolutionary, comparative history of the cultural techniques of the ancients. But in 1749, Buffon's *Theory of the Earth* (*Théorie de la terre*), to which he devotes a section of the first volume of the *Natural History* (*Histoire naturelle*), had, by going back to and reassessing William Whiston's cosmogony, already threatened all arguments that spoke in its favour. In his later *Epochs of Nature* (*Epoques de la nature*, 1778), Buffon admitted in public that the Earth was about 75,000 years old; his unpublished calculations added up to about 3 million years (Rossi 1979, p. 135). And, what is more, Buffon imitated in his fashion the framework of the cosmogony of

Lucretius; according to the second book of *De rerum natura* the process of nature, evolving out of chaos, arrives at a standstill which lasts for a certain term, until the 'walls of the creation' ('moenia mundi') collapse again in a process of self-destruction. Buffon's earth had – according to his published computations – consolidated in 3,000 years, after a comet had hit the sun and chipped off a part, which cooled down so as to enable life on earth to appear. He predicted that the world would last only 45,000 more years before the incessant process of losing warmth would lead to the complete freezing of the planet and the extinction of life. Moreover, Buffon shocked all scientists, who tried to maintain the conformity of modern science with the Bible, by declaring that the purity of scripture should not be polluted with uncouth physics (Rossi 1979, p. 126). This statement reopened the question of combining the problem of cosmogony with Galileo's mechanistic system of the universe, wherein Descartes had failed because of his chimerical system of whirls ('tourbillons'). Newton had refrained from making that attempt, even dabbling instead in a fruitless endeavour to retain and improve the antiquated chronology, as Herder remarked irreverently (*Ideas*, bk XII, iii: HW, III/1, p. 447).

Herder himself, in this respect, was siding with Buffon and the teachings of his former master Kant, in the *Universal Natural History and Theory of Heaven* (*Allgemeine Naturgeschichte und Theorie des Himmels*, 1755); so he basically had no scruples about acknowledging the antiquity of the earth beyond what was permitted by sacred chronology, and he firmly opposed the attempt of Jean-André de Luc to maintain the link between the literal text of the Bible and modern geological science (*Lettres physiques et morales sur l'histoire de la terre et de l'homme*, Physical and Moral Letters on the History of the Earth and Man, 1778–82). But he nevertheless hesitated to conjecture that the earth's first inhabitants might be as old as the planet itself. When he published the second volume of his *Ideas* in 1785, he withdrew the concluding chapter of book X from print at the very last moment. It had been inscribed *Revolution of the Earth According to the Oldest Traditions* (*Revolution der Welt nach den ältesten Traditionen*; cf. HW, III/1, pp. 1140–54). In this chapter on ancient chronicles, published posthumously in 1814, he was to advance a geological hypothesis about the Flood which challenged de Luc. Following Buffon, he sought to avoid the catastrophism or violent interruption of the natural processes of the earth which was integral to sacred history. From the moment when the 'gates of creation had been closed', as he said with Lucretius (*Ideas*, bk v, iii: HW, III/1, p. 163), Herder's mankind lives, tucked away safely in the folds of the Himalayas, in order to descend from Paradise, which Herder situated in Kashmir, so as to populate the globe – after a flood provoked by a shift of the axis of the earth (HW, III/I, pp. 1143–7). This hypothesis, vaguely based on that of Johann Heinrich Lambert, is obscured in the published version of the *Ideas* (p. 1143). If the revolutions that shaped the earth are of such remote antiquity as modern science and mythology together suppose, then mankind must be very young (*Ideas*, bk x, vi: HW, III/I, p. 379). Herder formulated a conception of history and culture as developed in two stages, framed in a horizontal and vertical pattern. The first stage, the 'geographic history', consists of mankind's spread over the whole earth and coming to live among its differing climates. Man is almost the only animal able to survive in all zones, thus conquering all continents, including the arctic as well as the torrid zones; and it is his technical ability to invent the means indispensable to his subsistence that guarantees his success. That is what 'culture' actually means for Herder; already in this early stage of human history we may speak of 'first, necessary, and general natural laws of humanity'; they are merely transformed in more elaborate stages of civilisation, even if fortified townships and the palaces of kings seem to belie their descent from nomadic camps and the primitive huts of leaves and straw of the patriarchs. It is only in mild climates, where nature's abundance frees mankind from the satisfaction of just the barest necessities, that more sophisticated forms of culture may initially develop (*Ideas*, bk VIII, iv: HW, III/I, p. 297). But this vertical pattern of cultural evolution may be continued even under less favourable conditions, when men's technical skills are developed to overcome rough climates. The cultures of ancient China, India, Mesopotamia, Egypt, Greece, and Rome could thereby be extended to northern Europe, creating the civilisation of modern times.

3   The history of the human mind

Still more damaging to the Christian rationalisation of history was the publication of Spinoza's *Tractatus theologico-politicus* in 1670, which greatly influenced Vico and Herder alike. In the sixteenth chapter of his work, Spinoza, in the wake of Grotius's Prolegomenon already mentioned, stated that the apparent arbitrariness of human nature was nonetheless subject to natural law. For, he observed, 'nobody will deprive himself of what he judges to be good and conducive to his welfare, if he should not be withheld by the expectation of something more useful or by the threat of a greater disadvantage'. 'This law is inscribed so *firmly* in the human breast, that it has to be placed among the immutable truths nobody is allowed to ignore' (Spinoza

1972, I, p. 472). Neither man's reason nor God's providence therefore regulated the course of history, which is determined rather in a totally arbitrary way by mankind's instincts and passions of self-preservation. God's assistance to man assumes two forms: outward, those natural resources that allow him, by exerting his own capacities or as free gifts of nature, to satisfy his wants; and inward, the dispositions of his mind. In this way, there can be no chance or contingency in nature; everything is preordained and occurs by necessity. 'I understand by "God's direction" that established and immutable order of nature . . . according to which everything . . . is determined . . . by God's decree and direction. . . . By "chance" I understand nothing else but God's direction' (pp. 102, 104). This singular interpretation of the world as governed by universal necessity, paradoxically embracing even the arbitrariness of human behaviour, was reinforced in 1689 by Locke's interpretation of the human mind. In chapters 20 and 21 of book II of his *Essay concerning Human Understanding* he argued that the sphere of liberty was divorced from the realm of instinct and its basic condition of 'uneasiness'. The will and actions of man are subject to the satisfaction of physical and moral desires and must not be presumed to constitute freedom of action, which according to Locke is a *petitio principii*, based on fundamental misinterpretations of the way the human mind works.

Spinoza's and Locke's interpretations of the human mind, combined with the key notion of 'imbecillitas' ('weakness' or 'deficiency') in Lucretius and Pufendorf, provided for Vico the clue that made it possible to understand the course of history, including the history of the gentiles, in a more general way. In Spinoza's *Tractatus* it was shown by this allegedly impious author that the Jewish nation had not been able to overcome the determined character of the human condition, despite its having been chosen by God and assisted by his presence and the revelation of his power. In his *Essay on the Mores and Spirit of Nations* (*Essai sur les moeurs et l'esprit des nations*, 1756) Voltaire was to mock such notions of universal necessity, particularly in opposition to Bossuet, while for his part Spinoza inferred that nature's assistance had been required to help the gentiles as well, in their endeavours to ensure their self-preservation. Following much the same train of thought, cast in the idiom of a theory of determinate cultural evolution drawn from book V of Lucretius's *De rerum natura*, Vico detected definite patterns of social development in mankind's history, leading from savagery and primitivism to the establishment of civic life through the enclosure of townships. Those patterns mapped the natural course of change of the human mind itself, which grew slowly but inevitably transformed its original domination by fancy and imagination into the rationality of civilisation and culture. If one followed the productions of the human mind and assumed their uniformity of function, the apparent gulf between man's state of nature and the condition of civil society could be bridged, despite the arbitrariness of the choices mankind had made. The invention of a contract, which implied the violation of natural equality as the foundation of law, would create an artificial gap intruding upon the regular patterns that marked the course of civilisation, Vico supposed. Already in the Prologue of his *Universal Right*, he had referred to a 'genuine eternal law, which has been received as law by all men, at any time and in any country', and he deemed that this law must derive from the constitution of man himself (Vico 1974, p. 31). His *New Science* of 1744, which embraces the 'Principles of a New Science regarding the Common Nature of Nations', was to adopt that point of view as its guiding principle. 'In that night of impenetrable darkness, which covers primeval . . . antiquity, there dawns this light of truth . . . which cannot be called into doubt'. He observed,

that this world of civil society certainly has been made by men. Therefore its principles may . . . be discovered within the modifications of the human mind . . . itself . . . . Philosophers . . . dedicated . . . to the acquisition of knowledge [have only studied] this physical world, a science . . . within God's reach because it is him who created nature. They neglected, however, to reflect on this world of nations or civil world, the science of which – because of its being made by mankind – was within the reach of men. (*New Science*, bk 1, ch. 3: Vico 1971, p. 461)

What was it that made Vico appear such a singular figure in his day? The tradition of Vico's isolation seems to be based on the judgement published in the *Acta Eruditorum* in 1727, in which an author – unknown to Vico himself – asserted that the first edition of the *New Science* of 1725 had met with greater disapproval than acclaim in Italy, because of the 'mass of lengthy conjectures' made by its 'more ingenious than truth-seeking author'. Vico reports this judgement in his violent *Vindications of Vico*, where he defends himself against the preposterous allegation of obscurity (*Vici vindiciae*, 1729: Vico 1971, pp. 342–7). As a matter of fact, he enjoyed a certain fame during his lifetime and in the second half of the century, although primarily on the grounds of the reputation he had gained as the author of the *Universal Right*. After his death, his pupil and professor of canon law at Rome, Emanuele Duni, drew strongly on his master's theory in his *Essay on Universal Jurisprudence* (*Saggio sulla giurisprudenza universale*, 1760), and his unmistakable influence upon the works of Antonio Genovesi, Ferdinando Galiani, and Mario Pagano has been established (de Mas 1969). Even in 1764 Finetti still calls Vico 'a famous philosopher, man of letters and jurist' ('celebris Philosophus, Philologus ac Jurisconsultus'; Finetti 1764 II, bk VIII, ch. 2, p. 113).

There were, however, three aspects of his work which helped to spread the impression of an isolated and original thinker – his methodology, his conception of truth, and his account of mankind's barbarian natural state, conceived by Vico paradoxically as an age of 'poetic wisdom'. As regards his methodology, it is often described as a late version of the Renaissance art of topic (that is, the science conceived as the foundation for both logic and rhetoric), but granted a new turn under the influence of Francis Bacon while remaining unaffected by the harsh critique of that tradition proffered by the school of Port Royal. Perhaps such a view neglects one aspect of Vico's method, growing out of the academic milieu with which he was completely familiar: the tradition of academic disputation that had given rise to a specific philosophical and literary genre, the 'conclusions'. In these conclusions one or several basic principles were, through a lengthy chain of propositions, applied to different fields of knowledge and their universal truth thereby definitively established. The most notorious conclusions had been published already in 1486 by Pico della Mirandola (*Conclusiones philosophicae*) whose public defence had been interdicted by the pope. Vico's concatenation of 'principles' ('degnità') is based on such disputations, still sustained with some vigour in the eighteenth century, but of course greatly influenced by Bacon's use of this method. Bacon, once again, stands at the crossroads of the complex theme of the relationship of idea and reality, philosophical truth, and empirical certainty in Vico's work, especially the *Thoughts and Conclusions on the Interpretation of Nature* (*Cogitata et visa de interpretatione naturae, sive de inventione rerum et operum*, 1607). This influence is intensely felt where Vico develops, in the first edition of his *New Science* (1725), his view of the order of human actions that presents itself in the world of history and which differs widely from the idea of logical order developed by Cartesianism. 'For thus was it disposed by nature: that men first did things through a certain human sense, without attending to them, and then, much later, they applied reflection to them and, by reasoning about their effects, contemplated their causes' (bk I, ch. 8: Vico 2002, pp. 21–2; cf. Vico 1971, p. 180). Bacon had diagnosed the problem of human ignorance in important matters of natural science as the principal reason for mankind's scant technical progress; his conclusion had been that it was indispensable to find a new way of reasoning that inverted the old abstractions of logical and classificatory proceedings, by applying itself first to the knowledge and handling of physical objects. This is a key topic for Vico's concept of a 'new science': knowledge can be derived only from handling objects ('fare') and the experience gained by this process. This knowledge may not be 'true' ('verum') in an absolute sense, because it is not general, but it is certain ('certum') because it derives from experience of what has been done, in operating upon the physical world ('factum'). When feeling despondent about formulating the tasks of a new natural science, Bacon had referred to ancient times, turning to the founders of laws, the killers of beasts, and the builders of towns who, as 'inventors of things', were rewarded with divine honours. These heroes of antiquity should be the models of the new scientists, he claimed.

Vico came to apply Bacon's logic of invention to what he conceived of as the rise of civilisation as a whole, progressing from arbitrary beginnings in the accumulation of certainties to the height of intellectual knowledge: 'The order of ideas must advance according to the order of real things', he concludes, in the third edition of the *New Science* (bk I, ch. 2, 'degnità' lxiv: Vico 1971, p. 447). This reversal of traditional logic, based on Bacon, was further enhanced by Spinoza and Gravina (cf. Pross 1987b, pp. 95–100). But the relationship between this concept of 'truth' and Vico's enquiry into the common nature of different peoples at different times that forms the basis of his 'new science' requires a more precise definition; it is a kind of 'philosophy' that relies on the authority of 'philology', as expounded in the *Universal Right*. The field on which this science is meant to operate can be excavated by antiquarian erudition in its reporting of the seemingly voluntary behaviour of the gentiles, outside the realm of the sacred history of the Jews. All other nations, therefore, are subjected to their own confused and bewildered notions of the savage world left behind by the Flood, from which protection can only be gained by barbarous and wilful acts of an authority based on the rule of the strongest. The key notions required to reconstruct this history must be taken from etymology, because the development of the mind follows a certain pattern that is best expressed in words:

Human mind is by its nature inclined to obey the senses when looking outside its body; and it is therefore only with difficulty that it can be aware of itself with the help of reflection. This principle serves as a universal axiom of etymology for all languages, because in language words are taken from bodies and their qualities in order to signify the objects of the mind and the spirit. (bk I, ch. 2, 'degnità' lxiii: Vico 1971, p. 447)

It is above all through words that the path of cultural evolution, leading from forests and huts to villages and townships and finally academies, may be reconstructed by this new science.

4 The anthropological history of man

One of the first attentive readers of Vico outside of Italy was to make use of his insight and method in explaining why and how it was possible to reconstruct the history of antiquity. In the third volume of his monumental *Primitive World* (*Monde primitif*, 1777), Antoine Court de Gébelin employed a method similar to Vico's in pointing to the need to assemble the scattered remnants and traces of mankind's self-made history contained in myths and fables. While to modern interpreters they might appear primitive, illogical, or even unintelligible, myths and fables expressed the basic needs ('besoins') of the cultures in which they were diffused and they were therefore to be considered as valuable documents of the history of the human mind, Gébelin maintained. Whereas Vico's philosophy was informed by the certainty that human history was accessible on account of its having been made by man, despite its arbitrariness in the primeval state of human ferocity, Gébelin and Herder sought to reconstruct the past in the light of the knowable needs that had shaped mankind's instruments of culture, no less in periods of remote antiquity than in contemporary civilisation. 'If one contemplated the remains of antiquity as the effects of a first cause, and searched for that cause in nature, which . . . will always be the only guide to the workings of the human mind, it would not be impossible to uncover the path pursued by the first generations and which might lead us back to them', observed Gébelin.

So as to retrieve all the links of this immense chain, it is imperative to identify an inherent principle in human nature, whose effects . . . would be invariably the same in all ages and climates and for all nations. . . . Everything is bred from our needs . . . whose persistence entails the perpetuation of the first means employed to satisfy them . . . It is enough to know man as he is at present in order to know mankind in all ages. The series of the physical and moral order are each necessary in themselves . . . Everything that . . . presents us with arts, laws, and customs has grown out of our wants and been improved by new needs; and it is because of their *refinement* that their roots can be traced to remotest antiquity . . . [whose] monuments are nothing other than the means formerly employed in order to satisfy humanity's needs, just as our own monuments bear testimony to our own needs and resources. If we confront that testimony with regard to both the present and the past . . . we will have grasped the true system and be masters of history in all ages . . . imagining ourselves as witnesses to the forging of a chain within which we constitute the last link. (Court de Gébelin 1773–82, III, pp. 3–4)

When in a draft of his *Pamphlet* of 1774 Herder asked whether any regular principle of mankind's physical and historical development could be formulated (HW, I, p. 685), he took up the same question that Vico had already treated, albeit only from a juridical and historical perspective, now reincorporating the 'physical' side of man with reference to our species' natural history or 'biological' existence as it would later be termed, integrating within Vico's scheme the dimension of anthropology. Such an approach had already been adopted by the English scholar, Richard Cumberland, in his *Laws of Nature* (*De legibus naturae*), published in 1672, the same year that had witnessed the appearance of Pufendorf's famous *Laws of Nature and Nations* (*De jure naturae et gentium*). Cumberland had directed his enquiry on the *Laws of Nature* mainly against Hobbes, advocating against the explanations of human behaviour which Hobbes had elaborated in *De corpore* and *De cive* the most recent physiological research of Thomas Willis and Richard Lower on the functions of the human heart and brain. In his second chapter Cumberland laid particular emphasis upon the physiological nature of man, which he took to favour our species' sociability, not only on the same level as other animals but also by virtue of the specific organisation that was unique to the human body (Cumberland 1672, ch. 2, §§ 23–4, pp. 132–40). The lack of any Galenic *rete mirabile* in the human brain, such as was to be found in most quadrupeds, and whose absence from the human species was regarded by Lower in his *Tractatus de corde* (1669) as evidence of higher organic development, comprised physiological proof, Cumberland supposed, that our imagination, memory, and mental faculties in general depended on the development of our brain and the rapid circulation of blood which was favoured by mankind's upright posture (Parkin 1999).

Cumberland had relied on anatomical testimony to advance his thesis that mankind was superior to animals by virtue of being anatomically and physiologically unencumbered in any particular way – a proposition he directed particularly against Hobbesian perspectives on the greater sophistication of animal instincts and the constitutional 'imbecility' of man. His arguments were to be revived in 1784 in the first volume of the *Ideas towards a Philosophy of the History of Mankind*, in which Herder takes issue with Rousseau's, Pietro Moscati's, and Kant's perspective upon man's upright posture, conceived as a sort of physical manifestation of original sin, unnaturally setting humanity apart from other animal species and thereby exposing it to ailments and diseases unique to our species (HW, III/1, p. 118). That controversy about the origins and benefits of human upright posture shows that two venerable dichotomies with respect to man's place in nature remained prevalent, notwithstanding the main thrust of Cumberland's critique of Hobbes more than a century earlier – in effect, the putative oppositions of mind and matter, on the one hand, and of civilisation and the savage state, on the other.

In 1756, Hermann Samuel Reimarus – who was to earn posthumous fame for his heretical views on Christianity – expounded, in one of the most widely circulated books of German popular philosophy of the eighteenth century, a traditionalist conception of man's position in this world. We may imagine the earth totally unpopulated, he remarked in his *The Foremost Truths of Natural Religion* (*Die vornehmsten Wahrheiten der natürlichen Religion*, 1756; ch. 3, § 2); for God could have created mankind without bodies cast in his image – that is, he might have created us purely as souls which require no solid place within which to reside. 'Are the maggots essential to the cheese?', Reimarus asked in a bizarre comparison of the relationship of men and their dwelling place, to which Herder opposed Cicero's adage about the world as 'the common house of gods and men', in which everything is made for the benefit of its inhabitants (*De natura deorum*, bk II, § 154). Nature brings forth life on this earth, which follows a pattern of development until it reaches the most complicated form of organisation, in man; human life, therefore, cannot be regarded as set apart from other forms of animate beings. This perspective on the naturalisation of humanity, without regard to religious scruples pertaining to the immateriality of the soul, Herder shared with Charles Bonnet, certainly a most godly man who, however, did not hesitate in his *Contemplation of Nature* to pronounce that, in order to conceive a notion of man's soul, one must first scrutinise his corporeal existence (*Contemplation de la nature*, 1770, I, p. lxxxviii: 'C'est toujours par le Physique qu'il faut passer pour arriver à l'âme'). The same recklessness characterises Herder's approach to the concept of 'culture', in his refusal to admit a distinction between 'culture' as means of self-preservation and as the framework of an enlightened 'civilisation'. Much of the evidence from missionaries and travellers since the discovery of the New World had contributed to an unshakeable belief that God had created two fundamental types of human beings fit for different forms of communal life: civilised and savage nations. By the grace of God it might one day prove possible for civilised tribes to attain enlightenment themselves and thereby scale the heights of European culture. According to this scenario, culture was conceived as having been bestowed on enlightened people, much in the manner that the Old Testament had been granted to God's chosen people. To lack culture or enlightenment was to be without the prospect of salvation. Whereas the German historian Christoph Meiners dangerously overstated this view in his *Elements of the History of Mankind* (*Grundriss der Geschichte der Menschheit*, 1785) by distinguishing between two fundamentally different 'races' of Celts and Mongols, of which only the first would be capable of civilisation, Herder insisted from the outset of his *Ideas* that there was no tribe or nation that did not have a claim to attribute to itself some 'culture', even in the most rudimentary stage of social organization (HW, III/1, Vorrede, p. 9).

Herder's philosophy of history, conceived as an account of the development of man as a natural and social being, is a combined elaboration, indeed, of the 'three histories' of Enlightenment, that is, natural history, the history of the human mind, and the history of society, as propounded by other commentators in the mid- to late eighteenth century. In so far as it concentrated upon the place of mankind, natural history in the age of Enlightenment – largely inspired by comparative anatomists of an earlier age, such as Claude Perrault and Edward Tyson, as well as by the contemporary physiology of Pieter Camper and Louis-Jean-Marie Daubenton – was chiefly devoted to establishing the human race's links with, or distinctions from, other species in the great *scala naturae* or 'chain of being'. As pursued in the *Natural History* of Buffon or by the philosopher Bonnet, definitions of man were taken to turn upon his relation to the next highest primates in that chain – the great apes – which, at least until the late 1770s, when the chimpanzee came to be identified as a different species, were collectively termed 'orang-utans', a Malay expression meaning 'men of the woods'. When arguments for the immortality of the human soul and the spirituality of man's understanding had come to seem less theologically compelling than in previous generations, it appeared, likewise, that neither reason nor language could any longer be regarded as the centrally distinguishing feature separating man from all other animals, in part because animals were also manifestly sentient creatures, in part because reason had come to be identified as a virtual rather than intrinsic faculty and language as a skill which had to be learned in society, in each case placing the burden of man's superiority over other animals more on his education than his nature. Descartes himself had paved the way to eighteenth-century materialism by describing animals as mere machines, and, in 1748, Julien Offray de La Mettrie adopted the same perspective with regard to the human race, sustaining in his *L'Homme machine* that man formed part of the animal kingdom and that the same natural laws governed all animate beings. Pursuing a theme he derived especially from Locke, La Mettrie contended that our apparently supernatural gifts of reason and language were only the consequences of the organisation of our faculties, whose development followed a prescribed pattern.

Starting from such premises eighteenth-century commentators on the *histoire de l'esprit humain* tried to explain that our cultures are neither the product of human reason nor the outcome of our unique spirituality, but are instead expressive of the emotional values attributed to external objects which persons try to manipulate and come to identify by ascribing arbitrary signs to them. The influence of Condillac in developing such ideas, originating ultimately in Locke, was decisive, and its principal contribution to the philosophy of history in the Enlightenment turned on its conception of the human understanding in terms of the development of signs – that is, its theory of language (Aarsleff 1982). First in his *Essay on the Origin of Human Knowledge* (*Essai sur l'origine des connoissances humaines*, 1746), then in the *Traité des systèmes* (1749), and finally in his *Traité des sensations* (1754), Condillac attempted to make plain that to engage in thinking or to have thoughts is just a consistent way of linking signs, which are themselves to be understood as the articulation of sensations. The analysis of every mental process, he argued, can trace its source ultimately to the first emotional impact – perhaps of desire or fear or interest – stirred by an external object, which would have inspired our forebears in the early childhood of human history to covet or recoil from it in an animistic way. In their respective courses of development both the mental faculties of children and the different stages of our civilisation should accordingly be understood in terms of the evolution of signs and the progress of language.

As constructed by Hume, Kames, Ferguson, Millar, Smith, and other luminaries of the Scottish Enlightenment, what came to be termed 'the history of civil society' was conceived in a similar way but with reference to other practices and institutions in addition to language, as a natural history of man which described our species' ascent from the state of nature to the domain of culture or civilisation. When couched in idioms drawn from the incipient science of political economy, conjectural histories of civilisation, particularly after the mid-eighteenth century, were conceived of as mankind's stadial passage from its original condition of barbarism by way of improvements of its modes of sustenance, first, in tribes characterised by hunting and fishing, then in pastoral and predominantly nomadic communities, then under regimes of agricultural production, and, finally, in commercial societies with their civil laws regulating property and trade. The refinement of arbitrary signs and the progress of the division of labour would thus each come to constitute a crucial measure of the progress of civilisation.

What Condillac had endeavoured to achieve was nothing less than the transformation of traditional metaphysics into a 'genetic epistemology' as Georges Gusdorf has termed it, or a 'temporalising' of the chain of being (Gusdorf 1971; Lovejoy 1936). Instead of attempting to fathom the essence of mind, Condillac maintained that he had instead sought to demonstrate the ways in which the mind works (*Essai sur l'origine des connoissances humaines*: Condillac 1973, p. 99). Instead of assuming the existence of parallel but unconnected worlds of physical reality on the one hand, and mind on the other, he tried to sketch a laboratory experiment of the awakening of human life and, with it, the development of the so-called faculties of mind, out of pure matter. The statue he portrays in his *Traité des sensations* passes from its condition of mere receptivity in becoming impressionable and sensitive, and subsequently reminiscent and reflective, through the retention of its first impressions by the sheer fact of being aware of them.

To remember, to compare, to judge, to distinguish, to imagine, to be astonished, to have abstract ideas . . . to know general and particular truths, are but different ways of being attentive. To have passions, to love . . . to hope, to abhor . . . are but different ways of desiring. Being attentive and to desire are originally just sensations. We must conclude that sensation embraces all the faculties of the mind. (*Traité des sensations*, I, vii, § 2: Condillac 1947–9, I, p. 239b)

Even the highest stages of abstract reasoning, Condillac believed, are nothing other than transformations of sensual impression. Herder was to take up this hypothesis, together with its elaboration in Diderot's *Lettre sur les aveugles* (Letter on Blindness, 1749), when in 1765, shortly after having abandoned his studies with Kant in Königsberg, he remarked that 'all philosophy must be reduced to anthropology' (cf. Pross, in HW, II, pp. 1133–4), adding that the fields of logic, aesthetics, and psychology should be encompassed within the boundaries of the *histoire de l'esprit humain*. Herder's interest in the physiology of sense-impressions and its implications for an anthropology that embraced the history of the human mind informed his projects on the human senses which he drafted in the late 1760s, together with the fourth of his *Critical Promenades* (*Viertes Kritisches Wäldchen*, 1769); the results of his reflections were the first version of his *Plastik* (1770) as well as his celebrated *Treatise on the Origin of Language* for which in 1771 he won the prize in a

Berlin Academy competition and in which for the first time he took up Cumberland's speculations on the physiological basis of our cognitive and social faculties. The same problem and the same themes were to be pursued in the three versions of his treatise on the relationship between cognition and sensitivity (*Vom Erkennen und Empfinden der menschlichen Seele*, 1774, 1775, 1778) and in the first and second part of his *Ideas* (1784–5).

The implications for comparative cultural history and ethnology of the study of the physical attributes of human nature had of course been central to Montesquieu's theory of the physiological effects of climate as elaborated principally in the fourteenth book of the *Spirit of the Laws*, based on the writings of Jean-Baptiste Dubos and John Arbuthnot, and they can be traced to Hippocrates. In 1723 Jean-François Lafitau had addressed the subject of men's moral relations in connection with their organic nature and physical environment by way of comparing cultures across continents and centuries, attempting to show in his *Moeurs des sauvages ameriquains, comparées aux moeurs des premiers temps* that the Hurons of North America bore great similarities to the Greek and Trojan heroes described by Homer. Lafitau's analogies and comparisons essentially implied that all cultures matured in similar ways and pursued similar trajectories of development, as evidenced by their tools, their artefacts, and their conventions and beliefs at comparable points of their evolution. Such perspectives were not only concerned with the interpenetration of physical and cultural anthropology which, after the age of Enlightenment, were to become separate disciplines taught in different university faculties. In addressing the totality of men's relations in their diverse geographical settings they also greatly contributed to the study of the roots of civic and ethnic cohesion which made nations and national allegiances possible, as well to the incipient science of social psychology.

5 The regularity and plurality of culture

For Enlightenment thinkers who supposed that mankind was basically everywhere the same, it was crucially important to account for diversity and the world's plurality of races and cultures. If the eighteenth-century discoveries of Australia and the islands of the Pacific had identified primitive cultures that appeared to resemble ancient tribes in European civilisation's own infancy, how, by contrast, could the transformation of the Mongols from imperialist warriors to peaceful nomads over several centuries, or, alternatively, the decay of the once majestic culture of China over a period of 2,000 years, be explained? In his *Enquiry concerning Human Understanding* (1748), David

Hume advocated the pursuit of a new kind of science, a *natural history of man*, to supplant the old histories of dynasties with their careers twisted in indeterminate ways by fortuitous and arbitrary actions. 'Mankind are so much the same, in all times and places, that history informs us of nothing new or strange in this particular', he remarked.

Its chief use is only to discover the constant and universal principles of human varieties of circumstances and situations, and furnishing us with materials from which we may form our observations and become acquainted with the regular springs of human action and behaviour. These records of wars, intrigues, factions, and revolutions, are so many collections of experiments, by which the politician or moral philosopher fixes the principles of his science, in the same manner as the physician or natural philosopher becomes acquainted with the nature of plants, minerals, and other external objects. (Hume 1975, pp. 83–4)

The sum of events that forms the history of mankind does not differ markedly from the material studied by the scientist or natural historian, who must rely on the constancy of natural forces in order to formulate the laws of matter. The facts recounted by historians and ethnographers, analogously, must be tested by scientists of human behaviour to establish the existence of uniformity in human actions and reasoning. The business and activities of men had to be closely examined in the rich variety of their cultural stratagems, Hume insisted. The science of human nature which he envisaged was not premised on narrow assumptions about men's universal conformity to a limited set of fixed principles; in establishing the diversity of the motives or springs of human action it was necessary to observe and record individuals' behaviour in all its complexity. 'We must not . . . expect that . . . all men, in the same circumstances, will always act precisely in the same manner, without making any allowance for the diversity of characters, prejudices, and opinions', he wrote.

Such a uniformity in every particular, is found in no part of nature. On the contrary, from observing the variety of conduct in different men, we are enabled to form a greater variety of maxims . . . I grant it possible to find some actions, which seem to have no regular connection with any known motives, and are exceptions to all the measures of conduct which have ever been established for the government of men. (Hume 1975, pp. 85–6)

In 1767 Ferguson developed a similar line of reasoning with respect to our comprehension of human motives, actions, and patterns of behaviour. 'Men, in general', he observed in his *Essay on the History of Civil Society*, are sufficiently disposed to occupy themselves in forming projects and schemes: but he who would scheme and project for others, will find an opponent in every person who is disposed to scheme for himself . . . Every step and every movement of the multitude, even in what are termed enlightened ages, are made with equal blindness to the future . . . No constitution is formed by concert, no government is copied from a plan. (Ferguson 1995b, pp. 119–20)

It was therefore plain, he concluded, that 'nations stumble upon establishments, which are indeed the result of human action, but not the execution of any human design'. Ferguson attributes this remark to the famous *Mémoires* of the Cardinal de Retz, published posthumously in 1717, and the philosophy of history it articulates was to catch wide attention in the second half of the nineteenth century by way of Marx's remark, in the opening section of his *Eighteenth Brumaire of Louis Bonaparte* (1852), to the effect that 'men make their own history but not of their own free will; not under circumstances they themselves have chosen but under the given and inherited circumstances with which they are directly confronted'. While morality pertains to what humans do rather than to how they are made, while 'the world of civil society is shaped by its own subjects', as Vico had remarked in the third edition of his *New Science* (bk 1, ch. 3: Vico 1971, p. 461), the science of human nature to which so many leading thinkers of the Enlightenment subscribed was addressed to causes and consequences rather than a narrative of intentions.

Herder's adoption of such perspectives on both the regularity of human behaviour and its variety in diverse regions and times accounts for the sometimes puzzling co-existence of universalism and conventionalism in his philosophy of history, generating, on the one hand, his insistence upon 'laws' of the historical process, based on human nature itself, and, on the other, his emphasis on the singularity and uniqueness of the life of nations, in their dependence upon peculiarly local habitats and conventions. According to his philosophy, cultures and the crafts associated with them formed patterns and methods of mankind's self-preservation, giving rise to appropriate rituals of social behaviour. Practitioners of the science of man as it came to be developed most particularly by Scottish thinkers of the mid- to late eighteenth century frequently addressed such questions with reference to systems of property and labour, technical innovations, and the tools of production characteristic of different forms of society and different historical epochs, out of which the science of economics, on the one hand, and what came to be termed 'historical materialism', on the other, were to arise. In France similar questions were to be posed by Goguet in his *De l'origine des loix, des arts, et des sciences,* and Goguet's account of the development of technical knowledge and its applications in antiquity from the Egyptians to the early Greeks was to influence both Winckelmann, in his *History of the Art of Antiquity* (*Geschichte der Kunst des Altertums,* 1764), and Herder, no less in the polemical pamphlet of his youth, *Another Philosophy of History* (1774), than in his mature *Ideas towards a Philosophy of the History of Mankind* (1784–91).

But Herder's invective against the Eurocentrism of his enlightened contemporaries, as it appears in both works, owed more to a related but somewhat different theme about the links between technology and morality, and about the interpenetration of the natural and the social world, propounded or implicit in the writings of Cumberland, Condillac, Hume, Ferguson, Goguet, and other Enlightenment philosophers of history. Like Montesquieu in his focus on the spirit of the laws, and upon the natural forces and psychological dispositions which determined the character of nations, Herder was anxious to describe the social systems of diverse peoples in their totality, with reference to the geographical and psychological factors which shaped their cultures in particularly distinctive ways, appropriate to local circumstances. 'Each state has its period of growth, maturity and decay to which its arts and sciences conform', he observed in his *Dissertation on the Influence of Government on Science and of Science on Government* (1779), which presents itself as a draft of the complex treatment of this theme in the *Ideas* (cf. Herder 1877–1913, IX, p. 375). 'The specific sciences and arts of Greece, unsurpassed by those of any other age or peoples after more than two thousand years, have been daughters of her legislation, of her political institutions, especially of the freedom . . . of common enterprise and competition' (Herder 1877–1913, IX, p. 328).

What, in his *Pamphlet* of 1774, he had objected to most in the philosophies of 'the so-called enlightenment and civilisation of the world' was the narrowness of their approach to particular cultures even while they traced the long trajectory of cultural progress as a whole (HW, I, p. 664). The 'general, philosophical, philanthropic tenor of our century' in the works of historians and philosophers, such as Voltaire, Robertson, or Iselin, whom he addressed explicitly in his *Pamphlet,* was, in its insistence on the achievements of the modern world, insensitive to the characteristic features of past ages (HW, I, pp. 618–19). That philosophy seemed to him incapable of comprehending, for example, the social meaning and function of corporations, guilds, craftsmen, scholarship, and the unsophisticated simplicities of late medieval (or early modern) cultures in which these institutions and professionals proudly thrived. Herder often expressed some dissatisfaction with the otherwise greatly estimable Montesquieu, whose generalisations about diverse peoples he took to be rather unspecific and unsystematic, husks of ideas plucked from their contexts. Yet he pursued themes that in Scotland and elsewhere were associated with Montesquieu above all other eighteenth-century thinkers, and Herder's censuring of Montesquieu was as much as anything else a lament on account of his not having been true to himself, on account of the – inevitable – deficiencies of commonplace summaries (HW, I, p. 611). Even while insisting, in his *Ideas*, that there is just one human race or species, Herder describes its nurture, maturation, and metamorphosis in terms already made popular before him by Montesquieu, and which, while borrowed ultimately from Lucretius, came to be cast by Montesquieu in an idiom which would shape the language of history of the late eighteenth century. Within that singular species of mankind, Herder, no less than Montesquieu, was convinced that language constituted the identity and coherence of each social group and formed barriers against even closely related neighbours and kinsmen (*Treatise on the Origin of Language*: HW, II, p. 345).

To explain national differences within the framework of one species whose members were all prompted by the same law of self-preservation, he sometimes concentrated upon migratory or seafaring peoples compelled to adopt new cultural patterns which would eventually lead to their forming a new nation. 'The Phoenicians . . . became, despite their affinity to the Egyptians, the contrary of their national culture', he observed in his *Another Philosophy of History* (1774). For

the Egyptians . . . hated the sea, hated foreigners, and just remained at home in order to develop all the . . . arts of their own country. The Phoenicians retired to a coast behind a mountain range and a desert, and they did so in order to create a new world on the sea. Suddenly human industry abandoned the heavy work of building pyramids and the tilling of the earth and stooped to the playfulness of petty occupations. Instead of shaping . . . obelisks, the art of masonry turned to useful ships. The mute, erect pyramid was transformed into the mobile, talking mast of the ship. (HW, I, pp. 603–4)

The Egyptian empire, defined by the borders of the Nile valley and threatened by nomads beyond them, had to create within its encircled and endangered space a political, religious, and cultural system that was of necessity monolithic, Herder believed. The Phoenicians, by contrast, having settled in a more confined area between the Lebanese mountains and the Mediterranean, had no option but to turn to the open sea and to navigating gods, their ships being made to serve the same symbolic function as the obelisk did for the Egyptians.

In pursuing not only the cultural but also the theological implications of the human race's task of survival under different conditions, Herder drew some inspiration from Charles de Brosses's *Du culte des dieux fétiches* (1760), in which the evolution of religious practice from fetishism to the worship of statues or saints was portrayed as preserving the original function of rites even while their objects of devotion were transformed. 'All the instruments invented or discovered by art or science, what else are they but signs or substitutions, denoting a peculiar feature or helping to achieve a premeditated aim?', he asked in a manuscript draft of his *Ideas* (Herder 1877–1913, XIII, p. 368). The words and symbols we employ, and the artefacts we manufacture, are nothing other than our own denotations or constructions of reality, in portraying our languages, arts, and social institutions in general as constitutive elements of what we term 'culture'. Herder's reputation as a Counter-Enlightenment thinker as portrayed by Isaiah Berlin is belied by his theory of culture and the sources upon which he drew (Berlin 1976). From d'Alembert, Condillac, Court de Gébelin, Monboddo, and especially James Harris and other eighteenth-century contributors to the *histoire de l'esprit humain*, he derived notions of the symbolic meanings of language and the essential human needs which language articulates. From Spinoza, Cumberland, and Hume, he adopted perspectives upon human nature in general which joined the moral dimensions of our behaviour to our physical constitutions and the pressures posed by our environments. From Ferguson he learned not only that men's social history reflects the unintended consequences of their actions, but also that nature and art are intermingled and often barely distinguishable in our conduct. 'Art itself is natural to man', Ferguson had asserted in his *Essay on the History of Civil Society*, adding that man 'is in some measure the artificer of his own frame, as well as his fortune . . . destined, from the first age of his being, to invent and contrive. . . . We may desire to direct his love of improvement to its proper object, we may wish for stability of conduct; but we mistake human nature, if we wish for a termination of labour, or a scene of repose' (Ferguson 1995b, pp. 12–13).

To overcome the breach between man's 'natural state' and the 'state of society', which Rousseau had attempted to bridge only by invoking our species' miraculous faculty of 'perfectibility', Herder turned to this definition of man as 'artificer of his own frame' which in Ferguson's formulation embraced a reference to Pico della Mirandola's celebrated treatise on human dignity (*De dignitate hominis*, 1485–6). But, unlike Ferguson, in assembling

The new light of reason

his own philosophy of history Herder laid special emphasis upon mankind's physiological constitution. Already, in his *Treatise on the Origin of Language* (1770), he had stressed the importance of understanding man's place in nature and the affinity of our species with others in the animal world. It is man's freedom from the constraints of animal instincts, he had argued in the *Treatise*, that makes possible our acquisition of speech and reason as manifested through our use of arbitrary signs in language and writing; in the *Ideas* he added that this transforms man into the 'first freeborn of creation' (*Ideas*, bk IV, iv: HW, III/1, p. 135). Herder's reflections on our species' superiority over the apes by virtue of our upright posture should be read within the context of European debates from the 1760s to the 1780s about the physical characteristics alleged to set man apart from all other creatures. This debate, enhanced by the discovery of the function of the occipital hole by Buffon's collaborator Daubenton (1764), Camper's studies on the anatomy of apes, and Goethe's discovery of the intermaxillary bone (1784), entailed for Herder the corollary of regarding man, physically, as an integrated part of the animal kingdom, albeit in the most complex form evolved by the general type of life whose existence Buffon had assumed. It is precisely the singularity of the upright posture of our species among the quadrupeds that frees man's hands and his mind from earthbound instincts. Human speech and what is commonly termed 'reason' are therefore nothing but substitutes for instincts that mankind lacks, even if they separate him henceforth from his 'elder brothers', the animals with which he shares the earth. The arbitrariness of human behaviour in the absence of compelling instincts facilitated for Herder man's adaptation to different environments, by forcing him to invent the means peculiar to his species – language, social codes, religions, and traditions – that enabled him to survive.

As distinct from Rousseau and from – the otherwise greatly admired – Lord Monboddo (*Of the Origin and Progress of Language*, 1773–92), and in vehement opposition to Moscati and Kant, Herder sought to establish the case for mankind's uniqueness as a species on naturalistic and physiological grounds alone, with reference to the structure and organisation of the human body. And as distinct from Henry Home's (Lord Kames's) polygenist account of the multiple races of man (*Sketches of the History of Man*, 1774), Herder put forward a monogenetic theory of humanity's origins, in the light of which the emergence of varieties within our species could be explained with reference to migrations and the accumulated effects of adjustments to diverse terrains, climates, and diets. Because he supposed that the rudiments of social life and institutions had been established to enable our forebears to achieve their aim of collective self-preservation, he thought there was a difference only of degree and not of kind between so-called 'enlightened' or 'civilised' nations, on the one hand, and 'primitive' nations, on the other. Montesquieu, in his *Spirit of the Laws*, had drawn a distinction between the peoples of the south, so bountifully supplied by nature that they felt no need to free themselves from its grip, as against those of the north, who, by dint of their industry in an inclement world, created cultures of emancipation from nature's control; his theory of the connections between commerce and republican government was, at bottom, climatological. Voltaire, in his *Essai sur les moeurs* of 1756, distinguished cultures in much the same manner as Montesquieu, except that he aligned the east with the south and the north with the west, along geographical axes that were also temporal, in so far, as he put it, that 'the fertile countries were the first to be peopled and civilized. The whole of the east, from Greece to the extremities of our hemisphere, was already famous, before we knew enough of this in order to recognize that we were barbarians' (Voltaire 1963a, I, p. 197).

In adopting these dichotomies between cultures in terms of climate and geography Herder placed particular emphasis upon their third dimension, time, describing the history of civilisation as comprised essentially of two stages, first, ancient history, tracing the growth and decay of empires from China, India, and Mesopotamia, to Egypt, Greece, and Rome; and, second, modern history, in effect, the emergence and development of European culture, with all its technical and institutional variations. Conceived in this fashion, perhaps the most crucial distinction that set modernity apart from both antiquity and the late middle ages in the wake of the Reformation turned on the notion of culture itself, in so far as the ancient world was mainly populated by nations whose peoples shared a collective identity with either civic or communal gods, whereas the modern world, from its beginning with the decline of the Roman Empire and the rise of Christianity, was threatened by the tendency towards absolute power of papal and feudal government. The systematic rule of the pope over each person's body and soul and the establishment of feudalism in Charlemagne's vast empire entailed the loss of the religious as well as intellectual freedom and patriotic devotion of their subjects. It was only in the aftermath of the Crusades that, with the collapse of the monolithic structures of church and feudal state, liberty and enterprise returned, in the communities of Italy, on the Rhine, or in the merchant-cities of the Hanse, only in order to give way, after a brief respite, once more to the complicated machinery of power of the contemporary absolutist state. Like Rousseau, but fundamentally at odds with most progressive thinkers of the age of Enlightenment, Herder espoused political ideals that were at once communitarian and republican; the state, therefore, held for him no value in itself. And, as passionately as Rousseau, Ferguson or, before them, Spinoza, Herder believed that 'the purpose of the state is, to maintain the liberty of its citizens' (Spinoza 1972, I, p. 604; HW, III/2, pp. 542–3). However much attached in his ethics to the liberating principle of autonomy, Kant, in his politics, seemed to Herder to subscribe to the venerable tradition of absolutist natural law, according to which, as his former teacher had put it in his *Universal History from a Cosmopolitan Perspective* (1784), 'man is an animal that needs a master' ('ein Tier, das einen Herrn nötig hat'). Herder, by contrast, believed that in this respect above all Kant had got his principles back to front, since it would have been much truer to say that 'a man who needs a master is an animal' (*Ideas*, bk IX, iv: 'der Mensch, der einen Herren nötig hat, ist ein Tier': HW, III/1, p. 337).

When the French Revolution in 1789 swept away the *ancien régime*, an occasion seemed to present itself for Herder's notion of liberty to be put into practice by political advocates. But Germany was not France, and Herder had not written a *Contrat social*. The enlightened absolutism of Frederick II of Prussia and of Emperor Joseph II had been ailing in the 1780s, and both monarchs died in quick succession, Frederick in 1786, Joseph in 1790, after having been forced to abandon or revise their reforms. Their successors were ready to turn the clocks back within their own countries and tried to stem the tide of their times in Europe: when Frederick William II of Prussia and Emperor Leopold II met in Pillnitz in 1791, by agreeing to restore the throne to Louis XVI they produced the revolutionary wars that were to be continued by Napoleon and were to wipe out the old Holy Roman Empire. Under such auspices, Herder's communitarian notions could not find much favour with political theoreticians, and the emerging German historical school of law, advocating the 'Volksgeist' as the basis of positive law, definitely took more from Justus Möser than from Herder, notwithstanding many appealing formulations in his writings. Such was the case, for instance, with regard to Friedrich Carl von Savigny in his *On the Vocation of our Time for Legislation and Jurisprudence* (*Vom Beruf unserer Zeit für Gesetzgebung und Rechtswissenschaft*, 1814). Barnard's opinion that political romanticism reversed Herder's political concepts should be considered in the light of Otto Dann's sobering diagnosis that 'as for the question of nationalism one might speak of a forgetfulness (or suppression?) of Herder' in the relevant political and juridical literature of the nineteenth century (Barnard 1964,

p. 187; Dann 1993, p. 309). German conservatism after the Congress of Vienna of 1815 is much more imbued with the ideology of obedience to the state, according to Kant's and Fichte's interpretation of the political meaning of liberty, embracing the sacrifice of their freedom by the members of a community in favour of a corporate state, ordained by God, according to the image drawn by Novalis in his *Christianity or Europe* (*Die Christenheit oder Europa*, 1799).

III

Natural jurisprudence and the science of legislation

9

German natural law

KNUD HAAKONSSEN

1   The reception of modern natural law

In order to appreciate the role of natural law in the eighteenth century, it is important to note that most Protestant Europeans saw it as a modern phenomenon. Seventeenth- and eighteenth-century thinkers were well aware that natural law was prominent in both ancient and medieval thought, but in their eyes it acquired a new role with the division of Christianity and the emergence of modern statehood. The concern of modern natural law was to find a basis for moral life that, without conflicting with the tenets of Christianity, was neutral with respect to confessional religion. Natural law was thus central to one of the defining debates of the Enlightenment, namely whether and to what extent the cognitive, including moral, powers of humanity were adequate to the conduct of life in this world. While all the sciences were invoked to this purpose, in discussions of the foundation, nature, and extent of natural law, that central issue was particularly explicit.

The debate ran deep in every Protestant community – Reformed, Lutheran, and episcopalian – for at issue was the basis for the social world. Natural law's replacement of revealed religion with natural religion led to a highly ambivalent view of morality and its institutional forms, ranging from the family and the economy to the state, as either the creation or the expression of natural man. Not least, the idea of religion as both a common bond and a shield between ruler and ruled was called into question, as was the status of the church.

The debate had to a large extent been provoked by Hobbes and Pufendorf, according to whom God had deposited humanity within a world in which moral characteristics were only instituted by the exertion of man's will.[1] The key question for such voluntarists was what guidance has humanity in this

---

[1] For general surveys of early modern natural law see Gierke 1934; Haakonssen 1996a, ch. 1; Haakonssen 2004; Hartung 1998, pt 1; Hinrichs 1848–52; Hunter and Saunders 2002; Ilting 1983; Schneewind 1998, pt 1; Stolleis 1988, ch. 6; Tarello 1976; Thieme 1954; Tuck 1999, chs. 1–5; Wolf 1963.

effort? According to Hobbes, it had a minimal natural law stating the rational precepts of self-interest, to which Pufendorf added humanity's natural sociability, though whether the latter was the expression of a moral faculty or an implication of self-interest is disputed (Palladini 1990). In the ensuing debate, which was significantly influenced by Richard Cumberland, attacks on the new natural law were generally to the effect that its voluntarism was tied to egoism (Cumberland 2005; Haakonssen 2000; Parkin 1999; Schneewind 1995). We find this, at the theological level, in both Anglican and Lutheran reactions and, at the philosophical level, in 'rationalistic' thinkers, such as Samuel Clarke and Leibniz, the latter of whom formulated a neo-scholastic theory of natural law (Beiser 1996, ch. 7; Riley 1996; Schneider 1967; Sève 1989). Equally universally, voluntarist natural law was defended through attempts to show that the exercise of will that is naturally enjoined on man encompasses the happiness of all humanity. The major defendant in this vein was Christian Thomasius, who formulated a theory of natural law as the specification and rule of the passions that make social life possible.

At the turn of the eighteenth century we find, then, a major European discussion forming a three-cornered contest between, first, a variety of traditional confessional standpoints according to which morality has its basis in revelation; secondly, the new, provocative voluntarism started by Hobbes and Pufendorf and continued by Thomasius; and, thirdly, a rationalist and realist view of natural law that owed significant debts to scholastic, especially Thomist, theory and typified by Clarke, Leibniz, and Christian Wolff. The interaction between these intellectual currents was, however, exceedingly complex, being often overdetermined by particular cultural and political circumstances. Hobbes's voluntarism was premised on a view of the divinity as so inscrutable that the sovereign could legislate for both religious and civil life. In the case of Pufendorf and Thomasius, voluntarism was accompanied by fideism, so that man was allowed access to the divine will in religious matters, while denied it in civil life, where convention and sovereign rule held sway. For their part, the rationalists could insist that natural reason was indeed capable of knowing the transcendent concepts and moral laws that issued from the divine mind, even if they thus imbued human reason with some of the key features of divine understanding. These fluid intellectual lines must be understood in their interaction with the religious and political circumstances in which they unfolded, as can be seen from the British and German instances (cf. Saunders and Hunter 2003).

Perhaps the most important contrast between Germany and Britain is that voluntarism of the Pufendorfian variety never became a dominant force in the latter. In fact, the line of thought represented by Pufendorf and Hobbes was diffused during the subsequent century. The idea of moral and political institutions as purely conventional was developed in an original manner by David Hume and Adam Smith, who made the conventions a matter of historical development. Mostly, however, English and Scottish thinkers were concerned to transform and undermine the voluntarist basis for Pufendorf's natural law system (Haakonssen 1996a, pp. 43–4n). England possessed within the Anglican Church an unbroken realist tradition in moral thought that variously sought inspiration from Thomist Aristotelianism, as with Richard Hooker and Nathaniel Culverwell, and from neo-Platonism, as with the Cambridge Platonists and the third earl of Shaftesbury (Beiser 1996; Greene and MacCallum 1971; Munz 1952; Passmore 1951; Rivers 1991–2000, II). To these lines of thought was added a strong revival of Stoicism (Oestreich 1982; Stewart 1991). When this tradition was challenged by Hobbesian and Pufendorfian voluntarism, a set of eclectic compromises was struck, beginning with the Cambridge Platonists but developed mainly by Scottish thinkers, most notably Francis Hutcheson (Haakonssen 1996a, chs. 2, 6–8). A line of argument was pursued that conceded to Platonism the idea of an inherently benevolent power in human nature, whilst at the same time accepting the voluntarist emphasis on the imposition of duties through the prescription of moral ends. The balancing of these two notions came to be conceived of as amenable to an empirical science of morality. It is possible to link these intellectual compromises to the broader movements to accommodate the Anglican Church in England to dissenting tendencies and to modernise the Presbyterian Kirk in Scotland, not least through new university curricula. In Germany, by contrast, the absence of a single politico-religious settlement, compounded by the multiplicity of polities, gave rise to a more fractured state of affairs. In Brandenburg-Prussia, for example, where there was no established church and the Calvinist dynasty had to rule over a powerful Lutheran church and estates, Pufendorf's and Thomasius's radically anti-metaphysical voluntarism was well entrenched in the law faculties, where it promised to deliver de-confessionalised officials to the state. Yet, in many philosophy and theology faculties, the metaphysical approach to ethics and law remained deeply entrenched, as we can see in the line that ran from Leibniz and the seventeenth-century Protestant scholastics through Wolff to Kant.

The Anglo-Scottish transformation of Pufendorf was due not only to the indigenous tradition but also to the way in which he was received in Britain via a 'Dutch–Swiss' filter. The Lutheran philosopher's work had been adopted as an ally by leading Huguenots in the debates about their perilous situation after the Revocation of the Edict of Nantes in 1685, as is apparent in Gershom Carmichael's Glasgow lectures of the 1690s and in his edition of Pufendorf's *De officio hominis et civis* (On the Duties of Man and Citizen). The crucial link was Jean Barbeyrac, whose French translations, with extensive introductions and annotations, of Pufendorf's *De jure naturae et gentium* (*Le droit de la nature et des gens* – The Law of Nature and Nations, 1706) and *De officio* (*Les Devoirs de l'homme et de citoyen*, 1707) were widely circulated and translated into several other languages. Both in Switzerland and Holland, Barbeyrac inspired a number of Reformed natural law thinkers, of whom one of lasting importance was Jean Jacques Burlamaqui.[2]

One cannot speak of a Barbeyrac school, but his voluntarist natural law, while underdeveloped, was marked by a distinctive core of historical and theoretical importance. In attempting to meet the challenge of the French king's assertion of a right to sovereignty over his subjects' religious beliefs, Huguenot opinion had polarised. On the one hand, Pierre Jurieu turned away from a traditional divine right theory of sovereignty and adopted a contractarian theory of monarchomach origin, combining an idea of resistance with faith in providential intervention of the kind that had apparently occurred in England in 1688. On the other hand, like Pufendorf's and Thomasius's, Pierre Bayle's scepticism about the possibility of moral and political knowledge led him to argue that religious toleration was a sovereign gift which, despite temporary setbacks, was most likely to be granted by governments that were the least influenced by changing opinion, namely absolute monarchies (Dreitzel 1997; Laursen 1989). The focus of these debates was conscience. Barbeyrac's importance lay in analysing this concept in order to rebut Bayle's scepticism and reach a more prudent political standpoint than Jurieu's.[3]

Conscience was the moral power that enabled people to live socially. It was the basis for political society and its institutions. Toleration of the free use of conscience was, therefore, essential; it had to be treated as a right;

---

2 For Carmichael see Carmichael 1724, 2002; Mautner 1996; Moore and Silverthorne 1983, 1984; and ch. 10 in the present volume Moore. For Barbeyrac see Barbeyrac 1709, 1728, 1996, 2003; Dufour 1976; Goyard-Fabre 1996a, pp. 11–74; Hochstrasser 1993, 1995. Cf. Brühlmeier 1995; Dufour 1976, ch. 2; Gagnebin 1944; Harvey 1937; Holzhey and Zurbuchen 1993; Korkman 2001; Larrère 1992, ch. 1; Luig 1972; Meylan 1937; Moore 1988; Othmer 1970; Rosenblatt 1997, pp. 93–101; Zurbuchen 1991, chs. 5–6. For Burlamaqui see Burlamaqui 1747, 1751, 1766–8, 1775, 2006; Brühlmeier 1995; Dufour 1976, ch. 2; Gagnebin 1944; Harvey 1937; Holzhey and Zurbuchen 1993; Larrère 1992, ch. 1; Rosenblatt 1997, pp. 93–101; Zurbuchen 1991, ch. 5.
3 Barbeyrac's arguments are spread throughout the annotations to his major editions, but he gives a concentrated brief exposition in 1749, pp. 1–14 and 71–5.

a right by which sovereignty was, consequently, limited. This meant that sovereign government was best understood as a conventional – contractual – device for protection, as opposed to a divine right. Further, unlike that of Hobbes and Pufendorf, Barbeyrac's political contract supported a residual right of resistance in the people, even if 'the people' had to be understood as the morally qualified, educated, upper magistracy and clergy. In short, Barbeyrac invoked both Lockean and traditional Calvinist resistance theory. While an unconstrained conscience was a right, according to Barbeyrac, it was, so to speak, an inescapable right which might as well be described as a duty: each person *had* to judge personally in moral and religious matters. Another construal was to call this right *inalienable*: it could be neither rightly removed nor renounced. This notion of an inalienable right was very clearly expounded by Burlamaqui, and it is likely that he had some influence on the development of the idea of rights in America (Haakonssen 1996a, pp. 322– 41, 2002; McConnell 1996; White 1978).

Under reference to Locke, Barbeyrac gave an account of the power of moral judgement as in principle veridical, that is, a power by which people were able to tell what is right and wrong. If so, why do we need natural law, considered as the law of God, to guide us? Because without divine decree, we would have no *obligation* to do right and avoid wrong: 'you will have only . . . *a speculative morality*, and you build upon the sand' (Barbeyrac 1749, p. 13). Without God's presence, our moral judgement would not constitute conscience. So, while Barbeyrac at one level presented a theory based upon natural right, the right to free conscience, at another level he offered a theory of a moral power that has a right use, namely that intended by God. This ambiguity of 'right' as freedom and as rightfulness became characteristic of most Scottish natural jurisprudence, and it persisted in the writers of the French Enlightenment, including Rousseau, notably in his discussion of the right to liberty.[4]

2 The political context of German natural law

For much of the eighteenth century, such ambiguity played little role in Germany, essentially because there moral realism was predominantly Aristotelian rather than Platonist in inspiration and, until the 1770s, generally lacked the British concern with moral agency. While Leibniz was influenced

4 Rousseau 1984, pp. 183–4; *SC*, 1.4, p. 188. Cf. Derathé 1950; Dufour 1976; Gordon 1994, pp. 54–73; Larrère 1992; Rosenblatt 1997; Wokler 1988a, 1994a; Zurbuchen 1991, chs. 4–6. For the Netherlands see Janssen 1987.

by Platonism, he did not set in train any equivalent to British speculations on Henry More's 'boniform power' and Hutcheson's moral sense. There was no comparable German attempt, until much later, to subvert the voluntarist idea of 'naked' acts of will as the foundation of morals. Instead Germany was dominated by confrontations with the new voluntarism, at first from orthodox Lutheran thinkers, and later from Leibniz and Wolff. The context for these debates is complex but vital, and may be sketched as follows.

At a political and juridical level, natural law was an important instrument in the transformation of German politics after the Peace of Westphalia which ended the catastrophic Thirty Years War in 1648, a war fought mainly along religious fronts and which was both civil and international. The peace treaty accelerated the formation of modern sovereignty in the form of centralised, mainly princely, rule in the territorial states into which Germany was divided. This required that the princes overcome the intricate corporatist as well as provincial diffusion of social, juridical, and political power that was part of the immediate post-Reformation settlement, often as remnants of late medieval arrangements. At the same time, the new system of sovereignty had to contend with the fact that it was being formed within the confederal constitutional framework of the Holy Roman Empire which encompassed Germany, Austria, and Bohemia. This was seen as the true heir to the Roman Empire through its adoption of Roman law, for a long time explained by the legislator-myth that Emperor Lothar III early in the twelfth century promulgated the law of Rome for Germany. This tale was discredited by Hermann Conring in 1643 (Stolleis 1983), and it was in any case more the medieval Italian glossators' version of Roman law that over the centuries penetrated into German law, but this did not make it a less potent weapon in the hands of Romanist lawyers and imperial officers; only slowly did it weaken (Stolleis 1988; Whitman 1990; Wieacker 1952). Faced with a long-standing internal devolution of power as well as an external diffusion of sovereignty in the name of a still evocative ancient constitution, the territorial princes welcomed natural law, seen as a theory of absolute sovereignty based on universal – 'natural' – values, without any need to invoke history, tradition, or confessional religion. In these endeavours the princes received some assistance from another dimension of Imperial law, namely, Imperial public law or *Staatsrecht*. Evolving through a series of Imperial statutes and international treaties – the most famous being the Treaty of Augsburg in 1555 and the Treaty of Westphalia in 1648 – Imperial public law helped to provide the framework of confessional co-existence within which princely territorial states could develop (Heckel 1992).

Appealing to the princes' rights to territorial governance which had, in fact, originally been framed by Imperial public law, natural law served as a means of disputing the Roman lawyers' claims for the institutions of the Empire and, during the eighteenth century, one state after another sought exemption from the right of appeal to the central Imperial court. However, while the Empire undoubtedly was weak in many respects in the Enlightenment, it remained a factor of some importance until its final demise in 1806 as a casualty of the Napoleonic wars; and the ideology of the ancient Roman constitution was revived as an integral part of the Romantic movement from the 1780s onwards. Since natural law, too, remained alive much longer than has often been thought (Dann and Klippel 1995), the intricate relationship between the two systems or approaches to law continued to be of importance well into the nineteenth century.

Internally in the states, natural law served as the underlying ideology in the many attempts to 'rationalise' and codify the legal systems through centralisation, in the drafting of constitutions, and in the education of princes and governing elites.[5] The eighteenth century's classic case of absolutism, France apart, was Denmark, whose *Lex regia* (1665) was deeply influenced by Hugo Grotius. The significant Swedish codification, the *Sveriges Rikes Lag* of 1734, was influenced by Pufendorfian natural law; and Pufendorf still played a role in the future Emperor Joseph II's education in politics and law twenty years later; Josephine law reforms were heavily indebted to natural law. Joseph's younger brother, Leopold II, was exposed to the ideas of Wolff, in the 'Catholicised' tenor given these ideas by Karl Anton von Martini; and it was the latter's student, Franz von Zeiller, who, inspired by Kant, drafted the code for all German parts of the Habsburg realm. The future Frederick the Great was steeped in Wolff's philosophy and he retained a basically Wolffian pattern of thought in his political ideas. The notable natural lawyer, Samuel von Cocceji, had already been involved in law reform in Prussia in the 1710s and 1720s, and he was the architect of Frederick's grand, if largely abortive, attempt to codify the Prussian legal system in the 1750s and 1760s. The great Prussian *Allgemeines Landrecht* of 1794 was significantly influenced by the systematics of natural law, which its main author, Carl Gottlieb Svarez, impressed upon the Prussian crown

---

5 Klippel 1987; for Denmark see Fabricius 1920; Jørgensen 1886. For Sweden: Peterson 1988; Picardi and Giuliani 1996; Skuncke 1992, pp. 127, 150–1; Wagner 1986a, 1986b. For the Habsburgs: Conrad 1961, 1964; Szabo 1994. For Prussia: Haakonssen 1996a, pp. 135–45; Johnson 1975, pp. 106–33; Klein 1977; Kleinheyer 1959; Reibstein 1962; Svarez 1960, pp. 3–624; Weill 1961; Wieacker 1952, pp. 322–47; cf. Gagnér 1960, ch. 1. For Hesse-Cassel: Ingrao 1987, pp. 13–16. For Geneva: Rosenblatt 1997, ch. 3.

prince in his private lectures in 1791–2, *Vorträge über Recht und Staat* (Lectures on Law and the State), while his co-author, Ernst Ferdinand Klein, debated the issues at length as a prominent member of the Berlin Enlightenment. Burlamaqui was tutor to the landgrave of Hesse-Cassel, Frederick II, and Gustav III of Sweden was fond of Burlamaqui's work. At the same time, in Geneva, Barbeyrac and Burlamaqui were invoked by the ruling patriciate in its struggle with the bourgeoisie about the true nature of the city's republican constitution.

Reflecting its growing political and legal importance, natural law became institutionalised. It became a major field of study. After the first university position to claim natural law as its domain, namely that held by Samuel Pufendorf in Heidelberg in the 1660s, the subject was introduced at nearly all the universities and other educational institutions of the German-speaking world as well as in many other parts of Europe. Along with professorial positions went the production of textbooks, often based on lectures, compendia, and commentaries on and translations of the major works (especially those of Grotius and Pufendorf), bibliographies, dissertations, etc. As is common when an area of study acquires 'disciplinary' status, natural law received its own historiography, which was commonly used as an introduction to the topic (Hochstrasser 2000). This literature was extensive and may be said to be the dominant form of moral and political thought in the Enlightenment in general, particularly so in Germany, aided by the fact that natural law was a loosely structured genre rather than a narrowly defined doctrine. It could be adapted to a wide variety of circumstances and purposes used across confessional and ideological divides, often as a tool for systematic organisation of material and as a vehicle for social knowledge which was in the process of dividing into separate academic disciplines, such as economics and demography (Brückner 1977; Klippel 1994; Larrère 1992; Tribe 1988).

It was, above all, its usefulness to the state governments that made natural law so prominent in German universities. This enabled natural lawyers to marginalise their Roman law colleagues in many places. Not least due to its non-confessional character, natural law could compete with theology for public prominence in the multiconfessional states of Germany. The Holy Roman Empire encompassed states that were Lutheran, Reformed, and Catholic. In some German states the ruling princes were of a different confession from that of their subjects; for example, Lutheran Brandenburg-Prussia was ruled by a Reformed (Calvinist) dynasty. There was, therefore, a strong interest in a supra-confessional natural law as a basis for social morality and positive law, and the princes tried to maintain a close alliance with, and control over, university faculties as the seedbeds for such ideas.

This portrait of secular, 'rational' natural law in the service of sovereign states, with a programme of bureaucratically organised modernisation of society, is commonly taken as an integral part of the Enlightenment in Germany. But tradition-based political and legal ideas and their decentralised institutional and individual proponents who were in conflict with the new natural law were not necessarily opposed to Enlightenment (Reill 1975). Provincial lawyers had their own ideas of enlightened reform in their local contexts and developed law and local governance by teaching, researching, and applying Roman law, Imperial law, state law, local common law, and natural law eclectically. The limited success of the grandiose codification projects by state governments may in part be explained by the circumstance that other reform movements were afoot (Lestition 1989).

Another complication in the nexus between Enlightenment and natural law was the lack of unity in natural law. It is a useful simplification to say that natural law theory in Germany in the eighteenth century was divided into two broad streams, one that developed the legacy of Pufendorf and one that emerged from Leibniz, while the rights theory that formed a third strand in European natural jurisprudence at the turn of the eighteenth century had little impact in the German-speaking world until late in the Enlightenment. The doctrinal differences of the two German traditions in the eighteenth century, represented by Thomasius and Wolff, will be discussed below, but their socio-political function will provide an introduction to those theoretical issues.

The two types of natural law possessed a number of common features. For example, they shared the same elaborate systematics and the same legal and political subject matters, and they derived these from the same sources, the Roman law tradition, the Spanish neo-scholastic natural law, and the major natural lawyers of the seventeenth century mentioned above. Similarly, both Thomasius's and Wolff's natural law were universalist and 'rational' in the sense of non-confessional. They were not primarily concerned with rights; rather, they were centred on the idea of law that imposes duties. They were also, in the common view, both theories of absolute sovereignty. For all these reasons, either form of natural law could fulfil several of the practical functions we have mentioned, and this has led to a long tradition of overlooking or down-playing their differences. However, there was a philosophical gulf between them which had important practical implications.

The core of the matter is that for thinkers in the Leibnizian tradition and especially for Wolff, law and politics were essentially concerned with the perfectibility of human nature as part of the general system of the world. In contrast, for those in the Pufendorfian line, and Thomasius in particular, law and politics were concerned with restraining and pacifying a human nature that was inherently passionate and tended to be ungovernable. According to the former view, the conventional political aim, *salus populi*, the people's welfare, meant the maximisation of happiness; in the latter, it meant the maintenance of peace and order. The former entailed that politics was all but limitless, and that sovereignty was in that sense justified in being absolute; the latter meant that politics was defined by its limited agenda and that sovereignty was absolute only within this sphere, since there was no safe common ground on which a limiting power could be justified. Against this background we can see that in the Leibnizian legacy it was philosophical insight into man's place in the world that qualified one for political rule. By contrast, the tendency in the Pufendorfian tradition was to exclude or limit the political invocation of ultimate things, whether religious or philosophical.

This contrast is reflected in the way in which the two lines of thought functioned socially and politically. Wolffian philosophy aspired to, and in considerable measure achieved, the status of a civic religion for the governing classes, especially in Prussia, where Wolff's natural law theory provided what has been analysed as the ruling bureaucracy's value scheme (Hellmuth 1985). Thomasius's philosophy never in this way aimed at being a politically entrenched *Weltanschauung*, but was much more concerned with a public ethos of delimiting religion, morals, law, and politics, and with the professional training of lawyers and administrators as the guardians of these boundaries. Accordingly, Wolffianism required that the universities' philosophical faculties become competitive with the traditionally 'higher' faculties of law and theology as seminaries for the new elite of bureaucrats, or that Wolffian philosophy was integrated into at least the legal training. In this, Wolff and his followers were remarkably successful. In contrast, the Thomasians tended to be most effective in the major new schools of law in Halle and Göttingen. Furthermore, for reasons that will become clear, Thomasius's ideas opened up historical and empirical studies of the law and thereby spread their influence widely but also much less perceptibly.

3   Christian Thomasius[6]

Thomasius's starting point was Pufendorf, with whom he was in close contact during the older man's last years. Thomasius's first major work, the *Institutions of Divine Jurisprudence* (1709 [1688a]; trans. forthcoming), was designed, as the title page proclaims, to prove and elaborate the principles of Pufendorf's natural law and to defend them against criticism. When he published his second attempt at a system of natural law seventeen years later, the *Foundations of the Law of Nature and Nations, Deduced from Common Sense* (1709 [1705a]; trans. forthcoming), Thomasius's ideas had undergone a dramatic change, although it might yet be possible to see the *Foundations* still building on Pufendorf.

The critics against whom Thomasius was offering Pufendorf a helping hand were the orthodox Lutherans, especially Valentin Alberti who was an influential professor of theology at Leipzig (Osterhorn 1962). In his *Compendium to Natural Law according to Orthodox Theology* (1678) and other writings, Alberti stated the orthodox case, that religious faith was doctrinal in character, i.e., that it was a matter of ideas about God's nature. These ideas were innate to the human mind, but they had been much obscured through original sin so that the clergy had the special role of 'declaring' – as opposed to interpreting – what was in a sense self-evident in scripture. The basis for morality, i.e. the law of nature, was thus to be extracted from the original human condition before the Fall when man could understand the divine prescriptions that derived from God's essence which, with reference to Thomas Aquinas, were called the eternal law. Pufendorf's core objection to this argument was that it mixed up two entirely different aspects of human life and that this mixture was immensely dangerous (Pufendorf 2002b, 2003, preface; Hunter 2001, ch. 4). Religion, or humanity's quest for living with God was one thing; morals and politics, people's striving to live with themselves and with each other in this world, quite another. What the orthodox were trying to do, in Pufendorf's eyes, was to lay claim to a special vantage point outside of all human morality and society from which they could judge the latter. This, however, was inconsistent with the simple fact that people are always and inevitably, given human nature and its condition, living in some sort of moral and social condition, though they do so with varying practical success (for Pufendorf even the imagined solitary

6 Ahnert 1999; Barnard 1965b, 1971, 1988b; Bienert 1934; Bloch 1961; Fleischmann 1931; Grunert 2000, pp. 169–288; Hochstrasser 2000, ch. 4; Hunter 2001, ch. 5; Kühnel 2001; Lieberwirth 1955; Lutterbeck 2002; Rüping 1968; Schneewind 1998, pp. 159–66; Schneiders 1971, 1989; Schröder 2001; Vollhardt 1997, 2001.

life in a state of nature is a moral condition under natural law). While it may make sense to ask why one should live in this or that particular moral or social arrangement, to claim a transcendent standpoint in relation to historical morality and society is nonsense, politically speaking, and very often dangerous nonsense, since by definition such a question sets itself above concern for the central point of moral and social living, namely peace. In Pufendorf's view, the relationship is of course symmetrical: just as salvational religion is irrelevant to the morality and politics of civil society, so the latter are, properly speaking, irrelevant to salvation.

Thomasius adopts this idea that we, as public persons (in contrast to our private roles in family and church), always see the world from inside some particular moral and socio-political position. Yet in the early *Institutions* he undermines the mentioned symmetry between morals/politics and religion. It is true that he, like Pufendorf, maintains that the law of nature which is the basis for morality and society is an expression of God's will, and that we know this law naturally through reasoning about ordinary human experience. However, by placing greater emphasis on human incapacity, he startlingly incorporates divine positive law – as found in scripture – into the discipline of jurisprudence, hence the title of the work. The difference between the two divine laws is the way in which we know of them: natural law through reason, God's positive law through scripture; but both are acts of divine will.

This move is commonly seen as half-hearted on the part of Thomasius; he appears to have wanted to accommodate both Pufendorfian natural law and more traditional Lutheran views of divine positive law. However, his point may be rather different and more daring. He treats the knowledge which scripture gives us of the pristine condition of humanity and its subsequent miseries as historical knowledge without any specially privileged status. Accordingly, it is subject to the standards of interpretation contained in natural law and may indeed be expounded by lay jurists. Such knowledge can only be formulated in human language which is directly bound up with mankind's fulfilment of the most basic edict of natural law, namely to live sociably, as we shall see. Thomasius is, therefore, in effect making the point that of the two manifestations of God's will – biblical law and natural law – the former is, for the purposes of social living, subject to the criteria of the latter; both laws are governed by the end of sociable living. The implication is, of course, that the claims of theologians to special insight into God's positive law should have no hearing outside the church and the theology faculty.

The Pufendorfian–Thomasian theory is profoundly voluntarist in the sense that it sees all moral values as directly or indirectly dependent on acts of will (Thomasius 1688a, 1.ii.74ff). No thing, such as a creature, no state of affairs, such as a relationship between creatures, and no event, such as an act of one creature towards another, has any *inherent* value. Human acts of will are in themselves nothing but natural events. In fact, in his late work, Thomasius came to understand the will in a somewhat Hobbesian sense, as a link in causal sequences of affections. Human acts of will only assume a moral aspect through their relationship to the law of nature, and the law of nature is only a moral law because it is God's will. Considerable intellectual energy was expended on the problem that this argument transforms the question of the foundation of morals into that of the goodness of God, and Thomasius's early work is a contribution to this debate. Put in modern terms, the gist of his reply is that it makes no sense to seek the foundations of morality if the latter is considered as a means of living with others qua human beings, as distinct from qua special relations in family, society, or religious faith. The reason is the 'internalist' point outlined above, namely that as persons of will and passion we are always inside a moral standpoint. Thomasius therefore denies that we can use our ideas of God to 'found' morality in general, and he underlines this by maintaining that, after the Fall, we really cannot have any reliable notions of God's nature or goodness that can direct our common behaviour. Our rational ideas of God are partly historical from scripture, partly analogical from human agency, and partly inferential from our experience of life in the world. Despite this lack of transcendent normative foundations, morality is a fact about our condition in the world that originates in a divine will we cannot scrutinise because we have no standpoint free of its effect – natural law – from which to make such judgement. This argument is underlined by the lapidary way in which Thomasius deals with the question of obligation to natural law. All law, including natural law, rests upon a 'first practical principle', namely, 'Obey the person who commands.' A commander is a person with power to oblige others; otherwise he would be no commander. A law is a commander's command that obliges others; if it did not, it would be no law. An obligation exists only because subjects have to obey a commander (1709 [1688a], 1.iii.34–7). In other words, law and obligation are facts about the human world which are subject to definition but, by implication, not subject to justification from within that world. Thomasius therefore sees no reason why he should take seriously the traditional 'Euthyphro' dilemma about the moral status of the natural law, a problem which Leibniz later tried to press on the Pufendorfians in an epistolary essay of 1706 (Leibniz 1988, pp. 45–64; cf. Barbeyrac 1718).

Since the content of natural law could be derived neither from God's nature, nor from his eternal law as the orthodox would have it, humanity had to rely on its own rationality and reflection on its experience of the world. The inevitable result of this reflection was our utter dependence upon others, both for physical survival and for mental development as persons. This is the core of Thomasius's argument and is a development of a similar point in Pufendorf that links rationality and sociability. The concept of reason upon which Thomasius relies is that of a dialogue or conversation. Reasoning consists of the manipulation of signs, and we only learn the use of signs in dealing with other people. So, without some minimum of social living, there could be no language and no ability to reason; these functions are interdependent. They are also unique to humanity, the means by which we alone can live under the guidance of natural law. It is through reason that we can reflect upon the fact that we would not have reason if we were not social, and that we could not be social if others were not reasoning likewise. Thomasius takes these undeniable facts as the best indication we have of God's will, namely that we should always act so as to benefit the whole of humanity considered as rational and social. This 'utilitas totius humani generis' ('benefit to the whole of the human race') is again to be understood as 'pax' or 'vita tranquilla', peace or the quiet life with others, and it can be characterised as the essence of temporal happiness, 'beatitudo'. This rational sociality ('socialitas' or 'Geselligkeit') is the basic natural law and thus the foundation for all society ('societas' or 'Gesellschaft').

In developing his early theory of natural law, Thomasius adopted a view of human nature according to which humanity is strongly influenced by the passions, but has the free will to apply reason to restrain the passions. At the centre of this rational restraint are natural law and its various institutionalisations. But within a few years of publishing the *Institutions of Divine Jurisprudence*, he began to make a fundamental change in this anthropology (Ahnert 1999, chs. 3–8; Hunter 2001, pp. 209–34). Through a string of major and minor works which we cannot discuss here (1688b, 1691a, 1691b, 1692, 1696, 1699a, 1699b), he developed the idea that the passions totally determine man's life and that there is no such thing as a free will to act upon rational understanding of experience. Restraint of the passions in the interest of social life would have to be sought in some way other than the kind of natural law originally put forward.

At the same time, there were reasons internal to the theory of natural law for seeking a change of doctrine. As Thomasius stresses in the *Foundations of the Law of Nature and Nations, Deduced from Common Sense*, much of which takes the form of a critical commentary on his earlier work, his former Pufendorfian concept of natural law did not fulfil the criterion for being a law proper. This is particularly so since humankind never receives the law of nature as a *command* of God because God does not tie specific sanctions to the law in the manner of a legislator; rather, the connection between action and sanction is what Thomasius calls a 'natural' one (1709 [1705a], cap. prooem./vorrede §§ 8–10; cf. Ahnert 1999, pp. 91–5). The common argument that the reward and punishment for our moral performance would be meted out in an afterlife was not available to him, since he did not think that such a life was ascertainable by natural reasoning. Furthermore, Thomasius's earlier, Pufendorfian understanding of natural law as a command with sanctions similar to positive law (divine and human) and only distinct from the latter in terms of the mode of understanding was, he now thought, the source of another serious mistake. By tying law to specifically imposed sanction, Thomasius had made all obligation external and ignored the internal 'which, after all, is the finest form of obligation' (§ 11). This, again, had prevented him, like everyone else, he thought, from distinguishing clearly between the various layers of morality which for him were three, namely what he called *justum*, *decorum*, and *honestum*, as we will see below. In fact, Pufendorf himself had thoroughly mixed up ethics and natural law (§ 12).

Thomasius's response to his extensive auto-critique in the *Foundations* included a significant change in legal theory. Natural law now lost its direct normative character and was only in an analogical sense law, not unlike Hobbes's conception of the matter. In effect, natural law pointed out the connection between certain forms of behaviour, especially the establishment of institutions and the conduct of the passions. Thomasius furthermore reduced the ultimate divine sanctions to the causal sequences that make up man's life on earth according to God's general providence for the species.

This leads us to investigate Thomasius's distinction between external and internal obligation and between the three layers of morals. The former is a distinction between two kinds of sanction; external obligation arises when the behaviour in question is subject to sanctions in our external actions, internal obligation when sanctions are suited for our inner life. The premise here is that the good which we naturally strive after is peace or quietness of life that can be either internal – peace of mind – or external – security of action. Furthermore, external peace can either be a purely negative matter of being left in peace, or a matter of having one's welfare actively secured or promoted. Actions that contribute to or are in accordance with the inner peace or balance of a person considered as a moral being make up *honestum*. This is the sphere of morality proper, for such actions are only obligatory internally, in conscience, and cannot be enforced; they are acts of love and would lose their specific moral character if enforced. Actions that simply avoid breaking the external peace comprise *justum*; they carry external obligation because they are enforceable and thus suitable objects of positive legislation. Actions that actively promote the external quiet of life, finally, form *decorum*. Although these actions relate to other people and in that sense are external, they only oblige internally and are not enforceable. They thus provide a middle way between *honestum* and *justum*, between morality and law; they have some similarities with those covered by Locke's 'law of opinion', and they are characterised as matters of prudence, or politics.

Thomasius's notion of internal obligation has nothing whatever to do with Kantian self-legislation, nor is the distinction between external and internal obligation the harbinger for one between heteronomy and autonomy. Obligation simply means the connection between behaviour and sanction. *Justum*, *decorum*, and *honestum* provide a typology for the forms of behaviour and their matching sanctions, delineated in the social theories of jurisprudence, prudence, and ethics.

While Thomasius in the *Foundations* was deeply critical of his earlier Pufendorfian theory, there is also significant continuity. It is the fundamental anti-metaphysical voluntarism that leads to the rejection of the 'spiritual' notion of a free will in favour of a supposedly empirical account of the passions. It is the same line of thought that takes away the idea that natural law is a command in the same sense as positive laws with an empirically ascertainable connection between legislative intent, action, and sanction. Thomasius accepts the consequences of the basic Pufendorfian idea that the law of nature is a fact about which it makes no sense to ask why we are obliged to it. Once that move is made, all specific content of the law of nature has to be derived from temporal sources, that is, from human acts of will that are guided by our limited understanding of our nature and place in the world. This procedure invites empirical methods, an invitation erratically accepted by Thomasius and yielding a combination of philosophical anthropology and moral, especially legal, history based upon his three spheres of *honestum*, *justum*, and *decorum*. Morals and law were thus seen as historical or cultural – 'conventional' – phenomena, and natural law lost its status as a metaphysically or religiously sanctified *Grundnorm*.

In view of that development of his views, it is hardly surprising that Thomasius's main influence, polemics apart, was in legal theory and its distinction from ethics and in legal history (Hochstrasser 2000, pp. 141–9; Rüping 1968, 1979). This influence was channelled through the law and, in part, philosophy faculties at the two great Enlightenment universities of Halle and Göttingen (Hammerstein 1972, chs. 4, 5, 7). In the former institution, N. H. Gundling (1715, 1734), J. P. von Ludewig (1727), and, after some peregrination, J. G. Heineccius (1737, 1744, 1748) were of significance. The last was perhaps Thomasius's most important follower who, on a similar philosophical basis, used natural law as a kind of systematic propædeutic to extensive studies of both Roman and German law (Heineccius 1741; Haakonssen 1996a, pp. 87–95). The founding father of Göttingen University in 1737, G. A. von Münchhausen, was a student of Gundling and the new faculty included several significant Thomasians, such as C. A. Heumann (1715–26), J. J. Schmauss (1748), and G. Achenwall (1750) who was also strongly influenced by Wolff. It was these historians of ethics and law who laid the foundations for the philosophical history that came to prominence in several academic disciplines in Göttingen, and was closely associated with similar British, especially Scottish, thought (Hochstrasser 2000, pp. 141–9; Oz-Salzberger 1995, ch. 10). These scholars also provided a link between Thomasian eclecticism and the cognate 'Popularphilosophie' of J. G. H. Feder, C. Meiners, and others in Göttingen (Bachmann-Medick 1989, ch. 1; van der Zande 1992, 1995). Outside Germany, Thomasius's influence was limited, but he did have a notable impact on the Norwegian–Danish playwright, historian, essayist, moralist, and cultural icon Ludvig Holberg, who compiled a textbook, mainly from Pufendorf and Thomasius, which helped ensure that natural law became a lasting influence at the University of Copenhagen and as a practical legal instrument (Foss 1934; Holberg 1716; Tamm 1986). Holberg's effort was followed by an anonymous translation of Barbeyrac's edition of the shorter Pufendorf (1742). In Sweden, the royal historiographer, John Wilde, was a Thomasian who influenced the debate leading to the codification in 1734. However, rival philosophical ideas were soon invading Scandinavia from the south.

4   Christian Wolff[7]

When Christian Wolff appeared in Halle at the turn of the eighteenth century, his philosophy immediately became the exemplary metaphysical opposition to Thomasius's eclectic and empirical programme. This opposition was to shape a great deal of German thought for more than half a century. The contest took place in a wider framework.[8] Two other factors were of particular importance, namely orthodox Lutheranism and the Pietist rebellion against orthodoxy also centered in Halle. All four movements vied for political influence. Lutheran orthodoxy upheld a view of faith and hence of morals as doctrinal, and of doctrine as a matter of scripture as declared by the church. The implication was a political status for the clergy which always led to accusations of 'Papalist' ambitions. In protest against such views, Pietism demanded a return to Luther's notion of every man as his own minister, which required that man's wilfulness be broken so that he could experience God's will directly. Such experience of conversion by the Almighty was the basis for all Christian living, but, in contrast to the theology of predestination, the individual could, according to Pietist Lutheranism, lose the effect of God's communication. Every moment of life, therefore, had to be devoted to proving one's worthiness of grace by showing its effectiveness in creating good in the world. As a consequence, the Pietists sought the princes' help to convert society more or less into one large workhouse with an associated asceticism.

While the Pietist emphasis on the will and passions as the dominant factor in human life was congenial to Thomasius and led to occasional alliances with their leaders, such as A. H. Francke, J. Lange, and J. F. Budde, especially in their fights with Wolff, there remained nevertheless a fundamental difference (Hunter 2001, pp. 270–1). For Thomasius, the Pietist focus on personal conversion was as much a claim to spiritual privilege as the claims put forward by orthodox theologians and metaphysicians; and, in the same way, it led to an effort to subsume politics under religion. Thomasius's fundamental endeavour was to keep religion private and out of politics. In contrast, Wolffianism became similar to a civic religion with significant appeal to ruling princes, but it did so on a rational metaphysical basis, and thus independently of both scriptural faith and immediate divine

---

7 Bachmann 1977; Hochstrasser 2000, ch. 5; Hunter 2001, pp. 265–73; Lutterbeck 2002; Schneewind 1990, I, pp. 331–50; 1998, pp. 431–42; Schneiders 1983; Schröer 1988; Schwaiger 1995; Stipperger 1984; Thomann 1977; Winiger 1992.
8 Bianco 1989; Erb 1983; Gawthrop 1993; Hinrichs 1971; Hinske 1989; Hope 1995, pt 1; Kramer 1880–2; Ratschow 1964–71; Sparn 1976; Stoeffler 1973; Stroup 1984; Ward 1992.

inspiration. In these battles, there were casualties on all sides, the most famous being Wolff's dismissal from Halle and expatriation at the instigation of the Pietists in 1723 and his triumphant reinstatement in 1740 by Frederick the Great.

Since his own lifetime, it has been common to consider Wolff's philosophy as an extension and systematisation of that of Leibniz.[9] Certainly Wolff was close to Leibniz in metaphysics and, not least, in his view of the public role of philosophy. Wolff also readily joined in the combat against voluntarist natural law and its implications. However, his source of inspiration was more the scholastic thinkers, especially Aquinas, than Leibniz. One reason for this was that Leibniz published little on these topics and certainly provided no systematic model for Wolff to follow in either ethics or politics, even though Wolff's central notion of happiness (*Glück*) was much influenced by Leibniz (Schwaiger 1995, ch. 3). He was a relatively independent thinker in practical philosophy, the area in which he published most.

Wolff was a prodigious and systematic writer who first worked out his philosophy in German and then rewrote the system in some thirty volumes in Latin. It is often assumed that the latter simply is an expression of German thoroughness, namely a rewriting for an international audience of the earlier German works, but that is a mistake (Stipperger 1984). Both the German and Latin series certainly move from a general theory of knowledge, through metaphysics to practical philosophy, but, in addition to significant rearrangements of the components of metaphysics (ontology, cosmology, empirical and rational psychology, and natural theology), there are important developments of practical philosophy in the Latin version that go to the heart of the political significance of Wolff's thought.

Put simply, while the German *Ethics* (*Rational Thoughts on Human Actions*, 1720) and the German *Politics* (*Rational Thoughts on the Social Life of Man*, 1721) contain a rather elementary and underdeveloped doctrine of natural law (*Naturrecht*), the Latin works elaborate natural jurisprudence (*ius naturae*), as a complete discipline. In making this change, Wolff worked out the relationship between the four central concepts of law (*lex*), obligation (*obligatio*), duty (*officium*), and right (*ius*). Behind the establishment of these relationships lay his speculations about innate rights (*iura connata*), especially the right to liberty, absent from the German work. The interpretation of these central features of Wolff's moral and political thought has become the

---

9 For Leibniz and Wolff, see Corr 1975; Schwaiger 1995, ch. 3. For Wolff and scholasticism, see Bianco 1989; Casula 1979; Ruello 1963. A selection from Wolff's moral thought is translated in Schneewind 1990, I, pp. 333–48.

subject of fundamental disputes, as scholars have looked afresh at the Latin work.

The central notion in Wolff's practical philosophy is not sociability but the perfectibility of humanity and its condition. This is the *summum bonum*, and pursuit of it is, therefore, our ur-duty, the most basic command of the natural law. The notion of human perfectibility is complex and can only be understood through Wolff's metaphysics, but three central characteristics indicate its nature. It is a gradual realisation of our natural abilities in such a way that they are in harmony with each other, both in ourselves and in others, which in turn is the same as our progress in happiness guided by the divine and transhuman ideal of perfect happiness, beatitude, and signalled to us through pleasure (Wolff 1733a, §§ 44, 49; Wolff 1738–9, I, §§ 374, 395). In order to have an obligation to natural law, people must have moral freedom, which consists in the realisation of one's moral objective or potential. If not, they are unfree, due to ignorance, illogical thinking, the sway of passions, and the like. In other words, Wolff gives a purely intellectualist account of moral freedom as action determined by correct moral insight. This is important for an understanding of the contractarian aspect of his theory.

With the natural law command to pursue perfection, or maximise happiness, we have an objective basis for morality entirely independent of God's will. It is true that humanity is contingent, and hence there would be neither humanity nor any law for its nature without God's voluntary act of creation. But the nexus between the nature of humanity and its moral law is purely conceptual and necessary, not something subject to any will, not even God's. Given human nature as it is created, natural law is therefore immutable and even 'God cannot prescribe for humans any law contrary to the natural' (1738–9, I, § 282; cf. 1736, § 29). Wolff can therefore also be explicit and blunt in his affirmation of Grotius's famous 'etiamsi daremus' proposition: the law of nature 'would be valid even if there were no God' (Wolff 1733a, § 20). Any denial of God's existence thus does not entail that there is no law of nature for atheists. The question is, why should they have any obligation to obey it?

Obligation to the law of nature is threefold. A natural obligation arises because the will is irresistibly drawn to perfection and natural law points the way to perfection by the actions it prescribes and prohibits. Since the human mind is able to see that this connection between free moral action and perfection is part of the divine intellect's scheme of possibilities for humanity, people will also see the obligation as divine in character. Finally, there is an additional source of obligation in that the divinity reinforces the law of nature by reward and punishment (1733a, §§ 28–31; 1738–9, I, cap. 3).

The law of nature is, simultaneously, descriptive of the connection between human action and human perfection and prescriptive of the moral necessity of realising this connection in our lives. It thus imposes the duties (sometimes *officia*, sometimes *obligationes*) of human life. In addition, it grants rights (*iura*), although Wolff is clear that 'right originates in duty (*obligatione*), duty is prior to right' (1740–8, I, § 24), where 'prior' refers to the order of justification. There are, then, rights given with human nature, i.e. which are innate (*connata*) and thus universal and equal. 'Natural right' and 'natural duty' are in fact complementary concepts, and 'natural rights and natural duties correspond mutually' (1740–8, I, prol. II). On the one hand, it would not make sense to ascribe duty without acknowledging the right to fulfil that duty. On the other hand, it would, for Wolff, be equally senseless to ascribe a right without acknowledging a duty, namely the duty to act in accordance with the law of nature. This is what 'right' means, according to Wolff, a power granted by the law of nature to pursue the goals set by that law, i.e. natural duties. So although natural rights are in a sense liberties, Wolff insists that they are not to be misunderstood as 'licence', i.e. areas of moral indifference.

Alongside this scholastic notion of *ius* as morally objective, Wolff has a subjective conception which bears similarity with the ideas of Grotius and Hobbes. Wolff sees natural rights as properties of the individual person; this is what he means by saying that they, along with the matching duties, are innate. A number of modern scholars have maintained that his idea of the innateness of rights makes him a grandparent of modern ideas of human rights as shields against the use of power, especially by governments (Bachmann 1977, pp. 100–14, 1983; Garber 1982; Thomann 1964, 1969, 1974, 1977, and introductions in Wolff 1740–8, 1749). In this connection, it has been suggested that Wolff had indirect influence on the declarations of rights of both the American and French Revolutions and on the development of constitutionalism (Goebel 1918–19; Thomann 1968). However, there is scant evidence for Wolff's impact on the Revolutions, and while he and his disciples clearly influenced German jurisprudence and its use in law reform, this was hardly characterised by the institutional entrenchment of individual rights (Klippel 1976, pp. 75–81, 1987, 1993). That is not surprising, for Wolff's idea of the innateness of rights was in fact very different from the modern idea.

Although basic rights are innate, this only means that they cannot be taken away, not that they cannot be given away. If rights could be withdrawn by one person from another, then the latter would not be a person, a moral agent, but simply a thing. Moral agency does include, however, the right to relinquish our rights, provided, of course, that such an action is in our best interests in pursuing the overall good, our perfection. A person cannot by such means stop being a moral agent, and in that sense one can speak of the basic right to moral freedom as a residual power; but a person can freely suspend the use of this power in any conceivable way. This is the basis for Wolff's endorsement of the right to submit to slavery. '*Libertas naturalis* is narrowed down to the liberty of making contracts to revoke that very liberty' and this is, for Wolff, the core of the moral life of the species (qu. Klippel 1976, p. 37). He schematises the moral career of humanity according to the types of trade-off people make of rights for security in the pursuit of perfectibility. The first great divider is the renunciation by some people of their right to complete control of their own persons and the right to equal access to the surrounding world. The former is the basis for (non-political) rule and thus for social groups, especially the household; the latter is the basis for private property. Before these contractual institutions, in the *status originarius*, people live with each other in both natural and moral equality (namely of innate duties to perfectibility), free from governance by others and free to protect themselves (and others) against attack, free to seek assistance from others, free to establish claims against others through contracts and to seek redress for injury, and free to lay claims to the use (not the ownership) of the surrounding world equally with others. These freedoms are humanity's innate natural rights, and the original condition defined by them and their matching innate duties is neither asocial and isolated nor hypothetical but experienced historically.

The lack of scope for perfection in the original state imposes a duty to seek beyond it, to the *status adventitius* characterised by private property and social hierarchies of authority. The same duty leads to the *status civilis*, the political society or state, and, eventually, to the *civitas maxima*, the international society. The original and the adventitious states together make up the state of nature, which is simply defined in contrast to the civic state, and the dividing line here is that the latter, the state, is not made by individuals but by the social groups in the adventitious state – typically households, represented by their (male) heads, and estates or communities based upon feudal tenure and represented by the lord. In other words, in the formation of the state, the relinquishing of rights is no longer in the hands of individuals.

The purpose of the state is to secure the common good through the most effective pursuit of perfection or happiness. This purpose can be divided into three areas, according to the classic scheme, namely the goods of the mind, the goods of the body, and external goods (*tranquilitas, securitas, vitae sufficientia*). Wolff sets about explaining how the state should provide for its citizens in all three areas, and the result is an extraordinary theory of the total welfare state. There is no theoretical limit to the state's pursuit of the welfare of its citizens, i.e. in making sure that they honour the three basic kinds of duties that make up morality; those to God, to others, and to ourselves. In this devotion to total human welfare, Wolff's state is the epitome of much traditional Lutheran political thought (Link 1979, pp. 137–8). He does, admittedly, take up the traditional *topos* of distinguishing between perfect and imperfect duties (and corresponding rights), but this is nothing more than a distinction into more and less urgent duties from the point of view of the pursuit of the common good; it is two different ways of pursuing happiness. It posits no barriers to state activity by distinguishing between law and morality or between a public and a private sphere. Nor does it offer anything like Pufendorf's and Thomasius's delimitation of the political sphere from all other spheres of life, such as religion. For Wolff there are only prudential, not principled, limits to the state. Frederick the Great's subjects may well have been relieved that he happened, as he said, to 'wish that in my territories everyone may pray and fornicate as they see fit', but at least some of them might have liked to enjoy such privileges on a more secure foundation than royal assent (qu. Blanning 1997, p. 544).

The institutions that characterise the adventitious and civic states are seen by Wolff as contractual, but this has little to do with contractualism as it is understood in modern political theory (cf. Reill 1975, ch. 4). The contracts in question need not involve any intentional acts by the parties to them, nor do they need to be actual events. They are often nothing more than the moral relationships in which people *de facto* happen to find themselves, i.e. quasi-contracts or implied contracts. All they presuppose is that the parties to them are moral agents, i.e. persons subject to the duties of natural law. When Wolff speaks of contractual institutions he is articulating a theory of social phenomena as rationally structured relations between individuals and groups in which the role of people's actual will and intentions

273

is entirely contingent. More particularly, he is avoiding a will theory of contracts: contracts may or may not be willed, or intentionally instituted, but what decides their obligation is whether or not they promote the *summum bonum*.

It is only on this understanding that we can make sense of one of the more puzzling features of Wolff's theory of natural law, namely its ability to justify historically given social formations such as feudalism or slavery. The question of whether such institutions infringe individuals' natural rights simply does not arise for Wolff because their very existence – which may have just or unjust *origins* – means that the people concerned do not live in the original state where moral life is characterised by natural rights and duties; they live in an adventitious state where authority, property, etc., produce adventitious duties and rights. Since any adventitious establishment by its very nature is the act of moral agents, its basis is contractual or quasi-contractual. While the parties to such contracts may have been morally misguided in entering into them, the existence of the resulting institutions creates a new moral situation. The only way of discussing the justifiability of such institutions, for example slavery or feudalism, is the same as for any social formation, namely in terms of its utility as a means to promote perfectibility. It is this basic thought that leads Wolff to view *ethica*, *oeconomica*, and *politica* as *techne*, in the classical sense as practical disciplines arranging means to the ends which are set by the theoretical discipline of *jus naturae*. This aspect of Wolff's practical philosophy as a discipline that gives a reasoned arrangement or classification of all the known features of the moral world should not be overlooked in our modern concern with the normative status of natural law as the moral law. It is an aspect that brings his and similar systems of natural jurisprudence closer to Enlightenment ideas of *histoire raisonée*.

The most significant (quasi-)contractual institution is civil society. Apart from the ideal of an international society governed by law, civil society is the apex of humanity's search for perfection-through-institution. The defining factor in civil society is governance, and Wolff presents a sophisticated theory of its foundation (Stipperger 1984). The presupposition is a social contract whereby the 'multitude' in the social state of nature becomes a people (*gens* or *Volk*; 1740–8, VIII.5). This body, in a further contract of governance, decides the most fundamental question concerning government, namely whether to keep it to themselves, in which case a pure democracy results, or to transfer it to somebody else. In the latter case, we have to distinguish between two things that can be transferred, either the ownership of persons and their goods, in which case we have a slave society (*imperium herile*), or an 'intangible thing' (*res incorporalis*) called authority (*imperium*) the transfer of which, in a contract of subjection, creates the authority of political government (*imperium civile*).

Having isolated slavery conceptually and thus prevented its confusion with absolute monarchy or the like, Wolff elucidates political government through some important distinctions. First, he distinguishes the right from its object, that is, that to which we have a right. The right itself can be more or less extensive; we can have full property right (*jus proprietatis*), or various degrees of dependent property rights, such as feudal rights and, even more dependent, *fideicommissum*, or we can have mere use rights (usufruct) (1740–8, VIII.39–40, 92, 95, 98–102). Similarly, the object of our right varies in completeness. It can be sovereign power (*summum imperium*), absolute power (*imperium absolutum*) in which the people may revoke exercises of power, or *imperium limitatum* in which the exercise of power is subject to constitutional law or the need for popular consent (1740–8, VIII.45, 65–74).

The point in these distinctions is that through them Wolff is able to provide an account of the full variety of forms of governance; he is not limited to the simple classical scheme of democracy, aristocracy, monarchy, and mixed forms. He is able to explain that a full sovereign power can be held by a less than full property right, his example being that of the Roman dictator's use right to total power (1740–8, VIII.70a). Similarly he can accommodate the various forms of less than full sovereign power which nevertheless are held in total property right, giving examples of separate powers as illustrations (1740–8, VIII.65, 69, 72, 74, 95).

The full significance of this formalistic theory of state and government in the Latin work can best be appreciated by briefly contrasting it with the German text. The German *Politics* (1736) is ambivalent. As has often been remarked, it appears, in many respects, quite Aristotelian. It sees the state as the fulfilment of the ethical life of the species, and it treats the state according to the Aristotelian forms of monarchy, aristocracy, democracy, and mixed forms. More fundamentally, it sees politics as a question of what is good and bad for the moral person whose nature is explained in the German *Ethics* (1733). Yet, on the other hand, Wolff presents the three basic forms of state as if they all in principle can be morally legitimate under natural law. This points to the formalism of the Latin work in which the fundamental question is not one of the moral goodness or badness of state forms but of juridical fact, namely, what can the parties in a given form of state be said to have 'agreed' to in a 'contract'? This is reflected in the different grounds on which slavery is assessed as a form of governance in the German and the Latin works. In the former, slavery may be legitimate if it furthers the common good of those governed, for example while they are too ignorant to benefit from other forms of governance. But in the Latin work, the primary question is whether or not people have the right to give away their rights of freedom.

The end of the latter road would be a complete questioning of the moral foundation of Wolff's practical philosophy, namely the idea of an objective standard of moral goodness in the form of moral perfectibility demanded as a duty by natural law. In the *Jus naturae* (Natural Right, 1740–8) this idea is severely threatened by, but never relinquished to, the contractarian aspect of his thought which really demands a notion of subjective rights as the primary feature of morality. Wolff was unable to break out of this dilemma between objective law and subjective right, but his transition from an Aristotelian civic humanism, in juridical guise in the German *Ethics* and *Politics*, to a highly formal natural law theory of society and its many forms of governance in the *Jus naturae* was one of the more dramatic, if ill-perceived, episodes in the reluctant modernity of early modern political thought.

While the potential for a subjectivist theory of rights in the *Jus naturae* remained obscure, it was clearly understood that the work's factual, non-judgemental treatment of all forms of governance meant that it could accommodate a historical approach to law and government and be adapted by those concerned with indigenous German laws and institutions in their historical particularity. This, and Thomasius's emphasis on history, means that it is often difficult to maintain the textbook division between universalist natural law – whether Thomasian or Wolffian – and particularist historical law and the associated division between reformist absolutism and traditionalist ideals of estate-based governance. However, while Wolff could *accommodate*, Thomasius *needed* a historical approach. The Wolffian legacy was blurred further by its sheer magnitude; Wolffians were teaching throughout Protestant Germany in the third quarter of the century. In time, the category of Wolffian became less precise, appealing both to philosophers and legal theorists even when they were not Wolffians in any strict sense (Hammerstein 1983). Moses Mendelssohn is an example of the former, Gottfried Achenwall and L. J. F. Höpfner of the latter (Altmann 1982; Höpfner 1795; Mautner 1994; Mendelssohn 1983 [1783], 1997, pp. 295–306; Plohmann 1992).

Even if not always distinct, the extraordinary extent of Wolff's influence is clear and of major significance. His pure doctrine was taught in many universities, including Halle and Frankfurt-an-der-Oder, the two premier universities in Prussia. In Wolff's own old university, the most faithful of his disciples, Daniel Nettelbladt, taught natural law for forty-five years; and in Frankfurt Joachim Georg Daries taught the subject with such regularity that by 1786 he had given his course one hundred times. Both wrote long-lasting textbooks in natural law (Nettelbladt 1772, 1777; Daries 1762–3; cf. Landsberg and Stintzing 1898–1910, I, pp. 284–6, 288–99 and II, pp. 192–3, 195–9). The extraordinary demand for this tuition arose not least from the need to train the Prussian bureaucracy. It is thus possible to delineate in detail how the basic 'value-scheme' of the Prussian bureaucracy in the second half of the century was formed by the Wolffian natural law theory of life as the discharge of duties for the sake of the common good (Hellmuth 1985; cf. Melton 1988). This has lent depth to the older interpretation of the great codifications of law as profoundly influenced by Wolffian natural law (see pp. 257–8 above; cf. Winiger 1992).

Wolff's system was readily adopted in the universities of Catholic Germany, Austria, and much of Italy, where his natural law was seen as modernising the late scholastics (Bianco 1993; Bruch 1997; Hammerstein 1985). At the same time Wolff gained a certain entry into French Enlightenment thought, albeit of a still undetermined nature (Carboncini 1993). Apart from Vattel (discussed below), the main vehicle for Wolff in France was the popular miscellany of his writings translated by the Huguenot secretary of the Berlin Academy, Formey, though it is difficult to gauge how much this 'Roman philosophique', as he described it, was used (Formey 1741–53, 1755, pp. 111–12; cf. Deschamps 1743–7; Hochstrasser 2000, p. 176). Formey's early translation of excerpts from Wolff's compendium, the *Institutiones*, seems to have had only limited impact (Wolff 1758).[10] It has, until recently, been thought that the article on 'Loi naturelle (morale)' in the *Encyclopédie* was cribbed by Diderot from Wolff, but we now know that its anonymous author took it nearly verbatim from Samuel Clarke's *Discourse concerning the Being and Attributes of God* (1704–5), and we can be sure that Wolff had no invisible hand in the events of 1789 (Burns 1984; Thomann 1968).

Like Grotius, Pufendorf, Thomasius, and many other early modern juridical philosophers, Wolff extended his *ius naturae* to *ius gentium*, and, with increasing clarity, the latter meant the moral–legal relationships between nations in the modern sense of sovereign states (cf. Cavallar 2002; Tuck 1999). However, this older *ius gentium* used the fiction of a *civitas maxima*, a

---

10 Rousseau nowhere mentions Wolff, though he knew Formey: Derathé 1950, pp. 99–100, cf. pp. 31–2. Elie Luzac published a translation of the full compendium, Wolff 1772.

universal political society, as the framework for understanding the international world; individual states were considered as members of this super-state in analogy with citizens of ordinary states. The analogy, of course, facilitated acceptance of *de facto* inequalities among states similar to those among citizens. It was Vattel's merit to change this perspective fundamentally.[11] He insisted on the equality of states considered as juridical (sovereign) entities, obviously drawing on his Swiss heritage (Barbeyrac and Burlamaqui) in formulating this view in terms of the equal rights of sovereign states. He rejected the patrimonial notion of the state that was pervasive in traditional natural law, including Wolff (Vattel 1916 [1758], preface, p. xvi; bk I, p. 61), and he even allowed that the people have residual rights of active resistance against tyranny (Vattel 1916 [1758], bk I, § 46; bk II, §§ 55–6; Vattel 1762, pp. 348–9, 429–30). However, Vattel accepted too much of Wolff's basic philosophy to have a coherent general theory of rights. He thought that the first moral law was to pursue perfection, and that this meant the contractual surrender of whatever rights were needed for the social purpose at hand. Publishing his work in the middle of the Seven Years War, to say nothing of debates about colonialism and empire, Vattel's ambition was to create a practical manual for the conduct of international affairs, and, as is well known, this was largely fulfilled (Vattel 1916 [1758], I, preface, pp. xiv–xv, xxiii; cf. Ruddy 1975). His *Law of Nations* (1758) had both immediate and lasting impact on international law and was popular well into the nineteenth century (Manz 1971, p. 55).

In Scandinavia, Wolff had a significant impact on university teaching, more with respect to theoretical than practical philosophy (Frängsmyr 1972; Koch 2003, pp. 21–31, 76–99, 235–40). The most notable contribution was Friedrich Christian Eilschov's lucid argument to include animals under natural law as full members of the moral community, on the basis that animals, *pace* Wolff, have reason that differs only in degree from that of humans (Eilschov 1747, 1748; cf. Koch 1976). In Dutch universities, Wolff's presence was limited (Janssen 1987). But he gained a significant voice through the French translation of his *Institutiones* by Elie Luzac (Wolff 1772), who saw his heavily annotated edition as a continuation of Barbeyrac's great work (Velema 1993, ch. 3). Wolff's influence in Switzerland was underscored by Vattel (Zurbuchen 1998).

11 Vattel 1916 [1758], 1762. Cf. Hochstrasser 2000, pp. 177–83; Jouannet 1998; Ruddy 1975; Whelan 1988.

5   Immanuel Kant

Histories of moral and political thought have commonly left the impression that natural law was killed off by Hume, Bentham, and Kant, and then buried by historicism, idealism, and positivism. This is a less than adequate view of the transition from the eighteenth to the nineteenth century, especially with regard to the German-speaking world (Klippel 1993, 1995; Schröder and Pielemeier 1995). The issue may be approached through a piece of contemporary evidence. In 1793 Karl Heinrich Heydenreich, professor of philosophy in Leipzig, wrote that if one considers the history of natural law theory from the point of view of the 'more or less pure and complete presentation of its principles, then one can only accept two periods, that of uncertain treatment which stretches until Kant and that of certain treatment which was begun with Kantian moral theory (*Sittenlehre*)' (Heydenreich 1793–6, I, p. 107).

Heydenreich's bombast was not simply the assertive triumphalism to be expected of a devoted Kantian but an opinion shared so widely that it made itself true (Kersting 1993, pp. 151–74; Klippel 1976, ch. 8). When Kant published his critical moral philosophy in 1785 and 1788, the categorical imperative was immediately taken as providing a new foundation of natural law theory. In fact, the *Groundwork of the Metaphysic of Morals* (1785) and the *Critique of Practical Reason* (1788) invigorated the genre to such an extent that when Kant at last published his own theory of law in 1797, a significant number of 'Kantian' works on natural law had already been published, and commentaries on Kant's *Doctrine of Right* (1797) appeared within months of its publication. These works were by thinkers ranging from Jacobins to conservatives.

Moreover, the debate about the shape of Kantian theory of law was taken up immediately in a lively manner in Denmark, where Anders Sandøe Ørsted's revision of Kant and temporary following of Fichte produced a liberal rights theory in tension with the absolute monarch, Frederick VI (Ørsted 1797; Tamm 1976, pt 2). One of the founders of the university in Christiania (later Oslo) and a statesman in Norway after its separation from Denmark and union with Sweden (1814), Nils Treschow, was inspired in his liberal philosophy by the debate about Kant while still teaching in Copenhagen (Treschow 1798). In Sweden the Uppsala philosopher Daniel Boëthius took up the Kantian renewal of natural law (Boëthius 1799).

The Kantian takeover of natural law can be seen as the outcome of a long struggle between the more or less direct heirs to the two 'schools' delineated here. More precisely, it can be seen as a victory for the metaphysical point of view of the Wolffians, though significantly transformed in the hands of Kant. The central change that took place was a shift from the metaphysics of natural *law* to that of natural *rights*, a process often obscured by the fact that both concepts in German commonly are denoted by the word *Naturrecht*. As the matter was clarified, *Menschenrecht(e)* (human right(s)) became the common word for the subjective concept, no doubt reinforced by the French *droits de l'homme*.

From the third quarter of the century, there had been an explosion of interest in 'anthropology', the broadly empirical study of all aspects of human life and culture which was commonly thought of in English as 'the science of human nature' (Zammito 2002). A major factor had been the indigenous tradition, originating in Pufendorf and Thomasius and subsequently much developed, for seeing the moral and political institutions of life as 'conventional' in character and subject to historical study. This kind of approach was reinforced by the influence of Anglo-Scottish ideas of the history of civil society (Oz-Salzberger 1995, ch. 8). As far as natural law was concerned, the study of human nature in society and history led to a rejection of the notion of a state of nature as an (historically or logically) 'original' condition of humanity just as the historicity of founding contracts came under pressure.

This turn towards historicism in political and legal matters was paralleled by a new interest in the empirical study of morality. In great part inspired by British moral and common-sense philosophy, German thinkers turned their attention to the problem of the mind's moral powers as both cognitive and active (Kuehn 1987; Waszek 1988, ch. 2; van der Zande 1998). In traditional Leibnizian and Wolffian theory, the active moral power was reduced to an intellectual love of perfection brought about by purely cognitive, or theoretical, activity; the moral life was a life of metaphysical understanding. When this model was compromised by the admission that moral feelings had a role, we have the beginning of a shift towards the idea that moral theory is concerned with powers of doing things towards the world, including other people, rather than with mere cognition of the world.

These two challenges to the German metaphysical tradition in terms of social historicism and anthropological empiricism were quashed by a series of reformulations of that tradition which culminated in Kant. The basic formula was to take over the new individualism and transform its empirical approach by focusing on a metaphysical view of the individual person. Thus the historicist rejection of the state of nature and the consequent historicisation of civil society could be avoided if one made the idea of a natural state into a conceptual component of human nature. That is to say, while the state of nature in the older natural law was a collective condition of humanity, in the new natural law of the later eighteenth century it became a condition of each person irrespective of time and place. In the older theories, the state of nature summarised those features of humanity (primarily our natural liberty and rights) which supposedly had to be discarded or transformed in order for political society to be possible. However, if these natural rights were part of each person's humanity, they had to play a continuing role in legitimating authority. This idea of right as each individual's natural liberty merged with the old idea of natural right as the right of free conscience, as had already occurred most strikingly in Rousseau, with whom more and more Europeans concurred in wondering how it was possible that 'man is born free, and everywhere he is in chains' (*SC*, 1.1, p. 41). However, as we saw in the first section of this chapter, the right of conscience was simultaneously the duty to the right use of conscience, and this idea that a natural right is not simply a freedom but one with a prescribed, morally right, use remained integral to the new theories of rights.

The second empirical challenge to the metaphysical tradition was met in similar fashion. The empirical study of the formation and function of moral sentiments can be set aside if man is naturally free. If the core of moral agency is the exercise of an inherent right grounded in a non-empirical ('pure') moral intellect, how the agent feels about it is of no relevance, let alone how it has come about. Irrespective of his actual circumstances, man as a rational being is a self-governing or autonomous agent.

The central question, however, was whether this metaphysical individualism could account for society between individuals. Why should the autonomous acts of one individual be of any relevance to the similar acts of another? On what ground can we assume that one person's rights entail another person's duties? How can the moral world, in the widest sense of that term, be well ordered? That was the fundamental issue with which German political thinkers, and especially the early Kantians, wrestled in the 1790s (cf. Beiser 1987, 1992). This line of thinking was similar to Leibniz's idea of universal harmony and to Wolff's of the maximum happiness in creation as the inherent *telos* of social life; all stand in sharp contrast to the Pufendorfian–Thomasian minimalist idea of civil society as the avoidance of violence. For those Kant-inspired thinkers who dealt with the problem before the appearance of Kant's own *Metaphysics of Morals* (1797), autonomy or self-legislation meant use of the categorical imperative as set out in the *Groundwork of the Metaphysics of Morals*. On this principle the moral world was divided into two broad spheres; those actions that were permitted because their maxims were universalisable; and those that were prohibited because their maxims were not universalisable. But this only said something definite about our duty in the negative sense, what not to do, while positive duties on the whole were left indefinite (for example, the duty to be charitable at best entails the vague injunction to consider giving something at some time to some charitable purpose). Outside the sphere of duty, the range of human action consisted of what was permissible, and for some thinkers, such as Fichte in his early work, this wide field was that of rights (Fichte 1796–7).

The young Fichte in particular saw the Hobbesian logic of this troubling conclusion with greater clarity than many political thinkers before or since. There might not be any principled entailment between right and duty; harmony between autonomous individuals might not be a moral but a purely prudential matter (or, for those who looked to Hume or Burke, a matter of slow adaptation through history). In order to sustain such views and retain a concept of rights, Fichte and his contemporaries would have had to develop a theory that gave the concept of rights moral standing independently of the concept of duty, so that rights were not only 'subjective' in the sense of being the characteristic of moral personality but also in the sense of not *presupposing* an objective and orderly correlation of right and duty. Most of these thinkers shied away from such ideas, often begging the question in the same way as subsequent scholarly commentators by insisting that 'right' *means* 'being owed something as a duty'.

Kant himself required more forceful measures than those of definition to keep the moral world well ordered and yet a matter of right. The core of the Kantian method was an appeal to common moral experience as being one that inherently involved freedom and an elaboration of what such freedom entailed. However, since the experience of freedom in moral decisions seemed impossible to ascertain empirically, the experience to which appeal was made had to be purified. To persons not already persuaded by Kant, this procedure has always appeared entirely question begging since the criterion of purification seems to be that one is free of ordinary 'sensuous' influences on one's decision-making. Indeed, it has been argued that the *Groundwork* is not so much an argument as an inculcation in a spiritual exercise to prepare the mind for the experience of freedom proper (Hunter 2002). Irrespective of how Kant's appeal to a supposedly 'pure' experience of moral freedom is interpreted, his assertion is the well-known claim that such experience entails our being both free and yet subject to ordinary causal influences;

and the most obvious way of reading it is as the metaphysical idea that our noumenal self is part of a realm outside time, space, and causation, while our empirical self is in the world of the senses (cf. Ameriks 2000a, intro. and pt 1). However flimsy these presuppositions may seem to the uninitiated, there can be no doubt that Kant's transformation of the metaphysical tradition condemned Leibniz and Wolff to the status of mere predecessors, and Pufendorf and Thomasius nearly to oblivion.

Kant's theory of law and the state in the *Doctrine of Right* was the outcome of more than thirty years' attention to the topic (XIX, 422–613, XXIII, 207–420, esp. 207–370).[12] He lectured repeatedly on natural law, using the textbook of Achenwall and Pütter (1750), and he foreshadowed his own book in correspondence and in the more famous critical works on moral philosophy. Yet the book significantly changed natural law and developed the critical moral philosophy in a way that surprised his followers.[13] At the heart of Kant's revision of the metaphysical natural law tradition was his notion of autonomy; natural law is not external to the moral agent; only self-legislation can be the source of legitimacy. However, in order for such self-legislation to yield a doctrine of right and a foundation for the state, the self in question must be conceived on empirical assumptions that had not been made in the *Groundwork* and the second *Critique*. According to the moral law, as stated in the *Groundwork*, 'a rational being must always regard himself as lawgiving in a kingdom of ends possible through freedom of the will, whether as a member or as sovereign' (IV, 434 [1785]). But what is required of a rational being's legislation when this kingdom of ends is considered as embodied in a world of empirical phenomena, in which people have an unknowable variety of goals ('ends')? Kant thinks we must divide this into two questions. First, what can reason tell us about the mode of pursuing our goals in abstraction from what those goals actually are? Secondly, are there any goals we ought to have, not as means to something else but as ends in themselves ('categorically')? The former of these practical questions is addressed in the 'Metaphysical First Principles of the Doctrine of Right', the latter in the 'Metaphysical First Principles of the Doctrine of Virtue', which together make up the *Metaphysics of Morals*.[14]

12 Kant's unpublished papers are referred to by the volumes and pages of the Akademie Ausgabe (Kant 1900–). In references to Kant's published works, the particular title is identified by its year of publication while volumes and pages are those of the Akademie Ausgabe; the translations all reproduce the Akademie Ausgabe's volume and page numbers.
13 Brandt 1982a; Busch 1979; Kersting 1993; Ludwig 1988; Ritter 1971.
14 The text of the *Doctrine of Right* is corrupt in several places and has been restored by B. Ludwig in Kant 1986. I refer to his edition but also to the pages of the Akademie Ausgabe. Ludwig's rearrangements

We may start from Kant's insistence that the embodied person, as a matter of rational necessity, has a right to his or her freedom (VI, 237–8 [1797a]).[15] This means the right to have possession (not property) in one's self, one's actions, and the positions in time and space that are entailed by being an embodied self in action – the ground one occupies, the space one fills, the air one breathes, and so on. To deny human beings these things would mean to deny their status as moral persons. However, this does not mean that one has a right to be in any particular place in the world for any particular span of time, holding on to any particular thing (Kant gestures towards Locke's example of picking an apple; VI, 250). Where, when, and how a person is in the world are entirely contingent matters, empirical questions. From the point of view of pure reason (as a matter of abstract principle), any part of the world – any constellation of things and events in time and space – is open as a possibility for any person. Furthermore, we must assume as a possibility – nothing stronger – that any person may have desires for another position (for other things) in the world than that which he or she happens to have. Finally, we must allegedly assume the empirical fact that the world is finite. Although we at any particular time may be able to go elsewhere, from the point of view of pure reason – in abstraction from the particular situation of specific individuals – humanity as a whole in its life tenure of the world must divide it up. The division provided by the vicissitudes of history – where one happens to find oneself – has no standing in reason: it might all have been entirely different 'with as much reason'. In other words, the empirical links between persons and the things in the world (such as physical control or addition of labour) have no rational standing and need replacement by the purely ideal links of reason.

If it is permissible to use force to prevent any other person from interfering in the relationship between oneself and an object of one's choice, then that object is one's property. Kant's concept of permissibility is here central (Brandt 1982a; Szymkowiak 2002). You need no special justification in defending your self, your actions, and their *immediate* objects against

---

are reflected in the English translation (Kant 1996a). For general commentary, see: Batscha 1976; Brandt 1974, pp. 180–201, 1982b; *Columbia Law Review*, 87 (1989): 'Symposium on Kantian Legal Theory'; Deggau 1983; Dreier 1986; Ebbinghaus 1986; Goyard-Fabre 1996b; Gregor 1963; Guyer 2000, ch. 7; Hunter 2001, ch. 6; *Jahrbuch für Recht und Ethik/Annual Review of Law and Ethics*, 5 (1997); Kaulbach 1982; Kühl 1984; Küsters 1988; Maus 1992; Mulholland 1990; Murphy 1970; Rosen 1993; Schneewind 1993, 1998, ch. 23.

15 This and the next paragraph attempt a reconstruction of the main argument in pt I, ch. I of the *Doctrine of Right* (VI, 245–57).

interference; the person who knocks the apple out of your hand is interfering with your basic right of liberty. But if you want to use force to keep others away from anything that you lay claim to outside this immediate sphere of your person, you need exemption from exactly the ban against interfering with the other's basic liberty. This exemption Kant calls the *Erlaubnisgesetz*, the law of permission (VI, 247 [1797a], cf. VIII, 348 n [1795]). The moral life of humanity considered only as occupiers of the empirical or phenomenal world consists of the search for ways of realising this law. The principle for this search is the principle of right; the method is the institution of the state and the universal society of the world.

We must understand the principle of right in comparison with the principle of virtue (VI, 218–21 [1797a], and VI, 379–413 [1797b]). The former regulates our actions, the latter the 'maxims' of our actions. When we deal with persons considered as members of the realm of freedom, reason demands that we respect the humanity of all, including ourselves, equally as an end of inherent value. The maxims upon which we act must, therefore, be equally applicable to all, for they must be maxims of respect for humanity. These fall into two broad categories of duties of virtue, namely the duty to self-perfection and the duty to seek the happiness of others. When we deal with persons considered only as joint occupiers of the world, we abstract from maxims and ends. Reason then demands that the exercises of our freedom in action be mutually compatible, which, more specifically, means that we are only permitted to use force against others when this could become a universal law. Just as the categorical imperative in its ethical or virtue aspect is a principle of reciprocity in the maxims we adopt, so in its juridical or rights aspect it is a principle of reciprocity in the actions we perform. Those are the basic thoughts behind Kant's division of the moral world into ethics or the doctrine of virtue and law or the doctrine of right; between what is not enforceable and what is; between internal and external.

A world in which the law of permission on every occasion of its use was truly universalisable would be a world without any conflict between people's claims on the things of the world, and this would constitute complete justice in the distribution of property. This is a utopian, limiting concept for humanity's moral striving; the most significant milestone on the way is the state. The rationale for the state is to ensure laws of permission that are universal for its members so that their takings from the world can be secured by being mutually compatible. Kant expresses this by saying that without the state – in the state of nature, to use the traditional language – all 'property' is merely *provisional*; the state makes it *peremptory* (though true finality would in fact only be achieved in the universal society) (VI, 255–7 [1797a]).

Before turning to Kant's theory of the state, we must consider the scope of the notion of property (VI, 258–96 [1797a, pt I, ch. 2]). While he has by far most to say about property in things (VI, 260–70), he includes in the concept of property the other part of our environment, other people. We cannot, of course, own others as persons since the notion of a person entails freedom or autonomy. We can, however, own aspects of other people, on condition that this does not infringe the autonomy of the other, and that means that the ownership in question has to be co-ownership. Kant divides such co-ownership into two types. We may unite our will with that of another about some *particular* aspect of that other person's behaviour (typically an individual action). Such a uniting of wills is a contract that creates a right against the other person (a 'personal' right) and its most important object is the transfer of property (VI, 271–6). Or, we may unite our will with the will of other persons about our control of some *general* aspect of their lives or mode of behaviour to the exclusion of such control by themselves or others. This form of contract creates the rights between spouses, parents, and children, and masters and servants (VI, 276–84 and 358–61). These rights do not take away the moral status of the persons against whom they are held (in effect, wives, children, and servants), and the husband, father, and master is not a moral representative of these persons. Consequently, Kant does not adhere to the traditional natural law idea that political society is composed of family societies through a contract of the heads of households (cf. Böhme 1993, pt I). The state is composed of individual property owners. This leaves a question mark over the political status of the propertyless.

Kant's theory of the state is a direct implication of his theory of property, which again is a specification of the principle of right that is a form of the categorical imperative. At the same time, Kant has the reputation of being a major representative of the idea of contract as the foundation for the state. What is the relationship between property and contract in the theory of the state (VI, 305–13)? Kant often employs the traditional language of a contract that bridges the state of nature and the political state, and this may tempt his readers into thinking in terms of a sequence, whether historical or hypothetical. But he did not think that there ever was, or could be, a 'state of nature' in the sense of a condition in which there was neither property nor power relations between people. From the hand of nature we have just one 'juridical' feature, namely the natural right to freedom without which we would not be persons but things. But the exercise of that right necessarily means occupation of parts of the world, as we have seen, and this again puts us into relationships with other people. The state of nature is therefore a rightful condition in the sense that the same principle of right applies there as in politically organised society. But in the non-political state, natural right rests on the individual will of each person, not on the will of humanity, although humanity holds the world collectively. Accordingly, whether there is peaceful harmony or war in the state of nature is a purely contingent, empirical matter. The point of the state (ultimately cosmopolitan society) is to remove this contingency (VIII, 349 [1795]).

We may say, then, that people inevitably live 'socially' and subject to the principle of right. To do so in accordance with rational principle is to live politically, and this can be encapsulated in the idea of a contract. The political contract is a requirement of pure reason not to be in conflict with itself and, since reason recognises no distinction between people, this means that there has to be unity of will among all members of the state about the distribution of property. The contract is a test or criterion for justice in the exercise of sovereign power by any state, not a founding act. It is best to think of the contract as a basic constitutional principle or principle of legitimacy, clearly inspired by Rousseau's notion of the general will (e.g. VI, 315–16 [1797a]). The united will of the people is not an empirical, historical concept which has to be ascertained through voting. It is a metaphysical prerequisite necessitated by the idea of right as a condition of complete reciprocity of rational owners of property, a prerequisite that can be presented as purely 'formal' once the speculative premise has been accepted. This requirement to the exercise of sovereignty can be honoured, in principle, by any type of government, including absolute monarchies.

Political society that is legitimated in this way is a purely rightful condition which can be explicated by three basic principles: '1. The *freedom* of every member of the society as a *human being*. 2. His *equality* with every other as a *subject*. 3. The *independence* of every member of a commonwealth as a *citizen*' (VIII, 290 [1793], cf. VI, 314 [1797a]). *Freedom* is stipulated as the moral condition of humanity, and this cannot be changed through political institution. That is the basis for Kant's severe criticism of all forms of paternalism in politics – but of course paternalism is defined as the absence of exactly this kind of freedom. *Equality* is implied by the idea of governance by universal law, which is the essence of the state. This is the premise for Kant's harsh rejection of all inherited status or office – naturally understood as the denial of this equality (VIII, 292 [1793], VI, 324–5, 328–9, 369–70

[1797a]). But what is meant by *independence* as a citizen, i.e. as a co-legislator with all other citizens? (VIII, 294–6 [1793], VI, 314–15 [1797a]).

Kant's explanation is that a person who has to sustain life exclusively by labour which is directed by others cannot be an 'active citizen', i.e. one who is considered part of the united will of the people. For this, property sufficient for living is required. 'Passive' citizens, by contrast, include wives and domestic servants, to whom only the civic principles of freedom and equality extend. Aside from the fact that he never provides any satisfactory explanation of the traditional notion of the man as master of the wife, Kant's argument seems problematic in two respects. He does not give any clear criterion for the degree of control over one's labour that is required for one to be considered independent. He does not stick consistently to the production of exchangeable goods as the criterion but seems to be bound by traditional ideas of household authority. More seriously, from a Kantian perspective, even if we could imagine a member of the commonwealth who held no property whatsoever, no external 'mine' but only the internal 'mine' that is unavoidable in the human condition, such a person would presumably be subject to the requirements of practical reason and thus surely have a duty/right to have his or her will counted in the rational exercise of sovereignty. While the Kantian state is in a sense based upon property, this does not entail that it has to be a corporation of property owners. If the state really is a requirement of reason – namely to live consistently or by universal law – then it must mean a requirement of *anyone's* reason, whatever property life may have brought them into.

The sovereign governance may be by the will of all, which is republicanism, and demanded by practical reason, or it may be by some particular will of one or more individuals, which is despotism and against reason (VIII, 349–53 [1795], VI, 340–1 [1797a]). However, any of the traditional forms of state – autocracy, aristocracy, or democracy – may govern in a republican manner – a kind of 'as-if' republicanism (cf. VII, 90–1 [1798]).[16] Whatever its form, the state's legitimacy stems from implementing the idea of the contract by governing as if there were a separation of powers (VIII, 351–2 [1795], VI, 313, 315–20 [1797a]). The legislative makes general laws in the name of the united will of the people, while the executive as an agent of the state applies law in particular circumstances, and the judiciary resolves conflicts through juries that determine guilt and judges that apply the law.

16 In *Perpetual Peace* (1795), democracy, meaning direct democracy, is ruled out as inherently despotic (VIII:351–2).

In a fully republican state, the executive is subject to the legislative in the sense that the latter can disempower or change the former, but the executive can never be subject to punishment since this would turn the legislative into an executive power. More generally, the legislative cannot be the executive government since the latter must be subject to law, which the former cannot be. In other words, politics is largely reduced to abstract legislation on the one hand, and administrative procedure on the other.

That is true, however, only of republican governance in abstract reason. Kant is well aware of, and has much to say about, politics in the historically given world, and the essence of his message is, not surprisingly, that such politics ought to be under the influence of the demands of reason he sets out. This implies his total rejection of revolutionary changes of state forms and it is the basis for his well-known theory of the role of publicity. Since practical reason claims governance by general law, the use of force is a contradiction: logically there cannot be a *right* to revolution (VI, 317–23, 370–2 [1797a]). There is, however, a right to passive resistance in situations where active compliance would imply that people deny their personal autonomy (autonomy being Kant's replacement of duty to God in traditional resistance theory) (VI, 371 [1797a]; cf. Arntzen 1996). Furthermore, since the life of reason is argument, freedom to argue is demanded as a basic right by our very condition as moral beings. A free public sphere of opinion, or publicity, is thus indispensable and cannot legitimately be obstructed (VIII, 33–42 [1784], VIII, 304–5 [1793], VIII, 381–4 [1795], VII, 17–75, 89–91 [1798]; cf. Brandt 1987; Habermas 1989; Laursen 1992, ch. 9; Lestition 1993; O'Neill 1989, ch. 2).

In the historical world, this sphere is the vehicle for political change, for it is here that kings and philosophers can meet, even if their roles cannot and should not be united (VIII, 369 [1795]). The process of creating a public sphere of reason encompassing both ruler and ruled was Kant's answer to the question, What is Enlightenment? (cf. Bödeker and Hermann 1987; Hinske 1989; Laursen 1989; Schmidt 1989, 1996; Schneiders 1974). This hallowed idea is, however, rather self-serving. For the point about the historically given world is, of course, that it does *not* consist of rational members of the realm of freedom, but of individuals and groups with all manner of temporal 'sensuous' interests, and the Kantian argument lends no legitimacy to the liberty of discussing such interests *per se*, or in their own right. The point of Kant's argument is to single out the pursuit of pure rationality and the postulated freedom; it is in the service of these particular values that the free public sphere is promoted. This was, in a sense, his particular interest as an educator and public intellectual and it has been argued that it was his sectarian propagation of that interest on behalf of the philosophical faculty against the theological and the juridical faculties that led the Prussian king to censor Kant's publishing activity (Hunter, 2005).

True to his presupposition that the moral world must by its nature be well ordered, Kant thought that conflict, even the possibility of conflict, is a sign of unreason, a sign that behaviour is not governed by principle (cf. Saner 1973, pt 3). Not least, this also applies to war. The formation of states is thus not enough to satisfy reason; we must pursue a legal order between states and, eventually, a cosmopolitan society and right that encompasses all states and individuals (VIII, 307–13 [1793], VIII, 383–5 [1795], VI, 352–3 [1797a]; cf. Cavallar 2002, ch. 6; Gerhardt 1995; Klemme in Kant 1992; Tuck 1999, pp. 207–25). Kant does not conceive of the latter as a world state; he rejects this because it would be impossible to have institutionalised enforcement of rights between states. Cosmopolitan right must be voluntary, and it is therefore crucially dependent upon the progress of republicanism in the world. This is so because despots, who by Kant's definition act on particular not general wills, cannot exercise voluntary adherence to an international legal order as a matter of principle, only as a matter of prudence. Furthermore, it is much more difficult for a republic than for other governments to go to war since war requires a united will to sacrifice life and property. Finally, the separation of powers in a republican government is in itself the kind of voluntary living by the principle of right that is required to secure a perpetual peace, which is the ultimate duty of right demanded by practical reason (VI, 354–5 [1797a], VII, 85–6 [1798]).

Kant's new 'tone of superiority in philosophy' – to echo one of his own titles – has been overwhelmingly successful in determining how the history of philosophy in general should be seen (Haakonssen 2006). In the philosophy of law, it has persuaded most commentators that his own enterprise was in an entirely different category from that of the Leibnizians and Wolffians and that the Pufendorfians and Thomasians were hardly philosophers at all.

10

Natural rights in the Scottish Enlightenment

JAMES MOORE

1 The context of Scottish natural jurisprudence

One of the notable achievements of recent scholarship on moral and political thought in eighteenth-century Scotland has been a recognition of the importance of the early modern natural rights tradition for what has come to be called the Scottish Enlightenment. The manner in which the natural rights theories of Grotius, Hobbes, Pufendorf, and Locke were received, adapted, criticised, and transformed has been narrated and interpreted from different points of view.[1]

It has become increasingly evident, in part as a consequence of this scholarship, in part as a result of research into the history of Scottish universities, that natural jurisprudence constituted an integral part of the moral philosophy curriculum at the universities of Glasgow, Edinburgh, and Aberdeen (only St Andrews was the exception) from the 1690s to the late eighteenth century (Emerson 1972, 1995; Sher 1985, 1990; Wood 1993). Gershom Carmichael, Francis Hutcheson, Adam Smith, and Thomas Reid at Glasgow; William Law, William Scott, John Pringle, and James Balfour at Edinburgh; and George Turnbull and David Verner at Aberdeen all lectured on natural rights theories. What led these professors, university councils, and noble patrons to conclude that students should be instructed in the literature and language of natural rights?

In the post-revolutionary world of the 1690s, there was the compelling practical political consideration that university students, the future political leaders of Scottish society, be made aware of the errors and dangers of pre-revolutionary political thought. In the natural rights theories of Grotius, Pufendorf, and, especially, Locke, students would find erroneous political theories – patriarchalism, the divine right of kings, indefeasible hereditary right – examined, analysed, and confuted. They would be directed by natural

---

1 Forbes 1975, 1982; Haakonssen 1981, 1989, 1996a; Hont 1987; Hont and Ignatieff 1983b; MacCormick 1982; Stein 1970, 1980.

rights theorists to a new range of questions, more consistent with the new order of things. Is there a law of nature, and, if so, how does it oblige? Is the natural condition of mankind a condition of sociability or of war? Do individuals have a natural right of self-defence, of liberty, of property? Is there a natural obligation to keep promises? Do governments have their origin in the consent, express or tacit, of the people? The persistence of patriarchal and feudal institutions in Scotland, and the threat that the pre-revolutionary order would be restored – a menace underlined by the Jacobite rebellions of 1715, 1719, and 1745 – presented recurrent challenges to Scottish moralists. In these circumstances, it is understandable that natural rights theories would be employed not only to expose the injustices of feudal societies but also to justify social change.

There were as well more academic reasons for the turn to natural rights theories. The moral philosophy taught in Scottish universities in the seventeenth century was typically a form of Aristotelian scholasticism.[2] In light of the experimental methods employed by natural scientists, the methods and arguments of Aristotelianism had fallen out of fashion. The systems of Grotius, Hobbes, Pufendorf, and Locke were all opposed to scholastic Aristotelianism. It remained a question for Scottish moralists to determine the moral psychology or motivation that might account for rights and virtues better than the scholastic theory that all men long for beatitude or lasting happiness. The differences that figure most prominently in the juridical debate engaged in by Carmichael, Hutcheson, Hume, Lord Kames, and Adam Smith turned upon their different understandings of the passions and sentiments deemed to prompt men to acknowledge and enforce the rights and obligations of men and citizens.

University chairs were coveted, in eighteenth-century Scotland, by some of the ablest individuals of that era. Smith observed that, whereas in France and England talented scholars and writers were frequently drawn to the church, in Scotland, and in the other countries of Reformed Europe, 'the most eminent men of letters . . . have, not all indeed, but the far greater part of them, been professors in universities' (*WN*, v.i.g.39, p. 811). The authority of university professors extended beyond the ranks of students formally enrolled in classes. Their lectures were attended, their books were read, and their presence solicited in select societies and clubs by men and women who were eager to be acquainted with their ideas and to engage

---

2 It was a requirement of the Visitation Commission at Glasgow in 1664 that 'Aristotle his text be diligently and succinctly gone through': Glasgow University Archives 26631 (1664) 12.

them in debate. But it is worth remarking that many of the same moral philosophers (including some of the most distinguished among them) who taught natural jurisprudence in the classrooms wrote in a different idiom for adult readers. Francis Hutcheson made it clear to readers of his Latin compendium of moral philosophy, where his treatment of natural law themes was adumbrated, that it was a work intended only for students in universities; when he wrote for mature readers, Hutcheson wrote on virtue, on moral affections, and the moral sense (Hutcheson 1747, p. iv). Smith's lectures on jurisprudence were never published in his lifetime; he gave priority to the moral sentiments when writing for publication. One may expect to discover accordingly evidence of tension in the natural jurisprudence of Hutcheson, Smith, and others, as they sought to reconcile their natural law theories with their other philosophical commitments.

David Hume, arguably the most eminent philosopher and man of letters in eighteenth-century Scotland, did not occupy a chair of moral philosophy in a university. The story of the endeavours of his friends to secure a university appointment for him has been told by his biographers (Emerson 1994; Stewart 1994). It has been remarked that Hume devoted a large part of his earliest work in moral philosophy to a consideration of natural rights theories (Forbes 1975, 1982; Haakonssen 1981, 1989, 1996a). It has also been observed that the character of his responses to the several questions posed by the natural jurists has much in common with the answers given by Epicureans and sceptics, both ancient and modern (Moore 1988, 1994). It is accordingly necessary to consider the problematic character of the relationship between natural rights theories and scepticism in the moral and political thought of Hume in what follows.

Students of civil law in eighteenth-century Scotland were understandably attracted to the study of natural law; for the law of Scotland was much indebted to Roman civil law, which was in turn agreed to be derived from principles of natural law (Stein 1963). Professorships of civil law were created at the Universities of Edinburgh and Glasgow in 1710 and 1714 respectively, but these professors were prevented from offering instruction in natural law, on the grounds that such teaching would invade the academic jurisdiction of moral philosophers (Cairns 1993, pp. 155–7). One jurist who was not inhibited in this way was Henry Home, Lord Kames, who made extensive use of natural law theories in his writings on jurisprudence and on moral philosophy (Lieberman 1983; 1989, pp. 144–75). He maintained that all his contemporaries had been pitifully deficient in their understandings of obligation. His writings on jurisprudence, together with the testimony of contemporaries, suggest that he was among the earliest, and arguably the first, Scottish thinker to elaborate the four stages theory which would come to be employed by so many Scottish moralists, jurists, and historians to explain the history of societies and their legal arrangements.

Among the most celebrated Scottish thinkers of the age of Enlightenment for his writings on ethics and political economy, Adam Smith must now be recognised to have been an accomplished theorist of natural jurisprudence (Cairns 1993; Haakonssen 1981; Hont and Ignatieff 1983b; Skinner 1993; Winch 1993). Although Smith distinguished the spheres of ethics and jurisprudence more sharply than his predecessors or contemporaries, he imported from his ethics to his jurisprudence his understanding of the passions and the sentiments that prompt men to seek justice and support enforcement of the natural and sacred rights of mankind. Like Kames, Smith was deeply impressed by the injustices of feudal society, and by the need to explain and justify what he took to be the natural course of social change. His teaching and writing on that subject would lead beyond natural rights theories to political economy.

Not all courses in moral philosophy offered in Scottish universities in the eighteenth century incorporated the intellectual agenda of natural jurisprudence. There were professors of moral philosophy who abjured the discourse of natural rights: William Cleghorn in Edinburgh; David Fordyce and James Beattie in Aberdeen. By the late eighteenth century, for a variety of reasons, the natural law tradition was superseded by a different range of questions and inquiries. It will be necessary to explain, briefly, how these enquiries came to replace natural jurisprudence in Scottish universities at the end of the eighteenth century.

The ensuing discussion will endeavour to answer the following questions. How did the early modern natural law tradition come to be established in the moral philosophy curricula of Scottish universities? How did moralists such as Hutcheson reconcile their natural rights theories with their commitment to the very different intellectual tradition of civic virtue? Is Hume's moral and political thought made more intelligible when it is located within a construction of the early modern natural rights tradition, or is it better understood as a sceptical response to that tradition? What considerations prompted Kames, Smith, and others to transform juridical speculation about the right of property and the right to punish into an enquiry concerning the history of societies? Finally, what were the factors that persuaded Scottish moral and political theorists to turn away from the natural rights tradition late in the eighteenth century?

2 Academic reform and the law of nature

In 1690 the Scottish parliament enacted a law which stipulated that all principals, professors, regents, and masters in universities, colleges, and schools in Scotland had to subscribe to the Confession of Faith of the newly established Presbyterian Church and swear allegiance to their majesties, King William and Queen Mary. In these circumstances, many resigned, or were obliged to resign, their positions. These professors had been appointed in an era – following the restoration of monarchy in 1660 and the imposition of a uniform liturgy in the Churches of England and Scotland in 1662 – when moral philosophy was taught in accordance with the principles of Aristotelian scholasticism. It was a system of morals which followed a four-fold division of the subject: the supreme good or final cause of moral life was conceived to be beatitude or lasting happiness; the formal causes of moral conduct were the intellect and the will, the faculties that direct our actions to beatitude; the material causes of lasting happiness were the appetites, passions, and affections; and the efficient causes, the effective means of attaining beatitude, were the virtues. This system was held to be consistent with the political principles of the Restoration crown and church: absolute monarchy, indefeasible hereditary right, and the duty of loyalty or passive obedience of subjects to their rulers. Only an absolute monarch could provide the single-minded direction of subjects so necessary for public happiness; the claims of hereditary right were consistent with the laws of inheritance of private estates and with the natural affection of parental love and filial respect; and, among the virtues, none was more important than obedience to sovereigns.

It was this controversial combination of scholastic ethics and divine right theory that moral philosophers attempted to counter in the post-revolutionary era by enlisting in opposition to it moral and political theories based upon the law of nature. The issue was joined in 1695 when representatives of the four Scottish universities found it impossible to agree upon a moral philosophy syllabus. The course had been proposed by a philosophy regent of the Restoration era, John Tran, appointed at Glasgow in 1669. He had been regarded with suspicion on political grounds by commissioners who visited the university in 1690 to administer the new oath of allegiance.[3] His approach to moral philosophy was equally suspect in the judgement of representatives from Edinburgh and St Andrews. In their opinion, the author had 'not at all distinctly treated of the law of nature

---

3 Glasgow University Archives 26631 (1690) 38.

though it be the great foundation of all ethics'; he was 'too much addicted to the old logical method of assigning efficient, material, formal, and final causes . . . which method seems not only needless, but often ridiculous'. The author had made passing references to the law of nature but he had made it part of the eternal law in the manner of Thomas Aquinas: 'he confounds *lex aeterna* and *naturalis*', whereas 'we think the eternal wisdom of God is improperly called a law, neither can we understand what our author means by an eternal law distinct from the law of nature'.[4]

The fundamental problem with the scholastic Aristotelian theory of natural law was theological. That theory of natural law supposed that human beings could participate, albeit imperfectly, in the Supreme Being, in the mind of God, or the eternal law. In Reformed or Presbyterian theology, no such participation was possible. Men and women do not participate in the real presence of God, which is merely signified. The mind of God is signified to us by revelation; but the same critics insist that to cite scripture is 'not at all to philosophize'. The mind of God is also made known to us by the nature of things. Such knowledge of the divine mind is properly called the natural law.

The principal critic of Aristotelian scholasticism in this debate was William Law, a regent at Edinburgh, and the first professor of moral philosophy at that university, from 1707 to 1729. Law urged his students to make use of the methods of experimental science in the study of the law of nature. He proposed that by such study we discover that we are obliged to observe that law by the rewards and punishments imposed by God. Law perceived his understanding of the law of nature to be consistent with Pufendorf's account of the rights and obligations which follow from the duty to cultivate sociability (Law 1705). In this respect, he concurred with the view of his colleague, William Scott, who held, with Pufendorf, that the fundamental duty of the law of nature is that every man ought to preserve and cultivate sociability. Scott maintained further that free men can only put themselves under government by their own consent, and that such was the case in Scotland in ancient times (Scott 1699). Scott also edited and annotated selections from Grotius in the expectation that he would be made professor of the law of nature and nations; he succeeded Law as professor of moral philosophy in 1729 (Walker 1985).

4 Edinburgh University Library, MS MC 1.4 TT (1695): 'Animadversions of the University of Edinburgh upon the Ethics of the University of Glasgow'; 'Animadversiones Facultatis Artium Universitatis Sancti-Andreae in Philosophiam Moralem Glasguensem'.

3   Gershom Carmichael: reformed scholasticism and natural rights

The moral philosopher who contributed most significantly to the establishment of the natural rights tradition in the universities of Scotland at the turn of the eighteenth century was Gershom Carmichael, a regent at Glasgow and its first professor of moral philosophy (Moore and Silverthorne 1983). Throughout his academic career, Carmichael identified the study of moral philosophy with the study of the natural rights theories of Grotius, Pufendorf, and Locke. His supplements and annotations to Pufendorf's *On the Duty of Man and Citizen* made Carmichael's ideas available to a wider readership in Britain and Europe (Carmichael 1724, 2002). The distinctive feature of Carmichael's adaptation of Pufendorf's natural jurisprudence was his insistence (with Grotius and Locke) on the natural rights of individuals. The manner in which he justified these rights would have implications for the work of his successors.

Like William Law and other philosophers of the post-revolutionary era, Carmichael repudiated the Aristotelian method of reasoning. In the preface to the last of his published works, he declared:

I have always avoided the forms of speaking of the Aristotelian school, which are obscure, ambiguous, and, as it were, deliberately fashioned for deception; nor did I think they were made any more sacred because they were blended into sacred matters, and for want of a better philosophy, applied to the explanation of the gravest topics of religion. (Carmichael 2002, p. 229)

Carmichael was in no sense an Aristotelian; but he was a scholastic, a Reformed or Presbyterian scholastic. He did not subscribe to the punitive conception of God found in more popular formulations of Reformed or Presbyterian theology: to the doctrines that sin must be punished; that God (in the person of Christ) has accepted this punishment for some (not all) of mankind; and that our obligation to God derives from our understanding that a debt has been paid on our behalf. Carmichael considered any punitive idea of God to be an unworthy conception of the deity. He arrived at his own understanding of man's relationship with God by reflecting upon those qualities or attributes or perfections of the deity which cannot be shared with mankind. He considered it impossible, given the imperfect conditions of human life, that beatitude or lasting happiness can ever be enjoyed in this life. But longing for such beatitude is inescapable; and this longing is most appropriately expressed in reverence for, or veneration of, God.

This was the first law of nature in Carmichael's natural jurisprudence, that every man signify his desire for lasting happiness in reverence for God.

One may signify such reverence directly, in worship; or it may be signified indirectly, in respect for God's creatures: in self-respect and respect for others. These were the second and third laws of nature: that one respect oneself and that one be sociable (Carmichael 2002, pp. 21–9, 46–53). There was no more appropriate way of signifying respect for persons, in Carmichael's view, than to acknowledge that every individual should be considered to enjoy certain natural rights, and it was the proper vocation of the moral philosopher to specify those rights and indicate how they applied to oneself and to others in various conditions of life.

Carmichael's understanding of the laws of nature permitted him an appreciably different perspective on social life from Pufendorf, who by contrast had argued that the cultivation and preservation of sociable living obliged all members of society to obey superior powers: husbands, fathers, masters, rulers. Carmichael thought otherwise. He maintained (with Grotius and Locke and against Pufendorf) that every individual has a natural right of self-defence. He concurred with Locke's reasoning that in the state of nature (in a world not yet occupied or appropriated, a negative community, as Pufendorf had conceived it) every man may have a right to property in things on which he has laboured (without waiting upon the agreement of others, as Pufendorf had maintained). He argued further, again on the authority of Locke, but putting the matter more unequivocally than Locke had ever done, that no man has the right to enslave another, 'for men are not among the objects which God has allowed the human race to enjoy dominion over'. He defended the theory, common to all the early modern natural jurists, that civil or political societies have their origin in an original contract, a theory which appealed to post-revolutionary Scottish thinkers, inasmuch as it excluded (particularly in Locke's formulation) any claim to political power on the grounds of hereditary right (Carmichael 2002, pp. 67–71, 92ff, 138–53).

Scottish jurists and legislators were also concerned, in the debates surrounding the Act of Union of 1707, with limitations on the powers that would be exercised by the government of Britain. Carmichael supported this demand for limitations, but he reinforced these arguments in a manner peculiar to his own understanding of natural law (Moore and Silverthorne 1995). In every properly constituted political society, limitations on the power of rulers already exist in the manner in which the original contract is made. Anyone who would exercise power over others, whether in civil society, or in the more immediate societies constituted by households and families, can do so legitimately only by recognising the rights or the claims of others. Such recognition generates a sense of obligation in others, a sense of obligation which endures as long as sovereigns, masters, husbands, and fathers continue to act in a spirit of reverence for the Creator and for His creatures. It will be evident that the obligatory force of natural law, in Carmichael's formulations, depended entirely upon his natural theology, upon a moral psychology which could assume that there is in all mankind a longing for beatitude which could be directed to veneration of God. It was a moral psychology which his successors would find problematic. Their search for an adequate substitute for this theory of rights and obligation would, however, prove to be no simple matter.

4   Francis Hutcheson: civic virtue and natural rights

The dogmas of Presbyterian theology, popular and scholastic, came under fire in various parts of Reformed Europe in the early eighteenth century (Moore 1990). In Ireland, there was an initiative, emanating from Belfast, which insisted on the right of Presbyterian ministers to decline subscription to the dogmatic theology of the Church of Scotland. In Dublin, a related campaign for reform of the Scottish universities was led by Viscount Molesworth, who encouraged his Scottish friends and followers to return to the teachings of the Stoic moralists of antiquity, to a love of virtue for its own sake. It was part of the genius of Francis Hutcheson as a moral philosopher that he attempted to bring these two movements together (Moore 1990). The results of his efforts were problematic: in part because of the intrinsic difficulties involved in reconciling the languages of rights and virtues; in part because Hutcheson situated his reconciling project in at least three quite different frames of reference.

In four treatises, written and published in Dublin in the 1720s, following the lead of Molesworth (and Molesworth's friend, the third earl of Shaftesbury), Hutcheson sought to identify in human nature a faculty or capacity which approved of virtue for its own sake. He called this faculty a moral sense, arguing that, whenever one perceives a character or an action that is prompted by benevolence or by kind affection, the moral sense brings to mind a sensation or a feeling of an idea of virtue (Hutcheson 1725, 1728). There was no need to suppose, with Carmichael, that moral conduct depended upon acting in a spirit of reverence for the deity; the motive to act virtuously, Hutcheson argued, is instinctive; it is benevolence (Hutcheson 1728, Illustrations, § 6). Thus the greater or more extensive the benevolence, the more virtuous the character that is so inspired or so motivated.

Hutcheson's idea of virtue had implications for his understanding of obligation and rights. He proposed that the idea of an obligation may be derived immediately from the moral sense and its idea of virtue as benevolence without the sanction of a law of nature. For the moral sense is so constituted that one cannot fail to feel a sense of obligation to act benevolently, quite apart from any law or rule. The same moral sense recognises a right to act from the same motive; so that whenever an action or a possession or a claim is prompted by benevolence one may say that 'any person in such circumstances has a right to do, possess or demand that thing'. It formed no part of the design of his English language writings of the 1720s to address the several questions posed by writers in the natural rights tradition. He did not neglect, however, to defend the right of private judgement, the right to serve God in the manner one believes to be most acceptable to the deity, the right insisted upon by non-subscribing clergymen of the Presbyterian Church in Ireland. He also defended the right of property derived from labour and industry; while acknowledging, paradoxically, that it is not the 'weak motive of general benevolence' which finds expression in this right, but rather the stronger motives of self-love and particular benevolence or family affection, friendship, and gratitude. This apparent contradiction in the moral psychology of Hutcheson's theory of rights was one that he attempted to resolve by employing a distinction first used by the natural jurists for very different reasons (Hutcheson 1725, § 7, pp. 256, 261–2, 264).

Grotius, Pufendorf, and Carmichael had distinguished between perfect rights, which are claims or actions so necessary for the preservation of sociable living that they must be enforced; and imperfect rights, which are claims or actions that may benefit others but are not necessary for social living and so need not be enforced. Hutcheson took over this terminology, but he put it to a different use. His determination to derive rights and obligations from the virtue of benevolence led him to adapt the perfect/imperfect distinction in a curious and paradoxical way. He argued that rights and obligations which are enforced do not require the exercise of much virtue; while rights and obligations which are unenforced require a greater exercise of virtue. He concluded that rights and virtues stand in an inverse relationship: perfect rights require little virtue, imperfect rights great virtue (1725, p. 268). It was a terminology that would prompt some to question Hutcheson's idea of virtue; and others, the descriptive value of his language of rights.

The tension between Hutcheson's commitment to virtue as benevolence and his treatment of natural rights theories is most conspicuous in his English-language treatises. In the pedagogical system of morals he prepared for students in universities and academies, his *Philosophiae moralis institutio compendiara* (1742), Hutcheson's exposition of natural rights theories closely followed Carmichael's, as Hutcheson generously acknowledged in his prefatory address. In this text, he writes of a 'divine natural law' which enjoins mankind that 'God is to be worshipped with all love and veneration', and that 'we ought to promote as we have opportunity the common good of all'. He did not hesitate to affirm that the natural condition of mankind is a sociable condition, which he interpreted to be a condition of innocence and beneficence. He reviewed the various perfect rights of individuals, the right of property, the obligation of promises, and the several sorts of contracts. He concurred with Carmichael's denunciation of slavery, and with his theory of the origin of government in an original contract (Hutcheson 1747, pp. 117, 119, 129, 275, 286). Some of the difficulties in reconciling rights with virtue or benevolence remained in Hutcheson's pedagogic system. He continued to maintain that imperfect rights require greater virtue than perfect rights and that the motivation that prompts respect for perfect rights is, in part at least, self-love.

These paradoxes, and others, became central features of Hutcheson's third construction of moral and political thought in the very large work that remained unpublished in his lifetime, *A System of Moral Philosophy* (1755). It was characteristic of the distinctive logic of this work that the very weaknesses of human nature, of our more ardent passions and desires, and the hardships and hazards of our natural condition, form parts of a divine plan, a theodicy, in which God has made provision for the happiness of the human race (Moore 2000). In this work, the various conflicts of the passions and affections are rendered harmonious by 'the moral faculty'; the disorders of the body politic must be reconciled by prudent legislators; divine providence will ensure that all things contribute to the happiness of the system as a whole. In this scheme, imperfect rights were now conceived as duties to the system: 'to show an example of all kindness, courtesy and inclination to oblige and assist any of our fellows'; 'to diffuse as far as we can the principles of virtue and piety'. These were duties, which we are obliged to perform not by law but by rights which belong to the happiness of the system of the whole human race (Hutcheson 1755, I, p. 74, II, pp. 111–12, 231).

In the successive systems of his moral philosophy, Hutcheson demonstrated various ways in which natural law theories might be reconciled with a commitment to civic virtue or benevolence. The tensions between rights and virtues are evident in Hutcheson's emphasis on imperfect rights and obligations and his insistence upon the greater benevolence signified by imperfect rights. The same tension appears in his pedagogic system, although it is allayed in some measure by his recourse to divine moral law to provide moral inspiration for natural rights and obligations. And in his last, unpublished system of moral philosophy, imperfect rights became duties to the system as a whole. Each one of Hutcheson's systems remains an illuminating illustration of the difficulties of bringing natural rights and civic virtue within the confines of a single system.

5 David Hume: natural rights and scepticism

In *A Treatise of Human Nature* (1739–40), book III, part II, David Hume addressed the sequence of questions posed by Pufendorf, Locke, Carmichael, and Hutcheson. How should one describe the state of nature? What is the origin of rights? What are the rules that determine property? How should one account for the obligation of promises? What is the origin of government? Natural rights theories clearly provided the intellectual agenda for Hume's treatment of justice in the *Treatise* (Forbes 1975, 1982; Haakonssen 1981, 1989, 1996a). But the manner in which he responded to the questions posed in the natural rights tradition reveals his scepticism concerning the answers typically provided by natural jurists. While Hume acknowledged that the rights of property and the obligations of promises provided the institutional arrangements of social life, he considered that these arrangements were artificial, not natural, in origin. The rules of justice might indeed be considered natural in the sense that they are indispensable for social life and are therefore co-existent with society. But he thought that justice, unlike other virtues, cannot be derived immediately from human passions. His reasons for thinking that the rules of justice, and the rights and obligations which follow from those rules, are artificial derive from his searching and extended reflections upon the passions and the understanding.

Unlike Grotius, Pufendorf, Carmichael, and Hutcheson, but, in this respect at least, like Hobbes, Hume found no natural instinct or passion which would motivate mankind to be naturally sociable. As Hume understood human nature, there is no instinct which would prompt us to leave others in possession of things they have occupied, or do what we have promised to do. The unrestrained passions of mankind, avarice and ambition, pride in property and riches, love of fame and esteem, naturally prompt individuals to seize the possessions of others and break promises. It is only by artificial restraint and redirection of these passions that the same passions countervail themselves. This artificial restraint is provided by a convention of abstinence from things which are connected to, or are associated with, others. Such a convention allows individuals to believe that others will be just in their behaviour, and this belief is further enlivened and reinforced by the sympathetic approval of others. The origins of justice, of rights, and of obligations, are not natural; law and legal arrangements are artificial or conventional in origin (*THN*, III.ii.2). Hume's general theory of the origin of justice would also have implications for his assessment of the most authoritative natural law theory of the right of property and the origin of government by the most noted natural jurist of the age, John Locke.

Locke's account of the right of property as having its origin in labour had been adopted by Carmichael and Hutcheson. Both philosophers had also embraced Locke's theory that legitimate governments had their origin in the consent, express or tacit, of the people. Hume disagreed with both theories. He argued against Locke and others that the activity of labouring upon or producing a thing confers no natural right of property in that thing. The connection between a person and a thing is never a necessary connection; it is at best a contingent connection. For property, Hume liked to claim, is 'a species of cause and effect', and in any causal relationship, it is possible to separate the cause from the effect. In the case of property, it is always possible to separate a person from a thing, at least in the imagination (*THN*, II.i.10, III.ii.3; Hume 1882, IV, p. 151). This is why rights of property must be determined artificially, by conventions and by general rules. Hume also rejected the natural law theory that legitimate governments have their origin in the consent, express or tacit, of a people. He found no evidence in history or in the experience of the founding of governments of an original contract or the consent of the people. He argued instead that governments have their origin in conquest or usurpation; the legitimacy of a government derives from the opinion of subjects that certain individuals have a right of power by virtue of long possession or inheritance; or a right to govern by virtue of their property; and ultimately governments derive their authority from the opinion of subjects that the institution of government is useful and in their interest.[5]

Hume's repudiation of natural rights theories of morals and politics was far-reaching, if not comprehensive. He did not consider mankind to be naturally sociable, rights and obligations were not natural but artificial or conventional in origin, the right of property did not have its origin in

---

5 'Of the Original Contract', 'Of the Origin of Government', and 'Of the First Principles of Government', in *Essays, Moral, Political, and Literary*. See Hume 1994a.

labouring or producing, and the authority of governments did not derive from the consent of the people. Hume's determination to make usefulness and agreeableness to oneself and others the principles of morals must also be recognised to have been opposed to the theory of natural rights. Hume told Hutcheson that he identified his theory of justice with the opinion of Horace, who had held that utility is the mother of justice and equity (Hume 1932, I, p. 33). Grotius and Pufendorf had identified this phrase of Horace's to have been the very position they were arguing against in their treatises on the law of nature (Moore 1994).

Hume retained, to be sure, the natural rights hypothesis of the state of nature and used it to illustrate the advantages of civil society: the prosperity, force, and stability which follow from observance of rules of justice and property (*THN*, III.ii.2). In the same vein, he described the condition of Europe before the recovery of Roman law as comparable with a state of nature; in the centuries that followed, the benefits of civil law became evident over time, in ecclesiastical as well as civil societies (Hume 1782, III, pp. 300–1). Hume's use of the state of nature hypothesis was not designed to establish a natural rights foundation for civil law; it was employed to underline the extraordinary utility of rules of justice and property. The principle of utility also permitted him to argue that what is considered useful and agreeable may vary across space and change over time, since different societies have different understandings of what is useful and agreeable ('A Dialogue', in Hume 1998, pp. 110–23; Moore 2002). This sceptical principle was relevant for Hume's work as a historian; one of his more notable insights was a recognition of different epochs in the constitution of England (Hume 1782, V, app. III, pp. 451ff). The scepticism of his moral and political thinking was not lost upon one of his oldest and most difficult friends, Henry Home.

6   Lord Kames: disquieting opinions and the law of nature

Henry Home, Lord Kames, must be considered a figure of pivotal importance in the history of natural rights in eighteenth-century Scotland (Lieberman 1983, 1989). He was not a systematic thinker in the manner of Hutcheson, Hume, or Smith. His intellectual interests were diffuse, his style of writing uneven. He did not attend a university and was educated at home by a Nonjuring minister. Kames told James Boswell late in life that he had been raised a Jacobite and an episcopalian. His appointment as a judge in the Scottish Court of Sessions was delayed by reports that his family had sympathy with the Jacobite cause (Ross 1972). Indeed it appears, from a letter written by him in 1745, that it was the Jacobite historian, Thomas Carte, who persuaded Home to take up the study of history.[6] But whatever may have been Home's political attachments prior to the Jacobite rebellion of 1745, it is remarkable that much of his later historical work was devoted to the repudiation of Jacobite and patriarchal principles. His arguments against patriarchy and hereditary right were based upon what he took to be the law of nature.

In the Introduction to his *Essays upon Several Subjects concerning British Antiquities* (1747) Kames advised his readers that this work was composed during 'our late troubles'. His hope was to 'raise a spirit among his countrymen of searching into their antiquities, . . . being seriously convinced that nothing will more contribute than this study to eradicate a set of opinions, which, by intervals have disquieted this island for a century and an half'. His essays on 'the introduction of the feudal law into Scotland', the 'constitution of parliament', 'honour [and] dignity', and 'upon succession or descent' were directed against the unnatural notions of property and government which had been fostered by the feudal law. The feudal law had been introduced in Scotland no earlier than the eleventh century, in imitation of English practice, and in order to consolidate power over land and vassals in the person of the king. At that time Scottish thanes surrendered their lands and their natural independence for feudal titles of honour. The effect of the feudal law was to withdraw property in land from commerce and attach land to families in perpetuity by the principle of primogeniture or the indefeasible hereditary right of succession of the eldest son. Nothing could be more contrary to the law of nature: 'For primogeniture, 'tis certain, is not a right of the law of nature, but a consequence only of the feudal law. Hence it is a principle embraced by the gravest writers, that all mankind are born free and independent of one another' (Kames 1747, p. 193). The unnatural condition of property and government under the feudal law could not long persist; industry, labour, and the natural demand for liberty led to the restoration of commerce in land and independence from feudal lords. It remained only to ensure that Scotland, with other nations, did not return to the feudal law. Such a retrograde step was unlikely as long as Scotsmen and others adhered to the law of nature. In an 'Appendix touching the Hereditary and Indefeasible Right of Kings', Kames reminded his readers that government is a trust, 'invented for the good of mankind'; that it would be unnatural indeed for a people 'to surrender their liberties to the

---

6 Bodleian Library, Oxford, MS Carte 128, fo. 267.

arbitrary will of any man. The act would be void as inconsistent with the great law of nature *salus populi, suprema lex*'; that people may always judge whether a government has betrayed the trust of the people. 'It is a fixed principle of the law of nature, that where there is no common judge to appeal to, the party injured may do himself justice' (Kames 1747, pp. 196–202).

Kames had become a natural law theorist; even though he did not, as yet, have a theory of natural law. He set out to create such a theory in his *Essays on the Principles of Morality and Natural Religion* (1751), where he argued that a law of nature is an affection or feeling that is experienced in a compulsory, law-like manner. Such feelings are implanted in human nature by divine providence; hence their compelling, irresistible nature. He disagreed entirely with Hume's theory that justice is an artificial virtue, regarding that theory as a personal idiosyncrasy of its author. 'That justice is an artificial virtue was a favourite doctrine of his, early adopted, as to become in him a sort of natural principle' (Kames 1779, p. 149). Kames passed over without notice Hume's argument that it is by adhering to a conventional manner of behaviour that individuals come to believe that others will abstain from injuring them and thereby come to have an interest, a natural obligation, to observe rules of justice. Kames perceived Hume's understanding of obligation to depend entirely upon sympathy, which was 'by far too faint a principle to control our irregular appetites and passions'. Conceived in this way, Hume's understanding of duty and obligation was as unsatisfactory as Hutcheson's theory that there is a feeling of obligation to act in a benevolent manner: 'upon this author's system, as well as Hutcheson's, the noted terms of duty, obligation, *ought* and *should*, are perfectly unintelligible' (Kames 1779, p. 58).

In contrast with Hutcheson and Hume, Kames held that there is a peculiar feeling of remorse that attends any breach or transgression of a duty or obligation: it was a 'sense of merited punishment and dread of its being inflicted upon us'. This feeling or principle is the foundation of what Kames called the law or laws of nature; it was the natural law source of positive law: there is 'not a characteristic of positive law which is not applicable in the strictest sense to these laws of nature'. The circumstance that we feel any breach of duty so painfully and acutely is evidence that justice is a natural virtue and that divine providence has implanted in mankind a sense of justice. And the sense of justice is the natural law source of the various duties of the law of nature: that one abstain from injuring others, that one keep promises, and acknowledge a natural right of property (Kames 1779, pp. 64, 72, 103–9). All of these duties are enforced effectively by the dread of apprehended and merited punishment.

In his insistence upon the universality of the feeling that transgressions of duty must be punished, that punishment is not only merited but necessary or unavoidable, Kames was restating, in his own idiom, the dogma of Reformed or Presbyterian theology that sin must be punished. He did not subscribe, however, to the Christian theological corollary of this dogma, that Christ, by His sacrifice, had made atonement for the sins of mankind. He considered the Christian doctrine of the atonement a primitive idea, and one productive of social mischief:

A notion prevailed in the darker ages of the world, of a substitute in punishment, who undertakes the debt and suffers the punishment that another merits. Traces of this opinion are found in the religious ceremonies of the ancient Egyptians and other ancient nations. Among them, the conceptions of a deity were gross, and of morality no less so. (Kames 1792, p. 15)

It was a source of regret to him that the Christian doctrine of the atonement should have continued to have an influence upon conduct, for it allowed guilty men to believe that bad behaviour might be redeemed by communion with Christ: 'Many men give punctual attendance at public worship to compound for hidden vices; many are openly charitable to compound for private oppression; and many are willing to give God good service in supporting his established church to compound for aiming at power by a factious disturbance of the state' (Kames 1792, pp. 19–20).

The Christians against whom Kames directed his natural law critique may well have included orthodox Presbyterians. Kames's writings, together with those of Hume, had narrowly escaped censure by the General Assembly of the Church of Scotland in 1755. But his allusion to seditious disturbers of the public peace suggests that he included in this general indictment Christians who had been responsible for more recent disturbances, episcopalians, and Jacobites. It was in the course of his natural law critique of Jacobitism that Kames and others associated with him advanced the theory of a natural succession of stages of society.

7   Adam Smith: the natural and sacred rights of mankind

The discovery in the 1890s and, more recently, in the 1950s, of student notes on Smith's lectures on jurisprudence has required scholars to recognise that natural rights theories formed a significant part of his system of thought (*LJA, LJB*). These lectures, delivered in 1762–4 at Glasgow, belong logically and chronologically between his lectures on ethics and his lectures on 'police' or political economy (Stein 1979). Smith distinguished jurisprudence from ethics; the proper scope of ethics was the delineation of the virtues, and of the several sentiments which prompt us to approve of particular virtues and disapprove of the corresponding vices. It did not belong to ethics to elaborate rules for the direction of conduct consistent with the virtues; indeed it had been the mistake of casuists and scholastic moralists that they had attempted to regulate moral conduct in this manner. Only justice permitted precise determination by rulers. Hence it belonged to a discipline distinct from ethics to elaborate rules of justice, a discipline which was 'what might properly be called natural jurisprudence' (*TMS*, vii.iv.37).

Smith located his lectures on jurisprudence in the natural rights tradition of Grotius, Hobbes, and Pufendorf, and the Prussian Reformed church illustrators of the work of Grotius, the father and son Heinrich and Samuel Cocceji (Haakonssen 1996a). The first five of the six volumes of student notes that comprise the 1762–3 lectures (*LJA*) may be seen to follow the agenda of the early modern natural rights tradition, adapted from Pufendorf's work by Carmichael and Hutcheson. The range of topics covered in Smith's jurisprudence included the right of property (volume i), the obligation of contracts (volume ii), the rights of members of households, including servants and slaves (volume iii), the origin and constitution of civil government (volume iv), and the rights of sovereigns and subjects (volume v).[7] The sixth and final volume advanced the argument beyond justice and the enforcement of rights to consideration of policy and the production of wealth. Unlike Carmichael and Hutcheson, Smith did not think it necessary to invoke a law of nature to explain the rights to life, liberty, self-defence, and reputation: 'the greatest part of what are called natural rights . . . need not be explained' (*LJA*, p. 13). But it is also notable that, unlike Hume, for whom all rights and obligations were artificial, dependent on conventions and their utility, Smith made allowance for a wide range of natural rights: 'in all about a dozen', including rights to life, body, reputation, property, and *jus commercii*, a right to engage in commerce, 'a right of trafficking with those who are willing to deal with him' (*LJA*, p. 8). Smith's confidence that he could account for natural rights without having recourse to a law of

---

7 The order of presentation of the lectures of 1763–4 (*LJB*) was different. See the comparative table of contents in Smith 1978, pp. 24–7.

nature or to utility may be explained by the circumstance that he had already lectured on the sentiments, natural and moral, that prompt men to seek and approve justice. His exposition of those sentiments and his differences with Hutcheson, Hume, Kames, and others on the subject of justice had been outlined in his lectures on ethics, revised for publication in *The Theory of Moral Sentiments* (1759).

It was the central contention of Smith's ethics that sympathy with the sentiments or feelings of others allows us to discover the sentiments that prompt men to observe and approve the virtues that are appropriate in different conditions of society and economic life. We sympathise in a particular way with the victim of injustice, with someone whose life, body, or reputation has been injured. We sympathise with the resentment felt by the victim, and we feel that the perpetrator of the injustice deserves or merits punishment (*TMS*, II.i.2.5). The sentiment that inspires the demand for justice is very different from benevolence. The difficulty with Hutcheson's theory that all virtue can be reduced to benevolence, public or private, general or particular, was that it could not account for other qualities of character which are also virtues. Some, like prudence, vigilance, constancy, or firmness, are prompted by self-love or a concern for self-preservation. Other virtues may be prompted by other sentiments; in the case of justice, for example, the relevant sentiment is the feeling that retaliation or retribution is appropriate; that justice, unlike other virtues, must be enforced (*TMS*, II.ii.3.3). Smith rejected the language of imperfect rights; all rights, properly speaking, must be considered perfect rights, enforceable by magistrates and governments (*LJA*, p. 9).

He also challenged 'the account commonly given of our approbation of the punishment of injustice', that injustice must be punished and rights enforced for the preservation of society (*TMS*, II.ii.3.7). It is not a sympathetic concern for society at large that enlists the sentiment that justice be enforced, in Smith's view; it is rather our sympathy with the sensibilities of assignable individuals who have been the victims of injustice that prompts us to approve the enforcement of justice. That justice and injustice are approved on account of their utility to society was Hume's theory, and Smith may have had Hume in mind as he composed this part of his ethics (*TMS*, II.ii.3.6). But his lectures on jurisprudence allow us to see that his argument was directed more broadly against natural rights theorists who also justified punishment on grounds of public utility. 'That which Grotius and other writers commonly allege as the original measure of punishments, viz. the consideration of the public good, will not sufficiently account for the constitution of punishments. So far they say as public utility requires . . . we will find the case to be otherwise' (*LJA*, p. 104).

Smith agreed with Kames that the sense of justice or the sentiment that prompts us to approve enforcement of the rights of mankind is a sense of merited punishment and dread of its being inflicted on us. He did not concur, however, with Kames's view that it was productive of mischief to believe that Christ had made atonement for the sins of mankind by his sacrifice and suffering. Smith's remarks on the subject of divine justice present a striking contrast with Kames's very sceptical reflections on this topic. Anyone, Smith wrote, who reflects upon the numberless violations of duty of which he has been guilty cannot imagine why

> the divine indignation should not be let loose, without restraint, upon so vile an insect, as he is sensible that he himself must appear to be . . . Some other intercession, some other sacrifice, some other atonement, must be made for him . . . before the purity of the divine justice can be reconciled to his manifold offences. The doctrines of revelation coincide, in every respect with those original anticipations of nature. (*TMS*, II.ii.3.12n)

Although this passage was deleted from the sixth and final edition of *The Theory of Moral Sentiments*, published in 1790, the year of Smith's death, it remains a graphic illustration of the religious aura that surrounds the sense of justice as he conceived it: 'The actions which this virtue requires are never so properly performed as when the chief motive for performing them is a reverential and religious regard to those general rules which require them' (*TMS*, III.6.10). He would later denounce as a violation of 'the most sacred rights of mankind' government interference in the affairs of 'a great people . . . employing their stock and industry in the way that they judge most advantageous to themselves' (*WN*, IV.vii.b.44).

The sentiments that prompt us to approve and enforce 'the sacred rights of mankind' are felt by people in all ages. But the manner in which those rights have been enforced in the laws and institutions of different nations have varied, depending upon the state or stage of that society.

8   Natural rights and the four stages of society

It has been a much-debated question as to how Kames, Smith, and others came to interpret the legal and political arrangements of the societies of the past as a sequence of stages: from societies of hunters, to societies of shepherds, to agricultural societies, and finally to commercial societies.[8]

8 Meek 1967, 1970, 1976; Pocock 1979; Stein 1980, 1988.

One of the lacunae that has bedevilled study of this matter in the Scottish Enlightenment is the absence of any satisfactory record of what Adam Smith may have taught in Edinburgh in the late 1740s and in Glasgow in the early 1750s. John Millar's description of Smith's lectures in Glasgow in 1751, and Smith's later claim that his views had never changed, and that his opinions had been misappropriated by others, have generated the supposition that Smith arrived at the four stages theory quite independently and prior to Kames's publication of the theory in 1758 in his *Historical Law Tracts* (Meek 1970, 1976). Another consideration, however, would seem to point to Kames as the Scottish jurist who brought the four stages theory to the attention of others. The first publication in the English language to make use of the four stages theory was John Dalrymple's *An Essay towards a General History of Feudal Property in Great Britain*, published in 1757. Dalrymple dedicated his book to Kames and acknowledged a particular debt to papers of Kames that were 'as yet unpublished, though they were open to me' (1757, pp. iii–iv). He also advised the reader that his work had been 'revised by the greatest genius of our age, President Montesquieu'; he does not tell us what revisions Montesquieu may have proposed. Dalrymple described the introduction of the feudal law in Scotland by King Malcolm III in the later eleventh century. The effect of the feudal law was its transformation of allodial land (held by the proprietor without obligation to a superior) into feudal land (held in leasehold or tenancy as a benefit conferred upon a vassal by a lord). In earlier societies there had been restrictions upon the alienation of land, but it was under the feudal law that restraints upon commerce in land were multiplied and strictly enforced (Dalrymple 1757, p. 24). In the earliest stages of society, he observed, following the sequence that Kames would elaborate in his *Historical Law Tracts*, in societies of hunters and fishermen, when property meant no more than possession of the catch or kill, there was little occasion for exchange of goods; exchanges would multiply in societies of herdsmen, and there would be little restraint upon alienation. It was feudal property which denied individuals their natural rights to property and its transference by consent. The feudal system was, as Kames put it, 'a violent and unnatural system, which could not be long supported in contradiction to love of independence and property, the most steady and industrious of all human appetites' (Kames 1792, p. 141).

Kames and Dalrymple described the decline of feudalism in Scotland during the sixteenth and seventeenth centuries, as vassals purchased land for themselves, and lords disposed of their lands to their own advantage. But this natural course of human affairs had been arrested by an act of the parliament of Scotland in 1685, which permitted landowners to entail their estates, making it impossible for heirs to alienate their land in perpetuity. Dalrymple thought that, with some modification of this law, entails would disappear altogether, that 'as in the case of many other branches of the feudal system, it will be remembered nowhere but in books of antiquities that such a species of conveyance ever existed' (Dalrymple 1757, p. 186). Kames was less sanguine in his expectation; he thought that the British parliament must act at once to repeal the practice of entailment, that failure to act would subvert not only industry and commerce, but also that 'liberty and independence, to which all men aspire, with respect to their possessions as well as their persons' (Kames 1792, p. 156).

The earliest published accounts of the four stages theory of society in Scotland followed directly, then, from Kames's natural law critique of feudal property. The practical concern underlying the theory was that property in land, the third stage of society, must be brought into commerce, the fourth stage of society. The first and second stages of society were introduced to affirm that property in these earliest stages had been in moveables; the mobility of property was its natural condition. What was lacking in Kames's emphatic assertion that land must be transferable or alienable was a clear articulation of the feeling or sentiment that prompts men to trade or transfer their property. That lacuna in Kames's natural law theory would be supplied by Adam Smith.

Smith's point of departure in his lectures on jurisprudence was Roman law. He thought that the civil law of the Romans provided an excellent foundation for the study of other legal systems: 'Anyone who has studied the civil law at least knows what a system of law is, what parts it consist of and how they ought to be arranged' (Smith 1987, p. 30). He chose to begin his lectures (of 1762–3) by reviewing the rules of ownership specified in the civil law: occupation, accession, prescription, succession, tradition, and voluntary transference of goods. The right of property derived, as might be expected from his general theory of justice, from the sympathy of a spectator with the resentment of a possessor that something had been 'wrongfully wrested out of his hands' (*LJA*, p. 17). But the occasion for this resentment or sense of injustice must vary depending upon the stage or condition of society. In a society of hunters, a spectator would sympathise with another only if the animal or fish that he had caught was snatched violently from his hands. In a society of shepherds, the spectator's sympathy would be aroused only if the animal bore some mark distinguishing it as belonging to the owner. It was in this second stage that property came to be differentiated from mere possession; in making this distinction, Smith was again on common ground with Dalrymple and with Kames. But in his observations upon the third stage of society, the agricultural stage, Smith elaborated a critique that exceeded, if possible, the warmth of the denunciation of feudal property by his fellow jurists. It was 'the tyranny of the feudal government and the inclination men have to extort all they can from their inferiors' that had removed land from individual appropriation (*LJA*, pp. 20, 23). Even wild animals and fish, *ferae naturae*, which should remain in common, available to be possessed (not yet appropriated) by anyone, had become the preserve of the king and his vassals.

Smith's most bitter comments on feudal property appear under the rubric of succession in discussion of the right of primogeniture. 'This method of succession, contrary to nature, to reason, and to justice, was occasioned by the nature of the feudal government' (*LJA*, p. 49). It took some time following the introduction of the feudal system for succession on the patriarchal principle of primogeniture to be fixed by law and custom. But the effect of this principle, combined with the practice of entailing estates in perpetuity, had led to arrangements as unjust as they were impolitic. It was consistent with natural rights, founded on sympathy with the natural sentiment of piety, for a dying man to dispose of his goods to persons alive at the time and for whom he has contracted an affection. But, as Smith put it, 'the utmost stretch of our piety' cannot reasonably extend to persons not yet born. Furthermore, it was impolitic.

This right is not only absurd in the highest degree but is also extremely prejudicial to the community, as it excludes land entirely from commerce. The interest of the state requires that lands should be as much in commerce as any other goods. This the power of making entails entirely excludes: I shall hereafter show more fully, only hinting at it now, that the right of primogeniture and the power of making entails have been the causes of the almost total bad husbandry that prevails in those countries where they are in use. (*LJA*, p. 70)

In his lectures on 'police' (in volume VI of the *Lectures on Jurisprudence*) and subsequently, in his great work on political economy, Smith explained how feudal estates had been broken up despite the persistence of primogeniture and entails. This had come about, not by recognition of the absurdity of those practices, or their inconsistency with 'the sacred rights of mankind', but by the silent and insensible operation of trade and commerce (*LJA*, pp. 331ff). It was the availability of commodities which the great feudal magnates could obtain without sharing them with their tenants and retainers:

'All for ourselves, and nothing for other people, seems, in every age of the world, to have been the vile maxim of the masters of mankind; . . . and thus, for the gratification of the most childish, the meanest and most sordid of all vanities, they gradually bartered their whole power and authority' (*WN*, III.iv.10). It was not a general recognition of the *jus commercii*, of the right to engage in commerce, which had led to the dismantling of feudal property; it was another sentiment or disposition, the disposition to truck, barter, and exchange which prompted feudal magnates to alienate their estates for the sake of commodities of negligible worth. Smith traced the disposition to truck, barter, and exchange to the still more basic propensity to persuade others to be of our own sentiment or opinion (*WN*, I.ii.1ff; *LJA*, pp. 352, 493–4). His explanation may point to an underlying coherence in his system of thought, centred upon his lectures on *belles lettres* and rhetoric, which he offered concurrently with his lectures on jurisprudence (Smith 1983; *LJA*, p. 352; *LJB*, pp. 493–4). But it is of some historic significance for the history of political thought in Scotland in the late eighteenth century that Smith chose to locate his compelling analysis of the break-up of feudal societies in lectures devoted to political economy or 'police', and not in the lectures concerned with natural rights. This decision must be considered to have been one of the factors that contributed to the displacement of natural rights theories by the science of political economy in the nineteenth century.

9   Dugald Stewart and the demise of the natural rights tradition

Adam Smith, Thomas Reid, and John Millar all chose not to publish their lectures on natural jurisprudence. All three made extensive use of the natural rights agenda, however, in their lectures on moral philosophy and civil law at Glasgow (Cairns 1995; Haakonssen 1986–7; Reid 1990). Adam Ferguson's lectures on moral philosophy at Edinburgh (1764–84), published some years after his retirement from teaching, included extended reflections on jurisprudence or compulsory law; his better known work on the history of civil society appears to exhibit (unlike the historical theories of Kames and Smith) no traces of dependence upon natural rights theories (Ferguson 1792, 1966, 1995). It was Ferguson's successor, Dugald Stewart, professor of moral philosophy at Edinburgh (1785–1810) whose teaching and writing presented an explicit repudiation of natural rights theories (Collini *et al.* 1983; Haakonssen 1996a). Stewart provided a variety of reasons for believing that natural jurisprudence should no longer be employed in the instruction of students in moral and political philosophy. His reasons were set out in his influential lectures on the active and moral powers, in his lectures on political economy, and in his *Dissertation: Exhibiting the Progress of Metaphysical, Ethical and Political Philosophy since the Revival of Letters in Europe* (1814).

Stewart's case against the natural rights tradition may be recapitulated under four sets of considerations. He maintained, first, that many of the duties of active life are immediately obligatory (Stewart 1854–60, I, p. 172, VII, p. 231). Justice is such a duty. The obligation to be just follows immediately from the promptings of conscience. There was no need therefore to specify the several duties of men and citizens in elaborate treatises, such as those of Grotius and Pufendorf. Moreover, commentaries on those treatises had become exercises in sterile scholasticism. Moral and political philosophers would do better to urge their readers and listeners to cultivate a sense of duty.

Second, natural jurists had attached undue importance to the rules of Roman law. They had made insufficient allowance for historical change and for the diversity of legal institutions. This might seem a curious criticism to direct against the writings of Kames and Smith. But Stewart does not seem to have appreciated the extent to which Kames and Smith made natural rights theories the point of departure for their writing and teaching. Indeed, Stewart conjectured that when Smith wrote in *The Wealth of Nations* that universities often provide a sanctuary for exploded systems of thought, he had in mind systems of natural jurisprudence (Stewart 1854–60, I, pp. 178n, 188).

Third, it is evident from Stewart's lectures on government that he was alarmed by the natural rights theory of Locke and the manner in which Locke's writings had been read in America, France, and England, by the friends of the Revolution in France. He deplored 'the mistaken notions concerning political liberty which have been so widely disseminated in Europe by the writings of Mr Locke' (Stewart 1854–60, VIII, p. 23). The great fallacy which Locke's writings encouraged was the idea that the people are capable of forming correct judgements concerning their rights and the policies of governments that would be conducive to their happiness. 'I do not think that in the present state of the world democratic constitutions in any form which it is possible to give them are favourable to the establishment of those systematic and enlightened principles of political economy which are subservient to the progressive happiness and improvement of mankind' (Stewart 1854–60, IX, p. 376).

Fourth, in Stewart's view, political economy should not be restricted to the study of wealth and population. Political economy should be extended to include 'all those speculations which have for their object the happiness and improvement of political society'. It should provide 'the standard by which the wisdom and expediency of every institution is to be established' (Stewart 1854–60, VIII, p. 10).

This chapter has traced the manner in which natural rights theories were introduced to the moral philosophy curriculum in Scotland in the 1690s, by Gershom Carmichael and others; how attempts were made to reconcile natural rights and theories of civic virtue in the second quarter of the eighteenth century, principally by Francis Hutcheson; how natural rights were subjected to sceptical scrutiny in the moral philosophy of David Hume; how an antithesis to Jacobitism was supplied by an understanding of the law of nature in the work of Lord Kames; how Adam Smith extended his theory of sympathy and the moral sentiments to comprehend the natural and sacred rights of mankind; how the juridical theories of Kames, Smith, and others gave rise to the four stages theory of society; and, lastly, how the natural rights tradition was repudiated and replaced by common-sense ethics and political economy in the work of Dugald Stewart. In the course of his review of reasons for dismissing natural rights theories, Stewart reminded his readers that natural jurisprudence was nonetheless 'a science which, for more than a hundred years constituted the whole philosophy, both ethical and political, of the largest portion of civilized Europe' (Stewart 1854–60, I, p. 193). As our understanding of natural rights theories advances, and we continue to learn more about how those theories were adapted to elucidate issues of moral and political life, we may be inclined to conclude that Stewart's epitaph for natural jurisprudence was somewhat premature.

11

The mixed constitution and the common law

DAVID LIEBERMAN

Accounts of England's constitution,[1] even in the more systematic treatments of the middle decades of the eighteenth century, followed the common early modern pattern in which political theory often comprised an uneven amalgam of classical maxims of government, narrow partisan polemics, antiquarian learning, historical researches, and technical legal doctrine. Nonetheless, 'the constitution of England', so constructed, enjoyed an extensive influence on liberal political philosophy and Western statecraft well beyond its place of origin and the particular circumstances of its first articulation. 'The eye of curiosity seems now to be universally turned' to this 'model of perfection', explained Jean Louis Delolme in the 1770s (Delolme 1834, p. 1). What was to be discovered in this model were the general principles of political freedom. ''Tis the Britannic Constitution that gives this kingdom a lustre above other nations', extolled Roger Acherley a half-century earlier, 'as it secures to Britons, their private property, freedom and liberty, by such walls of defence as are not to be found in any other parts of the universe' (Acherley 1727, p. vi).

The organising principle for much of the eighteenth-century celebration of the English constitution was the commonplace idea that structures of government could preserve political freedom only where they frustrated the abuse of political power. The extent to which the English enjoyed unique levels of political freedom was the result of a constitutional order which effectively prevented arbitrary or tyrannical acts of power. The achievement of this kind of political system, in turn, depended upon the existence and

---

1 The 1707 Act of Union created the single political entity of Great Britain from the previous separate kingdoms of England and Scotland, leaving a legacy of cumbersome terminology to describe what hitherto was called the 'English constitution'. After 1707, the basics of the constitutional structure were now British, not English. The law and the church, however, remained separate. Contemporary usage varied among 'English constitution', 'British constitution', and 'Britannic constitution'. For surveys of eighteenth-century constitutional developments, see Carter 1969 and Langford 1991, pp. 677–725; more detailed treatments are provided by Thomson 1938 and Williams 1960. The themes of the present chapter are explored in earlier contexts in ch. 2 above.

co-ordination of several distinct kinds of institutions and governmental procedures. Theorists of the English constitution differed over which of these institutions contributed most critically to the maintenance of political freedom, and disagreed sharply over which political forces and developments posed the most toxic threats to liberty's well-being. But there was a common supposition, challenged by only a minority of theorists, that public liberty was best served by institutional complexity. The English political system contained a dense patchwork of new and older legal and corporate structures, whose contemporary functions often differed significantly from those they originally performed. The first task for eighteenth-century constitutional analysis was the correct identification of the nature of this complex political order.

1   The mixed constitution

No characterisation of England's constitution was more pervasive than the claim that the kingdom comprised a mixed form of government, combining elements of rule by one, the few, and the many. The formula recalled the traditional meaning of constitution to refer to the basic composition or ordering of both political and natural bodies; and, no less conventionally, it centred the state's identity on the organisation of its sovereign legislature. The 'British constitution', William Blackstone explained in his renowned *Commentaries on the Laws of England* (1765–9), entrusted the 'legislature of the kingdom . . . to three distinct powers': the king ('a single person'), the Lords ('an aristocratical assembly'), and the Commons ('a kind of democracy'); which, by operating jointly, escaped 'the inconveniences of either absolute monarchy, aristocracy, or democracy', while uniting 'so well and so happily' the benefits of each pure form (Blackstone 1979, I, pp. 50–2). Most importantly – the 'true excellence' of this constitutional form – each component part provided a potential 'check' to the abuse of power committed by any other component part, which in turn secured a political order best equipped to sustain public liberty:

Like three distinct powers in mechanics, [king, Lords, and Commons] jointly impel the machine of government in a direction different from what either, acting by themselves, would have done; but at the same time in a direction partaking of each, and formed out of all; a direction which constitutes the true line of the liberty and happiness of the community (Blackstone 1979, I, p. 151).

The theory of England's mixed government, centred on the tripartite legislature of king-in-parliament, first attained prominence in Charles I's *Answer to the Nineteen Propositions* of 1642 (Weston 1965; Weston and Greenberg 1981). Eighteenth-century commentators continued to invoke this source, particularly in their efforts to clarify the 'limited or regulated' character of monarchy in this constitutional system (Mackworth 1701, pp. 2, 9). As in the case of the *Answer to the Nineteen Propositions*, their favoured presentation clearly echoed classical and Renaissance motifs concerning the superiority and durability of the 'mixed' political form. But in one crucial respect they distinguished their accounts from earlier formulations. Formerly the appeal to England's mixed government competed with other, more absolutist accounts of English kingship; now it enjoyed constitutional orthodoxy. 'The constitution of England had been seen in two very different lights for almost a century before the Revolution', Viscount Bolingbroke observed in 1733; but now 'our constitution is no longer a mystery'. 'It is by this mixture of monarchical, aristocratical, and democratical power, blended together in one system', he explained, 'that our free constitution of government hath been preserved' (Bolingbroke 1997b, pp. 77–8, 125–6).

The Glorious Revolution of 1688 was routinely credited, as by Bolingbroke, with this definitive clarification and vindication of the political order. To invoke 1688 and the mixed constitution was thus to distinguish plainly the character of kingship in Britain from the very different absolutist regimes which oppressed the subjects of Continental monarchies and which had, in earlier eras, threatened England's liberties too. One measure of the security furnished by the Glorious Revolution was the near complacency mid-century commentators displayed in treating once fiercely contested issues concerning the nature and authority of England's monarch and parliament (Pocock 1987; Weston 1991). Hume in his *History of England* (1754–62) acknowledged that it 'was once disputed . . . with great acrimony' whether the House of Commons formed a constituent part of the original parliament, but that the question 'by general consent' had been settled against the claims of the Commons (Hume 1983–5, I, p. 467). Blackstone in the *Commentaries* noted the same controversy 'among our learned antiquarians', but dismissed its relevance to current political arrangements. He was sure that 'whatever doubts might be formerly raised by weak and scrupulous minds' concerning 'the existence' of an 'original contract' between subjects and sovereign, such qualms 'must now entirely cease; especially with regard to every prince who has reigned since 1688' (Blackstone 1979, I, pp. 145, 226).

Such appeals to the consensus and stability which followed in the wake of the Glorious Revolution were, of course, a matter of tendentious exaggeration. Indeed, the most robust claims for constitutional certainty appeared in precisely those settings – such as Bolingbroke's writings – in which the legacy of 1688 underwent partisan dispute. The major enactments of the Revolution era – the 1689 Bill of Rights and Act of Toleration, the 1694 Triennial Act, the 1701 Act of Settlement – were all documents of political compromise and even purposeful ambiguity, which readily allowed for rival understandings of their constitutional meaning, novelty, or conservatism. As a recent generation of historians has shown, whatever the successes of the Revolution settlement and the Hanoverian succession, this political achievement did not lead to the silencing or eradication of the antagonistic doctrines of non-resistance and hereditary kingship, Jacobite loyalism, royal supremacy, or High Anglican ecclesiology (Clark 1985; Gunn 1983, pp. 120–93; Kenyon 1977).

Where, however, the legacy of 1688 seemed most emphatic was in its repudiation of the pretensions of Stuart absolutism, and the supporting doctrines of non-resistance and divine right kingship. 'The principal duty of the king', Blackstone explained, 'is to govern his people according to law' (Blackstone 1979, I, p. 226). Accordingly, the Revolution parliament had moved to regulate and restrain by statute just those practices of royal prerogative (such as the 'suspending' and 'dispensing' power) through which James II violated 'the laws and liberties' of the kingdom, threatened 'the Protestant religion', and undermined the constitutional order by governing 'without consent of parliament' (Blackstone 1979, IV, pp. 433–4; Williams 1960, pp. 26–7). Whereas James II had sworn a coronation oath to keep 'the ancient customs of the realm', William and Mary swore more precisely to govern 'according to the statutes in parliament agreed on, and the laws and customs of the same' (Williams 1960, p. 37). The 'continual struggle' of the first four Stuart reigns between 'the crown and the people' and between 'privilege and prerogative', Hume explained in the final chapter of his *History*, had been settled 'in favour of liberty'. 'The powers of the royal prerogative were more narrowly circumscribed and more exactly defined', and the 'great precedent of deposing one king and establishing a new family . . . put the nature of the English constitution beyond all controversy' (Hume 1983–5, VI, pp. 530–1).

2   Parliamentary sovereignty

If the theory of the mixed constitution thus clarified the limited nature of monarchic power in England, it proved less decisive in settling the extent of parliament's own institutional capacity. Eighteenth-century statements of parliamentary authority often retained the traditional formulation of parliament's powers in terms of its historical responsibilities as legislature, high court (*magna curia*), and place of counsel (*commune concilium regni*) (Atkyns 1734, pp. 69–70). But in the routinisation of parliamentary government in the decades following the Glorious Revolution, parliament's specifically legislative function, including its annual enactments governing taxation and finance, came to dwarf its other roles (Langford 1991, pp. 139–206; Thomas 1971, pp. 45–88). By this time it had become commonplace to analyse parliamentary power more abstractly in terms of a general theory of sovereignty (Dickinson 1977, pp. 121–42; Lieberman 1989, pp. 31–40, 49–55).

Blackstone, whose treatment in the *Commentaries* supplied the battle-ground for several important subsequent discussions, approached the topic through a brief summary of the nature of civil society and political obligation, drawn from the standard materials of natural jurisprudence. Political authority was created through a voluntary transfer of natural right; the aims of such political association were to secure individual liberty and the collective good; and, to achieve such purposes, every political society required 'a supreme, irresistible, absolute, uncontrolled authority in which . . . the rights of sovereignty reside' (Blackstone 1979, I, p. 49). The distinguishing mark of 'sovereign power' was 'the making of laws' (I, p. 49), which power, in Britain, was exercised by the king-in-parliament:

It hath sovereign and uncontrollable authority in the making, confirming, enlarging, restraining, abrogating, repealing, reviving, and expounding of laws, concerning matters of all possible denominations, ecclesiastical, or temporal, civil, military, maritime, or criminal; this being the place where that absolute despotic power, which must in all governments reside somewhere, is entrusted by the constitution of these kingdoms. (I, p. 156)

This, moreover, was a not a claim of pure conceptual abstraction. Parliament had confirmed its sovereign power by regulating 'the succession to the throne' ('as was done in the reigns of Henry VII and William III'); by altering 'the established religion of the land' ('as was done . . . in the reigns of Henry VIII and his three children'); and by changing 'even the constitution of the kingdom and of parliaments themselves' ('as was done by the Act of Union and the several statutes for triennial and septennial elections'). 'Some have not scrupled to call its power . . . the omnipotence of parliament', Blackstone reported (I, p. 156).

As the critics of this type of formulation argued, such legislative 'omnipotence' seemed to threaten the very fabric of liberty the English constitution was celebrated as protecting. The kingdom had simply defeated royal tyranny by enshrining parliamentary absolutism (Gunn 1983, pp. 7–42; Hamburger 1994). In its most extreme articulations – as in the case mounted by Thomas Paine in the *Rights of Man* (1791–2) – the criticism led to the dramatic conclusion that England, in fact, had no constitution: 'merely a form of government without a constitution' (Paine 1989, p. 131). A parliamentary supremacy which included the authority to revise the constitution itself entailed a reversal of a true system of constitutional government in which the constitution controlled the government, and the community itself controlled the constitution (pp. 81–3).[2]

Paine's was no doubt a self-consciously iconoclastic assault on English political orthodoxies. But he navigated a much-traversed eighteenth-century issue, which recalled and rehearsed the themes of earlier disputes concerning the nature and limits of political obligation. Notwithstanding the *Commentaries*' imposing itemisation of past parliamentary enactments that altered the basic structures of church and state, there were many who felt that the bald claim of parliament's 'uncontrollable' authority seriously distorted the nature of legislative power. One important line of speculation, dominated by jurists and university moralists, sought a more careful and discriminating treatment of the nature of sovereignty than that afforded by the Blackstonean language of 'absolute despotic power'. There was the need to distinguish 'sovereign power' and 'supreme power', and to differentiate the domestic from the external (or international) face of sovereignty (Rutherforth 1822, pp. 282–5). Similar was the injunction 'always carefully' to 'distinguish *juridical* from *moral* power' in the understanding of parliament's 'supreme jurisdiction' (Chambers 1986, I, p. 140). And there was the insistence that the frequently '*indefinite*' extent of sovereign authority in many states should not be confused, as by Blackstone, with the idea that sovereignty was therefore '*infinite*' (Bentham 1988, p. 97; Sedgwick 1800, p. 126).

2 Paine joined Blackstone in viewing the 1716 Septennial Act, which extended the maximum duration of parliaments to seven years, as the definitive modern example of parliament's ability to alter the constitution (Paine 1989, p. 83). The controversial statute was standardly given this constitutional significance by both defenders and critics of the Hanoverian political order.

In addition to the attempted clarification of the concept of sovereignty was a corresponding effort to elucidate the term 'constitution' more clearly. Blackstone, as was conventional, identified the constitution with the organisation of the legislature. As William Paley later put it, 'A government receives its denomination from the form of the legislature; which form is likewise what we commonly mean by the *constitution* of a country' (Paley 1838, III, p. 253). On this understanding, the constitution existed so long as the tripartite structure of king-in-parliament survived as sovereign; and any enactment issued by this legislative sovereign enjoyed legal validity (Blackstone 1979, I, pp. 51–2). But while the legislature furnished the core element of the English constitution, few commentators – Blackstone included – treated this structural form as exhausting the kingdom's system of constitutional norms and practices. In this manner, Bolingbroke maintained that 'by constitution we mean, whenever we speak with propriety and exactness, that assemblage of laws, institutions, and customs . . . that compose the general system, according to which the community hath agreed to be governed' (Bolingbroke 1997b, p. 88). On the basis of this more dense definition of the constitution, it was easy to identify a situation in which parliament's legislative product violated constitutional principles (Burns 1962). Paley more cautiously and hesitantly conceded that, although a parliamentary enactment 'in the strict and proper acceptation of the term' could not be 'unconstitutional', 'in a lower sense it may, viz. when it militates with the spirit, contradicts the analogy, or defeats the provision of other laws, made to regulate the form of government' (Paley 1838, III, p. 261).

Most weighty and controversial, however, was the characterisation of the constitutional resources available for dealing with an abuse or violation of the constitutional order. Blackstone, in setting out the case for parliament's 'sovereign and uncontrollable authority', acknowledged the arguments of 'Mr Locke and other theoretical writers' that 'there remains still inherent in the people a supreme power to remove or alter the legislative' when it violated 'the trust reposed in [it]' (Blackstone 1979, I, p. 157). Later, in treating the likely response of the community to severe 'unconstitutional oppressions', he noted that 'whenever necessity and the safety of the whole shall require it', future generations would mobilise 'those inherent (though latent) powers of society, which no climate, no time, no constitution, no contract, can ever destroy or diminish' (I, p. 238). But, throughout the *Commentaries*, Blackstone endeavoured to blunt any radical implications of his own appeal to natural rights and natural equality (Lieberman 1989, pp. 52–5). In the hypothetical case of morally legitimate political resistance, he insisted that this must involve an extra-legal exercise of individual moral capacity 'necessarily . . . out of the reach of any *stated rule* or *express legal provision*': 'No human laws will . . . suppose a case, which at once must destroy all law . . . nor will they make provision for so desperate an event, as must render all legal provisions ineffectual. So long therefore as the English constitution lasts . . . the power of parliament is absolute and without control' (Blackstone 1979, I, pp. 156–7).

It was this Blackstonean insistence that the constitution did not and could not specify in law the rights of popular sovereignty upon which it was ultimately based that more radical theorists of political liberty challenged most vehemently. 'Judge Blackstone', James Burgh charged in his *Political Disquisitions* (1774–5), 'seems to forget that the safety of the people *limits* all free governments'. 'The truth is', he had 'placed the sovereignty wrong, viz. in the government; whereas it should have been in the people' (Burgh 1774–5, I, p. 226, III, p. 278). In 1776, Richard Price, in his avowedly Lockean defence of civil liberty, dismissed as 'absurd' the doctrine 'which some have taught' concerning 'the omnipotence of parliaments'. All government was 'in the very nature of it, a trust'; and legislators exercised a 'subordinate and limited' authority according to the specific fiduciary powers the community had delegated to them. 'If they contradict this trust, they betray their constituents and dissolve themselves' (Price 1991, p. 28; Sheridan 1779; Wilson 1967, II, p. 23).

3 The balanced constitution

The classification of the English government as a mixed constitution and the debate over parliamentary sovereignty tended to focus on somewhat narrow, though fundamental, questions concerning the structure and extent of public power. Analysis of the English constitution rarely confined itself to these questions alone, and a more expansive treatment of constitutional arrangements proved especially critical to the theory of English liberty. Such explorations ranged widely and often repetitively over a varied stock of preoccupations, but two broad themes enjoyed particular prominence and influence. One of these concerned the relationship between English law and English liberty (considered in section 6 below); the other scrutinised the conduct and co-ordination of the principal institutions of governance, to which I now turn in this and in the following section.

The theory of mixed constitution itself supplied the framework for evaluating the conduct of government. The legislature not only mixed elements of each of the three simple forms of government, but also combined these elements in such a manner 'that all the parts form a mutual check upon each other' so as to frustrate the abuse of power. This, in turn, meant that the mixture demanded a sufficient 'equilibrium of power between one branch of the legislature and the rest' in order to sustain this checking process (Blackstone 1979, I, pp. 150–1). English liberty, in the more familiar contemporary formulation, depended upon 'the *balance* of the constitution'.

Once the necessity of constitutional balance was affirmed, it became possible to consider the particular powers and political functions of each branch of the legislature in terms of this requirement. Humphrey Mackworth, justifying the House of Commons's campaign to impeach several royal ministers over alleged illegalities in their conduct in foreign affairs in 1701, furnished a particularly lucid version of this kind of constitutional analysis. 'The great rule' of English government, he reported, was 'to preserve the just balance of the constitution' (Mackworth 1701, 'To the Lords'). The practice of ministerial impeachments supplied an exemplary instance of the manner in which the constitution fulfilled this maxim. The strength of the king was promoted by the crown's legal immunity, but his ministers and servants were held legally accountable in their public functions through the mechanism of parliamentary impeachment. The crown could not shield any favourite from impeachment, as the decision to prosecute fell entirely under the aegis of the Commons. The actual trial and conviction of those accused, however, was the exclusive judicial right of the Lords, which again could not be obstructed by either crown or Commons. Thus the constitution equipped each part of the legislature with 'particular powers' that served to 'assist each against the encroachments of the other' and to prevent 'any one' part from defeating 'the right or power that is lodged in any other' (Mackworth 1701, pp. 2, 4; cf. pp. 5–7, 18–21). The correct understanding of the practice was supplied by this general logic of distributed functions and cumulative balance; and the same logic disclosed the vital mechanism through which the 'absolute, supreme power' of the legislature came in its internal operations to be checked and regulated (Mackworth 1701, p. 3).

The form of analysis adopted by Mackworth became a staple of eighteenth-century political debate and speculation. The particular privileges of each legislative branch – the crown's powers of appointment, the House of Commons's control of fiscal legislation, the judicial authority of the Lords – were routinely assessed and defended in terms of how such authority equipped that institution with sufficient power to resist encroachments from the other branches. Similarly, reform projects and parliamentary machinations would predictably be defended and denounced in terms of their likely impact on constitutional balance. Nonetheless, throughout the century, until the era of the wars against revolutionary France, one formidable issue dominated the debate over the health of the mixed and balanced constitution: the relationship between the executive power of the crown and the independence of parliament, especially the House of Commons.

'Executive power', according to the conventional juridical categories, denoted the task 'of *enforcing*' (as opposed to '*creating*') the laws (Blackstone 1979, I, p. 142; Rutherforth 1822, pp. 83–5). In more common usage, the 'executive' referred to the potent list of 'discretionary powers . . . vested in the monarch', as Edmund Burke described it, 'for the execution of the laws, or for the nomination to magistracy and office, or for conducting the affairs of peace and war, or for ordering the revenue' (Burke 1884, I, pp. 469–70). Among the more delicate of the kingdom's constitutional arrangements was the placement of legislative power jointly in the hands of 'king, lords, and commons', and the granting of executive power to 'the king alone' (Blackstone 1979, I, p. 143).

The expansive eighteenth-century discussion of the relationship between executive and legislative authority engaged directly with the major changes in governance that had emerged in the decades following the Glorious Revolution. These included, first, the dramatic expansion of the size, costs, and revenues of statecraft: the large military establishment supporting a bellicose foreign policy; the new apparatus of public finance and national debt; the reliance on customs and excise; and the droves of crown appointees required to staff these structures. Second was the system of parliamentary management used to secure the annual legislative renewal of this statecraft: the techniques of ministerial direction of the crown's interests in parliament; and the extensive use of government offices, patronage, and electoral influence to garner support in the House of Commons.

Students of eighteenth-century political thought are now familiar with these developments, and the terms in which they were evaluated, defended, and especially condemned.[3] The critics' case received classic exposition in the journalist denunciations of Walpole's administration in the 1720s and 1730s through such widely disseminated vehicles as John Trenchard and Thomas Gordon's *Cato's Letters* (1720–3) and Bolingbroke's *Craftsman*

---

3 Pocock 1975, part 3, remains the most ambitious elucidation of eighteenth-century British political argument in terms of these developments. The relevant changes in statecraft received classic interpretation in Dickson 1967 and Plumb 1967, and more recent revision in Brewer 1989, Langford 1991, and O'Gorman 1989.

(1726–36). Bolingbroke, as we have seen, fully embraced the standard formulation of England's 'mixed constitution'; and further celebrated this constitution as the 'tree' which produced 'that delicious and wholesome fruit'
of 'liberty' (Bolingbroke 1997b, p. 118). Within this mixture, the 'essentials of British liberty' were sustained through 'parliamentary freedom'; and
throughout English history, attacks on liberty invariably took the form of
campaigns to subdue parliament (pp. 101, 98). What, in turn, ultimately sustained this vital parliamentary freedom was the mechanism of parliamentary
elections which enabled the community to ensure 'the integrity of their
trustees' in the Commons. 'As a bad king must stand in awe of an honest
parliament, a corrupt House of Commons must stand in awe of an honest
people' (p. 125).

In past ages, parliamentary freedom had been challenged by royal
prerogative; currently, it was undermined by the more subtle, but no less
malignant, forces of executive corruption. The unprecedented size of the
civil and military establishments, along with the inflated revenues of the
crown (which, no less menacingly, were attributable to equally unprecedented levels of public debt), supplied government with a vast network
of patronage through which to transform, through 'place' and 'office', the
trustees of English liberty into the pawns of executive power. At the same
time, the deployment of electoral patronage and the statutory extension of
the parliamentary term to seven years disabled the mechanisms of electoral
accountability. Superficially, the outward form of a constitution of king,
Lords, and Commons was maintained. In practice what prevailed was an
anti-constitutional regime of government 'by corruption' that placed parliament under the 'absolute influence of a king or his minister' (Bolingbroke
1997b, p. 94).

The understanding of the constitution offered by Bolingbroke and like-
minded opponents of the Hanoverian regime thus placed the fate of English
liberty squarely upon the virtue of the community (its capacity to hold parliament to its trust) and the independence of parliament (in its capacity to
combat the ever-present tendency of political power to corruption, abuse,
and aggrandisement). As such, the account – standardly adorned with the
appropriate classical maxims and examples from Roman history – constituted a distinctly 'republican' and 'commonwealth' reading of the British
constitution; or, in the more common contemporary usage, it furnished a
'Country' critique of Hanoverian 'Court' politics (Pocock 1975, pp. 467–
90). The positive 'commonwealth' or 'Country' strategy for restoring constitutional balance followed directly from its diagnosis of the current threats

to British liberty. The fiscal resources and scale of government were to be reduced through the elimination of public debt. The manipulation of parliamentary deliberations by the executive was to be destroyed by barring those with government offices ('placemen') or contracts from the House of Commons. The independence of parliament was to be restored through a strengthening of the electoral process: 'freedom of elections' (the elimination of electoral patronage and expenditures in the borough constituencies) and 'frequent elections' (the repeal of the Septennial Act). With the adoption of these measures, the constitution would be restored, and the community rescued from the party divisions and ministerial rivalries that had infested politics since the Glorious Revolution.

The response of the 'Court Whigs' to this indictment of British political practice was joined immediately by ministerial apologists and journalists in the 1720s and 1730s (Browning 1982; Burtt 1992; Pocock 1975, pp. 446–61). But what was to prove the most elegant and suggestive of the responses to the 'republican' interpretation of the constitution did not appear until 1741–2, when Hume presented the first of the several editions of his *Essays, Moral and Political* published in his lifetime.[4] In these essays, as in the later *History of England*, he tendentiously adopted 'the temper . . . of a philosopher', who properly recognised the 'infinitely complicated' texture of 'all political questions', and taught 'a lesson of moderation' to replace the 'violent animosities' of the 'party-zealots' (Hume 1994a, pp. 216, 12–13). He concurred in the commonplace judgement that England's mixed system of government produced unequalled levels of public liberty. 'The whole history of mankind', he reported, offered no comparable instance of a community governed 'in a manner so free, so rational and so suitable to the dignity of human nature' (p. 217). But, in reaching this conclusion, Hume distanced himself from many contemporary commentators by emphasising the historical novelty, institutional fragility, and considerable political risks of this distinctive form.

In his response to the 'Country' attack on Walpolean corruption, Hume maintained that what had there been treated as pathological features of post-Revolution politics instead needed to be acknowledged as the inevitable, though potentially dangerous, features of England's complex institutional structures. The political order secured through the Glorious Revolution and Protestant succession had ended the destructive constitutional conflicts of the Stuart era. Likewise, these developments had served to blur and attenuate

4 Hume's political theory was, of course, also to be found in his moral philosophy and 'philosophical' history. For broader treatment than given here see Forbes 1975, Haakonssen 1993, and Miller 1981. For other aspects of Hume see chs. 3, 5, 7, 10, and 12 in this volume.

the kingdom's earlier political divisions between the Whig and Tory parties. But it was wrong to expect that this clarification of the constitution simply eliminated political division and partisanship. The constitution's 'extremely delicate' combination of 'republican and monarchical parts' meant that 'different opinions must arise' over its proper balance, 'even among persons of the best understanding'. On any particular issue 'some will incline to trust larger powers to the crown', while others would fear the 'approaches of tyranny and despotic power'; and hence, partisan divisions had to be allowed as 'the genuine offspring of the British government' (Hume 1994a, pp. 40–1, 44–55). Moreover, since 'the power of the crown' was 'always lodged in a single person, either king or minister', the extent of this power would inevitably vary according to the ambition and capacity of the individual exercising it. Consequently, the constitutional structures could never 'assign to the crown such a determinate degree of power, as will, in every hand' serve the purposes of constitutional balance (p. 27; see also pp. 203–5).

If, for Hume, political division and constitutional ambiguity formed an 'unavoidable disadvantage' of England's system of 'limited monarchy' (p. 27), the mechanisms of constitutional balance themselves required similar re-examination and elucidation. Contrary to the conventional wisdom concerning the balance among king, Lords, and Commons, Hume maintained that the constitution in fact 'allotted . . . to the House of Commons' a 'share of power . . . so great that it absolutely commands all the other parts of the government' (p. 25). Neither the monarch's legislative veto, nor the privileges of the Lords, was sufficient to counter the strength of the Commons. The costs of modern statecraft, coupled with the House of Commons's settled control over the 'right of granting money', gave that body more than enough capacity to overwhelm the constitutional order (pp. 25–6).[5]

What, in fact, prevented this destruction of the mixed constitution were precisely those frequently condemned patronage resources of the crown which created a block of support in the House of Commons sufficient to maintain the crown's authority (p. 26). In this manner, Hume concluded, executive influence was revealed as the true saviour of the constitutional order: 'We may . . . give to this influence what name we please; we may call it by the invidious appellations of *corruption* and *dependence*; but some degree

---

5 For Hume, the power of the Commons was the political face of the social transformations of the Tudor and Stuart eras, which he identified with commerce and manufactures. These changes had undermined the power of the peerage and the feudal order. See Hume 1983–5, II, pp. 522–5, and 1994a, pp. 111–12.

and some kind of it are inseparable from the very nature of the constitution, and necessary to the preservation of our mixed government' (p. 26).

In the decades which followed, constitutional argument and programmes of reform routinely adhered to the script set out in these polemics of the early Hanoverian period. Apologists for the political order emphasised the manner in which 'executive influence' had simply replaced 'prerogative' as the main source of royal power in the scheme of constitutional balance (Blackstone 1979, I, pp. 322–5). But even the most complacent observers recognised that the scale of British government and its military establishment gave the executive, in Blackstone's phrase, 'an influence most amazingly extensive' (p. 324). Accordingly, the conduct of executive government and its impact on parliamentary independence necessarily remained a leading preoccupation (Burke 1884, I, pp. 444–50; Hume 1994a, pp. 26–7). This was an imperative that framed both moderate and radical projects of constitutional purification (Cannon 1973, pp. 47–97; Langford 1989, pp. 710–19).

Radical schemes of constitutional reform, developed in the contexts of the Wilkesite protests of the 1760s and the American resistance of the following decade, offered increasingly democratic versions of the 'Country' programme to block executive corruption by strengthening the mechanism of parliamentary election. The 'subversion of the constitution' at the hands of 'parliamentary corruption' received encyclopedic denunciation through the vehicle of Burgh's three-volume *Political Disquisitions*. The 'British government', he reported, had long ceased functioning as a mixed constitution, and now was 'really a juntocracy . . . or government by a minister and his crew' (Burgh 1774–5, I, pp. 49–50; see III, p. 267). The recovery of parliamentary independence required, as John Cartwright expressed the radical prescription, 'making our parliament *annual* and our representation *equal*' (Cartwright 1776, p. 15).[6]

Conservative critics of this approach to parliamentary reform, such as Josiah Tucker and Edmund Burke, returned to an analysis furnished by Hume, arguing that such schemes actually threatened to unbalance the constitution by overstrengthening its republican features, thereby exposing the kingdom to all the vices and instabilities correctly associated with pure democracy (Burke 1884, VII, pp. 71–87; Hume 1994a, pp. 31–2; Tucker 1781, pp. 257–74). But even the alternative, self-consciously moderated schemes of political reform adhered to much the same logic of constitutional

---

6 Burgh also supported the call for an extra-parliamentary 'Grand National Association' to lead the mobilisation for constitutional reform: see Burgh 1774–5, III, pp. 428–35. This movement is detailed in Black 1963 and Christie 1962.

balance. When in 1780 Burke presented to the House of Commons the Whig version of the popularly agitated plan for 'economical reform', he duly stressed that 'economy' itself merely constituted a 'secondary' goal of this plan for administrative retrenchment. Its primary purpose was to reduce 'the direct and visible influence' of the executive, and to extinguish 'secret corruption almost to the possibility of its existence' (Burke 1884, II, p. 356).[7]

The debates over corruption, influence, and constitutional balance formed the common coin of political argument in eighteenth-century Britain, and frequently involved little better than repetitive and even formulaic rehearsals of stock themes. Yet this material came to attain an intellectual impact far more substantial than the oftentimes narrowly partisan contexts of its rehearsal. In focusing so much attention on the relationship between executive power, on the one hand, and the integrity of the House of Commons, on the other, the debate tended to shift attention away from the conventional image of the mixed constitution and its combination of monarchic, aristocratic, and democratic elements.[8] This, as was perceived with special force by the author of the period's single most famous treatment of the English constitution, made possible an alternative explication of the nature of England's complex political structures. Not the least of Montesquieu's remarkable achievements in this account was to convince a large, cosmopolitan audience that the design of England's government, so described, revealed the foundational principles for the general theory of constitutional freedom.

4 The separation of powers

Montesquieu's renowned chapter 'On the Constitution of England' formed the centrepiece of the first of two books (XI and XII) of *The Spirit of the Laws* devoted to 'the laws that form political liberty'. The first of these considered liberty 'in its relation with the constitution'; a form of liberty, Montesquieu began by arguing, that was commonly wrongly identified with democratic self-government. Instead, political liberty was uniquely a property of those 'moderate governments' which made possible such a stable structure of law that their subjects were enabled 'to do everything the laws permit'. Such

---

7 On 'economic reform' and its connection with parliamentary reform, see Cannon 1973, pp. 75–84; Christie 1956; Harling 1996.

8 One by-product of this emphasis (ironic, in light of the actual political power of the peerage) was the marginalisation of the House of Lords in constitutional discussions. William Paley, for example, found it necessary to explain the 'little notice [that] has been taken of the House of Lords' in his own survey (Paley 1838, III, p. 272).

liberty could survive only under a government where 'power is not abused'; and the key mechanism for preventing the abuse of power, Montesquieu famously claimed, was a political form in which 'power' checked 'power by the arrangement of things' (*SL*, XI.1–4).

Having thus clarified in the abstract the nature of constitutional freedom, the French jurist invoked England as the sole 'nation of the world' whose constitution had 'political liberty for its direct purpose'. 'We are going to examine the principles on which this nation founds political liberty', he explained. 'If these principles are good, liberty will appear there as in a mirror' (*SL*, XI.6, p. 156).[9]

The detailed analysis of England's constitution (XI.6) centred on an account of how the 'three sorts of powers' exercised in every state – legislative power, executive power, and 'the power of judging' – were, in England, distributed into separate institutional hands. It was in terms of the complex distribution and co-ordination of these three powers that Montesquieu identified those features of England's political system designed to frustrate the principal forms of political and legal tyranny.[10] In the case of the 'power of judging', the separation meant that those responsible for creating law and for mobilising the resources of the state lacked the power of punishing particular 'crimes' or settling 'legal disputes between individuals'. English justice – in an oblique reference to common law juries and the system of semi-annual judicial assize circuits – placed the 'power of judging' in the hands of temporary tribunals 'drawn from the body of the people' (pp. 157–9).

The 'power of judging' was acknowledged to be the weakest of the three elements of state power (p. 160), which meant that the distribution and operation of legislative and executive powers required the most attention. Here Montesquieu's discussion reworked and revised topics already established in native debates over the balance of the constitution (Shackleton 1949). The division of parliament into two houses served the interests of political stability by giving those 'distinguished by birth, wealth, or honours' their own assembly serving their 'separate views and interests'. But the same bicameral structure also created an internal restraint on legislative power by requiring the agreement of two separate bodies in the making of law (*SL*, XI, 6, pp. 160, 164). The monopolisation of executive authority by a

9 The place of Montesquieu's discussion of England in his more general theory is explored in Baker 1990, pp. 173–85; Mason 1990; and Richter 1977, pp. 84–97. See also two substantial histories of the theory of separation of powers: Gwyn 1965 and Vile 1967.
10 Montesquieu's discussion in XI.6 concerned the *design* of England's constitution and not whether in practice this design was realised: see *SL*, XI, 6, p. 166.

hereditary monarch rendered explicit the institutional division between legislative and executive powers. The monarch's 'faculty of vetoing' proposed legislation meant that 'the executive power' could 'check the enterprises of the legislative body' when these tended to the aggrandisement of power (p. 162). The 'legislative power', in turn, could prevent executive abuse through its control over 'the raising of public funds' and through its power to accuse and impeach those officials who violated the law 'in matters of public business' (pp. 163, 164). The overall arrangement of 'these three powers', Montesquieu observed, 'forced' them 'to move in concert'; so that whenever public power was deployed, these institutional checks against the abuse of power were automatically mobilised (p. 164).

The reception of Montesquieu's analysis in Anglophone political thought proved rapid and, most often, enthusiastic. 'The celebrated Montesquieu', James Madison reported, was the 'oracle' whom 'enlightened patrons of liberty' invariably 'consulted and cited' in support of 'the political maxim' that 'the legislative, executive, and judicial departments ought to be separate and distinct' (Hamilton *et al.* 1981, pp. 138–9). There was, of course, much in Montesquieu's assessment to flatter his English readers, and it is striking how much less attention was directed to those other sections of *The Spirit of the Laws* which supplied far more critical and pessimistic assessments of England's political system (*SL*, XIX.27, XX.7; Baker 1990, pp. 173–85). But the chief importance of the discussion was due less to its praise for England than to its presentation of England's constitution as a basic institutional model which provided the correct framework and standard for understanding the logic of constitutional liberty more generally. In contrast with native discussions, Montesquieu's treatment of English structures and practices proceeded at a highly abstract level (even such basic nomenclature as 'House of Lords' and 'House of Commons' was absent), replete with comparisons to political arrangements in the states of the ancient and modern world. This comparative dimension was thereafter greatly extended in the remainder of book XI, which continued with three chapters on constitutional liberty in the case of modern monarchy (7–9) and ten chapters on ancient governments (10–19). Ironically, Montesquieu's overall account of political liberty in book XI devoted more space to the case of ancient Rome (12–19) than it did to contemporary England (6).

Montesquieu's more general and comparative concerns help explain what proved a particularly influential feature of his analysis: the prominence and importance ascribed to 'the power of judging'. The institutional power and political impacts of courts and legal practices had long been recognised in the political theory of European kingdoms. But the formal analysis of political power, particularly by jurists, tended to remain framed by the distinction between legislative and executive power. Montesquieu's departure from this convention received prompt notice.[11] Thomas Rutherforth, in his mid-century Cambridge University lectures on Grotius, thus lamented the growing fashion to distinguish civil power into 'three several parts, legislative, judicial, and executive'. 'Judicial power', he countered, was 'plainly . . . nothing else but a branch of the executive power' (Paine 1989, p. 139; Rutherforth 1822, p. 275).

Nonetheless, this separation and elevation of 'the power of judging' was absolutely critical to Montesquieu's comparative purposes. In the case of modern (Continental) monarchies, such as in France, the fact that the king left 'the power of judging' to 'his subjects' created a level of constitutional freedom in these states unknown in despotic governments, where 'the three powers' were 'united in the person' of a single prince. Furthermore, the common failure in republican states to achieve a stable institutional separation of 'the power of judging' helped clarify Montesquieu's initial claim in book XI that constitutional liberty could not be equated with self-government (*SL*, XI, 6, pp. 157–8). On the basis of this insight, Montesquieu explained the precariousness of political liberty in ancient Rome, and drew the striking, albeit reassuring, conclusion that 'the Italian republics' enjoyed 'less liberty than in our monarchies' (pp. 179–84, 157).

Most British commentators eagerly embraced Montesquieu's emphasis on 'the power of judging', though in a manner which often enlarged and significantly altered his own teaching. Montesquieu had focused his attention on the English jury and circuit assizes, and had consistently used the phrase *la puissance de juger* (and not *le pouvoir judiciare*) ('the power of judging', not 'judicial power') to refer to this third element of state power. His eighteenth-century English translator, Thomas Nugent, rendered the phrase as 'judicial power' and 'judiciary power', thus making easier the eventual mutation of Montesquieu's separated *la puissance de juger* into an independent judicial department or branch of government. Blackstone, whose analysis closely followed Montesquieu, thus spoke more broadly of the 'distinct and

11 The ambiguities of Montesquieu's own text reflect some of the difficulties attending this revision. At the outset of XI.6, he distinguished 'legislative power' from two different forms of 'executive power' ('over things depending on the right of nations' and 'over things depending on civil right'), before settling down to the now more familiar classification into legislative, executive, and judicial functions (*SL*, XI, 6, pp. 156–7). His initial formulation recalls Locke's distinction between legislative and two kinds of (analytically differentiated) executive power: executive power and federative power: Second Treatise, ch. 12.

separate existence of the judicial power' being 'one main preservative of the public liberty' (Blackstone 1979, I, p. 259). In explaining this vital – and now extended – constitutional feature, he emphasized recent legislative changes Montesquieu omitted. Formerly English judges held office 'at the pleasure of the crown' (*durante bene placito*); now they served 'during their good behaviour' and 'their full salaries are absolutely secured to them during the continuance of their commissions' (I, p. 258).[12]

English authors, such as Blackstone, found in Montesquieu's treatment of judging a convenient formula for accommodating already well-rehearsed precepts concerning the importance of independent courts and impartial judicial decision-making to English liberty. The condemnation of the English crown's earlier reliance on prerogative courts (Star Chamber, High Commission), along with the denunciation of the royal manipulation of the common law bench, formed a staple and central theme of the eighteenth-century indictment of Stuart absolutism. Likewise, legislative enactments designed to strengthen the integrity of common law process – such as the Habeas Corpus Act (1679), the Treason Trials Act (1696), the Act of Settlement (1701) – figured no less prominently in post-Revolution accounts of the basic structures preserving public freedom (Blackstone 1979, IV, pp. 431–3; Delolme 1834, pp. 46–8, 165–70).

Still, Montesquieu's more abstract thesis concerning the distribution of three powers stimulated an important shift in the English discussion of these familiar themes. In earlier discussions, concern for the impartial administration of justice focused on the threats posed by royal power and prerogative. Often the favoured case for establishing the *independence* of the judiciary from royal interference was to emphasise the courts' proper *dependence* on parliamentary authority. 'The judges', Roger Acherley urged, 'ought to give judgement in all cases before them without being obliged to resort to the king for advice, instructions or directions'. Instead, they should be 'accountable in parliament' (Acherley 1727, p. 86; Atkyns 1734, pp. 96–7). Once Montesquieu's distribution-of-powers thesis gained currency, it became common to celebrate a far more generalised version of judicial independence and institutional autonomy. Blackstone stressed the need for the separation of 'judicial power' from the 'legislative' no less than from 'the executive power' (Blackstone 1979, I, p. 259). Paley reported that 'the first maxim of a free state' was that 'the legislative and judicial characters be

---

12 The change, introduced after the Glorious Revolution, was made statutory in the 1701 Act of Settlement. Reference to this legislation became routine in discussions of the independence of English judges.

kept separate', thereby dropping the earlier preoccupation with interference from the crown (Paley 1838, III, p. 281). Finally, Burke expansively extolled independent judges 'wholly unconnected with the political world' (Burke 1884, II, p. 351).[13]

5 Delolme versus Price

The appropriation and adjustment of Montesquieu's 'power of judging' for domestic purposes was paralleled in the more general reception of his interpretation of the English constitution. His authority was standardly paraded to confirm Whiggish pieties about the exceptionalism of English liberty; and his formulation of separated 'power' checking 'power' was mobilised in partisan disputes over constitutional balance (Fletcher 1939; Vile 1967, pp. 111–21). In his own discussion, Montesquieu did not classify England's constitution as a mixture of monarchy, aristocracy, and democracy; in book XI, he reserved this formula for the government of ancient Rome (*SL*, XI, 6, p. 170).[14] English commentators, in contrast, frequently layered Montesquieu's separation of powers thesis on top of the older theory of England's mixed constitution (Adams 1998, pp. 58–61; Blackstone 1979, I, pp. 50–2, 149–51; Paley 1838, III, pp. 265, 269–71, 281–2). The combination implied two overlapping networks of institutional arrangements, both of which functioned to frustrate the abuse of political power. Analytically, however, each thesis was quite distinct: mixed government explaining the internal composition (and resulting restraints in the operation) of sovereign legislative power; the separation of powers treating the institutional distribution of three kinds of state power, of which legislative power was but one. The blending of the two theses followed readily, given their shared concern with the manner in which complex structures and balances helped produce political liberty. Nonetheless, it was possible to use the materials assembled in *The Spirit of the Laws* to propose a more substantial and ambitious recasting of established constitutional pieties. Such a task was undertaken by another influential continental author, Jean Louis Delolme, whose *Constitution de*

---

13 These fulsome theories of judicial independence strained against much of the settled routines of political patronage and recruitment attending judicial appointments and promotions; see Lemmings 1993.

14 Montesquieu in ch. 6 identified all the structural features relevant to England's 'mixed constitution', though he avoided the label. He regarded England as a largely anomalous political form, which explains some of his reticence in applying conventional political categories to its constitution. In v.19 England is described as 'a nation where the republic hides under the form of monarchy' (*SL*, p. 70).

l'Angleterre (1771), earned later praise as 'the best defence of the political balance of three powers that ever was written' (Adams 1797, I, p. 70).

Even more than Montesquieu, Delolme presented a detailed comparative canvass in order to confirm the commonplace judgement that England enjoyed unrivalled levels of political freedom. Of special concern to him was the effort to vindicate the English system of government from the strictures of those modern enthusiasts of 'the governments of ancient times' (in particular the judgement of his fellow Genevan, Rousseau), who 'cried up the governments of Sparta and Rome as the only fit ones for us to imitate' (Delolme 1834, p. 209). Thus, although Delolme pursued at length the fundamental ways in which the English monarchy and nobility differed from their Continental counterparts (pp. 33–40, 323, 335–8), he explored most pointedly the contrast between England's unique regime of modern liberty and the republican states of antiquity.

In the course of this ambitious survey, reference to England as a mixed government of monarchic, aristocratic, and democratic parts appeared almost as an afterthought (p. 431). Instead, Delolme emphatically anchored his constitutional analysis in 'the particular nature and functions' distributed to the 'constituent parts of the government', which gave to English government 'so different an appearance from that of other free states' (p. 171). The 'first peculiarity of the English government' was the crown's exclusive monopoly of 'executive power' (pp. 171, 335). Another 'capital principle' was identified in the provision 'that the legislative power belongs to parliament alone' (p. 49). Finally, it was the 'singular situation of the English judges' relative to the 'constituent powers of the state' which served to frustrate the abuse of both legislative and executive power, as well as to promote that 'strict and universal impartiality' of justice which formed yet another 'essential difference . . . between the English government and those of other countries' (pp. 326, 141–2, 192). Whereas previous commentators anxiously noted the delicacy and fragility of England's constitutional balance, Delolme instead emphasised the political system's 'resources', 'equilibrium', and overall strength (p. 171). It was precisely this 'solidity' and 'peculiar stability of the governing authority' which enabled the 'several essential branches of English liberty to take place' (p. 371).

Delolme's more detailed treatment explained the manner in which the constitution's distinctive distribution of governmental functions secured English liberty from the dangers and vices that typically afflicted free governments. The political capacity of the crown rested on its exclusive command of executive power, but this was effectively restrained by the House of Commons's control of supply. Such royal authority, denied 'the power of imposing taxes', was 'like a vast body which cannot of itself accomplish its motions' (p. 66). Conversely, the fact that executive authority was separated, and, even more, 'exclusively vested' in one institution, made for an extremely potent form of executive authority. The strength of English kingship, in this respect, contributed critically to 'the remarkable liberty enjoyed by the English nation' (p. 335). Historically, this 'indivisible and inalienable' executive power served to unify the Commons and Lords in common cause against the abuse of royal prerogative; currently, it proved easier to monitor and restrain than a more diffuse executive (pp. 16–17, 187–9, 244–8). More importantly, since executive power was wielded only by an hereditary monarch, even the most powerful and ambitious of private subjects was discouraged from attempting that kind of direct seizure of state power that afflicted the ancient republics. Instead, each English subject – knowing he must remain a subject – acquired a strong interest 'really to love, defend, and promote those laws which secure liberty to the subject' (pp. 185n; see pp. 183–8, 335).

In treating legislative power, Delolme similarly emphasised the efficacy of unique structural arrangements. The organisation of parliament into Lords and Commons – largely shorn of their conventional associations with 'aristocracy' and 'democracy' and the social divisions to which these were related – served its primary constitutional function by introducing an internal restraint on the operation of legislative power. So effective was each House in blocking the aggrandisement of power by the other, Delolme maintained, that the crown rarely needed to deploy its veto power to protect the executive from legislative encroachments (pp. 190–1, 349–50).

Of equally profound consequence were the unique arrangements governing the organisation and functions of the House of Commons. The people, acting through their representatives in the Commons, enjoyed a robust power of 'the *initiative* in legislation' that contrasted favourably with the less potent veto power allotted to the plebeian institutions of antiquity (p. 201; see pp. 223–8). This power, however, was restricted by being exercised 'only through' the community's 'representatives' (p. 232). These representatives – moderate in number, placed on an easily monitored political stage, and generally selected 'from those citizens who are most favoured by fortune' – were equipped with both experience and incentives for resisting the ambitions and intrigues of the powerful. Hence the absence in England of that kind of lethal political volatility and demagogic manipulation of the popular will which routinely destroyed liberty in the ancient world (pp. 220–3).

England's '*representative* constitution', Delolme triumphantly concluded, had thus achieved a structural 'remedy' for the perversions of republican government that had eluded previous 'popular constitution[s]' (p. 233).

In elucidating the history and operation of England's constitution, Delolme traversed well-rehearsed matters of political structures, government functions, and themes of balances and checks. Nonetheless, his study is indicative of how, by the mid-1770s, significantly divergent accounts had developed concerning the manner in which this system of government produced its celebrated benefit, political liberty. The spectrum of interpretation can be indicated through a brief comparison of the sharply contrasting positions adopted in Delolme's tendentious rendering of England's separation of powers and in Richard Price's no less substantial recasting of England's mixed constitution in his *Observations on the Nature of Civil Liberty* (1776).

Ultimately what divided the two theorists was a basic conflict over the nature of liberty, which by this time boasted a rich and distinguished pedigree (Pocock 1985, pp. 37–50; Skinner 1998). Price, who identified liberty in general with 'the idea of self-government or self-direction', identified civil freedom as the capacity of the members of a given community to govern and make laws for themselves (Price 1991, pp. 22, 23–4). Delolme (reacting here to the doctrines of Rousseau) directly repudiated this approach. 'To concur by one's suffrage in enacting laws' was to enjoy 'a share' of 'power'. 'To live in a state where the laws are equal . . . and sure to be executed' was 'to be free' (Delolme 1834, p. 212; Paley 1838, III, pp. 250–2).

Of greater concern here is the particular account each offered for the constitutional basis of England's freedom. Price, associating civil freedom with popular self-government, naturally turned to the elected body of legislative representatives as the appropriate vehicle of self-government in the circumstances of a large and populous state; such an assembly fulfilled the requirements of political liberty to the extent that it 'fairly and adequately represented' the community it served (Price 1991, pp. 24–5). Accordingly, England's claims for enjoying a 'free government' depended entirely on the representativeness and accountability of the House of Commons. When fashioning 'the most perfect constitution of government', Price acknowledged, excellent reasons might exist to introduce 'useful checks in the legislature' by adding a 'supreme executive magistrate' and an 'hereditary council' to the 'body of representatives' (thus creating a mixed form of government). Still, these institutional additions were, strictly speaking, irrelevant to the issue of liberty (Adams 1979, pp. 87–9; Price 1991, pp. 26–7, 43).

For Delolme, as we have seen, English freedom was not chiefly a function of political power's dependence on the community, much less the result of the people themselves immediately directing the government. Rather, the liberty England enjoyed was principally a product of separations and balances operating within the institutions of political power. Although Delolme recognised the 'right of election' as a basic 'remedy' against the abuse of parliamentary power (Delolme 1834, p. 249), his detailed treatment of the distinctive merits of England's '*representative*' (as opposed to '*popular*') constitution celebrated the House of Commons as much for its capacity to restrain as to facilitate the popular will. It was entirely in keeping with this conception of the function of representatives that Delolme went on to identify the 'democratical' features of English government with 'trial by jury' and 'liberty of the press'; instruments which respectively placed 'judicial power' and 'censorial power' directly 'in the people'.[15] These institutions, whose efficacy Delolme emphasised, rendered England 'a more democratical state than any other' (p. 381n; see pp. 250–69). But, the compliment additionally served neatly (if silently) to efface the democratic credentials of the House of Commons, and thereby destroy one of the major elements in the conventional depiction of England's mixed government.

6 The common law

The accounts of England's constitutional system considered thus far offered diverse explanations for the manner in which political structures frustrated the abuse of power; how England came emphatically to be blessed (in the frequently invoked Aristotelian formula) with a 'government of laws, not of men'. In principle, these treatments need not have attended in detail to the content of the specific law which governed the relations among individual subjects. Eighteenth-century jurists deployed several analytical categories to distinguish the issue of political or civil liberty (depending chiefly on the form of the state) from the issue of personal liberty or personal security (depending chiefly on the private rights secured by the body of domestic law) (P. N. Miller 1994, pp. 130–6). Furthermore, 'the law' which governed Britain actually comprised several distinct systems of rules and legal process,

---

15 Delolme was unusual in placing the press and public opinion under a distinct political function, 'censorial power', and in treating this power on a par with other leading powers (Delolme 1834, pp. 48, 250–61). Other commentators observed the contribution of the press and public discussion to the distinctiveness of British political culture, but tended not to accommodate this within their account of the constitution (*SL*, XIX.27, pp. 325–7; Paley 1838, III, p. 239).

Scots law and English law forming one obvious division, but, even within England, Roman law and canon law being used in specific jurisdictions, such as the ecclesiastical courts, military courts, and courts of admiralty (Blackstone 1979, I, pp. 79–84).

In fact, however, constitutional analysis attended at length to England's system of customary or common law. Just as most commentators found it virtually impossible to discuss English politics without reference to the mixed and balanced constitution, so they found it scarcely less difficult to consider the constitution without reference to the common law. 'The constitution', John Cartwright insisted, 'is a frame of government coeval with, erected upon, and regulated by, the spirit of the common law of England' (Cartwright 1776, p. 10).

The political importance ascribed to the common law followed several lines of argument, much of it replete with the same language of exceptionalism and triumphalism directed at the constitution itself. In the grand narrative of England's political development, the common law featured as parliament's key ally in the struggles for English liberty (Forbes 1975, pp. 233–60; Weston 1991). Royal absolutism and unchecked prerogative threatened the courts of common law no less than the mixed constitution; both had survived through an extended process of mutual support. 'Parliaments and the kingdom', the seventeenth-century jurist Matthew Hale had explained, had shown 'great regard' for the common law and 'great care . . . to preserve and maintain it' (Hale 1971, pp. 35–6). One momentous product of this historical process was the imposing series of declarations of basic 'rights and liberties' issued by parliaments at moments of political peril. Blackstone equipped the *Commentaries* with a particularly fulsome and uncritical catalogue of these enactments: beginning with the measures forced upon an unwilling King John – the *carta de foresta* (the Forest Charter) and Magna Carta (the latter, 'for the most part declaratory' of the more ancient common law); next, the confirmatory legislation of Edward I and his successors (Magna Carta having been renewed thirty-two times, according to Sir Edward Coke); then, 'after a long interval', the great monuments of the Stuart era – the 1628 Petition of Right, the 1679 Habeas Corpus Act ('a second *Magna Carta*'), the Bill of Rights of 1689, and, finally, the 1701 Act of Settlement, 'for better securing our religion, laws, and liberties . . . according to the ancient doctrine of the common law' (Blackstone 1979, I, pp. 123–4, IV, pp. 416–17, 431–4).[16]

16 Blackstone's catalogue disregarded the more critical historical scholarship on the origins of the common law as well as on the antiquity of the mixed constitution (see Forbes 1975, pp. 233–307; Weston

The historical symbiosis between the common law and the mixed constitution followed readily, since the two institutions shared the same goal of civil liberty. And the limitation of public power in England needed to be elucidated in terms of both structures. Just as the king could not alter the law except through the mechanism of parliamentary legislation, so he could not accuse a subject or punish him without mobilising the institutions of the common law. Thus, when Blackstone confidently boasted that 'the idea and practice of this political liberty flourish in their highest vigour in these kingdoms where it falls little short of perfection', he immediately referenced 'the legislature, and of course the laws of England'. 'This spirit of liberty is so deeply implanted in our constitution', he maintained, 'that a slave or a negro, the moment he lands in England, falls under the protection of our laws and . . . becomes *eo instanti* a freeman' (I, pp. 122–3).[17]

For common law jurists, English law's unrivalled devotion to personal liberty received its fullest manifestation in its protection of the rights of private property.[18] Property rights, particularly 'the law of real property', commanded special attention in light of its being 'the most important, the most extensive, and . . . the most difficult' part of English law (Sullivan 1772, p. 18). For the theory of the constitution, however, of greatest concern were those features of common law that most directly implicated issues of state power. Montesquieu, in treating the 'the power of judging', referred to trial by jury and legal protections against arbitrary imprisonment (*SL*, XI.6, pp. 158–9). Delolme predictably expanded this line of analysis through some lengthy reflections on England's practices of impartial and equal justice, and on the 'extreme mildness' of its criminal law (Delolme 1834, p. 329).

Criminal justice, Delolme revealingly reported at the outset of three chapters devoted to the topic, was strictly not 'part of the powers which are properly constitutional'; yet an area of law that so concerned 'the security of individuals' and 'the power of the state' had necessarily to be considered (pp. 135–6). In addition to the basic separation of judicial power (pp. 141–2,

1991). For examples of more restrained contemporary treatments, see Barrington 1769, p. 3; Delolme 1834, pp. 20–3; Hume 1983–5, I, pp. 442–6. On Blackstone's legal history, see Cairns 1985; Willman 1983.

17 Blackstone's generous formulation (later invoked by British abolitionists) exaggerated the common law's more limited and circumspect treatment of African slaves in England, and in later editions he revised the wording. On Blackstone's position and chattel slavery in eighteenth-century law, see Oldham 1992, II, pp. 1221–44.

18 Among his accomplishments in the *Commentaries* was Blackstone's success in presenting England's notoriously labyrinthine rules of property law and common law procedure as 'the genuine offspring of that spirit of equal liberty which is the singular felicity of Englishmen' (Blackstone 1979, III, pp. 422–3; see Lieberman 1989, pp. 39–48).

146–7), England's legal order included a full panoply of provisions further to ensure the liberty of the subject: public trials; protection against false imprisonment and false accusation; the elimination of judicial torture; written indictments; and a diligent strictness over procedural requirements in the interest of the accused (pp. 104, 147–53, 165–70). 'All branches of government are influenced', he enthused, 'from the spirit both of justice and mildness' which guided 'the laws for the security of the subject' as well as 'the manner in which they are executed' (p. 298).[19]

The heralded institutional centrepiece of the common law checks against the abuse of power was, of course, trial by jury – 'that part of their liberty', Delolme reported, 'to which the people of England are most thoroughly and universally wedded' (p. 164). What Hale extolled as 'the best trial in the world' figured prominently and unsurprisingly in the eighteenth-century catalogue of the antiquity and exceptionality of England's liberties (Hale 1971, p. 160). Blackstone's *Commentaries* (notwithstanding an initial reassurance 'not [to] misspend the reader's time in fruitless encomiums') supplied no less than three extended panegyrics detailing 'the glory of English law' and 'this *palladium*' of 'liberties' (Blackstone 1979, III, pp. 349–51, 379–81, IV, pp. 277–8, 342–4). In these treatments, moreover, the common law jury was often given an explicit and broad political purpose, which overshadowed its more specific function as one of several modes of trial in English law. Delolme, as we have seen, classified juries as part of the 'democratic' components of English government. Blackstone reported that juries not only restrained the 'prerogatives of the crown' in criminal cases by placing 'in the hands of the people' an appropriate 'share' in 'the administration of public justice', but they also equally served against 'the encroachments of the more powerful and wealthy citizens' (IV, p. 343, III, pp. 380–1). John Adams proposed that the English constitution could be thought of as embodying two distinct schemes of mixed government: a mixed legislature of king, Lords, and Commons; and a mixed executive of king, judges, and juries. On this basis, 'two branches of popular power' were revealed – 'voting for members of the House of Commons' and 'trials by juries' – which together helped sustain 'the balance and mixture of the government' (Adams 1998, pp. 58–60, 1979, pp. 88–92).

As Adams's testimony indicates, this specifically political treatment of the common law jury was by no means unique to establishment apologists,

19 Delolme's case for the mildness of criminal justice ignored the debate over the increased severity of penal sanctions which resulted from recent parliamentary legislation; see Beattie 1986, pp. 520–618; Lieberman 1989, pp. 199–215; and ch. 19 below.

such as Blackstone and Delolme. Indeed, throughout the course of the century, it was the radical critics of Hanoverian government who often pressed this characterisation most zealously. Wilkes and his propagandists in the 1760s celebrated the jury as a representative body against which to measure the failings of a now-corrupted assembly of parliamentary representatives (Brewer 1980b, pp. 153–7). In a series of notorious prosecutions for seditious libel then and in the following decades, political dissidents found ample confirmation of the continuing efficacy of juries in the battle to preserve English liberties. Following the lapse of the Licensing Act in 1695, the common law bench revised and adapted the law of seditious libel so that it became a leading (if often counter-productive) instrument for silencing public attacks on the government. The frustration of these efforts largely depended on the repeated unwillingness of jurors to accept the specific and limited legal task assigned them in such cases by government prosecutors and common law judges.[20] Such episodes, and their contemporary celebration, both confirmed and helped sustain the powerful 'constitutionist idiom' which remained so central to British radicalism through to the nineteenth century (Epstein 1994, pp. 3–5, 29–69). As in past eras, the battle against tyranny came armed with the appropriate common law weapons.

The common law's well-considered role in the restraining of public power did not, however, exhaust its contribution to the theory of England's constitutional freedom. Of no less importance was the fund of conceptual resources the law provided for defining the myriad relationships of authority and subordination that comprised the social order of the community. The same government structures, routinely described in the explicitly political terms of the theory of the mixed constitution or the theory of the separation of powers, were no less appropriately or commonly understood in the settled juridical categories of private right and legal title.

Burke made full use of this point in the ornate celebration of the English political experience which he pitted against the follies and wickedness of the French revolutionaries. Invoking the testimony of Coke and 'and indeed all the great men who follow him, to Blackstone', he emphasised how 'our lawyers' had taught the nation not only to regard its 'most sacred rights and franchises as an *inheritance*'; in so doing, they additionally had made it possible for all of 'the people' to conceive government power and their

20 Juries were expected to determine whether in fact an accused printer or author had produced the publication, while the judge determined whether the publication was or was not seditious libel. The distribution of responsibility between judge and jury was modified in Fox's Libel Act of 1792. See Green 1985, pp. 318–55; Hamburger 1985; Oldham 1992, II, pp. 775–808.

own rights under a unifying logic of prescriptive title. 'By a constitutional policy', Burke shrewdly and reassuringly observed, 'we receive, we hold, we transmit our government and our privileges, in the same manner in which we enjoy and transmit our property and our lives' (Burke 2001, pp. 182, 184; Pocock 1960).

While Burke's *Reflections on the Revolution in France* (1790) supplied what became the best-known statement of this common law orientation for later generations, for his contemporary audience its most complete rehearsal had appeared twenty-five years earlier in the first volume of the *Commentaries on the Laws of England*. Blackstone's celebrated volume furnished its readers with a uniquely detailed, elegant, and subsequently influential apology for Britain's constitutional order. But this learning did not come assembled in a discrete section on the 'constitution' or even on 'constitutional law'. Instead the book, devoted to 'the rights of persons', began with a chapter-length survey of 'the three great and primary rights' of English subjects: 'personal security, personal liberty, and private property'. The chapter concluded with an overview of the principal 'barriers' established 'to protect and maintain' the three rights, which Blackstone characterised as a scheme of 'auxiliary subordinate rights of the subject' (Blackstone 1979, I, p. 136). These 'auxiliary' rights comprised the right of self-defence, the right to petition the king or parliament, the right to apply 'to the courts of justice for redress of injuries', the 'limitation of the king's prerogative', and 'the constitution, powers, and privileges of parliament' (I, pp. 136–9). Blackstone's chapters on parliament and the king then followed, presenting 'the rights and duties of persons' who exercised 'supreme' magistracy. The *Commentaries* next treated, in turn, the 'rights of persons' exercising 'subordinate' magistracy (sheriffs, constables, etc.); the rights associated with particular social ranks and stations (clergy, nobility, military, etc.); the rights 'in private oeconomical relations' (master–servant, husband–wife, etc.); and the rights of 'artificial persons' (corporations).

This ordering of materials presented the central institutions of government as but one particular cluster of 'rights of persons' – rights which functioned to secure the 'auxiliary subordinate rights' of the subject, and which existed within a hierarchical system of personal rights that gradually reached down to the legal relations of the domestic household. The approach, which later English jurists found confused, served to erode the kind of organising boundary between state and society that featured in later treatments of constitutional law (Dicey 1939, p. 7; Lieberman 2002). But it properly reflected the manner in which the eighteenth-century state

continued to be conceptualised and debated both in terms of the categories
of customary law and in terms of the divisions of political science. Indeed,
the two overlapping registers appeared in descriptions of each of the main
components of England's constitutional system.

Thus the monarchy, from the perspective of constitutional analysis,
appeared in its executive capacity and in its power of legislative veto. But the
crown was equally conceived as a form of 'estate', an analogy that greatly
complicated and potentially constrained efforts to alter the royal succession
(Clark 1985, pp. 121–41; Nenner 1977, pp. 145–54, 178–90). Parliament's
constitutional function, as we have seen, centred on its control of supply and
its legislative supremacy. But when contests arose over parliamentary 'privilege', its traditional status as a 'high court', whose power and jurisdiction
were settled by 'custom and usage' (or *lex parliamenti*), regained prominence
(Blackstone 1979, I, p. 158; Thomson 1938, pp. 329–33; Williams 1960,
pp. 221–49). Again, the parliamentary franchise figured critically in the
political assessment of the independence of the House of Commons and its
credentials as a representative assembly. But the franchise was no less recognised to be a form of property for those who exercised it; and in disputed
elections it was the issue of an elector's good title to this property that often
proved paramount.[21]

The categories of the common law thus furnished a distinctive framework
for the elucidation and evaluation of constitutional structures – a framework,
moreover, which at the same time effectively deprived the constitution of
its convenient, if misleadingly limited, identification with the 'the form of
the legislature' (Paley 1838, III, p. 253). The gain in conceptual enrichment
and juridical accuracy, in this sense, came at the cost of definitional clarity
and precision. 'Some have said that the whole body of the laws' makes the
constitution; 'others that King, Lords, and Commons make the constitution', reported John Adams from Boston in 1766. But even though neither
definition seemed quite 'satisfactory', 'yet I cannot say that I am at any loss
about any man's meaning when he speaks of the British constitution, or of
the essentials and fundamentals of it' (Adams 1998, p. 57).

---

21 The understanding of the franchise as property appeared routinely in election disputes. The issue was
aired with particular thoroughness in the Oxfordshire election of 1754, which raised the question of
whether voters who held copyhold tenures were legally entitled to the franchise on the basis of these
tenancies (see Robson 1949, pp. 141–8).

12

Social contract theory and its critics

PATRICK RILEY

1 The historical background

At the heart of social contract theory is the idea that political legitimacy, political authority, and political obligation are derived from the consent of the governed, and are the artificial product of the voluntary agreement of free and equal moral agents. On this view, legitimacy and duty depend on a concatenation of voluntary individual acts, and not on 'natural' political authority, patriarchy, theocracy, divine right, necessity, custom, convenience, or psychological compulsion. Michael Oakeshott was thus right to call contractarianism a doctrine of 'will and artifice' (1975a, p. 7).[1]

While traces of contract theory can be found in ancient and medieval thought, and while the doctrine has recently been revived by John Rawls, it is generally agreed that the golden age of social contract theory was the period 1650–1800, beginning with Hobbes's *Leviathan* (1651) and ending with Kant's *Rechtslehre* (Metaphysics of Morals, 1797; Rawls 1972, pp. 11–13; Riley 1982, 1983). For at least the following century it was eclipsed by utilitarianism, Hegelianism, and Marxism. But between the mid-seventeenth and the early nineteenth centuries consent emerged as the leading doctrine of political legitimacy. Hobbes urges in chapter 42 of *Leviathan* that 'the right of all sovereigns is derived originally from the consent of every one of those that are to be governed', and in chapter 40 he insists that human wills 'make the essence of all covenants' (Hobbes 1991, pp. 395, 323). Locke in the second of his *Two Treatises of Government* argues that 'voluntary agreement gives . . . political power to governors' (*TTG*, II, §173, p. 383). Rousseau, in *The Social Contract* (1762), asserts that 'I owe nothing to those to whom I have promised nothing'; 'Civil association is the most voluntary act in the world; every man being born free and master of himself, no-one may on any pretext whatsoever subject him without his consent' (*SC*, II.6, p. 66, IV.2, p. 123). As for Kant, in the *Rechtslehre* he urges that all legitimate laws

---

1 For the background to the theme of this chapter see Barker 1947; Riley 1982, 1986; Ritchie 1893.

must be such that rational men *could* consent to them (Kant 1965, pp. 97, 112–13). Similarly, the American Declaration of Independence holds that governments derive their 'just powers' from the consent of the governed. The theme is stressed in most major thinkers of the period between Hobbes and Kant, though Hume and Bentham are important exceptions. Even Edmund Burke, who rejected consent as the basis of authority, thought it useful to say that society was grounded on a metaphorical contract of some sort (Burke 2001, p. 260). Hegel, though scarcely an 'atomistic individualist' or a contractarian, explicitly argued that while 'in the states of antiquity the subjective end was entirely identical with the will of the state', in modern times 'we make claims for private judgement, private willing, and private conscience'. When a social decision is to be made, Hegel continues, 'an "I will" must be pronounced by man himself' (Hegel 1991, pp. 285, 321).

Political philosophy since the seventeenth century was thus characterised by 'voluntarism', by an emphasis on the will of individuals. Why voluntarism came to hold such an important place in Western thought is debatable. It is probable that the introduction of Christianity facilitated a shift, from ancient theories of the good regime and the 'naturally' social end of man, to seeing politics as 'good acts', and hence requiring both knowledge of, and the will to do, the good. Politics now required moral assent, and the individual became implicated in politics by his own volition. The freedom to conform voluntarily to absolute standards had always been important in Christian doctrine; and the Reformation doubtless strengthened the element of individual choice and responsibility in moral thinking, while questioning the role of moral authority. It was natural enough that the 'Protestant' view of individual moral autonomy would pass from theology and moral philosophy into politics, forming the intellectual basis of social contract theory. By the end of the Reformation era, the mere excellence of an institution would no longer be sufficient to establish legitimacy: it would now require authorisation by individual men, understood, that is, as 'authors' of those institutions. However voluntarism and social contract theory arose, what is certain is that ideas of the good state increasingly gave way to ideas of the 'legitimate' state; and during the seventeenth century this legitimacy was often taken to rest on the notion of *willing*.

That shift represented a substantial break with much of ancient tradition, in which consent does not commonly function as a principle of legitimacy (perhaps because the concept of 'will' rarely has major moral significance in ancient philosophy) (Adkins 1960, pp. 2–4). While the need for consent to fundamental principles of political society in order to create a political construct through will and artifice is a doctrine characteristic of the 'idiom of individuality', the ancient conception of a highly unified and collective politics was dependent on a morality of the common good quite foreign to any insistence on individual 'will' as the creator of society (Oakeshott 1962, pp. 249–51). This is why Aristotle repudiates contractarian views of society: any true *polis*, he urges in the *Politics*, must devote itself to the encouragement of goodness if the city is not to sink into a mere 'alliance', a mere covenant that 'guarantees men's rights against one another' (*Politics*, 3.9.8.1280b). For Plato, with the exception of *Crito*, the will counts for even less: it is often simply assimilated to arbitrary caprice, as in the *Republic*, when Socrates refutes Thrasymachus' view that justice is the will of the stronger (*Republic* 1.338a–c).

The decisive turn in the voluntarisation of Western social thought came with Augustine, who appropriated the *bona voluntas* of Cicero and Seneca and deepened it into a central moral concept. In *De libero arbitrio* (Freedom of the Will) Augustine defines 'good will' as 'the will by which we seek to live honestly and uprightly and to arrive at wisdom' (3.1; 1968, 59:167; see Gilbert 1963). This is not to say that Augustine is a voluntarist or contractarian in his explicitly political writings, above all *The City of God*; but it is certainly true that he made important voluntaristic moral claims that later grew into political doctrines. In *De spiritu et littera*, for example, he insists that 'consent is necessarily an act of will' (Gilbert 1963, p. 33). Without the strong link that Augustine forged between consent and will, social contract theory would be unthinkable, since it defines consent in terms of will (Riley 1978, pp. 486–8).

The link between voluntarism and politics became more explicit in some of the Christian philosophers who followed Thomas Aquinas, particularly William of Ockham and Nicholas of Cusa. In the early fourteenth century Ockham urged in his *Quodlibeta* that 'no act is virtuous or vicious unless it is voluntary and in the power of the will', and this general moral doctrine finds political expression in his insistence that 'no-one should be set over a *universitas* of mortal men unless by their election and consent . . . what touches all ought to be discussed and approved by all' (Ockham 1957, pp. 145–6). For Ockham, then, Christian liberty is both the ground of virtue and the limiting condition of rightful politics. A political voluntarism is even clearer in the greatest of the conciliar theorists, Nicholas of Cusa, who argued in his *De concordantia catholica*, in an almost contractarian vein, that 'since all men are by nature free', legitimate rulership can come only 'from the agreement and consent of the subjects'. Such subjects, Nicholas insists, must not be 'unwilling', and whoever is 'set up in authority' by the 'common consent of the subjects' must be viewed 'as if he bore within himself the will of all' (qu. Sigmund 1963, pp. 96–7, 140).

But the most advanced and subtle form of political voluntarism before the social contract school itself is contained in Francisco Suárez's *On the Laws and God the Lawgiver* (1612). For Suárez free will and political consent are analogous or even parallel; will is the 'proximate cause' of the state. Suárez summarises his doctrine with the observation that 'human will is necessary in order that men may unite in a single perfect community', and that 'by the nature of things, men as individuals possess to a partial extent (so to speak) the faculty for establishing, or creating, a perfect community'. Plainly, for Suárez that faculty is will: men can be 'gathered together' into 'one political body' only by 'special volition, or common consent'; the people cannot 'manifest' consent 'unless the acts are voluntary' (Suárez 1944, pp. 66, 370, 375, 380, 383, 545).

It is possible to treat contractarianism as a narrowly political and secular idea, or as a theory of rational decision-making. But this would take inadequate account of the revolution introduced into political and moral philosophy by Christian ideas and thereby underemphasise the ethical components of contractarianism, such as autonomy, responsibility, duty, authorisation, and willing (Arendt 1978).

2   The equilibrium between consent and natural law in Locke

In the Second Treatise Locke argues that 'voluntary agreement gives . . . political power to governors for the benefit of their subjects' and that 'God having given man an understanding to direct his actions, has allowed him a freedom of will, and liberty of acting' (*TTG*, II, §173, p. 383, II, §58, p. 306). At first sight Locke appears to have taken up and extended the social contract doctrine of Hobbes; but there is disagreement as to what extent Locke was really a contractarian at all. He is sometimes represented as a consent and social contract theorist, sometimes as a theorist of natural law, sometimes as a theorist of natural rights (particularly natural property rights). The problem is that all three characterisations are correct; the difficulty is to find an equilibrium between them so that none is discarded in the effort to define Locke's complete concept of right.

Nevertheless, some writers urge that consent and contractarianism are not central in Locke because natural law is for him a sufficient standard of right, obviating the need for mere consensual arrangements. It is true that excluding from Locke's system the obligations and rights to which consent and contract give rise leaves a tolerably complete ethical doctrine based on natural law and rights. But natural law, though necessary for Locke, is not sufficient to define explicitly political rights and duties, for there is a distinction to be drawn between the general moral obligations that men have under natural law and the particular political obligations that citizens have through consent and the social contract. This is clear not only in the Second Treatise but also in the *Essay concerning Human Understanding* (1689) (Locke 1959, pp. 472–3).

In book 2, chapter 28 of the *Essay* Locke draws a careful distinction between the natural law, to which all men as men are obliged to conform their voluntary actions, and the civil law, to which all men as citizens are obliged to adhere because they have created a human legislative authority by consent. 'A citizen, or a burgher', Locke says, 'is one who has a right to certain privileges in this or that place. All this sort depending upon men's wills, or agreement in society, I call instituted, or voluntary; and may be distinguished from the natural.' In a commonwealth, which is what human wills institute, men 'refer their actions' to a civil law to judge whether or not they are lawful or criminal. Natural law, however, is not instituted by consent, not even by a Grotian 'universal' consent. Nor does it merely define 'certain privileges in this or that place'. It is rather the law 'which God has set to the actions of men', and is 'the only true touchstone of moral rectitude' (Locke 1959, pp. 472–3, 475–6). But the natural law defines only general moral goods and evils, only moral duties and sins; it cannot point out what is a crime, in the strict legal sense, in a commonwealth, in 'this or that place':

If I have the will of a supreme invisible lawgiver for my rule, then, as I supposed the action commanded or forbidden by God, I call it good or evil, sin or duty: and if I compare it to the civil law, the rule made by the legislative power of the country, I call it lawful or unlawful, a crime or no crime. (p. 481)

To say, then, that the natural law is a complete and sufficient standard of political right is for Locke to conflate sin and crime, the duties of man and citizen, what one owes to God with what one owes to the civil magistrate. As a result, the kind of objection to Lockean contractarianism that one finds, for example, in T. H. Green ('a society governed by . . . a law of nature . . . would have been one from which political society would have been a decline, one in which there could have been no motive to the establishment of civil government') is at best only half-right (Green 1941,

p. 72). It is partly wrong because a society governed by a law of nature would have had a motive to establish civil government – a motive based not merely on a desire to distinguish between sin and crime, divine and civil law, what one owes as a man and as a citizen, but also on a desire to set up some 'known and impartial judge' to serve as 'executor' of the law of nature, to avoid men's being the judges of their own cases. Locke, after all, states clearly that there are three good reasons for allowing the natural law to be politically enforced:

First . . . though the law of nature be plain and intelligible to all rational creatures; yet men being biased by their interest . . . are not apt to allow of it as a law binding to them in the application of it to their particular cases.
Secondly, In the state of nature there wants a known and indifferent judge, with authority to determine all differences according to the established law . . .
Thirdly, In the state of nature there often wants power to back and support the sentence when right, and to give it due execution. (*TTG*, II, §§124–6, p. 351)

But Green is certainly right in saying that the transition from a society truly and completely governed by natural law, if such a society could exist, to one under political government, would involve a decline. In section 128 of the Second Treatise Locke argues that under the terms of the law of nature every man 'and all the rest of mankind are one community, make up one society distinct from all other creatures'. If it were not for the 'corruption' and 'viciousness' of 'degenerate men', Locke goes on, 'there would be no need of any other' society; there would be no necessity 'that men should separate from this great and natural community, and by positive agreements combine into smaller and divided associations' (p. 352). If Green is right in pointing out that voluntarily instituted political society represents a decline, that does not mean that it is unnecessary, that there is no motive for setting it up. For Locke, as for Kant in *Perpetual Peace*, the mere fact that it would be better if natural law were universally observed, such that one could dispense with politics, does not make politics unnecessary, given human life as it is. The social contract, for Locke, is *necessitated* by natural law's inability to be literally 'sovereign' on earth, by its incapacity to produce 'one society'. Natural law and contractarianism, far from being simply antithetical in Locke, necessarily involve each other, at least given human imperfection and 'corruption'.

The most familiar contractarian arguments are found in the Second Treatise. Sometimes – indeed, repeatedly – Locke contents himself with the bare claim that consent creates political right, as in section 102 ('politic societies all began from a voluntary union, and the mutual agreement of men freely acting in the choice of their governors, and forms of government') and in section 192 (rulers must put the people 'under such a frame of government, as they willingly, and of choice, consent to') (pp. 335, 394). Occasionally, however, he provides a more elaborate argument, particularly when he wants to distinguish legitimate political power from both paternal and despotic power.

> Nature gives the first of these, viz. paternal power to parents for the benefit of their children during their minority, to supply their want of ability, and understanding how to manage their property . . . Voluntary agreement gives the second, viz. political power to governors for the benefit of their subjects, to secure them in the possession and use of their properties. (*TTG*, II, §173, p. 383)

It is never the case that consent and contract are treated as the whole of political right, that whatever happens to be produced by this process would *ex necessitatis* be correct. In Locke there is no general will that is always right. This is perfectly clear, for example, in section 95, which is one of Locke's best statements of an equilibrium between the naturally and the consensually right. Since men are naturally 'free, equal and independent', no-one can be subjected to the political power of anyone else 'without his own consent'. In giving up 'natural liberty', and accepting the 'bonds of civil society', men agree to 'join and unite into a community', not for the purpose of being controlled by any objective to which a group may happen to consent, but for the purpose of 'comfortable, safe, and peaceable living one amongst another, in a secure enjoyment of their properties, and a greater security against any that are not of it' (*TTG*, II, §95, pp. 330–1). Security, of course, is authorised by natural law, which protects the innocent by allowing defence against wrongful attacks, while property is a natural right derived partly from God's giving the earth to men and partly from human labour. A political order, created by consent, makes these things possible even given the 'inconvenience' of some men's 'corruption' and 'depravity'. In this passage there is an equilibrium between consent, natural law, and natural rights: it is because men are made free and equal by God, because they want to enjoy natural rights in the security of a political society in conformity with natural law, that they consent to become citizens, to conform their voluntary actions to the civil law as well as to the divine law and the law of reputation. Consent operates within a context for John Locke; it is a strand in a complex doctrine.

3   Bossuet and the challenge of divine right to contract theory

Before turning to contractarianism in the 'high' Enlightenment, we need to note that it was never unchallenged in the eighteenth century. One would not expect a partisan of divine right absolute monarchy to favour a view of government as the product of human 'will and artifice', set up between equals in a state of nature – that is, in the absence of any natural (especially paternal) authority. There is no trace of contractarianism in Bossuet's claim, in his *Politics Drawn from the Very Words of Holy Scripture* (1709), that 'there never was a finer state constitution than that which one sees in the people of God', which was 'formed' by Moses, who was instructed by 'divine wisdom' and inspired to construct a polity *vraiment divine* – a divine politics then sustained by 'two great kings of this people, David and Solomon . . . both excellent in the art of governing' (Bossuet 1990, p. 2).

Bossuet opposed contractarianism not just *en général* but *en particulier*, for he was deeply hostile to Pierre Jurieu, who spoke for French Protestant émigrés, and who had used contract theory radically to urge that the Edict of Nantes, which gave toleration to the Huguenots, was a contract between the Huguenots and the French monarchy, so that Louis XIV's Revocation of the Edict of Nantes in 1685 was, *inter alia*, a breach of contract. Jurieu tried to find a scriptural provenance for his contractarianism by 'locating' a contract in Jewish antiquity: more precisely in David's 'waiting' for popular approval before reassuming the throne after the revolt of Absalom. But Bossuet, anxious as he was to find a permanent model of perfect government in Hebrew monarchy, and to overturn any suggestion that the throne of David and Solomon arose out of popular concession or 'will', also offered 'secular' objections to contractarianism which showed an appreciation of Hobbes's turns of phrase, if not of his conclusions. Beginning with an attack on Jurieu, Bossuet soon broadened the argument of his *Cinquième avertissement aux protestants* to take in the whole contract tradition.

To consider men as they naturally are, and before all established government, one finds only anarchy, that is to say a savage and wild liberty in all men where each one can claim everything, and at the same time contest everything; where all are on guard, and in consequence in a continual war against all; where reason can do nothing, since each calls reason the passion that transports him; where even natural law itself remains without force, since reason has none; where in consequence there is neither property, nor domain, nor good, nor secure repose. (Bossuet 1815, IV, pp. 403–5)

Not only, in Bossuet's view, has Jurieu mistaken anarchy for 'popular sovereignty'; he has made the still worse mistake of imagining 'that it is against reason for a people to deliver itself up to a sovereign without some pact, and that such an agreement must be null and against nature'. Here Bossuet's sarcastic fury can barely contain itself: '"It is"', he says, '"against nature to deliver oneself without some pact" . . . It is as if he said: It is against nature to risk something to pull oneself out of the most hideous of all conditions, which is that of anarchy' (pp. 403–5). If Hobbes is right, then, that the state of nature is a state of war – here Christian 'charity' seems to be as vestigial for Bossuet as it had been for Hobbes – this does not mean that a 'social contract' is the means of peace and felicity. Here some broader comparisons between Bossuet and Hobbes may be instructive.

Bossuet as well as Hobbes gives prominence to the notion of covenant. But for Bossuet the covenant is 'there', on the opening page of *Politics Drawn from Scripture*, and is (or rather historically was) a pact between God and Abraham – from whom 'kings' then issue in an anointed patriarchal succession (Bossuet 1990, p. 3). For Hobbes, 'wills . . . make the essence of all covenants', and it is covenants expressive of everyone's will which endow sovereigns with legitimate authority (Hobbes 1991, ch. 40, p. 323); if there is not a popular 'sovereignty' in Hobbes, there is at least a transfer of popular natural right to a sovereign beneficiary by an act of will. For Bossuet there is one permanent covenant – in Genesis – which provides the world with monarchs for all time ('kings shall come out of you'); for Hobbes a covenant can arise – with the 'will' of all as its 'essence' – whenever escape from the state of nature is needed. The will of Abraham is replaced by the wills 'of every one of those that are to be governed' (Hobbes 1991, ch. 42, p. 395).

Hobbes, moreover, given his principles, had to give primacy to reason over revelation, because scripture (for him) has no 'intrinsic' meaning at all: the Bible must be made 'canonical' by legitimate sovereign authority. Inverting Bossuet, what Hobbes offers is a 'Holy Scripture drawn from the very words of politics'. For Hobbes, then, popular 'assent', which creates sovereignty, also 'creates' the Bible, as something 'canonical'. All of this confirmed Bossuet's belief that contractarianism is impious and dangerous – whether one tries to make King David into a Lockean *avant la lettre*, or uses the idea of 'contract' for modern times.

4   The anti-contractarianism of Hume and Bentham

The most formidable anti-contractarian in the middle of the eighteenth century was Hume, whose attack took the form of annihilating the 'Lockeanism' which had been transformed from questionable innovation into received orthodoxy in the half-century between 1690 and 1740 (enabling Voltaire to speak of *le sage Locke*). In book III of the *Treatise of Human Nature* (1739–40), and in the essay 'Of the Original Contract' (1748), Hume strove to sever the three intertwined strands of Locke's politics: its contractarianism, its voluntarism, and its natural law. He undercut Lockean natural law by arguing that neither 'reason' nor God could provide it: not reason, because it was 'passive' or 'inert', having no bearing on 'active' moral feeling or sentiment; not God, because his real existence was undemonstrable (*THN*, III.i.1). Lockean voluntarism he subverted by insisting that the will is no autonomous moral 'cause', but simply a fully determined datum of empirical psychology: 'It is a will or choice that determines a man to kill his parent; and they are the laws of matter and motion that determine a sapling to destroy the oak from which it sprung. Here then the same relations have different causes; but still the relations are the same' (*THN*, III.i.1). Clearly, Hume could not say, with Locke, that by 'voluntary agreement' we set up 'governors' whose principal function will be to protect the natural rights (of life and property) which flow from a 'natural law' provided by God or reason.

If, for Hume, government cannot reasonably be viewed as an artifice for the protection of a natural order – a set of voluntarily 'instituted' magistrates who 'give effect' to natural law in an 'inconvenient' world – one must hold that the principal social institutions (peace, civility, property, legality) are held up by nothing more than a 'sentiment of approbation' concerning them: just as, for Hume, a 'sentiment of disapprobation' arises in the breast of normally constituted persons at the sight of a murdered body, so too all social institutions are recommended and sustained by nothing more than our general, shared sense or feeling of their necessity and utility. Hence Lockean contractarianism is not merely historically false, in Hume's view, given that governments in fact began through force and violence, and only slowly acquired a veneer of acceptability; it is also philosophically ridiculous. Since the real reason for obedience to government is that without such obedience 'society could not otherwise subsist', it is useless to rest the duty of obedience on consent or a 'tacit promise' to obey. For we must then ask, 'Why are we bound to observe our promise?' And for Hume the only possible answer is that promise-observance is simply necessary because 'there can be no security where men pay no regard to their engagements'. Since a shared sense of actual usefulness is the ground of obedience in general, as well as of promises, it is foolish to base one on the other, to ground obligation in 'will': 'We gain nothing by resolving the one into the other', because 'the general interests or necessities of society are sufficient to establish both.' Sentiments must take the place of contract, will, reason, and God ('Of the Original Contract'; Hume 1994a, pp. 196–7).

Hume adds, in a caustic aside, that Plato's *Crito* was the exception to the rejection of contractarianism by Greek and Roman antiquity, and that even that small but significant work was anomalous within the Platonic canon, since Plato usually stressed not consent but a mathematics-based harmonious psychic order (*Republic*, 443 d-e) which is then 'writ large' in a non-dissonant *polis* (and then largest in the harmony of the spheres). And even *Crito*, Hume continued, has an unexpected conclusion:

> The only passage I meet with in antiquity, where the obligation of obedience to government is ascribed to a promise, is in Plato's *Crito*; where Socrates refuses to escape from prison, because he had tacitly promised to obey the laws. Thus he builds a Tory consequence of passive obedience on a Whig foundation of the original contract. (Hume 1994a, p. 201)

'New discoveries are not to be expected in these matters', Hume tartly concludes. 'If scarce any man, till very lately, ever imagined that government is founded on compact, it is certain that it cannot, in general, have any such foundation' (p. 201).

More than a generation after Hume's *Treatise*, Jeremy Bentham, in *A Fragment on Government* (1776), had occasion to lament that the Scottish philosopher's anti-contractarian efforts had not been sufficient to arrest the appearance of Sir William Blackstone's *Commentaries*: 'As to the original contract, by turns embraced and ridiculed by our author [Blackstone] . . . I was in hopes . . . that this chimera had been effectually demolished by Mr Hume.' For Hume had been simply right: 'the indestructible prerogatives of mankind have no need to be supported upon the sandy foundation of a fiction'. For Bentham, as for Hume, a sense of utility is the very thing that reveals the social contract as 'dangerous nonsense': 'It is the principle of utility, accurately apprehended and steadily applied, that affords the only clue to guide a man' in morals, politics, and (above all) law (Bentham 1988, pp. 51–2, 96).

It is no accident, indeed, that Bentham included contractarianism among dangerous 'anarchical fallacies', insisting that 'The origination of government from a contract is a pure fiction, or, in other words, a falsehood. It never has been known to be true in any instance; the allegation of it does mischief, by involving the subject in error and confusion, and is neither necessary or useful to any good purpose' (Bentham 1838–43, II, 501). Since, for Bentham in the *Principles of Morals and Legislation* (1789), mankind is 'fastened to the throne of pain and pleasure', not to Lockean 'will' and 'natural law', it is essential to avoid the kind of error which is displayed in the thought of the Abbé Sieyès during the French Revolution: the abbé's contractarian notion that 'every society cannot but be the free work of a convention entered into between all the associated [members]' must be firmly repulsed. 'From a man's being known to write such stuff', Bentham urges, 'it follows . . . that he is living either in Bedlam, or in the French convention' (Bentham 1838–43, II, 527). Bentham was as progressive (as a legal reformer) as Hume was conservative; nonetheless they shared the conviction that 'sentiments of utility' alone could underpin and justify social institutions. Hume used utility to recommend continuity and stability, Bentham to urge reform and change; what linked them was the conviction that Lockeanism was a tissue of fables.

5   French contractarianism before Rousseau

Before turning to Rousseau's radical transformation of contractarianism in the 1760s, it is important to know how *le contrat social* was viewed in the period between Bossuet's violently anti-contractarian *Politics Drawn from Scripture* and the advent of the *citoyen de Genève*. After the appearance of Bossuet's treatise (and of Fénelon's *Télémaque*, 1699), no commanding work of French political theory that was addressed to principles other than those applicable to French history alone materialised until Montesquieu's *Persian Letters* (1721), *Considerations on the Causes of the Greatness of the Romans and their Decline* (1734), and *The Spirit of the Laws* (1748); and even these contain no hint of a contractarian strand. To be a social contract theorist, after all, one must view the state as generated, or justified, or both, by 'voluntary agreement' – by will viewed as the 'essence' of covenants, as a moral 'cause' yielding legitimate government as an 'effect'. By contrast, Montesquieu was in search of physical and moral *causes générales* which could account for the *esprit*, the spirit, of a particular nation: 'Many things govern men: climate, religion, laws, the maxims of the government, examples of past things, mores, and manners – a general spirit is formed as a result' (*SL*, XIX.4). Despite the Malebranchian Platonic rationalism of book 1 of *The Spirit of the Laws*, which views justice as a 'relation' as eternal as the radii of a circle, Montesquieu's main effort is devoted to a proto-sociological uncovering of the 'causes' of (for example) English constitutionalism, or 'oriental despotism'.

It is revealing that, when Montesquieu discusses Hobbes in his (unpublished) *Pensées* (no. 615), he says not a word about 'will' and 'covenant', but instead repeats Malebranche's complaint (from the *Discourses on Metaphysics*) that Hobbesian notions of 'natural' human ferocity in a violent state of nature are simply mistaken: natural beings, for Montesquieu, are isolated, lonely, and timid, and inequality and domination begin only with the advent of society (cf. *SL*, 1.2–3). Montesquieu regards Hobbes (and Spinoza) as 'dangerous' – because of their egoistic psychology, not because of their contractarianism, which goes completely unremarked. To be sure, in *Pensée* number 616 he combines 'sociology' with voluntarism: 'Chance and the turn of mind of those who have agreed have established as many forms of government as there have been peoples: all good, because they were the will of the contracting parties'. But the first half of the sentence ('chance') cancels the force of the second half.

Of course voluntarism and contractarianism were present in French thought, if not in its most original and striking figures, such as Montesquieu, Helvétius, Condillac, or d'Alembert. For echoes of Locke one must turn to the *Encyclopédie* and to Jean Jacques Burlamaqui's *Principes du droit naturel* (Principles of Natural Law, 1747). Indeed, the radicalism of Rousseau's version of contractarianism becomes clear if one contrasts it with the orthodox Lockeanism of those contemporaneous articles in Diderot's *Encyclopédie* which treat of 'the social contract'. The essays by the chevalier de Jaucourt entitled *Etat*, *Etat de nature*, and *Gouvernement* are three of the least innovative pieces in a work which was frequently suppressed or delayed for its daring heterodoxy.

The essay *Etat de nature* repeats Locke verbatim, sometimes lifting the actual language of the French translation of the *Two Treatises*; and the article *Gouvernement* deviates not at all from the Second Treatise: 'All political societies began through a voluntary union of individuals, who have made the free choice of a form of government' (*Encyclopédie* 1756, VI, p. 22). Following Locke's critique of Filmer's patriarchalism *à la lettre*, the *Encyclopédie* urges that 'men have never regarded any natural subjection into which they were born . . . as a tie which obliges them without their own consent to submit themselves to it' (*Encyclopédie* 1757, VII, p. 788). For the chevalier de Jaucourt, as for Locke, politics derives not from the 'natural' subjection of children but from the artificial self-subjection of adult voluntary agents: 'At the age of reason', Jaucourt urges, a man 'is a free man, he is the master of his choice of the government under which he finds it good to live, and of uniting himself to that political body which most pleases him; nothing is capable of submitting him to the subjection of any power on earth, except his own consent' (*Encyclopédie* 1757, VII, p. 789). These lines could be invisibly woven into the *Two Treatises* – unsurprisingly, since they were drawn from it.

To be sure, in the article *Etat*, Jaucourt, while remaining essentially Lockean, introduces some slight quasi-Rousseauian notion of the general good of a *corps politique*.

One can consider the state as a moral person of which the sovereign is the head . . . This union of several persons in a single body, produced by the concourse of their wills and by the powers of each individual, distinguishes the state from a multitude: for a multitude is only an assemblage of several persons among whom each has his particular will (*volonté particulière*), instead of which the state is a society animated by a single soul which directs its movements in a constant way, with reference to the common utility. (*Encyclopédie* 1757, VI, p. 19)

The provenance of various phrases is clear enough: 'concourse of wills' is Hobbes's phrase from *De Cive* (1998, p. 72); *volonté particulière* used negatively (as it is here) descends from the *Pensées* of Blaise Pascal; 'constancy' of movement comes from Cartesian–Gassendian physics. Nonetheless, the heart of Jaucourt's thought is Lockean, despite the grafting on of phrases from different traditions; the *Encyclopédie* simply agrees that 'voluntary agreement gives political power to governors'.

If the *Encyclopédie* simply echoes Locke, Burlamaqui's *Principes du droit naturel* by contrast offers voluntarism without contractarianism, and says that sovereignty involves not merely power but wisdom and goodness as well – here following Leibniz's critique of Hobbes and Pufendorf. In the *Principes*, Burlamaqui develops an elaborate theory of free will, urging that human beings are not merely intelligent, but also 'spontaneous' and self-determining; following Malebranche's *Traité de la nature et de la grâce* (1680), he says that while we are determined to pursue *le bien général*, we have the power to 'suspend' our pursuit of any *bien particulier* while we determine what is intrinsically good (by the light of reason). The 'state of nature' he views as the juxtaposition of many such naturally equal, self-determining beings. The need for a 'common defence' necessitates the erection of 'civil government', in Burlamaqui's view; but, unlike Locke, he does not make civil government the outcome of a contract. Men 'will' the state (and sovereignty) in the sense that they see its sheer necessity; here Burlamaqui almost anticipates Hegel's notion that 'willing' the state really means recognising it as morally necessary.

The essential character of this [civil] society, which distinguishes it from the simple society of nature of which we have spoken, is subordination to sovereign authority, which takes the place of equality and independence.

Society is . . . the union of several persons for a certain end, which is some common advantage. The end is the effect or the advantage which intelligent beings propose to themselves, and which they want to procure; and the union of several persons is the concourse of their wills to obtain the end which they jointly propose to themselves. (Burlamaqui 1748, pp. 62, 119)

Here there is 'will' – indeed a 'concourse of wills' (*De Cive* again) – but not contract; the transition from nature (implying equality) to the 'civil' (involving subordination) mentions no intervening 'Lockean' stage of 'voluntary agreement' between natural equals. But if sovereignty is stressed as the hallmark of 'civil society', Burlamaqui avoids pure 'Hobbism' by saying that sovereignty involves 'superior power', wisdom, and goodness in *equal* measure (like the equal attributes of God in scholastic thought); here he mentions favourably Leibniz's *Opinion on the Principles of Pufendorf* (1706), which had insisted that adequate rulership must rest on *caritas sapientis*, the 'charity of a wise being', not just on 'irresistible' power (Burlamaqui 1747, pp. 134–5; Leibniz 1988, pp. 3ff).

Burlamaqui's thought, then, is a kind of compendium of Enlightenment doctrines: with Hobbes it insists on sovereignty; with Locke it stresses equality in the state of nature; with Malebranche it urges free will as suspension of particular desires; with Leibniz it insists on wisdom and goodness in addition to omnipotence; with Hegel subsequently it views 'real' will as recognition of the necessity of the state. None of the elements of Burlamaqui's argument was original, but together they formed an unusual combination; strikingly the *Principes* show that one could favour aspects of Hobbism, Lockeanism, and ethical voluntarism, and yet still not emerge as a full contractarian.

Before turning to Rousseau, it is worth remembering that one other eminent Franco-Swiss theorist, Jean Barbeyrac – best remembered as the translator and populariser of Grotius and Pufendorf – used (more-or-less Lockean) natural law theory in the radical way that Hume had feared, while subordinating what is merely 'willed' to natural justice. Beginning with the assertion that 'all that which is just is not of such a nature that it can be prescribed by civil laws', Barbeyrac goes on to say that 'from the moment that the most authentic laws of the most legitimate sovereigns are found to be in opposition . . . to these immutable [natural] laws', it is necessary, 'whatever it may cost, to disobey the first, in order not to taint the latter'. The submission of men to civil government, he continues, could not have extended 'to the point of placing a human legislator above God, the author of nature, the creator and the sovereign legislator of men' – even if 'men should have willed it' (Barbeyrac 1717, p. 18, 1716, p. 15). Barbeyrac's thought shows what happens if one radicalises natural law theory, then uses 'natural justice' to confine voluntarism (including both popular and 'sovereign' will).

6   Rousseau and the radicalisation of social contract theory

As has been remarked, political thought since the seventeenth century had been characterised by voluntarism, by an emphasis on individual will and consent as the standard of political legitimacy. Rousseau ordinarily upheld much of this tradition, sometimes even exaggerating his agreement with a voluntarist and contractarian such as Locke: the English philosopher, he said, had treated political matters 'with exactly the same principles as myself' (Rousseau 1962, II, p. 206). In the *Lettres de la montagne* (Letters from the Mountain, 1764), speaking of contract and consent, Rousseau admitted that the foundation of obligation had divided political theorists: 'according to some, it is force; according to others, paternal authority; according to others, the will of God'. All theorists, he said, establish their own principle of obligation and attack that of others. 'I myself have not done otherwise, and, following the soundest element of those who have discussed these matters, I have settled on, as the foundation of the body politic, the contract of its members.' And he concluded by asking, 'what more certain foundation can obligation among men have, than the free agreement of him who obligates himself?' (Rousseau 1962, II, pp. 200–6).

But while voluntarism took care of legitimacy, it could say nothing about the intrinsic goodness of what is willed. It was precisely here that Rousseau made a stand for a particular kind of will: he wanted voluntarism to legitimise what he conceived to be the unity and cohesiveness – the 'generality' – of the ancient polity, particularly of Sparta and of (republican) Rome. Indeed, his political ideal was the ancient polity, now willed by moderns who were as concerned with reasons for obligation as with perfect forms of government. Against the alleged 'atomism' of earlier contract theory, Rousseau wanted the generality – the non-individualism, or rather the pre-individualism – of antiquity to be legitimised by consent. Hence Rousseau made 'the general will' the heart of his political theory (Riley 1986).

Rousseau was a severe critic of modern political life – of its lack of a common morality and virtue, of its neglect of patriotism and civic religion, of its indulgence in 'base' philosophy and morally uninstructive arts. At the same time, he was a great admirer of the more highly unified political systems of antiquity, in which, as he thought, morality, civic religion, patriotism, and a simple way of life had made men 'one', wholly socialised and truly political. He thought that modern political life divided man against himself, leaving him, with all his merely private and anti-social interests, half in and half out of political society, enjoying neither the amoral independence of nature nor the moral elevation afforded by true socialisation.[2]

Why Rousseau thought unified ancient political systems preferable to modern ones is not difficult to understand. He conceived the difference between natural man and political man in very sharp terms; while for most contract theory political life was merely non-natural (a belief largely created to exclude arguments for natural political authority), for Rousseau it was positively unnatural, or anti-natural, requiring a complete transformation of the natural man. For Rousseau, the political man must be deprived of his natural powers and given others, 'which are foreign to him and of which he cannot make use without the help of others'; politics reaches a peak of perfection when natural powers are completely dead and extinguished, and man is given 'a partial and moral existence' (Rousseau 1962, I, pp. 325–6). The chief defect of modern politics, in Rousseau's view, was that it was insufficiently political; it compromised between the utter artificiality and communality of political life and the naturalness and independence of pre-political life, and in so doing caused the greatest misfortunes of modern man: self-division, conflict between private will and the common good, a sense of being neither in one condition nor another. 'What makes human misery', Rousseau said in *Le bonheur public* of 1762, 'is the contradiction which exists between our situation and our desires, between our duties and our inclinations, between nature and social institutions, between man and citizen'. To make man one, to make him as happy as he can be, 'give him entirely to the state, or leave him entirely to himself . . . but if you divide his heart, you will rip him apart; and do not imagine that the state can be happy, when all its members suffer' (Rousseau 1962, I, p. 326).

Ancient polities such as Sparta, Rousseau thought, with their simplicity, morality (or politics) of the common good, civic religion, moral use of fine

2 For these themes see particularly his *Discourse on the Origin of Inequality* (1755; in Rousseau 1997a, pp. 111–18; *Discourse on the Sciences and Arts* (1751; in 1997a, pp. 1–28); *Considerations on the Government of Poland* (1772; in 1997b, pp. 177–260); and *Letter to M. d'Alembert* (1758).

and military arts, and lack of extreme individualism and private interest had been political societies in the proper sense: in them man was 'part of a larger whole' from which he 'as it were receive[s] his life and his being' (*SC*, II.7, p. 69). Modern 'prejudices', 'base philosophy', and 'passions of petty self-interest', on the other hand, assure that 'the moderns no longer find within themselves anything of that vigour of soul which everything instilled in the ancients' (*Government of Poland*: Rousseau 1997b, pp. 180–2). And this spiritual vigour may be taken to mean the avoidance (through identity with a 'greater whole') of 'that dangerous disposition which gives rise to all our vices', self-love. Political education in an extremely unified state will 'draw us out of ourselves' before the human ego has 'there become actively engaged in the contemptible concerns that do away with all virtue and make up the life of petty souls' (*Economie politique*: Rousseau 1997b, pp. 20–1). It follows that the best social institutions 'are those best able to denature man, to take away his absolute existence and to give him a relative one, and to carry the *moi* into the common unity' (*Emile*: Rousseau 1962, II, p. 145). These social institutions, in ideal ancient polities, were always for Rousseau the creation of a greater legislator, a Numa or a Moses: they did not develop and perfect themselves in political experience, but were 'handed down' by the lawgiver (*Poland*: Rousseau 1997b, pp. 180–1).

But if Rousseau thought the highly unified ancient polity, and its political morality of the general or common good, superior to modern fragmented politics and its political morality of self-interest, at the same time he shared with modern individualist thought the conviction that all political life was conventional and could be made obligatory only through individual consent. Despite the fact that he sometimes treated moral notions as if they simply 'arose' in a developmental process, Rousseau often (and particularly when speaking of contract and obligation) fell back on a kind of moral theory in which the wills of free men were taken to be the causes of duties and of legitimate authorities. Thus in an argument against 'obligations' based on slavery in *The Social Contract*, Rousseau urged that 'to deprive one's will of all freedom is to deprive one's actions of all morality', that the reason one can derive no notion of right or morality from mere force is that 'to yield to force is an act of necessity, not of will' (*SC*, I.3–4, pp. 44–5). In the *Discourse on the Origin of Inequality*, in a passage which almost prefigures Kant, he insisted on the importance of 'free agency', arguing that while 'physics' might explain the 'mechanism of the senses', it could never make intelligible 'the power of willing or rather of choosing' – a power in which, he said, nothing could be found but 'purely spiritual acts about which nothing is explained by the laws of mechanics' (Rousseau 1997a, p. 141). It is this power of willing, he emphasised, which (rather than reason) distinguishes men from beasts.

Rousseau very definitely thought that he had derived political obligation and rightful political authority from this 'power' of willing: 'civil association is the most voluntary act in the world; since every individual is born free and his own master, no-one is able, on any pretext whatsoever, to subject him without his consent' (*SC*, IV.2, p. 123). Indeed, the first four chapters of *The Social Contract* are devoted to refutations of erroneous theories of obligation and right (paternal authority, the 'right of the strongest', and obligation derived from slavery). 'Since no man', Rousseau concluded, 'has a natural authority over his fellow man, and since force produce no right, conventions remain as the basis of all legitimate authority among men' (*SC*, 1.4, p. 44).

One may suspect, however, that for Rousseau contract theory was more a way of destroying erroneous theories of obligation and authority than of creating a comprehensive theory of what is politically right. Any political system which 'limits itself to obedience . . . will find difficulty in getting itself obeyed. While it is good to know how to use men as they are, it is much better still to make them what one needs them to be' (*Economie politique*: Rousseau 1997b, pp. 12–13). That, in a word, was Rousseau's criticism of all contract theory: it dealt too much with the form of obligation, with will as it is, and not enough with what one ought to be obligated to do, and with will as it might be.

His criticism of Hobbes is based on this point. Hobbes had, indeed, established rightful political authority on consent; he had made law the command of an artificial 'representative person' to whom subjects were 'formally obliged' through transfer of natural rights (save self-defence) by covenant. But Hobbes had done nothing to cure the essential flaw (in Rousseau's view) of modern politics; private interest was rampant, and indeed paramount, in Hobbes's system. The essential error of Hobbes, Rousseau thought, was to have read back into the state of nature all the human vices which half-socialisation had created, and thus to see culturally produced depravities as 'natural', with Hobbesian absolutism, rather than the creation of a feeling of the common good, as the remedy for these depravities. 'The error of Hobbes', Rousseau declared in *The State of War*, 'is to confuse natural man with the men they have before their eyes, and to move into one system a being that can thrive only in another.' Rousseau, who thought that a perfectly socialised state (like Sparta) could elevate men, and turn them from 'stupid and limited animals' into moral and intelligent beings, was bound to think Hobbesian politics incomplete, one which 'confines itself to mere obedience', one which did not attempt to make men 'what they ought to be', but which, through a system of mere mutual forbearance, did not undertake any improvement in political life. And the result was that while Hobbes knew 'well enough what a Londoner or Parisian is', he never saw a *natural* man (Rousseau 1997b, pp. 164–5; *SC*, I.8, p. 53).

Rousseau had another objection to traditional contractarianism – an objection which, however, he kept under control in *The Social Contract* – namely that a social contract might simply be a fraud imposed by the rich on the poor with a view to 'legitimising' a ruinous inequality. In the *Discourse on the Origin of Inequality* Rousseau suggests that the rich man, 'lacking valid reasons' which he can use to justify his unequal possessions, and fearful of being plundered by the many, 'at last conceived the most well-considered project ever to enter the human mind; to use even his attackers' forces in his favour . . . and to give them different institutions, as favourable to himself as natural right was contrary to him' (Rousseau 1997a, pp. 172–3).

'Let us unite', he told them, 'to protect the weak from oppression, restrain the ambitious, and secure for everyone the possession of what belongs to him: let us institute rules of justice and peace, to which all are obliged to conform, which favour no-one, and which in a way make up for the vagaries of fortune, by subjecting the powerful and the weak alike to mutual duties.' (1997a, p. 173)

Such an argument, Rousseau continues, would have worked quite well with 'crude' men who were 'easily seduced'; 'all ran towards their chains in the belief that they were securing their freedom'. Only the rich, who had something to lose, he urges, saw the danger involved since they were 'sensitive in every part of their goods' (1997a, p. 175).

It is worth noting, however, that in the published version of *The Social Contract*, where Rousseau wanted to *rely* on contractarian arguments, he very much mitigated the radicalism of this view: in the definitive version, indeed, he confined himself to the moderate observation that since 'laws are always useful to those who possess something and harmful to those who have nothing', the social state 'is advantageous for men only in-so-far as all have something and none has too much of anything' (*SC*, I.9, p. 56n). In this work Rousseau emphasises the benefits of the social contract, provided that 'conditions' are roughly equalised for all parties to the agreement: 'since each gives himself entirely, the condition is equal for all, and since the condition is equal for all, no-one has any interest in making it burdensome to the rest' (*SC*, ii.6, p. 50). But in *The Social Contract* the notion that a social contract is a rich man's confidence trick is distinctly subordinated.

Rousseau, in any case, held in his mind, at once, both the idea that the closely unified political systems of antiquity (as he idealised them) were the most perfect kinds of polity, and the notion that all political society is the conventional creation of individual wills through a social contract (at least when 'conditions' could be equalised). Holding both of these ideas created problems, for while the need for consent to fundamental principles of political society for the creation of a mere political construct through 'will and artifice' is a doctrine characteristic of the 'idiom of individuality', the ancient conception of a highly unified and collective politics was dependent on a morality of the common good quite foreign to any insistence on individual will as the creator of society and as the basis of obligation, and Rousseau sometimes recognised this, particularly in the *Discourse on Political Economy*.

He never really reconciled the tensions between his contractual theory of obligation and his model of political perfection. If Rousseau had cared to do so, he would have had to admit that his ancient ideal model, as the creation not of a contractual relation of individual wills, but of a great legislator working with political education and a common morality, is not 'obligatory' on citizens, is not founded in right. Moses, for example, 'executed the astonishing enterprise of instituting as a national body a swarm of wretched fugitives'; he gave them 'morals and practices'. Lycurgus 'undertook to institute a people' at Sparta; he 'imposed on it an iron yoke' (*Poland*: Rousseau 1997b, pp. 180–1). It is, really, only in *The Social Contract* that Rousseau makes much reference to consent or contract in ancient politics; the usual emphasis (as in the *Discourse on Political Economy* and *Government of Poland*) is on great men, political education, and the absence of a highly developed individual will. As Rousseau put it in an early prize-essay entitled *Discourse on Heroic Virtue* (1750),

men are governed [not] by abstract views; they are only made happy by being constrained to be so, and they have to be made to experience happiness in order to be made to love it: this is [the object of] the Hero's care and talents; often it is with force in hand that he puts himself in the position of receiving the blessings of men whom he begins by compelling to bear the yoke of the laws so that he might eventually subject them to the authority of reason. (Rousseau 1997a, p. 306)

However these tensions are treated, it remains to be said that Rousseau was consistently clear that modern calamities caused by self-interest must be avoided, and that the political systems created by ancient legislators were better than any modern ones. Although it did not always occur to him that both the merely self-interested 'particular' will which he hated, and the 'general' will necessary for consent to conventional society, were part of the same individualistic idiom of modern political thought, and perhaps inseparable, Rousseau always thought that mere will, as such, could never create a proper political society. For him, then, the problem of political theory, above all in *The Social Contract*, became that of reconciling the requirements of consent (which obligates) and perfect socialisation (which makes men 'one'); men must somehow choose the politically perfect, somehow will such complete socialisation as precludes self-division.

To retain the moral attributes of free will while doing away with will's particularity, selfishness, and 'wilfulness' – to generalise this moral 'cause' without causing its destruction – is perhaps the central problem in Rousseau's political, moral, and educational thought, and one which reflects the difficulty Rousseau found in making free will and rational, educative authority co-exist in his practical thought. Freedom of the will is as important to the morality of actions for Rousseau as for any voluntarist coming after Augustine's insistence that *bona voluntas* alone is good; but Rousseau was suspicious of the very 'faculty' – the only faculty – that could moralise. Thus he urges that 'the most absolute authority is that which penetrates to man's inmost being, and affects his will no less than it does his actions' (*Political Economy*: Rousseau 1997b, p. 13). Can the will be both an autonomous 'moral cause' and subject to the rationalising, generalising effect of educative authority? This is Rousseau's constant difficulty. Even Emile, the best educated of men, chooses to continue to accept the guidance of his teacher: 'Advise and control us; we shall be easily led; as long as I live I shall need you' (Rousseau 1974, p. 444). How much more, then, do ordinary men need the guidance of a 'great legislator' – the Numa, or Moses, or Lycurgus of whom Rousseau speaks so often – when they embark on the setting up of a system which will not only aid and defend but also moralise them. The relation of will to authority, of autonomy to educative 'shaping', is one of the most difficult problems in Rousseau. The general will is dependent on 'a union of understanding and will in the social body' (*SC*, ii.6, p. 68). But that understanding, which is provided (at least initially) by educative authority, is difficult to make perfectly congruent with 'will' as an autonomous 'moral cause'.

If will in Rousseau is generalised primarily through an educative authority, so that volition as 'moral cause' is not quite so free as he would sometimes prefer, it is at least arguable that any tension between will and the authority that 'generalises' it is only a provisional problem. Rousseau seems to have hoped that at the end of political time (so to speak) men would finally be citizens and would will only the common good in virtue of what they had learned over time; at the end of civic time, they might actually be free, and not just 'forced to be free' (*SC*, 1.7, p. 53). At the final point (of 'decision') there would be a 'union of understanding and will' in politics, but one in which 'understanding' is no longer the private possession of a Numa or a Lycurgus. At this point, too, 'agreement' and 'contract' would finally have real meanings: the 'general will', which is 'always upright', would be enlightened as well, and contract would transcend the mere rich man's confidence-trick (legalising unequal property) that it is in *Inequality*. At the end of political time, the 'general will [one] has as a citizen' would have become a kind of second nature (*SC*, 1.7, II.3, pp. 52–3, 59).

For Rousseau's theory to work, education must, therefore, lie at the heart of his thought. There are unavoidable stages in all education, whether private or public: the child, he says in *Emile*, must first be taught necessity, then utility, and finally morality, in that inescapable order; and if one says 'ought' to an infant he simply reveals his own ignorance and folly. This notion of necessary educational time, of *becoming* what one was not – Aristotelian potentially-becoming-actuality, transferred from *phusis* to the *polis* – is revealed perfectly in Emile's utterance, 'I have decided to be what you made me' (Rousseau 1974, p. 435). That is deliberately paradoxical (as are so many of Rousseau's central moral-political beliefs), but it shows that the capacity to 'decide' is indeed 'made'. It is education that 'forces one to be free' – by slowly 'generalising' the will. Similarly, Rousseau's 'nations' are at first ignorant: 'For nations as for men there is a time of maturity for which one has to wait before subjecting them to laws' (*SC*, II.8, p. 73). On this reading, Rousseau does not oscillate incoherently between Platonic education and Lockean voluntarism; if his notion of becoming-in-time works, then the *généralité* of antiquity and the *volonté* of modernity are truly fused by this 'modern who has ancient soul' (Rousseau 1962, I, p. 421; Riley 1991). Rousseau is the most complex contractarian of the eighteenth century.

7 Kant and the social contract as an ideal of reason

One cannot say that before Kant social contract theory flourished in Germany. Leibniz, the greatest pre-Kantian German philosopher, complained in the *New Essays concerning Human Understanding* (*c.* 1704) that English contractarianism was wrong in insisting on natural human equality, and in viewing the state of nature as a state of war: Hobbes, in particular, he accused of ignoring Aristotelian 'natural' sociability. For Leibniz an enlightened prince should rule the state through 'the charity of the wise'. This fusion of Pauline charity and Platonic wisdom has nothing to do with contract or 'voluntary agreement' (Riley in Leibniz 1988, Introduction). Much of the early German Enlightenment (including Thomasius and Wolff) placed its faith in the notion of enlightened monarchy – though Johann Jacob Brucker, the Augsburg polymath who wrote the first German history of philosophy – *Historia critica philosophiae* (1742–4 and 1766) – viewed Hobbes and even Algernon Sidney with some favour, saying that Hobbes had introduced genuine 'improvements' into 'moral and political science'. But the decisive turn came with Kant, whose admiration for Rousseau finally made contractarianism central in German political philosophy.

Kant's political writings of the 1790s are rightly viewed as completing and crowning the social contract tradition. Since, however, Kant's contractarianism enters his thought late and at an oblique angle, it is first essential to characterise the heart of his social theory. That heart rests on the notion that 'a true system of politics cannot therefore take a single step without first paying tribute to morality', and that morality (in its turn) involves respect for persons as 'ends in themselves' – indeed as members of a Kingdom of Ends who ought never to be used merely as 'means' to relative, arbitrary ends (Kant 1991, p. 125). Kant's contractarianism, when it arrives, must be related to this larger view of 'public legal justice' as a legal approximation to a Kingdom of Ends which 'good will' alone may be too feeble to attain (Kant 1960, pt 4). To be sure, Kant employs the Rousseauian vocabulary of 'general will' and 'the social contract' (Riley 1983, ch. 5). But Rousseau is a radically *civic* thinker for whom the 'general will of the citizen' (of Sparta, Rome, Geneva) is the highest social ideal; Kant by contrast is a universalist and cosmopolitan who aims at a Kingdom of Ends populated by 'persons' – all rational beings – and only reluctantly accepts contractarian politics as a mere approximation to a universal 'ethical commonwealth' (Kant 1960, pt 4).

Despite grounding politics on morals, Kant drew a strict distinction between moral motives (acting from good will or respect for the moral law) and legal motives, and insisted that moral and legal incentives must never be collapsed into each other. This is why he argued (in *The Contest of the Faculties,* 1798) that, even with growing 'enlightenment' and 'republicanism', there still will not be a greater quantity of moral actions in the world, but only a larger number of legal ones which roughly correspond to what pure morality would achieve if it could (Kant 1991, pp. 187–8). (At the end of time, a purely moral 'Kingdom of Ends' will not be realised on earth – though it ought to be – but one can reasonably hope for a better legal order which is closer to morality than are present arrangements.) Morality and public legal justice must be related in such a way that morality shapes politics – by forbidding war, by insisting on 'eternal peace' and the 'rights of man' – without becoming the motive of politics (since politics cannot hope for 'good will') (Kant 1923, pp. 162–5). Given this tension between a morality and a public legal justice which must be related but which equally must remain distinct, it may be that the notion of 'ends' can help to serve as a bridge: for public law certainly upholds some moral ends (e.g. the avoidance of murder), even though that law must content itself with a legal motive.

Using teleology as a bridge connecting the moral to the political-legal realm is not a very radical innovation, since Kant himself had already used 'ends' in the *Critique of Judgement* (1790) to unite his whole philosophy. He did this by arguing that nature can be estimated (though never known) through purposes and functions which mechanical causality fails to explain, that persons as free agents both have purposes which they strive to realise, and view themselves as the final end of creation, and that art exhibits a 'purposiveness without purpose' which makes it (not directly moral but) the symbol of morality. Surely, then, if ends can link – or be thought of as linking – nature, human freedom, and art, they can link (much more modestly) two sides of human freedom: namely the moral and the legal realms (Kant 1952, Intro. § ix; §§ 74ff, 84–6; Riley 1983, ch. 4).

Now if 'good will', in the moral realm, could mean never universalising a maxim of action which would fail to respect persons as ends in themselves, then morality and politics/law could be connected through Kantian teleology. If all persons had a good will, then they would respect all others as ends – indeed as members of a 'Kingdom of Ends'; but, although it ought to, this does not actually happen, thanks to the 'pathological' fact that man is 'radically evil'. If, in sum, good will means respect for persons as ends in themselves, and if public legal justice sees to it that some moral ends (such as avoiding murder) get observed, if not respected, then public legal justice in Kant might be viewed as the partial realisation of what would happen if all wills were good. In addition Kant frequently suggests that law creates a kind of environment for good will, by eliminating occasions for political sin (such as fear of others' domination) which might tempt (though never determine) people to act wrongly.

Perhaps Kant's whole position on politics as the legal realisation of moral ends is best summed up in two passages, the first from his *Metaphysical Principles of Virtue* (1797):

Man in the system of nature . . . is a being of little significance and, along with the other animals, considered as products of the earth, has an ordinary value . . . But man as a person, i.e. as the subject of a morally practical reason, is exalted above all price. For as such a one (*homo noumenon*) he is not to be valued merely as a means to the ends of other people, or even to his own ends, but is to be prized as an end in himself. (Kant 1964, pp. 96–7)

In *The Contest of the Faculties* Kant translated this passage – or so it seems – into the language of politics:

For man in turn is a mere trifle in relation to the omnipotence of nature, or rather to its inaccessible highest cause. But if the rulers of man's own species regard him as such and treat him accordingly, either by burdening him like a beast and using him as a mere instrument of their ends, or by setting him up to fight in their disputes and slaughter his fellows, it is not just a trifle but a reversal of the *ultimate purpose* of creation. (Kant 1991, p. 185)

On this teleological view, sovereigns deny the rights of man (or perhaps more properly the rights of persons) by treating men as mere means to a relative purpose (e.g. territorial aggrandisement). In Kant's view war, which necessarily treats men as mere means to an immoral purpose, causes the state to attack and subvert morality, when in fact the state and the legal order ought (as qualified goods) to provide a stable context of peace and security within which men can safely exercise the sole unqualified good, a 'good will'. So the notion that persons are ends who ought never to be used merely as means to arbitrary purposes provides 'good will' with an objective end which is the source of the categorical imperative, and it sets a limiting condition to what politics can legitimately do. Despite what Hegel says, then, Kantianism is not merely a formal doctrine in which (to quote Hegel's language) 'chill duty is the final undigested lump left within the stomach' (Hegel 1896, III, p. 461).

Kant is clear, moreover, that consenting *citizens* (not mere feudal subjects) in a 'republic' would dissent from war, out of the legal motive of self-love. Thus republicanism (internally) and eternal peace (externally) are interlocked and are absolutely inseparable. This is why Kant says that in 'a constitution where the subject is not a citizen, and which is therefore not republican, it is the simplest thing in the world to go to war' – despite the fact that 'moral-practical reason within us pronounces the following irre-sistible veto: *there shall be no war* . . . for war is not the way in which anyone should pursue his rights'. Therefore republican citizenship is instrumental to an essential moral end that good will alone may never realise, thanks to human pathology. For Kant, the outside is shaped by the inside; it is that which leads him to say that the first definitive article of eternal peace is that 'the civil constitution of every state shall be republican', that all just laws must be such that 'a people of mature rational powers' could consent to them (Kant 1991, pp. 99, 100, 104, 174, 187).

All of this is brought out in the last pages of the *Metaphysical Elements of Justice*, where it is asserted that it is morality itself that vetoes war (doubtless because war treats ends as mere means, persons as mere things); that peace as a moral end can be legally approached by establishing that constitution (namely 'republicanism in all states, individually and collectively') that may bring self-loving, consenting rational citizens to veto war; that to think that the moral law that forbids war might be misleading is to renounce reason and to fall back on the 'mechanism of nature'; that right, which legally realises some moral ends (even without good will), has universal and lasting peace as its 'entire ultimate purpose' (Kant 1991, p. 174). It is doubtful whether there is any other passage, anywhere in Kant, that so vividly and movingly fills out his notion of a politics that pays homage to the ends of morals. It is a passage whose visionary but sane breadth redeems the drier parts of the *Metaphysical Elements of Justice*. It confirms, in sum, what should never have been doubted: that Kant is a political philosopher of the first rank who fits contractarianism into a powerful general moral theory.

8 The decline of social contract theory

Kant's subtle and careful but oblique and attenuated contractarianism – shaped by the notion that a self-loving rational being would consent to life-saving eternal peace and dissent from war – might stand as the perfect illustration of Hegel's dictum that the Owl of Minerva takes flight only with the falling of dusk: that forms of thought perfect themselves at the moment they begin to vanish. Certainly Hegel himself, in the *Philosophy of Right* (publ. 1821), was contemptuous of mere contractarianism, and urged that modern men can be said to 'will' the state only in the sense that they 'recognise' it as the sufficient and satisfying 'realisation' of non-capricious rational freedom (Hegel 1991, preface, p. 22, and pp. 333–4). If, for Hegel, a person finds his 'subjective satisfaction' in willing membership in the modern state qua 'ethical' order, then one will be secured and freed up for the pursuit of what has 'absolute' value – art, religion, and (especially) philosophy. But this willingness has nothing to do with 'mere' consent or contract: rather one 'sees' the state for what it is (Kelly 1978, chs. 1–3). The 'recognition' which is so important in the *Phenomenology of Spirit* – in the servant's acknowledgement of the master – is now transferred to the citizen's *Anerkennung* (recognition) of 'the ethical world' (Kelly 1978, chs. 1–3; Riley 1992, ch. 1). Hegelianism simply severs the link between 'will' and 'consent' which had been in place since Augustine, and which had been made politically central by Hobbes, Locke, and Rousseau. Hegelianism then had enormous weight throughout the nineteenth century – together with utilitarianism, now flourishing and able to insist on Hume's argument that social institutions are justified by their necessity and utility alone, that it is useless to ground legitimacy in a contract whose utility will still have to be settled. It was for Bentham to say that the social contract is 'nonsense upon stilts'; but Hume had pulled out the first props (Bentham 1843, II, p. 501).

To be sure, one of the most celebrated paragraphs in Burke's *Reflections on the Revolution in France* (1790) uses contractarian imagery – but it is only a vestigial echo of a doctrine that Burke undercuts even while seeming to employ its customary rhetoric:

Society is indeed a contract. Subordinate contracts for objects of mere occasional interest may be dissolved at pleasure – but the state ought not to be considered as nothing better than a partnership agreement in a trade of pepper and coffee, callico or tobacco, or some other such low concern, to be taken up for a little temporary interest, and to be dissolved by the fancy of the parties. It is to be looked on with other reverence; because it is not a partnership in things subservient only to the gross animal existence of a temporary and perishable nature. It is a partnership in all science, a partnership in all art, a partnership in every virtue, and in all perfection. (Burke 2001, pp. 260–1)

Burke's real view, of course, was that social goods (including political rights) should be viewed as an historical 'entailed inheritance', not as dictates of 'reason' or products of 'will'; when he uses Lockean words it is with a view to subverting the Lockean world.

By the early 1800s, then, social contract theory was being displaced from its eminence by Burkean historical 'organicism', by various stripes of utilitarianism (whether Benthamite or Humean), and by the flowering of Hegelianism over a political spectrum stretching from far left to far right (Kelly 1978, ch. 5). With Hegel's death in 1831 and Bentham's in 1832 the death of contractarianism might also have been pronounced – except in America where a fairly unreconstructed Lockeanism continued to hold the field (Hartz 1955, ch. 1). Few in 1831–2 would, therefore, have predicted a new era of contractarianism in the late twentieth century, driven by a work, John Rawls's *Theory of Justice*, which avowedly built on Hobbes, Locke, Rousseau, and Kant (Rawls 1972, pp. 11–13).

IV
Commerce, luxury, and political economy

13

The early Enlightenment debate on commerce and luxury

ISTVAN HONT

1 The spectre of luxury

A spectre was haunting the modern world, wrote the Neapolitan Ferdinando Galiani in 1751, the spectre of 'luxury'. It 'wanders among us never seen in its true light, or recognised for its efficacy and it, perhaps, never occurs to the virtuous'. It was akin to the idea of 'terrestrial happiness', but 'no-one knows or dares to say', Galiani grumbled, 'what luxury might properly be' (Galiani 1977, p. 214). Denis Diderot was in a similar quandary. Defining the term in the *Encyclopédie*, he called for a 'discussion among those who show the most discrimination in their use of the term luxury: a discussion which has yet to take place, and which even they cannot bring to a satisfactory conclusion' (Diderot 1755, v, p. 635). The article on 'Luxury', published in 1762, and written by the marquis de Saint Lambert, was as much a summary of the luxury debates of the first half of the eighteenth century as an attempt to resolve them. The purpose of this chapter is to present the work of eight important contributors to these debates in France and Britain before 1748, the year of publication of Montesquieu's *Spirit of the Laws*, that supplied Saint Lambert with the resources he needed to try to say what luxury actually was.

As Saint Lambert presented it, luxury was not merely an economic phenomenon, but the central moral and political issue of modernity. The standard definition of 'luxury' was excessive individual consumption (Butel-Dumont 1771), but Saint Lambert followed the definition of Véron de Forbonnais (the author of the articles 'Commerce' and 'Agriculture' and the original assignee for 'Luxury'): '[Luxury] is the use men make of wealth and industry to assure themselves of a pleasant existence' (Forbonnais 1754, p. 221; Saint Lambert 1965, p. 202). This turned 'luxury' into a constituent part of 'self-love', a direct offspring of human instinct, a definition that is most familiar today in Adam Smith's *Wealth of Nations* (1776) as the 'desire of bettering our condition, a desire which, though generally calm and dispassionate, comes with us from the womb, and never leaves us till we go into

379

379

the grave' (*WN*, ii.iii.28; cf. Saint Lambert 1965, p. 204). The philosophical point of this definition of 'luxury' was to show self-love in a positive light, as a counter to Christian and republican moral rigorism. Saint Lambert ferociously attacked the Jansenists and the libertines of the seventeenth century (Nicole, Pascal, and Rochefoucauld) for making 'self-love a principle that is always vicious', and for finding 'no virtue in us because self-love is the principle of our actions'. Instead, Saint Lambert aligned himself with the third earl of Shaftesbury, not as a theorist who counted 'self-love in man for nothing' as he was often miscast, but as an innovative philosopher who regarded 'benevolence, love of order, and even the most complete self-sacrifice as the effects of our self-love' (Saint Lambert 1765a, p. 818).

Saint Lambert was a participant in two different luxury debates. The first revolved around the uncompromising critique of luxury by republicans and Christians. This was a debate between 'ancients' and 'moderns', echoing long-standing arguments originating in Greece, republican Rome, and early Christianity. For its critics, luxury was the product of extreme inequality, the sacrifice of the countryside for the cities, the cause of depopulation, the nemesis of courage, honour, and love of country. For its defenders, luxury was an engine of population growth, higher living standards, the circulation of money, good manners, the progress of the arts and sciences, and, last but not least, the power of nations and the happiness of citizens. Saint Lambert was desperate to draw a line under this ultra-polarised debate, and sided with the advocates of luxury. He had no truck with radical anti-luxury reforms, or the cult of ancient military states. It was better, he wrote, 'for a people to obey frivolous Epicureans than fierce warriors, and to feed the luxury of voluptuous and enlightened rascals rather than the luxury of heroic and ignorant robbers'. The historical record, Saint Lambert claimed, was so mixed that it proved nothing in particular. 'Luxury does not make the character of a nation', he wrote, 'but takes on that character' (Saint Lambert 1765a, p. 230). Its effects depended on bad and good government, on the balance between corruption and 'public spirit'.

The second debate was amongst the 'moderns' themselves. The issue for them was not whether to accept modern economic growth, but how to make it politically and morally benign. This was a controversy between the partisans of 'unregulated' and 'well-ordered' luxury. Here Saint Lambert was on the side of the critics of unfettered luxury, for he stood for 'patriotic' luxury firmly guided by civic spirit. As his allegiance to Shaftesbury demonstrated, he was not an Epicurean. But he still wanted a patriotic and democratic form of luxury as a source of national happiness, to benefit and motivate everyone. Virtuous states did not need to be poor, nor rich ones dissolute. 'If men use riches according to the dictates of patriotism they will seek other things besides their base personal interest and false and childish pleasures', he wrote. 'It is then that luxury is no longer in conflict with the duties of a father, a husband, a friend, and man' (p. 228). Luxury, Saint Lambert emphasised, was not a problem for societies 'founded on the equality and community of goods', where both economy and polity were equally communal (p. 204). It became an issue when the economy became 'private' (with private property and hence inequality) and less obviously compatible with the *esprit de communauté* (public spirit) (cf. Saint Lambert 1765b, pp. 357–8). Europe had long reached a level of inequality, Saint Lambert believed, that could not be suppressed. European states had to be monarchies, the political form of inequality *par excellence*. Saint Lambert's regime of 'well-ordered' luxury was a kind of monarchical equivalent of the regime prescribed for Geneva by Rousseau in his *Social Contract* (1762).

By describing luxury as an epiphenomenal product of inequality and private property, Saint Lambert indicated that the luxury debate of the 'moderns' was continuous with the property debates of the seventeenth century. The difference between the two was a matter of emphasis. As a contemporary commentator observed, the seventeenth-century discourse of the 'Law of Nations' was already a controversy about the consequences of luxury (Mackenzie 1691, 'Dedication'). However, while the property debate focused on the origins of private property, the luxury debate was about the political and economic feasibility of a fully developed property system. The luxury debate was the property debate at the fourth stage of social development, dealing with societies that had progressed beyond not only hunter-gathering and shepherding, but also agriculture. It addressed the fate of those who had been excluded from private property in land. The vital role of the luxury of the cities in creating employment for those whose livelihood depended on effective demand for their products and services was already recognised in the late seventeenth century. For property theorists like Locke and Pufendorf urban luxury was no longer a predominantly moral problem, but an issue of justice and even more of political prudence (Hont 2005; Hont and Ignatieff 1983b). The standard complaints of the 'ancients' against luxury seemed increasingly outdated, as their blindness to the economic limits to politics became more apparent. The 'modern' search was for a political and moral accommodation of luxury that would yield a positive answer to questions of social stability, population growth, and the misery of the working classes. Saint Lambert's 'patriotic luxury' was an attempt to reconcile the communal spirit of the ancients with modern economic growth as a solution to these dilemmas. The other side in the 'modern' debate looked for specifically modern forms of politics that could contain the ill effects of luxury. Both sides tended to be highly critical of the prevailing European state system, suggesting that it was living on borrowed time, neither fulfilling ancient political ideals, nor well adapted to modern luxury.

It is often assumed that Bernard Mandeville, the author of the *Fable of the Bees* (1714), was the central figure of the eighteenth-century luxury debate and that he was an apologist for luxury without qualification (Morize 1909). Neither assumption is accurate. Mandeville is often misunderstood because he is seen solely in the context of the debate between 'ancients' and 'moderns'. His chief targets, however, were neither republicans, nor Christian devotees of austerity. He attacked the 'frugal hive' as the ideal of those who wanted both economic growth and good moral order, including thinkers such as Locke, who wanted 'honest industry' and attacked 'evil concupiscence' (Dunn 1969a; Waldron 2002). Such a position, Mandeville argued, necessarily defaulted into poverty. Taming luxury required a more comprehensive approach to the phenomenon: psychological, moral, economic, and political. For Saint Lambert the central political problem of luxury involved facing up to the disastrous legacy of Louis XIV. But he distanced himself from the Sun King's most potent public critic, Archbishop Fénelon, who made the abolition of luxury the *sine qua non* of any prospects of France recovering from royal absolutism (Rothkrug 1965). Saint Lambert accepted Fénelon's anti-absolutist politics (particularly his renunciation of war and his emphasis on 'public spirit'), but rejected his radical antipathy to luxury. He signalled this by praising Colbert, Louis XIV's virtuous minister of finance, whose pro-urban, pro-manufacturing, and pro-luxury policies Fénelon found utterly repugnant (Cole 1939). It was Colbert, not Mandeville, who was the standard-bearer of the luxury party in France. There was, however, an affinity between Mandeville's ideas and those of the neo-Colbertists, for Mandeville was as much a critic of Fénelon's views on luxury as they were.

Fénelon and Mandeville represented the two poles of the early eighteenth-century luxury controversy, the purest and ablest formulations of the fundamental alternatives on offer. Mandeville was the first major critic of the project of 'honest' modernity. But he did not initiate the argument. The line of causation ran from Fénelon to Mandeville, rather than the other way round. The eighteenth-century debate began with Fénelon's presentation of a detailed scenario of how Europe's luxury could be destroyed and replaced with a virtually incorruptible economy. Thus this chapter begins with Fénelon, and continues with a discussion of Mandeville's counterblast. It then turns to Shaftesbury's critique of the psychology of luxury, and to the restatement of the idea of economic growth without luxury by two of Mandeville's Protestant Irish critics, Francis Hutcheson and Bishop Berkeley. The second part of the chapter deals with the highly influential French luxury debate of the 1730s, to show how Montesquieu, Voltaire, and Jean François Melon – whose *Political Essay upon Commerce* (1735) was at that point the most widely available French defence of luxury – forged a neo-Colbertist idiom of the politics of luxury, in opposition both to Fénelon's project and to attempts to resuscitate Louis XIV's project of universal monarchy. The two parts of the chapter together show how 'luxury' became a key issue in the European thought of the period not only for domestic, but also for international political theory.

2   Fénelon

Shortly after Fénelon was appointed tutor to Louis XIV's grandson in 1689, he wrote *The Bees*, a fable about luxury. It was written in the style of La Fontaine, echoing ancient examples and describing a well-ordered, meritocratic 'little republick' based on the principle of compulsory labour (Fénelon 1747b, pp. 52–3). The idea reappeared in Fénelon's most famous work, *Les aventures de Télémaque, fils d'Ulysse* (The Adventures of Telemachus, Son of Ulysses, 1699), a heroic prose poem purporting to be a continuation of the fourth book of Homer's *Odyssey*. It describes Telemachus's search for his father in the company of his tutor Mentor, who gradually teaches him the art of pacific and virtuous kingship. It became the most popular secular book of the entire eighteenth century (Cherel 1917). The central feature of *Telemachus* was the reform of the corrupt and warlike princely city-state of Salentum (an imaginary place) based on the template already laid down in *The Bees*. Mentor explained that two things were wrong with corrupt monarchy: despotism and luxury. The second was worse than the first since, while 'arbitrary power' was 'the bane of kings', 'luxury poisons a whole nation'. In Machiavellian fashion Fénelon described luxury as the corruption of the people. Under the yoke of luxury, Fénelon claimed, the 'whole nation goes to wreck; all ranks are confounded . . . all live above their rank and income, some from vanity and ostentation, and to display their wealth; others from false shame, and to hide their poverty'. It was a diseased condition of society in which 'even those who are poor will affect to appear wealthy, and spend as if they really were so' (Fénelon 1994, pp. 297–8). Technically, luxury was the consumption of 'superfluity', over and above what was 'necessary' for satisfying the 'real' (or 'true') needs of man (p. 109). Analogous to 'vain-glory', it was 'vain' need. Fénelon recognised that the notion of what constituted 'necessities' changed over time. A 'whole nation', he lamented, 'comes by degrees to look upon superfluities as necessary to life, and to invent such necessaries every day; so that they cannot dispense with what was counted superfluous thirty years before' (p. 297).

Fénelon blamed Colbert's economic policies for France's luxury. These were simply the economic side of Louis XIV's 'Italian policy' (reason of state), aimed at establishing a European universal monarchy. Fénelon knew the Colbertist apologia for luxury perfectly well: that luxury maintained 'the poor at the expense of the rich' and paved the way to a modern civilisation, to 'good taste, the perfection of arts, and the politeness of a nation' (p. 297). He found these arguments fallacious. The claim that luxury was the nursery of civility and politeness was irresponsible, because it sacrificed morality for its mere simulacrum and made luxury a veritable social contagion. Urbanisation and state support for trade and manufacturing were self-defeating policies that perverted the social order and caused the neglect of agriculture, the decline of rural population, and the undermining of the monarchy's tax base. Hence the constant need for conquests that might replenish the depleted coffers of the luxurious military state. France, Fénelon claimed, was bound to share Rome's fate. Luxury would lead to military defeat and domestic revolution. Instead of reducing the absolutist monarchy's power, he added, the revolution would most likely become uncontrollable and result in a total 'overthrow' of the state. The French monarchy's 'bow of power', Fénelon pleaded, had to be 'slackened' by skilful reform before it was too late (p. 297). Salentum was Fénelon's blueprint for preventing a violent revolution in France.

Telemachus offered a tripartite model of the history of luxury, by describing a pre-luxury community (Boetica), a luxurious and warlike state (Salentum unreformed), and a post-luxury society (Salentum reformed). Boetica was the highest stage of material civilisation without luxury, living frugally but comfortably from shepherding (with some agriculture and manufacturing) (Fénelon 1994, pp. 108–14). It had no political state, no private property, no inequality, and no system of ranks. By prohibiting permanent housing Boetica hoped to prevent urbanisation, and thus luxury. It self-consciously rejected the 'benefits' of the wealth of the pharaohs and the Greek states. Boetica is often seen as a semi-Platonic utopia of the Golden Age, with tinges of Sparta and borrowings from More's *Utopia* (1516). In fact, it was modelled on ancient Israel in the age of the patriarchs, a model borrowed from the Abbé Claude Fleury, Fénelon's deputy, in educating the duke of Burgundy, and author of *The Manners of the Ancient Hebrews* (1681). Israel, Fleury emphasized, provided an alternative to luxury that was not imaginary like the 'commonwealth of Plato', but a description of how 'the greatest part of the world lived during near four thousand years' (Fleury 1683, p. 34). Boetica was the strict equivalent of Locke's and Pufendorf's states of nature, both arguably also modelled on early Israel.

In Boetica luxury was ruled out, whereas Salentum was a model for the surgical correction of developed luxury. The reform programme involved three phases: the destruction of luxury, the transition to frugality, and the creation of 'public spirit' to make the regime of 'honesty' durable (Fénelon 1994, pp. 160–71, 295–302). First the urban economy of luxury was abolished by the shock therapy of a sumptuary law. Simultaneously, an agrarian law provided land for all the former workers in the luxury industries who were forced to re-settle in the countryside. Plot sizes reflected personal and family needs. To alleviate initial food shortages agricultural labourers were brought in from abroad, while the mountain of confiscated luxury goods was exported in exchange for cattle. Manufacturing was restricted to the level of 'real' needs, like agricultural implements. Fénelon also added to Salentum a commercial port modelled on Tyre (representing Holland). In *Telemachus* Tyre was described as an immensely rich maritime beehive, whose citizens were 'industrious, patient, laborious, clean, sober, and frugal' as well as 'constantly employed' (p. 37). Trade of this kind was morally safe and benefited both Salentum and mankind. The port was isolated from the rest of the economy, and subjected to draconian financial regulation. Its income provided the resources for Salentum's huge armament industry. Strong, but renouncing conquest, Salentum (reformed France) would be the arbiter of the European balance of power. Policing the order of the European state system, Fénelon emphasised, would allow Salentian troops to gain valuable battle experience for national defence.

The key issue was Salentum's longevity. Growth without luxury, or any superfluity, was the aim. The 'earth, if well cultivated, would feed a hundred times more men than now she does', Fénelon claimed (Fénelon 1713, p. 19). Farms could thus increase their production to facilitate population growth, and industry could expand in strict proportion. Comparison with Locke is instructive. He too (like Pufendorf) assumed that private land-holding should be limited to the real needs of the owner and also argued that labour could raise the productivity of land a hundred, or even a thousand fold. Locke also saw human labour as the key to honest wealth. A 'king of a large and fruitful territory' where labour is underused, 'feeds, lodges, and is clad worse than a day labourer in England' (*TTG*, II, §41, p. 297). When Locke listed the various labour-inputs needed for the production of the simplest foods, tools, and utensils or even of such complex objects as a ship, he was describing an economy of 'real needs', not praising luxury. Salentum was designed with similar ideas in mind. It was not supposed to be poor just because it proscribed luxury (Ehrard 1994, pp. 577–83). Locke's assessment of Europe's security resembled Fénelon's. 'Numbers of men are to be preferred to largeness of dominions', he wrote,

and . . . the increase of lands [hands?] and the right employing of them is the great art of government. And that prince who shall be so wise and godlike as by established laws of liberty to secure protection and encouragement to the honest industry of mankind against the oppression of power and narrowness of party will quickly be too hard for his neighbours. (*TTG*, II, § 42, pp. 297–8; cf. Locke 1993a, p. 136)

This was the same programme as that presented in *Telemachus*, but while Locke wanted reform to be instituted 'by the established laws of liberty', Salentum initially required the draconian use of arbitrary power.

Absolute power was needed during the transition. If the ground rules and proportions of the economy were first set in place correctly, the economy could then run unattended. The legislator was like a master architect designing a well-proportioned building. Once built, he could withdraw. Monarchs were like gardeners pruning excess vegetation or conductors keeping their orchestras in harmony. Salentum was to become a land of unprecedented liberty by delegating the authority needed to perform technical tasks to experts. In fully built Salentum the laws were in command, not the king. Salentum had to forget its former luxury completely, in order that frugality could become a national habit. Palaces had to be replaced by standardised utilitarian houses built on a new town plan. Furnishings and dietary habits were also regulated. Salentum could never become Boetica; competitive psychological needs and the legacy of pride could not be eliminated completely. A system of ranks, based on merit, ability, and contributions to society was retained, and ancient aristocratic lineage was rewarded with continued high status. To sever links between status and wealth a new hierarchy of seven ranks was organised, carefully calibrated, and made highly visible through a detailed prescription of codes in dress and ornament.

Fénelon did not trust human nature (Keohane 1980; Riley 2001a). In his religious writings he complained that even Christianity had come to be suffused with selfishness and luxury. He was a leading supporter of a French semi-mystical movement called quietism, which believed in silent prayer and a direct relationship with God that bypassed the use of language. Fénelon regarded the love of God tainted by self-love as mere hypocrisy (Fénelon 1746, pp. 6–10). He drew a parallel between Christian pure love and the ancient Greeks' love of their *polis*. Salentum needed the 'pure love of order' as the 'source of all political virtues' if it was to endure. The Salentinians became 'obedient without being slaves' and 'free without being licentious'. This was no domination of the individual by the community. Individuals were supposed to conquer themselves individually, while being members of the political community they loved. This did not have to be a self-standing and perfect version of pure love. A mixed love, a balance between the love of self and the pure love of the legal order was sufficient, reinforced by an educational system and other public institutions. Decorative arts would serve to celebrate heroic individuals and the great deeds of the state. The militia would act as a school of virtue. Fénelon's anti-luxury vision was comprehensive, grand, and virtuous. *Telemachus* captured the imagination of its readers from the moment it appeared.

3   Mandeville

In 1705 an immigrant Dutch physician, Bernard Mandeville, published a satirical pamphlet in London containing 423 lines of doggerel verse under the title of *The Grumbling Hive: Or, Knaves Turn'd Honest*, later republished with a substantial commentary as *The Fable of the Bees* (1714, 1723). Mandeville asserted that the foundation of national power was a flourishing economy and that luxury was the best bulwark against the danger of conquest. He ridiculed the example of virtuous and frugal bees. Making England a beehive, he claimed, was bound to lead to a sharp contraction in economic activity and catastrophic unemployment. Anybody who failed to see this was either deluded or a hypocrite. It was the charge of hypocrisy that provoked a ferocious legal and ideological counter-attack (particularly after the publication in 1723 of the viciously satirical *Essay on Charity, and Charity Schools*), making Mandeville famous both at home and in Europe. Hypocrisy was indeed fodder for Mandeville's satirical wit, but it was not his immediate political target. Although emblematic of the polite latitudinarian culture of Christian England, hypocrisy in itself was rarely associated with ambitious plans for economic reform. Fénelon's *Telemachus*, however, was.

The *Grumbling Hive* emerged when Queen Anne's government was preparing for war against France over the issue of the Spanish Succession, and in the midst of a general election (McKee 1988; Minto 1883). Mandeville viewed English politics as a spectator, a beneficiary, and supporter of the 'Dutch' regime established by the Glorious Revolution. In *The Pamphleteers: A Satyr* (1703) he supported the Protestant Succession and attacked the denigrators of William III. It was here that he first complained about 'a grumbling Nation, that was ne'er at ease' (an uneasiness Montesquieu later described as essential to English political culture). For Mandeville the Tories were crypto-Jacobites, and he feared the return of religious intolerance and a bloody civil war. The defection of the English could also open the door to French hegemony in Europe. In 'The Moral' of his translation of 'The Wolves and the Sheep' in his *Some Fables after the Easie and Familiar Method of Monsieur de la Fontaine* (1703), enlarged and re-titled in 1704 as *Aesop Dress'd*, Mandeville hinted at the danger of the English gullibly accepting Louis's peace overtures ('cunning Tyrants call 'em Friends / No longer than it serves their Ends') to 'avoid Expence' (Mandeville 1704, p. 45).

The *Grumbling Hive* expressed Mandeville's fear that with a further expensive war in train the English might be swayed by anti-war propaganda and abandon their Continental commitments. 'The Moral' suggested that 'T'enjoy the World's Conveniencies, / Be famed in War, yet live in Ease / Without great Vices, is a vain / EUTOPIA seated in the Brain' (Mandeville 1924, I, p. 36). The 'eutopia' in question was an adaptation of Fénelon's Salentum to England, to accompany the dynastic reversal of the Glorious Revolution of 1688. The opposition's campaign of 1705 targeted the corrupt regime of debt and luxury created by the so-called 'financial revolution' (Hont 1990, 2005; Pocock 1975). The English counter-revolution was not designed to make England resemble Louis XIV's 'luxurious' France, but the virtuous alternative outlined by Louis's opponents. *Telemachus* was published in English in 1699 and again in 1700, soon after its first appearance in France. Some believed that Idomeneus, king of Salentum, was modelled on James II, and soon an association arose between Fénelon and the Jacobite cause (which, through its connections with freemasonry, had a lasting effect through the entire eighteenth century). *Telemachus* thus attracted another royal pupil besides the duke of Burgundy: the 'king of England' in exile, whom Mandeville called the Pretender. The ideological nexus between the

Jacobites and *Telemachus* was laid bare in a poem by the Whig grandee, the duke of Devonshire, tellingly entitled, *The Charms of Liberty: A Poem in Allusion to the Archbishop of Cambray's 'Telemachus'* (Devonshire 1709). Mandeville confirmed the Jacobite association of the 'bees' project in his *Free Thoughts on Religion, the Church, and National Happiness* (1720), where he repeated his objection to the Jacobite 'eutopia'. The 'popish bigot' and his supporters might declaim about liberty and frugality, Mandeville wrote, but the real question remained

> whether we shall be contented with the present establishment, and the blessings, which it is in our power to enjoy under it in peace and tranquility, or renounce both to go in quest of an eutopia to be looked for in a revolution, that in all human probability will never be brought about, and of which the very attempt, whether the thing it self be compassed or not, cannot cost less, if made with any vigour or resolution, than the ruin of at least half the nation. (Mandeville 1720, p. 354)

Mandeville objected to the use of *Telemachus* (built on the 'seraphick' doctrine of pure love, as Devonshire commented dismissively) by the political opposition to William III and Anne. The *Grumbling Hive* was not an encomium of luxury as such, but a defence of the English economic and political regime created by the Glorious Revolution, and its foreign policy, against a Jacobite counter-revolution that promised to create an English 'Salentum' with James III as its virtuous pacific king.

The extended *Fable of the Bees* of 1714 contained a detailed commentary on twenty-three lines of the original poem (numbered alphabetically from A to Y). In these 'Remarks' Mandeville offered an ironical, but detailed description of the 'wholesome regulations' that were designed to make England a 'happy reformed kingdom', replicating the Salentum project step by step. The basic reform to banish 'fraud and luxury' was to 'enact sumptuary laws' and to 'knock down foreign trade', with the intended effect that 'the greatest part of the covetous, the discontented, the restless and ambitious villains would leave the land, vast swarms of cheating knaves would abandon the city, and be dispersed throughout the country'. The former employees of luxury were to resume life in the country: 'Artificers would learn to hold the plough, merchants turn farmers', as Mandeville summarised the reform project. Thus 'the sinful over-grown Jerusalem' that was London would 'without famine, war, pestilence, or compulsion, be emptied in the most easy manner, and ever after cease to be dreadful to her sovereigns'. The English Salentum would 'be crowded in no part of it, and every thing necessary for the sustenance of man be cheap and abound'. Imports having been prohibited, more expensive English 'manufacture unmixed [would] be promiscuously wore by the lord and the peasant'. Specie was to be melted down and re-made 'into sacred utensils' for the church; thus 'the root of so many thousand evils, money would be very scarce'. Without luxury and money, England was to become the land of justice 'where every man should enjoy the fruits of his own labour'. If everything proceeded according to plan, Mandeville noted sarcastically, 'from the next generation we might reasonably expect a more healthy and robust offspring than the present; an harmless, innocent and well-meaning people, that would never dispute the doctrine of passive obedience, nor any other orthodox principles, but be submissive to superiors, and unanimous in religious worship' (Mandeville 1924, I, pp. 231–3). Mandeville was filled with rage against this Tory-Jacobite vision of a counter-revolution and proceeded to ridicule every single item in it.

Modern society inevitably produced luxury that 'no government on earth' could 'remedy' (Mandeville 1924, I, p. 8). The 'crowning achievement of our century's politics' as Rousseau called it, was to understand how the 'beautiful machine' of a well-ordered society could be made to work by rendering 'the very vices of every particular person subservient to the grandeur and worldly happiness of the whole' (Rousseau 1997a, p. 100; Mandeville 1924, I, p. 7). Mandeville followed Hobbes's opening gambit in *De Cive* (1642), where he famously rejected the notion of man as a *zoon politikon*, a creature by nature political. The continuation, however, was un-Hobbesian (Hundert 1994). Instead of emphasising the process of authorisation, Mandeville concentrated on how a 'dextrous politician' (a legislator figure rather than a *politico*) could create peace by manipulating the passions. His wonderful piece of 'political wisdom' was the invention of morality itself. As Hobbes had shown, pride always sabotaged social cohesion. But instead of relying on fear, the trick was to goad pride into mimicking virtue. 'Morality' for Mandeville was a labelling system. Behaviour destructive to society was 'bad' (vice); behaviour useful for society 'good' (virtue). The 'clever' or manipulative element was to use selfishness to control itself (within a punitive political order), by rewarding 'virtue' with higher 'moral' status than the odium due to unregenerate egoists. Mandeville insisted that counterfeit virtue (vice) was perfectly able to create utility (benefits), but could never become true 'morality', which for Mandeville was strictly a matter of intentions. 'Men are not to be judged by the consequences that may succeed their actions, but . . . the motives which it shall appear they acted from' (Mandeville 1924, I, p. 87). As Mandeville explained, his intention was not to label mankind as cheats. The issue was rather the weakness of the human will. 'There is nothing left us, but to say what Mr Bayle has endeavoured to prove at large in his *Reflections on Comets*'. Mandeville wrote, 'that man is so unaccountable a creature as to act most commonly against his principle; and this is so far from being injurious, that it is a compliment to human nature, for we must say either this or worse' (p. 167; cf. Bayle 2000b, p. 229; Montaigne 1987). Mandeville's analysis of luxury followed from this contrast between true virtue (the suppression of self) and counterfeit virtue (artificial sociability).

Fénelon's distinction between necessary and superfluous consumption only made sense, Mandeville claimed, if it coincided with the distinction between nature and culture. Following the Epicurean tradition, Mandeville depicted early man as a mere animal that 'fed on the fruits of the earth, without any previous preparation, and reposed himself naked like other animals on the lap of their common parent' (Mandeville 1924, I, p. 169). Like animals, men were programmed to seek pleasure and avoid pain. Natural human needs were hunger and lust (but not raiment); once satisfied, men lapsed into inertness. Early human life was of 'natural innocence and stupidity', without morals or knowledge. 'Whatever has contributed since to make life more comfortable, as it must have been the result of thought, experience, and some labour', Mandeville explained, 'so it more or less deserves the name of luxury, the more or less trouble it required and deviated from the primitive simplicity' (p. 169). By this definition even the 'most simple and savage people on earth' were luxurious, for 'it is not probable that there are any but what by this time have made some improvements upon their former manner of living; and either in the preparation of their eatables, the ordering of their huts, or otherwise added something to what once sufficed them' (p. 107). This rigour was unavoidable: 'If we are to abate one inch of this severity, I am afraid we shan't know where to stop', Mandeville pointed out. 'If once we depart from calling every thing luxury that is not absolutely necessary to keep a man alive', we would only ever see the constant mutation of the 'superfluous' into the 'necessary' (p. 107). Nothing is ever completely superfluous, Mandeville claimed, even if some objects were regarded as 'necessary' by kings only. This was no frivolous assertion. Mandeville was simply restating Locke's dictum that the ordinary English worker lived better than the kings of simpler ages, or of contemporary America and Africa. 'So that many things, which were once looked upon as the invention of luxury', Mandeville concluded, 'are now allowed even to those that are so miserably poor as to become the objects of public charity, nay counted so necessary, that we think no human creature ought to want them' (p. 169).

Mandeville made 'luxury' coterminous with the entirety of human civilisation (Hundert 1994). Instead of being a slippery slope of corruption, 'luxury' was the ascent of mankind from animal-like poverty to modern welfare. Man was teleologically prepared for this, for humans could use their hands as tools and their brains to reason, unlike any other animal. Progress was through the division of labour and technical innovation, which created new human needs in an open-ended process. 'Luxury' developed in tandem with the arts and sciences. For the traditional meanings of luxury Mandeville substituted other terms. Individual excess was prodigality or avarice, both clearly vices. Legislators played them against each other, like doctors who administered poison against poison. Prestige consumption was not 'luxury' but 'ornamentation', which Mandeville distinguished from material and scientific progress. He deemed the application of the term 'luxury' to the excesses of entire nations to be even less useful. National 'luxury', he claimed, was almost invariably the consequence of 'bad politics, neglects, or mismanagements of the rulers' (Mandeville 1924, I, p. 117).

The counterpoint to 'luxury' was the desire to arrest the progress of material civilisation out of moral considerations. 'Frugality in ethics is called that virtue, from the principle of which men abstain from superfluities', Mandeville wrote, 'and despising the operose contrivances of art to procure either ease or pleasure, content themselves with the natural simplicity of things, and are carefully temperate in the enjoyment of them without any tincture of covetousness' (pp. 181–2). National frugality was feasible in societies with 'a fertile soil and a happy climate, a mild government, and more land than people' (p. 183). The 'best policy' to perpetuate it was 'to preserve men in their native simplicity, strive not to increase their numbers; let them never be acquainted with strangers or superfluities, but remove and keep from them every thing that might raise their desires, or improve their understanding' (p. 185). Frugality was for places like Boetica, or for the state of nature. But frugality implied self-denial. Without 'arts or sciences', Mandeville insinuated, 'all the cardinal virtues together won't so much as procure a tolerable coat or a porridge pot among 'em' (p. 184). What was not possible, according to the *Fable of the Bees*, was to have both frugality and the arts and sciences at the same time. Mandeville dismissed the apparent modern counter-example of Holland, whose famed frugality he regarded as temporary, and due to the exceptional circumstances created by the lengthy revolutionary war against the Spanish.

The great leap forward in 'luxury' was the establishment of private property. The outcome would be national wealth, 'and where they are', Mandeville added, 'arts and sciences will soon follow'. But what inner principle made private property the greatest productivity tool ever invented? Its purpose was to facilitate the abandonment of self-denial without creating immediate social war. 'Divide the land, though there be never so much to spare', Mandeville advised, 'and their [men's] possessions will make them covetous: rouse them, though but in jest, from their idleness with praises, and pride will set them to work in earnest' (p. 184). The novelty was not in claiming that envy and emulation promoted economic activity, but that trade and technology could not develop far without them. Many would 'allow that among the sinful nations of the times, pride and luxury, are the great promoters of trade', Mandeville claimed. But most refuse 'to own the necessity there is, that in a more virtuous age (such a one as should be free from pride) trade would in a great measure decay' (p. 124). The reason was not corruption, but human nature. Economic development, Mandeville claimed, was not as robust a process as some imagined. The development of knowledge was too slow, and pleasure seeking was an unreliable motor of the economy. The sensory pleasures of humans could easily be satiated, creating inertness. 'A favourable construction of our present circumstances, and a peaceful tranquillity' of mind could be a real obstacle to growth (p. 242).

An expanding economy required restlessness, a sort of industriousness (as Mandeville called it) that was rooted in 'a thirst after gain, and an indefatigable desire of meliorating our condition' (p. 244). Pride was just the incentive that the economy needed, both on the demand and the supply sides, for it was relentless and insatiable. Pride gave human passions a huge boost. 'Whilst they lie dormant, and there is nothing to raise them, [man's] excellence and abilities will be for ever undiscovered', Mandeville wrote. 'The lumpish machine' that was human society could not operate unless it was moved by pride. Without the desires and passions, society may be 'justly compared', in Mandeville's memorably Dutch metaphor, 'to a huge windmill without a breath of air' (p. 184). It was pride that created economic man (cf. Hollis 1981). The purpose of private property was to create an institutional pathway for connecting pride and utility. Thus modern politics depended on taking care of such apparently minor matters as economic incentives. A moral or honest economy was a defective idea, for it wilfully discarded the psychological underpinnings of truly dynamic economic growth.

Pride provided a huge spur to the entire economy (in the original *Grumbling Hive* Mandeville wrote that 'Luxury / Employ'd a Million of the Poor, / And odious Pride a Million more' (1924, I, p. 25)). The fashion industries provided pride with its lifeblood, and their dynamism rested precisely on their non-utilitarian character. The larger and richer society became, the more it relied on the visibility of ranks. The anonymity of large cities created the possibility of counterfeiting social standing by simply appearing with the appropriate ornaments of rank. This was the source of new pleasures. Social fakes had 'the satisfaction to imagine, that they appear what they would be', Mandeville wrote, 'which to weak minds is a pleasure almost as substantial as they could reap from the very accomplishments of their wishes' (p. 128). The ever more elaborate visual representation of inequality drove fashion along a path of incessant change. Mandeville vividly described how mimicking class and counterfeiting ethics (hypocrisy) jointly forged a society of mere appearances that nonetheless functioned better than ever (Dickey 1990). Pride and vanity provided employment for a vast number of those who were excluded from private property in land (and indirectly even to those who laboured in the 'honest' sectors of the economy). Mandeville consistently nominated full employment as the prime economic task of modern government. Cutting pride was cutting jobs.

Mandeville also emphasized the role of envy in modern society. Envy was a compound of pride with grief and anger. Both ugly and dangerous, it was 'that baseness in our nature', Mandeville wrote, 'which makes us grieve and pine at what we conceive to be a happiness in others' (p. 134). He accepted that modern society needed an underclass, for only those who were uneducated and poor would undertake the unpleasant labour without which the social machine could not operate. This underclass, however, had to be treated gingerly, for envy made them want a share of the benefits of a rich society, which in some circumstances they might demand violently. In his critique of hypocrisy Mandeville did not equate the positions of the rich and the poor. 'Virtue is made friends with vice' in modern society, not just because 'industrious good people, who maintain their families and bring up their children handsomely, pay taxes' while employed to serve the vices of the rich, but also because they do so without becoming an 'accessary to [such vices] any otherwise than by way of trade, as a druggist may be to poisoning, or a sword-cutler to bloodshed' (p. 85).

Pride and envy were permanent fixtures of human nature, but aristocracy and a fixed system of ranks were not. Mandeville denied that political authority required the flaunting of wealth. 'To say, that men not being so easily governed by their equals as by their superiors, it is necessary that to keep the multitude in awe, those who rule over us should excel others in outward appearance . . . to be distinguished from the vulgar', he wrote, was 'a frivolous objection' (p. 163). Mandeville wanted luxury generalised through all levels of society. The existing beneficiaries of luxury were stupid to be wary of pressure from below. It was what propelled society upwards on the path to civilisation. It had to be accommodated politically. If today's beggars could claim yesterday's luxuries as an entitlement, the same must be possible tomorrow. Fénelon complained that the corruption of the people was total when even the 'very dregs of the people' wanted the false dignity of luxury (Fénelon 1994, p. 297). For Mandeville the idea of suppressing this process was to court disaster. The political expediency of demotic, perhaps even democratic, luxury was the most Dutch part of Mandeville's political message, addressed to both critics and supporters of luxury, in England as much as in France. It made him an advocate of 'modern' republicanism (Blom 2002).

4 Shaftesbury

That the *Fable of the Bees* was the first 'Anti-Telemachus' has been forgotten because Mandeville is chiefly remembered now as the opponent of the third earl of Shaftesbury. Mandeville first presented himself as anti-Shaftesbury nine years after Shaftesbury's death in an essay entitled 'A Search into the Nature of Society' in the 1723 edition of the *Fable* (Primer 1975a). The sequel to the *Fable of the Bees*, the six dialogues published as volume II (1729) (Mandeville 1924, II) and the further two dialogues, *Inquiry into the Origin of Honour, and the Usefulness of Christianity in War* (Mandeville 1732), restated Mandeville's *oeuvre* as a debate with Shaftesbury, subtly transforming (but never abandoning) some of his earlier positions. Shaftesbury's original work was directly contemporaneous with *Telemachus*, predating even the *Grumbling Hive*. The unauthorised early version of the *Inquiry into Virtue, or Merit*, Shaftesbury's most cogent and important work, was published in 1699, while the official edition came out in a compendium called *Characteristics* in 1708 (amended in 1714) (Shaftesbury 1977). Shaftesbury's *Inquiry* was immensely influential in the eighteenth century because it contained a direct counterblast to Hobbes's ethics. Shaftesbury went for the jugular of Hobbes's *De cive* and asserted that humans were primarily and naturally social. Thus Shaftesbury's problems tended to be mirror images of Hobbes's. Instead of needing to show how isolated individuals could be joined artificially into society, he had to explain the artificial birth of the 'individual' from naturally social beginnings. Having defined sociability as natural, Shaftesbury saw any form of solitude as unnatural (he himself suffered from bouts of melancholy). Actual solitude and exile, he wrote, were unhappy choices dictated by necessity. The real evil of modern social existence, however, was moral solitude, the 'inward banishment', the 'real estrangement from human commerce'; the forced exile into the moral 'desert' of evil (Shaftesbury 1977, § 268). It was his cry against alienation, 'the horridest of solitudes, even when in the midst of society', that echoed so persistently in the intellectual world of the eighteenth century (albeit more in Germany and Switzerland than in England). Shaftesbury's theory of luxury was part and parcel of his conjectural history of individualism, and a major rival to Mandeville's account.

Shaftesbury (as Saint Lambert correctly noted) was not a Manichean theorist of sociability versus self-love. In Adam Smith's categorisation he was a propriety theorist, seeing morality, like Plato did, as the proper governance of the self, balancing other-regarding and self-regarding inclinations (*TMS*, VII.ii.1.48). For Shaftesbury 'self-passions' were integral and perfectly acceptable components of the 'self-system'. The 'self-system' of each individual was connected to a 'social-system' consisting of a nested hierarchy of groups to which the individual belonged, from the family to mankind. Propriety depended on the balance of the two systems. Human beings were like musical instruments which sounded best together (in harmony) when well tuned. Selfishness was an excess of 'self-passions', corresponding to the 'human instrument' being out of tune. Excess, however, was not nearly as dangerous as the emergence of harmful, mutant, and artificial passions that favoured neither the 'self-system' nor the 'social system'. Envy, Mandeville's great explanatory agent of modernity, was just one of the most conspicuous of these unnatural psychological phenomena; it went along with ultra-excessive versions of some natural 'self-passions', such as tyranny, that would 'leave nothing eminent, nothing free, nothing prosperous in the world'. The catalogue of horrors stretched even further, from cruelty to wanton mischievousness, sexual deviation, unprovoked malice, inhumanity in general, and the hatred of mankind and society. Compared to these aberrations luxury was less dangerous. Nonetheless, it was the harbinger of horrid artificiality insofar as it created the wholly unnatural condition of insatiability, the pre-condition of all further moral degradation.

Shaftesbury rejected the idea that human sociability stemmed from human weakness. Man was no less generously endowed for survival than animals. Humans were not 'thoroughly associating' or 'confederate' (political) animals, like bees (Shaftesbury 1999, II, § 234). Nonetheless, they were inherently sociable, a fact which could be demonstrated by showing that the human 'oeconomy' needed the presence of company to experience most pleasures. Shaftesbury interpreted virtue hedonistically: its presence was pleasurable, its absence a source of misery. Without social affections (virtue) the hedonism of the 'self-system' was liable to become dysfunctional. Humans were initially as much in equilibrium with nature as other animal species. However, because of their faculty of reason, men were capable of changing both positively and negatively: 'the highest improvements of temper are made in human kind; so the greatest corruptions and degeneracies are discoverable in this race' (Shaftesbury 1977, § 157). As society grew, man's natural 'oeconomy' lost its inner balance. Animals were forever busy with survival. Humans lost their natural balance of existence when economic progress made their material self-preservation easier. When an animal has 'the accommodations of life at a cheaper and easier rate than was at first intended him by nature', he 'is made to pay dear for them in another way; by losing his natural good disposition, and the orderliness of his kind or species' (§ 208). The growth of civilisation allowed individuals to develop a taste for 'good living', but their mental apparatus failed to adjust; 'their inward faculties' could not 'keep pace with these outward supplies of a luxuriant fortune' (§ 230). The origin of luxury lay in the gap that opened up between body and mind as a result of economic and technological progress.

The human desire to eat well, procreate pleasurably, and possess wealth stemmed from natural affections, and only their excessive pursuit turned them into luxury and avarice. The 'sole end' of honest industry was 'the advantage and promotion of the species', assisting the progress of the 'public as well as private system' (§§ 235, 241). But those who indulged in excess were bound to upset their 'self-system'. Luxury of this kind was a 'self-oppressor'. By endlessly seeking pleasure, the luxurious person made an error of hedonistic calculation, foolishly thinking that repeating the pleasurable act would create more and more pleasure. But humans are not pleasure machines: 'by urging nature, forcing the appetite, and inciting sense, the keenness of the natural sensation is lost' (§ 232). The result was insatiability, burnout, nauseating distaste, and finally illness. Once it broke out of its natural mode of operation, the human mind knew no limits. 'For where shall we once stop, when we are beyond this boundary?', Shaftesbury asked, just like Mandeville. 'How shall we fix or ascertain a thing wholly unnatural and unreasonable, or what method, what regulation shall we set to mere imagination, or the exorbitancy of fancy, in adding expense to expense, or possession to possession?' (§ 242). The trajectory Shaftesbury described was that of human imagination becoming destructive to society when detached from its natural moorings.

The economic origin of these psychological problems was inequality. 'We see the enormous growth of luxury in capital cities, such as have been long the seat of empire', he wrote. 'We see what improvements are made in vice of every kind, where numbers of men are maintained in lazy opulence, and wanton plenty' (§ 211). The mind grows diseased when the body is inactive. The working classes, Shaftesbury emphasized, were immune to the disease. While busy producing the material foundations of modern luxury, they remained healthy and enjoyed a better and more natural 'self-system' than their masters. The pursuit of urban luxury became truly limitless when pride took hold of it. The diminishing returns of sensual pleasure could be ignored when consumption was purely for prestige. This constituted the gateway to the world of artificial affections. Under the guidance of pride, 'rest and security as to what is future, and all peace, contentedness and ease as to what is present, is forfeited by the aspiring passions of this emulous kind'. The 'appetites towards glory and outward appearance' transformed luxury into pathological envy (§ 245).

Shaftesbury despised the pride and envy that accompanied inequality as engines of civilisation. He advocated two methods of countering them. If inaction harmed man's 'animal oeconomy', the cure was a physically active life. Sports were a potent antidote to luxury. Shaftesbury proposed to repair the 'social oeconomy' by increasing the frequency of social interaction in every possible institutional setting, and by inventing institutions dedicated to sociability. He was not an apostle of politeness, for he harboured intense suspicion of 'feigned carriage', and was convinced that 'the passions thus restrained will force their prison, and in one way or other procure their liberty, and find full employment' (§ 212). Rather, he recommended a sentimental education into sociability for its joy as much as for its obvious utility (Klein 1994). This required neither rational self-denial, nor the aping of Christian virtue. The fight against luxury first and foremost required a socialising therapy, erecting a barrier against individualism and its sickening mental consequences.

In 1723, Mandeville complained that Shaftesbury's advocacy of sociability opened a 'vast inlet of hypocrisy' (Mandeville 1924, I, p. 331). In the second volume of *The Fable of the Bees*, he presented Shaftesbury's theory as an over-reaction to Hobbes's extreme hostility to sociability. To steer a middle way, Mandeville re-wrote his account of self-love, by introducing a new 'technick word', self-liking, a more neutral instinct that was the source of pride. His purpose was to undermine Shaftesbury's key idea, the direct link between pleasure and sociability. Everybody must like themselves first before liking or loving others. Self-liking, not keeping company, was nature's antidote to melancholy. The entirely natural, automatic, and incurable tendency towards the over-valuation of one's worth was as important a part of the toolkit for self-preservation as hunger and thirst. Mandeville derived politeness from self-liking. Good manners served as much to obtain happiness as to make ourselves acceptable to others. By being polite 'we assist one another in the enjoyments of life, and refining upon pleasure; and every individual person is rendered more happy by it'. Mandeville presented this insight as a great lesson of history. In 'old Greece, the Roman empire, or the great eastern nations, that flourished before them', he wrote, 'we shall find, that luxury and politeness ever grew up together . . . to obtain happiness in this world' (Mandeville 1924, II, p. 147). This train of thought led to a major addition to Mandeville's theory of luxury. He developed a theory of fashion that was not directly connected to hierarchy, competition, and envy. Fashion was the material expression of polite sociability, a means to satisfy a genuine human yearning for self-esteem by impressing others through our outward appearance. Fashion was a vehicle of one's psychological well-being, not just an expression of social ambition. It was probably the least damaging instance of insatiability that could stimulate economic growth.

5 Hutcheson

Mandeville's English opponents readily recognised his foreign sources, the notorious Continental sceptics who were the experts on the 'weak and corrupt side of human nature', like Montaigne, La Rochefoucauld, Jacques Esprit, St Evremond, and, first and foremost, Pierre Bayle. Many also surmised that the *Fable of the Bees* was an illustration of Bayle's famous society of atheists in action. Mandeville ridiculed Christianity, and Christians who defended it often disregarded the finer points of his account of luxury

(Stafford 1997). The most able and important defenders of the 'honest hive' were two of the major moral philosophers of the period, Francis Hutcheson and George Berkeley, both writing from Ireland. Hutcheson was a moderate Christian and enemy of the orthodox Presbyterians in Scotland (Moore 1990). He was implacably hostile to Mandeville, because he saw his scepticism as a de-Christianised version of the worst kind of dogmatic Calvinism (Hutcheson 1997, p. 407). He refused to approve the Salentum project in any direct fashion for similar reasons. If land was to be 'divided to all, except a few artificers to prepare instruments of husbandry', he wrote,

the whole nation must want all the pleasure arising from other arts, such as fine convenient habitations, beautiful dress, furniture, and handy utensils. There would be no knowledge of arts, no agreeable amusements or diversions; and they must all be idle one half of their time, since much of the husbandman's time is now spent in providing materials for more curious arts. (p. 392)

Modern humans, Hutcheson claimed, had too many desires. The dilemma was that neither 'universal gratification', nor 'the universal suppressing or rooting them out' was feasible (p. 391). The only way forward was to separate the wheat from the chaff. We ought to learn, wrote Hutcheson, 'as much as possible, to regulate our desires of every kind, by forming just opinions of the real value of their several objects, so as to have the strength of our desires proportioned to the real value of them, and their real moment to our happiness' (p. 391). Hutcheson, like Mandeville, distinguished between nature and nurture. Appetites (like hunger and thirst), Hutcheson argued, were instinctive and practically unstoppable. But desires, or passions, were less directly connected to the experience of pain or pleasure, and required a previous recognition of objects as potential sources of pleasure.

Stern warnings about consequences were notoriously ineffective. 'Unless just representations be given of the objects of our passions', Hutcheson claimed, 'all external arguments will be but rowing against the stream; an endless labour' (Hutcheson 1993, pp. 104–5). Humans had the innate capacity to appreciate objects by aesthetic criteria, and this could then be judged by a moral sense, a specifically human organ (conceived analogously to seeing, hearing, and tasting). Hutcheson thus rejected Mandeville's view that the distinction between the 'necessary' and the 'superfluous' had to be either ultra-minimalist or incoherent. He resuscitated the theory of 'true' or 'real' needs, but supported the idea that the standard for 'necessaries' always had to be revised upwards. He argued that spending always had to be related to place, time, and income. What he called luxury was excess beyond one's means, a pathological case of individual ruin. Thus conspicuous consumption, once an individual paid his social dues (family, charity, taxes, etc.), was not inappropriate as such. Hutcheson attacked the (Protestant) scholastics who concentrated on the *summum bonum* and other 'beatific' visions. He believed that civilisation ought to be based on honest labour and moderate (that is, pleasurable) religion. Incentives had to come from willingness to work in exchange for higher living standards. Sloth or laziness had to be condemned. The leisured utopia of 'Arcadia or unactive Golden Age', he argued, was an entirely inappropriate ideal (p. 393). Hutcheson put his faith in the division of labour as a way to increase productivity, enabling population growth. Nonetheless, he was worried about the deflationary effects of a vigorous drive against luxury. The rich were neither to overspend, nor to save too much, but to spread their income around as widely as possible (lending it out at zero interest, providing a better life for family and friends, or for the lower classes in general). Instead of drinking, workers could dress their wives better and send their children to schools. In this way the new 'necessaries' of the age would reach a much wider circle of customers more quickly. The democratisation of consumption had an important economic function. It replaced the former demand for luxury with a comparable 'consumption of manufactures, and encouragement of trade' entirely consisting of 'necessaries', obviating Mandeville's objection that the 'vicious' incentive regime based on envy and pride was a precondition of economic progress.

6 Berkeley

Berkeley, who earned Mandeville's respect as a philosopher, attacked *The Fable of the Bees* in the 'Second Dialogue' of his *Alciphron* (Berkeley 1950). He characterised Mandeville as a follower of Bayle and listed Mandeville's philosophical crimes as moral relativism (morals were mere fashion), utilitarian hedonism, and elision of the difference between men and animals ('man is a mere engine, played upon and driven about by sensible objects') (Berkeley 1950, p. 82). He accused Mandeville of promoting an anarchist theory of society, based on a bastardised version of Epicureanism ('making men wicked upon principle, a thing unknown to the ancients'), in which vice (as opposed to a balance between virtue and vice) was the sole principle of community (p. 76). Such a society was bound to be entirely amoral: 'give them riches and they will make themselves happy, without that political invention, that trick of statesmen and philosophers, called virtue' (p. 80). The reason why 'vice produceth this effect', Berkeley explained, 'is because it causeth an extravagant consumption, which is the most beneficial to the manufacturers, their encouragement consisting in a quick demand and high price' (p. 71). A system of this kind required 'exorbitant and irregular motions in the appetites and passions' that were unimaginable without vanity playing a major role (p. 76). But if morality were just a fashion, Berkeley asked, 'why the fashion of a government should not be changed as easily as that of a garment'? 'Circulation' was the central social (as well as economic) institution of an Epicurean polity. Summing up Bayle's and Mandeville's system, Berkeley wrote that 'The perpetual circulating and revolving of wealth and power, no matter through what or whose hands, is that which keeps up life and spirit in a state' (p. 77). This was libertarianism, since its basis was the principle that all we need to do was to leave 'nature at full freedom to work her own way, and all will be well' (p. 78).

Berkeley himself was a fervent supporter of economic growth, but without the vices that Mandeville so vividly described. *The Querist* (whose three parts in the first edition of 1735–7 consisted of 895 pointed questions) was unashamedly a design for an Irish Salentum (Berkeley 1970). Berkeley's transition problem differed from Fénelon's. Ireland needed to create honest wealth from scratch. Creating potent incentives for growth was imperative. Berkeley was a ferocious critic of contentedness and the Irish love of sloth (their 'cynical content in dirt', he claimed, exceeded that of 'any other people in Christendom'). However, he recognised that man's 'natural appetites' were 'limited to their respective ends and uses', and only 'artificial appetites' were 'infinite' (Q. 304). There was an urgent need for awakening an appetite 'for a reasonable standard of living' in Ireland, but without generating luxury. As Berkeley recognised, appetites for economic growth were 'largely dependent on fashion'. He recommended that in Ireland the state should seek to control it, and thus direct the 'appetite' of the people. Foreign fashion as an incentive was inappropriate for this purpose; hence Berkeley hoped to turn the Irish gentry into creators of patriotic fashion by improving the standards and ornamentation of housing, thereby serving their own pride while creating new opportunities for employment. He was worried about the implications for liberty, but consoled the Irish with the idea that 'reasonable fashions' were no 'greater restraint on freedom than those which are unreasonable' (Q. 14). He was determined to keep out of Ireland that 'capricious tyrant which usurps the place of reason' and leads men (particularly stockjobbers and projectors) 'into endless pursuits and wild labyrinths' in order to accumulate luxurious objects 'without having a proper regard to the use, or end, or nature of things' (Q. 306, 308).

Berkeley, like Fénelon, advocated agrarian and sumptuary laws (the latter he planned to copy from Switzerland, particularly Berne) (Q. 420–2). In his private correspondence he explained his project: 'Luxury seems the real original root of those evils under which we groan, avarice, ambition and corruption.' To extirpate this 'national evil' agrarian and sumptuary laws were genuinely the most 'highly expedient' instruments. 'To attempt or even mention such things now would be madness', he commented, but 'a scheme the most perfect *in futuro* may take place in idea at present'. Plato's republic was a project akin to trying 'to square the circle'. Nonetheless, 'Plato's republic may be kept in view', Berkeley wrote, 'if not for a rule, yet for an incentive.' For 'what cannot be seized at once may be grasped successively' (Berkeley 1956, p. 262). There was one more reason for Berkeley's patience, namely, that he found a modern replacement for the 'agrarian law', which miraculously also solved his Mandevillian problem of incentives. He advocated not only state-controlled fashion, but also the creation of paper money by a national bank, along the lines of the ideas of John Law, the Scotsman who became the financial wizard of France under the Regency. Despite the system's spectacular failure, Berkeley (who visited Paris during the heyday of Law's 'system') saw the creation of paper money not only as the best way to stimulate a backward economy but also as a highly practical way of gaining control over the nation's money supply, and hence the entire Irish economy. The fast circulation of paper money was also bound to undermine the entrenched economic position of the traditional system of ranks, acting as an infinitely more ruthless leveller than any legislator ever could. This amounted to harnessing Mandeville's Epicurean economy of 'circulation' for Berkeley's Platonic purposes. Hence Berkeley's quizzical but entirely serious question: 'Whether a national bank may not be the true philosopher's stone in a state' (Q. 459). If so, suddenly Salentum was a lot closer to achieving reality than ever before.

Berkeley's French contemporaries were in a more difficult situation. The idea that John Law's paper money experiment was the best, and perhaps only, option to take over the command of an entire national economy and steer it towards the path of 'honesty', remained very attractive throughout the century. But the opportune moment created by the death of Louis XIV in 1715 to change the course of France's domestic economic order with one huge radical reform had passed (Kaiser 1991). The Regency's attempt to combine John Law's imaginative nationalist monetarism with some of the key ideas of Fénelon's Salentum reforms was an extraordinary event, but it also ended in a most spectacular failure. The flare-up of the luxury controversy in France in the 1730s was a result of the re-examination of the remaining options for restoring France to greatness and economic health. A new post-mortem of Louis's regime was conducted, in order to discover the precise causes of his failures. The rehabilitation of Colbert's economic policies emerged from the insight that it was not luxury but militarism that was the cause of France's ills. Leaving behind Louis's legacy in foreign policy, however, was not a simple affair and required a sustained intellectual and political effort (Childs 2000). The problems that Louis faced continued to exist, even if his specific answers were rejected. The idea of returning France to peaceful greatness required the solving of the entire European security problem with means other than 'universal monarchy'. This, the other face of Fénelon's vision, was also powerfully expressed in the Abbé de Saint-Pierre's project for permanent European peace (Fénelon 1720; Saint-Pierre 1714). The goal was to achieve European stability not through conquest but by making France (rather than England) the arbiter of the European balance of power. A prerequisite of this project was the completion of Europe's transformation into a stable state system within which the balance of power could operate optimally. The main problem areas were Germany and Italy, seen as sources of volatility because of their anarchic geopolitical structures. France's strategic aim was to consolidate these two regions into a small number of powerful modern states. The means could be entirely peaceful, but some wanted to provide military assistance to rearrange the European political map into a more rational pattern. In the French luxury debates of the 1730s neo-Colbertism became an alternative choice not only to Salentum but also to the military route to create a stable Europe. Montesquieu's *Considerations on the Causes of the Greatness of the Romans and their Decline* (1734), Melon's *Political Essay upon Commerce* (1735), and the *Anti-Machiavel* (1740) of the future Frederick II of Prussia and Voltaire, were, in this context, powerful apologies for luxury.

7 The early Montesquieu

Montesquieu had already developed the foundations of his position on luxury by the time of his *Persian Letters* (1721), which contained a more important and systematic political theory than is generally assumed. He rejected Epicurean and Hobbesian (and hence also Mandevillian) foundations, and Fénelon and John Law as guides to policy. The groundwork was laid in his

'Tale of the Troglodytes' (Montesquieu 1973, letters 10–14). These addressed two questions: whether sensual pleasure or virtue was the more pleasurable, and whether either virtue or justice was innate to man (letter 10). The question about justice was answered explicitly, by siding with Shaftesbury's critique of Hobbes (letter 83). Justice was not artificial but 'eternal and does not depend on human conventions'. Man was sociable, and the foundation of politics was not fear. Although self-interest often trumped justice decisively, Montesquieu conceded, nonetheless we should not 'walk about among men as if they were wild lions, and . . . never be sure for a moment of our possessions, our happiness, or our lives', as Hobbes had suggested. Instead, it was most comforting 'for us to know that all these men have in their hearts an inner principle which is on our side and protects us from any action they might undertake against us' (letter 83). This position was developed in detail by the 'moral painting' of the 'Tale', which probably drew upon Joseph Addison's *Spectator* (no. 588, written by Henry Grove), which contained a modern interpretation of Cicero's opposition to the Epicurean doctrine that 'all goodness and charity are founded in weakness'. Mr Spectator opposed this reductionist attempt to explain human behaviour from one cause (selfishness), and questioned whether 'a society . . . with no other bottom, but self-love in which to maintain a commerce, could ever flourish'. Presupposing that man had two instincts, working in opposite directions, was no contradiction. The planetary system was stable while 'the diurnal rotation of the earth is opposed to its annual; or its motion round its own centre, which may be improved as an illustration of self-love, to that which whirls it about the common centre of the world, answering in universal benevolence' (Grove in Addison and Steele 1965, v, p. 12). In the 'Tale of the Troglodytes' and in the *Spirit of the Laws* Montesquieu developed the implications of this doctrine to its end.

The 'Tale' began with a picture of Hobbesian anarchy, but rejected a Hobbesian exit. Montesquieu saw pure monarchy as too difficult to establish, even by force. The opposite model was a carbon copy of Fénelon's Boetica, a society based on the positive golden rule, believing that 'individual interest is always bound to the common interest' (Richter 1977, p. 40). The third installment depicted the voluntary and democratic exit of the Troglodytes from their happy paradise of natural sociability, pressurised by population growth, and discomforted by the awakening of material desires (the beginning of luxury). Private property was established, and natural justice exchanged for liberty under positive laws. This first state was a monarchy, not a republic. The Troglodytes, though born free, were willing

to submit to a master in the hope of gaining a richer life. The tale concluded on a tragic note. Montesquieu showed the new monarch weep-
ing over the people's decision to opt for wealth over virtue. The unpublished sequel discussed the precautions the Troglodytes had taken against
absolutism and luxury (Montesquieu 1977). They wished to move from
their 'Boetica' to the honest well-being of the new 'Salentum', but no further. Private property had to be so well regulated that neither avarice nor
profusion could raise its ugly head. Inequality had to be based on merit,
never on wealth. If any of these rules were breached, the monarchy would
become corrupt, requiring the king to amass wealth to retain authority.
This would entail high taxes, which would impoverish the Troglodytes,
the opposite of what they had hoped for. The monarchy depicted in the
Spirit of the Laws was just this kind of corrupt monarchy. Montesquieu used
the planetary metaphor (changing it to a Newtonian version), to show
how honour could act as the counterbalance to *amour propre*. Such honour could be false, based on a hierarchy of wealth, so modern monarchies
indeed worked as Mandeville described them. Guided by false honour, private vices were turned into public benefits, for 'each person works for the
common good, believing he works for his individual interests' (*SL*, III.7;
p. 27).

In the *Persian Letters* Montesquieu described Paris, as Fénelon had, as
a city of luxury where the 'superfluous' became the 'necessary', where
people lived under the sway of ever-rotating fashion and accepted wealth as
the measure of social standing (Sonenscher 1998b). Both king and people
were corrupt. Nonetheless Montesquieu resolutely rejected the Salentian
option (Ehrard 1994, p. 590). Its place was in the beginning, as in the
'Tale'; trying to restore it was to court catastrophe. To retain 'only the arts
absolutely necessary for the cultivation of the earth' and to banish 'everyone
serving only luxury or fancy' from the cities was a foolish idea, leading to
serious economic decay and a loss of national independence. People in the
countryside would live at near starvation levels, the circulation of goods and
services would stop, and the reciprocal ties of society would be destroyed.
Without industrial goods state revenue would be reduced to the net yield
of agriculture, halting and even reversing population growth. Any country
attempting to recreate Salentum, Montesquieu intoned, would end up as
'one of the most wretched on earth' (letter 106). The *Persian Letters* also
completely rejected Law's 'system', not only as a fraud, but also as a mortal
danger to the nobility because of its levelling effect. Montesquieu vented
his contempt in a satire entitled a 'Fragment of an Ancient Mythologist'

(letter 142), a parody of *Telemachus*. He placed John Law's fraud in Boetica. This pairing of Law (with his Scottish bagpipe spewing out air-money) and Boetica signalled Montesquieu's clear understanding of the explosive synergy that existed between the projects of Law and Fénelon (and the Jacobites). Montesquieu was quite clear about what the only viable direction had to be. 'For a king to remain powerful', he wrote, 'his subjects must live luxuriously' (letter 106). He drew up a balance sheet of civilisation and corruption for Europe since the military revolution of the Renaissance and the discovery of America. The gains, he claimed, outweighed the losses. No great polity had ever flourished without the arts and sciences, even if their excess had destroyed many. Primitivism was not an option. The 'loss of the arts' in Europe would simply recreate the 'unhappy life' of savages, 'among whom', Montesquieu sneered, even 'a reasonably well-educated ape could live and be respected' (letter 106).

Montesquieu's book on the causes of the greatness and decline of the Romans, published thirteen years later, was a crucial contribution to the luxury debate. The clear message was that Rome's fall had been caused not by luxury, as traditional wisdom had it, but by war, over-extension, and institutional confusion. The Romans' failure was political, caused by the loss of their 'public spirit'. Montesquieu had two stories to tell. The first grew straight out of the 'Tale of the Troglodytes'. Originally Rome was a backward urban settlement, ruled by virtuous monarchs, which subsequently went through three political revolutions. The monarchy first became hereditary, then absolute. In the third revolution the people overturned the monarchy and established a republic. Their motivations were those established in the 'Tale of the Troglodytes': the desire for a materially better life. The choice was stark: 'either Rome would change its government, or it would remain a small and poor monarchy' (Montesquieu 1965, p. 26). The principle of the new republic had to be war, because this was the only way to wealth that the Romans knew. Without commerce, 'pillage was the only means individuals had of enriching themselves' (p. 27). The republic's key economic institution was the 'equal partition of land' among citizen-soldiers. Once it abandoned this institution, the republic could be described as corrupt. Human nature, the avarice of some, and the prodigality of others led to inequality. The rise of the rich changed the population of the city, filling Rome with unpatriotic artisans (and slaves), whose task (and sole livelihood) was to serve the luxury of the wealthy. The egalitarian revolution of the Gracchi, which was intended to return Rome to its first principles, failed because it came too late: 'the old morals no longer existed, since individuals had immense riches, and since riches necessarily confer power' (p. 85). It was not social friction alone that destroyed Rome. Political union, Montesquieu claimed, was sustainable despite social conflict, just as the planetary system sustained itself in a dynamic equilibrium of antagonistic forces (this was the first version of the principle of monarchy announced in the *Spirit of the Laws*) (p. 94). At this stage Rome was a society, Montesquieu wrote, 'like the one we are in' (meaning eighteenth-century Europe) (p. 40). Rome should have become a post-republican, i.e. modern, monarchy, based on luxury and inequality.

Montesquieu's second story concerned Rome's protracted decline because of its failure to adapt its republican superstructure to its new inegalitarian socio-economic base. It was the story of the corruption of the army, which lagged well behind the initial corruption of the city. Once deprived of land rights, the citizen-soldiers left the city, and retained their original Roman ethos of despising commerce and the arts. Thus Rome's 'martial virtues remained after all the others were lost', allowing it to remain a mighty war machine (p. 99). Had it stopped conquering it might have survived. But the insatiability of the luxurious capital city made wars a necessity, leading to a colossal loss of manpower, and hence to the replenishment of the Roman state from vanquished peoples. This dissolved the 'public spirit of Rome' even further: 'Roman sentiments were no more'. Rome became a fragmented multicultural entity, not a 'complete whole' (p. 93). Corruption became total when the army also caught the bug of Asiatic luxury during the Syrian wars, marking the beginning of Rome's military decline. Ever higher military remuneration required more tributary income and higher taxes, fuelling further expansion. The solution was to have cheaper soldiers, even if they were not Romans. Eventually the uninterrupted military success of the Romans under the Republic turned into an uninterrupted sequence of reverses under the Empire. The Empire was an irregular or ambiguous political body. 'Rome was really neither a monarchy nor a republic', Montesquieu wrote, 'but the head of a body formed by all the peoples of the world' (p. 75). It was a monarchy because inequality and luxury constituted its social base. It was a republic because it preserved its ferocious republican military drive. Military government, Montesquieu explained, was by its nature always 'republican rather than monarchical' (p. 152).

It was the possible recurrence of just this kind of combination of corrupt monarchy and republican militarism that frightened so many political thinkers in the eighteenth century. In the companion piece to the *Romans*, entitled *Reflection on Universal Monarchy* (typeset at the same time but never distributed), Montesquieu addressed this danger, presenting luxury or commercial growth under the auspices of a peaceful modern monarchy as the only viable alternative (Larrère and Weil 2000). He hinted at the possibility that the republic of Berne might become a new Rome. But in all other respects he declared a Roman type of universal monarchy to be both impossible and undesirable in modern Europe for geographical and 'moral' reasons. Modern European states were monarchies, based on inequality and luxury. Nonetheless, they loved their liberty and were prepared to defend themselves. Standing armies were a more effective deterrent than the militias of the past. Communication in Europe was free, surprise was difficult, and the same military ideas and technology were available to everybody. The case of Holland showed that a small mercantile nation without significant territory could use its money to become a formidable military power. But the idea of lasting military superiority over other European states was obsolete. For four hundred years, Montesquieu remarked, no nation could change Europe's political map by means of war. Europe was in flux, but only through the dynastic rearrangements of borders. To stabilise it by establishing French hegemony over Europe was, Montesquieu thought, an uncommonly stupid project. He considered this idea of armed universal pacification to be a chimera as damaging as Law's 'system' (Browning 1994, pp. 46, 71–2; Montesquieu 1914, I, p. 371, 1991, p. 477). France had no need to stoke the fire of military supremacy; economic growth was a sufficient aim. Montesquieu addressed French fears of English commercial hegemony by explaining that it was impossible for any one nation to establish a permanent advantage in trade and navigation, because the influx of money would cause prices to rise in such a country, making its artisans luxurious, and hence expensive and uncompetitive (Montesquieu 2000, pp. 341–2). Monopolists like England would fail because poorer nations would be able to undersell their products. If all the states of Europe developed luxury and commerce the Continent would be safe.

8   Melon

In his *Political Essay upon Commerce* (1735, second edition with seven added chapters in 1737) Jean François Melon followed the same line of argument as Montesquieu had in the *Romans* and *Universal Monarchy*. They belonged to the same Bordeaux coterie and shared a common analytical framework in considering France's political and economic options. By the time

Montesquieu wrote his two long essays on empire he had also written his chapter on the English constitution, which later appeared in the *Spirit of the Laws*, and had started to work on the chapters about England's commerce (completed before 1741) (Shackleton 1961, pp. 238–9). In a similar fashion, Melon offered 'the Legislator' a complete set of policies to allow France to emulate England, and even to replace it as the dominant commercial power (Larrère 1992; Meysonnier 1989). Melon's first book, a short novel vaguely in the style of the *Persian Letters*, entitled *Mahmoud le Gasnévide* (Mahmud of Ghazni), offered a parable of the choice between peaceful and military methods of achieving national greatness through the example of a Muslim emperor in Afghanistan who conquered and plundered Persia and the Punjab (Melon 1729, esp. pp. 69–72). In the *Political Essay*, he also declared that historically states followed two different kinds of policies, the spirit of conquest and the spirit of preservation. The two were incompatible (Melon 1739, p. 136). In order to offer a viable modern version of the latter Melon distinguished three models of commercial policy (pp. 1–12). First, he assumed three islands of equal territory and population, each with a single product, corn, wool, etc. Such complementary economies could barter peacefully. Next, he looked at the case of monopolistic advantage, or of trade between a completely self-sufficient island and two islands that still had only a single product. Given French perceptions of England as a rising monopolist, this was a very important case. Melon steadfastly maintained that war against a commercial monopolist was both necessary and just. 'Wool' would lose, because its product was not essential for its enemies' survival. 'Corn' as a monopolist, on the other hand, would be practically invincible. Without food no army could fight. 'Corn' (France) would then become the master of the others. Monopolistic empire, however, was not Melon's choice. He wanted all nations to become self-sufficient, at least in food. This did not preclude the possibility of competitive (rather than monopolistic) hegemony. The rise or decline of nations depended on the wisdom of their economic policy. Mistakes could make nations fall behind, while the consistent application of correct economic policies could result in superiority. Military victory over an economic super-power had only a slim chance. Such a state could enhance its lead by benefiting from the labour of economic migrants. It could also hinder the trade of its direct rivals and assist nations that did not pose a direct competitive threat. By such economic policies, the security and 'tranquillity' of such a super-state 'will become equal to her power'. This was the alternative Melon offered to universal monarchy. Luxury was its very foundation.

Melon's theory of luxury rested on a three-stages theory of economic development, proceeding from absolutely necessary goods to luxuries (Melon 1983, p. 188; cf. pp. 515, 531, 651). Agriculture enjoyed absolute precedence, for without a secure food supply a state could be neither rich nor safe. Subsequent stages were possible if there was a surplus of basic goods. A commercial system consisted of reciprocal trade forming a circular flow from one sector to the next, using money as a means of exchange. Melon advocated free trade in grain and an inflationary recoinage to eliminate food shortages and reduce French debts (pp. 13–23, 207–17). Opponents of these monetary experiments advocated sumptuary laws to improve France's balance of trade (Dutot 1739, p. 259). Melon regarded such anti-luxury policies as completely mistaken. Individual luxury posed no problem once those involved had discharged their duties to humanity. Ranting against individual excess was the mission of the church, not of political economy (Melon 1739, p. 194). But he regarded the idea of political or national luxury as muddled. 'The term luxury', he wrote, 'is an idle name, which should never be employed, in considerations on polity, and commerce: because it conveyeth uncertain, confused and false ideas' (p. 180). Agriculture was the foundation of the economy, but national power came from industry. The key to economic growth was not land, but labour. Labour output could be increased either by population growth, or by raising productivity. Melon preferred the second.

The crucial step in the history of mankind was the invention of tools enhancing man's physical strength. Tools opened up a 'progress of industry' that 'hath no bounds', by creating a virtuous circle of 'new wants' and 'new skill and industry' to satisfy them (p. 145). In the competition between nations the one that used better tools and machines had to be the winner. By 'employing fewer men' to produce the same quantity of goods, such a nation could sell them more cheaply than anybody else. The introduction of new machines could indeed cause temporary unemployment. But avoiding them (as Montesquieu advocated) was the wrong answer. Changes in fashion had similar effects on employment, but nobody tried to save fashion jobs by legislation (pp. 148–9). The answer was in the constant redeployment and redevelopment of human skills: 'the same skill that serves for one, may, with ease, be turned to another, without the legislatures having occasion to intermeddle therein' (p. 148). Melon denounced the admirers of Sparta and early Rome, just as much as ancient constitutionalist eulogies of old France under the Merovingians (singling out for ridicule the Abbé Vertot's description of the healthy and luxury-free life of old France as comparable to that of the Iroquois and the Hurons) (pp. 166–8). He ridiculed the sumptuary laws of modern republics and, with a swipe at Fénelon, he denounced the 'project to make all France live in common' as quite inapplicable to a great monarchical state (p. 181).

For Melon, 'luxury' was an adequate incentive for economic growth, if sufficiently democratic. Military government was motivated by glory. Since men could be governed only by their passions, the replacement for glory in peacetime had to be happiness. This was a perfect 'spur for the multitude', for the 'expectation of being in a condition to enjoy an easy, voluptuous life' was an incentive without negative moral effects (p. 174). The common man could afford 'luxury' only if he also worked extremely hard, benefiting both himself and the state. Luxury in the traditional sense, Melon claimed, was the affliction of those who were inactive. 'Human imagination wanteth to be fed, and when true objects are not presented to it, it formeth to its self others, according to a fancy, that is directed by pleasure, or momentary advantages' (p. 155). It was not luxury but idleness, Melon claimed, that needed countervailing legislation. It was the opportunistic pampering of Rome's proletariat (with bread and circuses) for electoral gain that caused Rome's corruption, not the introduction of the arts in the city. Melon ended up with two definitions that he hoped would change the discourse of luxury. He reformulated the relationship between the necessary and the superfluous. 'Commerce', as he defined it, was 'the permutation of what is superfluous or superabundant, for what is necessary' (p. 8). Corn was a necessity, but its surplus could be exchanged only for something less necessary, or even an item of 'luxury'. Luxury was a relative concept, both in time and space, a natural and necessary stage in the progress of the economy. It was an 'extraordinary sumptuousness, proceeding from the riches and security of a government' that was 'attendant upon every well-governed society' (p. 174).

9   Voltaire

Voltaire's most direct contribution to the luxury debate was a poem entitled *Le Mondain* ('The Worldling'), a witty satire of 128 lines in decasyllabic verse, published a year after Melon's *Essay*. It described a day in the life of an *honnête homme* (an upright man of good sense) in Paris, enjoying modern architecture, sumptuous furniture, fine paintings (Poussin and Correggio), the opera, and finally a merry dinner with friends, enlivened by the popping of champagne corks. The political message lay in Voltaire's declared preference for the 'iron age' of Louis XIV to the Salentum of 'monsieur de *Télémaque*' (Voltaire 1901a, XXXVI, p. 88). The most famous line of the poem, 'Le superflu, chose très-nécessaire' ('the superfluous, that most necessary thing') was a direct inversion of Fénelon's own definition of luxury, rejecting the distinction between real needs and mere wants (p. 84, line 22). Voltaire had previously praised Pope's *Essay on Man* (1733–4) for jettisoning the idea of 'original sin'. There never was a paradise, Voltaire asserted. Eden was a place of the most primitive barbarism. Adam and Eve's lovemaking was an animal act, driven by instinct. Voltaire made the point memorably with his witty depiction of Adam's long and dirty nails (no implement yet made to manicure them), and how they would have frustrated his effort to embrace Eve (Cronk 1999). This image developed the general argument of Voltaire's 'Anti-Pascal' (that first appeared in the 1733 edition of the *Philosophical Letters*) (McKenna 1990, pp. 837–910). In it he asserted that

to look upon the universe as a dungeon, and all mankind as criminals who are going to be executed, is the idea of a fanatic. To believe that the world is a place of delight, where one should experience nothing but pleasure, is the dream of a sybarite. To think that the earth, men, and animals are what they must be, according to the law of providence, is, I believe, the part of a wise man. (Voltaire 1961b, p. 125)

Voltaire's claim in the *Mondain* that paradise was 'here and now' was an adaptation of Pope's axiom 'whatever is, is right', borrowing the corollary of Pope's theodicy that human nature had not been corrupted and that 'man always enjoys that measure of happiness which is suited to his being'.

Following the scandal caused by *Le Mondain*, Voltaire wrote *La Défense du mondain ou l'apologie du luxe* (Defence of the Worldling or an Apology for Luxury, 1737) and sent it from his temporary exile in Holland to his follower, the crown prince of Prussia. It also described a dinner conversation, in this case with a 'rank bigot' who upbraided Voltaire for his earlier insults to religion and his praise of luxury (Voltaire 1901a, XXXVI, p. 170). Voltaire had no difficulty crushing the bigot's personal hypocrisy. The real target was his political rhetoric. *La Défense* rounded out Voltaire's 'Anti-Telemachus' by delivering a withering attack on the favourite moral conceit of the age, the alleged association between poverty, virtue, and national greatness. The key argument (repeated in Voltaire's article on 'Luxury' in his *Philosophical Dictionary*, 1764) stated that 'luxury, which destroys a state that's poor, enriches one that's great' (Voltaire 1901a, XXXVI, p. 171). Without the division of labour and extensive trade, no hypocrite could possibly enjoy a high living standard. Early Rome might have been commendably virtuous, but it was no Paris. The original Roman agricultural citizen-soldiers were ridiculous provincial rustics involved in mayhems arising from local boundary disputes. By contrast, luxury was vital for the modern economies of Britain and France, converting the follies of the rich into much needed employment for the poor. Voltaire held up Colbert as the alternative to Fénelon. 'France flourished by wise Colbert's care / that minister, as wise as great, by luxury enriched the state' (p. 173).

Voltaire concluded *La Défense* with a new kingly ideal. He offered the ancient Jewish king Solomon as the appropriate model for consummating the alliance between wealth and virtue. Solomon was 'a Plato, while he filled the throne', at the same time as his luxury 'surpassed mankind' (p. 173). This was no mere rhetorical flourish. In his poem 'To the King of Prussia on his Accession to the Throne', Voltaire reminded Frederick that he was expected to become a 'northern Solomon', to enlighten the barbarians (rather than following his father's austere militarism and turning Prussia into the Sparta of the North) (p. 81). Fénelon had advocated Salentum as second best to Boetica. Voltaire recommended the next stage in the history of the Jews; not David's kingship, but Solomon's. Fleury equally presented Solomon's monarchy as luxurious, engaged in commerce, but still reasonably just and virtuous (Fleury 1683, pp. 197–201). In his *Political Essay* Melon also used Solomon of the Jews as the example of a virtuous but commercial king. Solomon was moreover an appropriate image of Montesquieu's good king in the sequel of the Troglodytes, who warned his subjects that his authority would need to be supported by great personal wealth. In the following years Voltaire found himself in a situation similar to Fénelon's regarding *Telemachus*, supplying Frederick with the details of how to be a 'Solomon of the North' in mid-eighteenth-century Europe (Mervaud 1985). This road led to the *Anti-Machiavel* (Bahner and Bergmann 1996). As Voltaire revealed in his 'auto-review' of the book, the aim was to replace *Telemachus* as the textbook of moral politics (Voltaire 1966, pp. 497–8). Voltaire's critical triptych of the 'Anti-Pascal', the 'Anti-Fénelon', and the 'Anti-Machiavel' defined the course of politics which he wished Europe to avoid.

The aim was not to dispense with Fénelon altogether, but to detach his thought from the advocacy of Salentum. In the *Philosophical Letters* Voltaire praised the English idea of limited monarchy in terms drawn directly from *Telemachus* (Voltaire 1961b, p. 31). Fénelon's idea of patriotic and pacific kingship was derived from the example of Henry IV. Voltaire supported this entirely, as is obvious from his *Henriade* (1723), the work that made him famous (Voltaire 1965, canto VII). But material culture in Europe had moved on a great deal since Henry's time. Thus Voltaire's second hero was Colbert, the best patriotic minister of finance that France ever had. In his histories Voltaire focused firmly on the condition of the arts and sciences as the true indicator of progressive and happy epochs. In *The Age of Louis* XIV (1751) he listed four progressive periods in Europe's history. The first three were classical Athens, Rome under Augustus, and the Renaissance in Italy. The fourth was France under Louis XIV, following Richelieu's founding of the French Academy in 1632 (Voltaire 1966, pp. 122–4; Pocock 1999–2003, I, pp. 84–7). Such flourishing would have been impossible if Colbert, despite the huge waste of Louis XIV's wars, had not provided the arts and sciences with the necessary economic support. This was the cornerstone of Voltaire's judgement of modern French luxury.

Voltaire agreed with Melon that the term 'luxury' was redundant. 'It is a word without any precise idea', he wrote, just as 'when we say the eastern and western hemispheres: in fact, there is no such thing as east and west; there is no fixed point where the earth rises and sets; or if you will, every point on it is at the same time east and west'. Either there was 'no such thing' as luxury, 'or else it is in all places alike' (Voltaire 1901b, p. 216). Voltaire also endorsed Melon's emphasis on industry and productivity. It was a mistake to see Colbert's time as one of economic decline, as Boisguilbert and other critics of Louis XIV had claimed. Looking at 'all the commodities and refinements which go by the name of luxuries, one would think that France is twenty times as rich as formerly' he wrote. But France did not have twenty times the revenue. The new wealth was the product of economic growth, the 'fruit of ingenious labour' and of 'the creative activity of the nation'. A house of Henry IV's time, he pointed out, was miserable compared to what the eighteenth century could build for only slightly more money (Voltaire 1966, p. 161). The apparent luxury of the modern age stemmed from the availability to the urban middle classes of hitherto exclusively aristocratic goods, at much lower prices than before. Voltaire's was an uncompromisingly modern and self-consciously bourgeois position. He dismissed the agrarian criticism of luxury as the hobbyhorse of a disaffected political opposition.

The *Anti-Machiavel* also criticised the spirit of conquest. Fénelon thought that banning luxury could dampen the desire for war. The *Anti-Machiavel* argued the opposite: 'If it occurred to some incompetent politician to banish luxury from a great state, that state would begin to languish' and would upset the balance of power, sowing the seeds of future war (Voltaire and Frederick 1981, p. 104). Voltaire and Frederick wanted to replace external territorial aggrandisement with domestic economic growth, which was 'more innocent, more just, and just as useful as the first' (p. 133). Modern states were not weakened but strengthened militarily by their 'luxury', which enabled them to wield up-to-date military technology and large standing armies. No state could hope for a lasting dominance over others. Republics were irrelevant, because they were small. As Voltaire suggested to Frederick, the task of the eighteenth century was to expel the shadow of Machiavelli from modern international politics (Tuck 1999). Adopting the policy of luxury (instead of conquest) as modern reason of state, and cleansing it of its imprecise, but clearly unsavoury, moral connotations was the key to the establishment of modern Europe. Its application required not heroic but 'practical virtue', since its principles were 'applicable to all the governments of Europe' (Voltaire and Frederick 1996, p. 498). The idea of a European commonwealth was the child of this redefinition of luxury. This message of the *Anti-Machiavel* must not be clouded by Frederick's subsequent record on war and peace. In the short term Frederick also learned from the French, from the Marquis d'Argenson and the Abbé de Saint-Pierre. Their view, that the anarchy of Germany had to be rectified before the modern European state system could become workable, Voltaire warmly recommended to Frederick (d'Argenson and Saint-Pierre 1737; Browning 1994, pp. 191–2, 199–202; Henry 1968). Nobody, and particularly not the French, recommended a wholly unified Germany, for, as Hume remarked, such a state would soon have become the master of Europe (Hume 1932, I, p. 126). Frederick surmised that France was keen on weakening Austria's stranglehold over the Holy Roman Empire and assisting Prussia to set out on the road to peace and prosperity. When Voltaire subsequently visited Frederick he discovered that it was in fact the message about luxury that Frederick initially neglected. Instead of becoming a new Solomon, Frederick became an austere patriot king, committed to the stamping out of all 'unregulated' luxury (Gay 1959).

Voltaire's *Traité de métaphysique* (Treatise on Metaphysics, 1734), particularly its concluding chapters on sociability and on the distinction between virtue and vice, supplied the moral theory for the politics of luxury he offered to Frederick before he wrote the *Anti-Machiavel* (Barber 1989; Edwards 1989, pp. 46–50). This is the only case where Mandeville's influence can be detected. Voltaire's lover, Emilie du Châtelet, made an attempt to translate *The Fable of the Bees*, and her amendments to Mandeville's text have parallels in the draft of Voltaire's *Traité* (Du Châtelet 1947; Wade 1947, pp. 22–114; Zinsser 2002). Nevertheless, on moral foundations even Voltaire took a middle position between Shaftesbury's line and Mandeville's (Aldridge 1975).

He rejected Mandeville's contention that pity was a purely selfish sentiment, and admitted to natural human goodness, even if he declared it significantly weaker than the selfish passions. On politics, however, Voltaire was more clearly with Bayle and Mandeville. Dismissing the passions as mere residues of the Fall, Voltaire thought, was mad. Eliminating them was no wiser than trying to prevent a heart attack by stopping the circulation of one's blood. Every game needed rules, thus society had laws. Conformity with the laws was 'virtue', breaking them was 'crime'. Clever men had discovered that selfish humans could be lured into contributing to common welfare if their pride was rewarded through flattery. There were four vices that could be exploited to create a system of luxury. First, pride could be converted into the desire to appear moral and sociable by dividing the population into two classes; the 'moral' or 'virtuous' class and the 'selfish' class. In the mad scramble for status even the most selfish would be happy to counterfeit morality in order to gain standing. Second, the desire for domination could be channelled into a clever deal, whereby ambitious men could talk the majority into accepting their leadership skills by pretending that all gained equally from the deal. Third, greed, 'the frantic acquisition of worldly goods', was a tool perfectly suited for generating social stability, as well as a 'daily improvement in all skills'. Fourth, envy, disguised as the spirit of competition, could make the incentive of greed permanent, so that the economy and public order remained stable even in the long run. It was the envy of our neighbours, rather than our love of them, that drove nations to extract more and more from the global resources available to mankind (Voltaire 1989b, pp. 90–2).

This was the moral world that Fénelon had tried to leave behind, but which Voltaire showed Frederick lay behind God's natural law (Voltaire 1989b, pp. 208–10). Voltaire's response to the alleged 'corruption of the people' was to re-describe luxury as the flourishing of the arts and sciences. Hume, facing the same dilemma, changed the title of his 1752 essay 'Of Luxury' into 'Of Refinement in the Arts' by 1760. Montesquieu's *Spirit of the Laws* inaugurated the second phase of the eighteenth-century luxury debate in 1748, by providing a spectacularly thorough and provocative analysis of luxury. Rousseau's *Discourse on the Origin of Inequality* of 1755 tried to prove, on the other hand, that the revolution against luxury that Fénelon predicted was inevitable despite Montesquieu's best efforts. Adam Smith, reviewing Rousseau, found the Genevan's essay perplexing. It was derived, Smith claimed, from volume II of the *Fable of the Bees*. But Rousseau, unlike Mandeville, wrote in a 'studiously elegant', and even 'sublime' style. 'It is by the help of this style, together with a little philosophical chemistry, that the principles and ideas of the profligate Mandeville seem in him to have all the purity and sublimity of the morals of Plato, and to be only the true spirit of a republican carried a little too far' (Smith 1980, p. 251). If Mandeville could be disguised as Plato by mere rhetoric, Smith recognised, then the issue of 'luxury' genuinely and urgently needed to be sorted out. No moral and political thinker worth his salt between Rousseau and the French Revolution failed to comment on luxury, by trying to advance either Fénelon's or Mandeville's side of the argument. In 1776 the *Wealth of Nations* announced that physiocracy in France was an over-reaction to the excesses of Colbert and his heirs, but also that Colbert's ideas with all their shortcomings suited modern Europe better than the grand economic reform against 'unproductive labour' promoted by the 'agricultural system' (*WN*, IV.ix 4; 50; Hont 1989, 2005). Connoisseurs of the luxury debate understood the context of Smith's political and moral message perfectly well.

14

Physiocracy and the politics of *laissez-faire*

T. J. HOCHSTRASSER

1 Physiocracy in its historical, intellectual, and political setting

Physiocracy, or 'rule of nature', was a largely, but not exclusively, French movement in political economy that prioritised agricultural productivity over manufacturing as the source of economic growth, and sought to move on from that analysis to provide a fresh model of the fiscal and administrative relationships that should operate between royal governments and the owners of property broadly defined.[1] It exercised intermittent influence on French administrations between the 1760s and 1780s and furthermore attracted vehement supporters and opponents outside France, especially in Italy and Spain, but also as far afield as the United States and Bengal.

However, physiocracy has not habitually been associated with innovative political theory, or indeed with any coherent political theory at all. From the days of early commentators such as the Abbé Galiani, Adam Smith, and, later, Jean Baptiste Say, it became conventional to argue that French physiocracy was mistaken in its economics and inept in its politics, partial in its understanding of the mechanisms of wealth creation, and ineffective in making its case before both the tribunal of emerging French public opinion and across the shoals of court politics. The first part of this condemnation, though not perhaps the most important in the eyes of contemporaries, has been conventionally turned into a textbook account, conveniently summarised by Robert Heilbroner in the following terms:

The trouble with physiocracy was that it insisted that only the agricultural classes produced true 'wealth' and that the manufacturing and commercial classes merely manipulated it in a sterile way. Hence Quesnay's system had but limited usefulness for practical policy. True it advocated a policy of laissez-faire – a radical departure for the times. But

---

1 For useful surveys that shed light on multiple aspects of French political economy in the eighteenth century see Fox-Genovese 1976; Kaplan 1976; Larrère 1992; McNally 1988; Perrot 1992; Steiner 1998; and Whatmore 2000a.

in denigrating the industrial side of life it flew against the sense of history, for the whole development of capitalism unmistakeably pointed to the emergence of the industrial classes to a position of superiority over the landed classes. (Heilbroner 1961, p. 42)

While this viewpoint is fairly familiar to us, though its detailed intellectual ancestry through Say and Smith may not be, it is not an accurate account of what Smith, at least, argued on this subject. In fact his position was much more generous, giving us a clearer sense already of why he originally proposed to dedicate *The Wealth of Nations* to Quesnay:

This system, however, with all its imperfections is, perhaps, the nearest approximation to the truth that has yet been published upon the subject of political oeconomy ... Though in representing the labour which is employed upon the land as the only productive labour, the notions which it inculcates are perhaps too narrow and confined; yet in representing the wealth of nations as consisting, not in the unconsumable riches of money, but in the consumable goods annually reproduced by the labour of the society; and in representing perfect liberty as the only effectual expedient for rendering this annual reproduction the greatest possible, its doctrine seems to be in every respect as just as it is generous and liberal. (*WN*, iv.ix.38)

When one recalls that Smith's direct dealings were exclusively with Quesnay and Mirabeau, and not Le Mercier de la Rivière, Turgot, Du Pont de Nemours, the Abbé Baudeau, or Guillaume Le Trosne – the distinctive second 'wave' of physiocratic thinkers, who were somewhat more sympathetic to the creative economic role of manufacturing and commerce – then further grounds for scepticism over the traditional 'economic' reading of physiocracy emerge.

Readings of the politics of physiocracy have been equally distorted, although for different reasons. The alleged political failure of physiocracy is conventionally assigned to the 1760s, to the initial failure to sustain grain liberalisation under Controller-Generals Bertin and Laverdy, and then to the collapse of the ministry of Turgot in 1776. But this interpretation has been based on a series of misinterpretations of what physiocracy intended in the political sphere, above all what it meant by 'legal despotism'; also omitted is a later intellectual contribution to the creation of fresh institutional and representative structures that would link the holders of land to the crown in a new fiscal and political relationship. This initiative was just beginning to bear fruit before the onset of the Revolution in the form of the experimental provincial assemblies (in part a physiocratic measure which Necker co-opted for his own purposes). In fact physiocracy bred a lively debate around the specifically political works written by the second generation of *économistes* listed above, and it needs to be regarded as part both of a creative reaction in the wake of France's crushing defeat in the Seven Years War and the general emergence among the administrative elite of a demand for a root-and-branch reappraisal of French political structures, in which the economics of physiocracy was only the starting point (Whatmore 2000a, pp. 46–56).

This summary in fact highlights what has become a central feature of recent research – namely the need to consider physiocracy as an evolving movement of distinct phases rather than as a uniform entity. In this regard its original proponents were often their own worst enemies; for, like later nineteenth-century 'scientific' socialists, they claimed a seamless immaculate precision for their system, and sought to explain its changing priorities and emphases through elaborations of detail and claims of derivation that were misleading. As a result of this static model many historians have overlooked the daring way in which physiocracy used the new impetus provided by defeat in the 1760s, and the failure of its own initial efforts to liberalise the grain trade, as a stimulus to further political enquiry. In fact physiocracy made a virtue out of necessity, and diverted its intellectual energies into developing a model of rational administration and qualified absolutist government that would provide the necessary framework for entrenching the new relationship between property holders and the crown, which it saw as the essential prerequisite to the implementation of the economic policies that had been rejected by the timorous governments of the early 1760s.

There is no opportunity here to explain the complex historiography that led to this blurring of the true contours of physiocratic political ideas and their impact, but one of the most significant contributors to this outcome was surely Tocqueville in *The Old Regime and the French Revolution* (1856). There is simultaneously in his commentary both much perceptive analysis of the later physiocrats, based on close reading of their works, and, alongside, a flawed overall attempt to assimilate their ideas to those of the revolutionaries, especially in what he calls the physiocratic denial of 'public freedom':

Thus it was not a question of destroying absolute power but of converting it . . . They did not merely count on the royal administration to reform the society of their own day; they borrowed from it, in part, the idea of a future government which they wanted to found. It was in looking at the one that they made themselves a picture of the other. The state, according to the physiocrats, was not only to rule the nation but to shape it in a certain way; it was for the state to form the citizen's mind according to a particular model set out in advance . . . In reality, there were no limits to its rights, nor bounds to what it might do; it not only reformed men, it transformed them . . . 'The state makes men whatever it wants', says Bodeau. This phrase sums up all their theories. (Tocqueville 1998–2001, I, p. 212)

After steeping himself during his researches in the papers of some of the leading physiocrats and the *intendants* who had sympathised with them, Tocqueville was very much alive to the sense in which the administration and those who staffed it provided the crucial mindset, with key strengths and weaknesses, for the development of a political theory based on a strong executive. But what is totally missing here is an account of 'legal despotism', a nuanced political theory, rather than a narrowly statist ideology, which sought to place new, unconventional restraints upon absolutism by arguing that the dangers of a robust executive could be qualified by a doctrine of judicial control and the power of public education expressed as opinion on the one hand, and the creation of a network of provincial assemblies that could link power and property in a new and mutually cohesive relationship on the other. It is the development and outline contours of that theory that it is most necessary to set out here.

While the physiocrats often presented themselves as a self-contained sect, owing little to contemporary work in political economy, in fact their contribution was deeply indebted both to discussions within France in the decades since the collapse of John Law's Mississippi Company, and to the example of England, seen as both an economic phenomenon and as a source of original work in political economy. Indeed, at the most obvious level, it needs to be noted that the key watchword 'laissez-faire, laissez-passer' originated not with any of the physiocrats, but with Vincent de Gournay, appointed *intendant de commerce* in 1751. Debates on the social effects of luxury, on how best to increase agricultural productivity, on the pricing and exporting of grain, and on redistributing the fiscal burden were underway, and had already broken the mould of mercantilist orthodoxy and initiated a wide-ranging attack on existing economic regulation and restriction. A brief examination of the work of three of the predecessors of physiocracy, Pierre Boisguilbert, Jean François Melon, and Richard Cantillon may indicate some of its foundations more clearly (Larrère 1992).

In reaction to the mercantilist policies of Louis XIV's minister Colbert, Boisguilbert had proposed in his *A Detailed Account of France* (1695) that it was the first duty of the state to promote agriculture ahead of manufacturing and commerce. This was not simply to argue for the priority of agriculture; instead he suggested that national wealth was more appropriately measured through agricultural export than by the influx of bullion. From this it followed that a free trade in grain should be adopted to allow agriculture to fulfil its role in wealth creation, and taxes should be equalised between town and country in the form of a poll tax. There is already here a sense of how free trade, grain liberalisation, and fiscal reform are intimately linked. For Melon, the basic focus on increasing the fertility of land and the size of the population were similar, but his *Political Essay on Commerce* (1734) went further in arguing against the old moral assumptions of mercantilism. From a toned-down Mandevillian perspective he offered an endorsement of luxury and free trade that significantly influenced many of the major figures of the French Enlightenment, notably Voltaire. But the key step towards the physiocratic synthesis was made by Richard Cantillon's *Essay on the Nature of Commerce in General* (1755), which gave a convincing account for the first time of why free markets offered a better and more secure outcome than traditional regulation (Murphy 1986).

Building on the theoretical insights of the late seventeenth-century English 'political arithmetician' William Petty about the nature of economic values, Cantillon gave more precision to the foundational economic position of agriculture by suggesting that the whole of society outside agriculture was dependent on the latter's surplus or 'overplus' for its survival, for without the spending of agricultural profits by landowners as well as the production of essential consumables the rest of society could not survive. From this there followed a number of conclusions: first, that landowners were the only true independent citizens (a view that would have a long trajectory in French debates down to the later provincial assemblies of the 1780s); secondly, that large-scale agriculture run on entrepreneurial lines, in imitation of English practice, was the best model for economic growth; and, thirdly, that there was a circular flow of wealth between different productive sectors based on the 'rents' earned by the farmer, a model which anticipates the key insights of Quesnay's famous *Tableau économique* (McNally 1988, p. 97).

While these contemporary writings provide the more immediate context for physiocracy, the study of and conflict with England in the mid-eighteenth century offer a more general backdrop against which the priorities of Quesnay and Mirabeau may be assessed. While it was England's constitutional and religious structures that had most interested Voltaire and Montesquieu in the 1720s, the emphasis shifted in later decades towards English agricultural improvement, now seen by French observers as the key factor in explaining that country's increasing imperial ascendancy. Writers such as Henry Patullo and Duhamel de Monceau had recommended practical measures such as crop rotation and enclosure on English models, but by the 1760s the theoretical writings of Locke, Child, and Davenant became better known, as also the recent contributions of Hume and Tucker. Thus in the wake of France's defeat in 1763 a range of possible responses and choices were available which covered the gamut of contemporary political economy: arguments were at hand to suggest either that France should seek to imitate Britain's foreign commerce and structures of public credit, or to urge a prior reform of French governmental structures to push French institutions in an English direction, or (finally) that *moeurs* and institutions operated so differently that a separate path altogether would have to be taken (Whatmore 2000a, p. 46). It was against this background that Quesnay proposed his crucial distinction between 'agricultural' and 'commercial' nations, which associated France with the former and inevitably placed greater weight on ensuring sustained investment in agriculture than on the riskier priorities of overseas commerce and state-managed instruments of credit.

Yet whatever view was taken of the best options for France in the 1760s, it was apparent to contemporaries (in a way it has not been to later historians of economic and political thought) that French theorists would have to concern themselves fundamentally with the role of the state, as much as with pure economics, to produce a political economy that balanced both halves of that equation. For there were two issues above all – tax and the grain trade, both already embedded in the pre-existing debates – which were essentially political in nature, and where any radical changes involved in turn concomitant far-reaching changes in the political theory on which the French political order was based. This meant that physiocracy would necessarily be an inherently political doctrine as much as a narrow and technical economic one.

On taxation, all of the available views carried with them vast political implications. There were those who followed the line recently articulated by Michael Mann in the following terms: 'In a pre-industrial society . . . it is not easy even to assess where landed wealth is, let alone extract it. The profits of trade are visible – they move. Hence the motto of almost all agrarian states: "If it moves, tax it!"' (Mann 1986–93, I, pp. 478–9). On this basis the effort involved in the kind of detailed cadastral survey required to ensure an accurate tax on land (such as Turgot attempted, for example, during his period as *intendant* of the Limousin) was never going to pay off. But on the other hand, with relatively few ports, an inadequate bureaucracy to manage collection of indirect taxes, and a highly disadvantageous jig-saw of internal tariff regulation, pursuit of movable goods within and outside France hardly seemed the solution either. Thus, even before physiocracy's inception the focus had turned back to ways of fine-tuning the disproportionate tax burden that fell most heavily on the rural producers (often the smallest ones too), so that the state could finance itself without sapping the strength of what was now perceived to be the most productive sector of the economy.

That in turn inevitably put the spotlight on the state's management of the grain trade, where government controls on price and movement reflected the old concept of *police* by which the state had a moral duty to take steps to avoid famines in times of crop shortfalls. The existing situation was open to criticism on a number of counts: first, and most obviously, because famines and shortages still took place at regular intervals in the eighteenth century despite regulation; and, secondly, because of an increasing sense that the government's concern with consumers rather than potentially dynamic producers was inhibiting economic growth for all. Even Forbonnais, later an arch-critic of the *économistes*, took the view that the government was in danger of crushing producers without actually assisting indigent consumers effectively. Surely there was little to be gained by preferring a mercantilist morality to the emerging consensus that agricultural productivity should be given its head? The crucial issue here was whether to sanction *foreign* export of grain by home producers, because this was the area in which market-profits could most effectively be maximised by free trade. Yet for this to work, the state had to hold its nerve when crops failed, and not reverse its policy. Once again we find that the initiative of the state rather than a capitalist class or order is absolutely central to the implementation and testing of economic theory, and it was therefore essential for the early physiocrats to produce a theory that not only reaffirmed the emerging economic consensus in favour of deregulation, but also provided a view of the moral role of government that could combat and supplant the old and still powerful moralising assumptions.

2   The development of physiocracy: from Quesnay to Turgot

François Quesnay was originally trained as a surgeon, before becoming Madame de Pompadour's personal doctor, and then medical adviser to Louis XV himself. He was a leading figure in contemporary salons in Paris and Versailles, where he recruited a series of gifted pupils and followers, who then acted as spokesmen and interpreters of his ideas. He published under his own name only a series of articles, though these were of fundamental importance to the later development of the ideas of the *économistes* as a whole. A sequence of pieces published in the *Encyclopédie* in 1756–7 ('Evidence', 'Fermiers', and 'Grains') established the leading themes of physiocratic economics, which were then consolidated within the famous zigzag of the *Tableau économique*, three versions of which were produced in 1758–9. At the same time he engaged the help of the marquis de Mirabeau, on the strength of his recent work *L'Ami des Hommes*, which had attempted to extrapolate the implications of Cantillon's *Essay*. They then worked together on three projects: an unpublished treatise on monarchy, and two works published under Mirabeau's name: a theory of taxation and *Rural Philosophy* (1763), which extended the reach of physiocracy into social and political life, making deft use of Mirabeau's rhetorical skills.

At this point they were joined by a group of younger, enthusiastic followers, and Quesnay repeated his earlier collaborative strategy, but this time applied more directly to political thought. He assisted Le Mercier de La Rivière between 1765 and 1767 in assembling a large work of purely abstract political and fiscal theory, *The Natural and Essential Order of Political Societies* (1767), which appeared alongside supporting articles on the political systems of Peru and China, this time under Quesnay's name alone. It was this *oeuvre* that expounded in detail the meaning of the term 'legal despotism'. At the same time Du Pont de Nemours began a long career as an indefatigable propagandist on behalf of physiocracy with a short summary of the school's doctrine, which used the familiar name for the first time: *Physiocratie* (1767–8). Not least, in terms of gaining wider public attention, the Abbé Baudeau's journal, *Les Ephémérides du citoyen*, provided a home for detailed exploration and debate of themes insufficiently treated so far, notably in the form of Turgot's most distinguished economic writings (Weulersse 1910).

The latter years of the 1760s represented the highest point of visibility for physiocracy as a movement in France and beyond. The Choiseul ministry was broadly sympathetic to its programme, and within the Enlightenment as a whole there were signs of acknowledgement that Quesnay and his followers might have formulated both a model for economic growth and a political model from which legal codification could proceed. For example, both Le Mercier and another expert on French administration, Le Trosne, were asked to participate in the discussions over Catherine II's proposed new code in Russia. However, this enthusiasm was short-lived, and undermined above all by two events: the return of famine conditions in 1769–70, which sapped public and government confidence in the policy of grain-trade liberalisation, and an intellectual demolition by the Abbé Galiani in his *Dialogues on the Grain Trade* (1770). Galiani exposed very effectively the tensions within physiocracy's social model between equality of individuals before the law and a retained social hierarchy still based on massive inequality of property holding. For Galiani, this undermined the crucial case (alluded to above) for grain to be considered 'an object of commerce' rather than, as traditionally held, 'an object of administration' (McNally 1988, p. 131). It was the reality of dearth, and the failure to make a new moral case on behalf of physiocracy's theories that persuaded key leaders of the Enlightenment in France, notably Diderot and Voltaire, to side with Galiani and against the physiocrats (Minerbi 1973).

The same issues arose in the ill-fated ministry of Turgot between 1774 and 1776, even though ideologically Louis XVI's first controller-general was far less dogmatic in his approach to reform than Quesnay's tightly knit circle of followers had been, and rather less wedded to a view of the economy that preferred agriculture to manufacturing. Once more a coalition of conservative secular and religious groups was able to join forces with popular concerns that the well-being of the population was being subjected to profiteering and pursuit of the abstract principles of political economy (Weulersse 1950). In part, what physiocracy had failed to take into account was that the strength of the old notion of political economy lay in its collusive organised hypocrisy. Though the needs of the indigent were real, the mind-set of contractors and consumers in the matter of grain combined a set of cheerfully sustained contradictions: between competitive entrepreneurship at the expense of others and a clamour for free trade, and alongside this an equally insistent demand for the retention of particular privileges, so that speculation could be cushioned by the government in case of harvest failure. This inconsistency and hypocrisy was typical of many who had to work through eighteenth-century French institutions, and the inevitable consequence of a clientage-system from which the government could not find a way to cut itself free. While the failure of the physiocrats' policies in the 'flour wars' were complete, they deserved credit for having recognised the centrality of these issues not just to political economy but also to the reform of the parasitism that was increasingly paralysing French government processes by the mid-eighteenth century.

Yet physiocracy had also brought this outcome on itself: for, despite its rhetoric in favour of shaping public opinion and a stated determination to promote public welfare, it failed to make an effective case to a wider public which was inevitably more engrossed in the consequences of changes in the organisation of the grain trade than in the details of a new system of political economy. In the many pamphlets generated by the so-called 'grain wars' two points emerged to which physiocracy never offered more than a theoretical response: first, it seemed something of a reckless gamble to put the welfare

427

of the needy at the mercy of future economic growth which could be derailed by a succession of poor harvests; and, secondly, even if this gamble could be justified, there was still concern that the largest property owners in France would be unduly rewarded, leaving little comfort or prospect of participation, economic or political, for the mass of smallholders who constituted the majority of French farmers.

This conundrum went to the heart of the shared assumptions of the French political, intellectual, and administrative elites as well as of the physiocrats themselves, and, to be fair to them, Galiani's critique offered no real answers either. To that extent it is right to regard the 'grain wars' as not merely a crisis for physiocracy, but 'a crisis of the Enlightenment as well' (Kaplan 1976, II, p. 610). What was doubly unfortunate, however, was that physiocracy did in fact have a concept of social and redistributive justice built into its system, but was never really able to articulate it in an accessible form.

Part of the problem was that 'the physiocrats were as much instruments of power as critics of it', which is true in two distinct senses (Jones 2002, p. 220). First, it was the case that physiocracy's rapid rise to influence in public policy was grounded as much in its excellent connections – at court, in the central administration, and among local *intendants* – as in the support of the *philosophes* or at the tribunal of public opinion. Many of the physiocrats themselves had first-hand experience of wielding power at different levels of authority, and therefore could write with inside knowledge about the complex relations between the centre and localities that lay at the heart of opaque yet important discussions of fiscal reform. But this was a weakness too; for it meant that they never fully mastered the task of talking to an audience beyond their own circle, of devising a rhetoric to explain the morality as well as the general profit that might be derived from their system. The appeal of physiocracy to its putative public opinion therefore remained more instrumental than visionary: it indeed offered the prospect of a recovery of France's international reputation and domestic prosperity with a minimum of social dislocation and administrative reordering; but more was required than the declaration through public education of the 'evidence' that endorsed the physiocratic 'natural order' if the real fears of famine conditions and associated social dislocation were to be addressed. Physiocracy always remained too much of an ideology for the experts.

Secondly, if we look forward to the continuing influence of physiocracy beyond Turgot and into the pre-revolutionary era, the period which in some ways is still most interesting and least studied, then again we see the *économistes* both remaining uneasily within the political establishment and criticising it from without. Du Pont, Le Mercier, and Baudeau accepted Necker's patronage, while continuously objecting to his measures. They assisted in his schemes for experimental local assemblies while complaining that the end-products were prevented from growing beyond mere consultative bodies. Physiocratic political theory gives out confusing signals at this point: it appears to centralise power under legal despotism, and it then decentralises it again through the creation of assemblies of the propertied. There is continuity between the two views, but this is never articulated as fully or as clearly as it might be: in fact sovereignty remained undiluted in the monarch, whereas administration was now to be largely handed over to new local authorities. Economies of scale were to be achieved without the dilution of absolute power. A further note of complexity is added, however, when the functions of the assemblies change quite sharply as we move into the later phase of physiocracy, dominated by Turgot and Condorcet, where the role of administration shades, as Keith Baker has noted, into 'social representation' (Baker 1990, pp. 238–43). Thus these forms of partial representation finally attain a political value in their own right, and are not (as in Mirabeau) simply a recognition of the local status as well as the economic dominance of the propertied landlord (Jones 1995, pp. 25–49).

3 From wealth creation to legal despotism

Let us now move from the specific engagements of physiocracy with politics to examine some of its core concepts in greater detail. While there is still scholarly dispute as to the precise degree to which Quesnay was indebted to natural law theory or vitalism, to Descartes or to Malebranche, for the inspiration of his system, the key aspects of his political economy are clearly articulated by the later 1750s (Sonenscher 2002). In his articles written for the *Encyclopédie*, Quesnay sets out clearly his social and political priorities: he wants to return the attention of governments to fostering the position of those who create wealth in society – pre-eminently farmers – because they are the most likely and reliable sources of state income. Unlike commerce and manufacturing, where productive outcomes are much more uncertain, and revenue possibilities weaker, agriculture meets basic needs, fosters population growth, and is amenable to taxation.

Moreover, if governments encourage farmers' efforts at wealth creation, then that wealth will itself be used – in the form of a proportion of the farmer's profit and the landlord's rent – to increase future crop yields and encourage further employment. The state should do all it can to increase demand in agriculture while discouraging spending on luxuries and manufactured goods. Behind this assertion lies a distinction between states whose primary resources lie in agriculture, and those lacking the capacity to produce a reliable agricultural surplus, which perforce must focus on trade to survive. Those states in the former category – such as France – should not try to emulate those in the latter, for that would be to risk a failure on both counts. Instead the French government should do all in its power to increase spending on agricultural products. Quesnay believes that this is a moral case too, for everyone benefits from the results:

> It must also be noted that all the kingdom's inhabitants should profit from the advantages afforded by proper cultivation, if the latter is to be maintained and made capable of producing a large revenue for the sovereign. It is by increasing the revenue of the proprietors and the profit of the farmers that it procures gains for all the other classes and supports a consumption and expenditure by which it is in turn maintained. (Quesnay 1962, p. 82)

Yet we should note that Quesnay's concerns, driven ultimately by his determination to overhaul and secure stable state revenues, lie first and foremost with the producers of wealth: he is clear that only large-scale capitalist farming will actually produce the substantial yields needed for significant economic growth; there is little scope within his proposals for the small-scale farmer or the peasant smallholder who would be best advised, on this analysis, to sell up and become a wage labourer. Part of the difficulty in convincing public opinion of the wider social benefits of physiocracy lay not merely in the rhetorical and presentational weaknesses which we have noted, but also in an embedded commitment to the creative role of one group in society, which was foundational in Quesnay at least. Though all in the wider economy could benefit from the successes of agricultural capitalism, the casualties of economies of scale within agriculture itself were not sufficiently examined – another point which Galiani and other critics were quick to make.

Finally, these early writings show how Quesnay also wishes to increase the liberty of the individual within the new economic order that he is proposing. It is evident that he regards human beings as primarily motivated by self-interest, which was imperfectly reflected in the pattern of rights currently available to them in society. He supports the need for free trade and a retreat from price-fixing in all states if the surplus of producers is to be enhanced, and shows no support for traditional restrictive practices. He is no friend to feudal, guild, or aristocratic privilege as such, and offers a justification of monarchy and social hierarchy that is functionally based on property holding, while also suggesting that monarchy's role lies above all in binding together sectional interests that would otherwise contend with one another. Many of these positions are simply asserted, rather than demonstrated: this was partly a matter of the format within which he was writing, but also – and more significantly – was in line with the argument of his earliest article 'Evidence', which held that once the natural order of economy and society had been revealed in a set of linked propositions that were self-evidently true, then public opinion would automatically fall in line with the physiocratic agenda. This confident assumption proved over-optimistic.

In the famous *Tableau économique*, Quesnay 'presented a model of the economy as a self-reproducing system, as an organic totality which creates and recreates itself' (McNally 1988, p. 110). This represented in diagrammatic form the central physiocratic thesis: once the internal flows of the economy are understood the state will gain a proper sense of the wealth of the kingdom, how it should be administered, and how taxes should best be extracted. The *Tableau* is not an end in itself but a prelude to a fresh analysis of the infrastructure and constitution of an agricultural nation, genuinely uniting the political and the economic. Once this is recognised, a number of its more curious features seem less bizarre: Quesnay's account does not dismiss the fruits of manufacturing out of hand; his point is more that the wealth it does produce is not of the kind that can be useful to and harnessed by a government, in the way that agricultural surplus can. It is this last link, demonstrated in the *Tableau*, that justifies the state's claim to be 'co-proprietor' of land with landowners, and evokes the critical importance of re-calibrating taxation so that it targets landowners rather than the farmers themselves (McNally 1988, pp. 118–19).

Important implications about the proper shape of the French state are revealed here. Quesnay believes that while society as a whole should allow for the free play of individual interests, the government's task must be that of reconciling and if necessary enforcing a common purpose, and this can only be done through an undivided sovereign. This sovereign needed, para-doxically, to be absolute to be effective, and yet also minimal in intervention so as to allow the economic machine to run unimpeded. The task of the sovereign was to clear away the present obstacles to free and unrestricted economic activity, while remaining on hand, rather like the deist concep-tion of God, to intervene in the disputes that were bound to arise among the contending self-interested factions, newly empowered within the state. Here in essence is the concept of 'legal despotism'.

It follows that the physiocratic political theory of this period can find little room for either feudal survivals or republican elements in its formulas. If the role of the state was to find and maintain the general interest when all other social groups were attempting to assert their particular interests, then a variety of partial associations could hold small appeal. Neither *parlements* nor traditional Estates offered a way forward; and republicanism too, in Mirabeau's opinion, often declined into oligarchic factionalism or popular anarchy. Within agricultural societies the only kind of representation that is appropriate and does not carry with it the danger of fragmentation of authority is representation of landowners within provincial assemblies, because that creates a precise nexus of interest and loyalty between the key creators of wealth and the state itself.

Much effort was expended by Le Mercier and Le Trosne, in the later 1760s and 1770s, in trying to establish a place for physiocracy's theory of monarchy that did not tilt too far towards either simple despotism on the one hand or particularism and mixed government on the other. Le Mercier put forward the notion in *The Natural and Essential Order* that the essential role of the physiocratic monarch was to be guardian of the laws. His executive role was largely restricted to ensuring that the rights of individuals to hold property, to live in security, and to trade freely were protected and secured. Once this was achieved, and an appropriate tax policy in place, the monarch should simply rely on a panel of judges to prevent the passage of laws that unjustly contradicted the natural order. In so doing they would protect the monarch himself from breaching the terms of that order. Le Trosne produced a variant of this check in the form of a royal council of advisers with similar powers. Neither was too concerned about the prospect of the monarch overriding such advice, for surely the inevitable acceptance of the natural order by statesmen and the public at large – through deliberate public education – would obviate this danger. In essence legal despotism was thus a classic form of enlightened despotism, but earthed in a holistic, systematic political economy, which created the possibility, in the view of its adherents, of a true science of administration.

But of course critics of the physiocrats were quick to allege that their theory of legal despotism was in these terms a pure rationalist utopia in which political theory had simply been logically extracted from economic doctrines, with scant reference to empirical practicalities. There seemed to be a real tension between the dramatic talk of despotic sovereignty on the one hand, and the assertion of a established *ordre naturel* on the other, which would be universally acknowledged through the power of *évidence*: either the power of the laws would need to be forcibly established as political order that was artificial, not natural, or talk of despotism represented a confusing and distracting rhetorical inflation (Gunn 1995, p. 265).

This key insight, best pinpointed by the Abbé Mably, shone light upon a major fissure within the coherence not only of physiocracy, but also of all contemporary notions of enlightened absolutism. The rational-deductive approach of Quesnay to economics had transferred itself unquestioned to politics, where it was far from clear that the logical need for legal despotism would be recognised at all widely in practice. For many interest groups within the fractured French political orders France was not China, and what was viewed as self-evidently in the common interest by the physiocrats was not inevitably seen in that consensual light. Instead, issues of fiscal apportionment and local representation were vital matters of contemporary political contest, not benign administration. No number of programmes in public education could overcome or wish away these empirical features of the contemporary French state.

Here the physiocrats are part of a general problem of false description in which a dynamic revision of the relations between central government and the provinces in the interests of greater uniformity of governance is presented as a tidying-up exercise in administration. While it was understandable that enlightened absolutism, whether in France or in the hands of the Emperor Joseph II, should aspire to be a natural vehicle for rational reform, it was not possible in the end to disguise the residual element of discretionary sovereignty on which it depended: promulgation of sweeping legal measures tended to mean not the transparent elevation of common sense, but the imposition of unpopular enlightened provisions targeted upon interest groups intent upon resistance. As Turgot was to find in 1776, an alliance between, on the one hand, smallholders, the indigent, and others adversely affected by physiocratic policy, and, on the other, court factions opposed to reform of feudal rights, could defeat the initiators and cast down their claims to have nature and truth on their side.

Thus legal despotism eventuated in an attempt to create a clear line of mutual self-interest between the monarchy and the holders of property within the state: each stood to benefit from a link in which the monarchy could shake off the shackles imposed upon it by the traditional social orders, and establish a simple but adequate fiscal basis for its operations.

In return, property holders would gain freedom from traditional stifling notions of social responsibility that interfered with the development of their full economic potential and win government support for the decisive administrative deregulation of the economy.

4   Critiques of physiocracy and later responses

Physiocrats writing in the final years of the Old Regime could not agree on how to respond to these objections. In part this was due to an uncertainty, as we have seen, as to the descriptive or prescriptive nature of their proposals. But there was also a deeper sense of perplexity about how to reach out and touch that 'opinion' whose support now seemed so necessary to the logic of legal despotism. Le Trosne, for example, argued that the experience of the natural order would be its own vindication: that, in other words, the fruits of wealth creation within physiocratic political economy would trickle down effectively, and convince the propertied of its validity. Mirabeau, Baudeau, and Le Mercier tended to favour more systematic educational outreach, though sensitive to the need to preserve and respect local custom and traditions. They were reluctant to go further because this was the very dilemma that they themselves had faced and had encountered in practice in the past as *intendants* and crown officials. Both theory and practice converged on a point of structural difficulty that could not be overcome, only stated.

It is not entirely clear whether what was offered here was a prescriptive or descriptive political theory. When Le Mercier used the term social 'class', was he using it as a neutral or evaluative category? In saying that the actions of the ruler would be saved from despotism by their conformity with the notion of 'natural order', was he offering a description of the world as it is, or as it might be once a physiocratic political economy was in place? Similarly, was the appeal to 'opinion' a reflection of a genuine desire to engage with the tribunal of public opinion, or simply a complacent expression of the self-evident truth of the doctrines the physiocrats wished wider society to espouse (Piguet 1996, pp. 37–65)?

It is concerns of this kind that run through Voltaire's critique of physiocracy, *The Man in the Street* (1768): he deplored what he saw as the utopian, abstract, dry, and schematic systematising of Quesnay and Le Mercier, and their apparent sympathy for a carelessly constructed model of despotism, while still remaining sympathetic to their free trade arguments. Diderot used his *Observations on the Nakaz* (1774) to delve deeper into the over-optimistic

434

assumptions of the physiocrats: here he built on his friend Galiani's critique of physiocracy to extend a more general scepticism over the practicality of physiocratic political economy and the adequacy of its account of human motivations:

I regard all modern works on politics as being like a watch made by a geometrician, which would take no account of friction, shock or gravity. Some have clearly seen the evil and not indicated the remedy, others have supposed the machine to be healthy and quite new; or, if they have been aware of the fault, they have not had enough sense of the difficulty of correcting it. On the one side, no remedy, on the other, no means of applying it. (Diderot 1992, p. 97)

However, it was Ferdinando Galiani who provided the most damaging critique of physiocracy, despite the fact that his *Dialogues on the Grain Trade* are a lively, discursive, highly emotive indictment, rather than a systematic analysis, of physiocracy's whole case. What Galiani did above all was provide a reserve of arguments, old and new, to combat Quesnay's system, presented in an accessible and effectively satirical rhetoric. Others could and later did develop alternative lines of attack on physiocracy through expanding different aspects of a critique which Galiani had sometimes only just sketched. Indeed the roots of Tocqueville's negative, unfair, but still plausible suspicion that the *économistes* sought to impose their order by *diktat* derive ultimately from this source.

The strength of Galiani's attack came from a combination of his deep understanding of the traditional 'moral economy' of the political regulation of food distribution, and his own careful study of the similarities and differences that existed between France and the Naples of his own background. In the first place the reality of continuing unpredictability in grain supplies meant that governments could not in practice abandon price and trading controls without provoking unrest and sapping confidence among the lower orders in the beneficial nature of the unequal allocation of property within the very society of orders that Le Mercier, Mirabeau, and their colleagues wished to preserve (Kaplan 1976, II, pp. 594–601). Famines in Naples and Tuscany in 1764 had offered the same lesson.

Moreover, if one stood back from the French case, it was possible to discern powerful arguments to refute that crucial distinction between agricultural and trading states that Quesnay had used to commence his whole analytical process. While there clearly *were* differences between the two, it did not follow that economic base could determine political superstructure in any rigid, uniform sense. Whatever the truth of Quesnay's flows of

435

circulation, to rely solely on agriculture as a source of wealth was to take a reckless gamble with repeated famine as the likely outcome; far better for governments also to foster manufactures alongside agriculture, and prevent the import of luxury goods from abroad (Robertson 1997, p. 694). Therein lay a truly rational political economy, as formerly practised in France under Colbert: to achieve what the physiocrats sought an interventionist rather than simply supervisory absolutism was necessary, which legal despotism certainly could not deliver (Venturi 1972, pp. 180–97).

Thus Galiani offered on one level the response to physiocracy that Montesquieu might have given had he lived to register it. The diversity of economic circumstances between states was matched by the unreliability of prosperous outcomes within them, which would always inhibit the growth of a truly uniform predictable political economy in both France and Naples. A prudent government's best recourse was to sponsor a diversity of commercial options, and the regulations controlling the trade in grain were a telling instance of the need for such local adjustments, operated at the discretion of provincial and state authorities. Political decisions could not simply be read off a logically prior economic template; there would always remain a role for reason of state.

The physiocrats never fully refuted this case for three reasons. First, the circumstances of dearth in the later 1760s seemed to offer proof positive that it was still wise for the state to regard grain as a subject best administered in line with traditional welfare provision rather than putative longer-term economic benefits. Secondly, the school was not blessed with a propagandist who could either match Galiani's rhetorical gifts or his grasp of telling comparative detail. This meant that they were unable to shake off the aura of extremist, over-rigorous system-building, and pseudo-religious enthusiasm that Galiani had successfully foisted upon them. Finally there was disagreement within their own number as to how the public ought to be addressed and won over. Baudeau, Le Trosne, and Le Mercier wished to persist with a programme of public education in the merits of physiocracy; whereas Turgot, Du Pont, and Condorcet were more concerned to reposition physiocracy within the pre-revolutionary debate about new forms of representation, and develop further the notion of government and property owners acting as *co-proprietors* of the resources of the state.

Works such as Baudeau's *Principles of Moral and Political Science Relating to Luxury* (1767), Le Mercier's *On Public Education* (1775), and *On Provincial Administration and Tax Reform*, written by Le Trosne in 1779, all offer useful technical refinements of earlier work by other physiocrats (while also showing an openness to Rousseau's ideas on education). However, it was Turgot and Condorcet who truly broke new ground. In their *Memorandum on Municipalities* (1775), Turgot and Du Pont de Nemours hoped to provide a balance between rationally organised, popular involvement in politics and government by experts (as did Condorcet in *Essay on the Constitution and Functions of Provincial Assemblies*, published in 1788). Turgot's *Memorandum* envisaged the creation in France of a pyramidal structure of assemblies that would rise from the level of the village up to a central, national assembly with landowners allocated one vote for each property owned that yielded income of 600 livres each year. While the assemblies would remain consultative, they would have powers to assess and collect taxes. Thus a real measure of decentralisation would be granted to localities in return for a secure and guaranteed tax income. A principle of co-ownership by the king and the propertied would create new bonds of loyalty based on the representation of interests defined according to political economy rather than feudal tradition; and the propertied would be directly implicated in the decision-making structures of the state without reference to *parlements* and other medieval survivals. An appeal to self-interest would sidestep the difficulties involved in offering education in the lineaments of the natural order, while still showing the appropriate responsible role of the 'tutelary authority' Turgot believed government should be. Condorcet's view was that Turgot was aiming for a kind of constitution 'in which all property owners have an equal right to participate in legislation, regulate the assemblies that draw up and promulgate the laws, give them sanction by their suffrage, and change the shape of all public institutions by a formal decision' (Condorcet 1847–9, v, pp. 209–10).

What is left unclear, though, is whether this proposal for limited social representation required the retention of absolutism. Just as his economic theory flirts with endorsing the inherent productive value of manufactures as much as agriculture, so in his writings about the United States after he left office, Turgot appeared to concede that such a state could be compatible with republican structures. As a king's minister, Turgot always claimed that he was trying to reconcile the monarchy with the social orders; but after his fall from office he was more than ready (in letters to Richard Price and others) to float the possibility of an ultimately republican orientation to his proposals.

In contrast, during the next decade, Turgot's leading disciples, Condorcet and Du Pont, both kept faith with the possibilities of legal despotism vested in monarchy, arguing that the provincial assemblies that were implemented

under Necker, Calonne, and Brienne (albeit in half-hearted fashion) offered
a final chance to rework the crown's troubled and fractured links, both fiscal
and jurisdictional, with the main property owners of the kingdom (though
this stance was quietly buried by the Revolution, not least by Condorcet and
Du Pont themselves, both of whom went on to serve within the National
Assembly). The two prototype assemblies implemented under Necker in
Berry and Haute-Guienne, and the later three-layered, general scheme that
emerged from the Assembly of Notables, fell far short of what was originally
proposed, and bore more relation to Mirabeau's original pre-physiocratic
proposals than to the work of those writing in the 1770s. Nevertheless, they
went some way towards offering representation by wealth rather than by
status, and offered real potential for further institutional development had
the Revolution not supervened (Renouvin 1921).

5   Physiocracy outside France

French physiocracy was read and studied with interest by many writers and
ministers within the broader European Enlightenment, and chapter 18 of
this volume treats its notable interaction with German cameralism; but there
were also important experiments and debates around physiocratic themes
in Spain and the Italian states, and elsewhere in Europe.[2] This wider resonance is partly accounted for by the way in which political economy in
general succeeded in crossing boundaries of geography, language, and culture to become a shared enlightened discourse (Robertson 1997, p. 672).
Moreover, as Franco Venturi above all has stressed, the combination of
cosmopolitan outreach and patriotic commitment to fostering reform and
domestic prosperity that was prevalent in Naples, Lombardy, and Tuscany
ensured that scrutiny of new theories of political economy – especially
of a grandly holistic kind – would be both sympathetic and rigorous
(Venturi 1969–90). Yet there were also cases of ministers and advisers,
innocent of knowledge of physiocracy, who nevertheless implemented
policies that could be called physiocratic simply because their current
economic circumstances demanded such responses in practice, regardless
of whether they were in line with contemporary best opinion. Spain offers
the best example of this.

2 The best general introduction to physiocracy outside France is Delmas, Delmas, and Steiner 1995; for
   guidance on specific Italian permutations see Carpanetto and Ricuperati 1987; Wahnbaeck 2004; and
   above all Venturi 1969–90.

Among the Italian states associated with the Habsburg monarchy, Tuscany under Peter Leopold (1765–90) was the most directly influenced by physiocracy: Mirabeau gave direct advice to the ruler, the port of Livorno was made a free port, grain liberalisation took place, tax farming was abolished, and a successful assault was mounted on the restrictive practices of the guilds. Yet these successes could not have taken place if the intellectual and political elite had not already been deeply imbued with the thought of Boisguilbert, through the writings of Ferdinando Paoletti and Sallustio Bandini, well before the accession of Peter Leopold. Physiocracy made progress here because so many of its proposals were already perceived to be inherently Tuscan (Wahnbaeck 2004).

A similar pattern may be observed in Naples and Milan, where physio-cratic ideas were welcomed, but only at points where they were most easily assimilable to debates that were already under way. For example, Antonio Genovesi's generally sympathetic reaction to physiocracy towards the end of his career was shaped by his response to the severe Neapolitan famine of 1764; for he believed that a freer international market in grain could have ensured a rapid response to the famine that the inflexible mechanism of the *annona* – the annual grain price – could not achieve. Likewise in Milan, the physiocratic agenda was subordinated to the increasingly divergent local visions of an agricultural or manufacturing future for Lombardy that were associated with the work of Cesare Beccaria and Pietro Verri respectively. However, for all the piecemeal discussion of physiocracy across the Italian states in the second half of the eighteenth century, its doctrinal influence was never as extensive as in France. The specifically political implications of its political economy, which have been stressed in this chapter, were not in general regarded as pressingly relevant to Italian conditions, where consideration of how to increase the size of the population and the abundance of commodities tended to weigh more heavily. Moreover, Galiani's critique of physiocracy (together with Forbonnais's *Eléments du commerce* of 1754) swayed opinion away from physiocracy by questioning its moral integrity and political reliability in tandem, and helped to direct attention towards consideration of Rousseau's political economy instead, especially his account of social inequality. These are some of the issues, alongside the role of public opinion and public education, that are treated with real sophistication by Gaetano Filangieri in his *Scienza della legislazione* (1780–5).

In Spain, Campomanes and his ministerial colleagues copied French grain liberalisation laws in 1765 in a similar attempt to reinvigorate the economy after defeat in the Seven Years War. When the harvest failed, this led to a serious riot in Madrid the next year, which threatened to overturn the monarchy. The ministry responded to this emergency with a series of measures which resembled physiocratic priorities in important ways: it instituted elections from among taxpayers to new offices at the municipal level that would seek to represent the public interest, and set up a series of 'Economic Societies of Friends of the Country' which could act like provincial academies, patriotically teaching and furthering political economy in all its forms (Herr 1989, p. 36; Noel 1990, p. 137). Yet the dominant philosophy of this group was regalism, not physiocracy, and no member of the government sought to extend the scope of large-scale capitalised agriculture at the expense of the traditional Spanish smallholder, who, for Campomanes, was still the key to continued prosperity and population growth, not an obstacle to be superseded (Herr 1989, p. 55).

But for the physiocrats themselves it was the prospective development of the fledgling United States of America that – France apart – most engaged their attention. The rapid population growth and largely agricultural basis of the thirteen colonies seemed to offer an excellent experimental case study of physiocratic theory in action, an interpretation that was encouraged by meetings with Franklin and Benjamin Rush in the late 1760s, and a translation into French of John Dickinson's *Letters from a Farmer in Pennsylvania* (1769). The physiocratic case against mercantilist subsidies for overseas commerce and manufactures seemed a relevant set of arguments to add to the colonists' mounting case against Britain, and was therefore accorded some attention in the years leading up to the War of Independence. Once independence had been achieved, Turgot (in retirement) and his leading follower, Du Pont, regarded America as the 'hope of humanity', likely to evolve in the direction of France rather than Britain, provided the remaining traces of British mixed government were removed, and the rights of the propertied were upheld. However, when Du Pont moved to America, and pressed his case on Jefferson and Madison in particular, he was to find that this second generation of American leaders, though sympathetic to the primacy of agriculture within the economy, did not share either his distrust of the encouragement of manufactures or his conviction that political rights should be reserved for landowners (McCoy 1980, pp. 228–32).

Perhaps the most surprising instance of physiocratic influence on public policy came in the 'permanent settlement' of British-controlled Bengal, initiated by Lord Cornwallis in 1793. In response to the economic damage created by the short-term leases on property administered by Warren Hastings, the governor-general instituted a complete freeze on the assessments payable on land, thus effectively conferring security of title. This was in part inspired by two physiocratic writers, Henry Patullo and Philip Francis, who had argued that such a measure would encourage investment in land and prompt the local landlords to move away from the exploitation of feudal privilege towards capitalist improvement. As Cornwallis wrote,

Although agriculture and commerce promote each other, yet in this country, more than in any other, agriculture must flourish before its commerce can be extensive. The materials for all the most valuable manufactories are the produce of its own lands. It follows therefore that the extent of its commerce must depend upon the encouragement given to agriculture, and that whatever tends to impede the latter, destroys the two great sources of its wealth. (qu. Guha 1963, p. 171)

Unfortunately the British administration's subsequent insistence on establishing a colonial market for British manufactured goods in Bengal prevented this promising analysis from reaching fruition, but such a case study provides powerful evidence in support of the view that physiocracy's best potential applications lay outside Europe, in countries where the case for the predominance of agriculture in sponsoring dynamic economic growth was hard to contest. When Quesnay had focused on China as a case study of an agricultural system in the 1760s, his analysis was in fact more pertinent for physiocracy and less appropriate for France than he had appreciated.

6   Conclusions

Any general evaluation of physiocracy needs to recognise that it was a movement with very specific origins in the concerns of the French administrative elite, from which fanned out a systematic model of how 'agricultural' and 'trading' states should best promote economic growth and foster political stability. What started as an attempt to investigate the different pattern of geopolitical development between Britain and France, and to reassess the French government's fiscal policy, grew into a 'unified field' theory of how states should manage prosperity, with which all contemporary commentators had to engage. Like many such elaborate systems, its strengths and weaknesses were bound up chiefly in the accuracy and validity of its initial assumptions; and, as Galiani above all others demonstrated, several of these, especially the core distinction between 'trading' and 'agricultural' states, were open to question. Yet as the system developed many unique insights and fruitful concepts were contributed to the vocabulary of eighteenth-century social and political thought that have had a distinguished subsequent career.

In particular, the physiocrats can be credited with the first serious usage of class-based social analysis which was grounded on economic role rather than social status; likewise their definitions of net surplus and how it might be peacefully extracted by government from the owners of land created a genuine bridge between economic theory and political realities; and, in the political field, their contribution to the analysis and definition of enlightened despotism is one of the most distinguished attempts to resolve the inherent contradictions of the concept. Behind these breakthroughs, as Michael Sonenscher has noted, is a genuine concern with moral justice that often goes unnoticed: for if the executive, educational, and redistributive functions of the state are funded entirely out of the net surplus produced from land, then the inequity of property distribution inherent in the *ancien régime* can once more emerge as ethically justified by its *end* if not by its *means*. So long as the units of production are large, and the farmer and proprietor are left their share of the surplus to ensure that it recurred, the single tax on land could be used, paradoxically, to restore justice, and not merely to protect the interests of landowners (Sonenscher 2002, pp. 337–8). Here is the basis of a moral riposte to Galiani's critique, and it may be regretted that the physiocrats never found an eloquent rhetorician in their ranks to express it more forcefully.

The historiography of physiocracy has done the movement a disservice in missing the grand, comprehensive sweep of its political economy in favour of critical scrutiny of either the technical aspects of its economic analysis or the exact nature of its relationship to absolutism. Ultimately what matters for the history of political thought about the work of the *économistes* is not that they represented an early and flawed example of liberal capitalism, but rather their collective insight as to what sort of framework, given the circumstances of a *society of orders*, would be needed for real economic individualism to flourish, while also preserving social harmony. That was and continues to be the nature of their challenge and interest.

15
Scottish political economy

DONALD WINCH

1 Adam Smith's pre-eminence

Whereas Scotland in the eighteenth century was already credited with the native talent of its metaphysicians and historians, its association with political economy owes more to hindsight than to contemporary perceptions. By the early decades of the nineteenth century the association was strong enough to become part of an English caricature of the 'Scotch pheelosopher', who was assumed to combine an interest in political economy with another Scottish habit of enquiry – the pursuit of the origins and development of civil society from 'rudeness to refinement' by means of a form of history in which universal psychological principles and socio-economic circumstances played twin illuminating roles.[1] By then of course an imposing work by a Scotsman that employed both of these modes, Adam Smith's *Inquiry into the Nature and Causes of the Wealth of Nations* (1776), had begun to make its way in the world. It was therefore appropriate that the first course of lectures on post-Smithian political economy in Britain should be given by Dugald Stewart, who for a decade after 1799 employed his chair of moral philosophy at Edinburgh for just that purpose. The result of Stewart's initiative was to produce for Smith a small band of Scottish-educated grandchildren in the shape of those who founded the *Edinburgh Review* in 1802, making it the main organ for disseminating the latest views on political economy for the next three decades. When David Buchanan produced the first critical edition of the *Wealth of Nations* in 1814 and two other Scottish economists, John Ramsay McCulloch and James Mill, emerged in the 1820s as popularisers of the new science, the early nineteenth-century association of political economy with Scotland was complete. What is equally significant, however, is that McCulloch and Mill were disciples of David Ricardo, the figure whose theories were reshaping Smith's legacy along narrower deductive lines. This

---

1 'Scotch pheelosopher' was the pejorative term coined by William Cobbett, but a better-informed version of the caricature can be found in Thomas Love Peacock's novel, *Crotchet Castle* (1831).

was a sign not merely that development was occurring, but that whatever had lent a distinctively Scottish flavour and breadth to the science during the latter half of the eighteenth century was already being diluted (Collini *et al.* 1983, pp. 23–126; Fontana 1985, pp. 1–111).

The early association of political economy with Scotland, therefore, did not last long. The attribution of special qualities to the Scottish version of the science that confirm its national origins by showing how it arose from particular Scottish circumstances and intellectual preoccupations during the eighteenth century belongs to a much later period. Indeed, the use of 'Scottish political economy' as a sophisticated term of interpretative art can largely be attributed to the last three decades of the twentieth century, when it acquired at least two different meanings, depending on whether it was employed by economists anxious to recapture historical, psychological, and sociological dimensions lost to modern economics, or by cultural historians and political theorists chiefly concerned with the collective characteristics of another fairly recent coinage, the Scottish Enlightenment.[2] Within the latter category falls what is by now a large and varied body of literature centring on those 'civic' themes that can be discerned in the writings of many educated Scots during the eighteenth century. In earlier social histories of the Scottish Enlightenment political economy and the associated stadial versions of the history of civil society were viewed as responses to an emergent or hoped-for capitalism, and as anticipations of Marx's materialist version of historical development (Meek 1976; Pascal 1938). In the newer literature we are still invited to see political economy as part of a provincial debate provoked by the problems of Scotland's relative economic backwardness, but the cultural and political background is given greater prominence, with stress being placed on the problems posed by the loss of national political institutions after the Act of Union of 1707. How far the economic and cultural improvement associated with commercial society – the prospect opened up by the Union – was compatible with, or could serve as a substitute for, those participatory qualities prized by classical ideals of active citizenship, became a major preoccupation in such a setting. The newer literature has certainly provided a richer ideological context within which it is possible to situate the work of those members of the Scottish literati who articulated positions on the moral and civic questions raised by the political economy of commercial society – with Adam Smith's work

2 See Mair 1990, especially the contributions by Macfie, Dow, and Hutchison. The usage by cultural historians will be considered further below.

being taken, problematically, either as an illustration of these themes, or as on the point of making them redundant.[3]

One of the difficulties in treating Smith within a provincial context is the sheer pre-eminence, let alone cosmopolitan scope, of the *Wealth of Nations*, a work that signals its comparative sweep in the plural form of the title. David Hume's sequence of penetrating essays on economic topics published in his *Political Discourses* (1752) and Sir James Steuart's *Inquiry into the Principles of Political Oeconomy* (1767) belie any thought that Scottish political economy can be regarded as a category designed to house a single Smith-shaped item. By broadening the connotations of political economy to encompass other features of cultural and political debate in eighteenth-century Scotland, particularly those arising out of the institutional problems of an expanding economy based on commerce and the division of labour, other figures who form part of the Scottish Enlightenment can be included – Francis Hutcheson, Adam Ferguson, Lord Kames, and John Millar. But there was more than conventional flattery in Ferguson's remark to Smith after publication of the *Wealth of Nations* that 'you are surely to reign alone on these subjects' (*Corr.*, p. 193).[4] Whether we take a broad or narrow view of the subject, Smith's work still looms so large that, whilst any enumeration of the characteristics of Scottish political economy which did not fit Smith in almost every particular would be a strange one, the same cannot be said of any of the writings of his compatriots – towards which, it must be said, Smith was not particularly generous in acknowledging shared aims and achievements.

It is well known that Smith unfairly dismissed Steuart by self-consciously choosing never to mention his name or work: 'I have the same opinion of Sir James Steuart's book that you have. Without once mentioning it, I flatter myself that every false principle in it, will meet with a clear and distinct confrontation in mine' (*Corr.*, p. 164). In the case of Hume's essays, though they subjected the ruling economic maxims of the day to critical scrutiny from a liberal and humane position that is often close to the one later developed by Smith, it has to be remembered that they were *essays*. As Dugald Stewart pointed out, although they must have been useful to Smith when he first began to prepare his lectures on economic subjects, Hume's

---

3 For the civic theme in general see Pocock 1975 and 1985. For some of its applications to Scotland see Phillipson 1973, and the essays by Phillipson, Pocock, and Robertson in Hont and Ignatieff 1983a; see also Robertson 1985 and Sher 1985.

4 In this chapter, *Corr.* stands for *Correspondence of Adam Smith*, ed. E. C. Mossner and I. S. Ross (Oxford, 1987).

essays contained 'some fundamental mistakes' on matters of theory, which showed that 'in considering a subject so extensive and so complicated, the most penetrating sagacity, if directed only to particular questions, is apt to be led astray by first appearances' (Smith 1980, pp. 320–1). That this was probably Smith's opinion is confirmed by the fact that explicit invocations of his friend's authority were chiefly reserved for Hume as historian and moral philosopher rather than for Hume as the source of economic doctrines – on which matters there were probably more differences of opinion than Smith wished to rehearse publicly.[5] From a Scottish perspective it would have been more fitting if Smith had wished to dedicate the *Wealth of Nations* to his dying friend rather than to the recently deceased François Quesnay, the founder of the physiocratic sect in France (Smith 1980, p. 304). With the notable exceptions of Hume, Francis Hutcheson, and, to a minor extent, Kames, in fact, Smith did not refer to other Scottish philosophers in either of his main published works, the *Theory of Moral Sentiments* (1759) and the *Wealth of Nations*. He even ignored contemporaries and pupils, such as Ferguson and Millar, who by 1776 had published works – respectively *An Essay on the History of Civil Society* (1767) and *Observations concerning the Distinction of Ranks* (1771) – that later commentators on the Scottish Enlightenment regard as having sufficiently close affinities with his own to justify a common label.

Whether we take this as a sign of congenital mean-spiritedness on Smith's part, or merely as evidence that he had a justifiable sense of his own original-ity as the architect of a substantially novel system, depends on the position one adopts towards the 'natural system of perfect liberty and justice' that is the centrepiece of the *Wealth of Nations*, whether considered as an analysis of the workings of commercial society or as a set of prescriptions. Smith's claims to early and independent enunciation of this system were certainly the ones he was most keen to register when he drew attention to the content of the lectures he gave first in Edinburgh and later as professor of moral philosophy in Glasgow from 1751 onwards (Smith 1980, pp. 321–2). He underlined this feature of his work by coining 'mercantile system' as a pejorative term to encompass the dominant features of existing economic thinking, and by signalling privately that he was intent on mounting a 'very violent attack' upon it (*Corr.*, p. 251). Smith's condemnation of those methods by which

---

5 The exceptions to this in *WN* are to be found in the neutral reference to Hume on paper money (II.ii.96) and the explicit endorsement of Hume on interest (II.iv.9). *LJB* contains fuller references to Hume's essays (e.g. p. 507), but they also register a doubt as to whether Hume, when writing on paper money, has not fallen into mercantile error.

merchants and manufacturers, acting in concert, had duped legislators into creating an illiberal programme of bounties, monopolies, and other exclusive privileges designed to serve their interest at the expense of the rest of society, is expressed, as Stewart noted, in 'a tone of indignation which he seldom assumes in his political writings' (Smith 1980, p. 316). It was this feature of the book too that several of Smith's Scottish friends remarked upon when the long-awaited work first appeared. In addition to registering their opinion that he had accomplished something without significant intellectual precedent or competition, they spoke of Smith as having overturned 'all that interested sophistry of merchants' (*Corr.*, pp. 186–94).

These congratulatory letters also refer to Smith's achievement as a contributor to 'political science' rather than to 'political economy'. In this respect they echo Smith's decision not to follow Steuart in using the term in his title and his sparing use of it in the body of his text. Where it does occur, it is mainly in book IV when discussing the policy implications of the two existing systems of political economy, mercantile and agricultural, thereby emphasising the connections with the art of legislation or its application to policy. Treated thus, Smith gave a fairly conventional definition of the practical objects of political economy, namely 'to provide a plentiful revenue or subsistence for the people, or more properly to enable them to provide such a revenue or subsistence for themselves; and secondly, to supply the state or commonwealth with a revenue sufficient for the public services' (*WN*, IV.1). But the fact that political economy was also defined as '*a branch of* the science of a statesman or legislator' is a reminder that the *Wealth of Nations* began life as those parts of Smith's lectures on natural jurisprudence that dealt with 'police, revenue and arms', and that for Smith there was a larger intellectual enterprise to which political economy was clearly subordinate.

Once more, the scope of Smith's work was recognised by his early Scottish readers. Ferguson had given the *Wealth of Nations* an advance notice in which he stated that 'the public will probably soon be furnished with a theory of national economy, equal to what has ever appeared on any subject of science whatever'. At the same time he took the opportunity to stress that Smith's book confirmed his own opinion that commerce and wealth did not constitute 'the sum of national felicity' and could not therefore be 'the principal object of any state' (Ferguson 1995b, p. 140n). That may seem an odd point to stress to potential readers of a comprehensive exposition of the principles underlying the growth of opulence, but it contains an insight as well as a piece of wishful thinking that will be considered more fully in the final section of this chapter.

For those to whom the creation of a narrower and more autonomous form of political economy during the first third of the nineteenth century represents a natural development of certain economic themes in the *Wealth of Nations* – one that does not call for any explanation – it is tempting to bypass the broader dimensions of Smith's enterprise. A great deal that is essential to an understanding of Smith's originality in the eighteenth-century context, however, is obscured when the *Wealth of Nations* is treated as a self-standing work of economic analysis. The discovery of an additional set of student notes on Smith's lectures on jurisprudence has made it possible to reconstruct, in outline at least, the 'theory and history of law and government' which Smith consigned to the flames along with other unpublished work at the end of his life. These lectures provide a bridge connecting the *Wealth of Nations* with those parts of the *Theory of Moral Sentiments* in which Smith expounds his theory of natural justice. The lectures not only provide an essential historical component to that theory – one that is couched in terms of the stages leading up to existing commercial society – but help to explain why considerations of justice so frequently fortify judgements based on expediency in the *Wealth of Nations*, and why the terminology of natural rights has a prominent part to play in defining the injuries it is possible for legislators to inflict on citizens and citizens to inflict on one another (see Haakonssen 1981; Winch 1983).

Far from being an atavistic survival from an uncompleted plan, Smith's science of the legislator, with its natural jurisprudential underpinnings, serves as a means of understanding the shape of Smith's enterprise and his confidence in its essential novelty. By operating from within this framework he was able to repossess and reposition much that had previously passed for wisdom in political economy (Winch 1992). Moreover, as with all seminal works, the process of repositioning was not confined to any single doctrine or perspective, but can be traced across a broad front – one that enables other influences of a non-jurisprudential character, economic, political, and 'civic', to be incorporated. The upshot of this series of moves was a work that departs from established models even when borrowing from them.

National labels serve to identify these models. They include what Smith referred to in a rare moment of generosity as 'the best English writers on commerce', as well as Quesnay and his French followers, whom he treated as the authors of an agricultural system that 'was the nearest approach to the truth that has yet been published upon the subject of political economy' (*WN*, IV.ix.38). Finally, one can also speak of the ways in which Smith

448

shares, responds to, or ignores the anxieties of those whom he called 'men of republican principles', some of them being his Scottish contemporaries whose opinions were close to those of Ferguson (Winch 2002).

2   Legislators versus politicians in a mercantile state

Any approach to Smith's political economy via the science of the legislator has to confront an initial paradox. Expressed in the French slogan *laissez-faire, laissez-passer*, which Smith did not choose to employ but later commentators found irresistible, the legislator appears to have precious little to do. The virtues he is asked to cultivate seem more like those of the contemplative philosopher or scientist than those of a purposive moulder of events and outcomes. That is why Smith has so often been seen by political theorists as the figure who pronounced a quietus upon politics in any genuine sense, partly through promotion of the economic at the expense of the political, partly through restriction of the public space available for the exercise of legislatorial will or active participation by citizens. The invisible hand of self-regulating markets harmonizes the decisions of private persons in the present and foreseeable future, just as unintended consequences of a beneficial kind explained major historical outcomes. Calculating reason, let alone political will or professed virtue in pursuing public good, are accorded little role in accounting for the revolution that Smith, following in Hume's footsteps, treated as the origin of modern civil liberty: the decline in power of the feudal barony and the rise of centralised monarchies capable of administering the rule of law impartially – 'a revolution of the greatest importance to the public happiness' which had created the conditions in which commercial society could begin to flourish (*WN*, III.iv.17).[6]

Much of the *Wealth of Nations* can rightly be read as a detailed case in favour of leaving a wide range of responsibilities to the 'natural course of things', where the contrast with Steuart's assumptions about the statesman or legislator is instructive and probably intentional. Steuart had said that 'in treating every question of political economy, I constantly suppose a statesman at the head of government, systematically conducting every part of it' (Steuart 1767, I, p. 122; see Eltis and Skinner in Mair 1990). And while he recognised that constitutions and economic forces placed limits on the statesman's conduct, Steuart endowed him with responsibilities in overseeing

---

6 The linkages between Smith and Hume on this subject were first examined in Forbes 1976.

and promoting the optimal distribution of the working population between
employments that were firmly repudiated by Smith:

> The statesman, who should attempt to direct private people in what manner they ought
> to employ their capital, would not only load himself with a most unnecessary attention,
> but assume an authority which could safely be trusted, not only to no single person, but
> to no council or senate whatever, and which would nowhere be so dangerous as in the
> hands of a man who had folly and presumption enough to fancy himself fit to exercise
> it. (*WN*, iv.ii.10)

Smith was not so much treating Steuart here as a proponent of the mercantile
system as emphasising that his legislator was moved by different principles
that entailed respecting the greater knowledge which economic agents have
of their own affairs – greater than any 'projector' or 'man of system', operating according to a plan, could ever possess. 'Common prudence' might
not characterise every individual on all occasions, but it was true of the
majority, and under conditions of 'tolerable security' where free competition ruled and the laws of justice were enforced, the cause of prosperity was
best served by leaving it to that 'desire to better our condition' with which
every individual was equipped from the cradle to the grave.

Benevolent inaction or negative action seem to describe these qualities of
Smith's legislator. His duties are to minimise injury, to avoid favouring one
order or group within society at the expense of others, and to remove all
those institutions and policies which explicitly license or tacitly encourage
combinations against the public interest. That these are not the only qualities
required of Smith's legislator will be shown later, but even at this stage
it is worth noting that a major legislative programme is entailed by the
advice to dismantle those misguided and unjust laws connected with the
mercantile state. The legislator is contrasted with 'that insidious and crafty
animal', the mere politician, who responds to the 'momentary fluctuations
of affairs' (*WN*, iv.ii.39). The politician is at the mercy of the 'clamorous
importunity of partial interests' surrounding the mercantile state, especially
one like Britain's, which offers scope for illegitimate extra-parliamentary
pressure groups to overawe legislators like an 'overgrown standing army'
(*WN*, iv.ii.43). If the world is ruled only by politicians, there would be
no scope for legislative wisdom of the kind implied by Smith's decision to
expound the principles that ought to rule conduct in one branch of the
science of the legislator that had become increasingly important during the
eighteenth century. In this respect Smith needed a statesman, if only as an
ideal type, just as much as Steuart.

Translated into economic arguments, as part of a dispute with the 'pretended doctors of the mercantile system' – that aggregation of opponents Smith created for polemical purposes – the attack has several prongs. First, there is the elevation of the interests of consumers over those of producers, an anti-corporatist move that Smith carried well beyond the assault on the 'monopolising spirit' of merchants and manufacturers to include the 'negligence, profusion and malversation' of bureaucrats and the indolence of teachers whose incomes derived not from serving their students well but from those corporate entities known as Oxford colleges. Secondly, there is the critique of the mercantile confusion of money with the real sources of a nation's wealth. Specie-fetishism had led to a systematic over-estimation of foreign trade at the expense of the far larger and more significant domestic trade that takes place between the town and country. It also makes a 'jealous' zero-sum indicator – a favourable balance of trade – the barometer of a nation's economic success in what ought to be seen as a world of multilateral gain and economic interdependence. Elimination of this fetish is essential in order to focus on labour as 'the ultimate price which is paid for everything', and hence on improvements in labour productivity through the division of labour as one of the most important ways in which real wealth is expanded. The quantity of labour embodied in commodities cannot explain exchange values in a modern society where labour takes on increasingly differentiated tasks requiring different levels of skill, and where the rewards to land (rent) and capital (profits) have to take their place alongside wages as components of the natural price. Nevertheless, for Smith the amount of labour or effort required to purchase commodities is still the best measure of welfare gains over time in a growing economy, as wages rise and the natural price of goods falls or remains constant.

Thirdly, combining the first two points, there is a shift of emphasis from profits to wages in the assessment of both wealth and welfare. Whereas under competitive conditions profits should fall with growth, real wages (along with rents) should rise: 'The liberal reward of labour . . . as it is the necessary effect, so it is the natural symptom of increasing national wealth' (*WN*, I.viii.27). Complaints about high wages, and the resulting diffusion of luxury goods and opportunities for leisure to wage-earners, based on their effect in raising costs and reducing effort was another mercantile fallacy: high wages encourage population and improve the health and hence productivity of labour. An increase in the absolute share of annual produce going to labour was one of the equitable side-conditions Smith placed on his definition of true opulence:

[W]hat improves the circumstances of the greater part can never be regarded as an inconvenience to the whole. No society can surely be flourishing and happy, of which the far greater part of the members are poor and miserable. It is but equity, besides, that they who feed, clothe and lodge the whole body of the people, should have such a share of the produce of their own labour as to be themselves tolerably well fed, clothed and lodged. (*WN*, I.viii.36)

3   The conditions of growth

One essential element needs to be added to the above sketch of Smith's economic model, and it further illustrates his capacity to borrow, modify, and reposition his subject. The improvements in the productivity of labour that are given such prominence in book I of the *Wealth of Nations* can only take place as markets widen if they are preceded by capital accumulation and accompanied by maintenance of the existing capital stock – the subject of book II. In the troublesome terminology Smith adapted from the French economists, growth depends not only on 'the skill, dexterity, and judgement with which labour is applied', but also on the proportion of the available labour force that is employed productively as opposed to unproductively. Within feudal society the latter could be readily identified with the unproductive expenditure of landlords – those entitled to receive any surplus left after subsistence needs are met – on 'menial servants' and the keeping of armed retainers. The difficulty comes with the application of the distinction to complex commercial societies, where the surplus may take the form of profits, rents, and even meagre savings made from wages, and where governments lay claim to an increasing share of the surplus through taxation and borrowing.

By assuming that under conditions which guarantee security of private property a man must be 'perfectly crazy' not to use his savings productively, that is by employing labour to produce profits or by lending at interest to others who will do so, Smith makes a bold distinction between the productive uses of private parsimony and the unproductive purposes to which public prodigality is generally devoted – with war continuing to serve as the best example of what is meant by unproductive. A strong argumentative device for warning against the way in which nations can be impoverished by public prodigality, however, runs into difficulty when it is recognised that some government spending for genuine public purposes is necessary and desirable. Further analytical difficulties arise from the attempt to employ what sounds like a normative distinction (one that Smith actually used for

452

normative purposes) in order to separate private expenditure on vendible and/or durable material goods, personal services, and old-fashioned private profligacy entailing running down one's own assets and going into debt. Faced with such difficulties the best construction that can be put on the productive/unproductive dichotomy is to say that Smith wishes to draw attention to the differences between activities such as private investment that are growth-inducing and other activities such as government spending, or private spending on services and durable items of consumption, that are merely income-circulating. The latter simply maintain the circular flow, the former lead to economic growth by employing labour in ways that add to the future productive capacity of the economy.

As part of the argument against the 'English' or mercantile model of political economy, Smith's emphasis on private parsimony and capital accumulation allowed him to substitute for the balance of trade a long-term and dynamic alternative as the proper barometer of growth and national prosperity. Nations that maintained a favourable balance of annual production over consumption were adding to their capacity to create wealth, regardless of the state of their balance of trade. They possessed the means by which their capital stock could be augmented, and, since this meant that the demand for labour would be rising, they were truly 'happy' or progressive states – those in which wages were likely to be high and rising, whatever the actual level of wealth that they had attained. By deploying this insight Smith could classify America as a more 'thriving' or prosperous society than Britain, though inferior in wealth, because wages depended on the rate of accumulation rather than on 'actual greatness of national wealth' (*WN*, I.viii.22). This innovation enabled him to justify the plural claims of his title by placing different nations on a scale of 'progressive', 'stationary', and 'declining' states, with America at one end of the spectrum and China and India standing as examples of 'stationary' and 'declining' states respectively.

The new emphasis on capital accumulation, on the productive use of the social surplus in all its forms, also enabled Smith to extend the time perspective according to which progress and decline were to be judged, where his target was not mercantile duplicity but contemporary jeremiads on luxury, depopulation, and imminent decay. Smith was more tolerant towards durable forms of private and public magnificence than some of his more puritanical-sounding remarks on the virtues of private parsimony might suggest. 'Noble palaces, magnificent villas, great collections of books, statues, pictures, and other curiosities, are frequently both an ornament and an honour, not only to the neighbourhood, but to the whole country to which they belong. Versailles is an ornament and honour to France, Stowe and Wilton to England' (*WN*, ii.iii.39). They were preferable to other forms of unproductive expenditure on servants and the waste associated with many of the activities of government. But the productive use of private parsimony was the key to the slow rise in each year's annual produce, where decades or centuries were the appropriate units of measurement. Concentration on particular branches of industry or districts, over shorter periods, accounted for the fact that 'five years have seldom passed away in which some book or pamphlet has not been published . . . pretending to demonstrate that the wealth of the nation was fast declining, manufactures decaying, and trade undone' (*WN*, ii.iii.33). A similar long-term view was contained in Smith's casual calming remark after Britain's defeat at Saratoga in 1777 to the effect that 'there was a great deal of ruin in a nation' (Winch 1997). The sage observer would not confuse evidence of potential or actual microeconomic disorder with the steadier macroeconomic signs of rising annual produce that Smith was recommending to the attention of legislators.

Smith did not directly join such fellow Scots as Robert Wallace, Hume, or Steuart in the long-standing debate on the connections between luxury, inequality, and populousness, though in the *Theory of Moral Sentiments* he employed the invisible hand image to show that luxury expenditure by the rich provided an antidote to inequality by creating employment and hence by redistributing income to the poor (*TMS*, iv.1.10). In book iii of the *Wealth of Nations* the same argument is used to explain why the pursuit of vanity through luxury expenditure brings about the downfall of the feudal barony. By seeking to gratify their taste for 'trinkets and baubles' the great proprietors were forced to grant independent tenancies to those who had previously lived in 'servile dependency' as feudal retainers (*WN*, iii.iv). But there is also the novel stress on frugality and the productive use of private parsimony that has already been noted. Smith's intervention ended the existing debate on luxury by shifting the focus from static circulation and redistribution towards expansion and growth, thereby marking another decisive reconfiguration of established lines of discussion.

Smith's borrowings from French economists in articulating the distinction between productive and unproductive labour for his own purposes, as well as the introduction of the tripartite division of an annually circulating total pro-duce between rents, profits, and wages, have often been treated as signs that the period he spent in France in the 1760s yielded considerable intellectual profit when he was transforming his lectures on police, revenue, and arms into the *Wealth of Nations*. His relationship with, and possible reliance on,

Turgot in particular has always aroused interest – another case where Smith has been suspected of inadequate acknowledgement of his debts.[7] Smith readily conceded the 'liberal and generous' character of the practical lessons taught by the French system; they were remarkably similar to his own. His attack on mercantile prejudices in favour of foreign trade, his arguments for multilateral free trade, and his demonstration of the way in which 'the policy of Europe' had inverted the 'natural progress of opulence' by developing commerce and manufacturing ahead of improvements in agriculture – all this had parallels in the French economists' attempt to undo Colbert's legacy of commercial regulation and encouragement of manufacturing. Yet the differences of outlook were still such as to justify Smith's belief that the *analysis* underlying his own system of natural liberty was distinctive and original.

Famously, Smith's main criticism of the physiocratic system was its erroneous supposition that only in agriculture, where man laboured directly with nature, was it possible to achieve a net surplus in the form of rent. It followed from this error that commerce and manufacturing were seen as barren or unproductive, only capable of yielding a return in the form of wages and profits that repaid the original expenses of production. Smith was prepared to recognise that agriculture was *more* productive and should occupy the topmost position in any natural hierarchy of employments for a nation's capital, but he could not accept that the application of capital and labour in commerce and manufacturing was merely a useful but unproductive appendage to agrarian pursuits. According to Smith's view, commerce and manufacturing were productive activities that yielded a net surplus which was just as available for future accumulation as rent. Indeed, since merchants and manufacturers were 'naturally more inclined to parsimony and saving than proprietors and cultivators', they were more likely to increase the annual produce of society through productive investment. Having argued at length in book I that manufacturing offered greater opportunities than agriculture for improvements in physical productivity through the division of labour, Smith could hardly accept any system in which it was treated as the inferior method of achieving growth.

Smith was also divided from his French colleagues by a profound difference in their respective conceptions of the role of the legislator. The agricultural system presupposed that 'only by a certain precise regimen' could any nation prosper: anything else involved a disease that might prove

7 See Groenewegen 1969 for a judicious survey of the literature on Turgot and Smith.

fatal. Hence Smith's description of Quesnay as a 'very speculative physician', where the charge of indulging in unwarranted jeremiad, though not
entirely out of place, is less applicable than another Smith had articulated
in the *Theory of Moral Sentiments*. Quesnay and his followers were guilty of
the arrogance of the 'man of system' who insisted upon establishing in its
entirety everything required by his 'idea of the perfection of policy and law'
(*TMS*, vi.ii.2.18). They overlooked the natural curative properties at work
in economic life which enabled the patient to recover in spite of the nos-
trums of doctor-legislators, whether well intentioned or not. By stressing
perfection the physiocrats had forgotten that 'if a nation could not prosper
without the enjoyment of perfect liberty and perfect justice, there is not in
the world a nation which could ever have prospered' (*WN*, iv.ix.28).

We may appear to have returned to the quiescent, almost will-less world in
which legislators adopt a purely contemplative stance. More appropriately,
Smith's criticisms of the French economists should be treated as evidence of
his realistic appreciation, not simply of the dangers of the 'spirit of system'
when applied to human affairs, but of the actual problems legislators face in
implementing change in an imperfect world. That Smith did not have high
hopes of his own system being enacted is well known. 'To expect, indeed,
that the freedom of trade should ever be entirely restored in Great Britain is
as absurd as to expect that an Oceana or Utopia should ever be established
in it' (*WN*, iv.ii.43). The guiding maxim for legislators should be the one
Smith mentioned in commending the Corn Law of 1772: 'With all its
imperfections . . . we may perhaps say of it what was said of the laws of Solon,
that, though not the best in itself, it is the best which the interests, prejudices,
and temper of the times would admit of. It may perhaps in due time prepare
the way for a better.'[8] Smith's regard for established interests and the existing
state of public opinion, even when they were abusive and ignorant, supports
gradualism and does not expect each generation to solve the problems of
the next. It imparts a decidedly conservative quality to Smith's thinking, the
sceptical qualities of which unite him with Hume in eschewing large-scale
extrapolation into an unknowable future. Another way of putting this is
to say that it is historically minded without being historicist. The kind of
speculations about the prospects of perfectibility through the application of
knowledge to social and political problems engaged in by Turgot's pupil,
Condorcet, and to a lesser extent by Dugald Stewart, lie outside its range.
Cautious and retrospective though it might be, however, it embodies a form

8 *WN*, iv.v.b.53; see also *TMS*, vi.ii.2.16; and see also Winch 1983.

of knowledge rather than a denial that wisdom has any part to play in the political life of commercial societies.

4   The positive duties of the legislator in commercial society

It would also be a mistake to infer that Smith's vision of limited government intervention in the economic sphere entails weak government or the setting of legislative goals that are purely economic in character. Ferguson's remark about not making private opulence 'the sum of national felicity' becomes apposite at this juncture. It also provides a means of returning to Smith's relationship with other members of the Scottish literati which reveals the wishful element in Ferguson's attempt to unite himself with Smith. For what was at stake here were the adverse moral and civic consequences of the kind of commercial society Smith had anatomised, and the institutional remedies that might be necessary in order to combat or minimise them. On these subjects Smith, usually in company with Hume, adopted a different political stance from Ferguson and those other compatriots who made up what has usefully been dubbed the Moderate literati in late eighteenth-century Scotland.

The purpose of book v of the *Wealth of Nations* was to show that in the fields of justice, defence, education, and public works, the legislator had positive duties to perform that could not be undertaken by any other agency. The duties were justified by the need to make good the shortcomings of private provision and to deal with those undesirable unintended by-products of commercial societies which required the 'serious attention of government'. Justice, the protection of 'every member of the society from the injustice or oppression of every other member of it', had special significance (*WN*, v.i.b.1). It was built into the original jurisprudential ground-plan of Smith's work and was confirmed by the belief, shared with Hume, that enforcement of the rules of commutative justice protecting person and property, rich against poor, was the foundation of social existence as well as the basis for post-feudal conceptions of civil liberty. Indeed, it was the chief justification for regular government of any kind. Since commercial societies create more complex forms of property, they multiply the number of ways in which it is possible for citizens to injure one another. In consequence the legislator may need to be more active in administering the laws of justice and more flexible in adapting institutions and laws to changing circumstances. Unlike some of his English successors as political economists, Smith was not burdened by visions of natural limits to growth and living standards. No country had yet

achieved 'that full complement of riches which the nature of its soil and climate, and its situation with respect to other countries allowed it to acquire'.
Even China in its stationary condition was only prevented from achieving
further growth by 'the nature of its laws and institutions' (*WN*, I.ix.14–15).
In these respects one could say that Smith is an advocate of purposive government, a preference equally marked in his attitude towards other essential
governmental functions, especially in matters of national security.

It is also clear that if Smith hoped – albeit without anticipating early
success – that the activities of legislators in the economic field would become
less extensive and detailed, he fully expected them to absorb a larger proportion of annual produce in rich commercial societies. Just as some forms
of durable magnificence were an 'ornament and an honour' to a nation,
so it should be anticipated that the cost of maintaining the dignity of the
monarch would rise with the wealth of his subjects. In his lectures, and
later in book v of the *Wealth of Nations*, Smith extended the scope of this
generalisation to include all aspects of government:

We may observe that the government in a civilized country is much more expensive
than in a barbarous one; and when we say that one government is more expensive than
another, it is the same as if we said that one country is farther advanced in improvement
than another. To say that the government is expensive and the people not oppressed is
to say that the people are rich. There are many expenses necessary in a civilized country
for which there is no occasion in one that is barbarous. Armies, fleets, fortified places,
and public buildings, judges, and officers of the revenue must be supported, and if they
be neglected, disorder will ensue. (*LJB*, pp. 530–1)

But, given the unproductive status accorded to government spending in the
Wealth of Nations, the problem was one of making effective provision for
expanding essential public services without allowing aggrandisement at the
expense of private sources of accumulation. With the capacity of modern
governments to supplement tax revenues by borrowing, the dangers arising
from public profligacy had increased. Britain had pioneered the debt technique, and Smith was in no doubt that it had 'never been blessed with a
very parsimonious government' (*WN*, II.iii.36). He suggested ways of min-
imising the effects of an increasing public debt, describing it conventionally
as this 'ruinous expedient'; but his tone is less alarmist than that of Hume
on the same subject, chiefly because Smith believed that economic growth
had made the debt burden easier to bear – another case of avoiding the conclusions of a jeremiad by adopting the longer view. As with his criticisms
of the perfectionism of the physiocrats, Smith held that the parsimony of
private persons based on the natural desire to better their condition was a

restorative principle that was generally strong enough to replace what was lost through the spendthrift proclivities of public agencies.

The rising debt associated with successive wars against France had been compounded by the difficulties experienced in making the American colonies bear their share of the cost of the imperial civil and military establishment. As Smith was putting the finishing touches to his work, a colonial revolt was in the offing with this issue at its centre. In contrast to Ferguson and other Scots who believed that failure to subdue the American colonies by military means would spell disaster, Smith consistently favoured pacific solutions to Britain's imperial difficulties. Abandoning the meretricious project of a mercantile empire was in fact to be one of the most sweeping practical proposals for accommodating British aims to the 'real mediocrity' of her economic circumstances. Events conspired to make this a reality without the intervention of statesmen, but that does not detract from Smith's ingenuity in devising an ambitious alternative scheme for a constitutional union combining transatlantic free trade with complete fiscal harmonisation between Britain and her North American colonies. He described this scheme as a utopian proposal, useful chiefly as an illustration of the requirements that would have to be met by any acceptable form of empire (see Winch 1978, ch. 7). But it also confirms a persistent feature of Smith's science of the legislator that he shares with Hume: a belief that institutional devices and constitutional machinery provide the best means of harnessing private interests to public purposes and preventing public interests from being sacrificed to private ones. Although such machinery does not function like clockwork – some degree of political 'management and persuasion' is always likely to be necessary and is certainly to be preferred to more 'violent' methods of governance – it provides better safeguards than any system that relies on virtue or public spiritedness alone. Smith was indeed remarkably fertile in suggesting practical institutional devices which would ensure that the services provided by corporate bodies or financed at the expense of the taxpayer were organised in such a way that reward was matched to diligent performance.[9] In this way his suspicions of corporate behaviour were translated into methods of dealing with defects of judicial, religious, bureaucratic, and educational organisations.

Military establishments posed rather different problems, central to the concerns of the Moderate literati in Scotland.[10] The campaign for a Scottish

---

9 See Rosenberg 1960 for an economic perspective, and Robertson 1983a for a political one.
10 See Robertson 1985; Sher 1985, chs. 5–6; and Winch 1978, ch. 5.

militia organised by the Edinburgh-based Poker Club, in which Ferguson was a leading light while Hume and Smith were more passive figures, was the focal point of many of their intellectual as well as political activities. As someone who described himself as a 'war-like philosopher' – much concerned with the preservation of those qualities within the populace at large that contributed to a nation's willingness and capacity to engage in defensive war – Ferguson shared Smith's opinion that commercial nations faced special difficulties in securing themselves against attack by increasingly jealous yet more primitive nations. He could have no quarrel with Smith's opinion that there were cases in which it was necessary to sacrifice opulence for the sake of national security: 'As defence . . . is of much more importance than opulence, the act of navigation is, perhaps, the wisest of all the commercial regulations of England' (*WN*, IV.ii.30). He would also have endorsed what Smith had to say in his sections on defence and education about the loss of martial spirit being one of the most serious problems associated with the division of labour in commercial societies. What Ferguson and his Poker Club friends could not stomach was Smith's conclusion that 'a militia . . . must always be much inferior to a well disciplined and well exercised standing army' (*WN*, v.i.a.23). The conclusion was based on an extension of the social division of labour to the increasingly costly and technical demands of modern warfare. Establishing professional armies required active intervention: without 'the wisdom of the state' it was impossible to create a counterweight to the interest of the private citizen in devoting himself single-mindedly to economic occupations that absorbed more of his time and natural inclinations.

Although Smith found himself at odds with his Scottish friends and 'men of republican principles' on the 'irresistible superiority' of standing armies, he continued to support the creation of militias, partly as a means of supplementing professional forces, but chiefly 'to prevent that sort of mental mutilation, deformity and wretchedness, which cowardice necessarily involves in it' from spreading throughout society (*WN*, v.i.f.60). Apart from their possible military benefits, therefore, militias formed part of Smith's remedy, along with publicly established parish schooling, for the debilitating effect on the 'intellectual, social, and martial virtues' of the mass of society. These unintended results of the division of labour were inescapable and incapable of being solved by improvements at the work-place. The state had a direct and indirect interest in overcoming the 'gross ignorance and stupidity which in a civilized society seem so frequently to benumb the understandings of all the inferior ranks of people'. Education was an antidote to 'faction and sedition'. It conferred that personal responsibility and respect for 'lawful superiors', as well as knowledge of public affairs, which was essential to the good order of 'free countries' (*WN*, v.i.f.61).

In dealing with defence and education in this way Smith was acknowledging that legislators have a duty to protect and improve the 'character' of the lower ranks among its citizenry. It was an example of what he referred to in the *Theory of Moral Sentiments* as 'imperfect rights', where political agency might be called upon to do more than enforce the negative yet perfect rights of commutative justice. In all civilised nations the legislator was entrusted with the power 'of promoting the prosperity of the commonwealth by establishing good discipline, and by discouraging every sort of vice and impropriety; he may prescribe rules, therefore, which not only prohibit mutual injuries among fellow-citizens, but command mutual good offices to a certain degree'. But it is also characteristic of Smith's position that he added immediately: 'Of all the duties of a law-giver, however, this, perhaps, is that which requires the greatest delicacy and reserve to execute with propriety and judgement. To neglect it altogether exposes the commonwealth to many gross disorders and shocking enormities, and to push it too far is destructive of all liberty, security and justice' (*TMS*, ii.ii.i.8). Ferguson, it can be suggested, would have reversed these priorities by stressing the moral qualities required of a society's leading citizens: 'If the pretensions to equal justice and freedom should terminate in rendering every class equally servile and mercenary, we make a nation of helots, and have no free citizens' (Ferguson 1995b, p. 177).

Equipping those most subject to the deleterious effects of the division of labour with more capacity to act responsibly does not necessarily prepare them for political liberty or a future democratic role (Robertson 1985). On this subject Smith, who died just as the French Revolution was about to give popular sovereignty a central place on the European political agenda, has little to say. What he does say suggests that representative institutions, by conferring a degree of legitimacy, make their chief contribution to stable government through reinforcing the commitment to civil liberty by constraining 'the interest of government' and 'the interest of particular orders of men who tyrannize the government, [and] warp the positive laws of the country from what natural justice should prescribe' (*TMS*, vii.iv.36). But along with his other remedies for allowing popular religious sects to proliferate, and for public support to the arts as a means of leavening the puritanical lump that bred fanaticism, Smith's educational ideas go well beyond preparing the lower ranks to be more effective in their occupations. Education assists them in understanding the way in which their interests are connected with the rest of society, and it could improve their grasp of those natural rights to which all were entitled. In this manner Smith once more joined Hume in believing that, since opinion was the foundation of all forms of government, especially those enjoying the benefits and running the associated risks of 'free' institutions, a populace capable of judging for itself was of benefit to the public interest.

There is a clear contrast here with Ferguson, who seems to have believed that the situation of the lower ranks in commercial society was so far beyond repair as to make them unfit for any political role, even by way of constituting a less pathological body of opinion. Most of his anxieties centred on the fatal immersion of those destined to provide political and military leadership in purely professional and other economic pursuits, and on the consequent dismemberment of the human character, with all the attendant risks of dissolving 'the common ties of society' and a descent into languor and despotism.[11] Smith, too, was interested in the character of the middle and higher ranks, despite his belief that their occupations and general standing in society offered satisfactory opportunities for its maintenance and improvement. Instead of wishing to insulate them from the corrupting effect of economic life, however, Smith proposed that the state should impose on them a meritocratic obligation to achieve a certified command of 'science and philosophy' before they were 'permitted to exercise any liberal profession', or could be 'received as a candidate for any honourable office of trust or profit' (*WN*, v.i.g.14).

By choosing to deal with this issue within an educational context Smith implicitly rejected Ferguson's diagnosis. His attitude towards the subject that most exercised Ferguson, energetic leadership by political elites, has to be assembled from a variety of other sources. Towards landowners as an economic class Smith was frequently more sympathetic than most of his successors as political economists found it possible to be after the Corn Laws became the battleground between landowners and the rest of society during the Napoleonic wars. Landowners were less prone to the spirit of monopoly than merchants and manufacturers, and the harmony between their interests as rent-receivers and that of the nation at large meant that 'when the public deliberates concerning any regulation of commerce or police, the proprietors of land never can mislead it' (*WN*, i.xi.8). Their main defect was lack of knowledge and application, the natural result of the

11 Ferguson 1995b, p. 208; see Forbes's introduction to Ferguson 1966 and Kettler 1965 and 1977.

indolence associated with the 'ease and security of their situation'. Smith was also highly critical of large landowners who benefited from those unjust feudal relics, the laws of primogeniture and entail, and who, in consequence, neglected their responsibilities for improving their patrimony. This problem was particularly acute in Scotland; it provoked Smith into angry condemnation of those noble engrossers who failed to regard themselves as 'answerable to God, their country and their posterity for so shameful as well as so foolish a neglect' (*Corr.*, p. 32). He proposed an interventionist device in the shape of a variable land tax designed to encourage cultivation by the landowner, although not at the expense of placing the management of all estate farms in the hands of 'idle and profligate bailiffs' rather than 'sober and industrious tenants', preferably those who had acquired experience in the school of commerce (*WN*, v.ii.c.15).

As this proposal indicates, Smith welcomed the way in which commercial society placed the management of national resources in the hands of more active and discerning decision-makers and employers, those less preoccupied with status and power, those 'who are naturally the most disposed to accumulate' as compared to those who are indolent (*WN*, IV.vii.c.61). Since Smith welcomed the wider diffusion of the spirit of commerce it is possible to conclude that he was more interested in seeing landowners perform their economic roles more effectively than in isolating them from those roles. There was certainly enough of the spirit of modernity and endorsement of social change about Smith to engage the later enthusiasm of Thomas Paine.

Most students of the Scottish literati now agree that neither Smith nor Hume shared the warmth of many of their compatriots on matters of public virtue (Robertson 1983a, 1983b; Sher 1985). Their vision was tainted in the eyes of Ferguson by a mixture of excessive scepticism and moral optimism. Ferguson saw a good deal less ruin in a nation than Smith was prepared to acknowledge: 'The gentlemen and peasants of this country do not need the authority of philosophers to make them supine and negligent of every resource they might have in themselves, in the case of certain extremities, of which the pressure, God knows, may be at no great distance' (*Corr.*, p. 194). Smith's long view was both less overtly didactic and more pragmatic; one could also say more contemplative, as long as that is not confused with determinism. The conservative label can be applied to both positions, but the version displayed by Smith and Hume has neither the mystery later associated with Edmund Burke, nor the apprehension of Ferguson.

In addition to its economic benefits, the commercial society in which 'every man . . . becomes in some measure a merchant' delivered greater independence and improved standards of honesty, punctuality, and civility. It was far better to be the most fawningly deferential of tradesmen than a vassal. But there were also serious drawbacks that went beyond the loss of various virtues so far mentioned. Prudence, the chief human motive brought into play, commanded only a 'cold esteem' when compared with the more generous, heroic, and noble of sentiments connected with non-commercial pursuits. A commercial society ruled solely by justice and the exact performance of contractual obligations might command respect, but it was not endearing (*TMS*, ii.ii.3.2). Any tendency towards nostalgia for a world ruled by benevolence and the comfort of the extended family, however, could not survive the memory of feudal dependence and disorder. The domain of family and friendship still offered scope for relationships not driven by prudence; and if benevolence and public spirit could not be relied upon in public settings, this did not mean that they should be discouraged or that they were not an embellishment to any civilised society.

The indefinite multiplication of wants through social emulation and the pursuit of the objects of vanity and refinement fed a corruption in moral sentiments, the propensity to admire the rich and powerful. It could not be defended by any philosopher in ascetic mood, but the public results were genuine enough to counter the kinds of fears expressed by Rousseau when condemning *amour propre*. Any acceptance of Rousseau's utopian and republican solutions to the problems he diagnosed, it can be conjectured, would have struck Smith (and Hume) as involving far too great a sacrifice of liberty in its civil or modern sense (Ignatieff 1984, ch. 4; Winch 1992). The lessons of Smith's science of the legislator are that commercial society is not precarious, that its defects can either be minimised or endured, that it offers, in short, a viable basis for social existence, the full potentialities of which had yet to be realised.

Smith chose to view this unfolding prospect from the provincial location of Scotland. Since 1707 it had provided a viewing point that was distant from 'the great scramble of faction and ambition', one that was better suited than London for the impartial stance he strove for in the *Wealth of Nations* (*WN*, v.iii.90). But Scotland was, in this respect, more a state of mind than a place. Judged by the auspicious outcome, Smith's branch of the science of the legislator fully merits its national adjective as a tribute to this state of mind.

16

Property, community, and citizenship

MICHAEL SONENSCHER

1   Prologue: Babeuf

Early in May 1793 François Noël Babeuf changed his name to Gracchus. By doing so, he committed himself to a conception of the relationship between property, community, and citizenship (and a particular claim about the place of justice in the modern world) that was to lead, exactly three years later, to his arrest and, in 1797, his execution for conspiring to overthrow the government of the first French republic. Gracchus Babeuf first used his new name in an open letter to the *procureur* (procurator) of the Paris commune, Nicolas Chaumette (who had changed his own name to Anaxagoras, after the sixth-century BCE Scythian leader, celebrated in Greek Cynic philosophy as a critic of Athenian luxury), on 7 May 1793, on the eve of an aborted Parisian insurrection on the night of 9–10 May 1793, when some of the leaders of the Paris commune and its forty-eight sections started, then abandoned, an armed attempt to force the French Convention to include the principle of 'real equality', as its advocates called it, in the articles dealing with the right to private property which were to be part of the new, republican, Declaration of the Rights of Man. In his letter, Babeuf called upon Chaumette to take the lead in convincing the Convention to accept the seven additional articles on the scale and scope of property rights which the Jacobin leader Maximilien Robespierre, in a speech to the Convention on 24 April 1793, had presented for incorporation into the new Declaration of Rights (Robespierre 1967, pp. 51–7). These additions (later included among the founding articles of the National Union of the Working Classes and Others in London in 1831 and the *Société des droits de l'homme* in Paris in 1832) stipulated that property was a right to dispose of those goods which were guaranteed to each citizen by the law, a right which could not be exercised in ways that were prejudicial to the security, liberty, existence, or property of others without being deemed unlawful and immoral (Lewis 1999; Prothero 1997, p. 126). Robespierre, according to Babeuf,

465

was a legislator comparable to Lycurgus and, in his speech, had presented the necessitous class, the class which made up the immense majority in the state, with a prospect of real, rather than purely ideal, equality. Once private property was subordinated to the needs of the great social majority, he concluded, the lives of all the members of the sovereign would no longer be prey to 'the voracity of the economist-monopolist-barbarians' (Babeuf 1935, pp. 142–7).

By singling out the physiocrats (or economists as they were usually known in the eighteenth century), personified in this instance by Marie Jean Antoine Nicolas Caritat, the former marquis de Condorcet, as those most responsible for what, in his view, was especially pernicious in the existing draft of the Declaration of the Rights of Man, Babeuf made it clear who he took his ideological enemies to be. The aim of this chapter is to identify who he took to be his ideological allies and, by doing so, to try to position what he took to be significant in Robespierre's revisions to the foundational principles of the new regime against a wider array of normative claims about the place of property in human affairs. None of these claims was peculiar to the period of the French Revolution. But all of them were given a heightened salience by contemporary assessments both of what the French Revolution might be and of how the various kinds of property that France had inherited from its ancient, feudal, and royal pasts might affect its future course and possible outcome. The view that private property was ultimately incompatible with the nature and purposes of human society was a very old one. But, as Babeuf's remark about the 'economist-monopolist-barbarians' suggests, it was a view that had resurfaced in the context of the debate about the freedom of the grain trade that began in France in the wake of the War of the Austrian Succession (1740–8) and continued into the period of the Seven Years War (1756–63) and beyond, not only in France, but all over Europe and the United States as well (Hont and Ignatieff 1983a). It did so because physiocracy was not just a claim about the positive relationship between free trade and economic development, but was also a more ambitious programme of social and political reform based upon an elaborate argument about the relationship between divine providence, the private ownership of land, and the material and moral improvement of mankind (Hont 1989; Sonenscher 2002). Countering physiocracy thus involved more than reviving long-established arguments about the limits to private property set by God's gift of the earth and its fruits to all mankind as described in Genesis 1:26, and more than simply reasserting humanity's ultimate moral right to revive that original positive community of goods in cases of extreme necessity. It also meant arguing that a different kind of property regime could match the potential for human improvement which the advocates of physiocracy associated with large-scale agriculture, free trade in grain, and a single tax on the income of the landowners.

Physiocracy was one of a large number of eighteenth-century attempts to develop or adapt the natural jurisprudence of the seventeenth century and its decisive rejection of a community of goods as a system incompatible with the large, populous sovereign states that, it was claimed, set Europe apart from the rest of the world. But older concerns with property's divisive character and its fundamental incompatibility with common humanity did not disappear. They remained the staples of innumerable sermons, moral treatises, and courses of jurisprudence throughout the eighteenth century, forming a largely forgotten counterpoint to the more controversially innovative products of eighteenth-century thought. The debate about the grain trade brought many of these concerns back to life. If, as with physiocracy, one way of thinking about property centred on how best to make a property-based system work, the controversy that it generated gave rise to several attempts to think of a set of institutional arrangements able to make something like common ownership work. Some, like the French barrister Simon Nicolas Henri Linguet, argued that the only genuine alternative to the economists' system had to be a state that was the full owner of both its territory and all the goods that it housed, because only a state that was directly responsible for its members' lives and goods was capable of restoring distributive justice to a world corrupted by private property (Levy 1980). Others, like the English Dissenter William Godwin, argued that only a world without any states at all would allow private judgement to resume its rightful place in human affairs, leaving property to revert to individual use and government to be carried out by temporary elected assemblies, similar in character to the dictatorships of the ancient Roman republic (Deane 1988; Godwin 1796). The position that Babeuf associated with Robespierre was different from either of these. It was based upon a limited amount of private ownership and an elaborate set of republican institutional arrangements. Robespierre's speech, with its strong claim about the communal limits to private property and its concluding peroration that 'nature' had given the earth to 'the immense family of the whole human race' as its 'dominion and abode', so that 'kings, lords and tyrants' were 'slaves' in rebellion against the 'sovereign of the earth', was followed immediately by a speech by Louis Antoine Saint-Just outlining a system of republican government commensurate with a world made up of nations, but no states. The two speeches formed a single argument. The 'political order', Saint-Just claimed, had been superimposed upon an already established 'social order'. Power which was first designed for use abroad had been turned upon society itself, gradually ensuring that the 'barbarous politeness invented by tyrants' would overwhelm the harmony of the social state. The new republican constitution which he went on to present was designed to redress the balance by establishing a rigid separation between internal and external affairs. By pushing the political order out of the social state, Saint-Just argued, the principles of property that Robespierre had described would be able to resume their rightful place in human affairs. Once 'the prince' (or all the members of the republic) was once again 'sovereign', the French republic would be able to live in peace and accord on the territory it occupied, like every other member of the whole human family (Saint-Just 1984, pp. 416–25).

The possibility that physiocracy might give rise to something like its mirror-image was not entirely unforeseen. As Jean Jacques Rousseau put it in an assessment of physiocracy which he sent to its most prominent advocate, Victor Riquetti, marquis de Mirabeau, in 1767, the economists' system was full of 'great and sublime truths'. But, he warned, it would lead to 'countries quite different' from those that the economists had in mind (Rousseau 1997b, p. 271). The Abbé Emmanuel Joseph Sieyès, the theoretical architect of the French Revolution of 1789, made a similar assessment in 1775 (Sieyès 1985, pp. 27–43). Both were warnings about the risks involved in using the morally opaque arrangements of an established property regime as the basis of a state's long-term ability to uphold law and justice. The force of these warnings soon became apparent after the fall of the Bastille. By the time of Robespierre's and Saint-Just's two speeches to the Convention in 1793, the problematic nature of property had split the patriot party of 1789 from top to bottom. The French National Assembly's attempts to promote political and economic stability by taking over responsibility for the national debt, by abolishing feudal property, and by confiscating the property of the church, rapidly gave it a range of financial and administrative responsibilities that went well beyond its self-proclaimed task of drafting a new constitution. Arguments about how best to meet those responsibilities, starting with the question of how to reconcile liberty at home with a slave-based colonial empire abroad, quickly turned into a series of vicious political fights over the scale and timing of political and social reform. While many of the critics of physiocracy (including Condorcet himself) argued that both the limited nature of the rural division of labour caused by the seasonal character of agricultural work and the local markets involved in the formation of prices for agricultural goods favoured the promotion of a small-scale property regime as the basis of a decentralised republican system of government, Babeuf himself finally came to advocate a system of genuinely common property. It was, he argued in his *Manifesto of the Plebeians*, published in issue 35 of the *Tribun du peuple* in November 1796 (notable also for transferring the word 'manifesto', normally used in declarations of war between states, to what he warned would be the civil war, or *Vendée civile*, between the rich and the poor), the only way to eliminate chance from human life, thus enabling every member of society to live independently of the vagaries of fortune or circumstance. In his final speech at his trial at Vendôme in 1797, Babeuf associated the claim with the work of four men whom he called 'those other levellers', Jean Jacques Rousseau, the Abbé Gabriel Bonnot de Mably, Claude Adrien Helvétius and Denis Diderot (Advielle 1884, II, p. 316).

Babeuf was thirty-six in 1797 (he was born on 23 November 1760). He was also almost entirely self-taught. But however odd the combination of the four individuals that he named may now seem, certain features of their work lent themselves to his assertion that a republic based on a system of common property was a genuine alternative to the property-based model of human improvement to be found in physiocracy. The first feature was a needs-based conception of human society and an age-based system of communal government. The second was an idea of the progress of the arts and sciences that was not causally dependent on the formation and development of private property. The third was a concern with the history and political institutions of republican Rome as an exemplary instance of the political dangers involved in conflict between the rich and the poor. The fourth was an interest in the modern funding system as a way to prevent the modern world from succumbing to the cycle of decline and fall that had led to the ruin of its ancient predecessor. These themes form the four parts into which this chapter is divided. As Babeuf's assertion about the French republic's need to opt for either communal property or civil war suggests, they were connected to one another by a heavily catastrophic conception of revolution, a conception that was one of the most glaring features of physiocracy. From this perspective, the 'old regime', as it came to be called, was neither backward nor archaic, but was hurtling instead towards a modern version of the cycle of class conflict, revolution, and military despotism that had destroyed the ancient world. Countering physiocracy thus meant adopting its apocalyptic vision of the future but rejecting its property-based solution to the threat of a revolution from which there might be no way back.

The name which Babeuf adopted had, therefore, a quite specific polit-ical significance as an emblem of both antiquity's failure and modernity's promise. The four individuals whose work he singled out offered four quite different conceptions of the kind of property regime consonant with the survival and development of a large and populous republic. The most prob-lematic of these was the one to be found in the works of Rousseau. But the conception of revolution that Rousseau set out at the end of his *Discourse on the Origin of Inequality* (1755) lent itself fairly readily to the projections of a largely non-political communal future which came to be superimposed upon his own political thought. Mably and Helvétius offered two models of how a large and populous republic might be established and maintained, the former by highlighting the abiding relevance of the imperatives of reason of state and the politics of necessity to circumstances of political crisis, even under a republican form of government, the latter by presenting an image of where the moral foundations of a prosperous territorial republic might be found once the extreme circumstances of a period of crisis had passed. But it was the figure who Babeuf took to be Diderot who supplied him with his model of a republican system of communal property. This model – and the conception of human nature on which it was based – was to be found in the *Code de la nature, ou du véritable esprit de ses lois* (The Code of Nature, or the True Spirit of its Laws), a work which Babeuf, like most of his contem-poraries, attributed to Diderot because it had appeared in at least two of the various editions of Diderot's collected works published before his death in 1783 (Morelly 1950). It was in fact by an obscure official in the French royal financial administration named (it would seem) Etienne Gabriel Morelly (Antonetti 1983, 1984). It had been published in 1755, partly (as its subti-tle indicated) as a reply to Montesquieu's *The Spirit of Laws*, and partly to elucidate the arguments in favour of a system of common property which Morelly had made in an earlier philosophical poem entitled the *Basiliade* (1753). It provided Babeuf with a simple but comprehensive alternative to the account of the ruin and recovery of mankind to be found in physiocracy and a natural foundation for the more elaborate conceptions of republican government to be found in Rousseau, Mably, and Helvétius. From the per-spective of the version of the history and future of human society which Babeuf came to adopt, it supplied him with a reason for thinking that the immense financial resources of the modern state could be used to give a new salience to need, possession, and occupation as the sole criteria governing the legitimate ownership of property, to virtue not the goods of fortune as the basis of genuine moral authority, and to merit, not inheritance, as the ultimate principle of the right to rule. Babeuf was not the last to find the combination irresistible.

2   Needs and society

The system of communal property described in the *Code de la nature* was predicated on a rejection of the idea of original sin. It was this that set it apart from what Morelly called 'the vulgar morality' underlying contemporary justifications of the unequal distribution of goods and, as he put it, the sociability of fear on which it was based (Morelly 1950, pp. 151, 196). This unnatural system, he wrote, relied on driving both the rich and the poor to be active and industrious because of their fear of losing, or hope of acquiring, goods that were privately owned. By this, Morelly was not referring to the justifications of private property to be found in the works of Pufendorf, Locke, or the other natural jurists of the seventeenth century, but those produced by the seventeenth-century French Jansenists Blaise Pascal, Pierre Nicole, and Jean Domat (as well as, according to Morelly, the Oratorian theologian Nicolas Malebranche). A popular version of their accounts of the relationship between fallen human nature, private property, and social inequality could be found in the multi-volume *Spectacle de la nature* (1732–50) by the Abbé Noël Antoine Pluche (and the title of Morelly's book suggests that Pluche may have been its immediate target). According to Pluche, the variety of conditions and the system of ranks which it entailed were part of a providential system devised to enable human society to withstand the effects of the Fall. Although, he wrote, summarising the claims of Nicole and Domat, God was not the author of 'human malice', he was the author of the arrangements devised to keep it in check. These included 'the severest meteors', the alternation of the seasons, the unequal distribution of natural resources, and the necessity that humans were under to meet their own needs by supplying the wants of others. The economy on which the preservation of human life depended thus served to force fallen human beings to restrain or disguise their malice in order to acquire the goods that they needed to satisfy their concupiscence. As Pluche put it, the disposition of nature visibly obliged men to work and to have a mutual regard for one another, however much self-love, not love, actually ruled their depraved hearts (Pluche 1732–50, VI, pp. 113–17).

The *Code de la nature* was a refutation of this conception of the ties that bind and an attack on the 'melancholy enthusiasts', as Morelly described them, responsible for the sombre view of both God and humanity on which it was based (Morelly 1950, p. 259). In this respect, it echoed some of the themes to be found in the works of seventeenth-century Christian Epicureans, sometimes described pejoratively as 'libertines', or those that had been revealed (to Voltaire's delight) in the recently published works of the heterodox French priest, Jean Meslier. Its starting point was a conception of human nature that was fundamentally at odds with the Jansenist claim that humans are slaves to their needs. Humans, according to Morelly, have no innate ideas or penchants. They are born in a state of total indifference, even to their own existence. Their first needs awaken a concern for their own survival and, by so doing, become the basis of their social capacity. Although intense, human needs are quite simple, varying only as men and women increase in bodily strength. The very elaborate range of needs and desires which humans now displayed was, Morelly argued, wholly unnatural and artificial in character and a product of the existence of private property. The natural parity of individual needs also meant that humans had an easy ability to feel the equality of their conditions and rights. This in turn produced a peculiarly human capacity for concord. It did so, Morelly argued, partly because humans cannot meet their needs without effort and partly because of the mixture of emotion and reason involved in human co-operation. If humans were to meet no obstacles in satisfying their needs, they would remain in their original state of indifference and would be no more sociable than brutes. Since the effort involved in meeting most basic needs usually exceeds any individual's ability, and since needs are experienced quite intensely, the feelings they produce come into conflict with humans' natural inclination towards idleness and rest, functioning as a natural stimulus to seek others' help in order to find a genuinely fixed point of rest. This, Morelly wrote, was why humans had an aversion to solitude and an inclination to meet their needs by seeking the company of others. This initial capacity for co-operation was then reinforced by a further set of emotions, since the most basic response to the satisfaction of a need was a feeling of contentment and gratitude, a feeling that was reinforced by the ability which humans had to use reason to identify the cause of the feeling itself. The result, according to Morelly, was that human society could be seen as a 'marvellous automaton'. Although it was made up of intelligent parts, it would work largely independently of conscious human choice, leaving reason, as Morelly (quoting Cicero's *De finibus*) put it, largely a 'spectator of what feeling effects' (Morelly 1950, pp. 169–70).

The communal system that Morelly envisaged would be managed by a patriarchal republican government in which all the members of the community would be divided into multiple units of ten, with the family forming the most basic unit. Ten families would form a tribe; ten tribes would form a city; ten cities would form a province; and ten provinces would make up a nation. Each tribe and city would contain a cross-section of the trades needed to meet their members' needs. All the trades would also be organised into corporate bodies, each headed by a number of permanent master artisans and an annually rotating corporate head. No-one, Morelly emphasised, would be able to become a master in any corporation without having first performed a ten-year period of agricultural labour. The government of this republic would be based on a system of patriarchal seniority. Every father of a family aged fifty or older would be a senator. Every tribe would have a life head (the oldest patriarch) and every tribal head would take it in turn to be the head of the city for a one-year period. Each city would supply an annually rotating head to each province and each province would supply a perpetual head of state to the generality of the nation. When the incumbent general head of state died, his successor would be the next head of the province in order of seniority, while his place as a provincial head would be taken by the most senior head of the city. There would also be a supreme national senate recruited annually by selecting two or more of the most senior members of the senates of each city. The heads of the cities, under the orders of the general head, would be responsible for implementing decisions by the local senates after they had been approved by the supreme senate. The function of the head of the nation was, in general, to enforce the law. He was also the general commander of all the corporations of the state involved in or attached to agriculture and was, furthermore, to have the general right of inspection of all public warehouses and the work of all the trade corporations. The same functions would be performed at the level of the provinces and cities by their respective heads.

The combination of communal property and a patriarchal republican government which Morelly described had a long pedigree. The prototype of the system was God's original government of the Jews, the model that the seventeenth-century English republican James Harrington had used in his *Oceana* (1656) to illustrate the original features of an agrarian, without which, he had argued, no government could last. The Jewish patriarchs were ministers, not monarchs, because the Jewish people lived under the sovereign power of God and were governed, under God's law, by the first-born males of every family. A century later, the Anglo-American radical Thomas Paine used the same model of the original form of human government in his *Common Sense* (1776). In France, it was one which could be found in the

Abbé Claude Fleury's *Moeurs des Israelites* (Manners of the Israelites, 1681), the work which served as the template for *The Adventures of Telemachus, Son of Ulysses* by Fleury's *protégé*, François de Salignac de la Mothe Fénelon, archbishop of Cambrai (Rothkrug 1965). As tutor to Louis XIV's grandson, Fénelon first wrote his epic continuation of Homer's *Odyssey* in 1695 in order to teach his royal pupil about the duties and qualities of a prince. The full version of *Telemachus* was published in 1715, the year of Fénelon's death. It soon became one of the eighteenth-century's best-selling books, with as many readers in Protestant as in Catholic Europe and as many admirers among republicans like Rousseau, Brissot, and Godwin as among reforming monarchs like Frederick II of Prussia, Joseph II of Austria, or Gustavus III of Sweden (Orcibal 1997). There was some discussion in the French republican Convention in October 1792 as to whether Fénelon's remains should be buried, along with Rousseau's, in the Panthéon, despite the fact that he had been an archbishop and that *Telemachus* had been written for a prince (an earlier proposal to the same effect was made by Paine's friend Nicolas Bonneville, the editor of the republican *Bouche de fer* (The Cast-Iron Oracle) in 1791) (Cherel 1917, p. 443; Rose 1978, p. 157).

The system of government outlined in *Telemachus* was designed to be compatible with a largely communal system of property. Fénelon transposed the combination of a rather remote sovereign and a patriarchal ministry that was the hallmark of the government of the Jews to the ancient world and used it in this setting to describe the institutional arrangements underpinning the two kinds of community, one pastoral, the other agricultural, to be found in Betica and Salentum. Even in Salentum, where agriculture was fully developed, property was held as a kind of usufruct and its possession was regulated by a strict agrarian law, designed to maintain the stability of the seven different classes into which the kingdom was divided by limiting the amount of land that any family could possess to no more than was absolutely necessary for its own subsistence. The whole model of reform laid out in *Telemachus* was based on three claims about the possibility for human improvement. The first was agriculture's huge potential for increasing the productivity of the land. Properly cultivated, as Fénelon had argued in an earlier *Demonstration of the Being and Attributes of God* (1712), the earth was capable of yielding a hundred times more than the seed sown upon it and could therefore provide for a very much larger population than it presently housed. The second was the impact that a fully developed system of agriculture and industry would have upon relations between nations. As Fénelon observed in an essay on the balance of power, promoting domestic prosperity and population growth would transform the international system more fully than war and conquest could ever do because it would reverse the direction of the internal and external mechanisms underlying the balance of power. Great states would grow from within, not from without. The third was a hostile view of the Jansenist interpretation of the Fall and its effects, a view which led to a flurry of accusations of Pelagianism aimed at his *Explanation of the Maxims of the Saints* (1697) and, two generations later, to the doctrine of universal regeneration put forward by his biographer and admirer, the Scottish Jacobite Andrew Michael Ramsay in his *Philosophical Principles of Natural and Revealed Religion*, published posthumously in 1748–9. For orthodox Christians, both Catholic and Protestant, the claim that God's will was, literally, a general will to save all was a heresy. But the idea found a receptive audience in the heterodox Catholic and Protestant circles in which the vogue for freemasonry began to grow. The claim that orthodox soteriology was a product of priestcraft, a claim made as readily by the devout as by sceptical freethinkers, served to form a bridge between heterodox Christian conceptions of human improvement, whether Catholic or Protestant, and the very much more ambiguous view of human improvement to be found in the works of Rousseau (Popkin 1996).

3 Property and the progress of the arts and sciences

For Morelly, the human capacity for communal life was inseparable from the dissipation of error and superstition produced by the progress of the arts and sciences. Accordingly, he took issue with Rousseau's answer, in the first *Discourse*, to the question posed by the Dijon Academy in 1749 on whether the re-establishment of the arts and sciences had purified manners. Rousseau, he commented, had given the wrong answer to the question. If property had not existed, the progress of the arts and sciences would undoubtedly have improved mankind. Even though there was property, that progress had still been enough to discredit a great deal of what Morelly called the nonsense once supported by the church and taught in the schools. Rousseau, he wrote, was a 'bold sophist' who had chosen to censor humanity on the basis of the vices caused by the existing property regime and had failed to acknowledge the way that the arts and sciences served to remove barbarism from society, and, by adding to the sum of human pleasure, to improve knowledge of society's true agreements.

Morelly's view was a simplified version of a long-established tradition of humanist argument about the relationship between human liberty and the arts and sciences and, in the light of the part that the latter were said to have played in promoting civility by polishing barbarous manners, about the decorative and ceremonial origins of morally acceptable regimes of communal and individual property. The place of this way of thinking about property in the eighteenth century has now been almost entirely forgotten, leaving the works of the only one of its exponents now remembered by posterity, Giambattista Vico, marooned in a highly specialised sub-branch of eighteenth-century historiography (Lilla 1993; cf. Chinard 1934; Manuel 1959; Rossi 1979). Its starting point (as the question posed by the Dijon Academy presupposed) was humanity's state of destitution after the Fall and the Flood. One way of explaining the development of culture and civility out of that original condition was to emphasise the parts played by necessity and poverty in stimulating human ingenuity and co-operation. In Protestant theology, this explanation was often connected to the idea of a covenant between God and Adam, a covenant that had been renewed as a covenant of works by Christ, the second Adam, after the Fall and the Flood. In Catholic theology, the idea of a covenant did not exist. This made it harder to justify the long-term material effects of making necessity the basis of the progress of the arts and sciences and difficult to explain why humans remained in society even after their needs had been met. One way of doing so was to follow the Jansenists and adopt a very purposeful idea of divine providence as the ultimate legitimating principle underlying an unequal distribution of goods and to place a very strong emphasis upon human depravity as the mechanism binding the members of human society together. But another way of doing so (one to be found in a great deal of Jesuit writing on natural morality and natural theology) was to drop necessity as a starting point altogether. Doing so involved placing more emphasis upon the uniquely human capacity for music, dance, and poetry, and the part that they played in forming ties based on something other than poverty and necessity (Lafitau 1724). Here, the arts and sciences were connected to a conception of human liberty that was Greek in origin, in which the emphasis fell on an idea of liberty as living in accordance with nature (and with the patterns, symmetries, and rhythms to which humans naturally respond) rather than on a Roman idea of liberty as living independently of someone else's will. From this perspective, one which was also a prominent feature of the *Code de la nature*, the *polis* and all of its members were free because they had all that they needed to perfect what nature had initially supplied.

This association between liberty and the arts and sciences encompassed several different ways of describing morally acceptable forms of property.

In some renditions, individual ownership began with shame, because shame had driven fallen humanity to cover its nakedness, and clothes, once worn, could not, without repugnance or impropriety, be worn by anyone else. In others, it began with death and the need to set land aside for ancestral graves. In yet others, it began with the digging of wells for water for livestock, or with the invention of proper names and the associations between persons, their progeny, and the things that they used, or with cave paintings and their testimony to the human propensity to embellish and decorate what other-wise would have been no more than temporary shelter. Clothes, graves, wells, paintings, or names were all, in a sense, property. But they were not easy to associate with the combination of need, indigence, and commercial reciprocity on which the conjectural histories of property-formation devel-oped by seventeenth-century natural jurists like Pufendorf and Locke had been based. They could co-exist with money, provided that money was also used mainly for decorative and ceremonial purposes and was not privately owned (Fénelon described the inhabitants of Betica as using gold in this way). They could be very simple or very ornate without necessarily gener-ating inequality in anything other than a moral sense. The first legislators, it was claimed, were often attired in ways that fitted the fact that they were also the best poets, warriors, or dancers.

This conception of the relationship between human improvement and the progress of the arts and sciences was deeply at odds with almost every-thing that Rousseau wrote. But Babeuf was not the only person to associate Rousseau with what he had found in Morelly (or Diderot, as he called him). Almost all the Jacobins who supported Robespierre in 1793 held a view of the arts and sciences that was nearer to Morelly's than Rousseau's (a view, incidentally, that was also compatible with the slogan that a republic had no need of *savants*). Although they admired and praised Rousseau's republican-ism, they rejected almost all the premises on which it was based. They did so mainly because they rejected Rousseau's radical claim that society was a state contrary to human nature and that only a very peculiar combination of a disembodied state and an indirectly elected government could prevent human needs from spiralling towards the kind of self-enslavement which the Jansenists had identified as the basis of society and, according to Rousseau, towards the despotism that a needs-based social system would ultimately pro-duce. Rousseau was no Jansenist. But he shared their view that there was no natural mechanism available to block the ordinary human need for survival (*amour de soi-même*) from turning into a more reflectively self-centred need for approval (*amour-propre*), just as there was no clear line of demarcation

477

between necessities, conveniences, and luxuries. The absence of the latter compounded the effects of the absence of the former. As Rousseau argued in both his first and second *Discourses*, even the earliest conveniences, by becoming habitual, would turn into real needs. Among these, he noted, were the use of language, the construction of huts for shelter, and the use of simple implements like bows, arrows, slings, or spears. Once the arts began to require the collaboration of several hands, human life was caught irretrievably in a web of its own making. Iron and wheat, Rousseau wrote, had civilised men, and ruined mankind. As long as survival was a purely individual matter, the relationship between the individual and the species would be a complementary one. But when individual survival became dependent on others, there was no escape from human society and the needs-based enslavement binding everyone to a society to which no-one had agreed to belong.

As several of his immediate contemporaries recognised, Rousseau's solution to the dilemmas created by the ratcheting up of human needs and the vicious system of hypocrisy which, he argued, it had to entail, grew out of a starting point that was quite similar to the one contained in the political thought of Hobbes (Trousson 2001). The only alternative to a society to which no-one had agreed to belong had, he argued, to be one to which everyone had agreed to belong. It had to be contractual all the way through, subjecting all of its members' goods as well as their lives to the sovereign power of the law. This meant that Rousseau began with a description of human nature that was as attenuated as anything to be found in Hobbes. But Rousseau went on to claim that Hobbes's starting point could be used to build up a theory of a very different kind of political society, with patriotism at its core. The way to keep needs within bounds, he argued, was to devise a purely artificial system of human association, whose only natural components, the feelings in its members' hearts, were to be transformed and ennobled by the moral beauty of the new object (the *patrie*) on which they would come to be fixed. Nothing else in Rousseau's system was natural. The kind of republic which he wrote about had no trace of the common property, the natural division of labour based on the production of durable and non-durable goods, or the age-based system of patriarchal government to be found in the *Code de la nature*. States, being artificial beings, do not have human needs. They may need money, but Rousseau was adamant that this was a sign of their corruption, not a measure of their wealth or power, arguing that voluntary service (or even something like the French *corvée* – the obligation to provide unpaid labour) was a far less dangerous resource for a state to rely on than anything involving the development of public finance.

There has never been a very convincing explanation of the extraordinary change that took place between the 1750s and the 1790s in descriptions of the content of Rousseau's political thought. When Babeuf placed him alongside Mably, Helvétius, and Diderot (or Morelly) as one of 'those other levellers' whose works heralded his own system of common property, he seems to have been entirely unaware that Mably, Helvétius, and Diderot had, a generation earlier, been among Rousseau's fiercest critics. In the 1750s, Rousseau was often taken to be very like Hobbes, mainly because of the similarity between their descriptions of human nature, rather than the more overtly political aspects of their thought (Adam Smith associated Rousseau as a political thinker with Mandeville) (Smith 1980, p. 250). By the 1790s, the Hobbes–Rousseau pairing had been almost entirely forgotten, or, if it was still remembered, it was usually to the advantage of a Hobbes redescribed in the light of Diderot's *Encyclopédie* article on 'Political Authority' and its anti-Hobbesian argument about the moral limits to the power of sovereign states set by the general society of all mankind. (A good example of this way of setting Hobbes against Rousseau can be found in the pamphlet entitled *Philosophie sociale* published in 1793 in the context of the debate about the French republican Declaration of the Rights of Man by the strange Moravian financier, Moses Dobruška, also known as Franz Thomas von Schönfeld and, when he wrote this, as the French Jacobin, Junius Frey.)

If Diderot's efforts to counter Rousseau's Hobbism by reinstating the general society of all mankind as a way of checking the otherwise arbitrary character of sovereign power was one reason for the change in what Rousseau was taken to stand for between the 1750s and the 1790s, a more direct cause was the effort to preserve his intellectual legacy after his death in 1778 by expanding upon, or modifying, the insistence upon patriotism as the emotional compound at the core of society that was the most striking feature of his thought. In most cases, this involved overlooking the amount of artifice involved in Rousseau's conception of patriotism and reinstating a more comprehensively natural principle of social integration. The result was that Rousseau's political thought was brought much closer into alignment with the thought of Mably, Helvétius, and Morelly than it had actually been. Writers like Jacques Henri Bernardin de Saint-Pierre (the author of the highly successful *Etudes de la nature* (Studies of Nature) which began to appear in 1784), the Abbé Gabriel François Brizard (the author of a eulogy of Mably and an avid collector of Rousseau relics who was also employed to verify the authenticity of noble genealogies, an oddly apt occupation in this context), or Louis Sébastien Mercier (the playwright, essayist and translator of the poems by the Swiss poet Salomon Gessner) all dropped the radically pared-down description of human nature that was the starting point of everything that Rousseau wrote, substituting for it a much more morally capacious account of natural human qualities and a very different idea of what a political society might be. Many of them also took their cue both from Rousseau's dismissive remarks about the modern theorists of natural law, particularly Grotius and Pufendorf, and his endorsement of Hobbes's assertion that theological speculation exceeded the capacities of human reason, to argue that it was *political* society (rather than society itself) that was the source of all human misfortune. Thus, after following the sequence of steps running from the state of nature to the 'hideous despotism' that Rousseau laid out in his *Discourse on the Origins of Inequality*, writers like Louis Claude de Saint-Martin or Dom Léger Marie Deschamps went on to argue that the revolution which Rousseau predicted would eventuate in a non-political, social state, more like the one described by Morelly than the law-governed republic of the *Social Contract* (Deschamps 1993). As the Abbé Barruel, Jacobinism's most relentless contemporary opponent noticed, there was a strong similarity between this kind of extrapolation from Rousseau's second *Discourse* and the antithesis between a social state and a political state which both Robespierre and Saint-Just used in their speeches to the Convention in April 1793 when setting out the fundamental principles of the new republican regime.

4   The Gracchi and their legacy

The question of what Rousseau really meant became a matter of intense political conflict during the French Revolution. At the same time as Robespierre was calling upon the Convention to add his articles on property and the rights of the human race to its new Declaration of the Rights of Man, and as Babeuf decided to change his name to Gracchus, another member of the Convention, Pierre Louis Roederer (a political ally of the Abbé Sieyès) was coming to the end of a course of public lectures in the Parisian Lyceum designed both to set out his view of the fundamental principles of the new regime and to rescue Rousseau's political thought from the interpretation put upon it by his Jacobin admirers. A central feature of Roederer's *Cours d'organisation sociale* (A Course of Lectures on the Organisation of Society) was the subject of an agrarian. His purpose in dealing with it was to show that Rousseau's vivid remark, in his *Discourse on the Origin of Inequality*, that the earth belonged to no-one and its fruits to everyone could not be used to justify a republican levelling policy because it presupposed the very opposite of the idea of common ownership on which any kind of redistributive policy had to be based. It was, he claimed, Mably not Rousseau who was the real source of republican justifications of an agrarian and the levelling policies that it implied.

According to Roederer, a great deal of what Mably had published, notably his *De la législation* (1776), had been written to refute Rousseau (Roederer 1853–9, VIII, p. 145). Mably himself had made his own hostility towards Rousseau quite clear by endorsing the description of human nature and the moral foundations of society set out in a book entitled *De la sociabilité* (1767) by his friend the Abbé François André Adrien Pluquet which (although it never mentioned his name) was a point-by-point refutation of Rousseau's second *Discourse*, serving, as one of its reviewers put it, to 'console' rather than to 'dismay' humanity as Rousseau had done (*Journal des beaux-arts et des sciences*, 1 (Paris, 1768), pp. 334–48). Although one of the major themes of Mably's work was the need to establish a republican system of government, the kind of republic that he envisaged was quite different from the small-scale republican state needed to create and maintain the intense emotional compound which Rousseau had argued would have to replace a personified representative sovereign for civil and political liberty to survive. Mably's republic was, instead, a very big territorial republic, modelled not so much on the ancient republics of Greece or Rome (morally admirable though they were) but on the huge federated republican system which, he argued, had once existed in Europe under Charlemagne. Although, he emphasised, the history of Greece and Rome was a vital source of information about the part played by property in human affairs because it contained the only surviving record of societies that had gone through the whole cycle of rise, growth, decline, and fall, the modern world was now far too heavily committed to a highly individuated property system for there to be any real possibility of finding a way back. The problem facing the modern world was, instead, to find a way of using the existing property regime to prevent a repetition of the cycle that had brought the ancient world to an end.

Mably had begun his own career by accepting the Machiavellian view that the cycle of rise and fall was largely governed by a state's size and by the difficulties involved in maintaining a republican system of government when a republic's territory increased (Wright 1997). His first book had been a parallel between modern France and imperial Rome based on the assumption that monarchy was the only regime compatible with a large territorial state. But the War of the Austrian Succession led him to change his mind. The combination of modern standing armies, the system of public debt, and the fiscal regime which it entailed led him to abandon the standard view. The modern world, he now came to argue, was committed to property, money, and trade in a way that the ancient world had never been. Under these inherently uncertain conditions, the centralised system of decision-making that was the hallmark of monarchy was no longer an advantage but a potentially fatal source of vacillation, inconsistency, and weakness. The system of absolute government that France had pioneered was the most pronounced example of the problem. From this perspective, Mably argued, the modern version of the cycle of decline and fall had begun with Henri IV and the consolidation of absolute royal sovereignty that had taken place in the early seventeenth century. The only way to prevent it from running its course was to devise a property-based system of republican government in a territory whose size and populousness would serve to make it largely self-sufficient.

As Mably presented it in his *Observations sur les Romains* (Observations on the Romans, 1751), the problem of extent had been the nemesis of the ancient republics because none of them had been able to devise constitutions capable of accommodating the multiplicity of competing interests and the unequal distribution of goods generated by large political associations. In this sense, he argued, the history of the Gracchi was an exemplary instance of the limits of ancient political science. As the republic stumbled towards its final crisis, the Romans simply did not have the conceptual resources needed to identify the underlying causes of the divisions and conflicts driving the republic towards its end. Among the many causes of their ruin, Mably wrote, all that the Romans could perceive was inequality, and the corruption of manners that it brought in its wake. Accordingly, they could do no more than echo Cato the Censor's lament about the corrosive effects of luxury, imagining that the impotent example of the virtue of a few honourable men might be enough to stem the flood. But all that this moralistic declamation served to do was to create conditions for ambitious demagogues to exploit popular misery. This, Mably observed, was what the brothers Tiberius and Caius Gracchus had done. Although, he wrote, some historians had said that Tiberius was motivated by patriotic zeal, it was more correct to think that ambition alone had been his inspiration. His campaign to fix the amount of land that anyone could possess served only to exacerbate the conflict between rich and poor. Had he been a genuine patriot, Mably commented,

Tiberius would have seen that the rich would be willing to sacrifice the whole republic to preserve their property, and would have abandoned the entire reckless enterprise. Instead, he allowed himself to be pushed into increasingly extreme political postures and, after threatening to take up arms, was assassinated as an enemy of the republic. His brother, Caius, was no better equipped for the task. His following, initially confined to the poor and dispossessed, grew massively when he offered Roman citizenship to several neighbouring Italian peoples and, had he been prepared to use them to fight a victorious civil war, he might have done what Augustus Caesar was later to do. But his reluctance to rely on force led to his own defeat, creating the conditions which led to the more ruthless politics of the ages of Marius, Sulla, and Julius Caesar which, finally, brought the republic to its end.

By the time of Caesar, Mably wrote, the only way to preserve the republic was to jettison the rule of law and do whatever was necessary to enable the republic to survive. Brutus, he observed, had been right to assassinate Caesar as a tyrant, but wrong to spare his allies and clients. His legalistic argument that Caesar's allies were entitled as Roman citizens to the benefits of the rule of law because, although they were planning to commit acts of tyranny, they had not actually done so, was, Mably argued, incompatible with the survival of the republic. In some desperate circumstances, he observed, politics calls for the punishment of intentions, or even the mere power, to do harm. Yet, he warned, even had this more prudent policy been followed, the republic would probably still have fallen. There was no liberty left for the Romans to aspire to unless some citizen, after making himself master of them all, were to change the form of the state from top to bottom and, by giving up all of Rome's conquests, would then go on to compel the Romans to readopt the manners and poverty of their ancestors. Even if such a reform had been practicable, Mably commented, it was unlikely that any Roman citizen would have been virtuous enough to usurp sovereign power and use it that way (Mably 1794–5, IV, pp. 314–24, 356–8).

Mably's remarks about the Gracchi and the conflicts that led to the demise of the Roman republic were aimed, in part, at a number of now little-known eighteenth-century historians of republican Rome (Raskolnikoff 1992). The most important of these was an Anglo-Irish Jacobite exile named Nathaniel Hooke, an admirer of Fénelon and the translator of *The Travels of Cyrus* by Fénelon's Scottish Jacobite disciple, the Chevalier Ramsay (Hooke also translated Ramsay's biography of Fénelon himself). Hooke made it clear that one of the purposes of his history of the Roman republic was to take the part of the 'commons', arguing when he came to write about the Gracchi that liberty and the republic were 'cant words' when the bulk of the people had neither property nor an opportunity to live by their labour. He compared the circumstances of Rome's plebeians to the English poor, arguing that if England's landowners were to import slaves to cultivate their farms, no-one would suggest that the poor did not have a right to revolt. Unlike Mably, Hooke argued that Tiberius Gracchus was 'the most accomplished patriot' that Rome had ever produced. Also unlike Mably, he went on to argue that the only power able to accomplish what the Gracchi had tried but failed to do was a reforming royal government, because only an absolute sovereign had the power to take on an aristocracy and win (Hooke 1738–71, I, p. iii, II, bk. 6, ch. vii, pp. 530–8; Raskolnikoff 1992, pp. 187–91; Ward 1964).

Mably's republican alternative to Hooke's Caesarism was a large, mixed, federated system, similar in size to the huge republic which, he claimed, Charlemagne had headed. If the Roman republic had fallen because it had been unable to withstand the combination of tensions between the centre and the periphery and between the rich and the poor to which every ancient republic had been subject, the modern world had a potential for neutralising these Machiavellian problems. As one of his critics pointed out, almost everything that Mably published was actually about one thing, the constitution of empires (Garat 1784, pp. 22–3). Here, Mably argued, the moderns did have an advantage, not only because of the examples supplied by the historical study of earlier societies, but also because they were equipped with a higher level of conceptual resources for dealing with the difficulties involved in switching from commonwealths based on expansion to those based on preservation than earlier ages had been. The art of the legislator consisted of finding ways to combine public frugality with enough private property for public and private interests to coincide. It was a distinctively modern art, since it relied heavily on prudence. This kind of knowledge, Mably argued, was not given by natural law but by history and, since human reason and the ability for abstract thought were slow to develop, the moderns were better placed than the ancients had been to solve the problems of constitutional design involved in finding a form of government compatible with the part that property had come to play in human affairs.

Property, according to Mably, was very much a case of an evil from which good could be extracted. Nature, he wrote, had not made man for the possession of wealth. Nor, he wrote a few years later (flatly contradicting Rousseau), was property the cause of the reunion of men into society.

People came together, he argued, because they had social qualities, and because their needs invited them to help and serve one another mutually. The first systems of property were, accordingly, communal in character. Even when nations ceased to be nomadic and, under the pressure of growing population, came to adopt a settled way of life, agriculture would have developed under a system of common ownership. In the absence of any privately owned agricultural surplus, there would have been no reason for the existence of avarice or ambition. But, Mably suggested, the idleness of some, or the partiality of the magistrates responsible for overseeing the allocation of goods, would in the end have caused this communal system to break down. Private property probably began, he wrote, when the most hardworking members of the community asserted their own claims to justice and persuaded the community to give up its responsibility for the distribution of goods, leaving the idle to fend for themselves. Privatisation then provided reasons for avarice and ambition. Once entrenched, these passions could never be eliminated. Instead, they had to be used for the common good.

To do so, Mably argued, it was essential that the state itself should have as few needs as possible, so that it would offer nothing to tempt its citizens away from hard-working self-reliance. The art of the legislator consisted of diminishing the needs of the state rather than in increasing its revenue to meet its needs more easily. The most fundamental rule to be followed was that political life had to be based on voluntary service. Every magistracy, Mably emphasised, should be unpaid. Once a government was rich because the needs of its state were few, it could, if necessary, act benevolently, by, for example, helping its citizens to repair damaged property, or by maintaining a corn reserve to bridge poor harvest years, or, like the aristocratic government of the Swiss republic of Berne, by paying invalids to go abroad to take the waters if they could not afford to do so themselves. The combination of modest private affluence and rigid public frugality was the key to the survival of equality under conditions of general private property. Frugality had to be maintained by sumptuary laws and strict proscriptions of financial speculation. Nothing was more necessary too, Mably argued, than for laws to regulate inheritance. The most admirable of these, he suggested, were the laws of the early Roman republic, both because they prevented anyone's estate from passing into the hands of another family, and because they placed strict limits on the faculty of making a will. The purpose of such legislation was not, he argued, to interfere with private property, but to ensure that it was always used in ways that were most advantageous to society. It was an error, he added, to believe that the agrarian laws had destroyed the Roman republic. It followed that an agrarian was also an essential component of a modern system of justice. The rudiments of an agrarian which was suitable for the modern world could, he claimed, be found in Sweden, where there were strict limits on the amount of property which the members of each of the kingdom's four estates could own (Mably 1774, pp. 139–46). By increasing the number of estates (to seven or more) and fixing the amount of property which each was entitled to own, a basis could be found for a system of government compatible with the range of occupations and activities which a property-based society would have to contain. Service, not money, would be its ruling principle.

Importantly (and again in opposition to Rousseau), Mably argued that there was no obstacle to establishing and maintaining a system of this kind in a large territorial state. Although, he argued, it could not be denied that abuses were more frequent in large states, this danger could be reduced by devising a federal system of republican government. Here Charlemagne supplied the model. He had divided his dominions into a hundred different provinces, each governed by elected assemblies open to every order of citizen. The result was an extensive system of republican government, headed by a prince who, Mably wrote, was simultaneously a philosopher, a legislator, a patriot, and a conqueror. Its constitutional core was a revived and more stable version of the ancient republican assemblies of the Franks. Under Charlemagne's aegis, and as the French people came to possess a very extensive territory, each county of the empire came to depute a dozen representatives every autumn to a closed meeting on the *Champ de Mars*, followed, in May, by a general assembly of the bishops, abbots, counts, lords, and deputies of the people, sometimes deliberating separately, sometimes as a single body, so that, as Mably put it, the legislative power resided in the body of the nation, with the king as its executive head.

Mably did not, however, expect France to play the part of a republican hegemon. He was appalled by the French government's decision in 1756 to form an alliance with the Holy Roman Empire. It confirmed his conviction that the corrupting combination of absolute government and public credit had eliminated the prospects for free government in France and would come to threaten the very survival of liberty in Europe as a whole. His fear was that the French alliance with Austria, instead of giving France a free hand to deal with Britain, amounted to a blank cheque to underwrite Habsburg ambitions in central, eastern, and southern Europe. France would then be even more exposed to the paralysingly divisive domestic effects of the combination of war, debt, and taxation, and acutely vulnerable to the possibility that the Empire might ditch its French ally and side with an even more heavily indebted and desperate Britain, forced, by the severity of its domestic political dissensions, to solve its debt problem at the expense of the rest of Europe. Mably pinned his hopes for Europe's future on Prussia – the Sparta of the North – as the only power uncontaminated by the modern funding system which was also able to defend itself with a patriotic, quasi-feudal, militia system. Prussia, he argued, would be Europe's only bulwark against despotism if the other states were to succumb to the Armageddon of a general bankruptcy.

Mably was no more confident about the prospects of the American insurgents after 1776. The best hope for liberty, he argued, would have been to leave the Americans to their own devices, forcing them to fight a long, bloody, but ultimately victorious war to establish their independence, while trapping Britain into a protracted military disaster in a distant country as the best way to promote a British revolution. A long-drawn-out war of liberation would serve to instil military virtue in the nascent republic and reinforce the moral and political authority of the Continental Congress over the selfish proclivities of the individual states, thus protecting the vulnerability of their mainly farming and trading populations from ambitious and unscrupulous political leaders. Having achieved liberty too easily, the republic would have, Mably wrote, to find a surrogate for virtue to neutralise ambition. This was why, as a short-term expedient, he was prepared to support that bugbear of republics and commonwealths, a standing army, arguing that the Congress should arm itself with a permanent body of troops directly under its power, to be assembled and used according to the needs of the moment. Terror, in some circumstances, had to stand in for republican virtue.

Dying in 1785, Mably did not live to see his advice about what the Americans ought to have done come home to roost in France, the country in which he expected it least. His bleak assessment of the prospects for French liberty once the love of money had taken root was shared by his literary executors, the Abbés Chalut and Arnoux. No political society ought to be subject to the threat of tyranny, they wrote to Thomas Jefferson in the spring of 1791, sending him two volumes of Mably's posthumous works. But, they warned, societies become corrupt as they grow old, and torrents of blood would have to be spilled to eliminate the almost universal love of riches and domination (Jefferson 1950-, xx, p. 428).

5   A modern agrarian

A great deal of the eighteenth-century interest in the power of public credit
was motivated by a desire to prevent exactly that. Much of that interest was
produced by the theories of money and trade set out in the early eighteenth
century by the Scottish Jacobite financier John Law, who took money to be
wealth, not a sign of wealth. It had originated as a pledge. Money came into
being when someone who needed to acquire something had nothing useful
to offer in exchange and, instead, offered something valuable as security for a
promise to make good the exchange in the future. Since money was wealth,
it was a permanent drain upon the productive potential of other kinds of
wealth, particularly if the returns from the land or industry and trade were
lower than the return from the possession of cash. Law's own concern was
to show how the creation of an artificial currency would be able to drive
up the rate of return from the land or industry and trade by removing the
attractions of keeping wealth tied up in money. The idea had a powerful
appeal in the immediate aftermath of the death of Louis XIV and became
the basis of the elaborate debt-reduction scheme put into practice in France
during the Regency. It rapidly turned into a speculative bubble, crashing
disastrously in 1720.

The failure of Law's system left a mixture of revulsion and regret. The
regret was particularly marked in Jacobite circles and those who identified
with them in France and other parts of Europe. In part, this was because
offering a way to extricate Britain from the cycle of war, debt, and debt-
induced taxation looked (as Old Whig critics of public credit like Charles
Davenant warned at the beginning of the eighteenth century) like a winning
card to play to promote a Stuart restoration. But even after the prospects
of a Stuart restoration had receded, variations on Law's scheme continued
to survive. They did so because implementing a debt-reduction scheme
looked, particularly from the outside, like the best way to eliminate the
imperial ambition and commercial aggression which, it was argued, successive British governments had been forced to adopt in order to generate the
flow of tax-revenue needed to service their debts. Once Britain was free from
public debt, it was claimed, a basis would then exist for an Anglo-French
rapprochement because the two country's respective economies and geopolitical situations were fundamentally too different to entail durable conflicts of interest. Properly managed, a co-ordinated debt-reduction scheme
would have the effect of cutting British external interests down to a scale
compatible with her size and still considerable domestic economic resources,

while simultaneously serving to bring the more backward French economy up to a level commensurate with her more exposed position on the European mainland.

The counterpart of a debt-reduction scheme to promote peace abroad was the use of public credit to promote equality at home. Like many of his contemporaries, Babeuf was captivated by this aspect of the modern funding system. He was an acquaintance of one of the many individuals to advocate using public credit in this way, a product of the Jacobite diaspora named James Rutledge who, Babeuf wrote in 1787, was someone he greatly esteemed (Babeuf 1961, p. 138). Rutledge himself was an admirer of James Harrington, claiming in a eulogy of Montesquieu published in 1786 that, properly understood, *The Spirit of Laws* actually amounted to a covert endorsement of Harrington's *Oceana*. He had established a minor literary reputation as a satirical playwright (mainly attacking Parisian salon-society) before turning his attention to political speculation. His most substantial work was an examination of international relations entitled *Essais politiques sur l'état actuel de quelques puissances* (Political Essays on the Present State of Several Powers) which was published in 1777. Its aim was to show that the impending conflict between Britain and France over the American Revolution (which Rutledge expected Britain to lose) could lead to the formation of a new world order to replace the system based upon the Treaties of Westphalia (1748) and Utrecht (1713). These, Rutledge wrote, were the products of political ideas based on the notion of self-preservation and, since they served to ratify inequalities between states established by force of arms, were the basis of the immoral system of the balance of power, a system which served to perpetuate misery and slavery among the impoverished peoples of modern Europe. The lynchpin of the new system, he argued, would be an Anglo-French common market designed to protect Europe from the long-term threat to civilisation represented by Russia in the east and the emerging New World in the west.

Rutledge argued that Law's ideas about public credit could be used to rebalance the international system and the distribution of property in France. This would involve promoting a virtuous circle of rising demand and increasing output based upon the credit made available by a land bank. Using public credit in this way was, like Law's original system, designed to eliminate the state's debt. Of the five classes into which France was divided – the landowners, tenants, agricultural labourers, urban artisans, and *rentiers* – the interest of the last, Rutledge argued, had to be sacrificed to those of the rest. The *rentiers*, he asserted, were the only idle group, and hence would not suffer particularly if its comforts were reduced. Increasing the resources available to the propertyless by establishing a land bank would make property and tenancy more profitable by causing the land to be subdivided and better cultivated. As individual wealth increased, the relationship between the wealth of the state and the wealth of its members would change to the latter's advantage. The long-term outcome of using public credit in this way would be a more popular system of government based upon the growing convergence between individual interests and the common interest. This, in turn, would produce a more stable international system. As the potential of the French economy came to be gradually realised, and the burden of England's public debt set increasingly severe limits upon her imperial ambitions, the two peoples would be able, finally, to co-exist in peace. The outcome of the entire process, Rutledge argued, would be a system of government based on merit, not property, and an international system based on commercial co-operation rather than the sordid scramble for commercial advantage (Rutledge 1777).

Rutledge was one of dozens of like-minded financial projectors writing about public credit's potential to reduce inequality. Similar schemes could be found in the marquis de Casaux's *Considérations sur les principes politiques de mon siècle* (Considerations on the Political Principles of the Age) of 1776 (a work which the younger Mirabeau set alongside the works of the French economists and Adam Smith) or in the Anglo-Swiss political economist Jean Herrenschwand's *De l'économie politique moderne* (On the Political Economy of the Modern Age, 1786), or in the proposals to use the property confiscated from the French church as the basis of a currency-backed debt-reduction scheme promoted by the Swiss banker and future finance minister of the first French republic, Etienne Clavière, or in the works of David Williams, the Welsh Dissenter and friend of the French Girondin leader Jacques Pierre Brissot (Dybikowski 1993). Williams coupled a strong preference for Harrington over Montesquieu (publishing an entire lecture course exposing the latter's shortcomings) with an equally strong admiration for the works of the Jacobite exile Sir James Steuart, singling out Steuart's remarks on public credit for particular attention, and highlighting the way that Steuart had shown how public debts made taxation a permanent necessity, and how taxation, in turn, served to prevent profits from being consolidated with price so that the fruits of industry might be brought to market on proper terms, leaving (as he put it) the artisan easy and the state with funds. He also accepted Steuart's projection of a continually increasing public debt (one which Steuart had taken over from Hume), arguing that the perpetual rotation of assets that would arise once the annuitants replaced the landed proprietors as the owners of the national income could become the basis of genuinely republican state. Since the annuitants would have to spend in order to live, the tax revenue raised from every other social class would circulate through the whole economy, while the tax burden would be equitably managed by a reformed system of political representation. Combining Harrington's republican system of government with Steuart's projections on public credit led, in this way, to a peculiarly democratic version of Hobbes's *Leviathan* (1651). As his late didactic poem, *Egeria* (1803), served to show, it was a position which Williams maintained throughout his life. As Williams presented it, the modern world had a unique potential to combine an ancient republican system of government with a modern system of public finance to form a unitary state with a unitary debt, based, ultimately, upon a unitary set of fundamental interests.

One reason for Babeuf's interest in this kind of speculation was that it seemed to open a way to promote justice by levelling up rather than levelling down, substituting what Tom Paine was later to call 'agrarian justice' for the old republican idea of an agrarian law (Wootton 1994a, 2000). It was probably this that allowed Babeuf to include Helvétius among 'the other levellers' whose ideas, he claimed, had preceded his own. Like Mably, Helvétius was an advocate of a large federal system of republican government. Unlike Mably, however, he did not claim that the key to preventing self-interest from undermining a republic's strength and stability lay in devising a system of government able to promote simplicity and self-reliance. Instead, in his controversial *De l'esprit* (1758), he followed through the argument about the relationship between property and the origin of political society which Hobbes had made in his *De cive* (1642) to claim that once a state had been established to maintain a system of private property, the property system itself would then become the cornerstone of a utility-based social system. Once human survival needs had been met, Helvétius argued, self-preservation gave way to a peculiar compound of love and vanity. Material goods were an important part of this compound, because the relationship between men and women which they involved included a self-centred appreciation of the pleasures associated with possessing – or being possessed by – someone whom others admired. The compound of love and vanity governing relations between men and women in a property-based society was, therefore, a product of prosperity, not frugality. Its reciprocal character presupposed a level of material well-being shared by both men and women and precluded the more pathological forms of love to be found in polygamy or polyandry.

Nor, Helvétius argued, could it be described as luxury because luxury was a purely relative term based on the prior existence of some other kind of inequality. Provided that there was no political or legal inequality, prosperity would serve to reinforce this sexual sociability by increasing the tact and discrimination involved in the sort of moral evaluations that, he argued, served to give the modern social system its strength and stability. It followed that what was important for Helvétius was not a political system based on the kind of moral and material austerity that Mably commended, but, as he suggested in his posthumously published *De l'homme* (1773), a decentralised republican system that would be able to prevent the development of the inequalities of power, privilege, and wealth that were the hallmark of the courts and capital cities of the absolute monarchies. Although Helvétius himself said nothing about the power of public credit to accelerate the process, it was not difficult for more communally minded republicans like Brissot and Clavière to push the argument of *De l'esprit* in this direction.

6   Conclusion

There was no straightforward continuity between the property theories produced during the seventeenth century by Grotius, Hobbes, Pufendorf, and Locke, and those of the eighteenth century. Much of the property theory taught in the universities and colleges of eighteenth-century Europe was a self-conscious reaction against the arguments about the origins of individual ownership to be found in the works of the great figures of seventeenth-century natural jurisprudence and the presuppositions about the limited natural human capacity for society and community on which, it was claimed, they were often too heavily based. In this respect, the reaction against the natural jurisprudence of the seventeenth century paralleled eighteenth-century scepticism about the irretrievable depravity of fallen human nature that was a common feature of seventeenth-century Augustinian thought in both its Protestant and Catholic guises. When, in the wake of the debates surrounding the first French Declaration of the Rights of Man in August 1789, Jefferson wrote his famous letter to James Madison asserting that the earth always belongs to the living generation, he was not reviving anything obscure, but was simply reaffirming what could readily be found in the mainstream of eighteenth-century thought, from the treatises of natural jurisprudence by his near contemporaries, Jean Jacques Burlamaqui and Emmerich de Vattel, to the work of the Scottish common-sense philosophers Thomas Reid and James Beattie (Jefferson 1999, pp. 593–8; Reid 1990; Rutherforth 1754, I.iii, pp. 51–2; Sloan 1995).

One final example of this way of thinking can be found in William Ogilvie's *Essay on the Right of Property in Land*, a work published in 1781 as a call for reform in the light of the impending British defeat in the American War of Independence and one which, in November 1791, an English friend of the French Revolution strongly urged the French republican Brissot to read. Ogilvie, who was professor of humanity at King's College, Aberdeen University, and a friend of both Beattie and Reid, based his *Essay* upon two premises. The first asserted that all right of property was founded on either occupancy or labour. Since, Ogilvie argued, the earth had been given to mankind in common occupancy, every individual seemed to have a natural right to possess and cultivate an equal share. The second, which was the starting point of the argument of the whole work, was that every state or community ought in justice to reserve for all its citizens the opportunities of, as Ogilvie put it, entering upon, or returning to, this birthright whenever they were inclined to do so. Occupancy, as he presented it, was not only the original title to property; it also modified the entitlements of labour. This, he argued, meant that Locke's efforts to circumvent the communal character of property was mistaken. Acquisition by labour was an individual right, sanctioned by positive law. As such, it was natural and just. But it could not negate the community's general right of occupancy to the territory of the state. The need now, Ogilvie wrote, was for the law to pay equal regard to both types of entitlement in order to bring the freedom and prosperity of the lower ranks into closer alignment with the improvement of the common stock and wealth of the community.

Three developments, he claimed, made this a real possibility. The first was the rise of the modern state and its power for general legislation. The second was the emergence of ever-larger standing armies and the progressive erosion of the distinction between civil and military life which this entailed. The third was the growth of the modern, debt-financed, funding system, and the potential it housed, beyond its immediate function of meeting the costs of war, for promoting the rotation of property by way of its impact upon relative asset prices over different periods of time. Together, he argued in the body of his work, they amounted to a powerful set of levers available to any reforming government to use the financial resources of the modern state to bring occupancy and labour, the two original sources of the right to property, into the sort of balance which earlier ages had been unable to achieve. Ogilvie maintained this position all his life, hoping, as he wrote in a letter to his former pupil, Sir James Mackintosh, in 1805, long after the latter had abandoned the views he had put forward in his *Vindiciae Gallica*, that Napoleon Bonaparte would not ultimately prove to be unfaithful to so glorious a cause (Macdonald 1891, p. 301).

From this vantage point, what now seems to be so odd in Babeuf was not quite so far from the eighteenth-century intellectual mainstream as it was once made to seem in nineteenth- and twentieth-century historiography. The content of that intellectual mainstream remains quite poorly understood. But the extraordinary transformation in what Rousseau was taken to stand for that took place between the third and the fourth quarters of the eighteenth century is one indication of the enduring appeal of conceptions of community that were nearer to Fénelon than to Hobbes, and of conceptions of property that owed more to notions of need, use, and occupation than to the idea of the sovereign state as the ultimate basis of legitimate ownership. These were the notions of community and property upon which Robespierre drew, not only in 1793, but also in 1789. 'Another sovereign', he had written, 'might limit his ambition to reviving and restoring those ancient and sacred maxims which protect the ownership of our goods.' But Louis XVI had a higher goal, namely to 'guide men to happiness by means of virtue and to virtue by means of a system of legislation based upon the immutable principles of immutable morality'. He would 'restore human nature to all its rights and all its original dignity' by rebinding 'the immortal chain linking man to God and to his fellows' and by destroying 'all the causes of oppression and tyranny and the fear, suspicion, pride, servility, egoism, hatred, cupidity, and all those vices they sow in their wake' (Robespierre 1910–59, I, pp. 669–70). By the spring of 1793, there was no longer the prospect of a patriot king. Instead, there was a republic, tottering, as the Roman republic once had, on the brink of ruin. If Robespierre had read Mably, he would have known what had to be done.

V

The promotion of public happiness

17
Philosophical kingship and enlightened despotism

DEREK BEALES*

1 The idea of the philosopher king

The notion of the philosopher king comes from Plato's *Republic*. After the Renaissance, Plato's influence declined, and none of the authors writing about the late sixteenth and seventeenth centuries in the previous volume of the *Cambridge History of Political Thought* found it necessary to mention this notion at all. But Hobbes concluded the second part of *Leviathan* (1651), in a characteristically sardonic passage, by placing the concept at the very heart of his political philosophy:

[C]onsidering how different this doctrine is, from the practice of the greatest part of the world, . . . and how much depth of moral philosophy is required, in them that have the administration of the sovereign power; I am at the point of believing this my labour, as useless, as the commonwealth of *Plato*; for he also is of opinion that it is impossible for the disorders of state, and change of governments by civil war, ever to be taken away, till sovereigns be philosophers. But when I consider again, that the science of natural justice, is the only science necessary for sovereigns, and their principal ministers; and that they need not be charged with the sciences mathematical, (as by Plato they are,) . . . ; and that neither Plato, nor any other philosopher hitherto, hath put into order, and sufficiently, or probably proved all the theorems of moral doctrine, that men may learn thereby, both how to govern, and how to obey; I recover some hope, that one time or other, this writing of mine, may fall into the hands of a sovereign, who will consider it himself, (for it is short, and I think clear,) without the help of any interested, or envious interpreter; and by the exercise of entire sovereignty, in protecting the public teaching of it, convert this truth of speculation, into the utility of practice. (Hobbes 1991, ch. 31, p. 254)

So Hobbes in the mid-seventeenth century, with an elaborate if back-handed acknowledgement to Plato, looked forward to the enthronement of a philosopher sovereign, asserting that only such a ruler, armed both

* The author is very grateful to T. C. W. Blanning, S. M. Dixon, M. Grečenková, T. J. Hochstrasser, H. B. Nisbet, and H. M. Scott for their comments on earlier drafts, and to Dorothea Link for generously sending him the quotation from Zinzendorf's diary. A version of this chapter appears in Beales 2005.

with absolute power and with the certainty of acquired wisdom, could rescue society from disorder and establish a state on true principles. Since he claimed that knowledge was power, Hobbes supposed that the rule of sovereigns might be strengthened if they were philosophically informed (Hobbes 1991, ch. 8, p. 53). But his imagined philosopher was to be trained very differently from Plato's. It was not simply that he could do without a mathematical education. What distinguished Plato's philosopher more than anything else was his supposed ability to see behind the evidence of the senses and the superficial realities of life and politics to a deeper reality of ideal 'forms'. This was an example of the metaphysical, quasi-theological thinking that Hobbes regarded as 'vain philosophy'. By contrast, he claimed, 'the science of natural justice' and his 'theorems of moral doctrine' were straightforwardly derived from the obvious realities of men's natures, passions, wills, behaviour, and historical experience.

Leibniz, on the other hand, profoundly admired Plato's *Republic*, his metaphysics, and even his mathematics. In 1701 Leibniz wrote that 'the end of monarchy is to make a hero of eminent wisdom and virtue reign' (Leibniz 1988, p. 23). But even he did not accept Plato's notion of a philosopher king in full. Nor was he thinking of a ruler with 'entire sovereignty' mounting a desperate rescue operation at a time of political disintegration. Leibniz envisaged a wise king ruling a well-established and stable state, preferably a mixed government rather than an absolute monarchy, and he generally had in mind German rulers whose sovereignty was limited by the framework of the Holy Roman Empire.

His widely influential follower, Christian Wolff, in his short tract *De rege philosophante et philosopho regnante* (Of Philosophical Rule and Ruling Philosophy, 1730), argued that an all-powerful monarch who, like a Chinese emperor, was also a philosopher could bring great benefits to his subjects; and, further, that any king was likely to be a better ruler if he had some philosophical training and competence. But, with his customary moderation or complacency, Wolff remarked that no-one could be a philosopher all of the time; and for him philosophy was concerned with rational analysis, which might encourage modest improvements. He clearly did not envisage philosophy as a fundamentally radical critique, or expect a philosopher king to desire, let alone achieve, a dramatic transformation of state and society (Hochstrasser 2000).

None of these notions of a philosopher king – Plato's, Hobbes's, or Leibniz's – was prominent or well developed in eighteenth-century political thought, although traces of all of them can be found, and although other aspects of Plato's thought did have considerable influence, especially on Rousseau (Beales and Hochstrasser 1993; Wokler 2001a). It is a quite different concept of a philosopher king that is characteristic of the period. This is best illustrated from the *Encyclopédie*. In the article 'Philosopher', which appeared in 1765, occurs this passage:

This love of society, so essential to the *philosopher*, demonstrates the truth of the emperor Antoninus' [Marcus Aurelius'] remark: 'How happy peoples will be when kings are *philosophers*, or when *philosophers* are kings!' So the *philosopher* is a gentleman (*honnête homme*) whose actions are always guided by reason, and who combines a reflective and judicious mind with sociable habits and qualities. Graft a sovereign on to a *philosopher* of such a stamp, and you will have a perfect sovereign.

This is a significant statement in a number of ways, especially placed in the context of the whole article. To begin with, the writer avoids attributing the notion of a philosopher king to its original author, Plato, ascribing it instead to Marcus Aurelius, who had been fond of using it, but had known very well where it came from. It is not hard to see why this attribution was preferred. A good part of the article is devoted to denying the value of metaphysical speculation and to freeing the word 'philosopher' from the meaning given to it by Plato. The article declares:

Truth for the *philosopher* is not a mistress who corrupts his imagination and who he believes can be found everywhere; he is content to be able to unravel it when he can perceive it. He certainly does not confuse it with plausibility. He takes what is true as true, what is false as false, what is doubtful as doubtful, and what is merely plausible as plausible.

'He founds his principles on an infinity of individual observations.' Nothing could be more completely opposed to Plato's method, or to the attitudes of the sort of philosopher he imagined as king. It is also, of course, totally opposed to the method of theologians. As Voltaire said, Plato 'was almost made a father of the Church on account of his trinitarian ideas, which no-one has ever understood' (Voltaire 1957, p. 1026). Marcus Aurelius, on the other hand, had been hostile to Christianity and professed a Stoic scepticism about metaphysical reasoning. The article emphasises the difference between the philosopher and the Christian: 'Reason is to the *philosopher* what grace is to the Christian. The Christian's decision to act comes from grace, the *philosopher's* from reason.' Furthermore, the philosopher is said to 'worship' civil society.

It is not only Platonic metaphysics and Christian theology that are objectionable to the author. So is any form of *esprit de système*, that is, any attempt to work out by deduction from first principles a complete explanation of the universe or of society – something of which Descartes and Hobbes, as well as Plato and Aquinas, had been guilty. Knowledge can only be gained by induction, by observation and experiment, and on this basis is necessarily incomplete. The same message, with insistent repetition of the words *philosophy* and *philosopher*, had dominated d'Alembert's preface ('Discours préliminaire') to the whole *Encyclopédie*, which appeared in 1751. For d'Alembert the core meaning of 'philosophy' was what we call natural science, and of the 'philosopher' what we would call a scientist, or at least a man of scientific bent (Grimsley 1963).

The article 'Philosopher' is also directed against a second common meaning of the word, generally identified with Stoicism, namely, a person who suffers pain and hardship uncomplainingly, perhaps withdrawing from the world: 'it is easy', declares the author, 'to infer how remote the unfeeling sage of the Stoics is from the perfection of our *philosopher*'. The latter, we are told, enjoys the pleasures of life and of company, and works for the good of society (Beales 1985, 2005).

This is only one article among the 72,000 in the *Encyclopédie*, not all of which sang the same tune. But the *Encyclopédie* sold very widely (Darnton 1979). The article was on a subject of special sensitivity, it attracted notice, and it was presumed by many to be the work of the general editor, Diderot. In fact it was a shortened version made by him of a piece first published in 1743, of which Voltaire said that 'it has been kept to hand by all enquiring persons; it dates from the year 1730'. In other words, this article stood for many decades as a standard definition of the new philosopher. The original was probably the work of César Dumarsais (Dieckmann 1948; Fairbairn 1972).

This new meaning of *philosopher*, first trumpeted by Bayle in his *Commentaire philosophique* of 1686, had by the mid-eighteenth century been proudly accepted as a title by a group of radical French thinkers, led by Voltaire and including the chief contributors to the *Encyclopédie*, who were, and are still, known as *les philosophes* (Diaz 1962; Lough 1973, 1975; Shackleton 1978). So far is this concept from the traditional meaning of the word that R. J. White could give to his book about them the title *The Anti-Philosophers* (1970), and it has become common in English writing to use the French form *philosophes* to describe them in order to distinguish them from philosophers in general.

By the time the *Encyclopédie* was launched, Voltaire and others had given additional connotations to this new meaning. The classic text here is Voltaire's *Letters concerning the English Nation* or *Lettres philosophiques*, first published in English in 1733 and then in French in 1734. A product of his visit to England from 1726 to 1729, this typically – and artfully – unsystematic work contains chapters on the thought of several English philosophers: on Francis Bacon, 'the father of experimental philosophy' and 'the precursor of philosophy'; on Locke, 'who ruined innate ideas'; and on Newton, 'the destroyer of Descartes's system' (Voltaire 1964c, pp. 57, 59, 64, 71). In addition, the book describes with relish the variety of British religious sects, placing special emphasis on the least orthodox, the Quakers, and praising the British state for tolerating them. Like most of the political writings of the *philosophes*, the *English Letters* was conceived as a critique of the French government, and in particular of the Catholic Church, which, since the Revocation of the Edict of Nantes in 1685, had been the only lawful church in France. Church as well as state authorities possessed and exercised the power to ban such publications and to punish their authors severely. Hence works like the *English Letters* had to be anonymous and published, ostensibly or in reality, outside France. Hence too the *philosophes* tirelessly advocated freedom of thought and writing, religious toleration, and state control over the activities of churches, which they regarded as a necessary corollary (Besterman 1969; Bien 1960; Wade 1938; Wilson 1972).

It must not be supposed that this new meaning of 'philosopher' supplanted all the others, nor that the word was used in precisely the same way by all *philosophes*, nor that any *philosophe* used it with complete consistency. The basic meaning of the word remained 'a seeker after truth' and Plato was not actually denied the title. It was very common too in all kinds of discourse to use the word in a loosely Stoic sense, meaning someone putting up with pain and misfortune – though the *philosophes* did their best to remove the Christian accretions of neo-Stoicism (Gay 1967–70). Descartes's system remained fundamental in French education until late in the eighteenth century (Brockliss 1987), and the *philosophes* themselves were distinctly less sceptical about ill-defined secular goals like 'happiness' and 'utility' than they were about religious concepts. But they certainly succeeded – at least in France – in popularising the new meaning of 'philosopher', thus deliberately subverting the traditional understanding of the word (Diaz 1962).

French was the international language of the age, and the upper classes in many countries outside France made a point of writing to each other in French; intellectuals everywhere conceded a prominent, if not dominant, role to French culture; and so the works of the principal French writers, such as Montesquieu, Voltaire, and Rousseau, were known throughout the Western world. But their concepts did not always travel well. In Britain, where the church authorities had limited power and where press freedom and religious toleration were already well developed, the new meaning of 'philosopher' with its full anti-clerical, anti-theological, and anti-establishment connotations never gained wide circulation, except, ironically, in a pejorative sense after the outbreak of the French Revolution, notably in Edmund Burke's *Reflections on the Revolution in France* (1790) (Lough 1971). But it was normal in English to use the word for what we would now term a 'scientist' to describe someone who tried to find out more about nature by experiment and observation (Gascoigne 1989). In Germany both metaphysics and theology remained highly respectable, if highly contentious, and in German the word *Philosoph* was rarely used in the new sense.

A further reason for this difference between France and other countries lies in yet another new connotation of the word *philosophe*. It has been discovered that Francophone printers and booksellers described all banned books – all those that were really dangerous to market, and in consequence fetched more per page than respectable volumes – as *livres philosophiques*. In other words, books that were condemned by the authorities because they were heterodox were lumped together with books that were condemned because they were pornographic. Although this terminology does not seem to have extended beyond the book trade, there were certainly works published with *philosophe* in their title that were pornographic as well as anti-clerical, most famously *Thérèse philosophe* (1748) (Darnton 1995). Some of the major *philosophes* contributed to the literature of pornography; and the idea of the *libertin*, which was closely associated with the new meaning of *philosophe*, also conflated the notion of a man of unorthodox opinions with that of a man of loose sexual morality (Keohane 1980). This aspect of the new meaning did not figure in elevated discussions of *philosophe* kings, but it helps to explain the hostility felt towards the *philosophes* and their attitudes by the more puritanical elements in society, especially outside France.

The remarks about philosopher kings in the *Encyclopédie*'s article on the 'Philosopher', brief though they are, are nonetheless telling. In many eighteenth-century writings on monarchy, headed by those of Montesquieu, and including other articles in the *Encyclopédie*, like Diderot's 'Autorité politique' and Louis de Jaucourt's group on 'Despotism' and on various types of 'Monarchy', discussion revolves around the need to limit royal power (Diderot and d'Alembert 1954; Lough 1970, 1973). But in the article on the 'Philosopher' a *philosophe* king is simply assumed, without argument or regret, to be in a position to give, or deny, his people happiness. This is one of numerous examples of eighteenth-century political thinkers putting their trust in princes – or, at the least, pinning their hopes on them.

No work that could be called a serious theoretical study of the idea of philosophical kingship was written during the eighteenth century, but admiring references to philosopher kings, in the sense of monarchs who are *philosophes*, are scattered through some of the more radical texts of the period (Pappas 1979). In *La voix du sage et du peuple* (The Voice of the Wise Man and of the People, 1750) Voltaire wrote: 'the best thing that can happen to mankind is to have a philosopher prince'. The Swiss publicist Joseph Lanjuinais began *Le monarque accompli* (The Complete Monarch, 1774) with the assertion that a philosophical monarch, concerned for men's happiness, is the most precious gift that heaven can bestow.

Political thinkers are always to some extent affected by the political practice of their day. But those who in the eighteenth century discussed philosophical kingship – and enlightened despotism – were influenced to an exceptional degree by the activities and attitudes of contemporary sovereigns. Apart from Britain, Holland, Poland, and a few decaying old republics, the states of Europe were governed by rulers who claimed more or less absolute power and who alone – short of a revolutionary upheaval such as few thinkers envisaged before the 1780s – could change the law and carry through reform. As a Saxon reformer wrote in 1762, 'if a prince is not prepared to plan the improvement of his territories himself, I doubt that, as things are, Estates will do much good or change what is bad' (Stievermann 1991). Hence many *philosophes* cherished hopes that their ideas would be endorsed and carried into effect by some sovereign. They also naturally looked to sovereigns for patronage and employment; and most rulers did something to encourage them. Many progressives were state employees before they became known as writers: Pietro Verri served Maria Theresa and Joseph II in Milan, as Joseph von Sonnenfels did in Vienna; in Germany professors like Immanuel Kant and most Protestant clergy, such as Johann Gottfried Herder, had been appointed by the ruler; in France Claude Helvétius was a tax-farmer. Other *philosophes* were given office partly because of their writings. Frederick the Great tried to make d'Alembert president of his Academy even though he would not reside in Berlin (Van Treese 1974); the physiocrat Turgot became Louis XVI's principal minister from 1774 to 1776 (Dakin 1939); and Cesare Beccaria was appointed to a chair (of 'cameral sciences') in Milan five years after the publication in 1764 of his *Dei delitti e delle pene* (On Crimes and Punishments) (Venturi 1969–90, v, pt 1). Even Voltaire became historiographer royal (Besterman 1969), and a galaxy of radicals served as secretaries to diplomatic legations or as special envoys: Voltaire again, Hume, Rousseau, and Beaumarchais (Beales and Hochstrasser 1993). Moreover, a few monarchs enhanced their claims to the status of *philosophe* by themselves publishing contributions to theoretical discussion.

The influence of practice on theory is highlighted by the fact that so many references to philosopher kings were to particular rulers. In the *English Letters* it was, surprisingly, George II's queen Caroline whom Voltaire called 'an amiable philosopher on the throne' (Voltaire 1964c, p. 51). In 1764 appeared a pamphlet by Joseph de Laporte called *The Spirit of the Philosopher Kings, Marcus Aurelius, Julian, Stanislas, and Frederick*. The Stanislas referred to was the former king of Poland, now duke of Lorraine, whose 'anodyne' *Oeuvres du philosophe bienfaisant* (Works of the Beneficent Philosopher) had been published in the previous year (Fabre 1963). Lanjuinais's *Le monarque accompli* of 1774 was a panegyric of Joseph II of Austria, which he followed up in 1776 by another praising Catherine II of Russia.

2   Frederick II, Catherine II, Joseph II

By far the most important and influential eighteenth-century claimant to the title of *philosophe* king was Frederick II of Prussia. His father and predecessor, Frederick William I (1713–40), though he governed with ferocious efficiency and economy, and tolerated more than one Protestant sect, was notorious for his coarse contempt of intellectual and artistic activity, and especially of French culture and language. He virtually closed down the Berlin Academy that his father, Frederick I, with Leibniz's collaboration, had founded in 1701. In educating his son, Frederick William sought by brutal methods to imbue him with his own rigid brand of Calvinism, to make him into a soldier, to suppress his interest in French culture, and to stifle his literary and musical tastes. Frederick, though he was even threatened at one point with execution, refused to conform and was eventually conceded a measure of independence (Baumgardt 1987). It was a landmark in the history of the notion of the philosopher king when in 1729, at the age of seventeen, he began to sign himself, in French, 'Frederick the philosopher'. He liked to write French poetry, and eagerly ordered and read the works of the *philosophes* as they appeared. In 1736, having failed to establish relations with Voltaire through diplomatic channels, he wrote personally to him, praising his genius and particularly his plays, and asking to be sent all his other works. He enclosed a translation he had made of one of the writings of

Wolff, whom Frederick William had exiled but whom Frederick admired. A flowery but brilliant correspondence ensued, the existence of which soon became public knowledge (Skalweit 1952). If they never quoted the precise words of Plato on philosopher kings, 'they continually paraphrased them': Voltaire regularly called Frederick a 'philosophical prince' (Mervaud 1985, pp. 37, 545–6).

Frederick soon conceived the idea of writing a refutation of Machiavelli's *Prince*. Voltaire commented exhaustively on the prince's draft, was permitted to improve its French and its argument, and then arranged its publication. *Anti-Machiavel* was published in the summer of 1740, with a preface by Voltaire, just after Frederick became king. Though it was anonymous, the identity of the author was easy to guess. The book, innocent of knowledge of Machiavelli's republican *Discourses*, denounced his immorality in a rather crude and unoriginal way, but made a great impression as a declaration of Frederick's philosophy of government. A king, he said, should not pursue glory and annexations of territory. As 'the first servant of the state', he must work for justice and for the happiness, the prosperity, and even the liberty of his people. While Frederick regarded 'Plato's man' as mythical, Marcus Aurelius, 'the crowned philosopher', was his hero (Frederick 1981, pp. 34, 136).

At the beginning of his reign, living up to his promise, Frederick recalled Wolff to Prussia, arranged a meeting with Voltaire, invited him and other *philosophes* to Berlin, and revived the Academy, filling it with French writers and scientists. He extended toleration to Catholics; he declared the freedom of the press; he gave asylum to writers threatened by prosecution in France; and he reformed the Prussian legal system to limit both the use of torture in legal proceedings and the number of crimes subject to the death penalty. These last measures later enabled him to assert, with some exaggeration, that he had anticipated the proposals of Beccaria's *Crimes and Punishments* (Maestro 1973). The accession, in Prussia of all countries, of a monarch who wrote poetry and philosophical tracts, who wished to consort with radical writers, and who introduced such progressive measures, caused a sensation. 'With Frederick', it was commonly said, 'philosophy ascended the throne' (Skalweit 1952).

In 1750 appeared the first of many editions of Frederick's *Works of the Philosopher of Sans Souci*, a substantial collection of poems and essays in French. (Sans Souci, 'free from care', was the name of the small but opulent palace he had built for himself at Potsdam.) It is clear that Frederick's use of the word 'philosopher' was somewhat different from the *philosophes*', especially at first. Voltaire soon weaned him from his early admiration for the writings of Wolff, and already in *Anti-Machiavel* he was denouncing Descartes, Leibniz, and all creators of metaphysical systems. But for Frederick the core meaning of *philosophe* was always Stoic. He had endured a ghastly upbringing, he saw it as his duty to work unremittingly for the state, he shared the hardships of his soldiers, and he often risked his life in battle. He profoundly believed in the play of chance and fully expected to be buffeted by fortune. He was even prepared to describe his philistine father as 'a philosopher on the throne' (Sagave 1987). Where the king and the *philosophes* found it easiest to agree was on religious questions, because they shared contempt for the church hierarchy, indifference to theological quarrels, and detestation of religious persecution.

Frederick proved far from perfect as a *philosophe* king (Blanning 1990). The connection between his literary and political activities was in reality slight. Poetry and philosophy, like music, were, as he said, his recreations, his distractions (Spranger 1942). Voltaire and others found him a capricious friend and host: the king even had Voltaire arbitrarily imprisoned for a few weeks in 1753 (Besterman 1969; Mervaud 1985). Frederick did not in fact allow the publication of many writings critical of his rule. He maintained the brutal discipline of his army and the barracks-like character of his state. He administered his territories – in German, of course – through the machinery established by his father. In the ordinary conduct of government cameralist principles were much more evident than any English or French influence (see ch. 18). Within months of the publication of *Anti-Machiavel* he showed himself a consummate Machiavellian in seizing Silesia from Maria Theresa of Austria, publicly justifying his actions by arguments he knew perfectly well to be specious. But, if this flagrant breach of treaties and international law initially blemished his reputation, the fact that he followed it up by showing himself a master general, winning battle after battle, and securing the permanence of his conquest, enhanced it. Many, though not all, of the *philosophes* accepted that war was a natural feature of the international system and that it was a necessary part of the duties of a sovereign to fight his corner and expand the boundaries of his state, rather than allow it to be defeated and reduced in size (Lortholary 1951; Perkins 1965, 1989; Skalweit 1952).

In 1770 Frederick published brilliant critiques of two radical works, the *Essai sur les préjugés* (Essay on Prejudices), which was probably the work of Baron d'Holbach, and *Le système de la nature* (The System of Nature), which certainly was. D'Holbach was one of the principal contributors to the *Encyclopédie*, especially on scientific subjects. He was a complete atheist and a

believer in the perfectibility of humanity through education and enlightenment (Cranston 1986; Lough 1968). These views were too much for
Frederick. He argued in his critiques that the mass of the people could
not be, and ought not to be, given the opportunity of an elite education,
and that religion and superstition were indispensable to them. He further
maintained that a God of some sort must exist. He thus separated himself
from the more extreme *philosophes*. Others thought he carried his religious
indifference too far when, after the suppression of the Jesuits in 1773, he
insisted on retaining them in his dominions (Van Treese 1974, pp. 148–53).
But he continued to commend himself, and to secure good publicity, by
publishing in a philosophical vein and by keeping up his correspondence
with the older and less radical *philosophes* including, despite a series of open
rows, Voltaire.

Frederick's success during a reign of forty-six years gave a shot in the
arm to the institution of hereditary monarchy, showing that, as well as kings
like the boorish Frederick William I, the voluptuary Louis XV, the boring
Hanoverians in Britain, the idle and dissolute rulers of Portugal, and the mad
Christian VII of Denmark, it could throw up a multifaceted genius who
insisted on governing his state personally and on commanding his armies
in the field, and who, astonishingly, had the transcendent ability to make a
resounding success of all these roles. His example showed too that a monarch
might himself be hostile to some of the assumptions of the *ancien régime*, and
hence that reform from above was a serious possibility. For more than two
decades he was the only serious contender as a *philosophe* king. But in 1759
Charles III became king of Spain, three years later Catherine II usurped the
throne of Russia, and in 1764 Stanislas Augustus was elected king of Poland.
Then in 1765 Joseph II succeeded as Holy Roman Emperor and co-regent
of the Austrian monarchy, while Leopold, his younger brother, the future
emperor Leopold II, became grand duke of Tuscany. In 1772 Gustavus III
re-established absolute monarchical rule in Sweden. All of these sovereigns
of major states, together with many lesser princes, had some claim to the
title of *philosophe* kings.

Among this group Catherine II was pre-eminent. As soon as she became
empress, she asked d'Alembert to be tutor to her son and heir (though he
was too prudent to accept), she began corresponding with Voltaire, and she
offered to publish the remaining volumes of the *Encyclopédie*, at that time
under the ban of French censorship, if the enterprise would move to Russia.
That proposal was not accepted, but in 1765 she bought Diderot's library for
more than the asking price, while allowing him to retain the use of it, and

giving him a handsome pension into the bargain. So far as her policies were concerned, she immediately reduced the power of the Orthodox Church and extended religious toleration (Lortholary 1951; Madariaga 1981). Then in 1767 she published a lengthy instruction (*Nakaz*) which she had given to a legislative commission summoned to review the Russian legal system. This extraordinary document, perhaps not originally composed with a legislative commission in mind (Sacke 1931), largely consisted of selections she had herself made from the writings of *philosophes*. Of 655 clauses, it has been calculated that 294 derived 'wholly or in substantial part' from Montesquieu's *Spirit of the Laws* (1748), 108 from Beccaria's *Crimes and Punishments* (1764), 35 from Baron Bielfeld's *Institutions politiques* (1760), 24 from J. H. G. von Justi's cameralist textbook, *Die Grundfeste zu der Macht und Glückseligkeit der Staaten* (Foundations of the Power and Prosperity of States, 1760–1), 20 from the *Encyclopédie* (completed only in 1765), and even a few, indirectly, from Adam Smith's lectures at Glasgow, long anticipating the publication of *The Wealth of Nations*. Some of the paragraphs are ludicrous:

48. The Chinese are guided by custom.
49. The severity of law tyrannises in Japan.
50. At one period morals formed the conduct of the Lacedemonians . . .
266. The peasants have generally from twelve to fifteen or twenty children by one marriage, but rarely does a fourth part of them attain to the age of maturity.

Other sections, however, embody serious political discussion. She endorses much of Beccaria's programme of penal reform:

200. In order that punishment may not appear to be the violence of one, or many rising up against a citizen, it ought to be public; conveniently speedy, useful to society, as moderate as circumstances will allow, proportional to the crime, and exactly such as is laid down in the laws.

It is astonishing not only that a sovereign should have been so up-to-date and progressive in her reading, even if she presented it in peculiar ways, but also that she should have been ready to publish this document and to make it available to a commission of more than 500 persons elected from all the provinces of Russia and almost all walks of life (Dukes 1977; Madariaga 1981). The text made a huge impression abroad, where it was believed to be a blueprint for a new law code. It highlighted the contrast with what most *philosophes* condemned as the confused, heterogeneous, and precedent-ridden legal arrangements of countries like France.

In the same year as the *Nakaz* was published, while Catherine and her court were floating lazily down the Volga, she organised and took part in the translation into Russian of Jean François Marmontel's *Bélisaire* (1767), a novel describing the work of a good king and advocating toleration. Marmontel expressed a widespread sentiment, at least among *philosophes*, when he wrote:

A wise man said that peoples would only be happy when philosophers were kings, or kings philosophers. There seemed little likelihood that either would ever occur. But we see in our own day that of all the orders of society the supreme rank is the one where, proportionally, there is the largest number of true friends of wisdom and truth. (Lortholary 1951, p. 108)

French censorship duly demonstrated its fatuity by banning both the *Nakaz* and *Bélisaire*.

Joseph II first made an impact at the beginning of his reign as Holy Roman Emperor with attempts to reform the imperial courts, but then became better known for his extensive travels 'as a philosopher' throughout his dominions, and also to Italy (1769, 1775, 1784), to France (1777, 1781), to the Netherlands (1781), and to Russia (1780, 1787) – fact-finding missions during which he avoided pomp and ceremony, made a point of visiting useful buildings like barracks, dockyards, hospitals, and prisons as well as courts, churches, and beauty-spots, and met artists, philanthropists, and entrepreneurs as well as kings and ministers. He conducted no correspondences with *philosophes*, evaded meeting Voltaire, seems not to have grasped the new meaning of *philosophe*, and published nothing which had not originated as an official document. But, on becoming ruler of the Austrian monarchy in 1780, he launched a frenetic programme of legislation which included granting toleration to the principal Protestant sects, the Orthodox Christians, and the Jews, and curbing the power and wealth of the Catholic Church, especially of its monasteries (Beales 2003; Blanning 1994; Bradler-Rottman 1973; Klueting 1995.) He was duly described as 'a philosopher on the throne' (Beales 1975, 1985, 1987, 1991, 2005).

Both Catherine and Joseph, like Frederick, troubled some of their admirers by their wars and annexations, especially the first partition of Poland in 1772. But Voltaire defended even that as giving to some of the backward, aggressively Catholic Poles the benefits of tolerant and enlightened rule. He and other *philosophes* rejoiced at Catherine's victories over the Turks and looked forward to her 're-establishing philosophy in Constantinople' (Lortholary 1951, pp. 112–14, 130–2). In the 1780s Joseph obtained the support of the most notorious French publicist of the decade, Simon Linguet, in his campaign to open the Scheldt to revive the economy of the Austrian

Netherlands; and some progressive writers saw his war of 1788 with Turkey as a crusade for toleration (Beales 1993, 2005; Levy 1980).

As grand duke of Tuscany (1765–90), Joseph's brother, Leopold, also imposed a vast range of similar reforms from above, but during the course of his reign his approach to government became increasingly different from Joseph's. He was determined to maintain neutrality in international affairs; he assisted the publication of a new edition of the French *Encyclopédie* in his dominions; and he enacted an exceptionally progressive criminal law code in 1786. He even wanted to introduce in Tuscany a constitution establishing representative government, and prepared himself to do so by studying the political writings of the past and of his own day, including documents of the American Revolution. But the project was vetoed by Joseph. Just after the latter had died, Leopold, who succeeded him as ruler of the monarchy, published an extraordinary manifesto, directed at the rebels against Austrian rule in the Netherlands, in which he declared:

I believe that even a hereditary sovereign is only a delegate and employee of the people . . . ; that in every country there must be a fundamental law or contract between the people and the sovereign which limits his power and authority; that when the sovereign fails to keep it, he forfeits his position . . . and people are no longer obliged to obey him; . . . that the orders of the sovereign do not acquire the force of law and need not be obeyed until after the Estates have consented to them. (Leopold II 1867, pp. 84–5)

As Leopold lived for only two more years, it is impossible to say how far he would have acted upon these principles. But his record inspired some writers to regard him as the best of all the *philosophe* kings (Valsecchi 1974; Wandruszka 1963–5).

Leopold was certainly the ruler who came nearest to the ideal imagined by Louis Sébastien Mercier in his well-known utopia of 1771, *L'an 2440* (The Year 2440). In Mercier's vision France has ceased to be oppressed by absolutism and has become a smiling land of liberty and prosperity.

Would you believe it? The revolution came about quite easily, by the heroism of a great man. A philosopher king, worthy of the throne because he disdained it, more concerned for the happiness of mankind than the appearance of power, concerned for posterity and wary of his own power, offered to restore to the Estates their ancient prerogatives. He sensed that a far-flung kingdom needed to unify its different provinces in order to be governed wisely . . . In this way, everything lives, everything flourishes. (Darnton 1995, p. 330)

For the sake of completeness, it should be added that, while in the last decades of the *ancien régime* an exceptional number of monarchs exercised their power personally, in important instances it was in effect delegated to enlightened or philosophical ministers (H. M. Scott 1996). In 1762 Voltaire said of Count Leopold Firmian, governor of Lombardy under Maria Theresa, 'All that is needed to transform a country is a minister' (Diaz 1962; Valsecchi 1931–4). Guglielmo Du Tillot in the duchy of Parma was another example (Benassi 1915–25). But by far the most notable was Sebastião Pombal in Portugal, who was the effective ruler of Portugal from 1750 to 1777. He brought about the expulsion of the Jesuits from his country in 1759 and so began the process that led to the suppression of the order throughout the world by the pope in 1773. He ruthlessly extended royal power over the church, censorship, and education, establishing a new system of secondary schools in the spirit of the Catholic Enlightenment (Maxwell 1995).

3   The idea of despotism

Despite the widespread use during the eighteenth century of the ancient concept of the 'philosopher king', if in perverted forms, modern scholarship has paid little attention to it (see Pappas 1979). In contrast, the notion 'enlightened despot', an eighteenth-century coinage but one only rarely used at the time (Bluche 1978), has been freely applied to the period by subsequent writers (e.g. Bluche 1968; Gershoy 1944; Krieger 1975). So has the closely related concept 'enlightened absolutism', although in this precise form it has not been traced in any text earlier than 1847 (Aretin 1974; Bazzoli 1986; Köpeczi *et al.* 1985; Reinalter and Klueting 2002; Roscher 1847, 1874; Scott 1990).

Let us start with eighteenth-century usage. Just as the new meaning of 'philosophical' was a deliberate perversion of an old term in order to remove from it its metaphysical content, the meanings of 'enlightened' in English and *éclairé* in French were perverted to remove from them their religious content. Before this period one of the commonest meanings of these adjectives was 'illuminated by faith'. Christ had brought 'a light to lighten the Gentiles'. 'Let your light so shine before men', urged the Book of Common Prayer. A convert was said to have 'seen the light'. In the new meaning the light was understood to come from the advance of secular philosophy, and in many contexts *éclairé* became indistinguishable from *philosophe*.

In the eighteenth century German was the only language to possess an abstract noun which can be directly translated as 'Enlightenment': *Aufklärung*. Paradoxically, this word did not have religious connotations and originally meant 'brightening up' or 'clearing up' rather than 'enlightening'. During the century its meaning gradually moved towards the modern acceptation, though at this time it always denoted a change of attitudes or a process, and was never used to describe a period (Nisbet 1982). In French the nearest equivalent noun was, as it still is, *les lumières*, the rays or sources of light, but *philosophie* was commonly employed instead. In German *Aufklärung* and *aufgeklärt* were used in this sense much more frequently than *Philosophie* and *philosophisch*. But a *philosophe* king may be regarded as virtually indistinguishable from an enlightened king, and a *philosophe* despot from an enlightened despot.

In 1784 Kant, answering the question *What is Enlightenment?* at a time when it was the subject of much debate in Prussia (Bahr 1974; Nisbet 1982) defined it as 'Man's emergence from his self-incurred immaturity', that is, from his dependence on the views of others, especially in religion. This is not exactly how the *philosophes* would have put it, but they would not have dissented. Kant went on to describe the age as 'an age of Enlightenment, the century of Frederick'. 'Only a ruler who is himself enlightened and has no fear of phantoms, yet who likewise has at hand a well-disciplined and numerous army to guarantee public security, may say what no republic would dare to say: *Argue as much as you like and about whatever you like, but obey!*' (Kant 1991, pp. 58–9). For Kant, Frederick, even at the close of his reign, is the enlightened king par excellence.

The meanings of the concepts 'despot' and 'despotism', together with 'absolute monarch(y)' and 'absolutism', present far greater difficulties than the meanings of 'enlightened' and 'Enlightenment'. Despotism in ancient Greece normally meant a master's dominion over his slaves, a fact not forgotten in eighteenth-century writing. But it had also been used by Aristotle as a variant of 'tyranny'. In his celebrated classification of regimes according to the number of persons ruling, monarchy was one-man rule that was responsible and beneficent, while tyranny was its corruption; rule by one man who exploited untrammelled power in his own interests and at his whim to the detriment of his subjects; and despotism was a form of government, especially suited to the East, in which the ruler treated his subjects like slaves. In the seventeenth century despotism was sometimes used more loosely, but always in a pejorative sense. This usage was the basis from which most eighteenth-century discussion started. In other words, when 'despotism' was being used in some other way, as it often was, it was in self-conscious divergence from this standard meaning (Koebner 1951).

However, the terminology had already been complicated by earlier writers. For example, Hobbes insisted that monarchy, despotism, and tyranny were indistinguishable because the people, when making their contract with their sovereign, had surrendered all power to him without conditions. The supposed differences, said Hobbes, were a matter of mere rhetoric: 'for they that are discontented under *monarchy*, call it *tyranny*' (Hobbes 1991, ch. 19, p. 130). Furthermore, from the sixteenth century the concepts of 'absolute monarchy', 'sovereignty', and 'arbitrary government' had been brought into play. Many proponents of monarchical rule, and most advocates of indivisible sovereignty, thought monarchs were or ought to be absolute, that is, above the law and able to change it on their own authority. This was the doctrine of Pufendorf and of most Continental theorists of natural law and natural rights, and also of the cameralists, commanding wide acceptance in the German and Italian states (Pufendorf 1991; Small 1909; Tribe 1988). Basically, they maintained that men had surrendered all, or almost all, their natural rights to the sovereign when they made their contract with him (Tuck 1979). Seventeenth- and eighteenth-century French kings too claimed to be absolute, partly on the basis of older traditions of thought. This claim justified their refusal to call the Estates General between 1614 and 1789, and their overriding in certain cases the remonstrances of the various *parlements*, whose members considered themselves constitutionally entitled to reject royal legislation. However, advocates of absolute monarchy usually claimed that it was quite distinct from 'arbitrary government' or despotism, alleging either that even absolute kings were bound by certain fundamental laws, or that they in fact used their power for the good of their state and people, or both. The great French preacher Bishop Bossuet, proponent of the Revocation of the Edict of Nantes, in his role as tutor to Louis XIV's heir took care to condemn arbitrary government and would never so much as mention despotism in his presence (Keohane 1980; Koebner 1951).

The text of *Anti-Machiavel* conveniently illustrates some of the inconsistencies of absolutist theory and some of the confusions of its terminology. Frederick insists that

justice . . . must be the principal object of a sovereign. It is thus the good of the people he governs that he must prefer to every other interest. It is thus their happiness and felicity that he must augment – or procure it if they do not have it. What becomes then of such ideas as interest, greatness, ambition, and despotism? The sovereign, far from being the absolute master of the people under his dominion, is nothing else but their first servant and must be the instrument of their felicity as they are of his glory. (Frederick 1981, pp. 34–5)

But he declares it essential for the good of the state and the people that the king should rule personally, without deferring to ministers. He has no time for the view that a monarch ought to be constrained by a constitution, the laws, ministers, parliaments, or any intermediary bodies. 'Just as kings can do good when they want to do it, they can do evil whenever they please' (p. 32). 'In every country there are honest and dishonest people just as in every family there are handsome persons along with one-eyed, hunchbacks, blind, and cripples; . . . there are and always will be monsters among princes, unworthy of the character with which they are invested' (p. 33). He thinks that the only sanction against a bad ruler is that he will acquire a bad reputation. But there is no suggestion that the views of his people should actually be sought, or deferred to, on this or any other issue. In discussing republics he maintains that they all in the long run degenerate into despotisms, while admitting that

no-one will ever persuade a republican . . . that monarchy is the best form of government when a king means to do his duty, since he has the will and power to put his good intentions into effect. I agree, they will say to you, but where can this phoenix of princes be found? He would be Plato's man . . . Your metaphysical monarchy, if any such existed, would be an earthly paradise; but despotism, as it really is, more or less changes this world into a living hell. (Frederick 1981, p. 73, retranslated)

For Frederick, it seems from some of these remarks, despotism is indistinguishable from absolute rule – in another place he talks of the 'absolute despotism in France' created by the seventeenth-century minister-favourites Richelieu and Mazarin (Frederick 1981, p. 47). But he also insists that the king, in order to do his job, must possess what appears to be absolute power, and yet that there is a great difference between beneficent monarchy on the one hand and despotism on the other. What makes the difference is purely the character and attitude of the prince himself.

4 The idea of the enlightened despot

Soon after the publication of *Anti-Machiavel*, the framework within which discussion of despotism had hitherto taken place was transformed by three developments. First, Montesquieu in *The Spirit of the Laws* (1748), as part of his attack on the absolute monarchy of France from the standpoint of a supporter of the *parlements*, deliberately challenged Aristotle's classification of forms of government, and defined monarchy and despotism as distinct species rather than opposed varieties of just one. In a monarchy, as he described it, there must be a constitution of sorts, including both a law of succession to the throne and the existence of countervailing forces like the aristocracy and the church, and/or of intermediary bodies like *parlements*, that the ruler was bound to consult about proposed legislation. Unless at least some of these conditions were satisfied, the state would be a despotism. On these premises France was or ought to be a monarchy, but its kings' absolutist theories and practices were in danger of turning it into a despotism. He further argued that despotism was an inherent characteristic of large and Oriental states, like Russia. Montesquieu nearly always avoided applying the word and concept 'absolute' to power and government, refusing to accept that there was a difference between absolute and despotic rule. With these views went his admiration for the English constitution and its balance or 'separation of powers'.

The Spirit of the Laws at once became one of those select books that all serious writers had to know and to take into account. Its new classification was rejected by many. Voltaire, for example, a consistent supporter of the French monarchy against the *parlements*, regarded the distinction as laboured (*L'ABC*, Voltaire 1994a, pp. 97–8). But the standing of Montesquieu's book led to its being drawn upon even by absolute rulers themselves. Catherine II's lavish borrowings from it for the *Nakaz* have been mentioned. But, despite her reverence for the book, she was determined to modify its message. She wished Russia to be regarded as European, and to qualify as a monarchy rather than a despotism, despite its lack of a law of succession, asserting that she had established adequate intermediary bodies. In the *Nakaz* she twisted Montesquieu's words in order to make this case:

9. The sovereign is absolute, for no other than absolute powers vested in one person, can be suitable to the extent of so vast an empire . . .

13. What is the object of absolute government? Certainly not to deprive the people of their natural liberty, but to direct their conduct in such manner that the greatest good may be derived from all their operations.

When Diderot was at last persuaded to visit her in 1773, he urged her, unsuccessfully, in his *Mémoires pour Catherine II* (Memoranda for Catherine II), to follow Montesquieu more thoroughly and establish stronger intermediary institutions. Not only Catherine II but also, more improbably, Joseph II admired aspects of Montesquieu's work. In Rome in 1769, he and his brother Leopold were painted together by Pompeo Batoni with *The Spirit of the Laws* on the table beside them. Joseph certainly did not accept Montesquieu's general scheme. But in the special circumstances of the Austrian monarchy one of Montesquieu's shibboleths, the separation of powers, proved useful to the centralising ruler. In many provinces Maria Theresa had found herself faced with the situation that much executive, some legislative, and most judicial power was in the hands of the local nobility, in their own right, or as members of the local Estates. In this context, to insist upon the separation of justice and administration, which was one of the planks in the empress's reform programme of 1749, was to enhance the power of the monarch and of her courts and administration over against the power of the provincial magnates. Montesquieu could be cited as supporting this separation even though he had specifically commended the exercise of judicial functions by local lords (Strakosch 1967).

The second development in discussions of despotism was that writers began to exploit it for their own purposes, to assert, for example, that the pope was a despot, or the Jesuits despotic, and that interfering bureaucrats or over-mighty nobles were petty despots, against whom the king with his absolute power intervened to protect his subjects. From the late 1750s French ministers were being described as despots whose machinations the supposedly absolute king was failing to control (Van Kley 1984, ch. 4).

Thirdly, some writers began to use 'despotism' in a positive sense. The first known example is the formulation of the Abbé de Saint-Pierre, according to Voltaire 'half philosopher and half mad', who insisted that 'when power is united to reason, it cannot be too great or too despotic for the greatest utility of society' (qu. Keohane 1980, p. 370). This sort of usage was often combined with calling subordinate authorities despotic in a negative sense. Joseph II, for example, liked to condemn lesser officials, such as the agents of landowners, as despots, and also to brand the pope as a despot, but in 1763 he recommended to his mother in a private paper that Hungary should be subjected to despotism for ten years in order to get rid of its absurd old constitution which, he claimed, was frustrating its development. This frank advocacy of 'despotism' was deemed so shocking that the document was suppressed (Beales 1980, 1991, 2005).

Beccaria made rather similar points in *Crimes and Punishments*, despite the fact that his argument started out from Rousseau's *Social Contract* (1762):

How happy humanity would be if laws were being decreed for the first time, now that we see seated on the thrones of Europe benevolent monarchs, inspirers of the peaceful virtues, of the sciences, of the arts, fathers of their peoples, crowned citizens. Their increased power serves the happiness of their subjects because it removes that crueller, because more capricious intermediary despotism, which suffocated the always sincere desires of the people which are always successful when they may reach the throne! If they leave the ancient laws in place, I say, it is because of the endless difficulty of removing the venerated and centuries-old rust. That is the reason for enlightened citizens to wish all the more fervently for their authority to continue to increase. (Beccaria 1995, pp. 71–2; translation adapted)

There is no clearer example of a radical humanitarian thinker of real stature recognising the potentiality of rule by enlightened monarchs, and demanding that their powers be increased to enable them to impose the major changes that are considered to be necessary. While attacking what he chose to describe as intermediate despotism, he was in fact recommending what would now be called enlightened despotism or absolutism. In an earlier passage he had written: 'the despotism of many individuals is only rectifiable by the despotism of a single person and the cruelty of the despot is proportional, not to his power, but to the obstacles he encounters' (Beccaria 1995, p. 16). No wonder his work was excerpted by Catherine II and he was given employment by Maria Theresa and Joseph II (Dukes 1977; Venturi 1969–90, v, pt 1). More surprising perhaps is that, to some degree, these rulers acted on his proposals for drastic reform of the criminal law.

Another positive use of 'despotism', but in a rather different sense, is to be found in certain works of the physiocrats: Quesnay's *Despotisme de la Chine* (Chinese Despotism, 1767) and especially Le Mercier de la Rivière's *L'ordre naturel et essentiel des sociétés politiques* (The Natural and Necessary Order of Political Societies, 1767), which was avowedly designed as the political manifesto of the group (Silberstein 1928; Weulersse 1910). These argued that government, society, and especially the economy are subject to laws which, like the laws of geometry, are indisputable and self-evident. It is the business of the good ruler to put these laws into effect, or – according to one formulation – to get rid of the existing counter-productive laws and then sit back, do nothing, and let the self-evident laws operate. These laws may, by a play upon words, be described, like Euclid's laws, as despotic, and the regime that enacts and sustains them as *despotisme légal*. This concept does not imply, as has sometimes been supposed, that the physiocrats approved of what is normally described and condemned as despotism, namely, the arbitrary rule of an individual. Confusingly, they too condemned despotism in this sense, while remaining strong advocates of absolute monarchy as the best form of government. For, far from acting wilfully or in his own interests, the ruler who enacts Le Mercier's laws will have no discretion; he will be doing the self-evidently right thing, not what he likes but what is natural and essential. Ironically, in the mid-1760s several governments introduced one of the physiocrats' laws, free trade in grain, thereby causing famine, and provoking violent opposition. The experiment had to be abandoned (Kaplan 1976; Venturi 1969–90, v, pt 1). Furthermore, the concept of 'legal despotism', though initially applauded by Diderot, Catherine II, and others, was attacked as absurd and self-contradictory, for example by Rousseau, and soon ceased to be taken seriously (Krieger 1975; Lortholary 1951; Spurlick 1986).

It was during these years when the concept of despotism was being widened, varied, and rehabilitated that the phrases 'enlightened despot' and 'enlightened despotism' were coined. The first unequivocal reference to an 'enlightened despot' which has so far been discovered dates from 1758. It comes from the *Correspondance littéraire*, a manuscript journal compiled in Paris by Friedrich Melchior Grimm, Diderot, Guillaume Raynal, and others from 1756 onwards, specifically in order to inform a handful of subscribing monarchs and princes about the writings and doings of the *philosophes* and matters of related interest. On 15 March 1758 Grimm refers to the Danish law of 1665 which gave absolute power to the king:

It is true that there is no government more perfect than that of a just, vigilant, enlightened, beneficent, despot, who loves the state and his people; but as such princes are rare and there are ten bad or incapable ones to one good, I leave you to judge if the Danish law is a masterpiece of prudence.

On 1 October 1767 Grimm used the same expression again: 'It has been said that the rule of an ENLIGHTENED DESPOT, active, vigilant, wise and firm, was of all regimes the most desirable and most perfect, and this is a true saying; but it was important not to take it too far. I passionately love such despots.' But this time he said that only one ruler in fifty could be expected to fulfil the role (Bluche 1978).

During his visit to Russia in 1773 Diderot and Catherine II held lengthy conversations, in preparation for which he wrote what are known as the *Memoranda for Catherine II*. One passage runs:

All arbitrary government is bad; I do not except the arbitrary government of a good, firm, just, enlightened master . . . A despot, even if he were the best of men, by governing in accordance with his good pleasure, commits a crime . . . One of the greatest misfortunes that could happen to a free nation would be two or three consecutive reigns of a just and enlightened despotism. Three sovereigns in succession like Elizabeth, and the English would have been imperceptibly led towards slavery for an indeterminate period . . . Let us work out the probabilities. The sovereign can be good and enlightened, but feeble; good and enlightened, but lazy; good, but without enlightenment; enlightened, but wicked. Out of five cases, the only favourable one is when he is enlightened, good, hard-working and firm, and only then will Your Imperial Majesty be able to hope that the good she has done will last and that her great aims will continue to be pursued. (Diderot 1966, pp. 115–18)

These remarks of Grimm and Diderot invite many comments. First, none of them was intended to be printed, and all of them were written as part of a private or very restricted dialogue between *philosophes* and rulers. In each it is accepted that an enlightened despot can exist, indeed that such rulers have existed, and do exist. But both writers express qualms about the phenomenon, that such rulers will inevitably be very rare, and in the case of Diderot that they cannot avoid doing harm and storing up trouble for the future even while doing good in the present.

Diderot first put such views into print in the 1774 edition of Raynal's best-selling *Deux Indes*. This radical anti-colonialist work contained much material which Raynal had commissioned from other authors, including many passages by Diderot, such as the following:

People say that the most fortunate kind of government would be that of a just, resolute and enlightened despot. What nonsense! Could it not be that the will of such an absolute master would contradict that of his subjects? Would he not then be wrong, in spite of all his justice and enlightenment, to deprive them of their rights, even if it were for their advantage? . . . A first despot who was just, resolute, and enlightened, would be a great evil; a second would be a greater evil; a third would be the most terrible scourge a nation could ever suffer. (Diderot 1992, pp. 207–8)

So, when Diderot finally went public with his concept of the enlightened despot – he used the abstract form 'enlightened despotism' even more rarely – it was to condemn it (Diderot 1992). Earlier, his attitude to the progressive rulers of his time had been less hostile. But he was shocked by Louis XV's *coup d'état* of 1770, when the king dismissed the *parlements* and asserted his absolute power, denouncing it as despotism. Then in his unpublished *Pages contre un tyran* (Pages Directed against a Tyrant) of 1771 he turned against Frederick the Great, replying to his attack on d'Holbach. However, his *Memoranda for Catherine II* make it clear that as late as 1773 he still had high hopes of persuading her to use her power in accordance with his advice. Only when she rebuffed him did he write his critical *Observations on the Nakaz* (1774), and even then he did not publish this work (Diderot 1992, pp. 77–164).

So the many historians who have denied that the precise concept of 'enlightened despotism' was known in the eighteenth century were mistaken (Behrens 1975; Derathé 1963; Gay 1967–70, II). But these rather offhand assertions of Grimm and Diderot hardly constitute a developed theory of enlightened despotism. There exists, however, one major work, admittedly by a second-rank thinker, from the same Milanese background as Beccaria, which makes an elaborate case for what amounts to enlightened despotism as normally understood, quite explicitly glorifying the despotic element. It is Giuseppe Gorani's *Il vero dispotismo* (True Despotism) of 1770. Despotism, he says, has been universally condemned as a monstrous form of government. He defines it as the operation of

that will which acts on its own without consulting others, which includes in itself the entire legislative and executive power, which by virtue of the strongest attraction joins and attracts to itself all the vigour and wide-ranging powers of the sovereign, the prince, the government, and the whole state, so that the movement of the entire political machine depends on his movement . . . Though above the laws, which he can create and destroy at his pleasure, he can through his absolute will arrive at laws as good or better than those existing, which generally and in most countries may be thoroughly bad.

This can yield 'a kind of despotism which ought to result in utility to the public' (Gorani 1770, I, pp. 6–7). Gorani sees rulers like Catherine II and Leopold of Tuscany as undertaking a beneficent 'total reform'. He calls upon 'philosophy, the support of thrones, the preserver of liberty, the joy of nations' to come to the aid of his imagined ruler (Gorani 1770, I, p. 97).

Gorani's work was not especially well known, but it is clear that ideas like these had a wider appeal. Pietro Verri, an economic and political writer, and an official of the Milanese government, who had given Beccaria substantial help in writing *Crimes and Punishments*, declared in 1781:

In my opinion, subjects ought never to fear the power of the sovereign when he himself exercises it and doesn't surrender any essential part of it into other hands . . . Only intermediate power is to be feared, and I think and feel that the best of all political systems will always be despotism, provided that the sovereign is active and in overall control and doesn't give up any portion of his sovereignty. (Venturi 1969–90, V, pt 1; Beales 1991, pp. 5–6)

Such views also found support from the bitter pen of Linguet, who was notorious for his defence of slavery as a necessary support to a civilised and enlightened elite (*Théorie des lois civiles*, 1767, esp. bk V). He said that he preferred to all other forms of government, for the happiness of the people, that is the most numerous and weakest part of a nation, [the form] that we improperly stigmatise with the odious name of despotism, namely, the one in which there are no intermediaries between the prince and his subjects powerful enough to stifle the complaints of the latter and to fetter the influence of the former. (Lortholary 1951, p. 138)

An extraordinary instance of the use of the very words 'enlightened despotism' is to be found in the writings of Stanislaw Staszic, who in 1787 actually recommended it to his fellow Poles, but in his mind the concept amounted only to an enhancement of royal power, checked by a representative assembly (Lukowski 2001).

It is hardly accidental that these resounding defences of enlightened or philosophical despotism came from men who, at the time they wrote them, were admirers of Joseph II. He was said to have inaugurated 'the era of enlightened South Germany' (Pezzl 1783). At the end of 1783 he issued to his officials and published what became known as his 'pastoral letter' in which he declared: 'I have weakened the obstructions resulting from prejudices and old, deep-rooted habits by means of Enlightenment (*Aufklärung*), and combated them with arguments.' He denounced those who put obstacles in the way of his avalanche of legislation, saying that he had enacted it for 'the general best' (*allgemeine Beste*) and for 'the utility and the greatest good of the greatest number'. He had convinced himself that his own inner light was the best guide to church reform, and so informed the pope. His personal identification with this anti-papal programme of Catholic Reform was so evident that it was later to be christened 'Josephism' (*Josephinismus*) (Beales 1987, 2002, 2003; Blanning 1994; Maass 1951–61; Valjavec 1945; Winter 1962). During the 1780s he carried out his earlier threat of subjecting Hungary to ten years of despotic rule. At the beginning of 1789 he told his recalcitrant subjects in the Netherlands: 'I do not need your permission to do good' (Beales 1987, 1991, 2005; Capra 1984). This was the apogee of enlightened despotism in practice.

By the time Joseph II died in February 1790, his troops had been driven out of Belgium, and he had been forced to abandon most of the reforms he had introduced in Hungary. A year after Leopold II had succeeded him, a minister who served both of them, Count Karl von Zinzendorf, wrote in his diary: 'What changes in principles and assumptions and decisions since then! Everything used to be directed towards concentration, uniformity; [now] everything is directed towards dispersion, diversity. It used to be all despotic monarchy, now it is all an anarchy of provincial Estates' (Haus-, Hof- und Staatsarchiv, Vienna).

5   Conclusion

It is not suggested here that the tradition of thought that has been described in this chapter was the only, or even the most important, thread in eighteenth-century political theory. In Britain absolute monarchy, seen as indistinguishable from despotism, had been definitively abolished, and hardly any thinkers saw it as a potentially creative force. One of the few exceptions was Bentham, who was much influenced by Beccaria, and whose early works, notably the *Fragment on Government* (1776), shared his expectations that reform would come from above, through the agency of enlightened absolute sovereigns. In the surviving republics, in parts of the Holy Roman Empire, in the southern Netherlands, and in Hungary, ancient mixed constitutions were stoutly defended. In France, although Voltaire and others had high hopes of strong enlightened rulers, Montesquieu and Rousseau were the most influential of the many who denounced absolute monarchy. Once the American Revolution had given an example of an alternative way of reform through revolution from below, and still more after the outbreak of the French Revolution, expectations of reform and revolution from above dwindled (Klippel 1990) – at least until the advent of Napoleon, when they emerged in a very different guise. Leopold II presents the extraordinary spectacle of a monarch proposing to use his absolute power to abolish absolutism.

However, as has been shown here, many *philosophes* and figures of the Continental Enlightenment, down to the 1780s, believed that the only chance, or the best hope, for the acceptance of their ideas was that they would be adopted by like-minded monarchs who would use their power to put them into practice. Especially after the accession of Frederick the Great, they thought that this process was under way. They sometimes deployed a modified version of the traditional concept of the philosopher king, sometimes talked of the absolute power of the enlightened or philosophical monarch, and occasionally of the enlightened or philosophical despot. Confusingly, despotism in its ancient meaning of corrupt, wilful tyranny was always condemned, though its emergence was sometimes admitted to be a risk inherent in an absolute regime. But a system in which the monarch possessed the full legislative power, under whatever name, was widely regarded as the best form of government and the best hope of securing rational reforms.

Those who took this view were influenced to varying degrees by the political situations of their time, yet general political theories also exercised differing amounts of sway over them. It is evident that the ideas of philosophical kingship and enlightened despotism fitted easily into the absolutist branch of the natural law tradition represented by Hobbes and Pufendorf. Moreover, thinkers who saw politics as a science and who believed that the same or a similar code of laws could and should be adopted in every country – the physiocrats and the utilitarians, for example – felt little difficulty in according full legislative power to an Enlightened sovereign (Wokler 1995b). Trust in such a ruler was consistent too with the view of history, most persuasively promoted by Voltaire, that the principal motive forces of history were ideas and great men. Writers who, on the contrary, emphasised the diversity of peoples and the deeper processes of history – such as Montesquieu, Rousseau, and Herder – looked to society as a whole rather than to the individual ruler to bring about beneficent change.

In the late nineteenth and twentieth centuries historians have set up the notion of 'enlightened absolutism' as a more appropriate description of eighteenth-century practice and theory than 'enlightened despotism' (Aretin 1974; Bazzoli 1986; Reinalter and Klueting 2002; Scott 1990). Those among them who maintained that to apply the notion of 'enlightened despotism' to the eighteenth century is anachronistic were mistaken. It is, rather, the concept of 'enlightened absolutism' which is absent in the eighteenth century. But it remains the case that many writers of the seventeenth and eighteenth centuries distinguished 'absolute' from 'despotic' monarchy, contending either that the absolute, unlike the despotic, ruler had good intentions, or that in an absolute system, as opposed to a despotic one, there existed some constitutional or legal restraints on him – or that both distinctions were valid. Ironically, an influential school of historians has described the French system of government in the eighteenth century as 'absolutism' while attributing to it the characteristics of Montesquieu's 'monarchy', a concept he had deliberately promoted in order to rebut the claims of absolute monarchy as he saw them (Mousnier 1974–80). Against this background it is worth considering the first formulation of the notion of 'enlightened absolutism', made by Wilhelm Roscher in 1847. He started by denouncing Montesquieu's classification of forms of government and reasserting the merits of Aristotle's. He continued: 'I call . . . those constitutions truly and completely monarchical . . . in which a single person, without being responsible in law, possesses, at least for his lifetime, the entire power of the state, or at any rate an overwhelming part of it' (Roscher 1847, p. 322). 'For absolute monarchies the king's will is the final earthly reason for everything that happens in the state' (Roscher 1847, p. 449). Roscher regarded such governments as the best of all forms, and as characteristic of the modern period. He argued that, broadly speaking, in the sixteenth century absolutism had been confessional and therefore weakened by religious influences; that in the seventeenth century court absolutism, typified by Louis XIV, had prevailed, and the ruler had been constrained by etiquette and his officials; but that the eighteenth century brought enlightened absolutism, which left the ruler untrammelled. It is hard to discern a difference between Roscher's notion of enlightened absolutism and the eighteenth-century idea of enlightened or philosophic despotism. As Hobbes would certainly have agreed, the problem is semantic. Historians need both to scrutinise eighteenth-century usage closely and to define their own terms with care. But there is no doubt that a concept close to the sort of philosophical kingship that Hobbes had envisaged commanded significant support in the eighteenth century, and that it was quite often described as enlightened or philosophic despotism.

18

Cameralism and the sciences of the state

KEITH TRIBE

1   The development of cameralism

Cameralism was a form of academic pedagogy aimed at the future administrators of the eighteenth-century German territorial states. As a written
discourse it was embodied in the several hundred textbooks produced for
use by students in German, Austrian, and Baltic universities between the
1720s and the 1790s. The first chairs dedicated to it were founded in 1727;
the period 1760–80 saw its consolidation and diffusion, but during the later
1790s it entered a phase of terminal intellectual and institutional decline.
The name persisted up to the end of the nineteenth century as a synonym
for the economics of state administration,[1] although its function had long
been displaced by faculties of law, and its substance by *Nationalökonomie*.[2]
Its very nature and purpose as a pedagogic discourse rendered it unsuitable
for contemporary translation into English, French, or Italian; consequently
it had no manifest resonances among those writers who provided the foundations of political economy. Moreover, commentary upon it has been to
this day largely confined to the German language, placing it therefore on
the margins of Anglo-French eighteenth-century studies.

From the standpoint of a modern literature of commentary, it thus represents a hermetic tradition in more ways than one – remote, esoteric,
and confined very much within a particular, though extensive, linguistic
zone. Traditionally, it has been the French Enlightenment, the French and
American Revolutions, and more recently also the Scottish Enlightenment
that have been identified as the leading sources of modern political theory.
In so far as the German Enlightenment was taken into account, it was

1 When Max Weber succeeded Knies as professor of *Nationalökonomie* at Heidelberg in 1897, the teaching
associated with this chair was located in the *Staats- und Cameralwissenschaften* section of the philosophy
faculty.
2 *Nationalökonomie* inherited the professorial chairs established in the course of the eighteenth century
for the teaching of cameralism and developed a form of economic discourse distinct from that of
the political economy practised in France and Britain. Tribe 1988, ch. 8, provides an outline of this
transformation.

generally viewed as a literary or philosophical phenomenon, of limited interest beyond a handful of key figures. From this perspective, cameralistic literature has appeared unexciting, ponderous, and without obvious relevance to the mainstream of European political thought. As a literature of economic administration it has likewise been shunned by historians of economic thought fixated upon locating the theoretical foundations of modern economic analysis.

This topology of political and social thought in eighteenth-century Europe has, since the later 1970s, been superseded by modern research which has shifted attention away from a preoccupation with the Great Traditions to a more differentiated understanding of the organisation and diffusion of enlightenment thought. In this process the role of universities in eighteenth-century German culture has been recognised, and consequently greater attention paid to the range of subjects that they taught. Coupled with this is a belated realisation that, while much of this teaching might not have been diffused by way of translation into English or French, the number of these universities and the area that they served was itself very large. The linguistic and cultural region within which cameralism was 'confined' reaches from the Baltic to the Atlantic, and from Amsterdam to Königsberg. Although it was primarily associated with the Protestant universities of North Germany, and especially with those of Prussia, two of its leading proponents, Johann Heinrich Gottlob von Justi and Joseph von Sonnenfels, were linked to the Austrian reform movement. In the absence of a reform-minded territorial ruler, Catholic universities tended to resist this new discipline, just as they resisted any other intellectual innovation until the hold of the Jesuit order on teaching was broken in the 1770s.

What, however, propelled this discourse of economic administration into the German universities? Simon Peter Gasser, appointed to the newly founded chair of 'Oeconomie, Policey und Cammersachen' at the University of Halle in 1727, had previously been involved in domain administration in Cleves, his success in this work being rewarded by Frederick William I with an appointment to a chair in law at Halle in 1721.[3] Despite Frederick William's evident contempt for academic affairs, his parallel foundation at the University of Frankfurt-an-der-Oder of a chair of 'Kameral-Ökonomie und Polizeiwissenschaft' indicates more than a passing concern with the training of future domain administrators. *Cammersachen* were, as in the Halle title,

3 Gasser did actually have a doctorate in law and had earlier been an extraordinary professor of law at Halle. On his appointment in 1721 the faculty protested, since there were only four posts and they were already filled: see Feist 1930, pp. 34–5.

'matters pertaining to the ruler's domains'.[4] Once developed in the university context, these various 'matters' became systematised into *Cameralwissenschaften*.[5] The cameralistic sciences became in turn part of the *Staatswissenschaften*, the 'sciences of the state', shifting the emphasis from the personal domains of the ruler to the lands and people, considered geographically, historically, and politically, of the territorial state as a whole. As the financial needs of the ruler increased, and as his conflicts with the estates over rights of taxation intensified, the fiscal base of the eighteenth-century territorial state shifted from a *Staatsökonomie*, dealing with the personal domains and monopolies of the ruler,[6] to a *Landesökonomie*, in which the entire territory and its population became the economic foundation for rule. In this way, principles first broached by court officials in the seventeenth century for the wise administration of a ruler's domains were systemised and translated into a discourse of academic instruction to officials concerning the rationale of state administration.

The basic principles involved did not undergo any great modification in the process. Johann Joachim Becher's *Politische Discurs*, first published in 1668 and dedicated to the Emperor Leopold I, opens with a section entitled 'Die Civil Societät wird definirt, daß sie seye eine Volkreiche Nahrhaffte Gemeind' ('Civil Society Is Defined, that it should be a Populous and Well-Nourished Community'). He continues: 'As I first seek to demonstrate wherein the advance of a land or city consists, I must beforehand bring to mind that man as the material of the republic is an *animal sociabile* and seeks society . . . Next to reason, it is human society alone that distinguishes human from animal life' (Becher 1688, *Erster Vorsatz*). Not only is the human person the 'material of the republic', but also the power of a ruler cannot be defended if he lacks people, and to attract people and maintain a population the ruler has to provide occupations and nourishment. In a populous country the people will 'help each other to gain their crust of bread through common trade and commerce'; a populous country thereby becomes a wealthy country, provided that proper attention is paid to the composition of the population. Becher offers to Leopold therefore a 'sceleton politicum' that provides an analysis of the various elements of society, their respective contributions to the common

4 Cf. *Kammermusik*, referred to in English as 'chamber music' and denoting court as opposed to church music.
5 It might be noted at this point that this plural form, the 'cameralistic sciences', is used here to cover both variations in terminology over time and the fact that 'cameralism' describes a number of linked 'sciences'.
6 *Staat* in this sense implies an identity with the person of the ruler and his court.

good, and the virtues required of a ruler and his officials (Becher 1688, pp. 3–4).

This emphasis on virtue draws attention to the manner in which Becher and many contemporaries composed texts that sought to persuade a patron of the principles to be adopted in the proper management of their states, and which implied that the writers of these texts would make suitable stewards. V. L. von Seckendorff, for example, presented his *Teutscher Fürsten Stat* (The German Princely State, 1656) as a treatise that could serve as a 'model after which each and every German principality, or any such not dissimilar province or dominion, may be described'. The text was arranged in three phases: first came a detailed description of the characteristics of the territory and its population; next came a survey of the spiritual and terrestrial government of the territory;[7] and, finally, a consideration of the best way that the ruler's own domains and monopolies should be administered so that his own subsistence be secured. A prudent ruler maintained everything in its proper social, spiritual, and legal place, while chief among his virtues was care for the welfare of his subjects and the heeding of mature advice from his officials (Seckendorff 1656, p. 59).

Within this framework it is evident that there is room for an elaboration of forms of rule and their consequences, as well as for a material assessment of the economic basis of rulership, whether this be in a discussion of taxation or in a consideration of the proper conduct of house, farm, and manufactory. It was possible to introduce a discussion of prudent rule by reviewing the various means for securing the position of the ruler: William von Schröder distinguished three basic approaches, the first by taking care of the wealthy, the second by taking care of the common man, and the third by plundering the rich and terrorising the rest. The first option was summarily dismissed as un-Christian, and nine distinct reasons for the advisability of the second course were advanced (Schröder 1686, 'Vorrede', §§ 3–7). There were in reality, he argued, two secure pillars of rule: a standing army and plenty of money in the chest. The merits of the first in maintaining peace and justice were evident, but without money nothing could be done. The principal concern of the responsible ruler was to raise sufficient money to maintain his power, and the only permanent way to ensure adequate finances was by linking the interest of the ruler with that of his subjects – for 'the welfare and well-being of subjects is the foundation upon which all happiness of

7 In a later edition the first was represented as 'a historical or geographical description', as opposed to the 'political description' of the second part (Seckendorff 1678, p. 17, § 4).

a ruler of such subjects must be based' (Schröder 1686, 'Vorrede', § 10). The political power of a ruler was therefore directly linked to the economic welfare of that ruler's subjects: the (political) happiness of a ruler rested upon the (economic) happiness of his subjects.[8]

> A prince is really like a father (*Hausvater*), and his subjects are, insofar as they have to be governed, his children . . . Now a husbandman (*Hausvater*) has to manure and plough his fields, if he wants something to reap . . . So a prince must first assist his subjects in their sustenance if he wishes to take something from them. (Schröder 1686, § 11)

In concluding his introductory remarks Schröder noted that his treatise was a utopia, but one which was Christian, blessed by God and directed against all principles of tyrannical rule derived from Machiavelli.

In this utopian state the resources of the prince were properly managed through the just distribution of expenditures, and in their increase.[9] Two quite separate administrative agencies were charged with these tasks: on the one hand the *Kameralisten* regulated the ruler's income and promoted his interest by accounting for it and seeing that it was not misused; the increase of a ruler's income was by contrast entrusted to a *Collegium*, a group of officials whose sole concern was to identify means of increasing revenue. Strictly speaking, then, the writings of Schröder and his contemporaries should not be labelled as 'cameralist', since this term, in so far as it was used by them, was still linked to the proper administration of the ruler's possessions. In separating off the agency charged with augmenting these possessions Schröder was simply echoing the best administrative practice of his time. It was only during the following century, when the competence of the *Kameralisten* was extended in parallel with the redefinition of the territorial state and its people as the proper object of administration and direct taxation,[10] that *Kameralismus* became synonymous with economic administration *per se*, and not simply domainal management.

---

8 The term used in the literature is *Glückseligkeit*, literally a state of 'feeling lucky and happy'. 'Fortunate' as used today is not emphatic enough; 'fortune' has fallen out of use but is closer in sense.
9 'Die menagie der Landesfürstlichen intraden bestehet in rechter distribuirung der ausgaben, und zum anderen in erweiterung und vermehrung derselben, das ist, in zwey worten, in *distribuendo et augmentando*' (Schröder 1686, pp. 11–12, § 3). 'Menagie' here means 'management', adopted from the French, but this usage failed to catch on, and in the absence of a suitable term the German language adopted the English 'management' first in the 1950s.
10 Direct in the sense that the right of the Estates to approve taxes was permanently displaced and the subjects of the ruler entered into a direct fiscal relationship with him. The genesis of the right to tax the property of subjects, argued by Grotius and Pufendorf in terms of the disposal on the part of the ruler over the rights of property of his subjects, is traced in Mann 1937.

2 'Oeconomy' and the *Hausvaterliteratur*

One important literary resource in effecting this transition – a transition which, it should not be forgotten, was closely related to a shifting balance of power between ruler and *Stände* (estates) in the territorial state – was the early modern revival of the doctrine of the house as an economic agency, and with it the patriarch as the co-ordinator and manager of the welfare of the household. It was this image that Schröder invoked when arguing that a ruler was like a *Hausvater*. In so far as this involved the delineation of relationships of authority between a patriarch and the members of his household, it recalled book 1 of Aristotle's *Politics*. But it was Xenophon's *Oikonomia* that was the classical source of this household as an economic entity, for Aristotle regarded all detail of the actual subsistence of the household as unimportant (Tribe 1988, pp. 22–8). It is possible to trace the transmission of this conception of the 'household' as a unity of authority, ethics, and economy from classical Greece and Rome through to the scholastics (Hoffmann 1959). But it was only at the beginning of the seventeenth century that a clear connection was made between the older political doctrine of the house, and the subsistence of the house as a form of 'oeconomy'.

Otto Brunner identifies the work of Johannes Coler as the inception of this new *Hausväterliteratur*, in which *Oeconomia* is treated as synonymous with householding. The conduct of household activity is here systemically itemised – starting with the relations of husband and wife, continuing through the preparation of food and drink, and then proceeding to the care and management of fields, vineyards, and crops (Brunner 1949; Coler 1604). In the course of the seventeenth century, the attention to relations of authority within the household that was typical of the classical sources became increasingly attenuated as the genre became more popular; so that, for example, Christoph Hering's *Oeconomischer Wegweiser* (Oeconomic Handbook, 1680), a work of several hundred pages, rapidly passes from the qualities necessary in the successful *Hauswirth* to the management of cattle and fields, concluding with the provision of a monthly calendar of work. Similar in emphasis were the works of Fischer (1690). Even in the most literary form of this genre, Wolf Helmhard von Hohberg's *Georgica Curiosa* (Oeconomic Inquiries, 1682), it is the practicalities of household and agricultural management that occupies the bulk of these texts' pages (Brunner 1949).

It was this more practical form of writing on the rural economy that provided a foundation for the development of the arguments of Schröder and Becher, counselling rulers on the path to wealth through a concern for the welfare of their subjects, into a more general discourse on economic management. During the first half of the eighteenth century there emerged a new literature of compendia, lexica, collections, and serial publications dealing with economic themes and addressed to an educated readership. This shift of address from nobility to *Bürger* underscored the parallel transition from *Staatsökonomie* to *Landesökonomie*, for the general reader was naturally more interested in the general economic affairs of town and country, and not just those relating to the ruler's domains and monopolies. The 'art of householding' became a generic term uniting the management of the prince's household with the conduct of rural holdings and urban trades. Julius Bernhard von Rohr, one of the most active composers of compendia in the early part of the century, still contrasted *Staats-Oekonomie* and *Lands-Oekonomie* as those relating to the ruler and the private person respectively. His *Compendieuse Haußhaltungs-Bibliothek* (Concise Library of Householding, 1716) nonetheless concentrated almost exclusively on the latter, arguing that the ruler also had his own *Privat-Oeconomie*, while the principles by which he operated his *Oeconomica Publica* had to take account of the welfare of his subjects: 'A rich man is someone who has a great deal of money in his chest, but a rich prince is one who has many wealthy subjects, who preserve his money just as well as it is preserved in his own treasury' (Rohr 1716, p. 46, § 2). In this text Rohr also entered a plea for the systematic teaching of the conduct of rural and urban economy in the universities, a plea similarly made by several other writers at this time.[11]

As already noted, the first such posts were created in 1727 at Halle and Frankfurt-an-der-Oder, and, at the installation of Gasser, the chancellor of the University of Halle composed a lengthy address emphasising the need for the teaching of practical economic matters in the university. He bemoaned the fact that while ethics, politics, and oeconomy were in fact taught under the banner of practical philosophy in the universities, the manner in which the last was dealt with left a great deal to be desired. Basing themselves on the teaching of Aristotle, the professors' conception of the oeconomy

remained almost entirely concerned with a doctrine of ethics based upon the *Hausvater* . . . What goes on in the fields, meadows, ponds, forests, gardens, and plants; how to look after cattle in their stalls; how the produce of the farm is to be increased; grain brewed and sold; what a *Hauswirth* has to do from day to day; what reserves one should

---

11 The best known example is Sincerus 1717. 'Sincerus' was C. H. Amthor, professor of law at Kiel.

have for fires, in the larder, in the bakery; what is needed in kitchen and cellar; how everything is to be acquired, maintained, and disposed of for the house: for all of these things Aristotle has not one syllable. (Ludewig 1727, pp. 142–3)

These, of course, are the concern of the *Privat-Oekonomie* outlined by Rohr, and Ludewig's endorsement of such matters as proper to university teaching reinforces the continuing shift in *Hausväterliteratur* away from the Aristotelian delineation of authority and ethics towards a discourse upon husbandry in the purely agricultural sense. But at this point a problem emerged that was to be of crucial importance for the literary dynamics of cameralism: given that this material was to be taught, where was a suitable textbook to be found?

Until the later nineteenth century, teaching in German universities almost exclusively took the form of lectures that systematically presented principles from a nominated textbook.[12] The professor was obliged to name the relevant text in announcing the course, and the lecture was conducted either as a point-by-point exposition of selected topics, or in some cases the professor simply read the book out, paragraph by paragraph. Academic literature was a literature of textbooks, compendia of principles more or less deliberately presented. The function of these texts as adjuncts to oral presentations dictated that they be internally organised by paragraph and chapter in a manner connected directly to a set number of lectures of a fixed length. Teachers naturally found fault with the length and substance of existing texts, and so then wrote their own, based upon previously delivered lectures. This is what Hegel did with the *Philosophy of Right*, for example (Tribe 1988, p. 12). Since these previous lectures were, however, necessarily delivered on an assigned textbook, the scope for innovation was limited. Both within and between texts there existed a marked emphasis on argument by accretion, turning upon the primacy of oral teaching and the subordination to this of written academic discourse. It is this imperative that lies at the heart of the sheer volume of cameralistic writing, for cameralism is nothing if not a literature of textbooks.

Gasser began teaching in the autumn of 1727, and nominated as his textbook Seckendorff's *Fürsten Stat*, with some apologies for selecting this not entirely suitable text (Gasser 1728, p. 3). However, he did at the same time announce that he would present a new set of lectures based upon the textbook that he was writing that was then published in 1729 as *Einleitung zu den*

---

12 The role of the lecture as the prime mode of teaching was modified with the introduction of the *Seminare* in the course of the nineteenth century. These first developed in the study of philology, but were not created for the *Staatswissenschaften* until the 1870s and 1880s.

Oeconomischen Politischen und Cameral-Wissenschaften (Introduction to Oeconomic, Political, and Cameralistic Sciences). This was the first cameralist
textbook – J. C. Dithmar's from Frankfurt did not appear until 1731. But
it must be said that in following Ludewig's guidelines it simply abandoned
the arguments of Seckendorff and opted for little more than a listing of the
various tasks of domain administration. This was, of course, Gasser's forte as
a domain official – valuing fields, breweries, and mills, setting up an inventory of cattle and lands, reviewing services due, listing the various modes of
taxation, and establishing rights of hunting and fishing – such are some of
the chapter headings in his *Einleitung*.

Not surprisingly, this first venture in teaching cameralistic subjects soon
slipped into obscurity. Gasser relinquished teaching by the early 1740s to an
undistinguished successor who, undeterred by lack of interest on the part of
the students, continued to teach the subject up to his death in 1772.[13] Frederick William's initiative at Halle thus generated neither adequate teaching,
nor a usable textbook, for even Gasser's successor, Stiebritz, had baulked at
using Gasser's *Einleitung* and nominated instead the textbook produced by
Dithmar for his Frankfurt lectures. Although the fate of teaching in Frankfurt was little better than that in Halle, Dithmar's textbook was a marked
success, being republished in several editions even after his death in 1737.[14]

Unlike Gasser's *Einleitung*, Dithmar's opens with a series of definitions
that are then used to organise the subsequent chapters. The first of these
definitions runs as follows: 'Oeconomic science or the art of house oeconomy and householding teaches the manner in which livelihood and wealth,
promoting temporal happiness, can be attained through proper conduct of
industry in town and country.'[15] *Oeconomie, Wirtschaft*, and *Haushaltung* are
used synonymously here as descriptive of the activity of gaining a living,
the purpose of which is general welfare and happiness. This lexical habit
of freely interchanging terms is illustrated by Georg Heinrich Zincke, an
assiduous contemporary composer of popular compendia on oeconomic
affairs, who directs the reader searching for a definition of *Oeconomie* in
his dictionary of economic terminology to 'see householding', which entry

13 Kathe 1980, pp. 86–7. Gasser's successor was Stiebritz, a specialist in Hebraic languages and the New
Testament.
14 Dithmar 1731. This was republished in 1745 and is today available as a reprint. Despite its claim to be
a 'new and enlarged edition', it is virtually identical to the 1731 text. A fifth edition was published
in 1755 with additional comments by D. G. Schreber, who at this time taught at Halle.
15 'Die Oeconomische Wissenschafft oder Hauß-Wirthschaffts-und Haußhalthungs-Kunst lehret wie
durch rechtmäßige Land- und Stadt-Gewerbe Nahrung und Reichthum zu Beförderung der
Zeitlichen Glückseligkeit mögen erlanget werden' (Dithmar 1731, *Einleitung*, § 1, p. 2).

runs in part as follows: 'The art of householding or the art of keeping house, oeconomy, oeconomic science, is a practical science, wherein the wisdom, prudence, and art of nearly all learned sciences are applied to the end of rightful concern for provisioning and economy' (Zincke 1744, col. 1099). This synonymity of oeconomy with householding has obvious roots in the *Hausväterliteratur* of the seventeenth century, but it extends to the analogous *Wirtschaft*, the term of Middle High German origin for the activity of providing food and drink for guests of the *Wirt*.[16] 'Keeping house' or 'householding' was thereby described as *wirtschaften*; it could be done well or badly, hence *gut oder schlecht wirtschaften*, emphasising an association of economy with good order (rather than parsimony as in English) that has persisted in the German language up to the present day.[17]

Accordingly, oeconomic practices were to be judged by standards embodied not in an ethics, as in the teaching of the Aristotelians, but rather by their practical consequences for the happiness and welfare of the people. That such practices could be systematically taught, like other disciplines, is also affirmed by Dithmar; but they were nonetheless treated as technical matters, subordinate to the work of *Polizei* which comprehended the general ordering of activity in the territorial state (Dithmar, 1731, §§ 2, 5, pp. 2–4). The boundaries of the regulatory activity of *Polizei* remained vague, as Dithmar candidly admitted; but this was not so much evidence of a lack of rigour, as a consequence of the cameralistic conception of the bases of social order and economic welfare.

Both Dithmar and Zincke sought to differentiate *Oeconomie-*, *Polizei-* and *Kameral-Wissenschaften* as distinct bodies of knowledge that had a definite relationship with each other. In Dithmar's *Einleitung* the outcome was a presentation first of *Oeconomische-Wissenschaft* dominated by an itemisation of a rural economy; second of *Polizei-Wissenschaft*, conceived as knowledge of the sources of order in a state, but which in enumerating the state's constituent parts recapitulates much of the material from the preceding part; and finally of *Cameral-Wissenschaft*, concerned only with the improvement of the ruler's income from landed and fiscal properties. This therefore involves a reprise of the established distinction of *Landes-* from *Staats-Oeconomie* that can be found in Rohr and others, with the difference that the former now dominates. *Polizei-Wissenschaft* does clearly belong with the *Landes-Oeconomie* since it involves principles for the creation of order and therefore wealth;

16 Grimm, *Deutsches Wörterbuch*, Bd. 14/2, p. 662, and pp. 662–86 for *Wirtschaften*.
17 An inn or a restaurant is still referred to in Southern Germany as a *Wirtschaft*, an innkeeper as a *Wirt*.

but there is a marked lack of success in identifying principles, as distinct from descriptions, of practical affairs. Zincke sought to produce a greater degree of system than was evident in Dithmar, but managed only to generate greater prolixity, for his writing lacked the rigid constraints of set lectures and a teaching programme. He did nevertheless introduce a concept linking the three spheres – *Nahrungs-Geschäfte*, or 'nourishment-business'. The pursuit of 'nourishment-business' is dubbed by him 'economising' (Zincke 1751, pp. 31–2). This conception was to play a part in Sonnenfels's account of the cameralistic sciences that began to appear in the 1760s.

By mid-century the elements for the development of elaborated cameralistic sciences were in place, but there were few chairs in existence from which it was systematically taught. William Stieda notes that in 1755 the calendar for the German universities listed only three cameralistic chairs among thirty-two German, Scandinavian, Dutch, Swiss, and Austrian universities: at Abo (i.e. Turku), Göttingen, and Rinteln (Stieda 1906, p. 65). In fact, of these three it is only certain that some teaching was done at Rinteln, where C. G. Fürstenau was professor of 'the art of householding'.[18] This underestimates contemporary teaching activity, as Stieda acknowledges, besides excluding the teaching that took place in academies – some teaching was done at the universities of Halle and Frankfurt-an-der-Oder, Justi had lectured from 1750 to 1754 at the *Collegium Theresianum* in Vienna, Zincke was teaching in Brunswick, and a chair had been founded at Uppsala in 1741 by Anders Berch. It is nevertheless true that during the 1750s teaching was still patchy compared with the situation that developed in the course of the 1760s, with the appointment of D. G. Schreber at Leipzig and Sonnenfels in Vienna.

Simply counting up the number of chairs and professors is, of course, a very partial way of assessing the impact of cameralism. For one thing, universities were of differing size and composition – so, for example, Halle had an average attendance of 988 students over the period 1700–90, while that of Frankfurt-an-der-Oder was 175. Student numbers attending thirty-two German universities declined from almost 9,000 in 1750 to an annual average of 7,494 in the period 1786–90. This decline, however, was not evenly distributed. Göttingen numbers increased from 625 to 816 over the same period, while those at Jena fell from 1,010 to 783, the latter itself a recovery from a low point of 472 on average in the period 1766–70 (Eulenburg 1904,

---

18 Rinteln was a small university near Hanover that closed in 1809; J. H. Fürstenau wrote the third cameralistic textbook, *Gründliche Anleitung zu der Haushaltungs-Kunst* (Complete Guide to the Art of Householding, Lemgo, 1736); see Tribe 1988, pp. 44–5, for an outline of this text.

pp. 153, 164–5). Within the hierarchy of the four faculties – theology, law, medicine, and philosophy – the cameralistic sciences were generally taught in philosophy, and since appointments to this faculty carried no automatic right to teach in the others, it was difficult to penetrate the numerically stronger faculties of law. The establishment of cameralistic teaching as a condition of state employment akin to the qualification of a law degree was hindered by the greater prestige of legal studies within the universities. Throughout the century chairs were founded, like those originally in Halle and Frankfurt-an-der-Oder, by rulers seeking to reform their administrations and make the study of cameralistic sciences compulsory for recruits. None of these attempts was successful. In the one university which did play a consistent role in the training of state officials, Göttingen, there was never any serious attempt to introduce cameralistic teaching. This is not to say that the *Staatswissenschaften* were poorly represented. On the contrary, Göttingen was where Johann Beckmann, Gottfried Achenwall, August Ludwig Schlözer, and Georg Sartorius taught, all leading representatives of various aspects of the *Staatswissenschaften*. Justi, on the other hand, when he taught there between 1755 and 1757, did so in a part-time capacity, his actual appointment being as councillor for mines and police director. The general principle of a specific course of training leading to qualification for appointment to the work of state administration only became established during the nineteenth century, and even then the major element in such qualification was a training in law, not economics.

Although the function of cameralistic sciences was firmly embedded within a conception of the administrative needs of the territorial state, and as such was located within the university curriculum, it failed to fulfil its assigned pedagogic function, and was in most cases marginal to university teaching. The evident regularities of cameralistic discourse cannot thus be accounted for simply by pointing to this assigned function or its pedagogic correlate.[19] The discursive regularities of cameralistic discourse are repeated over a period of one hundred years and are expressed in several hundred texts. The stability of the basic figures repeated through these texts is to some extent an effect of the incremental dynamics of the literature, each text setting itself up to recapitulate its recognised forerunners, while at the same time introducing some kind of variation.

Cameralistic literature does not so much inform us about the actual concepts applied by administrations as displays to us *in extenso* the problematic

---

19 Schiera 1968 remains the most systematic attempt to relate the administrative imperatives of the territorial state to the actual structure of cameralistic texts.

within which they operated. The conceptual repetitions already noted in the early development of cameralistic literature provide us with an image of the ruling conceptions of economic order and wealth in early modern Central Europe. It does not matter that this or that individual text is inconsistent, nor that the delivery of lectures on the subject in the universities was sporadic, or conducted by persons lacking adequate knowledge of the subject. We can note the failure of rulers to persuade their administrators of the necessity of recruiting 'qualified' university graduates; we can note the uneven distribution of chairs and their occupation. These factors do not weaken the consistency with which textbooks repeat their 'principles of oeconomic order', nor the force with which they are thereby endowed. Seeking explanatory reference outside the text is a distraction from a proper confrontation with textual structure. As has been shown, up to the midpoint of the eighteenth century there had been no generally acknowledged successful presentation of a cameralistic system. This situation was soon rectified by the writings of Justi; but he was neither an academic nor were his texts concise enough to serve as textbooks. Nonetheless, it is to Justi that we must look if we are to gain an insight into the mid-century systematisation of cameralistic principles.

3   Justi

Justi was an atypical figure by the mid-eighteenth century, in that his career bore all the marks of a seventeenth-century projector in the mould of a Schröder or a Becher. Born in 1720 in Thuringia, he saw service in the Saxon army, and then studied law at Wittenberg in 1742–4. During 1745–7 he edited a literary journal at Leipzig, after which he spent three years as legal counsellor to the duchess of Saxe-Eisenach. His literary career took off in 1747 when he won a prize from the Prussian Academy of Sciences for an essay on Leibniz's doctrine of monads, and in 1750 he moved to Vienna and was appointed to teach rhetoric at the *Theresianum*. He also delivered a series of lectures on economic matters, dealing with finance, trade, taxation, and manufacture from an administrative viewpoint. A hurried departure from Vienna followed, most probably resulting from the failure of his speculation in silver mining; two years were then spent in journalistic activity in Leipzig, before he moved again to Göttingen in 1755. Once more his departure from Göttingen was swift, this time because of a possible occupation by French troops allied to the Austrians, and thereby a threat to his continued liberty. A period spent in Hamburg, where he, among other things, sketched a plan for a canal linking the Baltic to the North Sea, was followed in 1760 by a move to Berlin. Here he became involved in various financial projects, all of which failed, before Frederick the Great appointed him Prussian inspector of mines in 1765. In 1768 he was imprisoned because of financial irregularities in his administration, and he died, blind, still incarcerated in the fortress of Küstrin, in 1771 (see Adam 2003, 2004).

Throughout this hectic life Justi wrote and wrote, 'a literary manufacturer in the greatest style' as Dreitzel rightly dubs him (Dreitzel 1987, p. 163). In 1754 he published his inaugural lecture at the *Theresianum*; in 1755 his *Staatswirthschaft* (second edition 1758) and his Göttingen lectures; in 1756 his *Grundsätze der Policey-Wissenschaft* (Principles of Police Science); in 1759 his *Grundriss einer Guten Regierung* (Outline of Good Government) and *Systematischer Grundriss allen Oeconomische und Cameral-Wissenschaften* (Systematic Outline of all Oeconomic and Cameralistic Sciences); and then in 1760–1 the two-volume work *Grundfeste zu der Macht und Glückseligkeit der Staaten* (Foundations of State Power and Happiness). Some of these are very bulky tomes indeed, and moreover represent only a selection of his writings relevant here – and there are also writings on politics, history, aesthetics, and the natural sciences. On the other hand, large sections of the above titles are simply copied from one book to another; and it is, in fact, quite feasible to expose Justi's basic cameralistic themes through a discussion of the *Staatswirthschaft* alone, based as it is upon his Vienna lectures, and the second edition of which is marked by the reception of Montesquieu's ideas.

From the background sketched above there is little reason for anticipating that Justi's cameralistic writings should have become standard works. But as we shall see, Sonnenfels, who composed the most generally used cameralistic textbook of the later eighteenth century, had likewise a singularly inauspicious background. The manner in which these two parvenus could compose such widely accepted textbooks is suggestive: first, that cameralistic textbooks could be easily assembled out of the discursive elements that lay readily to hand; and, secondly, that this itself indicates that authorial originality, as opposed to a talent for composition, is here heavily discounted. Given that Justi had more than enough to do and sought to make his living by writing and advising, his dedication to the production of a whole series of cameralistic texts suggests that he, as well as his bookseller, thought that readers existed who would readily buy them. Prosaic it might seem, but this supposition, in the light of his dogged production of these tomes, tells us a great deal about the provenance of cameralistic discourse.

Justi dubbed his first major foray into this area *Staatswirthschaft*. Significantly, although the scope of this 'state economy' is not immediately clear, it is evident that it involves more than a consideration of the ruler's domains, since the first volume bears the subtitle 'On the Maintenance and Increase of the Entire Property of the State, for which the Principles of *Staatskunst, Polizei* and Commercial Science, as well as Oeconomy, are Necessary'. *Staat* here then is synonymous with what elsewhere was referred to as *Bürgerliche Gesellschaft*, 'civil society'.[20] The correlate of the activity of 'good government', the happiness of the people, is described by Justi as 'the good order and condition of a state such that each is able, by his own efforts, to attain those moral and temporal goods that are necessary for a pleasant life according to his respective *Stand*' (Justi 1755, I, 56). The 'comfort of the inhabitants of a state' does not therefore require that entitlements be equally distributed; they are distributed according to the requirements of the *Stände* (estates), and a principal objective of administration is, moreover, the maintenance of *ständisch* differences. This was certainly a preoccupation of the regulations issued under the auspices of *Polizei*. The subject of a ruler is first of all a member of a particular *Stand*, and a human subject second. What then of the wealth of a state? This is defined as those goods required to maintain this ordering of subjects according to *Stände*, and it is recognised that no country is in a position to supply all these from its own resources. Exchanges between states are necessary, effected by stocks of gold and silver – hence the flows of these precious metals are themselves an indicator of a country's actual wealth. If this is to be increased, it must, so the argument goes, first be maintained; measures have to be taken to ensure that this wealth then is kept at home. These measures involve the increase of inhabitants, the development of foreign trade, and the exploitation of gold and silver mines. The inhabitants of a country must be a population of hard-working subjects. The ruler has to ensure that each pursues his own ascribed ends and is thus in a position to pay the dues and obligations owed to the state. A subject who does not do so reneges on an obligation laid upon him, and an apparatus of educational institutions and workhouses is required to correct this.

It is evident that this conception of good order and the relation of ruler and subject is a long way from the 'system of natural liberty' to be exposed

20 The casual equation of these two concepts was commonplace until the latter part of the century, and is indicative of their synonymity. Cf. J. G. Sulzer's usage: '*Staatswissenschaft*, or *Politik*, contains the theory of the happiness of entire states or civil societies, and demonstrates the means by which it can be attained' (1759, p. 180). See also Riedel 1975, pp. 754–5.

by Adam Smith just twenty-one years later. But it would be incorrect to regard that difference as one between a 'liberal' and an 'absolutist' regime. While Justi equates the property of the ruler with that of the state in general, he explicitly rejects the idea that the ruler has a property in his subjects – that his right of taxation, for instance, is based on his ultimate ownership of the economic capacities of his subjects. The ruler, suggests Justi, is charged with the economic government of the territorial state, and the welfare of all depends absolutely on the effectiveness of this work of governing. The subjects of this state are not inactive in the absence of the active work of government; it is rather that their activities require definite direction and limitation if welfare is to be maximised. Without the conscious regulative activity of government there would be chaos, which is what collections of human beings create spontaneously in their natural state in the absence of government. The work of regulation is consequently ever extending, and this itself contributes to the expansion of cameralistic literature. Regulation of the diverse activities of a ruler's subjects is the task of *Polizei*, but although this is ever more detailed and imaginative in foreseeing potential zones of disorder, Justi is adamant that the work of economic government cannot involve the direct supervision of individual subjects in the conduct of their households. The state would soon require as many supervisors as households once it embarked upon this route, and, in addition to this, supervisors to supervise the supervisors. It was not beyond the bounds of possibility that *Polizei* regulation could be brought to bear on poorly run households, but this would itself involve a degree of compulsion which fitted ill with the axiom of human freedom:

> But above all it is not possible to judge whether someone economises well or ill if one has no insight into his condition, property, and household affairs, an insight that must account for the most precise detail; and this is not possible in itself and in terms of good principles. All manner of impossibilities therefore stand in the way of forcing the subject to a good economy by means of compulsion; instead each is in this respect left to his own devices, whether he will observe his duty to himself and his associated obligation to the state, or not. (Justi 1755, I, 377)

The state does not therefore possess the capacity, let alone the moral author- ity, required to direct in detail the rational conduct of the subject. On the other hand, the subject is not thought capable of contributing spontaneously, in association with other subjects, to the welfare of the state. This is the fun- damental problem that economic government has to resolve. It does so by the ruler providing a rational framework within which the subject can conduct his activities in a purposive manner. The pedagogic task of the cameralistic sciences is the identification of this rational framework; although this framework must needs take account of the propensities of the human subject, these do not provide the dynamic in the system. This comes from the work of regulation on the part of *Polizei*, channelling the inchoate vitality of the human subject.

Polizei is quite clearly central to the cameralistic conception of wealth and order, and in the year following the publication of the *Staatswirthschaft* Justi published what he described as the first text to present its subject matter in a systematic fashion, it previously having been treated merely as part of *Staatskunst*, the art of state management.

> By contrast with that, *Polizei* concerns itself with nothing but the maintenance and increase of the entire property of the state through good internal organisation, lending the republic all inner power and strength of which it is capable according to its condition. To this end it seeks to cultivate the lands, improve the state of subsistence, and maintain discipline in the common weal. (Justi 1756, 'Vorrede')

Justi sought to develop both general and specific definitions of *Polizei*, but, as later writers were to find, such attempts fail to produce any greater degree of clarity. *Polizeiwissenschaft* was in truth as inchoate as the *Polizeiordnungen* that it purported to systematise. It sought to regulate human activity in the absence of any idea that sociability generated its own form of purposive order; the work of *Polizei* was therefore in principle never ending and ever extending, defying any clear demarcation other than the practical limitation of supervision noted by Justi. Here it is sufficient to note that Justi's textbook on *Polizei* covers the health and welfare of urban and rural populations, the standardisation of weights and measures, the proper conduct of cultivation, the restriction of free movement between occupations, the proper conduct of internal and external trade, the maintenance of social discipline, the proscription of displays of luxury, and the promotion of education and religion. Coupled with the *Staatswirthschaft*, Justi produced the key cameralistic textbooks upon which Sonnenfels was then able to build in the following decade. Sonnenfels did not have such a turbulent life as Justi, and quickly secured and maintained a position within the Austrian reform movement; but the route by which he came to compose the leading textbook of late eighteenth-century cameralism was every bit as unpromising as that taken by his predecessor.

4 Sonnenfels

Sonnenfels was born in 1733, but owing to the modesty of his father's income spent five years in the army before entering Vienna University in 1754 to study law. By the time he graduated in 1758 he was principally interested in literary work, joining the *Deutsche Gesellschaft* in 1761 and applying, without success, for a chair in rhetoric at the university in 1762. At the end of the same year he discovered that there was interest at court in the establishment of teaching on cameralism, and so he delivered a memorandum to the empress suggesting the establishment of a periodical devoted to commercial issues, and an associated chair in the cameralistic sciences. As far as the former proposal went, he suggested that translations of sections relevant to Austria could be made directly from the *Journal de commerce*, published in Brussels and Paris between 1759 and 1761.

Examinations of the *Journal* and a consideration of the existing available literature suggest that Sonnenfels had at this time a marginal acquaintance with cameralistic and commercial writings (Kremers 1988, pp. 171–90; Tribe 1988, pp. 79–84). There was little in the *Journal* that could conceivably be seen as relevant to Austria, while the fact that Sonnenfels cited a French language publication indicates his lack of familiarity with existing German literature. The conclusion must follow that, at this stage in his career, Sonnenfels's primary qualifications for a chair in the cameralistic science were a desire for a secure position, a willingness to masquerade as a suitable candidate for any available position, and some literary talent.

This last ability was decisive, for Sonnenfels was appointed professor of *Polizei-* and *Cameral-Wissenschaften* in the autumn of 1763 and had a lot of reading to catch up on. The trial essay that he had submitted in June 1763 was a discussion of the section of Justi's *Staatswirthschaft* dealing with the increase of population in a country, and this was in fact the text that he at first used for his lectures, combined, it appears, with François Forbonnais's *Elémens du commerce*. In 1765, however, Sonnenfels published the first volume of his own textbook, which he had decided to write because of the lack of a text suitable for the ten-month course that he taught. This three-volume textbook dealt in turn with *Polizei*, commercial science and financial science. In one form or another it remained the assigned textbook for the Austrian universities until 1848, and was also the basis for a series of teaching outlines.[21]

---

21 Sonnenfels 1765–76. The title was altered to *Grundsätze* . . . with the third volume, by which time the first two volumes had already been reprinted. The most commonly available edition is the fifth, published in 1787; although the text went through eight German editions to 1819, translation into

The priority given to *Polizei* in this sequence reverses the sequence of Justi's textbooks, but lends emphasis to the relationship between Sonnenfels's teaching and the efforts to reform Austrian society through the introduction of new regulations. Sonnenfels was personally involved in these efforts, being responsible for the introduction of street lighting into Vienna, serving as a book censor, and being closely involved in controversies over the role of the theatre (Melton 1988, pp. 86–90; Ogris 1988b, pp. 11–92). The first volume of the *Sätze* reviews in detail the sources of potential disorder within the state, and identifies the task of *Polizei* as being the maintenance of a proper equilibrium in society. The execution of this task involved the collection of information on the size and structure of the population, and the conformity of the work of *Polizei* with existing moral institutions such as the family and the church. The economic purpose of *Polizei* is the prevention of want through the regulation of markets and trading. If a shortage is attributable to poor cultivation then this is a problem for householding as a subordinate part of commercial science; but shortages resulting from too high prices or catastrophes were to be prevented by *gute Polizei*. Whereas in Justi the conception of *Polizei* was one that generally ordered economic life, in Sonnenfels there is a greater emphasis on social and moral questions, resulting perhaps from the continuing development of Austrian *Polizeiordnungen*. Moreover, since Sonnenfels exposed the functions of *Polizei* first in his thematic sequence, it was correspondingly difficult to treat *Polizei* as an instrument of economic welfare, which was the more orthodox position in the late eighteenth century.

The key idea in the second volume of Sonnenfels's textbook is that the economic progress of a nation is a process in which 'means of subsistence multiply' – the *Vervielfältigen der Nahrungswege und der Beschäfftigungen*, recalling Zincke's association of economising with 'nourishment-business', *Nahrungs-geschäfte* (Sonnenfels 1765–76, II, pp. 21–2, 170). Mutual need is the basis of exchange, and these needs and their means of satisfaction multiply with the advance of commercial relations.[22] The multiplication of occupations that arises from the increase of mutual exchange is linked to the increase of population. Sonnenfels, then, judges welfare not simply by the standards of happiness and populousness, but by conceiving a population as an entity actively pursuing ever more complex wants. Exports and imports

---

Latin in 1808 and three Italian editions from 1784 to 1806, few material changes were introduced to the original text.

22 It is notable that Hegel uses the same conception of needs and the multiplication of the means for their satisfaction in his discussion of the system of needs: *Philosophy of Right*, § 191.

are also judged by this standard, so that advantageous commerce involves the export of as much as is commensurate with the satisfaction of domestic needs.

The discussion of agriculture in this second volume is notable for the absence of any direct consideration of agricultural production or good practice. Instead, Sonnenfels concentrates on the mechanisms that will ensure that agriculture flourishes, such as the regulation of prices, the supervision of cultivation, the balance of occupations as between rural and urban trades, and the balance of supply of, and demand for, produce. The same approach is adopted when considering manufacture: here the focus of discussion is upon guilds and monopolies, the levels of wages and prices, and the role of machinery in the multiplication of occupations. If, for example, the introduction of machinery reduces the number of occupations, then this is harmful to the state, argues Sonnenfels, and must be checked. There could be no clearer instance of the dominating role that the conception of populousness and activity plays in this assessment of economic organisation: they are needs in themselves, and not part of the wider assessment of the forms of the generation of wealth that political economy was to undertake.

The third volume of *Sätze* deals with finance, and almost exclusively with a review of the sources of revenue in the state, without, at the same time, treating the needs of the state in any more than a cursory fashion in the introductory pages. One feature of this volume is some discussion of physiocratic fiscal ideas, but this, as much else in Sonnenfels's *Grundsätze*, is taken almost directly from Forbonnais (Sonnenfels 1765–76, III, §§ 128–48, pp. 300–17). Whereas the first two volumes of the *Sätze* expose definite conceptions of politico-economic order and its maintenance and development, the third volume simply lists sources of finance without any systematic conception of their impact on the welfare of the state. This is because the leading idea involves regulation and the promotion of activities; there is no independent motor of wealth separate from the functioning of *Polizei*, and this itself requires finance from a variety of sources.

When they were finally complete, there were over 1,100 pages in the three volumes of Sonnenfels's textbook; as so often, the original ambition of replacing one text with another more concise and comprehensive version went astray in the execution. The centralised nature of the Austrian university system, and Sonnenfels's role within it, did however ensure that his textbook became assigned for use in all universities under Austrian influence: among these were Prague, Linz, Graz, Freiburg, and Buda (Osterloh 1970, p. 124). In addition, it seems that from 1770 it was made a requirement that those entering state service had at least attended lectures on cameralism. A series of condensed versions were written by teachers in these universities, reducing the 1,100 pages to a series of maxims and lists of questions. I. De Luca's *Leitfaden* (Guide, 1776) for example had sixty-two pages of questions, while L. B. M. Schmid's *Ausführliche Tabellen* (Comprehensive Tables, 1785) took the form of a systematic precis of Sonnenfels. Evidently some of these versions of Sonnenfels were quite successful; F. X. Moshammer's 500 page compendium went into a third edition in 1820, indicating the manner in which cameralistic routines persisted in Austrian universities well after they had been abandoned elsewhere (De Luca 1776; Moshammer [Sonnenfels] 1820; Schmid 1785).

If anything, the systematising efforts of Justi and Sonnenfels stimulated, rather than forestalled, a wave of production of cameralistic textbooks. This did not, however, involve further significant elaboration. Any substantial alteration from one textbook to another involved differing emphases between the component parts of the conceptual apparatus already laid out by Justi and Sonnenfels. This is again a quite usual phenomenon in textbook literature.

The textbooks of the late eighteenth century were largely impervious to developments in political economy elsewhere. The reception of physiocracy in Germany and Austria during the 1770s largely left the universities, and thus cameralistic argument, untouched. A brief but intense wave of discussion and publication took place among members of provincial societies and academies that formed the basis of the German Enlightenment. Since much of this reception focused on the *impôt unique* there existed recognisable avenues along which a cameralistic critique could be made; and, accordingly, so far as physiocracy was at all registered in the cameralistic textbooks, the reaction was overwhelmingly negative.

The transmission of cameralism through translation was also very limited. Where more than a handful of translations were made, this was into languages which shared in some way the cultural imperatives that shaped cameralism.[23] Diffusion into French and English through translation was almost non-existent, if one excludes Jacob Friedrich von Bielfeld's *Lehrbegriff der Staatskunst* (Doctrine of Statecraft, 1764), which was in effect a French text written in German and published in both languages. The composition of just

---

23 During the period 1766–1800 fourteen economic works were translated from German into Danish: see Carpenter 1977, p. 34. The translations were of texts on trade, technology, and agriculture, not on the cameralistic sciences. Justi's *Grundfeste zu der Macht und Glückseligkeit der Staaten* was translated into Russian in four parts (Moscow, 1772–8), as were also extracts from Sonnenfels.

one major eighteenth-century treatise on political economy was marked by cameralistic argument – Sir James Steuart's *Inquiry into the Principles of Political Oeconomy* (1767), books I and II of which were drafted while he was in exile in Germany, for in Tübingen he became familiar with elements of the *Staatswissenschaften*. Read in this context, Steuart's *Inquiry* gains a new coherence, and in translation it was frequently cited in cameralistic literature. In Britain, on the other hand, Steuart's work was quickly eclipsed by Adam Smith's *Wealth of Nations* (1776) and has subsequently always been regarded simply as 'pre-Smithian'.

When change did come to the *Staatswissenschaften*, with the reception of Smith in the 1790s, and Jean Baptiste Say in the early 1800s, it involved a complete reconceptualisation of the problematic of state and social order, a reordering that robbed cameralism of its inner logic. The emergence of civil society from its lexical identification with the state involved a recognition of the autonomous dynamic of subjects within this society, and the consequent restriction of state activity. Initially identified with the management of a ruler's domains, cameralism had extended its scope with the changing balance within the territorial state to comprehend the entirety of economic life within the state. The emancipation of civil society as a realm of freedom, separated from state activity, brought with it a new conceptualisation of the generation of needs and their satisfaction within society. The set of principles which addressed these issues was initially dubbed a *Wirtschaftslehre*, but it very quickly became known as *Nationalökonomie*, spawning a whole new set of textbooks that completely displaced those of the cameralistic tradition. By the 1820s in Germany, although not in Austria, the vast literature of cameralism had fallen into disuse; and within a few decades it had become a curiosity whose regularities and dynamism were scarcely intelligible. The emergence of a new conjunction of law, economics, and political science at the end of the nineteenth century completed this process of occlusion, displacing the sciences of the state with the new science of the social.

19

Utilitarianism and the reform of the criminal law

FREDERICK ROSEN*

The first object of this chapter is to chart the development of philosophical thought about crime and punishment in the latter half of the eighteenth century, with special emphasis on the writings of Montesquieu, Beccaria, and Bentham. It will be shown that the common thread running through their writing is the application of a doctrine of civil and political liberty to this aspect of state power. A second object is to relate the philosophical arguments of these influential thinkers to the more practical discussions, mainly in Britain, regarding the abolition of the death penalty and the use of various alternative forms of punishment such as transportation and imprisonment. It will be shown that intellectual debate was not simply between 'reformers' and 'conservatives' but instead proceeded in a more complex manner on philosophical and ideological levels and was directed towards different objects.[1]

* In preparing this chapter I am indebted to Stephen Conway, Philip Schofield, Simon Renton, and the late Janet Semple for useful comments and advice. A version of this chapter also appears in Rosen 2003, ch. 9.

1 Although the term 'utilitarianism' is given a prominent place in the title of this chapter, no attempt will be made here to trace the development of the doctrine in the eighteenth century (see Rosen 2003). Both consequentialism and hedonism, two important elements of modern utilitarianism (Quinton 1973, p. 1), were, Baumgardt suggests, 'probably as old as human thought itself' and well-known to the philosophers of antiquity (Baumgardt 1952, p. 35). Opinions differ as to the origin of modern utilitarianism. It is possible to see elements of the doctrine in Hobbes and Locke (Plamenatz 1958, pp. 1–21, 162–2; Stephen 1876, II, pp. 80ff), though other scholars trace its origins variously to Richard Cumberland's *De legibus naturae* (1672, 1727) (see Albee 1902, p. 11; Quinton 1973, p. 16) or to John Gay's 'Dissertation' (1731) (see Halévy 1952, p. 7), while recognising the importance of Hume in its development. But the idea of utility is closely related to the ancient and modern Epicurean traditions, the latter of which begins with Pierre Gassendi (see Rosen 2003, pp. 19ff). Although utilitarian arguments feature in numerous political debates throughout the century (see Molivas 1994, pp. 105–34), utilitarianism as a *system* of thought appears latterly in the writings of Paley and Bentham (see Sidgwick 1906, pp. 225ff). Both Paley and Bentham recognised the importance of earlier writers, with Paley (1785, pp. xiii–xiv) acknowledging the influence of Abraham Tucker's *The Light of Nature Pursued* (1768) and Bentham referring most often to Helvétius (1758), Beccaria (1766), Priestley (1768), and Hume (*THN*) (see Baumgardt 1952, pp. 37ff). The Greatest Happiness Principle, the foundation of Bentham's system (see Rosen 1983, pp. 200–20), has been traced to Beccaria (1766, p. 3; 1767, p. 2); Priestley (1768, p. 17); Hutcheson (1725, pp. 163–4; and even to Leibniz (Hruschka 1991, pp. 165–77) (Shackleton 1972; see Stephen 1900, I, pp. 177–9).

1   Liberty and the criminal law

Montesquieu was the first major writer to place the reform of the criminal law on the agenda of the Enlightenment.[2] As early as the *Persian Letters* (1721) (especially no. 80, but also nos. 76 and 102), but mainly in books VI and XII of the *The Spirit of the Laws* (1748), he contended that severe punishments did not necessarily deter crime. Following his typology of constitutions he argued that mild punishments were appropriate to moderate governments and severe ones only to despotisms (*SL*, VI.9, 11–13). In moderate governments the wise legislator attempted to prevent crime by the adjustment and use of customs and traditions. Where penalties were needed, they could be mild with the use, for example, of fines which could also be made proportionate to wealth (*SL*, VI.18). Torture had no place in moderate governments, and he even hesitated to recommend the practice as being suitable for despotisms (*SL*, VI.17).

The theme of a proportion between crimes and punishments was invoked by Montesquieu on several occasions in book VI. 'It is essential for penalties to be harmonious among themselves', he wrote, 'because it is essential that the greater crime be avoided rather than the lesser one' (*SL*, VI.16). To punish robbery and murder with the same penalty would not encourage the robber to avoid committing murder. Montesquieu praised the use of transportation in England for robbers (though not for murderers), as a way of distinguishing between crimes. But he did not explain in book VI how punishments could be 'harmonious among themselves', beyond several examples and anecdotes where the lesser penalty was or was not provided as an encouragement to the reduction of crime. However, he returned to the theme of proportion in book XII where he approached this problem from the perspective of individual liberty.

Montesquieu's celebrated discussion of constitutional liberty is usually presented in terms of the doctrine of the separation of powers in book XI, and little attention has been devoted to what he called political liberty in its relation to the citizen, discussed more fully in book XII.[3] Political liberty was defined as 'that tranquillity of spirit which comes from the opinion each one has of his security, and in order for him to have this liberty

---

2 See Gay 1967–70, II, pp. 427–33; Radzinowicz 1948–86, I, pp. 269–76. This is not to suggest that the reform of the criminal law was confined to the Enlightenment. See, for example, Beattie 1986, pp. 450–637; Green 1985; Langbein 1977. As for the state of the criminal law prior to and during the eighteenth century, see the brief discussion in Maestro 1942, pp. 1–22.

3 Despite an examination of the theme of liberty, Shackleton 1961, pp. 284–301, virtually ignores the material in book XII. But see Pangle 1973, pp. 139–42; Richter 1977, pp. 94–6.

the government must be such that one citizen cannot fear another citizen' (*SL*, XI.6). Constitutional liberty was obviously connected to political liberty in that the separation of powers would prevent the abuse of power by government and encourage government under law. These in turn would enhance the security of the individual citizen. But Montesquieu also distinguished between constitutional and political liberty, as he thought that it was possible to have one without the other. The citizen could enjoy freedom in the sense that life and property were in fact secure in a constitution where no separation of powers existed (*SL*, XII.1). But the two were closely related, and the *de facto* security enjoyed by a citizen in an unfree state, depending mainly on customs, manners, and some purely civil laws regarding the individual and his property, would not be sufficient to maintain freedom. Montesquieu then looked, in addition, to the criminal law to establish that political liberty which complemented the separation of powers.

When Montesquieu defined liberty as security, he gave his definition an individual orientation in saying that liberty 'consists in security or in one's opinion of one's security' (*SL*, XII.1; see XII.2). Security, for Montesquieu, was established by governments only with reference to the individual citizen. The importance of this perspective as well as the definition of liberty as individual security will be seen in his discussion of penalties and the use of proportion in book XII, which clearly differed in scope and application from the earlier discussion in book VI. Montesquieu began his analysis with the following declaration: 'It is the triumph of liberty when criminal laws draw each penalty from the particular nature of the crime. All arbitrariness ends; the penalty does not ensue from the legislator's capriciousness but from the nature of the thing, and man does not do violence to man' (*SL*, XII.4).

Montesquieu was not initially concerned here (as he was in book VI) with how penalties harmonized with different offences (e.g. murder and robbery), but he turned to examine the different sorts of offences to which punishment should be attached. He began by distinguishing four sorts of crimes: those (a) against religion; (b) against mores; (c) against tranquillity; and (d) against the security of citizens. In crimes against religion, such as sacrilege, witchcraft, etc., Montesquieu knew that traditional penalties in many societies, and especially in France, were horrendous. He simply rejected most of these so-called offences in so far as they did not violate individual liberty. As crimes, they had the lowest and not the highest priority. The same argument was applied to the second category of crimes against public mores. In this category, he tended to include mainly sexual offences. He distinguished between sexual crimes, such as rape or kidnapping, which threatened individual security and those which were more simply based on the pursuit of pleasure. For the latter, he suggested a number of mild penalties and argued that such offences were based less on wickedness than on 'forgetting or despising oneself' (*SL*, xii.4). In the third category were crimes against tranquillity, by which he meant public order offences which did not threaten the security of other individuals. Here again, no great penalties were proposed. These were reserved for the final category of crimes against security, where the idea of proportion entered at still another level. For these offences, punishment was needed and Montesquieu conceived of it as 'a kind of retaliation'. The punishment 'is derived from the nature of the thing and is drawn from reason and from the sources of good and evil' (*SL*, xii.4).

Despite these vague phrases, Montesquieu clearly sought to proportion punishment to the severity of the offence (in terms of the violation of individual security), with death envisaged as the appropriate punishment for murder, and lesser penalties for lesser crimes. He believed that offences against property should not be punished as severely as offences against persons, and while he could conceive of some capital offences involving the theft of property, he thought that loss of goods for those who had them and corporal punishment for those who did not were preferable (*SL*, xii.4). What was significant in Montesquieu's analysis was the way in which the idea of liberty as security formed the basis of his examination of proportion in the relationship between crimes and punishments. Proportion was no longer a formal idea suggested in the traditional phrase depicting justice as 'to each his due'. The basis of 'his due' was to be calculated in terms of individual security, with those acts which posed the greatest threat to security receiving the greatest punishment. Montesquieu developed his idea in skilful assaults on existing offences such as magic, heresy, and homosexuality ('crimes against nature') (*SL*, xii.5–6). From his point of view these often capital offences were virtually dismissed as not being crimes at all.

He criticised at length the crime of high treason for its vagueness (*SL*, xii.7) and for the tendency to include within the offence a variety of actions including forgery and counterfeiting (*SL*, xii.8). Even worse was the extension of the offence of high treason to thought, speech, and writing, which he rejected as not being crimes except when part of the preparation of an actual criminal act (*SL*, xii.9–13, 16). 'How, then, can one make speech a crime of high treason? Wherever this law is established, not only is there no longer liberty, there is not even its shadow' (*SL*, XII.12).

In suggesting that Montesquieu set the agenda for the reform of the criminal law during the Enlightenment, it should now be clear that he went further than an opposition to severe penalties and to punishment based more on religious enthusiasm than on actual injuries to individuals. He called for a careful definition of offences based on the idea of individual liberty as security; he sought to proportion punishments to the severity of the threat to security; he attempted to link punishment to the nature of the crime itself (as a kind of 'retaliation'); and he called attention to the link between customs, mores, and forms of government on the one hand and crime and punishment on the other, in order to encourage a more varied approach to criminality which placed considerable emphasis on prevention rather than strictly on punishment.

2   Crime and punishment in Beccaria

The importance of Montesquieu was readily recognized in discussions of criminal law throughout the latter half of the eighteenth century, and no less so than by one of his most important disciples, Cesare Beccaria, whose celebrated *Dei delitti e delle pene* (Of Crimes and Punishments) was published in 1764, sixteen years after *The Spirit of the Laws*. Although Beccaria freely acknowledged his great debt to Montesquieu (Beccaria 1958, I, p. 46, 1995, pp. 8, 10), he developed a more consistent critical argument, the method of which was taken perhaps more from Helvétius than from Montesquieu, and which was clearly utilitarian. The object of legislation should be 'la massima felicità divisa nel maggior numero' (in the English translation of 1767, p. 2: 'the greatest happiness of the greatest number') (1995, pp. 7, 141; see Shackleton 1972; Venturi 1971, p. 102). His prescriptions were universally applicable and he introduced into his arguments for the first time, as Bentham later noted, 'the precision and clearness and incontestableness of mathematical calculations' (Bentham 1838–43, III, pp. 286–7; Hart 1982, p. 40). This 'mathematical' approach was combined with a passionate attack, especially in the chapters on torture and the death penalty, on the cruelty and folly of the criminal law and its enforcement in eighteenth-century Europe (1958, I, pp. 66–72, 79–87, 1995, pp. 39–44, 66–72). Both the passion and the calculation of Beccaria's treatise differed from the 'satirical, witty, urbane, irreverent' approach of Montesquieu (Cranston 1986, p. 9), so characteristic of the Enlightenment itself, but Beccaria's work came to be widely read, translated, and admired throughout Europe.[4]

Like Montesquieu, Beccaria took the theme of individual liberty as the basis of his treatise, though he followed Rousseau in employing the doctrine of the social contract. To escape from a state of war, where liberty had ceased to have value, free and equal individuals sacrificed part of their liberty to establish peace and security (Beccaria 1958, I, pp. 47–9, 1995, pp. 10–11). The portion of liberty which was given up was used by the sovereign to defend the liberty of members and the bond of society itself, and punishment played a key role in this defence. Punishments were then seen as providing motives influencing individual actions so as to discourage behaviour which might cause anarchy and chaos.

Beccaria agreed with Montesquieu that every punishment which was not based on the absolute necessity to defend the security of members of society was tyrannical, and this limited power of punishment was the sole, legitimate use of that liberty which was given up by individuals to the sovereign. 'No man has made a gift of part of his freedom', he wrote, 'with the common good in mind' (Beccaria 1958, I, p. 48, 1995, p. 10). By justice he meant simply the maintenance of the bond on which society was based. 'Punishment that goes beyond the need to preserve this bond is unjust by its very nature' (1958, I, p. 49, 1995, p. 11). The 'justice of God', he noted, was a very different idea concerned only with rewards and punishments in the next world (1958, I, p. 49n, 1995, p. 11).

On a number of themes, Beccaria restated Montesquieu's position and then built on it. For example, he favoured mild rather than severe punishments and used several arguments already developed by Montesquieu such as the importance of encouraging criminals to choose the lesser crime, and the diminishing value of severe penalties, such as the wheel, which, when generally accepted, no longer deterred. But Beccaria stressed, in addition, the importance of the certainty of punishment as opposed to its severity. To the argument that the prospect of severe punishment deterred crime, he replied (in the English version of 1767) that 'crimes are more effectually prevented by the *certainty*, than the *severity* of punishment'. 'The certainty of

---

4 André Morellet (Beccaria 1766), urged on by d'Alembert, translated the work into French, and this version was soon translated into English (Beccaria 1767) and into other languages. Beccaria received the admiration of many writers, including Diderot, Helvétius, Buffon, Rousseau, and Hume. Voltaire wrote a commentary (*Commentaire sur le livre des délits et des peines*, 1766) which was often published with Beccaria's treatise. See Maestro 1942, *passim*, 1973, pp. 38ff; Voltaire 1994a, pp. 244–79. For the influence of Beccaria throughout Europe, see the materials provided by Venturi in Beccaria 1965. See also Draper 2000, pp. 177–99; Maestro 1942, pp. 124–51.

a small punishment', he continued, 'will make a stronger impression, than the fear of one more severe, if attended with the hopes of escaping' (Beccaria 1767, p. 8; see 1958, I, pp. 92–4, 1995, pp. 63, 67). Beccaria applied a utilitarian calculation which led him to conclude that the expectation of pain to follow the crime from immediate apprehension, trial, and punishment would be sufficient to prevent crime and would enable the legislator to avoid the use of severe punishments. He was anxious to see crime and punishment closely associated (as closely as cause and effect), with the punishment inflicted as soon as possible after the crime was committed. This emphasis on the certainty of punishment led him, like Rousseau and Kant (though for different reasons), to criticise the use of pardons in the enforcement of the criminal law (1958, I, p. 93, 1995, pp. 111–12; *SC*, II.5, p. 65; Kant 1991, p. 160). The code itself should display clemency through the employment of mild punishments, and clemency by judges or sovereigns would then not be necessary. To encourage the hope of a pardon would be to encourage the avoidance of punishment.

Like Montesquieu, he believed that 'there must, therefore, be a proper proportion between crimes and punishments', but he too did not work out such a proportion with any precision (Beccaria 1958, I, p. 97, 1995, pp. 19–21, 64). He conceived of a scale of crimes with those that threatened the bond of society itself at the top and the smallest injustice to the individual at the bottom. Punishments would then be ranked to match the crimes. Such a scale, once established with scientific precision, could even be used to provide a 'common measure' to assess the degrees of liberty and slavery, and humanity and cruelty in various nations (1958, I, p. 97, 1995, p. 20). The stage of civilisation achieved by various states could be assessed by the various punishments they employed.

Beccaria provided few clues as to how any precise relationship between crimes and punishments might be established. The object of having mild punishments, applied with certainty, based on a clearly defined code, and serving to prevent crime, would go part of the way towards establishing the guiding principles of such a scale. At one point he called for punishments to be as analogous as possible to particular crimes (Beccaria 1958, I, p. 91, 1995, p. 49). In explanation, he saw the punishment as leading the criminal to see the particular crime in a different and less advantageous light than seen at the time the criminal act was committed. He thought that 'public punishment', especially of small crimes, would serve to prevent larger crimes, and for this reason he opposed imprisonment or transportation for such crimes because they removed the criminal from immediate public gaze (1958, I, p. 92, 1995,

p. 49). Yet, the 'public' character of such punishments was never explored. He clearly intended to employ calculations of pleasure and pain as ways of measuring punishments and adjusting them to the scale of crimes, though he did not develop this calculus to any extent (1958, I, p. 97, 1995, p. 20).

Both Beccaria and Montesquieu, as we have seen, did little to develop such ideas as proportional and analogous punishments or even the idea of using mild punishments to prevent crime. What was perhaps more important was their use of these concepts to *exclude* other and more traditional means of approaching crime and punishment. They strongly opposed the intermingling of the ideas of crime and sin, and reserved for the former a narrow definition and a minimal range of punishments. As for the latter, sinful acts were not necessarily considered crimes at all (Beccaria 1958, I, pp. 98–100, 1995, pp. 24–5).

In the brief chapters of his treatise, Beccaria covered a wide range of topics. He was eloquent in rejecting the cruelties of excessive punishments currently employed and especially common punishments for suicide, sodomy, infanticide, bankruptcy, so-called crimes against religion such as heresy, sorcery, and witchcraft, and crimes against property. He was also eloquent in his opposition to the death penalty, for which he could find virtually no justification except for extreme necessity where a powerful figure in the state not only threatened it with destruction but whose very existence would certainly succeed in destroying it. Such times of threatened anarchy would, however, be rare (Beccaria 1958, I, pp. 79–87, 1995, pp. 66–72).

Beccaria presented two sorts of arguments to support his position: the first was based on his conception of the social contract, and the second was founded on utilitarian considerations. As for the social contract, he asked whether or not any person had ever given up to the sovereign the right of taking one's life. He had in fact prepared to answer this question negatively in his earlier account of the terms of the contract. If each person joined with every other only to protect themselves from the invasion of their lives and property, it did not necessarily follow that the sovereign could take life to provide that protection. Indeed, if the contract was for the protection of life and property, there was nothing that one might do to have this protection withdrawn.

Beccaria clearly differed from Rousseau on the connection between sovereignty and the death penalty (*SC*, II.5). Although in a practical sense Rousseau believed that the death penalty should not be used if the criminal was no danger to society, he held in principle that under the social contract 'it is in order not to become the victim of an assassin that one consents to die if one becomes an assassin oneself' (*SC*, II.5, p. 64). Furthermore, in breaking the law, the wrongdoer ceased to be a member of society and could be considered as having made war against it. Beccaria denied that the sovereign possessed the authority to punish with death, and, turning Rousseau's formulation around, he asserted that the offender remained a citizen against whom the whole nation had wrongly declared war (Beccaria 1958, I, p. 80, 1995, p. 66).

Nevertheless, Beccaria did not rely wholly on arguments connected with his account of the social contract. He followed this analysis with a series of utilitarian arguments to show that other forms of punishment made the death penalty unnecessary as a deterrent to others. His first general argument was that the intensity of pain felt when a criminal was executed had a less powerful effect on the mind of the observer than the repeated feeling of lesser pains following the observation of the criminal suffering imprisonment at hard labour. To the spectator, then, the continued spectacle of a prisoner deprived of liberty and condemned to hard labour perhaps for the rest of his life was, according to Beccaria, a more powerful deterrent to crime than the brief experience of intense pain in watching an execution (Beccaria 1958, I, p. 81, 1995, pp. 67–9).

In this somewhat artificial argument, Beccaria went to the heart of the debate over the death penalty in attempting to counter the widespread belief that it was the only certain deterrent of crime, and especially of violent crimes such as murder. That Beccaria adopted a utilitarian form of argument perhaps corresponded to the fact that the problem itself, the degree of deterrence of certain punishments, was one posed in terms of the calculation of consequences, that is to say, the consequences of certain forms of punishment in deterring crime. As we shall see, Bentham rejected the argument concerning the relationship between the intensity and duration of pain and conceded that the death penalty did in fact have one advantage over other forms of punishment in being widely perceived as the most effective deterrent. In this sense he regarded it as a 'popular' punishment. Furthermore, Beccaria failed to deal with an obvious problem in recommending hard labour as an alternative punishment, in that the condition of most free labour at the time did not differ much from penal servitude. For most of the population of most countries hard labour on its own was not a punishment at all (see Venturi 1971, p. 106).

Secondly, Beccaria argued that an execution aroused both compassion and indignation in the spectator, and not simply the terror of oneself possibly suffering a similar fate. In enduring penal servitude only terror would be aroused and hence this latter punishment would prove more effective. To the objection that perpetual slavery and hard labour were as cruel a penalty as death, Beccaria replied that while that might appear to be the case to the spectator, it would not be the same for the person sentenced to this loss of liberty, because the pains of the prisoner were not focused on to one point but were scattered throughout his life. In addition, Beccaria argued that the death penalty was a barbarous punishment and one that encouraged the taking of life. In this respect, it was an imperfect deterrent and even an incitement to murder.

Beccaria's treatise 'made the idea of reform popular, palatable, respectable, almost fashionable' (Gay 1967–70, II, p. 446). But it was criticised, and not just by those who preferred a penal system based on vengeance and the widespread use of the death penalty. His arguments against the death penalty were not generally accepted; even Voltaire did not wholly support its clear abolition. In the two codes influenced by Beccaria (those of Leopold, grand duke of Tuscany, and Joseph II of Austria) which did abolish the death penalty, this was implemented not because it was believed that the state had no right to punish with death, but because capital punishment had failed to deter crime. In some respects, what replaced capital punishment was even more severe and brutal. Flogging, branding, and very long periods of imprisonment under atrocious conditions meant that the savagery against which Beccaria had protested most strongly remained in spite of the abolition of capital punishment (see Radzinowicz 1948–86, I, pp. 297–8).

Another sort of criticism was developed by Kant who dismissed Beccaria's account of the right of punishment as 'pure sophistry' (Kant 1991, p. 158). Kant sought to establish a strict relationship between crime and punishment, so that the punishment for murder would be death. Without this sort of retribution there could not be justice in the state. For Beccaria to argue that the pact of society precluded the use of the death penalty on the grounds that a person could not have consented to give to others what he had not in his power to do by right to himself was, for Kant, to confuse the right of punishment with extraneous considerations. According to Kant, the right to punish, including the death penalty for murder, was established when the individual as co-legislator authorised the penal law. As a subject, he agreed to live within the framework of the law, and, as a criminal, accepted punishment according to it. In comparison with Beccaria, the criminal, as an individual, had less control over his destiny and had to submit to the legislator's justice. Although Kant's theory was retributive, it was not based on vengeance; he referred to the *jus talionis* (the right of retaliation) in terms of sin, but he did not confuse crime and sin (Fleischacker 1988, pp. 436, 442; Williams 1983, pp. 97–109). Beccaria and Kant had developed two thoroughly modern, though incompatible, theories of punishment. But if Kant rejected Beccaria's argument regarding the death penalty, he did not forgo entirely the use of utilitarian arguments in his discussion of punishment (Williams 1983, p. 106; see also Hare 1993, pp. 1–20).

3 Bentham's theory of proportion

Jeremy Bentham was influenced by Montesquieu and especially by Beccaria, influences visible particularly in his *Introduction to the Principles of Morals and Legislation* (1789). Beccaria had made the first attempt to apply the principle of utility to the reform of the criminal law, and Bentham, having already been attracted to such an approach from his reading of Helvétius, found in Beccaria important ideas to develop (Bentham 1968, II, p. 99). These ideas consisted of more than an early statement of the 'greatest happiness' principle. Both Bentham and Beccaria believed that punishment was a subject that could be analysed rationally and critically, and not left to feelings, prejudice, and the justification of existing practices (Hart 1982, pp. 42–4). They believed that a system of punishments could be devised which would reduce existing crime and prevent numerous offences. At a minimum, such a system could contribute to human happiness in reducing the terrible suffering and brutality of existing punishments which had also apparently failed to reduce the great suffering caused by crime.

Despite Beccaria's acknowledged influence on Bentham, and Bentham's apparent adoption of Beccaria's ideas regarding certainty of punishment and the use of proportion and analogy in devising a scale of punishments, Beccaria, like Montesquieu, had done no more than set an agenda. For example, with regard to the much discussed proportion between crimes and punishments, Bentham noted: 'Establish a proportion between crimes and punishments, has been said by Montesquieu, Beccaria, and many others. The maxim is, without doubt, a good one; but whilst it is thus confined to general terms, it must be confessed it is more oracular than instructive' (Bentham 1838–43, I, p. 399).

Bentham's discussions of proportion, though written in the 1770s, were substantially more advanced than anything attempted at that time, and arguably might be seen as putting this key topic in the theory of punishment on a different level (see Draper 1997, pp. 218–60). He did so by working up a number of rules to govern the relationship between crimes and punishments which were based on assumptions or arguments he had already worked out. The first rule was that 'the value of the punishment must not be less in any case than what is sufficient to outweigh that of the profit of the offence' (*IPML*, p. 166). This rule assumed several key aspects of Bentham's penology. The initial idea was that of an economic model that allowed him to write of the 'value' of the punishment and the 'profit' of the offence (see Hart 1982, p. 46). Bentham was well aware that the language of political economy had not yet been applied to punishment, and he saw in this language the possibility of the greater use of reason and calculation. Besides very crude and largely intuitive notions such as that a thief should not receive the same punishment as a murderer, no-one had devised a way to relate punishments to crimes, or, for that matter, crimes to crimes and punishments to other punishments. Bentham believed that his economic model would enable him to do so. He regarded the pain of punishment as (quasi-economic) capital, which was invested with the expectation of profit. The profit was the prevention of crime in the future; loss, the continuation or increase in crime. The idea of an economic punishment was one that produced its desired effect with the least possible cost of suffering.

The profit of the offence would have to be weighed against the profit of the punishment, with the latter profit having to be greater than the former. There were several interests at stake. The first was that of the offender who profited from the offence. The second was that of the person or persons who suffered from the offence and who had an interest in the punishment. The third was that of the public at large whose interest in the prevention of crime gave it an interest in the punishment. The economic model depended on the calculation of these interests which might each be physical, financial, or psychological, but which were all expressible in terms of pleasure and pain. Indeed, the economic model was a model about pleasures and pains and only indirectly about profit and loss in any financial sense. The question then arises: does the model make the scale of punishment any more accessible than before? To answer this question it is necessary to see how Bentham used it in his rules to measure what ought to be the proportion between crimes and punishments.

As for the two terms in the first rule – the profit of the offence and the value of the punishment – Bentham meant by the former the force which urged the person to commit the offence, i.e. what one got from doing so, and by the latter, the force employed to prevent the crime. Even where the offence was easily quantifiable, Bentham was aware that the calculation was not a simple one. If an offender stole a pound, the first rule would indicate that he should at least be forced to repay the pound plus the costs of obtaining it from him. But such a simple equation of crime and punishment might not be adequate. If the offender had little reason to believe that he would be caught, he might be willing to steal again. A low detection rate might allow him to steal several pounds before having to repay only one. Furthermore, the offender might have stolen a pound but so alarmed others by the audacity of his theft that he forced them to purchase expensive locks. This expense, plus the psychological pain suffered by the increased expectation of theft, might make the repayment of only one pound too slight a punishment for the offence committed. On the other hand, the person who stole the pound might be very poor and at the point of starvation. The money might be needed to feed his family, and the punishment to repay the one pound might be not only far beyond his grasp but also no deterrent, because he was impelled to steal more by the pain of hunger and extreme suffering than by the fear of punishment.

How is one to decide when the 'value of punishment' exceeds the 'profit from an offence'? Some assistance comes from other rules which Bentham devised. The second was that 'the greater the mischief of the offence, the greater is the expense, which it may be worthwhile to be at, in the way of punishment' (*IPML*, p. 168). Bentham believed that this rule needed little argument in its support, though he admitted that so-called crimes against religion, like sacrilege, witchcraft, and sorcery, were often severely punished though they caused little mischief. His rule would oppose that trend, but it did not in itself reveal how mischief was to be understood.

For Bentham, mischief was constituted by acts which produced pain or diminished pleasure. He considered mischief a highly complex idea even within the framework of a system of offences. He first distinguished between primary and secondary mischief. Primary mischief (divided into original and derivative mischief) consisted of mischief sustained by assignable individuals. Secondary mischief (divided into 'alarm' and 'danger') consisted of mischief suffered by unassignable individuals as a result of the primary mischievous act (*IPML*, pp. 143–4). For example, the person who suffered loss in a robbery was in receipt of primary mischief. As a consequence of being robbed, other assignable individuals might suffer, e.g. a person to whom he was about to pay some money when it was taken from him. This is some of the derivative mischief arising from the initial robbery, though not part of the robbery itself. Secondary mischief was also of two kinds: the first (called 'alarm') was the pain of apprehension which spread throughout the community that life and possessions were increasingly under threat. The amount of pain suffered by people in general upon learning about the robbery would depend on the circumstances of the robbery itself. If it was particularly cruel and brutal, a greater alarm would be felt. The second part of secondary mischief (called 'danger') consisted of the apprehension in the whole society of the chance that one might suffer at the hands of the same robbers or similar ones as a result of the robbery that had been committed.

The third rule was that 'when two offences come in competition, the punishment for the greater offence must be sufficient to induce a man to prefer the less' (*IPML*, p. 168). This rule was first devised by Montesquieu (*SL*, VI.16), but Bentham criticized Montesquieu for his praise of England, where the possibility of transportation contributed to the effect sought by the rule. For Bentham, the English practice depended on an arbitrary act by the sovereign rather than on a rule embodied in a scale of punishments. He clearly favoured a scale of crimes where the effect would operate more definitely and surely (Bentham 1838–43, I, pp. 400–1nn). The fourth rule was that 'the punishment should be adjusted in such manner to each particular offence, that for every part of the mischief there may be a motive to restrain the offender from giving birth to it' (*IPML*, p. 168n). This rule, which Bentham believed had been violated 'in almost every page of every body of laws I have ever seen' (*IPML*, p. 168n), would give offenders every incentive to limit or reduce the magnitude of the offence. If a person was given the same punishment for stealing ten shillings as for stealing five, he argued, the second group of five shillings was taken without the offender receiving any punishment. Thus punishments would have to be carefully graduated so that increases in the mischief of the offence could receive a corresponding punishment.

If the first four rules were designed to prevent punishments from being too small, rules five and six were intended to prevent them from being too great (see *IPML*, p. 169). Bentham believed that punishments which were too small were fairly obvious as they would fail to deter crime. But there was a strong tendency to punish with undue severity, because it was not easy to make the correct estimation of what punishments would in fact succeed in preventing crimes. If rule five aimed at curbing the severity of punishments by requiring them to fall within the rules requiring inexpensive punishments for offences, rule six introduced a whole range of factors to be considered in doing so. Bentham knew that certain punishments, while severe to some, were not so to others. A fine which was nothing to a rich man would ruin a poor man. 'The same imprisonment that would be ruin to a man of business, death to an old man, and destruction of reputation to a woman', he wrote, 'would be nothing, or next to nothing, to persons placed in other circumstances' (Bentham 1838–43, 1, p. 401). Bentham's approach required that various factors influencing sensibility (such as age, sex, rank, wealth, etc.) should be taken into account in the actual imposition of punishments so that some were not too severe and others too mild. This calculation could not, however, be embodied in the code itself and would require considerable latitude in the imposition of punishments (within the maximum and minimum frame established for each offence) to be placed in the hands of judges.

After completing the first six rules, Bentham added three additional ones to fill out and elaborate the first rule which was that the value of a punishment must not be less than the profit from an offence (*IPML*, p. 170). If there was less of a certainty of punishment for any given offence, the punishment must be increased in proportion to the uncertainty. Similarly, if the punishment was remote in time from the offence, it would have a diminished deterrent effect and hence would have to be increased in proportion. Finally, if a number of offences had been committed by the same offender (e.g. fraud in weights and measures) it was necessary that the punishment should reflect all the instances of the offence so that the punishment was greater than the profit from the offence. Otherwise, an offender would find it profitable to pay a small penalty and continue committing the offence.

Bentham's economic model tended to assume that the relationships between crimes and punishments could be established and adjusted largely in quantitative terms, especially in the adjustment of the amount of punishment to the profit from the offence. But he also realised that given a variety of forms of punishment, there was no exact way to quantify their deterrent capacity and that where certain punishments seemed most appropriate to particular crimes, they might not necessarily be the cheapest to prevent the crime. Like Montesquieu and Beccaria, Bentham was interested in the idea of linking punishment to a crime in a way that would dramatically reduce the motivation to commit it. For example, he favoured castration as opposed to the death penalty as a punishment for rape. Not only would it be the less drastic punishment but it might also 'produce a strong impression on the mind at the moment of temptation' (Bentham 1838–43, 1, p. 418; see Williams 1983, p. 106). He rejected the idea of punishment based strictly on retaliation, due to both its tendency towards severity and its highly limited applicability. To find a punishment that exactly mirrored a crime would be difficult and the only merit that Bentham could see in the idea was its simplicity and the popularity of the idea of punishing murder with death.

Analogous punishments were another matter, especially where their use seemed to reduce the quantity of punishment traditionally employed (Bentham 1838–43, I, pp. 407–11). But in establishing a proportion between crimes and punishments, he admitted that these qualitatively different punishments would be difficult to relate quantitatively to each other (see *IPML*, p. 171).

When Bentham felt that he had set forth the basic groundwork for his theory of punishment, he then proceeded to establish various 'properties' of punishment to be used by the legislator to establish a system within the rules of proportion (*IPML*, pp. 175ff). The 'properties' of punishment were necessary to make the system work. Among the eleven 'properties' listed and discussed were variability, equability, and commensurability. Bentham emphasized the quantitative aspect of punishments in holding that for every variation in the severity of an offence (see rules one and four), there should be different degrees of punishment. Otherwise, there would be needless or inefficacious punishment. The second property, equability, was related to the first. Although a punishment might allow for variability, it might not be adjustable to fit a variety of circumstances so that for one person it would fall heavily and be severe, while for another it might be overly mild. The forfeiture of property was an example used by Bentham, where, despite the possibility of variability in the parcels to be forfeited, the severity of punishment would depend on whether or not the prisoner possessed that kind of property and to what extent. Bentham noted that under English law certain offences required the forfeiture of moveable property (money, goods, etc.) but not immoveable property (land, buildings, etc.). If a person's fortune was in moveable property, all would be lost; if in immoveables, he would not suffer any loss. A third 'property' of punishment was called commensurability. This was necessary to implement the third rule of proportion which would lead the offender always to choose the lesser of two related offences. For two punishments to be commensurable, all persons in various circumstances should be willing to choose the lesser offence over the greater. This 'property' differed from equability, in so far as it was mainly concerned with relating punishments to each other, while equability was a matter of relating punishments to individual crimes.

As Bentham spun his web of offences and punishments into ever more complex patterns, he was well aware that he risked making it unworkable (*IPML*, p. 171). At the same time the rules of proportion and the various 'properties' of punishment seem fairly remote from an actual scale of crimes and punishments as envisaged by Montesquieu and Beccaria. Etienne

Dumont, Bentham's Genevan editor (see Blamires 1990), referred to this material as the 'logical apparatus': 'the scaffold which ought to be taken down when the building is erected'. Once the actual penal code was constructed, the rules of proportion would no longer have any direct utility in relating punishment to crimes, except, as Dumont put it, as 'a machine for thought – *organum cogitativum*' (Bentham 1838–43, I, p. 407n).

4 The debate over the death penalty

Due to their philosophical character, Bentham's writings on punishment stood apart from the numerous discussions of various aspects of crime and punishment which continued into the early decades of the nineteenth century. In the debate over the death penalty in Britain, there was a general acceptance by all the main parties of 'rational principles' regarding punishment (see Gatrell 1994). These were for the most part utilitarian in being concerned with preventing and deterring crime and not with the guilt or sinfulness of the criminal. Even so extreme a writer as Michael Madan, who favoured a rigid executive justice whereby all who were convicted of capital offences would suffer the death penalty, declared that the end of punishment was the prevention of crime, held (like Montesquieu and Beccaria) that certainty of punishment was more important than severity, and argued from a general concern with the consequences of existing and proposed policies (Madan 1785, pp. 11, 62–3nn, 131–2ff). Madan believed that the death penalty provided the only satisfactory deterrent to crime, although at one point he thought that transportation might work were this punishment strictly enforced (1785, p. 76). Given the importance of self-preservation, he argued that criminals would do and suffer virtually anything rather than die (1785, pp. 108ff). Madan regarded the current situation in England as wholly unsatisfactory, with numerous capital offences, but juries unwilling to convict and judges all too willing to exercise mercy.

If Madan believed that the way to prevent crime was to enforce the law with certainty so that the criminal would know what to expect, William Paley took a different view. Like Madan, he believed that the end of human punishment was not the 'satisfaction of justice' but 'the prevention of crimes' (Paley 1785, p. 526), and that the death penalty was the only available punishment with sufficient terror to deter crime. If a crime was difficult to prevent, it should be more severely punished and for this reason he could justify making theft from a shop a capital offence (pp. 527ff). Similarly, Paley justified the English practice of making sheep-stealing, horse-stealing, stealing cloth, etc., capital offences by arguing that these crimes were more difficult to prevent than others and required the 'terror of capital punishment' to protect the public (p. 529). The death penalty for non-violent crimes like forgery and perjury was justified in terms of the consequences of these offences in threatening commerce and civilisation itself (pp. 538–41). Unlike Madan, however, Paley supported current English practice which assigned capital punishment to numerous offences, but only inflicted it on a few (pp. 531–4). He opposed torture and was opposed to spectacles of human agony which tended only to harden and deprave. Yet he wanted the horror of the death penalty fully felt by the populace in order for it to deter crime and suggested at one point that murderers should be cast into a den of wild beasts, but that such an execution should be concealed from the public so as not to deprave them. Such a suggestion was based on Paley's calculation of the consequences of the punishment for the prevention of crime (pp. 546–8). In the same vein, he opposed transportation on the grounds that it did not contain sufficient terror, especially for those without property, friends, and other ties to the community (p. 543).

These utilitarian arguments for the retention of the death penalty by Madan and Paley were opposed by other arguments of a similar form but towards differing ends in two pamphlets by Samuel Romilly.[5] Unlike Beccaria, whom he generally admired, Romilly was not wholly opposed to the death penalty, but he did oppose it for offences against property (Romilly 1786, pp. 24–5). He set forth a series of arguments in criticism of Madan's contention that the death penalty was the only effective deterrent for theft. He pointed to other countries where milder punishments deterred crime, and argued that the spectacle of frequent executions eventually ceased to deter people from crime, as they grew hardened to it and corrupted by it (p. 30). He cited Sir William Blackstone's argument that to deter crime by any means was not justifiable (pp. 32–3). He rejected the view, adopted by Madan, that the sacrifice of one guilty person to preserve thousands was justifiable on the grounds that it assumed that the death penalty was a valid means of deterrence. Madan's position, he argued, would also justify the sacrifice of an innocent person.

5 Romilly 1786, 1810. Romilly was a close friend of Bentham to whom he was introduced in 1784 (Bentham 1981, p. 17n). Bentham claimed that Romilly 'was among the earliest, and, for a time, the only efficient one of my disciples' (Bentham 1993, p. 257), and his speech and pamphlet against Paley drew on Bentham's unpublished work, 'Law versus arbitrary power:- or, A Hatchet for Dr Paley's Net' (University College, London, Bentham MSS, cvii. 199–266). On Bentham and Paley, see Crimmins 1987 and Schofield 1987.

At the heart of Romilly's critique of Paley were two doctrines. The first was based on Paley's belief in Beccaria's maxim that certainty of punishment was of more consequence than severity. Romilly used this against Paley to argue that Paley's faith in the discretionary power of magistrates to impose the death penalty or to grant pardons and his belief in the death penalty for theft in fact led to uncertainty of punishment (Romilly 1810, pp. 33–5). The second doctrine, also originating in Montesquieu and Beccaria, was that there should be a proportion between crimes and punishments with the most severe punishments reserved for the worst crimes (pp. 21, 49–50). Both Madan and Paley rejected this doctrine as it would lead to a major reduction in the use of the death penalty.

The idea of a proportion between crimes and punishments or a scale of punishments was based on the doctrine of liberty adopted by Montesquieu, Beccaria, and Bentham. For these writers, liberty meant individual security, and the establishment of a proportion between crimes and punishments should work towards a condition in society where arbitrary and unnecessary punishments would be abolished. Neither Madan nor Paley were enthusiastic about liberty. Madan thought that justice and liberty were in conflict, and that the security of the public was more important than the security of the individual (Madan 1785, pp. 12, 15–16). Paley rejected Montesquieu's idea of liberty as the security of the individual (Rosen 1992, pp. 32–4), and believed that too much liberty in Britain was in fact the cause of crime and a reason why the death penalty was needed. Paley seemed to argue that in despotic societies there was less crime, because legal rights protecting the individual were not observed and punishments were both severe and certain (Paley 1785, pp. 541ff). He rejected the maxim that it was better for ten guilty persons to escape rather than that one innocent man should suffer (pp. 552–3). Paley took the view that one might regard the sacrifice of an innocent man in terms of a person giving his life for his country.

As we have seen, Bentham adopted Montesquieu's idea of liberty and embedded it in his own theory of punishment. He became a firm opponent of the death penalty (see Jackson 1991), although at first he accepted its use for the crime of murder. He also recognised some positive features about the death penalty: it prevented the offender from doing further injury; it was analogous to the offence of murder and could be seen as the appropriate penalty; it was popular with the public in general; and, contrary to the view of Beccaria who argued that the prospect of life imprisonment was more painful than the prospect of death, Bentham believed that the death penalty made a deep and lasting impression, and served as an example to deter others (Bentham 1838–43, I, pp. 444–5). Yet, there were also numerous disadvantages: it could not be 'convertible to profit' in the sense that compensation might be obtained from the labour of the criminal; it represented a loss of 'frugality' because society was deprived of the labour and strength of the person executed; it did not affect different people in the same way, as some feared death and others did not, or at least not to the same degree; it was not remissible and hence the innocent might be killed; and it paradoxically produced a tendency in juries not to convict and judges to show mercy, hence producing arbitrary punishment and even contempt for the law (pp. 445–50).

Bentham at first agreed with Beccaria that the death penalty might be justified where rebellion threatened society and where, by destroying the leader, one could destroy the rebellion (Bentham 1838–43, I, pp. 449–50). When he returned to the theme of the death penalty at the end of 1830, he was even more strongly opposed to it, and could see no place for its continuation (pp. 525–32). He then felt that imprisonment was a fully viable and superior alternative to capital punishment. He had also become more radical in his political opinions and could readily sympathise with the view that the law 'grinds' the poor, because it was made and enforced by the rich. The example of milder punishments in the United States, especially for minor crimes like theft, provided further evidence that the continuation of the use of the death penalty for stealing sheep or theft from a private house would only cease when radical political reform took place in England (p. 532). Bentham looked forward to a fully representative democracy which would provide the engine for reform, including the reform of the criminal law (see Rosen 1983).

5   Transportation and imprisonment

The attack on severe punishments and the widespread use of the death penalty led to a search for alternatives to such cruelty and inhumanity and to the development of secondary punishments (Beattie 1986, pp. 450–1). Transportation, which had ceased abruptly with the American War of Independence but began again in 1787 with the first voyage to Botany Bay, was favoured by some. Montesquieu had viewed it favourably as an alternative to the death penalty. In his *Enquiry concerning Political Justice* (1793), the libertarian William Godwin, opposed to all forms of punishment, found it least objectionable if not combined with a regime of slavery (Godwin

1976, p. 679). Nevertheless, most writers were suspicious of transportation. William Eden tended to oppose it as a loss of manpower to the country (Eden 1771, p. 28). Romilly thought transportation a severe punishment, but also that it seemed mild when compared with the death penalty (Romilly 1810, p. 63). Bentham's critique of transportation was perhaps more thorough but not less critical (Bentham 1838–43, I, pp. 490–7).

The only serious alternative to transportation was imprisonment, which, of course, existed throughout the period in question. But few who read John Howard's *The State of the Prisons in England and Wales* (1777) doubted that there was an urgent need for considerable reform. Howard was not initially concerned with prison as an alternative to the death penalty or to transportation. As high sheriff of Bedfordshire he had responsibility for the county gaol. He became interested in the people who languished in prison awaiting trial and found that even if they were acquitted or if the prosecution did not proceed with its case, they were often unable to leave prison, as they were liable to exorbitant gaoler's fees. He was also deeply distressed by the widespread disease and general squalor in prisons (Howard 1777, pp. 1–3). Howard influenced the passage of the Gaols Act of 1774 and his own proposals for an ideal prison were 'in many ways the forerunner of [Bentham's] panopticon' (Semple 1993, p. 72).[6] Bentham thought highly of Howard's work and at one point planned to dedicate his book on the theory of punishment to him (if he managed to complete it) (Semple 1993, p. 74). In later editions of his treatise Howard acknowledged the influence of writers such as Beccaria and Eden (Howard 1792, pp. 9n, 14n, 15, 19, 42n, 43n, 118n).

Together with William Blackstone, Howard assisted a small group of reformers, including Eden, Charles Banbury, and Gilbert Elliot, to draft and see through parliament the Penitentiary Act of 1779. When the bill was about to be published Bentham was prompted to write his *View of the Hard Labour Bill* which started him on the road to the panopticon prison (Semple 1993, pp. 42–61; Bentham 1838–43, IV, pp. 3–35). Bentham apparently favoured a more lenient regime than that proposed in the bill. Nevertheless, he accepted initially one aspect of contemporary penology which was hardly lenient in its effects on the prisoner. The use of solitude (or solitary confinement) was not necessarily part of the reforms inspired by the Enlightenment, but it became associated with both imprisonment and the reform

---

6 The panopticon was a circular prison which allowed surveillance of all prisoners from a single vantage point. Bentham devised his panopticon scheme in the mid-1780s and pressed it upon the government in the 1790s.

of prisoners. Partly inspired by the desire to keep prisoners apart to prevent prisons becoming seminaries for thieves or other criminals, partly by a desire to save Christian souls, and partly to protect prisoners from intimidation by other prisoners, the emphasis on solitary confinement became common-place in eighteenth-century writings on penology (Semple 1993, pp. 78ff). Among influential writers in favour of solitary imprisonment were Samuel Denne (1771), John Jebb (1786), and Jonas Hanway (1775, 1776, 1781).

Although Howard initially favoured solitary confinement, he soon changed his mind (Semple 1993, p. 89). In his *An Account of the Principal Lazarettos in Europe* (1789, pp. 169n, 192n), he recognised the dangers of the use of solitary confinement for more than two or three days. Nevertheless, Howard's name became associated with this regime, and a writer like God-win could call attention to 'the well intended, but misguided, philanthropy of Mr. Howard' in creating prisons where 'the prisoners . . . spend a large proportion of their time shut up in silent and dreary cells, like so many madmen' (1976, p. 679n).

Bentham accepted solitary confinement in the original panopticon *Letters*. By 1790 he began to have doubts, and these doubts were fully expressed in the *Postscripts* (Bentham, 1838–43, IV, pp. 47, 59, 71–6; Semple 1993, p. 130). He cited Howard's new position and referred to solitary confinement as enabling one 'to screw up the punishment to a degree of barbarous perfection never yet given to it in any English prison, and scarcely to be given to it by any other means' (Bentham 1838–43, IV, p. 71). He favoured two, three, or possibly four prisoners placed together in double or larger cells. The change of view, though 'not a trifling one', revealed the extent to which he was not overly concerned with the cure of souls through solitude and contemplation in any religious sense. His concern was more simply to prevent the commission of crime when the prisoner was released from prison and to develop the productive use of labour. He argued that the productivity of labour was actually enhanced with more than one person working in a cell, and he believed that the panopticon prison scheme could lead to the prevention of crime by means other than solitary confinement.

6 Enlightenment and reform

The legacy of the Enlightenment to the reform of the criminal law was the insistence on humanity in the face of cruelty and on liberty in place of despotism. For the former, the life and writings of Voltaire provide an important example; his efforts in the Calas, Sirven, and La Barre cases testify to his humanitarianism (Gay 1959, pp. 273–94). A comparison of his *Commentaire sur le livre des délits et des peines* (1766) with the text of Beccaria's treatise, on which it comments, reveals in Voltaire's work less of a theory and more of a sense of outrage at the unjust, inhumane, and pernicious character of the legal systems of most European states, and particularly France.

The concern with liberty was more complex and clearly began with Montesquieu and Beccaria upholding the liberty of the individual citizen and seeing that liberty closely connected to the reform of the criminal law. But it was difficult to see how liberty entered into any theory of punishment except in the sense that members of society were protected from various crimes, and the system of criminal procedure prevented arbitrary accusations, trials, and punishments. The theory of liberty not only encouraged reflection on these important aspects of the criminal law, but also penetrated into the very idea of punishment itself, which might otherwise be defined in broad terms as being concerned with the deprivation of liberty.

The idea of a scale of punishments was one major attempt to bring liberty to bear on this aspect of state power. The scale of punishments, in the language of liberty, meant that each person had a right to security from interference by others, but that if this right was violated, punishment would be limited to the prevention of profit from the offence and would aim to deter others from committing a similar offence. Any greater amount of punishment beyond these two objects would be a deprivation of liberty. In the hands of Beccaria and especially Bentham the doctrine was clearly utilitarian, but both placed the idea of liberty at the heart of their utilitarianism. Liberty rested on the calculation of the consequences of the minimum exercise of state power, and hence pain, necessary to deter certain actions which were deemed criminal by their effects on individual security and could be prevented by no other means than by punishment.

During the eighteenth century there was no understanding of or even a consensus of opinion about what kinds and amounts of punishment would deter criminal action. But there were numerous writers willing to express an opinion, and some of these opinions were based on utilitarian calculations. Paley's argument is a good example, and the deep differences between Paley and Bentham arose not from their commitment to utilitarianism as an ethical theory but to Bentham's incorporation of the idea of liberty into that theory.

But can the panopticon prison system be regarded as the product of an Enlightenment theory of liberty applied to punishment? Recent social history and Marxist theory would tend to answer this question negatively and see in the panopticon prison the failure of the Enlightenment to do little more than replace one system of terror with another (see Foucault 1977; Hay 1975; Ignatieff 1978, 1983b; cf. Langbein 1983; Semple 1993). Such views have tended to interpret the movement towards imprisonment with hard labour less in terms of an advancement of liberty and more as the development of systems of discipline and control within capitalist society. But, for Bentham, widespread inspection, especially from the central core of the prison, was designed to prevent abuses of power by prison officers and other prisoners and to enhance the security of the prisoner. His inspection principle would remove the prison from seclusion and open it to 'the great *open committee* of the tribunal of the world' (Bentham 1838–43, IV, p. 46). Inspection would enable a considerable leniency to be introduced into prison life. He believed that the inmates would approve of the regime, as, for example, irons and chains, widely used in most prisons, would not be employed (p. 47; cf. Ignatieff 1978, pp. 34–5). The use of contract management and life insurance based on average mortality rates were intended to provide the governor with every incentive to keep prisoners alive, well, and actively engaged in productive labour (see Halévy 1952, p. 85). It is important to distinguish Bentham's panopticon scheme from the practices employed in many prisons in the nineteenth century. When Sir John Bowring, Bentham's friend and literary executor, examined prison labour in 1865, he could still praise Bentham as 'the most profound and philanthropic writer on Prison Discipline' while at the same time condemning such common practices as 'the crank, the treadmill, water lifting, stone breaking, oakum picking, absolute isolation – unremunerative, hopeless, heartless toil' (Bowring 1865, pp. 1–2).

Some recent historians have also dismissed the tendency to emphasize the so-called movements to reform the criminal law in the eighteenth century as a 'Whig interpretation' of this period, in that it assesses the eighteenth century in terms of progress made towards the humanitarian ideals of a later period (Emsley 1987, pp. 200–1; see Innes and Styles 1986; Philips 1985). Nevertheless, this criticism tends to assume that a debate between 'reformers' and 'conservatives' took place at this time (Hay 1975, p. 56 and n). But such a view underestimates the complexity of varying initiatives to reform the criminal law in the eighteenth century.

A major objective of movements for reform in many countries, including England, was the abolition of severe penalties for so-called religious offences. In England, this issue united Paley with Romilly, and Blackstone with Bentham. Blackstone could confidently declare (citing Beccaria) that 'all crimes ought therefore to be estimated merely according to the mischiefs which they produce in civil society' (Blackstone 1765–9, IV, p. 41). By the time he wrote these words criminal prosecutions for offences against God and religion were in decline and would cease to be a major issue, at least in England, by the end of the eighteenth century. But the movement to assess the seriousness of offences 'according to the mischiefs they produce in civil society', and hence to separate crime from sin, represented a major development in legal theory.

Only Bentham made any major advance on the ideas of Montesquieu and Beccaria on a philosophical level. His analysis was highly complex, even technical, largely because it was a more complex issue than Montesquieu and Beccaria could appreciate when they called for punishments in proportion to crimes. Although the theory was developed in the later chapters of the *Introduction to the Principles of Morals and Legislation* (originally drafted as an introduction to a penal code), published in 1789 but with limited circulation, the full statement of his ideas on penal law appeared in French in 1802 and 1811, but not in English until 1830 and in the posthumously published edition of his works, edited by Bowring between 1838 and 1843 (see Bentham 1802, 1811, 1830, 1838–43). This important development of the ideas of Montesquieu and Beccaria was part of Bentham's legacy to the nineteenth century.

It is difficult to discover any sort of public 'debate' between 'reformers' (like Eden, Bentham, and Romilly) and 'conservatives' (e.g. Madan and Paley) beyond Romilly's critique of both Madan and Paley on the death penalty. Beccaria's influence, for example, seemed everywhere (Draper 2000, pp. 177–99). Of greater importance perhaps was the fact that writing was developing on different levels and towards different objects. For example, both Eden and Bentham might be regarded as major reformers of the criminal law in England (Draper 2001, pp. 106–30; Holdsworth 1903–72, XII, pp. 364–5), but the differences between them are striking. Bentham stated some of these in a candid note in his manuscripts:

I write from system: and it is the fashion to hate systems. I labour to learn and to instruct: he writes secure of pleasing. He swims with the current: my struggle is to turn it . . . He is one of the ornaments of a court. I have long sequestered myself from the face of men, in the fond hope that I might one day do them service.[7]

Bentham was well aware of the need for allies in the uphill struggle to reform the criminal law, but Eden, though a reformer and despite Bentham's

---

7 University College, London, Bentham MSS, xxvii. 107, qu. Semple 1993, p. 59.

approaches, would not become one (see Bentham 1968, II, pp. 90–3). Eden's achievement was more like Blackstone's, to show how far the criminal law had already progressed since an earlier and less civilised period, and to suggest areas where further reform was necessary (see Lieberman 1989). Bentham's philosophical approach looked first towards a system which might resolve the numerous difficulties and puzzles so easily passed over by Eden. Bentham's work was closer, perhaps, to that of Paley, who also devised a system and used it to consider the criminal law. Both Paley and Bentham were utilitarians, and to see them simply as a 'conservative' and a 'reformer' respectively falsifies the historical experience of the eighteenth century, and seriously underestimates the role of philosophical thought in this period (see Hay 1975, pp. 56–63).

20

Republicanism and popular sovereignty

IRING FETSCHER*

1   Rousseau

A Protestant among Catholics, a proud citizen of the tiny republic of Geneva among cosmopolitan fellow travellers of monarchical imperialism, a critic of modernity at its most fashionable eighteenth-century shrine, Rousseau was spiritually estranged from the intellectual circles in Paris to which he had previously been drawn when, in 1750, he won the prize offered by the Academy of Dijon by responding in the negative to its question, 'Has the restoration of the arts and sciences contributed to the purification of morals?' With the publication of this work, his *First Discourse*, he immediately became a celebrity and thereby launched his literary career as chief critic of the age of Enlightenment. When, in 1755, in addressing the same academy's question, for another prize competition, on 'What is the origin of inequality among men, and is it authorised by natural law?', he condemned both the loss of innocence and lack of virtue prevalent in refined society. Private property, he asserted in his *Second Discourse*, was the principal source of that form of unnatural inequality which gives rise to governments, rulers, and violence.

The first man who, having enclosed a piece of ground, to whom it occurred to say *this is mine*, and found people sufficiently simple to believe him, was the true founder of civil society. How many crimes, wars, murders, how many miseries and horrors mankind would have been spared by him who, pulling up the stakes or filling in the ditch, had cried out to his kind: Beware of listening to this impostor; You are lost if you forget that the fruits are everyone's and the earth no-one's. (Rousseau 1997a, p. 161)

Rousseau here, as well as in his *Essay on the Origin of Languages* largely drafted some years later (and first published posthumously in 1781), sketches a theory of historical development according to which mankind must originally have lived in a purely animal and unsociable state of nature, driven by hunger and sexual appetite alone. In that condition man's only inclinations would

* Translated from the German by George St Andrews and adapted by Robert Wokler.

have been self-love and compassion, Rousseau argues, but as the human race multiplied, this simple form of life would have disappeared. Hunting and fishing would have made co-operation necessary, thereby giving rise to rudimentary forms of social life. Mankind would then have passed through successive stages, from nomadic shepherding to settled agriculture and the invention of metallurgy, he claims, with each stage unleashing ever greater luxury, the passions of egoism, the despotism of rich over poor, and increasingly sophisticated forms of social power. These stages trace what Rousseau regarded as the downfall and corruption of natural man by way of a speculative history that not only denied his contemporaries' faith in progress but also the Augustinian doctrine of original sin. According to Rousseau's re-reading of the Book of Genesis, sin had been manufactured in the course of human history and civilisation and had reached its zenith in the transformation of agricultural into commercial society.

In his *Social Contract* of 1762 he depicts not so much the social origins of vice as the political characteristics of ancient virtue, deemed appropriate to all legitimate republics wherein the people as sovereign do not run headlong into their chains but rather achieve a kind of equality in which every man remains 'as free as before' (*SC*, 1.6, p. 50). The freedom a man gains under republican rule is, however, different from the 'natural independence' which he gives up when entering into a contractual relation with his fellow citizens. Rousseau here endeavours to answer the question, what can render legitimate the chains which bind men everywhere? It is, he contends, the idea of contract or covenant, which can only be legitimate if the 'person' to which the will of everyone is submitted is the 'association of all'. Only an association of citizens who rule themselves can pretend to sovereignty. A state in which that self-governing sovereign constitutes the legislative will is, according to Rousseau, a republic.

The 'act of association involves a reciprocal engagement between the public and the private individuals', whereby each individual, he maintains, 'contracting, so to speak, with himself, finds himself engaged in a two-fold relation: namely, as a member of the sovereign towards private individuals, and as an individual member of the state towards the sovereign' (*SC*, 1.7, p. 51). The seeming paradoxes of this formula are explained by Rousseau's dualistic conception of human nature. As a virtuous citizen every man wills the 'general will' (*volonté générale*) which promotes the common good, but as an individual with private interests he is at the same time a 'subject' of the laws which, as a citizen, he has prescribed to all. 'The people's deliberations', as constituted in the legislative sovereign to which they individually bind themselves, are always upright, but only on condition that they are united by their shared concern for the whole community. Their laws, conceived not as the 'will of all' which is the mere sum of their disparate particular wills but as the expression of their general will, must pertain to all citizens of the republic (*SC*, II.3, pp. 59–60). The sovereign cannot have an interest contrary to the collective interests of its citizens, for sovereignty, 'by the mere fact that it is, is always everything it ought to be' (*SC*, I.7, p. 52). When a people is united and virtuous, its sovereign will is inalienable and indivisible (*SC*, II.1–2). Of course Rousseau admits that the *volonté générale* seldom prevails in actual societies. The will of all, or of the majority when compounded of citizens' individuals wills, often errs, for 'what generalizes the will is not so much the number of voices, as it is the common interest which unites them'. What is required is an 'agreement between interest and justice' (*SC*, II.3, II.4, pp. 60, 62).

How can such a concordance be achieved? Through education, through the prohibition of partial societies within the state which produce their own private wills in contradiction with the general will, and through the erosion of social differences in order to create a more homogeneous society (*SC*, II.3, p. 60). In order to attain greater equality or homogeneity of interests, there ought either to be no political parties, corporations, or unions in the state (such as was sought through the *loi* Le Chapelier of 1791, justified with reference to Rousseau), or as many as possible, each roughly equal to the others, as Solon, Numa, and other great legislators of antiquity had sought. Recalling the central theme of his *Second Discourse* (that is, his *Discourse on Inequality*), Rousseau reports that the social state is always advantageous to those who have possessions and harmful to those who have none. While he allows that social and economic inequalities are inevitable, he insists that the republic must prevent citizens who are sufficiently rich from buying the will of others and those who are poor from selling their votes and thereby enslaving themselves (*SC*, I.9, II.11). Neither wage-earners nor great capitalists could flourish in a republic such as he portrays, which would, ideally, form an agrarian society comprised of independent producers.

Rousseau, moreover, draws a sharp distinction between a republic's sovereign and its government. The sole authority of the sovereign citizenry is to make laws. The administration and application of the laws in particular instances is a matter for the state's government, 'magistrate', or 'prince', but not its sovereign. The relationship between legislative and executive power may be likened to that which determines the two causes of human action in general – a spiritual or moral cause, and a material or physical cause, in effect, a will which determines and a power which executes (*SC*, III.I). Government provides the connection between the sovereign and the subject, a *corps intermédiaire*. It may be an individual or a group, but what is crucial, according to Rousseau, is that the functions of sovereignty and government must never be exercised by the same body. As much as he insisted, like Hobbes, upon the need for absolute sovereignty, he also stipulated, like Montesquieu, that there must be a separation of powers in the state, sovereigns never possessing the authority to enforce their own laws and governments never having the authority to make them.

Just as the particular will incessantly acts against the general will, so the government makes a constant effort against sovereignty. The greater this effort grows, the more adulterated does the constitution get, and since there is here no other corporate will to resist the will of the prince and so to balance it, it must sooner or later come to pass that the prince ends up oppressing the sovereign and breaking the social treaty. (*SC*, III.10, p. 106)

In that mounting clash of government and sovereignty lies the old age and death of the social organism. It was to be found in Rousseau's lifetime in the usurpation of the powers of Geneva's sovereign General Council by the Small Council that comprised its government, the patriciate wresting the authority of Geneva's bourgeoisie as if to illustrate the iron law of oligarchy two centuries before Robert Michels had invented it. The development of royal sovereignty in France in the seventeenth century had pursued a similar evolution.

While sovereignty always took only one legitimate form, according to Rousseau, he allowed, in classical Aristotelian fashion, that governments might take different forms, appropriate to different circumstances, generally in inverse correlation with a state's population, monarchical power prevailing in large states, democratic rule and popular liberty in small ones, with hereditary aristocracies constituting what he terms 'the worst of all governments' and elective aristocracies, provided offices are there determined by merit, the best (*SC*, III.5, p. 93). It is in this context that Rousseau's deprecating remarks about democracies – in particular their tendency to anarchy, faction, and civil war – should be understood. 'If there were a people of gods, they would govern themselves democratically. So perfect a government is not suited to men', he contends (*SC*, III.4, p. 92).

In the *Social Contract*, if not everywhere throughout his political writings, democracy is described merely as a form of government that purports to be sovereign, a confusion equally characteristic, from the opposite end of the spectrum, of oligarchy and tyranny. The radically democratic hue of Rousseau's political theory is nonetheless displayed in this work's defence of the idea of popular sovereignty and especially in its hostility to the idea of representation. 'Sovereignty cannot be represented', Rousseau insists, for laws require the direct and unmediated mandate of all citizens. 'The deputies of the people therefore are not and cannot be its representatives, they are merely its agents; they cannot conclude anything definitively. Any law which the people has not ratified in person is null; it is not a law' (*SC*, III.15, p. 114). This formula does not confine Rousseau's vision just to the face-to-face citizen assemblies of the ancient city-state; it points as well to systems of mandated delegates, dismissible at will, and to the ratifications of legislation through referenda. In his *Government of Poland*, drafted in the early 1770s, he proposes mandated deputies for the diet of an independent Polish state, which would be too large for an assembly of all citizens. The debates about the nature of popular mandates which took place in the French National Assembly in 1789 and thereafter were much influenced by his reflections on this subject in his *Government of Poland*. But in condemning representation in the *Social Contract*, he pours scorn above all on the British constitution, contending that 'The English people thinks it is free; it is greatly mistaken, it is free only during the election of members of parliament; as soon as they are elected, it is enslaved, it is nothing' (*SC*, III.15, p. 114).

Commentators have often remarked upon the contrasts between the apparent utopianism of the *Social Contract* and Rousseau's more nuanced and pragmatic schemes for Poland, Corsica, and Geneva. Those contrasts must not be exaggerated. The ideal type of republican rule which he outlines suits only a small and Spartan society comprised of virtuous citizens. In practice, and even in the *Social Contract*, he warns his readers against any swift alteration of ancient and venerable laws. Legislation should follow the customs and practices of a people, he insists, rather than the dogmatic maxims of intellectuals. In a corrupt world, ancient laws can be a sound guide.

2 Mably

The Abbé Gabriel Bonnot de Mably, elder brother of Condillac whom Rousseau encountered in Lyons in 1741, came from a wholly different background, having been born into prosperity as a member of France's provincial *noblesse de robe*. By virtue of his inheritance and education he was destined for an ecclesiastical, diplomatic, or political career which, however, he abandoned to become a writer. His first book, the *Parallèle des romains et des français* (Comparison of the Romans and the French) of 1740 offered a defence of Dubos's monarchical philosophy and a rejection of Boulainvillier's contrary *thèse nobiliaire*, showing how feudal government in medieval France had paved the way towards a perfected form of monarchy under the Bourbons which, unlike the Republic of Rome, had proved incapable of degenerating into despotism.

But Mably did not continue to subscribe to such views for long. On the occasion, in 1747, of Cardinal Pierre Guérin Tencin's decision to authorise the annulment of a Protestant marriage over his and other objections, and more generally on account of his perception of the abuse of monarchical power and its mismanagement of the public purse in the War of the Austrian Succession, he broke with the court circles to which he had come to be allied and repudiated his own earlier doctrines. First, in his *Observations sur les grecs* (Reflections on the Greeks) of 1749, and then, more decisively, in his *Observations sur l'histoire de France* (Observations on the History of France) of 1765, he appealed to both Spartan and Roman models of constitutional government which he contrasted with the practice of arbitrary rule under France's monarchy, like Rousseau, and indeed with a substantially wider range of historical sources and references at his disposal, turning to classical antiquity as a guide to the defects of modern absolutism. Rome's republic had been modelled on that of Sparta, he asserted, its perfection, as Polybius had explained, residing in its mixed character, embracing monarchical, aristocratic, and democratic components, its fundamental framework of popular sovereignty secured by the introduction of the tribunate, which had protected the interests of Rome's plebeian classes. The accumulation of wealth through trade that in the contemporary world was so central to the prosperity of commercial societies fostered the corruption of morals and public spiritedness such as had drawn the more egalitarian citizens of Sparta and Rome together in common service to the state.

In his *Entretiens de Phocion* (Conversations of Phocion) of 1763, a dialogue purporting to be a translation of a recently discovered Greek manuscript that won him great acclaim and proved the most widely circulated of all his writings, Mably couched his praise of ancient republican virtue in the language of justice, prudence, and right reason, adopting perspectives and the terminology invoked by Stoics to keep the passions of avarice and ambition at bay. An invincible nation was one defended selflessly by all its citizens, he claimed, and they shared that objective because the passions that would otherwise divide them, including contempt and envy arising from extremes of wealth and poverty, would have been successfully suppressed. Unlike some utopian writers of the eighteenth century, such as Jean Meslier or Morelly, who hoped that the abolition of private property might lead to the dissolution of all forms of despotic power in its wake, Mably, like Rousseau, attached importance to the idea of private property as, at least in principle, a measure of self-reliance, and like Rousseau, too, he portrayed images of citizens' public engagement as exemplified by ideals prevalent in the Republic of Rome. He showed little patience, however, for Rousseau's interest in a fictitious state of nature, for his critique of the idea of sociability, and for his supposition that collective self-rule was only possible in small states. Yet these differences are less striking than their similarities. Mably's egalitarianism, decried by Benjamin Constant as similar to Rousseau's attempt to transform France into Sparta, was, on account of its concentration on political solidarity, closer to classical republicanism than to that of most strains of nineteenth-century socialism that were more akin to anarchism (Wright 1997).

3   Diderot

Ever since it became known that almost all the politically radical passages in the later editions of the Abbé Raynal's *Histoire philosophique et politique des deux Indes* (Philosophical and Political History of the Two Indies) are by Diderot himself, as well as in the light of the publication from hitherto unknown manuscripts of his *Entretiens avec Catherine II* (Conversations with Catherine II) in 1899, his *Observations sur le Nakaz* (Observations on [Russia's] Code of Laws) in 1920, and his *Pages contre un tyran* (Pages against a Tyrant) in 1937, Diderot must be reckoned among the most significant political writers of the eighteenth century. The *Encyclopédie*, which he edited and brought out almost single-handedly, contains a considerable number of political texts, though they do not follow a consistent line. Diderot secured among his contributors on political and economic subjects many luminaries of the day, including Turgot and other leading physiocrats, while the indefatigable chevalier de Jaucourt proved the most assiduous collaborator of all. The general tenor not only of his own contributions but of the whole enterprise which he supervised may be described as one of enlightened and optimistic rationalism, not least with respect to its portrayal of the natural sciences, arts, crafts, and technical industries, as well as its (cautious) critique of religion. The *Encyclopédie* undoubtedly helped to undermine conservative ideologies prevalent under the *ancien régime*, but neither by design nor effect was it a revolutionary text, and the Empress Catherine II not only sought Diderot's company in St Petersburg but also offered to have the *Encyclopédie* printed in Russia if French censors put too many obstacles in the way of its chief editor.

Diderot's most forthright political views are by and large to be found in places other than the *Encyclopédie*. His critical judgement of the English constitution derived chiefly from his contact with John Wilkes, who in 1763–4 was an exile in France. Diderot urged Wilkes to defend the American cause in parliament. Obliquely in the 1782 edition of his *Essai sur les règnes de Claude et de Néron* (Essay on the Reigns of Claudius and Nero), comprising a revision of his account of the life and writings of Seneca published four years earlier, and more directly in his contribution to the *Histoire des deux Indes*, he enthusiastically acclaimed the American 'insurrection' and urged the New Englanders not to falter in their struggle against oppression. In freeing themselves they had given all the inhabitants of Europe a refuge from fanaticism and tyranny, and taught their rulers a lesson in the legitimate use of their authority, Diderot suggested, adding his hope that the manners of these brave fighters and their descendants would not be corrupted 'by the enormous growth of wealth and its uneven division' in America.

In the *Essai*, which appeared towards the end of his life under his name, he defends a right of popular insurrection, going far beyond his more character-istically cautious advocacy of reform. But it is in his (anonymous) additions to Raynal's commentary on the two Indies that can be found Diderot's most revolutionary pronouncements. Although the work is mainly about colonial history, Diderot's words are easily transferrable to domestic conditions. 'You should know that an empire cannot endure . . . without morals and virtue', he remarks in directly addressing France's Louis XVI with regard to the corruption of his court. 'Do you intend to go on condoning the insatiable greed of your courtiers . . . or to allow the nobility and magistrates . . . to continue to keep far from them the burden of taxation and make it fall on the people?' (Diderot 1992, pp. 172–3). Sooner or later justice must pre-vail, Diderot insisted, even if this should mean that a nation can only be reborn through a bloodbath. From evidence provided by history itself, it was plain that 'all arbitrary power rushes towards its own destruction, and that everywhere revolutions . . . bring back the reign of liberty' (p. 174).

In transmitting its principles of freedom to its American colonies, England had recently witnessed its own enlightenment invoked against itself as those principles had taken root there. Through the American Revolution Euro-pean philosophy had spread abroad, while the corruption of political power in France beckoned its return to the Old World as well (p. 198). 'Wherever the sovereign does not allow people to express themselves freely . . . he provides the most convincing evidence of his inclination to tyranny.' 'When the horrors of tyranny and the instincts of liberty put weapons into the hands of bold men', there is more moral strength among the few citizens who bring about this 'fortunate upheaval' than in the most populous nations (pp. 182, 174).

With the empress of Russia Diderot of course adopted a milder tone. Her reform of her nation's legal code, itself apparently inspired by Montesquieu, excited the admiration of many *philosophes*, and Diderot heaped praise on this attempt to bring philosophy and kingship together. At the same time, through a series of incisive comments in his *Observations sur le Nakaz*, he endeavoured to promote more radical change out of Catherine's proposed programme.

His use of the word *souverain* in this text is not consistent. In a passage which appears in the preface he seems to offer his unequivocal support for popular sovereignty: 'There is no true sovereign except the nation; there can be no true legislator but the people.' Here Diderot seems plainly to be following Rousseau. The people is sovereign, and its task is to provide binding laws for all. Russia could be seen as a republic in Rousseau's sense, if its monarch were merely the people's magistrate. Yet, in most passages of the *Observations*, Diderot speaks of the empress herself as sovereign. He declares that the 'first line of a well made Code . . . should begin thus':

We the people and we sovereign of this people swear conjointly to obey these laws by which we will be equally judged; and if it should happen that we, the sovereign, [thereby becoming] enemy of our people, should change them or infringe them, it is just that our people should be released from the oath of loyalty, and that they should pursue us, depose us and even condemn us to death if the case demands it. (Diderot 1992, p. 81)

The people are here clearly distinguished from the sovereign, over whom they are granted 'supreme authority' (p. 82). They do not create the republic; there is at best a contract of rulership and subjection between people and sovereign. What Diderot most frequently stressed is not so much popular sovereignty as the rule of law. He is less concerned with the ultimate source of legislation than a monarchy's subjection to the same laws as all its citizens. Without the rule of law, the empress is a despot.

In his *Observations sur le Nakaz* Diderot proceeded to recommend the creation, or election, of a representative body, to meet every five years so as to judge whether the sovereign had observed the laws. If necessary this body, he suggested, could determine a punishment or terminate the sovereign's office. Reform must begin with the unequivocal renunciation of autocracy. Whatever good might be achieved by unlimited power, enlightened absolutism must engender popular passivity, and at worst a good ruler was likely to be succeeded by a tyrannical despot. A limited monarchy, or *monarchie tempérée*, by contrast, should be so constituted that the monarch is free to do good, but prevented from doing ill.

When the empress declared that 'it is more advantageous to obey the laws under a single master than to depend on several masters', Diderot agreed on condition that the master himself 'is the first subject of the laws' (1992, p. 88). The natural tendency of all monarchs was to slide towards despotic rule. 'The king of England does all he can to establish a French government; and the king of France all he can to introduce an Asiatic government'(p. 90). Diderot had in mind and here alludes to the regime of Maupeou, between 1768 and 1771, which had contravened the constraining power of the *parlement* of Paris and the Cour des Aides. The fate of the *parlements* showed that law courts formed no adequate safeguard against despotism. There must, Diderot thought, be a better guarantee of the 'fundamental laws of Russia'. Even the English House of Commons could be weakened by corruption. What was required was a sufficiently powerful countervailing force, *un corps dépositaire*, to balance the monarch. Who shall be the repository of the laws? 'A body representing the nation.' It must be a body elected by the people which, when not seduced by political munificence, will choose the most upright and best informed among them.

What should be the prerogative of this body? To revise, approve or disapprove the wishes of the sovereign, and to convey them to the people. Who should make up this body? Owners of large property (*grands propriétaires*). How should this body be given some strength? That is a matter of time, of public consideration . . . of the permanence of those members. (Diderot 1992, p. 100)

Diderot's identification of this body with the *grands propriétaires* must have struck quite a number of his readers as odd, bearing in mind his advocacy elsewhere of the abolition of privilege and his insistence upon laws of inheritance that would make the division of estates compulsory.

The *Observations* are also marked by excursions on the need for universal schooling, a liberal divorce law, and a restrained legal code (with a preference for reparation over imprisonment and the death penalty). Diderot urges the separation of church and state and the necessity of not favouring any particular religion, since priests seduce monarchs by preaching that they are accountable to God alone, and feed upon ignorance, the foundation of their wealth and position. 'The priests have been much more cunning than sovereigns', he remarks. 'They made us drink in the dogmas of religion with our mothers' milk . . . When you establish laws you should not put them under the sanction of religion' (1992, pp. 114–15). In the same text Diderot calls for serfdom to be abolished (pp. 126–7). That is necessary if economic development is to be promoted, he insists. With the exception of foreign trade, there should be full freedom of trade and competition. Though Diderot held, like Rousseau, that gross inequalities of wealth were dangerous, he embraced freedom as appropriate to economic progress. Wealth was not of itself harmful if it contributed to the welfare of all and if taxes reflected the ability to pay of those over whom they were levied.

If Diderot sometimes reflected Rousseauian republicanism, he nowhere imagined a Russia formed out of a federation of small virtuous republics, and in his eyes, as against Rousseau's pessimism, he came to see in Russia an optimistic progressivism, in the light of which Russia might in time even overtake the 'most modern states' of Europe.

4   Venice and Geneva

Rousseau remarks in his *Confessions* that his *Institutions Politiques*, as he initially conceived what would have been his magnum opus in political theory and of which the *Social Contract* was to be the sole surviving fragment, had been inspired by his stay in Venice in 1743–4, when he had been secretary of the French ambassador to that republic. Its similarity to the contemporary government of the republic of Geneva had struck him, the bourgeoisie of his native city being exactly equivalent to the Venetian patriciate, he observed. He held that it was wrong 'to take the government of Venice for a genuine aristocracy'; it should rather be understood as a 'mixed government', like Geneva's. 'While the people has no share in the government, the nobility is itself of the people. A multitude of poor Barnabites never came close to any magistracy, and all they get for being noble is the empty title of Excellency and the right to be present at the Great Council' (*SC*, IV.3, p. 126). The constitution of Venice would correspond to the ideas of the *Social Contract* if its government had not long ago become an hereditary aristocracy. 'It is very important to regulate by laws the form of electing magistrates; because if it is left to the will of the prince, hereditary aristocracy is the inevitable consequence, as it was in the republics of Venice and of Berne' (*SC*, III.5,

p. 93). Venice's practice of election by lot in the manner of ancient Athens could not be masqueraded as democracy since in Venice the doge ruled for life.

Jaucourt was the author of the *Encyclopédie* article 'Venise, gouvernement de', in which he summarised the history of the Venetian state from the establishment of its republican constitution in 709, recounting its transformation into an aristocracy of the higher nobility from virtually the time of its inception and then formally in 1172. But even while its republican foundations were subverted, a countervailing force, he explained, remained in Venice, residing in the body of the twelve tribunes, who could oppose ordinances of the 'prince' and annually chose forty citizens from each section of the city to serve on its Grand Council, comprised in all 240 members. This constitution survived until 1289, when the doge established a 'true aristocracy', by restricting membership of the Grand Council just to citizens of the day and their descendants, in perpetuity thereafter electing the members of Venice's Small Council or government.

The republic's population came to be divided hierarchically by ranks, including three orders of nobility distinguished by the length of their genealogy, below which resided a largely undifferentiated class of townsmen (*cittadini*) eligible for such public offices that were beneath the dignity of the nobility but excluded from the franchise that determined other roles. If the constitution gave the impression of a *gouvernement mixte* by way, respectively, of monarchy (the doge), aristocracy (the Small Council), and democracy (the Grand Council), 'in reality the state is a pure aristocracy', he claimed. Raynal, in his *Histoire des deux Indes*, was equally critical of the Venetian constitution. Like Rousseau, however, he maintained that its government might appear the best if its aristocracy were not the worst. All branches of the ruling power are there divided amongst the nobility and balanced with admirable harmony, he suggested. The great rule effortlessly like shining stars in a spectacle which pleases the people, who console themselves for their lack of power with aspirations of wealth that, with diligent application, is within their grasp.

Rousseau himself, especially in his *Lettres de la montagne* (Letters from the Mountain) of 1764, supplied a far more detailed account of the republican constitution of Geneva. He identified the five or six classes of persons that comprised the state in Geneva and defined their political rights, though he neglected the population's lowest class, the *sujets*, forming around one third of the city's inhabitants. The first two classes, the citizens and the bourgeois, were the only ones entitled to take part in legislation, and the most important offices of state were reserved for the *citoyens* themselves, a status Rousseau shared and which he proudly proclaimed on the title-page of most of his major works until he renounced it himself in objecting to the corruption of Geneva's constitution, and was in any case stripped of it by Geneva's government, mainly for the seditious character of his theology. *Citoyens* were sons either of *citoyens* or of bourgeois, provided that they had been born in the city. A bourgeois resided in the city and could be admitted to all trades, subject to expulsion only by the verdict of a court. The number of *citoyens* and bourgeois together never exceeded 1,600. Below them in political status were the *habitants* who formed a class of foreigners entitled to live and work in but not vote on the affairs of the republic. Their children counted as *natifs* and enjoyed certain rights, among them of access to certain professions, which their parents did not possess. *Habitants* and *natifs* were more highly taxed than *citoyens* and bourgeois. The *sujets* or subjects generally lived outside the walls of the city but within the territorial orbit of the state, bound by its laws but taking no part in its political life.

From Rousseau most famously but also other sources in the eighteenth century it was known that Geneva's republic was comprised of the following institutions. (1) The *Petit Conseil*, or Small Council of twenty-five members, sometimes called the Senate, consisting of members nominated for life, which settled political and constitutional questions and could initiate legislation to be brought before other councils, as well as serving as a supreme court. (2) The *Syndici* or Syndics, who administered public policy in all branches of government, chosen annually by the *Conseil Général* or General Assembly of all citizens from among the members of the *Petit Conseil*. (3) The Council of Two Hundred, responsible for appointing members of the *Petit Conseil*. (4) The Council of Sixty, consisting of members of the *Petit Conseil* and thirty-five delegates of the Council of Two Hundred. And (5) the *Conseil Général* itself, bringing together all *citoyens* and bourgeois, thereby forming the legislative body of Geneva's republican constitution. Although Rousseau sometimes described Geneva as a democracy, in the *Social Contract* he reserved that term to define a form of government in which the people, in administering the laws to themselves, rendered their state's general will particular. No more than ancient Athens, whose democracy he portrays as providing its citizens' freedom only by way of an institution of slavery that made their leisure possible, Genevan democracy, consisting of around 5 per cent of the republic's 30,000 inhabitants, bore little resemblance to the idea of genuinely popular self-government of which Rousseau was the eighteenth-century's chief advocate.

He objected fiercely to the *Petit Conseil*'s progressive metamorphosis, accelerated in his own lifetime, into a hereditary governing body dominated by a few families, regarding this tendency as 'le vice principal' of the Genevan constitution. But the restriction of full citizenship and all its rights to a small percentage of the population disturbed him less. In response to the efforts of the city's public prosecutor, Jean Robert Tronchin, to defend the prerogatives and indispensability of the power wielded by its *Petit Conseil* against its critics who accused it of usurping the authority of the people, Rousseau championed the sovereign status of the *Conseil Général* in his *Lettres de la montagne*. These tensions had arisen before on several occasions in the eighteenth century, but their resurgence in the early 1760s was due in no small measure to the influence of the *Social Contract* itself upon radical circles which thereafter couched their opposition to Genevan oligarchy in the language of popular sovereignty he employed, even though Rousseau had in his fashion merely recapitulated principles invoked by earlier generations of democrats who regarded their state's original constitution as having been subverted by its government. Tronchin had traded on the ambiguities of the meaning of the term *gouvernement* to obscure the *de facto* usurpation of sovereignty by the *Petit Conseil*. Rousseau responded that in a republic, sovereignty resided in and with the people, while the 'government' merely carried out the laws which expressed the sovereign's will. If the best possible form of government was that in which the best persons – that is, an aristocracy – ruled, it was also the case that hereditary aristocracy was the most dreadful form of sovereignty. Aristocratic sovereignty was in principle even worse than monarchical sovereignty, allowing that the congruence of a state's general will with the will of an enlightened prince was more probable than with a political body comprised of mixed elements. While an individual might come to subordinate private interest to the common good, the consciences of the members of a council come to be soothed effortlessly by their conviction that in acting together they have put private interest aside – but they were nevertheless engaged in their common interest, a particular interest compared to that of the whole community.

In propounding such claims Rousseau sharply differentiated his own political philosophy from that of d'Alembert in his article on 'Geneva' published in 1757 in the the seventh volume of the *Encyclopédie*. 'Geneva knows no hereditary dignities: the son of a first magistrate remains undistinguished from the mass, unless by his own merit', d'Alembert insisted. Rousseau's critique of oligarchy and indeed the concept of representation not only of the people but on the stage – a common theme that joined his philosophies of the state and the arts together – owes much to his disenchantment with Genevan politics and culture and his opposition to those, who like Voltaire and d'Alembert, sought to refine and prepare for the challenges and promise of the modern world the character of the people of that austere republic. Unless it was in his posthumously published *Government of Poland*, which first appeared in print in 1782, and would come to inspire some of the central debates about sovereignty and representation in the course of the French Revolution, nowhere would these populist themes in defiance of modernity play a greater role in his writings than in his critique of d'Alembert's essay, his *Lettre sur les spectacles* (Letter on the Theatre) of 1758, which occasioned more commentaries and replies from his admirers and detractors alike than his *Discourse on Inequality* and *Social Contract* together.

5 Kant

In the course of a long life Immanuel Kant hardly ever set foot outside the city of Königsberg in East Prussia. But there was nothing provincial about the tastes and interests of perhaps the most cosmopolitan of all eighteenth-century philosophers. Through immensely broad reading in several languages and by way of entertaining widely travelled visitors he engaged with world events as if he had witnessed them first hand. This was above all true with respect to the American and French Revolutions. As a university professor employed by the Prussian state, Kant was obliged to show caution and reserve in pronouncing on religion and politics, but his passionate support for the American colonists in not just their grievances but their uprising is evident, and he regarded the intellectual sympathy which French revolutionary events evoked abroad as a sign of humanity's moral progress.

While Hume had aroused him, as he famously remarked, from the 'dogmatic slumbers' into which German philosophy had sunk in the metaphysical wake of Leibniz and Wolff, it was to Rousseau that Kant owed his abandonment of philosophical elitism and conversion to a 'democratic' way of thinking. As he remarks in a celebrated fragment, 'I am myself by inclination a seeker after truth.'

I feel a consuming thirst for knowledge and a restless passion to advance it, as well as satisfaction in every forward step. There was a time when I thought that this alone could constitute the honour of mankind, and I despised the common man who knows nothing. Rousseau set me right. This blind prejudice vanished; I learned to respect human nature, and I should consider myself far more useless than the ordinary working-man if I did not believe that this view could give worth to all others to establish the rights of man (cited in Cassirer 1945, pp. 1–2).

Kant no more subscribed to Rousseau's philosophies of history and the state than he did to Hume's scepticism, but the only adornment that could be found in his modest study was a portrait of Rousseau, from whom he drew insights into the nature of society and of *sinnlichen Mensch* (sentient man) tempered by his altogether different conception of the links between political theory and practice in the light of which, unlike Rousseau, he sought to develop his political philosophy (forming only a small and relatively minor part of his corpus as a whole) entirely from the principles of 'pure reason'.

By contrast with Rousseau, Kant did not assume that mankind is by nature good or perfectible, nor did he agree with those materialists of his day who, following Locke, supposed that human nature was at bottom largely formless and elastic and that, as Helvétius put it, 'L'éducation peut tout' ('Education can achieve everything'). On the contrary, in accord with Christian theology, he accepted that mankind had fallen from grace, and in a passage in his *Idee zu einer allgemeinen Geschichte* (Idea for a Universal History, 1784), which Isaiah Berlin was to make the cornerstone of his own philosophy, he declared that 'nothing straight can be constructed from such warped wood as that which man is made of' (Kant 1991, p. 46). Likewise in contrast with Rousseau he believed that a gradual moral improvement of humanity was possible, and that *natura naturans* or creative nature had ensured that mankind should aspire to and procure higher things by its own reason, unconditioned by instinct. The dignity or worth of persons lay in their each being ends in themselves, which Kant supposed was even the purpose of Creation itself. From this notion stemmed his conception of the categorical imperative, in its second formulation the idea that every rational being should treat every other 'always at the same time as an end, never merely as a means' (*Groundwork of the Metaphysics of Morals*: Kant 1998, p. 38). From the man who is capable of reason, a reasonable being can be made. It is because of the antagonism of human instincts, because of man's 'unsociable sociability', that there can be cultural progress, whose trajectory, because it is compelled by his own nature, is not of his making as are the moral choices by which he enacts that nature. Rousseau subscribed to virtually the opposite perspective with respect to mankind's evolution, convinced as he was that cultural progress ensured only moral regression. In the seventh proposition of his *Idea for a Universal History* Kant, however, maintained that

We are *cultivated* to a high degree by art and science. We are *civilised* to the point of excess in all kinds of social civilities and proprieties. But we are still a long way from the point where we could consider ourselves *morally* mature. For while the idea of morality is indeed present in culture, an application of this idea which only extends to the semblance of morality, as in love of honour and outward propriety, amounts merely to civilisation. (Kant 1991, p. 49)

While, by and large, Kant accepted Rousseau's critique of contemporary moral deficiencies, he took the exercise of the faculty of reason with which human beings were endowed to mark not only prospective but already achieved stages of gradual moral progress, thereby rejecting one of the central contentions of the *Discourse on Inequality* in which Rousseau had contended that human history had marked the abuse and not the refinement of mankind's perfectibility or capacity for self-improvement. One of the chief hindrances to this progress, as Kant remarked in the same passage, was the concentration of states upon external expansion rather than on 'the slow and laborious efforts of their citizens to cultivate their minds'. In the eighth proposition of his *Idea for a Universal History* he asserted that 'the history of the human race as a whole can be regarded as the realisation of a hidden plan of nature to bring about an internally – and for this purpose also externally – perfect political constitution as the only possible state within which all natural capacities of mankind can be developed completely' (Kant 1991, p. 50). If this goal were to be reached or approached, then the adoption of the categorical imperative, which as a matter of conscience stipulates a rule prescribed to itself by *homo noumenon* or a rational human being, would be possible without endangering man's self-preservation. On this point Kant may appear not to differ markedly from Rousseau, but his guide was perhaps less Rousseau than Adam Smith, who, like him, believed in both moral progress and civilisation, occurring by a design that was not consciously intended by human agency and thus not of human origin, manifesting the achievement of an 'invisible hand'.

Kant took as empirical evidence for such 'philosophical chiliasm' the widespread acclaim which greeted the achievements of the French Revolution on the part of individuals not directly interested in its outcome. 'This revolution has aroused in the hearts and desires of all spectators who are not themselves caught up in it a *sympathy* which borders almost on enthusiasm, although the very utterance of this sympathy was fraught with danger. It cannot therefore have been caused by anything other than a moral disposition within the human race', he asserted in *Der Streit der Facultäten* (The Contest of the Faculties, 1798: Kant 1991, p. 182). By way of disinterested condemnation of the *ancien régime* it can be recognised that inequality among men institutionalised as hereditary dependency is irreconcilable with the categorical imperative. Whoever does not personally profit from this injustice is in a position to recognise its immorality. This 'sympathetic participation' goes beyond mere passive observation and implies readiness to take an active part. The moral cause at work here is comprised of two elements, he wrote.

Firstly, there is the *right* of every people to give itself a civil constitution of the kind that it sees fit, without interference from other powers. And secondly, once it is accepted that the only intrinsically *rightful* and morally good constitution which a people can have is by its very nature disposed to avoid wars of aggression (i.e. that the only possible constitution is a republican one, at least in its conception), there is the *aim*, which is also a duty, of submitting to those conditions by which war, the source of all evils and moral corruption, can be prevented. If this aim is recognised, the human race, for all its frailty, has a negative guarantee that it will progressively improve or at least that it will not be disturbed in its progress. (Kant 1991, pp. 182–3)

To these remarks is attached an odd footnote expressly rejecting the establishment of a republican regime in a territorially extended monarchy – from the context of Kant's work, plainly Prussia – whose population 'may feel that monarchy is the only kind of constitution which can enable it to preserve its own existence between powerful neighbours'. If their subjects should complain of their government's discouragement of republicanism abroad, this does not prove they are dissatisfied with their own constitution, for, on the contrary, it proves 'that they are profoundly attached to it; for it becomes progressively more secure from danger as more of the other nations become republics'. If republics are inherently peaceful, then – at least after the transformation of all neighbouring states into republics – Prussia too could become a republic, because it would no longer need to be defended against foreign aggression. Kant's remarks were of course shrouded in prudent caution.

For Kant, a republic is a polity whose laws articulate the united will of the people, whereby each decides the same for all and all for each. As he put this point in 1795 in *Zum ewigen Frieden* (Perpetual Peace), 'The civil constitution of every state shall be republican', by which he meant, as he explained, that in separating executive from legislative power the government was not despotic, since he took the arbitrariness of despotic rule to be most conspicuous when a state's laws were made and executed by the same power (Kant 1991, pp. 99, 101). For republicanism to prevail, such separation of power he deemed as important as Montesquieu and Rousseau had done before him. No less than Rousseau he judged democracy to be pernicious and indeed despotic when it was a form of government, just in so far as it grants an executive power to the whole people, enabling citizens to decide against single individuals or groups among them without their consent, rendering 'the general will . . . in contradiction with itself' (Kant 1991, p. 101). In insisting that this separation of powers required that government be representative, he stressed the importance of a concept with respect to government that Rousseau had been at pains to reject with respect to sovereignty, not least in his condemnation of the parliamentary system by which the British people's representatives masqueraded their own wills for the general will of the nation as a whole. Rousseau may not have noticed that in rejecting the idea of representation as an abuse of the unmediated sovereignty of the people he had left scant room to reintroduce the principle with respect to government in its separation from the people's legislative power, but that idea did not escape Kant's attention, and in his political philosophy it opened the prospect for a form of government that Rousseau decried, in the person of Frederick II, who at least *said* that he was the highest servant of the state, his own will according with the *spirit* of a representative system. By way of the concepts of representation and the separation of powers, enlightened despotism could appear to coincide with the republican constitution of a state in which the people were nominally sovereign.

To be a citizen of a republic, three conditions – freedom, the dependence of citizens as subjects of common rules, and legal equality – were required, in Kant's judgement (Kant 1991, p. 99). Like Rousseau he thought that only persons who disposed of their own means of production and were not dependent on the grace or favour of other individuals could be recognised fully as citizens, a proposition which, however, led him, and in the course of the French Revolution the Abbé Sieyès as well, to draw a clear distinction between active and passive citizenship of a kind that Rousseau had never drawn himself and which Jacobin populists who turned to him for inspiration deplored. Women, servants, and others who might be classed as dependants could only be granted the status of passive citizens, supposed Kant, enjoying the protection of the law but not contributing to its promulgation. Free and equal with respect to their humanity, they were not entitled to vote because not independent, although Kant allowed that passive citizens might in time or through their endeavours become truly active. Following Locke, Kant held that private property is generated by labour, by industriousness.

That prospect could never be achieved in feudal societies, which Kant deplored most of all for the privileges they granted to the nobility, rendering the dependence and therefore the lack of true freedom of others permanent.

While Kant (notwithstanding his endorsement of the American and French Revolutions) never allowed that subject peoples in feudal societies might possess a natural right to overthrow their governments, he always decried the privileges that the nobility enjoyed in such societies. The idea of rank, when associated with political entitlements, invariably excluded the notion of merit, he supposed. It presumed a prerogative based on descent. It entrusted authority to persons unfit for it, unaccountable to any electors, denying to those who were not born to it the freedom to partake of it themselves. Kant's critique of the idea of privilege bears a striking resemblance to Paine's plea for the rights of all citizens to choose their own governors in his condemnation of Burke's critique of the French Revolution.

Whereas Rousseau, at least in principle, took the totality of a nation's citizens to be sovereign, Kant instead held the state's legislative authority to be comprised of only those among its citizens who by virtue of their independence could be termed 'active'. An optimist as against Rousseau's pessimism with regard to the human race's prospects for moral improvement, but on the other hand more sceptical in his perception of human nature's failings than Rousseau, who thought mankind was by nature good, Kant shared Rousseau's judgement that economic inequalities formed a threat to moral liberty. He believed, however, that concentrations of power based on wealth might be disaggregated through the introduction of compulsory partible inheritance, the abolition of privilege, and the growth of enlightened public opinion.

6 Fichte

Fichte has sometimes been described as a Jacobin like Saint-Just or Robespierre, a claim which no doubt exaggerates the truth, although if Sieyès may be portrayed as a French revolutionary similar to Kant, Fichte does indeed appear to resemble French revolutionary democrats. His anonymous first composition, the *Kritik aller Offenbarung* (Critique of all Revelations) of 1792, was cast with a Kantian title in Kant's style and was regarded by many readers to be Kant's own work, making Fichte an overnight celebrity, and in consequence no doubt reinforcing the passion for freedom proclaimed in Kant's moral philosophy by which he had already been seized. But while he denied that there was a popular right of revolution, Fichte soon asserted its legitimacy. In *Zurückforderung der Denkfreiheit von den Fürsten Europens* (A Reclamation of Freedom of Thought from the Princes of Europe, 1793), a speech signed at 'Heliopolis in the last year of the old darkness', he proclaims,

with Kant, the 'freedom of the pen' as the 'palladium of the people's freedom', a proposition which would later figure at the heart of Ernst Cassirer's
Philosophy of the Enlightenment, whose first publication, in German, dates
from 1932. But the rhetorical passion of Fichte's work recalls Robespierre
more than Kant. 'The times of barbarism are over', he lamented.

You peoples, in which men dared to proclaim to you, in the name of God, that you were
herds of cattle . . . set upon the earth to carry the burdens of a dozen sons of gods, to
minister to their comfort as servants and maidservants, finally to be slaughtered . . . you
know . . . that God has stamped his divine seal deep in your breasts and that you should
belong to no-one but yourselves. (Fichte 1962–, II.2, p. 202)

The 'inner voice' of conscience whispers to every man that he can be no-
one's property and that he must be 'freed from an alien power'. 'He is free
and must remain free.' 'Man has a right to those conditions under which
alone he can act dutifully, and to those actions which his duty demands'
(1962–, II.2, pp. 203–5).

The state arises from a (conjectural) contract, which places the parties to it
under an obligation that extends only to their external actions and not their
inner sentiments. According to this contract, every signatory member gives
up some of his alienable rights, on condition that the others also relinquish
theirs. The contract prescribes no Rousseauian *aliénation totale*, however, but
only a Lockean limited relinquishing of certain rights. Freedom of expression
and an individual's right to judge truth and error remain inviolable. There
can be no legitimate contract which passes a right of *confessio* to a state's
ruler. An unrestricted right to investigate every possible object of thought
is acknowledged as belonging to all humanity. Anything which aspires to
less is 'mental slavery'. Anyone advising a prince to 'hinder the progress of
enlightenment among his people' must presume that kingly rule can only
be maintained in darkness (1962–, II.2, pp. 204, 210). True princes know
that no light can hurt them.

Fichte's *Beitrag zur Berichtigung der Urtheile des Publikums über die französische
Revolution* (Contribution to Rectifying the Public's Judgement of the French
Revolution) of 1793 was provoked by August Wilhelm Rehberg's *Inquiry
into the French Revolution*, which had been published earlier in the same year
and which, while endorsing political reforms, had rejected revolutionary
claims to popular sovereignty. The French Revolution, Fichte proclaimed,
had been of momentous importance for the whole of humanity. It had
shown that most existing constitutions were unjust in denying what were
actually inalienable rights to their subjects. To change this state of affairs 'the

worthiness of freedom' must be appreciated 'from below', although Fichte
still welcomed the endeavours on behalf of his people of a wise prince, for
'liberation can only occur without disorder if it comes from above' (Fichte
1962–, I.1, 203, 207, 208). He held that no legitimate assessment of the
justice of the French Revolution could be proferred by either the oppressed
or the oppressors, as intimately interested parties. Only an unprejudiced
external observer, well disposed to mankind as a whole, could be warranted
to make such a judgement.

Fichte rehearsed familiar arguments for political legitimacy in terms of
an original contract and repeated the Rousseauian principle that only the
people (albeit through their representatives such as Rousseau disallowed)
were entitled to frame laws, binding the magistrates of their government,
even if it was monarchical. He placed special emphasis on the fact that
the people's contract must be alterable, on the grounds that its original
parties could not bind their descendants. The right to formulate and adopt
a constitution belonged to each generation as sovereign, he claimed, and
likewise every citizen in each generation retained a right to withdraw from
his civil association and to transport his own property abroad. Under the
law of nature, groups of citizens must also be free to secede and form new
communities, Fichte maintained (Fichte 1962–, I.1, pp. 229, 240).

In a striking excursus to this work, Fichte argued that some groups within
a state – among them Jews, the military, or the nobility – in fact possess an
identity shaped by their own laws, such that a 'state within a state' need
not be regarded as factious. No state becomes dangerous just by virtue of
its occupying space within another state, he insisted. It constitutes a threat
only when its interests come to be opposed to the others' (Fichte 1962–, I.1,
pp. 188–9, 294). Revolutionary withdrawal from a regime deemed illegitimate and unendurable is complete when the old regime loses all its adherents
who join together to form a new pact. 'When the old association finally
has no more supporters, and all have voluntarily removed themselves to the
new one, the whole revolution has been rightfully carried out' (p. 296).

Fichte next proceeded to examine the question of privileged estates. Following Kant, he denied that the privileges of the nobility or the church could
be reconciled with practical reason. It was, he suggested, legitimate to suppress those privileges without compensation, although just for a transitional
period he recommended state stipends to allow the dispossessed sufficient
time to readjust and acquire new skills. Not only hereditary privilege but
hereditary serfdom of the peasantry as well, together with primogeniture
and preferential access to high office, should be swept away. Accession to

public offices ought henceforth to be based on ability and achievement alone. Once instituted, a system of partible inheritance would increase the number of independent farmers and also the ranks of the citizenry, whom Fichte (like Rousseau and Kant) judged capable of political participation only when having economic independence.

In his *Grundlage des Naturrechts* (Foundations of Natural Right) of 1796 he explained that the highest 'absolute inalienable property of all human beings' consisted of their being able to flourish through their own work (Fichte 2000, pp. 185–7). Whenever someone cannot survive through the proceeds of his own labour, the social contract by which he would otherwise be obliged is fully dissolved, and from that moment he is no longer legally bound to recognise the sanctity of another man's property. Anyone suffering destitution was entitled, by the law of nature, to take whatever he required to remain alive. In a free commonwealth, therefore, the right to live through one's own labour or in the performance of one's occupation must be guaranteed to all. The rational state consisted of citizens whose economic existence (which formed the foundation of their freedom) must be ensured and upheld by it. This entailed a political ramification which had been a prerogative of ancient Sparta's ephors (the term Fichte himself employed) and the Roman Republic's tribunes, recapitulated by Rousseau in book III, chapter 14, of the *Social Contract*, to the effect that *in extremis* executive power could be interdicted or suspended and the law itself might be judged unlawful, there being a need in a rightful state for 'an *absolutely negative* power to be posited alongside the *absolutely positive* one' (Fichte 2000, p. 151).

In *Der geschlossene Handelstaat* (The Closed Commercial State) of 1800, Fichte developed such thoughts further. The state had to ensure that every one of its labouring or professional citizens received an appropriate share of leisure as compensation for his efforts. Work and leisure were to be fairly distributed. This proposal has been portrayed as Fichte's sketch of 'socialism', but it would be better described as a planned economy of an egalitarian utopia.

The conception of the state that Fichte was to elaborate in his *Reden an die deutsche Nation* (Addresses to the German Nation) of 1807–8 constitutes a variation of Rousseau's republic transported to another culture, taking up themes already developed in *Die Grundzüge des gegenwärtigen Zeitalters* (The Characteristics of the Present Age) of 1806. Fichte's claim in that earlier work to the effect that 'in this constitution each person's individuality is entirely and absolutely swallowed up in the genius of all and each receives in return his share of the contribution to the state's general strength augmented by the strength of all others' is a paraphrase of a passage in book 1, chapter 6 of the *Social Contract* (Fichte 1962–, 1.8, p. 309). As with Rousseau, Fichte here identifies a complete 'alienation' and 'restitution', though he goes on to claim that the 'absolute state' so constituted would contribute to a 'perfection of all the relations of the human species', in which 'love of the good' would produce a pure coincidence of human will with perfect law. In the glow of such perfection basks an idea of community founded upon love and reason rather than power (p. 328). In the *Reden an die deutsche Nation* he proceeds to speak of the 'mission of the Germans' to point this way equally to other nations, which if they accept these progressive principles are 'of our race, and belong to us, but which if they do not, show themselves to be alien' (Fichte 1978, pp. 228–31).

7 Humboldt

While Fichte came from a poor petty bourgeois family and insisted on every citizen's acquiring his own property, Wilhelm von Humboldt, born in Potsdam in 1767 and scion of a recently ennobled family, wholly excluded the question of property ownership from his conception of a free state. Later a reforming minister in Prussia who would become the chief author of its educational system and the founder of the University of Berlin, in the early 1790s he reflected, like Fichte, on the significance of the French Revolution, which he saw at first hand in Paris. His first thoughts, dedicated to Friedrich von Genz and published in the *Berlinischer Monatsschrift* in 1791, appeared in *Thoughts on Constitutions, Occasioned by the French Constitution* and contained passages that were to be taken up again in his *Ideen zu einem Versuch die Grenzen der Wirksamkeit des Staates zu bestimmen* (Some Ideas concerning the Attempt to Define the Limits of State Action) drafted shortly afterwards but unpublished until 1851. To the question of whether an entirely new state can be constructed 'on the principles of reason alone as is now being attempted in France', Humboldt replied firmly in the negative, claiming that chance was stronger than reason. In many respects sympathetic to the ambitions of the French revolutionaries, he shared none of their confidence in an ideal of popular sovereignty, which he saw not as promoting citizens' freedom but as risking the substitution of one form of despotism for another.

Humboldt was in many respects himself a profound admirer of Rousseau, no less than Kant and Fichte had been, but it was to *Emile* and not the *Social Contract* that he turned for inspiration, rejecting most of Rousseau's contractarian language of rights and his images of the general will in favour of his portrait of an education according to nature that promoted the self-development of individuals rather than their collective discipline under a state's rules allegedly of their own making. Humboldt's chief debt to Rousseau, like Herder's, turned around his notions of organic growth, maturation, and spontaneity, which came to inform a German conception of the formation of character as *Bildung*. Instead of a Rousseauist state designed to promote public fraternity and social solidarity, he advocated the idea of voluntary associations which encouraged self-help and diversity. The state, in his philosophy, threatened its citizens' liberties even when through positive solicitude it sought to protect them. Humboldt's liberalism prescribed that modern republics should not emulate the republics of antiquity so much as keep all state authority at bay. His was a form of romantic liberalism that in the nineteenth century came to underpin the ideals of John Stuart Mill's *On Liberty* and Herbert Spencer's *The Man versus the State*. As much as any other political thinker of the eighteenth century, he was to identify true freedom not in the form of governance of the state but in its depoliticised interstices. In subscribing to one dimension of Rousseau's philosophy Humboldt made it appear the enemy of another which had failed in the course of the French Revolution.

VI
The Enlightenment and revolution

21

The American Revolution

GORDON S. WOOD

The American Revolution transformed thinking about politics. Its significance goes beyond the creation of the United States of America. 'The
independence of America, considered merely as a separation from England,
would have been a matter of little importance', wrote Thomas Paine in
1791, 'had it not been accompanied by a revolution in the principles and
practice of government' (Paine 1989, p. 152). The era of the Revolution was
undoubtedly momentously creative in its political thought, but the contributions were collective, not individual; they were the products not of closet
philosophising but of contentious political debate. The Revolution spawned
no great theorists of the stature of Hobbes, Locke, or Montesquieu; no
Rousseau, not even a Burlamaqui or a Pufendorf. The revolutionary leaders were widely read and thoughtful men, but they were not philosophers,
and they did not work out their theories in the quiet of a study (though
some like James Madison tried to do so). They were experienced, pragmatic political leaders who competed for power, lost and won elections,
served in colonial and state legislatures and in the national congress, became
governors, judges, even presidents. Yet they were also intensely interested in
ideas and concerned with making theoretical sense of what they were doing.
Because they were so intimately involved in politics, much of their thinking
was polemical and of the moment. They usually had to extemporise in the
heat and urgency of debate. Most of their many political writings took the
form of pamphlets and newspaper essays, and only occasionally large treatises, such as John Adams's sprawling *Defence of the Constitutions of Government
of the United States* (1787–8). In these circumstances the degree of originality
and coherence which their political thought achieved is remarkable.

1   The English constitution

To appreciate properly the originality and creativity of the American revolutionaries' contribution to political theory between the end of the Seven

Years War in 1763 and the making of the constitution in 1787 we have to understand the character of their thinking about government at the outset, before the revolutionary crisis began. The American colonists in the early 1760s thought of themselves not as Americans but as Britons. They were provincials living on the edges of a great pan-British world, and were all the more British for that. They were proud of being part of the British empire and of living under a free government, and they shared fully the enlightened eighteenth-century's enthusiasm for the English constitution – 'this beautiful system' as Montesquieu called it (*SL*, xi.6).

The English constitution was the source of England's liberty, and Englishmen of every social rank and on both sides of the Atlantic revelled in their worldwide reputation for liberty. Unlike the poor enslaved French, the English people, they told themselves, had no standing army, no *lettres de cachet*; they had their rights of habeas corpus and trial by jury, their freedom of speech and conscience and to trade and travel; they were free from arbitrary arrest and punishment; their homes were their castles; their property could not be taken from them without their consent. These English liberties were individual and private; they were the rights of persons to pursue their ends free from governmental obstruction, essentially 'negative' liberties, as we call them today.

Against these ancient rights and liberties were set the prerogative powers of the crown, those vague and discretionary but equally ancient rights the king possessed in order to carry out his responsibility for governing the realm. Indeed, the whole of English history was seen as a perennial struggle between these two conflicting rights – between a centralising monarchy trying to fulfil its obligation to govern on the one hand and local-minded nobles and people trying to protect their liberties on the other. Each of the great events of England's past, from Magna Carta to the Glorious Revolution, marked a moment defining the proper relationship between these two sets of conflicting rights – between power and liberty. The crown, in other words, with its ancient inherited legal rights and prerogatives was an independent constitutional being with which the people had to bargain and contract in order to protect their own rights and liberties. Indeed, by the eighteenth century the relationship was often compared to a mercantile contract or agreement between two mistrustful agents in which allegiance and protection were the considerations. To bargain collectively with the crown the people relied on the institutions of the House of Commons or their various colonial legislatures.

These representative bodies were the means by which the people participated in government and protected their liberties from royal encroachment.
For most Englishmen the House of Commons or the separate colonial
assemblies were identical to what was commonly referred to as the people's
public or political liberty. As yet there was no perceived incompatibility or
conflict between this public liberty and the people's personal liberties. Participation by the people in government, ancient civic virtue, or what we
today call 'positive' liberty, was considered to be essential for the protection
of the people's private liberty. Hence liberty was often used synonymously
with self-government by the civic community.

Liberty was thus important to Englishmen, so much so that it gave their
constitution a reputation for being more republican than monarchic. Indeed,
the relative egalitarianism and mobility of English society, in apparent contrast to that of France, made many Englishmen feel themselves republican in
spirit. In a world seemingly full of absolute monarchies Englishmen stressed
the limited and liberty-loving nature of their own monarchy. But liberty,
participation by the people in government, could never be enough for a
proper constitution. The constitution also had to be mixed or balanced.
Indeed, the beauty of the English constitution in many eyes was that it had
achieved the ideal kind of balance or mixture. Not only did the English constitution fully embody the social interests or estates of the realm – the king,
the nobility, and the people – in the crown, House of Lords, and House
of Commons, but also the three parts of this balanced government corresponded marvellously with the classical categories of monarchy, aristocracy,
and democracy.

When the Americans eventually revolted from this English constitution,
justifying it in their Declaration of Independence of 4 July 1776 by the
crown's breaking of the implicit contract with the colonists, most of them
had no intention of repudiating the classical ideal and assumptions behind
the constitution. Nor did they believe that this ideal of balanced or mixed
government was incompatible with republicanism. A mixed elective republic
was as possible as a mixed hereditary monarchy, since independence from
Britain and the elimination of a king did not alter the basic postulates of the
science of politics. After all, wrote John Adams, who had much to do with
designing the new revolutionary state constitutions of 1776, 'the republics
of Greece, Rome, Carthage were all mixed governments' (Adams 1961, II,
p. 58). The American constitution-makers thus thought they could have
monarch-like single governors and aristocratic-like senates of wise men,

even within an elective system. How the governors or senators were chosen, even when elected directly by the people, did not thereby determine their essential nature. Only the several houses of representatives in the Americans' new state constitutions were initially designed to represent the people and incorporate the principles of democracy in their classical republican mixed governments.

The Americans' quarrel with the English constitution was not with its theory but its current practice. They believed that the ideal English constitution had degenerated and become corrupted. Hence the Americans could quite intelligibly claim as late as 1776 that they were revolting not against the English constitution but on behalf of it and were in fact simply preserving what Englishmen had historically valued.

Yet the English constitution that the colonists perceived was not the same constitution that Englishmen at home experienced. Many of the constitutional principles that the colonists invoked were not the 'true principles' held by establishment England in the mid-eighteenth century but, as Tories and royal officials tried to indicate, 'Revolution principles' outside the mainstream of English thought. Since the colonists were reading much the same literature, law books, and history as other Englishmen, they were scarcely aware that they were seeing the English heritage differently. Amid their breadth of reading and references, however, the colonists concentrated on particular strains of thought that ultimately gave them a radically critical perspective on English life (Bailyn 1967, pp. 22–54).

The English literature of the first half of the eighteenth century, both *belles lettres* and political polemics, which the colonists read and imitated, and by which they evaluated English life, was above all a literature of social and political criticism. Most of the English writers of the Augustan age – whether notables or coffee-house hacks, whether Tory satirists like Alexander Pope or Jonathan Swift, or radical Whigs like John Trenchard and Thomas Gordon – wrote out of deep and bitter hostility to the great social, economic, and political changes taking place in the wake of the Glorious Revolution. The rise of banks, stock markets, and powerful trading companies, the growing commercialisation of agriculture, the emergence of new moneyed men, and the increasing public debt all threatened traditional values and made many English intellectuals pessimistic about the fate of England (Kramnick 1968).

At the heart of this criticism lay an intense fear that excessive monarchical power was threatening English liberty. Both ends of the political spectrum – radical Whig, with its libertarian heritage from the seventeenth century, and extreme Tory, with its nostalgic image of an older rural England of independent gentry – came together in shrill opposition to the changes Sir Robert Walpole and his ministries were making in government under the Hanoverian monarchs, particularly in the use of money and influence to manipulate or 'corrupt' the electorate and parliament. Radical critics of Walpole made ringing proposals to control and reduce what seemed to be the enormously inflated powers of the crown in order to recover the original principles of the English constitution. Stock proposals included prohibiting government salaried puppets ('placemen') from sitting in the House of Commons, reducing the public debt, obtaining more equal representation, constituency instructions to members of parliament, and more regular elections. All were designed to restore the proper balance in the constitution.

The king, it seemed, was using his power to appoint men to crown offices in order to bribe and influence members of the Lords and Commons. The monarchical or executive part of the constitution was, in other words, unsettling the balance among the three supposedly independent ruling forces of crown, peers, and people, absorbing all power to itself. This Hanoverian tyranny seemed subtler than the monarchical aggrandisement of the Stuart kings, for it did not rely on the independent prerogative powers of the king, but instead had infiltrated and corrupted parliament and insidiously turned that ancient bulwark of the people's liberty into an instrument of tyranny.

The colonists tended to take this critical opposition literature more seriously than Englishmen themselves. Precisely because it made such good sense of both the many ways in which American life had deviated from that of the mother country and of the colonists' habitual antagonism to their royal governors, Americans from the early decades of the eighteenth century had published, republished, read, cited, and plagiarised much of that literature. By the middle of the eighteenth century this opposition or 'Country' ideology, with its intense mistrust of monarchical power and suspicion of growing English corruption, had become central to American thinking about politics. When in 1776 Americans declared their independence from the British crown, they were determined to apply what they had learned to their own revolutionary state constitutions and to prevent any semblance of this monarchical tyranny from reappearing in their new mixed republics.

Most of the new state constitutions created in 1776–7 were meant, therefore, to be republican copies of what the English constitution should have been. Although elected, the governors, senates, and houses of representatives of the several states were supposed to resemble the king, Lords, and Commons of the English constitution. But in order to prevent their balanced governments from degenerating in the way the English constitution had, Americans in 1776 meant to apply what they had learned from political science and to institute reforms in their new state constitutions that British radicals had been talking about for decades – broadening the suffrage, increasing the size of the legislatures, equalising the representation, establishing annual elections for most officers of government including the governors, and more.

The American revolutionaries, in their ambitious desire to root out tyranny, went far beyond what Englishmen in 1688–9 had attempted; they were not content merely to erect higher barriers against prerogative power or to formulate new and more explicit charters of the people's liberties. They sought to abolish all prerogative powers outright. They consequently took away from their governors or chief magistrates and gave to the legislatures most of the powers that the monarch had historically exercised; not only those to declare war and make peace, to assent to legislation, and to control the meeting of the legislatures, but also the power to pardon criminals. In most of the American states the governors remained, but not as independent magistrates with an independent right to rule but simply as executives, as they were now increasingly and appropriately called.

In order to root out the most insidious and dangerous source of eighteenth-century monarchical tyranny and corruption, the constitution-makers abolished or severely limited the power of the governors to appoint men to magisterial office. And, crucially, in all the states they forbade members in both houses of the legislature and the judiciary from simultaneously holding office in the executive branch. By excluding legislators from executive or administrative office, the constitution-makers sharply separated America's constitutional tradition from that of the mother country and prohibited the development in America of a cabinet form of government.

In justifying this exclusion of the legislators from participation in the executive, some of the revolutionaries invoked a doctrine, made famous by Montesquieu, of separating the executive, legislative, and judicial powers from each other. This triad of functional powers was not the same as the classical mixture of ruling elements – governors, senates, and houses of representatives – but the goal of the two triads, the prevention of corruption, was the same. Since the separation of the functional powers of government was subsequently used to justify the independence and proper balance of the ruling parts of the government, there was a likelihood that separating the executive, legislative, and judicial powers of government and balancing

606

the governors, senates, and houses of representatives would blend in people's minds, which is eventually what happened. Such a blurring of what had once been distinct ideas was made possible by what Americans did to the conception of representation. Indeed, it was ultimately their transformation of the traditional meaning of representation, of the way the people participated in government, that enabled Americans to make their most important and radical contributions to political theory.

2   Virtual and actual representation

The imperial debates of the 1760s and 1770s exposed for the first time just how different Americans' conceptions of representation were from those of Britain. With the passage of the Stamp Act in 1765, parliament's first unmistakable tax levy on the colonists, the Americans immediately raised their resistance to the highest plane of principle. 'It is inseparably essential to the freedom of a people, and the undoubted rights of Englishmen', the Stamp Act Congress declared in 1765, 'that no taxes should be imposed on them, but with their own consent, given personally, or by their representatives.' And since 'the people of these colonies are not, and from their local circumstances, cannot be represented in the House of Commons of Great Britain', the colonists could be represented and taxed only by persons who were known and chosen by themselves and who served in their respective colonial legislatures. That statement defined the American position at the outset, and despite subsequent confusion and stumbling in the debate with Britain the colonists never abandoned this essential point.

Once the British ministry sensed a stirring of colonial opposition to the Stamp Act, a number of government pamphleteers set out to explain and justify parliament's taxation of the colonies. These writers all agreed that Americans, like Englishmen everywhere in the realm, were subject to acts of parliament through the principle called 'virtual' representation. It was true, they said, that the colonists, like 'nine-tenths of the people of Britain', did not in fact vote for any representatives to the House of Commons; nevertheless, they were undoubtedly 'a part, and an important part of the Commons of Great Britain: they are represented in parliament in the same manner as the inhabitants of Britain are who have not voices in elections' (Whately 1765, p. 112).

The British electorate made up only a small proportion of the nation; probably only one in six British adult males held the parliamentary franchise. In addition Britain's electoral districts were of many sizes and used different qualifications for the franchise. Some constituencies had thousands of voters, while other 'rotten' boroughs had only a handful, and were often in the pocket of a single landowner. Some of England's largest but recently grown cities, such as Manchester and Birmingham, had no representatives of their own. Yet many Englishmen, sharing the judgement of Edmund Burke in his speech to his Bristol constituents in 1774, justified this hodgepodge system by claiming that each member of parliament represented the whole British nation, and not just the particular locality he came from. According to this conception, virtual representation was proper and effective not because of election, which was incidental to the process of representation, but because of the mutual interests that members of parliament were presumed to share with all Englishmen for whom they spoke – including those like the colonists who did not actually vote for them.

The Americans emphatically rejected claims that they were 'virtually' represented in parliament in the same way that the non-voters of cities like Manchester and Birmingham were, and set out a contrasting conception of 'actual' representation. If the people were to be properly represented in a legislature, many colonists claimed, they not only had to vote directly for the members of the legislature but had to be represented by members whose numbers were proportionate to the size of the population they spoke for. What purpose was served, asked James Otis of Massachusetts in 1764, by the continual attempts of Englishmen to justify the lack of American representation in parliament with reference to the examples of Manchester and Birmingham, which returned no members to the House of Commons? 'If those now so considerable places are not represented, they ought to be' (Otis 1765, p. 6).

The colonists' faith in actual representation grew out of their peculiar historical development. In the New World electoral districts were not the products of centuries, but were instead recent and regular creations that were related to changes in population and the formation of new towns and counties. The American belief in actual representation made election and voting not incidental but central to representation. Many believed that the interests of the people in a political community were so local, so individual, and so personal that, as one American put it in 1765, 'the only ground and reason why any man should be bound by the actions of another who meddles with his concerns is, that he himself choose that other to office' (*Boston Evening Post*, 24 June 1765).

This desire for the most explicit form of consent was in fact based on mistrust. It was the constituents' suspicion of what their elected agents might do once they were away in a distant legislature that led them to want the closest possible connection between themselves and their representatives. The representatives thus ought to be residents of the localities they spoke for; the people of the localities ought to have the right to instruct their representatives, even to bind them with instructions; and the localities ought to be represented in the legislature in proportion to their population. In short, in the greatly enlarged popular assemblies of the revolutionary state constitutions of 1776–7, the American belief in actual representation led to the fullest and most equal participation of the people in the process of government that modern history had yet seen.

In the years following the Declaration of Independence the mistrustful character of actual representation, with its resort to binding instructions by constituents in place of traditional petitions, ate away at the independent authority of the representatives and indeed threatened to undermine the very conception of representation. The people were repeatedly 'cautioned against acquiescing in the sentiment of placing implicit confidence in the representatives' (Austin 1786, pp. 44–5). They were told that they were the real legislators in the society and that they could take back at any time the power they had given to their representatives. The radical Pennsylvania constitution of 1776 actually recognised this right of the people 'out-of-doors' to legislate. It provided for all bills passed by the unicameral assembly to be printed for consideration by the people-at-large before they could become law at the next legislative session – in effect turning the elective assembly into a kind of aristocratic upper house restrained only by the 'grand legislative council, the people who had a right to approve or disapprove every bill'. 'In a word', noted one perceptive critic, 'the new system of government for Pennsylvania destroys all ideas of representation' (*Pennsylvania Packet*, 5 Oct. 1776).

Pennsylvania's radicalism was only a logical extension of what occurred elsewhere in America. In all the states individuals and groups were participating in all sorts of extra-legal associations, forming numerous committees and conventions, and appealing continually to various alternative bodies and even to the nebulous will of the people in a state of nature. Such activity rendered suspect all institutions set above the people and made it increasingly difficult for anyone to think of any part of the American state governments, even the so-called houses of representatives, as fully representative of the people. Evidently in America the people could never be completely embodied in any part of their governments (as, for example, the people of Britain were said to be in the House of Commons). Instead they stood outside all the institutions of government, which they regarded as their limited and temporary agents.

Taking the people out of the government in this way tended to blur the once important distinction among representatives, senators, and governors or magistrates. All became the equally mistrusted agents of the people. Actual representation with its assumption that voting was the criterion of representation only enhanced this development. Suddenly, it was possible to think of all elected officials, including governors and senators, simply by the fact of their election, as just as equally 'representative' of the people as the lower houses of the legislatures were. Consequently, the several houses of representatives, which in the revolutionary state constitutions of 1776–7 had been created in order to embody the people or the democratic element of mixed government, lost their representational exclusiveness. What this would mean for the Americans' attempt in 1776 to incorporate and balance the ancient categories of government – monarchy, aristocracy, and democracy – within a republican or elective political system was not immediately apparent.

3 Constitutionalism

Although the Americans' developing ideas about representation were fundamental to their eventual fashioning of a new understanding of politics, it was their constitution-making of 1776–80 that captured attention across the Atlantic. Their revolutionary state constitutions were published, republished, and endlessly debated in several European languages. The enlightened everywhere recognised that something new in politics was being created.

First of all, the American revolutionaries virtually established the modern idea of a written constitution. There had, of course, been written constitutions before in Western history, but the Americans did something new and different. They made written constitutions a practical and everyday part of governmental life. They showed the world how written constitutions could be made truly fundamental and distinguishable from ordinary legislation and how such constitutions could be interpreted on a regular basis and altered when necessary. Furthermore, they offered concrete and useable governmental institutions for carrying out these constitutional tasks.

Before the era of the American Revolution a constitution was rarely distinguished from the government and its operations. In traditional English thought a constitution referred not only to fundamental rights but also to the way the government was put together or constituted. 'By constitution', wrote Viscount Bolingbroke in 1733, 'we mean, whenever we speak with propriety and exactness, that assemblage of laws, institutions and customs, derived from certain fixed principles of reason, directed to certain fixed objects of public good, that compose the general system, according to which the community hath agreed to be governed' (Bolingbroke 1997b, p. 88). The English constitution, in other words, included both fundamental principles and rights and the existing arrangement of governmental laws, customs, and institutions.

By the end of the revolutionary era, however, the Americans' idea of a constitution had become very different from that of the English. A constitution was now seen to be no part of the government at all. A constitution was a written document distinct from and superior to all the operations of government. It was, as Thomas Paine said in 1791, 'a thing antecedent to a government, and a government is only the creature of a constitution'. And, said Paine, it was 'not a thing in name only; but in fact'. For Americans a constitution was like a Bible, possessed by every family and every member of government. 'It is the body of elements, to which you can refer, and quote article by article; and [which] contains . . . everything that relates to the complete organization of a civil government, and the principle on which it shall act, and by which it shall be bound' (Paine 1989, p. 81). A constitution thus could never be an act of a legislature or of a government; it had to be the act of the people themselves, declared James Wilson, one of the principal framers of the federal constitution, in 1790, and 'in their hands it is as clay in the hands of a potter: they have the right to mould, to preserve, to improve, to refine, and to finish it as they please' (Wilson 1967, I, p. 304). If the English thought this new idea of a constitution resembled, as Arthur Young caustically suggested in 1792, 'a pudding made by a recipe', the Americans had become convinced that the English no longer had a constitution at all (qu. McIlwain 1947, pp. 1–2). It was a momentous transformation of meaning in a short time, precipitated, like so much else, by the controversy with Britain.

Like all Englishmen, the eighteenth-century colonists had thought of power as inhering in the crown and its prerogatives. Time and again they had been forced to defend their liberties against the intrusions of royal authority. They relied for their defence on their colonial assemblies – the democratic element of their mixed governments – and invoked their rights as Englishmen and what they called their ancient charters as barriers against crown power. In the seventeenth century many of the colonies had been established by crown charters, corporate or proprietary grants made by the king to groups like the Massachusetts Puritans or to individuals like William Penn and Lord Baltimore to found colonies in the New World. In subsequent years these written charters gradually lost their original purpose in the eyes of the colonists and took on a new importance, both as prescriptions for government and as devices guaranteeing the rights of the people against their royal governors. In fact, the whole of the colonial past was littered with such charters and other written documents of various sorts to which the colonial assemblies had repeatedly appealed in their quarrels with royal power.

In appealing to written documents as confirmations of their liberties the colonists acted no differently from other Englishmen. From almost the beginning of their history, Englishmen had continually invoked written documents and charters in defence of their rights against the crown's power. 'Anxious to preserve and transmit' their liberties 'unimpaired to posterity', the English people, observed one colonist in 1775, had repeatedly 'caused them to be reduced to writing, and in the most solemn manner to be recognized, ratified and confirmed', first by King John with Magna Carta, then by Henry III and Edward I, and 'afterwards by a multitude of corroborating acts, reckoned in all, by Lord Coke, to be thirty-two from Edw. Ist to Hen. 4th and since, in a great variety of instances, by the bills of rights and acts of settlement' (Mather 1775, pp. 8–9). All of these documents, from Magna Carta to the Bill of Rights of 1689, were merely written evidence of those 'fixed principles of reason' from which Bolingbroke had said the English constitution was derived.

Although eighteenth-century Englishmen talked about the fixed principles and the fundamental law of the constitution, few of them doubted that parliament, as the representative of the nobles and people and as the sovereign law-making body of the nation, was the supreme guarantor and interpreter of those fixed principles and the fundamental law. Parliament was in fact the defender of the people's liberties against the crown's encroachments; it alone protected and confirmed the people's rights. The Petition of Right, the Act of Habeas Corpus, and the Bill of Rights were all acts of parliament, mere statutes not different in form from other laws passed by parliament.

For Englishmen, therefore, as Sir William Blackstone, the great eighteenth-century jurist, explained, there could be no distinction between the 'constitution or frame of government' and 'the system of laws' (Blackstone 1765–9, I, p. 126). All were of a piece: every act of parliament was part of the English constitution and all law, customary or statute, was thus constitutional. 'Therefore', concluded William Paley, 'the terms *constitutional* and *unconstitutional*, mean *legal* and *illegal*' (qu. Wilson 1967, 1, p. 310).

Nothing could be more strikingly different from what Americans came to believe. Indeed, it was precisely on this distinction between 'legal' and 'constitutional' that the American and British constitutional traditions most obviously diverged at the Revolution. During the 1760s and 1770s the colonists came to realise that although acts of parliament like the Stamp Act might be legal, that is, in accord with the acceptable way of making law, such acts could not thereby be automatically considered constitutional, that is, in accord with the basic rights and principles of justice that made the English constitution the palladium of liberty. It was true that the English Bill of Rights and Act of Settlement were only parliamentary statutes, but surely, the colonists insisted, they were of 'a nature more sacred than those which established a turnpike road' (*The Crisis* 1775, no. 11, pp. 81–7). Under the pressure of events Americans came to believe that the fundamental principles of the English constitution had to be lifted out of the law-making and other processes and institutions of government and set above them. 'In all free states', said the revolutionary leader Samuel Adams in 1768, 'the constitution is fixed; and as the supreme legislature derives its powers and authority from the constitution, it cannot overleap the bounds of it without destroying its own foundation' (Adams 1904–8, 1, p. 185). Thus in 1776, when Americans came to frame their own constitutions, they sought to make them fundamental and to write them out explicitly in documents.

It was one thing, however, to define the constitution as fundamental law, different from ordinary legislation and circumscribing the institutions of government; it was another to make such a distinction effective. In the years following the Declaration of Independence many Americans paid lip-service to the fundamental character of their state constitutions, but like eighteenth-century Britons they continued to believe that their legislatures were the best instruments for interpreting and changing these constitutions. The state legislatures represented the people, and the people, it seemed, could scarcely tyrannise themselves. Thus in the late 1770s and the early 1780s several state legislatures, acting on behalf of the people, set aside parts of their constitutions by statute and interpreted and altered them, as one American observed, 'upon any occasion to serve a purpose' (Warren and Adams 1917–25, II, p. 219). Time and again the legislatures interfered with the governors' legitimate powers, rejected judicial decisions, disregarded individual liberties and property rights, and in general, as one victim complained, violated 'those fundamental principles which first induced men to come into civil compact'.

By the mid-1780s many American leaders had come to believe that the democratic element of their mixed republics, the state assemblies – and not the monarchical element, the governors, as they had thought in 1776 – were the political authority to be most feared. Legislators were supposedly the representatives of the people who annually elected them; but '173 despots would surely be as oppressive as one', wrote Thomas Jefferson. 'An *elective despotism* was not the government we fought for' (Jefferson 1999, p. 326). It increasingly seemed to many that the idea of a constitution as fundamental law had no practical meaning at all. 'If it were possible it would be well to define the extent of the legislative power, but', concluded a discouraged James Madison in 1785, 'the nature of it seems in many respects to be indefinite' (Madison 1962–91, VIII, p. 351).

Nobody wrestled more persistently with this problem of distinguishing between statutory and fundamental law than Jefferson. In 1779 Jefferson knew from experience that assemblies 'elected by the people for the ordinary purposes of legislation only, have no power to restrain the acts of succeeding assemblies'. Thus he realised that to declare his great Act for Establishing Religious Freedom in Virginia to be 'irrevocable would be of no effect in law'. He wrote into the bill in frustration that the legislators 'do declare, that the rights hereby asserted are of the natural rights of mankind, and that if any act shall be hereafter passed to repeal the present or to narrow its operations, such act will be an infringement of natural right' (Jefferson 1999, pp. 391–2). But such a paper declaration was obviously not enough. By the mid-1780s both he and Madison were eager 'to form a real constitution' for Virginia; the existing one enacted in 1776 was merely an 'ordinance' with no higher authority than the other ordinances of the same session. They wanted a constitution that would be 'perpetual' and 'unalterable by other legislatures'. But how? If the constitution were to be truly fundamental and immune from legislative tampering, somehow or other it would have to be created, as Jefferson put it, 'by a power superior to that of the legislature' (Jefferson 1999, p. 339).

By the time Jefferson came to write his *Notes on the State of Virginia* in the early 1780s the answer had become clear. 'To render a form of government unalterable by ordinary acts of assembly', said Jefferson, 'the people must delegate persons with special powers. They have accordingly chosen special conventions to form and fix their governments' (Jefferson 1999, p. 331). In 1775–6 conventions or congresses had been legally deficient legislatures made necessary by the refusal of the royal governors to call together the regular and legal representatives of the people. Now, however, because of what had happened since 1776 to the Americans' understanding of representation, these conventions were seen to be special alternative representations of the people temporarily given the exclusive authority to frame or amend constitutions. When Massachusetts and New Hampshire wrote new constitutions in the early 1780s, the proper pattern of constitution-making and constitution-altering was set: constitutions were formed or changed by specially elected conventions and then placed before the people for ratification. Thus in 1787 those who wished to change the federal government knew precisely what to do: they called a convention in Philadelphia and sent the resultant document to the states for approval. Even the French in their own revolution several years later followed the American pattern. Conventions and the process of ratification made the people the actual constituent power. And this was made possible because Americans had come to believe that the people could never be fully embodied or represented in any institution of government; they simply delegated parts of their power to a variety of governmental institutions, no one of which any longer spoke with complete popular authority.

But the new ideas about constitutions and conventions were only part of the Americans' constitutional achievement. With the conception of a constitution as fundamental law immune from legislative authority more firmly in hand, some state judges in the 1780s began cautiously moving in isolated cases to impose restraints on what the assemblies were enacting as law. In effect they said to the legislatures, as George Wythe, judge of the Virginia Supreme Court did in 1782, 'Here is the limit of your authority; and hither shall you go, but no further' (Call 1833, IV, pp. 8, 17–18). These were the hesitant beginnings of what would come to be called judicial review – that remarkable American practice by which judges in the ordinary courts of law have the authority to determine the constitutionality of acts of the state and federal legislatures.

The development of judicial review came slowly. It was not easy, even for those who were convinced of the injustice and unconstitutionality of many acts of the state legislatures, to believe that unelected judges could set aside acts of the popularly elected assemblies; this clearly seemed to be an undemocratic judicial usurpation of power that rightly belonged to the people. But as early as 1787 James Iredell of North Carolina, soon to be appointed a justice of the newly created Supreme Court, saw that the new meanings Americans had given to a constitution and to representation had clarified the responsibility of judges to determine the law. A constitution in America, said Iredell, was not only 'a fundamental law' but also a special popularly created 'law in writing . . . limiting the powers of the legislature, and with which every exercise of those powers must necessarily be compared'. Judges were not arbiters of the constitution or usurpers of legislative power. They were, said Iredell, merely judicial officials, simply another kind of agent of the people, fulfilling their duty of applying the proper law. When faced with a decision between 'the fundamental unrepealable law' made specially by the people in their conventions and an ordinary statute enacted by a legislature contrary to the constitution, they must simply determine which law was superior. Judges could not avoid exercising this authority, concluded Iredell, for in America a constitution was not 'a mere imaginary thing, about which ten thousand different opinions may be formed, but a written document to which all may have recourse, and to which, therefore, the judges cannot wilfully blind themselves' (Iredell 1857–8, II, pp. 172–6). Although Iredell may have been wrong in believing that a written document would generate fewer different opinions than an unwritten constitution, he was certainly right about the direction judicial authority in America would take. Through the subsequent development of judicial review judges in America came to exercise a power over governmental life unparalleled by any other judiciary in the world.

4   The extended republic

All these new and radical ideas about representation and constitutionalism developed rapidly in the decade following independence, but neither deliberately nor evenly; for they were not the products of systematic philosophy but polemical responses to fast changing reality. Rarely before 1787 were these fragments of principle comprehended as a whole. It took the pressure of creating and justifying the new federal constitution to bring them together into a new conception of politics.

On one level the new federal constitution of 1787 was a response to the widely acknowledged weakness of the Articles of Confederation, the original league or union of the states, composed in 1777 and ratified in 1781. On another, more fundamental level, however, the creation of the new national constitution was the climax of general efforts to reform the state constitutions created in 1776 and to curb the extraordinary powers that had been given to the state legislatures, particularly the lower houses, which were presumed to be the spokesmen for the people. Since the state legislatures, which were the most democratic and representative in the world, were the true testing ground of the Americans' revolutionary experiment in popular republican government, their unexpected abuses of power in the years since 1776 were no simple practical matter: they struck at the heart of what the Revolution was about. For abuses by popularly elected legislatures, said Madison, brought 'into question the fundamental principle of republican government, [that] the majority who rule in such governments are the safest guardians both of public and private rights' (Jefferson 1950–, xiv, p. 19). In other words, the public liberty of the people, their participation in government, suddenly seemed incompatible with their personal liberty or rights.

Only such an arresting recognition could have led Americans to create the remarkably powerful national government embodied in the constitution of 1787. This government was no longer a league of independent states, as the Articles of Confederation had envisaged, but a continental-wide republic in its own right with a single executive, a bicameral legislature, an independent judiciary, and the authority to operate directly on individuals. A decade earlier no American patriot had even dreamed of such strong central government. The colonists had too much despairing experience with the far-removed governmental power of the British empire to think about erecting a powerful distant government for themselves. If they had learned anything under the empire it was that the closer government was to the people, the safer and less tyrannical it was likely to be. Besides, the best minds, including Montesquieu, had repeatedly told them that republics had to be small in territory and homogeneous in character. Monarchies were long-lasting and designed for large states; they could maintain order from the top down over large, diverse, and even corrupt populations through their use of fear, patronage, hereditary privilege, unitary authority, standing armies, and religious establishments. But republics, such as the American states, were fragile and often short-lived polities; they had to be held together from below, through civic virtue, from the consent and sacrifice of the people themselves. The only surviving republics – the Netherlands and the Italian and Swiss city-states – were small and compact. Large heterogeneous states that had tried to establish republics – as England had in the seventeenth century – were bound to lead to chaos resulting in some sort of military dictatorship, like that of Oliver Cromwell. Too great a geographical extent, and too many diverse interests, and a republic would fly apart.

Explaining and justifying the new powerful national republic of 1787, the like of which had not been conceived of ten years earlier, would therefore not be easy. In defending and making sense of the new government, the Federalists, as the supporters of the constitution were called, were compelled to formulate a new and original understanding of American politics. The opponents of the constitution, the Anti-federalists, immediately grasped the unprecedented nature of this new enlarged republic and invoked Montesquieu's dictum to bolster their opposition. It was impossible, they argued, for a republican government to comprehend both Georgia and Massachusetts. The very idea of a single republic 'on an average one thousand miles in length, eight hundred in breadth, and containing six million of white inhabitants all reduced to the same standard of morals, or habits, and of laws, is in itself an absurdity, and contrary to the whole experience of mankind' (Ford 1888, pp. 64–5).

These were outmoded assumptions, said Madison, who quickly emerged as not only the principal drafter of the constitution but also its most theoretically minded defender. Americans in 1776, he said, in a series of letters, speeches, and working papers, culminating with his essays in *The Federalist*, had thought that the people composing a republic 'enjoy not only an equality of political rights, but that they have all precisely the same interests and the same feelings in every respect', which was why they assumed republics had to be small in size (Jefferson 1950–, XII, p. 277). They had thought that in such small republics 'the interest of the majority would be that of the minority also; the decisions could only turn on mere opinion concerning the good of the whole of which the major voice would be the safest criterion; and within a small sphere this voice could be most easily collected and the public affairs most accurately managed'. Now, however, to Madison and other Federalists, with a decade's experience behind them, these assumptions about republicanism seemed 'altogether fictitious'. No society, no matter how small, 'ever did or can consist of so homogeneous a mass of citizens'. All 'civilised societies' were made up of 'various and unavoidable' distinctions and interests: rich and poor, creditors and debtors, farmers and manufacturers, merchants and bankers, and so on (Jefferson 1950–, XII, p. 277; *Federalist*, no. 10). In small republics, such as the several states were, it was sometimes possible for one of these competing factions or interests to gain a majority, control the legislature, and become oppressive. This problem of tyrannical majority factions was precisely what had plagued most of the states since 1776, and it was the cause of the crisis that had led to the formation of the new national constitution. 'To secure the public good and private rights against the danger of such a faction, and at the same time to preserve the spirit and the form of popular government', wrote

Madison, was 'the great object to which our inquiries are directed' (*Federalist*, no. 10).

Madison and other Federalists solved the problem by turning the assumptions about the size of republics on their head. Instead of trying to keep the republics small and homogeneous, Madison seized on and ingeniously developed Hume's radical suggestion that a republican government operated better in a large territory than in a small one (Hume 1994a, p. 232). The republic, said Madison, had to be so enlarged, 'without departing from the elective basis of it', that 'the propensity in small republics to rash measures and the facility of forming and executing them' would be stifled. In a large republican society 'the people are broken into so many interests and parties, that a common sentiment is less likely to be felt, and the requisite concert less likely to be formed, by a majority of the whole' (Jefferson 1950–, XII, p. 2778). Madison and the Federalists, in other words, accepted the reality of diverse competing partial interests in American society and were willing to allow them free play in the society.

But not, it was hoped, in the new national government. Madison was not a modern-day pluralist. He did not expect the new federal government to be neutralised into inactivity by the competition of these numerous diverse interests. Nor did he see public policy or the common good emerging naturally from the give-and-take of such clashing interests. He did not expect the new national government to be an integrator and harmoniser of the different interests in the society; instead he expected it to be a 'disinterested and dispassionate umpire in disputes between different passions and interests in the state' (Madison 1962–91, IX, p. 384). And it would be able to play that role because the men holding office in the new central government would by their fewness of numbers and the largeness of the electoral districts most likely be 'men [who] possess the most attractive merit, and the most diffusive and established characters' (*Federalist*, no. 10).

The new central government would combine the best of monarchy and republicanism. In monarchies the king was sufficiently neutral towards his subjects, but often he sacrificed their happiness for his personal avarice or ambition. In small republics the government had no selfish will of its own, but it was never sufficiently neutral towards the various interests of the society. What the new extended and elevated republic would do, said Madison, was combine the good qualities of each. The new government would be 'sufficiently neutral between the different interests and factions, to control one part of the society from invading the rights of another, and at the same time sufficiently controlled itself, from setting up an interest adverse to that of the whole society' (Madison 1962–91, IX, p. 357).

In other words, Madison was willing to allow ordinary people to pursue their partial selfish interests in the expectation that they would be so diverse and clashing that they would rarely be able to combine and enter into the government as tyrannical majorities. This competitive situation would then allow those with 'enlarged' and 'liberal' outlooks to dominate government and promote the common good. It seemed to have worked that way in American religion, which was a common analogy for Madison. The multiplicity of religious sects in America prevented any one of them from dominating the state and permitted the enlightened reason of philosophers like Jefferson and himself to shape public policy concerning religion and church–state relations. 'In a free government', wrote Madison in *The Federalist*, 'the security for civil rights must be the same as for religious rights. It consists in the one case in the multiplicity of interests, and in the other, in the multiplicity of sects' (Hamilton *et al.*, 2003, p. 254).

5   The sovereignty of the people

The extended size of the new republic was not, however, the only reason the Anti-federalists opposed the constitution. More important was its likelihood of becoming what the Anti-federalists called a 'consolidation', which they thought would eventually weaken and probably destroy the separate state governments. 'Instead of being thirteen republics, under a federal head', wrote the 'Federal Farmer', in a widely expressed Anti-federalist opinion, the constitution 'is clearly designed to make us one consolidated government' (Ford 1888, p. 282).

What gave force to the Anti-federalist argument that the individual states would sooner or later succumb to the centralising authority of the national government was the conventional eighteenth-century British theory of sovereignty – a theory most notably affirmed by Blackstone in his *Commentaries on the Laws of England* (1765–9). This was the notion the British government expressed repeatedly in its quarrel with the colonies – that in every state there had to be one final indivisible and incontestable law-making authority to which all other authorities must be ultimately subordinate, and in the British empire that final sovereign authority was parliament. When by 1774 the colonists replied that this supreme law-making authority lay not in parliament but in their separate colonial legislatures, the issue that would break the empire was drawn. The doctrine of sovereignty was the most important conception of politics in the eighteenth-century Anglo-American world, and it dominated the polemics of the entire revolutionary generation.

So when the Anti-federalists in 1787–8 declared that there could be but one supreme legislative power in every state, they were invoking the logic of the standard political science of the day. 'I never heard of two supreme co-ordinate powers in one and the same country before', said Anti-federalist William Grayson of Virginia; 'I cannot conceive how it can happen' (Elliot 1854, III, p. 281). The logic of sovereignty demanded that either the state legislatures or the national Congress must predominate. There could be no compromise: 'It is either a federal or a consolidated government, there being no medium as to kind' (Philadelphia *Independent Gazetteer*, 15 Apr. 1788). And the Anti-federalists had no doubt that the federal government under the proposed constitution, with its great sweeping power and its authority as 'supreme law of the land . . . must eventually annihilate the independent sovereignty of the several states'. Once the constitution was established 'the state governments, without object or authority, will soon dwindle into insignificance, and be despised by the people themselves' (Elliot 1854, II, pp. 312–13).

The Anti-federalists had a formidable argument. At first the Federalists tried to evade, refine, or deny the concept of sovereignty. They attempted to delineate 'joint jurisdictions' and 'co-equal sovereignties' and to work out some way of sharing sovereignty between the national and state governments. But such efforts were doomed to fail. The idea that there must in every state be one supreme law-making power was too firmly entrenched to be denied or avoided. In the end James Wilson in the Pennsylvania ratifying convention found the best answer to the Anti-federalist argument. More boldly and originally than anyone else, Wilson developed the position that became the basis of all Federalist thinking, indeed, of all thinking about American government. Wilson challenged the Anti-federalist case for the logic of sovereignty not by attempting to divide sovereignty or to deny it altogether, but by locating that power 'from which there is no appeal, and which is therefore called absolute, supreme, and uncontrollable' only in the people at large (qu. McMaster and Stone 1888, p. 229). It seemed a simple solution, but it was not, and its implications were momentous.

Sovereignty exists, conceded Wilson, but it cannot be located in either the federal government or the state legislatures; 'it resides in the PEOPLE, as the fountain of government'. The people never give up this sovereignty; it always stays with them. 'They can delegate it in such proportions, to such bodies, on such terms, and under such limitations, as they think proper.' Thus the people gave some of their power to the institutions of the national government, some to the various state governments, and some at other extraordinary times to constitutional conventions for the specific purpose of making or amending constitutions. But unlike the British people in relation to their parliament, the American people never surrendered to any political institution or even to all political institutions together their full and final sovereign power. Always they retained their rights and their ultimate authority. Wilson was not saying, as theorists had long said, that all governmental power was *derived* from the people. Instead, he was saying that all governmental power was only a temporary and limited agency of the people – out, so to speak, on a short-term, always revocable, loan. This was the principle underlying the new federal system, Wilson told the delegates in the Pennsylvania ratifying convention, and unless they grasped it, they would never be able to understand how the people 'may take from the subordinate governments powers with which they have hitherto trusted them, and place those powers in the general government' (qu. McMaster and Stone 1888, pp. 316, 302).

Although no Federalist seized and wielded this principle of the sovereignty of the people with more authority than Wilson, other Federalists in the ratification debates were inevitably pressured by persistent Anti-federalist references to consolidation into invoking the same principle. Indeed, once the defenders of the constitution saw the political and intellectual advantages of locating sovereignty in the people as a whole, they could scarcely restrain their excitement. Now they had a ready-made justification both for the Philadelphia Convention's bypassing the Confederation Congress and for the reliance on special state conventions in place of the state legislatures as instruments of ratification. Only by conceiving of sovereignty literally remaining with the people could the Federalists explain the emerging idea of 'federalism', where, contrary to the prevailing thought of the eighteenth century, both the state and national legislatures could be equally and simultaneously representative of the people, 'both possessed of our equal confidence – both chosen in the same manner, and equally responsible to us' (Elliot 1854, III, p. 301).

The Federalists now realised that government in America was different from government anywhere else in the world. It was not something that belonged to a king, consul, duke, or any ruler whatsoever. For Americans there could be no pre-existing rights of government inhering in anyone, no prerogative powers that the people had to bargain with and try to limit.

In America, the Federalists concluded in wonderment at their own audacity, there no longer existed the age-old, seemingly permanent, distinction between rulers and ruled. Almost at a stroke, the Federalists created the theoretical basis for modern representative democracy. A constitution in America could no longer be regarded as it still was in England, as a contract or agreement between two hostile parties, between rulers and people. 'In Europe', wrote Madison in 1792, 'charters of liberty have been granted by power. America has set the example and France has followed it of charters of power granted by liberty' (Madison 1900–10, VI, pp. 83–5). In America the people created not only constitutions but governments – in all their parts. They temporarily granted some of their sovereign power to their governmental agents, and those agents were now diverse and numerous. As the developing logic of actual representation had made evident, the people were no longer represented exclusively in the houses of representatives. All parts of America's governments at both the state and national levels – senates, governors, congress, the president, even judges – could now intelligibly be described as limited agents of the people. Government was simply the aggregation of some of the people's parcelled-out power, with the remainder of their power – their rights and liberties – kept in their own hands. All parts and all levels of this delegated aggregate governmental power were in some sense equally representative of the people.

Thinking about government and political power in America would never again be the same. Separation of powers, checks and balances, constitutions, limited government, federalism – all almost at once took on their modern meanings. With all governmental institutions regarded equally as the people's limited representatives, it no longer made sense to talk about mixing the classical categories of government and balancing social entities in the institutions of government (though a few like John Adams stubbornly tried), and the ancient theory of mixed government became meaningless for most Americans. Undoubtedly most of the framers at Philadelphia in 1787 thought they were creating a balanced government much in the manner of the several state governments – only with a stronger chief executive and senate than in most of the states. Although the model for this structure was the ideal English constitution, by 1787 few American political leaders felt comfortable any longer saying so in public – again Adams was a conspicuous exception. Referring to the chief executive as the monarchical element and the senate as the aristocracy in a balanced government became politically impossible in the populist atmosphere of the 1780s. Thus the Federalists had to find justifications for their two-house legislature and their strong, independent, king-like president somewhere other than the English constitution and the classical ideal of mixed government.

What they did was to exploit the radical implications of actual representation and the sovereignty of the people, which turned all parts of government into agents of the people, and then to collapse the older theory of balanced or mixed government into the notion of the division of the functional powers of government – executive, legislative, and judicial – and to appeal to the need to separate power in order to justify the now fragmented and countervailing character of America's political system. From a once minor maxim the separation of powers was suddenly elevated into the paramount principle of American constitutionalism. 'The constant aim', wrote Madison, who summed up the Federalists' thinking on the parcelling of power, 'is to divide and arrange the several offices in such a manner as that each may be a check on the other.' Bicameralism, the presidential power of veto, the independent judiciary, even federalism itself – the apportioning of authority between the national and state governments – all became various means of dividing, checking, and balancing a mistrusted political power. It was now assumed that all power, whether in the hands of governors, the president, Congress, or the state houses of representatives, no longer bore any relationship to any social estate or category of government but was essentially indistinguishable, all a delegation by the people. Such an assumption made possible reform not only of the national government but of the state governments, taking away some of the extraordinary power the revolutionary state constitutions had granted to the lower houses of the legislatures and giving it to the governors, senates, and judges.

Despite the haste and the polemical manner in which the Federalists often spoke and wrote, the monumental significance of their intellectual achievement was almost immediately grasped. Their ideas were so popularly based, so related to the debates of the previous two decades, and indeed so embodied what Americans had been groping for from the beginning of their history, that they were soon taken up even by their opponents and made the basis for all subsequent discussion of American politics. The creation of a government that was, as one American put it in 1791, 'perhaps without example in the world', could not long remain an exclusively Federalist achievement (Sullivan 1791, p. 38). 'As this kind of government', wrote Samuel Williams in 1794, 'is not the same as that which has been called monarchy, aristocracy, or democracy; as it had a conspicuous origin in America, and has not been suffered to prevail in any other part of the globe, it would be no more than just and proper, to distinguish it by its proper name, and call it, *The American System of Government*' (Williams 1794, p. 346). Just and proper perhaps, but not entirely correct; for similar changes in political thought were at the same time taking place, under similar pressures of logic and circumstances, elsewhere in the Western world.

22

Political languages of the French Revolution

KEITH MICHAEL BAKER

Although they were preceded by several decades of political contestation, the debates of the French Revolution can reasonably be said to have begun on 5 July 1788, when Louis XVI agreed to summon the Estates General after a lapse of almost two centuries.[1] Declaring the royal archives inadequate to determine how that body had once been convened, the king invited his subjects to investigate the precedents for calling an assembly that would be 'truly national, both in its composition and in its results' (Baker 1987b, pp. 143–5).[2] This was a remarkable pronouncement in what was still thought to be an absolute monarchy, since it invited public enquiry not only into the entire history of the realm but also the ultimate definition of the 'truly national'. No earlier constitutional crisis in France had unleashed a response comparable in force and magnitude to the torrent of political argument that was now to sweep the country.

1   Competing discourses of the Old Regime

Participants in this debate could draw upon a variety of discourses forged in the course of several decades of political contestation. A discourse of justice drew on the conceptual resources of a French constitutional tradition dramatically revived and reworked by defenders of the *parlements* in opposition to the royal 'despotism' which was increasingly their target after

1 The literature on the French Revolution is immense; no justice can be done to it here. Caldwell 1985 provides the fullest bibliography, but many crucial works have since appeared; some of the English ones are listed in Doyle 1988. Further exploration of events, persons, and ideas discussed in this chapter might begin with general works on the Revolution, e.g., Doyle 1989, 1999; Furet 1992; C. Jones 1988; Palmer 1941; Schama 1989; dictionaries devoted to it, e.g., Furet and Ozouf 1989b; Scott and Rothaus 1985; Soboul 1989; or recent interpretations of its political culture, e.g., Baker 1987b, 1990, 1994b; Furet 1981; Gauchet 1989, 1995; Guéniffey 2000; Higonnet 1998; Hunt 1984, 1992; Jaume 1989; Ozouf 1988; Singer 1986. These latter will lead the reader back to the classic interpretations of Burke, Marx, and Tocqueville.
2 Quotations are from English translations collected in Baker 1987b whenever possible. Other translations from French sources are the author's, unless otherwise stated.

1750. Juxtaposing the lawful (justice) with the arbitrary (will), it upheld the
principles of a society comprised of orders and Estates, governed according
to regular legal forms, secured by magistrates exercising their functions of
judicial review and registration of laws in the *parlements*. As political conflict
escalated, however, the more radical pro-*parlement* theorists had also come
to argue that fundamental laws constraining the exercise of royal sovereignty
belonged to a fundamental constitution alterable only by the consent of a
nation endowed with a political identity and collective rights independent
of the crown. Moving beyond the assertion that registration of laws by the
parlements symbolised such consent in matters of legislation, they had called
for the convening of the Estates General as the only and ultimate institutional
expression of the national will. From within the framework of a discourse
of justice, therefore, *parlementaire* constitutionalism had been driven towards
a conception of the sovereignty of the nation, albeit an essentially defensive
one, understood as the ultimate limiting condition upon the exercise of
royal power (Baker 1990; Van Kley 1996).

But it was also possible to defend the constitutional claims of the *parlements*
in a more explicitly political discourse of will drawing on such writers as
Rousseau and Mably – and, with them, upon the language of classical
republicanism. In this idiom, collective order and identity were defined
not in terms of justice, law, prescription, and adjudication, but in terms of
will, liberty, contingency, choice, and participation. As early as 1775, in a
desperate response to Maupeou's coup against the *parlements*, the *Catéchisme
du citoyen* of Guillaume Joseph Saige had offered a version of *The Social
Contract* in question-and-answer form, using it to insist that the status of
the historical constitution was absolutely contingent upon the will of the
nation, which alone could 'modify [it], or annihilate it totally, in order to
form a new one' (Saige 1775, qu. Baker 1990, pp. 143–4).

The discourse of will, nevertheless, was more usually invoked against
both *parlementaire* and royal claims. In Mably's account of French history,
parlementaire constitutionalism was exposed as a sham concealing the fact
that the nation had lost its fundamental laws along with its desire for liberty.
Arguing more abstractly, Rousseau set aside historical facts and juridical titles
to imagine freedom secured by the general will of a political community
comprising citizens equal before the law. Both Rousseau and Mably, in
their different ways, fused the language of classical republicanism into a
potent combination with the idiom of natural rights theory deriving from
the tradition of natural jurisprudence. Rousseau's reworking of the concept
of the social contract was a way of radicalising the arguments for popular

sovereignty within the discourse of classical republicanism, one possible solution to the problem of securing the autonomy of individual subjectivity in a commercial society. Mably appropriated the language of rights even as he sought to contest the political passivity frequently preached by the doctors of natural jurisprudence (Baker 1990; Rosenblatt 1997; Wright 1997).

But the language of individual rights appeared in its most distinctively French form before the Revolution in a discourse of reason associated with the physiocrats. In this idiom, the ancient constitution was a present contradiction and royal will no more than arbitrary. Both had to give way to the enlightened rule of reason in a social order reconstituted according to natural law and the principles of political economy. In contrast to the discourse of will which frequently appealed to the model of the ancient city-states against the institutions of modern commercial society (and to the discourse of justice, which preferred to seek its principles of continuity in the earliest laws and customs of the Franks), the discourse of reason was an idiom of modernity emphasising the growth of commerce and the progress of civil society. In the last years of the Old Regime, it sustained the modernising reform programme of the monarchy for greater administrative uniformity, commercial expansion, civil rights, and fiscal equality, and for the representation of social interests through the participation of property owners in the rational conduct of local government (Baker 1990, 1994b). If no single one of these competing discourses entirely defined the language of the French Revolution, it was nevertheless forged in a process of creative improvisation drawing upon all of them.

2 Revolutionary improvisation

A crucial response to the royal announcement of 5 July 1788 came from the *parlement* of Paris, which stipulated that the Estates General be 'regularly convoked and composed', in the manner of its last meeting of 1614 (Egret 1977, p. 197). It quickly became clear that this was a formula for a tricameral assembly with each Estate voting separately. Intended to counter 'ministerial despotism' (long the target of *parlementaire* protest) by eliminating the opportunity to manipulate the forms and procedures of the Estates General, the *parlementaire* declaration was immediately denounced as a reactionary defence of 'aristocracy' (the more recent target of defenders of governmental reform policies). There followed countervailing demands for a convocation that would allow the Third Estate the same number of representatives as the two other orders combined, within a common assembly where each representative would have an equal vote.

This programme for the 'doubling' of the Third Estate was presented by the first minister, Necker, to a special Assembly of Notables convened in the autumn of 1788. To Necker's surprise, the Notables refused it and upheld the *parlement*'s insistence on the constituted forms of 1614. The conflict between 'despotism' and 'aristocracy' had thus reached an impasse. Necker proceeded to call the Estates General in a way that doubled the representatives of the Third Estate and organised their election on the basis of a broad (male) suffrage (at least outside the towns, which retained elements of corporate representation). But in doing so, he left undecided the critical question of whether the three Estates would vote by head in a common assembly or separately by order, thus ensuring that the meeting would open with a conflict between the principles of democracy and those of aristocracy. The issue of making government accountable to the nation had become secondary to the more fundamental question of the definition of the nation to which the government might be accountable. This question was answered systematically, and with radical implications, by the most celebrated pamphlet of the revolutionary period, the Abbé Sieyès's *Qu'est-ce que le Tiers-Etat?* (What is the Third Estate?, 1789).[3]

Sieyès began as a student of political economy. His was a discourse of reason, a scientific discourse of the social investigating the nature of production and wealth, the implications of the division of labour, and the reorganization of society according to principles of a rational social art. His *Essai sur les privilèges* (1788), declaring exchange rather than hierarchy the true bond of society, denounced privilege as economic sterility 'gobbling up capital and persons' (Sieyès 1982, p. 24). It followed that the nation, as a social body actively engaged in useful and productive functions, simply could not contain an entire class of citizens who gloried in 'inactivity amidst the general movement', consuming 'the best part of the product without having in any way helped to produce it'. Such a class, Sieyès insisted in *Qu'est-ce que le Tiers-Etat?* had, by definition, to be excluded from a society of 'useful and industrious citizens'; it was 'foreign to the nation because of its idleness' (Baker 1987b, pp. 155–7). Nor were the privileged less absolutely excluded by the second definition of the nation Sieyès adduced in his famous pamphlet, one configured within a political discourse of will. The essence of the

---

3 Forsyth 1987 gives a broad exposition of Sieyès's political thought. However, there has been an explosion of interest in Sieyès's thinking in recent years. Among the most interesting perspectives are those offered by Hont 1994a, Sewell 1994, and Sonenscher 1997, 2003.

nation in this definition lay in the equality of citizens and the universality inherent in their exercise of a common will. Those who refused a common civic status excluded themselves automatically from the political order: 'the general will . . . cannot be *one* as long as you retain three orders and three representations' (Baker 1987b, p. 178).

Put together, these arguments produced a devastating repudiation of appeals to an ancient constitution and a fundamental law. Even if such a constitution had existed, Sieyès insisted, the nation could not be bound by it for a moment longer. No present constitution, no fundamental laws, no putative previous contract between the nation and its ruler, no prior decision of the body of the nation or of its representatives, could henceforth bind the nation in the exercise of its inalienable sovereign will, or constrain the expression of that will within particular forms. 'The nation is prior to everything. It is the source of everything. Its will is always legal; indeed, it is the law itself' (Baker 1987b, p. 171). With this utterance, Sieyès transformed the historical effect that was the nation into a primordial political reality, the metaphysical ground of all collective existence. A radical doctrine of national sovereignty had been invented.

Sieyès thus gave revolutionary discourse its earliest form by dissolving claims for privilege and *parlementaire* constitutionalism in a rhetorical blending of a discourse of reason and a discourse of political will. Against it the discourse of justice would have relatively little force in future revolutionary debates. But this compound was itself an unstable one. Its binding element lay in Sieyès's notion of representation – and in a fundamental departure from Rousseau on this point. Rousseau had seen the practice of representation as a feudal legacy fundamentally inconsistent with the exercise of the general will, which would cease to exist the moment it was alienated or represented. When faced with the necessity of representation, he insisted on the binding mandate (also a traditional feature of the assemblies of the Estates General) as an essential device for subjecting the will of the deputies to the general will. Sieyès, by contrast, saw representation as the quintessentially modern form of government: the only possible mechanism for the expression of political rationality in a complex modern society organised on the principle of the division of labour, and the only means of expressing a unitary general will in a polity too numerous to allow for the direct participation of the entire body of the citizens. Its operation in both respects required precisely that each deputy act as the representative of the totality of the nation, entirely unrestrained by any mandate binding him to the particular will of his constituents. This latter condition was to become a crucial matter of political contention (Furet 1981; Gauchet 1989, 1995; Guéniffey 1993).

The opening of the Estates General in May 1789, with its coded formalities of dress and precedence, signified the essential differentiation within a juridically constituted society of orders made one by the presence of the monarch. But when Louis XVI ordered the deputies of the three Estates to begin their deliberations by verifying their credentials in separate chambers, the representatives of the Third Estate baulked at this differentiation, refusing to take any action until the deputies of the clergy and the nobility had joined them in a common assembly. In the struggle that resulted when the privileged orders declined this call, the notion of an ancient monarchical constitution, central to the discourse of justice, finally disintegrated. The power of the historical repertoire exhausted by competing claims, the century-long search for secure precedents upon which to reconstitute the French monarchy reached its end (Van Kley 1994a).

The decisive moment occurred in June when the deputies of the Third Estate, after long and difficult debates over alternative formulations, declared themselves a 'National Assembly' which alone could 'interpret and set forth the general will of the nation'. In doing so, the deputies of the Third Estate broke with the past by virtue of the principle of national sovereignty. Resisting the claims of the privileged orders, they implicitly denied the king's authority to sustain such claims. Furthermore, by asserting that 'representation is one and indivisible', they made the nation that was represented one and indivisible too. Three days later, in defiance of the crown, they swore in the famous Tennis Court Oath not to disband until the constitution of the realm had been 'established and secured on solid foundations' (Baker 1987b, pp. 199–201).

This formulation allowed for a crucial ambiguity. Had the deputies sworn to strengthen a traditional constitution, or to establish a new one where none existed? The question proved to be critical as the Assembly sought to formulate constitutional principles. To stake out some middle ground became the goal of Mounier, whose efforts involved identifying the barest rudiments of an ancient constitution – notably monarchical government and the principle of consent to taxation – to be salvaged from the rubble of French history. In his view, the deputies could neither restore an existing constitution nor create one *de novo*. Instead, they had to build a complete constitutional order on fragmentary historical foundations, separating and limiting powers to prevent the arbitrary exercise of will and to protect the rights of individual citizens. From this initial definition of the Assembly's task, Mounier was to develop the constitutional programme modelled on British government taken up by the group of his allies that became known as the Monarchiens (Egret 1950).

But there were other models. The deputies were far from blind to American examples, particularly in the matter of a declaration of rights. It quickly became clear in their debates that differences over the necessity or desirability of such a declaration were intimately bound up with disagreements over whether the deputies were creating a new constitution or building upon an old one. Those who aimed at strengthening an existing constitution feared that an abstract declaration of individual rights issued in advance of any positive constitutional provisions would throw a traditional society into chaos. Their fears deepened when the Assembly received news of widespread social disorder in the countryside. Those who sought an entirely new constitutional order derived from rational principles and instituted by a sovereign act of constituent power – the position made most explicit by Sieyès – held, by contrast, that a prior declaration of rights was the indispensable first step towards the social peace to be achieved by enlightened reform (Baker 1994b; Gauchet 1989; Rials 1988).

The issue came to a head on 4 August. First, the clerical deputies forced a vote on their demand that any declaration of rights also include a statement of duties, lest 'egoism and pride' be consecrated at the expense of religious and moral obligations. Repudiating this argument – endorsing, in effect, the proposition that duties were simply the corollary of rights in an individualistic order – the Assembly decided that the constitution would indeed be preceded by a Declaration of the Rights of Man and of the Citizen. But, with the countryside in flames, immediate action was necessary to restore peace. Some deputies were anxious to implement the principle of individual rights, others to limit its implications; all were eager to protect legitimate property. The latter now required some definition. It came, dramatically, that same evening, when weeks of frustration suddenly gave way to a transforming moment. After bitter attacks on feudal practices now rendered shameful in an enlightened age, deputies from the nobility began to offer a sacrifice of their seigneurial rights, only to be followed, in a crescendo of collective renunciation, by deputies abandoning the privileges of their clerical orders, their towns, or their provinces. Before the celebrated Night of the Fourth of August was over, not only feudal dues but also all the traditional privileges and prerogatives of a corporate society had been cast aside (Fitzsimmons 1994).

Whatever doubts followed this 'holocaust of privileges', a decree confirmed the Assembly's decisions by announcing the complete destruction of the 'feudal regime'. Property was saved by disengaging it from personal privilege, abolishing outright all seigneurial exactions held to derive from personal relations of domination and dependence, and allowing the redemption of other peasant obligations as part of a new, implicitly contractual, relation between landlord and tenant. More fundamentally, the entire administrative, financial, legal, and judicial order of what was soon to be called the 'Old Regime' was dismantled in favour of a new society of individuals before the law, one in which private activities would be freed from corporate constraints and public functions would be open to all. In June the National Assembly had claimed to represent national sovereignty; now it acted on that authority to sweep away an entire traditional order in the name of reason. Careful to implicate the king in its action by celebrating him as 'The Restorer of French Liberty', it had, in repudiating the corporate conception of society, nevertheless severed the spiritual taproot that fed the absolute monarchy. It had inaugurated a philosophical and psychological dynamic of national regeneration.

Returning to contentious debates over a declaration of rights that would serve as a preamble to the constitution, the deputies arrived by late August at a draft theoretically subject to modification once the constitution itself had been written.[4] Almost immediately, however, the draft Declaration of the Rights of Man and of the Citizen assumed a virtually sacred status. The document finally gave the National Assembly the legitimation conferred by a statement of eternal principles regarding the imprescriptible rights of individuals, the inalienable sovereignty of the nation, and the natural order of society. Truths held to be universal were now invoked against the despotism of any arbitrary, particular will, against the injustices and vicissitudes of an ancient political order forever emptied of the authority of historical prescription.

Yet the Declaration bore all the marks of a difficult birth in linguistic compromise and conceptual ambiguity. The deputies had produced a text that blended competing discourses into a volatile mixture. By prohibiting arbitrary acts of power, by upholding the principles of representation and consent to taxation, and by insisting on the necessity of a clear separation of

4 Text translated in Baker 1987b; Baecque *et al.* 1988; Baker 1994b; Gauchet 1989; debates analysed in Rials 1988.

powers, the document achieved goals long expressed within the discourse of justice. By promising that its statement of 'natural, inalienable, and sacred rights' would create a transparent political order in which acts of the legislative body could 'at each moment' be compared against the rational goals of political society, it embraced a discourse of reason. By maintaining that 'the law is the expression of the general will', it adhered to a discourse that gave political will a priority over the exercise of individual rights.

This 'legicentrism' of the Declaration has long been noted. It was forged in the confrontation between those deputies determined to contain despotism and those fearing anarchy and disorder. The latter insisted on the necessary power of the law to protect society from the dangers emanating from abstract principles of individual rights. The former insisted on the principle that rights, remaining free from abridgement by any arbitrary personal power, could be limited *only* by the law, understood as that impersonal collective power emanating from all and applying to all. By virtue of this *'only'* the two sides could agree. The law, but *only* the law, could fix the point at which liberty became dangerous. By the same token, however, the law, and *only* the law, could decide the limits of the law (Baker 1994b, pp. 192–3; Rials 1988, pp. 236, 369–73, 396–403).

This being the case, much depended on the precise institutional expression to be given to two key phrases: the 'separation of powers', which the Declaration held to be a defining characteristic of any proper constitution, and the 'general will' it identified as the source of the law. Was the 'separation of powers' to be configured as a separation of legislative, executive, and judicial powers, a system of checks and balances on the British model favoured by Mounier and the Monarchiens, in which legislative will might be restrained (and rights protected) by an independent judiciary? Or was it, on the contrary, to be construed in terms of a Rousseauian separation between a superior legislative power and a subordinate executive power, the former consisting of the formal expression of the general will by the sovereign body of the people, the latter its application to particular persons and cases by the act of government? Was the statement that 'the law is the expression of the general will' to be interpreted as implying the strong Rousseauian notion of a direct and immediate sovereignty that could ultimately have no limits other than those inherent in its very generality? Or might it allow some less demanding conception of sovereignty?

Ambiguity was compounded by the fact that the Declaration, having identified the law as the expression of the general will, gave all citizens the right to participate, either personally or through their representatives, in the formation of this will. How was this statement to be understood, given Rousseau's repudiation of representation as incompatible with the general will? Little clarification could be found in the insistence that 'the source of all sovereignty resides essentially in the nation'. To assert that the nation was the ultimate *source* of all sovereignty was not necessarily to say that the nation must *exercise* that sovereignty directly and immediately. Such indeed was the specific virtue of this formulation in the eyes of its originator, Mounier. Nor were the Monarchiens to wait long in their attempt to contain the potential implications of what their leader rather exasperatedly called 'this so frequently repeated expression, *the general will*' (Mavidal *et al.* 1862–1913, VIII, p. 563).

The vision Mounier and his allies now offered drew heavily on the interpretation of the British constitution formulated by Delolme and John Adams in reaction to Rousseau's idealisation of direct democracy. It included a strong executive authority, unitary in the person of the monarch; a divided legislative power, shared among the monarch, a senate (with members chosen for life), and an elected house of representatives; and an absolute royal veto in matters of legislation. With the adoption of these provisions, the Monarchiens insisted, the legacy of French history would be perfected by philosophy and an improved constitution built upon traditional foundations. Monarchical and democratic despotism alike would be made impossible by virtue of a system of checks and balances.

The key to this system of dividing and balancing power lay in the provision for an absolute royal veto. Without this share in legislative power, Mounier maintained, the king would be merely a magistrate following orders and 'the government would no longer be monarchical but republican' (Mavidal *et al.* 1862–1913, 1862, VIII, p. 586). This was the issue around which the constitutional debate condensed. Two theoretical positions were clearly articulated in opposition to the Monarchiens' proposals. One, drawing on Rousseau, maintained a strong interpretation of the principle of national sovereignty. It dismissed the British constitution as a feudal accident, incoherent in itself and quite incompatible with the unitary character of the general will, and it argued for a unitary legislature and a strict distinction between legislative and executive power. This clearly precluded any absolute monarchical veto. But the Rousseauians in the Assembly still faced the essential problem of combining the theory of the general will with the practice of representation, which they acknowledged to be the only feasible form of political decision-making in a large modern society. What guarantee could there be that the particular decisions of a representative assembly would express the general will of an entire nation? The traditional device of the binding mandate, which Rousseau himself had favoured, had already been rejected in the course of transforming the Estates General into the National Assembly. Hence, some Rousseauians now opted for a suspensive royal veto that would trigger an immediate appeal to the people in the primary assemblies whenever the king (acting not as a co-legislator but in his capacity as executive) judged a legislative decision to be potentially contrary to the general will.

The Monarchiens were not slow to ridicule the idea of an appeal to the people. But the most telling argument against it came from another of their opponents, Sieyès, in whose analysis representation – in this case, the division of political labour between the more and less enlightened – was the very essence of modern society. In his view, the general will could not be held to exist as an aggregate of the particular wills of primary assemblies brought to the legislature by deputies acting as mandataries of particular constituencies. Instead, it took shape only through the deliberation of representatives sent to act for the entire nation in a common assembly. The idea of appealing a decision of the legislature back to the primary assemblies was as dangerous as it was absurd. It would tear into separate little republics a nation that was only now recovering its unity from the dismemberment that had been the Old Regime.

The National Assembly, thus presented with three quite distinct theoretical models, opted for none in their entirety. Repudiating the Monarchiens' proposals as too redolent of aristocratic and monarchical power, the deputies voted for the unitary legislature favoured by Sieyès and the Rousseauians as the only form consistent with the principles of universality, equality, and national sovereignty. Opting, against Sieyès's arguments, for a suspensive royal veto, they implicitly endorsed the Rousseauian distrust of representation as the sole means of expressing the general will in a modern society. But when it came to deciding the mechanics of the royal veto they showed a converse distrust of the Rousseauians' idea of an immediate appeal to the people in the primary assemblies, decreeing instead that the suspensive veto could stand against the will of two legislatures (each lasting two years) before it could be overturned by the majority vote of a third. In effect, this vote repudiated the notion that the general will could be revealed by the direct expression of a popular vote and endorsed the (Sieyèsian) principle that it was formulated only by the deliberation of the representative body itself.

These decisions left the logic of the suspensive veto fundamentally incoherent. It was to be a veto exercised against the legislative assembly's will by a hereditary monarch declared by the new constitution to be a 'representative' of the French nation: a monarch entrusted with the right of veto as an executive authority, in which capacity he was also deemed to be subject to the legislative power rather than sharing in it; yet one authorised, nevertheless, to delay the action of the legislature for an extended period of time, in an appeal to the nation that allowed the latter no direct means of endorsing or repudiating this action. This incoherence was to place great pressure on the principle of representation itself. The suspensive veto had been proposed by the Rousseauians as an immediate and definitive means of closing the gap between sovereignty and representation. The new constitution effectively kept that gap open – indeed, it institutionalised it at the heart of the political order – by allowing for a period of sustained uncertainty in which the king, the Assembly, and those outside the Assembly who claimed to speak for the people could maintain competing claims to express the general will. Within this site of uncertainty, the political theory of the Revolution was to become profoundly radicalised, and the constitutional monarchy destroyed.

There remained, in the decisive debates of September 1789, a final question that went to the heart of the Assembly's conception of its task: could the king now refuse the constitutional changes upon which the deputies had decided? The issue was joined amidst the turmoil of the October Days, when Louis XVI gave his 'accedence' to the Declaration of the Rights of Man and the constitutional articles so far decided, but only on condition that the completed constitution preserve the monarch's full possession of executive power. This challenge to the Assembly's claim to constituent power drew an immediate and vigorous response from the deputies, who voted to require the king to submit his 'pure and simple acceptance'. Their ultimatum was delivered with the support of the women (and others) who had marched from Paris to demand bread, invading the Assembly on their way to the royal château. The king immediately yielded under the threat of popular violence.

The Assembly debates thus made clear that a constitution would be instituted *de novo* in the name of reason and national sovereignty. The National Assembly could now appropriately claim the title of 'Constituent Assembly'. But nobody would forget that this title had finally been secured by the direct insurrectionary force of the sovereign people embodied as a crowd. The taking of the Bastille had already displayed the power of this 'embodied' people; the October Days turned its intervention from a unique event into an action to be repeated whenever the Parisian crowd might choose to express a popular will directly. As a result, the constitution could be fixed against the king, but it could not be fixed against the people. Popular insurrection had been inscribed within a revolutionary process (Baker 1990).

The October Days also brought into clear relief other ambiguities within the Declaration of the Rights of Man and of the Citizen: those surrounding the very definitions of the terms 'man' and 'citizen'. None of the women and few of the men who marched in protest from Paris to Versailles would have met the conditions for active citizenship that had already been proposed to the National Assembly by its Constitutional Committee. The Committee's report simply assumed that women, servants, and others 'lacking the independence necessary for the exercise of political rights' would enjoy the protection of the law without participating in its formulation. In the following months, however, it became obvious that the Declaration of Rights had raised more questions than it resolved. Did the rights of man pertain to all human beings, as individuals? Did they entitle all adults to equal status as full and active citizens, whatever their economic status or profession, or simply to the equal protection of the laws? Did they pertain equally to women as to men? To Protestants as to Catholics? To Jews as to Christians? Did they require the abolition of slavery, or at least of the slave trade, in the French colonies? (Hunt 1996).

If answers to all these questions were pressed in the direction of a universalist conception of individual rights, revolutionary legislation frequently foundered on fears of their radical implications. Conflict over the application of the distinction between active and passive citizens was to be a constant feature of the revolutionary dynamic until it was abolished (with the Constitution of 1791) by the revolution of August 1792. If the claims of Protestants were clearly acknowledged as early as December 1789, the question of civil rights for Jews evoked bitter debates until the matter was abruptly settled in their favour during the last days of the Constituent Assembly. Claims for equal rights for women – both political and social, in the sense of equality in matters of marriage, divorce, and inheritance – were quickly advanced, most notably in Olympe de Gouges's *Declaration of the Rights of Women* (1791) (partial translation in Baker 1987b; J. W. Scott 1996). But if the revolutionary assemblies legalised divorce and equal inheritance, and sought to introduce greater equality into marriage (now conceptualised as a civil contract), they consistently rejected arguments for women's political rights. The Convention, in particular, also suppressed women's political participation in the name of a strictly gendered conception of republican virtue (Hunt 1996; Levy *et al.* 1979). When it came to the complexities of the French colonies, the issue of rights became even more explosive. Claims on behalf of free blacks or mulattoes were resisted, as well as arguments for the abolition of slavery, with predictions of economic disaster, slave revolt, or racial warfare – all of which were brought to fulfilment before slavery was (only briefly) abolished in French colonies in 1794. Slave revolt continued in Saint Domingue until it secured the free black republic of Haiti in 1804 – a logical outcome of the principles of the Declaration of the Rights of Man, but linked to it only by a bloody chain of events (Blackburn 1988).

3 Two languages of liberty

The Constituent Assembly took almost two years to complete the work of a constitution making France 'one and indivisible'. In the process, the administrative and judicial patchwork of a particularist social order was swept away: new divisions of the territory into *departements*, districts, and communes replaced ancient provinces and traditional local jurisdictions in town and country; the privileges of the nobility, of corporations, and of guilds were destroyed in the name of equality and universality; the administration of the church was nationalised by the Civil Constitution of the Clergy, making the practice of the Catholic religion a public function and its ministers elected officials. By these actions, the constituted society of the Old Regime was destroyed, and with it the essential historical referent for the pre-revolutionary discourse of justice. Still more fundamentally at issue was the entire nature of the modern European form of society that eighteenth-century theorists had increasingly distinguished from others (Hont 1983; Pocock 1975). The political thinking of the French Revolution remained profoundly shaped by the tension between arguments framed within a discourse of will derived from classical republicanism and those framed within a discourse of reason offering a theory of modern commercial society.

As exemplified by Sieyès, the discourse of reason was essentially a language of the social. Rooted in a tradition of natural jurisprudence that had been slowly transformed into the idiom of political economy, it began with a conception of society as an association among individuals for the satisfaction of needs and the pursuit of happiness. In Sieyès's political thinking, however, the distinction between the natural state of humankind and its social state is almost entirely elided; the notion of the social contract is generalised into the principle of constant exchange underlying the logic of the division of labour and the progress of society towards greater complexity. In this idiom, freedom is not secured against domination by a single contractual act; instead it is indefinitely extended by a constantly proliferating system of contracts/exchanges generating an ever-increasing satisfaction of human needs. Liberty inheres in the expansion of the means to happiness through the progressive advance of civil society from simple to more complex forms of interdependence, from ignorance to enlightenment, and from direct and immediate to more indirect and representative forms of action.

It was an essential implication of this expansionist conception of freedom that 'liberty often consists less in doing than in getting done' (qu. Forsyth 1987, p. 122). Viewed in this light, Sieyès's distinction between active and passive citizenship involved an allocation of function rather than an abridgement of rights. To passive citizens belonged the equal enjoyment of all the rights and benefits of individuals in society; to active citizens was assigned direct responsibility for the political decision-making and administration of public functions that secured those rights and expanded those benefits. Active citizenship was thus necessarily linked to the possession of property, since property owners alone possessed the time and knowledge to articulate and implement rational political decisions.

In Sieyès's analysis, then, everything hinged on the distinction between representative government and democratic government. The latter, the model of the Ancients, was appropriate to a simpler society, or one based on slavery. Only representative government could serve the needs of all individuals seeking to live as equals in the complex, differentiated, commercial society of the Moderns. This distinction remained a central one in the Constituent Assembly's closing debates in the summer of 1791 over the right to vote, and in efforts to defend the Constitution of 1791 thereafter. Barnave, among others, drew on it repeatedly in his defence of a property-based criterion for active citizenship, accusing his opponents of mindlessly invoking the example of those slave-based societies, Athens and Sparta. Misled by abstract theorists (namely Rousseau, a constant referent in the debates), these critics, he charged, had forgotten that in such societies 'the pure democracy of one part of the people can only exist because of the civil, political, effective, absolute enslavement of the other' (Mavidal *et al.* 1862–1913, XXXIII, p. 366). Representative government, by contrast, would secure the liberty and the interests of all citizens, and it would do so by entrusting the key function of active citizens – electing or serving as deputies – to those individuals most closely attached to the social interest by their ownership of property.

Eventually, in his *De la Révolution et de la Constitution* (1792), an account that owed much to Scottish thought, Barnave defended the Constitution of 1791 by embedding its meaning within a sociological understanding of the

long-term transformation of a feudal order through the growth of a commercial society: a process that required, and had finally received, appropriate
legal and political consummation by the creation of a representative regime
secured by property (Barnave 1988; partial translation in Barnave 1971). His
views coloured by the need to understand why that constitution had failed
so dramatically within a few months, Barnave gave the discourse of modern
society a distinct, retrospective, and increasingly conservative cast.

Others would open up the logic of history in ways more alive to its possibilities for the continuing expansion of liberty in modern society. The best-
known, and ultimately most influential, statement of this theme appeared
in Condorcet's *Esquisse d'un tableau historique des progrès de l'esprit humain*
(Sketch of an Historical View of the Progress of the Human Mind, 1795),
which – like Barnave's reflections – was written in the shadow of the guillotine and only published posthumously (Condorcet 1955). But the same
vision had already been given powerful expression in revolutionary debates
by Condorcet's *Mémoires sur l'instruction public* (1791)[5] and by the subsequent
report and proposals for a system of public instruction which he presented
to the Legislative Assembly early in 1792.

Condorcet, like Sieyès, was above all a political rationalist. Heirs to the
physiocrats, each aspired to the creation of a 'social art' (or 'social science')
that would provide the basis for rational political decisions. Hence their
shared emphasis on rational deliberation as an essential ingredient of representative government, and on the search for constitutional devices to ensure
that the common will would also be a rational will. They found common
ground in their hopes for a rational, individualistic, and expansionist liberty
in modern society. But Condorcet was prepared to push the implications
of individual equality further, particularly in favour of the rights of women.
In this regard, the argument of his *Sur l'admission des femmes au droit du cité*
(On the Admission of Women to the Rights of Citizenship, 1790) was simple (Condorcet 1976). To exclude women from the exercise of equal rights
not only contravened the principle of equality but deprived society of the
potential for progress to be derived from the enlightened participation of
half of humanity in advancing its destiny.

Public instruction was for Condorcet an essential element of liberty.
He repudiated as incompatible with individual rights in a modern society any conception of 'education' on the communal model of the Ancients,
the inculcation of values, beliefs, and attitudes through total control of a

---

5 Condorcet 1847–9, VII, pp. 169–437; partial translation in Condorcet 1976.

pedagogical environment. 'Instruction', by contrast, implied the communication of the knowledge and critical skills necessary for the conduct of everyday life in a society where the distinction between slave and free had been replaced by the postulate of equality and the aspiration to individual happiness, on the one hand, and by the complex differentiation of social functions and economic rewards on the other.

To public instruction thus defined Condorcet assigned two tasks: the maintenance of equal rights, and the maximisation of the sum of knowledge and ability available to society as a whole. Equal in their rights, he argued, human beings are nonetheless unequal in their abilities. Public instruction cannot diminish the intellectual superiority of particular individuals; indeed it must foster such superiority for the advancement of society as a whole. Condorcet therefore proposed a hierarchical system of instruction offering progressively more advanced and specialised knowledge to all in proportion to their means and abilities, and enabling each individual to acquire the knowledge and skills of which he or she is capable. Knowledge would thereby increase, enlightenment would become widespread, and human progress would continue indefinitely.

While exploiting natural inequalities for the benefit of all, however, it was also the task of public instruction, as Condorcet conceived it, to eliminate the pattern of domination and subjection such inequalities had always hitherto implied. Knowledge, in his analysis, had always been power; ignorance had always implied subordination – in daily life, in religion, and in politics. The progress of equality therefore required the distribution throughout society of knowledge adequate to eliminate this form of dependence. This knowledge had to consist of positive facts, critical reasoning, and calculation; it had to emphasise science and technology, rather than the literary learning of the classics. The public power could inculcate no opinions as established truths, impose no beliefs as dogmas; it had no warrant to decide what constituted truth and error. The latter could only be decided independently and provisionally by an independent intellectual body ultimately accountable to the scientific community. An enlightened people is a free people, Condorcet argued. With the spread of enlightenment, power would wither away, and social and political conduct would express the informed choices of free individuals in a representative system of government. Politics would finally become both rational and democratic (Baker 1975).

Condorcet's proposals for public instruction were quickly denounced, when the Convention took up the matter in December 1792, by opponents who preferred to invoke ancient models of education in calling for an egalitarian system to inculcate republican virtue in a regenerated social order. Seven months later, Robespierre too replied by presenting the Convention with a very different project for a system of communal education clearly modelled on the Spartan example (Vignery 1965). Drafted by the republican martyr, Michel Lepelletier, this plan would have placed all boys (aged five to twelve) and girls (aged five to eleven) in compulsory state boarding schools where new bodies would be formed through physical exertion and new minds by moral training. There a regime of physical work and the inculcation of manual skills would form individuals for a life of productive labour with the rigorous collective discipline the Spartans had once devoted to forming hoplites. By the time this scheme was proposed to the Convention in July 1793, the Constitution of 1791 had been overthrown by popular insurrection, the Republic had been proclaimed, the king executed, and the moderate Girondins purged from the National Assembly. With these developments, notions of representation in an individualistic modern society had been increasingly challenged by conceptions of popular sovereignty and political virtue framed within a discourse of will drawing on the idiom of classical republicanism.

This idiom was most powerfully and directly injected into the political arguments of the French Revolution by Marat, the future 'Ami du peuple', who had received his political apprenticeship in England, where his first political work, *The Chains of Slavery*, appeared anonymously in London in 1774. Vitriolic, hyperbolic, and inflammatory in its rhetoric, it drew heavily on classical republican themes to provide a panoramic denunciation of the devices by which princes had constantly sought, with inevitable success, to deprive peoples of their always fragile liberty. And it carried a particular exhortation to English voters to use the opportunity of an approaching election to throw out the pensioners and placemen corrupting the independence of the House of Commons. From the beginning, then, the susceptibility of representative bodies (indeed, of all public officials) to corruption was the central theme in Marat's political thinking.

The remarkable feature of Marat's journal *L'Ami du Peuple* (The People's Friend) when it began to appear in 1789 was that in revolutionary Paris its author deployed the same classical republican arguments as he had in Wilkite London. Active vigilance and endless suspicion were now demanded of a people barely waking from slavery, a people all too prone to slip back into its ancient lethargy before the work of transformation had been completed. The attack on placemen and pensioners was now directed at the National Assembly, a body still filled with remnants of the Old Regime even as its arrogation of sovereign authority in the name of the nation had given it the power to betray the people. Throughout the National Assembly's initial constitutional debates, and consistently thereafter, Marat protested against the notion that in a modern society the general will could only be expressed through representation. He saw the claim that each deputy represented the whole nation, not just his particular constituents, as simply a device of the representatives to evade the people's control. To the contrary, he insisted, individual deputies must be subject to recall by their constituents at will, and their collective decisions must receive popular ratification before they could be regarded as binding. Above all, their actions had to be subject to constant surveillance.

In Marat's journal, accordingly, hyper-vigilant patriotic watchfulness is constantly opposed to the dangers of a civic slumber that is blind to despotic machinations, whether those be of the executive power and its agents, of the rich and corrupt, or of the representative body itself. Calls for intense revolutionary action are constantly directed against the lethargy of a people still disabled by the experience of centuries of oppression. The abyss yawns ever deeper before the nation's feet; counter-revolutionary enemies spring up ever more frenetically before the advance of liberty. In this conception, the denunciation of the corrupt becomes a patriotic duty, the denouncer the 'eye of the people' against those who would destroy it. Above all, revolutionary action becomes the necessary means of purging the people of its enemies. The numbers of potential suspects escalated in the course of Marat's revolutionary career, but the language remained consistent.

This version of revolutionary discourse was taken up by the more radical political clubs, especially the Cordelier Club, whose action it made essential for the preservation of liberty (Hammersley 2004). Marat insisted upon their role early in 1791, against Le Chapelier's argument that collective petitions by popular societies or other groups contravened the principles of equality and universality (as, more famously, did efforts at collective bargaining by groups of workers in his view) (Sewell 1980, pp. 86–91). Within the political body of the nation, Le Chapelier insisted, there could be only individuals or the representative assembly that gave form to their common sovereignty. Marat took a very different view. When it was a question of opposing the machinations of the enemies of the Revolution, of repressing conspirators, or saving the *patrie* from destruction, his journal proclaimed, the popular societies had the right to be 'not only deliberating societies, but acting societies, repressing, punishing, and massacring societies' (Marat 1989–95,

IV, p. 2419). To think otherwise, he contended, was to deny the sacred right of resistance to oppression.

In September 1791 Le Chapelier led another charge against the clubs, introducing a bill that would deny popular societies any active political existence in the new constitution. The entire debate was coloured by the history of the king's attempted flight from the country the previous June, his subsequent capture at Varennes, and his forced return to the capital. Espousing republican themes, the more radical popular societies had demanded the monarch's replacement according to the will of the people. Their calls had been met by the repression of popular activism that began with the Champs de Mars Massacre, by the concerted efforts of the leaders of the Constituent Assembly to restore Louis XVI to executive authority, and by hasty revision of the constitution in ways that would preserve it from popular pressure for change.

Against this backdrop, Le Chapelier now insisted that the suppression of political clubs was an essential step in bringing the Revolution to a close. Brissot defended the clubs as exemplifying ideals of open discussion and rational deliberation in a free society; he placed them among the essential media of communication through which public opinion was formed and translated into political will (Brissot 1791). But Robespierre opted for a more explicitly classical republican language in assigning to the clubs 'the watchfulness that reason imposes even on people who have enjoyed liberty for centuries'. Efforts to deny them this role, he maintained, could only derive from the selfish interests of the corrupt and the ambitious, those who had set their personal interests above the common good. 'Only virtue can unearth this kind of conspiracy against the patriotic societies. Destroy them, and you will have eliminated the most powerful restraint against corruption' (Baker 1987b, pp. 278–86).

Virtue, corruption, conspiracy: this lexicon was to permeate Robespierre's language during the coming months as he called from the Jacobin Club for constant surveillance of the Legislative Assembly. In the most general terms, this distrust of the representative body derived from a classical republican identification of liberty with active political participation. In particular, it was coloured by his opposition to the property-based regime under which the new deputies had been elected. That the vote was a function rather than a right, and could thus be exercised more rationally by some citizens than others, was a proposition utterly antithetical to the republican conception of freedom. Marat had attacked it bitterly, as had the radical democrats in the Cordelier Club. Robespierre had been no less adamant that the right to vote inhered in citizens by virtue of their membership in the sovereign body of the nation, not as a binary function of their individual capacities. 'There are not two ways of being free', he insisted, 'one must either be entirely free or become enslaved again' (Robespierre 1910–59, VII, p. 164).

Accordingly, Robespierre constantly warned during the life of the Legislative Assembly of a crisis that would lead to the return of despotism. Celebrating *défiance* as the watchword of a people who could never sleep with impunity, he denounced the war plans of the Brissotin leaders of the Assembly as serving only the ministerial ambition, financial corruption, and military turpitude that would destroy liberty. War would only breed ambition among generals while fostering the power of the court to corrupt. It would create 'a crisis that can lead to the death of the political body' (Robespierre 1910–59, VIII, p. 86).

Create a crisis it did, exacerbating all the political tensions that had been built into the Constitution of 1791. As the king exercised his veto power against measures to punish counter-revolutionaries (*émigrés* and recalcitrant priests) and attempts to organise the defence of Paris by revolutionary activists summoned from the provinces (*fédérés*), so the veto was pilloried as the means by which a hostile monarch was now frustrating the will of the people. As the Legislative Assembly itself hesitated to respond to demands for the king's suspension or replacement, or for an appeal to the people in the primary assemblies, so it too was accused of betraying the general will by the Parisian *sections* – the assemblies of voters within Paris which declared themselves in permanent session. By the time Robespierre announced to the Jacobins in July 1792 that 'the great crisis we have reached is the conspiracy of the majority of the deputies of the people against the people', he was following, rather than leading, a popular movement to which he and Marat had offered a powerful language (Robespierre 1910–59, VIII, p. 417). The attack on the Legislative Assembly was clear: 'the source of all our evils is the absolute independence in which the representatives have placed themselves in regard to the nation', Robespierre proclaimed. 'They have recognized the sovereignty of the nation, and they have annihilated it. They . . . have made themselves sovereigns, which is to say despots. For despotism is nothing but the usurpation of sovereign power' (Robespierre 1910–59, VIII, p. 416). This was a call to popular insurrection – not simply against the monarch, but against the Representative Assembly as well. That insurrection came in August as the crowd invaded the Tuileries Palace to force the king's dismissal.

The overthrow of the constitutional monarchy, the subsequent declaration of a republic, the replacement of the Legislative Assembly by a National Convention charged to draw up a new constitution, demands for (and, in the case of the September Massacres, dramatic popular acts of) revolutionary justice against those who had defended the king, betrayed the people, or could otherwise be suspected of conspiring to destroy the Revolution: all of these could be seen as logical implications of the Parisian uprising of August 1792, understood as the decisive intervention of a people to save itself from a crisis of the political body issuing only in liberty or death. The debate over whether to try the king was also, in part, a debate over the legitimacy of the insurrection that had overthrown him (Walzer 1974). Against the Girondins, who were eager to preserve some vestige of constitutionalism, Robespierre insisted that punishing the king had to derive from an act of political will rather than any judicial decision. The king had been tried and condemned by an act of insurrection, carried out in the name of *salus populi*. To discuss further the monarch's culpability was to allow the possibility of his innocence, thus admitting the potential guilt of the sovereign people that had overthrown him by insurrectionary action. It was to put the Revolution itself on trial. Instead, Robespierre declared, Louis must die that the *patrie* might live. His new disciple, the young Saint-Just, stated the republican theme even more succinctly: 'No man can reign innocently . . . Every king is a rebel and a usurper' (Baker 1987b, p. 306).

The language of revolutionary will escalated once the Convention decided to try Louis XVI, and especially once the Girondins, fearing the domination of a minority within the Assembly whose power derived from the support of Paris activism, started talking of an appeal to the entire people to ratify the deputies' judgement. 'I do not recognize majority and minority here', Robespierre exclaimed in condemnation of this idea.

The minority retains an inalienable right to make heard the voice of truth, or what it regards as such. Virtue is always in the minority on this earth . . . Hampden and Sidney were of the minority, for they died on the scaffold[6] . . . Socrates belonged to the minority, for he swallowed the hemlock. Cato was of the minority, for he tore out his bowels. (Baker 1987b, p. 317)

The reign of virtue was about to begin.

---

6 Robespierre here invokes seventeenth-century English patriots, inaccurately: John Hampden, who resisted Charles I over Ship Money in 1635, was not executed; Algernon Sidney, the republican, was, under Charles II in 1683.

4 The people's two bodies

For the Convention, as for previous National Assemblies, the issues raised by the initial yoking of the practice of representation to the theory of the general will remained paramount. Sieyès had solved the problem theoretically by arguing that a common will simply did not exist until formulated by the representatives on behalf of a nation of individuals who could never meet directly. This same theory underlay Le Chapelier's insistence that there could be no intermediary political bodies between the nation and its representatives. But it was decisively repudiated when the insurrection of August 1792 overthrew the Legislative Assembly (with the king) in the name of a general will embodied in the people as a whole. Henceforth, any decision of the representatives (or any other agents of government) could be indicted as expressing a particular rather than a general will. Accordingly, the will of the deputies had to be made identical with that of the nation in some way or another. The difficulty of achieving this end was further compounded, however, by the fact that the people found its most direct and immediate embodiment, vis-à-vis the National Assembly, in the Parisian crowd – whose will might or might not be deemed that of the people as a whole. As a result, the question of the relationship between sovereignty and representation necessarily entailed that of the relationship between Paris and the provinces.

The Girondins opted, in effect, for the provinces; they hoped to maintain the principle of representation by appealing to the principle of the sovereignty of the entire nation in the primary assemblies. This was the underlying goal of the constitutional project, drafted by Condorcet, behind which they put their declining political weight in the spring of 1793. As dictated by the insurrection of 10 August 1792, this Girondin Constitution was republican (proposing the replacement of the king by a council of ministers directly elected by the people) and democratic (at least to the degree that it would institutionalise universal male suffrage and eliminate the distinction between active and passive citizens). Consistent with the decisions of 1789, it also located the exercise of legislative power in a unicameral assembly free of those Anglo-American checks and balances that had been dictated elsewhere by 'the fear of innovation, one of the most fatal scourges of the human race' (Condorcet 1976, pp. 156–7).

Condorcet was radical, however, in his proposed manner of linking sovereignty and representation, which eliminated all forms of indirect representation (and their coincident possibilities for the development of particular corporate interests) in favour of primary assemblies that would choose members of the National Assembly and the Council of Ministers, censure the legislative body at any time, decide issues submitted to popular referendum (including constitutional revisions), and initiate demands for legislative action or a constitutional convention. His constitution also bore the mark of his continuing search for ways to transform political decisions from acts of arbitrary will into expressions of collective reason. His aim was to prevent any portion of the people from taking action that would subvert the sovereignty of the whole. Insurrection would be rendered redundant on the one hand, and usurpation of power by the representatives impossible on the other, by allowing as few as fifty citizens to set in motion the formal process by which the primary assemblies could require the legislative body to take up a particular issue or to summon a constitutional convention.

Condorcet thus sought to eliminate the threat of popular insurrection by institutionalising revolution: frequent recourse to the vote would provide that '*legal* means of resisting oppression' which he declared to be among the rights of man (Mavidal *et al.* 1862–1913, LVIII, p. 602). But this effort to produce a constitution that would resolve the political two-body problem found little favour in the Convention. For Saint-Just, its implementation of the notion of the general will was too abstract, denying expression to the 'material will of the people, its simultaneous will' (Saint-Just 1984, pp. 422–3); for Robespierre, it was simply a perfidious scheme to undermine popular sovereignty through a surfeit of elections. Its main fault, though, was its identification with the Girondins. Supported by them, it was condemned with them – appropriately enough by precisely that insurrectionary popular action it (and they) had aimed to prevent. Marching on the Convention as May turned into June 1793 the Parisian crowd sought, by purging the Assembly, to impose upon the legislative body the unity without which it could not be held to represent the general will inhering in the people. The Girondins once expelled, the Jacobins wasted little time in improvising a constitutional plan of their own. It was adopted by the Convention within a fortnight and ratified by popular referendum the following month.

Although it was immediately suspended in favour of the emergency government of the Terror, two features of this Montagnard Constitution are nevertheless worth noting: its consecration of the right of insurrection in the name of popular sovereignty, and its treatment of property. To ensure subordination of the legislative body to the popular will, it allowed the submission of legislation to popular referendum on the demand of a proportion of the primary assemblies. It also upheld insurrection, now declared 'the most sacred of rights and the most indispensable of duties', as the ultimate means of safeguarding the people from oppression by the deputies (Mavidal *et al.* 1862–1913, LXVII, p. 107). The *Conventionnels* sought to forestall the dangers of representation by a doctrine of real political presence: 'the people is always there'.

Metaphysical though it was in some respects, this political presence was also a physical presence, and one increasingly insistent in its demands for controlled prices on bread and flour, the essential means of subsistence. The Girondins had not wavered in upholding economic liberty in a free market as an undeniable consequence of the right of property. Robespierre, to the contrary, had insisted that property be understood not as a natural right but as a social institution guaranteed by the law, and hence subject to conditions established by it. Though he was careful to dismiss absolute social equality as a chimera, he clearly yearned for a society in which citizens would have that modicum of property assumed in the classical republican tradition to be the condition of civic virtue (Gross 1997).

The Montagnard Declaration of Rights retained property as a natural right, even as it made provision of subsistence an obligation of society. For the moment, however, subsistence was less an issue of rights than of revolutionary will. 'Food, and to get it, force for the law', became the watchword of the Parisian popular movement in the summer of 1793. It was a watchword effectively imposed upon the Convention by yet another popular demonstration, on 5 September, which urged the Assembly to 'make terror the order of the day' (Baker 1987b, pp. 342–3). Both the Law of Suspects and the General Maximum, the twin pillars of the Terror in its first phase, emerged as logical consequences of this act. In the language of the popular movement, the link between bread and the revolutionary exercise of sovereign will was an essential one. Indeed, it lay at the heart of the conception of the general will as inhering in a real physical body of the people.

The language of the Parisian popular movement, of the activists who gloried in the title of *sans-culottes* – signifying that they wore the trousers of the common man rather than the silken breeches of the aristocrat – was essentially one of physical embodiment, corporeal vitality, and active political energy (Sewell 1980; Soboul 1972; Sonenscher 1984). Sovereignty was seen to inhere in the people as a political body, the entire body of citizens bound together in the unanimity of its common will. But it also inhered in the people as a social body, as those whose common existence was defined by the physicality of their relation to material nature and the immediacy of their need for subsistence. In this common relation to nature, the people was consubstantial not only physically but also politically: each member, each *section*, could speak for the whole. By this common relation to nature, the people was also delimited from other segments of the population. Accordingly, the *sans-culottes* now directed against the rich and idle the logic of exclusion first used against the privileged by Sieyès in *Qu'est-ce que le Tiers-Etat?* As a social body sustained by its work upon physical nature, the sovereign nation consisted of those who were actively engaged in that work. As a political body, it comprised only those who were actively identified with the general will – meaning those energetically committed to the Revolution. The 'aristocrat' to be expelled from the nation was now defined in terms not of his social status but of the energy and orientation of his will; suspected counter-revolutionaries, as defined by the Commune of Paris in October 1793, now included all 'those who, having done nothing against liberty, have also done nothing for it' (Baker 1987b, p. 339).

It followed from these arguments that sovereign power inhered, directly, immediately, and inalienably, in the body of citizens permanently assembled in the *sections*. There, its unity unimpaired by factitious distinctions between active and passive citizens and its will unimpeded by devious systems of indirect elections, the people could be found in the physicality of its existence and in the positivity of its will. This conception of inalienable popular sovereignty had several implications, not least of which was the demand that legislative acts be submitted to the sanction of direct popular approval prior to their acceptance as law. More immediately relevant to revolutionary politics, it entailed insistence upon the status of the deputies as mandataries sent to the Assembly not to decide on the people's behalf but to bear its sovereign will. Their fidelity to that will was to be assured by perpetual popular surveillance.

Hence the right now claimed for the people in the *sections* to address, control, and censure decisions of the Assembly. Hence the people's right to call individual deputies to account at the end of each session, or whenever such action seemed required; to revoke, dismiss, discipline, and replace unfaithful mandataries at will. Hence, ultimately, the people's right to rise in insurrection; to impose the popular will upon a divided assembly, as in August 1792; to purge refractory deputies, and to restore the representative body to the unity it must necessarily possess as a reflection of that will, as in June 1793. Hence, too, the people's right to demand and assert the use of terror to save the Republic by eliminating its enemies. 'Representatives, the days of mercy are past', the William Tell *section* warned the Convention in

November 1793. 'Let the avenging blade fall upon every guilty head, let no criminal be spared . . . Never forget the sublime words of the prophet, Marat: *Sacrifice 200,000 heads, and you will save 1,000,000*' (Baker 1987b, p. 340).

The Terror thus instituted at popular insistence was seen as a response to emergency conditions. But the idiom in which these circumstances were identified drew deeply on the classical republican language of 'crisis', with its images of the life and death of the body politic, of the need for energy and vigour in defence of the public safety, and of the imperative to regenerate a political organism threatened with annihilation. Billaud-Varenne, one of the chief architects of the government of the Terror, had already sounded the essential tones in a speech given to the Jacobin Club in June 1793. In 'the decisive moment of a violent crisis', he argued, the fatal half-measures of the past were no longer tolerable. It was essential to mobilise the 'energy of the people' to save the Republic, essential, above all, to 'excise from the political body the heterogeneous or decayed parts which enfeeble and infect it, and which lead it to annihilation'. In this view, the elimination of all those hostile or apathetic towards the Revolution was no more than 'the amputation of a gangrened limb which leads to death if the operation is too long delayed' (Billaud-Varenne 1793, pp. 25–7). The logic of the Terror, however, required more than the vigour of the people in the face of crisis; it demanded concentrated authority to direct the people's force. The popular movement, even as it imposed its energy on the Convention, opened the way for the representative body to control and channel that energy in the name of a unitary political will. Popular activism was to be increasingly curtailed and controlled as the Terror was put into place.

Billaud-Varenne made this clear in his speech of November 1793 introducing the legislation that established the detailed organisation of revolutionary government. The details added up to the extreme centralisation of power in the Convention and, more particularly, in the Committee of Public Safety that became its executive authority. Despotism, Billaud now argued, had established itself through 'that unity of action and of will resulting from an imperative and simultaneous execution'. Liberty had now to be established by the same means. The statement was a remarkable one, coming as it did from a figure who had dreamt two years earlier of a society in which power would be entirely diffused through the political body. But this switch from the ideal of a radical dispersal of power to that of its radical concentration simply highlights the essential contradiction within the logic of revolutionary discourse. The essential problem remained the same – 'to leave no more separation between the legislator and the people'. This time it seemed solvable only by making 'legislative centrality . . . the pivot of government' (Mavidal *et al.* 1862–1913, LXXIX, pp. 452, 454–5). To achieve a *volonté pulsatrice* (pulsating will) all intermediary governmental authorities had to be purged to eliminate resistance within the medium of executive power. Following Billaud's exhortation to 'restore robust health to the political body at the expense of its gangrened members', the Committee of Public Safety ordered all government bodies purged and placed under its immediate surveillance and direction (Mavidal *et al.* 1862–1913, LXXIX, p. 457). The same measures were applied to the popular movement itself. 'The political body, like the human body, becomes a monster if there are many heads', the Committee declared as the government of the Terror was put in place: 'the only one that must govern its movements is the Convention. Beyond the sphere it traces there lies the void and an infinite chaos where roam the frightening spectres of anarchy and despotism, dragging behind them this monster with its bloody chains' (Aulard 1889, IX, p. 168; Jaume 1989, pp. 343–7).

Understood in this way, the Terror marked a last, extreme effort to resolve the fundamental contradiction in revolutionary political theory by making the will of the people coincide with that of its representative body. In establishing a government that would be 'revolutionary until the peace', as Saint-Just demanded in October 1793, the Convention sought to eliminate all that impeded the immediacy and transparency of a unitary general will, all that separated the people from its representatives on the one side, and all that stood between the people and its enemies on the other. This was the meaning of Saint-Just's attack on government itself as the most dangerous enemy of all, since in the very act of executing the laws the agents of government could destroy the immediacy of the political will through inertia, corruption, or passivity (Baker 1987b, pp. 354–62). The impossible simultaneity in the formulation and execution of revolutionary laws for which Saint-Just called was needed to save the republic from its enemies. But it was also necessary to save the republic from its own logical contradictions.

5 Virtue, regeneration, and revolution

The law organising revolutionary government proposed by Billaud-Varenne was adopted in December 1793. In effect, all agents of government were made directly responsible to the Committee of Public Safety in a manner that sought to monopolise and control the exercise of revolutionary violence. Deputies who had resorted to the most extreme measures to suppress counter-revolutionary resistance in the provinces, and to wipe out the religious 'superstition' which they saw as sustaining it, were now to be brought under stricter central control. Agencies of local government were to be purged and the resulting vacancies filled by administrative mandate: 'Electoral assemblies are monarchical institutions', asserted Barère; 'it is particularly necessary to avoid them in a moment of revolution' (Mavidal *et al.* 1862–1913, LXXX, p. 636). No less importantly, the most radical vehicles of popular revolutionary extremism were to be either eliminated or radically curtailed. In short, in the hope of establishing liberty by emulating the model of despotism, as Billaud-Varenne had urged, the Convention brought all executive power into the hands of the Committee. Was this concentration of power to be feared? Not as long as the Committee was accountable to the Convention itself, argued Billaud-Varenne, for 'a large assembly can never become despotic' (Mavidal *et al.* 1862–1913, LXXX, p. 635). Not as long as the deputies were virtuous, proclaimed Robespierre. 'The greater the power of [revolutionary government]', he insisted, 'the freer and more rapid will be its action; the more it must be directed by good faith. The day that it falls into impure and perfidious hands, liberty will be lost' (Robespierre 1910–59, X, p. 277). Thus the reign of terror had necessarily to be the reign of virtue. Power had to assume the mantle of incorruptibility, rectitude the burden of power.

This was all the more true in so far as the Terror, in addition to resolving the contradictions of the revolutionary conception of sovereignty, had a second fundamental purpose: the regeneration of an entire people. Powerful throughout the Revolution, the language of regeneration was also extremely ambiguous (Ozouf 1989, pp. 116–57). The term could mean the miraculous resuscitation that would spring more or less immediately from the recovery of liberty, in which case the people needed only to rise from its chains. But it could also denote the necessary – and necessarily coercive – process of social refashioning to be undergone by a people that had been corrupted by centuries of despotism and superstition: for this purpose, excision of gangrened members of the body politic was imperative but not sufficient; a period of re-socialisation was also necessary to transform former subjects into active citizens. If these two notions of regeneration continued to co-exist throughout the Revolution, it was, nevertheless, the latter that came to the fore in 1793. It found its most dramatic initial expression in the radical de-Christianising movement announced by Chaumette to the *sans-culotte* activists in the Paris Commune and spread throughout the provinces by the bands of revolutionary extremists organised as revolutionary armies. Destruction of sacred images, closing of churches or their conversion into Temples of Reason, renunciation (often forced) of priestly vows and celebration of priestly marriages on the one hand, rituals of mockery and the improvisation of revolutionary cults on the other, were the principal manifestations of this movement. In the capital, it reached its height early in November when Jean Baptiste Gobel, the constitutional bishop of Paris, was pressured into renouncing his functions, and the cathedral of Notre Dame became the setting for a festival of the goddess Reason.

A principal instrument in this project of regeneration was the revolutionary calendar which was given shape along with the other institutions of the Terror in the autumn of 1793. The new calendar symbolised above all the revolutionary ambition to reshape humanity by transforming all social institutions – even those of time and space, which the Revolution now refused to share with its enemies. Time itself was to be cleansed of the crimes of history. The calendar would begin anew, shattering the baleful power of the sabbath by instituting a ten-day week, purging days of the stain left upon them by the memory of saints and kings, freeing them for commemorations of the Revolution, even imposing upon them a more rational (decimal) organisation of hours, minutes, and seconds.

Romme presented the calendar as the vehicle for recording and celebrating the regeneration of France. Fabre d'Eglantine, the poet who embellished its nomenclature of days and months, was more direct in conceiving it as an active instrument of de-Christianisation. Priests, he insisted, had used the power of images 'to subjugate the human species and enslave it under their dominion' (Baker 1987b, p. 366). The Revolution would use this same means to restore humanity to reason and nature. Henceforth the natural rhythms of the seasons and the cycle of agricultural labour would structure the experience of time and the meaning of action in the French Republic, while celebration of the Revolution, its events, virtues, achievements, and martyrs, would enliven days of feast and festival. Strikingly, at the moment of its most extreme assertion of political will, the Revolution still sought the rational reassurance of Nature; six months later, although he repudiated the de-Christianising passion of a Fabre d'Eglantine, Robespierre deployed similar naturalistic themes in his Festival of the Supreme Being. In this version of a Rousseauian civil religion, political duties were ritualised in terms of a natural gender differentiation and the stages of a natural progression of human life. In the rhythms of Nature, a people still in the process of revolution was offered relief from the terrible logic of revolutionary events and an image of the peaceful, regenerated social existence that was to come (Ozouf 1988).

For it now fell to Robespierre, dubbed the 'Incorruptible', to fix the reign of virtue and to chart the path towards regeneration; to give, in short, the ultimate definition of the Terror. To do so, he had to set a course between two options and eliminate the competing factions that pressed for them: the Hébertists, who combined their programme of de-Christianisation with calls for continuing popular activism, the social agenda of the *sans-culottes*, and an intensification of the Terror against all suspected enemies of the people; and the Dantonists, who argued for a relaxation of the Terror and a return to constitutional rule and the principles of the Declaration of Rights.

Among the Dantonists, no voice was more passionate in calling for a restoration of liberty than that of Camille Desmoulins. First published in December 1793, his journal, *Le Vieux Cordelier*, flaunted the revolutionary credentials of its author and the authority of its classical republican inspiration. Glorying in the task of offering the 'lessons of history' as revealed by Tacitus and Machiavelli, 'the greatest political analysts who have ever existed', it immediately took as its target the fundamental notion underlying the Terror: that liberty could be established by resorting to the methods of despotism. Conjuring up a Tacitean vision of the rivers of blood unleashed by the despotism of the Caesars, *Le Vieux Cordelier* left little doubt that its true target was the dangerous conflation of liberty with 'terror, the sole instrument of despots, [as] Machiavelli said' (Desmoulins 1987, pp. 40, 55). The words rankled with Robespierre. He remembered them when he gave to the Convention the most celebrated of all his speeches, in February 1794, defining the principles of political morality guiding revolutionary government. Repudiating those who believed 'that the plan of the French Revolution was written out in full in the books of Tacitus and Machiavelli', he accused them of failure to recognise the great task that had now to be accomplished: 'to fulfil nature's desires, accomplish the destiny of humanity, keep the promises of philosophy, absolve providence from the long reign of crime and tyranny' (Baker 1987b, pp. 369–70). This is revealing language. It suggests that, while he did not altogether abandon the idiom of classical republicanism in conceptualising the Terror, Robespierre was forced to reach far beyond its register.

For Robespierre, as for others, the idea of the Terror was intimately bound up with the classical republican notion of crisis. Indeed, by the end of 1793, as the Terror was being given its form, he was reviewing the entire Revolution as a series of 'crises', each of which had suspended the political body between life and death before finally propelling it forward. The problem confronting the Convention, he now insisted, was that of sustaining and intensifying republican virtue; it was necessary to 'ceaselessly rewind the sacred spring of republican government, instead of letting it slip'. But, even as the Incorruptible adopted classical republican language in speaking of the virtue that would secure the fate of the Revolution, this language underwent an important transformation. The virtue to which he referred was not simply a political effect of good laws that restrained human passions by identifying individual interest with the public good. It was innate in human nature. 'Happily, virtue is natural to the people, despite aristocratic prejudices', he insisted. 'Moreover, one can say, in a sense, that to love justice and equality, the people has no need of a great virtue; it is enough for it to love itself' (Robespierre 1910–59, X, pp. 355–6).

Paradoxically, this assertion of the natural goodness of the people allowed Robespierre to expand and moralise the Terror. The more good the people were, the more evil their enemies had to be, and the more ruthlessly directed against them the instruments of terror must be. The Terror, it might be said, was the coerced recovery of the natural goodness of the people. In Robespierre's speech advocating the cult of the Supreme Being, he marked the line between two kinds of egoism: one, the basis of despotism, was 'vile and cruel, isolating man from his fellows, which seeks an exclusive well being purchased at the cost of the misery of another'; the other, the essence of the republic, was 'generous and beneficent, conjoining our own happiness with that of all, attaching our own glory to that of the *patrie*' (Robespierre 1910–59, X, p. 446). This was a reworking of Rousseau's distinction between the natural *amour de soi* which the Citizen of Geneva found in every individual heart – and which he imagined could be preserved in society, and extended to the political body as a whole, through the operation of the general will – and the depraved *amour propre* he saw appearing as individuals in society became corrupted by their dependence one upon another. In Robespierre's late speeches, however, the corrupting force of society – the contamination that is shot through modern civilisation in Rousseau's analysis – is focused and given a face, albeit a hidden one, in the guise of the counter-revolutionary.

In Robespierre's discourse, the Terror was moralised. Civic virtue was no longer to be understood as an artificial identification of private interest with the public good; it could not be achieved unless and until natural virtue had been recovered and humanity returned to its true nature. In a profound shift, the classical republican discourse of will had thus been infused with the language of natural morality. Moreover, it had been rendered messianic by its placement within the world-historical framework of the Enlightenment. Ancient liberty had been local, the institutional achievement of certain polities only for so long as they could sustain that liberty against the force of human passions. The new freedom, by contrast, would be universal and emancipatory. The French Revolution was not one more engagement in a losing battle against political entropy. Instead it was a great leap forward in the progress of humankind.

This messianism of the French Revolution found no more ecstatic prophet than Saint-Just, for whom revolutionary government meant 'not war or a state of conquest, but the passage from evil to goodness, from corruption to probity, from bad maxims to good' (Saint-Just 1984, p. 809). In Saint-Just's speeches the mythical legislator of the classical republican tradition became the world-historical revolutionary working to regenerate human nature. 'Those who make revolutions, those who wish to do good, must sleep only in the tomb', he proclaimed to the Convention. 'A revolution is a heroic undertaking whose authors walk between perils and immortality. The latter is yours if you know how to immolate enemy factions' (Saint-Just 1984, pp. 761, 526). No longer the trait of the austere patriot of classical republicanism, who remained all too aware that the passions could never be controlled indefinitely, republican virtue had become metaphysical exhaltation, the sheer exhilaration of transforming a world.

Saint-Just's sentiments brought to completion the transformation of the idea of revolution that had been occurring since mid-century. By that date, 'revolution' no longer had as its primary meaning the astronomically inspired idea of a cycle bringing things back to their point of departure. When Rousseau proclaimed in 1762 that 'we are approaching the state of crisis and the century of revolutions' (Rousseau 1979, p. 194), he invoked an already conventional meaning of the term to describe radical mutations and disorders erupting within the flow of affairs. Linking this meaning to the notion of a state of crisis, the point at which the very existence of the body politic hung in the balance simply gave it added resonance from within a classical republican discourse attuned to the spectre of destructive forces within modern society. But 'revolution' had also been appropriated by the *philosophes* as they celebrated the very development of modern society. In their lexicon, the term was increasingly given a more positive and expansive meaning oriented towards a future of indefinite progress; it applied to the dynamic processes and effects of social and cultural transformation ameliorating the human condition.

In the course of the French Revolution – indeed, in the very conceptualisation of the 'French Revolution' – these competing notions were fused in an explosive combination. When Revolution was simultaneously experienced as a crisis and reoriented towards the future, when it became the awesome passage towards universal transformation, even to think of ending it was to lapse into counter-revolution. The Revolution could not be closed before the work of philosophy – the regeneration of humanity – was completed. The notion was a powerful one, destined for a momentous future.

23
British radicalism and the anti-Jacobins

IAIN HAMPSHER-MONK

1 Nostalgia and modernity

British radicals of the later eighteenth century derived their ideas from the various 'outs' excluded from the Revolution Settlement of 1689 and the Whig triumph of the early Hanoverian era: the 'Country' Whigs and city Tories, the supporters of the 'Good Old Cause' disappointed by the half-revolution of 1688, the Dissenters, and the deists (Colley 1981; Dickinson 1977, ch. 6; Pocock 1985, ch. 11; Robbins 1959). It was during the controversies surrounding John Wilkes, the continued imposition of religious tests, the American War of Independence, and, most spectacularly, the French Revolution that radical ideas developed.

The languages used – versions of classical republicanism, ancient constitutionalism, natural jurisprudence and contract, Dissenting tolerationism, and millenarianism – had been well established in the conflicts of the seventeenth and early eighteenth centuries. In the context of a new political and economic order characterised by the growth of empire, a military establishment, the explosion of commerce and credit, a court-dominated Commons, urbanisation, rural enclosure, and a creeping if never secure secularism, such 'radicalisms' were dispositionally nostalgic (Pocock 1984, 1985, ch. 11). An important feature of the period is the attempt by radicals to accommodate their inherited patterns of thought to new and irreversible features of society and to the aspirations of the growing urban middle and lower orders. This involved integrating received vocabularies with those derived from the philosophical psychology wrought by Locke and elaborated by Hume and David Hartley, and with the largely Scottish development of political economy and historical sociology (Claeys 1990; Hampsher-Monk 1991; Pocock 1985, chs. 2, 11; ch. 15 above).

A fragmentation and attempted resynthesis of discourses is characteristic of the period. Some syntheses were widely deployed: natural rights, conceived of aboriginally, were readily identified with those of an 'Ancient' or

660

specifically Anglo-Saxon constitution; both Tories and Whigs insinuated the operations of divine providence into the otherwise secular processes of constitutional development (or, in the case of 1688–9, disjuncture). Syntheses of natural rights and utility were often asserted, less often elaborated: whilst Joseph Priestley appealed to their providential coincidence (Canovan 1984), Sir James Mackintosh essayed a rule-utilitarian basis for rights (Mackintosh 1791, pp. 216–17). Less rigorously, Joseph Towers defended natural rights against Josiah Tucker as a means to society's and mankind's greatest happiness (Towers 1782, pp. 13, 45), whilst the Dublin United Irishmen innocently asserted, as one and the same thing, 'The rights of man in Ireland, the greatest happiness of the greatest number in this island' (qu. de Paor 1985, p. 166).

Confusingly, particular discourses were not the exclusive property of either radicals or conservatives. Thomas Paine invoked that patriarchalist trump card, the book of Genesis, in his startling claim that each generation had the same right as the first to order government as it saw fit (Paine 1989, pp. 76–7), natural rights were deployed to defend the *status quo* (Plowden 1792, pp. 19–28), a seemingly radical utilitarianism was used to urge political quietism (Paley 1837, pp. 132, 168), and ancient constitutionalism was brought to the defence of aristocratic and propertied privilege (Lee 1982).

Some scholars identify a pervasive Anglican political theology growing in strength at the end of the century (Bradley 1989; Clark 1985, pp. 216–34, 247–76). High Church Anglicans indeed insisted on a duty of absolute non-resistance, and, particularly in sermons commemorating the anniversary of Charles I's ('the martyr's') execution on 30 January, that God had ordained monarchy and a particular Anglican creed and form of church organisation (Hole 1989, ch. 1). Criticisms of contractualism derived from the high priest of seventeenth-century patriarchalism, Sir Robert Filmer, reappeared, citing the works of Nonjurors in their support. A small group even championed, on theological grounds, John Hutchinson's anti-Newtonian cosmology (Gunn 1983, pp. 164ff). High Church Anglicans stressed the importance of apostolic episcopal succession and trinitarianism in providing sacral underpinnings to the otherwise secular establishments of church and state (Clark 1985, pp. 216ff; Waterman 1996).

Theorists defending social and political order certainly recognised the fundamental need to motivate subjects' political (and moral) obedience in order to maintain any order, and especially the new commercial one, through the keeping of oaths and contracts. The most 'liberal' Anglican bishop of the period, Richard Watson, emphasised that 'the belief [in] a God governing the affairs of this present world, and a future state of rewards and punishments is among the most powerful means' which governments had at their disposal (Paley 1837, pp. 24, 129; Watson 1791, p. 10). Secular theories of obligation, always suspect, were perceived after 1789 as politically destabilising (Aldridge 1951). Paine's deistic *Age of Reason* (1794–5) confirmed to its enemies the long association between republicanism and an anticlericalism invariably construed as atheism, and it seriously undermined his support amongst radicals (Champion 1992, ch. 6; Claeys 1989b, ch. 7).

However, recent scholarship has suggested a broader Anglican consensus according to which, as Bishop Robert Lowth put it, 'Government in general is the ordinance of God, [but] the particular form of government is the ordinance of man' (Hole 1989, p. 150). Accepting that the moral authority of governments and their motivational efficacy derived from God left wide scope for differences about the mode and limits of that derivation. Bishop Watson combined a belief in the individual's divinely derived obligation to obey government with an affirmation of its popular appointment and a right of resistance where there was widespread popular dissatisfaction (Hole 1989, p. 20). Such a (Lockean) view amalgamated the disparate ideological stances required to legitimate both present constitutional stability and the undeniable constitutional violence of its establishment in 1688–9. Still, as another bishop astutely observed, the church too was committed, on Biblical grounds, to two contradictory principles, the right of resistance to tyranny and the duty of obedience to the powers that be (Markham 1774, pp. 8–13). Some, perhaps a majority at the start of the 1770s, saw human prudence settling the scope of each of these principles, the best expression of which, for Englishmen, was the constitution itself, making justifiable resistance paradoxically a question of constitutional precedent. For others, such as Edmund Burke, recourse to resistance, as in 1688, marked a deviation enacted in response to a necessity so extraordinary that no positive principle could capture it (Burke 1989, pp. 70–1, 2001, pp. 167–8).

The increased political instability of the 1790s produced heightened, and unusually widespread, millenarian expectations. Amongst others, the rationalist Priestley (1794) and the visionary William Blake (1791b) saw revolutionary events presaging the millennium (Fruchtman 1983; Garret 1975, ch. 6; Morton 1952). Others claimed themselves to be divine instruments. In 1794 Richard Brothers announced he was the 'nephew of the Almighty', identified the French as the instrument of God's millennial wrath, and sought to lead England's converted Jewry to a new Jerusalem (Brothers 1794; Harrison 1979, ch. 4). Even the anticlerical and agnostic Wolfe Tone saw in the French expulsion of the pope from Rome 'a special providence guiding the affairs of Europe . . . to . . . the emancipation of mankind from the yoke of religious and political superstition under which they have too long groaned' (Tone 1826, ii, p. 464).

2 The Wilkites and pro-American radicalism

The first phase of radicalism emerged from the affair of John Wilkes in a series of issues – liberty of the press, the right of individuals to due process of law, the right of electors to choose their representative, and the right to publish reports of parliamentary proceedings – which all entailed mobilising support for a politics projected beyond a parliamentary elite. The Wilkite movement established a vital extra-parliamentary political space for popular national politics. Wilkes was no theorist, but his personalisation of radical struggle was an effective literary and political device going back to John Lilburne and John Bunyan.

His struggles focused controversy upon the question of whether the House of Commons carried its own inherent legitimacy, or whether (and if so how) it derived its legitimacy conditionally and revocably from 'the people' (Brewer 1976, ch. 9; Cannon 1973, p. 61). Wilkes asserted a popular basis to government and the existence of entrenched popular rights, both of which undermined a strictly parliamentary sovereignty:

Many things are so closely woven with the constitution, like trial by jury, that they cannot be separated, unless the body of the people expressly declare otherwise . . . there are fundamental inalienable rights, landmarks of the constitution which cannot be removed. The omnipotence of parliament therefore, which is contended for, seems to me a false and dangerous doctrine. (*Parliamentary History* (1806–20), xix, p. 570)

Wilkes presented his claims as traditional 'Englishmen's rights' and shared with his opponents the assumption that precedent would identify them. When the Society of Supporters of the Bill of Rights sought to instruct candidates in the 1774 election, Burke denounced the practice to his Bristol electors as one 'utterly unknown to the laws of this land', a denunciation itself contemptuously dismissed by James Burgh as 'a novel Doctrine . . . a mere innovation' ('Speech at the Conclusion of the Poll': Burgh 1774–5, i, p. 186; Burke 1886, p. 447; Sharp 1775). Later radicals would shift the balance of their claims to more abstract and individual principles, yet Wilkite radicalism had already become decidedly demotic, urban, and commercial, organising new social groups on a larger scale, deploying fresh and often 'commercial' methods of political mobilisation – subscriptions, tokens, emblems – suited to a wider public, with a new language, more strident, assertive, and dismissive of the custodial character claimed for national institutions (Brewer 1976, p. 276; McKendrick *et al.* 1982, ch. 5).

The debate on the American War supervened upon the Wilkite agitation. Whilst Americans owed much to English 'Country' opposition (Bailyn 1967; Wood 1969), there was important ideological traffic in the other direction. The American Revolution was both a colonial rebellion and one of British subjects against their parliament in which the intellectual and political battles were fought on both sides of the Atlantic (Derry 1976, pp. 3–4; Pocock 1985, ch. 4). For example, Thomas Hollis had distributed, and John Almond had republished, the American James Otis's famous *Vindication of the British Colonies* (1765), to support British reformers at home.

Otis's aspirations were mild enough – the representation of the American colonies in a parliament which, together with common law, he recognised as the source of the colonists' rights. Yet his case propounded a thoroughly abstract Lockean argument, suggesting that James II's flight in 1688 had created a state of nature from which the Convention Parliament ('there was neither time for nor occasion to call the whole people together') had redeemed the nation and colonies by a kind of 'virtual' social contract (Otis 1764, pp. 33, 15). Three important texts for British radicalism derived from this American context: James Burgh's *Political Disquisitions* (1774–5) ('the reformers' Bible'), Richard Price's *Observations on the Nature of Civil Liberty* (1776), and 'Major' John Cartwright's *Take Your Choice!* (1776).

The most immediate issue in the American conflict – the conditions of legitimate taxation – raised, in an imperial context, questions with important domestic constitutional undertones. These involved considerations of the relationship between the parts (constitutional as well as geographical) of the empire, of the concept of representation, and of the location of sovereignty.

One view saw the king-in-parliament as sovereign over imperial provinces as it was over Britain; but viewing the king as separate and co-ordinate with Lords and Commons allowed the theoretical possibility of equal and co-ordinate provincial parliaments. If the English (British) parliament was a purely local body, the American colonies ought to possess such parliaments too (Koebner 1961, pp. 206ff). Taxation was otherwise illegal, since there could be 'no taxation without representation'.

The case of Ireland was ominously parallel. Granville Sharp reasserted William Molyneux's claim to Ireland's legislative independence as a constitutional precedent for America (Sharp 1775, pt II). The Irish volunteer defence mobilisation during the American War became a political spearhead and forced the granting of nominal legislative independence in 1782. A National Convention held in Dublin in 1783 demanded electoral reform, which Henry Flood unsuccessfully moved in the Irish Commons. Franchise reform, nervously promoted by Lord Charlemont and Henry Grattan, continually foundered on the Catholic question (Cannon 1973, pp. 98ff).

These modest initial reforming aims were driven by a classical analysis of corruption which stressed the independence of the legislature from the executive within a mixed and balanced constitution. The imperial context complicated, without invalidating, this analysis. In Ireland in the 1790s, Tone argued that the submission of Irish legislators to English avarice was 'the indispensable condition of office'. The price exacted was 'to surrender . . . the commerce, the manufactures, the liberty, and independence of Ireland'. In a striking adaptation of the classical republican analysis to the conditions of commercial imperialism, Tone argued that, whilst in England political corruption advanced commercial ends, in Ireland politicians had traded the commercial development of their nation for the dubious privileges of a kept aristocracy (Tone 1796, pp. 12–15). Tone's case for Irish emancipation rested not only on 'nationalist' aspirations, but also on a constitutional analysis which revealed the full independence of Ireland to be the only means of achieving true legislative independence (formally granted in 1782) from the pervasive influence of the (British) executive (Dunne 1982, pp. 47–8).

If representation had to be not only independent of the executive but inclusive of all those represented, many domestic communities were clearly no better represented than those in America. Claims that they were 'virtually' represented in parliament (a concept of representation widely denigrated by radicals, but with a pedigree going back to the Elizabethan theorists Sir Thomas Smith and Richard Hooker), got the response: 'that our brethren and fellow subjects . . . ought not to be deprived entirely of their natural rights and liberties, merely because our own liberties are not entirely perfect!' (Sharp 1775, pp. 8–9).

A focus on the link between taxation and representation led not only to demands for the representation of nations within the empire and new communities within the nation, but also from new classes within the community. If representation was virtual, so ought taxation to be, observed Cartwright wryly (1782, p. 17). More insistently since, via the excise, every man paid taxes, so every man ought to be enfranchised (Brewer 1976, p. 20). By contrast, reformers seeking the recovery of legislative independence could not support extensions of the franchise beyond the point at which voters were independent enough – propertied enough – to be themselves free from being influenced. There was certainly universalist potential in the widely cited Roman Law maxim that laws that affect all should be agreed by all, yet unequivocal support for universal manhood suffrage was still rare. Major Cartwright was almost alone in championing the undiluted and (at this stage somewhat eccentric) claim that 'personality is the sole foundation of the right of being represented: and that property has nothing to do with the case' (Cartwright 1776, p. 35).

Even moderate reformism crystallised the distinctly Augustinian anti-radicalism of Soame Jenyns, who saw human nature as necessarily fallen, and, following Hume, defended parliamentary and political corruption as a necessary means of political control. 'Every governor', he thought, 'is in the situation of a gaoler, whose very office arises from the criminality of those over whom he presides.' Purging corruption would destroy the operation of self-interest, leaving the politician without 'attractive influence, to enable him to draw together the discordant particles' (Jenyns 1790, III, p. 276, II, p. 245). Some radicals worried about the competence of an independent Commons within or without a balanced government. Absolute parliamentary sovereignty, apparently claimed over America, was, wrote Sharp tellingly, 'a kind of popery, in politics' (Sharp 1775, pt II). For Burgh, the principles of 1688 required that 'the king and government are in all cases responsible to the people, and that a majority of the people can at any time change the government' (Burgh 1774–5, I, p. 200), a position which Paine would advocate in *Common Sense* (1776), and which raised the issue of how governments could be balanced and limited without kings or lords.

An important legacy of this period was the creation of extra-parliamentary associations, a force for the dissemination of pamphlets, 'political education', and political mobilisation. The 'association' was public opinion emerging in and through political practice (Black 1963; Parssinen 1973). In articulating the relationship of the people to government, the association's status was as equivocal as that relationship was perceived to be. For Wyvill and most county associators outside London, it was merely a particularly active and concerted form of petitioning. Even Burke momentarily, *in extremis*, conceded resort to that 'most unpleasant remedy', 'the interposition of the body of the people itself' (Burke 1993, p. 181). Others, particularly in Westminster, and in the Society of Supporters of the Bill of Rights, invoked claims of a direct and popular sovereignty. Burgh likened the relationship between people and government to proprietors and directors of a company. Like proprietors, the associated people could discipline their trustees, and even 'new-model the whole government' (Burgh 1774–5, I, p. 222). John Jebb declared a national convention of county associations competent to override a corrupt Commons (Jebb 1787, pp. 479–80).

Yet, despite apparently universalist formulations, these ideas were enmeshed in traditional assumptions about the political incapacity of ordinary people and the persistence and inviolability of existing constitutional arrangements. Although Burgh thought all, even 'wretched', householders had a right to vote, his proposed convention was to be summoned by 'all men of property'. He thought it 'not safe to teach [the people] to unite, and to give them the means of knowing their own strength' (Burgh 1774–5, I, pp. 43, 435). Jebb, whose convention superseded the corrupt Commons, nevertheless regarded it as co-ordinate with the king and lords (Parssinen 1973, pp. 506, 509). Articulating positions from which truly subversive conclusions would later be drawn, radicals before 1789 were still predominantly 'nostalgic' and constitutionalist, seeking the restoration of an original polity or some essential dimension of it – purity, independence, balance – or some ancient equivalent in representation for new taxpayers.

The most ingenuous arguments invoked an 'ancient constitution', bequeathed by sturdy yet entirely fanciful Anglo-Saxon democrats who elected both their king and an annual witenagemote (the purportedly ancestral House of Commons), reinforcing liberty through the jury system and a citizen militia. English constitutional history was a progressive corruption of that golden age, beginning with the notorious 'Norman Yoke', and pursued through such tyrannies as the Septennial Act (1716), and the maintenance of a war economy (Cartwright 1776; Hulme 1771). Innovating through appeal to the past was congenial to a political culture with a 'powerful prepossession to antiquity' (Burke 1989, p. 82), yet it bound radicals to primitivist and historically naive thought patterns, inhibiting their full engagement with issues raised by new political and economic contexts.

Such arguments would not disappear with the French Revolution; indeed they enabled radicals to pursue reform whilst rejecting French ideas – a possibility anti-Jacobins sought to deny them by exposing Anglo-Saxon realities. However, arguments based essentially around individuals, often their 'rights', but especially, as opponents noted with alarm, involving the 'right of individual judgement', became increasingly prevalent. Vital sources of such arguments were the ideas already emerging from 'Rational Dissent'.

3   Rational Dissent

'Rational Dissent' emerged via Arminian and Socinian defection from old Presbyterian Dissent, joined by some notable Calvinist Independents such as Price and Priestley, and by Unitarian exiles from the Anglican ministry (Haakonssen 1996b). The leader of these last, Theophilus Lindsay, having unsuccessfully petitioned in 1771 (the Feathers Tavern Petition) to abolish clerical subscription to the creed of the Church of England contained in the Thirty-Nine Articles, established the first openly Unitarian congregation. Such reinvigorated Rational Dissent revived the toleration debate, provoked the paranoia of some Anglicans who saw the constitution of church and state under threat, and encouraged leading Dissenters in turn to fear revived persecution (Fitzpatrick 1990; Seed 1985, p. 316).

Doctrinally, socially, and in tone and orientation, Rational Dissent contributed hugely to the development of radical political ideas (Haakonssen 1996b). Its non-trinitarian theology, purged of 'mystery', negated as false or irrelevant those tenets which established empirical connections between the godhead and forms of ecclesiastical and political authority, particularly the link between the divinity of Christ and the apostolic succession of priests in the state religion (Waterman 1996). This left secular magistracy, in the view of many opponents, dangerously exposed. Dissenting stress on free and rational methods of enquiry challenged the fideism of High Church Anglican theology and politics alike (Clark 1985, pp. 279–89, 315–35; Watts 1978, pp. 464ff).

Such intellectual traits also brought secular success, and Dissenters' commercial, academic, and intellectual prominence gave them an influence disproportionate to their numbers (Seed 1985). Evincing a predilection for rationalist philosophy and Lockean politics, they commonly adopted natural rights or consequentialist theories of political authority, and their account of political obligation, like their theology, stressed the quality of the individual's own judgement (Stafford 1992). Their focus on personal conviction and self-examination – a fundamental tenet of their religious position, leading to heterodox practices even within congregations – was, as opponents feared, carried into secular politics, and towards demands for universal toleration and a personal, not propertied, basis for representation.

With non-trinitarianism still technically illegal (Barlow 1962; Furneaux 1770, pp. 5–7) it was, thought Priestley, 'hardly possible that we should be other than friends to the civil liberty of our fellow citizens' (Priestley

1817, XXII, p. 263). Yet Dissent, originally a means to a religious end, had now become a civil principle in itself. Unlike their puritan forebears, late eighteenth-century Dissenters claimed to dissent not 'on account of scruple with regard to certain ceremonies . . . nor liturgy and offices . . . [but] because we deny the right of any body of men, whether civil or ecclesiastical, to impose human tests, creeds or articles' (Kippis 1772, pp. 25–6). Priestley urged universal toleration, and invited even 'persons who disbelieve Christianity, and revelation in general' to contribute to his *Theological Repository* (Priestley 1769, p. x). Such eager heterodoxy confirmed Burke's suspicion that some Dissenters pursued toleration from a zeal 'not for the diffusion of truth, but for the spreading of contradiction' (Burke 1989, p. 63, 2001, p. 158).

Richard Price's *Observations on the Nature of Civil Liberty*, the most famous and theoretically self-conscious English work of the American rebellion, was a product of this milieu. It had fifteen London editions in 1776 alone. Followed by a second tract, *Additional Observations* (1777), it was reprinted with further material in 1778 as *Two Tracts on Civil Liberty*, also much reprinted (Thomas *et al.* 1993). Price was already famous for his *Review of the Principal Questions and Difficulties in Morals* (1758) where, drawing on Ralph Cudworth's Platonism, he defended a moral intuitionist position, both against those (characteristically High Church Anglicans) who derived morality from God's will, and against the naturalistic 'moral sense' ethics of Francis Hutcheson and emergent utilitarianism.

Two features of Price's ethics exemplified his Dissent and structured his politics: the extensive claims of moral obligation and the requirement to act from sincere individual conviction. These two principles made political involvement a matter of pervasive duty and precluded deferential or unreflective habitual activity. Under these conditions, and where liberty allowed, moral and political progress was possible. This in turn grounded important assertions of inalienable rights: 'no people can lawfully surrender or cede their liberty', and even if they did 'they have a right to emancipate themselves as soon as they can' (Price 1991, pp. 89, 33).

Price's conception of liberty was 'self-direction, or self-government' (Price 1991, p. 22). Any extraneous power over self-directed action was slavery. Yet moral liberty was freedom to pursue a higher self, identified with our rational, moral natures. Price's Socratic belief in the impossibility of freely and knowingly doing wrong (p. 81) epitomised the axiom of moral perfectibility under conditions of true freedom and reason to be found, in varying degrees of philosophical precision, from Paine to William Godwin, and contrasted with the sense of the individual's moral fragility which characterised the opposition to Jacobinism.

Identifying government with corruption, intrigue, and hereditary privilege, Price, like most radicals, advocated a minimal role for it. Properly considered, it was 'nothing but an institution for guarding against the invasion' of properties and lives, and properly constituted it does 'not take away the rights of mankind, but protects and confirms them'. Price argued that true civil liberty existed only where there was 'security for the possession of it' (Price 1991, pp. 81–2), and, against the Whigs' custodial view of politics, this required that 'every independent agent in a free state [has] a share in the government of it, either . . . personally, or by . . . representatives'. Representation had to be complete, not restricted spatially or socially, freely chosen, freely acting, and of short duration (pp. 80, 78–9).

Both the *Two Tracts'* 'conclusion', assessing the state of liberty in Britain, and Price's later assessment of the prospects for the newly independent United States, showed how easily thinkers moved from the language of natural rights to the language of virtue and corruption, which in this case had both puritan and republican valencies (Price 1991, pp. 9–10). England evoked irresistible parallels with Rome, which 'sunk into slavery in consequence of enlarging its territories, becoming the centre of wealth . . . and the seat of universal empire'. Without strenuous moral effort 'by a common and natural progress' Britain may expect to go 'the round of other nations once free' (pp. 99–100). Like other radicals Price thought that simplicity of manners, an independent yeomanry, and equality of property promised as well for American liberty as their absence threatened British. Yet even simplicity and virtue could yield to depravity, equality could be lost, liberty languish, and civil government degenerate (p. 208).

Price correctly identified two prevailing accounts of civil government. The first was that 'civil government is an expedient contrived by human prudence for gaining security against oppression', so that 'the people (that is the body of independent agents in every community) are their own legislators [and] . . . governors are only public servants'. The second saw government as 'an ordinance of the Deity'. On this latter dangerous and growing view, the people are 'placed by their Maker in the situation of cattle on an estate', and the power of those in government 'is a commission from heaven, unbounded in its extent, and never to be resisted' (Price 1991, p. 15).

Responses to Price confirmed his analysis. John Wesley typified the political conservatism of the evangelical movement by posing Filmerian objections: whether 'the people' included women, children, and the poor; and how an individual's consent could be the source of a civil community's right to punish with death, or compatible with the majority principle. Price's principles, Wesley concluded, would 'unhinge all government, and plunge every nation into total anarchy', because although government is a trust, it is a trust from God, not from the people (Peach 1979, pp. 248–52). In response to his critics, Price claimed his principles were 'the same with those taught by Mr Locke' (Price 1991, p. 20).

Joseph Priestley, the other Dissenting political theorist of comparable stature, exemplified the optimistic, radical, progressive individualism which Burke would so anathematize. Celebrated as a scientist, the polymath Priestley saw an intimate connection between the practice and culture of science and that of the state of true civil and political liberty (Kramnick 1986). The methods that had already brought success in science – free enquiry, distrust of inherited knowledge, empirical investigation – were to be the redemptive agents of a transformation of religious and political life, achieved through the progress of the intellect. The reformers, 'laying gunpowder, grain by grain, under the old building of error and superstition', would overturn 'in a moment . . . that edifice, the erection of which has been the work of ages' (Priestley 1791a, p. 100). Whilst government was a 'great instrument of the progress of the human species', its task was to free individuals to do for themselves everything except in that small area 'in which the public can make better provision' (Priestley 1993, p. 134).

Although often linked with Price, important differences separated Priestley from his contemporaries. Priestley emphasised the benefits of free trade, which Price had warned the Americans against. Priestley invoked both natural rights and utility, which to some earlier commentators indicated confusion (Lincoln 1938, p. 159). However, his argument presumed a God concerned with the fulfilment of His creation, to which end natural rights and social utility were congruent means: 'the very idea . . . of right is founded upon a regard to the general good of the society'. He happily ascribed natural rights to individuals whilst warning that 'all claims of individuals inconsistent with the public good are absolutely null and void' (Priestley 1993, pp. 25, 31). He was confident that the observance of individual rights would optimise progressively defined utility (Canovan, 1984). From the early 1770s Priestley became a materialist and determinist, a difference aired with Price in a famous pamphlet exchange (Priestley 1778). Their defences of civil liberty accordingly rested on different grounds. For Price, political liberty was an analogue and an entailment of the moral liberty of the will. Priestley's necessitarianism precluded this: civil liberty was instead a precondition for moral and general progress, justified on instrumental and consequentialist grounds.

This led to what has been perceived to be an important difference in their political analysis. Civil liberty for Price entailed political participation, 'by every independent agent', directly or through election of representatives. Priestley drew a distinction between political liberty – the right of exercising magistracy – and civil liberty – freedom from political interference, a distinction well rehearsed by 'scientific Whigs' (Priestley 1993, p. 12). Nevertheless, whilst Priestley laid greater stress on civil liberty as a means to progress, both men acknowledged political liberty as a safeguard of civil, seeing the threat of tyranny in confining magistracy or the election of representatives in a few hands. Although Price supported the principle of universal suffrage, in practice he joined Priestley in considering personal independence a condition of political agency.

In this they were not unusual: many radicals supporting universal suffrage in principle tacitly excluded not only women but also other groups on the grounds of their lack of independence, ethical probity, education, or responsibility. Here, civic arguments, rich in discriminations concerning the circumstances affecting political personality, were widely invoked, even in conjunction with foundational natural rights (Hampsher-Monk 1979; Wyvill *et al.* 1782, pp. 27–8, 83–4).

Indeed, before the French Revolution, opponents of radicalism were generally clearer about the implications of universalist principles than were the reformers, who usually had limited aims. During the American debate, Burke already saw universal individual rights as a dangerous hostage to fortune: 'When you come to examine this claim of right, founded on self-government in each individual, you find the thing demanded infinitely short of the principle of the demand' (Burke 1888, III, p. 146).

Josiah Tucker's *Treatise concerning Civil Government* (1781) was a sustained critique of natural right and contractualism, which he had already denounced as essentially 'the resolves of the Cromwellian Levellers worked up into a system' (Tucker 1773, p. 96). A strict adherence to the right of individual judgement in matters political produced anarchy, rendering majority decisions illegitimate, and allowing men and women to pay or not pay taxes, obey or disobey laws as they pleased (Tucker 1781, pp. 36, 49, 33). Praising, like Burke, the English lack of inquisitiveness 'concerning the original title of the reigning powers', Tucker opposed to individual rights and consent a 'quasi-contract', and the associated doctrines of 'implicit consent, tacit agreement, implied covenant, virtual representation, and the like' (Tucker 1781, pp. 85, 139). Humans were naturally sociable and unequal, yet mutually needy, some naturally submissive, some not; this was quite enough to account for and legitimate the emergence of both political society and hierarchy without 'tedious [and] uncertain experiments' in contractualism (Tucker 1781, pp. 124–8, 134, 137).

The 'quasi-contract' retained some critical reach over arbitrary or absolute government without the awkward populism seemingly entailed by individual consent. Tucker, like Burke, resolved the tensions in the Revolution Settlement by combining a right of resistance with an insistence on the inscrutability of its precise application. In this, he claimed, scripture and constitutional theory were at one: 'the boundary line between resistance and obedience is no more marked out by the laws of England, than it is in the Gospel of Christ', such imprecision being a just and proper caution against demagogy and popular licentiousness (Tucker 1781, p. 421).

4   Edmund Burke and the debate on the French Revolution

Price's famous anniversary sermon for the Glorious Revolution supervened upon an already extensive debate about the right of individual judgement. Although the French Revolution itself provoked deep divisions in attitudes, it was Burke's celebrated response to Price's sermon, *Reflections on the Revolution in France* (1790), linking it with English politics, that shaped the ensuing argument. Price insisted on the status of magistrates as 'public servants', supposedly established in 1689 through declaring the following rights: 'First, the right to liberty of conscience in religious matters. Secondly, the right to resist power when abused. And thirdly, the right to choose our own governors, to cashier them for misconduct, and to frame a government for ourselves' (Price 1991 [1789], pp. 189–90). Price broached subjects which became central to the debate between radicals and anti-Jacobins: the identification of the nation with its people, not its land, the contingency and partiality of our patriotic affection (and by implication other partial and unexamined sentiments) in comparison with a more universal benevolence, and the contested character of the Revolution of 1688 (Price 1991, pp. 178, 190ff). These were themes taken up by Paine, Wollstonecraft, Mackintosh, and Thelwall.

The exchange between Price and Burke reinforced the emblematic yet ambiguous status of 1688 as the link between the French Revolution and domestic reform. Burke saw Price's radical account of 1688 as a Trojan horse insinuating dissatisfaction with the Revolution Settlement, 'a great [but] . . . by no means perfect work' (Burke 1989, pp. 64–5, 2001, p. 160; Price 1991, p. 191). Yet, in claiming that French principles were those of 1688 perfected, radicals risked, and continually found themselves arguing on the basis of, appeals to precedent. Instead of themselves asserting the popular basis of government, they were continually diverted into discussing whether or not such a basis had already been established in 1688.

Natural rights arguments, whilst vulnerable to charges of primitivism, evaded and challenged preoccupation with the constitutional past. Although not prominent in Price's sermon, they epitomised French aspirations and were at the centre of Burke's attack and radical responses (Pendleton 1982). They moved the debate on to a higher level of abstraction in pitting the rights of each individual to exercise political judgement against the authority of history embodied in established institutions, customs, and the family. Even when advanced for domestic use in France such arguments had universal implications. As Burke stressed, abstractly formulated claims of right were implicitly applicable to all countries regardless of circumstance. The French Revolution was thus essentially an international ideological crusade: 'a revolution of doctrine and theoretic dogma. It has a much greater resemblance to those changes which have been made upon religious grounds, in which a spirit of proselytism makes the essential part. The last [such] revolution . . . in Europe, is the Reformation' ('Thoughts on French Affairs', 1791: Burke 1989, p. 341). The Jacobins, by forcing men into adopting their system, or to live 'in perpetual enmity', sought to make a 'violent breach in the community of Europe' ('Letter on a Regicide Peace', 1796: Burke 1991, p. 249).

Earlier commentators stressed Burke's debt to a broadly Thomist natural law tradition (Canavan 1960; Stanlis 1958; Wilkins 1967). However, his reasons for anticipating the Revolution's 'departure from every one of the ideas and usages, religious, legal, moral, or social of this civilized world' ('Regicide Peace': Burke 1889, p. 215) drew on the modern rights tradition of Grotius, Selden, and Hobbes. Burke endorsed assertions of the incompatibility of natural rights with social life (Burke 1989, p. 110; 2001, p. 218). Natural rights could only be realised through the utter destruction of society, which rests instead on painfully acquired conventions, a kind of continuing social contract 'between those who are living, those who are dead and those who are to be born' (Burke 1989, pp. 110–11, 2001, p. 261). The revolutionary assertion of natural rights would effectively reintroduce the state of nature, from which civilised life would have laboriously to be recreated ('Appeal from the Old Whigs': Burke 1992, p. 164).

Burke also stressed the Hobbesian implications in the epistemological indeterminacy of natural rights – social institutions could not be derived unequivocally from pure reason. Even so apparently obvious a device as the majority principle was 'one of the most violent fictions of positive law' ('Appeal': Burke 1992, p. 164). Convention and artifice were not deductions from reason, nor the product of 'rude' nature, but they were, nevertheless, vital to us: in this sense 'art is man's nature' (p. 169). States fortunate enough to have settled institutions, ruled by custom and precedent, not coercion, would be foolish to undermine them through disadvantageous comparison with abstract principles. Moreover, abstract secular ideas, as well as religion, could become the object of unstable 'enthusiasm' (pp. 164, 169, 182).

In 1791 Burke already saw the French undoing everything and having to set out on the long historical road from man's natural condition again. By 1795 this quasi-anarchy had become a system of government that 'has never been hitherto seen, or even imagined in Europe', whose unprecedented institutions were 'not explained by any common acknowledged rule of moral science'. He denounced the proposers of a 'regicide peace' for not recognising the *'peculiar* nature' of the war, not grounded in interests, but in which the enemy was 'an armed doctrine' that could not be opposed by the normal diplomatic means ('Regicide Peace': Burke 1889, pp. 206, 164).

Claims to a radically individualised natural right highlighted the qualities of the individual judgement required to exercise it, about which Burke had always harboured deep reservations. Drawing on Sir Edward Coke's and Matthew Hale's defence of English common law as the refined embodiment of an inarticulable collective historical experience, Burke, in a series of arresting images, defended the superiority of actual, extant institutions ('corporations') and psychological dispositions ('prejudices') as a product of collective reason far superior to that of any individual (Pocock 1960; Postema 1986, chs. 1–2). His reasons lay partly in a sceptical empiricist epistemology and partly in a belief, well explored by Hume and others, in the incapacity of reason or its products to engage our emotional or moral commitment: 'what would become of the world', he had asked, in his first published work, *A Vindication of Natural Society* (1756), 'if the practice of all moral duties . . . rested upon having their reasons made clear and demonstrative to every individual?' (Burke 1993, p. 11). For Burke, not only were the practical properties of rational schemes unpredictable, but also, in failing to elicit people's loyalty, they would, to be implemented, require coercion.

Burke defended constitutional continuity in general – without it 'no one generation could link with the other'. Men would become 'like flies of a summer', and so too would the established church and the constitutional settlement of 1689. Many radicals followed Price in identifying 1688 as a constitutional discontinuity which enacted the rights to choose, cashier, and frame government. Burke, conceding that it might then, if ever, have been possible, denied it had been done; moreover, 'Its not being done at that time is a proof that the nation was of the opinion that it ought not to be done at any time', but should, rather, retain the peculiarly providential form of a co-ordination of king, Lords and Commons (Burke 1989, pp. 145, 68, 2001, pp. 259, 165). He particularly defended the royal and aristocratic family as a vehicle of cultural transmission, and the need for large heritable landed properties as a 'sluggish' principle to balance the more energetic ones of ability and commerce.

This last enterprise recast the old connection between the monarchy and the authoritarian patriarchal family into an identity between a monarchical political culture and a newly emerged conception of domesticity and domestic virtue. The family was the nursery of sentiments upon which political and wider loyalties relied. Burke denounced 'universal benevolence' because he believed we necessarily 'begin our public affections in our families . . . our neighbourhoods, and our habitual provincial connections' as 'a sort of elemental training to those higher and more large regards' (Burke 1989, p. 244, 2001, p. 366). Only localised sentiments could generate that sustained commitment that ultimately, through wider circles of attachment, linked us to the state. Many anti-Jacobins stressed the reliability and honesty of untutored (loyalist) sentiment. By contrast, the professed and abstract internationalism of Price, Paine, and Godwin, the universalism of their arguments, the radicals' provocative adoption of republican styles ('comrade', 'citizen'), and their open communication with the French, especially after the war began, enabled its opponents to present radicalism as an emotionally cold creed, ignorant, careless, and ultimately destructive of local affections, familial and national (*Anti-Jacobin* 1798; Deane 1988, pp. 31, 53ff). Burke's portrayal of the revolutionaries as alchemical patricides boiling up their dismembered parents in a kettle, or rapaciously (even incestuously) invading the bedroom of their lady queen, entered popular loyalist consciousness, inspiring several famous cartoons. It enabled the drawing of a successful contrast with the constitutional piety of the English, and it established the identity Burke insinuated between familial affections and political duty: 'binding up the constitution of our country with our dearest domestic ties' (Burke 1989, pp. 121–84, 2001, pp. 260, 232, 185). At another level it confronted rationalist ethics with a popular ethical sentimentalism based on natural feeling.

Despite its scepticism about abstract analysis, *Reflections* can be read as reasserting a widespread mid-eighteenth-century paradigm – famously associated with Hume, although for Burke providentially underpinned – concerning the relationship between political and economic institutions and an epistemology which determined the nature and stability of the moral beliefs and public opinion supporting them. The established (especially Protestant) religion was believed best to support those beliefs, and a responsible (and suitably well-bred) government guaranteed both property rights and a church establishment.

The French National Assembly's lack of political experience, its litigiousness, enthusiasm for abstract schemes of government and finance, and its appropriation of church property, had, Burke thought, destroyed this always precarious balance, threatening to loose political power to those lower orders whom he famously called the 'swinish multitude'. Yet the Revolution was no accident. Jacobinism was 'the revolt of the enterprising talents of a country against its property' (Burke 1991, p. 241). Entrepreneurs, both intellectual and economic – philosophers and financiers – had engineered it, the former recruited by the latter to destroy the moral authority of an indebted *ancien régime* about to default. Worse for Burke, the new economic forces mortally threatened an irrecoverable moral culture, originating in feudal manners and on which civil life and the very possibility of modern commercial society depended (Pocock 1982). The church was vital in sustaining these moral standards. By seizing its capital, the 'monied men' both secured their loans and weakened moral resistance to their actions. The sale of French church lands to finance state debt violated virtually every shibboleth of eighteenth-century mainstream Whig statecraft, undermining the stability of property rights, the representatives' control over government revenues, and the security which the church needed to condition public moral opinion. By issuing *assignats* – the Revolution's paper credit – as both a unit of currency and a share in the as-yet-unrealised value of church lands, the French had implicated everyone in the desecration and turned every transaction into a financial speculation. In a single stunning metaphor Burke epitomised eighteenth-century horror at the volatility, and catastrophic social, economic, and epistemological effects, of unconstrained speculation. The French were 'the first who have founded a commonwealth on gaming'; they sought 'to metamorphose France into one great play table; to turn its inhabitants into a nation of gamesters; to make speculation as extensive as life . . . and to divert the hopes and fears of the people from their usual channels, into the impulses, passions, and superstitions of those who live on chances' (Burke 1989, p. 240, 2001, p. 362). Because his analysis derived from well-worn patterns of eighteenth-century discourse, Burke could substitute images for argument in relating economics to moral psychology. Yet evoking both epistemological and economic instability through 'speculation' and 'credit' was no pun where perceptions were shaped by social reality.

Burke's deep sense of the vulnerability of human institutions to both economic and philosophical rationalism renders his scepticism much more unsettling than any mid-century Toryism. His insight into the rationally ungrounded character of social institutions was ultimately rescued only by a faith in the providential ordering of the history which produced them. This highlighted the role of Christianity, the truth of which we must suppose 'in every transaction in life' ('Fourth Letter . . . Regicide Peace': Burke 1991, p. 119). In customs and manners, as well as doctrinally, Christianity underpinned European civilisation. To a century which prided itself on the rational moderation of religious enthusiasm, the Jacobins were a terrifying hybrid: rationalist atheistical fanatics. The revolutionary war was a showdown between irreligious barbarism and Christian civility.

The *Reflections* provoked extensive debate (Butler 1984; Cobban 1950; Pendleton 1982). Radicals, frustrated at the diffuse character of Burke's attack, particularly disputed two of his claims: first, that the capacities of individual reason, and particularly of the 'swinish multitude', were insufficient to master political complexities; secondly, that the assertion of individual natural rights would undo modern commercial society and civilised manners, returning society to a primitive economy, even to a Hobbesian state of nature. The first claim was widely attacked from the start; answering the second increasingly led radicalism into social and economic terrain.

Two early responses, Mary Wollstonecraft's *Vindication of the Rights of Men* (1790–2) and Paine's *Rights of Man* (1791–2), re-enforced 'natural rights' as the dominant radical discourse. Each attacked Burke's claim that natural and civil rights were incompatible. Far from being antithetical, 'every civil right has for its foundation some natural right pre-existing in the individual', the enjoyment of which needs protection (Paine 1989, p. 78). Natural right was 'such a degree of liberty, civil and religious, as is compatible with the liberty of every other individual . . . and the continued existence of [the social] compact' (Wollstonecraft 1995, p. 7).

Burke's praise for a prescriptive constitution so disfigured by violence and conquest – either Norman (Paine 1989, p. 87) or the more general 'rebellions . . . cabals, feuds, vices, superstition which shaped it' (Wollstonecraft 1995, p. 76) – was incomprehensible or sinister. If the British had a constitution, it was established 'not out of society' but by conquest 'over the people' (Paine 1989, p. 82). Paine and Wollstonecraft opposed their presumption of progress to Burke's claims of precedent, attempting a generalised deconstruction of the reverence he urged for inherited institutions, which were in fact 'settled in the dark days of ignorance . . . prejudices and most immoral superstition' (Wollstonecraft 1995, p. 11). Precedent – that vain 'presumption of governing beyond the grave' – epitomised lost freedom. State-of-nature and Biblical origins established the freedom and the moral and political equality of man, and every age was 'as free to act for itself, in all cases' as the first. Mankind was 'all of one degree', aristocratic distinctions being 'a sort of foppery' which are outgrown on reaching maturity, as first America and now France had shown (Paine 1989, pp. 55, 77, 89).

The principle of hereditary subordination, with monarchy as its institutional symbol, was conspicuously opposed to natural rights. Paine and Wollstonecraft both denounced Burke's meretricious identification of the natural family with the institutions of primogeniture and hereditary property, which in reality violated natural familial affection, sacrificing younger children to the eldest: 'Aristocracy has never but one child. The rest are begotten to be devoured' (Paine 1989, p. 91). Concentrating property, thought Wollstonecraft, inhibited early marriage; the repressed desires that ensued encouraged libertinage and coquetry (Wollstonecraft 1995, pp. 22–3).

Her argument contributed to a growing debate about the political implications of the family and domestic character formation. Wollstonecraft sought to recruit connections between gender and political morality for the radical cause. In her *Vindication of the Rights of Woman* (1792) she stressed the political character of the domestic arena and of women's confined roles there. The structure of the home reflected the flawed – because unequal – relations of the parents and so formed flawed characters in their children. The prevailing model of femininity – weakness and vulnerability – prevented women from realising a fulfilling role or even eliciting respect from their husbands (Wollstonecraft 1995, pp. 142–3). A projected second volume was intended directly to address women's claims to political rights (Wollstonecraft 1995, pp. 69–71).

However, the issue was captured by the anti-Jacobins and the apostates from radicalism, who stressed the family as the school of those natural sentiments upon which morality relied, and weak femininity and female chastity as the bases of the family. Pre-revolutionary sexual laxity and post-revolutionary easy divorce of the French (exemplified also in Wollstonecraft's own sexual career) were held responsible, through undermining the family, for the excesses of the Revolution (*Anti-Jacobin* 1798). Looking back, Mackintosh reflected, 'Purity is the sole school of domestic fidelity and domestic fidelity is the only nursery of the affections between parents and children, from children towards each other, and through these affections, of all the kindness that renders the world habitable' (Deane 1988, pp. 53ff; Mackintosh 1851, p. 119).

A further target of the radicals was Burke's overblown rhetoric – with more than a suggestion that support for the *ancien régime* was a self-delusion, a linguistic effect – 'living within the bastille of a word' – which could be dissolved through ridicule or plain speaking (Paine 1989, p. 89; Wollstonecraft 1995, p. 80). Scholars have increasingly echoed the participants in noting the rhetorical and linguistic dimension of the debate (Boulton 1963; Hampsher-Monk 1988; Lock 1985; Smith 1984). Several reformers made sustained analyses of the political power of linguistic codes and sought linguistic reform (Spence 1775a; Tooke 1786) or education for effective speaking (Burgh 1761; Cobbett 1820, Letter 1; Priestley 1763; Thelwall 1808). Paine's contribution to this subject was practical. Like Wilkes, he constituted his audience by invoking and inviting, through his tone as much as by his content, subscription to a demotic republic of political discourse (Boulton 1963; Philp 1989, p. 118).

Wollstonecraft, although less successful polemically than Paine, provided a more sustained theoretical analysis of Burke's rhetoric, linking his defence of family relationships and female vulnerability to two long-standing issues in eighteenth-century moral philosophy. She attacked as 'sentimental jargon' his claim, which she ascribed to 'common-sense' philosophy, that feelings could be uncritically identified with moral truth (Wollstonecraft 1995, p. 30). She pointed out the political significance of his own aesthetic distinction between the beautiful (the smooth, the soft, and the vulnerable) and the sublime (the rugged, awesome, and unfathomable). The identification of the political virtues with the sublime, and the domestic with the beautiful, became a justification for a separate morality for woman. Burke had argued in effect 'that nature, by making women little, smooth, delicate, fair creatures, never designed that they should exercise their reason to acquire the virtues that produce the opposite, if not contradictory, feelings'. His aesthetic was not only gendered, but also perpetuated a polarity between virtuous and sublime austerity, and corrupt beauty and refinement. On this view of virtue, respect for either beauty or women was impossible. Wollstonecraft rejected this opposition: 'there is a beauty in virtue, a charm in order'. This beauteous–virtuous–respectful nexus can only be achieved through liberty, since inequality 'impede[s] the growth of virtue by vitiating the mind that submits or domineers' (Wollstonecraft 1995, pp. 47–9). Wollstonecraft not only sought to politicise the undervalued domestic realm, but also attacked the gendered moral aesthetic polarity which re-enforced 'weak' female confinement to it. More widely, her argument can be seen as part of a quest for a republicanism consistent with modern conditions and sensibilities, cultured, polite, and commercial, cognisant of the contribution of the private to the public realm and the domestic construction of political personality.

In responding to Burke's claims about the perceptual and motivational inadequacy of individual reason, radicals initially denied that political needs, properly understood, were complex. Arguments parallelling the rational deists' attacks on religious mystery (some reprinted at the time) were deployed against the defenders of political 'mystery'. Priestcraft and kingcraft, mutually supportive, had recourse to the same paraphernalia of intellectual obfuscation. They created the ostensible complexity over which their expertise claimed to offer mastery. At the street level this point was made through ridicule (Eaton 1793–5; Spence 1793–5).

A second argument concerned a demotic 'progress of enlightenment'. Joel Barlow claimed that the 'the spirit of investigation, which the French Revolution has awakened . . . is stimulating people to pursue the enquiry, and will frequently lead them to pursue the remedy' (Barlow 1795). The light of political truth emanating from America, thought Paine, only needed, like the sun, to be seen to distinguish itself from darkness (Paine 1989, p. 120). The radicals could be regarded as secular enthusiasts, believing that rational conviction itself could achieve emancipation from their historical conditions (Pocock 1989, p. 26). It was precisely this possibility that Burke paradoxically both denied and feared.

Godwin's *Enquiry concerning Political Justice* (1793) provided the most theoretically elaborate claim that individual reason could indeed achieve emancipation both for the individual and, eventually, for society. Its target audience was not the artisanal debating clubs at which the works of Paine and John Thelwall were read and discussed, when the authorities and 'church and king' mobs allowed, but the rationalist culture of the theological and metropolitan margins (Philp 1986; Thale 1989). Substantially revised over its three editions, there is controversy even about the work's central positions. Godwin's criterion of both political justice and private virtue was 'the greatest sum of pleasure or happiness' (Godwin 1976, pp. 76, 185). He supported a strict act-utilitarianism, to which all obligations arising from promises, familial duty, and conventional institutions, such as marriage and political society, were immediately vulnerable. Nevertheless, this principle was accompanied by, and frequently in tension with, two others which owed much to his Dissenting background. One was the absolute obligation of sincerity and veracity, and the other was that the 'conviction of a man's understanding is the only legitimate principle imposing on him the duty of adopting any species of conduct' (Godwin 1976, pp. 311, 208). Godwin sought to harmonise his principles by claiming that the latter were necessary means to the maximisation of utility. Contemporary society relied on a variety of motives – habit, deference, reluctance to cause offence, fear – all of which inhibited individuals from that rational scrutiny of actions by which alone total utility could be increased.

It was in accounting for the possibility of altruistic utilitarian calculations that Godwin made the most extensive claims for reason's capacity to transcend its context of personal experience. He endorsed the empiricist faculty psychology argument that reason was incapable of motivating action, able only to compare experiences. However, we were 'able in imagination to go out of ourselves, and become impartial spectators', comparing our own sensations with those of others, and preferring the greatest happiness even to our own (Godwin 1976, p. 381). Reason, given full imaginative rein, could abstract us from ourselves and establish a society based on individual judgements about what would conduce to universal benevolence, rather than reliance on rules, authority, habit, or localised affections. 'Universal philanthropy' became a favoured target of anti-Jacobin propaganda, preaching, it was claimed 'benevolence to the whole species and want of feeling for every individual' (Burke 1889, p. 537).

Godwin originally indeed intended such a position. It was the very decisiveness of habit and feeling in motivating action so praised by Burke, rendering 'a man's virtue his habit' (Burke 1989, p. 158, 2001, p. 252), which for Godwin inhibited and foreclosed the intervention of reflective reason, the development of individual judgement, and social progress. He criticised all collective activity not resulting from conscious and continuing individual conviction, expressing serious reservations even about theatrical and orchestral performances. In anticipating the eventual 'euthanasia of government', he is often invoked as the founder of modern anarchism (D. Miller 1984; Woodcock 1963). Historically, however, he is better seen as utilising a secularised rationalist Protestantism to construct a theory of progressive republicanism, in which the dynamic is not the potentially vulnerable one of external economic and social forces, but the individual and idealist one of rational self-critique and cultivation.

Properly applied, the pursuit of the greatest happiness, would, Godwin thought, even lead to a conception of property as mere stewardship, which could not (and eventually would not) be asserted against those whose possession of it would increase the total sum of happiness – a tendency to equality in at least basic possessions. Existing property rights comprised a system 'by which one man enters into the faculty of disposing of the produce of another man's industry' (Godwin 1976, p. 711). Godwin joined a number of radicals in rejecting claims that labourers had benefited – or under existing conditions could benefit – from the advent of commercial and refined society. Great as would be the advantage of an economic and political transformation, he consistently held that this must result from the conviction of the understanding: a 'revolution of opinions is the only means of attaining this inestimable benefit' (Godwin 1976, p. 716). Godwin's absolute rejection of forceful change led him to side with Prime Minister William Pitt against his radical colleague Thelwall and the London Corresponding Society, presaging his increasingly Burkean sensitivity to the value and nuance of 'things as they are' (Godwin 1796; Kramnick 1972, pp. 124ff).

5 Radical political economy

Radicals were always vulnerable to charges that they undermined property rights, the stability of which was a crucial plank in the progressive commercial state. John Reeves mobilised fear of 'levelling' – with some assistance from the authorities – through his Association for the Preservation of Property and Liberty from Republicans and Levellers, founded in 1792. The issue also formed a focus for 'Crown and Anchor' associations and other popular loyalist societies, who opposed, in prose, verse, and cartoon, the miserable egalitarianism of the trouserless, frog-eating French to the benefits which a propertied society showered on an idealised hearty lower order: 'Long may old England possess good cheer and jollity / Liberty and Property and no Equality.'[1] The poor were deluged with tracts and sermons, notably including those by Hannah More, stressing the benefits of order, 'reasons for contentment', and the danger destabilisation posed even to those of very little property (Hole 1991; Pedersen 1986).

---

1 Anonymous loyalist handbill: British Library, Add. MS 16922, f. 45.

The charge that natural rights threatened the new economic order seemed borne out by the writings of agrarian radicals (Chase 1988, chs. 1–3). William Ogilvie, professor at Aberdeen University, advanced Locke's authority for the view that there remained, even in society, a 'Natural law right to an equal share with others in the land', which each state ought to guarantee to every citizen. Whilst recognising that only primitive economies could in fact ensure this, he hoped 'if possible' to combine it with the order and refinement of cultivated ages, assisted by a certain nostalgic civic deprecation of luxury (Ogilvie 1781).

Whilst Ogilvie successfully stressed the innocently speculative character of his ideas, they became notoriously subversive when recruited by the artisan Thomas Spence, drawing attention to the political sensitivity of the social status of both writer and intended audience (Spence 1793–5). Spence argued that a right to life entailed a natural right to a sufficiency of property since 'there is no living but on land and its productions' (Spence 1982, p. 1). For Spence, as for many radicals of the 1790s, the crucial issue was the relationship between personal and property rights, epitomised in the claim that a franchise based on personality would violate the 'properties' of existing voters. As he told his trial judge: 'The laws are made by property; and all for property. Men then, are out of the question except as appendages to this same property' (Spence 1982, p. 98). Spence envisaged an essentially agrarian community (variously called Crusonia or Spensonia), organised in parish units acting as landlords of their territory and guaranteeing to every individual that amount of land to which, in the natural state, they could have laid claim (Spence 1982, pp. 54, 104). Strikingly, in one version, the administrators of the parish are to be women (Spence 1982, p. 46).

In Spence, as in Ogilvie, there are elements of virtuous republicanism, and strong Harringtonian echoes in the universal right to bear arms (Spence 1982, p. 88). Like Ogilvie, Spence could repudiate charges of economic primitivism only by assertion: a visitor to Spensonia is astonished to find 'instead of anarchy, idleness, poverty and meanness, the natural consequences, as I narrowly thought, of a ridiculous levelling scheme, . . . nothing but order, industry, wealth, and magnificence' (Spence 1982, p. 81). Although his influence in the next century inspired truly insurrectionary politics, Spence's agrarianism may account for his marginalisation in the 1790s (Chase 1988, chs. 3–4; McCalman 1988, ch. 5).

By then, the essentially urban, commercial, and proto-industrial context was leading radicals to consider the potential inherent in the new society rather than the need to return to an earlier one. Paine, who originally harboured traditional republican reservations about commerce, now, along with Priestley, Mackintosh, Godwin, John Millar, and others, saw in it an equalising and liberalising force, undermining aristocratic privilege and discouraging war (Claeys 1989b, p. 46; Godwin 1976, p. 791; Mackintosh 1791, p. 136; Millar 1806, p. 271). Nevertheless, despite growing acceptance of such aspects of commercial regimes, radicals increasingly realised that commerce and manufacturing generated their own forms of inequality. Concerns about this were argued out differently within natural rights and civic languages.

Within natural jurisprudence, Paine and Thelwall both sought to construe a persisting natural property right without raising agrarian threats to the developed exchange economy or the property rights on which it depended. Thelwall (1796) used Locke and Smith to argue that a complex wage labour economy denied labourers both their original entitlement to land and the current just reward of their labouring activity, going beyond Paine in seeking profit-sharing for labourers. Part of Paine's *Rights of Man* had argued for the redistribution of existing taxation, but only through an intuitive appeal to fairness. In *Agrarian Justice* (1797), however, he joined Thelwall in proposing a money bounty for all non-property-holders in lieu of lost natural rights to land. Both men also claimed that the unpropertied had a right to the *increased* wealth produced by private property (which is not individual but 'the effect of society'), landed or otherwise (Claeys 1989b, ch. 8; Hampsher-Monk 1991; Philp 1989, pp. 84ff).

Parallelling Thelwall's and Paine's adaptation of radical natural jurisprudence to the new economy were radical excursions from Scottish Smithian and civic traditions. Whilst the aggregative focus of political economy conflicted with radical natural jurisprudence, civic elements within it sustained a concern for the moral and temperamental effects of socio-economic change on individuals, epitomised in Adam Smith's worries about the detrimental effects on individuals of the increasing division of labour. Lord Lauderdale and Dugald Stewart both claimed that the substitution of machinery would allay such effects, leaving for humans 'the nobler departments of industry and talent'. However, as Lauderdale noted, the deployment of machine production relied on demand which was sensitive to distributional effects, thus raising the issue of poverty and the need for redistributive taxation (Hont 1983, pp. 310ff).

John Millar came to such issues from firmly within a civic tradition. His *Origin of the Distinction of Ranks* (1771) had sought to synthesise an understanding of familial and household practices, national economy, and politics, to answer recognisably civic questions about the interplay between private manners and public law. Millar, professor of law at Glasgow and a member of the reforming Society of the Friends of the People, retained civic concerns about the growth of the state apparatus which seemed to accompany that of a commercial economy. In the pervasiveness of contractual relations, he recognised a new sense of 'independence' with *prima facie* political claims. Although originally complacent about Hanoverian politics, the rise of Pitt in defiance of the Commons, 'Treasury influence' on the 1784 election, and the corruption fostered by a war economy, led Millar to re-examine Smith's and Hume's indifference between the rule of law and political liberty, and to propose a significant extension of the franchise. Yet Millar remained pessimistic about reform, seeing, in the very pervasiveness of the market exchange which extended 'independence', an engine for spreading calculating individualism into the family – the necessary reservoir of that selfless virtue on which political life was drawn (Ignatieff 1983a, pp. 336ff). Such fears of calculating reason's effects on sentiment were expressed by many later retrospectives of eighteenth-century moral and political philosophy, such as those of Coleridge and Hazlitt (Mackintosh 1851). Persistent doubts about political economy's resolution of civic worries provided one conduit for an emerging conservative romanticism (Deane 1988, chs. 3–4; Morrow 1990, ch. 2).

Similar analyses could, however, lead in different directions. The *Letters of Crito*, probably by John Craig, pupil and biographer of Millar, sought to answer both Lauderdale's worries about demand deficiency and Millar's about the political effects of individualistic inequality, to establish the possibility of a radical Whig political economy based on a redistributive inheritance tax. Craig deployed a Humean associative account of the status of property rights in order to stress their weakness at the point of inheritance, and urged the harmless effect of such taxes on the stability of both property and expectation ('Sidney' [Craig] 1796, esp. letters 9–15).

Whilst the figures discussed here were all recognisably political thinkers, the range of *forms* in which political ideas were expressed during the 1790s qualify conventional notions of the 'political treatise' as a genre characterised by a certain systematic structure of argument (Epstein 1994). Daniel Eaton, in his rumbustious journal *Pig's Meat*, and 'Citizen Lee', cheerfully pillaged ancient and modern writers for radical 'sound bites' with complete disregard for theoretical coherence or authorial intention. Supporting radical plebeian political aspirations by mining the Whig canon suggests their incorporation within the dominant political value system, yet the ridicule

and satire, the subversive dictionaries, and the eager embracing of the swinish identity offered them by Burke, all have overtones of charivari and the
incipient instauration of a counter-culture. Some modern commentators
have deployed the notion of 'bricolage' to describe these efforts (McCalman
1988; Paulson 1983). In at least one case – the sophisticated radicalism of
Blake – there was a deliberate attempt to theorise *from outside* in order to dis-
rupt traditional and 'hegemonic' discourses (Mee 1992, p. 8). 'I must create
a system or be enslaved by another man's / I will not reason and compare:
my business is to create' (Blake 1927, p. 564). Yet Blake's reactionary appeal
was personal, indeed prophetic, and only problematically political (Pocock
1987, p. 21).

By contrast, the ostentatiously published 'proceedings', 'records', and
'correspondence' of plebeian organisations, such as the London Corresponding Society, are a significant new and undeniably civic genre (Thale
1983). The fact and facility of such 'electric' communication (a favoured
neologism), uniting hitherto unpoliticised and dispersed people, were
widely remarked. It was in the very act of assembling, in person or in
print, to debate national politics as something properly subject to a broadly
construed 'public opinion', that radicals both defined themselves and transformed their erstwhile loyal opposition.

24
Ideology and the origins of social science

ROBERT WOKLER

1   The invention of the modern nation-state

The American and French Revolutions of the late eighteenth century were each preceded and accompanied by lofty debates about constitutional principles, whose prospects of imminent enactment lent a sense of urgency to the fulfilment of philosophical ideals. Notions of a state of nature and a social contract had long been decried as illusions that could not account for the complexity of even our most primitive associations, but in overthrowing the trappings of government in two widely separated continents, legislators of modern republicanism in the United States and France made such abstractions appear credible, as if through their endeavours an earthly paradise might be regained and the first liberated citizens of large and durable republics since the demise of classical Rome could aspire to genuine self-rule. No less than in England around the time of its Civil War of the 1640s, there appeared, in America for about a decade before 1787 and in France for a similar period from 1789, a collection of classic works, some by leading statesmen or major figures in public life, each of which sought to plot a fresh path for civil institutions that had still to be born. These include Paine's *Common Sense* (1776), Hamilton, Madison, and Jay's *Federalist Papers* (1787–8), and, in France, Sieyès's *Qu'est-ce que le Tiers-Etat?* (What is the Third Estate?, 1789) and Condorcet's *Esquisse d'un tableau historique des progrès de l'esprit humain* (Sketch of an Historical View of the Progress of the Human Mind, 1795). While such texts highlighted both the promise and risks of the circumstances they addressed, they also drew upon earlier writings of the Enlightenment, whose innovative terminology or more discursive treatments of law and justice these revolutionary tracts and treatises often distilled. The establishment by way of franchise of a federal constitution for the first republic of the New World, and, on the other hand, the creation of a new social order in France which levelled not just the state but the whole of the *ancien régime*, gave special purchase, among the Enlightenment's most central doctrines, to Montesquieu's notion of a democratic republic and Rousseau's ideal of popular sovereignty. Allowing for a great many other debts and sources, it is around the civic imagery these doctrines inspired, as well as the institutions deemed necessary to realise them in practice, that the modern state in its most conspicuous configurations still prevalent today came to be formed.

The institutions and central concepts associated with the modern state are, of course, not only attributable to the great political revolutions of the late eighteenth century. They owe much to both earlier and subsequent developments – on the one hand to transfigurations of the language of *status* and *civitas* in fifteenth- and sixteenth-century Europe into the modern terminology of *état* or *state* (Skinner 1989) as well as to the sixteenth-century crystallisation of hegemonic rule within territorial limits that came to be known as *raison d'état* (Foucault 1991); and on the other to the nationalist movements that inspired the unification of Italy and Germany in the nineteenth century, to the financial and industrial enterprises of both England and the United States that in each case shaped the direction of public policy, and to the development of political parties and party governments throughout the world. No account of the theoretical genesis of the modern state could ignore the immense contributions, in particular, of the notions of sovereignty formulated by Bodin and Hobbes and the latter's account of representation, dating from the late sixteenth and mid-seventeenth centuries respectively. But since the end of the eighteenth century the modern state has required for its formation at least one principle absent from all these earlier prefigurations. In addition to establishing undivided rule over its subjects, the genuinely modern state has characteristically, if by no means universally, further demanded that those who fall under its authority be united themselves, that they form one people morally bound together by a common identity. Hobbes had conceived a need for a unitary sovereign in his depiction of the artificial personality of the state, but he had not supposed that the multitude of subjects which authorised that power could be identified as having a collective character of its own. Joined to his conception of the unity of the representer, as outlined in the sixteenth chapter of *Leviathan* (1651), the modern state generally requires that the represented be a moral person as well, the unity of all subjects going hand in hand with the political unity of the state, thereby superimposing upon a modern framework of sovereignty an at once ancient and medieval conception of corporate personality in the *status rei publicæ* of citizens linked by a common purpose. While it speaks with only one voice in the manner imputed to absolutist monarchy, the modern state has seldom, if ever, taken the form of a monarchical *civitas* along any lines set forth by Bodin or Hobbes. It is instead conceptually an invention of the age of Enlightenment and politically a creation of the American and French Revolutions. As it has been known since the late eighteenth century, in the language of Montesquieu adopted by Paine to describe how America was just Athens writ large, the modern state is, in most of its manifestations, a democratic republic. It bears the essential attributes of Herder's notion of *das Volk* articulated in the language of Hegel's conception of *der Staat*.

In the case of France and the republics of both Europe and Latin America, followed by much of the world whose political discourse was thus crucially framed in the late eighteenth century, the modern democratic state is of its essence a *nation-state*, in which nationality is defined politically and political power is held to express the nation's will. That achievement owes much to the third article of the Declaration of the Rights of Man, drafted by Lafayette, according to which the nation is the source of all sovereignty, but it may owe still more to the endeavours of the Abbé Sieyès, who on 17 June 1789 successfully steered the resolution which transformed the Estates General into the National Assembly, more than two months before its endorsement of the Declaration. By virtue of their reconstituting themselves from a collection of deputies convoked at the monarch's behest into a unicameral political system comprised of agents representing the national will, the people's delegates standing for the nation as a whole came to exercise sovereignty, even while the French king remained on his throne. These developments ensured that the French revolutionary nation-state, which Sieyès had largely invented, joined the rights of man to the sovereignty of the nation, in a spirit profoundly at odds with Enlightenment cosmopolitanism, thereby giving warrant to modern nationalism by defining human rights in such a way that only the state could enforce them and only members of the nation could enjoy them. As Hannah Arendt rightly noted in her *Origins of Totalitarianism*, it has been a characteristic feature of the nation-state since the French Revolution that the rights of man and the rights of the citizen are the same (1958, pp. 230–1; cf. Hont 1994a; Wokler 2000a).

2   The French revolutionary invention of social science

If *Qu'est-ce que le Tiers-Etat?* may be regarded as the chief blueprint of the modern nation-state, the same text also heralded the development of a new science of society that, as interpreted by others after the Terror of

1793–4, would come to discredit the political campaign on behalf of the people of France which the establishment of the National Assembly had launched. No recorded use of the term 'social science' in any European language prior to the publication of this pamphlet in January 1789 has yet been traced, although in adopting his fresh terminology Sieyès appears to have been uninterested in such conceptual innovation as he achieved in the same work's treatment of politics. The expression *la science sociale* figured only in the initial issue of *Qu'est-ce que le Tiers-Etat?*, and Sieyès in fact thought so little of his neologism that in subsequent editions of his text he replaced it with the expression *la science de l'ordre social* (Sieyès 1970, p. 151; see Head 1982). His meaning seemed plain enough not only to him but also to his readers, and in neither case did his choice of words occasion comment from them, for they apparently grasped, correctly, that what he had in mind was nothing other than the principles of social order which France's Third Estate, representing the nation as a whole, divorced from all particular or factional interests, sought to realise in practice. Reflecting on his own purpose and achievement in that work in a conversation with Etienne Dumont a few months after the publication of *Qu'est-ce que le Tiers-Etat?*, Sieyès remarked that politics was a science he believed he had already completed (Bénétruy 1962, p. 399). He might well have said the same of social science, for he imagined that, with his encouragement, the political system of France would be empowered to put into practice the science of society he had himself set out in theory, having elaborated its first principles so as to ensure its public enactment, thereby making it real.

Subsequent appearances of the expression *la science sociale* in its earliest articulations have been traced to Pierre Louis Lacretelle's *De l'établissement des connoissances humaines* (The Formation of Human Knowledge) of 1791, to a pamphlet by Dominique Joseph Garat addressed to Condorcet in December of that year, and to Condorcet's own *Rapport et projet de décret sur l'organisation générale de l'instruction publique* (Report and Plan of a Decree for the General Organisation of Public Instruction) presented in January 1792. It is very likely that the words *la science sociale* gained a certain currency in the fertile political literature of the period from 1789 to 1792 and that other instances of their use in those years have yet to be uncovered. But, with respect to the expression's previously ascertained pioneering examples, two points in particular bear emphasis. The first is that every one of its thus far identified authors was a member of the short-lived *Société de 1789*, a club formed to commemorate the launch of the Revolution and to ensure the success of its reconstruction of French society and dissolved in 1791 after its membership had splintered into just such sectarian groups, representing different interests of the nation, which Sieyès had sought to prevent. The second is that the initial users of the term spoke of *la science sociale* more or less interchangeably with other human sciences, such as *la morale* and *la politique*, in the terminology of Lacretrelle, or even with *l'art social*, in the language of Condorcet, the aim of which, as he put it in his draft prospectus of the *Société de 1789*, was to promote political stability through constitutional reform, based upon the prevailing *sciences morales et politiques* (see Baker 1964; Iggers 1959; Senn 1958).

Garat supposed that such political principles as Montesquieu's conception of the division of powers and Rousseau's notion of popular sovereignty could become constitutive elements of *la science sociale* if they were put into practice by enlightened states, while Condorcet believed that *la science sociale*, as embraced within *les sciences morales et politiques* and indeed the human sciences in general, was set to advance on the model of the physical sciences, thereby making truly scientific such social change and educational reforms as France's constitutional upheaval had rendered politically possible. In its first printed articulations in the most politically explosive period at the dawn of the establishment of the modern state, *la science sociale* was introduced, innocuously, as a term roughly equivalent to politics in general. By the early nineteenth century, when the term had achieved quite widespread currency in France and was poised to become fashionable in England as well, Antoine Louis Claude Destutt de Tracy could remark in his commentary on Montesquieu's *The Spirit of the Laws* that, in the course of the French Revolution's first endeavours to establish a new order, social science meant much the same as the new politics (1819, p. vii).

After the rise and fall of the Jacobins and the passing of their Terror, the new term, *science sociale*, was to undergo an epistemic break or *décalage* such as was proclaimed by Michel Foucault on behalf of all the human sciences, precisely in 1795, his designated year of the conceptual guillotine marking the passage, he imagined, of *l'âge classique* into *l'âge moderne*, as if men's minds could only be changed after their heads had already been severed (see Foucault 1966, pp. 238, 263). While anticipating more recent research devoted to the *idéologues* of the 1790s, and drawing special attention to a decade in which terms such as *démocrate*, *révolutionnaire*, and *terroriste*, as well as *idéologie*, erupted into European political discourse, Foucault's thesis has generally failed to carry conviction, if only because the examples he cites often stray from his pivotal year by many decades. If he had concentrated instead on both the practice and terminology of *la science sociale* his account of relatively abrupt epistemic change in the course of the French Revolution would have had greater plausibility.

In the summer and autumn of 1795 the Convention planned, and in November the Directory established, the *Institut national des sciences et des arts*, thereby launching an academy already proposed by Talleyrand in 1792 and foreshadowed still earlier in Condillac's vision of scientific integration and by Condorcet's pedagogical programmes cast in the same image. Within the *Institut* was established the *Classe des sciences morales et politiques*, the third of whose six sections was called *Science sociale et législation*. The stipulated conjunction of social science with legislation in this name, and the election of Sieyès and Garat to other sections of the *Classe des sciences morales et politiques* and later of Lacretelle to another *Classe*, might appear to make Foucault's notion of an epistemic metamorphosis with regard to *la science sociale* relatively tame, articulated as it was by at least the survivors of a cast of already familiar characters. After 1795, however, the expression *science sociale* came progressively to acquire a fresh meaning, all the more explosive on account of its divorce from, rather than conjunction with, politics and legislation. From the time of Foucault's *annus mirabilis* of the human sciences in general, social science in particular came to acquire the meanings now associated with it as the central science of modernity.

The creation of the *Institut national* after the coup of 9 Thermidor on 27 July 1794 was prefigured by several attempts in the course of the French Revolution to reform the academies of the *ancien régime* and to promote a national scheme of public education which might make the diffusion of knowledge appear centrally instrumental to the promotion of happiness, virtue, progress, and prosperity along lines envisaged for their *Encyclopédie* by Diderot and d'Alembert more than four decades earlier. In 1774, the young Condorcet, d'Alembert's protégé, already permanent secretary of the *Académie des sciences* as was his mentor of the *Académie française*, launched a scheme which would link France's provincial scientific academies to their hub in Paris, by way of this network hoping to foster scientific exchanges, collaborative research projects, and, through such intellectual ventures, ultimately the rejuvenation of the nation's civic life and culture. Condorcet had been inspired in that aim not only by the *Encyclopédie* but also by Condillac's endeavour to construct a unified plan bringing together all the sciences as outlined in his *Traité des systèmes* (1749) and other writings; more than any other figure of the French Revolution it was Condorcet who in the early 1790s was to carry the mantle of these Enlightenment ideals. Not long before his death in 1791 the marquis de Mirabeau also advocated the reform of the academies as part of a similar project of encouraging education, while in September of that year Talleyrand conceived the creation of what he himself called an *Institut national* as part of a still wider programme of public instruction which would enlist France's professoriate to the *Encyclopédistes'* cause as second-generation *philosophes*.

Talleyrand had taken careful note of a memoir on educational reform which Condorcet had published in the *Bibliothèque de l'homme public* in 1790–1, but consideration of both schemes was deferred following France's declaration of war against Austria and Prussia in the spring of 1792, and these delays were at once prolonged and complicated by the Legislative Assembly's demise and its replacement by the National Convention in the autumn of 1792, followed in August 1793 by the Convention's abolition of all Parisian academies. Only after Thermidor would they fall under political scrutiny again, and by the summer of 1795 Condorcet's proposed structure of an alternative and multidisciplinary scientific academy, albeit bearing Talleyrand's name, would come to be implemented in virtually every detail, including the establishment of a *Classe des sciences morales et politiques* with its six sections. In 1798 a member of the third section, Jean Jacques Régis de Cambacérès, later to become Napoleon Bonaparte's second consul, delivered a *Discours sur la science sociale*, probably the first work ever published to contain the term 'social science' in its title, which discipline, as he conceived it, would embrace a science of interests, or political economy; a science of authority, or legislation; and a science of sentiments, that is, ethics.

The transformation of the expression *science sociale* into a fresh concept, however, was not achieved by either Condorcet or Cambacérès. It was made possible by the intellectual predominance within the *Classe des sciences morales et politiques* of another section, the first, devoted to the analysis of sensations and ideas, the specially recognised domain of the so-called *idéologues*, led by Destutt de Tracy and Cabanis, until the dissolution of the entire *Classe* in 1803 by the first consul, Napoleon, who thereby demonstrated a more decisive manner of effecting epistemic change. Their collective strength and the coherence of their scientific agenda owed much to the system of patronage by which they were selected, largely under the auspices of their chief sponsor and patriarch, the Abbé Sieyès. Much as the Baron Georges Cuvier achieved or, rather, manipulated the appointment of his preferred candidates for the first *Classe* of the *Institut* devoted to mathematical and physical sciences, Sieyès, by sponsoring as candidates for the second *Classe* the *idéologues* and other members of the circle over which he presided at Auteil in the suburbs of Paris, managed to plot, if not entirely to control, the direction that French social science would take in its incipient phase.

Principal architect of the modern nation–state and author of the expression *la science sociale*, Sieyès, by virtue of his promotion or endorsement of select candidates to the *Institut national*, was also the godfather of *idéologie*. Once admitted to the second *Classe*, the *idéologues* sponsored by Sieyès attempted to delineate a new science of human nature which was more deeply rooted in the psychology of the human mind and the physiology of the human body than any conception of *la science sociale* as the art of politics could ever be. Destutt de Tracy's coinage of the term *idéologie* in the memoir on the science of the formation of our ideas which he presented to the *Classe* on 2 Floréal of the year IV (21 April 1796) was itself patterned from a similar mould. 'Ideology', drawn from the Greek *eidos* or image, was the true science of thought, Destutt de Tracy claimed, and it exactly described his section's objective of analysing ideas and sensations. As such it was distinct from metaphysics which, by contrast, was abstract and esoteric, as different from speculative knowledge as was astronomy from astrology. Its aim would be to cleanse our moral and political sciences of centuries of encrusted prejudice, which Marxists would later define as the proper signification of the term 'ideology' when portraying it as pseudo-scientific 'false consciousness', thereby inverting Destutt de Tracy's meaning. Thomas Jefferson, as he confessed in a letter to John Adams in 1816, found Destutt de Tracy's *Eléments d'idéologie* insubstantial and vacuous, as distinct from the later *Commentaire sur 'L'Esprit des lois'* to which he warmed greatly, not least because he judged that its author there subscribed to his own political priorities and philosophy of education (Jefferson 1999, pp. 295–6). Jefferson, however, had not been attentive to Destutt de Tracy's main interest in promoting ideology as the only social science appropriate to a post-Jacobin age.

3   The *idéologues* and their distrust of politics

The *idéologues* had learned the dreadful lessons of the Terror and, following the Constitution of the year 1795, they were less disposed than their precursors had been to proclaim the dangerously egalitarian doctrine of the natural rights of man, preferring instead to defend such rights as mankind could only enjoy in society. Distrustful of the critical character of the revolutionary programmes which had inspired the establishment of the *Société de 1789*, they were convinced that the problems of social disorder and derangement which the Revolution itself had generated were as striking as the despotism of the *ancien régime* had appeared to the aspiring legislators of the National Assembly. Wholesale constitutional reform had proved a remedy as harmful as the disease itself, because it was in part too drastic, in part too superficial, engendering political violence without producing social change. While they were men of predominantly liberal temperament whose outlook remained, by and large, as secular as was the anticlericalism of their precursors, their new conception of the science of society was more historical, more preservative, and more solidly situated, they supposed, in the concrete world of real experience.

Together with most of the *idéologues* Destutt de Tracy himself was by disposition republican, but he was more deeply stirred by anxieties about the consequences of revolutionary violence than by the attractions of his preferred constitutional principles, and in contributing to an *Institut* prize competition on the subject of inculcating morality in 1798 he advocated strong and even repressive police powers to counteract the degeneration of public opinion so as to restore traditional values. Ideology might be a true science, but both the need for it and the means of its enforcement made it appear a secular substitute for religion. It served Destutt de Tracy's purposes well that the *Classe des sciences morales et politiques* came to regard itself as having not only a pedagogical but also a politically consultative role, for instance with respect to government policy in connection with poor relief and the care of orphans, thereby attempting by way of social science to match the achievements of the *Classe des sciences mathématiques et physiques* which had successfully promulgated and then gained political endorsement for the metric system of measurement. It may have been frustrating for the *idéologues* to find that Condillac's philosophy of language and signs would also have greater public impact through the endeavours of physical scientists, who in the light of it promoted the semaphore signal device for cross-Channel communication, than through the efforts of social scientists; but they should not have been surprised when the Directory's Interior Ministry only sought out select individual members of the *Institut* rather than any of its committees when embarking on a reform of the curriculum of the *lycées*. Not for the first or last time did social scientific experts and aspiring consultants thus languish in deprecating obscurity. Several were to escape the marginalisation from public policy that might, in so far as they comprised an intellectual class, have been regarded as their due, by demonstrating their enthusiasm for Napoleons's *coup d'état* of November 1799 and then engineering their own service to, and recognition by, the new regime.

In the fifth section, devoted to the study of history, congregated some of the most politically conservative members of the second *Classe*, including Jean Baptiste Delisle de Sales, Pierre Charles Lévesque, and Paul Philippe Gudin de la Brenellerie. A royalist rather than a republican, Delisle de Sales would, after the Revolution, come to call for the restoration of a religious sanction to underpin the authority of civil laws, and he was in many respects suspicious of the *idéologues* within the *Institut* because of what he took to be their atheism. Together with Lévesque he challenged populist accounts of the enduring significance of the Third Estate in French history, while Gudin sought to show that no assembly embracing *sans-culottes*, or indeed the common people as a whole (however that amorphous mass might be identified), had ever articulated the nation's general will. Not only, according to Lévesque, were there few medieval sources for eighteenth-century French republicanism; there were in fact no reliable ancient precedents either, since the Spartan constitution had actually been aristocratic rather than egalitarian, while Athenian democracy had shown itself to be unstable and prone to tyranny (Staum 1996, pp. 145–9).

However disinclined to share, or even unable to comprehend, some of the philosophical and psychological presuppositions of the *idéologues*, these historians of the *Institut*, nevertheless, bore a notable political resemblance to the luminaries who dominated the first section of the *Classe des sciences morales et politiques*. They were no less hostile to abstract notions of the people than were the *idéologues* to metaphysical ideals. They were anti-utopian, suspicious of the chimeras of equality and democracy, as sceptical of arguments from precedent as were *idéologues* of the illusions of first principles. The Revolution's descent into anarchy, they believed, had been made possible by philosophical misconstruals of the real facts of French history. They had scant admiration for what they took to be the dogmatism of Voltaire and Rousseau, who, they imagined, had together provided the conspirators of the French Revolution with much inspiration and thereby prompted some of its worst excesses, not only its violence but also its declarations of the rights of man. From virtually all the pre-eminent political theories of the age of Enlightenment with which they were acquainted, and most particularly those couched in the abstract language of liberty, sovereignty, and other utopian values associated with the state, the *idéologues* and their allies at the *Institut national* felt themselves estranged.

Above all, perhaps, the *idéologues* sought to explain mental and moral phenomena scientifically by retracing them to their physical roots, a task particularly congenial to those among them, like Constantin François Volney, who were trained in statistical geography. Volney, a founding member of the first section of the *Classe des sciences morales et politiques*, was especially well placed there, not only as an *idéologue* and member of the circle of Auteil but also as a political nominee of the Directory, subsequently serving as director of Napoleon's *Bureau de statistique*. His earlier *Loi naturelle, ou catéchisme du citoyen français* (Natural Law, or the French Citizen's Catechism), commissioned by the Convention's Interior Ministry in 1793, had depicted ethics not in the language of old religions or newly acquired liberties but as 'a physical and geometric science'. While he there occasionally referred to every person's 'equal right' of self-preservation, he insisted that rights in general were not derived from a social contract but could instead be deduced from the 'physical attributes that are inherent in human organisation' (Staum 1996, pp. 121, 174). Pierre Louis Roederer, by training a lawyer, but with Sieyès and Talleyrand elected to the fourth section of the *Classe*, devoted to political economy, insisted both throughout his writings and in public lectures that politics and ethics were reducible to rules as demonstrably true as those of mathematics and the natural sciences.

In emphasising the social significance of physical attributes Volney attempted to account for their impact upon the production of cultural institutions, including political systems and religious beliefs, whose characteristics were largely shaped, he believed, by features of the physical geography in which diverse populations lived. In commentaries on the modes of sustenance of native Americans he was partly inspired by Jean François Lafitau's study of the *Mores of the Savages of America* dating from 1723 and also derived some material from William Robertson's *History of America* of 1777, employing a stadial theory of human development similar to Robertson's to criticise both Rousseau's conception of the innocence of natural man and the contrasting account given by Cornelius de Pauw, whose widely read *Recherches philosophiques sur les américains* (Philosophical Investigations of the Americans, 1768–9) had instead followed Buffon in portraying the degenerative bodily characteristics of Americans. From Robertson's work, which embraced perhaps the first social scientific questionnaire, Volney no doubt also drew encouragement for his own proposed survey, drafted in 1795, designed to establish the topographical, climatological, and other physical roots of the local character and customs of diverse populations. In his *Leçons d'histoire* (delivered when he was professor of the *Ecole normale* in 1795 and subsequently published in 1799), he adopted a global historical approach that would prove fashionable in France as early as the end of the eighteenth century and would come to be still further emulated by French social historians of the mid- to late twentieth century.

Cabanis, moreover, in his *Rapports du physique et du moral* (1802), first delivered as a set of readings to the *Classe des sciences morales et politiques*, expounded a doctrine of the science of man conceived as a synthesis of physiology, morals, and the science of ideas – in this work, perhaps above all others produced by any of the *idéologues*, establishing the physicalist, vitalist, and sensationalist foundations of what they took to be *la science sociale*. Cabanis was particularly concerned with the organic roots of human dispositions and sentiments, and he sought to show how medicine and physiology could provide ethics with principles that were cultivated out of natural temperaments, conceiving the medical profession as a kind of priesthood of sanitary magistrates that would superintend public morals by extirpating disease. Cabanis's close identification of the moral with the physical dimensions of human affairs was shared, if not in every detail, by virtually all the *idéologues* of the circle of Auteil and the *Classe des sciences morales et politiques* to whom he was both professionally and personally tied. Their understanding of societal forces and of the broad currents of historical change inclined them to emphasise the significance of material culture over what they took to be the ethereal realm of philosophical ideals (see Staum 1980a, 1996). If they had produced their writings in the twentieth century, they would have been warmly received as fellow travellers of the contemporary school of the French *Annales*; in the eighteenth century theirs was already a social science of *mentalités*. Unlike Condorcet and Sieyès they could never have confused the nature of that science with the art of politics.

There were, no doubt, other factors besides their distrust of politics and legislation which made the *idéologues* conspicuously less incendiary than had been the inventors of a more critical notion of *la science sociale*. It may even be the case that their membership of the *Classe des sciences morales et politiques*, described by Keith Baker as the embodiment of Condorcet's dream of a social sciences academy, lent a more conservative character to the discipline than had been conceived by their patron saint, simply on account of its institutionalisation in an academic setting made possible by patronage of another kind (Baker 1975, pp. 371–2, 388–90). At any rate, in adopting holistic methodologies of social explanation different from those that had figured in the notions of Condorcet and Sieyès, they parted company from their ideological precursors and could even appear to have made common cause with a number of profoundly reactionary critics of the whole French

Revolution, including Bonald, Chateaubriand, and de Maistre, who likewise supposed, and indeed stressed even more, that the political manipulation of French society had fractured it. In France after 1795, the idea of a genuine social science, or *science de la société*, as Bonald sometimes termed it, could be appropriated by romantic conservatives no less than by progressive liberals or socialists. In every case, however, it excluded the political tampering of naively enthusiastic legislators and metaphysicians, now placed in the same rogues' gallery as the clerics and despots reviled by the *philosophes*. Following the failure of *la science sociale* as originally conceived by Sieyès to prevent the Jacobin disintegration of the achievements of 1789, its revision by sceptics more attentive to the pathology of the French body politic and to the systemic nature of its disorders led them to a fresh understanding of that new science and, in practising it, to concentrate upon society's organisation, infrastructure, and internal functions.

To ensure order and stability, social science would henceforth require not the constitutions of legislators but regulation by administrators and engineers. When embarking for Egypt in June 1798 Napoleon himself invited Destutt de Tracy to join his expedition as a *maréchal de camp*. Although Destutt de Tracy declined and was even suspicious of that honour, most of his associates in the circle of Auteil, where both he and Madame de Condorcet held court, endeavoured to serve Napoleon or enlist his support for their own schemes when the conquering hero of France returned and settled triumphantly in Paris on 16 October 1799. In place of the political power sought on behalf of the public good by the first social scientists, after its epistemic metamorphosis the new science of society as conceived by Destutt de Tracy, the *idéologues*, and the circle of Auteil, would promote social hygiene. Rather than aiming to achieve the enfranchisement of all citizens, it would be designed to fulfil the prognosis of Alexander Pope's couplet from *An Essay on Man* (1733; epistle III, lines 303–4),

> For Forms of Government let fools contest;
> Whate'er is best administer'd is best.

In turning their attention to the underlying forces which shaped human nature rather than to the principles which ought to govern it, the *idéologues* were plainly more committed to deep structural explanations of the conduct of men and women than they imagined had been most of the *philosophes* of pre-revolutionary France, whose pragmatism, it was suggested, had inclined them to promote wholesale political and economic reforms such as might avert what they took to be the impending cataclysm of a corrupt *ancien régime*. No less anti-theological than the *philosophes* and for the most part still largely liberal in their political perceptions, the *idéologues* ought by no means to be regarded as reactionary critics of the Enlightenment. Their chief opponents were not only partisans of Enlightenment deism who recoiled from their apparent lack of faith in any principles of cosmic order, but also theological and political conservatives who, at least when focusing on their republicanism rather than their notions of social science, regarded them essentially as disciples of the *philosophes* in undermining the authority of both church and state. Their epistemologies – empiricist, associationist, and utilitarian – bore striking resemblances to the materialism of Helvétius and the psychology of Condillac in particular, whose hostility to Cartesian dualism and to the doctrine of innate ideas they shared. But while they were just as hostile to metaphysical abstractions as their precursors of the mid-eighteenth century, and accordingly no less sceptical of the great seventeenth-century cosmologies decried by d'Alembert in distinguishing the systematic spirit of his own age from the spirit of system that had prevailed a century earlier, their focus of criticism was markedly different after the overthrow of the Jacobin tyranny.

Because of its destructive zeal and excessive concentration of political power the French revolutionary state under the Convention had devised blunt, and in effect intolerable, cures for the illnesses of the nation. It had ministered France's last sacraments on behalf of a civil religion no less damaging to the people's true spirit than Christianity's endeavours to cleanse the soul of France by way of the Revocation of the Edict of Nantes and its sequels, through which Louis XIV had sought to expunge toleration for the Huguenots. Constitutional changes that were too rapid and police powers that were too great to protect the citizens of France seemed to discredit the political science of the *philosophes'* disciples among French legislators of the period from 1789 to 1794, so that even after the first French Republic supplanted the monarchy the Revolution's failures were held to mark the demise of the radical Enlightenment's overweening ambitions. The *idéologues* largely spurned what they took to be the political science of the *philosophes* on account of its proving too dangerous when put into practice. In substituting a deep structural *social* science for the reformist zeal of *political* science they became the pre-eminent technicians and regulators of order throughout the nation which they sought to improve diagnostically and incrementally, rather than by way of violent upheaval and constitutional purge.

4   The origins of social science in Britain

Both the terminology and practice of social science in Britain were drawn from these French precedents, but without the conservative implications that followed from the need, in France after Thermidor, to replace wholesale political change with piecemeal improvements (Burns 1959; Claeys 1986b, 1989a; Collini *et al.* 1983; Goldman 1983). In his *Enquiry concerning Political Justice* of 1793 Godwin continued to stress the importance of political ideals and institutions in the manner of the revolutionary zealots elected to the French National Assembly in 1789 whom he viewed as sharing his belief that politics only arises from a need to remedy injustice or oppression. But he also drew the attention of his readers to his own philosophical precursors across the channel – especially Rousseau and Helvétius – who like him, he supposed, held political institutions to be fundamentally linked with the happiness and morality of individuals and their society's organisation. That connection between politics and society Godwin regarded as all the more crucial because it had been overlooked, he imagined, less by the *philosophes* of the Enlightenment than by radicals of an earlier age, such as Locke and Algernon Sidney, who had placed too much stress upon the values of individual liberty, security, and property. These seventeenth-century thinkers had lacked, he remarked, 'a consciousness of the intimate connection of the different parts of the social system' (bk 1, ch. 1).

In the early nineteenth century Robert Owen frequently invoked the expression 'social system' to characterise what he took to be, in essence, the need for a conjunction of self-love with social benevolence, and that idea of a co-operative social system underpinned the Owenites' critique of irrational competition, or the 'individual system', such as was allegedly prescribed by the eighteenth-century science of political economy. Thus far the earliest published English-language reference to the expression 'social science' has been traced to (the Irishman) William Thompson's *Inquiry into the Principles of the Distribution of Wealth Most Conducive to Human Happiness* of 1824 (see pp. viii–ix). From his remarks both there and frequently in his subsequent writings, it is plain that Thompson had in mind the application of what he also termed 'the art of social happiness', regulated by a principle of utility that required the science of political economy to promote not only the accumulation of wealth but also human contentment. In introducing social science as a corrective to individualist political economy Thompson appears thereby to have subscribed both to the idea of a social system inspired directly by Owen and originally by Godwin, as well as to Bentham's utilitarianism.

For British thinkers of the late eighteenth and early nineteenth centuries who would come to be described as socialist, the terms 'social system' and subsequently 'social science' were largely connected with philosophies conceived as correctives to commercial relations under a manufacturing system which was deemed to have failed most of its members on account of its lack of a co-operative framework. Addressed mainly to the shortcomings of an economic system rather than to the revolutionary excesses of a political system, social science or the new science of society did not in Britain, in contrast to France, so promptly lose its political character or radical zeal. French social science after 1795 appears to have been generated and institutionalised within a new academy whose members largely subscribed to what might be termed a Hegelian interpretation of the Revolution's descent from absolute freedom to terror and who were determined to strike a new course that promised stability by way of promulgating a syllabus of depoliticised and deradicalised human sciences. The epistemic break in France between political science and social science which marked the Thermidorean reaction to the upheavals and constitutional changes of the whole period between 1789 and 1794 was, for this reason, absent from a nation whose revolution a century earlier had restored its monarchy and Protestant succession so that, according to its chief domestic adversaries, it was manifestly England's economy rather than its polity that now appeared to be in need of social scientific healing.

Yet Foucault's perception of the intellectual volatility which he believed had largely generated the human sciences in their modern forms around the year 1795 has some bearing upon fractionally later developments in England as well, with reference to the longer *durée* of the Industrial as distinct from the political French Revolution. The terror in England that incipient British social science sought to explain stemmed not from the state but from the world's most progressive manufacturing system. Its development addressed abuses of political economy rather than of Jacobin dictatorship. Its early adherents could be wedded to political programmes which facilitated ideals of communitarian government. Thanks to the editors of his correspondence, we now know that Bentham invoked the term 'social science' in his personal letters more than a decade before Thompson first employed it in print. But Thompson may originally have had the expression drawn to his notice by way of the circle of Condorcet or even through Condorcet himself, whom he cited in his *Inquiry*. By the 1830s, when John Stuart Mill also used the term in his *Essays on Economics and Society*, Thompson's definition of 'social science', meaning a more co-operative form of the science of political economy, had virtually become common currency (see Claeys 1986b, 1989a).

5 Saint-Simon and the legacy of Enlightenment political thought

In contemplating the legacy of Enlightenment political thought at least two striking paradoxes need to be borne in mind. The first is that the commitment of late eighteenth-century *philosophes* to what came to be termed the unity of theory and practice inspired many of them to conceive programmes of political reform designed to avert the upheavals of a great revolution which several had foreseen but virtually none of them had advocated, believing it to be a remedy worse than the disease. When, however, at the dusk of the age of Enlightenment that revolution descended upon France, it soon came to be perceived, by its advocates and critics alike, as cast in moulds patterned by the *philosophes*' doctrines, prefigured in their diverse images of the state and its constitutional and administrative framework. The reputation as a political thinker of Rousseau in particular has, since 1789, been profoundly coloured by such judgements of his influence. As Madame de Staël remarked at the turn of the nineteenth century, 'He discovered nothing but he inflamed everything' – the passions, the senses, and indeed ultimately the Terror (1800, II, 33).

By way of the Jacobin and Bonapartist dictatorships, Rousseau's collectivist precepts as articulated in *The Social Contract* (1762), the *Considerations on the Government of Poland* (1772), and some of his other writings have come, above all other doctrines of the age of Enlightenment, to be identified as the fount of totalitarian democracy. The political philosophy of modern liberalism was devised by its proponents in the early nineteenth century largely as a corrective to revolutionary claims, couched in the language of Rousseau, to the effect that popular sovereignty was the only means of securing the liberty of all citizens. Through its precipitous descent from freedom to terror and dictatorship, the broken promise of 1789, as if in anticipation of the collapse of communism in 1989, appeared only to recapitulate mankind's original fall from innocence to vice. Of course Rousseau had himself, in his *Discourse on the Origin of Inequality* (1755), portrayed the history of civilisation in similar terms, albeit sketched on a much broader canvas, as humanity's long day's journey into night. After the French Revolution, however, his philosophy of history, so hostile to widely prevalent Enlightenment conceptions of progress and of mankind's ascent from barbarism, came to be judged as less important than his political philosophy, which thereafter was deemed by most commentators to be the prophetic harbinger of a false dawn. The principles of *The Social Contract*, embraced by his revolutionary admirers themselves as if they had been the ten commandments of republican France, were held responsible for its decomposition. The ancient ideals of civil and moral liberty he invoked were judged to be no safeguard at all for personal freedom, which required not the political engagement of citizens such as he had prescribed but the protection of individuals against the state. At its source much of modern liberalism, mediated by the French Revolution, is in effect a rejection of Enlightenment, and mainly Rousseauian, republicanism.

The second paradox about Enlightenment political philosophy engendered by the Revolution follows from the first and turns upon the fact that, through its conspicuous abuse of power, the modern state, in the patterns it adopted after 1789, has seemed to discredit Enlightenment programmes of legislative and constitutional reform, however oblique the *philosophes'* political influence might have been. The pioneers of modern social science around the year 1795 were of course also indebted to certain eighteenth-century thinkers and traditions which did not centrally address governments' first principles or indeed any agendas of political reform. While Sieyès held Condillac's theory of the senses to be distorted because it rendered the mind passive and devoid of purposive direction such as could be determined by an active faculty of judgement, virtually all the *idéologues* he sponsored whose use of the term *science sociale* differed from his own were in fact drawn to the sensationsalist philosophy of Condillac and especially to his sketches, in his *Traité des systèmes* and *Traité des sensations* (1754), of a unified science of human nature which would be free of the metaphysical abstractions associated with seventeenth-century notions of the soul. By way of Condillac, they were also influenced by Locke's epistemology; and they agreed with Maupertius, La Mettrie, and d'Holbach, among Condillac's contemporaries, that the moral attributes of human nature could be explained with reference to man's physical constitution alone, and with Helvétius that the central task of a system of education was to shape the pliant clay of human nature. In their physiological conception of a social science the *idéologues* owed a certain debt to Théophile de Bordeu and Paul Joseph Barthez, indirectly perhaps even to Albrecht von Haller, taking particular stock of such features of the Montpellier school of physiology as had inspired Diderot's writings on the subject and were to come to the notice of Claude Henri de Saint-Simon mainly by way of Marie François Bichat and Jean Burdin.

Above all, perhaps, they were spiritual descendants of Montesquieu's *Spirit of the Laws*, less with respect to its constitutionalism and republicanism than its attempt to formulate what might be termed deep structural explanations of human behaviour, interpreting laws in terms of manners and mores, and even religions by way of mental dispositions which reflected the influence of climate and other external factors upon the nerve fibres of the body. Historians of social science, sometimes inspired by the seminal studies on the Scottish Enlightenment of Gladys Bryson, George Davie, Duncan Forbes, and their successors, have frequently traced the origins of that discipline to the writings of Hutcheson, Hume, Smith, Adam Ferguson, John Millar, and Dugald Stewart in particular (Bryson 1945; Davie 1961; Forbes 1975). No genealogical study of the roots of modern social science can ignore with impunity that great current which swelled in Scotland's cities and universities throughout the mid- to late eighteenth century and then came to feed tributaries in Germany, France, America, and elsewhere. But in the conceptual revolution that succeeded both the invention of the term and the upheavals of the Jacobin Reign of Terror, the progenitors of modern social science drew inspiration from Scottish precursors in large measure by way of a French source who thus himself profoundly influenced the development and trajectory of the Scottish Enlightenment.

In claiming that the human sciences first arose around 1795 Foucault was, in a fundamental sense, mistaken, since the epistemic metamorphosis he traced to that period of European intellectual history actually had a longer period of gestation throughout the eighteenth century than his notion of a *rupture épistemologique* allowed. In its materialist philosophy it may indeed be said to have issued, through the Enlightenment, from some central elements of seventeenth-century Cartesian science itself, and ultimately from Democritus and especially Lucretius. But, however we interpret its nature and pedigree, it remains the case that the transformation of the human sciences around 1795, or, indeed, their invention, as Foucault describes it, was marked by the removal of politics from the scientific scrutiny of human nature – by the elimination of the spheres of legislation and political action from *la science sociale* and their redescription as abstract, utopian, metaphysical, and, after the Terror, dangerous to know. Nothing was to prove so destructive of that central feature of Enlightenment political thought, which throughout the latter half of the eighteenth century had been conceived as a science of legislation for the promotion of human happiness, than the birth, by Cæsarean section plucked from the womb of the old society, of genuinely modern social science. The proponents of the fresh disciplines that arose

from around 1795 were far less committed than their predecessors to changing the world. They sought instead, by interpreting its internal functions,
to preserve it.

While the expression 'social science' gained currency in England later
than in France, it appeared in both cases, although for different reasons, and
despite the hostility to theological dogmas professed by its advocates in each
country, to evoke profound religious convictions and values, including mystical notions of corporate identity and collective faith, as distinct from the
guidelines of political reason and the market's impersonal rules of exchange.
To their critics in France who charged them with having fomented violence, and to their adversaries in England who accused them of promoting
competition only, progressive thinkers of the eighteenth century came in
each instance to seem, in the light of the French and Industrial Revolutions
respectively, to have dispensed with the bonds of social cohesion and to have
cast aside the consolidating ties of religious belief. In demystifying Christianity and thereby toppling the superstitions which had, through priestcraft
and feudalism, sustained its empire over gullible believers, the *philosophes* and
their 'party of humanity' had apparently shorn society of its communal soul.
So as to enable it to heal itself, they had dissected the body politic and uncovered its skeletal core without ever detecting its marrow. Romanticism, in so
far as it may be described as a philosophy of the Counter-Enlightenment,
arose in the last two or three decades of the eighteenth century as a voice
of just such reactionary disenchantment. Modern social science around the
turn of the nineteenth century in both France and England was similarly
inspired by hostility towards the zeal of the age of Enlightenment for a world
freed of the baggage of all religions, apart from – and that only in certain
instances – a patriotic devotion to the state. Socialism likewise would in the
nineteenth century come to articulate the vengeance of religious populism
and medieval corporatism against the presuppositions and goals of a naively
secular age.

In large measure modelled upon the *idéologues'* attempt to sketch a new
science de l'homme, the first great synthesis of a post-Revolutionary science of
society was to be the scheme elaborated by Saint-Simon in several writings
of the early nineteenth century, culminating in his *Introduction aux travaux scientifiques du XIXe siècle* (Introduction to the Scientific Writings of the Nineteenth Century) of 1807–8 and his *Mémoire sur la science de l'homme* (Memoir
on the Science of Man) of 1813. While Saint-Simon perceived himself to
be a disciple of the Enlightenment, inspired in his revolutionary ardour by
its critical spirit, its commitment to science, and its *Encyclopédie*, he came as

well to put the case for a positive science of human nature and society which had as its aim the synthesis of the anatomy of Félix Vicq-d'Azyr, the physiology of Bichat, the psychology of Cabanis, and the philosophical history of Condorcet. That *science de l'organisation sociale*, as he sometimes termed it, was to lead Saint-Simon to inspect the internal constitution and morphology of the social body in a fresh idiom, different from the perspectives adopted by the *philosophes* of the Enlightenment he admired, even including Montesquieu, who above all other major eighteenth-century thinkers came closest to sharing his conception of a social science.

Saint-Simon was convinced that, following both its achievement and its failure, the critical and revolutionary philosophy of the eighteenth century must be superseded in the nineteenth by a reconstructive science or applied philosophy of organisation. The predominantly physiological perspective which inspired him to give precedence to the cohesion of a civil community's internal structure over the pursuit of overarching principles helps to account for why this precursor of socialism, no less than the *idéologues* before him, sometimes found himself in agreement with conservative critics of both the Enlightenment and the Revolution, who likewise complained of the abstractions of eighteenth-century philosophy and the political excesses to which it was prey. The same perspective was also to inform Saint-Simon's view of religion, so radically different from what he termed the *anti-théologie* of the *Encyclopédistes*. The supposition of Condorcet and other eighteenth-century *philosophes* that the middle ages had marked a retrograde step in the development of the human mind he deemed absurd. Quite the contrary. The medieval world, he argued, had witnessed both the progress of scientific knowledge under the Saracens and the advance of social organisation – indeed the foundation of European society itself – through the bond of religious association Charlemagne had formed with Rome. With the end of the age of Enlightenment, the hostility to theological dogma and superstition which had been embraced in so many of its leading doctrines, and their all too frequent conjunction of barbarism and religion, came to be widely supplanted by theologically inspired notions of community and a more sympathetic understanding of Europe's 'dark ages'.

In putting his account of the internal organisation of society in physiological terms, Saint-Simon showed much the same distrust of legislative and political solutions to social problems of disorder and derangement as was felt by the *idéologues* of the *Classe des sciences morales et politiques*. Rather like Burke and other opponents of the French Revolution of an earlier generation, he deplored the immense influence exercised over the government of France by lawyers and jurists, which had proved calamitous both under Robespierre and the Committee of Public Safety and again when the despotism of Napoleon had overnight converted republican lawyers into proselytes of his supreme authority. The *industriels*, or class of entrepreneurial scientists, engineers, and businessmen whose cause he championed, had not played an active part in the Revolution, he complained; they had, indeed, been among its principal victims, and French society had suffered as a consequence. In the age of organisation and reconstruction, intercessionist rule would come to be superseded by prophylactic management alone, the government of men in effect giving way to the administration of things. Through the influence of Saint-Simon's principal disciple, Auguste Comte, this new positive science of society, soon to be known by the word *sociologie* – which Comte invented – was to become the pre-eminent science of modernity itself, while political economy, the deism of commercial or capitalist society in the late eighteenth century and subsequently destined to become the 'dismal science' of a post-Enlightenment age, was, through an invisible hand or power that steered an impersonal market, to become modernity's new religion (see Gouhier 1933–41; Wokler 1987d).

The idea of a social system, which in the course of the French Revolution had given rise to the first academic formulations of the discipline of social science, would by way of its positivist interpreters of the nineteenth century thereafter come to refer to societal patterns that were at once organised and organic, in each sense intricately structured from within while nevertheless subject to regulation not by the people themselves, nor even by politicians, but by expert social engineers. An alternative clerisy would arise with appropriate technical knowledge and spiritual powers to replace the priestcraft of the old theologies whose authority the age of Enlightenment had undermined. And while a much cherished Revolutionary Declaration of the Rights of Man and the Citizen would come to be enshrined in the constitution of Europe's first genuine nation-state, neither natural nor civil rights would subsequently figure prominently as the centrally guiding principles of nineteenth-century social science. Even if they were not positivists, social scientists would henceforth be less interested in human rights than were their Enlightenment precursors, and many socialists among them would in time come to follow Friedrich Engels in advocating the abolition or withering away of the state.

Biographies

These notes provide outline biographies of many of the political writers of the eighteenth century. Details of modern editions of some of their chief works are given in the 'Bibliography of primary sources'. At the end of most entries there is a guide to scholarly literature, details of which can be found in the 'Bibliography of secondary sources'. (For the dozen most prominent authors only books are noted: further literature may be found in the Bibliography.) The principle of inverse proportion has been applied: major figures do not necessarily have longer entries than minor ones, since they can more readily be traced in standard reference works. Foreign language titles are translated, except where their meaning will be readily understood by Anglophone readers. Further biographical information can be explored in the reference works listed in the 'Bibliography of general works'.

ABBADIE, JACQUES

c. 1654–1727. French Huguenot theorist of resistance. Born in Nay near Pau, and educated at Saumur and Sedan, he fled France and became pastor in Berlin, *c.* 1680. He accompanied William of Orange's invasion of England, 1688, and Marshal Schomberg's campaign in Ireland, 1689–90. He was an Anglican minister in London, 1690–9, then dean of Killaloe, Ireland, 1699–1727. His theological works softened Calvinism with Christian rationalism and optimism. His principal political work was a defence of the Glorious Revolution: *Défense de la nation britannique* (1692; partly repr. 1775). He grounded political power in contract and the protection of natural rights.

ACHENWALL, GOTTFRIED

1719–72. German jurist. Born in Elbing, he became professor of law at Göttingen University, was a student of comparative politics, and travelled to England and Holland. In 1749 he published a survey of contemporary politics in the principal European monarchies and republics. His principal legal work was *Jus naturae* (The Law of Nature, 1750). He was responsible for the key textbooks in law and ethics studied at Göttingen in mid-century, which broadly followed a Thomasian account of legal obligation.
• Hruschka 1986.

ACHERLEY, ROGER

c. 1665–1740. English lawyer. Born in Stottesden, Shropshire, and called to the bar, 1691. He strongly advocated the Hanoverian succession, but met with little reward, despite lobbying Leibniz. Of his numerous political, legal, and constitutional works, the most significant is *The Britannic Constitution* (1727, repr. 1741, 1759). It applauded the Ancient Constitution, denied that William I conquered the English, and summed up Magna Carta as 'a renewal of the original contract'. It was admired by John Adams and Jefferson, and crops up in colonial American libraries.
• Colbourn 1965.

Biographies

ADAMS, ABIGAIL

1744–1818. American revolutionary. Born Abigail Smith in Weymouth, Massachusetts, she married John Adams, 1764, and became the wife and the mother of presidents. She had no formal schooling, but learnt Latin. Her friends included Jefferson and Mercy Otis Warren. Her political thinking emerged in prolonged correspondence with her husband and others. She has acquired considerable *éclat* because of a remark made in a letter to John in 1776: 'Remember the ladies . . . do not put such unlimited power into the hands of husbands. Remember all men would be tyrants if they could. If particular care and attention is not paid to the ladies, we are determined to foment a rebellion, and will not hold ourselves bound by any laws in which we have no voice, or representation.'
• Gelles 1992; Keller 1994.

ADAMS, JOHN

1735–1826. American revolutionary. Born in Braintree, now Quincy, Massachusetts, he was educated at Harvard University, and practised law in Boston. He served in the Continental Congresses, 1774–7, helped draft the Declaration of Independence, 1776, and drafted the Massachusetts constitution, 1779. He was US ambassador to Britain, 1785–8, served under Washington as the first vice-president, 1789–97, and was second president, 1797–1801. His works include *A Dissertation on the Canon and Feudal Law* (1765), which collected his essays against the Stamp Act from the *Boston Gazette*; *Thoughts on Government* (1776); *A Defence of the Constitutions of Government of the United States of America* (1787–8); and *Discourses on Davila* (1791), which argued that a monarchic and aristocratic government was suited to France.
• Howe 1966; McCullough 2001; Wood 1969; Zvesper 1977.

ADAMS, SAMUEL

1722–1803. American revolutionary. Born in Boston, Massachusetts, a cousin of John Adams, he failed in business, practised as a lawyer, and made his name as a journalist and pamphleteer against British rule. He helped organise the Boston Tea Party, 1773, and by 1774 was calling for resistance; he signed the Declaration of Independence, 1776. He was governor of Massachusetts, 1794–7. His newspaper articles during the 1760s drew from a variety of sources, including the English republican tradition, Locke, and Vattel.
• Colbourn 1965; Schlesinger 1958.

ADDISON, JOSEPH

1672–1719. English moral essayist, poet, classicist, and politician. Born in Amesbury, Wiltshire, and educated at Oxford University, he went on the Grand Tour, 1699–1703. He was a Member of Parliament, 1709–19, and Whig secretary of state, 1717–18. With Steele, he wrote essays for the *Tatler* (1709–11), the *Spectator* (1711–12, 1714), and the *Guardian* (1713). He also produced the *Free-holder* (1715–16) and the *Old Whig* (1719). His highly influential essays helped define the 'polite' culture of eighteenth-century Britain and models of virtue for citizens of a commercial society. His tragedy, *Cato* (1713), celebrating the Roman republican patriot, was a great success on the London stage.
• Bloom and Bloom 1971; Bloom, Bloom, and Leites 1984; Walker 2003.

ALEMBERT, JEAN BAPTISTE LE ROND D'

1717–83. French philosopher and mathematician. Born in Paris, he was educated at a Jansenist school and the Sorbonne. He published extensively on mathematics and mechanics, and was elected to the *Académie des sciences*, 1741, of which he became permanent secretary, and to the *Académie française*, 1754. During 1746–58 he was co-editor with Diderot of the *Encyclopédie*. He composed this work's 'Discours préliminaire' (1751), a manifesto for empiricism as the

712

foundation for the advancement of humanity. He wrote many articles, mostly on mathematical subjects, but also that on Geneva. He declined Frederick II's offer to become president of the Berlin Academy. Among his tracts was *Sur la destruction des Jésuites* (On the Destruction of the Jesuits, 1765).
• Grimsley 1963; Hankins 1970; Lough 1968; Pappas 1962; Paty 1977; Van Treese 1974.

ALFIERI, VITTORIO

1749–1803. Italian poet and dramatist, self-proclaimed enemy of tyranny, whose work influenced the Risorgimento. Born in Asti, Piedmont, and educated at Turin, he was much travelled and wrote voluminously, most notably nineteen tragedies, 1775–89. He had a long affair with the wife of the Stuart 'Young Pretender' to the British thrones, living with her in Paris in the 1780s. Alfieri applauded the American Revolution (*L'America libera* (Free America, 1781–3)), and the French (he wrote an ode on the fall of the Bastille), but fled France for Italy, 1792. He was influenced by Montesquieu's admiration for British liberty. His tragedies celebrated heroes (such as Brutus) and deprecated tyrants (such as Philip II of Spain). His political essays include *Della tirannide* (On Tyranny, 1789), and *Del principe e delle lettere* (On the Prince and Literature, 1786), the latter arguing for literary freedom.
• Santato 1988.

AMO, ANTON WILHELM

c. 1703–56. Ghanaian jurist, and the first European-trained African philosopher. Educated at Halle, Wittenberg, and Jena Universities, he was influenced by Leibniz and Wolff. At Halle he wrote a dissertation on the relationship between the Roman law of slavery and the position of Africans in Europe. He wrote on a wide variety of other topics in international law, psychology, and metaphysics.
• Abraham 1964.

ARBUTHNOT, JOHN

1667–1735. Scottish journalist and satirist. Born in Arbuthnot, Kincardineshire, and educated at Aberdeen and St Andrews Universities, he became a physician and mathematician, settled in London, was elected a Fellow of the Royal Society, 1704, and appointed physician to the queen, 1705. He published on statistics, numismatics, and medicine, as well as satires on the more absurd aspects of contemporary scientific speculation. He co-wrote with Pope and Swift the *Memoirs of Martin Scriblerus* (1741). His philosophical poem *Know Your Self* (1734) is a resigned Christian meditation on fallen humanity. His principal political work is the satire *The History of John Bull* (1712).
• Aitken 1892; Condren 2000; Levine 1977.

ARGENSON, RENÉ LOUIS DE VOYER, MARQUIS D'

1694–1757. French statesman and author. Born in Paris, he belonged to the Club de l'Entresol, a literary salon which included Voltaire. A civil servant who briefly held high office, he was foreign minister during the War of the Austrian Succession, 1744–7. His chief work was *Considérations sur le gouvernment ancien et présent de la France* (written in 1739 but not published until 1764). Monarchic but egalitarian, its critique of economic and social injustice influenced later theorists of property.
• Henry 1968; Israel 2001; Johnston 1928; Ogle 1893.

ASTELL, MARY

1666–1731. Sometimes called 'the first English feminist'. Born in Newcastle-upon-Tyne, she settled in Chelsea near London and turned to authorship. Her principal work was *A*

Serious Proposal to the Ladies (1694), a challenge to patriarchalism, which offered a scheme for a secular convent devoted to intellectual, moral, and pious education. In the preface to the third edition (1706) of her *Some Reflections upon Marriage* (1700) appears her most often quoted remark: 'If all men are born free, how is that all women are born slaves?' Astell was a Tory and High Church Anglican, and her later pamphlets, such as *A Fair Way with the Dissenters* (1704) and *An Impartial Enquiry into the Causes of Rebellion* (1704), were assaults on Whigs and Dissenters. She also published an extended work of philosophical theology, *The Christian Religion* (1705), which challenged Locke's friend Damaris Masham.
• Kinnaird 1979; McCrystal 1993; Pateman 1988; Perry 1986, 1990; Springborg 1995.

ATTERBURY, FRANCIS

1662–1732. English Tory churchman. Born in Milton, Buckinghamshire, he was educated at Oxford University. He became a clergyman, 1687, chaplain to King William and Queen Mary, and rose to be bishop of Rochester, 1713. He turned to Jacobitism after the Hanoverian succession, and the conspiracy of 1722 is known as the Atterbury Plot. Attainted for treason, he was deposed from his bishopric and banished, 1723. He died in Paris. In the 1690s he began a literary campaign in defence of the Church of England against its enemies. His chief tracts were *A Letter to a Convocation Man* (1697), *The Rights, Powers, and Privileges of an English Convocation* (1700), *The Mitre and the Crown* (1711), and *A Representation of the State of Religion* (1711).
• Bennett 1975.

ATWOOD, WILLIAM

c. 1661–c. 1705. English Whig lawyer and constitutional theorist. He became chief justice of New York, 1701, but was suspended on charges of corruption, 1702, and returned to England. In *Jani anglorum facies nova* (New Face of the English Janus, 1680) and *Jus anglorum ab antiquo* (English Law from the Beginning, 1681) he attacked Robert Brady's theory of the medieval monarchical origins of parliament, asserting instead its Saxon origins and legislative supremacy over the crown. In the *Fundamental Constitution of the English Government* (1690) he presented a Whig account of the Revolution of 1688, albeit taking issue with Locke's *Two Treatises*, insisting that government had devolved upon the Convention and not the community at large. Later, he defended the sovereignty of the British parliament over Ireland and Scotland, against Molyneux and the Scottish patriots.
• Franklin 1978; Ludington 2000; Pocock 1987; R. J. Smith 1987.

BABEUF, FRANÇOIS NOËL (GRACCHUS)

1760–97. French communist and revolutionary. Born in Saint-Quentin, of poor parents, he began as a clerk, but during the Revolution came to prominence as a virulent journalist. After the fall of Robespierre in 1794, he attacked the government in his newspaper, *Tribun du peuple* (Tribune of the People). In issue 35 he published his *Manifesto of the Plebeians*. He organised a 'Conspiracy of the Equals', and in 1796 was arrested for treason. He attempted suicide before his execution.
• Advielle 1884; Rose 1978; Thamer 1973.

BACKUS, ISAAC

1724–1806. American defender of religious toleration and the separation of church and state. Born in Norwich, Connecticut, he had little formal education. Experiencing religious conversion during the Great Awakening, 1741, he founded a New Light Church, and then joined the Baptists, 1751, becoming pastor at Middleborough, Massachusetts. He presented

a memorial to the Continental Congress, 1774, in favour of full religious liberty. His chief works are: *A Seasonable Plea for Liberty of Conscience* (1770), *An Appeal to the Public for Religious Liberty* (1773), and *Government and Liberty Described, and Ecclesiastical Tyranny Exposed* (1778).
• Maston 1962.

BARBEYRAC, JEAN DE
1674–1744. French jurist and philosopher of natural law. Born in Béziers of Protestant parents, he fled to Switzerland, 1686, where he studied law. After teaching in Switzerland and Germany, 1697–1710, he became professor of law at Groningen in the Netherlands, 1717. He is known chiefly as the translator and editor of Grotius, of Cumberland, and especially of Pufendorf's *De jure naturae et gentium* (1706), the notes to which cite Locke extensively. An English translation, *Of the Law of Nature and Nations*, appeared in 1717.
• Brühlmeier 1995; Goyard-Fabre 1996a; Hochstrasser 1993, 1995; Korkman 2002; Mautner 1996; Merk 1937; Othmer 1970; Saunders 2003.

BARKER, JANE
1652–1732. English Jacobite poet and novelist. Born in Blatherwick, Northamptonshire, she converted to Catholicism, 1685, and entered the London literary world. *Poetical Reflections* (1688) reflected her spiritual and intellectual concerns. After the Revolution she fled and lived in proximity to the Jacobite court in France. *Poems Referring to the Times* (1701) was presented to the Jacobite prince of Wales. After returning to England, 1704, she dramatised Jacobite loyalism in a series of novels and romances, notably the *Amours of Bosvil and Gelasia* (1713), *Exilius: or The Banish'd Roman* (1714), and *A Patch Work Screen for the Ladies* (1723). *The Christian Pilgrimage* (1718) translated Fénelon's Lenten meditations.
• King 2000.

BARLOW, JOEL
1754–1812. American lawyer, diplomat, poet, and author. Born in Reading, Connecticut, and educated at Dartmouth and Yale University, he served in the militia during the War of Independence. He became a military chaplain and later a lawyer. He edited *The American Weekly* (1784–5). His national epic, *The Vision of Columbus* (1787) brought him fame. He lived in Europe, 1788–1805, joining Paine's circle in London, and arranging publication of Paine's *Age of Reason*. His *Advice to the Privileged Orders in the Several States of Europe, Resulting from the Necessity and Propriety of a General Revolution in the Principle of Government* (1792) was a reply to Burke. His *Letter to the National Convention of France* (1792) brought him French citizenship, and he became a delegate in the Assembly. He exhorted the Piedmontese to revolt, and acted as diplomatic intermediary between America and France. He returned to America, 1805, was US ambassador to France, 1811, and died during Napoleon's retreat from Moscow.
• Ball 1967; Cantor 1958; Durden 1951; Woodress 1958.

BARNAVE, ANTOINE PIERRE JOSEPH MARIE
1761–93. French revolutionary. Born in Grenoble, a Protestant, he became a lawyer, was elected to the Estates General, 1789, and became president of the National Assembly. His pro-slavery defence of French colonial interests was opposed by Brissot, and he became increasingly detached from the Jacobins. A defender of constitutional monarchy, he was guillotined during the Terror. While in prison in 1792 he wrote his *Introduction à la Révolution française*, published in 1843. This is a remarkable attempt at a social or 'philosophical' history of the Revolution, showing the evolution of society toward the hegemony of the bourgeoisie.
• Webster 1993.

BARRINGTON, JOHN SHUTE, FIRST VISCOUNT

1678–1734. English lawyer and theorist of religious toleration. Born at Theobalds, Hertfordshire, he was educated at a Dissenting academy and Utrecht University. In 1704 he befriended Locke. He was sent to Edinburgh to help persuade the Scots to support the Union with England. His appointment as a customs commissioner, 1708, made him the highest ranking Dissenter in public office. He was elected a Member of Parliament, 1715 and 1722, and made an Irish peer, 1720. He and Calamy were the principal early eighteenth-century defenders of toleration on behalf of the Dissenters, both deploying Locke's *Letter concerning Toleration*. His publications include *An Essay upon the Interest of England* (1701), *The Rights of Protestant Dissenters* (1704–5), *A Dissuasive from Jacobitism* (1713), and *The Revolution and Anti-Revolution Principles Stated and Compared* (1714).
• Hunt 1961.

BASNAGE (DE BEAUVAL), JACQUES

1653–1723. French Huguenot cleric and theorist of toleration. Born in Rouen, and educated at Saumur, Geneva, and Sedan. After the Revocation of the Edict of Nantes, he settled in the Dutch Republic, ministering to congregations at Rotterdam, 1685–1709, and The Hague, 1710–23. He was a prominent member of Bayle's circle at Rotterdam. He wrote an innovative history of the Jews, *Histoire des Juifs* (1706), histories of the French Reformed church, and a defence of religious toleration, *Traité de la conscience* (1696). His brother, Henri, was a journalist, who wrote *Tolérance des religions* (1684).
• Adams 1991; Cerny 1987; Mailhet 1880.

BAUDEAU, ABBÉ NICOLAS

1730–92. French political economist. Born in Amboise, he became a monk and taught theology, but was called to Paris in the 1760s by the archbishop of Paris to challenge the physiocrats, which he did in his journal *Les Ephémérides du citoyen* (The Citizen's Almanac), founded in 1765. However, he changed his mind and became an accomplished defender of physiocracy, notably in his *Première introduction à la philosophie économique* (1771).
• Hensmann 1976.

BAYLE, PIERRE

1647–1706. French Protestant encyclopedist and defender of toleration. Born in Le Carla in the Pyrenees, he studied at Toulouse University, went to Geneva, taught there, and then became professor of philosophy at the Huguenot academy at Sedan, 1675. After its closure by Louis XIV in 1681, he settled in Rotterdam, where he taught in the Huguenot college. His earliest polemics were the *Lettre sur la comète* (Letter on the Comet, 1682) and *Critique générale de l'Histoire du Calvinisme de M. Maimbourg* (1682). In 1684 he launched a periodical, *Nouvelles de la république des lettres* (News of the Republic of Letters, 1684–7), which pioneered the essay-review journal. In his *Commentaire philosophique* (1686) he defended toleration and became embroiled in controversy with Jurieu. His principal work was the *Dictionnaire historique et critique* (1697; English trans. *An Historical and Critical Dictionary*, 1710), a large and influential encyclopedia of historical and contemporary philosophical opinions, marked by a strain of scepticism.
• Jenkinson 2000; Kilcullen 1988; Labrousse 1963–4, 1983; Mason 1963; Rétat 1971; Rex 1965; Schneewind 1997; Simonutti 1996.

BEAUMARCHAIS, PIERRE AUGUSTIN CARON DE

1732–99. French playwright. Born in Paris. He was by turns a clockmaker, court official, and music teacher. He was involved in numerous ventures, intrigues, and court cases. He published for Voltaire. He is best known for two satirical comedies, *Le Barbier de Séville* (1775) and *Le Mariage de Figaro* (1784), both rich in social commentary, particularly at the expense of the aristocracy.

BECCARIA, CESARE BONESANA, MARCHESE DE

1738–94. Italian legal theorist. Born in Milan, he studied at Pavia University. With the brothers Pietro and Alessandro Verri he formed a salon in Milan, adopted Enlightenment ideals, and published a journal, *Il Caffè* (The Coffee-House, 1764–6). In 1768 he took the chair of cameralist science in Milan, and from 1771 he was a member of the Milanese government, introducing legal and monetary reforms. His chief work was *Dei delitti e delle pene* (On Crimes and Punishments, 1764; French trans. by Morellet 1766; English trans. 1767). Grounded on the premise, articulated for the first time, that the aim of society is to secure the greatest happiness of the greatest number, it set out a scheme for reducing both crime and punishment, through a defined legal code. It urged the abolition of torture and the death penalty. It was extremely influential, Bentham being a signal admirer. Beccaria's lectures of 1769–70, *Elementi di economia pubblica* (Elements of Public Economy) were published in 1894.
• Draper 2000; Maestro 1942, 1973; Venturi 1969–90, 1971, 1972.

BECHER, JOHANN JOACHIM

1635–82. German cameralist and chemist. Born in Speyer, he was largely self-educated and in youth travelled widely in Northern Europe and Scandinavia. From 1660 he was court physician in Mainz, where he converted to Catholicism, and married the sister of Philip von Hörnigk (1640–1714), author of the early cameralist treatise, *Österreich über alles* (Austria Above All, 1677). In 1664 Becher entered Bavarian service, and wrote his principal works in Munich: *Methodus didactica* (1668), *Politische Discurs* (1668), and *Physica subterranea* (1669). He returned to Vienna, 1670, where he was alchemical and economic adviser to Leopold I. His last years were spent wandering in the Low Countries and England.
• Frühsorge and Strasser 1993.

BENTHAM, JEREMY

1748–1832. English jurist, penal reformer, and philosopher. Born in London, he was educated at Oxford University and the Inns of Court, London, but did not practise law. An associate of the earl of Shelburne, 1781, he visited Russia, 1785–8, and became an honorary citizen of France, 1792. In *A Fragment on Government* (1776) he attacked the shibboleths of the common law and defended the systematic codification of law, through an attack on Blackstone's *Commentaries*. He assailed the ideas of natural law and the social contract. His *Introduction to the Principles of Morals and Legislation* (1789) laid the philosophical groundwork of utilitarianism, building an ethical and penal theory on sensationalist psychology. His theory of punishment rested on deterrence and rehabilitation rather than retribution. He later campaigned for prison reform, and became famous for his proposed 'Panopticon' prison. Towards the end of his life he advocated a democratic franchise. He inspired the 'Philosophical Radicals' of the 1830s and 1840s, whose ideas were promoted in the *Westminster Review*, founded in 1824.
• Baumgardt 1952; Bonner 1995; Dinwiddy 1989; Halévy 1928; Harrison 1983; Hart 1982; Hume 1981; Kelly 1990; Long 1977; Lyons 1973; Mack 1962; Manning 1968; Parekh 1974; Postema 1986; Rosen 1983, 1992; Rosenblum 1978; Semple 1993; Steintrager 1977.

BERINGTON, JOSEPH

1746–1827. English Catholic advocate of religious toleration. Born in Shropshire, he was educated at the Jesuit college of Saint-Omer, France, and ordained priest. Returning to

England, 1786, he served in Staffordshire and later in Berkshire. A leading figure of the English Catholic Enlightenment, friendly with Protestant Dissenters, he was fiercely 'Gallican' and anti-papal. He was censured by Catholic authorities for his liberal theology. His *Letters on Materialism* (1776) opposed Hartley and Priestley. He defended toleration and civil liberties for Catholics and Dissenters in *The State and Behaviour of the English Catholics* (1780), *An Address to the Protestant Dissenters* (1787), and *The Rights of Dissenters from the Established Church, in Relation, Principally, to English Catholics* (1789).
• Chinnici 1980.

BERKELEY, GEORGE
1685–1753. Irish philosopher and political writer. Born in Thomastown, Kilkenny, he was educated at Trinity College, Dublin. He travelled abroad during the 1710s. Ordained in 1710, he became dean of Derry, 1724, and bishop of Cloyne, 1734. In London in 1713, he met Addison, Steele, Swift, and Pope, and wrote for Steele's *Guardian*, attacking philosophical materialism. He wrote on epistemology, mathematics, cosmology, optics, politics, and theology. His *Treatise concerning the Principles of Human Knowledge* (1710) offers a theory of philosophical idealism. In *Three Dialogues between Hylas and Philonous* (1713) he attacked religious sceptics and deists. His early political writing was on *Passive Obedience* (1712). Later he devised a scheme for a college at Bermuda, and visited New England, 1728–31. His other main works were an *Essay towards a New Theory of Vision* (1709), *Alciphron, Or, the Minute Philosopher* (1732), *Analyst* (1734), and *The Querist* (1736).
• Berman 1986; Gausted 1979; Olscamp 1970; Pappas 2000; Rozbicki 2001; Warnock 1986.

BERNARDIN DE SAINT-PIERRE, JACQUES HENRI
1737–1814. French utopian. Born in Le Havre, he was much travelled – in Martinique, Holland, Russia, and Mauritius – and he served as an engineer during the Seven Years War, 1756–63. His novel *Paul et Virginie* (1788), set in Martinique, is an idyll on the theme of natural religion and harmony with nature. Anticlericalism and opposition to slavery are the themes of his play *Empsaël et Zoraide* (*c.* 1789–92). He was elected to the Convention, 1792, and later supported Napoleon.
• Davies 1994.

BILLAUD-VARENNE, JACQUES NICOLAS
1756–1819. French revolutionary. Born in La Rochelle, he studied in Paris and Poitiers and became a lawyer and pamphleteer. At the Revolution he joined the Jacobins, and was the chief author of the resolution for a republic, 1792. He led the attack on the Girondins and, as a member of the Committee of Public Safety, was one of the architects of the Terror, 1793–4, though he contributed to Robespierre's downfall. He sought to turn the Revolution toward the claims of the *sans-culottes*. His *Eléments du républicanisme* (1793) promoted the ideas of Hébert for full employment and the redistribution of wealth. In 1795 he was deported to the West Indies, and died in Haiti. Other works include *Despotisme des ministres de France* (The Despotism of the Ministers of France, 1789), and *L'Acéphocratie, ou le gouvernement fédératif* (Acephocracy, or Federative Government, 1791).
• Guilaine 1969.

BLACKBURNE, FRANCIS
1705–87. English latitudinarian cleric. Born in Richmond, Yorkshire, and educated at Cambridge University, he became rector of Richmond, 1739–87, and wrote a number of theological works. His chief political contribution was *The Confessional, Or, A Full and Free Inquiry*

into the Right, Utility, Edification, and Success of Establishing Systematical Confessions of Faith and Doctrine in Protestant Churches (1766), which rejected the requirement of subscription to the doctrines of the Church of England, and was a key text in the campaign for a wider tolera-tion. He celebrated the 'Commonwealth' political tradition in his *Memoirs of Thomas Hollis* (1780).

• Barlow 1962; Clark 1985; Fitzpatrick 1993; Gascoigne 1986.

BLACKSTONE, SIR WILLIAM
1723–80. English jurist and exponent of the common law. Born in Wallingford, Oxfordshire, he was educated at Oxford University and the Inns of Court, London, being called to the bar in 1746. He became a Tory Member of Parliament, 1761, solicitor-general to the queen, 1763, and a judge, 1770. He gave the first university lectures on English law, 1753, and was the first Vinerian professor of English law at Oxford, 1758–66. His chief work, based on lectures, was his *Commentaries on the Laws of England* (1765–9), translated into French, German, Russian, and Italian. This became a standard textbook, setting out the principles of the common law in systematic fashion. Though holding that the common law was a local application of natural law, Blackstone made the relationship between natural and positive law appear ambiguous, not least because of his strong doctrine of the illimitable sovereignty of parliament. The book was the target of Bentham's *Fragment on Government*.

• Cairns 1985; Cross 1976; Lieberman 1988, 1989; Lobban 1987; Milsom 1981; Raeff 1974; Willman 1983.

BLAND, RICHARD
1710–76. American revolutionary. A native of Virginia, he studied at William and Mary College. He was a landowner, scholar, and politician, becoming a key figure in the Vir-ginia House of Burgesses, 1742–75. He protested against colonial taxation in *The Colonel Dismounted* (1764), where he accused his enemies of being 'Filmer's disciples'. During the Revolution he was a delegate to the Continental Congress, 1774. His key work was *An Enquiry into the Rights of the British Colonies* (1766), which challenged the doctrine of 'vir-tual' representation, denying that Americans could be construed as being represented in the imperial parliament. It argued that the Americans are a 'distinct people', already in a 'distinct state': the early colonists, by withdrawing from England, had 'quit' the English polity and had begun new ones.

• Bailyn 1967; Rossiter 1953.

BOISGUILBERT, PIERRE LE PESANT, SIEUR DE
1646–1714. French political economist. Born in Rouen, he was an official there from 1689. He proposed reforms to the fiscal system in order to rescue the regime from bankruptcy. His principal tracts were *Le détail de la France* (A Detailed Account of France, 1695) and *Le factum de la France* (The Case of France, 1707). He was briefly exiled in 1707.

• Roberts 1935.

BOLINGBROKE, HENRY ST JOHN, VISCOUNT
1678–1751. English Tory politician, theorist, and historian. Born in Wiltshire. He went on the Grand Tour, 1698–1700. A member of parliament, 1701–12, until raised to the peerage, he rose to be secretary of state, 1710–14. The Treaty of Utrecht, 1713, was largely his achievement: it ended war with France, but brought the ire of the Hanoverian dynasty and the Whigs. At the Hanoverian succession, he was attainted for Jacobite treason, and fled to France. After rejecting Jacobitism he was allowed to return home, 1723, but exclusion from the House of Lords forced him to lead the Country opposition to Prime Minister Walpole

with his pen. He led a brilliant circle, among them Pulteney, Swift, Pope, and Gay, and was host to Montesquieu on his visit to England, 1729–31. His essays for *The Craftsman* used the 'Commonwealth' tradition to fuse Tories and dissident Whigs in an assault on corrupt and overweening executive power. He retired to France again in 1734. The *Dissertation upon Parties* (1733–4) and *Remarks on the History of England* (1743) reworked *Craftsman* essays from the early 1730s. *The Idea of a Patriot King* (1749) argued for a liberty-loving monarch who would transcend partisan divisions. For all his Toryism, his *Letters on the Study and Use of History* (1752) exhibit the 'Whig' theory of history as the struggle of parliaments for liberty.
• Armitage 1997; Barrell 1988; Burns 1962; Cottret 1995; Dickinson 1970; Hart 1965; Kramnick 1968; Mansfield 1965; Rogers 1970; Shackleton 1949; Skinner 1974; Varey 1984.

BONALD, LOUIS GABRIEL AMBROISE, VICOMTE DE
1754–1840. French counter-revolutionary, philosopher, and critic. Born at Millau, he studied in Paris, became a soldier, and then mayor of Millau. In 1791 he joined the émigré army in Germany. He published a series of indictments of Enlightenment and revolutionary principles, particularly the presuppositions of individualism: *Théorie du pouvoir politique et religieux dans la société civile* (Theory of Political and Religious Power in Civil Society, 1796); *Essai analytique sur les lois naturelles de l'ordre social* (Analytical Essay on the Natural Laws of the Social Order, 1800); *Législation primitive* (1802). With Chateaubriand and Maistre, he was a principal ideologist of aristocratic and royalist reaction. During the 1820s he was a minister under the restored monarchy.
• Godechot 1972; McMahon 2001; Spaemann 1959.

BOSSUET, JACQUES BÉNIGNE
1627–1704. French Catholic orator, theologian, and philosopher of absolutism. Born in Dijon and educated at the Sorbonne, he became bishop of Condom, 1669, and of Meaux, 1681, and was tutor to the Dauphin, 1670–81. Bossuet gained renown for the eloquence of his funeral orations. His ecclesiastical outlook was Gallican, but his theology orthodox. He defended the Four Articles of 1682 which asserted the rights of the French church and of the general council of the church against the papacy. He approved the Revocation of the Edict of Nantes, 1685, which accelerated the persecution of the Huguenots. His *Exposition de la foi catholique* (Exposition of the Catholic Faith, 1671) shared something of Jansenist puritanism. His writings include the *Discours sur l'histoire universelle* (Discourse on Universal History, 1681), a providentialist account of history. His main political work, the *Politique tirée des propres paroles de l'écriture sainte* (Politics Drawn from the Words of Scripture), begun in 1677, was published in 1709. It drew on Stoic, Augustinian, and Hobbesian pessimism, asserting the necessity of absolute monarchical sovereignty.
• Calvet 1968; Martimort 1953; Meyer 1993; Ranum 1976; Rébelliau 1900; Riley 1990.

BOUCHER, JONATHAN
1738–1804. Anglo-American Tory. One of the most prominent loyalists who opposed the Revolution. Born in Bromfield, Cumberland, son of an English alehouse keeper, he migrated to America, 1759. Ordained an Anglican minister, he took up a parish in Annapolis, 1770, and bought a tobacco plantation. He preached against rebellion and fled to England, 1775, where he became vicar of Epsom, Surrey, 1785. His sermons and commentaries, including 'On Civil Liberty, Passive Obedience, and Non-Resistance' (1775), were gathered in *A View of the Causes and Consequences of the American Revolution* (1797), replete with footnotes influenced by his reading of Burke. His *Reminiscences of an American Loyalist* were published in 1925.
• Bailyn 1967; Benton 1969; Nelson 1961; Zimmer 1978.

BOULAINVILLERS, HENRI, COMTE DE

1658–1722. French historian and defender of aristocracy. Born in Saint-Saire, Normandy, he was educated by the Oratorian order, became a soldier, and turned to authorship. He wrote on history, antiquity, and scripture, the last under the influence of Spinoza and Richard Simon. His chief political work was a defence of the French aristocracy against absolute monarchy (the *thèse nobiliaire* against the *thèse royale*): *Histoire de l'ancien gouvernement de France* (1727). In similar vein were the *Etat de la France* (State of France, 1727) and *Essai sur la noblesse de France* (Essay on the French Nobility, 1732). These treatises argued against the monarchic thesis of Dubos. Boullainvilliers claimed that the Frankish chiefs (ancestors of the modern French nobility) had conquered Roman Gaul and elected their own king. Dubos, by contrast, claimed that the Franks were heirs of the Romans and inherited Roman institutions, not least the *imperium* of the Caesars. Montesquieu would pursue a middle way between the two.
• Ellis 1988; Keohane 1980.

BRISSOT (DE WARVILLE), JACQUES PIERRE

1754–93. French revolutionary. Born in Chartres, he studied law, and, in the 1780s, became a journalist. He was jailed in the Bastille, 1784, for pamphlets attacking the court, and fled to London, 1787. He visited the United States, where he advocated abolition of the slave trade. His works include *Théorie des lois criminelles* (Theory of Criminal Law, 1781) and *De la France et des Etats Unis, ou l'importance de la Révolution de l'Amérique pour le bonheur de la France* (France and the United States, Or the Importance of the American Revolution to the Happiness of France, 1787). At the Revolution, he returned to France, his faction acquiring the name of Girondins. He edited *Le Patriote Français* and sat in the Convention. He attacked the Jacobins in *A tous les républicains de France* (To All French Republicans, 1792). Defeated by them, he was guillotined during the Terror.
• Darnton 1982; Whatmore 2000a.

BROOKE, HENRY

1703–83. Irish author. Born in Co. Cavan, he was educated at Trinity College, Dublin, and the Inns of Court, London. He published poems, plays, novels, and essays for journals. In London he joined the circle around Frederick, prince of Wales. His best-known work was the anti-Walpolean tragedy, *Gustavus Vasa, Deliverer of his Country* (1739), banned by the theatre censor in London, but staged in Dublin. He settled in Dublin, *c.* 1740. At the time of the Jacobite rebellion he published an anti-Catholic tract, *A Farmer's Letters to the Protestants of Ireland* (1745), but later he wrote in defence of toleration of Catholics, notably *The Tryal of the Roman Catholicks* (1761).

BROWN, JOHN

1715–66. English moralist. Born in Rothbury, Northumberland, and educated at Cambridge University. Ordained a minister, he became rector of an Essex parish, 1756, and then in Newcastle, 1761. He published odes, epics, essays, and sermons, among them, *Essays on Shaftesbury's moral philosophy* (1751). He is chiefly known for *An Estimate of the Manners and Principles of the Times* (1757), a jeremiad on national luxury, corruption, and degeneracy. Later he published *Thoughts on Civil Liberty* (1765). He committed suicide.
• Roberts 1996.

BRUCKER, JOHANN JAKOB

1696–1770. German historian of philosophy. Born in Augsburg, he was educated at Jena University and ordained a pastor, 1731. His major work was the *Historia critica philosophiae* (Critical History of Philosophy, 1742–4), upon which the *Encyclopédie* drew heavily. It sketched an

intellectual history of humankind, and applauded the achievements of Bacon, Descartes, Locke, and Newton, as laying foundations for an adequate understanding of God's natural order and intentions for the social world.
• Schmidt-Biggemann and Stammen 1998.

BUFFON, GEORGES LOUIS LECLERC, COMTE DE
1707–88. French natural historian. Born at Montbard, he studied law, then turned to science. As director of the king's garden in Paris, 1739–88, he planned a comprehensive 'natural history'. His most influential work, *Histoire naturelle* (1749–66), discussed the history of the earth, classified the natural world, and offered an anthropology of man and the animals. It was followed by *Histoire naturelle des oiseaux* (1770–83) and *Histoire naturelle des minéraux* (1783–8).

BURGH, JAMES
1714–75. Scottish moralist and political reformer. A Presbyterian minister, born in Perth, and educated at St Andrews University, he founded Stoke Newington Academy, 1747, and became an Arian. He excelled in jeremiads on the nation's corruption, notably in *The Dignity of Human Nature* (1754), *The Art of Speaking* (1761), and articles in the *General Evening Post*. Disillusionment with George III radicalised him, leading to his utopian *Account of the First Settlement, Laws, Form of Government, and Police, of the Cessares, a People of South America* (1764), an essay, *Crito* (1766), and campaigns for constitutional reform and in favour of Wilkes and America. His *Political Disquisitions* (1774–5) was an influential compilation of radical arguments. An inveterate 'associator' and mobiliser of propertied groups, he convoked a National Association of Free Britons to restore the constitution.
• Handlin 1961; Hay 1979a, 1979b, 1982; Kramnick 1990; Robbins 1959; Zebrowski 1991.

BURKE, EDMUND
1729–97. Anglo-Irish political philosopher and politician. Born in Dublin of an Anglo-Irish family (his father Protestant, his mother Catholic), he was educated at Trinity College and at the Inns of Court, London. His early produced a treatise on aesthetic psychology, *A Philosophical Enquiry into the Origin of our Ideas of the Sublime and the Beautiful* (1757) and a satirical *Vindication of Natural Society* (1756). He became secretary to Lord Rockingham, 1765, and pamphleteer and speech writer for the Whigs (*Observations . . . on a Late State of the Nation* (1769), *Thoughts on the Cause of the Present Discontents* (1770)). He sat in parliament, 1765–94, and became a close associate of Charles James Fox. He sought British reconciliation with the American colonies: *Speech on American Taxation* (1775); *Speech . . . on . . . Conciliation with the Colonies* (1775). He promoted reform of national finances, 1780; was appointed postmaster general, 1782; defended Irish commercial rights and the civil rights of Catholics (*Letter to Sir Hercules Langrishe*, 1792); and pursued the impeachment of Warren Hastings for his exploitation of India. His lifelong reputation as a reforming Whig was reversed by his attack on revolutionary France in his *Reflections on the Revolution in France* (1790), which shaped modern conservatism in its opposition to rationalism in politics and its defence of prejudice and custom. He followed with *An Appeal from the New to the Old Whigs* (1791). The *Reflections* met with a torrent of responses, including Paine's *Rights of Man* and Wollstonecraft's *Vindication of the Rights of Men*. Burke pursued his French themes in *Two Letters . . . On the Proposals for Peace with the Regicide Directory of France* (1796).
• Boulton 1963; Butler 1984; Cameron 1973; Canavan 1995; Chapman 1967; Cone 1957–64; Courtney 1975; Crowe 1997; Dreyer 1979; Fennessy 1963; Freeman 1980; Kramnick 1977; Lock 1985, 1999; Macpherson 1980; Mansfield 1965; O'Brien 1992; O'Gorman 1973; Parkin 1956; Whale 2000; White 1994; Wilkins 1967.

BURLAMAQUI, JEAN JACQUES

1694–1748. Swiss jurist and philosopher of natural law. Born in Geneva, where he taught law, he travelled widely in Europe. He joined Geneva's ruling council, 1740. His chief works were *Principes du droit naturel* (Principles of Natural Law, 1747) and *Principes du droit politique* (Principles of Political Law, 1751). He was influenced by Barbeyrac's translations of Grotius and Pufendorf and, in turn, his own work helped familiarise European readers with their thought. He was read by Rousseau and by Hamilton and other American revolutionaries.
• Brühlmeier 1995; Gagnebin 1944; Harvey 1937; Zurbuchen 1991.

BURNET, GILBERT

1643–1715. Scottish-English Whig, a principal ideologist of the Revolution of 1688. Born in Aberdeenshire, he was educated at Aberdeen University and ordained a minister in the episcopal Church of Scotland. A distinguished preacher, much travelled in Western Europe, and a political intriguer, he came to London, 1673, and was close to the leading Whigs. He thought it prudent to go abroad, 1685, returning as chaplain to William of Orange's invading army, 1688, and was made bishop of Salisbury, 1689. He is best known for his *History of the Reformation* (1679–1714) and *History of his Own Time* (1724–34). A series of tracts and sermons in 1688–9 developed 'revolution principles' and led eighteenth-century commentators to place him alongside Locke, Sidney, Hoadly, and Somers in the Whig canon. The chief tract was *An Enquiry into the Measures of Submission* (1688).
• Claydon 1996.

BURNETT, JAMES, *see* MONBODDO

CABANIS, PIERRE JEAN

1757–1808. French *idéologue*. Born in Brive, Limousin, he trained in medicine at Reims, and published several medical treatises. In 1797 he became a senator. He was involved in the Brumaire coup that brought Napoleon to power. Building on the theories of Condillac, he attempted a science of man in his *Rapports du physique et du moral de l'homme* (On the Physical and Moral Aspects of Man, 1802).
• Staum 1980a; and see under Destutt de Tracy.

CALAMY, EDMUND

1671–1732. English Dissenting minister and defender of toleration. Born in London, he was educated at Dissenting academies and Utrecht University. He was a Presbyterian minister in London, 1692 until his death, and inherited Richard Baxter's mantle as leader of the English Presbyterians. His account of the Puritan ministers ejected from the Church of England in 1662 became the standard Dissenting martyrology. His *Defence of Moderate Nonconformity* (1704) marked the final abandonment of Presbyterian ambitions for a national Calvinist religious settlement, defended denominational status, and deployed Locke's *Letter concerning Toleration* in defence of liberty for Dissenters.

CAMPOMANES, PEDRO RODRÍGUEZ, CONDE DE

1723–1803. Spanish politician, reformer, and political economist. Born in Santa Eulalia de Sorriba, he rose to be a minister under Charles III, became president of the Council of Castile, 1783, and of the Cortes, 1789. He took a leading part in the suppression of the Jesuits, who were expelled in 1767. He wrote on economic reform under the influence of the physiocrats, pressed for free trade, and, from 1774, promoted the Economic Societies of Friends of the Country. The themes of his *Discurso sobre el fomento de la industria popular* (Discourse on the Encouragement of Popular Industry, 1774) and *Discurso sobre la educacion*

popular de los artesanos (Discourse on the Popular Education of Artisans, 1775) were putting the idle to work, developing manufacturing in the countryside, creating an artisan class independent of the nobility, and making the clergy useful as practical educators. His *Tratado de la regalía de amortización* (Treatise on the Royal Prerogative of Amortization, 1765) argued for limitations on the alienation of secular land to the church: his 'Gallican' views were influenced by Febronius and van Espen. He recommended publication of suitably censored parts of the *Encyclopédie*. He fell from power in 1790.
• Castro 1996; Diaz 1975; Herr 1958, 1989.

CANTILLON, RICHARD
1680–1734. Irish-French political economist. Born in Co. Kerry, he became a merchant in London and Paris, and assisted John Law. His chief work was an *Essai sur la nature du commerce en général* (1755; trans. as *The Analysis of Trade, Commerce, Coin, Bullion, Banks, and Foreign Exchanges*, 1759). He was murdered by his cook.
• Murphy 1986.

CARMICHAEL, GERSHOM
1672–1729. Scottish jurist. Born in London, he was educated at Edinburgh University, and taught at St Andrews, transferring to Glasgow as professor of philosophy, 1694. In 1727 he became the first professor of moral philosophy at Glasgow, therein preceding Hutcheson, Smith, and Reid. From 1694 Carmichael incorporated the natural law school of Grotius, Pufendorf, and Locke into his lectures. His chief work was an edition of Pufendorf's *De officio hominis et civis* (On the Duty of Man and Citizen, 1718). He also wrote on theology and logic.
• Mautner 1996; Moore and Silverthorne 1983, 1984.

CARTWRIGHT, 'MAJOR' JOHN
1740–1824. English political reformer. Born in Marnham, Nottinghamshire, he left school at fourteen, and served in the navy and county militia. A writer and activist, his views remained tied to notions of the Saxon Ancient Constitution, in which he gave a key role to freeholder-militiamen, yet also championed universal male suffrage. *Take your Choice!* (1776) went through many editions: it advocated annual parliaments, universal suffrage, and a secret ballot. He defended American independence, and was a member of the Society for Constitutional Information, 1780, and the Society of Friends of the People, 1792. His tracts include *A Letter to Edmund Burke, Controverting the Principles of American Government* (1775), and *Give us our Rights!* (1782). Attempts to enter parliament were unsuccessful. He founded the Hampden Club, 1812, and stood trial for conspiracy, 1819. His last work was *The English Constitution Produced and Illustrated* (1823). His causes included the abolition of slavery and the emancipation of Greece and Spain.
• Bonwick 1977; Osborne 1972.

CASAUX, CHARLES, MARQUIS DE (ALEXANDRE CAZAUD)
1727–96. French political economist and revolutionary. Born in Angoulême, he became the owner of a sugar plantation in Grenada, and thereby became a British subject when the island was conquered in 1759. He returned to Europe, 1777, lectured on sugar cultivation, and was elected a Fellow of the Royal Society, 1780. His *Considérations sur quelques parties du méchanisme des sociétés* (Considerations of Some Parts of the Mechanism of Societies, 1785) quarrelled with Quesnay's ideas on taxation. By 1788 the self-styled marquis was publishing a string of pamphlets in Paris; soon he joined Mirabeau and the revolutionaries. Mirabeau approved of his *Simplicité de l'idée d'une constitution* (1789). In 1792 he returned to London,

where he published *Considérations sur les effets de l'impôt dans les differents modes de taxation* (Considerations of the Effects of Tariffs in Two Different Modes of Taxation, 1794).

CATHERINE II ('THE GREAT'), EMPRESS OF RUSSIA

1729–96. Born Princess Sophie of Anhalt-Zerbst at Stettin, Prussia, she married the future Czar Peter III, who, after a brief reign in 1762, was deposed in her favour. She broadened her education by reading works of the French Enlightenment, especially Montesquieu. After her accession she invited *philosophes* to Russia, including d'Alembert (who declined), Le Mercier de la Rivière, Diderot, Bentham, and Grimm. Her interest in and generosity towards these writers and her correspondence with Voltaire, together with the publication of her *Nakaz* (Instruction, 1767), enhanced her reputation in the West. She enacted many anticlerical, educational, and humanitarian measures. In her last years, under the impact of the French Revolution, she veered away from the *philosophes*.
• Dukes 1977; Gleason 1981; Lortholary 1951; Madariaga 1981; Raeff 1974; Sacke 1931; Venturi 1979.

CHARRIÈRE, ISABELLE DE (BELLE VAN ZUYLEN)

1740–1805. Dutch novelist and epistolary commentator. Born near Utrecht, she settled near Neuchâtel, Switzerland, 1771. From 1787 to 1795 she corresponded with the young Constant. She published a series of novels, notably *Caliste* (1786). Her *Lettres trouvées sous la neige* (Letters Found beneath the Snow, 1794) were critical of inequality and aristocratic privilege and showed the influence of Diderot and Rousseau.
• Courtney 1993a; Trousson 1994.

CHASTELLUX, FRANÇOIS JEAN, MARQUIS DE

1734–88. French military adventurer and commentator on America. Born in Paris, he became a soldier at the age of fourteen, and, while serving, wrote plays and political works, notably *De la félicité publique* (On Public Happiness, 1772), and was elected to the *Académie française*, 1755. He served in North America during the War of Independence. He travelled extensively in New England, 1780–2, met Jefferson and Washington, and took notes on the history and character of the new republic. The result was *Voyages dans l'Amérique* (1788).

CHATEAUBRIAND, FRANÇOIS RENÉ, VICOMTE DE

1768–1848. French Counter-Enlightenment moralist, politician, and novelist. Born in Saint-Malo, he went to Paris, 1788, travelled in North America, 1791, and joined the French émigrés in England, 1793. He published *Essai historique, politique et moral sur les révolutions anciennes et modernes* (An Historical, Political, and Moral Essay on Revolutions Ancient and Modern, 1797), but is chiefly known for his *Génie du christianisme* (The Genius of Christianity, 1802), written during English exile, which became a foundation of the conservative Catholic revival. He served as ambassador to London, 1822–4.
• Bénichou 1973, 1977; McMahon 2001; Painter 1977.

CLAVIÈRE, ÉTIENNE

1735–93. Swiss financier and political economist. Born in Geneva, from where he was expelled, 1782, for political agitation. He had been a banker there, and continued so in Paris, mastering the stock market. He was close to Brissot, Mirabeau, and Dumont. His economic ideas are contained in his *Opinions d'un créancier de l'état sur quelques matières de finance importantes* (Opinions of a State Creditor on Certain Important Financial Matters, 1789). With Brissot he wrote *De la France et des Etats-Unis, ou l'importance de la Révolution de l'Amérique pour le bonheur de la France* (France and the United States, Or the Importance of the American Revolution to the Happiness of France, 1787), and also the revolutionary journal, *Patriote français*. He was briefly Girondin minister of finance, 1792. Arrested by the Jacobins, he chose suicide over the guillotine.

• Bénétruy 1962; Whatmore 2000a.

CLOOTS, JEAN BAPTISTE DU VAL-DE-GRACE (ANACHARSIS), BARON

1755–94. French revolutionary atheist. An itinerant German nobleman, born in Gnadenthal near Clèves, he settled in Paris at the Revolution, became a journalist for the Jacobins, and was elected to the Convention. He adopted his Greek name in 1790. He advocated war upon Europe in order to export the Revolution, and as well as French thinkers he admired foreign theorists of freedom, including Bentham, Paine, Priestley, Schiller, and Washington. A militant atheist, his works assailed Christianity, and he was a chief architect of the Cult of Reason. He was guillotined. His works include *L'Orateur du genre humain* (The Orator of Mankind, 1791), *La République universelle, ou addresses aux tyrannicides* (The Universal Republic, or Addresses to Tyrannicides, 1792), and *Bases constitutionelles de la république du genre humain* (Constitutional Foundations of the Republic of Mankind, 1793).

COCCEJI, HEINRICH VON

1644–1719. German jurist. Born in Bremen. He succeeded to Pufendorf's chair at Heidelberg and then in 1690 became professor at Frankfurt-on-the-Oder. An influential scholar of natural and public law, his principal works were *Iuris publici prudentia* (Public Jurisprudence, 1695), *Prodromus juris gentium* (Prolegomena to the Law of Nations, 1719), and, with his son Samuel, *Grotius illustratus* (Commentary on Grotius, 1744–8).

COCCEJI, SAMUEL VON

1679–1755. German jurist. Born in Heidelberg, the son of Heinrich von Cocceji. Following his father, his doctoral dissertation, *Disputatio de principio juris naturalis unico, vero, et adaequato* (Disputation concerning the One, True, and Sufficient Origin of Natural Law, 1699), expounded the idea of natural law as the will of God. He became professor at Frankfurt-on-the-Oder. Latterly he was occupied in judicial activity and reforms in Prussia under Frederick I and II. His chief works were *Tractatus juris gentium* (Treatise on the Law of Nations, 1702), *Elementa justitiae naturalis et Romanae* (Elements of Natural and Roman Justice, 1740), and *Project des Corporis juris fridericinis* (Project for the Frederican Code of Law, 1749).

• Haakonssen 1996a, ch. 4; Weill 1961.

COLLINS, ANTHONY

1676–1729. English deist. Born in Heston, Middlesex, and educated at Cambridge University. He was close to Locke, 1703–4, and followed the materialist implications of Locke's 'thinking matter' hypothesis. His *Essay concerning the Use of Reason* (1707) attacked the distinction between things 'contrary to' and 'above' reason. *Priestcraft in Perfection* (1710) attacked church authority. His notoriety rested chiefly on his *Discourse of Free-thinking* (1713), which popularised the term 'freethinking'. His *Philosophical Inquiry concerning Human Liberty* (1717) defended determinism. The *Discourse of the Grounds and Reasons of the Christian Religion* (1724) assaulted the veracity of scripture. Collins visited Holland, 1711 and 1713.

• Berman 1975; Jacob 1981; O'Higgins 1970.

CONDILLAC, ÉTIENNE BONNOT DE

1715–80. French philosopher, logician, and economist. Born in Grenoble, he was ordained priest, 1741. From 1758 to 1767 he was tutor to the prince of Parma. His treatises popularised

Locke in France and promoted sensationalism (the thesis that knowledge derives purely from sense experience). His chief works are *Essai sur l'origine des connaissances humaines* (Essay on the Origin of Human Knowledge, 1746), *Traité des systèmes* (1749), *Traité des animaux* (1755), and *Traité des sensations* (1754). They influenced Rousseau, Herder, and the *idéologues*.
• Aarsleff 1982; Knight 1968.

CONDORCET, MARIE JEAN ANTOINE NICOLAS DE CARITAT, MARQUIS DE

1743–94. French philosopher, mathematician, and feminist. Born in Nyons, Picardy, and educated at the Jesuit College of Navarre, he became a mathematician and was appointed Inspecteur des Monnaies, 1774, and became permanent secretary of the *Académie des sciences*, 1785. His friends included Voltaire, d'Alembert, and Turgot. After the Revolution he was elected to the National Assembly. Opposed to the Jacobins, he tried to flee in 1793, was captured, and died in captivity. His *Esquisse d'un tableau historique des progrès de l'esprit humain* (Sketch for a Historical Account of the Progress of the Human Mind, 1795) offers an account of human development and a classic statement of the idea of progress and perfectibility. He defended the rights of women in *Essai sur l'admission des femmes au droit de cité* (On the Admission of Women to the Rights of Citizenship, 1790).
• Badinter and Badinter 1988; Baker 1975; Duchet 1971; Manuel 1962; Popkin 1987b, 1989; Rothschild 1996, 2001; Schandeler 2000.

COOPER, ANTHONY ASHLEY, *see* SHAFTESBURY

COXE, TENCH

1755–1824. American political economist. Born in Philadelphia, he was educated at Philadelphia College, then joined his father's business. At first neutral during the Revolution, he turned to its support, and sat in the Constitutional Convention, 1787. *An Examination of the Constitution for the United States of America* (1788) was a Federalist defence of the constitution. Coxe held national office in the 1790s and early 1800s. His chief economic work was *An Enquiry into the Principles on which a Commercial Economic System for the United States of America should be Founded* (1787). He argued for the development of manufacturing (especially cotton textile) industry, for tariffs against British goods, and for American ships to have exclusive carriage of import and coastal trade.
• Cook 1978; Nelson 1987.

CRÈVECOEUR, MICHEL GUILLAUME JEAN DE ('J. HECTOR ST JOHN DE')

1735–1813. Franco-American writer, surveyor, and diplomat. Born in Caen, Normandy, he emigrated to America during the Seven Years War, 1756–63, and became a land surveyor and farmer in New York. Neutral during the Revolution, he fled to England. His *Letters from an American Farmer* (1782) form a philosophical travel narrative in the tradition of Montesquieu's *Persian Letters*. Crèvecoeur's celebration of America's agrarian utopia of religious and political equality, in contrast to the tyranny and feudalism of Europe, is balanced by a prediction of decline as a result of war, slavery, and commercial luxury.
• Allen and Asselineau 1987.

CUMBERLAND, RICHARD

1631–1718. English philosopher of natural law. Born in London, he became a Fellow of Magdalene College, Cambridge, 1656, and was a friend of Samuel Pepys and Sir Orlando Bridgeman, to whom his work of natural jurisprudence was dedicated. He was made bishop

of Peterborough, 1691. *De legibus naturae* (1672), translated as *A Treatise of the Laws of Nature* (1727), had a considerable influence on eighteenth-century ethical theory and jurisprudence. Cumberland was, broadly, a 'theological utilitarian', and despite criticising Hobbes, shared many of his premises.
• Haakonssen 2000; Kirk 1987; Parkin 1999.

DALRYMPLE, SIR JOHN
1726–1810. Scottish lawyer and historian. Born in Cranston near Edinburgh, he was educated at Edinburgh and Cambridge Universities, and rose to be a judge in the Exchequer court, 1776. He discovered the art of making soap from herrings. His political works include *An Essay towards a General History of Feudal Property in Great Britain* (1757), which Hume admired, and *The Rights of Great Britain Asserted against the Claims of America* (1776). His *Memoirs of Great Britain and Ireland* (1771) was a significant history of the early Whigs.

DARIES, JOACHIM GEORG
1714–91. German jurist. He was professor of moral and political philosophy at Jena, 1744, and moved to Frankfurt-on-the-Oder, 1763. He published extensively on metaphysics and ethics, law and politics, notably his *Institutiones jurisprudentiae universalis* (Principles of Universal Jurisprudence, 1740).

DAVENANT, CHARLES
1656–1714. English political economist. Born in London, the son of the poet Sir William Davenant, he was educated at Oxford University and qualified in civil law. Davenant was elected a Tory Member of Parliament, 1685, 1698, and 1700. His service as commissioner for excise, 1678–89, and inspector general of imports and exports, 1703–14, gave him great experience in fiscal matters. A series of tracts addressed economic questions: *Essay on the East-India-Trade* (1696), *An Essay upon Ways and Means* (1695), *An Essay on the Probable Methods of Making a People Gainers in the Ballance of Trade* (1699), *Essays upon the Balance of Power* (1701), *Essays Upon Peace at Home, and War Abroad* (1704). More pungent was *The True Picture of a Modern Whig* (1701), which excoriated the Court Whigs for reneging on the Country principles they had held at their creation twenty years before.
• Multamäki 1999.

DEFOE, DANIEL
1661–1731. English journalist, political writer, and novelist. A butcher's son, born in London, he was educated at a Dissenting academy. After failing in trade, he turned to writing, published *An Argument Shewing that a Standing Army . . . is not Inconsistent with a Free Government* (1698), and achieved prominence with his populist *Legion's Memorial* (1701). This was followed by *The Original Power of the Collective Body of the People of England* (1701), its themes also expressed in verse in *The True-Born Englishman* (1701) and *Jure divino* (Divine Right, 1706). His numerous publications included defences of religious toleration and commerce, and a series of novels, among them *Robinson Crusoe* (1719), *Moll Flanders* (1722), and *Roxana* (1724). His journal *The Review* (1704–13) assailed Tory politics, and popularised ideas of the state of nature and the original contract. Other works included *A Journal of the Plague Year* (1722), and *A Tour through the Whole Island of Great Britain* (1724–6).
• Backscheider 1988, 1989; Penovich 1995; Schonhorn 1991.

DELOLME, JEAN LOUIS
1741–1806. Swiss political theorist. Born and educated in Geneva, he came to England, *c.* 1769, and earned a precarious living by his pen, publishing a stream of political and

historical works. He befriended but fell out with the London literati. His key work is *La Constitution d'Angleterre* (1771; English trans. *The Constitution of England*, 1775); it had seven English and eight French editions within twenty years. It was an admiring analysis of its subject, applauding the combination of freedom with strength of government, upholding representative over popular assemblies, and extolling the balance of powers. Isaac D'Israeli called Delolme 'the English Montesquieu'. He returned to Geneva, *c.* 1800, and became a member of the Geneva Council.
• Machelon 1969.

DESCHAMPS, LÉGER MARIE

1716–74. French utopian communist. Born in Rennes, he became a Benedictine monk at Saint-Maur. His main publications were the anonymous, and highly metaphysical, *Lettres sur l'esprit du siècle* (Letter on the Spirit of the Age, 1769) and *La Voix de la raison contre la raison du temps et particulièrement contre celle de l'auteur du 'Système de la nature'* (The Voice of Reason against the Reason of the Times and especially that of the 'System of Nature',1770). The latter attacked the materialist system of Holbach and offered a pantheist alternative. Deschamps advocated a complete social and moral revolution which entailed abolishing laws, property, and authority; he contrasted the existing corrupt 'state of laws' with 'the state of morals'. Diderot admired his work.
• Puisais 2001.

DESMOULINS, LUCIE CAMILLE SIMPLICE

1760–94. French revolutionary. Born in Guise, he was a schoolfriend of Robespierre, and, like him, trained as a lawyer. At the Revolution he became a street agitator, urging the storming of the Bastille. In *La Philosophie du peuple français* (The Philosophy of the French People, 1788) and *La France libre* (Free France, 1789) he defended popular participation and the resort to physical force. His newspaper, *Les Révolutions de France et de Brabant*, served the Jacobin cause. He was elected to the Convention and voted for the king's death. By late 1793 his newspaper *Le Vieux Cordelier* (named for the Franciscan friary where Danton and Desmoulins established their club) sought to moderate the Terror. He was guillotined.
• Hammersley 2004.

DESTUTT DE TRACY, ANTOINE LOUIS CLAUDE, COMTE

1754–1836. French *idéologue*. Born in Bourbonnais, he served in the French army. At the Revolution he abandoned his title and was elected to the Estates General. Though jailed during the Terror, he survived. Under Napoleon he was a senator, and under the restored monarchy a nobleman. He coined the term *idéologie* (ideology) in 1796 for his science of ideas, which drew upon Condillac's sensationalism. His principal work is *Eléments d'idéologie* (1801–15). He wrote a *Commentaire sur 'L'Esprit des lois' de Montesquieu* (1808), which Jefferson, with whom he corresponded, translated in 1811.
• Baker 1973; Challamel 1895; Goetz 1993; Gusdorf 1978; Head 1985; Kennedy 1978; Picavet 1891; Simon 1885; Staum 1996; Welch 1984.

DICKINSON, JOHN

1732–1808. American revolutionary. Born in Maryland, he became a lawyer in Philadelphia. He wrote two of the most powerful tracts against British rule: *Letters from a Farmer in Pennsylvania to the Inhabitants of the British Colonies* (1769, derived from essays in the *Pennsylvania Chronicle* and widely syndicated, 1767–8) and *An Essay on the Constitutional Power of Great Britain over the Colonies in America* (1774). He declined to sign the Declaration of

Independence, but served in the Revolution militia and represented Delaware in the Constitutional Convention, 1787. His collected political writings were published in 1801.
• Flower 1983.

DIDEROT, DENIS

1713–84. French encyclopedist and prolific author. Born in Langres, Champagne, he was educated by the Jesuits and at the Sorbonne. He settled in Paris, *c.* 1728, and lived by his pen. With d'Alembert, he began the *Encyclopédie* in 1745, which absorbed him for twenty years; the first volume was published in 1751, the final text volume in 1765. He was briefly jailed in 1749 for his *Lettre sur les aveugles* (On the Blind). He visited Russia, 1773–4, at the invitation of the Empress Catherine. Besides many contributions to the *Encyclopédie*, he wrote on science and philosophy, as well as plays and novels. He moved from deism to atheism, and came to defend determinist materialism. His *Supplément au voyage de Bougainville* (1772, publ. 1796), which drew on Louis Antoine de Bougainville's account of his Pacific voyage (1771), extolled the primitive virtues and sexual freedom of the Tahitians in contrast with Christian morality. Diderot contributed to Raynal's *Histoire des deux Indes* (History of the Two Indies, 1770), which attacked colonialism and the slave trade. Other key works include *Le Rêve de d'Alembert* (D'Alembert's Dream, 1769, publ. 1782), and the posthumous *Le Neveu de Rameau* (Rameau's Nephew, 1805, begun *c.* 1762) and *Jacques le Fataliste* (1796).
• Blum 1974; Bremner 1983; Davison 1985; Duchet 1978; France 1983; Furbank 1992; Gordon and Torrey 1947; Lough 1968, 1971; J. Hope Mason 1982; Proust 1962, 1965; Schwab *et al.* 1971–3; Strugnell 1973; Venturi 1988; Wilson 1972.

DITHMAR, JUSTUS CHRISTOPH

1678–1737. German cameralist. Born in Rotenberg, Fulda, he studied history and law at Marburg University, after which he spent several years at Leiden University. In 1709 he became professor of history at Frankfurt-on-the-Oder. He published a commentary to Tacitus' *Germania* (1724). In 1727 he took the newly founded chair of *Kameral-, Ökonomie und Polizeiwissenschaft*, which he held until his death.

DOBBS, FRANCIS

1750–1811. Irish patriot. Born in Co. Dublin, and educated at Trinity College, he was called to the Irish bar, 1773. He published a play, *The Patriot King, or Irish Chief: A Tragedy* (1774). In the 1780s he enthusiastically supported the autonomy of the Irish parliament and the Volunteer movement, in such tracts as *Thoughts on Volunteers* (1781). In the 1790s he vehemently opposed the union of Ireland with Britain. He was elected a member of the last Irish parliament, 1799, where he denounced the Union Bill as unscriptural.

DORIA, PAOLO MATTIA

1662–1746. Italian philosopher. Born in Genoa, he spent most of his intellectual life in Naples. His greatest political work was the *Vita civile* (1709), which Le Clerc compared to the works of Grotius and Pufendorf. Drawing upon Machiavelli, it delineated the origins of society and social change, grappled with the problem of the division of powers within the state, and provided perceptive opinions upon republics and monarchies. His unpublished *Massime* provided a severe criticism of Spanish Habsburg rule in southern Italy. In his work in natural philosophy, Doria was an opponent of the innovations of Galileo, Locke, Descartes, and Newton. He and his friend Vico were pivotal figures in the academy *degli Oziosi* founded to counter their philosophical principles. Doria's last major political work, *Idea di una republica perfetta*, took a decisively republican turn. It was never printed, was burnt by the authorities, and no copies survive.
• Ferrone 1995; Ricuperati 1987.

DRAYTON, WILLIAM

1742–79. American revolutionary. Born in St Andrews, South Carolina, the son of a planter, and educated at Oxford University. He was at first a loyalist, writing articles for the South Carolina *Gazette*, which he collected in *The Letters of a Freeman* (1771), but, frustrated by lack of government recognition, he joined the revolutionists, denouncing Britain's 'despotic power' in *A Letter from a Freeman* (1774) and *The Genuine Spirit of Tyranny* (1778). Drayton was a member of the Continental Congress, 1778, became chief justice of South Carolina, and helped shape that state's new constitution.
• Dabney and Dargon 1962.

DRENNAN, WILLIAM

1754–1820. Irish patriot and poet. Born in Belfast, the son of a Presbyterian minister, he was educated at Glasgow University, where he was a pupil of Dugald Stewart, and at Edinburgh. He returned to Ireland, *c.* 1778. *Letters of Orellana, an Irish Helot* (1784) allegorised the suffering condition of Ireland. He was among the founders of the United Irishmen, 1791, and drafted several of their early manifestos. After being tried for sedition, 1794, he retreated to writing poetry.
• Dickson *et al.* 1993.

DUBOS, JEAN BAPTISTE, ABBÉ

1670–1742. French historian and diplomat. Born in Beauvais, he was educated at the Sorbonne. He undertook several embassies for France. He corresponded with Bayle and Locke, and became secretary of the *Académie française*, 1720. His vigorous defence of absolute monarchy, the *thèse royale*, in his *Histoire critique de l'établissement de la monarchie française dans les Gaules* (A Critical History of the Establishment of the French Monarchy in Gaul, 1734) was challenged by Boulainvilliers.
• Ford 1953; Mackrell 1973.

DULANEY, DANIEL

1685–1753. Irish-American defender of colonists' rights. Born in Queens Co., and educated at Trinity College, Dublin, he emigrated to Maryland, 1703, as an indentured servant. He became a prosperous lawyer in Annapolis in the 1720s, and in time a wealthy land speculator and slave trader. He was attorney general, 1720–5, 1734–44, member of the general assembly, 1722–44, and member of the governing council, 1742. In the 1720s he led the Country or anti-proprietary party, against the powers of Lord Baltimore. *The Right of the Inhabitants of Maryland to the Benefit of the English Laws* (1728) deployed ammunition from Magna Carta, the Petition of Right, Coke, Locke, Grotius, Pufendorf, and Trenchard. But in 1732 Dulaney took office under Baltimore and was thereafter loyal to the proprietor.

DUMARSAIS, CÉSAR CHESNEAU

1676–1756. French philosopher and grammarian. Born in Marseilles, and educated by the Oratorians, his attempt at a legal career failed. He became a tutor in noble households and for the financier John Law. His writings against papal claims made some impact, but his literary reputation rests on his works on grammar, on which he contributed articles to the *Encyclopédie*. Believed to be an atheist, he was seen by the younger *philosophes* as a bold precursor. He was probably the author of *Le Philosophe* (1743), from which Diderot adapted the article 'Philosophe' for the *Encyclopédie*. After his death, Dumarsais was the subject of an *Eloge* by d'Alembert at the beginning of vol. VII of the *Encyclopédie*. The *Essai sur les préjugés* (Essay on Prejudices, 1770), which so irritated Frederick II, is sometimes

attributed to him (but is now usually ascribed to Holbach), so too are other works critical of religion.
• Diaz 1962; Dieckmann 1948; Douay-Soublin 1988; Fairbairn 1972; Wade 1938.

DUPONT DE NEMOURS, PIERRE SAMUEL
1739–1817. French physiocrat, born in Paris. He advised Turgot, who appointed him editor of the physiocratic journal *Les Ephémérides du citoyen* (The Citizen's Almanac). At the Revolution he became a deputy in the Estates General, and produced the journal *Correspondance patriotique* (1790–2). He was arrested during the Terror, but survived, and moved to the United States, 1799, returning to France under Napoleon, and settling in America again in 1815, dying at Wilmington, Delaware. For Jefferson he drafted a plan of education. His chief work was the *Tableau raisonnée des principes de l'économie politique* (Analytical Scheme of the Principles of Political Economy, 1773). Other works include *Physiocratie, ou Constitution naturelle du gouvernement le plus avantageux au genre humain* (Physiocracy, or the Natural Constitution of the Most Advantageous Government for Mankind, 1767–8) and *Du pouvoir législatif et du pouvoir exécutif* (On Legislative and Executive Powers, 1795). He edited Quesnay's works under the title *Physiocratie,* and also Turgot's works.
• Bouloiseau 1972; Joly 1956; Schelle 1888.

EATON, DANIEL ISAAC
d. 1814. English democrat. By profession a bookseller, he was prosecuted for selling Paine's *Rights of Man* (1791–2). He published a populist tract, *Politics for the People: Or, a Salmagundy for Swine* (1793), the reference being to Burke's remark on the 'swinish multitude'. After several prosecutions, he fled to America and was outlawed, 1796. He translated Helvétius's *System of Nature* (1810), and was apparently involved in the production of *Ecce Homo* (1813), a translation from Holbach. He was frequently prosecuted for these and other publications.

EDEN, SIR FREDERICK MORTON
1766–1809. Writer on the poor. Educated at Oxford University, he was a nephew of the next, and became the manager of an insurance company. He applied Adam Smith's principles to investigations of the condition of the poor. His chief work, *The State of the Poor, Or an History of the Labouring Classes of England* (1797) was admired by Marx.

EDEN, WILLIAM, LORD AUCKLAND
1744–1814. English penal reformer, politician, and diplomat. Born in Co. Durham, he was educated at Oxford University, became a barrister, and was elected a Member of Parliament, 1774. He was appointed to the Board of Trade, 1776, and established the National Bank of Ireland. Created Baron Auckland, 1789, he served as ambassador to the Netherlands during the French Revolution, and was a member of the cabinet, 1806–7. His principal work was *Principles of Penal Law* (1771).
• Draper 2001.

EYBEL, JOSEPH VALENTIN
1741–1805. Austrian canonist. Born in Vienna and educated by the Jesuits, he was a member of that society until 1765. He held the post of professor of church law at Vienna, 1773–9. A follower of Febronius, he served the cause of Joseph II's reform of the relations between church and state through his textbook of canon law, *Introductio in jus ecclesiasticum Catholicorum* (Introduction to Catholic Ecclesiastical Law, 1777), which was condemned by the papacy in 1784. The work was influential among the Gallican-inclined in Spain and elsewhere in Catholic Europe. After the easing of censorship, 1781, Eybel published a series of intensely

anti-papal pamphlets, the most successful of which was *Was ist der Papst?* (What is the Pope?, 1782), which argued for the equality of all bishops.
• Bernard 1971.

FAUCHET, FRANÇOIS CLAUDE

1744–93. French revolutionary. Born in Durnes, Nivernais, he was ordained priest. A leader in the attack on the Bastille, 1789, he was a member of the Paris Commune, the Legislative Assembly, and the Convention, and became bishop of Calvados in the Constitutional Church. He established a populist journal, *La Bouche de fer* (The Iron Mouth, 1790–1), for which he wrote commentaries on Rousseau's *Social Contract*; Roland, Condorcet, and Nicolas Bonneville were also contributors. He sided with the Girondists and was guillotined.

FEBRONIUS, *see* HONTHEIM

FEIJÓO Y MONTENEGRO, BENITO JERÓNIMO

1676–1764. An instigator of the Enlightenment in Spain. Born in Galicia, he was educated at Salamanca University, and became a Benedictine monk. For most of his career he taught theology at Oviedo. In the fourteen volumes of *Teatro crítico universal* (1726–39) and *Cartas eruditas* (1742–40), a melange of literature, philosophy, theology, science, history, and politics, he introduced Spain to Descartes, Newton, and Locke, and assailed superstition and ignorance. In 1750 the king prohibited attacks on his writings.
• Delpy 1936; Herr 1958, 1989.

FÉNELON, FRANÇOIS DE SALIGNAC DE LA MOTHE

1651–1715. French theologian and political writer. Born in the château of Fénelon, Périgord, he was ordained priest. After serving as tutor to Louis XIV's grandson he was appointed archbishop of Cambrai, 1695. Later he was attacked by Bossuet and condemned by the pope for his defence of the mystical 'Quietist' heresy. He defended the education of women in his *Traité de l'éducation des filles* (Treatise on the Education of Girls, 1687). His chief political work was his hugely popular novel, *Les Aventures de Télémaque* (The Adventures of Telemachus, 1699). In Rousseau's *Emile* it is the only book given to the pupil Emile by his tutor when he reaches adulthood. Fénelon also published the *Dialogues des morts, composés pour l'éducation d'un prince* (Dialogues of the Dead, Composed for the Education of a Prince, 1712). His views were propagated by Ramsay in his *Essai sur le gouvernement civil, selon les principes de Fénelon* (1723).
• Carcassonne 1946; Davis 1979; Gilroy 1979; Goré 1957; Gouhier 1977; Keohane 1980; Riley 1994.

FERGUSON, ADAM

1723–1816. Scottish social theorist. Born in Logierait, Perthshire, a Gaelic-speaking son of a clergyman, he was educated at St Andrews University, and was chaplain to (and fought with) the Black Watch regiment, 1745–54. He tutored at Groningen and Leipzig, 1754–6. He succeeded Hume as librarian of the Advocates Library, 1757, and was tutor to Lord Bute's sons and to the earl of Chesterfield. He was appointed to the chair of natural philosophy at Edinburgh, 1759, the chair of moral philosophy, 1764, and the chair of mathematics, 1785. He was an active campaigner for a Scottish militia. He was secretary of a commission to negotiate with the American colonies, 1778. He visited Voltaire at Ferney, 1775, and was in Prussia, 1793–4. His principal works were *Reflections Previous to the Establishment of a Militia* (1756), the *Essay on the History of Civil Society* (1767), *Institutes of Moral Philosophy* (1769), *History of the Progress and Termination of the Roman Republic* (1783), and (based on

his Edinburgh lectures) *Principles of Moral and Political Science* (1792). Ferguson outlined a 'conjectural history' of social evolution from barbarism to commercial society.
• Berry 1997; Forbes 1966; Hill 1997; Kettler 1965, 1977; Lehmann 1930; Mason 1988; Oz-Salzberger 1995; Robertson 1985; Sher 1985; Small 1864.

FICHTE, JOHANN GOTTLIEB

1762–1814. German philosopher. Born in Rammenau, Lusatia, he was educated at Jena University, and taught at Zurich, Leipzig, Jena, and finally at Berlin, where he became rector, 1811. He was an early follower of Kant and came to prominence with *Versuch einer Kritik aller Offenbarung* (Essays Towards a Critique of all Revelation, 1792). Fichte greatly influenced the ensuing generation of German Romantics. He was a republican, supporting the French Revolution and opposing Napoleon. Early works included *Zurückforderung der Denkfreiheit von den Fürsten Europas* (Demand for Return of Free Thought from Europe's Princes, 1793), *Grundlage des Naturrechts* (Foundations of Natural Law, 1796), and *Der geschlossene Handelstaat* (The Closed Commercial State, 1800). After Prussia's defeat by Napoleon he issued the patriotic *Reden an die deutsche Nation* (Addresses to the German Nation, 1807–8).
• Adamson 1881; Baumanns 1990; Beiser 1987.

FIELDING, HENRY

1707–54. English novelist and political journalist. Born in Glastonbury, Wiltshire, he was educated at Leiden University. His satirical stage plays, especially *Pasquin* (1736) provoked Prime Minister Walpole to introduce censorship of the stage, 1737. Fielding wrote numerous fusillades against the government, from a standpoint of populist Toryism, in *The Champion* (1739–43), *The True Patriot* (1745–6), *The Jacobite's Journal* (1747–8), and *The Covent-Garden Journal* (1752–3). He is best known as a novelist, notably for *Joseph Andrews* (1742), *Jonathan Wild* (1743), and *Tom Jones* (1749)
• Cleary 1984; Rogers 1979.

FILANGIERI, GAETANO

1752–88. Italian political economist. Born in Naples, he practised as a lawyer, and became a member of the treasury council, 1787. His *Riflessioni politiche* (Political Reflections, 1774) dwelt on legal reform, while *Scienza della legislazione* (Science of Legislation, 1780–5) called for economic and penal reform and reform of the church. Indebted to the natural law tradition and to Montesquieu, he professed to place legislation on a scientific basis, general principles being related to local circumstances. He sought means to increase national wealth and its equitable distribution. Other works include *Morale de' principi fondata sulla natura e sull'ordine sociale* (The Morality of Princes Grounded in Nature and the Social Order, 1771).
• Venturi 1972.

FLETCHER, ANDREW

1655–1716. Scottish patriot and republican. Born in Saltoun in East Lothian. He joined Monmouth's rebellion, 1685 (for which he was attainted for treason), served in Hungary against the Turks, and joined William of Orange's invasion of England, 1688. In the Scottish parliament in the early 1700s he led the 'patriot' opposition to English rule, and opposed the Union of 1707. He was briefly jailed in 1708 on suspicion of Jacobite conspiracy. He was much travelled on the Continent. His main tracts were *A Discourse of Government with Relation to Militias* (1698), *A Discourse concerning the Affairs of Spain* (1698), *Two Discourses Concerning the Affairs of Scotland* (1698), *An Account of a Conversation concerning a Right Regulation of Governments for the Common Good of Mankind* (1703), and *State of the Controversy Betwixt United and Separate Parliaments* (1703).
• Mackenzie 1935; Omond 1897; Robertson 1987b; Rozbicki 2001; Scott 1992.

FLOOD, HENRY

1732–91. Irish patriot. Born in Dublin, and educated at Trinity College, Oxford University, and the Inns of Court, London. As a member of the Irish parliament, from 1759, he championed a Country platform. He opposed the Townshend administration in essays in the *Freeman's Journal* and *Baratariana* (1772). His appointment as an Irish privy councillor undermined his Country credentials, but he continued to campaign for parliamentary reform and religious toleration (but not political representation) for Catholics. With Grattan he secured the autonomy of the Irish parliament, 1782. He was elected a member of the British parliament, 1783, where he proposed a bill to extend the franchise, 1790.
• Kelly 1998.

FONSECA PIMENTAL, ELEANORA

1752–99. Neapolitan republican journalist. Born in Rome of a Portuguese gentry family, she settled in Naples. Influenced by Pombal and Giannone, she supported the reformist movement of the 1780s, and admired the principles of the French Revolution. She was jailed, 1794–8, and then was active in the short-lived Neapolitan republic, 1798–9. At its crushing, she was executed. She edited *Il Monitore Napoletano* which debated political questions, including the propensity of the plebeians to conspire with Bourbon monarchy to defeat the republic.

FONTENELLE, BERNARD LE BOVIER DE

1657–1757. French philosopher. Born in Rouen, he studied and practised as a lawyer. He was elected to the *Académie française* and became permanent secretary of the *Académie des sciences*. He was a populariser of modern natural philosophy; his critique of superstition and miracles, and his anticlericalism, ensured that the *philosophes* revered him. In his *Dialogues des morts* (Dialogues of the Dead, 1683) and *Digression sur les anciens et les modernes* (Digression on the Ancients and Moderns, 1688), he defended the moderns and attacked veneration of the classical world. *Entretiens sur la pluralité des mondes* (Conversations on the Plurality of the Worlds, 1686) explained the Copernican system and its implications. *Histoire des oracles* (History of Oracles, 1686) and *Histoire des fables* (History of Fables, 1724) dismissed ancient myths and fables as absurd chimeras.
• Duchet 1971.

FORBONNAIS, FRANÇOIS VÉRON DUVERGER DE

1722–1800. French political economist. Born in Le Mans, he was educated in Paris and worked for his father's textile business. In about 1747 he settled in Paris, became inspector-general of the French coinage, 1752, and began to write. His first major publication was a critical commentary on the *Esprit des lois* (1750), arguing that Montesquieu overvalued the English constitution and exaggerated English religious toleration. He soon became a prominent economist, particularly in his *Considérations sur les finances d'Espagne* (1753) and *Recherches et considérations sur les finances de la France* (1758). He drew on his many articles for the *Encyclopédie* in his *Elémens du commerce* (1754). He admired Quesnay but opposed the physiocrats on the basis of their perceived hostility to manufacturing, their condemnation of tariffs, and (in his view) inflexible fiscal policy. For some decades he advised the government, including after the Revolution, during which he sat as a deputy in the Estates General, although he withdrew before the fall of the monarchy.
• Airiau 1965; Fleury 1915.

FORDYCE, DAVID

1711–51. Scottish philosopher. Born at Broadford near Aberdeen, the son of a provost of Aberdeen, he studied at Marischal College, obtaining his MA in 1728. He was professor of moral philosophy at Aberdeen from 1742 until his early death by drowning in the North Sea, upon his return from a Continental tour. He published *Dialogues concerning Education* (1745–8) and *Elements of Moral Philosophy* (1754), which reached its fourth edition in 1769 and was translated into German in 1757.

FORMEY, JEAN HENRI SAMUEL

1711–97. Franco-German *savant*. Born in Berlin, where his Huguenot father had settled, he became a Calvinist pastor of the French church in Berlin, but turned increasingly to journalism and polemic. He became a professor at the French college and a member (eventually secretary) of the Berlin Academy, and served as royal translator. He wrote popularisations and defences of Leibniz and Wolff, and a series of apologies for, and panegyrics of, Frederick I and II. His papers intended for a philosophical dictionary were sold to the publishers of the *Encyclopédie*, and many of its articles derived from them. His literary output was enormous. He wrote attacks on Rousseau, including *Anti-Emile* (1763); his *La Belle Wolfienne* (1741–53) may have been the source of Voltaire's *Candide*.
• Marcu 1953; Velema 1993.

FRANKE, AUGUST HERMANN

1663–1727. German Pietist. Born in Lubeck, he studied at Erfurt and Kiel, then taught at Leipzig, 1685. He turned to Pietism under the influence of Spener. He was a founding professor at the Pietist Halle University. He countered both the orthodoxy of the Lutheran church and the Enlightenment of Wolff, whose dismissal in 1723 he helped secure.
• Beyreuther 1956.

FRANKLIN, BENJAMIN

1706–90. American publisher, scientist, diplomat, inventor, and moralist. Born in Boston, he had little formal education, but built up a printing business in Philadelphia and published newspapers. His scientific work was chiefly on electricity and lightning. In the 1750s and 1760s he represented the American colonies in negotiations with Britain and France. He was a signatory of the Declaration of Independence, 1776, and a member of the Constitutional Convention, 1787. He founded the American Philosophical Society. He gathered his essays in *Political, Miscellaneous, and Philosophical Pieces* (1779). *Poor Richard's Almanack* (1733–58) was a popular compendium of useful knowledge and moral aphorisms. His vision was of incremental practical progress, self-sufficiency, and egalitarianism. He supported universal male suffrage and a unicameral legislature, his democratic instincts tempered by fear of faction and the mob.
• Conner 1965; Middlekauff 1996; Wood 2004; Wright 1986.

FREDERICK II ('THE GREAT'), KING OF PRUSSIA

1712–86. Born in Berlin, he educated himself in Enlightenment philosophy, and music, despite his Calvinist, martinet father, Frederick I, who preferred a military education. Before he came to the throne in 1740 he began a relationship with Voltaire which was to endure, with interruptions, until the latter's death. His military training proved effective. He seized Silesia from Austria and retained it through two wars, 1740–5, 1756–63. After 1763 Prussia was treated as a great power. Frederick was an agnostic and contemptuous of theology. His rule was notorious for maintaining the pre-eminence of the army, but also for religious toleration, the mitigation of torture and the penal code, educational reform, and the encouragement of French intellectual influences. He published tracts and poems, including *Considérations sur l'état présent du corps politique de l'Europe* (Considerations on the Present State of the Body Politic of Europe, 1738), *Anti-Machiavel* (1740), *Testament Politique* (Political Testament, 1752),

Histoire de mons temps (History of My Own Times), and *Essai sur les formes du gouvernement et sur les devoirs des souverains* (Essay on the Forms of Government and on the Duties of Sovereigns, 1777).
• Bazzoli 1986; Blanning 1990, 1997; Hubatsch 1973; Ingrao 1987; Maestro 1973; Melton 1988; Mervaud 1985; Schieder 1983; Skalweit 1952; Spranger 1942; Van Treese 1974; Weill 1961.

FURNEAUX, PHILIP
1726–83. English defender of religious toleration. Born in Totnes, Devon, and educated at a Dissenting academy in London, he was ordained to the Presbyterian ministry and served as pastor in or near London. He was a leader of the Dissenting campaign against subscription to the doctrinal articles of the Church of England, and against the Test Acts, which excluded Dissenters from public office. His *Letters to . . . Mr Justice Blackstone* (1770) attacked Blackstone's *Commentaries* for holding that the Act of Toleration of 1689 merely suspended the penalties and not the crime of religious nonconformity. His *Essay on Toleration* (1773) opposed penal laws in matters of conscience.
• Haakonssen 1996b.

GALIANI, FERDINANDO
1728–87. Italian political economist. A Neapolitan, who, as secretary of the embassy in Paris, became an intimate of Holbach's circle, as well as a friend of Diderot and Grimm. His chief work was *Dialogues sur le commerce des blés* (Dialogues on the Grain Trade, 1770), which cautioned against the policy of free export of grain. Diderot wrote in its defence, and Morellet and Le Mercier de la Rivière attacked it. An earlier work of his was *Della moneta* (On Money, 1751).
• Davison 1985; Kaplan 1976; Venturi 1969–90.

GARVE, CHRISTIAN
1742–98. German literary critic and moral philosopher, born in Breslau. Briefly professor of philosophy at Leipzig, he suffered from poor health and spent most of his life on his family estate near his native city. Best known for his translation of Cicero's *De officiis* (On Duties, 1784), he was also a noted commentator on British authors. Garve greatly admired the polished style and versatility of British literature and urged Germans to follow that country's example. He believed English to be well attuned for the purpose of social improvement and public education. He translated Adam Smith's *Wealth of Nations* (1794–6).
• Oz-Salzberger 1995; Van der Zande 1995; Van Dusen 1970.

GENOVESI, ANTONIO
1713–69. Italian political economist. A Neapolitan, born in Castiglione, he was ordained priest, 1737. Failing to secure a chair in theology, he turned to political economy, in which he obtained a chair at Naples, 1754, the first university chair in political economy in Europe. An admirer of British and French ideas and commerce, he advocated reform in his *Discourse on the True End of the Arts and Sciences* (1753) and *Lezioni di commercio* (Lessons on Commerce, 1765). Other works included *Principia theosophiae naturalis; De principiis legis naturalis* (On the Principles of Natural Law, 1747–52), and *Discorso sull'agricoltura* (Discourse on Agriculture, 1764).
• Bellamy 1987; Robertson 1987a; Venturi 1972.

GERDIL, GIACINTO SIGISMONDI
1718–1802. Italian critic of Enlightenment. A native of Savoy, Gerdil became professor of philosophy at Macerato, 1737, and then at Turin, 1749. He was made a cardinal in 1777.

Only old age prevented his election as pope in 1798. He was a disciple of Malebranche, a critic of Locke's epistemology, and of Rousseau's *Emile*. His books include *L'Immatérialité de l'âme démontrée contre M. Locke* (The Immateriality of the Soul Demonstrated against Locke, 1747), *Anti-Contrat social* (1764), and *Réflexions sur la théorie et la pratique de l'éducation, contre les principes de J. J. Rousseau* (1764).

GIANNONE, PIETRO
1676–1748. Italian jurist and historian. Born in Ischitella, Capitanate, he studied law at Naples. His *Dell' istoria civile del regno di Napoli* (Civil History of the Kingdom of Naples, 1723) dwelt on the contest between church and state in Neapolitan history. Excommunicated in 1724, he fled to Vienna and then settled in Venice. Induced to enter Savoy, he was arrested, and spent the last twelve years of his life in jail in Turin. His work was admired by Montesquieu, Voltaire, and Gibbon.
• Ajello 1980; Carpanetto and Ricuperati 1987; Ricuperati 1970; Trevor Roper 1996.

GIBBON, EDWARD
1737–94. English historian. Born in London, he studied at Oxford University but left when he converted to Catholicism, 1753. To cure him, his father sent him to a Calvinist minister in Lausanne, where he stayed five years, 1753–8, and acquired the basis for his future scholarship. The Grand Tour, 1764–5, took him to Rome, where he conceived the idea for his master work. He settled in London, 1772, was elected a Tory Member of Parliament, 1774, but gave this up, and migrated to Lausanne, 1783, remaining there ten years, returning to England shortly before his death. *The History of the Decline and Fall of the Roman Empire* appeared in six volumes between 1776 and 1788, to great acclaim. It is a masterpiece of history in the secular, philosophic manner, giving a naturalistic rather than providentialist account of early Christianity. Its anticlericalism shocked the orthodox.
• Baridon 1977; Burrow 1985; McKitterick and Quinault 1997; Momigliano 1966; O'Brien 1997; Pocock 1999–2003; Porter 1988; Womersley 1997.

GODWIN, WILLIAM
1756–1836. English radical political writer and novelist. Born of a Dissenting family at Wisbech, Cambridgeshire, and educated for the Presbyterian ministry, he abandoned Christianity, left his congregation in 1782, and turned to authorship and journalism. He achieved a reputation for his *Enquiry concerning Political Justice* (1793) and his philosophical novel, *Caleb Williams* (1794), which influenced a generation of radicals. He subjected all institutions, including marriage, to a synthesis of extreme act-utilitarianism and to the absolute sanctity of individual judgement. He is claimed as a founder of modern anarchism. In 1797 he married Mary Wollstonecraft; their child was Mary Shelley, author of *Frankenstein*. His candid *Memoirs of the Author of a Vindication of the Rights of Woman* (1798) linked sexual scandal with revolutionary politics and provoked a reaction which damaged the reputation of both authors. Later works included novels, plays, books on history and education, and (against Malthus) on population.
• Butler 1984; Claeys 1986a; Clark 1977; Locke 1980; Marshall 1984; Morrow 1991; Philp 1986; Stafford 1980.

GOGUET, ANTOINE YVES
1716–58. French historian. The son of a wealthy lawyer in Picardy, he studied at Beauvais, Plessis, and Harcourt, and himself became a successful lawyer, and chancellor of the *parlement* of Paris. His chief work is *De l'origine des loix, des arts, et des sciences, et de leurs progrès chez les ancien peuples* (1758) – there is an English edition (1976): *The Origin of Laws, Arts, and Sciences, and their Progress among the Most Ancient Nations*.

738

GORANI, GIUSEPPE

1740–1819. Italian political writer. Born in Milan, he enlisted in the Austrian army, 1757, but spent four years of the Seven Years War as a prisoner in Prussia. There he studied under the guidance of members of the Berlin Academy, met Kant, and became an admirer of Frederick II. He visited nearly every Continental country before returning to Lombardy, 1767, and then went to Vienna, where he was given official assignments in Holland and England. He soon lost his job and returned to Milan where, with the advice of Beccaria, he wrote *Il vero dispotismo* (The True Despotism, 1770), allegedly published in London but actually in Geneva. His hopes of reform by an Enlightened monarch were eventually dispelled by Joseph II's actions. He published *Ricerche sulla scienza dei governi* (Researches on the Science of Government, 1790). He was in France, 1790–6, and took an active part in revolutionary politics. His liveliest work is his *Memoirs* (1794), published posthumously.
• Bazzoli 1986; Capra 1989; Venturi 1969–90.

GORDON, THOMAS

c. 1691–1750. Scottish 'Commonwealthman', born in Kirkcudbright. He began his polemical career in the 1710s with tracts against high churchmen. He assailed Toryism, Jacobitism, and religious credulity. He collaborated with Trenchard to produce the anticlerical *Independent Whig* (1720–1) and *Cato's Letters* (1720–3). These went through several editions, the former translated into French by Holbach. Gordon voiced Country Whig refrains against ministerial corruption, stock-jobbing, standing armies, and placemen, but later became Prime Minister Walpole's press adviser. *Cato's Letters* echoed Locke on natural rights, but combined this with a 'neo-Harringtonian' preoccupation with money and credit, and the impact of commerce. He also wrote an *Essay on Government* (1747), and translated Tacitus and Sallust.
• Bailyn 1967; Dworetz 1990; Hamowy 1990; McMahon 1990; Pocock 1975; Zuckert 1994.

GOUGES, MARIE OLYMPE DE

1755–93. French feminist. Born near Montauban, the daughter of a butcher, her true name was Marie Gouze. Though having little formal education, she went to Paris to live by her pen. Her first play was produced in 1784. A stream of plays, novels, and political tracts followed. Her proposals included schemes for relief of the poor and the abolition of slavery. Her main work was *Déclaration des droits de la femme et de la citoyenne* (Declaration of the Rights of Woman and the Female Citizen, 1791). She declared that if a woman can mount the scaffold, she also has 'the right to mount the tribune'. Defending the king and attacking the Jacobins, she demanded a plebiscite on the government of France: *Les Trois urnes, ou le salut de la patrie* (The Three Ballot Boxes, or the Salvation of the Fatherland). She was guillotined.
• Blanc 1989; Hesse 2001; Hunt 1992; Landes 1988; Roessler 1996; Scott 1996.

GOURNAY, VINCENT DE

1712–58. French economist. He worked first as a businessman in Cadiz and was later appointed as *intendant de commerce,* 1751–8. The supposed author of the catch-phrase *laissez-faire, laissez-passer*, he presided over and sponsored the translation into French of a number of English and Scottish works of political economy in the 1740s, for instance by Josiah Child and Joshua Gee, collaborated in works by Morellet and Forbonnais, and himself wrote *Observations sur l'agriculture, le commerce et les arts de la Bretagne* (1757). He was the mentor of Turgot, who celebrated his achievements in a well-known *éloge*. Credited by Dupont de Nemours with founding 'the science of political economy' alongside Quesnay, he differed from the physiocrats in his advocacy of free trade for all commodities and not merely the products of the land, of whose unique productivity he remained unconvinced.
• Schelle 1897.

GRATTAN, HENRY

1746–1820. Irish patriot. Born in Dublin, he was educated at Trinity College, and the Inns of Court, London. He made his name in journalism, in articles for the *Freeman's Journal*, collected in *Baratariana* (1772). Elected a member of the Irish parliament, 1775, he worked with Flood for the independence of the Irish parliament from executive control by London. He criticised placemen and the imperial tax and trade regime. The parliament of 1782 is known as 'Grattan's Parliament'. He pressed for franchise reform and Catholic relief. Though he spoke vehemently against the Union in 1800, he became a member of the united parliament at Westminster, 1805, where he continued to campaign for Catholic emancipation. His collected speeches encapsulate the Irish Whig patriotism of the 1770s–80s.
• Boyce *et al.* 2001; McDowell 2001.

GRAVINA, GIAN VINCENZO

1664–1718. Italian jurist. Born at Rogiano (Cosenza), he studied philosophy, the classics, and jurisprudence at Naples. He moved to Rome and became secretary to Cardinal Pignatelli, 1689. He was there appointed to the chair of civil law, 1696, and then canon law, 1703. His principal juridical work was *Originum juris civilis* (1708), which was translated into French and German, and admired by Montesquieu and Gibbon. He also published critiques of Jesuit moralism, a number of plays, and works on poetry.

GRÉGOIRE, ABBÉ HENRI BAPTISTE

1750–1831. French Gallican and revolutionary. Born near Lunéville, Lorraine, of a peasant family, he became a Jansenist priest. At the Revolution he served in the Estates General and the National Assembly. He promoted the union of the clergy with the Third Estate and accepted the Civil Constitution of the Clergy, under which he became bishop of Loir et Cher, 1791–1801. In the Convention he opposed the execution of the king, 1793. He opposed Napoleon and supported the Bourbon restoration of 1815. His works defended Gallicanism and a vision of moral reformation under state Catholicism. In 1788 he wrote an essay on the emancipation of the Jews. *Histoire des sectes* appeared in 1810. He championed racial equality in *De la littérature des Nègres* (1808).
• Herman-Blot 2000; Plongeron 1989; Popkin and Popkin 2000.

GRIMALDI, FRANCESCO ANTONIO

1749–84. Neapolitan statesman, philosopher, and historian. Grimaldi took his degree in law from Naples University. Strongly influenced by the thought of Vico, his *Riflessioni sopra l'ineguaglianza tra gli uomini* (Reflections on the Inequality of Mankind, 1779) reacted against Rousseau and attempted to demonstrate that inequality was both inevitable and morally justified. He later wrote *Annali del regno di Napoli* which described the succession of civilisations in southern Italy. In 1783, Grimaldi became minister for war for the Kingdom of Naples.

GRIMM, FRIEDRICH MELCHIOR, BARON VON

1723–1807. German diplomat, author, and critic. Born in Ratisbon, the son of a Lutheran pastor, he served in Paris as representative of several states, and then as secretary to the duke of Orleans. He befriended the *philosophes*, contributed to the *Encyclopédie*, and maintained an extensive correspondence. Through him, French work became known in Germany. His *Correspondence littéraire, philosophique et critique*, originally circulated in manuscript, was written between 1753 and 1769 and published in 1813.
• Lizé 1979.

Biographies

GUNDLING, NICOLAUS HIERONYMUS
1671–1729. German jurist. Son of a clergyman, he trained for the church, turned to law under the influence of Thomasius, and became professor of natural and international law at Halle. His prolific output included *Jus naturae et gentium* (The Law of Nature and Nations, 1715). His work on the philosophy of history is also of note.
• Mulsow 1997.

GUSTAV III
1746–92. King of Sweden, 1771–92. Born in Stockholm. An admirer of Beccaria, Le Mercier, Marmontel, and Voltaire. In 1772 he staged a bloodless coup to overthrow the 'Age of Liberty' and restored absolute rule. He promoted agriculture, commerce, and the arts and sciences, granted religious toleration, and reduced the number of capital offences. Another coup in 1789 enhanced further his powers of legislation, limited the aristocracy, and opened public offices to commoners. He was assassinated at a masked ball.
• Barton 1986.

HAMANN, JOHANN GEORG
1730–88. German critic of Enlightenment, born in Königsberg. He opposed Kant and critical philosophy for its separation of reason from language, experience, and tradition. He stressed instead the historical, social, and cultural contexts of ideas. A founder of the *Sturm und Drang* (Storm and Stress) movement, his aesthetics celebrated creative genius and the power of art.
• Berlin 1993, 2000; Merlan 1954.

HAMILTON, ALEXANDER
1757–1804. American revolutionary. Born on Nevis Island, West Indies, he came to America in 1772. He wrote pamphlets in defence of colonial autonomy against the loyalist Seabury – *A Full Vindication of the Measures of the Congress* (1774) and *The Farmer Refuted* (1775) – and served as aide-de-camp to Washington. He was a member of the Continental Congress, 1782–3, and the Constitutional Convention, 1787. He co-authored with Madison and Jay *The Federalist Papers* (1787–8), the authoritative vindication of the federal constitution. Of the eighty-five papers he wrote fifty-one, and co-authored three with Madison. He was first secretary of the treasury, 1789–95. He led the Federalist party against Jefferson's Democratic Republican party. A proponent of strong central government, he held that a large and diverse but united republic would weaken local faction. In his *Report on Manufactures* (1791) he favoured an economic policy supportive of industrialisation. He was killed in a duel by Aaron Burr, Jefferson's vice-president.
• Kenyon 1958; McCoy 1980; McDonald 1979; Miller 1959; Mitchell 1957–62; Nelson 1987; Read 2000; Rossiter 1964; Stourzh 1970.

HAYS, MARY
1760–1843. English feminist. Born in London of a Dissenting family, in the 1780s she joined the radical circle that included Priestley, Paine, Godwin, and Wollstonecraft. She published essays, novels, and memoirs. Her feminist works were *An Appeal to the Men of Great Britain in Behalf of Women* (1798), *The Victim of Prejudice* (1799), and *Female Biography* (1803).
• Kelly 1993.

HEIBERG, PETER ANDREAS
1758–1841. Danish–Norwegian political critic. Born in Vordingborg, he wrote plays and songs. His *Rigsdalersedlens Haendelser* (Dealings in Six-Dollar Notes, 1789–93) attacked

corruption in politics and religion, as well as absolute monarchy and aristocracy. In 1798 he was banished. He settled in Paris, where he died.

HEINECCIUS (HEINECKE), JOHANN GOTTLIEB
1681–1741. German jurist, born in Eisenberg. He became professor of law at Halle and elsewhere. His chief works were *Elementa juris naturae et gentium* (1737, English trans. *A Methodical System of Universal Law*, 1741), *Praelectiones academicae in Hugonis Grotii de jura belli ac pacis* (Lectures on Grotius's Law of War and Peace, 1744), *Praelectiones academicae in S. Pufendorfi de officio hominis et civis* (Lectures on Pufendorf's Duty of Man and Citizen, 1748). The adaptation of Heineccius by George Turnbull ensured that he was the most influential of Thomasius's pupils outside Germany. He was admired for his historically sensitive application of the principles of natural law to the study of German customary law.
• Bergfeld 1996; Haakonssen 1996a.

HELVÉTIUS, CLAUDE ADRIEN
1715–71. French philosopher and civil servant. Born in Paris, he was educated at the Collège de Louis-le-Grand. He served as a tax farmer, 1738–51, thereafter retiring to his country estate. His chief work was *De l'esprit* (1758; English trans. *Essays on the Mind*, 1759), a defence of 'sensationalism', materialism, and determinism, for which he was condemned by the Paris *parlement*. His *De l'homme, de ses facultés intellectuelles et de son éducation* (1772; English trans. *A Treatise on Man*, 1777) was published posthumously. His analysis of man as driven by the pleasure–pain principle, his emphasis on environment in shaping our nature, and his confidence in education, made his work attractive to Bentham, James Mill, and the *idéologues*. Helvétius's emphasis on the uniformity of human nature led to a strong egalitarianism, which he carried through to a call for subdivision of land so that every family could be self-sufficient.
• Andlau 1939; Cumming 1955; Horowitz 1954; Smith 1965.

HERDER, JOHANN GOTTFRIED VON
1744–1803. German philosopher. A native of Mohrungen, East Prussia, he studied under Kant at Königsberg. He taught at Riga from 1764, and was ordained. He embarked on travels in France, 1769. Through Goethe he became court preacher at Weimar, 1776–1803. His literary and aesthetic theory influenced the Romantics and encouraged a native German literature. *Ursprung der Sprache* (On the Origin of Language, 1772) emphasised cultural specificity against Enlightenment universalism. *Auch eine Philosophie der Geschichte* (Yet Another Philosophy of History, 1774) marked a further break with Kant. His principal work of historical theory was *Ideen zur Philosophie der Geschichte der Menscheit* (Ideas for the Philosophy of the History of Mankind, 1784–91), which argued for a teleological view of history, each nation following its own organic pattern of development, according to its specific cultural and geographical circumstances. He is credited as a source for modern nationalism and cultural relativism.
• Barnard 1965a, 1983, 1988a; Berlin 1976, 2000; Clark 1955; Pross 1987a, 1987b; Redekop 2000; Rouché 1940.

HERRENSCHWAND, JEAN FRÉDÉRIC
1728–1812. Born in Switzerland, he apparently served in Swiss regiments in French service, but little is known of his life. His principal work, *De l'économie politique et morale de l'espèce humaine* (The Political and Moral Economy of Humankind, 1796), was a late defence of physiocracy.

HIPPEL, THEODOR GOTTLIEB VON

1741–96. German jurist, novelist, and feminist. Born and educated at Königsberg, of which city he was mayor, 1780–96. A close friend of Kant, Hamman, and Herder. He advocated equality for women in *Über die Ehe* (On Marriage, 1774) and *Über die bürgerliche Verbesserung der Weiber* (On the Civil Emancipation of Women, 1793).

• Hull 1996; Kohnen 1987.

HOADLY, BENJAMIN

1676–1761. English Court Whig. Born in Westerham, Kent, and educated at Cambridge University, Hoadly came to prominence with his defence of 'Revolution principles'. He deployed natural right and the social contract against Leslie's crypto-Jacobite revival of monarchic patriarchialism and hereditary right. Through assiduous support for Whig governments, Hoadly rose through four bishoprics, Bangor, Hereford, Salisbury, and Winchester. His *Nature of the Kingdom, or Church of Christ* (1717) sparked the Bangorian Controversy, a paper war over the relationship of church and state. He dissolved all claims of ecclesiastical authority independent of secular power. Under Prime Minister Walpole, Hoadly was a regular contributor to *The London Journal* (1721), where he defended the constitutional necessity of executive influence over the legislature. His works included *The Measures of Submission to the Civil Magistrate Considered* (1706) and *The Original and Institution of Civil Government* (1710).

• Bailyn 1967; Browning 1982; Kenyon 1977; Schochet 1975.

HOLBACH, PAUL HENRI DIETRICH, BARON D'

1723–89. French atheist, philosopher, and political commentator. Born in Edesheim in the Palatinate, he was educated in Paris and Leiden. He became a French subject and settled in Paris, 1749, where, until the 1780s, he hosted a distinguished salon of *philosophes*. He translated scientific works into French, which gave an impetus to French chemistry. He contributed hundreds of articles on science, religion, and politics to the *Encyclopédie*. In 'Représentans' he recommends the reduction of royal power and the summoning of national assemblies with a broad representation. In articles on non-Christian religions he argued the absurdity of religion. His best-known work is the materialist and determinist treatise *Système de la nature* (1770). In the 1760s there appeared increasingly atheistic writings, including *De l'imposture sacerdotale* (Priestly Imposture, 1767). *La Politique naturelle* (1773), *Système social* (1773), and *L'Ethocratie, ou le gouvernement fondé sur la morale* (Ethnocracy, or Government Founded in Morality, 1776) defended a monarchy moderated by representative assemblies of landowners.

• Kors 1976; Naville 1967; Topazio 1956; Wickwar 1935.

HOLLIS, THOMAS

1720–74. English 'Commonwealthman'. Born in London, he attended Amsterdam University. His tours of the Continent, 1748–50, reinforced his republican principles. He inherited an estate, and settled in Lincoln's Inn, where he became an antiquary, book collector, and promoter of 'Commonwealth' causes. A supporter of Catherine Macaulay's historical writing, he defended the Americans, and was violently anti-Catholic. He founded the Society for Constitutional Information, and suggested to Thomas Hardy the idea for the London Corresponding Society. He is significant for 'canonising' the republican tradition through a programme of republication. He issued editions (adorned with caps of liberty) of Toland's *Life of Milton* (1760), Sidney's *Discourses concerning Government* (1763), Neville's *Plato Redivivus* (1763), Locke's *Two Treatises* (1764), and *Letters concerning Toleration* (1765). In 1772 Hollis recommended to the Swedes the following authors in the Calvinist–Whig revolutionary tradition: Ponet, Goodman, the *Vindiciae contra tyrannos*, Hotman, Buchanan, Milton,

Harrington, Nedham (*Excellency of Free Government*), Molesworth (*Account of Denmark*), and Trenchard (*Short History of Standing Armies*). He declared his political creed to be embodied in Molesworth's preface to Hotman's *Francogallia* (1710).

• Bailyn 1967; Bond 1990; Bonwick 1977; Robbins 1950.

HOME, HENRY, *see* KAMES

HONTHEIM, JOHANN NIKOLAUS VON (JUSTINIUS FEBRONIUS)
1701–90. German conciliarist. Born in Trier, where he spent most of his life, he was ordained priest, 1728, and became bishop, 1748. His chief work, influenced by Van Espen, was *De statu ecclesiae et legitima potestate Romani Pontificis* (On the State of the Church and the Legitimate Power of the Roman Pontiff, 1765–74), the guiding text of Febronianism. Here he assailed the authority of the papacy and defended Gallican and conciliarist positions. He was forced to make a formal retraction in 1778.

HOOKE, NATHANIEL
d. 1763. Irish Jacobite, and nephew of the Jacobite of the same name (1664–1738). He was admitted to the Inns of Court, London, 1702. A friend of Pope, and a disciple of Fénelon. He produced the English translation of Ramsay's *Voyages de Cyrus* (*Travels of Cyrus*, 1739). His chief work was his *Roman History* (1738–71). Its democratic commitments indicate the paradoxical transition between Jacobitism and Jacobinism.

HOPKINS, STEPHEN
1707–85. American revolutionary. Born in Cranston, Rhode Island, he had no formal education. From the 1730s he held local office, and from the 1740s had a shipping business. He was a member of the Rhode Island Assembly, 1744–54, chief justice, 1751, and held the annual office of governor nine times between 1755 and 1768. He was a member of the Continental Congress, 1774, and signatory of the Declaration of Independence, 1776. His tracts, including *An Essay on the Trade of the Northern Colonies* (1764) and *Rights of the Colonies Examined* (1764), upheld the principles of 'no taxation without representation' and the limited jurisdiction of the imperial parliament. The latter was widely reprinted, and Otis's *Vindication* was a defence of it.

• Bailyn 1967.

HORNE, GEORGE
1730–92. English Tory. Born near Maidstone, Kent. He spent most of his life as a Fellow and then as president, 1768, of Magdalen College, Oxford. He was chaplain to the king, 1771–81, and bishop of Norwich, 1790. Hostile to the claims of political reformers, Dissenters, and American revolutionaries, he reached back to seventeenth-century Toryism. His sermons, particularly 'The Origins of Civil Government' (1769) assailed Lockean Whiggery, ridiculing the notion of a pre-political state of nature. The posthumous compilation, *The Scholar Armed against the Errors of the Time* (1795), did service in the Burkean onslaught on the French Revolution.

• Aston 1993a, 1993b; Clark 1985; Gunn 1983; Sack 1993.

HORSLEY, SAMUEL
1733–1806. English Tory. Born in London, he was educated at Cambridge University and taught at Oxford University. Ordained a minister, he became a mathematician and edited Newton's works (1779–85). Bishop of St David's, 1788, Rochester, 1793, and St Asaph, 1802. Following controversy with Priestley over the Trinity and, drawing upon patristic scholarship, he championed a high Anglican position, including the apostolic succession of bishops and

the real presence of Christ in the eucharist (*Letters from the Archdeacon of Saint Albans . . . to Dr Priestley*, 1784). He preached a notoriously authoritarian sermon to the House of Lords, 30 January 1793, declaring that he 'did not know what the mass of the people in any country had to do with the laws, except to obey them'. He vigorously opposed the slave trade.
• Hole 1989; Mather 1992.

HOWARD, JOHN
c. 1726–90. English philanthropist and penal reformer, born probably in Hackney, London. He was imprisoned in France, 1756. Appointed sheriff of Bedfordshire, though a Dissenter, 1773, he reformed the county prisons. From his extensive tours of inspection of prisons in Britain, Ireland, France, Holland, Germany, and Switzerland, 1775–6, arose *The State of the Prisons* (1777; enlarged 1784). He visited Denmark, Sweden, Russia, 1781; Spain, Portugal, 1783; Italy, Turkey, 1785–6; and published accounts of his travels. He died in a Russian military camp.

HUMBOLDT, KARL WILHELM VON
1767–1835. German theorist of liberalism, and educationalist. Born in Potsdam of a Prussian aristocratic family, he studied at Göttingen, and was a friend of Schiller and Goethe. His chief work was *Ideen zu einem Versuch die Grenzen der Wirksamkeit des Staates zu bestimmen* (Some Ideas concerning the Attempt to Define the Limits of State Action, partly published, 1792, fully, 1851), which was given prominence in J. S. Mill's *On Liberty* (1759). Here Humboldt developed the idea that state intervention inhibited the conditions for self-development of the personality. As Prussian minister of education, 1808–10, he helped establish the tradition of the humanistic *Gymnasium*.
• Beiser 1992; Krieger 1957; Sweet 1978–80; Vogel 1982.

HUME, DAVID
1711–76. Scottish philosopher and historian. Born and educated in Edinburgh, he lived mainly at his ancestral home, Ninewells, in the Scottish Borders, until the mid-1740s. He lived in France, 1734–7, and travelled on the Continent later, particularly during 1763–6 when he was secretary to the British embassy in Paris. He failed to gain the chair of moral philosophy at Edinburgh, 1745, and a chair at Glasgow, 1752. From 1752 to 1757 he was librarian of the Advocates Library, Edinburgh, where he lived 1751–63, 1769–76. He served briefly as under-secretary of state in London, 1767–9. He died in Edinburgh. His principal philosophical work was his *Treatise of Human Nature* (1739–40; written 1734–7; revised as the *Enquiry concerning Human Understanding* (1748) and *Enquiry concerning the Principles of Morals* (1751), and *A Dissertation on the Passions* (1757)). He argued that the passions, rather than reason, are the motives for action. An atheist, his critique of religion appeared in *The Natural History of Religion* (1757) and *Dialogues concerning Natural Religion* (1779). His main political reflections occur in *Essays Moral and Political* (1741–2). He was most familiar to contemporaries as author of the *History of England* (1754–62).
• Ayer 1980; Berry 1997; Bongie 1965; Buckle 1991; Cohon 2001; Dunn and Harris 1997; Forbes 1975; Haakonssen 1981, 1996a; Harrison 1981; Hope 1989; Miller 1981; Morice 1977; Mossner 1954; Norton *et al.* 1979; Norton 1993; Noxon 1973; Phillipson 1989; Pompa 1990b; Stewart 1963; Stewart and Wright 1994; Whelan 1985.

HUTCHESON, FRANCIS
1694–1746. Irish-Scottish philosopher. Born in Drumalig, Co. Down, of a Presbyterian family, he studied at Glasgow University, was ordained, and taught at an academy in Dublin, 1721–30. He succeeded Carmichael as professor of moral philosophy in Glasgow, 1729–46.

He developed Shaftesburian moral sense theory against Mandevillian egoism in his *Inquiry into the Original of our Ideas of Beauty and Virtue* (1725). He coined the phrase later made famous by Bentham, 'that action is best, which procures the greatest happiness for the greatest numbers'. His works include *Essay on the Nature and Conduct of the Passions and Affections* (1728); *Philosophiae moralis institutio compendiaria* (1742; English trans. *A Short Introduction to Moral Philosophy*, 1747), and *A System of Moral Philosophy* (written 1734–7, publ. 1755).
• Brown 2002; Cairns 1991; Gobetti 1992; Hope 1989; Horne 1986; MacIntyre 1988; Miller 1995; Moore 1990, 1994; Rivers 1991–2000; Rozbicki 2001.

HUTCHINSON, THOMAS

1711–80. American loyalist. Born in Boston, Massachusetts, a descendant of the Puritan Anne Hutchinson. As chief justice of Massachusetts he upheld the Stamp Act, 1765, and as governor, 1771–4, defended British rule. He was widely vilified as epitomising British tyranny and in 1774 retreated to Britain. His chief published work was a history of Massachusetts, but his significant contribution to political thought was his unpublished 'Dialogue between an American and a European Englishman' (1768), written in response to Dickinson's *Farmer's Letters*. It is a subtle consideration of parliamentary supremacy and the nature of empire, and includes a debate on how Livy and Locke might have interpreted the Revolution. It was printed in 1975.
• Bailyn 1974; Pencak 1982.

ICKSTATT, JOHANN ADAM VON

1702–76. German jurist, in the service of Bavaria, and professor of *jus oeconomicocamerale* at Ingolstadt. He published *Opuscula juridica varii argumenti* (Juridical Essays on Diverse Themes, 1747–59).

INGLIS, CHARLES

1734–1816. Irish-American loyalist. Born in Glencolumbkille, Co. Donegal, Ireland, he was too poor for a university education and was largely self-taught. He emigrated to Pennsylvania, *c.* 1754, became a teacher, was episcopally ordained, and became a pastor. He wrote in defence of the establishment of an episcopate in America. During the Revolution he published some thirty tracts denouncing revolutionary principles, including *The True Interest of America Impartially Stated* (1776, against Paine's *Common Sense*), and *Letters of Papinian* (1779, against the Continental Congress). Inglis served as chaplain to the British army, 1778, was attainted by the revolutionaries, 1779, and withdrew to Britain. He returned to North America in 1787 as the first bishop of Nova Scotia.

IREDELL, JAMES

1751–99. American revolutionary. Born in Lewes, Sussex, and brought up in Bristol, the son of a merchant, he was sent to America in 1768 to take up a post as a customs official in North Carolina. He trained as a lawyer and became successful. He defended the American cause in *To the Inhabitants of Great Britain* (1774) and *The Principles of an American Whig* (1776), where he argued that parliament had no jurisdiction over the colonies, since the colonies were the king's personal dominions and not part of Britain; he proposed a federation of independent legislatures under the monarch. Iredell served as attorney general for North Carolina in 1779–81, and in 1790 was appointed to the Supreme Court. He was one of the first to argue for the Court's power of judicial review of the constitutionality of legislation.

ISELIN, ISAAK

1728–82. Swiss political and economic theorist, born in Basle where he studied philosophy and law. Iselin met Rousseau at Paris in 1752 and was initially impressed by his work. Nevertheless, he disagreed with the pessimism of Rousseau's second *Discourse* (1755). Iselin set forth a refutation in *Philosophische und Patriotische Träume eines Menschenfreundes* (Philosophical and Patriotic Dreams of a Lover of Mankind, 1755). Dissatisfied with this piece, it was in his *Geschichte der Menschheit* (History of Mankind, 1764) that he gave his most comprehensive reply to Rousseau's social analysis. He argued that moral improvement was encouraged by opportunities for social interaction, and that commercial progress and intercourse, far from leading to moral decadence, allowed humans to take full advantage of their social faculties.
• Kapossy 2001.

JAUCOURT, LOUIS, CHEVALIER DE

1704–79. Born in Paris, a Huguenot aristocrat of nominal Catholic parentage. He was educated at Geneva and Leiden Universities, gaining a doctorate in medicine. He turned to literary work, publishing an edition of Leibniz's *Theodicy*, and a life of Leibniz (1734). He became the most prolific contributor (1,700 articles) to the *Encyclopédie*, writing on religion, politics, law, economics, medicine, and literature. His comments on politics are largely derived from Montesquieu and Locke, praising England's supposed separation of powers, and France's monarchy balanced by nobility.
• Lough 1971; Morris 1979; Rapp 1965.

JAY, JOHN

1745–1829. American revolutionary, diplomat, and jurist. Born in New York. He was a member of the Continental Congress, 1774, and published *An Address to the People of Great Britain* (1774), against taxation without consent. Initially he opposed independence, but changed his mind. He drafted the constitution of New York State, 1777, and was president of the Continental Congress, 1778–9. With John Adams and Benjamin Franklin he negotiated the Treaty of Paris which ended the War of Independence, 1783. He was secretary for foreign affairs, 1784–9, and first chief justice of the Supreme Court, 1789–95. His principal political writing was his contribution to the *Federalist Papers* (1787–8, co-authored with Hamilton and Madison).
• Morris 1967, 1985.

JEBB, JOHN

1736–86. English political and theological writer. Educated at Cambridge University, where he later taught divinity. Ordained a minister, he held parishes in Suffolk until 1775. A Unitarian, he campaigned for abolition of subscription to the articles of the Church of England, 1771. He campaigned with Cartwright for franchise reform. After leaving the ministry, 1775, he became a physician. His works (collected in three volumes in 1787) include *Letters . . . to the Volunteers of Ireland on . . . Parliamentary Reform* (1784) and *Thoughts on the Construction and Polity of Prisons* (1785).
• Page 2003.

JEFFERSON, THOMAS

1743–1826. American revolutionary and politician. Born in Shadwell, Virginia, and educated at William and Mary College, he was a wealthy plantation owner. In *A Summary View of the Rights of British America* (1774) he argued a federal theory of empire, each legislative body free, equal, and independent under the crown. He was the principal author of the

Declaration of Independence, 1776, and of the Virginia statute for religious freedom, 1777. He was ambassador to France, 1784–9, secretary of state, 1789–93, vice-president, 1797–1801, and third president, 1801–9. He led the anti-Federalist party, preferring an agrarian to a commercial vision for the United States, and defending states' rights against central power. He envisioned a revived *polis*, enriched by local direct democracy. He published *Notes on the State of Virginia* (1787; written 1781) and founded the University of Virginia, 1819.
• Banning 1978; Becker 1958; Fliegelman 1993; Koch 1957; Lehmann 1985; McCoy 1980; Malone 1948–81; Matthews 1984; Mayer 1994; Read 2000; Sheldon 1991; Sloan 1995; White 1978; Wills 1978.

JENYNS, SOAME

1704–87. English conservative. Born in Bottisham, Cambridgeshire, and educated at Cambridge University. He sat in parliament as a Whig, 1742–80, was a member of the Board of Trade, 1755–80, and a county justice of the peace. He was widely admired as a prose stylist. Stressing the incompatibility of political idealism and the Christian view of sinfulness, he defended political 'corruption' from 'virtuous' reforming principles (*Free Inquiry into the Nature and Origin of Evil*, 1757; *Thoughts on Parliamentary Reform*, 1784). He robustly defended Britain against the American colonies (*The Objections to the Taxation of our American Colonies . . . Considered*, 1765). His *View of the Internal Evidence of the Christian Religion* (1776) ran to many editions.

JOHNSON, SAMUEL

1709–84. English moralist, lexicographer, biographer, novelist, journalist, and critic. Born in Lichfield, the son of a bookseller, he was educated at Oxford University. He settled in London and began a literary career, 1737. His prodigious output included journalism, plays, novels, biographies, poems, editions, and, most famously, his *Dictionary of the English Language* (1755). He produced a journal, the *Rambler* (1750); his best known fiction is *Rasselas, Prince of Abissinia* (1759). He was renowned for his conversation and wit, recorded by James Boswell in his *Life of Samuel Johnson*. His political tracts include the anti-American *Taxation no Tyranny* (1775), *The False Alarm* (1770), and *The Patriot* (1774).
• Cannon 1994; Clark 1994b; DeMaria 1993; Greene 1990.

JONES, SIR WILLIAM

1746–94. Orientalist. Born in Westminster, he was educated at Oxford University and the Inns of Court, London. He became a barrister, and acquired phenomenal erudition in Oriental languages. He was a friend of Adam Smith, Burke, and Gibbon. In 1783 he was appointed a judge in Bengal, and died in Calcutta. He wrote on linguistics, literature, law, religion, and Asian society. He pressed for a comparative treatment of legal systems as between East and West, and for deference to Indian legal culture. His principal legal works were *An Essay on the Law of Bailments* (1781) and *Digest of Hindu Law* (posth., 1797–8). His *Principles of Government* (1782) summarised Lockean natural law and politics, in a tract designed for common readers, and was the subject of a notorious trial for seditious libel.
• Cannon 1990.

JOSEPH II, EMPEROR

1741–90. Born in Vienna. He succeeded his father, Francis I, as Holy Roman Emperor in 1765, when he also became co-regent with his mother, Maria Theresa, of the Austrian monarchy, succeeding his mother as sole ruler in 1780. He imbibed the political theory of the natural law school, with emphasis on the advantages of personal rule, but also received instruction about the diverse provinces he would govern, to which he reacted by determining

748

to make them uniform. He knew little of the *philosophes*. He considered himself an orthodox Catholic, but seemed a Jansenist to papalists and was committed to drastic reform of the church. During the 1780s he subordinated church to state, freed the press, and introduced toleration for some Protestants and Jews. Many of his laws were directed as much towards strengthening his power as towards reform, and provoked violent opposition, particularly in Belgium and Hungary.
• Barton 1978; Bazzoli 1986; Beales 1975, 1980, 1985, 1987, 1991, 1993; Birtsch 1987; Blanning 1970, 1994; Bradler-Rottmann 1973; Hammerstein 1983; Karniel 1986; Klueting 1995; Kovács 1979; Mitrofanov 1910; O'Brien 1969; Press 1988; Sashegyi 1958; Szabo 1994; Valjavec 1945; Venturi 1969–90; Wangermann 1969; Winter 1962.

JOVELLANOS, GASPAR MELCHIOR DE
1744–1811. Spanish reformer, politician, and author, born in Gijon, Asturias. He studied law, and became a judge in Seville, 1767, and Madrid, 1778. In 1797 he became minister of justice, but was imprisoned in Minorca, 1801–8, for his anticlericalism and defence of the independence of the church from Rome. His main political work was *Informe de la sociedad económica de Madrid al real supremo consejo de Castilla en el expediente de ley agraria* (Report on the Agrarian Law, 1795), which argued for agrarian reform, economic deregulation, and the enclosure of common land. An eclectic work, it drew on Locke for the rights of people to the product of their labour, on Adam Smith for the free play of private interest, on the physiocrats in its stress on agriculture, and on the Jansenists for its critique of church property. His speech to the Real Academia de la Historia, 1780, gave a Tacitean account of Spain's Visigothic ancient constitution, arguing a decline from primeval liberty through the rise of an over-mighty and oppressive nobility.
• Herr 1958, 1989; Varella 1988.

JURIEU, PIERRE
1637–1713. Huguenot theorist of political resistance and religious intolerance. Born in Mer near Orleans, he was educated at the Protestant academy of Saumur. He was professor of theology at Sedan, 1674, until the college's forced closure, when he went into exile in Holland, becoming pastor at Rotterdam, 1681. He wrote many works against Catholicism. His *Lettres pastorales aux fidèles de France qui gémissent sous la captivité de Babylone* (Pastoral Letters to the Faithful of France who Groan under the Babylonian Captivity, 1686–8) savaged Louis XIV and looked forward to the overthrow of the French Antichrist. He engaged in a prolonged controversy with his fellow Huguenot Bayle over religious toleration.
• Dodge 1947; Knetsch 1967; Labrousse 1996.

JUSTI, JOHANN HEINRICH GOTTLOB VON
1720–71. Austrian cameralist. Born in Brücken, Saxony, he served as a soldier and studied at Wittenburg University. Although chiefly remembered for his economic and political treatises, his career was punctuated by financially unsuccessful projects. His literary pursuits began in 1745, first editing a journal at Leipzig, and then in 1747 winning a prize from the Prussian Academy of Sciences for an essay on monads. He taught at the Theresianum in Vienna, 1750–4, returned to Leipzig, and became director of police at Göttingen, 1755–8. He next entered Danish service, but from 1760 lived in Berlin. In 1765 Frederick II appointed him director of mines and supervisor of glass and steel factories, but these soon faced financial difficulties. He was dismissed and died in prison. He produced a systematic exposition of cameralism in *Grundfoste zu der Macht und Glückseligkeit der Staaten* (Foundations of the Power and Prosperity of States, 1760–1).
• Adam 2003, 2004; Dreitzel 1987; Frensdorff 1903; Hull 1996.

KAMES, HENRY HOME, LORD

1696–1782. Scottish social theorist. Born in Berwickshire, he was called to the Scottish bar, 1742, and became a lord of session (judge of the Supreme Court) in 1752. He was a friendly patron and opponent of Hume and Adam Smith. He published a series of legal and historical works. The chief are *Historical Law Tracts* (1758), *Principles of Equity* (1760), and *Sketches of the History of Man* (1774). His *Essays on the Principles of Morality and Natural Religion* (1751), written against Hume, brought accusations of heresy.

• Berry 1997; Haakonssen 1996a; Lehmann 1971; Lieberman 1983, 1989; Ross 1972; Wokler 1988b.

KANT, IMMANUEL

1724–1804. The pre-eminent German philosopher of the eighteenth century. He was born, lived, and died in Königsberg in East Prusia. From a poor and Pietist background, he attended the university, studying philosophy, theology, the classics, and natural philosophy. He worked as a tutor, 1746–55, was appointed *privatdozent* (lecturer) in 1755, and became professor of logic and metaphysics in 1770. Later he served as rector. His earliest work was in natural philosophy. His 'critical' phase began in 1769, and led to his principal works, the *Kritik der reinen Vernunft* (Critique of Pure Reason, 1781), the *Kritik der praktischen Vernunft* (Critique of Practical Reason, 1788), and the *Kritik der Urteilskraft* (Critique of Judgement, 1790). The first critique was popularised in the *Prolegomena zu einer jeden Künftigen* (Prolegomena to any Future Metaphysics, 1783). His principal ethical work was the *Grundlegung zur Metaphysik der Sitten* (Groundwork of the Metaphysic of Morals, 1785). As David Hume famously awoke him from his 'dogmatic slumber' in metaphysics, so his reading of Rousseau's *Social Contract* and *Emile* awoke him to the liberalism and republicanism evinced in his later political writings. His work on politics is scattered through a series of essays, including *Was ist Aufklärung* (What is Enlightenment, 1785); *Idee zu einer allgemeinen Geschichte in Weltbürgerlicher Absicht* (Idea of Universal History from a Cosmopolitan Point of View, 1784), *Über den Gemeinspruch: Das mag in der Theorie richtig sein, taugt aber nicht für die Praxis* (On the Common Saying: This May Be True in Theory, but it Does not Apply in Practice, 1793). Important too are *Die Religion innheralb der Grenzen der blossen Vernunft* (Religion within the Limits of Reason Alone, 1793), which is sceptical of established religions; *Zum Ewigen Frieden* (Perpetual Peace, 1795), a theory of international relations; the *Die Metaphysik du Sitten* (The Metaphysics of Morals, 1797); and *Der Streit der Facultäten* (The Contest of the Faculties, 1798). Kant ceased lecturing in 1797.

• Allison 1990; Beiser 1992; Cassirer 1981; Guyer 1992; Kelly 1969; Kuehn 2001; Mulholland 1990; Riley 1983; Shklar 1984; Scruton 1982; Sullivan 1989; Wolff 1967.

KING, WILLIAM

1650–1729. Irish theologian and political writer. Born in Antrim, he was educated at Trinity College, Dublin. Ordained in 1674, he rose to be chancellor, 1679, and dean of St Patrick's Cathedral, Dublin, 1689, bishop of Derry, 1691, and archbishop of Dublin, 1703. His *De origine mali* (1702; trans. *An Essay on the Origin of Evil*, 1731) was a significant essay in theodicy, known to Bayle, Leibniz, and Wolff. His main political work was *The State of the Protestants of Ireland* (1691), an influential vindication of the Williamite Revolution in Ireland and of the Protestant Ascendancy.

• Boyce *et al.* 2001; Kelly 1989a; O'Regan 2000.

KNOX, WILLIAM

1732–1810. Anglo-Irish-American defender of the British empire. Born in Monaghan, Ireland, he was educated at Trinity College, Dublin. He was provost marshal of Georgia,

1756–62, acquiring a plantation and slaves. He returned to Britain as agent for Georgia, 1762, and thereafter advised British governments on American policy, serving as under-secretary in the American Department, 1770–82, after which he lost office in Britain as well as his estates in America. His *The Claim of the Colonies* (1765) defended parliament's right to tax the colonies; *The Present State of the Nation* (1768) defended the idea of commercial empire, advocating concessions to America under the umbrella of parliamentary supremacy, and proposing that the colonies be given seats in the imperial parliament. His *Controversy between Great Britain and her Colonies Reviewed* (1769), against Dickinson, was more intransigent in defence of parliamentary sovereignty. Later he defended slavery on evangelical Christian grounds, foreshadowing later arguments used in the American South: *Three Tracts respecting the Conversion and Instruction of the Free Indians and Negroe Slaves* (1768, repr. 1789) and *A Letter from W. K. Esq. to W. Wilberforce* (1790).
• Bellot 1977; Greene 1986; Koebner 1961.

LA METTRIE, JULIEN OFFRAY DE
1709–51. French philosopher, the best-known Enlightenment defender of materialism. Born in Saint-Malo, he trained in medicine at Paris and Leiden. He published medical works and then turned to expositions of materialist philosophy. Following the appearance of *L'Histoire naturelle de l'âme* (Natural History of the Soul, 1745) he was forced to leave France for Holland. His *L'Homme machine* (1748) applied his philosophic materialism to human beings. In consequence, he was forced to leave Holland and found asylum in Prussia at the court of Frederick II, where he died.
• Vartanian 1960; Wellman 1992.

LANJUINAIS, JOSEPH
1730–1808. French philosopher. Born in Brittany, he became a Benedictine monk, but fled his monastery and established himself as a Protestant minister and teacher in Switzerland. His writings included works on Necker, Linguet's imprisonment, and the iniquities of Pope Clement XIV, but *Le Monarque accompli* (The Accomplished Monarch, 1774), ostensibly about Joseph II, was the most famous. All his writings were vehicles for scathing criticism of the Catholic Church and for advocacy of enlightened attitudes, especially religious toleration.
• Lortholary 1951.

LAW, JOHN
1671–1729. Scottish financier and political economist. Born in Edinburgh, the son of a goldsmith, he urged the Scottish parliament to establish a state bank. He fled to France after killing a man in a duel. Becoming rich by gambling, he travelled in Europe, 1708–15. His *Money and Trade Considered, with a Proposal for Supplying the Nation with Money* (1705) advocated the issuance of paper money as a stimulus to trade and industry. His *Considérations sur le numéraire et le commerce* (Considerations on Specie and Commerce, 1715) is a mercantilist work in the tradition of Petty, Davenant, and Vauban. He created a bank in France, 1716, which soon gained control of Louisiana and effective control of French overseas trade and French taxation. He was appointed controller-general of finances, 1720, but the bank collapsed, causing financial devastation and unrest. He fled, and died in poverty in Venice.
• Murphy 1997.

LAW, WILLIAM
1686–1761. English theologian. Born in Stamford, Lincolnshire, he was educated at Cambridge University and was ordained, 1711. He was a Nonjuror, who rejected the Church of England because it was fatally compromised by the Revolution of 1688. He wrote many

theological and polemical works defending the Catholicity of the church and attacking Erastianism. These included *Three Letters to the Bishop of Bangor* (1717–19). He attacked Mandeville in *Remarks upon the Fable of the Bees* (1724). His semi-mystical *Serious Call to the Devout and Holy Life* (1732) achieved an enduring readership.
• Walker 1973; Young 1994.

LE CLERC, JEAN (JOANNES CLERICUS)
1657–1736. Swiss theologian and advocate of Lockeanism. Born in Geneva, he studied at Grenoble and Saumur, where he abandoned strict Calvinism for Arminianism. In 1684 he became professor at the Remonstrant college in Amsterdam. He was close to Locke and to the circle of Dutch and Huguenot defenders of toleration. His periodicals *Bibliothèque universelle* (1686–93), *Bibliothèque choisie* (1703–8), and *Bibliothèque ancienne et moderne* (1714–26) were major vehicles for the Republic of Letters. His many works on religion and the Bible place him alongside Locke in the campaign for a 'rational Christianity'.
• Barnes 1938.

LEE, ARTHUR
1740–92. American revolutionary. Born in Westmorland, Virginia, and educated at Edinburgh University and the Inns of Court, London. He served as Maryland's agent in London, 1770. He published many newspaper articles, under the name 'Junius Americanus', 1768 onward, in defence of colonial rights. *An Appeal to the Justice and Interests of the People of Great Britain* (1774) and other tracts put the American case, from Britain, where he mixed in the circle of Wilkes, Catharine Macaulay, Price, Priestley, and Franklin. He was in France and Spain, 1776–7, seeking recognition for the independent colonies. He was a member of the Continental Congress, 1781–4. Brother of the next.
• Potts 1981.

LEE, RICHARD HENRY
1732–94. American revolutionary. Born in Westmorland, Virginia, he studied in England at Wakefield Dissenting Academy, returned to qualify as a lawyer, and inherited his parents' plantation. He sat in the Virginia House of Burgesses, 1758–75. He strongly opposed the Stamp Act and spoke against black slavery. Elected to the Continental Congress, 1774, he became a great orator, framed the bill that broke ties with England, and was a signatory of the Declaration of Independence, 1776. Though he opposed the federal constitution, he was chosen senator for Virginia, 1788–92. His anti-federalist tracts appeared as *Letters from the Federal Farmer to the Republican* (1787–8).
• Chitwood 1967.

LEIBNIZ, GOTTFRIED WILHELM VON
1646–1716. German philosopher, born in Leipzig. He was official historian at the court of the elector of Hanover. He engaged with Catholics in a scheme to reunite Christendom; he quarrelled with Newton over which of them discovered calculus; and he undertook a philosophical correspondence with Samuel Clarke. Leibniz differed from Descartes, Hobbes, Spinoza, and Locke (all of whom he criticised) in his determination to rescue what was valuable in Aristotle, Plato, and scholasticism, and somehow to synthesise them with modern materialist and sceptical insights. His *Essai de théodicée* (Theodicy, 1710), adopted a position of philosophical optimism, and is the object of Voltaire's satire in *Candide*. Most of his political writing took the form of short essays, among the most important of which are 'Meditation on the Common Concept of Justice' (c. 1702–3) and 'Opinion on the Principles of Pufendorf' (1706).

• Aiton 1985; Barber 1955; Corr 1975; Hostler 1975; Jolley 1975, 1984; Rescher 1967; Riley 1973, 1996; Schneider 1967; Sève 1989.

LE MERCIER DE LA RIVIÈRE, PIERRE PAUL

1719–1801. French physiocrat. Born in Saumur, he became counsellor to the Paris *parlement*, 1747, and was *intendant* of Martinique in the West Indies, 1759–64. He came to prominence with his *L'Ordre naturel et essentiel des sociétés politiques* (The Natural and Essential Order of Political Societies, 1767), which elaborated Quesnay's views. He attacked Galiani in *L'Intérêt général de l'état* (1770). Other works include *De l'instruction publique* (1775) and *Essai sur les maximes et les lois fondamentales de la monarchie française* (1789).
• May 1975–8; Silberstein 1928.

LEOPOLD, DUKE OF TUSCANY, EMPEROR LEOPOLD II

1747–92. Born in Vienna, the younger brother of Emperor Joseph II. Grand duke of Tuscany, 1765–90, Holy Roman Emperor and ruler of the Austrian monarchy, 1790–2. In Tuscany he embarked on a programme of legal, administrative, and religious reforms which procured him a reputation for enlightenment. He kept in touch with enlightened thought and wished to establish a constitutional regime influenced by British and American models. In the 1780s he encouraged what seemed to be a Jansenist movement within the Tuscan church, culminating in the Synod of Pistoia, 1786. However, when it provoked violent opposition he repudiated it. As emperor, he carried out a brilliant damage-limitation exercise in the wake of his brother's rule, making concessions to calm Hungary, recover Belgium, and bring the Turkish war to an end.
• Bolton 1969; Cochrane 1973; S. J. Miller 1994; Wandruszka 1963–5; Wangermann 1969.

LE PAIGE, LOUIS ADRIEN

1712–1802. French Jansenist anticlerical. A native of Paris, he became a lawyer. Librarian to, and supporter of, the prince de Conti, he played a prominent role in the Paris *parlement*, leading the Jansenist attack on the Jesuits. His many essays in the *Nouvelles ecclésiastiques* denounced priestcraft and defended toleration for the Huguenots, while his *Lettres historiques sur les fonctions essentielles du parlement* (1753–4) summarised earlier French criticism of absolute monarchy.
• Adams 1991; Van Kley 1975, 1996.

LESLIE, CHARLES

1650–1722. Irish Jacobite political theorist and theologian. Born in Dublin, and educated at Trinity College. Ordained a minister, 1680, he was ejected from ecclesiastical office at the Revolution. He published a series of attacks on the Revolution regime, and on the theology of its church leaders; as well as against Dissenters, Whigs, Quakers, Deists, and Jews. Among his works are: *An Answer to a Book, Intituled, The State of the Protestants in Ireland* (1692, against William King), *The Case of the Regale and the Pontificat* (1700), *The New Association* (1703), and *The Finishing Stroke: Being a Vindication of the Patriarchal Scheme of Government* (1711). His weekly journal, *The Rehearsal* (1704–9) attacked Lockeanism and Whiggery, and specifically Defoe's *Review*, and provided fuel for Tories and Jacobites alike. Leslie fled to France, 1711, and served in the household of the Jacobite pretender to the throne, 1713.
• Clark 1985; Daly 1979; Dunn 1969b; Goldsmith 1992; Schochet 1975.

LESSING, GOTTHOLD EPHRAIM

1729–81. German philosopher. Born in Kamenz, Saxony, the son of a Lutheran pastor, he abandoned a career in the church for literature. He wrote plays and essays on aesthetics. His

theological writings pushed at the boundaries of Lutheran liberalism, equating true religion with morality, independent of historical revelation. His key work of rationalist theology and advocacy of toleration was *Nathan der Weise* (Nathan the Wise, 1779), depicting the ideal Jew of serene benevolence and tolerance.
• Allison 1966; Redekop 2000.

LE TROSNE, GUILLAUME FRANÇOIS

1728–80. French administrator and physiocrat. After an early career as a magistrate in Orleans and possibly as a grain speculator, he became a major publicist for physiocracy. His chief works were *De l'ordre social* (1777) and *De l'administration provinciale et de la réforme de l'empôt* (On Provincial Administration and Tax Reform, 1788), written under the influence of the ideas of Turgot. He offered a distinctive vision of physiocratic 'legal despotism' that stressed the role of positive law over *moeurs* in shaping public opinion.
• Gunn 1995; Mille 1971.

LINGUET, SIMON NICOLAS HENRI

1736–94. French lawyer and journalist. Born in Reims, he was educated at the college at Beauvais, and made a reputation as a vigorous defence lawyer. He became an advocate in the *parlement* of Paris, 1764, but was expelled. His *Théorie des lois civiles, ou principes fondamentaux de la société* (Theory of Civil Laws, 1767) attacked Montesquieu and defended despotism as a necessary instrument to uphold property rights. He edited the *Annales politiques, civiles et littéraires* (1777–92, for a time based in Brussels), which became notorious for its criticism of the regime and predictions of its downfall. In 1780, on a visit to France, he was arrested and imprisoned in the Bastille. Released after twenty months, he published *Mémoires sur la Bastille* (1783), a violent assault on the government, which established the prison as the symbol par excellence of Bourbon repression. Linguet was guillotined during the Terror.
• Darnton 1971, 1996; Godechot 1970; Levy 1980; Lortholary 1951; Mackrell 1973; Schama 1989; Thamer 1973; Venturi 1984.

LOCKE, JOHN

1632–1704. English philosopher. Born in Wrington in Somerset and educated at Oxford University. In 1667 he joined the household of the earl of Shaftesbury and was drawn into political activity. He wrote the *Two Treatises of Government* during or shortly after the Exclusion Crisis, 1679–81, and the *Letter concerning Toleration* while in exile in Holland in 1685. Upon his return to England both works were published anonymously, 1689. His chief philosophical work, a defence of empiricism, *An Essay concerning Human Understanding*, appeared in the same year. Other principal works were *Thoughts concerning Education* (1693) and *The Reasonableness of Christianity* (1695). In the 1690s Locke served on the Board of Trade and wrote a series of economic tracts.
• Aarsleff 1982; Bonno 1955; Chaudhuri 1977; Dunn 1969a; Dworetz 1990; Gobetti 1992; Harris 1994; Horton and Mendus 1991; Hutchinson 1991; Huyler 1995; Jolley 1984; Marshall 1994; Pangle 1988; Riley 1982; Stewart 2000; Vernon 1997; Waldron 2002.

LUCAS, CHARLES

1713–71. Irish patriot, born in Ballingaddy, Co. Clare. He campaigned for municipal reform in Dublin on behalf of the citizenry against the city oligarchy, his populist case expressed in *Divelina Libera: An Apology for the Civil Rights and Liberties of the Commons and Citizens of Dublin* (1744). He is sometimes called the 'Wilkes of Ireland'. He stood for parliament for Dublin city, and was arrested for sedition, 1748. He fled to London, and latterly practised

medicine in Paris, Reims, and Leiden. Returning to Ireland, he sat as Member of Parliament for Dublin, 1761–71. From 1763 he contributed to the *Freeman's Journal*.
• Smyth 2001.

LUZAC, ELIE

1721–96. Dutch publisher, historian, and economic and political commentator. Born in Noordwijk to an émigré Huguenot family, and educated at Leiden. Luzac was a prolific writer in Dutch and French, coming to attention as publisher of La Mettrie's materialist tract *L'homme machine* (1747). He edited the journal *Nederlandsche Letter-Courant*, 1759–63. Although favourable to Enlightenment philosophy, he believed that over-enthusiasm for Lockean empiricism had led to a neglect of rationalism and metaphysics. His French edition of Wolff's *Institutiones iuris naturae et gentium* (On the Law of Nature and Nations, 1772) was his most respected scholarly publication. *Hollands Rijkdom* (Holland's Wealth, 1780–3) was the first serious history of Dutch commerce and attempted to explain her economic decline. Luzac's belief in freedom of the press was expressed in his *Mémorie* (1770). He rejected the Dutch Patriotic movement's demand for popular sovereignty and defended the powers of the *stadholder* in a series of pamphlets of the 1780s–90s.
• Popkin 1989; Velema 1993.

MABLY, ABBÉ GABRIEL BONNOT DE

1709–85. French diplomat, moralist, historian, and utopian socialist. Born in Grenoble, the elder brother of Condillac. He studied at the Jesuit college of Saint-Sulpice. He became secretary to Cardinal de Tencin, with whom he travelled abroad, 1741–6. In the 1750s he wrote *Des droits et des devoirs du citoyen* (The Rights and Duties of Citizens, 1789), and in 1763 published *Entretiens de Phocion sur la morale et la politique* (Conversations of Phocion on Morality and Politics), commentaries on the evils of private property and the prospects for a republican future. In *Observations sur l'histoire de France* (1765) he traced the growth of despotism. Other works included *De la législation, ou des principes des lois* (1776) and *Principes de morale* (1784). He became, with Rousseau, one of the heroes of Revolutionary republicanism.
• Baker 1990; Coste 1975; Thamer 1973; Wright 1997.

MACAULAY (GRAHAM), CATHERINE

1731–91. English republican historian. Born Catherine Sawbridge at Wye, Kent, she came from a London commercial family, and settled in Bath, 1774. On a visit to America, 1784–5, she met Washington. She moved in 'Real Whig' circles and belonged to the radical movement surrounding Wilkes. Her *History of England* (1763–83), covering 1603–1714, was a radical response to Hume's *History*. Mirabeau had it translated into French to counter Hume's 'servile principles' (1791–2). She denounced Burke's *Present Discontents* as an apology for a corrupt aristocratic faction (*Observations*, 1770). She attacked Britain's American policy as destructive of liberty (*Address to the People of England*, 1775). Her *Observations* on Burke's *Reflections* (1790) rejected his interpretation of the Revolution of 1688, and asserted a popular right to change the constitution. Other essays include *Loose Remarks on . . . Hobbes's Philosophical Rudiments of Government and Society* (1769), and *A Short Sketch of the Democratical Form of Government, in a Letter to Signior Pauli* (1767).
• Gunther-Canada 1998; B. Hill 1990, 1995; Pocock 1998; Schnorrenberg 1992.

MACKINTOSH, SIR JAMES

1765–1832. Scottish lawyer and radical theorist. Born in Inverness, he was educated at Aberdeen, Edinburgh, and Leiden Universities, trained in medicine, but turned to law and

became a barrister. He was a judge in Bombay, 1806–11, elected a Member of Parliament, 1813, and appointed professor at Haileybury College, 1818. His *Vindiciae Gallicae* (1791) defended the early, moderate phase of the French Revolution and its British admirers against Burke's *Reflections*. He subsequently moved closer to Burke's views, in *Lectures on the Law of Nature and Nations*, delivered in 1799. He briefly held government office under Prime Ministers Canning and Grey. He was a contributor to the *Edinburgh Review*. Other principal works include a *Review of the Causes of the Revolution of 1688* (1834), and an extended retrospect on moral and political philosophy since Grotius, his *Dissertation on the Progress of Ethical Philosophy* (1830).
• Christian 1976; Deane 1988; Haakonssen 1984.

MACKWORTH, SIR HUMPHREY

1657–1727. English Tory politician and pamphleteer. Born in Betton Grange, Shropshire, and educated at Oxford University and the Inns of Court, London, he became a businessman with mining interests, as well as owning a landed estate. He was a Member of Parliament, 1701–13. In a series of political and economic pamphlets he adapted Toryism to post-Revolution circumstances, attacking Whig populism in the name of parliamentary sovereignty. These included *A Vindication of the Rights of the Commons* (1701), *Peace at Home* (1703), and *Free Parliaments* (1704).

MADISON, JAMES

1751–1836. American revolutionary and politician. Born in Port Conway, Virginia, and educated at the College of New Jersey (later Princeton University). He held office in Virginia from 1774. As a member of the Constitutional Convention, 1787, he was a chief framer of the Constitution and of the Bill of Rights. He supported strong central government and, with Hamilton and Jay, authored *The Federalist Papers* (1787–8). Accepting the dangers conventionally attributed to democracy – instability, and oppression by majorities – he argued that a large republic, with indirectly elected representatives standing for the people as a whole, was better than a small state for obviating these dangers. The diversity of parties and interests at national level would overcome local faction and petty despotism. He later turned against Hamilton's centralising and pro-industrial policies, organising the Republican party and promoting Jefferson's election as president in 1800. He was secretary of state, 1801–9, and succeeded Jefferson as fourth president, 1809–17.
• Banning 1995; Epstein 1984; Ketcham 1971; McConnell 1996; Rakove 1990; Read 2000; G. Rosen 1999.

MAFFEI, FRANCESCO SCIPIONE

1675–1755. Italian political economist, historian, and theologian. Born in Verona, he studied under the Jesuits, fought in the War of the Spanish Succession, and befriended Pope Benedict XIV. He attacked the Jansenists, and published editions of the Church Fathers. His defence of the levying of interest on loans, *Dell' impiego del danaro* (On the Employment of Money, 1744), helped change official Catholic attitudes to usury and commerce.
• Marchi 1992; Silvestri 1954.

MAISTRE, JOSEPH MARIE, COMTE DE

1753–1821. Savoyard ultramontane political theorist. Born in Chambéry in Savoy, he studied law at Turin University. He fled Savoy when the French invaded in 1792, was the chief judicial officer in Sardinia, 1800–3, and for many years represented the Savoyard crown in Russia, 1803–17. He became a leader of counter-revolutionary thought, and has been called a French Burke. His *Lettres d'un royaliste savoisien* (1793) defended the virtue and utility of monarchy against revolutionary anarchy. *Considérations sur la France* (1797) accounted for the French Revolution as a divine punishment and national purification. *Du pape* (1819) and *Les Soirées de Saint-Pétersbourg* (1821, begun 1809) asserted the need for unquestioning obedience and the maintenance of tradition. Maistre voiced a revulsion against Enlightenment ideas and sought to renew the authority of the Catholic Church.

• Bayle 1945; Berlin 1990; Bradley 1999; Lebrun 1965, 1988a, 1988b; Lefage 1998; McMahon 2001; Triomphe 1968.

MALESHERBES, GUILLAUME CHRÉTIEN DE LAMOIGNON DE

1721–94. French politician and commentator, born in Paris. Director of publications, 1750–63. His regime as official censor was relatively liberal, and facilitated the appearance of the *Encyclopédie*. He became a member of the *Académie française*, 1775. His *Très humbles et très respectueuses rémontrances que présentent au roi notre très honoré et souverain seigneur les gens tenants sa cour des aides* (Humble and Respectful Remonstrances Presented to the King and the Gentlemen of his Court, 1775) warned of a slide toward despotism. His *Mémoire sur le mariage des protestants* (1785–6) argued for civil liberties for the Huguenots. He urged renewal of rights of representation, and wrote a tract on press freedom, *Mémoire sur la liberté de la presse* (1790). After the Revolution, he defended the king in the Convention and was guillotined during the Terror.

• Baker 1987, 1990; Grosclaude 1961; Kelly 1982.

MALTHUS, THOMAS

1766–1834. English political economist. Born in Wooton, Surrey, and educated at several Dissenting academies and Cambridge University. Ordained a minister in the Anglican church, 1789, he taught history and political economy at Haileybury College from 1805. He was absentee rector of a Lincolnshire parish, 1803–34. In *An Essay on the Principle of Population* (1798, enlarged in later editions) he argued that population will tend to grow geometrically whereas the means of subsistence will grow arithmetically, so that population will outstrip resources and drastically reduce living standards – unless famine or birth control arrest the process. Malthus supported schemes for drastic curtailment of Poor Law provision.

• Hollander 1997; James 1979; McNally 2000; Winch 1987, 1996.

MANDEVILLE, BERNARD (DE)

1670–1733. Anglo-Dutch social theorist and satirist. Born in Dort near Rotterdam, he was educated at Leiden University, settled in London, 1692, and practised medicine. His poem *The Grumbling Hive* (1705) was republished with an 'Inquiry into the Origin of Moral Virtue' and with a series of prose commentaries, as *The Fable of the Bees, or Private Vices, Public Benefits* (1714), under which title it is best known. He sought to show that vice, or at least self-interest, had economic benefits, ought largely to be unimpeded, and was the mainspring of a prosperous and happy society. The book was condemned by the Middlesex grand jury in 1723, when a new edition carried 'An Essay on Charity and Charity Schools'. His later tracts included *Free Thoughts on Religion, the Church, and National Happiness* (1720).

• Carrive 1983; Dekker 1992; Dumont 1977; Goldsmith 1977, 1985; Gunn 1983; Hirschman 1977; Horne 1978; Hundert 1994, 1995; Jack 1987; Kerkhof 1995; Monro 1975; Primer 1975; Prior 2000.

MANLEY, MARY DELARIVIERE

c. 1670–1724. English Tory playwright and novelist. Born in Jersey, the daughter of a governor of the Channel Islands. Her early plays of the 1690s place her alongside Aphra Behn among popular female dramatists. She was arrested for libel for her attack on the Whigs in *The Secret*

Memoirs (1709), and succeeded Swift as author of *The Examiner*, 1711. She is best known for *New Atalantis* (1709), an allegory, perhaps inspired by Fénelon, dedicated to exposing the corrosive effects of aristocratic greed and lust on government and society. She published further satires on the Whigs.
• Herman 2003.

MANSFIELD, WILLIAM MURRAY, EARL OF

1705–93. Scottish jurist. Born in Scone, and educated at Oxford University, he became a barrister at Lincoln's Inn, 1730. After his election as a Member of Parliament, 1742, he rose through the ranks to senior legal office: solicitor general, 1742, attorney general, 1754, lord chief justice, 1756, and a peerage, 1756. He favoured coercing America. He reversed Wilkes's outlawry and presided over a series of seditious libel cases. A considerable legal innovator, he showed the possibilities for evolution of the common law, through judicial development of commercial law and the law of evidence, and the procedure of the courts. His house was ransacked by the anti-popish Gordon rioters, 1780.
• Lieberman 1989; Oldham 1992.

MARAT, JEAN PAUL

1743–93. Swiss/French revolutionary and journalist. Born at Boudry near Neuchâtel, Switzerland, he became a physician, and practised in Britain in the 1760s and 1770s. He published his *Essay on the Human Soul* (in English, 1772), which was revised as *A Philosophical Essay on Man* (1773), and translated into French as *De l'homme* (1775). This was followed by *The Chains of Slavery* (1774). At the outbreak of the Revolution, he turned to journalism, publishing *L'Ami du peuple* (1789), later called *Journal de la République française* (1792). He was elected a deputy to the Convention, 1792, became president of the Jacobin clubs, and was murdered by the Girondist Charlotte Corday. He then became the focus of a republican cult, immortalised in Jacques David's painting *The Death of Marat*.
• Coquard 2003; Darnton 1982; Gottschalk 1927.

MARMONTEL, JEAN FRANÇOIS

1723–99. French author. Born in Bort-les-Orgues, he became secretary of the *Académie française*, and was appointed royal historiographer, 1772. He published novels, plays, poetry, and journalistic essays. *Bélisaire* (1767), set in the late Roman Empire, provided a critique of French decline, and defended toleration. *Les Incas* (1767–8, publ. 1777) echoed Raynal's critique of colonialism. *Mémoires* (1793–6) deplored revolutionary populism in the name of enlightened monarchy.
• Renwick 1974.

MAULTROT, GABRIEL NICOLAS

1714–1803. French Jansenist. Born in Paris, he became an advocate in the *parlement* of Paris, an expert in canon law, and a collector of documents used by historians of Jansenism. He supported the *parlements* as a check upon monarchy. He was the co-author of *Maximes du droit public français* (Maxims of French Public Law, 1772), and of *Questions sur la tolérance* (1758; later republished as *Essai sur la tolérance*), which argued that Protestants were no threat to civil society. At the Revolution, Maultrot and Mey diverged from Le Paige, seeking to separate church and state and resisting the Erastianism of the Civil Constitution of the Clergy.
• Adams 1991; Van Kley 1975, 1996.

Biographies

MAYHEW, JONATHAN
1720–66. American defender of religious toleration. Born in Martha's Vineyard, Massachusetts, and educated at Harvard College, he became a Congregationalist pastor in Boston, 1747. He opposed Calvinist predestinarianism, and preached several sermons, notably *The Snare Broken* (1766), against the despotism of the seventeenth-century English monarchy and against the current imposition of unjust law under the Stamp Act. Earlier, he defended a right of resistance in *A Discourse concerning Unlimited Submission and Non-resistance to the Higher Powers* (1750).
• Akers 1964; Corrigan 1987.

MELON, JEAN FRANÇOIS
1675–1738. French political economist. Born in Tulle. While practising as an advocate at Bordeaux he helped established the academy there. He became secretary in Paris to the council of finance, and served d'Argenson and John Law. His economic writings, notably *Essai politique sur le commerce* (Political Essay on Commerce, 1734), are seen as forerunners of physiocracy. The *Essai* included a summary of Mandeville, and was read by Montesquieu and Rousseau.
• Fox-Genovese 1976; Hundert 1994; Larrère 1992.

MENDELSSOHN, MOSES
1729–86. German Jewish philosopher. Born in Dessau, where he was rabbinically trained, he settled in Berlin, where he absorbed Leibniz, Locke, Shaftesbury, and Wolff. Much of his work lay in aesthetics, scriptural studies, and natural theology, and in the promotion of what was to become Reform Judaism. He translated Rousseau's second *Discourse* (1764). In *Jerusalem* (1783) he advocated religious toleration, defined the delimited sphere of the state, and offered a rationalist version of Judaism. The central character in his friend Lessing's *Nathan the Wise* is modelled on him.
• Altmann 1973, 1982.

MERCIER DE LA RIVIÈRE, PIERRE PAUL, *see* LE MERCIER

MERCIER, LOUIS SÉBASTIEN
1740–1814. French historian, utopian, critic, novelist, and dramatist. Born in Paris, he pursued a literary career. He is chiefly known for his utopian novel, *L'An 2440* (The Year 2440, 1771). He wrote tragedies on the theme of religious toleration, including *Jean Henauyer* (1772) and *La Destruction de la Ligue* (1782). His *Tableau de Paris* (1782–8) comprises a series of brief philosophical reflections, social commentary, satire, and gossip. At the Revolution he became a journalist, editing *Les Annales patriotiques et littéraires* (1789–97). He sat as a deputy in the Convention for the Girondin party. Arrested in 1793, he escaped the guillotine.
• Chisick 2001.

MESLIER, JEAN
1664–1729. French agrarian communist. Born in Mazerny in the Ardennes. He studied at the Reims seminary, was ordained, 1689, and became a parish priest in the Champagne. His *Mémoire*, which circulated in manuscript after his death, was communistic, materialistic, and atheistic. He envisioned self-governing village communities, free of private property. A bowdlerised version was published by Voltaire as *Extrait* (1762); it did not appear in full until 1864.
• Kors 1990; Martin 1962; Spink 1960; Verona 1975; Wade 1938.

759

MEY, ABBÉ CLAUDE

1712–96. Franch Jansenist cleric. He became a lawyer, and an expert on canon law. He published an attack on the pope's bull *Unigenitus*, and collaborated with Maultrot in writing the strongly Gallican *Apologie de tous les jugemens rendus par les tribunaux séculiers en France contre le schisme* (1752). At the Revolution, Mey and Maultrot diverged from Le Paige, seeking to separate church and state and resisting the Erastianism of the Civil Constitution of the Clergy.
• Adams 1991; Van Kley 1975, 1996.

MILLAR, JOHN

1735–1801. Scottish historian and philosopher. Born in Shotts near Edinburgh, he was educated at Glasgow University, where he was a pupil of Adam Smith. He became tutor in Lord Kames's household, befriended Smith and Hume, was called to the bar, and was appointed professor of civil law at Glasgow, 1761. He acquired a reputation as a radical Whig during the French Revolution, and was a member of the Society of Friends of the People. He advocated parliamentary reform and the abolition of the slave trade. His principal work was *Observations concerning the Distinction of Ranks in Society* (1771), which explored the relationship between economic development and egalitarian principles. Author also of *An Historical View of the English Government* (1787); *Letters of Sidney on Inequality of Property* (1796); and *Letters of Crito, on the Causes, Objects, and Consequences, of the Present War* (1796).
• Berry 1997; Bowles 1986, 1990; Cairns 1993; Carrithers 1995; Francis and Morrow 1988; Haakonssen 1985a; Ignatieff 1983a; Lehmann 1960.

MIRABEAU, VICTOR RIQUETI, MARQUIS DE

1715–89. French physiocrat. Born in Perthuis of a recently ennobled Provencal family. He first pursued a military career and later turned to authorship and journalism. A leading member of the physiocratic school, in economic theory he generally deferred to Quesnay, with whom he collaborated, but his writings on the spheres and functions of central and local government, on fiscal policy and public opinion were influential. He acquired a reputation for radicalism by insisting on the role of public opinion and on the rights of property rather than privilege. His works include *L'Ami des hommes ou traité sur la population* (1756); *Théorie de l'impôt* (Theory of Taxation, 1760); *Lettres sur le commerce des grains* (1768); *Lettres économiques* (1769). He was the father of the revolutionary politician Honoré Mirabeau (1749–91).
• Fox-Genovese 1976; Gunn 1995; McNally 1988.

MOLESWORTH, ROBERT

1656–1725. Irish 'Commonwealthman'. Born in Dublin, of an Anglo-Irish family. He came to prominence with *An Account of Denmark* (1694), a country he had visited two years earlier as envoy and where he had been dismayed at the negative social and economic consequences of absolutism. He warned of the danger of regime change by stealth. His other principal contribution to political thought was his preface to an English translation of François Hotman's *Francogallia* (1711). He was a member of the Irish parliament, 1695–1705, and the English, 1705–8, a privy councillor in Ireland, 1697–1714, and became a peer, as Viscount Molesworth, 1719. He led a circle of Irish patriots in the 1720s: Swift dedicated one of his *Drapier's Letters* to him.
• Robbins 1959.

MOLYNEUX, WILLIAM

1656–98. Irish philosopher and patriot. Born in Dublin, where he studied at Trinity College. A student of philosophy and mathematics, he founded the Dublin Philosophical Society,

1683, and held the post of surveyor general of the king's buildings in Ireland, 1684–8. He was a member of the Irish parliament, 1692 and 1695. A correspondent of Locke, the two men discussed philosophical questions. Molyneux's *The Case of Ireland's Being Bound by Acts of Parliament in England* (1698), which cited Locke's *Two Treatises*, defended the autonomy of the Irish parliament by claiming that Ireland was a co-equal kingdom with England. It was much cited by American patriots in the 1760s.
• J. Hill 1995; Kelly 1988; Simms 1982.

MONBODDO, JAMES BURNETT, LORD

1714–99. Scottish jurist, philosophical historian, and anthropologist. Born in Monboddo, Kincardineshire, he studied at Aberdeen, Edinburgh, and Groningen Universities. He became a judge in Court of Session, the Scottish supreme court, 1767. He hosted a salon of the Edinburgh literati, and authored *Of the Origin and Progress of Language* (1773–92) and *Antient Metaphysics* (1779–99), in each of which he lauded ancient Greece and lamented the modern world. The former is important for its ideas on the origins of society and its anthropological treatment of human origins.
• Cloyd 1972; Wokler 1988b.

MONTESQUIEU, CHARLES LOUIS DE SECONDAT, BARON DE LA BRÈDE ET DE

1689–1755. French philosopher and jurist. Born in La Brède near Bordeaux, he studied at the college of Juilly and Bordeaux University. He practised law, became a judge, 1714, and inherited his title and the post of *président à mortier* in the *parlement* of Bordeaux. He was often in Paris in the 1720s, and visited Italy, 1728–9, and England, 1729–31. *Les Lettres persanes* (Persian Letters, 1721), an allegorical and satirical romance at the expense of Christianity and the hypocrisies of civilisation, made him famous. This was followed by *Considérations sur les causes de la grandeur des Romains et de leur décadence* (Considerations on the Causes of the Greatness of the Romans and their Decline, 1734). His magnum opus, *L'Esprit des lois* (The Spirit of the Laws, 1748) explored the relationship between the spirit of a people, its culture and *mores*, and the economy, geography, religion, government, and laws of nations. It articulated a defence of moderate French monarchy, in which nobility counterbalanced crown and people. The book was one of the most influential works of political theory of its century.
• Baum 1979; Carcassonne 1927; Carrithers *et al.* 2001; Durkheim 1966; Fletcher 1939; Hampson 1983; Hulliung 1976; Keohane 1980; Merry 1970; Pangle 1973; Richter 1977; Shackleton 1961, 1988; Shklar 1987; Waddicor 1970.

MORE, HANNAH

1745–1833. English conservative moralist, dramatist, and educator. Born in Stapleton near Bristol, she was educated by her father, a schoolteacher. She wrote plays until she decided it was immoral to do so. Her *Strictures on the Modern System of Female Education* (1799) went through thirteen editions; it argued the moral superiority and otherwise inferiority of women. She deplored Wollstonecraft's *Rights of Woman* and had no more time for the 'rights' of men. Against the French she wrote *Remarks on the Speech of M. Dupont, Made in the National Convention of France* (1793), against Paine *The History of Mr Fantom, the New-Fashioned Philosopher* (1797). Her most prominent work, *Village Politics* (1792), directed the poor to be content and enjoined the avoidance of radical ideas. Her many works of popular moralism and on Christian duty were bestsellers.
• Hopkins 1947; Jones 1952; Stafford 2002.

MORELLET, ABBÉ ANDRÉ

1727–1819. French philosopher. Born in Lyons, he was educated in Paris for the church, and became a tutor. He contributed articles on religion to the *Encyclopédie*. In such tracts as *Le Manuel des inquisiteurs* (1762) he inveighed against religious intolerance. A series of writings, among them *Réflexions sur les avantages de la liberté d'écrire* (Reflections on the Benefits of Freedom of Writing, 1775), and *Mémoire sur la situation actuelle de la Compagnie des Indes* (Memoir on the Present State of the East India Company, 1769), promoted the free trade ideas of Vincent de Gournay and Turgot, and criticised Galiani. Morellet translated Beccaria's *Dei delitti e delle pene* and Jefferson's *Notes on the State of Virginia* into French. In 1792 he wrote indictments of Brissot and narrowly escaped the guillotine. He supported Napoleon.
• Merrick and Medlin 1995.

MORELLY, ETIENNE GABRIEL

c. 1715–78. French utopian theorist and novelist. Little is known about his life. He was perhaps born in Vitry-le-François. His *Code de la nature* (1755) is an egalitarian exploration of a society governed by a patriachal system, without property, marriage, a church, or police. An important communistic work, which influenced Babeuf and later socialists, it was published anonymously, and often attributed to Diderot. Morelly wrote two books on education, *Essai sur l'esprit humain* (1743), and *Essai sur le coeur humain* (1745), as well as a critique of Montesquieu, *Le Prince, les délices des coeurs, ou traité des qualités d'un grand roi et système d'un sage gouvernement* (The Prince, the Delights of the Heart, or, A Treatise on the Qualities of a Great King and Wise Government, 1751).
• Coe 1961; Martin 1962.

MOSER, FRIEDRICH CARL VON

1723–98. German politician and publicist. Born in Stuttgart, the son of the next. He was in government service in south Germany and Austria, serving as chief minister of Hesse Darmstadt, 1772, until his dismissal, 1782. He implemented reforms in commerce and education. His political writings offered a programme of enlightened princely rule and dwelt on the education of the prince. They include *Der Herr und der Diener* (Master and Servant, 1759), in which he criticised misgovernment in the smaller German states, *Von dem deutschen Nationalgeist* (On the German National Spirit, 1765), which took the Imperial side against Frederick II of Prussia, and *Patriotische Briefe* (Patriotic Letters, 1767).

MOSER, JOHANN JAKOB

1701–85. German jurist. Born in Stuttgart, he studied at Tübingen, where he became professor of law. He took a chair at Frankfurt-on-the-Oder, 1736, but resigned under pressure from Frederick I of Prussia. He retired to private study and prepared his fifty-two-volume *Teutsches Staats-Recht* (German Public Law, 1737–54). In 1751 he returned to Wurtemberg as a councillor, but was imprisoned for opposition to the arbitrary rule of the duke, 1759–64. His voluminous writings addressed the development of European international law; they included *Neues deutsches Staatsrecht* (1766–75) and *Grundriss der heutigen Staatsverfassung von Deutschland* (Outline of the Present German Constitution, 1731).
• Walker 1981.

MÖSER, JUSTUS

1720–94. German political essayist and historian. Born in Osnabruck, Munster, he studied law at Jena and Göttingen Universities. He served the state of Osnabruck, becoming in effect its head of government, 1764. He edited a moral weekly, *Ein Wochenblatt* from 1746, contributed

to *Die deutsche Zuschauerin* (The German Female Spectator, 1748), and wrote a history of Osnabruck (1768). His major work was *Patriotische Phantasien* (Patriotic Fantasies, 1775–86), a collection of some 300 essays on social, economic, and historical topics. His affirmation of the uniqueness of cultures, societies, and social groups, and of historical circumstances, appealed to the German Romantics.
• Knudsen 1986; Sheldon 1970.

MOUNIER, JEAN JOSEPH

1758–1806. French revolutionary. Born in Grenoble, where he became a royal judge. At the Revolution he sat as president of the National Assembly and argued, in *Nouvelles observations sur les Etats Généraux de France* (1789) that his country had never possessed a constitution and that the Assembly should frame one. He initiated the tennis court oath of 20 June 1789, to the effect that the deputies would remain united until a constitution had been established. In *Considérations sur les gouvernements, et principalement sur celui qui convient à la France* (Considerations on Governments, and Principally those which suit France, 1789), he advanced a form of government modelled upon the British parliamentary system, with the monarch's prerogatives bounded by law. Mounier was no democrat. He fled to Switzerland, 1790, not returning to France until 1801. In 1805 Napoleon named him a councillor of state.
• Bourgeois 1998; Egret 1950; Furet and Ozouf 1990.

MOYLE, WALTER

1672–1721. English 'Commonwealth' Whig. Born in St German, Cornwall, Moyle was educated at Oxford University and the Inns of Court, London. In the 1690s he belonged to the circle of Commonwealthmen who met at the Grecian and Will's coffee-houses in London. Elected member of parliament, 1695, he joined the Country Whig assault on the Junto (ministerial) Whigs. He co-authored with Trenchard *An Argument, Shewing that a Standing Army is Inconsistent with a Free Government* (1697). His main work appeared posthumously: *An Essay upon the Constitution of the Roman Government* (1726). It was republished by Thelwall (1796) and by Bertrand Barrière in French (1801). His collected *Works* appeared in 1726.
• Pocock 1975; Robbins 1959.

NETTELBLADT, DANIEL

1719–91. German jurist. A pupil of Wolff at Marburg, he followed him to Halle, later becoming professor of law there. His legal expositions appeared as *Systema elementare universae jurisprudentia naturalis* (Elementary System of Universal Natural Jurisprudence, 1749), and *Systema elementare jurisprudentiae positivae Germanorum generalis* (Elementary System of German Positive Jurisprudence, 1781).

NOODT, GERARD

1647–1725. Dutch jurist, born in Nijmegen. He was appointed professor of law at Nijmegen, 1671, at Franeker, 1679, at Utrecht, 1684, and at Leiden, 1686, remaining at Leiden until his death. His views were developed in lectures on Roman law and legal history. His most influential publications were his rectorial addresses: *De jure summi imperii et lege regia* (On the Law of Sovereignty and the Lex Regia, 1699), which grounded sovereignty in the people, and *De religione ab imperio jure gentium libera* (On the Freedom of Religion from Supreme Power According to the Law of Nature, 1706). These were translated into Dutch, French, English, German, and Swedish.
• Bergh 1988.

NORDENSKJÖLD, AUGUST

1754–92. Swedish critic of slavery. Born in Sibbo, Finland, and educated at Turku, Finland, he came under the influence of Swedenborgianism in Stockholm. Close to court circles, he was involved in an attempt, supported by Gustav III, to found a colony on Africa's west coast, shaped by Swedenborgian hostility to slavery. In London he published (in English), with Carl Bernhard Wadström and others, the anti-slavery *Plan for a Free Community at Sierra Leona* (1792). He died in Sierra Leone.

• Lenhammar 1966.

NORDENSKJÖLD, CARL FREDRIK

1756–1828. Swedish radical. Brother of August, he was born in Sibbo and studied at Turku, moving to Stockholm, 1772, where he entered the civil service and became an influential Swedenborgian. He lived in London, 1783–6. A member of the *riksdag* (diet), 1789 and 1792. His journal *Medborgaren* (The Citizen), 1788–93, was suppressed for its support of the French Revolution. After Gustav III's assassination, he published a Swedish translation of Paine's *Rights of Man* (1792) and was involved in a translation of Locke's *Letter concerning Toleration* (1793). He died at Rostock.

• Lenhammar 1966.

O'CONNOR, ARTHUR

1763–1852. Irish patriot. Born in Mitchelstown, Co. Cork, educated at Trinity College, Dublin, and called to the Irish bar, 1782. He sat in the Irish parliament, 1791–5, and joined the United Irishmen, 1796. A string of pamphlets defended republicanism and promoted Catholic emancipation, including *Speech on the Catholic Emancipation* (1795). Imprisoned for seditious libel, 1797, he was again arrested and later deported to France, where Napoleon made him a general. He married Condorcet's daughter and published an edition of Condorcet's works, 1847–9.

• Dickson *et al.* 1993; Hayter Hames 2001.

O'CONNOR, CHARLES

1710–91. Irish advocate of toleration for Catholics. Born in Kilmactranny, Co. Sligo. He was one of the first political voices on behalf of Irish Catholics during the Protestant Ascendancy, and co-founder of the Catholic Committee, 1757. He published *The Case of the Roman Catholics* (1755), *The Principles of the Roman Catholics* (1756), and *Observations on the Popery Laws* (1771). His younger brother turned Protestant and sued to seize his lands, thus exemplifying the Catholics' lack of civil liberties.

OGILVIE, WILLIAM

1736–1819. Scottish advocate of common property in land. Born in Elgin, he was educated at Glasgow, Aberdeen, and Edinburgh Universities, and, after school teaching, returned to university teaching, at Glasgow, 1761–2, and Aberdeen, where he was professor of philosophy, 1764–5, and of humanity, 1765–1817. His interests included natural history, antiquities, numismatics, and farming, devoting much effort to improving his estates. He is known for his *Essay on the Right of Property in Land* (1781), which argued that everyone had a natural right to sufficient land for their subsistence. It influenced nineteenth-century agrarian socialists.

• Beer 1920; Menger 1899.

O'LEARY, ARTHUR

1729–1802. Irish advocate of religious toleration for Catholics. Born in Fanlobbus, Co. Cork, he became a Capuchin monk at Saint-Malo, then settled in Ireland, 1771. He wrote

pamphlets urging Catholics to be loyal to British rule, and published *An Essay on Toleration* (1780). He was chaplain to the Irish National Volunteers, 1782–4, and published *An Address to the Common People of the Roman Catholic Religion* (1779). His willingness to press Catholics to remain loyal on promises of emancipation earned him a secret pension from the British government. He settled in England, 1789, where he preached in London and assisted the Catholic Committee.
• Hayter Hames 2001.

OTIS, JAMES
1725–83. American revolutionary. Born in Cape Cod, Massachusetts, and educated at Harvard College, he became a lawyer in Boston. In the campaigns against British taxation and general warrants, he wrote influential critiques of British rule: *A Vindication of the Conduct of the House of Representatives of the Province of Massachusetts Bay* (1762), *The Rights of the British Colonies Asserted* (1764), and *Considerations on Behalf of the Colonists* (1765). His leadership of Massachusetts politics ended abruptly when he was badly injured by a British soldier in 1769.
• McIlwain 1923; Breen 1998.

PAGANO, FRANCESCO MARIO
1748–99. Italian jurist. Born in Brienza, Basilicata, he studied under Genovesi at Naples, and became professor of moral philosophy and jurisprudence. His *Saggi politici* (Political Essays, 1783–5) provides a philosophical history of the Kingdom of Naples. It stands alongside the work of Filangieri and Beccaria in its advocacy of more benign penal codes, arguing against torture and capital punishment. He fled Naples in 1796, returned in 1799, helped draft the short-lived republican constitution, and was executed at the republic's fall.

PAINE, THOMAS
1737–1809. Anglo-American revolutionary. Born in Thetford, Norfolk, of a Quaker farming family, he left school at thirteen, went to sea, and worked as a corsetmaker, shopkeeper, and excise officer, 1757–74. At the encouragement of Franklin, whom he met in London, he emigrated to America, 1774. In 1775 he wrote his influential incitement to the Americans to break with Britain, *Common Sense* (1776); there were twenty-five editions in a year. He served in the revolutionary army, and helped draw up the Pennsylvania constitution. He returned to Europe, 1787, lived in France, 1789–90, and in 1791–2 published his *Rights of Man* against Burke's *Reflections*. This caused him to flee to France, 1792, where he was made a citizen and elected to the National Assembly. He narrowly escaped the guillotine during the Terror. His increasing concern with social justice emerged in *Agrarian Justice* (1797). His deist *Age of Reason* (1794) was denounced as atheistical and lessened his popularity in America, to which he returned in 1802. Other works include *The Crisis* (1776–83), *Letters to Abbé Raynal* (1782), and *Dissertation on the First Principles of Government* (1795).
• Aldridge 1984; Butler 1984; Claeys 1989b; Fennessy 1963; Foner 1977; Fruchtman 1994; Keane 1995; Philp 1989.

PALEY, WILLIAM
1743–1805. English moral philosopher and theologian. Born in Peterborough, he was educated at Cambridge University, where he taught at Christ's College, 1766–76. An ordained clergyman, he held parish appointments, and became archdeacon of Carlisle, 1782. His *Principles of Moral and Political Philosophy* (1785), based on Cambridge lectures, articulated a theological basis for political and social life which incorporated Smithian economics and a coincidence between God's will and human happiness and utility. His *Reasons for Contentment Addressed to the Labouring Part of the British Public* (1792) were purely secular.

His defence of Christianity, *A View of the Evidences of Christianity* (1794), which drew chiefly on the 'Argument from Design', was for decades a keystone of the English religious curriculum.
• Clark 1974; Clark 1985; Hole 1989; Horne 1985; Le Mahieu 1976; Schofield 1987.

PANCKOUCKE, CHARLES JOSEPH

1736–98. French publisher, bookseller, and journalist. Born in Lille, the son of a bookseller, he settled in Paris, 1762, where he compiled and published enyclopedias, reference works, and journals, notably the *Journal des savans* and *Mercure de France*. He was principal publisher of the *Encyclopédie méthodique* (1781–1832) which reorganised the content of the *Encyclopédie*. He published for Voltaire, Buffon, and Raynal. In the 1770s and 1780s he dominated the publication of French journals; his newspapers supported the Revolution.
• Darnton 1979.

PLOWDEN, FRANCIS

1749–1829. English Catholic theorist. Born in Plowden, Shropshire, he was educated at the Jesuit college at Saint-Omer, and taught at the Jesuit college at Bruges, 1771–3. He trained at the Inns of Court, London, but, as a Catholic, was limited to conveyancing until 1796, when he was called to the bar. Oxford awarded him an honorary degree for his *Jura Anglorum* (The Rights of Englishmen, 1792), a conservative formulation of natural rights and contract theory. Further defences of the *status quo* followed: *A Friendly and Constitutional Address to the People of Great Britain* (1794), *The Constitution of the United Kingdom, Civil and Ecclesiastical* (1795). Following prosecution for his *Historical Review of the State of Ireland* (1801–3), he went to Paris, 1813, where he became professor at the Scots College.
• Chinnici 1980; Hole 1989.

POMBAL, SEBASTIÃO JOSÉ DE CARVALHO E MELHO, MARQUES DE

1699–1782. Portuguese statesman and patron of enlightened policies. He was born in Lisbon of a gentry family, and studied law at Coimbra University. He entered the diplomatic service, serving in London, 1739–43, and Vienna, 1745–50. He was appointed secretary of state for foreign affairs, 1750, and within a few years dominated the administration of Jose I, becoming chief minister in 1756. He restrained the Inquisition and the property of the church, suppressed the Jesuits, abolished slavery, and initiated commercial as well as educational reforms such as the teaching of Newtonianism in the universities. He was made marquis in 1769, but fell from power at the accession of Maria I in 1777.
• Carvalho dos Santos 1984; Maxwell 1995.

POPE, ALEXANDER

1688–1744. English poet, satirist, and moralist. A Catholic, he was born in London, largely self-educated, and lived most of his life at Twickenham. He was a friend of Swift and Arbuthnot. He achieved literary fame through translations of Homer's *Iliad* (1715–20) and *Odyssey* (1725–6). He was close to Bolingbroke, and took part in the literary assault on Walpolean Whiggery. He satirised English life and literary culture in *The Dunciad* (1728) and *The Rape of the Lock* (1714). Jacobitism has been detected in *Windsor Forest* (1713). His most sustained piece of social theory was his verse *Essay on Man* (1733–4).
• Brown 1985; Erskine-Hill 1975, 1998; Gerrard 1994; Mack 1969; Nicholson 1994; Nuttall 1984; Rivers 1973.

Biographies

POWNALL, THOMAS
1722–1805. American political theorist and colonial administrator, known as 'Governor Pownall'. Born in Lincolnshire, and educated at Cambridge, he served on the Board of Trade, before removing to New Jersey as lieutenant-governor, 1755, then to Massachusetts as governor, 1757–60. He left America, 1760, and sat in the British parliament, 1767–80. He published some twenty-five works, mostly on politics and economics. The most significant is *The Administration of the Colonies* (1764), in which he advocated a self-governing union of the American colonies, warned of the dangers of taxing the colonists without their consent, and envisaged a future *translatio* whereby America rather than Britain would be the seat of the English-speaking empire. During the War of Independence he was among the first to insist that British sovereignty over America was lost and that the government should negotiate.
• Bailyn 1967; Greene 1986.

PRÉVOST, ANTOINE FRANÇOIS, ABBÉ
1697–1763. French novelist and editor of travel and anthropological material. Born in Hesdin, Artois, he became a Benedictine monk, left the order, rejoined it, abandoned monastic life again, fled to London and then Holland, returned to France and rejoined his order once more. He travelled widely, befriended the *philosophes*, and made a living by writing novels, journalism, and translations. His novel *Manon Lescaut* (1728–31) has been the subject of several operas. Politically he is known chiefly for his sixteen-volume collection, *Histoire générale des voyages* (1745–59), which was consulted by Rousseau and Diderot.
• Gilroy 1979; Singerman 1987.

PRICE, RICHARD
1723–91. Welsh Dissenting radical. Born in Tynton, Glamorgan, and educated at Welsh Dissenting academies and Moorfields Academy, London, he was ordained a Presbyterian minister, and served as pastor at Stoke Newington and Hackney from 1744. His *Review of the Principal Questions and Difficulties in Morals* (1758) was an expression of rationalist intuitionism that established his reputation. He produced a Lockean defence of American independence, *Observations on the Nature of Civil Liberty . . . and . . . the Justice and Policy of the War with America* (1776), which saw more than twenty editions. His sermon commemorating the English Revolution of 1688, *A Discourse on the Love of our Country* (1789), occasioned Burke's *Reflections on the Revolution in France*. His actuarial work *Observations on Reversionary Payments* (1772) established a foundation for life insurance and pension schemes. Other chief works are *Observations on the Importance of the American Revolution* (1784) and *The Evidence for a Future Period of Improvement in the State of Mankind* (1787).
• Cone 1952; Fitzpatrick 1995; Fruchtman 1983; Laboucheix 1982; Peach 1979; Thomas 1977.

PRIESTLEY, JOSEPH
1733–1804. English scientist and radical Dissenter. Born in Birstall, Yorkshire, he became a Presbyterian minister, taught at the Dissenting academy in Warrington, and served as minister in Birmingham from 1780. Abandoning his youthful Calvinism, he turned to Unitarianism. In philosophy, he became a determinist and materialist. He wrote on rhetoric, grammar, law, theology, philosophy, history, education, and biography. He conducted experiments on electricity and gas in his Birmingham laboratory, which was ransacked by a Church and King mob, 1791. In his philosophical writings he defended Lockean and Hartleyan associationism against the Scottish Common Sense School. He wrote a series of tracts on civil liberty: *Essay on the First Principles of Government* (1768), *Essay on Civil Liberty* (1768), *The Present State of Liberty* (1769), *Reflections on Free Enquiry* (1785), and *Letters to the Right Honourable*

767

Edmund Burke (1791). He was awarded French citizenship in 1792. Despairing of England, he emigrated to America, 1794. His *Works* appeared in twenty-six volumes, 1817–32.
• Canovan 1984; Fitzpatrick 1977, 1990; Fruchtman 1983; Kramnick 1986, 1990; Lincoln 1938.

PROAST, JONAS

c. 1642–1710. English critic of Locke's *Letter concerning Toleration*. Born probably in Colchester, Essex, and educated at Oxford University, he became chaplain of All Souls College, 1677, from which post he was expelled, 1688, an Anglican victim of James II's Catholic policies. The post-Revolution church would not, however, reinstate him, because of his aggressively High Church views. His only published works were three critiques of Locke: *The Argument of the Letter concerning Toleration, Briefly Considered* (1690), *A Third Letter concerning Toleration* (1691), and *A Second Letter to the Author of the Three Letters for Toleration* (1704). Locke's *Second* (1690), lengthy *Third* (1692), and unfinished *Fourth* (1704) *Letters* are replies. Proast revived the Augustinian argument for coercion of belief.
• Goldie 1993b; Nicholson 1991; Vernon 1997; Waldron 1991.

QUESNAY, FRANÇOIS

1694–1774. French surgeon and physiocrat. Born in Méré, Ile-de-France, he studied medicine, taught surgery in Paris, 1737–47, became physician to Mme de Pompadour and Louis XIV, and was elected to the Académie des Sciences, 1751. He contributed articles on economic matters to the *Encyclopédie*, arguing in favour of freedom of the grain trade, and emphasising land and agriculture as the source of national wealth. Through his *Tableau économique* (1758) he was a principal creator of the school of physiocracy, which acquired considerable influence in the 1760s. He published a series of articles, especially on political economy, in the mid-1760s in the journal *Les Ephémérides du citoyen* (The Citizen's Almanac).
• Fox-Genovese 1976; Meek 1962; Vaggi 1987.

RADICATI DI PASSERANO, ALBERTO

1698–1737. Savoyard freethinker and republican. Born into the Piedmontese aristocracy in Turin, he travelled widely, acquiring deistic views in England and Holland. He served Victor Amadeus II in 1725–6 during his conflict with the papacy, but was soon forced to exile, in England and then Holland. He was deeply anticlerical. In his social thought he was egalitarian and republican. His major work, however, *Twelve Discourses concerning Religion and Government* (1734), probably written in the 1720s for Victor Amadeus, is a scheme for reformed princely rule.
• Carpanetto and Ricuperati 1987; Jacob 1981; Venturi 1971.

RAMSAY, ANDREW MICHAEL

1686–1743. Franco-Scottish Jacobite, known as the Chevalier Ramsay. Born in Ayr, Scotland, the son of a baker, he was educated at Edinburgh University. Under the influence of Fénelon, whose biography he wrote (1723), he converted to Catholicism, 1710. He was tutor to the Jacobite Pretender Prince Charles Edward, 1724. His *Voyages de Cyrus* (1727) was strongly influenced by Fénelon's *Télémaque*. Other works include *Essai philosophique sur le gouvernement civil* (1721) and *Philosophical Principles of Natural and Revealed Religion* (1748–9).
• Baldi 2002; Childs 2000; Henderson 1952.

RAPIN (RAPIN-THOYRAS), PAUL DE

1661–1725. Huguenot historian. Born in Castres, France, he fled to England, 1686. He then went to Holland, joined William of Orange's army of invasion, 1688, and fought against the Jacobites in the English army in Ireland. He was tutor to the duke of Portland's son. His

Whiggish *History of England* (1725) became the standard work on the subject until Hume's *History*.
• Bailyn 1967; Forbes 1975.

RAYNAL, ABBÉ GUILLAUME THOMAS FRANÇOIS

1713–96. French historian of colonialism. Born in La Panouze, he was ordained priest, 1743, and settled in Paris, 1746, where he joined the salons of Holbach and Necker, and became a protégé of the statesman Choiseul. He edited and contributed to journals, including the *Mercure de France*. His chief work, in collaboration with Diderot, was the *Histoire philosophique et politique des établissements et du commerce des Européens dans les deux Indes* (History of the Settlements and Commerce of the Europeans in the Two Indies, 1770), usually called the *Histoire des deux Indes*, which had many editions. The book provides a wealth of information about the mores of non-European peoples and attacks slavery and colonialism. He also wrote *Histoire du parlement d'Angleterre* (1748).
• Bancarel and Goggi 2000; Lüsubrink and Strugnell 1995; Lüsubrink and Tietz 1991; Salmon 1999; Wolpe 1957.

REID, THOMAS

1710–96. Scottish philosopher. Born in Strachan, Kincardineshire. Educated at Aberdeen University, he was ordained a minister, and became librarian and, in 1751, professor of philosophy there, before moving to the chair of moral philosophy at Glasgow, 1764. His *Inquiry into the Human Mind* (1764), in answer to Hume, *Essay on the Intellectual Powers of Man* (1785), and *Essay on the Active Powers of Man* (1788), laid out his 'Common Sense' epistemology, arguing for the reality of intuitive knowledge common to rational beings.
• Haakonssen 1986–7.

REIMARUS, HERMANN SAMUEL

1694–1768. German philosopher and theologian. A native of Hamburg, he studied at Jena, and was a student of J. A. Fabricius. He was appointed a teacher at Wittemberg, 1716, visited the Netherlands and England, 1720–1, became rector of a school at Mecklenburg, 1723, and settled as professor of Hebrew and Oriental languages at Hamburg, 1727. He published an edition of Dio Cassius, and books on logic and theology. The chief of these was *Die vornehmsten Wahrheiten der natürlichen Religion* (The Foremost Truths of Natural Religion, 1755). He was a deist and his philosophical position was Wolffian. His most heretical work, on the historical Jesus, was published posthumously.

RESTIF DE LA BRETONNE, NICOLAS EDME

1734–1806. French satirist. Born in Sacy near Auxerre, of peasant parents, he became a printer in Paris, and entered upon a life of notoriety. He wrote several novels which scandalised by their libertine views. Though he briefly worked in, of all things, the ministry of police, the Revolution brought about the collapse of his celebrity, and he died in obscurity and poverty. Over 200 works are attributed to him. They include Rousseauesque reveries on the idyll of rural life and the corruption of the city.
• Coward 1991; Poster 1971; Wagstaff 1996.

RICCI, SCIPIONE DE

1741–1810. Italian conciliarist. Born at Rignana near Florence, in 1780 he was made bishop of Pistoia-Prato in Tuscany by Duke Leopold. He pursued a Josephinist reform programme, designed to limit the excesses of Catholic spirituality, monasticism, and the influence of

the papacy, culminating in the Synod of Pistoia, 1786. He was forced to resign his see in 1791.
• Miller 1994; Rodolico 1920.

ROBERTSON, WILLIAM
1721–93. Scottish historian. Born in Borthwick, Midlothian, he was educated at Edinburgh University, ordained a minister, and rose to be principal of the university, 1762–92, Moderator (president) of the General Assembly of the Church of Scotland, 1763–90, and historiographer royal, 1763–90. He began his *History of Scotland* (1759) in 1753; this was followed by *The History of the Reign of the Emperor Charles V* (1762–71), and *The History of America* (1777). He was a leader of the Moderate party in the Scottish Presbyterian church.
• Brown 1997; O'Brien 1997; Sher 1985.

ROBESPIERRE, MAXIMILIEN FRANÇOIS ISIDORE
1758–94. French revolutionary. Born in Arras, he studied law in Paris, and practised in Arras. At the Revolution he was elected to the Estates General. In the Assembly and the Convention he pressed democratic and populist positions. He became leader of the Jacobins, and the most powerful figure in France during the Terror, of which he was a chief architect, 1793–4. His enemies eventually outmanoeuvred him and he was himself guillotined. He founded the journal *Le Défenseur de la Constitution*.
• Hampson 1974; Haydon and Doyle 1999.

ROEDERER, PIERRE LOUIS, COMTE DE
1754–1835. French *idéologue*. Born in Metz, he became councillor to the *parlement* there, 1780, was elected to the Estates General, 1789, and wrote for the *Journal de Paris*. He went into hiding when the Girondins were persecuted. He was appointed professor of political economy at the *école centrales*, 1796, and founded the *Journal d'économie publique, de morale, et de politique*. He was a senator and held several offices under Napoleon, including minister of finance in the Kingdom of Naples, 1806.

ROHR, JULIUS BERNHARD VON
1688–1742. German cameralist. Son of a landowner, he studied law, mathematics, physics, and chemistry at Leipzig. After travelling with his father he returned to Leipzig, 1712, where he completed a dissertation on economics. He moved to Halle, 1713, where he studied with Wolff and composed a dissertation on the utility of the mathematical sciences. From 1714 he occupied a number of positions in local administration, and completed several important economic compendia, 1715–30.

ROLAND DE LA PLATIÈRE, MARIE JEANNE (MANON PHILPON), MADAME
1754–93. French revolutionary. Born in Paris, the daughter of a Parisian engraver, she studied the classics, especially Plutarch, and the *philosophes*, including Montesquieu, Voltaire, and Rousseau. In 1781 she married Jean Marie Roland, and assisted his literary work on commercial policy, soon writing journal articles under his name, in *Le Courier de Lyon*. The Rolands settled in Paris in 1791 where she conducted a salon for the revolutionaries, among them Robespierre and Brissot. Her husband was briefly minister of the interior, 1792, and she drafted some of his directives. The Rolands sided with the Girondins. In 1793 she was imprisoned, and wrote her memoirs, an apostrophe to revolutionary patriotism. 'Oh Liberty! What crimes are committed in your name' were her last words at the guillotine.
• Chaussinand-Nogaret 1985; May 1964, 1970.

ROMAGNOSI, GIAN DOMENICO
1761–1835. Italian jurist and philosopher, a native of Parma, where he studied law. He became a prominent lawyer and in 1791 published *Genesi del diritto penale* (The Origins of Penal Law), which went through three editions in his lifetime. He was a magistrate at Trent during the French occupation of the 1790s and consequently spent fifteen months in prison after the Austrians took the city in 1799. He was reinstated as a senior civil servant in Trent after the French reoccupation of 1801, and later was professor of public law at Parma. He published works on mathematics and logic as well as law.

ROMILLY, SIR SAMUEL
1757–1818. English law reformer. Born in Westminster, he became a barrister and rose to be solicitor-general, 1806, and Member of Parliament, 1806–18. An early convert to Rousseau, he supported penal reform, Catholic emancipation, and the abolition of slavery. In France in the 1780s he met Diderot, d'Alembert, Franklin, and Raynal, and in London, Mirabeau. His chief works are *Observations on 'Thoughts on Executive Justice'* (by Martin Madan) (1786), and *Observations on the Criminal Law of England* (1810). He committed suicide on the death of his wife.
• Follett 2001.

ROUSSEAU, JEAN JACQUES
1712–78. French philosopher and moralist. Son of a Genevan watchmaker, and largely self-educated, he wrote on politics, education, and music, as well as producing an opera, an autobiography, and pre-Romantic fiction. He led a life of wandering and exile. He moved to Paris, 1742, befriended Diderot, but later broke with him. He came to public attention as the author of the *Discours sur les sciences et les arts* (Discourse on the Sciences and the Arts, 1751). This was followed by the 'Second Discourse', *Discours sur l'origine de l'inégalité* (Discourse on the Origin of Inequality, 1755). In the name of nature, simplicity, and virtue, both essays attacked civilisation as fostering artificial needs, *mores*, and inequalities. *Du contrat social* (The Social Contract, 1762) addressed the principles of popular sovereignty. His other chief works are *Emile* (1762), on education, *Julie, ou la Nouvelle Héloïse* (1761), and the autobiographical *Confessions* (1781–2, written 1764–70). His other principal political writings are the article on 'Political Economy' for the *Encyclopédie* (1755), *Lettres écrites de la montagne* (Letters Written from the Mountain, 1764); *Projet de Constitution pour la Corse* (drafted, *c.* 1765); and *Considérations sur le gouvernement du Pologne* (written 1772).
• Baczko 1974; Barnard 1988a; Blum 1986; Cameron 1973; Cassirer 1945, 1963; Charvet 1974; Cranston 1983, 1991b; Cranston and Peters 1972; Dent 1988; Derathé 1950; Fetscher 1960; Fralin 1978; Grimsley 1973; Hampson 1983; Hobson *et al.* 1992; Hulliung 1994; Kelly 1987; Leduc 1974; Masters 1968; Miller 1984; Riley 1982, 1986, 2001b; Rosenblatt 1997; Shklar 1969; Starobinski 1957, 1988; Vaughan 1925; Viroli 1988; Wokler 1975, 1987b, 1995a; Zurbuchen 1991.

RUTHERFORTH, THOMAS
1712–71. English jurist. Born in Papworth, Cambridgeshire, he was educated at Cambridge University, where he became regius professor of divinity, 1756. He was appointed chaplain to Frederick, prince of Wales, and archdeacon of Essex, and published works on science, ethics (*An Essay on the Nature and Obligation of Virtue*, 1744), and jurisprudence. His *Institutes of Natural Law* (1754–6) drew upon lectures on Grotius's *Laws of War and Peace*. They argued that natural law decrees the happiness of the species, and that the rights and duties of humankind are grounded in the divine will discernible in the workings of nature. In treating of the theory of property, he cautions against Locke's dangerous leanings towards the rights of labour.
• Haakonssen 1996a; Horne 1990.

RUTLEDGE, JAMES

1742–94. Franco-Irish Jacobite turned Jacobin. Born in Dunkirk, of an Irish Jacobite father and French mother, he served briefly in the Irish brigade of the French army. He settled in Paris and made a living by his pen, mainly translating English literary works into French. He was prominent in Paris during the Revolution, plastering the streets with anti-Necker posters. He was a member of the Cordeliers Club until 1791, but was refused admission to the Jacobin Club. His journal, *Le Creuset, ouvrage politique et critique*, was a Cordelier organ. He discussed the English republican tradition, especially in another journal, *Calypso*. His chief political work is *Essais politiques sur l'état actuel de quelques puissances* (Political Essay on the Present State of Certain Powers, 1777), a meditation on the likely outcome of the probable defeat of Britain in its war with America, and on the reform of the French economy.
• Hammersley 2004; Las Vergnas 1932.

SADE, DONATIEN ALPHONSE FRANÇOIS, MARQUIS DE

1740–1814. French philosopher and pornographer. Born in Paris, he served in the army, 1754–63. Condemned to death for cruelty and sexual deviation, 1772, he escaped, but was later imprisoned in the Bastille, 1784–9. He was later incarcerated in the asylum at Charenton. Author of *120 Days of Sodom* (*c.* 1784) and *Justine* (1791). Sade deduced his reveries of orgiastic and transgressive sex from the mechanistic materialism and irreligion of the Enlightenment; he was a reader of Holbach, Helvétius, Diderot, and La Mettrie. From his name is derived 'sadism'.

ST JOHN, HENRY, *see* BOLINGBROKE

SAINT-JUST, LOUIS ANTOINE LÉON

1767–94. French revolutionary. Born in Decize, central France, the son of a soldier, he took a law degree at Soissons, 1788, and then moved to Paris. His epic poem *Organt* (1789) was characteristic of the erotic-subversive underground literature of the period. He was elected to the Convention, 1792, became an energetic administrator and soldier, and, as a member of the Committee of Public Safety, was a chief architect of the Terror, 1793–4. He introduced the decrees for confiscating the property of the enemies of the Revolution. In his *L'Esprit de la révolution et de la constitution de la France* (1791) he argued that the Revolution was incomplete, and in *Fragments sur les institutions républicaines* (1792, publ. 1800) he envisioned a Revolution realised in communalism and egalitarianism. He was guillotined.
• Curtis 1935; Hampson 1991; Soboul 1968.

SAINT-PIERRE, CHARLES IRÉNÉE CASTEL, ABBÉ DE

1658–1743. French diplomat and political writer. Born in Saint-Pierre, Normandy. Author of many projects of political and economic reform. He published his *Projet de paix perpètuelle* (Project for Perpetual Peace, 1713), after assisting negotiations for the Treaty of Utrecht, 1712. It proposed a league of sovereign states which would resolve disputes through an international congress and court. The scheme served as a model for Rousseau and Kant.
• Martin 1962; Perkins 1959.

SAINT-SIMON, CLAUDE HENRI DE ROUVROY, COMTE DE

1760–1825. French social theorist and Christian socialist. Born in Paris of an impoverished noble family, he served in the French army during the American War of Independence. After the Revolution he became rich from nationalised land, but was imprisoned during the Terror, and returned to poverty in later years. His principal works were *L'Industrie* (1816–18),

Système industriel (1820–3), and *Nouveau Christianisme* (1825). He envisioned an industrialised society managed by scientists and engineers.

• Ansart 1970; Baker 1987; Manuel 1956; Wokler 1987d.

SCHILLER, JOHANN CHRISTOPH FRIEDRICH

1759–1805. German poet, dramatist, and moralist. Born in Marbach, southern Germany, the son of an army doctor. His years in a military academy instilled an enthusiasm for freedom. His rebellious play, a keynote text of the *Sturm und Drang* (Storm and Stress) movement, *Die Räuber* (The Robbers, 1781), won him honorary citizenship of revolutionary France, 1792. He developed an idea of freedom achieved through self-development, the cultivation of character and the faculties, notably in *Über die aesthetische Erziehung des Menschen* (On the Aesthetic Education of Man, 1795). He looked to ancient Greece for an ideal of social harmony which the modern fragmentation of labour, reason, and feeling disrupted.

• Miller 1970; Reed 1991.

SCHLÖZER, AUGUST LUDWIG VON

1735–1809. German historian, mathematician, and educationalist. Born in Hohenlohe-Kirchberg, he studied at Wittenberg and Göttingen Universities. He taught in Sweden, 1755–9, and Russia, 1761–7, and then returned to Göttingen. His chief works were *Essay on the General History of Trade and of Seafaring in the Most Ancient Times* (1758), and *Allgemeines Staatsrecht und Staatsverfassungslehre* (General Public Law and the Theory of Constitutions, 1793).

• Hennies 1985.

SCHRÖDER, WILHELM VON

1640–88. German cameralist. Born in Königsberg and educated at the court of Duke Ernst of Saxe Gotha and at the Gotha *gymnasium*. He studied law at Jena, but broke off to travel to England, where he met Hobbes, William Petty, and Robert Boyle. He returned to Germany, 1663, and presented a dissertation influenced by Hobbes. This was rejected, and he travelled the European courts, converted to Catholicism, and found favour with Emperor Leopold I, who sent him to England to study political economy. On his return to Vienna he was appointed successor to Becher as director of the manufactory, where he introduced woollen manufacture on the English model. He published several treatises on politics, 1663–86, ending his life in Hungarian service.

SEABURY, SAMUEL

1729–96. American loyalist. Born in Groton, Connecticut, he was educated at Yale and Edinburgh Universities. Taking Anglican ordination, he was pastor in New Jersey, 1754–7, and New York, 1757–66, becoming rector of Westchester, New York, 1766–76. Arrested by a Whig mob, 1775, he served as chaplain in a loyalist American regiment, 1776–83. He became the first American bishop (Connecticut), 1785–96. His pamphlets, under the name A Westchester Farmer, denounced the Revolution: *Free Thoughts on the Proceedings of the Continental Congress* (1774), *The Congress Canvassed* (1774), and *A View of the Controversy between Great Britain and her Colonies* (1775).

• Steiner 1971.

SECKENDORFF, VEIT LUDWIG VON

1626–92. German jurist. Born in Erlangen and educated at the court of Duke Ernst of Saxe Gotha and at the Gotha *gymnasium*. He studied law from 1642 in Strasburg, became librarian to Ernst, 1646, being later promoted to councillor and judge in Jena. He became privy councillor to Frederick II of Brandenburg, 1691, and chancellor of the new Halle University, 1692. He published a series of historical and political works in German and Latin from 1656 to his death, including *Fürsten-Staat* (Sovereign State, 1656). These were widely read by the cameralists.

• Roscher 1874; Small 1909; Stolleis 1977.

SHAFTESBURY, ANTHONY ASHLEY COOPER, THIRD EARL OF

1671–1713. English moralist. Born in London, the grandson of the Whig leader the first earl of Shaftesbury, his education was supervised by Locke. He took the Grand Tour, 1686–9, was a Member of Parliament, 1695–8, and succeeded to the peerage, 1699. He lived in Holland, 1703, where he met Bayle and Le Clerc. He died in Naples. Shaftesbury's moral essays were grounded in a thesis about human moral sensibility and the sociable self, encouraged the ethic of 'politeness' and moderation, and promoted the value of wit and irony. They were collected as *Characteristics of Men, Manners, Opinions, Times* (1711), and include his *Enquiry Concerning Virtue* (1699) and *Letter concerning Enthusiasm* (1708). They were translated into French by Diderot.

• Aldridge 1951; Klein 1994; Rivers 1991–2000; Voitle 1984.

SHEBBEARE, JOHN

1709–88. English Tory polemicist. Born in Bideford, Devon, he was apprenticed to a surgeon in Exeter. He moved to Bristol, turned to chemistry, visited Paris, then settled in London and, from *c.* 1754, made a living by writing. A stream of political novels, satires, and pamphlets followed. *Letters on the English Nation, by Batista Angeloni, a Jesuit* (1755) and *Letters to the People of England* (1757) assailed the duke of Newcastle's government; for the latter he was jailed for sedition. *The History of the Excellence and Decline of the Institutions, Religion, Laws, Manners, and Genius, of the Sumatrans, and of the Restoration thereof in the Reign of Amurath the Third* (1763) defended George III and his ministers against the Whigs, and won him a government pension. His *Essay on the Origin, Progress, and Establishment of National Society* (1776) attacked Price and the Americans, in 'justification of the legislature in reducing America to obedience by force'.

• Sack 1993.

SHERIDAN, THOMAS

1646–1712. Irish Jacobite. Born at St Johns near Trim, Co. Meath, and educated at Trinity College, Dublin. He came to England, 1677, was elected a Fellow of the Royal Society, 1679, and rose rapidly in the circle of the future James II. He converted to Catholicism, 1686, was made chief secretary of Ireland, 1687, and went into exile with James, 1689. *A Discourse of the Rise and Power of Parliaments* (1678) defended toleration, including for Catholics. Later works, which exist only in manuscript, defended James's kingship, Catholic absolutism, and religious intolerance: *The King of Great Britain's Case* (1692) and *Political Reflections on the History and Government of England* (1709).

• Geoghegan 2001.

SHERLOCK, WILLIAM

c. 1641–1707. English theologian and Tory polemicist. Born in Southwark, London, and educated at Cambridge University, he was ordained an Anglican minister. A defender of the divine right of kings and passive obedience in the 1680s, he at first repudiated the Revolution of 1688; his later conformity caused a storm of controversy, but was rewarded with appointment as dean of St Paul's. His *Case of Allegiance* (1691) was a 'de facto' defence of the Revolution, parallel to similar Hobbesian tracts of 1649–51. Locke wrote a manuscript

attack on it, and Leibniz produced a more favourable essay in which he too came close to a Hobbesian stance.
• Jolley 1975; Riley 1973.

SHUTE, JOHN, *see* BARRINGTON

SIEYÈS, EMMANUEL JOSEPH, ABBÉ

1748–1836. French revolutionary and constitutional theorist. Born in Fréjus and educated by the Jesuits, he was ordained a priest. His principal work is the tract *Qu'est-ce que le Tiers-Etat?* (What is the Third Estate?, 1789), which had great impact in the first revolutionary year. It was accompanied by other tracts, *Essais sur les privilèges* (Essay on Privileges), and *Vues sur les moyens d'exécution dont les représentans de la France pourront disposer* (Views of the Executive Means Available to the Representatives of France). He was elected to the Estates General and was the principal author of its transformation into the unicameral National Assembly. His constitutional expertise was called upon in drafting the constitutions of 1791, 1795, and 1799, as well as the Declaration of the Rights of Man. His other works include the *Discours sur la liberté des cultes* (1791), which defended religious toleration. Avoiding death in the Terror, he later achieved high office under the Directorate and sought to instal Napoleon in the coup of 18th Brumaire 1799, under whom he served as president of the senate. He was exiled to Brussels after the emperor's fall.
• Bastid 1939; Forsyth 1987; Sewell 1994; Sonenscher 2003; Van Deusen 1932.

SMITH, ADAM

1723–90. Scottish political economist and moral philosopher. Born in Kirkcaldy, the posthumous son of a civil servant. Educated at Glasgow University, where his teacher was Hutcheson, and at Oxford University, where he was self-taught. Appointed to the chair of logic at Glasgow, 1750, but switched to the chair of moral philosophy, 1752, a position he held until 1764, when he accompanied the duke of Buccleuch on the Grand Tour as tutor, 1764–6. *The Theory of Moral Sentiments* (1759) contains his ethical teaching and emphasises sympathy in the formation of the moral sense. His chief work is the *Inquiry into the Nature and Causes of the Wealth of Nations* (1776), an expanded version of lectures on jurisprudence. It promoted free trade and a limited role for government, urged that market economies will in the long run make everyone better off, inequalities notwithstanding, and explored the transition of societies from agriculture to commerce and manufacture. Smith was appointed commissioner of customs, 1778.
• Campbell 1971; Campbell and Skinner 1982a; Dwyer 1998; Fitzgibbon 1995; Griswold 1999; Haakonssen 1981, 1998; Hollander 1973; Hont and Ignatieff 1983a; Hope 1989; Mizuta and Sugiyama 1993; Raphael 1985; Ross 1995; Rothschild 2001; Skinner 1993; Skinner and Wilson 1975; Teichgraeber 1986; Vivenza 2001; Winch 1978.

SONNENFELS, BARON JOSEPH VON

1733–1817. Austrian cameralist. Born in Moravia of Jewish parents who later converted to Christianity. He entered military service, 1749–54, then studied law in Vienna. He was appointed to the newly founded chair of administrative science (*Cameralwissenschaft*) at Vienna, 1763. In addition he became a book and theatre censor, 1770, and secretary of the Academy of Arts, 1772. He devoted much attention to penal reform and the abolition of torture, and served on Joseph II's reform commissions. He was an active journalist, launching several periodicals. He was ennobled in 1797. His chief work is the *Grundsätze der Polizei- Handlungs- und Finanzwissenschaft* (Basic Principles of the Science of Administration, Business, and Finance, 1765–76).
• Kremers 1988; Ogris 1988b; Osterloh 1970; Reinalter 1988; Tribe 1984.

SPENCE, THOMAS

1750–1814. English radical journalist. Born in Newcastle of impoverished but literate parents, he became a schoolmaster. He was expelled from the Newcastle Philosophical Society for his lecture proposing agrarian communalism (*The Rights of Man*, 1775). He moved to London, became a bookseller and publisher, and joined the London Corresponding Society. He was prosecuted in 1793 for selling Paine's *Rights of Man*, in 1794 and 1798 for treason, and in 1801 for seditious libel. During the 1790s he published a weekly called *Pig's Meat* (a reference to Burke's remark on the 'swinish multitude'). In *The End of Oppression* (1795) and *The Restorer of Society to its Natural State* (1801) he declared the need for economic as well as political equality. In several tracts he described a utopia called Spensonia. Five 'Spenceans' were executed for the Cato Street Conspiracy of 1820.
• Ashraf 1983; Chase 1988; Horne 1990; Thompson 1998.

SPENER, PHILIPP JAKOB

1635–1705. German Pietist. Born in Alsace, he studied at Strasburg, was ordained, and practised his ministry in Dresden and Berlin. Influenced by German and English evangelicals, he became a leader of the Pietist movement. His accent on personal, inner religious life, in place of the formulae of dogma and ritual, put him at odds with orthodoxy, but he had the support of Frederick I of Prussia. Halle University was founded chiefly under his influence. He wrote prolifically.

STAËL, ANNE LOUISE GERMAINE NECKER, MADAME DE

1766–1817. French novelist, critic, and political commentator. Born in Paris, the daughter of Jacques Necker, French director of finance, 1777–88. In youth she absorbed Montesquieu, Rousseau, and Voltaire. During the Terror she fled to Switzerland. A critic of Napoleon, she lived in exile in Germany, 1803–13. Through her novels, literary criticism, and meditations she attacked absolute monarchy, clericalism, and the excesses of the Revolution, defending the British model of constitutional monarchy and the separation of powers. Among her works are *Lettres sur les écrits de Jean Jacques Rousseau* (Letters on the Writings of Rousseau, 1788), *Réflexions sur le procès de la reine* (Thoughts on the Trial of the Queen, 1793), *Des circonstances actuelles qui peuvent terminer la révolution* (Present Circumstances which may lead to an end of the Revolution, 1798–9), *Delphine* (1802), *Considérations sur la révolution française* (1818), and *Dix années d'exil* (Ten Years of Exile, 1818).
• Balayé 1979.

STANISLAS I LESZCZYNSKI

1677–1766. King of Poland, 1704–9, 1733–5. Born in Lwow, of Polish nobility. He was deposed in 1709 by Czar Peter the Great of Russia, and in 1735 he abdicated after military defeat by Russia. Thereafter he was duke of Lorraine. His court at Lunéville was a centre of culture. He composed objections to Rousseau's first *Discourse*.
• Lukowski 1991.

STEELE, SIR RICHARD

1672–1729. Anglo-Irish journalist and playwright. Born in Dublin and educated at Oxford University. After a brief military career he became an influential essayist. Together with Addison he produced the *Tatler* (1709–11), *Spectator* (1711–14), and *Guardian* (1713). His pseudonym was Isaac Bickerstaff. He was a Whig Member of Parliament, 1713, until expelled for the *Crisis* (1714). Later he wrote stage comedies. Other journals include the *Englishman* (1713–14) and the *Plebeian* (1719).
• Bloom, Bloom, and Leites 1984.

Biographies

STEUART (also DENHAM), SIR JAMES

1713–80. Scottish political economist. Born in Edinburgh, and educated at the university there, he joined the Scottish bar, 1735. He travelled on the Continent and met the Old Pretender to the Stuart throne in Rome. During the Jacobite Rebellion of 1745 he was Prince Charles's ambassador in Paris. He returned from exile, 1763, but was not given a formal pardon until 1771. He was a friend of Hume. His chief work is *An Inquiry into the Principles of Political Oeconomy* (1767), which provided a principal source for Hegel's political economy.

• Hont 1983; Hutchison 1988; Sen 1957; Skinner 1966; Tortajada 1999; Waszek 1988; Winch 1993.

STEWART, DUGALD

1753–1828. Scottish philosopher and political economist. Born in Edinburgh, he studied at the university there, where he became professor of mathematics, 1775, and of moral philosophy, 1785. An influential teacher, he mounted the first separate course on political economy in Britain, and his pupils included the founders of the *Edinburgh Review*, and two future prime ministers, Palmerston and Russell. He supported the French Revolution at first, visiting France in 1788–9, wrote Adam Smith's life, and wrote on moral philosophy in the tradition of Reid. His chief works are *Elements of the Philosophy of the Human Mind* (1792–1827), *Outlines of Moral Philosophy* (1793), and *Lectures on Political Economy* (1800).

• Collini *et al.* 1983; Fontana 1985; Haakonssen 1996a; Winch 1983.

SWIFT, JONATHAN

1667–1745. Irish satirist, journalist, and novelist. Born in Dublin and educated at Trinity College, he was ordained into the Anglican ministry, but sought a literary career. In the *Contests and Dissensions in Athens and Rome* (1701) he commented on Whig–Tory quarrels. *A Tale of a Tub* (1704), which included *The Battle of the Books*, satirised abuses in learning and religion. Until 1710 his main associates were Whig, but he then moved towards the Tories, becoming a propagandist for Prime Minister Robert Harley, 1710–14, for whom he produced *The Conduct of the Allies* (1711), to promote peace with France, and the newspaper, *The Examiner*, 1710–11. He belonged to the Scriblerus Club alongside Pope and Gay, and his *Journal to Stella* (1710–13) records these years. His hopes of a bishopric were dashed by the accession of the Whigs in 1714. Latterly he lived in Dublin, where he was dean of St Patrick's, writing in defence of Ireland against English landowners and placemen, especially in *Drapier's Letters* (1725). *Gulliver's Travels* (1726) was a brilliant political satire, its first book, the Voyage to Lilliput, directed against Prime Minister Walpole.

• Boyce *et al.* 2001; Cook 1967; Downie 1984; Ehrenpreis 1962–83; Lock 1983; Nokes 1985; Rogers 1970.

TALLEYRAND-PÉRIGORD, CHARLES MAURICE DE

1754–1838. French revolutionary and counter-revolutionary. Born in Paris into a noble family, he was ordained priest, 1775, and became bishop of Autun, 1788. Elected a deputy to the Estates General, he was a key influence in the appropriation of church lands by the state and the passage of the Civil Constitution of the Clergy. During the Terror he removed to England and America. He became foreign minister under the Directory, 1797, a post he held until 1807, continuing under Napoleon. In 1814 he orchestrated the deposition of Napoleon, and became foreign minister under Louis XVIII. At the Congress of Vienna he preserved the place of France in the concert of Europe. He was ambassador to Britain, 1830–4.

• Orieux 1970.

TAMBURINI, PIETRO

1737–1827. Italian advocate of toleration. Born in Brescia. A Jansenist theologian, he taught at the Irish College in Rome and then took a chair at Pavia University, where he remained. His chief work was *On Ecclesiastical and Civil Tolerance* (1783). His advocacy of the separation of church and state influenced the decrees of the Synod of Pistoia, 1786.
• Bolton 1969; Davidson 2000; Jemolo 1928.

THELWALL, JOHN

1764–1834. English radical pamphleteer. Born in London, he left school at thirteen. He published poetry and edited the *Biographical and Imperial Magazine* (1789–). He became a prominent member of the London Corresponding Society and the Society of Friends of the People, was an enthusiast for the French Revolution, and was charged with treason, 1794. His (undelivered) defence was published as *The Natural and Constitutional Rights of Britons* (1795). His major work, *The Rights of Nature* (1796), was written against Burke's *Letters on a Regicide Peace*. He sought to evade suppression of his political meetings by ostensibly lecturing on Roman history. He republished Moyle's essay on the Roman republic.
• Cestre 1906; Chase 1988; Claeys 1994b, 1995; Gallop 1986; Hampsher-Monk 1991; Horne 1990; Schneewind 1998; Thompson 1998.

THOMASIUS, CHRISTIAN

1655–1728. German jurist. Born in Leipzig, Saxony, he studied law at Frankfurt-on-the-Oder, and pursued a varied career in Leipzig as advocate, private lecturer, author, and founder of a journal *Monatsgespräche* (Monthly Conversations). His satires against religion and the clergy and denial of divine right kingship caused him to move to Halle, 1690, where he helped found the university, of which he became president, 1710. Here he established himself as the leading German philosopher, synthesising natural law with Francke's Pietism. Despite tensions, his ideas became the official ideology of Frederick I's Prussia. His principal work was *Fundamenta juris naturae et gentium* (Foundations of the Law of Nature and Nations, 1705).
• Ahnert 2002; Barnard 1965b, 1971, 1983, 1988b; Bienert 1934; Bloch 1961; Engfer 1989; Fleischmann 1931; Hochstrasser 2000; Hunter 2001; Lieberwirth 1955; Reill 1975; Rüping 1968, 1979; Schmidt 1995; Schneiders 1971, 1989; Spaeting 1971.

TINDAL, MATTHEW

1657–1733. English deist and anticlerical. Born in Devon and educated at Oxford University, he became a Fellow of All Souls College, 1678. After briefly converting to Catholicism under James II, he veered steadily towards heterodoxy. *The Rights of the Christian Church* (1706) was a frontal assault on clerical authority, publicly burnt in 1710. *Christianity as Old as the Creation* (1730) summed up a generation of deist publications. His early *Essay concerning the Law of Nations and the Rights of Sovereigns* (1694), *Essay concerning Obedience to the Supreme Powers and the Duties of Subjects in all Revolutions* (1694), and *Essay concerning the Power of the Magistrate and the Rights of Mankind in Matters of Religion* (1697) all defended Whig 'Revolution principles' and show the influence of both Hobbes and Locke.
• Reventlow 1984; Rivers 1991–2000; Torrey 1930.

TOLAND, JOHN

1670–1722. Irish deist and radical Whig. Born near Londonderry of Catholic parentage. He converted to Protestantism and studied at Glasgow, Edinburgh, Leiden, and Oxford Universities. His deism, scriptural criticism, and critique of priestcraft appeared in *Christianity not Mysterious* (1696), *Letters to Serena* (1704, for Princess Sophie Charlotte of Hanover), *Nazarenus* (1718), and *Pantheisticon* (1720). The first of these brought him notoriety and condemnation. In 1705 he coined the word 'pantheism'. During 1698–1700 he published editions of the works of Civil War republicans, James Harrington, Algernon Sidney, and Edmund Ludlow, together with a life of John Milton, establishing a canon of 'commonwealth' texts which armed generations of critics of executive power. He was active in the campaign against standing armies, in which he collaborated with Moyle and Trenchard. His political tracts include *The Militia Reform'd* (1698), *Anglia Libera* (1701), and *The Art of Governing by Partys* (1701).

• Bailyn 1967; Champion 1992, 2003; Daniel 1984; Jacob 1981; Sullivan 1982.

TONE, THEOBALD WOLFE

1763–98. Irish revolutionary. Born in Dublin of Protestant parents, he was educated at Trinity College and the Inns of Court, London. He founded the Society of United Irishmen, 1791, to promote parliamentary reform on a non-sectarian property-holding basis. *An Argument on Behalf of the Catholics of Ireland* (1791) sought to persuade Protestant Dissenters of a common cause with Catholics in pursuit of toleration. He was secretary to the Catholic Committee and campaigned to secure the Catholic Relief Act. In 1795–6 he visited America and France. He conspired with France during the 1798 rebellion, was captured and tried, and committed suicide while awaiting execution. At his trial he claimed the object of his life had been 'the independence of my country'.

• Dickson *et al.* 1993; Dunne 1982; Elliot 1989; McBride 1988.

TOOKE, JOHN HORNE

1736–1812. English radical. Born in Westminster and educated at Cambridge University, he became a clergyman but resigned and turned to the law. He opposed the American war and was imprisoned for seditious libel, 1775. His *Diversions of Purley* (1786) was a work on language and etymology, in defence of plain English. He was prominent in the Society of Supporters of the Bill of Rights, 1769, the Society for Constitutional Information, founded 1780, and the London Corresponding Society, founded 1792, working with Thelwall and Francis Burdett. He was convicted of seditious libel, 1777, for pro-American remarks, and acquitted of treason for organising democratic clubs, 1794. He stood unsuccessfully for parliament, 1790 and 1796, was returned in 1801, but was disqualified as a clergyman. His tracts include *The Petition of an Englishman* (1765) and *A Letter to Lord Ashburton* (1782; retitled *Letter on Parliamentary Reform,* 1789).

• Bewley and Bewley 1998; Goodwin 1979.

TOUSSAINT L'OUVERTURE (FRANÇOIS DOMINIQUE TOUS-SAINT)

1746–1803. Haitian revolutionary. Born a slave in Haiti (then San Domingo), in 1791 he joined a rebellion against French rule, and by 1797 was ruler of an independent nation – a successful slave revolt. He took inspiration from Raynal. He died in a French prison after capture by Napoleon. Haiti achieved final liberation from France in 1804.

• James 1980.

TOWERS, JOSEPH

1737–99. English radical Dissenter. Born in Southwark, London, he was apprenticed to a printer, and ordained a Dissenting minister, 1774, serving congregations in London, where he was co-pastor with Price. He campaigned for repeal of the Test Act, 1780s, and was a member of the Revolution Society and the Society for Constitutional Information. Besides works on theology, he wrote a life of Frederick II of Prussia (1788), which attacked autocracy, and a tract on Hume's *History*, which denounced his defence of Stuart tyranny. His Wilkite

Observations on Public Liberty (1769) assailed George III and Prime Minister Bute, and argued that members of parliament were delegates of the people. He also published *Tracts on Political and Other Subjects* (1796).
• Donelly 1987.

TRACY, ANTOINE LOUIS CLAUDE, COMTE DE, *see* DESTUTT

TRENCHARD, JOHN

1662–1723. Anglo-Irish radical Whig. Educated at Trinity College, Dublin, he became a lawyer. With Moyle he wrote *An Argument, Shewing that a Standing Army is Inconsistent with a Free Government* (1697) and *A Short History of Standing Armies* (1698). With Thomas Gordon he produced the anticlerical newspaper *The Independent Whig* (1720–1). His critique of priestcraft emerges also in *The Natural History of Superstition* (1709). His most important work was *Cato's Letters* (1720–3), weekly essays in the classical republic tradition which appeared in the *London Journal* and *British Journal*, and were then collected. He was elected to parliament, 1722.
• Hamowy 1990; McMahon 1990; Pocock 1975; Zuckert 1994.

TUCKER, JOSIAH

1713–99. Welsh political economist. Born in Laugharne, Carmarthenshire, and educated at Oxford University, he became an Anglican clergyman, serving in Bristol, where he attacked Methodism. In 1749 he published *A Brief Essay on Trade*, a critique of mercantilism, arguing that labour, not money, is the basis of national wealth. His *Elements of Commerce* (1755) was read by Marx. He was made dean of Gloucester, 1758. A tract on trade, *The Case of Going to War for the Sake of . . . Trade* (1763), was translated into French by Turgot. In *Cui Bono?* (1781), addressed to Necker, he argued that the American war was a mistake for all concerned. In 1781 he published his *Treatise concerning Civil Government* 'against Locke and his followers', perhaps the most profound eighteenth-century British confrontation with Locke. Tucker attacked political reformers in *Four Letters on Important National Subjects, Addressed to . . . the Earl of Shelburne* (1783).
• Pocock 1985; Shelton 1981; Young 1996.

TURGOT, ANNE ROBERT JACQUES, BARON DE L'AULNE

1727–81. French physiocrat and politician. Born in Paris, and destined for the church, he became a civil servant and member of the Paris *parlement*, 1753–61. He held a series of political offices, rising to be finance minister, 1774–6. His reforms – free trade in grain and abolition of artisanal guilds – led to his forced resignation and replacement by Necker, who had attacked him in *Sur la législation et le commerce des grains* (On Legislation and the Grain Trade). His principal physiocratic text is *Réflexions sur la formation et la distribution des richesses* (Reflections on the Formation and Distribution of Wealth, 1766). His letter to Price of 1778 in the latter's *Observations* provoked John Adams's *Defence of the Constitution of the United States*. He also wrote *Lettres sur la tolérance* (1753).
• Dakin 1939; Groenewegen 1969; Hill 1999; Manuel 1965; Meek 1970; Popkin 1987b; Weulersse 1950.

TURNBULL, GEORGE

1698–1748. Scottish moral philosopher. Born in Alloa and educated at Edinburgh and Aberdeen Universities. He taught at the latter, but for a period was a peripatetic tutor on the Continent, at Groningen and elsewhere, 1725–35. He wrote on theology, ethics, education,

and natural jurisprudence. His main work, *The Principles of Moral Philosophy* (1740), sought to derive moral science from natural philosophy. An idea of civic virtue emerges in his *Discourse upon the Nature and Origin of Moral and Civil Laws*, appended to Heineccius's *A Methodical System of Universal Law* (1741).
• Haakonssen 1996a.

TYRRELL, JAMES
1642–1718. English Whig polemicist and historian. Born in London, and educated at Oxford University, he became a barrister, 1666, and justice of the peace in Buckinghamshire. A close friend of Locke. His *Patriarcha non monarcha* (1681) was, with Algernon Sidney's *Discourses concerning Government* and Locke's *Two Treatises of Government*, one of the major ripostes to the Tories' ideological flagship, Sir Robert Filmer's *Patriarcha*. Tyrrell's book included remarks on Hobbes and revealed a debt to Pufendorf. In the 1690s he wrote a massive compendium of Whig constitutional theory, *Bibliotheca politica* (1692–4). Later he wrote a history of England (1697–1704), extolling the Ancient or Gothic Constitution. He also published *A Brief Disquisition of the Law of Nature* (1693), an English abridgement of Cumberland's *De legibus naturae* (1672).
• Gough 1976; Rudolph 2002.

ULLOA, BERNARDO DE
d. 1740. Spanish political economist. Author of *Restablecimiento de las fabricas y comercio espanol* (Re-establishment of Factories and Commerce in Spain, 1740), which aimed to reorientate the Spanish economy away from dependence on Latin American gold. The work of Ulloa and Uztáriz was taken up by later political economists, in Bernardo Danvila y Villarrosa's *Lecciones de economia civil* (1779), a stadial theory of economic history, Juan Sempere y Guarinos's *Historia del luxo* (1788), a defence of the economic role of luxury, and Vicente Alcalá Galiano's *Sobre la necesidad y justicia de los tributos* (1788), which used Adam Smith against the physiocrats.
• Herr 1958, 1989.

UZTÁRIZ (USTARIZ), GERÓNIMO DE
1670–1732. Spanish political economist. His *Theoria y práctica de comercio y de marina* (Theory and Practice of Commerce and Shipping, 1724) promoted mercantilist policies, urging state support for industry and protective tariffs against foreign imports. Beccaria cited him alongside Genovesi, Ulloa, and Montesquieu as a founder of political economy.
• Hamilton 1935; Herr 1958, 1989.

VAN ESPEN, ZEGER BERNHARD
1646–1728. Belgian conciliarist. Born in Louvain, he became a priest, 1673, and professor of canon law at the university, 1675. He soon became an adviser to princes and bishops. His ecclesiology, chiefly expressed in his *Jus ecclesiasticum universum* (Universal Ecclesiastical Right, 1700), was strongly Gallican and conciliarist. He was dismissed in 1728 and retreated to a Jansenist community. All his works were placed on the papal index of forbidden books.
• Nuttinck 1969.

VATTEL, EMERICH DE
1714–67. Swiss jurist. Born in Couvet, Neufchâtel (then Prussian). He served as Saxon minister in Berne, 1746–58, and at Dresden. His main work was *Le droit des gens* (The Law of Nations, 1758), which drew heavily on Christian Wolff's *Jus gentium* (Law of Nations,

1749). The book was widely read by the American revolutionaries and used to argue for the pre-existing statehood of the colonies.
• Bailyn 1967; Béguelin 1929; Brühlmeier 1995; Jouannet 1998; Manz 1971; Remec 1960; Whelan 1988; Zurbuchen (forthcoming).

VELESTINLIS, RIGAS

1757–98. Greek revolutionary. Born at Velestino in Thessaly, he lived his adult life mostly in Constantinople and Bucharest. In Vienna in the 1790s he absorbed Rétif de la Bretonne and other French authors. His own works sought to awaken Greek national spirit and antique purity. In *The New Political Constitution of the Inhabitants of Rumeli [Turkey in Europe], Asia Minor, the Archipelago, Moldavia, and Wallachia* he envisaged a new Byzantine empire, but having republican institutions and free of theocracy; Greek would be the unifying culture but all inhabitants would be equal citizens, the Christian, Muslim, and Jewish religions all tolerated. He plotted revolution and was executed by the Ottomans in Belgrade. An edition of his complete works has recently been published.

VERRI, PIETRO

1728–97. Italian political economist. Born in Milan, he was educated at Monzi, Milan, Rome, and Parma. He led a salon of Milanese intellectuals, edited a journal, *Il Caffè* (The Coffee House, 1764–6), and persuaded Beccaria to write *Dei delitti delle pene* (Crimes and Punishments). He served the Milanese government. He produced a series of writings on economics: *Considerazioni sul commercio* (1763); *Riflessioni sulle leggi vincolanti* (Reflections on Binding Laws, 1769); *Meditazioni sulla economia politica* (Meditations on Political Economy, 1771). His *Meditazioni sulla felicità* (1763; retitled *Discorsi sulla felicità*, Discourses . . . on the Nature of Pleasure, Pain, Happiness, and on Political Economy, 1781) and *Osservazioni sulla tortura* (Observations on Torture, 1770) share Beccaria's outlook.
• Capra 1999, 2002; Limoli 1958; Venturi 1969–90.

VERSÉ, NOEL AUBERT DE

c. 1642/5–1714. French advocate of religious toleration. Born in Le Mans. He converted to Protestantism, 1662, and studied at the academy at Sedan, but reverted to Catholicism, 1670, after being ejected from the ministry for alleged Socinianism. After the Revocation of the Edict of Nantes, he once more rejected Catholicism; but, denounced for anti-Trinitarianism and harassed in the Dutch *refuge* by Jurieu's supporters, he returned once more to Catholicism in 1690. He tried settling in Hamburg and Danzig, visited England in 1689, and returned to France, where he renounced Socinianism. His chief tolerationist works are *Le Protestant pacifique* (1684) and *Traité de la liberté de la conscience, ou de l'autorité des souverains sur la religion des peuples opposé aux maximes impies de Hobbes et de Spinosa adopteé par le sieur Jurieu* (1687), both directed against Jurieu.
• Dodge 1947; Morman 1987.

VICO, GIAMBATTISTA

1668–1744. Italian jurist and philosopher of history. Born in Naples, he was educated by the Jesuits, and studied law at Naples University, where he became professor of rhetoric, 1699–1741. After reading Grotius, he turned to jurisprudence, and wrote *Il diritto universale* (Universal Right, 1720–2). His principal work is *Scienza nuova* (begun 1723, publ. 1725, enlarged editions, 1730, 1744), its full title in English being *The Principles of a New Science of the Nature of Nations through which the Principles of a New System of Natural Law of Peoples are Discovered*. Here he explored the relationship between natural law and the social contingencies of past societies, and put forward a distinction between scientific facts and truths of human manufacture which had great influence upon later philosophers of the social sciences.

• Berlin 1976, 2000; Burke 1985; Croce 1913; Haddock 1986; Lilla 1993; Mali 1989; Pompa 1990a, 1990b; Stone 1997; Tagliacozzo 1981; Tagliacozzo and Verene 1976.

VOLNEY, CONSTANTIN FRANÇOIS DE CHASSEBOEUF, COMTE DE

1757–1820. French *idéologue* and cultural historian. Born in Craon, Anjou. After studying medicine, he travelled in the Middle East and North Africa. He wrote on geography and history. During the Revolution he was a Girondin. Arrested in 1793, he avoided the guillotine. Later he was allied to Cabanis and the *idéologues*. He became a senator, 1799, and a count, 1808. His chief works are *Les Ruines, ou, méditations sur les révolutions des empires* (1791), and *Catéchisme du citoyen français* (1793).

• Gusdorf 1978; Roussel 1988.

VOLTAIRE (FRANÇOIS MARIE AROUET)

1694–1778. French philosopher and essayist, perhaps the chief protagonist of the French Enlightenment. Born in Paris, he studied at the Jesuit college Louis-le-Grand, and quickly became prominent in Parisian society. As early as 1717 he spent a year in the Bastille because of his writing. He adopted the name Voltaire in 1718. He was in England, 1726–8, which resulted in his *Lettres philosophiques* (first published in English as *Letters on the English Nation*, 1734), which praised liberty, religious tolerance, commerce, and Lockean empiricism; it was condemned by the Paris *parlement*. He lived at Cirey with Madame du Châtelet, 1734–49, was briefly historiographer royal, 1745–7, and served at the court of Frederick II of Prussia at Potsdam, 1750–3, whose *Anti-Machiavel* he published in 1740. He moved to Geneva, 1755, then to Ferney on the Swiss border, 1759, and there remained. He waged a campaign to clear the name of the Protestant Jean Calas, wrongly executed for murdering his Catholic son, 1762, assaulting *l'infâme*, the injustices of clerical power. His vast output included poetry, plays, histories, philosophy, and polemical tracts. Among his chief works are *La Henriade* (The Epic of Henry IV, 1723), *Zadig* (1747), *Le siècle de Louis XIV* (The Age of Louis XIV, 1751), *Essai sur les moeurs* (1756), *Candide* (1759), *Traité sur la tolérance* (1763), *Dictionnaire philosophique* (1764), *L'A B C* (1768, a series of dialogues on politics), *Les droits des hommes et les usurpations des autres* (The Rights of Men and the Usurpation of Others, 1768), and *Questions sur l'Encyclopédie* (1770–2).

• Badir 1974; Besterman 1969; Brumfitt 1970; Gargett 1980; Gay 1988; Hadidi 1974; Howells *et al.* 1985; Maestro 1942; Mason 1963, 1975, 1981; Mervaud 1985; Naves 1938; O'Brien 1997; Pappas 1962; Perkins 1965; Pomeau 1995; Schilling 1950; Torrey 1930; Wade 1959, 1969.

WARBURTON, WILLIAM

1698–1779. English theologian and ecclesiologist. Born in Newark, Nottinghamshire, he was largely self-educated. Ordained, 1723, he rose to become bishop of Gloucester, 1759. Highly disputatious, he quarrelled incessantly with critics of his works. His best-known book was *The Divine Legation of Moses* (1738–41), read by Condillac, Rousseau, and Herder, which argued that the Mosaic books provide no charter for modern legislation, because the Jewish system was *sui generis* and directly secured by providence. He was a friend and editor of Pope. His key political work was *The Alliance between Church and State, or the Necessity and Equity of an Established Religion and Test Law Demonstrated from the Essence and End of Civil Society* (1736), which argued that an established national church was dictated by natural law and the civil contract.

• Clark 1985; Evans 1932; Taylor 1992; Young 1998.

WARREN, MERCY OTIS

1728–1814. American revolutionary, dramatist, poet, and historian. Born in Barnstable, Massachusetts, the sister of James Otis. Her play *The Adulateur* (1773) was an allegorical attack on the despotic rule of Governor Thomas Hutchinson (Rapatio), who is contrasted with the patriot hero, Brutus. Several more plays attacking government corruption followed. Warren was at first sceptical of the US constitution, her fear of 'aristocratic tyranny' reflected in *Observations on the New Constitution* (1788) and in plays of the 1790s. Although she upheld the new regime in her *History of the Rise, Progress, and Termination of the American Revolution* (1805), she always stressed the importance of a virtuous citizenry above the mechanics of constitutions.
• Cohen 1980; Richards 1995.

WATSON, RICHARD

1737–1816. English latitudinarian bishop. Born in Heversham, Westmorland, he was educated at Cambridge University, where he became professor of chemistry, 1764, and regius professor of divinity, 1771, as well as bishop of Llandaff, 1782. A loyal Anglican, his liberal views nonetheless shocked contemporaries and made him appear an odd bishop. He defended the American and French Revolutions, though turned against the latter after the regicide. He defended Christianity against Paine and Gibbon. His Lockean Whiggery is evident in *The Principles of the Revolution Vindicated* (1776) and *Answer to the Disquisitions on Government and Civil Liberty* (1782), against Jenyns. He argued for civil liberties for Dissenters (*A Charge Delivered to the Clergy*, 1791) and Roman Catholics (*Charge*, 1805).
• Brain 1978.

WIELAND, CHRISTOPH MARTIN

1733–1813. German philosopher, poet, dramatist, and novelist. Born in Oberholzheim near the Swabian city of Biberach. Briefly professor of philosophy at Erfurt, 1769–72; then tutor to Duke Karl August in Weimar, where he settled. Pietistic emotionalism combined with Shaftesbury's moral philosophy to produce a distinctive philosophy of sentiment. His literary career spanned six decades and he became the best-known writer in German. His translations of Horace, Lucian, and Shakespeare were admired. *Der goldene Spiegel* (The Golden Mirror, 1772) was a meditation on enlightened absolutism. In 1773 he commenced the literary journal *Der Teutsche Merkur* (The German Mercury). There he reported the French Revolution with enthusiasm, but the events of 1793 disillusioned him. He concluded that only an absolute ruler could extricate France from her troubles. Wieland was prolific and executed a collected edition of his works in forty-two volumes.
• Sahmland 1990.

WILKES, JOHN

1727–97. English radical. Born in London, he travelled in Europe, served in the militia, and entered parliament, 1757. He successfully challenged the illegality of his arrest for seditious libel for remarks in his *North Briton*, no. 45 (1763). He was subsequently outlawed and expelled from parliament for seditious and obscene libel, as publisher of the *North Briton* and the *Essay on Woman*. He was elected to parliament for Middlesex, 1768, but three times was denied his seat. Wilkes skilfully exploited this contest to highlight the threat to the right of the electorate to choose its representatives, and eventually prevailed. He became lord mayor of London, 1774. A legacy of his campaign was the Society of Supporters of the Bill of Rights. Wilkes supported the American colonists but opposed the French Revolution. His tracts include *A Letter to the Worthy Electors of the Borough of Aylesbury* (1764), *English Liberty* (1769), and *Speeches . . . in the House of Commons* (1786).
• Boulton 1963; Brewer 1976; Christie 1962; Colley 1981; Rudé 1962; Thomas 1996.

WILLIAMS, DAVID

1738–1816. Welsh radical. Born in Watford, Glamorganshire, he studied at a Dissenting academy, and was ordained a minister, 1758. He ministered and taught in Exeter and London, and founded the Royal Literary Fund, 1812. He applauded the French Revolution, was a friend of Brissot, and called for a British national constitutional convention, but was appalled at the regicide. He wrote extensively on religion, politics, and education. His main political works were *The Nature and Extent of Intellectual Liberty* (1779), *Letters on Political Liberty* (1782), *Lectures on Political Principles* (1789), *Lessons to a Young Prince* (1790), and *Observations sur la dernière constitution de la France* (1793).
• Dybikowski 1984, 1993.

WILLIAMS, ELISHA

1694–1755. American advocate of toleration. After graduating from Harvard, 1711, he became a Congregationalist clergyman. He farmed, preached, taught, and studied law. He served as rector of Yale College, 1726–39, and sat in the Connecticut General Assembly. In response to restrictions on the freedom of itinerant preachers, he wrote his *Essential Rights and Liberties of Protestants* (1744), a classic defence of toleration. It combined Lockean theory with traditions of Puritan evangelicalism and the claims of conscience, and argued against the legitimacy of any 'legal establishments' of religion.
• Bonomi 1986.

WILSON, JAMES

1742–98. American revolutionary. Born in St Andrews, Scotland, he studied at St Andrews, Glasgow, and Edinburgh Universities. He emigrated to America, 1765, and became a leading lawyer and land speculator in Philadelphia. His *Considerations on the Nature and the Extent of the Legislative Authority of the British Parliament* (1774) denied that parliament could legislate for the colonies, arguing for federated equality with Britain under a common sovereign. He was a signatory of the Declaration of Independence, 1776, and a key figure in the Constitutional Convention, 1787. He became one of the first justices of the Supreme Court, 1789, and in 1793 wrote a judgement arguing that the United States was a single sovereign nation and not a confederacy of sovereign states.
• Read 2000.

WOLFF, CHRISTIAN, FREIHERR VON

1679–1754. German philosopher, mathematician, and jurist. Born in Breslau, Silesia. A pupil of Leibniz, he was educated at Breslau, Jena, and Leipzig Universities. He became professor of mathematics, 1707, and later of philosophy at Halle, then Marburg, 1723–40, and Halle again, 1740, where he became chancellor of the university, 1743. Gradually, and against opposition from the Pietistic establishment, Wolff branched out from mathematics to physics, logic, metaphysics, and moral philosophy. He lectured in German rather than Latin. Under pressure from the orthodox, he was sacked from Halle by Frederick I, 1723, after a lecture in which he defended natural morality independent of revealed religion. His return to Halle was part of Frederick II's revenge against his father. Wolff's principal juristic works were *Vernünfftige Gedancken von dem gesellschaftlichen* (Rational Thoughts on the Social Life of Mankind, 1721), and *Institutiones juris naturae et gentium* (1750; *Grundsätze des Natur- und Volkerrechts*, 1754; Principles of the Law of Nature and Nations).
• Arndt 1989; Bachmann 1977; Bianco 1989, 1993; Biller 1983; Casula 1979; Corr 1975; Frängsmyr 1972; Goebel 1918–19; Hammerstein 1983; Hochstrasser 2000; Hunter 2001; Lach 1953; Menzel 1996; Schneiders 1983; Thomann 1964, 1968, 1970, 1977; Winiger 1992.

WOLLASTON, WILLIAM

1660–1724. Moral philosopher. Born in Coton Clanford, Staffordshire, and educated at Cambridge University, he was ordained a minister. He published treatises on ethical, philological, and religious questions, adopting an intellectualist or rationalist theory of morality. His views were close to those of Samuel Clarke, and opposed by Hume. He aimed to reduce moral judgements to truth statements: actions express propositions which may be true or false: the wrongdoer lives a lie. His chief work was *The Religion of Nature Delineated* (1724).

WOLLSTONECRAFT, MARY

1759–97. English feminist. Born in London, she pursued a career as a governess and then as an author. A member of Price's Dissenting circle, she wrote *Thoughts on the Education of Daughters* (1787), articles for the *Analytical Review*, and the novels *Mary* (1788) and *Maria: Or, The Wrongs of Woman* (1799). Her major works, *A Vindication of the Rights of Men* (1790) (a response to Burke) and *A Vindication of the Rights of Woman* (1792), which extended the radicals' arguments to the role of women, particularly in relation to morality and education. Wollstonecraft travelled in France, 1792, and bore a child by Gilbert Imlay. She published *An Historical and Moral View of the Origin and Progress of the French Revolution* (1794). Deserted by Imlay, she returned from France, 1794, and toured Scandinavia, 1795, writing *Letters Written during a Short Residence in Sweden, Norway, and Denmark* (1796). She settled in London with William Godwin, whom she married in 1797, and died giving birth to Mary Godwin (Mary Shelley). Her reputation was damaged by the frank exposure of her troubled life in Godwin's *Memoirs* (1798).
• Barker-Benfield 1989; Conniff 1999; Gunther-Canada 2001; Kelly 1992; McCrystal 1993; Sapiro 1992; Stafford 2002; Taylor 2003; Todd 2000; Tomalin 1974.

ZINCKE, GEORG HEINRICH

1692–1769. German jurist. He studied theology at Jena, then law at Erfurt and Halle, was employed as a Prussian state official and taught at Halle University. He moved to Weimar, where he fell into disfavour, was stripped of his property and imprisoned for six years. He delivered lectures on cameralism in Leipzig, 1740–5, and began publication of his *Leipziger Sammlungen von Wirtschafftlichen- Policey- Cammer- und Finantz-Sachon* (Leipzig Papers concerning Matters of Economy, Police, and Finance, 1742–67). He became curator of the Collegium Carolinium in Brunswick, 1746. Between 1742 and 1759 he published and edited a number of cameralistic compendia.
• Roscher 1874.

ZUBLY, JOHN JOACHIM

1724–81. American patriot turned loyalist. Born in St Gallen, Switzerland, he was ordained in London and emigrated to South Carolina, 1744. Moving to Georgia, 1760, he became a Presbyterian pastor in Savannah, Georgia. In a series of tracts he defended American rights, notably *The Stamp Act Repealed* (1766), *An Humble Enquiry* (1769), and *The Law of Liberty* (1775). A member of the Continental Congress, 1775, he opposed a complete break with Britain, was arrested and banished, 1776–7. He returned to Savannah under the protection of the British army, 1779. His early tracts combined the English republican tradition with a vision of America as a new Canaan, particularly in their defence of a citizenry endowed with virtuous simplicity. Later, *To the Grand Jury* (1777) and a series of articles in the *Royal George Gazette* (1790), signed 'Helvétius', expressed alarm at oppression by majoritarian democracy.
• Introduction to Zubly 1982.

Bibliography

GENERAL WORKS

Appleby, J. (1992). *Liberalism and Republicanism in the Historical Imagination* (Cambridge, MA).

Bailyn, B. (1967). *The Ideological Origins of the American Revolution* (Cambridge, MA).

Baker, K. M. (1990). *Inventing the French Revolution* (Cambridge).

Black, J., and Porter, R., eds. (1994). *The Penguin Dictionary of Eighteenth-Century History* (London).

Cassirer, E. (1951). *The Philosophy of the Enlightenment* (Princeton). 1st publ. in German in 1932.

Craig, E., ed. (1998). *The Routledge Encyclopedia of Philosophy*, 10 vols. (London).

Cranston, M. (1986). *Philosophers and Pamphleteers: Political Theorists of the Enlightenment* (Oxford).

Delon, M., ed. (1997). *Dictionnaire européen des lumières* (Paris).

Elshtain, J. B. (1981). *Public Man, Private Woman: Women in Social and Political Thought* (Princeton).

Fitzpatrick, M., Jones, P., Knellwolf, C., and McCalman, I., eds. (2004). *The Enlightenment World* (London).

Foucault, M. (1977). *Discipline and Punish: The Birth of the Prison* (London). 1st publ. in French in 1975 (Paris).

Gay, P. (1954). *The Party of Humanity: Essays in the French Enlightenment* (New York). 2nd edn 1964.

Gay, P. (1967–70). *The Enlightenment: An Interpretation*, 2 vols. (London).

Gierke, O. (1934). *Natural Law and the Theory of Society, 1500–1800*, trans. E. Barker, 2 vols. (Cambridge). 1st publ. 1913.

Gwyn, W. B. (1965). *The Meaning of the Separation of Powers* (New Orleans).

Haakonssen, K. (1996). *Natural Law and Moral Philosophy: From Grotius to the Scottish Enlightenment* (Cambridge).

Haakonssen, K., ed. (2006). *The Cambridge History of Eighteenth-Century Philosophy* (Cambridge).

Habermas, J. (1989). *The Structural Transformation of the Public Sphere*, trans. T. Burger (Cambridge, MA). 1st publ. in German in 1962.

Hampsher-Monk, I. (1992). *A History of Modern Political Thought: Hobbes to Marx* (Oxford).

Hazard, P. (1953). *The European Mind, 1680–1715* (New Haven). 1st publ. in French in 1935 (Paris).

Hazard, P. (1954). *European Thought in the Eighteenth Century* (London). 1st publ. in French in 1946 (Paris).

Hont, I., and Ignatieff, M., eds. (1983). *Wealth and Virtue: The Shaping of Political Economy in the Scottish Enlightenment* (Cambridge).

Israel, J. I. (2001). *Radical Enlightenment: Philosophy and the Making of Modernity, 1650–1750* (Oxford).

Jones, C., ed. (1988). *The Longman Companion to the French Revolution* (London).

Kafker, F. A., and Kafker, S. (1988). *The Encyclopedists as Individuals: A Biographical Dictionary of the Encyclopédie* (Oxford).

Keohane, N. O. (1980). *Philosophy and the State in France: The Renaissance to the Enlightenment* (Princeton).

Kors, A. C., ed. (2003). *Encyclopedia of the Enlightenment*, 4 vols. (Oxford).

Koselleck, R. (1988). *Critique and Crisis: Enlightenment and the Parthenogenesis of Modern Society* (Cambridge, MA). 1st publ. in German in 1959.

Kuehn, M., ed. (2004). *Dictionary of Eighteenth-Century German Philosophers* (Bristol).

Manuel, F. E. (1962). *The Prophets of Paris* (Cambridge, MA).

Melton, J. H. (2001). *The Rise of the Public in Enlightenment Europe* (Cambridge).

Miller, D., ed. (1987). *The Blackwell Encyclopedia of Political Thought* (Oxford).

Passmore, J. A. (1970). *The Perfectibility of Man* (London).

Plamenatz, J. (1992). *Man and Society*, II: *From Montesquieu to the Early Socialists*, ed. M. E. Plamenatz and R. Wokler, 2nd edn (London).

Pocock, J. G. A. (1975). *The Machiavellian Moment: Florentine Political Thought and the Atlantic Republican Tradition* (Princeton).

Pocock, J. G. A. (1985). *Virtue, Commerce and History: Essays on Political Thought and History, Chiefly in the Eighteenth Century* (Cambridge).

Pocock, J. G. A. (1999–2003). *Barbarism and Religion*, 3 vols. (Cambridge).

Pocock, J. G. A., ed. (1993). *The Varieties of British Political Thought, 1500–1800* (Cambridge).

Porter, R. (2000). *Enlightenment: Britain and the Making of the Modern World* (London).

Porter, R., and Teich, M., eds. (1981). *The Enlightenment in National Context* (Cambridge).

Rahe, P. A. (1992). *Republics Ancient and Modern*, 2 vols. (Chapel Hill).

Riley, P. (1982). *Will and Political Legitimacy: A Critical Exposition of Social Contract Theory in Hobbes, Locke, Rousseau, Kant and Hegel* (Cambridge, MA).

Rutherford, D., ed. (2004). *Dictionary of British Economists* (Bristol).

Scott, S., and Barry, R., eds. (1985). *Historical Dictionary of the French Revolution, 1789–1799*, 2 vols. (Westport, CT).

Stephen, L. (1876). *History of English Thought in the Eighteenth Century*, 2 vols. (London). Many later editions.

Van Kley, D. (1996). *The Religious Origins of the French Revolution: From Calvin to the Civil Constitution, 1560–1791* (New Haven).

Vaughan, C. E. (1925). *Studies in the History of Political Philosophy before and after Rousseau*, 2 vols. (Manchester). Revised edn, New York, 1960.

Venturi, F. (1971). *Utopia and Reform in the Enlightenment* (Cambridge). 1st publ. in Italian in 1970.

Viguerie, J. de (1995). *Histoire et dictionnaire du temps des lumières* (Paris).

Vile, M. J. C. (1967). *Constitutionalism and the Separation of Powers* (Oxford).

Wootton, D., ed. (1994). *Republicanism, Liberty, and Commercial Society, 1649–1776* (Stanford).

Yolton, J. W., ed. (1991). *The Blackwell Companion to the Enlightenment* (Oxford).

Yolton, J. W., Price, J. V., and Stephens, J., eds. (1999). *Dictionary of Eighteenth-Century British Philosophers* (Bristol).

PRIMARY SOURCES

This bibliography provides references for works quoted and cited in the text, together with a range of other works, especially those that are available in modern editions. Abbreviations are used for leading series of eighteenth-century political texts, as follows:

CTHPT   Cambridge Texts in the History of Political Thought
H   Hackett (Indianapolis)
LF   Liberty Fund (Indianapolis)
P   Penguin (London)
P&C   Pickering and Chatto (London)
T   Thoemmes (Bristol)
VF   Voltaire Foundation (Oxford)

Achenwall, Gottfried, and Pütter, Johann Stephan (1750). *Elementa iuris naturae* (Göttingen). Latin text with German trans. in *Anfangsgründe des Naturrechts*, ed. and trans. J. Schröder, 1995 (Frankfurt).

Acherley, Roger (1727). *The Britannic Constitution, Or, the Fundamental Form of Government in Britain* (London).

Adams, John (1797). *A Defence of the Constitutions of Government of the United States of America*, 3 vols. (Philadelphia). 1st publ. 1787–8.

Adams, John (1851–6). *Works*, 10 vols. (Boston, MA).

Adams, John (1961). *Diary and Autobiography of John Adams*, ed. L. H. Butterfield *et al.*, 4 vols. (Cambridge, MA).

Adams, John (1979). *Thoughts on Government*, in *Papers of John Adams*, IV, ed. R. J. Taylor (Cambridge, MA). 1st publ. 1776.

Adams, John (1998). 'The Earl of Clarendon to William Pym', in *Declaring Rights*, ed. J. N. Rakove (Boston, MA). 1st publ. 1766.

Adams, John (2000). *The Revolutionary Writings*, ed. C. B. Thompson (Indianapolis: LF).

Adams, John (2003). *The Political Writings*, ed. G. A. Peek (Indianapolis: H).

Adams, Samuel (1904–8). *The Writings of Samuel Adams*, ed. H. A. Cushing, 2 vols. (New York).

Addison, Joseph (1713). *Cato: A Tragedy* (London).

Addison, Joseph (1979). *The Freeholder*, ed. J. Leheny (Oxford).

Addison, Joseph, and Steele, Richard (1965). *The Spectator*, ed. D. F. Bond, 5 vols. (Oxford). 1st publ. 1711–12, 1714.

Alembert, Jean Le Rond d' (1821–2). *Oeuvres*, 5 vols. (Paris). Repr. 1967.

Alembert, Jean Le Rond d' (1963). *Preliminary Discourse to the Encyclopedia of Diderot*, ed. R. Schwab and W. Rex (Indianapolis). 1st publ. 1751. Republ. Chicago, 1995.

Alembert, Jean Le Rond d'. *See also* Diderot.

Amo, Anton Wilhelm (1968). *Antonius Guilielmus Amo Afer of Axim in Ghana: Translation of his Works*, ed. D. Siegmund-Schultze, trans. L. A. Jones and W. E. Abraham (Halle).

Amthor, Christoph Heinrich ('Anastasio Sincerus') (1717). *Project der Oeconomie in Form einer Wissenschaft*, 2nd edn (Frankfurt).

Anon. (1690). *Political Aphorisms* (London). Repr. in Goldie 1999, I.

Anon. (1696). *Some Considerations about the Raising of Coin* (London).

Anon. (1709). *Vox populi, vox dei* (London).

Anon. (1748). *Thérèse philosophe* (Paris).

Anon. (1994). *Trattato dei tre impostori* (c. 1706), ed. S. Berti, intro. R. H. Popkin (Turin).

Anti-Jacobin (1798). *The Anti-Jacobin Review* (London).

Antraigues, Emmanuel Louis de Launay, comte d' (1791). *Dénonciation aux François catholiques, des moyens employés par l'Assemblée nationale, pour détruire en France, la religion catholique* (London).

Argenson, René Louis de Voyer, marquis d', and Saint-Pierre, Charles de (1737), *Autre traité des principaux intérêts de la France* . . . , ed. J. M. Gallanar, <http://home.ptd.net/~gallanar/d'argenson/argenson.htm>

Argenson, René Louis de Voyer, marquis d' (1764). *Considérations sur le gouvernement ancien et présent de la France* (Amsterdam).

Aristotle (1996). *The Politics*, ed. S. Everson, trans. J. Barnes (Cambridge: CTHPT).

Arnall, William (1727). *Clodius and Cicero* (London).

Arnold, Gottfried (1699–1700). *Unparteiische Kirchen- und Ketzerhistorie, von Anfang des Neuen Testaments biss auf des Jahr Christi 1688*, 2 vols. (Frankfurt).

Astell, Mary (1704). *Moderation Truly Stated* (London).

Astell, Mary (1706). *Some Reflections upon Marriage*, 3rd edn (London). 1st publ. 1700. Repr. in Astell 1996; extract in Goldie 1999, II.

Astell, Mary (1986). *The First English Feminist: 'Reflections upon Marriage' and Other Writings*, ed. B. Hill (Aldershot).

Astell, Mary (1996). *Political Writings*, ed. P. Springborg (Cambridge: CTHPT).

Astell, Mary (1997). *A Serious Proposal to the Ladies*, ed. P. Springborg (London: P&C). 1st publ. 1694 and 1697.

Atkyns, Robert (1734). *The Power, Jurisdiction and Privilege of Parliament*, in *Parliamentary and Political Tracts* (London). 1st publ. 1689.

Atterbury, Francis (1697). *A Letter to a Convocation Man* (London).

Atterbury, Francis (1700). *The Rights, Powers, and Privileges of an English Convocation* (London).

Atwood, William (1690). *The Fundamental Constitution of the English Government* (London). Extract in Goldie 1999, I.

Atwood, William (1698). *The History and Reasons of the Dependency of Ireland upon the Imperial Crown of the Kingdom of England* (London).

Atwood, William (1704). *The Superiority and Direct Dominion of the Imperial Crown of England over the Crown and Kingdom of Scotland* (London).

Augustine, St (1968). *The Free Choice of the Will*, in *Selections*, trans. R. P. Russell (Washington, DC).

Aulard, François Alphonse, ed. (1889). *Recueil des Actes des Comités du Salut public*, completed by M. Bouloiseau, 28 vols. (Paris).

Austin, Benjamin (1786). *Observations on the Pernicious Practice of the Law* (Boston, MA).

Babeuf, François Noël (Gracchus) (1935). *Pages choisies de Babeuf*, ed. M. Dommanget (Paris).

Babeuf, François Noël (Gracchus) (1961). *Correspondance de Babeuf avec l'Académie d'Arras*, ed. M. Reinhard (Paris).

Babeuf, François Noël (Gracchus) (1977). *Oeuvres*, ed. V. Saline, A. Saitta, and A. Soboul (Paris).

Backus, Isaac (1968). *Isaac Backus on Church, State, and Calvinism: Pamphlets, 1754–1789*, ed. W. G. McLoughlin (Cambridge, MA).

Bagehot, Walter (2001). *The English Constitution*, ed. P. Smith (Cambridge: CTHPT).

Bahr, Erhard, ed. (1974). *Was ist Aufklärung? Thesen und Definitionen* (Stuttgart).

Bailyn, Bernard, ed. (1965). *Pamphlets of the American Revolution* (Cambridge, MA).

Baker, K. M., ed. (1987a). *The Old Regime and the French Revolution* (Chicago).

Barbeyrac, Jean (1709). *Traité du jeu*, 2 vols. (Amsterdam).

Barbeyrac, Jean (1716). *Discours sur la permission des loix* (Amsterdam).

Barbeyrac, Jean (1717). *Discours sur le bénéfice des loix* (Amsterdam).

Barbeyrac, Jean (1718). 'Judgment of an Anonymous Writer on the Original of this Abridgment', in Pufendorf 2003.

Barbeyrac, Jean (1728). *Traité de la morale des pères de l'Eglise* (Amsterdam).

Barbeyrac, Jean (1749). 'An Historical and Critical Account of the Science of Morality', in Pufendorf 1749, pp. 1–75.

Barbeyrac, Jean (1996). *Ecrits de droit et de morale*, ed. S. Goyard-Fabre (Paris).

Barbeyrac, Jean (2003). 'Two Discourses and a Commentary', in Pufendorf 2003.

Barlow, Joel (1792). *Advice to the Privileged Orders in the Several States of Europe* (London).

Barlow, Joel (1795). *Advice to the Privileged Orders in the Several States of Europe, Part II* (London).

Barlow, Joel (1970). *Works*, intro. W. K. Bottorff and A. L. Ford, 2 vols. (Gainesville, FL).

Barnave, Antoine (1971). *Power, Property, and History: Barnave's Introduction to the French Revolution and Other Writings*, trans. E. Chill (New York).

Barnave, Antoine (1988). *De la Révolution et de la Constitution*, ed. P. Gueniffey (Grenoble). 1st publ. 1792.

Baron, Richard, ed. (1768). *The Pillars of Priestcraft and Orthodoxy Shaken*, 4 vols. (London). 1st publ. 1752.

Barrington, Daines (1769). *Observations on the More Ancient Statutes, from Magna Charta to the Twenty-first of James I Cap. XXVII* (London). 1st publ. 1766.

Barrington, John Shute (1704–5). *The Rights of Protestant Dissenters*, 2 vols. (London).

Barrington, John Shute (1714). *The Revolution and Anti-Revolution Principles Stated and Compared* (London).

Barruel, Augustin (1790). *Question nationale sur l'autorité et sur les droits du peuple dans le gouvernement* (Paris).

Basnage, Jacques (1715). *Histoire des juifs* (Amsterdam). 1st publ. 1706.

Baudeau, Nicolas (1763). *Idées d'un citoyen sur l'administration des finances du roi* (Amsterdam).

Baumeister, Friedrich Christian (1739). *Vita, fata et scripta Christiani Wolffii philosophi* (Leipzig).

Bayle, Pierre (1686). *Commentaire philosophique sur ces paroles de Jésus Christ 'Contrains-les d'entrer'* (Amsterdam).

Bayle, Pierre (1697). *Dictionnaire historique et critique* (Amsterdam).

Bayle, Pierre (1730). *Dictionnaire historique et critique*, 4th edn, 4 vols. (Amsterdam).

Bayle, Pierre (1737). *Oeuvres diverses*, 4 vols. (The Hague). 1st publ. 1723–31.

Bayle, Pierre (1965). *Historical and Critical Dictionary: Selections*, ed. R. H. Popkin and C. Brush (Indianapolis: H). 1st publ. 1695–7.

Bayle, Pierre (1987). *Pierre Bayle's Philosophical Commentary*, trans. A. G. Tannenbaum (New York).

Bayle, Pierre (2000a). *Political Writings*, ed. S. L. Jenkinson (Cambridge: CTHPT).

Bayle, Pierre (2000b). *Various Thoughts on the Occasion of a Comet*, trans. R. C. Bartlett (Albany).

Bayle, Pierre (2001–). *Correspondence*, ed. E. Labrousse *et al.* (Oxford: VF).

Bayle, Pierre (2005). *A Philosophical Commentary on the Words of Jesus Christ, 'Compel Them to Come In'*, ed. C. Kukathas and J. Kilcullen (Indianapolis: LF).

Beccaria, Cesare (1766). *Traité des délits et des peines*, trans. André Morellet (Paris). 1st publ. 1764.

Beccaria, Cesare (1767). *An Essay on Crimes and Punishments* (London).

Beccaria, Cesare (1958). *Opere*, ed. S. Romagnoli, 2 vols. (Florence).

Beccaria, Cesare (1965). *Dei delitti e delle pene*, ed. F. Venturi (Turin).

Beccaria, Cesare (1984). *Dei delitti e delle pene*, ed. G. Francioni (Milan).

Beccaria, Cesare (1984–). *Edizione nazionale delle opera di Cesare Beccaria*, ed. L. Firpo, 8 vols. (Milan).

Beccaria, Cesare (1986). *On Crimes and Punishments*, ed. D. Young (Indianapolis: H).

Beccaria, Cesare (1995). *On Crimes and Punishments and Other Writings*, ed. R. Bellamy, trans. R. Davies (Cambridge: CTHPT).

Becher, Johann Joachim (1688). *Politische Discurs, von den eigentlichen Ursachen deß Auff- und Abnehmens der Stadte / Länder unde Republicken*, 3rd edn (Frankfurt). 1st publ. 1668.

Beck, Christian August von (1964). *Recht und Verfassung des Reiches in der Zeit Maria Theresias. Die Vorträge zum Unterricht des Erzherzogs Joseph im Natur- und Völkerrecht sowie im deutschen Staats- und Lehnrecht*, ed. H. Conrad (Cologne).

Beck, Jacob Sigismund (1798). *Commentar über Kants Metaphysik der Sitten* (Halle). Repr. Brussels, 1970.

Beiser, Frederick, ed. (1996a). *The Early Political Writings of the German Romantics* (Cambridge: CTHPT).

Bentham, Jeremy (1789). *An Introduction to the Principles of Morals and Legislation* (London).

Bentham, Jeremy (1802). *Traité de législation, civile et pénale*, ed. E. Dumont, 3 vols. (Paris).

Bentham, Jeremy (1811). *Théorie des peines et des récompenses*, ed. E. Dumont, 2 vols. (London).

Bentham, Jeremy (1830). *The Rationale of Punishment* (London).

Bentham, Jeremy (1838–43). *Works*, ed. J. Bowring, 11 vols. (Edinburgh).

Bentham, Jeremy (1843). *A Fragment on Government*, in Bentham 1838–43, II (Edinburgh).

Bentham, Jeremy (1968). *The Correspondence*, II (1777–80), ed. T. L. S. Sprigge (Collected Works, London).

Bentham, Jeremy (1968–). *Collected Works*, general eds. J. H. Burns, J. R. Dinwiddy, F. Rosen and P. Schofield (London).

Bentham, Jeremy (1977). *A Fragment on Government*, in *A Comment on the Commentaries and A Fragment on Government*, ed. J. H. Burns and H. L. A. Hart (Collected Works, London). 1st publ. 1776.

Bentham, Jeremy (1981). *The Correspondence*, IV (1788–93), ed. A. T. Milne (Collected Works, London).

Bentham, Jeremy (1988). *A Fragment on Government*, ed. J. H. Burns and H. L. A. Hart, intro. R. Harrison (Cambridge: CTHPT).

Bentham, Jeremy (1993). *Official Aptitude Maximized; Expense Minimized*, ed. P. Schofield (Collected Works, Oxford).

Bentham, Jeremy (1996). *An Introduction to the Principles of Morals and Legislation*, ed. J. H. Burns and H. L. A. Hart, intro. F. Rosen (Oxford).

Bentham, Jeremy (2001). *Writings on the Poor Laws*, I, ed. M. Quinn (Collected Works, Oxford).

Bentham, Jeremy (2002). *Rights, Representation, and Reform: Nonsense upon Stilts and Other Writings on the French Revolution*, ed. P. Schofield, C. Pease-Watkin, and C. Blamires (Collected Works, Oxford).

Bergk, Johann Adam (1796). *Untersuchungen aus dem Natur-, Staats- und Völkerrechte mit einer Kritik der neuesten Konstitution der französischen Republik* (Leipzig).

Bergk, Johann Adam (1797). *Briefe über Immanuel Kants metaphysische Anfangsgründe der Rechtslehre* (Leipzig). Repr. Brussels, 1968.

Berkeley, George (1712). *Passive Obedience* (London). Repr. in Goldie 1999, II.

Berkeley, George (1948–57). *Works*, ed. A. A. Luce and T. E. Jessop, 9 vols. (London).

Berkeley, George (1950). *Alciphron: Or the Minute Philosopher*, in Berkeley 1948–57, III, ed. T. E. Jessop (London). 1st publ. 1732.

Berkeley, George (1956). 'Letter to Sir John Percival, 26 March 1742', in *Letters*, in Berkeley 1948–57, VIII, ed. A. A. Luce (Edinburgh).

Berkeley, George (1970). *The Querist*, in *Bishop Berkeley's Querist in Historical Perspective*, ed. J. Johnston (Dundalk).

Berkeley, George (1988). *Principles of Human Knowledge, and Three Dialogues between Hylas and Philonous*, ed. R. Woolhouse (London: P).

Bernasconi, Robert, ed. (2001). *Concepts of Race in the Eighteenth Century*, 8 vols. (Bristol: T).

Berruyer, Isaac Joseph (1728–55). *Histoire du peuple de Dieu, depuis son origine jusqu'à la naissance du Messie*, 12 vols. (Paris).

Bielfeld, Jacob Friedrich von (1760). *Institutions politiques*, 4 vols. (Paris).

Bielfeld, Jacob Friedrich von (1764). *Lehrbegriff der Staatskunst*, 2nd edn (Breslau).

Billaud-Varenne, Jacques Nicolas (1793). *Discours . . . sur des mesures de salut public indiqués par les circonstances, prononcé a la Société des amis de la liberté et d'égalité dans la séance de 9 juin 1793* (Paris).

Blackall, Offspring (1705). *The Subject's Duty* (London).

Blackburne, Francis (1766). *The Confessional, Or, A Full and Free Inquiry into the Right, Utility, Edification, and Success of Establishing Systematical Confessions of Faith and Doctrine in Protestant Churches* (London).

Blackburne, Francis (1780). *Memoirs of Thomas Hollis*, 2 vols. (London).

Blackstone, William (1979). *Commentaries on the Laws of England*, 4 vols. (Oxford). Facs. repr. Chicago, 1979. 1st publ. 1765–9.

Blake, William (1791a). *The Marriage of Heaven and Hell* (Lambeth).

Blake, William (1791b). *The French Revolution: A Poem in Seven Books* (London).

Blake, William (1927). *Poetry and Prose of William Blake*, ed. G. Keynes (London).

Blake, William (1966). *The French Revolution: A Poem*, in *Complete Writings*, ed. G. Keynes (Oxford). 1st publ. 1791.

Bland, Richard (1766). *An Enquiry into the Rights of the British Colonies* (Williamsburg). Repr. in Goldie 1999, III.

Blount, Charles (1683). *Miracles, no Violations of the Laws of Nature* (London).

Boëthius, Daniel (1799). *Försök till en lärobok uti natur-rätten* (Uppsala).

Bohun, Edmund (1689). *The History of the Desertion* (London).

Boisguilbert, Pierre de (1695). *Le Détail de la France*. Republ. as *Testament politique* under the name of Sébastien de Prestre de Vauban, Maréchal de France (Paris, 1707).

Bolingbroke, Henry St John, Viscount (1743). *Remarks on the History of England* (London). Written 1730–1.

Bolingbroke, Henry St John, Viscount (1749). *The Idea of a Patriot King* (London). Written 1739.

Bolingbroke, Henry St John, Viscount (1752). *Letters on the Study and Use of History* (London). Written 1738.

Bolingbroke, Henry St John, Viscount (1754). *Works*, ed. D. Mallet, 5 vols. (London).

Bolingbroke, Henry St John, Viscount (1844). *Dissertation on Parties*, in *Works*, 4 vols. (London). 1st publ. 1733–4.

Bolingbroke, Henry St John, Viscount (1972). *Historical Writings*, ed. I. Kramnick (Chicago).

Bolingbroke, Henry St John, Viscount (1982). *Contributions to The Craftsman*, ed. S. Varey (Oxford).

Bolingbroke, Henry St John, Viscount (1997a). *Bolingbroke's Political Writings: The Conservative Enlightenment*, ed. B. Cottret (London).

Bolingbroke, Henry St John, Viscount (1997b). *Political Writings*, ed. D. Armitage (Cambridge: CTHPT).

793

Bonald, Louis de (1796). *Théorie du pouvoir politique et religieux dans la société civile* (Paris).

Bonald, Louis de (1800). *Essai analytique sur les lois naturelles de l'ordre social* (Paris).

Bonnet, Charles (1770). *Contemplation de la nature* (Amsterdam). 1st publ. 1764–5.

Bonola, Rocco (1789). *La lega della teologia moderna colla filosofia a' danni della chiesa di Gesù Cristo* (Rome). Spanish trans. (1798): *La liga de la teología con la filosofia en daño de la iglesia de Jesucristo* (Madrid).

Bossuet, Jacques Bénigne (1815). *Cinquième avertissement aux protestants*, in *Oeuvres complètes*, IV (Versailles).

Bossuet, Jacques Bénigne (1961). *Discours sur l'histoire universelle*, in *Oeuvres*, ed. Abbé Velat and Y. Champailler (Paris) (at pp. 657–1027). 1st publ. 1681.

Bossuet, Jacques Bénigne (1967). *Politique tirée des propres paroles de l'écriture sainte*, ed. J. Le Brun (Geneva). 1st publ. 1679.

Bossuet, Jacques Bénigne (1990). *Politics Drawn from the Very Words of Holy Scripture*, ed. P. Riley (Cambridge: CTHPT).

Boucher, Jonathan (1797). *A View of the Causes and Consequences of the American Revolution* (London). Extract in Goldie 1999, III.

Boulainvilliers, Henri, comte de (1727). *Histoire de l'ancien gouvernement de France et de l'Etat de la France* (The Hague).

Boulainvilliers, Henri, comte de (1727). *Etat de la France*, 3 vols. (London).

Boulainvilliers, Henri, comte de (1732). *Essai sur la noblesse de France* (Amsterdam).

Boulanger, Nicolas Antoine (1761). *Recherches sur l'origine du despotisme oriental* (Geneva). Publ. by d'Holbach.

Bowles, John (1798). *Thoughts on the Origin and Formation of Political Constitutions*, in *The Retrospect* (London). Repr. in Goldie 1999, IV.

Bowring, John (1865). *On the Remunerative Prison Labour, as an Instrument for Promoting the Reformation and Diminishing the Cost of Offenders* (Exeter and London).

Brissot (de Warville), Jacques Pierre (1791). *Discours sur l'utilité des sociétés patriotiques et populaires . . . prononcé à la société des amis de la Constitution séante aux Jacobins . . . le 28 septembre 1791* (Paris).

Brissot (de Warville), Jacques Pierre (1792). *De la vérité, ou méditations sur les moyens de parvenir à la vérité dans toutes les connoissances humaines* (Paris). 1st publ. 1782.

Brooke, Henry (1739). *Gustavus Vasa, Deliverer of his Country* (Dublin).

Brooke, Henry (1753). *The Spirit of Party* (Dublin).

Brooke, Henry (1759). *The Interests of Ireland* (Dublin).

Brooke, Henry (2000). *The Tryal of the Roman Catholicks*, ed. N. Lee (Bristol: T). 1st publ. 1761.

Brothers, Richard (1794). *A Revealed Knowledge: Of the Prophecies and Times* (London).

Brown, John (1757). *An Estimate of the Manners and Principles of the Times* (London).

Brown, John (1765). *Thoughts on Civil Liberty: On Licentiousness and Faction* (London).

Brown, John (1969). *An Estimate of the Manners and Principles of the Times*, ed. D. D. Eddy (New York).

Brucker, Johann Jakob (1742–4, 1766). *Historia critica philosophiae*, 6 vols. (Leipzig).

Burgh, James (1761). *The Art of Speaking* (London).

Burgh, James (1774–5). *Political Disquisitions*, 3 vols. (London).

Burke, Edmund (1756). *A Vindication of Natural Society* (London). Repr. in Burke 1993.

Burke, Edmund (1770). *Thoughts on the Cause of the Present Discontents* (London). Repr. in Burke 1993.

Burke, Edmund (1780). *A Speech . . . in Bristol, Previous to the Late Election* (London).

Burke, Edmund (1791a). *An Appeal from the New to the Old Whigs* (London).

Burke, Edmund (1971b). *Thoughts on French Affairs* (London).

Burke, Edmund (1796). *Two Letters . . . On the Proposals for Peace with the Regicide Directory of France* (London).
Burke, Edmund (1884). *Works*, 12 vols. (Boston, MA).
Burke, Edmund (1886). *Works*, I (London).
Burke, Edmund (1888). *Works*, III (London).
Burke, Edmund (1889). *Works*, V (London).
Burke, Edmund (1969). *Reflections on the Revolution in France,* ed. C. C. O'Brien (London: P). 1st publ. 1790.
Burke, Edmund (1982). *A Vindication of Natural Society,* ed. F. N. Pagano (Indianapolis: LF).
Burke, Edmund (1987). *Reflections on the Revolution in France,* ed. J. G. A. Pocock (Indianapolis: H).
Burke, Edmund (1989). *Writings and Speeches of Edmund Burke,* VIII, ed. L. G. Mitchell (Oxford).
Burke, Edmund (1991). *Writings and Speeches of Edmund Burke,* IX, ed. R. B. McDowell (Oxford).
Burke, Edmund (1992). *Further Reflections on the Revolution in France,* ed. D. E. Ritchie (Indianapolis: LF).
Burke, Edmund (1993). *Pre-Revolutionary Writings,* ed. I. Harris (Cambridge: CTHPT).
Burke, Edmund (1998). *A Philosophical Enquiry into the Origin of our Ideas of the Sublime and Beautiful, and Other Pre-Revolutionary Writings,* ed. D. Womersley (London: P).
Burke, Edmund (1999). *Select Works,* 3 vols. (Indianapolis: LF).
Burke, Edmund (2001). *Reflections on the Revolution in France,* ed. J. C. D. Clark (Stanford).
Burlamaqui, Jean Jacques (1747). *Principes du droit naturel* (Geneva).
Burlamaqui, Jean Jacques (1751). *Principes du droit politique* (Amsterdam).
Burlamaqui, Jean Jacques (1766–8). *Principes du droit de la nature et des gens,* 8 vols. (Yverdon).
Burlamaqui, Jean Jacques (1775). *Elémens du droit naturel* (Lausanne).
Burlamaqui, Jean Jacques (2006). *The Principles of Natural and Politic Law,* ed. P. Korkman (Indianapolis: LF).
Butel-Dumont, Georges Marie (1771). 'Dissertation sur le sens primordial du mot luxe', in *Théorie de Luxe: ou traité dans lequel on entreprend d'établir que le luxe est un ressort non-seulement utile, mais même indispensablement nécessaire à la prospérité des états,* 2 vols. (Paris), II, pp. 177–201.
Cabanis, Pierre Jean (1802). *Rapports du physique et du moral de l'homme* (Paris).
Cabanis, Pierre Jean (1956). *Oeuvres philosophiques,* ed. J. Cazeneuve and C. Lehec (Paris).
Cabanis, Pierre Jean (1981). *On the Relation between the Physical and Moral Aspects of Man,* ed. G. Mora (Baltimore).
Calamy, Edmund (1704). *A Defence of Moderate Nonconformity, Part II* (London).
Call, Daniel, ed. (1833). *Reports of Cases Argued and Decided in the Court of Appeals of Virginia,* 4 vols. (Richmond, VA).
Cambacérès, Jean Jacques Régis de (1798). 'Discours sur la science sociale', in *Mémoires de l'Institut national: Sciences morales et politiques,* III (Paris).
Campomanes, Pedro Rodríguez (1774). *Discurso sobre el fomento de la industria popular* (Madrid).
Cantillon, Richard (1755). *Essai sur la nature du commerce en général* (Paris). Eng. trans.: *The Analysis of Trade, Commerce, Coin, Bullion, Banks, and Foreign Exchanges* (London, 1759).
Carmichael, Gershom (1699). *Theses philosophicae* (Glasgow).
Carmichael, Gershom (1724). *S. Puffendorfii De Officio hominis et civis, juxta legem naturalem. Supplementis et observationibus in academicae juventutis usum auxit et illustravit Gerschomus Carmichael* (Edinburgh). 1st publ. 1718.

Carmichael, Gershom (1729). *Synopsis theologiae naturalis, sive notitiae, de existentia, attributis et operationibus, summi numinis, ex ipsa rerum natura haustae, studiosae juventutis usibus accommodata* (Edinburgh).

Carmichael, Gershom (2002). *Natural Rights on the Threshold of the Scottish Enlightenment: The Writings of Gershom Carmichael*, ed. J. Moore and M. Silverthorne (Indianapolis: LF).

Carte, Thomas (1747–55). *A General History of England*, 4 vols. (London).

Cartwright, John (1776). *Take your Choice!* (London).

Cartwright, John (1782). *Give us our Rights!* (London).

Cary, John (1698). *An Answer to Mr Molyneux* (London).

Casaux, Charles, marquis de (1776). *Considérations sur les principes politiques de mon siècle* (London).

Casaux, Charles, marquis de (1785). *Considérations sur quelques parties de méchanisme des sociétés* (London).

Casaux, Charles, marquis de (1786). *Thoughts on the Mechanism of Societies* (London).

Catherine the Great, Empress (1977). *Catherine the Great's Instruction (Nakaz) to the Legislative Commission, 1767*, ed. P. Dukes (Newtonville, MA).

Chamberlayne, Edward (1700). *Angliae notitia, Or, The Present State of England* (London). 1st publ. 1669.

Chambers, Robert (1986). *A Course of Lectures on the English Law*, ed. T. M. Curley, 2 vols. (Oxford). Lectures delivered 1767–75.

Charrière, Isabelle de (Belle van Zuylen) (1784). *Lettres neuchâteloises* (Amsterdam).

Chastellux, François Jean de (1772). *De la félicité publique* (Amsterdam).

Chateaubriand, François René de (1797). *Essai historique, politique et moral sur les révolutions anciennes et modernes* (London).

Chateaubriand, François René de (1802). *Génie du christianisme* (Paris).

Chaupy, Bertrand Capmartin de (1756). *Réflexions d'un avocat sur les remonstrances du Parlement, du 27 novembre 1755, au sujet du Grand Conseil* (London).

Claeys, Gregory, ed. (1994a). *Utopias of the British Enlightenment* (Cambridge: CTHPT).

Claeys, Gregory, ed. (1995). *Political Writings of the 1790s*, 8 vols. (London: P&C).

Claeys, Gregory, ed. (1997). *Modern British Utopias, 1700–1850*, 8 vols. (London: P&C).

Cloots, Anacharsis (1980). *Oeuvres*, 7 vols. (Munich).

Cobbett, William (1820). *A Grammar of the English Language* (London).

Cocceji, Heinrich von (1719). *Prodromus juris gentium* (Frankfurt).

Cocceji, Heinrich von (1744–52). *Grotius illustratus, seu commentarii ad Hugonis Grotii De jure belli et pacis*, 4 vols. (Bratislava).

Cocceji, Samuel von (1748). *Introductio ad Henrici L. B. de Cocceji . . . Grotium Illustratum* (Halle).

Cocks, Sir Richard (1996). *The Parliamentary Diary of Sir Richard Cocks, 1698–1702*, ed. D. W. Hayton (Oxford).

Coler [Colerus], Johannes (1604). *Calendarium perpetuum, et Libri oeconomici* (Wittenberg).

Collins, Anthony (1713). *A Discourse of Free-thinking* (London). Facs. repr. New York, 1976.

Condillac, Etienne Bonnot de (1746). *Essai sur l'origine des connoissances humaines* (Amsterdam).

Condillac, Etienne Bonnot de (1749). *Traité des systèmes* (The Hague).

Condillac, Etienne Bonnot de (1754). *Traité des sensations*, 2 vols. (Paris).

Condillac, Etienne Bonnot de (1775). *Cours d'études pour l'instruction du Prince de Parme* (Parma).

Condillac, Etienne Bonnot de (1776). *Le Commerce et le gouvernement considérés relativement l'un à l'autre* (Amsterdam).

Condillac, Etienne Bonnot de (1947–9). *Oeuvres philosophiques*, ed. G. le Roy, 3 vols. (Paris).

Condillac, Etienne Bonnot de (1971). *Essay on the Origin of Human Knowledge*, trans. T. Nugent (Gainsville, FL).

Condillac, Etienne Bonnot de (1973). *Essai su l'origine des connoissances humaines*, ed. J. Derrida (Auvers-sur-Oise).

Condillac, Etienne Bonnot de (1982). *Philosophical Writings*, trans. F. Philip (Hillsdale, NJ).

Condillac, Etienne Bonnot de (1997). *Commerce and Government Considered in their Mutual Relationship*, ed. S. Eltis and W. Eltis (Cheltenham).

Condillac, Etienne Bonnot de (2001). *Essay on the Origin of Human Knowledge*, ed. H. Aarsleff (Cambridge).

Condorcet, Jean Antoine, marquis de (1786). *Influence de la Révolution de l'Amerique sur l'Europe* (Amsterdam).

Condorcet, Jean Antoine, marquis de (1792). *Rapport et projet de décret sur l'organisation générale de l'instruction publique* (Paris).

Condorcet, Jean Antoine, marquis de (1795). *Esquisse d'un tableau historique des progrès de l'esprit humain* (Paris).

Condorcet, Jean Antoine, marquis de (1847–9). *Oeuvres*, ed. A. Condorcet-O'Connor and M. F. Arago, 12 vols. (Paris). Repr. 1968.

Condorcet, Jean Antoine, marquis de (1955). *Sketch for a Historical Picture of the Progress of the Human Mind*, trans. J. Barraclough, ed. S. Hampshire (London).

Condorcet, Jean Antoine, marquis de (1976). *Selected Writings*, ed. K. M. Baker (Indianapolis: H).

Condorcet, Jean Antoine, marquis de (1988). *Esquisse d'un tableau historique des progrès de l'esprit humain,* ed. A. Pons (Paris).

Condorcet, Jean Antoine, marquis de (1999). *Selected Writings* (Indianapolis: H).

Conrad, Hermann, ed. (1964). *Recht und Verfassung des Reichs in der Zeit Maria Theresias: Die Vorträge zum Unterricht des Erzherzogs Joseph im Natur- und Völkerrecht sowie im Deutschen Staats- und Lehnsrecht* (Cologne).

Cook, John (1794). *Monarchy no Creature of God's Making*, preface by Daniel Eaton (London). 1st publ. 1651.

Costa, Uriel da (1993). *Examination of Pharasaic Traditions*, ed. H. P. Saloman (Leiden).

Court de Gébelin (1773–82). *Monde primitif, analysé et comparé avec le monde moderne*, 9 vols. (Paris).

Coxe, Tench (1787). *An Enquiry into the Principles on which a Commercial System for the United States of America should be Founded* (Philadelphia).

Coxe, Tench (1788). *An Examination of the Constitution for the United States of America* (Philadelphia).

Coxe, Tench (1792). *Reflexions on the State of the Union* (Philadelphia).

Crèvecoeur, J. Hector St John de (1981). *Letters from an American Farmer*, ed. A. E. Stone (London: P). 1st publ. 1782.

Cudworth, Ralph (1678). *The True Intellectual System of the Universe* (London). Repr. Stuttgart-Bad Cannstatt, 1964.

Cumberland, Richard (1672). *De legibus naturae* (London).

Cumberland, Richard (2005). *A Treatise of the Laws of Nature*, ed. J. Parkin (Indianapolis: LF). 1st publ. 1727, translating the Latin 1st edn of 1672.

Custodi, Pietro, ed. (1803–16). *Scrittori classici italiani di economia politica*, 50 vols. (Milan).

Dalberg, Karl Theodor von (1787). *The Connection between Moral and Political Philosophy* (London).

Dalrymple, John (1757). *An Essay towards a General History of Feudal Property in Great Britain* (London).

Daries, Joachim Georg (1740). *Institutiones jurisprudentiae universalis* (Jena).

Daries, Joachim Georg (1762–3). *Discours über sein Natur- und Völkerrecht*, 3 vols. (Jena).

Davenant, Charles (1699). *An Essay upon the Probable Methods of Making a People Gainers in the Ballance of Trade* (London).

Davenant, Charles (1701a). *Essays upon the Balance of Power; the Right of Making War, Peace, and Alliances; Universal Monarchy* (London).

Davenant, Charles (1701b). *The True Picture of a Modern Whig* (London).

Davis, Michael T. *et al.*, eds. (2002). *London Corresponding Society, 1792–1799*, 6 vols. (London: P&C).

Defoe, Daniel (1698). *An Argument Shewing that a Standing Army, with Consent of Parliament, is not Inconsistent with a Free Government* (London).

Defoe, Daniel (1701a). *The True-Born Englishman* (London).

Defoe, Daniel (1701b). *Mr S – r. The Enclosed Memorial . . . on the Behalf of Many Thousands of the Good People of England* (London). I.e. *'Legion's Memorial'*.

Defoe, Daniel (1701c). *The Original Power of the Collective Body of the People of England* (London). Repr. in Goldie 1999, I.

Defoe, Daniel (1965). *Selected Writings of Daniel Defoe*, ed. J. T. Boulton (London).

Defoe, Daniel (1997). *The True-Born Englishman and Other Writings*, ed. P. N. Furbank and W. R. Owens (London: P).

Defoe, Daniel (2000). *Political and Economic Writings*, ed. W. R. Owens and P. N. Furbank, 8 vols. (London: P&C).

Defoe, Daniel (2001). *Robinson Crusoe*, ed. J. Richetti (London: P). 1st publ. 1719.

Defoe, Daniel (2003–). *Defoe's Review, 1704–1713*, ed. J. McVeagh, 18 vols. (London: P&C).

Delolme, Jean Louis (1771). *La Constitution d'Angleterre* (Amsterdam). 1st Eng. trans. 1775.

Delolme, Jean Louis (1834). *The Constitution of England*, ed. W. H. Hughes (London).

Delolme, Jean Louis (forthcoming). *The Constitution of England*, ed. D. Lieberman (Indianapolis: LF).

Denne, Samuel (1771). *A Letter to Sir Robert Ladbroke . . . with An Attempt to Shew the Good Effects which may Reasonably be Expected from the Confinement of Criminals in Separate Apartments* (London).

Desaguliers, John (1728). *The Newtonian System of the World the Best Model of Government* (London).

Deschamps, Jean (1743–7). *Cours abrégé de la philosophie Wolfienne*, 3 vols. (Amsterdam and Leipzig). In Wolff 1962–, III.

Deschamps, Léger Marie (1993). *Oeuvres philosophiques*, ed. B. Delhaume, 2 vols. (Paris).

Desmoulins, Camille (1987). *Le Vieux Cordelier*, ed. P. Pachet (Paris). 1st publ. 1793.

Destutt de Tracy, Antoine Louis Claude, Comte (1801–15). *Eléments d'idéologie* (Paris).

Destutt de Tracy, Antoine Louis Claude, Comte (1819). *Commentaire sur 'L'Esprit des lois' de Montesquieu*, 2nd edn (Paris). 1st publ. 1811.

Destutt de Tracy, Antoine Louis Claude, Comte (1969). *A Commentary and Review of Montesquieu's Spirit of Laws*, trans. W. Duane (New York).

Destutt de Tracy, Antoine Louis Claude, Comte (1970). *A Treatise on Political Economy*, trans. T. Jefferson (New York). Trans. 1st publ. 1817.

Devonshire, William Cavendish, 2nd duke of (1709). *The Charms of Liberty: A Poem* (London).

Dickinson, John (1774). *An Essay on the Constitutional Power of Great Britain over the Colonies in America* (Philadelphia).

Dickinson, John (1801). *Political Writings of John Dickinson*, 2 vols. (Wilmington).

Dickinson, John (1895). *The Writings of John Dickinson*, ed. P. L. Ford (Philadelphia).

Dickinson, John, and Lee, Richard Henry (1999). *Empire and Nation: Letters from a Farmer in Pennsylvania (John Dickinson) and Letters from the Federal Farmer (Richard Henry Lee)*, ed. F. McDonald, 2nd edn (Indianapolis: LF).

Diderot, Denis (1755). 'Encyclopédie', in *Encyclopédie ou Dictionnaire raisonné des sciences, des arts et des metiers*, v (Paris), pp. 635–49.

Diderot, Denis (1875–7). *Oeuvres complètes*, ed. J. Assézat and M. Tourneux (Paris).

Diderot, Denis (1877–82). *See* Grimm 1877–82.

Diderot, Denis (1955). *Supplément au voyage de Bougainville*, ed. H. Dieckmann (Geneva). Written 1772, 1st publ. 1796.

Diderot, Denis (1963a). *Lettre sur les aveugles*, ed. R. Niklaus (Geneva). 1st publ. 1749.

Diderot, Denis (1963b), *Oeuvres politiques*, ed. P. Vernière (Paris).

Diderot, Denis (1966). *Mémoires pour Catherine II*, ed. P. Vernière (Paris).

Diderot, Denis (1967). *Oeuvres philosophiques*, ed. P. Vernière (Paris).

Diderot, Denis (1969–73). *Oeuvres complètes*, ed. R. Lewinter, 15 vols. (Paris).

Diderot, Denis (1976). *Rameau's Nephew and D'Alembert's Dream*, trans. L. Tancock (London: P).

Diderot, Denis (1992). *Political Writings*, ed. J. H. Mason and R. Wokler (Cambridge: CTHPT).

Diderot, Denis (1999). *Jacques the Fatalist and his Master*, ed. D. Coward (Oxford). 1st publ. 1796.

Diderot, Denis (2001). *Rameau's Nephew and Other Works*, ed. J. Barzun and R. H. Bowen (Indianapolis: H).

Diderot, Denis (2004). *Contes et romans*, ed. M. Delon *et al.* (Paris).

Diderot, Denis, and d'Alembert, Jean, eds. (1751–80). *L'Encyclopédie, ou Dictionnaire raisonné des sciences, des arts et des métiers*, 35 vols. (Paris).

Diderot, Denis, and d'Alembert, Jean, eds. (1954). *The Encyclopédie of Diderot and d'Alembert: Selected Articles*, ed. J. Lough (Cambridge).

Diderot, Denis, and d'Alembert, Jean, eds. (1984). *L'Encyclopédie ou Dictionnaire raisonné des sciences, des arts et des métiers: textes choisis*, ed. A. Soboul and P. Goujard (Paris).

Dieckmann, Herbert, ed. (1948). *Le Philosophe: Texts and Interpretation* (St Louis, MO).

Dithmar, Justus Christoph (1731). *Einleitung in die Oeconomische-, Policey- und Cameralwissenschaften* (Frankfurt a. O.).

Dobbs, Francis (1774). *The Patriot King, or Irish Chief: A Tragedy* (London).

Dobbs, Francis (1781). *Thoughts on Volunteers* (Dublin).

Dobbs, Francis (1782). *A History of Irish Affairs from . . . 1779 to . . . 1782* (Dublin).

Dodwell, Henry (1692). *A Vindication of the Deprived Bishops* (London).

Drennan, William (1784). *Letters of Orellana, an Irish Helot* (Dublin).

Dubos, Jean Baptiste (1703). *Les Intérêts de l'Angleterre mal-entendus dans la guerre présente* (Amsterdam).

Dubos, Jean Baptiste (1734). *Histoire critique de l'établissement de la monarchie française dans les Gaules* (Amsterdam).

Du Châtelet, Gabrielle Emilie, marquise (1740). *Institutions de physique* (Paris).

Du Châtelet, Gabrielle Emilie, marquise (1746). *Discours sur le bonheur* (Paris).

Du Châtelet, Gabrielle Emilie, marquise (1947). 'Unpublished Papers of Madame du Châtelet', in *Studies on Voltaire*, ed. I. O. Wade (Princeton).

Dumarsais, César Chesneau (1988). *Des tropes ou des différents sens, figures et vingt autres articles de l'Encyclopédie, suivis de l'Abrégé des tropes de l'Abbé Ducros*, ed. F. Douay-Soublin (Paris).

Dupont de Nemours, Pierre Samuel (1767–8). *Physiocratie, ou Constitution naturelle du gouvernement le plus avantageux au genre humain*, 2 vols. (Leiden and Paris).

Bibliography

Dupont de Nemours, Pierre Samuel (1979). *Oeuvres politiques et économiques*, ed. E. Fox-Genovese, 10 vols. (Nendeln).

Dutot, — (1739). *Political Reflections upon the Finances and Commerce of France* (London).

Earbery, Matthias (1716). *Elements of Policy, Civil and Ecclesiastical, in a Mathematical Method* (London).

Eaton, Daniel Isaac (1793–5). *Hog's Wash, or, a Salmagundy for Swine* (London). Later title: *Hog's Wash, or Politics for the People.*

Eden, Frederick Morton (1797). *The State of the Poor, Or an History of the Labouring Classes of England*, 3 vols. (London). Repr. 1994.

Eden, William (1771). *Principles of Penal Law* (London).

Eilschov, Friederich Christian (1747). *Philosophiske Skrifter* (Copenhagen).

Eilschov, Friederich Christian (1748). *Philosophiske Breve* (Copenhagen).

Elliot, Jonathan, ed. (1854). *The Debates in the Several State Conventions, on the Adoption of the Federal Constitution*, 3 vols. (Washington).

Erb, Peter C., ed. (1983). *Pietists: Selected Writings* (New York).

Espen, Zeghert Bernhard van (1700). *Jus ecclesiasticum universum hodiernae disciplinae, praesertim Belgii, Galliae, Germaniae, et vicinarum provinciarum accommodatum*, 2 vols. (Brussels and Louvain).

Evelyn, John (1669). *The History of the Three Late Famous Impostors* (London).

Febronius, Justinus. *See* Hontheim.

Feder, Johann Georg Heinrich (1770). *Lehrbuch der praktischen Philosophie* (Göttingen).

Fénelon, François de Salignac de la Mothe (1712). *Dialogues des morts, composés pour l'éducation d'un prince* (Paris).

Fénelon, François de Salignac de la Mothe (1713). *A Demonstration of the Existence, Wisdom, and Omnipotence of God* (London).

Fénelon, François de Salignac de la Mothe (1720). 'Sentiments on the Balance of Europe', in *Two Essays on the Balance of Europe* (London).

Fénelon, François de Salignac de la Mothe (1725). *Les Aventures de Télémaque, fils d'Ulysse* (Rotterdam). 1st publ. 1699.

Fénelon, François de Salignac de la Mothe (1746). *Letters to the Duke of Burgundy* (Glasgow).

Fénelon, François de Salignac de la Mothe (1747a). *Examen de conscience pour un roi. Ecrit pour l'usage de Mons. Le duc de Bourgogne, puis dauphin de France* (London). 1st publ. 1734.

Fénelon, François de Salignac de la Mothe (1747b). *The Tales and Fables of the Late Archbishop and Duke of Cambray, Author of Telemachus*, trans. N. Gifford (London). 1st publ. 1738.

Fénelon, François de Salignac de la Mothe (1810). *Dialogues des morts anciens et modernes, avec quelques fables, composés pour l'éducation d'un prince* (Paris). 1st publ. 1692.

Fénelon, François de Salignac de la Mothe (1964). *Letters*, ed. J. McEwen and T. Merton (London).

Fénelon, François de Salignac de la Mothe (1972–2000). *Correspondance*, ed. J. Orcibal *et al.*, 17 vols. (Geneva).

Fénelon, François de Salignac de la Mothe (1983–97). *Oeuvres*, ed. J. Le Brun, 2 vols. (Paris).

Fénelon, François de Salignac de la Mothe (1990). *Démonstration de l'existence de Dieu*, ed. J. L. Dumas (Paris). 1st publ. 1712.

Fénelon, François de Salignac de la Mothe (1994). *Telemachus*, ed. P. Riley (Cambridge: CTHPT). 1st publ. 1699.

Ferguson, Adam (1783). *The History of the Progress and Termination of the Roman Republic* (London).

Ferguson, Adam (1792). *Principles of Moral and Political Science*, 2 vols. (Edinburgh).

Ferguson, Adam (1966). *An Essay on the History of Civil Society*, ed. D. Forbes (Edinburgh). 1st publ. 1767.

800

Ferguson, Adam (1995a). *Correspondence*, ed. V. Merolle and J. B. Fagg, 2 vols. (London: P&C).

Ferguson, Adam (1995b). *An Essay on the History of Civil Society*, ed. F. Oz-Salzberger (Cambridge: CTHPT).

Feuerbach, Paul Johann Anselm (1796). *Kritik des natürlichen Rechts als Propädeutik zu einer Wissenschaft der natürlichen Rechte* (Altona). Repr. Darmstadt, 1963.

Feuerbach, Paul Johann Anselm (1797). *Anti-Hobbes, oder über die Grenzen der höchsten Gewalt und das Zwangsrecht der Bürger gegen den Oberherrn* (Gießen). Repr. Darmstadt, 1967.

Fichte, Johann Gottlieb (1793a). *Zurückforderung der Denkfreiheit von den Fürsten Europens* (Heliopolis [Danzig]).

Fichte, Johann Gottlieb (1793b). *Beitrag zur Berichtigung der Urtheile des Publikums über die französiche Revolution* (n.p.).

Fichte, Johann Gottlieb (1796). *Grundlage des Naturrechts nach Prinzipien der Wissenschaftslehre* (Jena and Leipzig). Repr. in Fichte 1845–6, III, pp. 1–385.

Fichte, Johann Gottlieb (1798). *System der Sittenlehre nach den Prinzipien der Wissenschaftslehre* (Jena and Leipzig). Repr. in Fichte 1845–6, IV, pp. 1–365.

Fichte, Johann Gottlieb (1800). *Der geschlossene Handelstaat* (Tübingen).

Fichte, Johann Gottlieb (1807–8). *Reden an die deutsche Nation* (Berlin and Leipzig).

Fichte, Johann Gottlieb (1845–6). *Sämmtliche Werke*, ed. J. H. Fichte, 8 vols. (Berlin).

Fichte, Johann Gottlieb (1847). *The Characteristics of the Present Age*, trans. W. Smith (London). 1st publ. 1806.

Fichte, Johann Gottlieb (1962–). *Gesamtausgabe der Bayerischen Akademie der Wissenschaften* (Stuttgart).

Fichte, Johann Gottlieb (1968). *Addresses to the German Nation*, ed. G. A. Kelly (New York). 1st publ. 1808.

Fichte, Johann Gottlieb (1978). *Reden an die deutsche Nation* (Hamburg).

Fichte, Johann Gottlieb (1987). *The Vocation of Man*, ed. P. Preuss (Indianapolis: H).

Fichte, Johann Gottlieb (1994). *Introductions to the Wissenschaftslehre and Other Writings, 1797–1800*, ed. D. Breazeale (Indianapolis: H).

Fichte, Johann Gottlieb (2000). *Foundations of Natural Right*, trans. M. Baur, ed. F. Neuhouser (Cambridge: CTHPT). 1st publ. 1796.

Filangieri, Gaetano (1774). *Reflessione politiche sull'ultima legge sovrana che riguarda l'amministrazione della giustizia* (Naples).

Filangieri, Gaetano (1780–5). *La scienza della legislazione*, 4 vols. (Naples).

Filangieri, Gaetano (1982). *Riflessioni politiche* (Naples).

Filangieri, Gaetano (1984). *Scienza della legislazione*, ed. V. Frosini (Naples).

Filleau, Jean (1654). *Relation juridique de ce qui s'est passé à Poitiers touchant la nouvelle doctrine des jansénistes* (Poitiers).

Filmer, Robert (1991). *Patriarcha and Other Writings*, ed. J. P. Sommerville (Cambridge: CTHPT).

Finetti, Germano Federigo (1764). *De principiis juris naturae et gentium*, 2 vols. (Venice). Publ. under his brother's name, Joannis Francisci Finetti.

Fischer, Christoph (1690). *Fleissiges Herren-Auge, oder wohl-, ab-, und angeführter Haus-Halter* (Frankfurt).

Fitzhugh, George (1854). *Sociology for the South, Or the Failure of Free Society* (Richmond, VA). Extract in Goldie 1999, VI.

Fletcher, Andrew (1698). *A Discourse of Government with Relation to Militias* (Edinburgh).

Fletcher, Andrew (1703). *An Account of a Conversation concerning a Right Regulation of Governments for the Common Good of Mankind* (London).

Fletcher, Andrew (1732). *Political Works* (London).

Fletcher, Andrew (1997). *Political Works*, ed. J. Robertson (Cambridge: CTHPT).

Fleury, Claude (1681). *The Manners of the Israelites* (London).

Fontenelle, Bernard de (1686). *Histoire des oracles* (Paris).

Forbonnais, François Véron de (1754). *Elémens du commerce* (Leiden).

Ford, Paul L., ed. (1888). *Pamphlets on the Constitution of the United States* (Brooklyn, NJ). Repr. New York, 1968.

Fordyce, David (2003). *The Elements of Moral Philosophy*, ed. T. D. Kennedy (Indianapolis: LF). 1st publ. 1754.

Formey, Jean Henri Samuel (1741–53). *La Belle Wolfienne*, 5 vols. (The Hague).

Formey, Jean Henri Samuel (1755). *Conseils pour former une bibliothèque peu nombreuse, mais choisie*, 3rd edn (Berlin).

Fownes, Joseph (1773). *An Enquiry into the Principles of Toleration* (Shrewsbury).

Franklin, Benjamin (1733–58). *Poor Richard's Almanack* (Philadelphia).

Franklin, Benjamin (1779). *Political, Miscellaneous, and Philosophical Pieces* (London).

Franklin, Benjamin (1960–83). *The Papers of Benjamin Franklin*, ed. L. W. Lebaree and W. B. Willcox *et al.*, 23 vols. (New Haven).

Franklin, Benjamin (1965). *The Political Writings*, ed. R. Ketchum (Indianapolis: H).

Franklin, Benjamin (1985). *Autobiography, and Other Writings*, ed. K. A. Silverman (London: P).

Franklin, Benjamin (1987). *Writings*, ed. J. A. L. Lemay (New York).

Franklin, Benjamin (2004). *The Autobiography and Other Writings on Politics, Economics, and Virtue*, ed. A. Houston (Cambridge: CTHPT).

Frederick the Great (1740). *Anti-Machiavel*. See Voltaire and Frederick.

Frederick the Great (1846–57). *Oeuvres*, ed. J. D. E. Preuss, 31 vols. (Berlin).

Frederick the Great (1913). *Werke*, ed. G. B. Volz, 10 vols. (Berlin).

Frederick the Great (1920). *Die politischen Testamente*, ed. G. B. Volz (Berlin).

Frederick the Great (1960). *Die 'Rêveries Politiques' in Friedrichs des Grossen Politischen Testament von 1752*, ed. E. Bosbach (Cologne).

Frederick the Great (1980). *Philosophische und Staatswissenschaftliche Schriften* (Munich).

Frederick the Great (1981). *Anti-Machiavel*. See Voltaire and Frederick.

Frederick the Great (1985a). *Friedrich II, König von Preußen, und die deutsche Literatur des 18 Jahrhunderts: Texte und Dokumente*, ed. H. Steinmetz (Stuttgart).

Frederick the Great (1985b). *Oeuvres philosophiques* (Paris).

Fredersdorff, Leopold Friedrich (1790). *System des Rechts der Natur auf bürgerliche Gesellschaften, Gesetzgebung und das Völkerrecht angewandt* (Braunschweig).

Furneaux, Philip (1770). *Letters to the Honourable Mr. Justice Blackstone concerning his Exposition of the Act of Toleration* (London).

Furstenau, Johann Hermann (1736). *Gründliche Anleitung zu der Haushaltungs-Kunst* (Lemgo).

Galanti, Giuseppe Maria (1779). *Con un discorso intorno alla costituzione delle società ed al governo politico* (Naples).

Galiani, Ferdinando (1751). *Della moneta* (Naples).

Galiani, Ferdinando (1770). *Dialogues sur le commerce des blés* (London).

Galiani, Ferdinando (1975). *Opere*, ed. F. Dinz and L. Guerci (Milan).

Galiani, Ferdinando (1977). *On Money*, ed. P. R. Toscano (Chicago). 1st publ. 1751.

Garat, Dominique Joseph (1784). In *Le Mercure de France*, 6 Mar. 1784, pp. 22–3.

Garat, Dominique Joseph (1791). *Membre de l'Assemblée Constituante à Monsieur Condorcet, membre de l'Assemblée Nationale, Seconde Législature* (Paris).

Garve, Christian (1788). *Abhandlung über die Verbindung der Moral mit der Politik* (Breslau).

Gasser, Simon Peter (1728). *Programma publicum* (Halle).

Primary sources

Gasser, Simon Peter (1729). *Einleitung zu den Oeconomischen Politischen und Cameral-Wissenschaften* (Halle).

Gay, John (1731). 'Preliminary Dissertation', in William King, *An Essay on the Origin of Evil* (London).

Gay, John (1986). *The Beggar's Opera*, ed. B. Loughrey and T. O. Treadwell (London: P). 1st publ. 1728.

Genovesi, Antonio (1765). *Delle lezione di commercio o sia d'economia civile* (Milan).

Genovesi, Antonio (1984). *Scritti economici*, ed. M. L. Perna, 2 vols. (Naples).

Gerrald, Joseph (1793). *A Convention the Only Means of Saving us from Ruin* (London).

Gerson, Jean (1706). *Opera omnia*, ed. Louis Ellies du Pin, 5 vols. (Antwerp).

Giannone, Pietro (1723). *Dell' istoria civile del regno di Napoli* (Naples).

Giannone, Pietro (1729–31). *The Civil History of the Kingdom of Naples*, 2 vols. (London).

Giannone, Pietro (1968). *Opere*, ed. S. Bertelli and G. Ricuperati (Milan).

Gibbon, Edward (1814). *The Miscellaneous Works*, ed. Lord Sheffield, 3 vols. (London).

Gibbon, Edward (1909–14). *The History of the Decline and Fall of the Roman Empire*, ed. J. B. Bury, 6 vols. (London). 1st publ. 1776–88.

Gibbon, Edward (1970). *An Essay on the Study of Literature* (New York). 1st publ. 1761.

Gibbon, Edward (1994). *The History of the Decline and Fall of the Roman Empire*, ed. D. Womersley, 3 vols. (London: P). Abridged edn in 1 vol., 2003.

Godwin, William (1793). *An Enquiry concerning Political Justice*, 2 vols. (London).

Godwin, William (1796). *Considerations on Lord Grenville's and Mr. Pitt's Bills concerning Treasonable and Seditious Practices and Unlawful Assembly* (London).

Godwin, William (1976). *Enquiry concerning Political Justice*, ed. I. Kramnick (London: P).

Godwin, William (1993). *Political and Philosophical Writings*, ed. M. Philp, 7 vols. (London: P&C).

Godwin, William (2002). *History of the Commonwealth of England*, ed. J. Morrow (Bristol: T).

Godwin, William, and Wollstonecraft, Mary (1987). *A Short Residence in Sweden, Norway, and Denmark, and Memoirs of the Author of the Rights of Woman*, ed. R. Holmes (London: P).

Goldie, Mark, ed. (1999). *The Reception of Locke's Politics*, 6 vols. (London: P&C).

Gorani, Giuseppe (1770). *Il vero dispotismo*, 2 vols. ('London' [Geneva]).

Gorani, Giuseppe (1790). *Recherches sur la science du gouvernement*, 2 vols. (Lausanne).

Gorani, Giuseppe (1793). *Lettres sur la Révolution française* (Paris).

Gorani, Giuseppe (1794). *Mémoires secrets et critiques des cours, des gouvernemens, et des moeurs des principaux états d'Italie*, 3 vols. (Paris).

Gordon, Thomas. *See* Trenchard.

Gouges, Olympe de (1986). *Oeuvres*, ed. B. Groult (Paris).

Gouges, Olympe de (1993). *Oeuvres*, ed. F. M. Castan (Montauban).

Grattan, Henry (1772). *Baratariana* (Dublin).

Grégoire, Henri (1789). *Essai sur la régénération physique, morale et politique des Juifs* (Metz).

Grégoire, Henri (1791). *Essay on the Physical, Moral, and Political Reformation of the Jews* (London).

Grégoire, Henri (1793). *Discours sur la liberté des cultes* (Paris).

Grégoire, Henri (1977). *Oeuvres*, ed. A. Soboul, 14 vols. (Nendeln).

Grégoire, Henri (1988). *Essai sur la régénération physique, morale et politique des Juifs*, ed. R. Badinter (Paris). 1st publ. 1789.

Grégoire, Henri (1996). *On the Cultural Achievements of Negroes*, ed. J. F. Brière and T. Cassirer (Amherst, MA). 1st publ. 1808.

Grimaldi, Francesco Antonio (1779). *Riflessioni sopra l'ineguaglianza tra gli uomini*, 3 vols. (Naples).

Grimm, Friedrich Melchior (1877–82). *Correspondance littéraire, philosophique et critique par Grimm, Diderot, Raynal, Meister, etc.*, ed. M. Tourneux, 16 vols. (Paris). 1st publ. 1813.

Grotius, Hugo (1724). *Du droit de la guerre et de la paix*, trans. Jean Barbeyrac (Amsterdam). 1st publ. 1625.

Gundling, Nicolaus Hieronymus (1715). *Jurisprudentia naturalis* (Halle).

Gundling, Nicolaus Hieronymus (1734). *Discours über das Natur- und Völkerrecht* (Frankfurt).

Hale, Matthew (1971). *The History of the Common Law of England*, ed. C. M. Gray (Chicago). 1st publ. 1713.

Hamann, Johann G. (1821–43). *Schriften*, 8 vols. (Berlin).

Hamilton, Alexander, Madison, James, and Jay, John (1981). *The Federalist Papers*, ed. R. P. Fairfield (Baltimore, MD). 1st publ. 1787–8.

Hamilton, Alexander, Madison, James, and Jay, John (1987). *The Federalist Papers*, ed. I. Kramnick (London: P).

Hamilton, Alexander, Madison, James, and Jay, John (2001). *The Federalist*, ed. G. W. Carey and J. McClellan, 2nd edn (Indianapolis: LF).

Hamilton, Alexander, Madison, James, and Jay, John (2003). *The Federalist, with The Letters of Brutus*, ed. T. Ball (Cambridge: CTHPT).

Hamilton, Alexander, Madison, James, and Jay, John (2004). *The Federalist*, ed. J. R. Pole (Indianapolis: H).

Hanway, Jonas (1775). *The Defects of Police, the Cause of Immorality* (London).

Hanway, Jonas (1776). *Solitude in Imprisonment, with Profitable Labour and a Spare Diet, the Most Humane and Effectual Means of Bringing Malefactors . . . to their Right Sense and Condition* (London).

Hanway, Jonas (1781). *Distributive Justice and Mercy: Shewing that a Temporary Real Solitary Imprisonment of Convicts, Supported by Religious Instruction, and Well-Regulated Labour, is Essential to their Well-Being, and the Safety, Honour, and Reputation of the People* (London).

Harrington, James (1700). *The Oceana of James Harrington and his Other Works*, ed. John Toland (London). *Oceana* 1st publ. 1656.

Hay, William (1728). *An Essay on Civil Government: Treating Summarily of its Necessity, Original, Dissolution, Forms, and Properties* (London).

Hays, Mary (1793). *Letters and Essays, Moral and Miscellaneous* (London). Repr. 1974.

Hays, Mary (1798). *Appeal to the Men of Great Britain in Behalf of Women* (London). Repr. 1974.

Hegel, Georg Wilhelm Friedrich (1896). *Lectures on the History of Philosophy*, III, trans. E. S. Haldane and F. H. Simson (London).

Hegel, Georg Wilhelm Friedrich (1942). *The Philosophy of Right*, trans. T. M. Knox (Oxford). 1st publ. 1821.

Hegel, Georg Wilhelm Friedrich (1991). *Elements of the Philosophy of Right*, ed. A. W. Wood, trans. H. B. Nisbet (Cambridge: CTHPT).

Hegel, Georg Wilhelm Friedrich (1999). *Political Writings*, ed. L. Dickey, trans. H. B. Nisbet (Cambridge: CTHPT).

Heineccius, Johann Gottlieb (1737). *Elementa juris naturae et gentium* (Halle). German trans. P. Mortzfeld, ed. C. Bergfeld, *Grundlagen des Natur- und Völkerrechts*, Frankfurt, 1994.

Heineccius, Johann Gottlieb (1741). *A Methodical System of Universal Law: Or, the Laws of Nature and Nations Deduced from Certain Principles and Applied to Proper Cases*, trans. George Turnbull, 2 vols. (London).

Heineccius, Johann Gottlieb (1744). *Praelectiones academicae in Hugonis Grotii de jure belli et pacis* (Berlin).

Heineccius, Johann Gottlieb (1748). *Praelectiones academicae in S. Pufendorfii de officio hominis et civis* (Berlin).

Heineccius, Johann Gottlieb (2006). *A Methodical System of Universal Law*, ed. P. Schröder (Indianapolis: LF).

Helvétius, Claude Adrien (1758). *De l'esprit*, 2 vols. (Paris).

Helvétius, Claude Adrien (1772). *De l'homme, de ses facultés intellectuelles, et de son éducation* ('London' [The Hague]).

Helvétius, Claude Adrien (1967–9). *Oeuvres* (Hildesheim).

Helvétius, Claude Adrien (1981). *Correspondance*, ed. D. W. Smith *et al.*, 5 vols. (Toronto).

Herder, Johann Gottfried (1774). *Auch eine Philosophie der Geschichte* (n.p.).

Herder, Johann Gottfried (1784–91). *Ideen zur Philosophie der Geschichte der Menschheit* (Riga and Leipzig).

Herder, Johann Gottfried (1877–1913). *Sämmtliche Werke*, ed. B. L. Suphan, 33 vols. (Berlin).

Herder, Johann Gottfried (1969). *J. G. Herder on Social and Political Culture*, trans. and ed. F. M. Bernard (Cambridge).

Herder, Johann Gottfried (1984–2002). *Werke*, vols. I–III, ed. W. Pross (Munich).

Herder, Johann Gottfried (2004). *Another Philosophy of History and Selected Political Writings*, ed. I. D. Evrigenis and D. Pellerin (Indianapolis: H).

Hering, Christoph (1680). *Oeconomischer Wegweiser* (Jena).

Herrenschwand, Jean (1786). *De l'économie politique moderne: Discours fondamental sur la population* (London).

Hervás y Panduro, Lorenzo (1789–90). *Historia de la vida del hombre*, 7 vols. (Madrid).

Hervey, John, Lord (1734). *Ancient and Modern Liberty Stated and Compar'd* (London).

Heydenreich, Karl Heinrich (1793–6). *Originalideen über die kritische Philosophie*, 3 vols. (Leipzig). Vols. II and III entitled *Originalideen über die interessantesten Gegenstände der Philosophie*.

Heydenreich, Karl Heinrich (1794–5). *System des Naturrechts nach kritischen Prinzipien*, 2 vols. (Leipzig).

Heydenreich, Karl Heinrich (1795). *Grundsätze des natürlichen Staatsrecht und seiner Anwendung*, 2 vols. (Leipzig).

Hickes, George (1716). *The Constitution of the Catholick Church* (London).

Hinske, N., and Albrecht, M., eds. (1977). *Was ist Aufklärung?: Beiträge aus der Berlinische Monaatschrift* (Darmstadt).

Hippel, Theodor Gottlieb (1979). *On Improving the Status of Women*, ed. T. F. Sellner (Detroit). 1st publ. 1793.

Hippel, Theodor Gottlieb (1994). *On Marriage*, ed. T. F. Sellner (Detroit). 1st publ. 1774.

Hoadly, Benjamin (1710). *The Original and Institution of Civil Government* (London).

Hoadly, Benjamin (1717). *The Nature of the Kingdom, or Church of Christ* (London). Repr. in Goldie 1999, V.

Hobbes, Thomas (1949). *De cive*, ed. S. P. Lamprecht (New York). 1st publ. 1642.

Hobbes, Thomas (1957). *Leviathan*, ed. M. Oakeshott (Oxford). 1st publ. 1651.

Hobbes, Thomas (1991). *Leviathan*, ed. R. Tuck (Cambridge: CTHPT). 2nd edn 1996.

Hobbes, Thomas (1998). *On the Citizen*, ed. R. Tuck and M. Silverthorne (Cambridge: CTHPT).

Hoffman, Leopold (1792). *Wiener Zeitschrift* (Vienna).

Hohberg, Wolfgang Helmhard von (1682). *Georgica curiosa aucta. Das ist: Umständlicher Bericht und klarer Unterricht von dem adelichen Land- und Feld-Leben*, 2 vols. (Nuremberg).

Holbach, Paul Henri, baron d' (1761). *See* Boulanger 1761.

Holbach, Paul Henri, baron d' (1770). *Essai sur les préjugés* ('London' [Amsterdam]).

Holbach, Paul Henri, baron d' (1773). *La Politique naturelle, ou discours sur les vrais principes du gouvernement*, 2 vols. ('London' [Amsterdam]).

Holbach, Paul Henri, baron d' (1820). *Le Système de la nature*, 2 vols. (London). 1st publ. 1770.

Holbach, Paul Henri, baron d' (1998–2001). *Oeuvres philosophiques*, ed. J. P. Jackson, 3 vols. (Paris).

Holberg, Ludvig (1716). *Moralske Kierne eller Introduction til Naturens og Folkerettens Kundskab* (Copenhagen).

Home, Henry. *See* Kames.

Hontheim, Johann Nikolaus von (Justinus Febronius) (1765–74). *De statu ecclesiae et legitima potestate Romani Pontificis*, 4 vols. (n.p.). 1st publ. 1763.

Hooke, Nathaniel (1738–71). *The Roman History, from the Building of Rome to the Ruin of the Commonwealth*, 4 vols. (London).

Höpfner, Ludwig Julius Friedrich (1795). *Naturrecht des einzelnen Menschen, der Gesellschaften und der Völker* (Gießen). 1st publ. 1790.

Horne, George (1787). 'The Origin of Civil Government', in *Discourses on Several Subjects and Occasions*. Written 1769. Repr. in Goldie 1999, III.

Hourwitz, Zalkind (1789). *Apologie des Juifs* (Paris).

Howard, John (1777). *The State of the Prisons in England and Wales, with Preliminary Observations, and an Account of some Foreign Prisons* (Warrington).

Howard, John (1789). *An Account of the Principal Lazarettos in Europe* (Warrington).

Howard, John (1792). *The State of the Prisons in England and Wales, with Preliminary Observations, and an Account of some Foreign Prisons and Hospitals*, 4th edn (London).

Huet, Pierre Daniel (1723). *Traité philosophique de la foiblesse de l'esprit humain* (Amsterdam).

Hulme, Obadiah. *See* Ramsay 1771.

Humboldt, Wilhelm (1851). *Ideen zu einem Versuch die Grenzen der Wirksamkeit des Staates zu bestimmen* (Breslau). Written 1792.

Humboldt, Wilhelm (1969). *The Limits of State Action*, ed. J. W. Burrow (Cambridge).

Hume, David (1739–40). *A Treatise of Human Nature*, 3 vols. (London).

Hume, David (1741–2). *Essays, Moral and Political*, 2 vols. (Edinburgh).

Hume, David (1752). *Political Discourses* (Edinburgh).

Hume, David (1754–62). *The History of England, from the Invasion of Julius Caesar to the Revolution of 1688*, 6 vols. (London).

Hume, David (1757). *The Natural History of Religion*, in *Four Dissertations* (London).

Hume, David (1782). *The History of England*, 8 vols. (London).

Hume, David (1874). *The Philosophical Works*, ed. T. H. Green and T. H. Grose, 4 vols. (London).

Hume, David (1882). 'A Dissertation on the Passions', in *Philosophical Works*, IV, ed. T. H. Green and T. H. Grose (London). 1st publ. 1757.

Hume, David (1884). *The History of England*, 6 vols. (London).

Hume, David (1932). *The Letters of David Hume*, ed. J. Y. T. Greig, 2 vols. (Oxford).

Hume, David (1951). *Hume: Theory of Politics*, ed. F. Watkins (Edinburgh).

Hume, David (1975). *Enquiries concerning Human Understanding and concerning the Principles of Morals*, ed. L. A. Selby-Bigge, 3rd edn, revised by P. H. Nidditch (Oxford).

Hume, David (1978). *A Treatise of Human Nature*, ed. L. A. Selby-Bigge, 2nd edn, revised by P. H. Nidditch (Oxford).

Hume, David (1980). *Dialogues concerning Natural Religion*, ed. R. H. Popkin (Indianapolis: H). 1st publ. 1779.

Hume, David (1983). *An Enquiry concerning the Principles of Morals*, ed. J. B. Schneewind (Indianapolis: H). 1st publ. 1751.

Hume, David (1983–5). *The History of England from the Invasion of Julius Caesar to the Revolution in 1688*, 6 vols. (Indianapolis: LF).

Hume, David (1985). *A Treatise of Human Nature*, ed. E. C. Mossner (London: P).

Hume, David (1987). *Essays, Moral, Political, and Literary*, ed. E. F. Miller (Indianapolis: LF).

Hume, David (1990). *Dialogues concerning Natural Religion*, ed. M. Bell (London: P). 1st publ. 1779.

Hume, David (1994a). *Political Essays*, ed. K. Haakonssen (Cambridge: CTHPT).

Hume, David (1994b). *Political Writings*, ed. S. D. Warner and D. W. Livingston (Indianapolis: H).

Hume, David (1998). *An Enquiry concerning the Principles of Morals*, ed. T. L. Beauchamp (Oxford).

Hume, David (2000a). *A Treatise of Human Nature*, ed. D. F. Norton and M. J. Norton (Oxford).

[Hume, David] (2000b). *Early Responses to Hume's Moral, Literary and Political Writings*, ed. J. Fieser, 2 vols. (Bristol: T).

[Hume, David] (2002). *Early Responses to Hume's History of England*, ed. J. Fieser, 2 vols. (Bristol: T).

Hunt, Lynn, ed. (1996). *The French Revolution and Human Rights: A Brief Documentary History* (Boston, MA).

Hutcheson, Francis (1725). *An Inquiry into the Original of our Ideas of Beauty and Virtue in Two Treatises* (London).

Hutcheson, Francis (1728). *An Essay on the Nature and Conduct of the Passions and Affections with Illustrations on the Moral Sense* (Dublin).

Hutcheson, Francis (1742). *Philosophiae moralis institutio compendiaria* (Glasgow).

Hutcheson, Francis (1747). *A Short Introduction to Moral Philosophy* (Glasgow). An English trans. of Hutcheson 1742.

Hutcheson, Francis (1755). *A System of Moral Philosophy*, 2 vols. (Glasgow).

Hutcheson, Francis (1969). *Collected Works* (Hildersheim).

Hutcheson, Francis (1993). 'Reflections on the Common Systems of Philosophy', in letters to *The London Journal*, 1724, in Francis Hutcheson, *On Human Nature: Reflections on our Common Systems of Morality; On the Social Nature of Man*, ed. T. Mautner (Cambridge).

Hutcheson, Francis (1997). 'Three Letters to *The Dublin Weekly Journal*', in [Mandeville] 1997b.

Hutcheson, Francis (2002). *An Essay on the Nature and Conduct of the Passions and Affections, with Illustrations on the Moral Sense*, ed. A. Garrett (Indianapolis: LF).

Hutcheson, Francis (2004). *An Inquiry into the Original of our Ideas of Beauty and Virtue*, ed. W. Leidhold (Indianapolis: LF).

Hutcheson, Francis (2006). *Logic, Metaphysics, Natural Sociability of Mankind*, ed. J. Moore and M. Silverthorne (Indianapolis: LF).

Hutcheson, Francis (forthcoming). *The Correspondence and Occasional Writings*, ed. J. Moore and M. A. Stewart (Indianapolis: LF).

Hutcheson, Francis (forthcoming). *The Meditations of the Emperor Marcus Aurelius Antoninus*, ed. J. Moore and M. Silverthorne (Indianapolis: LF).

Hutcheson, Francis (forthcoming). *Philosophiae moralis institutio compendiaria, with a Short Introduction to Moral Philosophy*, ed. L. Turco (Indianapolis: LF).

Hutcheson, Francis (forthcoming). *A System of Moral Philosophy*, ed. K. Haakonssen (Indianapolis: LF).

Hutchinson, Thomas (1768). 'A Dialogue between an American and a European Englishman'. Repr. in Goldie 1999, III.

Hyland, P., Gomez, O., and Greensides, F., eds. (2003). *The Enlightenment: A Sourcebook and Reader* (London).

Hyneman, C. S., and Lutz, D. S. (1983). *American Political Writing during the Founding Era, 1760–1805*, 2 vols. (Indianapolis: LF).

Ickstatt, Johann Adam (1747–59). *Opuscula juridica varii argumenti*, 2 vols. (Ingolstadt).

Iredell, James (1857–8). *Life and Correspondence of James Iredell*, ed. G. J. McRee, 2 vols. (New York).

Jay, John. *See* Hamilton.

Jebb, James (1787). *An Address to the Freeholders of Middlesex*, in *Works*, 3 vols. (London), II. 1st publ. 1779.

Jebb, John (1786). *Thoughts on the Construction and Polity of Prisons, with Hints for their Improvement* (London).

Jefferson, Thomas (1774). *A Summary View of the Rights of British America* (Williamsburg).

Jefferson, Thomas (1787). *Notes on the State of Virginia* (London).

Jefferson, Thomas (1950–). *Papers*, ed. S. P. Boyd, L. H. Butterfield *et al.* 27 vols. (Princeton).

Jefferson, Thomas (1955). *Notes on the State of Virginia*, ed. W. Peden (Chapel Hill).

Jefferson, Thomas (1970). *The Democratic Republic*, ed. M. Diamond (Chicago).

Jefferson, Thomas (1984). *Writings*, ed. M. D. Peterson (New York).

Jefferson, Thomas (1999). *Political Writings*, ed. J. Appleby and T. Ball (Cambridge: CTHPT).

Jenyns, Soame (1757). *Short but Serious Reasons for a National Militia* (London).

Jenyns, Soame (1765). *The Objections to the Taxation of our American Colonies . . . Considered* (London).

Jenyns, Soame (1782). *Disquisitions on Several Subjects* (London). Repr. in Goldie 1999, IV.

Jenyns, Soame (1784). *Thoughts on Parliamentary Reform* (London).

Jenyns, Soame (1790). *Works*, 4 vols. (London).

Johnson, Samuel (1774). *The Patriot* (London).

Johnson, Samuel (1775). *Taxation no Tyranny* (London).

Johnson, Samuel (1958–). *The Yale Edition of the Works*, 16 vols. (New Haven).

Johnson, Samuel (2000). *Political Writings*, ed. D. J. Greene (Indianapolis: LF).

Joseph II (1834). 'Briefwechsel Kaiser Josephs II mit Clemens Wenzel, Churfürst von Trier', ed. D. G. Mohnike, *Zeitschrift für die historische Theologie*, 4:263–90.

Joseph II (1895). 'Das Lehrbuch der Metaphysik für Kaiser Joseph II, verfasst von P. Josef Frantz', ed. T. M. Wehofer, *Jahrbuch für Philosophie und spekulative Theologie*, II (Paderborn).

Joseph II (1950). *Die österreichische Zentralverwaltung: Die Zeit Josephs II und Leopolds II: Aktenstücke*, ed. F. Walter. In *Veröffentlichungen der Kommission für neuere Geschichte Österreichs*, 36:123–32. (The 'pastoral letter' of 1783.)

Joseph II (1964). *See* Beck 1964.

Joseph II (1980). 'Joseph II's "Rêveries"', ed. D. Beales, *Mitteilungen des österreichischen Staatsarchivs*, 33:97–106.

Jurieu, Pierre (1686–8). *Lettres pastorales*, 3 vols. (Rotterdam). Eng. edn 1689.

Jurieu, Pierre (1696). *La Religion du latitudinaire, avec l'apologie pout la Sainte Trinité* (Rotterdam).

Justi, Johann Heinrich Gottlob von (1755). *Staatswirthschaft*, 2 vols. (Leipzig).

Justi, Johann Heinrich Gottlob von (1756). *Grundsätze der Policey-Wissenschaft* (Göttingen).

Justi, Johann Heinrich Gottlob von (1759a). *Der Grundriss einer Guten Regierung* (Frankfurt).

Justi, Johann Heinrich Gottlob von (1759b). *Systematischer Grundriss allen oeconomische und Cameral-Wissenschaften* (Frankfurt).

Justi, Johann Heinrich Gottlob von (1760–1). *Die Grundfeste zu der Macht und Glückseligkeit der Staaten*, 2 vols. (Leipzig).

Kames, Henry Home, Lord (1747). *Essays upon Several Subjects concerning British Antiquities* (Edinburgh).

Kames, Henry Home, Lord (1760). *Principles of Equity* (Edinburgh).

Kames, Henry Home, Lord (1774). *Sketches of the History of Man*, 2 vols. (Edinburgh).

Kames, Henry Home, Lord (1779). *Essays on the Principles of Morality and Natural Religion* (Edinburgh). 1st publ. 1751.

Kames, Henry Home, Lord (1792). *Historical Law Tracts* (Edinburgh). 1st publ. 1758.

Kames, Henry Home, Lord (2005a). *Elements of Criticism*, ed. P. Jones (Indianapolis: LF).

Kames, Henry Home, Lord (2005b). *Essays on the Principles of Morality and Natural Religion*, ed. B. Moran (Indianapolis: LF).

Kames, Henry Home, Lord (forthcoming). *Historical Law Tracts*, ed. B. Moran (Indianapolis: LF).

Kames, Henry Home, Lord (forthcoming). *Principles of Equity*, ed. S. Dickson (Indianapolis: LF).

Kames, Henry Home, Lord (forthcoming). *Sketches of the History of Man*, ed. I. Harris (Indianapolis: LF).

Kant, Immanuel (1784). 'Beantwortung der Frage: Was ist Aufklärung?', (*Berlinische Monatsschrift* 4). In Kant 1900–, VIII, pp. 33–42. Trans. in Kant 1996a.

Kant, Immanuel (1785). *Grundlegen zur Metaphysik der Sitten*, Riga. In Kant 1900–, IV, pp. 385–463. Trans. in Kant 1996a.

Kant, Immanuel (1788). *Kritik der praktischen Vernunft*, Riga. In Kant 1900–, V, pp. 1–163. Trans. in Kant 1996a.

Kant, Immanuel (1793). 'Über den Gemeinspruch: Das mag in der Theorie richtig sein, taugt aber nicht für die Praxis' (*Berlinische Monatsschrift* 22). In Kant 1900–, VIII, pp. 273–313. Trans. in Kant 1996a.

Kant, Immanuel (1795). *Zum ewigen Frieden. Ein philosophischer Entwurf* (Königsberg). In Kant 1900–, VIII, pp. 341–86. Trans. in Kant 1996a.

Kant, Immanuel (1797a). *Metaphysische Anfangsgründe der Rechtslehre* (Königsberg). As Part I of *Die Metaphysik der Sitten*, in Kant 1900–, VI, pp. 203–372. Trans. in Kant 1996a.

Kant, Immanuel (1797b). *Metaphysische Anfangsgründe der Tugendlehre* (Königsberg). As Part II of *Die Metaphysik der Sitten*, in Kant 1900–, VI, pp. 373–493. Trans. in Kant 1996a.

Kant, Immanuel (1798). *Der Streit der Facultäten* (Königsberg). In Kant 1900–, VII, pp. 1–116. Trans. in Kant 1996b.

Kant, Immanuel (1838). *Religion within the Boundary of Pure Reason*, ed. J. W. Semple (Edinburgh). 1st publ. 1793.

Kant, Immanuel (1900–). *Kant's gesammelte Schriften*, ed. Preußische Akademie der Wissenschaften (Berlin).

Kant, Immanuel (1923). *Kritik der reinen Vernunft*, ed. B. Erdmann (Berlin).

Kant, Immanuel (1952). *The Critique of Judgement*, trans. J. C. Meredith (Oxford). 1st publ. 1790.

Kant, Immanuel (1960). *Religion within the Limits of Reason Alone*, trans. T. M. Greene and H. H. Hudson (New York).

Kant, Immanuel (1964). *Metaphysical Principles of Virtue*, trans. J. Ellington (Indianapolis). 1st publ. 1797.

Kant, Immanuel (1965). *The Metaphysical Elements of Justice*, trans. J. Ladd (Indianapolis).

Kant, Immanuel (1978). *Lectures on Philosophical Theology*, trans. A. Wood and G. M. Clark (Ithaca, NY).

Kant, Immanuel (1983). *Perpetual Peace and Other Essays on Politics, History, and Morals*, ed. T. Humphrey (Indianapolis: H).

Kant, Immanuel (1986). *Metaphysische Anfangsgründe der Rechtslehre* (*Metaphysik der Sitten*, Part I), ed. B. Ludwig (Hamburg). Trans. in Kant 1996a.

Kant, Immanuel (1990). *Metaphysische Anfangsgründe der Tugendlehre*, (*Metaphysik der Sitten*, Part II), ed. B. Ludwig (Hamburg). Trans. in Kant 1996a.

Kant, Immanuel (1991). *Political Writings*, ed. H. Reiss, trans. H. B. Nisbet (Cambridge: CTHPT). 1st edn, 1970.

Kant, Immanuel (1992). *Über den Gemeinspruch: Das mag in der Theorie richtig sein, taugt aber nicht für die Praxis; Zum ewigen Frieden; Ein philosophischer Entwurf*, ed. H. F. Klemme (Hamburg).

Kant, Immanuel (1993). *Grounding for the Metaphysics of Morals*, ed. J. W. Ellington (Indianapolis: H).

Kant, Immanuel (1996a). *Practical Philosophy*, trans. and ed. M. J. Gregor, intro. A. Wood (Cambridge).

Kant, Immanuel (1996b). *Religion and Rational Theology*, trans. and ed. A. Wood and G. di Giovanni (Cambridge).

Kant, Immanuel (1998). *Groundwork of the Metaphysics of Morals*, ed. M. Gregor and C. M. Korsgaard (Cambridge).

Kant, Immanuel (1999). *Metaphysical Elements of Justice*, ed. J. Ladd (Indianapolis: H).

Kant, Immanuel (2000). *Kant on Freedom, Law, and Happiness*, ed. P. Guyer (Cambridge).

King, William (1691). *The State of the Protestants of Ireland* (London).

Kippis, Andrew (1772). *A Vindication of the Protestant Dissenting Ministers* (London).

Klein, Ernst Ferdinand (1797). *Grundsätze der natürlichen Rechtswissenschaft nebst einer Geschichte derselben* (Halle).

Klein, Ernst Ferdinand (1977). 'Über Denk- und Druckfreiheit', in Hinske and Albrecht 1977. 1st publ. 1784.

Knox, William (1769). *The Controversy between Great Britain and her Colonies Reviewed* (London). Extract in Goldie 1999, III.

Kreittmayr, W. X. A. von (1770). *Outline of General and of German Public Law* (Munich).

Kurland, P., and Lerner, R. (1987). *The Founders' Constitution*, 5 vols. (Chicago).

Lacratelle, Pierre Louis (1791). *De l'établissement des connoissances humaines et de l'instruction publique dans la constitution française* (Paris).

La Fare, Etienne Joseph de (1730). *Mandement de monseigneur l'évêque duc de Laon, second pair de France, Comte d'Ainsy, etc., sur la soumission due à la constitution Unigenitus, sur la fidélité indispensable des sujets envers leurs souverain, et sur les droits sacrez de l'épiscopat* (Laon).

Lafitau, Joseph François (1723). *Moeurs des sauvages ameriquains comparées aux moeurs des premiers temps* (Paris).

Lafitau, Joseph François (1974–7). *Customs of the American Indians Compared with the Customs of Primitive Times*, ed. W. M. Fenton and E. L. Moore, 2 vols. (Toronto).

La Mettrie, Julien Offray de (1748). *L'Homme machine* ('London' [Amsterdam]).

La Mettrie, Julien Offroy de (1994). *Man a Machine and Man a Plant*, ed. R. Watson and M. Rybalka (Indianopolis: H).

Lamoine, Georges, ed. (1992). *Charges to the Grand Jury, 1689–1803* (London).

Languet de Gergy, Jean Joseph (1719). *Instruction pastorale de monseigneur J.-Joseph Languet, évêque de Soissons, contenant un troisième avertissement à ceux de son diocèse qui se sont déclarés appellans de la constitution Unigenitus* (Paris).

Languet de Gergy, Jean Joseph (1729). *La Vie de la vénérable mère Marguerite-Marie, religieuse de la Visitation Sainte-Marie du monastère de Paray-le-Monial* (Paris).

Lanjuinais, Joseph (1774). *Le Monarque accompli, ou Prodiges de bonté*, 2 vols. (Lausanne).

Lanjuinais, Joseph (1776). *Eloge historique de Catherine II* (Lausanne).

Laporte, Abbé Joseph de (1764). *L'Esprit des monarques philosophes, Marc-Aurele, Julien, Stanislas et Frederic* (Amsterdam).

Law, John (1720). *The Present State of the French Revenues and Trade, and of the Controversy betwixt the Parliament of Paris and Mr Law* (London).

Law, William (1705). *Theses philosophicae* (Edinburgh).

Law, William (1717–19). *Three Letters to the Bishop of Bangor* (London).

Law, William (1724). *Remarks upon a Late Book, Entitled, the Fable of the Bees* (London).

Le Clerc, Jean (1987–97). *Epistolario*, ed. M. Grazia and M. Sina, 4 vols. (Florence).

Le Corgne de Launay, Abbé J. B. J. (1760). *Les Droits de l'épiscopat sur le second ordre, pour toutes les fonctions du ministère ecclésiastique* (Paris).

Lee, Richard Henry (1978). *Letters from the Federal Farmer to the Republican*, ed. W. H. Bennett (Alabama). 1st publ. 1787–8.

Lee, Richard Henry. *See also* Dickinson and Lee.

Legros, Charles François (1786). *Examen des systèmes de J. J. Rousseau et de M. Court de Gébelin* (Geneva).

Legros, Charles François (1787). *Analyse et examen du système des philosophes économistes* (Geneva).

Legros, Charles François (1788). *Analyse et examen de l'antiquité dévoilée, du despotisme oriental et du Christianisme dévoilé* (Geneva).

Leibniz, Gottfried Wilhelm von (1875–90). *Die philosophischen Schriften*, ed. C. I. Gerhardt, 7 vols. (Berlin). Repr. Hildersheim, 1965.

Leibniz, Gottfried Wilhelm von (1951). *Theodicy*, ed. A. Farrer, trans. E. M. Huggard (London). 1st publ. 1710.

Leibniz, Gottfried Wilhelm von (1969). *Philosophical Papers and Letters*, ed. L. E. Loemker (Dordrecht).

Leibniz, Gottfried Wilhelm von (1988). *Political Writings*, ed. P. Riley (Cambridge: CTHPT).

Leibniz, Gottfried Wilhelm von (1996). *New Essays concerning Human Understanding*, ed. P. Remnant and J. Bennett (Cambridge). Written *c.* 1704.

Le Mercier de la Rivière, Pierre Paul (1767). *L'Ordre naturel et essentiel des sociétés politiques* (Paris).

Leopold II, Emperor (1867). *Leopold II und Marie Christine. Ihr Briefwechsel (1781–1792)*, ed. A. Wolf (Vienna). (The manifesto of 2 Mar. 1790 at pp. 84–6.)

Le Paige, Louis Adrien (1753–4). *Lettres historiques sur les fonctions essentielles du parlement, sur le droit des pairs, et sur les loix fondamentales du royaume* (Amsterdam).

Leslie, Charles (1700). *The Case of the Regale and of the Pontificat* ([Oxford]).

Leslie, Charles (1703). *The New Association of those called Moderate Churchmen with the Modern Whigs and Fanatics*, Part II, Supplement (London).

Leslie, Charles (1704–9). *The Rehearsal* (London). Extracts in Goldie 1999, II.

Leslie, Charles (1711). *The Finishing Stroke: Being a Vindication of the Patriarchal Scheme of Government* (London).

Leslie, Charles (1715). *A Short and Easie Method with the Jews* (London).

Lessing, Gotthold Ephraim (1779). *Nathan der Weise* (Berlin).

Lessing, Gotthold Ephraim (1970–9). *Werke*, ed. H. G. Göpfert *et al.*, 8 vols. (Munich).

Lessing, Gotthold Ephraim (1985). *Werke*, ed. K. Bohnen *et al.*, 12 vols. (Frankfurt).

Levi, David (1789). *Letters to Dr Priestley in Answer to his Letters to the Jews* (London).

Lichtenberg, Georg Christoph (1967–92). *Schriften und Briefe*, ed. W. Promies, 4 vols. (Munich).

Limborch, Phillip van (1687). *De veritate religionis Christianae: amica collatio cum erudito Judaeo* (Gouda).

Limborch, Phillip van (1731). *The History of the Inquisition*, trans. S. Chandler, 2 vols. (London).

Linguet, Simon Nicolas Henri (1767). *Théorie des lois civiles, ou principes fondamentaux de la société* (London). Repr. Paris, 1984.

Linguet, Simon Nicolas Henri (1771). *La tête leur tourne* (n.p.)

Linguet, Simon Nicolas Henri (1774). *Oeuvres*, 6 vols. (London).

Linguet, Simon Nicolas Henri (1777–92). *Annales politiques, civiles, et littéraires du dix-huitième siècle*, 19 vols. (London). Repr. 1970.

Linguet, Simon Nicolas Henri (1779). *La tête leur tourne* (n.p.)

Linguet, Simon Nicolas Henri (1788). *Réflexions sur la résistance opposée à l'exécution des ordonnances promulgués le 8 mai; suivies de la différence entre la révolution passagère de 1771, et la réforme de 1788, dans l'ordre judiciaire en France* (Brussels).

Linguet, Simon Nicolas Henri (1927). *Memoirs of the Bastille*, trans. J. and S. F. Whithorn (London). 1st publ. 1783.

Locke, John (1692). *Some Considerations of the Consequences of the Lowering of Interest* (London). Repr. in Locke 1991.

Locke, John (1959). *An Essay concerning Human Understanding*, ed. A. C. Fraser (New York). 1st publ. 1689.

Locke, John (1975). *An Essay concerning Human Understanding*, ed. P. H. Nidditch (Oxford).

Locke, John (1983). *A Letter concerning Toleration*, ed. J. H. Tully (Indianapolis: H). 1st publ. 1689.

Locke, John (1988). *Two Treatises of Government*, ed. P. Laslett (Cambridge: CTHPT). 1st publ. 1689 (but bearing date 1690). This edn 1st publ. 1960.

Locke, John (1991). *Locke on Money*, ed. P. H. Kelly, 2 vols. (Oxford).

Locke, John (1993a). *Two Treatises of Government*, ed. M. Goldie (London).

Locke, John (1993b). *Political Writings*, ed. D. Wootton (London: P).

Locke, John (1997). *Political Essays*, ed. M. Goldie (Cambridge: CTHPT).

[Locke, John] (1999). *The Reception of Locke's Politics,* ed. M. Goldie, 6 vols. (London: P&C).

Luca, Ignaz. de (1776). *Leitfaden in die Polizeywissenschaft des Joseph von Sonnenfels* (Vienna).

Lucas, Charles (1748). *To the Free Citizens and Free-holders of Dublin* (Dublin).

Lucas, Charles (1770). *The Rights and Privileges of Parlements Asserted* (Dublin).

Lucretius (1959). *De rerum natura*, 3rd edn by W. H. Rouse (Cambridge, MA).

Ludewig, Johann Peter von (1727). *Die, von Sr. Königlichen Majestät unserm allergnädigstem Könige auf dero Universität Halle* (Halle).

Ludlow, Edmund (1698). *Memoirs*, ed. John Toland, 3 vols. (London).

Maass, Ferdinand, ed. (1951–61). *Der Josephinismus. Quellen zur seiner Geschichte in Österreich, 1760–1850*, 5 vols. (Vienna).

Mably, Gabriel Bonnot de (1740). *Parallèle des romains et des français par rapport au gouvernement* (Paris).

Mably, Gabriel Bonnot de (1748). *Le droit public de l'Europe* (Amsterdam and Geneva).

Mably, Gabriel Bonnot de (1749). *Observations sur les grecs* (Geneva).

Mably, Gabriel Bonnot de (1763). *Entretiens de Phocion sur la morale et la politique* (Amsterdam).

Mably, Gabriel Bonnot de (1765). *Observations sur l'histoire de France*, 2 vols. (Geneva).

Mably, Gabriel Bonnot de (1768). *Doutes proposés aux philosophes économistes sur l'ordre naturel des sociétés* (The Hague).

Mably, Gabriel Bonnot de (1769). *Phocion's Conversations or the Relation between Morality and Politics* (London).

Mably, Gabriel Bonnot de (1774). *De la législation, ou, principes des loix* (Amsterdam).

Mably, Gabriel Bonnot de (1784). *Observations on the Government and Laws of the United States of America* (Amsterdam).

Mably, Gabriel Bonnot de (1789). *Des droits et des devoirs du citoyen* (n.p.).Written 1758.

Mably, Gabriel Bonnot de (1794–5). *Oeuvres*, 15 vols. (Paris). Repr. Aalen, 1977.

Macaulay, Catherine (1763–83). *The History of England*, 8 vols. (London).

Macaulay, Catherine (1769). *Loose Remarks on . . . Hobbes's Philosophical Rudiments of Government and Society* (London).

Mackenzie, Sir George (1691). *The Moral History of Frugality* (London).

Mackintosh, James (1791). *Vindiciae Gallicae: Defence of the French Revolution and its English Admirers* (London).

Mackintosh, James (1799). *Discourse on the Study of the Law of Nature and Nations* (London).

Mackintosh, James (1851). *A Dissertation on the Progress of Ethical Philosophy*, in *Miscellaneous Works* (London). 1st publ. 1830.

Mackintosh, James (2005). *Vindiciae Gallicae: A Defence of the French Revolution and its English Admirers, against the Accusations of the Right Hon. Edmund Burke*, ed. D. Winch (Indianapolis: LF).

Mackworth, Humphrey (1701). *Vindication of the Rights of the Commons of England* (London).

McMaster, John B., and Stone, Frederick D., eds. (1888). *Pennsylvania and the Federal Constitution, 1787–1788* (Philadelphia).

Madan, Michael (1785). *Thoughts on Executive Justice, with Respect to our Criminal Laws* (London).

Madison, James (1900–10). *Writings*, ed. G. Hunt, 9 vols. (New York).

Madison, James (1962–91). *Papers*, ed. W. T. Hutchinson and W. M. E. Rachal, 17 vols. (Chicago).

Madison, James. *See also* Hamilton.

Maffei, Scipione (1744). *Dell'impiego del danaro* (Verona).

Mairobert, Mathieu François Pidanzat de (1774–6). *Journal historique de la révolution opérée dans la constitution de la monarchie françoise*, 7 vols. (London).

Maistre, Joseph de (1793). *Lettres d'un royaliste savoisien à ses compatriotes* (Annecy).

Maistre, Joseph de (1797). *Considérations sur la France* (London).

Maistre, Joseph de (1819). *Du pape*, 2 vols. (Lyon).

Maistre, Joseph de (1965). *Selected Works*, ed. J. Lively (London).

Maistre, Joseph de (1974). *Considerations on France*, ed. R. A. Lebrun, intro. I. Berlin (Cambridge: CTHPT).

Maistre, Joseph de (1975). *The Pope*, intro. R. A. Lebrun (New York).

Maistre, Joseph de (1993). *St Petersburg Dialogues: Or, Conversations on the Temporal Government of Providence*, ed. R. A. Lebrun (Montreal).

Maistre, Joseph de (1996). *Against Rousseau: On the State of Nature, and On the Sovereignty of the People*, ed. R. A. Lebrun (Montreal).

Mallet, David (1739). *Mustapha* (London).

Malthus, Thomas (1986). *Works*, ed. E. A. Wrigley and D. Souden, 8 vols. (London: P&C).

Malthus, Thomas (1992). *An Essay on the Principle of Population*, ed. D. Winch (Cambridge: CTHPT). 1st publ. 1798.

[Malthus, Thomas] (1994). *Works on Malthus and the Population Controversy*, 10 vols. (Bristol: T).

Malthus, Thomas (1996). *An Essay on Population: The First Six Editions*, 11 vols. (Bristol: T).

Mandeville, Bernard (1703). *The Pamphleteers: A Satyr* (London).

Mandeville, Bernard (1704). *Aesop Dress'd, or A Collection of Fables writ in Familiar Verse* (London). Facs. repr. Los Angeles, 1966.

Mandeville, Bernard (1714). *The Fable of the Bees: Or, Private Vices, Publick Benefits* (London).

Mandeville, Bernard (1720). *Free Thoughts on Religion, the Church, and National Happiness* (London).

Mandeville, Bernard (1732). *An Enquiry into the Origin of Honour, and the Usefulness of Christianity in War* (London).

Mandeville, Bernard (1924). *The Fable of the Bees: Or, Private Vices, Public Benefits*, ed. F. B. Kaye, 2 vols. (Oxford). Repr. 1988.

Mandeville, Bernard (1970). *The Fable of the Bees*, ed. P. Harth (London: P).

Mandeville, Bernard (1988). *The Fable of the Bees: Or, Private Vices, Public Benefits*, ed. F. B. Kaye (Indianapolis: LF). Repr. of 1924 edn.

Mandeville, Bernard (1997a). *The Fable of the Bees and Other Writings*, ed. E. J. Hundert (Indianapolis: H).

Mandeville, Bernard (1997b). *Private Vices, Publick Benefits?: The Contemporary Reception of Bernard Mandeville*, ed. J. M. Stafford (Solihull).

Mandeville, Bernard (1999). *By a Society of Ladies: Essays in The Female Tatler*, ed. M. M. Goldsmith (Bristol: T).

Manley, Mary Delariviere (1991). *New Atalantis*, ed. R. Balaster (London: P&C; reissued London: P, 1992). 1st publ. 1709.

Marat, Jean Paul (1774). *The Chains of Slavery* (London).

Marat, Jean Paul (1989–95). *Oeuvres politiques, 1789–1793*, ed. J. de Cock and C. Goetz, 10 vols. (Brussels).

Markham, William (1774). *A Sermon Preached before the House of Lords . . . January 31, 1774* (London).

Marmontel, Jean François (1767). *Bélisaire* (Paris).

Marmontel, Jean François (1972). *Mémoires*, ed. J. Renwick, 2 vols. (Clemont-Ferrand). 1st publ. 1793–6.

Marmontel, Jean François (1994). *Bélisaire*, ed. R. Granderoute (Paris).

Martini, Karl Anton von (1755). *Ordo historiae iuris civilis* (Vienna). 2nd edn 1757.

Martini, Karl Anton von (1767). *De lege naturali positiones* (Vienna).

Martini, Karl Anton von (1783–4). *Lehrbegriff des Natur-, Staats-, und Völkerrechts* (Vienna).

Martini, Karl Anton von (1788). *Allgemeines Recht der Staaten* (Vienna).

Mather, Moses (1775). *America's Appeal to the Impartial World* (Hartford, CN).

Maultrot, Gabriel Nicolas, and Mey, Abbé Claude (1752). *Apologie de tous les jugemens rendus par les tribunaux séculiers en France contre le schisme*, 2 vols. (n.p.)

Maultrot, Gabriel Nicolas, and Mey, Abbé Claude (1775). *Maximes du droit public français*, 2 vols., 2nd edn (Amsterdam). 1st publ. 1772.

Maultrot, Gabriel Nicolas, and Mey, Abbé Claude (1788). *Dissertation sur le droit de convoquer les Etats-généraux, tirée des capitulaires, des ordonnances du royaume, et des autres monuments de l'histoire de France* (n.p.).

Mavidal, Jérôme, *et al.*, eds. (1862–1913). *Archives parlementaires de 1787 à 1860: première série, 1787–1799*, 82 vols. (Paris).

Maxwell, Henry (1703). *An Essay towards an Union of Ireland with England* (London).

Meek, R. L., ed. (1962). *The Economics of Physiocracy: Essays and Translations* (London).

Melon, Jean François (1729). *Mahmoud le Gasnévide: histoire orientale, fragment traduit de l'arabe* (Rotterdam).

Melon, Jean François (1734). *Essai politique sur le commerce* (Amsterdam).

Melon, Jean François (1739). *A Political Essay upon Commerce*, trans. D. Bindon (Dublin).

Melon, Jean François (1983). *Opere I*, ed. O. Nicastro and S. Perona, 2 vols. (Pisa).

Mendelssohn, Moses (1983). *Jerusalem, or, On Religious Power and Judaism*, trans. A. Arkush, ed. A. Altmann (Hanover, NH). 1st publ. 1783.

Mendelssohn, Moses (1997). *Philosophical Writings*, ed. D. O. Dahlstrom (Cambridge).

Mercier, Louis Sébastien (1771). *L'An deux mille quatre cent quarante* (London).

Meslier, Jean (1970–2). *Oeuvres complètes*, ed. J. Deprun, R. Desné, and A. Soboul, 3 vols. (Paris).

Middleton, Conyers (1741). *The History of the Life of Marcus Tullius Cicero* (London).

Milbourne, Luke (1707). *The People not the Original of Civil Power* (London).

Millar, John (1771). *Observations concerning the Distinction of Ranks in Society* (London). Revised as *The Origin of the Distinction of Ranks*, 1779.

Millar, John (1787). *An Historical View of the English Government* (London).

Millar, John (1796). *Letters of Sidney on Inequality of Property* (Edinburgh).

Millar, John (1806). *The Origin of the Distinction of Ranks* (London). 1st publ. 1771, under this title 1779. Repr. Bristol, 1990.

Millar, John (1984). *Letters of Crito e Letters of Sidney*, ed. V. Merolle (Rome).

Millar, John (2006a). *An Historical View of the English Government*, ed. M. Phillips and D. Smith (Indianapolis: LF).

Millar, John (2006b). *The Origin of the Distinction of Ranks*, ed. A. Garrett (Indianapolis: LF).

Millar, John (forthcoming). *Letters and Occasional Writings*, ed. J. Cairns and A. Garrett (Indianapolis: LF).

Milton, John (1699). *Works*, ed. John Toland, 3 vols. (London).

Mirabeau, Victor de (1756). *L'Ami des hommes, ou, traité de la population* (Paris).

Molesworth, Robert (1694). *An Account of Denmark* (London).

Molyneux, William (1698). *The Case of Ireland's Being Bound by Acts of Parliament in England* (London). Repr. in Goldie 1999, I.

Monboddo, James Burnett, Lord (1773–92). *Of the Origin and Progress of Language*, 6 vols. (Edinburgh).

Montagu, Mary Wortley (1994). *Turkish Embassy Letters*, ed. M. Jack (London).

Montagu, Mary Wortley (1997). *Selected Letters*, ed. I. Grundy (London: P).

Montaigne, Michel de (1987). *An Apology for Raymond Sebond*, trans. M. A. Screech (London: P).

Montesquieu, Charles de Secondat, baron de (1914). *Correspondance*, ed. F. Gébelin and A. Morize, 2 vols. (Paris).

Montesquieu, Charles de Secondat, baron de (1950–5). *Oeuvres complètes*, ed. A. Masson, 3 vols. (Paris).

Montesquieu, Charles de Secondat, baron de (1958). *Oeuvres complètes*, ed. R. Caillois (Paris).

Montesquieu, Charles de Secondat, baron de (1964). *Oeuvres complètes*, ed. D. Oster and G. Vedel (Paris).

Montesquieu, Charles de Secondat, baron de (1965). *Considerations on the Causes of the Greatness of the Romans and their Decline*, trans. D. Lowenthal (Ithaca, NY). Repr. Indianapolis: H, 1999. 1st publ. 1734.

Montesquieu, Charles de Secondat, baron de (1973). *Persian Letters*, trans. C. Betts (London: P). 1st publ. 1721.

Montesquieu, Charles de Secondat, baron de (1977). *The Political Theory of Montesquieu*, ed. M. Richter (Cambridge).

Montesquieu, Charles de Secondat, baron de (1989). *The Spirit of the Laws*, ed. A. M. Cohler, B. C. Miller, and H. S. Stone (Cambridge: CTHPT). 1st publ. 1748.

Montesquieu, Charles de Secondat, baron de (1990). *Selected Political Writings*, ed. M. Richter (Indianapolis: H).

Montesquieu, Charles de Secondat, baron de (1991). *Pensées; Le Spicilège*, ed. L. Desgraves (Paris).

Montesquieu, Charles de Secondat, baron de (1999). *Persian Letters*, ed. G. R. Healy (Indianapolis: H).

Montesquieu, Charles de Secondat, baron de (2000). *Réflexions sur la monarchie universelle en Europe*, ed. F. Weil, in *Oeuvres complètes de Montesquieu*, II (Oxford: VF).

Montesquieu, Charles de Secondat, baron de (2000–). *Oeuvres complètes* (Oxford: VF). In progress.

More, Hannah (1801). *Works*, 8 vols. (London).

Morellet, André (1990). *Traité de la propriété*, ed. E. di Rienzo and L. Campos Boralevi (Florence).

Morellet, André (1998). *Mémoires sur le dix-huitième siècle et sur la révolution*, ed. J. P. Guicciardi (Paris). 1st publ. 1821.

Morelly, Etienne Gabriel (1743). *Essai sur l'esprit humain* (Paris). Repr. Geneva 1971.

Morelly, Etienne Gabriel (1751). *Le Prince, les délices des coeurs, ou traité des qualités d'un grand roi et système d'un sage gouvernement* (Amsterdam).

Morelly, Etienne Gabriel (1950). *Code de la nature, ou du véritable esprit des lois*, ed. G. Chinard (Paris). 1st publ. 1755.

Morelly, Etienne Gabriel (1971). *Essai sur l'esprit humain* (Geneva).

Moser, Friedrich Carl von (1759). *Der Herr und der Diener* (Frankfurt).

Moser, Friedrich Carl von (1765). *Von dem deutschen Nationalgeist* (Frankfurt).

Moser, Friedrich Carl von (1784). *Über Regentun, Regierung und Ministers* (Frankfurt).

Moser, Johann Jakob (1737–53). *Teutsches Staats-Recht*, 51 vols. (Nuremberg).

Möser, Justus, ed. (1768). *Osnabrückishe Geschichte*, 3 vols. (Osnabrück).

Möser, Justus (1775–86). *Patriotische Phantasien* (Berlin).

Moshammer, Franz Xavier von [J. von Sonnenfels] (1820), *Grundsätze der Polizei, Handlung und Finanzwissenschaft*, 3rd edn (Tübingen).

Moyle, Walter (1727). *An Essay on the Lacedaemonian Government*, in *Works* (London). Written 1698. Repr. in Goldie 1999, I.

Moyle, Walter, and Trenchard, John (1697). *An Argument, Shewing, that a Standing Army is Inconsistent with a Free Government* (London). Repr. The Rota, Exeter, 1971

Muratori, Lodovico Antonio (1747). *Della regolata divozione de' Cristiani* (Venice).

Muratori, Lodovico Antonio (1749). *Della pubblica felicità, oggetto de' buoni principi* (Lucca).

Muratori, Lodovico Antonio (1996). *Della pubblica felicità, oggetto de' buoni principi*, ed. C. Mozzarelli (Rome).

Necker, Jacques (1781). *State of the Finances of France* (London).

Nettelbladt, Daniel (1772). *Abhandlung von dem gantzen Umfange der natürlichen und der in Teutschland üblichen positiven gemeinen Rechtsgelahrtheit* (Halle).

Nettelbladt, Daniel (1777). *Systema elementare universae jurisprudentia naturalis* (Halle). 1st publ. 1749.

Newton, Isaac (1959). *Correspondence*, III, ed. H. W. Turnbull (Cambridge).

Novalis (Hardenberg, Friedrich von) (1799). *Die Christenheit oder Europa* (n.p.).

Ockham, William of (1957). *Philosophical Writings*, ed. and trans. P. Boehner (London).

O'Connor, Arthur (1795). *Speech . . . in the House of Commons of Ireland upon the Important Question of Catholic Emancipation* (London).

O'Connor, Arthur (1798). *State of Ireland* (Dublin).

O'Conor, Charles (1753). *Dissertations on the Antient History of Ireland* (Dublin).

O'Conor, Charles (1755). *The Case of the Roman Catholics of Ireland* (Dublin).

O'Conor, Charles (1771). *Observations on the Popery Laws* (Dublin).

Ogilvie, William (1781). *An Essay on the Right of Property in Land* (London). Extract in Goldie 1999, VI.

O'Leary, Arthur (1777). *Loyalty Asserted . . . With an Enquiry into the Pope's Deposing Power* (Cork).

O'Leary, Arthur (1779). *An Address to the Common People of the Roman Catholic Religion* (Cork).

O'Leary, Arthur (1780). *An Essay on Toleration* (Dublin).

Orobio de Castro, Isaac (1770). *Israel vengé, ou exposition naturelle des prophéties hébraïques* (London).

Ørsted, Anders Sandøe (1797). *Over sammenhængen mellem dydelærens og retslærens princip, et akademisk prisskrift* (Copenhagen). Repr. in Ørsted, *Skrifter i Udvalg*, 7 vols., ed. T. G. Jørgensen, VII: *Moralfilosofiske Skrifter*, 1936 (Copenhagen).

Otis, James (1764). *The Rights of the British Colonies Asserted* (Boston, MA). Extract in Goldie 1999, III.

Otis, James (1765). *Considerations on behalf of the Colonists* (Boston, MA).

Pagano, Francesco Mario (1993). 'Saggi politici', in *Opere complete*, ed. L. Firpo and L. S. Firpo (Naples). 1st publ. 1783–5.

Paine, Thomas (1795a). *The Age of Reason* (London). Repr. in Paine 1945. Pt I 1st publ. 1794.

Paine, Thomas (1795b). *Dissertation on the First Principles of Government* (London).

Paine, Thomas (1797). *Agrarian Justice* (London). Repr. in Paine 1945.

Paine, Thomas (1945). *The Complete Writings*, ed. P. S. Foner, 2 vols. (New York).

Paine, Thomas (1969). *Rights of Man*, ed. E. Foner and H. Collins (London: P). 1st publ. 1791–2.

Paine, Thomas (1982). *Common Sense*, ed. I. Kramnick (London: P). 1st publ. 1776.

Paine, Thomas (1989). *Political Writings*, ed. B. Kuklick (Cambridge: CTHPT).

Paine, Thomas (1992). *Rights of Man*, ed. G. Claeys (Indianapolis: H).

Paley, William (1785). *The Principles of Moral and Political Philosophy* (London). Extracts in Goldie 1999, IV, VI.

Paley, William (1792). *Reasons for Contentment Addressed to the Labouring Part of the British Public* (Carlisle).

Paley, William (1837). *Works*, ed. D. S. Wayland (London).

Paley, William (1838). *The Principles of Moral and Political Philosophy*, in *Works*, ed. E. Paley, 4 vols. (London).

Paley, William (1860). *Works*, ed. E. Paley (London).

Paley, William (1998). *Works*, intro. V. Nuovo, 6 vols. (Bristol: T).

Palmieri, Giuseppe (1789). *Pensieri economici relative al regno di Napoli* (Naples).

Palmieri, Giuseppe (1792). *Della ricchezza nazionale* (Naples).

Parliamentary History (1806–20). *The Parliamentary History of England*, 36 vols. (London).

Pauw, Cornelius de (1768–9). *Recherches philosophiques sur les américains* (Berlin).

Picardi, N., and Giuliani, A., eds. (1996). *Codex legum Svecicarum* (1734) (Milan).

Plato (1961). *Collected Dialogues*, ed. E. Hamilton and H. Cairns (New York).

Plowden, Francis (1792). *Jura Anglorum: The Rights of Englishmen* (London).

Plumard de Dangeul, Louis Joseph (1754). *Remarques sur les avantages et les désavantages de la France et de la Grande-Bretagne, par rapport au commerce et aux autres sources de la puissance des états* (Dresden [Paris]).

Pluquet, François André Adrien (1767). *De la sociabilité*, 2 vols. (Paris).

Pompignan, Jean Georges Lefranc de (1769). *Défense des actes du clergé de France, concernant la religion, publiés en l'assemblée de 1765* (Louvain).

Pope, Alexander (1950). *An Essay on Man*, ed. M. Mack, 2 parts (London). 1st publ. 1733–4.

Pope, Alexander (1963–). *Poems*, ed. J. Butt, 6 vols. (London).

Pope, Alexander (1986). *Prose Works*, ed. N. Ault and R. Cowler, 2 vols. (Oxford).

Price, Richard (1759). *Britain's Happiness and the Proper Improvement of it* (London). In Price 1991.

Price, Richard (1772). *An Appeal to the Public on the Subject of the National Debt* (London).

Price, Richard (1776). *Observations on the Nature of Civil Liberty, the Principles of Government, and the Justice and Policy of the War with America* (London). Repr. in Price 1991, and Goldie 1999, III.

Price, Richard (1777). *Additional Observations on the Nature and Value of Civil Liberty* (London).

Price, Richard (1778). *The General Introduction and Supplement to the Two Tracts on Civil Liberty* (London).

Price, Richard (1784). *Observations on the Importance of the American Revolution*. Repr. in Price 1991.

Price, Richard (1789). *A Discourse on the Love of our Country* (London). Repr. in Price 1991.

Price, Richard (1974). *A Review of the Principal Questions and Difficulties in Morals*, ed. D. D. Raphael (Oxford). 1st publ. 1758.

Price, Richard (1979). *Richard Price and the Ethical Foundations of the American Revolution: Selections from his Pamphlets*, ed. W. B. Peach (Durham, NC).

Price, Richard (1983–94). *The Correspondence*, ed. W. B. Peach and D. O. Thomas, 3 vols. (Durham, NC).

Price, Richard (1991). *Political Writings*, ed. D. O. Thomas (Cambridge: CTHPT).

Priestley, Joseph (1763). *A Course of Lectures on the Theory of Language and Universal Grammar* (Warrington).

Priestley, Joseph (1768). *An Essay on the First Principles of Government* (London). Repr. in Priestley 1993, and Goldie 1999, III.

Priestley, Joseph (1769). *Theological Repository*, no. 1 (London).

Priestley, Joseph (1771). *An Essay on the First Principles of Government* (London). 1st publ. 1768.

Priestley, Joseph (1778). *A Free Discussion of the Doctrines of Materialism, and Philosophical Necessity* (London).

Priestley, Joseph (1791a). *Letters to the Right Honourable Edmund Burke, Occasioned by his Reflections on the Revolution in France* (Birmingham).

Priestley, Joseph (1791b). *A Political Dialogue, On the General Principles of Government* (London).

Priestley, Joseph (1791c). 'Reflections on the Present State of Free Enquiry in this Country', in *Sermons by Richard Price D. D. F. R. S. and Joseph Priestley Ll.D. F. R.S.* (London). 1st publ. 1785.

Priestley, Joseph (1794). *The Present State of Europe Compared with Antient Prophecies* (London).

Priestley, Joseph (1817). 'A Free Address to Protestant Dissenters', in *The Theological and Miscellaneous Works*, ed. J. T. Rutt, 25 vols., XXII. Repr. Bristol: T, 1999. 1st publ. 1769.

Priestley, Joseph (1993). *Political Writings*, ed. P. N. Miller (Cambridge: CTHPT).

Pufendorf, Samuel von (1672). *De jure naturae et gentium* (London).

Pufendorf, Samuel von (1698). *Of the Nature and Qualification of Religion in Reference to Civil Society* (London).

Pufendorf, Samuel von (1706). *Le Droit de la nature et des gens*, trans. J. Barbeyrac, 2 vols. (Amsterdam).

Pufendorf, Samuel von (1707). *Les Devoirs de l'homme et du citoyen*, trans. J. Barbeyrac (Amsterdam).

Pufendorf, Samuel von (1718). *De officio hominis et civis juxta legem naturalem libri duo*, ed. G. Carmichael (Edinburgh). 2nd edn 1724.

Pufendorf, Samuel von (1742). *Et Menneskis og en Borgers Pligter efter Naturens Lov*, trans. C. Brugman (Copenhagen).

Pufendorf, Samuel von (1749). *The Law of Nature and Nations*, trans. Basil Kennet, 5th edn (London).

Pufendorf, Samuel von (1991). *On the Duty of Man and Citizen According to Natural Law*, ed. J. Tully, trans. M. Silverthorne (Cambridge: CTHPT). 1st publ. 1673.

Pufendorf, Samuel von (1996). *Briefwechsel*, ed. D. Döring (Berlin). In Samuel von Pufendorf, *Gesammelte Werke*, ed. W. Schmidt-Biggemann, 1.

Pufendorf, Samuel von (2002a). *The Divine Feudal Law*, trans. T. Dorrington, ed. S. Zurbuchen (Indianapolis: LF).

Pufendorf, Samuel von (2002b). *Of the Nature and Qualification of Religion in Reference to Civil Society*, ed. S. Zurbuchen (Indianapolis: LF).

Pufendorf, Samuel von (2003). *The Whole Duty of Man According to the Law of Nature*, ed. I. Hunter and D. Saunders (Indianapolis: LF).

Pufendorf, Samuel von (forthcoming). *Introduction to the History of the Principal Kingdoms and States of Europe*, ed. M. Seidler (Indianapolis: LF).

Pufendorf, Samuel von (forthcoming). *Of the Law of Nature and Nations*, ed. K. Haakonssen (Indianapolis: LF).

Pufendorf, Samuel von (forthcoming). *The Present State of Germany*, ed. M. Seidler (Indianapolis: LF).

Quesnay, François (1767). *Le Despotisme de la Chine* (Paris).

Quesnay, François (1962). 'Corn', in Meek 1962.

Quesnay, François (1972). *Tableau économique*, ed. M. Kuczynsko and R. Meek (London). 1st publ. 1758.

Radicati, Alberto (1734). *Twelve Discourses concerning Religion and Government* (London).

Ramsay, Allan (1771). *An Historical Essay on the English Constitution* (London).

Ramsay, Andrew (1721). *An Essay upon Civil Government* (London).

Ramsay, Andrew (1727a). *Les Voyages de Cyrus* ('Paris' [London?]).

Ramsay, Andrew (1727b). *The Travels of Cyrus*, 2 vols. (London).

Ramsay, Andrew (1748–9). *The Philosophical Principles of Natural and Revealed Religion*, 2 vols. (Glasgow).

Rapin, Paul (1725). *Acta regia* (London).

Rautenstrauch, Franz Stephan, *et al.* (1781). *Was ist der Papst?* (Vienna).

Raynal, Guillaume Thomas François, Abbé (1770). *Histoire philosophique et politique des établissements et du commerce des Européens dans les deux Indes*, 6 vols. (Amsterdam and The Hague). 2nd edn, 7 vols., The Hague, 1774. 3rd edn, 10 vols., Geneva, 1780.

Raynal, Guillaume Thomas François (1776). *A Philosophical and Political History of the Settlements and Trade of the Europeans in the East and West Indies*, 4 vols. (London).

Raynal, Guillaume Thomas François (1780). *See* Raynal 1770.

Raynal, Guillaume Thomas François (1877–82). *See* Grimm 1877–82.

Reid, Thomas (1990). *Practical Ethics: Being Lectures and Papers on Natural Religion, Self-Government, Natural Jurisprudence, and the Law of Nations*, ed. K. Haakonssen (Princeton).

Reimarus, Hermann Samuel (1756). *Die vornehmsten Wahrheiten der natürlichen Religion* (Hamburg).

Reiss, Hans Siegbert, ed. (1955). *The Political Thought of the German Romantics, 1793–1815* (Oxford).

Richelieu, Armand Jean du Plessis, cardinal de (1933). *Oeuvres*, ed. R. Gaucheron (Paris).

Richer, Edmond (1611). *Libellus de ecclesiastica et politica potesta* (Paris).

Ridpath, George (1703). *An Historical Account of the Antient Rights and Power of the Parliament of Scotland* (Edinburgh).

Robertson, William (1769). *History of the Reign of Charles v*, 3 vols. (London).

Robertson, William (1777). *The History of America*, 2 vols. (London).

Robertson, William (1791). *An Historical Disquisition concerning the Knowledge which the Ancients had of India*, 2 vols. (London).

Robertson, William (1972). *The Progress of Society in Europe*, ed. F. Gilbert (Chicago). 1st publ. 1769.

Robespierre, Maximilien (1789). 'Mémoire pour le Sieur Louis Marie Hyacinthe Dupond', in Robespierre 1910–59.

Robespierre, Maximilien (1910–59). *Oeuvres complètes*, ed. V. Barbier *et al.*, 10 vols. (Paris).

Robespierre, Maximilien (1967). *Robespierre*, ed. G. Rudé (New York).

Roederer, Pierre Louis (1853–9). *Oeuvres*, ed. A. M. Roederer, 8 vols. (Paris).

Roederer, Pierre Louis (1989). *The Spirit of the Revolution of 1789 and Other Writings on the Revolutionary Epoch*, ed. M. Forsyth (Aldershot).

Rohr, Julius Bernhard von (1716). *Compendieuse Haußhaltungs-Bibliothek* (Leipzig).

Roland, Marie (1937). *Un voyage en Suisse*, ed. G. R. de Beer (Neuchâtel).

Roland, Marie (1986). *Mémoires*, ed. P. de Roux (Paris).

Romilly, Samuel (1786). *Observations on a Late Publication, Intitled, Thoughts on Executive Justice* (London).

Romilly, Samuel (1810). *Observations on the Criminal Law of England: as it Relates to Capital Punishments* (London).

Rousseau, Jean Jacques (1911). *Emile*, trans. B. Foxley (London) 1st publ. 1762.

Rousseau, Jean Jacques (1915). *Political Writings*, ed. C. E. Vaughan, 2 vols. (Cambridge). Repr. Oxford, 1962.

Rousseau, Jean Jacques (1948). *Lettre à M. d'Alembert sur les spectacles*, ed. M. Fuchs (Lille). 1st publ. 1758.

Rousseau, Jean Jacques (1950). *Discourse on the Arts and Sciences*, in *The Social Contract and Discourses*, trans. G. D. H. Cole (New York). 1st publ. 1751.

Rousseau, Jean Jacques (1953a). *Political Writings*, ed. F. Watkins (Edinburgh).

Rousseau, Jean Jacques (1953b). *Confessions*, ed. J. M. Cohen (London: P). 1st publ. 1781–2.

Rousseau, Jean Jacques (1959–95). *Oeuvres complètes*, ed. B. Gagnebin, M. Raymond *et al.*, 5 vols. (Paris).

Rousseau, Jean Jacques (1962). *Political Writings*, ed. C. E. Vaughan, 2 vols. (Oxford).

Rousseau, Jean Jacques (1965–98). *Correspondance complète de Jean-Jacques Rousseau*, ed. R. A. Leigh, 52 vols. (Geneva and Oxford).

Rousseau, Jean Jacques (1968). *The Social Contract*, trans. M. Cranston (London and New York: P). 1st publ. 1762.

Rousseau, Jean Jacques (1971). *Oeuvres complètes*, ed. M. Launay, 3 vols. (Paris).

Rousseau, Jean Jacques (1974). *Emile*, trans. B. Foxley (London).

Rousseau, Jean Jacques (1979). *Emile, or, On Education*, ed. A. Bloom (New York).

Rousseau, Jean Jacques (1984). *A Discourse on the Origin of Inequality*, ed. and trans. M. Cranston (London: P). 1st publ. 1755.

Rousseau, Jean Jacques (1985). *The Government of Poland*, ed. W. Kendall (Indianapolis: H). 1st publ. 1772.

Rousseau, Jean Jacques (1987). *Basic Political Writings*, trans. and ed. D. A. Cress, intro. P. Gay (Indianapolis: H).

Rousseau, Jean Jacques (1988). *On the Social Contract*, ed. D. A. Cress (Indianapolis: H).

Rousseau, Jean Jacques (1992). *Discourse on the Origin of Inequality*, ed. D. A. Cress and J. Miller (Indianapolis: H).

Rousseau, Jean Jacques (1997a). *The Discourses and other Early Political Writings*, ed. V. Gourevitch (Cambridge: CTHPT).

Rousseau, Jean Jacques (1997b). *The Social Contract and other Later Political Writings*, ed. V. Gourevitch (Cambridge: CTHPT).

Rutherforth, Thomas (1754–6). *Institutes of Natural Law*, 2 vols. (London). Extract in Goldie 1999, VI.

Rutherforth, Thomas (1822). *Institutes of Natural Law* (Chicago). 1st publ. 1754.

Rutherforth, Thomas (1832). *Institutes of Natural Law* (Baltimore).

Rutledge, James (1777). *Essais politiques sur l'état actuel de quelques puissances* ('London', [Geneva]).

Sade, Donatien Alphonse, marquis de (1986–91). *Oeuvres*, ed. J. J. Pauvet and A. Le Brun, 15 vols. (Paris).

Sade, Donatien Alphonse, marquis de (1990–). *Oeuvres complètes*, ed. M. Delan, 3 vols. (Paris).

Saige, Guillaume Joseph (1775). *Catéchisme du citoyen, ou, Elémens du droit public français, par demandes et réponses* (Geneva). Repr. Paris, 1987.

Saint-Just, Louis Antoine (1984). *Oeuvres complètes*, ed. M. Duval (Paris).

Saint-Lambert, Jean François, marquis de (1765a). 'Intérêt', in *Encyclopédie*, VIII (Paris).

Saint-Lambert, Jean François, marquis de (1765b). 'Législateur', in *Encyclopédie*, IX (Paris).

Saint-Lambert, Jean François, marquis de (1766). *An Essay on Luxury* (London).

Saint-Lambert, Jean François, marquis de (1798). *Principes des moeurs chez toutes les nations*, 3 vols (Paris).

Saint-Lambert, Jean François, marquis de (1965). 'Luxury', in *Encyclopedia: Selections*, ed. N. S. Hoyt and T. Cassirer (Indianapolis). 1st publ. 1765.

Saint-Pierre, Charles Irénée Castel, Abbé de (1714). *A Project for Settling an Everlasting Peace in Europe* (London). 1st publ. Paris, 1713.

Saint-Simon, Claude Henri, comte de (1966a). *Introduction aux travaux scientifiques du XIXe siècle*, in *Oeuvres de Saint-Simon*, VI (Paris). 1st publ. 1807–8.

Saint-Simon, Claude Henri, comte de (1966b). *Mémoire sur la science de l'homme*, in *Oeuvres de Saint-Simon*, V, pt 2 (Paris). 1st publ. 1813.

Sandoz, Ellis, ed. (1991). *Political Sermons of the American Founding Era, 1730–1805*, 2 vols. (Indianapolis: LF). Repr. 1998.

Sauvage, Henri Michel (1787). *La Réalité du projet de Bourg-Fontaine, démontrée par l'exécution*, 2 vols. (Paris).

Schiller, Friedrich (1967). *On the Aesthetic Education of Man*, ed. and trans. E. M. Wilkinson and L. A. Willoughby (Oxford). 1st publ. 1795.

Schlözer, August Ludwig von (1793). *Allgemeines Staatsrecht und Staatsverfassungslehre* (Göttingen). Repr. n.p., 1970.

Schmalz, Theodor (1792). *Das reine Naturrecht* (Königsberg).

Schmalz, Theodor (1794). *Das natürliche Staatsrecht* (Königsberg).

Schmalz, Theodor (1795a). *Das natürliche Familienrecht* (Königsberg).

Schmalz, Theodor (1795b). *Das natürliche Kirchenrecht* (Königsberg).

Schmid, Carl Christian Erhard (1795). *Grundriß des Naturrechts* (Jena and Leipzig).

Schmid, Ludwig Benjamin Martin (1785). *Ausführliche Tabellen über die Policey, Handlungs- und Finanzwissenschaft* (Mannheim).

Schneewind, Jerome B., ed. (1990). *Moral Philosophy from Montaigne to Kant: An Anthology*, 2 vols. (Cambridge).

Schröder, Wilhelm von (1686). *Fürstliche Schatz- und Rentkammer* (Leipzig).

Schwab, Johann Christoph (1798). *Neun Gespräche zwischen Christian Wolff und einem Kantianer über Kants metaphysische Anfangsgründe der Rechtslehre und der Tugendlehre* (Berlin and Stettin). Repr. Brussels, 1968.

Scott, William (1699). *Disputatio juridica* (Edinburgh).

Seabury, Samuel (1930). *Letters of a Westchester Farmer, 1774–1775*, ed. C. H. Vance (White Plains, NY).

Seckendorff, Veit Ludwig von (1656). *Teutscher Fürsten-Staat* (Frankfurt).

Seckendorff, Veit Ludwig von (1678). *Teutscher Fürsten-Staat*, 5th edn (Frankfurt).

Sedgwick, James (1800). *Remarks, Critical and Miscellaneous, on The Commentaries of Sir William Blackstone* (London).

Seller, Abednego (1689). *The History of Passive Obedience* (London).

Shaftesbury, Anthony Ashley Cooper, third earl of (1977). *An Enquiry concerning Virtue or Merit*, ed. D. Walford (Manchester). 1st publ. 1699.

Shaftesbury, Anthony Ashley Cooper, third earl of (1995). *Characteristics of Men, Manners, Opinions, Times*, ed. L. Klein (Cambridge). 1st publ. 1711.

Shaftesbury, Anthony Ashley Cooper, third earl of (1999). *Characteristics of Men, Manners, Opinions, Times*, ed. P. Ayres, 2 vols. (Oxford).

Shaftesbury, Anthony Ashley Cooper, third earl of (2001). *Characteristics of Men, Manners, Opinions, Times*, 3 vols. (Indianapolis: LF).

Sharp, Granville (1775). *A Declaration of the People's Natural Right to a Share in the Legislature*, 2nd edn (London). 1st publ. 1774.

Sheehan, C. A., and McDowell, G. L., eds. (1998). *Friends of the Constitution: Writings of the 'Other' Federalists, 1787–1788* (Indianapolis: LF).

Sheridan, Charles (1779). *Observations on the Doctrine Laid down by Sir William Blackstone, respecting the Extent of the Power of the British Parliament* (London).

Sherlock, William (1691). *The Case of the Allegiance due to Soveraign Powers* (London). Facs. repr. The Rota, Exeter, 1979.

Sherlock, William (1691). *Their Present Majesties Government Proved to be Thoroughly Settled, and that we may Submit to it, without Asserting the Principles of Mr Hobbs* (London).

Sibbald, Sir Robert (1702). *The Liberty and Independency of the Kingdom and Church of Scotland* (Edinburgh).

Sidney, Algernon (1990). *Discourses concerning Government*, ed. T. G. West (Indianapolis: LF). Written *c.* 1683. 1st publ. 1698.

'Sidney' [Craig, John?] (1796). *Letters of Sidney* (Edinburgh).

Sieyès, Emmanuel (1789). *Qu'est-ce que le Tiers-Etat?* (Paris).

Sieyès, Emmanuel (1791). *An Essay on Privileges, and Particularly on Hereditary Nobility* (London).

Sieyès, Emmanuel (1970). *Qu'èst-ce que le Tiers-Etat?*, ed. R. Zappieri (Geneva).

Sieyès, Emmanuel (1982). *Essai sur les privilèges*, in Sieyès, *Qu'est-ce que le Tiers-Etat?*, ed. E. Champion (Paris). 1st publ. 1788.

Sieyès, Emmanuel (1985). *Ecrits politiques*, ed. R. Zappieri (Paris).

Sieyès, Emmanuel (2003). *Political Writings*, ed. M. Sonenscher (Indianapolis: H).

Sincerus, Anastasio (pseud.). *See* Amthor.

Smith, Adam (1970). *The Wealth of Nations*, Books I–III, ed. A. Skinner (London: P).

Smith, Adam (1976a). *The Theory of Moral Sentiments*, ed. D. D. Raphael and A. L. Macfie (Works, I, Oxford). 1st publ. 1759.

Smith, Adam (1976b). *An Inquiry into the Nature and Causes of the Wealth of Nations*, ed. R. H. Campbell, A. S. Skinner, and W. B. Todd, 2 vols. (Works, II, Oxford). 1st publ. 1776.

Smith, Adam (1978). *Lectures on Jurisprudence*, ed. R. L. Meek, D. D. Raphael, and P. G. Stein (Works, V, Oxford). Report A written 1762–3; Report B written 1763–4.

Smith, Adam (1980). *Essays on Philosophical Subjects*, ed. W. P. D. Wightman, J. C. Bryce, and I. S. Ross (Works, III; Oxford).

Smith, Adam (1981). *The Wealth of Nations*, ed. R. H. Campbell, A. S. Skinner, and W. B. Todd (Indianapolis: LF). 1st publ. 1776.

Smith, Adam (1982). *Lectures on Jurisprudence*, ed. R. L. Meek, D. D. Raphael, and P. G. Stein (Indianapolis: LF).

Smith, Adam (1983). *Lectures on Rhetoric and Belles Lettres*, ed. J. C. Bryce (Works, IV, Oxford).

Smith, Adam (1984). *The Theory of Moral Sentiments*, ed. D. D. Raphael and A. L. Macfie (Indianapolis: LF). 1st publ. 1759.

Smith, Adam (1987). *Correspondence of Adam Smith*, ed. E. C. Mossner and I. S. Ross, 2nd edn (Works, VI, Oxford).

Smith, Adam (1993). *The Wealth of Nations*, abr. and ed. L. Dickey (Indianapolis: H).

[Smith, Adam] (1997). *On Moral Sentiments: Contemporary Responses to Adam Smith*, ed. J. Reeder (Bristol: T).

[Smith, Adam] (1998). *On the Wealth of Nations: Contemporary Responses to Adam Smith*, ed. I. S. Ross (Bristol: T).

Somers, John (?) (1701). *Jura populi Anglicani* (London).

Sonnenfels, Joseph von (1765–76). *Grund sätze aus der Polizei-, Handlungs- und Finanzwissenschaft*, 3 vols. (Vienna). Third volume title begins *Grundsätze*.

Sonnenfels, Joseph von (1970). *Grundsätze der Polizey, Handlungs- und Finanz*, 3 vols. (Rome).

Sonnenfels, Joseph von. *See also* Moshamm.

Spedalieri, Nicola (1791). *De' diritti dell'uomo* (Assisi).

Spence, Joseph (1966). *Observations, Anecdotes, and Characters of Books and Men*, ed. J. M. Osborn, 2 vols. (Oxford).

Spence, Thomas (1775a). *The Grand Repository of the English Language* (Newcastle).

Spence, Thomas (1775b). *The Rights of Man* (Newcastle). Later edns entitled *The Real Rights of Man* and *The Whole Rights of Man*.

Spence, Thomas (1782). *The Real Reading Made Easy* (Newcastle).

Spence, Thomas (1792). *Burke's Address to the Swinish Multitude* (London).

Spence, Thomas (1793–5). *Pig's Meat, Or, Lessons for the Swinish Multitude* (London).

Spence, Thomas (1982). *The Political Works*, ed. H. T. Dickinson (Newcastle).

Spener, Philipp Jakob (1676). *Pia desideria; oder hertzliches Verlangen nach gottgefälliger Besserung der wahren evangelischen Kirchen* (Frankfurt).

Spener, Philipp Jakob (1963). *Pious Desires, or Heartfelt Longings for a Reformation of the True Evangelical Church*, trans. A. C. Deeter (Ann Arbor).

Spinoza, Benedict de (1670). *Tractatus theologico-politicus* (Amsterdam).

Spinoza, Benedict de (1958). *Political Works*, ed. A. G. Wernham (Oxford).

Spinoza, Benedict de (1972). *Opera*, 4 vols. (Heidelberg).

Spinoza, Benedict de (1991). *Tractatus theologico-politicus*, ed. S. Shirley (Leiden).

Spinoza, Benedict de (1996). *Ethics*, ed. E. Curley (London: P).

Spinoza, Benedict de (2000). *Ethics*, ed. G. H. R. Parkinson (Oxford).

Staël, Anne Louise Germaine Necker, Mme de (1800). *De la littérature considérée dans ses rapports avec les institutions sociales*, 2 vols. (Paris).

Staël, Anne Louise Germaine Necker, Mme de (1987). *An Extraordinary Woman: Selected Writings*, trans. V. Folkenflik (New York).

Staël, Anne Louise Germaine Necker, Mme de (1995). *Delphine*, trans. A. H. Goldberger (De Kalb, IL). 1st publ. 1802.

Stafford, J. M., ed. (1997). *Private Vices, Publick Benefits?: The Contemporary Reception of Bernard Mandeville* (Solihull).

Stanislas, King of Poland (1763). *Oeuvres du philosophe bienfaisant* (Paris).

Steele, Richard, ed. (1965). *The Spectator*, ed. D. F. Bond, 5 vols. (Oxford).

Steele, Richard, ed. (1982). *The Guardian*, ed. J. C. Stephens (Lexington, KY).

Steele, Richard, ed. (1987). *The Tatler*, ed. D. F. Bond, 3 vols. (Oxford).

Stephens, William (1696). *An Account of the Growth of Deism in England* (London).

Steuart, Sir James (1767). *An Inquiry into the Principles of Political Oeconomy*, 2 vols. (London).

Steuart, Sir James (1805). *Works*, 6 vols. (London). Repr. Bristol: T, 1995.

Steuart, Sir James (1998). *Principles of Political Oeconomy*, ed. A. S. Skinner, N. Kobayashi, and H. Mizuta, 4 vols. (London: P&C).

Stewart, Dugald (1854–60). *The Collected Works*, ed. Sir W. Hamilton, 11 vols. (Edinburgh). Repr. Bristol: T, 1994.

Stewart, Dugald. *See also* Smith 1980.

Stillingfleet, Edward (1662). *Origines sacrae* (London).

Suárez, Francisco (1944). *A Treatise on Laws and God the Law Giver*, in *Selections from Three Works*, ed. G. L. Williams, 2 vols. (Oxford).

Sullivan, Francis Stoughton (1772). *An Historical Treatise on the Feudal Law, and the Constitution and Laws of England* (London).

Sullivan, James (1791). *Observations upon the Government of the United States of America* (Boston, MA).

Sulzer, Johann Georg (1759). *Kurzer Begriff aller Wissenschaften* (Leipzig).

Svarez, Carl Gottlieb (1960). *Vorträge über Recht und Staat*, ed. H. Conrad and G. Kleinheyer (Cologne). Lectures 1791–2.

Swift, Jonathan (1701). *A Discourse of the Contests and Dissensions between the Nobles and the Commons in Athens and Rome* (London).

Swift, Jonathan (1725). *A Compleat Collection of all the Drapier's Letters* (Dublin).

Swift, Jonathan (1939–68). *Prose Works*, ed. H. Davis *et al.*, 14 vols. (Oxford).

Swift, Jonathan (1967). *A Discourse of the Contests and Dissensions between the Nobles and the Commons in Athens and Rome*, ed. F. H. Ellis (Oxford). 1st publ. 1701.

Swift, Jonathan (2003). *Gulliver's Travels*, ed. R. De Maria (London: P). 1st publ. 1726.

Tamburini, Pietro (1794). *Lettere teologico-politiche sulla presente situazione delle cose ecclesiastiche*, 4 vols. (n. p.).

Thale, Mary, ed. (1983). *Selections from the Papers of the London Corresponding Society, 1792–1799* (Cambridge).

Thelwall, John (1795). *The Natural and Constitutional Right of Britons to Annual Parliaments, Universal Suffrage, and the Freedom of Popular Association* (London). Repr. in Thelwall 1995.

Thelwall, John (1796). *The Rights of Nature, against the Usurpations of Establishments* (London). Repr. in Thelwall 1995. Extract in Goldie 1999, VI.

Thelwall, John (1808). *Mr Thelwall's Plan . . . for the Cure of Impediments of Speech . . . Cultivation of Oratory* (London). In Thelwall 1995.

Thelwall, John (1995). *The Politics of English Jacobinism: Writings of John Thelwall*, ed. G. Claeys (University Park, PA).

Thomasius, Christian (1688a). *Institutiones jurisprudentiae divinae* (Frankfurt). German trans., *Göttlichen Rechtsgelahrheit* (Halle, 1709).

Thomasius, Christian (1688b). *Introductio ad philosophiam aulicam* (Leipzig). German trans., *Einleitung zur Hof-Philosophie* (Leipzig, 1710).

Thomasius, Christian (1691a). *Einleitung zu der Vernunfft-lehre* (Halle).

Thomasius, Christian (1691b). *Auszübung der Vernunfft-lehre* (Halle).

Thomasius, Christian (1692). *Von der Kunst vernünftig und Tugendhaft zu lieben* (Halle).

Thomasius, Christian (1696). *Von der Artzeney wider die unvernünftige Liebe* (Halle).

Thomasius, Christian (1699a). *Versuch vom Wesen des Geistes* (Halle).

Thomasius, Christian (1699b). *Summarischer Entwurf des Grundlehren* (Halle). Repr. Aalen, 1979.

Thomasius, Christian (1705a). *Fundamenta juris naturae et gentium ex sensu communi deducta* (Halle). German trans.: see Thomasius 1709.

Thomasius, Christian (1705b). *Kurtzer Entwurff der politischen Klugheit* (Frankfurt).

Thomasius, Christian (1709). *Grundlehren des Natur- und Völkerrechts* (Halle).

Thomasius, Christian (1719). *Paulo plenior, Historia juris naturalis* (Halle). Repr. Stuttgart-Bad Cannstatt, 1972.

Thomasius, Christian (1995–). *Ausgewählte Werke*, 20 vols., ed. W. Schneiders (Hildesheim).

Thomasius, Christian (forthcoming). *Essays on the Church, State, and Politics*, ed. I. Hunter, M. Grunert, and T. Ahnert (Indianapolis: LF).

Thomasius, Christian (forthcoming). *Institutes of Divine Jurisprudence, with Selections from Foundations of the Law of Nature and Nations*, ed. T. Ahnert (Indianapolis: LF).

Thompson, William (1824). *An Inquiry into the Principles of the Distribution of Wealth most Conducive to Human Happiness* (London).

Thomson, James (1740). *Alfred: A Masque* (London).

Tindal, Matthew (1694). *An Essay concerning the Laws of Nations and the Rights of Soveraigns* (London).

Tindal, Matthew (1706). *The Rights of the Christian Church* (London).

Tindal, Matthew (1730). *Christianity as Old as the Creation* (London).

Tocqueville, Alexis de (1998–2001). *The Old Regime and the Revolution*, trans. A. S. Kahan, ed. F. Furet and F. Mélonio, 2 vols. (Chicago). 1st publ. 1856.

Todd, Janet, ed. (1996). *Female Education in the Age of Enlightenment*, 6 vols. (London: P&C).

Toland, John (1696). *Christianity not Mysterious* (London).

Toland, John (1697). *An Apology for Mr Toland* (London).

Toland, John (1698). *The Militia Reform'd* (London).

Toland, John (1701a). *The Art of Governing by Partys* (London).

Toland, John (1701b). *Anglia Libera* (London). Extract in Goldie 1999, I.

Tone, Wolfe (1791). *An Argument on Behalf of the Catholics of Ireland* (Belfast).

Tone, Wolfe (1796). *An Address to the People of Ireland* (Belfast).

Tone, Wolfe (1826). *Life of Theobald Wolfe Tone*, ed. W. T. Tone, 2 vols. (Washington).

Tone, Wolfe (1998). *Life of Theobald Wolfe Tone*, ed. T. Bartlett (Dublin).

Tone, Wolfe (1998–). *Writings*, ed. T. W. Moody, R. D. McDowell, and C. J. Woods (Oxford).

Tooke, John Horne (1765). *The Petition of an Englishman* (London).

Tooke, John Horne (1786). *Diversions of Purley* (London). Repr. Bristol: T, 2002.

Towers, Joseph (1782). *A Vindication of the Political Principles of Mr Locke, in Answer to the Objections of the Rev. Dr. Tucker* (London). Repr. in Goldie 1999, IV.

Trenchard, John (1698). *A Short History of Standing Armies* (London).

Trenchard, John, and Gordon, Thomas (1995). *Cato's Letters*, ed. R. Hamowy, 2 vols. (Indianapolis: LF). 1st publ. 1720–3. Extract in Goldie 1999, II.

Trenchard, John, and Moyle, Walter (1697). *An Argument, Shewing that a Standing Army Is Inconsistent with a Free Government* (London). Repr. The Rota, Exeter, 1971.

Treschow, Niels (1798). *Forelaesninger over den kantiske Philosophie* (Copenhagen).

Tucker, Josiah (1773). *Letters to the Rev. Dr. Kippis* (Gloucester).

Tucker, Josiah (1781). *A Treatise concerning Civil Government* (London). Repr. in Goldie 1999, IV.

Tucker, Josiah (1783). *Four Letters on Important National Subjects* (Gloucester).

Turgot, Anne Robert Jacques (1753). *Lettres sur la tolérance* (Paris).

Turgot, Anne Robert Jacques (1766). *Réflexions sur la formation et la distribution des richesses* (n.p.).

Turgot, Anne Robert Jacques (1973). *Turgot on Progress, Sociology, and Economics*, ed. and trans. R. L. Meek (Cambridge).

Turnbull, George (1740). *The Principles of Moral Philosophy*, 2 vols. (London). Facs. repr. Hildesheim, 1976.

Turnbull, George (2003). *Observations upon Liberal Education*, ed. T. O. Moore (Indianapolis: LF).

Turnbull, George (2005). *The Principles of Moral and Christian Philosophy*, ed. A. Broadie (Indianapolis: LF).

Turnbull, George (forthcoming). *Education for Life: Correspondence and Writings on Religion and Practical Philosophy*, ed. J. Moore and M. A. Stewart (Indianapolis: LF).

Tyrrell, James (1692–4). *Bibliotheca politica* (London). Repr. 2 vols., New York, 1979. Extract in Goldie 1999, I.

Uztáriz, Gerónimo de (1751). *The Theory and Practice of Commerce and Maritime Affairs*, 2 vols. (London). 1st Spanish edn 1724.

Vattel, Emerich de (1758). *Le Droit des gens, ou principes de la loi naturelle appliqués à la conduite et aux affaires des nations et des souverains*, 3 vols. (Leiden). Facs. repr. with English trans. by C. G. Fenwick, *The Law of Nations or the Principles of Natural Law Applied to the Conduct and to the Affairs of Nations and Sovereigns*, 3 vols. (Washington, 1916; New York, 1964).

Vattel, Emerich de (1762). *Questions de droit naturelle et observations sur le traité du droit de la nature de M. le Baron de Wolf* (Berne).

Vattel, Emerich de (forthcoming). *The Law of Nations, and the Duties of Citizens*, ed. T. Hochstrasser (Indianapolis: LF).

Vélez, Rafael de (1818–25). *Apología del altar y del trono*, 3 vols. (Madrid).

Venturi, Franco, ed. (1958). *Illuministi italiani*, III: *Riformatori lombardi, piemontesi e toscani* (Milan).

Venturi, Franco, ed. (1962). *Illuministi italiani*, V: *Riformatori napoletani* (Milan).

Venturi, Franco, and Torcellan, G., eds. (1965). *Illuministi italiani*, VII: *Riformatori delle antiche repubbliche, dei ducati, dello stato pontificio e delle isole* (Milan).

Verri, Pietro (1771). *Meditazioni sulla economia politica* (Livorno).

Verri, Pietro (1781). *Discorsi . . . sull'indole del piacere e del dolore, sulla felicità, e sulla economia politica* (Milan).

Verri, Pietro (1985). *Osservazioni sulla tortura*, ed. G. Barbarisi (Milan). 1st publ. 1770.

Verri, Pietro (1910–42), *Carteggio di Pietro e di Alessandro Verri*, ed. E. Greppi, A. Giulini, and G. Seregni, 12 vols. (Milan).

Verri, Pietro (1993). *Il Caffè (1764–1766)*, ed. G. Francioni and S. Romagnoli (Turin).

Vico, Giambattista (1725). *Scienza nuova* (Naples).

Vico, Giambattista (1744). *Scienza nuova*, 3rd edn (Naples).

Vico, Giambattista (1971). *Opere filosofiche*, ed. N. Badaloni and P. Cristofolini (Florence).

Vico, Giambattista (1974). *Opera giuridiche*, ed. N. Badaloni and P. Cristofolini (Florence).

Vico, Giambattista (1990). *Opere*, ed. A. Battistini (Milan).

Vico, Giambattista (2002). *The First New Science*, ed. L. Pompa (Cambridge: CTHPT).

Volney, Constantin François de (1791). *Les Ruines, ou, méditations sur les révolutions des empires* (Paris).

Volney, Constantin François de (1793). *La Loi naturelle, ou Catéchisme du citoyen français* (Paris).

Volney, Constantin François de (1795). *The Ruins, or, A Survey of the Revolutions of Empires* (London).

Volney, Constantin François de (1796a). *The Law of Nature, or, Catechism of French Citizens* (London).

Volney, Constantin François de (1796b). *An Abridgement of the Law of Nature, or, Catechism of French Citizens* (London).

Volney, Constantin François de (1799). *Leçons d'histoire prononcées à l'Ecole normale en l'an III de la République française* (Paris).

Voltaire (François Marie Arouet) (1740). Review of *Anti-Machiavel*, in *La Nouvelle Bibliothèque* (Paris).

Voltaire (François Marie Arouet) (1750). *La Voix du sage et du peuple* ('Amsterdam', [Paris]).

Voltaire (François Marie Arouet) (1763). *Traité sur la tolérance, à l'occasion de la mort de Jean Calas* (Geneva).

Voltaire (François Marie Arouet) (1766). *Commentaire sur le livre des délits et des peines* (Geneva).

Voltaire (François Marie Arouet) (1769). *Histoire du parlement de Paris* (Amsterdam).

Voltaire (François Marie Arouet) (1782). *An Essay on Universal History, the Manners and Spirit of Nations*, trans. T. Nugent, 2 vols. (Edinburgh).

Voltaire (François Marie Arouet) (1877–85). *Oeuvres complètes*, ed. L. Moland, 52 vols. (Paris).

Voltaire (François Marie Arouet) (1901a). *The Works of Voltaire: A Contemporary Version with Notes*, 36 vols. (New York).

Voltaire (François Marie Arouet) (1901b). *On Commerce and Luxury*, in *The Works of Voltaire: A Contemporary Version*, XXXVIII (New York).

Voltaire (François Marie Arouet) (1953–65). *Voltaire's Correspondence*, ed. T. Besterman, 107 vols. (Geneva).

Voltaire (François Marie Arouet) (1957). *Oeuvres historiques*, ed. R. Pomeau (Paris).

Voltaire (François Marie Arouet) (1961a). *The Age of Louis XIV*, trans. M. P. Pollack (London). 1st publ. 1751.

Voltaire (François Marie Arouet) (1961b). 'On the Pensées of M. Pascal', in *Philosophical Letters*, ed. E. Dilworth (Indianapolis). 1st publ. 1733.

Voltaire (François Marie Arouet) (1962). *Philosophical Dictionary*, ed. P. Gay (New York). 1st publ. 1764.

Voltaire (François Marie Arouet) (1963a). *Essai sur les moeurs et sur l'esprit des nations*, ed. R. Pomeau, 2 vols. (Paris). 1st publ. 1756.

Voltaire (François Marie Arouet) (1963b). *Politique de Voltaire*, ed. R. Pomeau (Paris).

Voltaire (François Marie Arouet) (1964a). *Lettres philosophiques*, ed. G. Lanson, 2 vols. (Paris) 1st publ. 1734.

Voltaire (François Marie Arouet) (1964b). *Lettres philosophiques*, ed. R. Pomeau (Paris).

Voltaire (François Marie Arouet) (1964c). *Lettres philosophiques, ou Lettres anglaises*, ed. R. Naves (Paris).

Voltaire (François Marie Arouet) (1964d). *Zadig, L'Ingénu*, trans. J. Butt (London: P). 1st publ. 1747.

Voltaire (François Marie Arouet) (1964–). *Correspondence*, ed. T. Besterman (Paris).

Voltaire (François Marie Arouet) (1965). *La Henriade*, ed. O. R. Taylor (Oxford: VF). 1st publ. 1723.

Voltaire (François Marie Arouet) (1966). *The Age of Louis XIV and Other Selected Writings*, trans. and ed. J. H. Brumfitt (London). 1st publ. 1751.

Voltaire (François Marie Arouet) (1968–). *The Complete Works*, ed. T. Besterman (Geneva and Oxford).

Voltaire (François Marie Arouet) (1969). *La Philosophie de l'histoire*, 2nd edn by J. H. Brumfitt, in *The Complete Works of Voltaire*, ed. T. Besterman *et al.*, LIX (Geneva). 1st publ. 1765.

Voltaire (François Marie Arouet) (1974). *Candide*, trans. J. Butt (London: P). 1st publ. 1759.

Voltaire (François Marie Arouet) (1979). *Philosophical Dictionary*, trans. T. Besterman (London: P).

Voltaire (François Marie Arouet) (1980). *Letters on England*, trans. and intro. L. Tancock (London: P).

Voltaire (François Marie Arouet) (1989a). *Selections*, ed. P. Edwards (London).

Voltaire (François Marie Arouet) (1989b). *Traité de métaphysique*, ed. W. H. Barber, in *Oeuvres complètes de Voltaire*, XIV (Oxford: VF). 1st publ. 1734.

Voltaire (François Marie Arouet) (1994a). *Political Writings*, ed. D. Williams (Cambridge: CTHPT).

Voltaire (François Marie Arouet) (1994b). *Letters concerning the English Nation*, ed. N. Cronk (Oxford).

Voltaire (François Marie Arouet) (1994c). *The Calas Affair: A Treatise on Toleration*, ed. B. Masters (London, 1994).

Voltaire (François Marie Arouet) (2000). *Candide*, ed. D. Wootton (Indianapolis: H).

Voltaire (François Marie Arouet) (2000–). *Les Oeuvres complètes*, ed. H. Mason (Oxford: VF).

Voltaire (François Marie Arouet) (2005). *Histoire du parlement de Paris*, ed. J. Renwick (Oxford: VF).

Voltaire (François Marie Arouet), and Frederick II of Prussia (1981). *The Refutation of Machiavelli's Prince or Anti-Machiavel*, trans. P. Sonnino (Athens, OH). 1st publ. 1740.

Voltaire (François Marie Arouet), and Frederick II of Prussia (1996). *Anti-Machiavel*, ed. W. Bahner and H. Bergmann, in *Oeuvres complètes de Voltaire*, XIX (Oxford).

Wake, William (1697). *The Authority of Christian Princes over their Ecclesiastical Synods Asserted* (London).

Walzer, Michael, ed. (1974). *Regicide and Revolution: Speeches at the Trial of Louis XVI* (Cambridge).

Warburton, William (1736). *The Alliance between Church and State* (London). Repr. in Goldie 1999, v.

Warburton, William (1788–94). *Works*, 7 vols. (London).

Warren, James, and Adams, John (1917–25). *Warren-Adams Letters*, 2 vols. (Boston, MA).

Warren, Mercy Otis (1989). *History of the Rise, Progress, and Termination of the American Revolution*, ed. L. H. Cohen, 2 vols. (Indianapolis). 1st publ. 1805.

Watson, William (1791). *A Charge Delivered to the Clergy of the Diocese of Llandaff* (London).

Wesley, John (1979). *Some Observations on Liberty*, in *Richard Price and the Ethical Foundations of the American Revolution*, ed. W. B. Peach (Durham, NC).

Wesley, John (1998). *Political Writings*, ed. G. Maddox (Bristol: T).

Whately, Thomas (1765). *The Regulations Lately Made concerning the Colonies, and the Taxes Imposed upon them, Considered* (London).

Wildman, John (?) (1689). *Some Remarks upon Government* (London).

Wilkes, John (1762–3). *The North Briton* (London).

Wilkes, John (1786). *The Speeches of Mr Wilkes in the House of Commons* (London).

Williams, David (1782). *Letters on Political Liberty* (London).

Williams, David (1789). *Lectures on Political Principles* (London).

Williams, David (1790). *Lessons to a Young Prince* (London).

Williams, E. Neville, ed. (1960). *The Eighteenth-Century Constitution* (Cambridge).

Williams, Samuel (1794). *The Natural and Civil History of Vermont* (Walpole, NH).

Wilson, James (1967). *Considerations on the Nature and Extent of the Legislative Authority of the British Parliament*, in *Works*, ed. R. G. McCloskey, 2 vols. (Cambridge, MA). 1st publ. 1774.

Wolff, Christian (1703). *Philosophia practica universalis* (Leipzig).
Wolff, Christian (1726). *Oratio de sinarum philosophia practica* (Frankfurt). German trans. by
  M. Albrecht (1985): *Rede über die praktische Philosophie der Chinesen* (Hamburg).
Wolff, Christian (1729–41). *Horae subsecivae Marburgenses*, 3 vols. (Frankfurt).
Wolff, Christian (1733a). *Ausführliche Nachricht von seinen eigenen Schriften* (Frankfurt).
Wolff, Christian (1733b). *Vernünfftige Gedancken von der Menschen Thun und Lassen* (Frankfurt).
  1st publ. 1721.
Wolff, Christian (1736). *Vernünfftige Gedancken von dem gesellschaftlichen Leben der Menschen*
  (Frankfurt).
Wolff, Christian (1738–9). *Philosophia practica universalis*, 2 vols. (Frankfurt).
Wolff, Christian (1740–8). *Jus naturae methodo scientifica pertractatum*, 8 vols. (Frankfurt).
Wolff, Christian (1749). *Jus gentium, methodo scientifica pertractatum* (Halle).
Wolff, Christian (1750a). *Institutiones juris naturae et gentium* (Halle).
Wolff, Christian (1750b). *The Real Happiness of a People under a Philosophical King Demonstrated*
  (London).
Wolff, Christian (1750–3). *Philosophia moralis, sive ethica*, 4 vols. (Halle).
Wolff, Christian (1758). *Principes du droit de la nature et des gens*, ed. J. H. S. Formey (Amster-
  dam).
Wolff, Christian (1770). *Logic: or Rational Thoughts on the Powers of the Human Understanding*
  (London).
Wolff, Christian (1772). *Institutions du droit de la nature et des gens*, trans. and ed. E. Luzac
  (Leiden).
Wolff, Christian (1962–). *Gesammelte Werke*, ed. J. Ecole, J. E. Hofmann, M. Thomann *et al.*
  (Hildesheim).
Wolff, Christian (1963). *Preliminary Discourse on Philosophy in General*, trans. R. J. Blackwell
  (Indianapolis).
Wolff, Christian (1992). *Moral Enlightenment: Leibniz and Wolff on China*, ed. J. Ching and
  W. G. Oxtoby (Nettetal).
Wollaston, William (1724). *The Religion of Nature Delineated* (London).
Wollstonecraft, Mary (1975). *A Vindication of the Rights of Woman*, ed. M. B. Kramnick
  (London: P). 1st publ. 1792.
Wollstonecraft, Mary (1989). *Works*, ed. J. Todd and M. Butler, 7 vols. (London: P&C).
Wollstonecraft, Mary (1995). *A Vindication of the Rights of Men, with A Vindication of the Rights
  of Woman*, ed. S. Tomaselli (Cambridge: CTHPT).
Wollstonecraft, Mary, and Godwin, William (1987). *A Short Residence in Sweden, Norway,
  and Denmark*, and *Memoirs of the Author of the Vindication of the Rights of Woman*, ed. R.
  Holmes (London: P).
Wyvill, Christopher, *et al.* (1782). *A Collection of Letters on the Proposed Reformation of the
  Parliament of Ireland*, 4 vols. (York).
Zedler, Johann Heinrich (1733–64). *Grosses vollständiges Universal-Lexicon*, 68 vols.
  (Leipzig).
Zincke, Georg Heinrich (1744). *Allgemeines oeconomisches Lexicon*, 2nd edn (Leipzig). 1st publ.
  1731.
Zincke, Georg Heinrich (1751). *Cameralisten-Bibliothek*, 4 vols. (Leipzig).
Zincke, Georg Heinrich (1755). *Anfangsgrunde der Cameralwissenschaften* (Leipzig).
Zinzendorf, Nicolaus Ludwig von (1962). *Hauptschriften*, ed. E. Beyreuther and G. Meyer,
  6 vols. (Hildesheim).
Zubly, John Joachim (1982). *'A Warm and Zealous Spirit': John J. Zubly and the American
  Revolution: A Selection of his Writings*, ed. R. M. Miller (Macon, GA).

Bibliography

SECONDARY SOURCES

Abbreviations

AHR   *American Historical Review*
BJECS   *British Journal for Eighteenth-Century Studies*
DHS   *Dix-huitième siècle*
ECS   *Eighteenth-Century Studies*
HEI   *History of European Ideas*
HJ   *Historical Journal*
HPT   *History of Political Thought*
JBS   *Journal of British Studies*
JHI   *Journal of the History of Ideas*
JMH   *Journal of Modern History*
PT   *Political Theory*
RHLF   *Revue d'histoire littéraire de la France*
SVEC   *Studies on Voltaire and the Eighteenth Century*
WMQ   *William and Mary Quarterly*

Aarsleff, H. (1982). *From Locke to Saussure: Essays on the Study of Language and Intellectual History* (Minneapolis).

Abraham, W. (1964). 'The Life and Times of Anton Wilhelm Amo', *Transactions of the Historical Society of Ghana*, 7:60–81.

Adam, U. (2003). 'Nobility and Modern Monarchy: J. H. G. Justi and the French Debate on Commercial Nobility at the Beginning of the Seven Years' War', *HEI*, 29:141–57.

Adam, U. (2004). 'Modern Monarchy and Commerce in the Writings of J. H. G. Justi' (doctoral thesis, Cambridge).

Adams, G. (1991). *The Huguenots and French Opinion, 1685–1787: The Enlightenment Debate on Toleration* (Waterloo, ON).

Adamson, R. (1881). *Fichte* (Edinburgh).

Adkins, A. W. H. (1960). *Merit and Responsibility: A Study in Greek Values* (Oxford).

Adorno, T. W., and Horkheimer, M. (1972). *Dialectic of Enlightenment* (New York). 1st publ. in German in 1947.

Advielle, V. (1884). *Histoire de Gracchus Babeuf et du babouvisme*, 2 vols. (Paris). Repr. Geneva, 1978.

Agesta, L. S. (1953). *El pensamiento politico del despotismo ilustrado* (Madrid). Repr. Seville, 1979.

Ahnert, T. (1999). *Christian Thomasius's Theory of Natural Law in its Religious and Natural Philosophical Context* (doctoral thesis, Cambridge).

Ahnert, T. (2002). 'The Prince and the Church in the Thought of Christian Thomasius', in Hunter and Saunders 2002.

Airiau, J. (1965). *L'Opposition aux physiocrates à la fin de l'ancien régime* (Paris).

Aitken, G. A. (1892). *The Life and Works of John Arbuthnot* (Oxford).

Aiton, S. J. (1985). *Leibniz: A Biography* (Bristol).

Ajello, R., ed. (1980). *Pietro Giannone e il suo tempo* (Naples).

Ajello, R., *et al.*, eds. (1985). *L'età dei lumi*, 2 vols. (Naples).

Akers, C. W. (1964). *Called unto Liberty: A Life of Jonathan Mayhew, 1720–1766* (Cambridge, MA).

Albee, E. (1902). *A History of English Utilitarianism* (London).

830

Albrecht, M., Engel, E. J., and Hinske, N., eds. (1994). *Moses Mendelssohn und die Kreise seiner Wirksamkeit* (Tübingen).

Aldridge, A. O. (1951). 'Shaftesbury and the Deist Manifesto', *Transactions of the American Philosophical Society*, 41:297–385.

Aldridge, A. O. (1975). 'Mandeville and Voltaire', in Primer 1975.

Aldridge, A. O. (1984). *Thomas Paine's American Ideology* (Newark, NJ).

Allan, D. (1993). *Virtue, Learning and the Scottish Enlightenment* (Edinburgh).

Allen, G. W., and Asselineau, R. (1987). *St John de Crèvecoeur: The Life of an American Farmer* (New York).

Allison, H. E. (1966). *Lessing and the Enlightenment* (Ann Arbor).

Allison, H. E. (1990). *Kant's Theory of Freedom* (Cambridge and New York).

Altmann, A. (1973). *Moses Mendelssohn: A Biographical Study* (Tuscaloosa, AL).

Altmann, A. (1982). 'Moses Mendelssohn über Naturrecht und Naturzustand', in A. Altmann, *Die trostvolle Aufklärung: Studien zur Metaphysik und politischen Theorie Moses Mendelssohns* (Stuttgart).

Ambrasi, D. (1979). *Riformatori e ribelli a Napoli nella seconda metà del settecento* (Naples).

Ameriks, K. (2000). *Kant and the Fate of Autonomy* (Cambridge).

Anderson, M. S. (1979). *Historians and Eighteenth-Century Europe, 1715–1789* (New York).

Anderson, P. (1974). *Lineages of the Absolutist State* (London).

Angermann, E., *et al.* (1972). 'Religion, Politik, Gesellschaft im 17. und 18. Jahrhundert', *Historische Zeitschrift*, 214:26–9.

Anon., ed. (1975). Atti del convegno internazionale di studi Muratoriani (Florence).

Ansart, P. (1970). *Sociologie de Saint-Simon* (Paris).

Antonetti, G. (1983). 'Etienne-Gabriel Morelly, l'homme et sa famille', *RHLF*, 83:390–402.

Antonetti, G. (1984). 'Etienne-Gabriel Morelly: l'écrivain et ses protecteurs', *RHLF*, 84:19–52.

Appleby, J. (1982). 'What Is Still American in the Political Philosophy of Thomas Jefferson?', *WMQ*, 39:287–309.

Appleby, J. (1984). *Capitalism and a New Social Order: The Republican Vision of the 1790s* (New York).

Appleby, J. (1986). 'Republicanism in Old and New Contexts', *WMQ*, 43:20–34.

Appleby, J. (1992). *Liberalism and Republicanism in the Historical Imagination* (Cambridge, MA).

Appleby, J. (2000). *Inheriting the Revolution: The First Generation of Americans* (Cambridge, MA).

Appolis, E. (1960). *Le 'tiers parti' catholique au XVIIIe siècle: entre jansénistes et zelanti* (Paris).

Appolis, E. (1966). *Les Jansénistes espagnols* (Bordeaux).

Arendt, H. (1955). *The Origins of Totalitarianism* (New York). 1st publ. 1951.

Arendt, H. (1978). *The Life of the Mind*, 2 vols. (London).

Arendt, H. (1982). *Lectures on Kant's Political Philosophy*, ed. R. Beiner (Chicago).

Aretin, K. O. von, ed. (1974). *Der aufgeklärte Absolutismus* (Cologne).

Aris, R. (1936). *History of Political Thought in Germany from 1789 to 1815* (London).

Arkush, A. (1994). *Moses Mendelssohn and the Enlightenment* (Albany, NY).

Armitage, D. (1997). 'A Patriot for Whom? The Afterlives of Bolingbroke's Patriot King', *JBS*, 36:397–418.

Armitage, D. (1998). *Theories of Empire, 1450–1850* (Aldershot).

Armitage, D. (2000a). 'Edmund Burke and Reason of State', *JHI*, 61:617–34.

Armitage, D. (2000b). *The Ideological Origins of the British Empire* (Cambridge).

Arndt, H. W. (1989). 'Erste Angriffe der Thomasianer auf Wolff', in Schneiders 1989.

Arntzen, S. (1996). 'Kant on Duty to Oneself and Resistance to Political Authority', *Journal of the History of Philosophy*, 34:409–24.

Ashraf, P. M. (1983). *The Life and Times of Thomas Spence* (Newcastle).

Aston, N. (1993a). 'The Dean of Canterbury and the Sage of Ferney: George Horne Looks at Voltaire', in Jacob and Yates 1993.

Aston, N. (1993b). 'Horne and Heterodoxy: The Defence of Anglican Beliefs in the Late Enlightenment', *English Historical Review*, 108:895–919.

Aston, N. (2003). *Christianity and Revolutionary Europe, 1750–1830* (Cambridge).

Atherton, H. A. (1974). *Political Prints in the Age of Hogarth* (Oxford).

Atwell, J. E. (1986). *Ends and Principles in Kant's Moral Thought* (Dordrecht).

Avenel, G. (1865). *Anacharsis Cloots, l'orateur du genre humain* (Paris). Repr. 1976.

Ayer, A. J. (1980). *Hume* (New York).

Ayres, P. J. (1997). *Classical Culture and the Idea of Rome in Eighteenth-Century England* (Cambridge).

Bachmann, H. M. (1977). *Die naturrechtliche Staatslehre Christian Wolffs* (Berlin).

Bachmann, H. M. (1983). 'Zur Wolffschen Naturrechtslehre', in Schneiders 1983.

Bachmann-Medick, D. (1989). *Die ästhetische Ordnung des Handelns: Moralphilosophie und Ästhetik in der Popularphilosophie des 18. Jahrhunderts* (Stuttgart).

Backscheider, P. R. (1988). 'The Verse Essay, John Locke and Defoe's *Jure divino*', *English Literary History*, 55:99–124.

Backscheider, P. R. (1989). *Daniel Defoe: His Life* (Baltimore).

Baczko, B. (1974). *Rousseau: solitude et communauté* (Paris). 1st publ. in Polish in 1970.

Baczko, B. (1978). *Lumières de l'utopie* (Paris).

Baczko, B. (1988). 'The Social Contract of the French: Sieyès and Rousseau', *JMH*, 60:98–125.

Baczko, B. (1989). *Utopian Lights: The Evolution of the Idea of Social Progress*, trans. J. L. Greenberg (New York).

Badinter, E., and Badinter, R. (1988). *Condorcet 1743–1794: un intellectuel en politique* (Paris).

Badir, M. G. (1974). *Voltaire et l'Islam, SVEC*, 125.

Baecque, A. de, Schmale, W., and Vovelle, M., eds. (1988). *L'An 1 des droits de l'homme* (Paris).

Baehr, S. L. (1991). *The Paradise Myth in Eighteenth-Century Russia* (Stanford).

Bahlman, D. (1957). *The Moral Revolution of 1688* (New Haven).

Bahner, W., and Bergmann, H. (1996). 'Introduction' to *Anti-Machiavel*, in *The Complete Works of Voltaire*, XIX (Oxford).

Bailyn, B. (1967). *The Ideological Origins of the American Revolution* (Cambridge, MA).

Bailyn, B. (1974). *The Ordeal of Thomas Hutchinson* (London).

Baker, K. M. (1964). 'The Earliest History of the Term "Social Science"', *Annals of Science*, 20:211–26.

Baker, K. M. (1973). 'Politics and Social Science in Eighteenth-Century France: The Société de 1789', in Bosher 1973.

Baker, K. M. (1975). *Condorcet: From Natural Philosophy to Social Mathematics* (Chicago).

Baker, K. M. (1978a). 'French Political Thought at the Accession of Louis XVI', *JMH*, 50:279–303.

Baker, K. M. (1978b). 'State, Society and Subsistence in Eighteenth-Century France', *JMH*, 50:701–11.

Baker, K. M. (1981). 'Enlightenment and Revolution in France', *JMH*, 53:281–303.

Baker, K. M. (1990). *Inventing the French Revolution* (Cambridge).

Baker, K. M. (1994a). 'The Idea of a Declaration of Rights', in Van Kley 1994b.

Baker, K. M. (2001). 'Transformations of Republicanism in Eighteenth-Century France', *JMH*, 73:32–53.

Baker, K. M., ed. (1987). *The French Revolution and the Creation of Modern Political Culture*, I: *The Political Culture of the Old Regime* (Oxford).

Baker, K. M., ed. (1994b). *The French Revolution and the Creation of Modern Political Culture*, IV, *The Terror* (Oxford).

Bakos, A. E. (1997). *Images of Kingship in Early Modern France: Louis XI in Political Thought, 1560–1789* (London).

Balayé, S. (1979). *Madame de Staël: lumières et liberté* (Paris).

Baldi, M. (2002). *Verisimile, non vero: filosofia e politica in Andrew Michael Ramsay* (Milan).

Ball, K. R. (1967). 'A Great Society: The Social and Political Thought of Joel Barlow' (doctoral thesis, Wisconsin).

Ball, T., Farr, J., and Hanson, R., eds. (1989). *Political Innovation and Conceptual Change* (Cambridge).

Ballestrem, K. G., ed. (1993). *Naturrecht und Politik* (Berlin).

Bancarel, G., and Goggi, G., eds. (2000). *Raynal, de la polémique à l'histoire*, *SVEC*, 12.

Banning, L. (1978). *The Jeffersonian Persuasion* (Ithaca, NY).

Banning, L. (1995). *The Sacred Fire of Liberty: James Madison and the Founding of the Federal Republic* (Ithaca, NY).

Barber, G., and Courtney, C. P., eds. (1988). *Enlightenment Essays* (Oxford).

Barber, W. H. (1955). *Leibniz in France: From Arnauld to Voltaire* (Oxford).

Barber, W. H. (1989). 'Introduction' to Voltaire, *Traité de métaphysique*, in *The Complete Works of Voltaire*, XIV (Oxford).

Baridon, M. (1977). *Edward Gibbon et le mythe de Rome* (Paris).

Barker, E. (1947). *The Social Contract* (Oxford).

Barker-Benfield, G. J. (1989). 'Mary Wollstonecraft: Eighteenth-Century Commonwealthwoman', *JHI*, 50:95–116.

Barlow, R. B. (1962). *Citizenship and Conscience: A Study in the Theory and Practice of Toleration in England during the Eighteenth Century* (Philadelphia).

Barnard, F. M. (1964). *Zwischen Aufklärung und politischer Romantik* (Berlin).

Barnard, F. M. (1965a). *Herder's Social and Political Thought* (Oxford).

Barnard, F. M. (1965b). 'Christian Thomasius: Enlightenment and Bureaucracy', *American Political Science Review*, 59:430–8.

Barnard, F. M. (1971). 'The Practical Philosophy of Christian Thomasius', *JHI*, 32:221–46.

Barnard, F. M. (1983). 'Self-Direction: Thomasius, Kant and Herder', *PT*, 11:343–68.

Barnard, F. M. (1988a). *Self-direction and Political Legitimacy: Rousseau and Herder* (Oxford).

Barnard, F. M. (1988b). 'Fraternity and Citizenship: Two Ethics of Mutuality in Christian Thomasius', *Review of Politics*, 50:582–602.

Barnard, F. M. (2003). *Herder on Nationality, Humanity, and History* (Montreal).

Barnes, A. (1938). *Jean Le Clerc et la république de lettres* (Paris).

Barny, R. (1974). 'Jean-Jacques Rousseau dans la Révolution', *DHS*, 6:59–98.

Barny, R. (1988). *L'Eclatement révolutionnaire du Rousseauisme* (Paris).

Barrell, R. A. (1988). *Bolingbroke and France* (Lanham, MD).

Barry, B. (1972). 'Warrender and his Critics', in Cranston and Peters 1972.

Bartlett, T. (1995). 'Protestant Nationalism in Eighteenth-Century Ireland', *SVEC*, 335:79–88.

Barton, H. A. (1986). *Scandinavia in the Revolutionary Era, 1760–1815* (Minneapolis).

Barton, P. F. (1978). *Jesuiten, Jansenisten, Josephiner: Eine Fallstudie zur frühen Toleranzzeit: Der Fall Innocentius Fessler* (Vienna).

Bastid, P. (1939). *Sieyès et sa pensée* (Paris).

Batscha, Z. (1981). *Studien zur politischen Theorie des deutschen Frühliberalismus* (Frankfurt).

Batscha, Z., ed. (1976). *Materialien zu Kants Rechtsphilosophie* (Frankfurt).

Battaglia, F. (1936). *Cristiano Thomasio: filosofo e giurista* (Bologna).

Baudet, H. (1988). *Paradise on Earth* (New Haven). 1st publ. 1965.

Baum, A. (1979). *Montesquieu and Social Theory* (Oxford).

Baumanns, P. (1990). *J. G. Fichte: Kritische Gesamtdarstellung seiner Philosophie* (Freiburg).

Baumgardt, D. (1952). *Bentham and the Ethics of Today* (Princeton).

Baumgardt, P. (1987). 'Kronprinzenopposition: Friedrich und Friedrich Wilhelm I', in Hauser 1987.

Bayle, F. (1945). *Les Idées politique de Joseph de Maistre* (Paris).

Bazzoli, M. (1986). *Il pensiero politico dell'assolutismo illuminato* (Florence).

Beales, D. E. D. (1975). 'The False Joseph II', *HJ*, 18:467–95.

Beales, D. E. D. (1980). 'Joseph II's "Rêveries"', *Mitteilungen des österreichischen Staatsarchivs*, 33:97–106.

Beales, D. E. D. (1985). 'Christians and *Philosophes*: The Case of the Austrian Enlightenment', in Beales and Best 1985.

Beales, D. E. D. (1987). *Joseph II*, 1: *In the Shadow of Maria Theresa, 1741–1780* (Cambridge).

Beales, D. E. D. (1991). 'Was Joseph II an Enlightened Despot?', in Ritchie and Timms, 1991.

Beales, D. E. D. (1993). *Mozart and the Habsburgs* (Reading).

Beales, D. E. D. (2002). 'Joseph II und der Josephinismus', in Reinalter and Klueting 2002.

Beales, D. E. D. (2003). *Prosperity and Plunder: European Catholic Monasteries in the Age of Revolution, 1650–1815* (Cambridge).

Beales, D. E. D. (2005). *Enlightenment and Reform in Eighteenth-Century Europe* (London).

Beales, D. E. D., and Best, G., eds. (1985). *History, Society and the Churches* (Cambridge).

Beales, D. E. D., and Hochstrasser, T. J. (1993). 'Un intellettuale piemontese a Vienna e un'inedita storia del pensiero politico' (1766), *Bolletino storico-bibliografico subalpino*, 91:248–309.

Beattie, J. M. (1986). *Crime and the Courts in England, 1660–1800* (Princeton).

Beck, L. W. (1971). 'Kant and the Right of Revolution', *JHI*, 32:411–22.

Becker, C. (1932). *The Heavenly City of the Eighteenth-Century Philosophers* (New Haven).

Becker, C. (1958). *The Declaration of Independence: A Study in the History of Political Ideas* (New York). 1st publ. 1922.

Becker, M. B. (1994). *The Emergence of Civil Society in the Eighteenth Century* (Bloomington, IN).

Beddard, R. A., ed. (1991). *The Revolutions of 1688* (Oxford).

Beer, M. (1920). *Pioneers of Land Reform* (London).

Béguelin, E. (1929). *En souvenir de Vattel, 1714–1767* (Neuchâtel).

Behrens, C. B. A. (1975). 'Enlightened Despotism', *HJ*, 18:401–8.

Behrens, C. B. A. (1985). *Society, Government and the Enlightenment* (New York).

Beik, P. (1956). *The French Revolution Seen from the Right* (Philadelphia).

Beiser, F. C. (1987). *The Fate of Reason: German Philosophy from Kant to Fichte* (Cambridge, MA).

Beiser, F. C. (1992). *Enlightenment, Revolution, and Romanticism: The Genesis of Modern German Political Thought, 1790–1800* (Cambridge, MA).

Beiser, F. C. (1996b). *The Sovereignty of Reason: The Defense of Rationality in the Early English Enlightenment* (Princeton).

Belcham, J. (1991). 'Republicanism, Popular Constitutionalism and the Radical Platform in Early Nineteenth-Century England', *Social History*, 6:1–32.

Bell, D. A. (1994). *Lawyers and Citizens: The Making of an Elite in Old Regime France* (Oxford).

Bell, D. A. (2001a). *The Cult of the Nation in France: Inventing Nationalism, 1680–1800* (Cambridge, MA).

Bell, D. A. (2001b). 'The Unbearable Lightness of Being French: Law, Republicanism and National Identity at the End of the Old Regime', *AHR*, 106:1215–35.

Bellamy, R. (1987). '"Da metafisico a mercatante": Antonio Genovesi and the Development of a New Language of Commerce in Eighteenth-Century Naples', in Pagden 1987.

Bellot, L. J. (1977). *William Knox: The Life and Thought of an Eighteenth-Century Imperialist* (Austin, TX).

Benassi, U. (1915–25). 'Guglielmo du Tillot, un ministro riformatore del secolo XVIII', *Archivio storico per le province parmensi*, new series, 15–16, 19–25.

Ben-Atar, D., and Oberg, B., eds. (1998). *Federalists Reconsidered* (Charlottesville).

Bene, E., ed. (1971). *Les Lumières en Hongrie, en Europe centrale et en Europe orientale* (Budapest).

Bénétruy, J. (1962). *L'Atelier de Mirabeau: quatre proscrits genevois dans la tourmente révolutionnaire* (Paris).

Bennett, G. V. (1975). *The Tory Crisis in Church and State, 1688–1730: The Career of Francis Atterbury, Bishop of Rochester* (Oxford).

Benot, Y. (1970). *Diderot: de l'athéisme à l'anticolonialisme* (Paris).

Benot, Y. (1991). 'Traces de l'*Histoire des deux Indes* chez les anti-esclavistes sous la Revolution', in Lüsebrink and Tietz 1991.

Bentley, M., ed. (1993). *Public and Private Doctrine* (Cambridge).

Benton, W. A. (1969). *Whig-Loyalism: An Aspect of Political Ideology in the American Revolutionary Era* (Rutherford, NJ).

Bergfeld, C. (1996). 'Pufendorf und Heineccius', in Palladini and Hartung 1996.

Bergh, G. C. J. J. van den (1988). *The Life and Work of Gerard Noodt, 1647–1725: Dutch Legal Scholarship between Humanism and Enlightenment* (Oxford).

Berlin, I. (1969). *Four Essays on Liberty* (London). 2nd edn Oxford, 2002.

Berlin, I. (1976). *Vico and Herder* (London).

Berlin, I. (1981). *Against the Current: Essays in the History of Ideas*, ed. H. Hardy (Oxford).

Berlin, I. (1990). *The Crooked Timber of Humanity* (London).

Berlin, I. (1993). *The Magus of the North: J. G. Hamann and the Origins of Modern Irrationalism* (London).

Berlin, I. (2000). *Three Critics of the Enlightenment: Vico, Hamann, Herder* (London).

Berman, D. (1975). 'Anthony Collins's Essays in the *Independent Whig*', *Journal of the History of Philosophy*, 13:463–9.

Berman, D. (1986). 'The Jacobitism of Berkeley's *Passive Obedience*', *JHI*, 47:309–20.

Berman, M. (1970). *The Politics of Authenticity* (New York).

Bernard, P. P. (1971). *Jesuits and Jacobins: Enlightenment and Enlightened Despotism in Austria* (Urbana, IL).

Berry, C. J. (1977). 'From Hume to Hegel: The Case of the Social Contract', *JHI*, 38:691–704.

Berry, C. J. (1994). *The Idea of Luxury* (Cambridge).

Berry, C. J. (1997). *Social Theory of the Scottish Enlightenment* (Edinburgh).

Besterman, T. (1969). *Voltaire* (London).

Betts, C. J. (1984). *Early Deism in France* (The Hague).

Bewley, C., and Bewley, D. (1998). *Gentleman Radical: A Life of John Horne Tooke, 1736–1812* (London).

Beyreuther, E. (1956). *August Hermann Francke, 1663–1727* (Marburg).

Bianchi, L. (1993). 'Nécessité de la religion et de la tolérance chez Montesquieu', in Mass and Postigliola 1993.

Bianco, B. (1989). 'Freiheit gegen Fatalismus: Zu Joachim Langes Kritik an Wolff', in Hinske 1989.

Bianco, B. (1993). 'Wolffianismus und katholische Aufklärung', in Klueting *et al.* 1993.

Bickart, R. (1932). *Les Parlements et la notion de souveraineté nationale au XVIIIe siècle* (Paris).

Bien, D. (1960). *The Calas Affair: Persecution, Toleration and Heresy in Eighteenth-Century Toulouse* (Princeton).

Bienert, W. (1934). *Der Anbruch der christlichen deutschen Neuzeit Dargestellt an Wissenschaft und Glauben des Christian Thomasius* (Halle).

Biller, G. (1983). 'Die Wolff-Diskussion 1800 bis 1982: Eine Bibliographie', in Schneiders 1983.

Birks, P., ed. (1993). *The Life of the Law* (London).

Birn, R. (1967). 'The French Language Press and the *Encyclopédie*, 1750–1759', *SVEC*, 55:263–85.

Birtsch, G. (1987). 'Der Idealtyp des augeklärten Herrschers: Friedrich der Große, Karl Friedrich von Baden und Joseph II im Vergleich', *Aufklärung*, 2:9–47.

Bitterli, U. (1976). *Die 'Wilden' und die 'Zivilisierten'* (Munich).

Black, E. C. (1963). *The Association: British Extraparliamentary Political Organization, 1769–1793* (Cambridge, MA).

Blackburn, R. (1988). *The Overthrow of Colonial Slavery, 1776–1848* (New York).

Blamires, C. (1990). 'Etienne Dumont: Genevan Apostle of Utility', *Utilitas*, 2:55–70.

Blanc, O. (1989). *Olympe de Gouges: une femme de libertés* (Paris)

Blanning, T. C. W. (1970). *Joseph II and Enlightened Despotism* (London).

Blanning, T. C. W. (1974). *Reform and Revolution in Mainz, 1743–1803* (Cambridge).

Blanning, T. C. W. (1990). 'Frederick the Great and Enlightened Absolutism', in Scott 1990.

Blanning, T. C. W. (1994). *Joseph II* (London).

Blanning, T. C. W. (1997). 'Frederick the Great and German Culture', in Oresko *et al.* 1997.

Blanning, T. C. W., and Cannadine, D., eds. (1996). *History and Biography* (Cambridge).

Bloch, E. (1961). *Christian Thomasius: Ein deutscher Gelehrter ohne Misere* (Frankfurt). 1st publ. Berlin, 1953.

Blom, H. W. (2002). 'The Republican Mirror: The Dutch Idea of Europe', in Pagden 2002.

Bloom, E. A., and Bloom, L. D. (1971). *Joseph Addison's Sociable Animal* (Providence, RI).

Bloom, E. A., Bloom, L. D., and Leites, E., eds. (1984). *Educating the Audience: Addison, Steele and Eighteenth-Century Culture* (Los Angeles).

Bluche, F. (1968). *Le Despotisme éclairé* (Paris).

Bluche, F. (1978). 'Sémantique du despotisme éclairé', *Revue historique de droit français et étranger*, 56:79–87.

Blum, C. (1974). *Diderot: The Virtue of a Philosopher* (New York).

Blum, C. (1986). *Rousseau and the Republic of Virtue* (Ithaca, NY).

Bödeker, H. E. (1993). 'Aufklärung als Kommunikationsprozeß', *Aufklärung*, 2:89–111.

Bödeker, H. E., and Hermann, U., eds. (1987). *Aufklärung als Politisierung: Politisierung der Aufklärung* (Hamburg).

Bödeker, H. E., Reill, P. H., and Schlumbohm, J., eds. (1999). *Wissenschaft als kulturelle Praxis, 1750–1900* (Göttingen).

Bödeker, H. E., and Steinbrügge, L., eds. (2001). *Conceptualizing Women in Enlightenment Thought: conceptualiser la femme dans la pensée des lumières* (Berlin).

Bodi, L. (1995). *Tauwetter in Wien: Zur Prosa der österreichischen Aufklärung, 1781–1795*, 2nd edn (Vienna).

Böhme, H. J. (1993). *Politische Rechte des einzelnen in der Naturrechtslehre des 18. Jahrhunderts und in der Staatstheorie des Frühkonstitutionalismus* (Berlin).

Bolgar, R. R., ed. (1979). *Classical Influences on Western Thought, 1659–1870* (Cambridge).

Bolton, C. A. (1969). *Church Reform in Eighteenth-Century Italy: The Synod of Pistoia, 1786* (The Hague).

Bond, W. H. (1990). *Thomas Hollis of Lincoln's Inn: A Whig and his Books* (Cambridge).

Bongie, L. (1961). 'Hume: "*Philosophe*" and Philosopher in Eighteenth-Century France', *French Studies*, 15:213–27.

Bongie, L. (1965). *David Hume: Prophet of the Counter-Revolution* (Oxford). 2nd edn Indianapolis, 2000.

Bonner, J. (1995). *Economic Efficiency and Social Justice: The Development of Utilitarian Ideas in Economics from Bentham to Edgeworth* (Aldershot).

Bonno, G. (1955). *Les Relations intellectuelles de Locke avec la France* (Berkeley).

Bonomi, P. (1986). *Under the Cope of Heaven: Religion, Society and Politics in Colonial America* (New York).

Bonwick, C. (1977). *English Radicals and the American Revolution* (Chapel Hill).

Boroumand, L. (1999). *La Guerre des principes: les assemblées révolutionnaires face aux droits de l'homme et à la souveraineté de la nation* (Paris).

Bosher, J. F., ed. (1973). *French Government and Society, 1500–1850* (London).

Boulton, J. T. (1963). *The Language of Politics in the Age of Wilkes and Burke* (London).

Bourgeois, R. (1998). *Jean-Joseph Mounier: un oublié de la Révolution* (Grenoble).

Bourke, R. (1999). 'Sovereignty, Opinion and Revolution in Edmund Burke', *HEI*, 25:99–120.

Bourke, R. (2000a). 'Edmund Burke and Enlightened Sociability: Justice, Honour and the Principles of Government', *HPT*, 21:632–56.

Bourke, R. (2000b). 'Liberty, Authority and Trust in Burke's Idea of Empire', *JHI*, 61:453–72.

Bowen, R. H. (1969). 'The *Encyclopédie* as a Business Venture', in Warner 1969.

Bowie, K. (2003). 'Public Opinion, Popular Politics, and the Union of 1707', *Scottish Historical Review*, 82:226–60.

Bowles, P. (1985). 'The Origin of Property and the Development of Scottish Historical Science', *JHI*, 46:197–210.

Bowles, P. (1986). 'John Millar, the Legislator and the Mode of Subsistence', *HEI*, 7:237–52.

Bowles, P. (1990). 'Millar and Engels on the History of Women and the Family', *HEI*, 12:595–610.

Boyce, D. G., Eccleshall, R., and Geoghegan, V., eds. (1993). *Political Thought in Ireland since the Seventeenth Century* (London).

Boyce, D. G., Eccleshall, R., and Geoghegan, V., eds. (2001). *Political Discourse in Seventeenth- and Eighteenth-Century Ireland* (London).

Bracken, H. (1984). *Mind and Language: Essays on Descartes and Chomsky* (Dordrecht).

Brading, D. A. (1983). *Classical Republicanism and Creole Patriotism: Simon Bolivar (1783–1830) and the Spanish American Revolution* (Cambridge).

Brading, D. A. (1991). *The First America: The Spanish Monarchy, Creole Patriots and the Liberal State, 1492–1867* (Cambridge).

Bradler-Rottmann, E. (1973). *Die Reformen Kaiser Josephs II* (Göppingen).

Bradley, J. E. (1989). 'The Anglican Pulpit, the Social Order, and the Resurgence of Toryism during the American Revolution', *Albion*, 21:361–88.

Bradley, J. E. (1990). *Religion, Revolution and English Radicalism: Nonconformity in Eighteenth-Century Politics and Society* (Cambridge).

Bradley, J. E. (2001). 'The Religious Origins of Radical Politics in England, Scotland, and Ireland, 1662–1800', in Bradley and Van Kley 2001.

Bradley, J. E., and Van Kley, D. K., eds. (2001). *Religion and Politics in Enlightenment Europe* (Notre Dame, IN).

Bradley, O. (1999). *A Modern Maistre: The Social and Political Thought of Joseph de Maistre* (Lincoln, NE).

Bradshaw, B., and Morrill J., eds. (1996). *The British Problem, c. 1534–1707* (London).

Brady, C., ed. (1989). *Worsted in the Game: Losers in Irish History* (Dublin).

Brain, T. J. (1978). 'Richard Watson and the Debate on Toleration in the late Eighteenth Century', *Price-Priestley Newsletter*, 2:4–26.

Brandt, R., ed. (1974). *Eigentumstheorien von Grotius bis Kant* (Stuttgart).

Brandt, R. (1982a). 'Das Erlaubnisgesetz, oder: Vernunft und Geschichte in Kants Rechtslehre', in Brandt 1982b.

Brandt, R., ed. (1982b). *Rechtsphilosophie der Aufklärung: Symposium Wolfenbüttel 1981* (Berlin).

Brandt, R. (1987). 'Zum "Streit der Fakultaten"', in Brandt and Stark 1987.

Brandt, R., and Stark, W., eds. (1987). *Kant-Forschungen*, 1 (Hamburg).

Brantlinger, P. (1996). *Fictions of State: Culture and Credit in Britain, 1694–1994* (Ithaca, NY).

Braubach, M. (1961). *Maria Theresias jüngster Sohn Max Franz* (Vienna).

Breen, T. H. (1998). 'Subjecthood and Citizenship: The Context of James Otis's Radical Critique of John Locke', *New England Quarterly*, 71:378–403.

Bremner, G. (1983). *Order and Chance: The Pattern of Diderot's Thought* (Cambridge).

Brender, N., and Krasnoff, L., eds. (2004). *New Essays on the History of Autonomy* (Cambridge).

Brewer, J. (1976). *Party Ideology and Popular Politics at the Accession of George III* (Cambridge).

Brewer, J. (1980a). 'English Radicalism in the Age of George III', in Pocock 1980.

Brewer, J. (1980b). 'The Wilkites and the Law, 1763–1764', in Brewer and Styles 1980.

Brewer, J. (1982). 'Commercialisation and Politics', in McKendrick *et al.* 1982.

Brewer, J. (1989). *The Sinews of Power: War, Money and the English State, 1688–1783* (New York).

Brewer, J., and Styles, J., eds. (1980). *An Ungovernable People: The English and their Law in the Seventeenth and Eighteenth Centuries* (London).

Broadie, A., ed. (2003). *The Cambridge Companion to the Scottish Enlightenment* (Cambridge).

Brockliss, L. W. B. (1987). *French Higher Education in the Seventeenth and Eighteenth Centuries* (Oxford).

Brockliss, L. W. B. (2002). *Calvet's Web: Enlightenment and the Republic of Letters in Eighteenth-Century France* (Oxford).

Brown, K. C., ed. (1965). *Hobbes Studies* (Oxford).

Brown, L. (1985). *Alexander Pope* (Oxford).

Brown, M. (2002). *Francis Hutcheson in Dublin, 1719–1730: The Crucible of his Thought* (Dublin).

Brown, R. (1984). *The Nature of Social Laws: Machiavelli to Mill* (Cambridge).

Brown, S. C., ed. (1996). *British Philosophy and the Age of Enlightenment* (London).

Brown, S. J., ed. (1997). *William Robertson and the Expansion of Empire* (Cambridge).

Brown, V. (1994). *Adam Smith's Discourse* (London).

Brown, W. (1969). *The Good Americans: The Loyalists in the American Revolution* (New York).

Browning, R. (1982). *Political and Constitutional Ideas of the Court Whigs* (Baton Rouge).

Browning, R. (1994). *The War of the Austrian Succession* (New York).

Bruch, R. (1997). *Ethik und Naturrecht im deutschen Katholizismus des 18. Jahrhunderts* (Tübingen).

Brückner, J. (1977). *Staatswissenschaften, Kamerlismus und Naturrecht: Ein Beitrag zur Geschichte der politischen Wissenschaft im Deutschland des späten 17. und frühen 18. Jahrhunderts* (Munich).

Brühlmeier, D. (1995). 'Natural Law and Early Economic Thought in Barbeyrac, Burlamaqui and Vattel', in Laursen 1995.

Brumfitt, J. H. (1970). *Voltaire: Historian* (London). 1st publ. 1958.

Brumfitt, J. H. (1972). *The French Enlightenment* (London).

Brunner, O. (1949). *Adeliges Landleben und europäischer Geist: Leben und Werk W. Helmhards von Hohberg, 1612–1688* (Salzburg).

Brunner, O., Conze, W., and Koselleck, R., eds. (1972–97) *Geschichtliche Grundbegriffe*, 8 vols. (Stuttgart).

Bryson, G. (1945). *Man and Society: The Scottish Inquiry of the Eighteenth Century* (Princeton). Repr. New York, 1968.

Buckle, S. (1991). *Natural Law and the Theory of Property: Grotius to Hume* (Oxford).

Buckle, S., and Castiglione, D. (1991). 'Hume's Critique of the Contract Theory', *HPT*, 12:457–80.

Buranelli, V. (1957). 'The Historical and Political Thought of Boulainvillers', *JHI*, 17:475–94.

Burchell, G., Gordon, C., and Miller, P., eds. (1991). *The Foucault Effect: Studies in Governmentality* (London).

Burg, P. (1974). *Kant und die französische Revolution* (Berlin).

Burgelin, P. (1952). *La Philosophie de l'existence de J.-J. Rousseau* (1952).

Burke, P. (1985). *Vico* (Oxford).

Burkhardt, J. (1992). 'Wirtschaft', in Brunner *et al.* 1972–97, VII.

Burns, A. (1984). 'The Source of the *Encyclopédie* Article "Loi naturelle (morale)"', *BJECS*, 7:39–48.

Burns, J. H. (1959). 'J. S. Mill and the Term "Social Science"', *JHI*, 22:431–2.

Burns, J. H. (1962). 'Bolingbroke and the Concept of Constitutional Government', *Political Studies*, 10:264–76.

Burns, J. H. (1986). *Absolutism: The History of an Idea* (London).

Burns, J. H., and Goldie, M., eds. (1991). *The Cambridge History of Political Thought, 1450–1700* (Cambridge).

Burrow, J. W. (1985). *Gibbon* (Oxford).

Burtt, S. (1992). *Virtue Transformed: Political Argument in England, 1688–1740* (Cambridge).

Bury, J. B. (1955). *The Idea of Progress* (New York). 1st publ. London, 1920.

Busch, W. (1979). *Die Entstehung der kritischen Rechtsphilosophie Kants, 1762–1780* (Berlin).

Butler, M. (1984). *Burke, Paine, Godwin and the Revolution Controversy* (Cambridge).

Butterwick, R. (1998). *Poland's Last King and English Culture: Stanislaw August Poniatowski, 1732–1798* (Oxford).

Butterwick, R., ed. (2001). *The Polish-Lithuanian Monarchy in European Context, c. 1500–1795* (Basingstoke).

Cairns, J. (1985). 'Blackstone, the Ancient Constitution and the Feudal Law', *HJ*, 28:711–17.

Cairns, J. (1991). 'Rhetoric, Language and Roman law: Legal Education and Improvement in Eighteenth-Century Scotland', *Law and History Review*, 9:31–58.

Cairns, J. (1993). 'The Origins of the Glasgow Law School', in Birks 1993.

Cairns, J. (1995). '"Famous as a School for Law, as Edinburgh . . . for Medicine": Legal Education in Glasgow, 1761–1801', in Hook and Sher 1995.

Caldwell, R. (1985). *The Era of the French Revolution: A Bibliography*, 2 vols. (New York).

Calhoon, R. M. (1994). *Dominion and Liberty: Ideology and the Anglo-American World, 1660–1801* (Arlington Heights, IL).

Calhoun, C., ed. (1992). *Habermas and the Public Sphere* (Cambridge, MA).

Callahan, W. J. (1972). *Honor, Commerce and Industry in Eighteenth-century Spain* (Cambridge, MA).

Calvet, J. (1968). *Bossuet* (Paris). New edn of *Bossuet: l'homme et l'oeuvre* (1941).

Cameron, D. (1973). *The Social Thought of Rousseau and Burke* (London).

Campbell, R. H., and Skinner, A. S. (1982a). *Adam Smith* (London).

Campbell, R. H., and Skinner, A. S., eds. (1982b). *The Origins and Nature of the Scottish Enlightenment* (Edinburgh).

Campbell, T. D. (1971). *Adam Smith's Science of Morals* (London).

Campbell, T. D. (1990). *Law and Enlightenment in Britain* (Aberdeen).

Canavan, F. (1960). *The Political Reason of Edmund Burke* (Durham, NC). Repr. 1982.

Canavan, F. (1995). *The Political Economy of Edmund Burke* (New York).

Cañizares-Esguerra, J. (2003). 'Eighteenth-Century Spanish Political Economy: Epistemology and Decline', *Eighteenth-Century Thought*, 1:295–314.

Cannon, G. (1990). *The Life and Mind of Oriental Jones* (Cambridge).

Cannon, J. (1973). *Parliamentary Reform, 1640–1832* (Cambridge).

Cannon, J. (1994). *Samuel Johnson and the Politics of Hanoverian England* (New York).

Canovan, M. (1978). 'Two Concepts of Liberty, Eighteenth-Century Style', *Price-Priestley Newsletter*, 2:27–43.

Canovan, M. (1984). 'The Un-Benthamite Utilitarianism of Joseph Priestley', *JHI*, 45:435–50.

Cantor, M. (1958). 'Joel Barlow, Lawyer and Legal Philosopher', *American Quarterly*, 10:165–74.

Capra, C. (1984). 'Il Settecento', in Sella and Capra 1984.

Capra, C. (1985). 'Il "Mosé della Lombardia": la missione di Carlo Antonio Martini a Milano, 1785–1786', in Mozzarelli and Olmi, eds., 1985.

Capra, C. (1989). 'Presentazione', in G. Gorani and A. Tarchetti, eds., *Storia di Milano dalla sua fondazione fino all'anno 1796* (Milan).

Capra, C. (2002). *I progressi della ragione: vita di Pietro Verri* (Bologna).

Capra, C., ed. (1999). *Pietro Verri e il suo tempo* (Milan).

Carboncini, S. (1989). 'Die thomasianisch-pietistische Tradition und ihre Fortsetzung durch Christian August Crucius', in Schneiders 1989.

Carboncini, S. (1993). 'Christian Wolff in Frankreich: Zum Verhältnis von französischer und deutscher Aufklärung', in Schneiders 1993.

Carcassonne, E. (1927). *Montesquieu et le problème de la constitution française au XVIIIe siècle* (Paris).

Carcassonne, E. (1946). *Fénelon: l'homme et l'oeuvre* (Paris).

Carpanetto, D., and Ricuperati, G. (1987). *Italy in the Age of Reason, 1685–1789* (London).

Carpenter, K. (1977). *Dialogue in Political Economy: Translations from and into German in the Eighteenth Century* (Boston, MA).

Carpenter, K. (2002). *The Dissemination of the Wealth of Nations in French and in France, 1776–1843* (New York).

Carroll, R. T. (1975). *The Common-sense Philosophy of Bishop Edward Stillingfleet* (The Hague).

Carrithers, D. W. (1991). 'Not so Virtuous: Montesquieu, Venice and the Theory of Aristocratic Republicanism', *JHI*, 52:245–68.

Carrithers, D. W. (1995). 'The Enlightenment Science of Society', in Fox et al. 1995.

Carrithers, D. W. (2001a). 'Introduction: An Appreciation of 'The Spirit of Laws', in Carrithers et al. 2001.

Carrithers, D. W. (2001b). 'Democratic and Aristocratic Republics: Ancient and Modern', in Carrithers et al. 2001.

Carrithers, D. W. (2001c). 'Montesquieu and the Liberal Philosophy of Jurisprudence', in Carrithers et al. 2001.

Carrithers, D. W., Mosher, M. A., and Rahe, P. A., eds. (2001). *Montesquieu's Science of Politics* (Lanham, MD).

Carrive, P. (1983). *La Philosophie des passions chez Bernard Mandeville* (Lille).

Carruthers, B. G. (1996). *City of Capital: Politics and Markets in the English Financial Revolution* (Princeton).

Carsten, F. L. (1959). *Princes and Parliaments in Germany from the Fifteenth to the Eighteenth Century* (Oxford).

Carter, J. (1969). 'The Revolution and the Constitution', in Holmes 1969.

Carvalho dos Santos, M. H., ed. (1984). *Pombal revisitado*, 2 vols. (Lisbon).

Cassirer, E. (1916). *Freiheit und Form* (Berlin).

Cassirer, E. (1945). *Rousseau, Kant, Goethe* (Princeton).

Cassirer, E. (1951). *The Philosophy of the Enlightenment* (Princeton). 1st publ. in German in 1932.

Cassirer, E. (1955). *The Philosophy of Symbolic Forms*, II: *Mythical Thought*, trans. R. Manheim (Oxford). 1st publ. in German, Berlin, 1923–9.

Cassirer, E. (1963). *The Question of Jean-Jacques Rousseau*, trans. and ed. P. Gay (Bloomington). 1st publ. in German, 1932.

Cassirer, E. (1981). *Kant's Life and Thought* (New Haven). Trans. of 2nd German edn Berlin, 1921.

Castiglione, D., and Sharpe, L., eds. (1995). *Shifting the Boundaries: Transformation of the Languages of Public and Private in the Eighteenth Century* (Exeter).

Castro, C. de (1996). *Campomanes: estado y reformismo ilustrado* (Madrid).

Casula, M. (1979). 'Die Beziehungen Wolff-Thomas-Carbo in der Metaphysica latina: Zur Quellengeschichte der Thomas-Rezeption bei Christian Wolff', *Studia Leibnitiana*, 11:98–123.

Caton, H. (1988). *The Politics of Progress: The Origins and Development of the Commercial Republic, 1600–1835* (Gainesville, FL).

Cavaciocchi, S., ed. (2000). *Il ruolo economico delle minoranze in Europa, secc. XIII–XVIII* (Prato).

Cavallar, G. (2002). *The Rights of Strangers: Theories of International Hospitality, the Global Community and Political Justice since Vitoria* (Aldershot).

Cerny, G. (1987). *Theology, Politics and Letters at the Crossroads of European Civilization: Jacques Basnage and the Baylean Huguenot Refugees in the Dutch Republic* (Dordrecht).

Cestre, C. (1906). *La République française et les poètes anglais* (Paris).

Chadwick, O. (1981). *The Popes and European Revolution* (New York and Oxford).

Challamel, J. B. (1895). *Les Clubs contre-révolutionnaires: cercles, comités, sociétés, salons, réunions, restaurants et librairies* (Paris).

Champion, J. A. I. (1992). *The Pillars of Priestcraft Shaken: The Church of England and its Enemies, 1660–1730* (Cambridge).

Champion, J. A. I. (2003). *Republican Learning: John Toland and the Crisis of Christian Culture, 1696–1722* (Manchester).

Chapman, G. W. (1967). *Edmund Burke: The Practical Imagination* (Cambridge, MA).

Chapman, P. (1984). 'Jacobite Political Argument in England, 1714–1766' (doctoral thesis, Cambridge).

Chartier, R. (1987). *The Cultural Uses of Print in Early Modern France* (Princeton).

Chartier, R. (1988). *Cultural History* (Ithaca).

Chartier, R. (1990). *Les Origines culturelles de la Révolution française* (Paris).

Chartier, R. (1991). *The Cultural Origins of the French Revolution*, trans. L. G. Cochrane (Durham, NC).

Chartier, R., and Martin, H. J., eds. (1984). *Le Livre triomphant* (Paris).

Charvet, J. (1974). *The Social Problem in the Philosophy of Rousseau* (Cambridge).

Chase, M. (1988). '*The People's Farm': English Radical Agrarianism, 1775–1840* (Oxford).

Châtellier, L. (1987). *L'Europe des dévots* (Paris).

Chaudhuri, J., ed. (1977). *The Non-Lockean Roots of American Democratic Thought* (Tucson).

Chaussinand-Nogaret, G. (1985). *Madame Roland: une femme en révolution* (Paris).

Cherel, A. (1917). *Fénelon au XVIIIe siècle en France (1715–1820)* (Paris).

Cherry, G. L. (1950). 'The Legal and Philosophical Position of the Jacobites, 1688–1689', *JMH*, 22:309–21.

Childs, N. (2000). *A Political Academy in Paris, 1724–1731: The Entresol and its Members* (Oxford).

Chinard, G. (1934). *L'Amérique et le rêve exotique dans la littérature française au XVIIe et au XVIIIe siècle* (Paris).

Chinnici, J. P. (1980). *The English Catholic Enlightenment* (Shepherdstown, VA).

Chisick, H. (1981). *The Limits of Reform in the Enlightenment: Attitudes Towards the Education of the Lower Classes in Eighteenth-Century France* (Princeton).

Chisick, H. (1991). 'The Ambivalence of the Idea of Equality in the French Enlightenment', *HEI*, 13:215–41.

Chisick, H. (2001). 'Utopia, Reform and Revolution: The Political Assumptions of L. S. Mercier's *L'An 2440*', *HPT*, 22:648–68.

Chitnis, A. (1986). *The Scottish Enlightenment and Early Victorian Society* (London).

Chitwood, O. P. (1967). *Richard Henry Lee, Statesman of the Revolution* (Morgantown, WVA).

Christian, W. (1973). 'James Mackintosh, Burke and the Cause of Reform', *ECS*, 7:193–206.

Christie, I. R. (1956). 'Economical Reform and "the Influence of the Crown", 1780', *Cambridge Historical Journal*, 12:144–54.

Christie, I. R. (1962). *Wilkes, Wyvill and Reform* (London).

Claeys, G. (1986a). 'William Godwin's Critique of Democracy and Republicanism and its Sources', *HEI*, 7:253–70.

Claeys, G. (1986b). '"Individualism", "Socialism" and "Social Science"', *JHI*, 47:81–93.

Claeys, G. (1989a). *Citizens and Saints: Politics and Anti-Politics in Early British Socialism* (Cambridge).

Claeys, G. (1989b). *Thomas Paine: Social and Political Thought* (London).

Claeys, G. (1989c). 'Republicanism versus Commercial Society: Paine, Burke and the French Revolution Debate', *Bulletin of the Society for the Study of Labour History*, 54:4–13.

Claeys, G. (1990). 'The French Revolution Debate and British Political Thought', *HPT*, 11:59–80.

Claeys, G. (1994b). 'The Origins of the Rights of Labor: Republicanism, Commerce and the Construction of Modern Social Theory in Britain, 1796–1805', *JMH*, 66: 249–90.

Clark, J. C. D. (1985). *English Society, 1688–1832: Ideology, Social Structure and Political Practice during the Ancien Regime* (Cambridge). 2nd edn 2000.

Clark, J. C. D. (1994a). *The Language of Liberty, 1660–1832: Political Discourse and Social Dynamics in the Anglo-American World* (Cambridge).

Clark, J. C. D. (1994b). *Samuel Johnson: Literature, Religion and English Cultural Politics from the Restoration to Romanticism* (Cambridge).

Clark, J. P. (1977). *The Philosophical Anarchism of William Godwin* (Princeton).

Clarke, M. L. (1974). *Paley: Evidences for the Man* (London).

Clarke, P., and Trebilcock, C., eds. (1997). *Understanding Decline* (Cambridge).

Claydon, T. (1996). *William III and the Godly Revolution* (Cambridge).

Cleary, T. R. (1984). *Henry Fielding, Political Writer* (Waterloo, ON).

Clément, P. P. (1976). *Jean-Jacques Rousseau: de l'éros coupable à l'éros glorieux* (Neuchâtel).

Cloyd, E. L. (1972). *James Burnett, Lord Monboddo* (Oxford).

Cobban, A. (1960). *Edmund Burke and the Revolt against the Eighteenth Century* (London). 1st publ. 1929.

Cobban, A. (1964). *Rousseau and the Modern State*, 2nd edn (London). 1st publ. 1934.

Cobban, A., ed. (1950). *The Debate on the French Revolution* (London).

Cochrane, E. (1973). *Florence in the Forgotten Centuries, 1527–1800* (Chicago).

Codignola, E. (1947). *Illuministi, giansenisti e giacobini nell'Italia del settecento* (Florence).

Coe, R. N. (1961). *Morelly: Ein Rationalist auf dem Wege sum Sozialismus* (Berlin).

Cohen, H. (1986). 'Diderot and China', *SVEC*, 242:219–32.

Cohen, L. (1980). 'Explaining the Revolution: Ideology and Ethics in Mercy Otis Warren's Historical Theory', *WMQ*, 37:200–18.

Cohen, S., and Scull, A., eds. (1985). *Social Control and the State* (Oxford).

Cohler, A. M. (1970). *Rousseau and Nationalism* (New York).

Cohler, A. M. (1989). 'Introduction' to Montesquieu, *The Spirit of the Laws*, ed. A. M. Cohler, B. C. Miller, and H. S. Stone (Cambridge).

Cohon, R., ed. (2001). *Hume: Moral and Political Philosophy* (Aldershot).

Colbourn, T. (1965). *The Lamp of Experience: Whig History and the Intellectual Origins of the American Revolution* (Chapel Hill). Repr. 1998.

Cole, C. W. (1939). *Colbert and a Century of French Mercantilism*, 2 vols. (New York).

Cole, L. (2000). 'Nation, Anti-Enlightenment and Religious Revival in Austria: Tyrol in the 1790s', *HJ*, 43:475–97.

Coleman, P., Hofmann, A., and Zurbuchen, S. (1998). *Reconceptualizing Science, Nature and Aesthetics: contribution à une nouvelle approche des lumières helvétiques* (Geneva).

Coleman, W. O. (1996). 'How Theory Came to English Classical Economics', *Scottish Journal of Political Economy*, 42:207–28.

Colley, L. (1981). 'Eighteenth-Century English Radicalism before Wilkes', *Transactions of the Royal Historical Society*, 31:1–19.

Colley, L. (1992). *Britons: Forging the Nation, 1707–1837* (New Haven).

Collini, S., Whatmore, R., and Young, B., eds. (2000a), *Economy, Polity and Society: British Intellectual History, 1750–1950* (Cambridge).

Collini, S., Whatmore, R., and Young, B., eds. (2000b), *History, Religion and Culture: British Intellectual History, 1750–1950* (Cambridge).

Collini, S., Winch, D., and Burrow, J. (1983). *That Noble Science of Politics: A Study in Nineteenth-Century Intellectual History* (Cambridge).

Collins, H. (1954). 'The London Corresponding Society', in Saville 1954.

Columbia Law Review (1989). Vol. 87. Symposium on Kantian Legal Theory.

Combes-Malavialle, J. F. (1988). 'Vue nouvelle sur l'abbé de Prades', *DHS*, 20:377–96.

Commager, H. S. (1977). *The Empire of Reason: How Europe Imagined and America Realized the Enlightenment* (New York).

Condren, C. (1997). *Satire, Lies and Politics: The Case of Dr Arbuthnot* (Basingstoke).

Cone, C. B. (1952). *Torchbearer of Freedom: The Influence of Richard Price on Eighteenth-Century Thought* (Lexington, KY).

Cone, C. B. (1957–64). *Burke and the Nature of Politics*, 2 vols. (Lexington).

Conner, P. (1965). *Poor Richard's Politicks: Benjamin Franklin and the New American Order* (New York).

Conniff, J. (1999). 'Edmund Burke and his Critics: The Case of Mary Wollstonecraft', *JHI*, 60:299–318.

Conrad, H. (1961). *Rechtsstaatliche Bestrebungen im Absolutismus Preußens und Österreichs am Ende des 18. Jahrhunderts* (Cologne).

Cook, J. E. (1978). *Tench Coxe and the Early Republic* (Chapel Hill, NC).

Cook, R. I. (1967). *Jonathan Swift as a Tory Pamphleteer* (Seattle).

Cookson, J. E. (1982). *The Friends of Peace: Anti-War Liberalism in England, 1793–1815* (Cambridge).

Coquard, O. (2003). *Marat* (Paris).

Corr, C. A. (1975). 'Christian Wolff and Leibniz', *JHI*, 36:241–62.

Corrigan, J. (1987). *The Hidden Balance: Religion and the Social Theories of Charles Chauncy and Jonathan Mayhew* (New York).

Coste, B. (1975). *Mably: pour une utopie du bon sens* (Paris).

Cottret, B. (1995). *Bolingbroke's Political Writings: The Conservative Enlightenment* (London).

Cottret, B., ed. (2002). *Du patriotisme aux nationalismes, 1700–1848* (Grânes).

Cottret, M. (1984). 'Aux origines du républicanisme janséniste', *Revue d'histoire moderne et contemporaine*, 31:98–115.

Cottret, M. (1998). *Jansénismes et lumières: pour un autre XVIIIe siècle* (Paris).

Courtney, C. P. (1975). *Montesquieu and Burke* (Westport, CT). 1st publ. Oxford, 1963.

Courtney, C. P. (1988). 'Montesquieu and the Problem of *la diversité*', in Barber and Courtney 1988.

Courtney, C. P. (1993a). *Isabelle de Charrière (Belle de Zuylen): A Biography* (Oxford).

Courtney, C. P. (1993b). 'Montesquieu and Revolution', in Mass and Postigliola 1993.

Courtney, C. P. (2001a). 'Montesquieu and Natural Law', in Carrithers *et al.* 2001.

Courtney, C. P. (2001b). 'Montesquieu and English Liberty', in Carrithers *et al.* 2001.

Coward, D. (1991). *The Philosophy of Restif de la Bretonne*, *SVEC*, 283.

Cox, I. (2001). 'Montesquieu and the History of Laws', in Carrithers *et al.* 2001.

Cragg, G. R. (1964). *Reason and Authority in the Eighteenth Century* (Cambridge).

Crahay, R., ed. (1982). *La Tolérance civile* (Brussels).

Cranston, M. (1983). *Jean-Jacques: The Early Life and Work of Jean-Jacques Rousseau, 1712–1754* (London).

Cranston, M. (1986). *Philosophers and Pamphleteers: Political Theorists of the Enlightenment* (Oxford).

Cranston, M. (1991a). *The Noble Savage: Rousseau, 1754–1762* (London).

Cranston, M. (1991b). 'John Locke and the Case for Toleration', in Horton and Mendus 1991.

Cranston, M., and Peters, R. S., eds. (1972). *Hobbes and Rousseau* (New York).

Crimmins, J. (1987). 'Strictures on Paley's Net: Capital Punishment and the Power to Pardon', *The Bentham Newsletter*, 11:23–34.

Crimmins, J. (1990). *Secular Utilitarianism: Social Justice and the Critique of Religion in the Thought of Jeremy Bentham* (Oxford).

Crimmins, J. (1994). 'Bentham's Political Radicalism Re-examined', *JHI*, 55:259–81.

Croce, B. (1913). *The Philosophy of Giambattista Vico*, trans. R. G. Collingwood (London).

Croce, B. (1970). *History of the Kingdom of Naples* (Chicago). 1st publ. in Italian, 1925.

Crocker, L. (1959). *An Age of Crisis: Man and World in Eighteenth-century French Thought* (Baltimore).

Crocker, L. (1968). *Rousseau's Social Contract: An Interpretive Essay* (Cleveland).

Crocker, L. (1985). 'Interpreting the Enlightenment: A Political Approach', *JHI*, 46:211–30.

Cronk, N. (1999). 'The Epicurean Spirit: Champagne and the Defence of Poetry in Voltaire's *Le Mondain*', *SVEC*, 371:53–80.

Cross, R. (1976). 'Blackstone versus Bentham', *Law Quarterly Review*, 92:516–27.

Crowe, I., ed. (1997). *Edmund Burke: His Life and Legacy* (Dublin).

Crowther-Hunt, N. C. (1961). *Two Early Political Associations: The Quakers and the Dissenting Deputies in the Age of Sir Robert Walpole* (Oxford).

Cruickshanks, E., ed. (1982). *Ideology and Conspiracy: Aspects of Jacobitism, 1689–1759* (Edinburgh).

Cumming, I. (1955). *Helvetius* (London).

Curti, M. (1937). 'The Great Mr Locke, America's Philosopher, 1783–1861', *Huntington Library Bulletin*, 11:107–52.

Curtis, E. N. (1935). *Saint-Just* (New York). Repr. 1973.

Dabney, W. M., and Dargan, M. (1962). *William Henry Drayton and the American Revolution* (Albuquerque).

Dabydeen, D. (1987). *Hogarth, Walpole and Commercial Britain* (London).

Dagen, J. (1977). *L'Histoire de l'esprit dans la pensée française de Fontenelle à Condorcet* (Paris).

Daiches, D. (1977). *Scotland and the Union* (London).

Dakin, D. (1939). *Turgot and the Ancien Régime in France* (London). Repr. 1965.

Daly, J. (1979). *Sir Robert Filmer and English Political Thought* (Toronto).

Daniel, S. H. (1984). *John Toland: His Methods, Manners, and Mind* (Kingston, ON).

Dann, O. (1987). 'Herder und die Deutsche Bewegung', in Sauder 1987.

Dann, O. (1993). *Nation und Nationalismus in Deutschland, 1770–1990* (Munich).

Dann, O., and Klippel, D., eds. (1995). *Naturrecht – Spätaufklärung – Revolution* (Hamburg).

Darnton, R. (1968). *Mesmerism and the End of the Enlightenment in France* (Cambridge, MA).

Darnton, R. (1971). 'The High Enlightenment and the Low-Life of Literarature in Pre-Revolutionary France', *Past and Present*, 51:81–115.

Darnton, R. (1973). 'The *Encyclopédie* Wars of Prerevolutionary France', *AHR*, 78:1331–52.

Darnton, R. (1979). *The Business of Enlightenment: A Publishing History of the Encyclopédie, 1775–1800* (Cambridge, MA).

Darnton, R. (1982). *The Literary Underground of the Old Regime* (Cambridge, MA).

Darnton, R. (1996). *The Forbidden Best-Sellers of Pre-Revolutionary France* (London).

Dascal, M. and Gruengard, O., eds. (1989). *Knowledge and Politics: Case Studies in the Relationship between Epistemology and Political Philosophy* (Boulder, CO).

Davidson, N. (2000). 'Toleration in Enlightenment Italy', in Grell and Porter 2000.

Davie, G. (1961). *The Democratic Intellect: Scotland and her Universities in the Nineteenth Century* (Edinburgh).

Davies, S. (1994). '*Paul et Virginie*, 1953–1991: The Present State of Studies', *SVEC*, 317:239–66.

Davis, D. B. (1975). *The Problem of Slavery in the Age of Revolution, 1770–1823* (Ithaca, NY).

Davis, D. B. (1984). *Slavery and Human Progress* (New York).

Davis, J. H. (1979). *Fénelon* (Boston, MA).

Davison, R. (1985). *Diderot et Galiani*, *SVEC*, 237.

Deane, S. (1988). *The French Revolution and Enlightenment in England, 1789–1832* (Cambridge, MA).

Deggau, H. G. (1983). *Die Aporien der Rechtslehre Kants* (Stuttgart).

Dekker, R. (1992). '"Private Vices, Public Virtues" Revisited: The Dutch Background to Bernard Mandeville', *HEI*, 14:481–98.

Delmas, B., Delmas, T., and Steiner, P., eds. (1995). *La Diffusion internationale de la physiocratie (XVIIIe–XIXe)* (Grenoble).

Delon, M. (1971). 'Candide au service de Joseph II', in Bene 1971.

Delpy, G. (1936). *L'Espagne et l'esprit européen: l'oeuvre de Feijóo (1725–1760)* (Paris).

DeMaria, R. (1993). *The Life of Samuel Johnson* (Oxford).

Dent, N. J. H. (1988). *Rousseau: An Introduction to his Psychological, Social and Political Theory* (Oxford).

Dent, N. J. H. (1992). *A Rousseau Dictionary* (Cambridge, MA)

de Paor, L. (1985). 'The Rebel Mind: Republican and Loyalist', in Kearney 1985.

Deppermann, K. (1961). *Der hallesche Pietismus und der preussische Staat unter Friedrich III* (Göttingen).

Derathé, R. (1950). *Jean-Jacques Rousseau et la science politique de son temps* (Paris). Later edns 1970, 1979, 1988.

Derathé, R. (1963). 'Les *Philosophes* et le despotisme', in Francastel 1963.

Derry, J. (1976). *English Politics and the American Revolution* (London).

Desgraves, L. (1993). 'Aspects de la correspondance de Montesquieu en 1749', in Mass and Postigliola 1993.

Diaz, F. (1962). *Filosofia e politica nel settecento francese* (Turin). 2nd edn 1973.

Diaz, F. (1966). *Francesco Maria Gianni* (Milan).

Diaz, L. R. (1975). *Reforma e ilustración en la España del siglo XVIII* (Madrid).

Dicey, A. V. (1939). *Introduction to the Study of the Law of the Constitution* (London). 1st publ. 1885.

Dickey, L. (1986). 'Historicizing the "Adam Smith Problem": Conceptual, Historiographical and Textual Issues', *JMH*, 58:579–609.

Dickey, L. (1990). 'Pride, Hypocrisy and Civility in Mandeville's Social and Historical Theory', *Critical Review*, 4:387–429.

Dickey, L. (1995). 'Power, Commerce and Natural Law in Daniel Defoe's Political Writings, 1698–1707', in Robertson 1995.

Dickinson, H. T. (1970). *Bolingbroke* (London).

Dickinson, H. T. (1976). 'The Eighteenth-Century Debate on the Glorious Revolution', *History*, 61:28–45.

Dickinson, H. T. (1977). *Liberty and Property: Political Ideology in Eighteenth-Century Britain* (London).

Dickinson, H. T. (1985). *British Radicalism and the French Revolution, 1789–1815* (New York).

Dickson, D., *et al.*, eds. (1993). *The United Irishmen: Republicanism, Radicalism, and Rebellion* (Dublin).

Dickson, P. G. M. (1967). *The Financial Revolution in England* (London).

Diggins, J. P. (1984). *The Lost Soul of American Politics* (New York).

Dinwiddy, J. (1971). 'Christopher Wyvill and Reform, 1790–1802', *Borthwick Papers*, 39:1–32.

Dinwiddy, J. (1974). 'Utility and Natural Law in Burke's Thought', *Studies in Burke and his Time*, 16:105–28.

Dinwiddy, J. (1975). 'Bentham's Transition to Political Radicalism, 1809–10', *JHI*, 36:683–700.

Dinwiddy, J. (1989). *Bentham* (Oxford).

Dodge, G. H. (1947). *The Political Theory of the Huguenots of the Dispersion* (New York).

Domínguez Ortiz, A. (1988). *Carlos III y la España de la Ilustración* (Madrid).

Domínguez Ortiz, A. (1990). *Las claves del despotismo ilustrado, 1715–1789* (Barcelona).

Donelly, F. K. (1987). 'Joseph Towers and the Collapse of Rational Dissent', *Enlightenment and Dissent*, 6:31–9.

Dorn, W. L. (1940). *Competition for Empire, 1740–1763* (New York).

Douthwaite, J. V. (2002). *The Wild Girl, Natural Man and the Monster: Dangerous Experiments in the Age of Enlightenment* (Chicago).

Downie, J. A. (1984). *Jonathan Swift: Political Writer* (Boston, MA).

Doyle, W. (1988). *The French Revolution: A Bibliography of Works in English* (London).

Doyle, W. (1989). *The Oxford History of the French Revolution* (New York and Oxford).

Doyle, W. (1999). *Origins of the French Revolution*, 3rd edn (Oxford). 1st publ. 1980.

Dozier, R. R. (1983). *For King, Constitution, and Country: The English Loyalists and the French Revolution* (Lexington, KY).

Draper, A. J. (1997). 'Bentham's Theory of Punishment' (doctoral thesis, University College London).

Draper, A. J. (2000). 'Cesare Beccaria's Influence on English Discussions of Punishment, 1764–1789', *HEI*, 26:177–99.

Draper, A. J. (2001). 'William Eden and Leniency in Punishment', *HPT*, 22:106–30.

Dreier, R. (1986). *Rechtsbegriff und Rechtsidee: Kants Rechtsbegriff und seine Bedeutung für die gegenwärtige Diskussion* (Frankfurt).

Dreitzel, H. (1987). 'Justis Beitrag zur Politisierung der deutschen Aufklärung', in Bödeker and Hermann 1987.

Dreitzel, H. (1991). 'Zur Entwicklung und Eigenart der "eklektischen Philosophie"', *Zeitschrift für historische Forschung*, 18:281–343.

Dreitzel, H. (1997). 'Christliche Aufklärung durch fürstlichen Absolutismus', in Vollhardt 1997.

Dreitzel, H. (2003). 'The Reception of Hobbes in the Political Philosophy of the Early German Enlightenment', *HEI*, 29:255–89.

Dreyer, F. A. (1979). *Burke's Politics: A Study in Whig Orthodoxy* (Waterloo, ON).

Dreyer, F. A. (1983). 'Faith and Experience in the Thought of John Wesley', *AHR*, 88:12–30.

Duchet, M. (1978). *Diderot et l'Histoire des deux Indes* (Paris).

Duchet, M. (1985). *Le Partage des savoirs* (Paris).

Duchet, M. (1991). '*L'Histoire des deux Indes*: sources and structures d'un texte polyphonique', in Lüsebrink and Tietz 1991.

Duchet, M. (1995). *Anthropologie et histoire au siècle des lumières* (Paris). 1st publ. 1971.

Dufour, A. (1976). *Le Mariage dans l'Ecole romande du droit naturel au XVIIIe siècle* (Geneva).

Dukes, P. (1977). *Russia under Catherine the Great* (Newtonville, MA).

Dumont, L. (1977). *From Mandeville to Marx: The Genesis and Triumph of Economic Ideology* (Chicago).

Duncan, C. M. (1995). *The Anti-Federalists and Early American Political Thought* (De Kalb, IL).

Dunn, J. (1969a). *The Political Thought of John Locke* (Cambridge).

Dunn, J. (1969b). 'The Politics of Locke in England and America in the Eighteenth Century', in Yolton 1969. Repr. in Dunn 1980.

Dunn, J. (1980). *Political Obligation in its Historical Contexts* (Cambridge).

Dunn, J. (1991). 'The Claim to Freedom of Conscience', in Grell *et al.* 1991.

Dunn, J., ed. (1990). *The Economic Limits to Modern Politics* (Cambridge).

Dunn, J., ed. (1995). *Contemporary Crisis of the Nation State?* (Oxford).

Dunn, J., and Harris, I., eds. (1997). *Hume*, 2 vols.(Cheltenham).

Dunne, T. (1982). *Theobald Wolfe Tone, Colonial Outsider* (Cork).

Dunthorne, H. (1999). 'Beccaria and Britain', in Howell and Morgan 1999.

Durden, R. F. (1951). 'Joel Barlow and the French Revolution', *WMQ*, 8:327–54.

Durkheim, E. (1966). *Montesquieu and Rousseau: Forerunners of Sociology* (Ann Arbor, 1960). Doctoral thesis, 1892. 1st publ. in French in 1953 (Paris).

Dworetz, S. M. (1990). *The Unvarnished Doctrine: Locke, Liberalism and the American Revolution* (Durham, NC).

Dwyer, J. (1987). *Virtuous Discourse: Sensibility and Community in Late Eighteenth-Century Scotland* (Edinburgh).

Dwyer, J. (1998). *Age of the Passions: An Interpretation of Adam Smith and Scottish Enlightenment Culture* (East Linton).

Dybikowski, J. (1984). 'David Williams and the Eighteenth-century Distinction between Civil and Political Liberty', *Enlightenment and Dissent*, 3:15–39.

Dybikowski, J. (1993). *On Burning Ground: An Examination of the Ideas, Projects and Life of David Williams*, *SVEC*, 307.

Dziembowski, E. (2001). 'The English Political Model in Eighteenth-Century France', *Historical Research*, 74:151–71.

Ebbinghaus, J. (1986). *Sittlichkeit und Recht: Praktische Philosophie, 1929–1954* (Bonn).

Eccleshall, R. (1993). 'Anglican Political Thought in the Century after the Revolution of 1688', in Boyce *et al.* 1993.

Echevarria, D. (1972). 'The Pre-Revolutionary Influence of Rousseau's *Contrat social*', *JHI*, 33:543–60.

Echeverria, D. (1985). *The Maupeou Revolution: A Study in the History of Libertarianism* (Baton Rouge).

Edling, M. (2003). *A Revolution in Favor of Government: Origins of the US Constitution and the Making of the American State* (New York).

847

Edwards, P. (1989), 'Introduction' to *Voltaire: Selections* (London).

Eger, E., Grant, C., Gallchoir, C. O., and Warburton, P., eds. (2001). *Women and the Public Sphere: Writing and Representation, 1700–1830* (Cambridge).

Egret, J. (1950). *La Révolution des notables: Mounier et les monarchiens* (Paris). 2nd edn 1989.

Egret, J. (1970). *Louis XV et l'opposition parlementaire, 1715–1774* (Paris).

Egret, J. (1977). *The French Prerevolution, 1787–1788*, trans. W. D. Camp (Chicago). 1st publ. in French in 1962 (Paris).

Ehrard, J. (1994). *L'Idée de la nature en France dans la première moitié du XVIIIe siècle* (Paris). 1st publ. 1963.

Ehrenpreis, I. (1962–83). *Swift: The Man, his Works, and the Age* (3 vols., London).

Eigeldinger, M. (1962). *Rousseau et la réalité de l'imaginaire* (Neuchâtel).

Elliott, M. (1989). *Wolfe Tone: Prophet of Irish Independence* (New Haven).

Ellis, H. A. (1988). *Boulainvilliers and the French Monarchy* (Ithaca, NY).

Ellis, H. A. (1989). 'Montesquieu's Modern Politics: The *Spirit of the Laws* and the Problem of Modern Monarchy in Old Regime France', *HPT*, 10:665–700.

Ellison, C. E. (1991). 'The Moral Economy of the Modern City: Reading Rousseau's *Discourse on Wealth*', *HPT*, 12:253–61.

Elshtain, J. B. (1981). *Public Man, Private Woman: Women in Social and Political Thought* (Princeton).

Emerson, R. L. (1977). 'Scottish Universities in the Eighteenth Century, 1690–1800', *SVEC*, 167:453–74.

Emerson, R. L. (1994). 'The "Affair" at Edinburgh and the "Project" at Glasgow: The Politics of Hume's Attempts to Become a Professor', in Stewart and Wright 1994.

Emerson, R. L. (1995). 'Politics and the Glasgow Professors, 1690–1800', in Hook and Sher 1995.

Emsley, C. (1987). *Crime and Society in England, 1750–1900* (London).

Engfer, H. J. (1989). 'Christian Thomasius: Erste Proklamation und erste Krise der Aufklärung in Deutschland', in Schneiders 1989.

English, G. B. (1813). *The Grounds of Christianity Examined by Comparing the New Testament with the Old* (Boston, MA).

Epstein, D. F. (1984). *The Political Theory of the 'Federalist'* (Chicago).

Epstein, J. A. (1994). *Radical Expression: Political Language, Ritual and Symbol in England, 1790–1850* (New York).

Epstein, K. (1966). *The Genesis of German Conservatism* (Princeton).

Erskine-Hill, H. (1975). *The Social Milieu of Alexander Pope* (New Haven).

Erskine-Hill, H. (1979). 'Literature and the Jacobite Cause', *Modern Language Studies*, 9:15–28.

Erskine-Hill, H. (1983). *The Augustan Idea in English Literature* (London).

Erskine-Hill, H. (1996). *Poetry of Opposition and Revolution: Dryden to Wordsworth* (Oxford).

Erskine-Hill, H. (1998). *Alexander Pope: World and Word* (Oxford).

Etudes sur le Contrat social *de Jean-Jacques Rousseau* (1964). Publications de Université de Dijon, 30 (Paris).

Eulenburg, F. (1904). *Die Frequenz der deutschen Universitäten* (Leipzig).

Evans, A. W. (1932). *Warburton and the Warburtonians* (London).

Evans, R. F. (1968). *Pelagius: Inquiries and Reappraisals* (New York).

Every, G. (1956). *The High Church Party, 1688–1718* (London).

Fabre, J. (1963). 'Stanislas Leszczynski et le mouvement philosophique en France au XVIIIe siècle', in Francastel 1963.

Fabricius, K. (1920). *Kongeloven: Dens tilblivelse og plads i samtidens natur- og arveretlige udvikling* (Copenhagan).

Fairbairn, A. W. (1972). 'Dumarsais and *Le Philosophe*', *SVEC*, 87:375–95.

Feaver, G., and Rosen, F., eds. (1987). *Lives, Liberties, and the Public Good* (London).

Febvre, L. (1930). *Civilisation: le mot et l'idée* (Paris).

Feist, B. (1930). *Die Geschichte der Nationalökonomie an der Friedrichs-Universität zu Halle* (Saale) *im 18. Jahrhundert* (Halle).

Fennessy, R. R. (1963). *Burke, Paine and the Rights of Man* (The Hague).

Ferguson, W. (1964). 'The Making of the Treaty of Union of 1707', *Scottish Historical Review*, 43:89–110.

Ferguson, W. (1974). 'Imperial Crowns: A Neglected Facet of the Background to the Treaty of Union of 1707', *Scottish Historical Review*, 53:22–44.

Ferrone, V. (1995). *The Intellectual Roots of the Italian Enlightenment* (Atlantic Highlands, NJ).

Festenstein, M., and Burgess, G., eds. (2005). *English Radicalism, 1550–1850* (Cambridge).

Fetscher, I. (1960). *Rousseaus politische Philosophie* (Neuwied). Repr. 1968.

Fetscher, I. (1962). 'Rousseau's Concepts of Freedom in the Light of his Philosophy of History', in Friedrich 1962.

Fetscher, I. (1965). 'Rousseau, auteur d'intention conservatrice et d'action révolutionnaire', in *Rousseau et la philosophie politique*, ed. Institut international de philosophie politique, v (Paris).

Fetscher, I. (1976). *Herrschaft und Emanzipation, Zur Philosophie des Bürgertums* (Munich).

Fetscher, I. (1996). 'Kants friedliebende Republiken und der (populistische) Nationalismus', in Kodalle 1996.

Fetscher, I., and Münkler, H. (1985). *Pipers Handbuch der politischen Ideen*, III (Munich).

Feugère, A. (1922). *Un précurseur de la Révolution: l'abbé Raynal* (Angoulême).

Finsen, H. C. (1983). *Das Werden des deutschen Staatsbürgers* (Copenhagen).

Fitzgibbons, A. (1995). *Adam Smith's System of Liberty, Wealth and Virtue* (Oxford).

Fitzpatrick, M. (1977). 'Joseph Priestley and the Cause of Universal Toleration', *Price-Priestley Newsletter*, 1:3–30.

Fitzpatrick, M. (1990). 'Heretical Religion and Radical Ideas', in Hellmuth 1990.

Fitzpatrick, M. (1993). 'Latitudinarianism at the Parting of the Ways', in Walsh *et al.* 1993.

Fitzpatrick, M. (1995). 'Patriots and Patriotism: Richard Price and the Early Reception of the French Revolution in England', *SVEC*, 335:231–50.

Fitzsimmons, M. (1994). *The Remaking of France: The National Assembly and the Constitution of 1791* (Cambridge).

Fleischacker, S. (1988). 'Kant's Theory of Punishment', *Kant-Studien*, 79:434–49.

Fleischacker, S. (1996). 'Values behind the Market: Kant's Response to the *Wealth of Nations*', *HPT*, 17:379–407.

Fleischacker, S. (2004). *On Adam Smith's Wealth of Nations* (Princeton).

Fleischmann, M. (1931). *Christian Thomasius: Leben und Lebenswerk* (Halle).

Fletcher, D. (1985). 'Guides, Philosophers and Friends: The Background of Voltaire's *Discours en vers sur l'homme*', in Howells *et al.* 1985.

Fletcher, F. (1939). *Montesquieu and English Politics (1750–1800)* (London).

Fleury, G. (1915). *François Véron de Forbonnais* (Mamers).

Fliegelman, J. (1993). *Declaring Independence: Jefferson, Natural Language and the Culture of Performance* (Stanford).

Flikschuh, K. (1999). 'Freedom and Constraint in Kant's *Metaphysical Elements of Justice*', *HPT*, 20:250–71.

Flower, M. E. (1983). *John Dickinson: Conservative Revolutionary* (Charlottesville).

Follett, R. R. (2001). *Evangelicalism, Penal Theory and the Politics of Criminal Law Reform in England, 1808–1830* (Basingstoke).

Foner, E. (1977). *Tom Paine and Revolutionary America* (Oxford).

Fontana, B. (1985). *Rethinking the Politics of Commercial Society: The Edinburgh Review, 1802–1832* (Cambridge).

Fontana, B., ed., (1994). *The Invention of the Modern Republic* (Cambridge).

Forbes, D. (1966). 'Introduction' to Adam Ferguson, *An Essay on the History of Civil Society* (Edinburgh).

Forbes, D. (1975a). *Hume's Philosophical Politics* (Cambridge).

Forbes, D. (1975b). 'Sceptical Whiggism, Commerce and Liberty', in Skinner and Wilson 1975.

Forbes, D. (1978). 'The European, or Cosmopolitan, Dimension in Hume's Science of Politics', *BJECS*, 1:57–60.

Forbes, D. (1982). 'Natural Law and the Scottish Enlightenment', in Campbell and Skinner 1982b.

Force, J. (1985). *William Whiston, Honest Newtonian* (Cambridge).

Force, P. (2003). *Self-Interest before Adam Smith* (Cambridge).

Ford, F. (1953). *Robe and Sword: The Regrouping of the French Aristocracy after Louis XIV* (Cambridge, MA).

Forsyth, M. (1987). *Reason and Revolution: The Political Thought of the Abbé Sieyès* (Leicester).

Foss, K. (1934). *Ludvid Holbergs Naturrett på idéhistorisk bakgrunn* (Oslo).

Foucault, M. (1966). *Les Mots et les choses* (Paris).

Foucault, M. (1977). *Discipline and Punish: The Birth of the Prison* (London). 1st publ. in French in 1975 (Paris).

Foucault, M. (1991). 'Governmentality', in Burchell *et al.* 1991.

Fox, C., Porter, R. S., and Wokler, R., eds. (1995). *Inventing Human Science: Eighteenth-century Domains* (Berkeley).

Fox, J. H., Waddicor, M. H., and Watts, D. A., eds. (1975). *Studies in Eighteenth-century French Literature* (Exeter).

Fox, R., and Turner, A., eds. (1998). *Luxury Trades and Consumerism in Ancien Régime Paris* (Aldershot).

Fox-Genovese, E. (1976). *The Origins of Physiocracy: Economic Revolution and Social Order in Eighteenth-Century France* (Ithaca, NY).

Fraisse, G. (1994). *Reason's Muse: Sexual Difference and the Birth of Democracy* (Chicago).

Fralin, R. (1978). *Rousseau and Representation* (New York).

França, J. A. (1965). *Une ville des lumières: la Lisbonne de Pombal* (Paris).

Francastel, P., ed. (1963). *Utopie et institutions au XVIIIe siècle: le pragmatisme des lumières* (Paris).

France, P. (1983). *Diderot* (New York).

Francis, M., and Morrow, J. (1988). 'After the Ancient Constitution: Political Theory and English Constitutional Writings, 1765–1832', *HPT*, 9:283–302.

Frängsmyr, T. (1972). *Wolffianismens genombrott i Uppsala* (Uppsala).

Freedman, J. (2002). *A Poisoned Chalice* (Princeton).

Freeman, M. (1980). *Edmund Burke and the Critique of Political Radicalism* (Chicago).

Freeman, M., and Robertson, D., eds. (1980). *The Frontiers of Political Theory* (Brighton).

Frensdorff, F. (1903). *Über das Leben und die Schriften des Nationalökonom J. H. G. von Justi* (Göttingen).

Friedland, P. (2002). *Political Actors, Representative Bodies and Theatricality in the Age of the French Revolution* (Ithaca, NY).

Friedrich, C. J., ed. (1962). *Nomos, IV: Liberty* (New York).

Fritz, P., and Williams, D., eds. (1973). *City and Society in the Eighteenth Century* (Toronto).

Fruchtman, J. (1983). *The Apocalyptic Politics of Richard Price and Joseph Priestley* (Philadelphia).

Fruchtman, J. (1994). *Thomas Paine: Apostle of Freedom* (New York).

Frühsorge, G., and Strasser, G. F., eds. (1993). *Johann Joachim Becher (1635–1682)* (Wiesbaden).

Fulbrook, M. (1983). *Piety and Politics: Religion and the Rise of Absolutism in England, Württemberg and Prussia* (Cambridge).

Furbank, P. N. (1992). *Diderot: A Critical Biography* (London).

Furet, F. (1981). *Interpreting the French Revolution*, trans. E. Forster (Cambridge). 1st publ. in French in 1978 (Paris).

Furet, F. (1992). *Revolutionary France, 1770–1880*, trans. A. Nevill (Oxford).

Furet, F., ed. (1965). *Livre et société dans la France du XVIIIe siècle* (Paris).

Furet, F., and Ozouf, M., eds. (1989a). *The French Revolution and the Creation of Modern Political Culture*, III: *The Transformation of Political Culture, 1789–1848* (Oxford).

Furet, F., and Ozouf, M., eds. (1989b). *A Critical Dictionary of the French Revolution*, trans. A. Goldhammer (Cambridge, MA).

Furet, F., and Ozouf, M. eds. (1990). *Terminer la Révolution: Mounier et Barnave dans la Révolution Française* (Grenoble).

Furet, F., Ozouf, M., and Baker, K. M., eds. (1993). *Le Siècle de l'avènement républicain* (Paris).

Fusil, C. A. (1932). *La Contagion sacrée* (Paris).

Gagliardo, J. G. (1967). *Enlightened Despotism* (New York).

Gagnebin, B. (1944). *Burlamaqui et le droit naturel* (Geneva).

Gagnér, S (1960). *Studien zur Ideengeschichte der Gesetzgebung* (Stockholm).

Gallagher, C. (1988). 'Embracing the Absolute: The Politics of the Female Subject in Seventeenth-Century England', *Genders*, 1:24–39.

Gallop, G. (1986). 'Ideology and the English Jacobins: The Case of John Thelwall', *Enlightenment and Dissent*, 5:3–20.

Garber, J. (1982). 'Vom "ius connatum" zum "Menschenrecht"', in Brandt 1982b.

García-Villoslada, R., ed. (1979–82). *Historia de la Iglesia en España*, 5 vols. (Madrid).

Gareth Jones, W. (1984). *Nikolay Novikov, Enlightener of Russia* (Cambridge).

Gargett, G. (1980). *Voltaire and Protestantism*, *SVEC*, 188.

Gargett, G., and Sheridan, G., eds. (1999). *Ireland and the French Enlightenment, 1700–1800* (Basingstoke).

Garin, E. (1990). *Dal Rinascimento all'Illuminismo* (Pisa).

Garret, C. (1975). *Respectable Folly: Millenarians and the French Revolution in France and England* (Baltimore).

Gascoigne, J. (1986). 'Anglican Latitudinarianism and Political Radicalism in the Late Eighteenth Century', *History*, 71:22–38.

Gascoigne, J. (1989). *Cambridge in the Age of Enlightenment* (Cambridge).

Gatrell, V. A. C. (1994). *The Hanging Tree: Execution and the English People, 1770–1868* (Oxford).

Gauchet, M. (1989). *La Révolution des droits de l'homme* (Paris).

Gauchet, M. (1995). *La Révolution des pouvoirs: la souveraineté, le peuple et la représentation, 1789–1799* (Paris).

Gausted, E. S. (1979). 'George Berkeley and New World Community', *Church History*, 48:5–17.

Gawthrop, R. L. (1993). *Pietism and the Making of Eighteenth-Century Prussia* (Cambridge).

Gay, P. (1954). *The Party of Humanity: Essays in the French Enlightenment* (New York). 2nd edn 1964.

Gay, P. (1959). *Voltaire's Politics* (Princeton).

Gay, P. (1967–70). *The Enlightenment: An Interpretation*, 2 vols. (London).

Gay, P. (1988). *Voltaire's Politics*, 2nd edn (New Haven). 1st edn, 1959 (Princeton).

Gazier, A. (1922). *Histoire générale du mouvement janséniste*, 2 vols. (Paris).

Gelles, E. B. (1992). *Portia: The World of Abigail Adams* (Bloomington).

Geoghegan, V. (2001). 'Thomas Sheridan: Toleration and Royalism', in Boyce *et al.* 2001.

Geras, N., and Wokler, R., eds. (2000). *The Enlightenment and Modernity* (Basingstoke).

Gerbi, A. (1973). *The Dispute of the New World: The History of a Polemic, 1750–1900* (Pittsburgh). 1st publ. in Italian in 1955 (Milan).

Gerhardt, V. (1995). *Immanuel Kants Entwurf 'zum ewigen Frieden'* (Darmstadt).

Gerrard, C. (1994). *The Patriot Opposition to Walpole* (Oxford).

Gershoy, L. (1944). *From Despotism to Revolution, 1763–1789* (New York).

Giarrizzo, G. (1981). *Vico: la politica e la storia* (Naples).

Gierke, O. (1934). *Natural Law and the Theory of Society, 1500–1800*, trans. E. Barker, 2 vols. (Cambridge). 1st publ. 1913.

Gilbert, N. W. (1963). 'The Concept of the Will in Early Latin Philosophy', *Journal of the History of Philosophy*, 1:17–35.

Gildin, H. (1983). *Rousseau's Social Contract* (Chicago).

Gilley, S. (1981). 'Christianity and Enlightenment: An Historical Survey', *HEI*, 1:103–22.

Gilroy, J. P. (1979). 'Peace and the Pursuit of Happiness in the French Utopian Novel', *SVEC*, 176:169–87.

Glassey, L. K. J., ed. (1997). *The Reigns of Charles II and James VII and II* (London).

Gleason, W. J. (1981). *Moral Idealists, Bureaucracy and Catherine the Great* (New Brunswick, NJ).

Gobetti, D. (1992). *Private and Public: Individuals, Households and Body Politic in Locke and Hutcheson* (London).

Godechot, J. (1965). *France and the Atlantic Revolution of the Eighteenth Century, 1770–1799* (London). 1st publ. in French in 1963.

Godechot, J. (1970). *The Taking of the Bastille* (London).

Godechot, J. L. (1972). *The Counter Revolution: Doctrine and Action, 1789–1814* (London).

Goebel, J. (1918–19). 'Christian Wolff and the Declaration of Independence', *Deutsch-amerikanische Geschichtsblätter*, 18/19:69–87.

Goetz, R. (1993). *Destutt de Tracy: philosophie du language et science de l'homme* (Geneva).

Goggi, G. (1991). 'La Collaboration de Diderot', in Lüsebrink and Tietz 1991.

Goggi, G. (1994). 'Galiani et l'Angleterre', *DHS*, 26:295–316.

Golden, R. M., ed. (1982). *Church, State and Society under the Bourbon Kings of France* (Lawrence, KS).

Goldgar, A. (1995). *Impolite Learning: Conduct and Community in the Republic of Letters, 1680–1750* (New Haven).

Goldgar, B. (1977). *Walpole and the Wits: The Relation of Politics to Literature, 1722–1742* (Lincoln, NE).

Goldie, M. (1977). 'Edmund Bohun and *Jus Gentium* in the Revolution Debate, 1689–1693', *HJ*, 20:569–86.

Goldie, M. (1978). 'Tory Political Thought, 1689–1714' (doctoral thesis, Cambridge).

Goldie, M. (1980a). 'The Roots of True Whiggism, 1688–1694', *HPT*, 1:195–236.

Goldie, M. (1980b). 'The Revolution of 1689 and the Structure of Political Argument', *Bulletin of Research in the Humanities*, 83:473–564.

Goldie, M. (1982). 'The Nonjurors, Episcopacy and the Origins of the Convocation Controversy', in Cruickshanks 1982.

Goldie, M. (1991a). 'The Political Thought of the Anglican Revolution', in Beddard 1991.

Goldie, M. (1991b). 'The Scottish Catholic Enlightenment', *JBS*, 30:20–62.

Goldie, M. (1991c). 'The Theory of Religious Intolerance in Restoration England', in Grell *et al.* 1991.

Goldie, M. (1992). 'Common Sense Philosophy and Catholic Theology in the Scottish Enlightenment', *SVEC*, 302:281–320.

Goldie, M. (1993a). 'Priestcraft and the Birth of Whiggism', in Phillipson and Skinner 1993.

Goldie, M. (1993b). 'John Locke, Jonas Proast and Religious Toleration, 1688–1692', in Walsh *et al.* 1993.

Goldie, M. (1996). 'Divergence and Union: Scotland and England, 1660–1707', in Bradshaw and Morrill 1996.

Goldie, M. (1997). 'Restoration Political Thought', in Glassey 1997.

Goldie, M. (2001). 'The Unacknowledged Republic: Officeholding in Early-Modern England', in Harris 2001.

Goldman, L. (1983). 'The Origins of British "Social Science": Political Economy, Natural Science and Statistics, 1830–1835', *HJ*, 26:587–616.

Goldmann, L. (1973). *The Philosophy of the Enlightenment* (London).

Goldschmidt, V. (1974). *Anthropologie et politique: les principes du système de Rousseau* (Paris).

Goldsmith, M. M. (1977). 'Mandeville and the Spirit of Capitalism', *JBS*, 17:63–81.

Goldsmith, M. M. (1979). 'Faction Detected: Ideological Consequences of Robert Walpole's Decline and Fall', *History*, 64:1–19.

Goldsmith, M. M. (1985). *Private Vices, Public Benefits: Bernard Mandeville's Social and Political Thought* (Cambridge).

Goldsmith, M. M. (1992). '"Our Great Oracle, Mr Lock": Locke's Political Theory in the Early Eighteenth Century', *Eighteenth-Century Life*, 16:60–75.

Goldsmith, M. M. (1994). 'Liberty, Virtue and the Rule of Law, 1689–1770', in Wootton 1994a.

Gooch, G. P. (1920). *Germany and the French Revolution* (London).

Goodman, D. (1991). 'Governing the Republic of Letters: The Politics of Culture in the French Enlightenment', *HEI*, 13:183–99.

Goodman, D. (1994). *The Republic of Letters: A Cultural History of the French Enlightenment* (Ithaca, NY).

Goodwin, A. (1979). *The Friends of Liberty: The English Democratic Movement in the Age of the French Revolution* (Cambridge, MA).

Gordon, D. (1994). *Citizens without Sovereignty: Equality and Sociability in French Thought, 1670–1789* (Princeton).

Gordon, D. E., and Torrey, M. L. (1947). *The Censoring of Diderot's Encyclopédie and the Re-established Text* (New York).

Gordon, F. (1999). '*Vues législatives pour les femmes*, 1790: A Reformist-Feminist Vision', *HPT*, 20:649–73.

Goré, J. L. (1957). *L'Itinéraire de Fénelon: humanisme et spiritualité* (Paris).

Gottschalk, L. R. (1927). *Jean-Paul Marat: A Study in Radicalism* (London and New York).

Gough, J. W. (1936). *The Social Contract* (Oxford). 2nd edn 1957.

Gough, J. W. (1955). *Fundamental Law in English Constitutional History* (Oxford).

Gough, J. W. (1976). 'James Tyrrell, Whig Historian, and Friend of John Locke', *HJ*, 19:581–610.

Gouhier, H. (1933–41). *La Jeunesse d'Auguste Comte et la formation du positivisme*, 3 vols. (Paris).

Gouhier, H. (1977). *Fénelon philosophe* (Paris).

Gouhier, H. (1983). *Rousseau et Voltaire* (Paris).

Goyard-Fabre, S. (1996a). *La Philosophie du droit de Kant* (Paris).

Goyard-Fabre, S. (1996b). 'Introduction' to J. Barbeyrac, *Ecrits de droit et de morale* (Paris).

Graham, J. (1989–90). 'Revolutionary Philosopher: The Political Ideas of Joseph Priestley (1733–1804)', *Enlightenment and Dissent*, 8:43–68; 9:14–46.

Gray, J. N., and Pelczynski, Z., eds. (1984). *Conceptions of Liberty in Political Philosophy* (London).

Green, T. A. (1985). *Verdict according to Conscience: Perspectives on the English Criminal Trial Jury, 1200–1800* (Chicago).

Green, T. H. (1941). *Lectures on the Principles of Political Obligation* (London). 1st publ. 1895.

Greene, D. J. (1990). *The Politics of Samuel Johnson* (Athens, GA). 1st edn 1960 (New Haven).

Greene, J. P. (1986). *Peripheries and Center: Constitutional Development in the Extended Polities of the British Empire and the United States, 1607–1788* (Athens, GA).

Greene, R. A., and MacCallum, H. (1971). 'Foreword' to N. Culverwell, *An Elegant and Learned Discourse of the Light of Nature* (Toronto).

Greengrass, M., Leslie, M., and Raylor, T., eds. (1994). *Samuel Hartlib and Universal Reformation* (Cambridge).

Gregor, M. (1963). *Laws of Freedom: A Study of Kant's Method of Applying the Categorical Imperative in the Metaphysik der Sitten* (New York).

Grell, O. P., Israel, J., and Tyacke, N., eds. (1991). *From Persecution to Toleration: The Glorious Revolution and Religion in England* (New York).

Grell, O. P., and Porter, R., eds. (2000). *Toleration in Enlightenment Europe* (Cambridge).

Grice, G. R. (1967). *The Grounds of Moral Judgement* (Cambridge).

Grimsley, R. (1963). *Jean d'Alembert, 1717–83* (Oxford).

Grimsley, R. (1973). *The Philosophy of Rousseau* (London).

Griswold, C. L. (1999). *Adam Smith and the Virtues of Enlightenment* (Cambridge).

Groenewegen, P. D. (1969). 'Turgot and Adam Smith', *Scottish Journal of Political Economy*, 16:71–87.

Grosclaude, P. (1961). *Malesherbes: témoin et interprète de son temps* (Paris).

Gross, H. (1990). *Rome in the Age of Enlightenment* (Cambridge).

Gross, J. P. (1997). *Fair Shares for All: Jacobin Egalitarianism in Practice* (Cambridge).

Grossmann, W. (1976). *Johann Christian Edelmann: From Orthodoxy to Enlightenment* (The Hague).

Grossmann, W. (1979). 'Toleration – *exercitium religionis privatum*', *JHI*, 40:129–34.

Grossmann, W. (1982). 'Religious Toleration in Germany, 1684–1750', *SVEC*, 201:115–41.

Grunert, F. (2000). *Normbegründung und politische Legitimität: Zur Rechts- und Staatsphilosophie der deutschen Frühaufklärung* (Tübingen).

Guéniffey, P. (1993). *Le Nombre et la raison: la Révolution française et les élections* (Paris).

Guéniffey, P. (2000). *La Politique de la Terreur: essai sur la violence révolutionnaire* (Paris).

Guha, R. (1963). *A Rule of Property for Bengal: An Essay on the Idea of Permanent Settlement* (Paris).

Guilaine, J. (1969). *Billaud-Varenne: l'ascete de la Révolution (1756–1919)* (Paris).

Guillois, A. (1894). *Le Salon de Mme Helvétius: Cabanis et les idéologues* (Paris).

Guimerá, A., ed. (1996). *El reformismo borbónico: una visión interdisciplinar* (Madrid).

Gunn, J. A. W. (1968). 'The Civil Polity of Peter Paxton', *Past and Present*, 40:42–57.

Gunn, J. A. W. (1972). *Factions no More: Attitudes to Party in Government and Opposition in Eighteenth-Century England* (London).

Gunn, J. A. W. (1983). *Beyond Liberty and Property: The Process of Self-Recognition in Eighteenth-Century Political Thought* (Kingston, ON).

Gunn, J. A. W. (1995). *Queen of the World: Opinion in the Public Life of France from the Renaissance to the Revolution*, *SVEC*, 328.

Gunther-Canada, W. (1998). 'The Politics of Sense and Sensibility: Mary Wollstonecraft and Catharine Macaulay Graham on Edmund Burke's *Reflections*', in Smith 1998.

Gunther-Canada, W. (2001). *Mary Wollstonecraft and Enlightenment Politics* (DeKalb, IL).

Gusdorf, G. (1971). *Les Principes de la pensée au siècle des lumières* (Paris).

Gusdorf, G. (1978). *La Conscience révolutionnaire: les idéologues* (Paris).

Guy, B. (1963). *The French Image of China, before and after Voltaire* (Geneva).

Guyer, P. (2000). *Kant on Freedom, Law, and Happiness* (Cambridge).

Guyer, P., ed. (1992). *The Cambridge Companion to Kant* (Cambridge).

Gwyn, W. (1965). *The Meaning of the Separation of Powers* (New Orleans).

Haakonssen, K. (1981). *The Science of a Legislator: The Natural Jurisprudence of David Hume and Adam Smith* (Cambridge).

Haakonssen, K. (1982). 'What Might Properly be Called Natural Jurisprudence', in Campbell and Skinner 1982b.

Haakonssen, K. (1984). 'The Science of a Legislator in James Mackintosh's Moral Philosophy', *HPT*, 5:245–80.

Haakonssen, K. (1985a). 'John Millar and the Science of a Legislator', *Juridical Review*, 41:41–68.

Haakonssen, K. (1985b). 'Hugo Grotius and the History of Political Thought', *PT*, 13:239–65.

Haakonssen, K. (1986–7). 'Reid's Politics: A Natural Law Theory', *Reid Studies*, 1:10–27.

Haakonssen, K. (1989). 'Natural Jurisprudence in the Scottish Enlightenment', in MacCormick and Bankowski 1989.

Haakonssen, K. (1990). 'Natural Law and Moral Realism: The Scottish Synthesis', in Stewart 1990.

Haakonssen, K. (1993). 'The Structure of Hume's Political Theory', in Norton 1993.

Haakonssen, K. (1996a). *Natural Law and Moral Philosophy: From Grotius to the Scottish Enlightenment* (Cambridge).

Haakonssen, K., ed. (1996b). *Enlightenment and Religion: Rational Dissent in Eighteenth-Century Britain* (Cambridge).

Haakonssen, K. (2000). 'The Character and Obligation of Natural Law According to Richard Cumberland', in Stewart 2000.

Haakonssen, K. (2002). 'The Moral Conservatism of Natural Rights', in Hunter and Saunders 2002.

Haakonssen, K. (2003). 'Natural Jurisprudence and the Theory of Justice', in Broadie 2003.

Haakonssen, K. (2004). 'Protestant Natural Law Theory: A General Interpretation', in Brender and Krasnoff 2004.

Haakonssen, K. (2005). 'The History of Eighteenth-Century Philosophy: History or Philosophy', in Haakonssen 2006.

Haakonssen, K., ed. (2006). *The Cambridge History of Eighteenth-Century Philosophy* (Cambridge).

Haakonssen, K., ed. (1998). *Adam Smith* (Aldershot).

Haakonssen, K., ed. (1999). *Grotius, Pufendorf and Modern Natural Law* (Aldershot).

Habermas, J. (1989). *The Structural Transformation of the Public Sphere*, trans. T. Burger (Cambridge, MA). 1st publ. in German in 1962.

Haddock, B. (1986). *Vico's Political Thought* (Swansea).

Hadidi, D. (1974). *Voltaire et l'Islam* (Paris).

Halévy, E. (1928). *The Growth of Philosophic Radicalism* (London). 1st publ. in French in 1901–4.

Halévy, E. (1952). *The Growth of Philosophic Radicalism* (London).

Hall, T. E. (1969). 'Thought and Practice of Enlightened Government in French Corsica', *AHR*, 74:880–95.

Hamburger, P. (1985). 'The Development of the Law of Seditious Libel and the Control of the Press', *Stanford Law Review*, 37:661–765.

Hamburger, P. (1994). 'Revolution and Judicial Review: Chief Justice Holt's Opinion in *City of London v. Wood*', *Columbia Law Review*, 94:2091–153.

Hamilton, E. J. (1935). 'The Mercantilism of Gerónimo de Uztáriz', in N. E. Himes, ed., *Economics, Sociology and the Modern World* (Cambridge, MA).

Hammersley, R. (2001). 'Camille Desmoulin's *La Vieux Cordelier*: A Link between English and French Republicanism', *HEI*, 27:115–32.

Hammersley, R. (2004). 'English Republicanism in Revolutionary France: The Case of the Cordelier Club', *Journal of British Studies*, 43:464–81.

Hammersley, R. (2005). *French Revolutionaries and English Republicans: The Cordeliers Club, 1790–1794* (Woodbridge, Suffolk).

Hammerstein, N. (1972). *Jus und Historie: Ein Beitrag zur Geschichte des historischen Denkens an deutschen Universitäten im späten 17. und im 18. Jahrhundert* (Göttingen).

Hammerstein, N. (1983). 'Christian Wolff und die Universitäten: Zur Wirkungsgeschichte des Wolffianisumus in 18. Jahrhundert', in Schneiders 1983.

Hammerstein, N. (1985). 'Besonderheiten der österreichischen Universitäts- und Wissenschaftsreform', in Plaschka 1985.

Hamowy, R. (1982). 'Jefferson and the Scottish Enlightenment', *WMQ*, 36:503–23.

Hamowy, R. (1987). *The Scottish Enlightenment and the Theory of Spontaneous Order* (Carbondale).

Hamowy, R. (1990). '*Cato's Letters*, John Locke and the Republican Paradigm', *HPT*, 11:273–94.

Hampsher-Monk, I. (1979). 'Civic Humanism and Parliamentary Reform: The Case of the Society of the Friends of the People', *JBS*, 18:70–89.

Hampsher-Monk, I. (1988). 'Rhetoric and Opinion in the Politics of Edmund Burke', *HPT*, 9:455–84.

Hampsher-Monk, I. (1991). 'John Thelwall and the Eighteenth-Century Radical Response to Political Economy', *HJ*, 34:1–20.

Hampsher-Monk, I. (1998). 'Burke and the Religious Sources of Skeptical Conservatism', in Zande and Popkin 1998.

Hampsher-Monk, I. (2005). 'Edmund Burke's Changing Justification for Intervention', *HJ*, 48:65–100.

Hampsher-Monk, I. (2006). 'On not Inventing the British Revolution', in Festenstein and Burgess 2005.

Hampson, N. (1968). *The Enlightenment* (Harmondsworth).

Hampson, N. (1974). *The Life and Opinions of Maximilien Robespierre* (London).

Hampson, N. (1978). *Danton* (London).

Hampson, N. (1983). *Will and Circumstance: Montesquieu, Rousseau and the French Revolution* (London).

Hampson, N. (1991). *Saint-Just* (Cambridge, MA).

Handlin, O., and Handlin, M. (1961). 'James Burgh and American Revolutionary Theory', *Proceedings of the Massachusetts Historical Society*, 73:38–57.

Hankins, T. L. (1970). *Jean d'Alembert: Science and the Enlightenment* (Oxford).

Haour, P. (1995). 'Antoine Court and Refugee Political Thought, 1719–1752', in Laursen 1995.

Hardy, G. (1925). *Le Cardinal de Fleury et le mouvement janséniste* (Paris).

Hare, R. M. (1993). 'Could Kant have been a Utilitarian?', *Utilitas*, 5:1–10.

Harling, P. (1996). *The Waning of 'Old Corruption': The Politics of Economical Reform in Britain, 1779–1846* (New York).

Harpham, E. J. (1999). 'Economics and History: Books II and III of the *Wealth of Nations*', *HPT*, 20:438–55.

Harris, I. (1993). 'Paine and Burke: God, Nature and Politics', in Bentley 1993.

Harris, I. (1994). *The Mind of John Locke* (Cambridge).

Harris, I. (1996). 'Rousseau and Burke', in Brown 1996.

Harris, R. (1996). *Politics and the Rise of the Press: Britain and France, 1620–1800* (London).

Harris, T., ed. (2001). *The Politics of the Excluded, c. 1500–1850* (Basingstoke).

Harrison, J. (1981). *Hume's Theory of Justice* (New York).

Harrison, J. F. C. (1979). *The Second Coming: Popular Millenarianism, 1780–1850* (London).

Harrison, P. (1990). *'Religion' and the Religions in the English Enlightenment* (Cambridge).

Harrison, R. (1983). *Bentham* (Boston, MA).

Hart, H. L. A. (1982). *Essays on Bentham: Studies in Jurisprudence and Political Theory* (New York).

Hart, J. (1965). *Viscount Bolingbroke: Tory Humanist* (London).

Hartung, G. (1998). *Die Naturrechtsdebatte: Geschichte der Obligatio vom 17. bis 20. Jahrhundert* (Freiburg).

Hartz, L. (1955). *The Liberal Tradition in America* (New York).

Harvey, R. F. (1937). *Jean Jacques Burlamaqui: A Liberal Tradition in American Constitutionalism* (Chapel Hill, NC).

Harvey, S., and Hobson, M., eds. (1980). *Reappraisals of Rousseau* (Manchester).

Harzer, R. (1994). *Der Naturzustand als Denkfigur moderner praktischer Vernunft* (Frankfurt).

Hatch, N. O. (1977). *The Sacred Cause of Liberty: Republican Thought and the Millennium in Revolutionary New England* (New Haven).

Hauser, O., ed. (1987). *Friedrich der Grosse in seiner Zeit* (Cologne).

Hay, C. H. (1979a). *James Burgh: Spokesman for Reform in Hanoverian England* (Washington).

Hay, C. H. (1979b). 'The Making of a Radical: The Case of James Burgh', *JBS*, 18:90–117.

Hay, D. (1975). 'Property, Authority and the Criminal Law', in Hay *et al.* 1975.

Hay, D. (1982). 'War, Dearth and Theft in the Eighteenth Century', *Past and Present*, 95:117–60.

Hay, D., *et al.*, eds. (1975). *Albion's Fatal Tree: Crime and Society in Eighteenth-Century England* (London).

Haydon, C., and Doyle, W., eds. (1999). *Robespierre* (Cambridge).

Hayter Hames, J. (2001). *Arthur O'Connor: United Irishman* (Cork).

Hazard, P. (1953). *The European Mind, 1680–1715* (New Haven). 1st publ. in French in 1935 (Paris).

Hazard, P. (1954). *European Thought in the Eighteenth Century* (London). 1st publ. in French in 1946 (Paris).

Head, B. (1982). 'The Origins of "La science sociale" in France, 1770–1800', *Australian Journal of French Studies*, 19:115–32.

Head, B. (1985). *Ideology and Social Science: Destutt de Tracy and French Liberalism* (Boston, MA).

Heath, J. (1963). *Eighteenth-Century Penal Theory* (Oxford).

Heckel, M. (1992). 'Religionsbann und landesherrliches Kirchenregiment', in Rublack 1992.

Heilbroner, R. (1953). *The Worldly Philosophers: The Lives, Times, and Ideas of the Great Economic Thinkers* (New York).

Heilbroner, R. L. (1961). *The Worldly Philosophers: The Lives, Times, and Ideas of the Great Economic Thinkers* (New York).

Hellmuth, E., ed. (1985). *Naturrechtsphilosophie und bürokratischer Werthorizont* (Göttingen).

Hellmuth, E., ed. (1990). *The Transformation of Political Culture: England and Germany in the Late Eighteenth Century* (London).

Hendel, C. W. (1934). *Jean-Jacques Rousseau: Moralist* (Indianapolis). 2nd edn, 1962 (Indianapolis).

Henderson, G. D. (1952). *Chevalier Ramsay* (London).

Hennies, W. (1985). *Die politische Theorie August Ludwig von Schlözers zwischen Aufklärung und Liberalismus* (Munich).

Henriques, U. (1961). *Religious Toleration in England, 1787–1833* (London).

Henry, N. O. (1968). 'Democratic Monarchy: The Political Theory of the Marquis d'Argenson' (doctoral thesis, Yale).

Hensmann, F. (1976). *Staat und Absolutismus im Denken der Physiokraten* (Frankfurt).

Herman, R. (2003). *The Business of a Woman: The Political Writings of Delarivier Manley* (London).

Herpel, O. (1925). *Zinzendorf: über Glauben und Lehren* (Berlin). 1st publ. 1920.

Herr, R. (1958). *The Eighteenth-Century Revolution in Spain* (Princeton).

Herr, R. (1989). *Rural Change and Royal Finances in Spain at the End of the Old Regime* (Berkeley).

Hersche, P. (1977). *Der Spätjansenismus in Österreich* (Vienna).

Hersche, P. (1990). 'Les Jansénistes en Autriche et en Allemagne face à la Révolution', in Maire 1990.

Hertzberg, A. (1968). *The French Enlightenment and the Jews* (New York).

Hesse, C. (2001). *The Other Enlightenment: How French Women Became Modern* (Princeton).

Higonnet, P. (1988). *Sister Republics: The Origins of French and American Republicanism* (Cambridge, MA).

Higonnet, P. (1998). *Goodness beyond Virtue: Jacobins during the French Revolution* (Cambridge, MA).

Hildesheimer, F. (1991). *Le Jansénisme en France aux XVIIe et XVIIIe siècles* (Paris).

Hill, B. (1990). *The Republican Virago: The Life and Times of Catharine Macaulay, Historian* (New York).

Hill, B. (1995). 'Reinterpreting the Glorious Revolution: Catharine Macaulay and Radical Response', in MacLean 1995.

Hill, J. (1995). 'Ireland without Union: Molyneux and his Legacy', in Robertson 1995.

Hill, L. (1997). 'Adam Ferguson and the Paradox of Progress and Decline', *HPT*, 18:677–706.

Hill, M. (1999). *Statesman of the Enlightenment: The Life of Anne-Robert Turgot* (London).

Himmelfarb, G. (1984). *The Idea of Poverty: England in the Early Industrial Age* (London).

Himmelfarb, G. (2004). *The Roads to Modernity: The British, French and American Enlightenments* (New York).

Hinrichs, C. (1971). *Preussentum und Pietismus* (Göttingen).

Hinrichs, H. F. W. (1848–52). *Geschichte der Rechts- und Staatsprinzipien seit der Reformation bis auf die Gegenwart in historisch-philosophischer Entwicklung*, 3 vols. Repr. Aalen, 1962.

Hinske, N., ed. (1989). *Halle: Aufklärung und Pietismus* (Heidelberg).

Hirschman, A. O. (1977). *The Passions and the Interests: Political Arguments for Capitalism before its Triumph* (Princeton).

Hobson, M., Leigh, J. T. A., and Wokler, R., eds. (1992). *Rousseau and the Eighteenth Century* (Oxford).

Hochstrasser, T. J. (1993). 'Conscience and Reason: The Natural Law Theory of Jean Barbeyrac', *HJ*, 36:289–308.

Hochstrasser, T. J. (1995). 'The Claims of Conscience: Natural Law Theory, Obligation and Resistance in the Huguenot Diaspora', in Laursen 1995.

Hochstrasser, T. J. (2000). *Natural Law Theories in the Early Enlightenment* (Cambridge).

Hoffmann, J. (1959). *Die 'Hausväterliteratur' und die 'Predigten über den christlichen Hausstand'* (Weinheim).

Hoffmann, P. (1977). *La Femme dans la pensée des lumières* (Paris).

Holdsworth, W. (1903–72). *A History of English Law*, 17 vols. (London).

Hole, R. (1989). *Pulpits, Politics and Public Order in England, 1760–1832* (Cambridge).

Hole, R. (1991). 'English Sermons and Tracts as Media of Debate on the French Revolution, 1789–1799', in Philp 1991.

Hollander, S. (1973). *The Economics of Adam Smith* (Toronto).

Hollander, S. (1997). *The Economics of Thomas Robert Malthus* (Toronto).

Hollis, M. (1981). 'Economic Man and Original Sin', *Political Studies*, 29:167–80.

Holmes, G., ed. (1969). *Britain after the Glorious Revolution, 1689–1714* (London).

Holzhey, H., and Zurbuchen, S. (1993). 'Die Schweiz zwischen deutscher und französischer Aufklärung', in Schneiders 1993.

Hone, J. A. (1982). *For the Cause of Truth: Radicalism in London, 1796–1821* (New York).

Honigsheim, P. (1952). 'The American Indian in the Philosophy of the Enlightenment', *Osiris*, 10:91–108.

Hont, I. (1983). 'The "Rich Country – Poor Country" Debate in Scottish Classical Political Economy', in Hont and Ignatieff 1983a. Repr. in Hont 2005.

Hont, I. (1987). 'The Language of Sociability and Commerce: Samuel Pufendorf and the Theoretical Foundations of the Four Stages Theory', in Pagden 1987. Repr. in Hont 2005.

Hont, I. (1989). 'The Political Economy of the "Unnatural and Retrograde" Order: Adam Smith and Natural Liberty', in M. Berg, ed., *Französische Revolution und politische Ökonomie* (Trier). Repr. in Hont 2005.

Hont, I. (1990). 'Free Trade and the Economic Limits to National Politics: Neo-Machiavellian Political Economy Reconsidered', in Dunn 1990. Repr. in Hont 2005.

Hont, I. (1993). 'The Rhapsody of Public Debt: David Hume and Voluntary State Bankruptcy', in Phillipson and Skinner 1993. Repr. in Hont 2005.

Hont, I. (1994a). 'The Permanent Crisis of a Divided Mankind: "Contemporary Crisis of the Nation State" in Historical Perspective', *Political Studies*, 42:166–231. Repr. in Hont 2005.

Hont, I. (1994b). 'Commercial Society and Political Theory in the Eighteenth Century: The Problem of Authority in David Hume and Adam Smith', in Melching and Velema 1994.

Hont, I. (2000). 'Irishmen, Scots, Jews, and the Interest of England's Commerce', in Cavaciocchi 2000.

Hont, I. (2005). *Jealousy of Trade: International Competition and the Nation-State in Historical Perspective* (Cambridge, MA).

Hont, I., and Bödeker, H. E. (1995). 'Naturrecht, Politische Ökonomie und Geschichte der Menschheit', in Dann and Klippel 1995.

Hont, I., and Ignatieff, M. (1983b). 'Needs and Justice in the *Wealth of Nations*', in Hont and Ignatieff 1983a. Repr. in Hont 2005.

Hont, I., and Ignatieff, M., eds. (1983a). *Wealth and Virtue: The Shaping of Political Economy in the Scottish Enlightenment* (Cambridge).

Hook, A., and Sher, R. B., eds. (1995). *The Glasgow Enlightenment* (East Linton).

Hope, N. (1990). 'The View from the Provinces: A Dilemma for Protestants in Germany, 1648–1918', *Journal of Ecclesiastical History*, 41:606–21.

Hope, N. (1995). *German and Scandinavian Protestantism, 1700–1918* (Oxford).

Hope, V., ed. (1984). *Philosophers of the Scottish Enlightenment* (Edinburgh).

Hope, V. (1989). *Virtue by Consensus: The Moral Philosophy of Hutcheson, Hume and Adam Smith* (New York).

Höpfl, H. (1978). 'From Savage to Scotsman: Conjectural History in the Scottish Enlightenment', *JBS*, 17:19–40.

Höpfl, H., and Thompson, M. P. (1979). 'The History of Contract as a Motif in Political Thought', *AHR*, 84:919–44.

Hopkins, J. K. (1982). *A Woman to Deliver her People: Joanna Southcott and English Millenarianism in an Era of Revolution* (Austin, TX).

Hopkins, M. A. (1947). *Hannah More and her Circle* (New York).

Horne, T. A. (1978). *The Social Thought of Bernard Mandeville* (London).

Horne, T. A. (1980). 'Politics in a Corrupt Society: William Arnall's Defence of Robert Walpole', *JHI*, 41:601–14.

Horne, T. A. (1985). '"The Poor Have a Claim Founded in the Law of Nature": William Paley and the Rights of the Poor', *Journal of the History of Philosophy*, 23:51–70.

Horne, T. A. (1986). 'Moral and Economic Improvement: Francis Hutcheson on Property', *HPT*, 7:115–30.

Horne, T. A. (1990). *Property Rights and Poverty: Political Argument in Britain, 1605–1834* (Chapel Hill).

Horowitz, I. L. (1954). *Claude Helvétius: Philosopher of Democracy and Enlightenment* (New York).

Horton, J., and Mendus, S., eds. (1985). *Aspects of Toleration* (London).

Horton, J., and Mendus, S., eds. (1991). *John Locke: 'A Letter concerning Toleration' in Focus* (London).

Horton, J., and Mendus, S., eds. (1994). *After MacIntyre* (Cambridge).

Hostler, J. (1975). *Leibniz's Moral Philosophy* (London).

Houston, A. C. (1991). *Algernon Sidney and the Republican Heritage in England and America* (Princeton).

Howe, J. R. (1966). *The Changing Political Thought of John Adams* (Princeton).

Howell, D. W., and Morgan, K. O., eds. (1999). *Crime, Protest and Police in Modern British Society* (Cardiff).

Howells, R. J., ed. (1985). *Voltaire and his World* (Oxford).

Hruschka, J. (1986). *Das deontologische Sechseck bei Gottfied Achenwall im Jahre 1767* (Göttingen).

Hruschka, J. (1991). 'The Greatest Happiness Principle and Other Early German Anticipations of Utilitarian Theory', *Utilitas*, 3:165–77.

Hubatsch, W. (1973). *Frederick the Great: Absolutism and Administration* (London).

Hubert, R. (1923). *Les Sciences sociales dans l'*Encyclopédie (Paris). Repr. Geneva, 1970.

Hughes, M. (1988). *Law and Politics in Eighteenth-Century Germany* (Woodbridge, Suffolk).

Hull, I. V. (1996). *Sexuality, State and Civil Society in Germany, 1700–1815* (Ithaca, NY).

Hulliung, M. (1976). *Montesquieu and the Old Regime* (Berkeley).

Hulliung, M. (1994). *The Autocritique of Enlightenment: Rousseau and the Philosophes* (Cambridge, MA).

Hume, L. J. (1981). *Bentham and Bureaucracy* (Cambridge).

Hundert, E. J. (1986). 'Bernard Mandeville and the Rhetoric of Social Science', *Journal of the History of the Behavioral Sciences*, 22:311–20.

Hundert, E. J. (1988). 'The Thread of Language and the Web of Dominion: Mandeville to Rousseau and Back', *ECS*, 21:169–91.

Hundert, E. J. (1994). *The Enlightenment's Fable: Bernard Mandeville and the Discovery of Society* (Cambridge).

Hundert, E. J. (1995). 'Bernard Mandeville and the Enlightenment's Maxims of Modernity', *JHI*, 56:577–94.

Hundert, E. J. (2000). 'Sociability and Self-love in the Theatre of Moral Sentiments: Mandeville to Adam Smith', in Collini *et al.* 2000a.

Hunt, L. A. (1984). *Politics, Culture and Class in the French Revolution* (Berkeley).

Hunt, L. A. (1992). *The Family Romance of the French Revolution* (Berkeley).

Hunt, N. C. (1961). *Two Early Political Associations: The Quakers and the Dissenting Deputies in the Age of Sir Robert Walpole* (Oxford).

Hunter, I. (2001). *Rival Enlightenments: Civil and Metaphysical Philosophy in Early-Modern Germany* (Cambridge).

Hunter, I. (2002). 'The Morals of Metaphysics: Kant's *Groundwork* as Intellectual *Paideia*', *Critical Inquiry*, 28:908–29.

Hunter, I. (2005). 'Kant's Religion and Prussian Religious Policy', *Modern Intellectual History*, 2:1–27.

Hunter, I., and Saunders, D., eds. (2002). *Natural Law and Civil Sovereignty: Moral Right and State Authority in Early Modern Political Thought* (Basingstoke).

Hunter, M., and Wootton, D., eds. (1992). *Atheism from the Reformation to the Enlightenment* (New York).

Hursthouse, R. (1996). 'Hume's Moral and Political Philosophy', in Brown 1996.

Hutchison, R. (1991). *Locke in France, 1688–1734*, SVEC, 290.

Hutchinson, T. (1988). *Before Adam Smith: The Emergence of Political Economy, 1662–1776* (New York).

Huyler, J. (1995). *Locke in America: The Moral Philosophy of the Founding Era* (Lawrence, KS).

Iggers, G. G. (1959). 'Further Remarks about the Early Uses of the Term "Social Science"', *JHI*, 20:433–6.

Ignatieff, M. (1978). *A Just Measure of Pain: The Penitentiary in the Industrial Revolution, 1750–1850* (London).

Ignatieff, M. (1983a). 'John Millar and Individualism', in Hont and Ignatieff 1983a.

Ignatieff, M. (1983b). 'State, Civil Society and Total Institution', in Sugarman 1983.

Ignatieff, M. (1984). *The Needs of Strangers* (London).

Ihalainen, P. (1999). *The Discourse on Political Pluralism in Early Eighteenth-Century England* (Helsinki).

Ilting, K. H. (1983). *Naturrecht und Sittlichkeit* (Stuttgart).

Ingrao, C. W. (1987). *The Hessian Mercenary State: Ideas, Institutions and Reform under Frederick II, 1760–1787* (Cambridge).

Innes, J., and Styles, J. (1986). 'The Crime Wave: Recent Writings on Crime and Criminal Justice in Eighteenth-Century England', *JBS*, 25:380–435.

Isaac, J. C. (1988). 'Republicanism *vs.* Liberalism? A Reconsideration', *HPT*, 9:349–77.

Israel, J. I. (1985). *European Jewry in the Age of Mercantilism, 1550–1750* (New York).

Israel, J. I. (2001). *Radical Enlightenment: Philosophy and the Making of Modernity, 1650–1750* (Oxford).

Israel, J. I., ed. (1991). *The Anglo-Dutch Moment* (Cambridge).

Jack, M. (1987). *The Social and Political Thought of Bernard Mandeville* (New York).

Jackson, A. (1991). 'Jeremy Bentham's Views on Capital Punishment' (MA in Legal and Political Theory, University College, London).

Jacob, M. (1976). *The Newtonians and the English Revolution, 1689–1720* (Hassocks, Sussex).

Jacob, M. (1981). *The Radical Enlightenment: Pantheists, Freemasons and Republicans* (Boston, MA).

Jacob, M. (1992). *Living the Enlightenment: Freemasonry and Politics in Eighteenth-Century Europe* (Oxford).

Jacob, M., and Jacob, J., eds. (1984). *The Origins of Anglo-American Radicalism* (Boston, MA).

Jacob, W. M., and Yates, N., eds. (1993). *Crown and Mitre: Religion and Society in Northern Europe since the Reformation* (Woodbridge, Suffolk).

Jahrbuch für Recht und Ethik / Annual Review of Law and Ethics (1997). Vol. 5: 200th Anniversary of Kant's *Metaphysics of Morals*.

James, C. L. R. (1980). *The Black Jacobins: L'Ouverture and the San Domingo Revolution* (London). 1st publ. 1938.

James, P. (1979). *Population Malthus: His Life and Times* (Boston, MA).

Janssen, C. J. H. (1987). 'Over de 18e eeuwse docenten naturrecht aan Nederlandse universiteiten en de dor hen gebruikte leerboeken', *Tijdschrift voor Rechtsgeschiedenis*, 55:103–15.

Janssens, J. (1973). *Camille Desmoulins, le premier républicain de France* (Paris).

Jaume, L. (1989). *Le discours jacobin et la démocratie* (Paris).

Jemolo, A. C. (1928). *Il giansenismo in Italia prima della rivoluzione* (Bari).

Jenkinson, S. L. (2000). 'Introduction' to Pierre Bayle, *Political Writings* (Cambridge).

Jennings, J. (1992). 'The *Déclaration des droits de l'homme et du citoyen* and its Critics in France', *HJ*, 35:839–59.

Johnson, H. C. (1975). *Frederick the Great and his Officials* (New Haven).

Johnston, E. (1928). *Le Marquis d'Argens: sa vie et ses oeuvres* (Paris). Repr. Geneva, 1971.

Jolley, N. (1975). 'Leibniz on Hobbes, Locke's *Two Treatises* and Sherlock's *Case of Allegiance*', *HJ*, 18:21–35.

Jolley, N. (1984). *Leibniz and Locke: A Study of the New Essays on Human Understanding* (New York).

Jolley, N., ed. (1995). *The Cambridge Companion to Leibniz* (Cambridge).

Joly, P. (1956). *Du Pont de Nemours, soldat de la liberté* (Paris).

Jones, C., ed. (1988). *The Longman Companion to the French Revolution* (London).

Jones, C. (2002). *The Great Nation: France from Louis XV to Napoleon, 1715–99* (London).

Jones, D. W. (1988). *War and Economy in the Age of William III and Marlborough* (New York).

Jones, M. G. (1952). *Hannah More* (Cambridge).

Jones, P., ed. (1988). *Philosophy and Science in the Scottish Enlightenment* (Edinburgh).

Jones, P. M. (1995). *Reform and Revolution in France: The Politics of Transition, 1774–1791* (Cambridge).

Jorgensen, C. D., ed. (1886). *Kongeloven og dens forhistorie* (Copenhagen). Repr. 1973.

Jouannet, E. (1998). *Emer de Vattel et l'émergence doctrinale du droit international classique* (Paris).

Jouvenel, B. de (1957). *Sovereignty: An Inquiry into the Political Good*, trans. J. F. Huntington (Cambridge). 1st publ. in French in 1955.

Joyce, P., ed. (2002). *The Social in Question: New Bearings in History and the Social Sciences* (London).

Jüttner, S., and Schlobach, J., eds. (1992). *Europäische Aufklärungen* (Hamburg).

Kafker, F. A. (1976). 'The Fortunes and Misfortunes of a Leading French Bookseller-Printer: A. F. Le Breton', *Studies in Eighteenth-Century Culture*, 5:371–85.

Kafker, F. A. (1981). *Notable Encyclopedias of the Seventeenth and Eighteenth Centuries* (Oxford).

Kafker, F. A. (1996). *The Encyclopedists as a Group*, SVEC, 345.

Kafker, F. A., ed. (1994). *Notable Encyclopedias of the Late Eighteenth Century* (Oxford).

Kafker, F. A., and Kafker, S. (1988). *The Encyclopedists as Individuals: A Biographical Dictionary of the Encyclopédie*, SVEC, 257.

Kaiser, G. (1961). *Pietismus und Patriotismus im literarischen Deutschland* (Wiesbaden).

Kaiser, T. E. (1991), 'Money, Despotism and Public Opinion in Early Eighteenth-Century France: John Law and the Debate on Royal Credit', *JMH*, 63:1–18.

Kamen, H. (1967). *The Rise of Toleration* (London).

Kann, R. A. (1960). *A Study in Austrian Intellectual History; From Late Baroque to Romanticism* (New York).

Kaplan, S. L. (1976). *Bread, Politics and Political Economy in the Reign of Louis XIV*, 2 vols. (The Hague).

Kaplan, Y. (1989). *From Christianity to Judaism: The Story of Isaac Orobio de Castro* (New York).

Kapossy, B. (2001). 'The Sociable Patriot: Isaak Iselin's Protestant Reading of Jean-Jacques Rousseau', *HEI*, 27:153–70.

Karniel, J. (1986). *Die Toleranzpolitik Kaiser Josephs II* (Gerlingen).

Karsten, P. (1978). *Patriot Heroes in England and America* (Madison, WI).

Kathe, H. (1980). 'Geist und Macht im absolutistischen Preußen: Zur Geschichte der Universität Halle von 1740 bis 1806' (doctoral thesis, Halle-Wittenberg).

Kaulbach, F. (1982). *Studien zur späten Rechtsphilosophie Kants und ihrer transzendentalen Methode* (Würzburg).

Keane, J. (1995). *Tom Paine: A Political Life* (Boston, MA).

Kearney, H. F. (1959). 'The Political Background to English Mercantilism, 1695–1700', *Economic History Review*, 11:484–96.

Kearney, R., ed. (1985). *The Irish Mind: Exploring Intellectual Traditions* (Dublin, 1985).

Keller, R. (1994). *Patriotism and the Female Sex: Abigail Adams and the American Revolution* (Brooklyn, NY).

Kelley, D. R. (1970). *Foundations of Modern Historical Scholarship: Language, Law and History in the French Renaissance* (New York).

Kelley, D. R. (1990). *The Human Measure: Social Thought in the Western Legal Tradition* (Cambridge, MA).

Kelley, D. R., ed. (1997). *History and the Disciplines: The Reclassification of Knowledge in Early Modern Europe* (Rochester, NY).

Kelly, C. (1987). *Rousseau's Exemplary Life: The Confessions as Political Philosophy* (Ithaca, NY).

Kelly, G. (1992). *Revolutionary Feminism: The Mind and Career of Mary Wollstonecraft* (Basingstoke).

Kelly, G. (1993). *Women, Writing and Revolution, 1790–1827* (New York).

Kelly, G. A. (1968). 'Rousseau, Kant and History', *JHI*, 29:347–64.

Kelly, G. A. (1969). *Idealism, Politics and History* (London).

Kelly, G. A. (1978). *Hegel's Retreat from Eleusis* (Princeton).

Kelly, G. A. (1982). *Victims, Authority and Terror: The Parallel Deaths of d'Orléans, Custine, Bailly and Malesherbes* (Chapel Hill).

Kelly, G. A. (1986). *Mortal Politics in Eighteenth-Century France* (Waterloo, ON).

Kelly, J. (1998). *Henry Flood: Patriots and Politics in Eighteenth-Century Ireland* (Dublin).

Kelly, P. (1988). 'William Molyneux and the Spirit of Liberty in Eighteenth-Century Ireland', *Eighteenth-Century Ireland*, 3:133–48.

Kelly, P. (1989a). 'Archbishop William King and Colonial Nationalism', in Brady 1989.

Kelly, P. (1989b). 'Perceptions of Locke in Eighteenth-Century Ireland', *Proceedings of the Royal Irish Academy*, 89:17–35.

Kelly, P. J. (1990). *Utilitarianism and Distributive Justice: Jeremy Bentham and the Civil Law* (New York).

Kendrick, T. D. (1956). *The Lisbon Earthquake* (London).

Kennedy, E. (1978). *A Philosophe in the Age of Revolution: Destutt de Tracy and the Origins of Ideology* (Philadelphia).

Kennedy, E., and Mendus, S. (1987). *Women in Western Political Philosophy: Kant to Nietzsche* (Brighton).

Kenyon, C. (1958). 'Alexander Hamilton: Rousseau of the Right', *Political Science Quarterly*, 73:161–78.

Kenyon, J. P. (1977). *Revolution Principles: The Politics of Party, 1689–1720* (Cambridge).

Keohane, N. O. (1980). *Philosophy and the State in France: The Renaissance to the Enlightenment* (Princeton).

Kerber, L. K. (1980). *Women of the Republic: Intellect and Ideology in Revolutionary America* (Chapel Hill).

Kerkhof, B. (1995). 'A Fatal Attraction?: Smith's *Theory of Moral Sentiments* and Mandeville's *Fable*', *HPT*, 16:219–33.

Kersting, W. (1982). 'Das starke Gesetz der Schuldigkeit und das schwächere der Gültigkeit: Kant und die Pflichtenlehre des 18. Jahrhunderts', *Studia Leibnitiana*, 14:184–220.

Kersting, W. (1993). *Wohlgeordnete Freiheit: Immanuel Kants Rechts- und Staatsphilosophie*, 2nd edn (Frankfurt). 1st publ. 1984 (Berlin).

Ketcham, R. L. (1971). *James Madison: A Biography* (New York).

Kettler, D. (1965). *The Social and Political Thought of Adam Ferguson* (Columbus, OH).

Kettler, D. (1977). 'History and Theory in Ferguson's Essay on the History of Civil Society', *PT*, 5:437–60.

Kidd, C. (1993). *Subverting Scotland's Past: Scottish Whig Historians and the Creation of an Anglo-British Identity, 1689–c. 1830* (Cambridge).

Kilani, M. (1992). *Le Discours anthropologique à la fin des lumières* (Lausanne).

Kilcullen, J. (1988). *Sincerity and Truth: Essays on Arnauld, Bayle and Toleration* (New York).

King, C. S. (1975). 'Philosophy and Science in the Arts Curriculum of the Scottish Universities in the Seventeenth Century' (doctoral thesis, Edinburgh).

King, K. R. (2000). *Jane Barker, Exile: A Literary Career, 1675–1725* (New York).

Kingston, R. E. (2001). 'Montesquieu on Religion and on the Question of Toleration', in Carrithers *et al.* 2001.

Kinnaird, J. K. (1979). 'Mary Astell and the Conservative Contribution to English Feminism', *JBS*, 19:53–75.

Kirk, L. (1987). *Richard Cumberland and Natural Law* (Cambridge).

Kirk, L. (1994). 'Genevan Republicanism', in Wootton 1994a.

Kitromilides, P. (1992). *The Enlightenment as Social Criticism: Iosipos Moisiodox and Greek Culture in the Eighteenth Century* (Princeton).

Klaits, J. (1976). *Printed Propaganda under Louis XIV* (Princeton).

Klein, L. E. (1989). 'Liberty, Manners and Politeness in Early Eighteenth-Century England', *HJ*, 32:583–606.

Klein, L. E. (1994). *Shaftesbury and the Culture of Politeness* (Cambridge).

Kleinheyer, G. (1959). *Staat und Bürger im Recht: Die Vorträge des Carl Gottlieb Svarez vor dem preußischen Kronprinzen, 1791–1792* (Bonn).

Kliger, S. (1972). *The Goths in England* (New York). 1st publ. 1952 (Cambridge, MA).

Klingenstein, G. (1970). *Staatsverwaltung und kirchliche Autorität* (Vienna).

Klingenstein, G. (1975). *Der Aufstieg des Hauses Kaunitz* (Göttingen).

Klippel, D. (1976). *Politische Freiheit und Freiheitsrechte im deutschen Naturrecht des 18. Jahrhunderts* (Paderborn).

Klippel, D. (1987). 'Naturrecht als politische Theorie', in Bödeker and Herrmann 1987.

Klippel, D. (1990). 'Von der Aufklärung der Herrscher zur Herrschaft der Aufklärung', *Zeitschrift für Historische Forschung*, 17:193–210.

Klippel, D. (1993). 'Naturrecht und Politik im Deutschland des 19. Jahrhunderts', in Ballestrem 1993.

Klippel, D. (1994). 'Johann August Schlettwein and the Economics Faculty at the University of Giessen', *HPT*, 15:203–27.

Klippel, D. (1995). 'Naturrecht und Rechtsphilosophie in der ersten Hälfte des 19. Jahrhunderts', in Dann and Klippel 1995.

Klueting, H. (1986). *Die Lehre von der Macht des Staaten* (Berlin).

Klueting, H., ed. (1995). *Der Josephinismus* (Darmstadt).

Klueting, H., Hinske, N., and Hengst, K., eds. (1993). *Katholische Aufklärung* (Hamburg).

Knetsch, F. R. J. (1967). *Pierre Jurieu* (Kampen).

Knight, I. F. (1968). *The Geometric Spirit: The Abbé de Condillac and the French Enlightenment* (New Haven).

Knott, S., and Taylor, B., eds. (2005). *Women, Gender and Enlightenment, 1650–1850* (Basingstoke).

Knudsen, J. B. (1986). *Justus Möser and the German Enlightenment* (Cambridge).

Koch, A. (1957). *The Philosophy of Thomas Jefferson* (New York). 1st publ. 1943.

Koch, C. H. (1976). 'Man's Duties to Animals: A Danish Contribution to the Discussion of the Rights of Animals in the Eighteenth Century', *Danish Yearbook of Philosophy*, 13:11–28.

Koch, C. H. (2003). *Dansk oplysningsfilosofi* (Copenhagen).

Kodalle, K. M., ed. (1996). *Der Venunftideen: Kants Entwurf im Widerstreit* (Würzburg).

Koebner, R. (1951). 'Despot and Despotism: Vicissitudes of a Political Term', *Journal of the Warburg and Courtauld Institutes*, 14:275–302.

Koebner, R. (1961). *Empire* (Cambridge).

Kohnen, J. (1987). *Theodor Gottlieb von Hippel, 1741–1796* (Berne).

Köpeczi, B., Soboul, A., Balázs, E., and Kosáry, D. (1985). *L'Absolutisme éclairé* (Budapest).

Korkman, P. (2001). 'Barbeyrac and Natural Law' (doctoral thesis, Åbo Academy).

Korkman, P. (2002). 'Civil Sovereigns and the King of Kings: Barbeyrac on the Creator's Right to Rule', in Hunter and Saunders 2002.

Korner, S. (1967). 'Kant's Conception of Freedom', *Proceedings of the British Academy*, 53:193–217.

Kors, A. C. (1976). *D'Holbach's Coterie* (Princeton).

Kors, A. C. (1990). *Atheism in France, 1650–1729* (Princeton).

Kosáry, D. (1987). *Culture and Society in Eighteenth-Century Hungary* (Budapest).

Koselleck, R. (1985). *Futures Past: On the Semantics of Historical Time*, trans. and ed. K. Tribe (Cambridge, MA). 1st publ. in German in 1965.

Koselleck, R. (1988). *Critique and Crisis: Enlightenment and the Parthenogenesis of Modern Society* (Cambridge, MA). 1st published in German in 1959.

Kovács, E., ed. (1979). *Katholische Aufklärung und Josephinismus* (Munich).

Kovács, I., ed. (1971). *Les Lumières en Hongrie, en Europe centrale et en Europe orientale* (Budapest).

Kramer, G. (1880–2). *August Hermann Francke*, 2 vols. (Halle).

Kramnick, I. (1968). *Bolingbroke and his Circle* (Cambridge, MA).

Kramnick, I. (1972). 'On Anarchism and the Real World: William Godwin and Radical England', *American Political Science Review*, 66:114–28.

Kramnick, I. (1977). *The Rage of Edmund Burke: Portrait of an Ambivalent Conservative* (New York).

Kramnick, I. (1982). 'Republican Revisionism Revised', *AHR*, 87:629–64.

Kramnick, I. (1986). 'Eighteenth-Century Science and Radical Social Theory: The Case of Joseph Priestley's Scientific Liberalism', *JBS*, 25:1–30.

Kramnick, I. (1990). *Republicanism and Bourgeois Radicalism: Political Ideology in Late Eighteenth-Century England and America* (Ithaca, NY).

Krause, S. (2000). 'The Spirit of Separate Powers in Montesquieu', *Review of Politics*, 62:231–65.

Krause, S. (2001). 'Despotism in *The Spirit of the Laws*', in Carrithers *et al.* 2001.

Kreiser, B. R. (1978). *Miracles, Convulsions and Ecclesiastical Politics in Early Eighteenth-Century Paris* (Princeton).

Kremers, H. (1986). 'L'Oeuvre de Joseph von Sonnenfels et ses sources européennes', *Francia*, 14:331–68.

Kremers, H. (1988). 'Das kameralistische Werk von Joseph von Sonnenfels', in Reinalter 1988.

Kremers, H. (1994). *Joseph von Sonnenfels: Aufklärung als Sozialpolitik* (Vienna).

Krieger, L. (1957). *The German Idea of Freedom* (Boston, MA).

Krieger, L. (1970). *Kings and Philosophers, 1689–1789* (New York).

Krieger, L. (1975). *An Essay on the Theory of Enlightened Despotism* (Chicago).

Kuehn, M. (1987). *Scottish Common Sense in Germany, 1768–1800* (Kingston, ON).

Kuehn, M. (2001). *Kant: A Biography* (Cambridge).

Kühl, K. (1984). *Eigentumsordnung als Freiheitsordnung: Zur Aktualität der Kantischen Rechts- und Eigentumslehre* (Freiburg).

Kühnel, M. (2001). *Das politische Denken von Christian Thomasius* (Berlin).

Küsters, G. W. (1988). *Kants Rechtsphilosophie* (Darmstadt).

Laboucheix, H. (1982). *Richard Price as Moral Philosopher and Political Theorist* (Oxford).

Labrousse, E. (1963–4). *Pierre Bayle*, 2 vols. (The Hague).

Labrousse, E. (1982). 'The Political Ideas of the Huguenot Diaspora', in Golden 1982.

Labrousse, E. (1983). *Bayle* (New York).

Labrousse, E. (1996). *Conscience et conviction: études sur le XVIIe siècle* (Paris).

Labrousse, E. (1985). *Essai sur la révocation de l'Edit de Nantes* (Geneva).

Lacey, M. J., and Furner, M. O., eds. (1993). *The State and Social Investigation in Britain and the United States* (Cambridge).

Lacey, M. J., and Haakonssen, K., eds. (1991). *A Culture of Rights: The Bill of Rights in Philosophy, Politics and Law, 1791–1991* (Cambridge).

Lach, D. F. (1953). 'The Sinophilism of Christian Wolff', *JHI*, 14:561–74.

Lafage, F. (1998). *Le Comte Joseph de Maistre (1753–1821)* (Paris).

Lagny, A., ed. (2001). *Les Piétismes à l'âge classique* (Villeneuve-d'Ascq).

Lamioni, C., ed. (1991). *Il Sinodo di Pistoia del 1786* (Rome).

Landau, N., ed. (2002). *Law, Crime, and English Society, 1660–1840* (Cambridge).

Landes, J. B. (1988). *Women and the Public Sphere in the Age of the French Revolution* (Ithaca, NY).

Landsberg, E., and Stintzing, R. (1880–1910). *Geschichte der deutschen Rechtswissenschaft*, 3 vols. (Berlin).

Langbein, J. H. (1977). *Torture and the Law of Proof: Europe and England in the Ancien Régime* (Chicago).

Langbein, J. H. (1983). 'Albion's Fatal Flaws', *Past and Present*, 98:96–120.

Langford, P. (1988). 'Property and "Virtual Representation" in Eighteenth-Century England', *HJ*, 31:83–115.

Langford, P. (1989). *A Polite and Commercial People: England 1727–1783* (New York).

Langford, P. (1991). *Public Life and the Propertied Englishman* (New York).

Langsam, W. C. (1949). *Francis the Good: The Education of an Emperor, 1768–1792* (New York).

Larrère, C. (1992). *L'Invention de l'économie au XVIIIe siècle: du droit naturel à la physiocratie* (Paris).

Larrère, C. (1999). *Actualité de Montesquieu* (Paris).

Larrère, C. (2001). 'Montesquieu on Economics and Commerce', in Carrithers *et al.* 2001.

Larrère, C., and Volpilhac-Auger, C. (1999). *1748, l'année de l'Esprit des lois* (Paris).

Larrère, C., and Weil, F. (2000), 'Introduction' to Montesquieu, *Réflexions sur la monarchie universelle en Europe*, in *Oeuvres complètes de Montesquieu*, II (Oxford).

Las Vergnas, R. (1932). *Le Chevalier Rutledge, gentilhomme anglais, 1742–1793* (Paris).

Launay, M. (1971). *Jean-Jacques Rousseau: écrivain politique (1712–1762)* (Cannes).

Laursen, J. C. (1986). 'The Subversive Kant: The Vocabulary of "Public" and "Publicity"', *PT*, 14:584–603.

Laursen, J. C. (1989). 'Skepticism and Intellectual Freedom: The Philosophical Foundations of Kant's Politics of Publicity', *HPT*, 10:99–133.

Laursen, J. C. (1992). *The Politics of Skepticism: In the Ancients, Montaigne, Hume and Kant* (Leiden).

Laursen, J. C., ed. (1995). *New Essays on the Political Thought of the Huguenots of the Refuge* (Leiden).

Lebrun, R. (1965). *Throne and Altar: The Political and Religious Thought of Joseph de Maistre* (Ottawa).

Lebrun, R. (1988a). *Joseph de Maistre: An Intellectual Militant* (Kingston, ON).

Lebrun, R., ed. (1988b). *Maistre Studies* (Lanham, MD).

LeDonne, J. P. (1984). *Ruling Russia: Politics and Administration in the Age of Absolutism, 1762–1796* (Princeton).

Leduc, F. (1974). *Jean-Jacques Rousseau et le mythe de l'antiquité* (Paris).

Lee, J. (1982). 'Political Antiquarianism Unmasked: The Conservative Attack on the Myth of the Ancient Constitution', *Bulletin of the Institute of Historical Research*, 55:166–79.

Leeb, I. L. (1973). *The Ideological Origins of the Batavian Revolution* (The Hague).

Lehmann, K. (1985). *Thomas Jefferson, American Humanist* (New York).

Lehmann, W. C. (1930). *Adam Ferguson and the Beginnings of Modern Sociology* (London).

Lehmann, W. C. (1960). *John Millar of Glasgow, 1735–1801* (London).

Lehmann, W. C. (1971). *Henry Home, Lord Kames, and the Scottish Enlightenment* (The Hague).

Leighton, C. D. A. (1994). *Catholicism in a Protestant Kingdom: A Study of the Irish Ancien Regime* (Basingstoke).

LeMahieu, D. L. (1976). *The Mind of William Paley* (Lincoln, NE).

Lemmings, D. (1993). 'The Independence of the Judiciary', in Birks 1993.

Lenhammar, H. (1966). *Tolerans och bekännelsetvång: studier i den svenska swedenborgianismen, 1765–1795* (Uppsala).

Lenman, B. P. (1992). 'The Poverty of Political Theory in the Scottish Revolution of 1688–1690', in Schwoerer 1992.

Lestition, S. (1989). 'The Teaching and Practice of Jurisprudence in Eighteenth-Century East Prussia', *Ius commune*, 16:27–80.

Lestition, S. (1993). 'Kant and the End of the Enlightenment in Prussia', *JMH*, 65:57–112.

Letwin, S. (1965). *The Pursuit of Certainty* (Cambridge).

Letwin, W. (1963). *The Origins of Scientific Economics: English Economic Thought, 1660–1776* (London).

Levack, B. P. (1987). *The Formation of the British State: England, Scotland and the Union, 1603–1707* (New York).

Levine, J. M. (1977). *Dr Woodward's Shield: History, Science and Satire in Augustan England* (Berkeley).

Levinger, M. (1996). 'Kant and the Origins of Prussian Constitutionalism', *HPT*, 19:241–63.

Levy, D. G. (1980). *The Ideas and Careers of Simon-Nicolas-Henri Linguet* (Urbana, IL).

Levy, D. G., Applewhite, H. B., and Johnson, M. D., eds. (1979). *Women in Revolutionary Paris, 1789–1795* (Urbana, IL).

Lewis, G. (1999). 'Robespierre through the Chartist Looking Glass', in Haydon and Doyle 1999.

Liebel, H. (1965). *Enlightened Bureaucracy versus Enlightened Despotism in Baden, 1750–1792* (Philadelphia).

Lieberman, D. (1983). 'The Legal Needs of a Commercial Society: The Jurisprudence of Lord Kames', in Hont and Ignatieff 1983a.

Lieberman, D. (1988). 'Blackstone's Science of Legislation', *JBS*, 27:117–49.

Lieberman, D. (1989). *The Province of Legislation Determined: Legal Theory in Eighteenth-Century Britain* (Cambridge).

Lieberman, D. (1999). 'Jeremy Bentham: Biography and Intellectual Biography', *HPT*, 20:187–204.

Lieberman, D. (2000). 'Economy and Polity in Bentham's Science of Legislation', in Collini, et al. 2000a.

Lieberman, D. (2002). 'Mapping Criminal Law: Blackstone and the Categories of English Jurisprudence', in Landau 2002.

Lieberwirth, R. (1955). *Christian Thomasius* (Weimar).

Lilla, M. (1993). *G. B. Vico: The Making of an Anti-Modern* (Cambridge, MA).

Limoli, D. A. (1958). 'Pietro Verri, a Lombard Reformer under Enlightened Absolutism and the French Revolution', *Journal of Central European Affairs*, 18:254–80.

Lincoln, A. (1938). *Some Political and Social Ideas of English Dissent, 1763–1800* (Cambridge). Repr. New York, 1971.

Lindberg, B. (1976). *Naturrätten i Uppsala, 1655–1720* (Uppsala).

Link, C. (1979). *Herrschaftsordnung und bürgerliche Freiheit* (Cologne).

Linton, M. (1999). 'The Unvirtuous King?: Clerical Rhetoric on the French Monarchy, 1760–1774', *HEI*, 25:55–74.

Linton, M. (2000a). 'Virtue Rewarded? Women and the Politics of Virtue in Eighteenth-Century France', *HEI*, 26:35–49, 51–65.

Linton, M. (2000b). 'Citizenship and Religious Toleration in France', in Grell and Porter 2000.

Linton, M. (2004). *The Politics of Virtue in 18th-Century France* (Basingstoke).

Lizé, E. (1979). *Voltaire, Grimm, et la correspondance littéraire*, *SVEC*, 180.

Llombart, V. (1992). *Campomanes, economista y politico de Carlos III* (Madrid).

Lobban, M. (1987). 'Blackstone and the Science of Law', *HJ*, 30:311–35.

Lock, F. P. (1983). *Swift's Tory Politics* (London).

Lock, F. P. (1985). *Burke's Reflections on the Revolution in France* (Boston, MA).

Lock, F. P. (1999). *Edmund Burke, i: 1730–1784* (New York).

Locke, D. (1980). *A Fantasy of Reason: The Life and Thought of William Godwin* (Boston, MA).

Loftis, J. (1963). *The Politics of Drama in Augustan England* (Oxford).

Long, D. G. (1977). *Bentham on Liberty* (Toronto).

Lortholary, A. (1951). *Le Mirage russe en France au XVIIIe siècle* (Paris).

Lough, J. (1968). *Essays on the Encyclopédie of Diderot and d'Alembert* (London).

Lough, J. (1970). *The Encyclopédie in Eighteenth-Century England and Other Studies* (Newcastle).

Lough, J. (1971). *The Encyclopédie* (London).

Lough, J. (1973). *The Contributors to the Encyclopédie* (London).

Lough, J. (1975). 'Who Were the *Philosophes*?', in Fox *et al.* 1975.

Lough, J. (1982). *The 'Philosophes' and Post-Revolutionary France* (Oxford).

Lough, J. (1985). 'Reflections on Enlightenment and Lumières', *BJECS*, 8:1–15.

Lovejoy, A. O. (1936). *The Great Chain of Being* (Cambridge, MA).

Lucas, C., ed. (1988). *The French Revolution and the Creation of Modern Political Culture, ii: The Political Culture of the French Revolution* (Oxford).

Ludington, C. C. (2000). 'From Ancient Constitution to British Empire: William Atwood and the Imperial Crown of England', in Ohlmeyer 2000.

Ludwig, B. (1988). *Kants Rechtslehre* (Hamburg).

Luig, K. (1972). 'Zur Verbreitung des Naturrechts in Europa', *Tidjschrift voor Rechtsgeschiedenis*, 40:539–57.

Lukowski, J. T. (1991). *Liberty's Folly: The Polish-Lithuanian Commonwealth in the Eighteenth Century* (London).

Lukowski, J. T. (1994). 'Recasting Utopia: Montesquieu, Rousseau and the Polish Constitution of 3 May 1791', *HJ*, 37:65–88.

Lukowski, J. T. (2001). 'The Szlachta and the Monarchy', in Butterwick 2001.

Lüsebrink, H. J., and Strugnell, A. (1995). *L'Histoire des deux Indes: réécriture et polygraphie*, *SVEC*, 333.

Lüsebrink, H. J., and Tietz, M., eds. (1991). *Lectures de Raynal: L'Histoire des deux Indes en Europe et en Amérique au XVIIIe siècle*, *SVEC*, 286.

Lutterbeck, K. G. (2002). *Staat und Gesellschaft bei Christian Thomasius und Christian Wolff* (Stuttgart).

Lutz, D. (1980). *Popular Consent and Popular Control: Whig Political Theory in the Early State Constitutions* (Baton Rouge).

Lutz, D. (1988). *The Origins of American Constitutionalism* (Baton Rouge).

Lynd, S. (1968). *Intellectual Origins of American Radicalism* (New York).

Lyons, D. (1973). *In the Interest of the Governed: A Study of Bentham's Philosophy of Utility and Law* (Oxford).

McBride, I. R. (1993). The School of Virtue: Francis Hutcheson, Irish Presbyterians and the Scottish Enlightenment', in Boyce *et al.* 1993.

McBride, I. R. (1998). *Scripture Politics: Ulster Presbyterians and Irish Radicalism in the Late Eighteenth Century* (New York).

McCalman, I. (1988). *Radical Underworld: Prophets, Revolutionaries and Pornographers in London, 1795–1840* (Cambridge).

McClelland, C. E. (1980). *State, Society and University in Germany, 1700–1914* (Cambridge).

McConnell, T. (1996). 'The Inalienable Right of Conscience: A Madisonian Argument', *Social Theory and Practice*, 22:397–416.

MacCormick, N. (1982). 'Law and Enlightenment', in Campbell and Skinner 1982b.

MacCormick, N., and Bankowski, Z., eds. (1989). *Enlightenment, Rights and Revolution: Essays in Legal and Social Philosophy* (Aberdeen).

McCoy, D. (1980). *The Elusive Republic: Political Economy in Jeffersonian America* (Chapel Hill).

McCrystal, J. (1993). 'Revolting Women: The Use of Revolutionary Discourse in Mary Astell and Mary Wollstonecraft Compared', *HPT*, 14:189–203.

McCullough, D. (2001). *John Adams* (New York).

MacDonald, D. C., ed. (1891). *Birthright in Land* (London).

McDonald, F. (1979). *Alexander Hamilton: A Biography* (New York).

McDonald, F. (1985). *Novus ordo seclorum: The Intellectual Origins of the Constitution* (Lawrence, KA).

McDonald, J. (1965). *Rousseau and the French Revolution, 1762–1791* (London).

McDowell, G. L. (1998). 'The Language of Law and the Foundations of American Constitutionalism', *WMQ*, 55:375–98.

McDowell, P. (1998). *The Women of Grub Street: Press, Politics and Gender in the London Literary Marketplace, 1678–1730* (New York).

McDowell, R. B. (2001). *Grattan: A Life* (Dublin).

Machelon, J. P. (1969). *Les Idées politiques de J. L. de Lolme* (Paris).

McIlwain, C. H. (1923). *The American Revolution: A Constitutional Interpretation* (Ithaca, NY).

McIlwain, C. H. (1947). *Constitutionalism, Ancient and Modern* (Ithaca, NY).

MacIntyre, A. (1981). *After Virtue* (London).

MacIntyre, A. (1988). *Whose Justice? Which Rationality?* (London).

Mack, M. (1969). *The Garden and the City: Retirement and Politics in the Later Poetry of Pope, 1731–1743* (Toronto).

Mack, M. P. (1962). *Jeremy Bentham* (London).

McKee, F. (1988). 'Early Criticism of *The Grumbling Hive*', *Notes and Queries*, 233:176–7.

McKendrick, N., ed. (1974). *Historical Perspectives* (London).

McKendrick, N., Brewer, J., and Plumb, J. H. (1982). *The Birth of a Consumer Society* (Bloomington, IN).

McKenna, A. (1990). *De Pascal à Voltaire*, 2 vols., *SVEC*, 276–7.

McKenzie, L. A. (1981). 'The French Revolution and English Parliamentary Reform: James Mackintosh and the *Vindiciae Gallicae*', *ECS*, 14:264–82.

Mackenzie, W. C. (1935). *Andrew Fletcher of Saltoun* (Edinburgh).

McKitterick, R., and Quinault, R. (1997). *Edward Gibbon and Empire* (New York).

Mackrell, J. Q. C. (1973). *The Attack on 'Feudalism' in Eighteenth-Century France* (London).

MacLean, G., ed. (1995). *Culture and Society in the Stuart Restoration* (Cambridge).

McLellan, J. E. (1985). *Science Reorganized: Scientific Societies in the Eighteenth Century* (New York).

McLynn, F. J. (1985). 'The Ideology of Jacobitism on the Eve of the Rising of 1745', *HEI*, 6:1–18, 173–88.

McMahon, D. M. (2001). *Enemies of the Enlightenment: The French Counter-Enlightenment and the Making of Modernity* (New York).

McMahon, M. P. (1990). *The Radical Whigs, John Trenchard and Thomas Gordon* (Lanham, MD).

McManners, J. (1969). *The French Revolution and the Church* (London).

McManners, J. (1981). *Death and the Enlightenment* (New York).

McManners, J. (1998). *Church and Society in Eighteenth-Century France*, 2 vols. (Oxford).

McNally, D. (1988). *Political Economy and the Rise of Capitalism: A Reinterpretation* (Berkeley).

McNally, D. (2000). 'Political Economy to the Fore: Burke, Malthus and the Whig Response to Popular Radicalism in the Age of the French Revolution', *HPT*, 21:427–47.

McPhail, B. (1993). 'Scotland's Sovereignty Asserted: The Debate over the Anglo-Scottish Union of 1707', *Parergon*, 11:27–44.

Macpherson, C. B. (1980). *Burke* (New York).

Madariaga, I. de (1981). *Russia in the Age of Catherine the Great* (London).

Madariaga, I. de (1982). 'Autocracy and Sovereignty', *Canadian American Slavic Studies*, 16:369–87.

Maestro, M. (1942). *Voltaire and Beccaria as Reformers of Criminal Law* (New York). Repr. 1972.

Maestro, M. (1973). *Cesare Beccaria and the Origins of Penal Reform* (Philadelphia).

Magnusson, L., Wittrock, B., and Heilbron, J., eds. (1998). *The Rise of the Social Sciences and the Formation of Modernity: Conceptual Change in Context, 1750–1850* (Dordrecht).

Mailhet, E. A. (1880). *Jacques Basnage, théologien, controversiste, diplomate et historien* (Geneva). Repr. 1978.

Mair, D., ed. (1990). *The Scottish Contribution to Modern Economic Thought* (Aberdeen).

Maire, C. (1981). 'L'Eglise et la nation: du dépôt de la vérité au dépôt des lois: la trajectoire janséniste au XVIIIe siècle', *Annales: Economies, Sociétés, Civilisations*, 5:1177–1205.

Maire, C. (1998). *De la cause de Dieu à la cause de la nation: le jansénisme au XVIIIe siècle* (Paris).

Maire, C., ed. (1990). *Jansénisme et Révolution* (Paris).

Malcolm, J. L. (1994). *To Keep and Bear Arms: The Origins of an Anglo-American Right* (Cambridge, MA).

Mali, J. (1992). *The Rehabilitation of Myth: Vico's New Science* (Cambridge).

Mali, J. (1989). 'The Poetics of Politics: Vico's "Philosophy of Authority"', *HPT*, 10:41–69.

Mali, J., and Wokler, R., eds. (2003). *The Counter-Enlightenment of Isaiah Berlin* (Philadelphia).

Malone, D., (1948–81). *Jefferson and his Time*, 6 vols. (London).

Mandrou, R. (1980). *La Raison du prince: l'Europe absolutiste, 1649–1775* (Verviers).

Manicas, P. T. (1981). 'Montesquieu and the Eighteenth-Century Vision of the State', *HPT*, 2:313–47.

Mann, F. K. (1937). *Steuerpolitische Ideale* (Jena).

Mann, M. (1986–93). *The Sources of Social Power*, 2 vols. (Cambridge).

Manning, D. J. (1968). *The Mind of Jeremy Bentham* (London).

Mansfield, H. C. (1965). *Statesmanship and Party Government: A Study of Burke and Bolingbroke* (Chicago).

Mansfield, H. C. (1978). *The Spirit of Liberalism* (Cambridge, MA).

Manuel, F. E. (1965). *The New World of Henri Saint-Simon* (Cambridge, MA).

Manuel, F. E. (1959). *The Eighteenth Century Confronts the Gods* (Cambridge, MA).

Manuel, F. E. (1962). *The Prophets of Paris* (Cambridge, MA).

Manz, J. (1971). *Emer de Vattel: Versuch einer Würdigung* (Zurich).

Marchi, G. P. (1992). *Un italiano in Europa: Scipione Maffei tra passione antiquaria e impegno* (Verona).

Marcu, E. (1953). 'Un encyclopédiste oublié: Formey', *RHLF*, 53:296–305.

Margerison, K. (1983). *P.-L. Roederer: Political Thought and Practice during the French Revolution* (Philadelphia).

Marshall, J. (1994). *John Locke: Resistance, Religion and Responsibility* (Cambridge).

Marshall, P. H. (1984). *William Godwin* (New Haven).

Marshall, P. J., and Williams, G. (1982). *The Great Map of Mankind: British Perceptions of the World in the Age of Enlightenment* (London).

Martimort, A. G. (1953). *Le Gallicanisme de Bossuet* (Paris).

Martin, K. (1962). *French Liberal Thought in the Eighteenth Century* (London). 1st publ. 1929.

Martin, V. (1929). *Le Gallicanisme politique et le clergé de France* (Paris).

Mas, E. de (1969). 'Vico and Italian Thought', in Tagliacozzo and White 1969.

Mason, J. Hope (1979). *The Indispensable Rousseau* (London).

Mason, J. Hope (1982). *The Irresistible Diderot* (London).

Mason, H. T. (1963). *Pierre Bayle and Voltaire* (London).

Mason, H. T. (1975). *Voltaire* (London).

Mason, H. T. (1981). *Voltaire: A Biography* (Baltimore).

Mason, H. T. (1982). *French Writers and their Society, 1715–1800* (London).

Mason, H. T., and Doyle, W., eds. (1989). *The Impact of the French Revolution on European Consciousness* (Gloucester).

Mason, P. A. (1993). 'The Genevan Republican Background to Rousseau's *Social Contract*', *HPT*, 14:547–72.

Mason, R. A., ed. (1987). *Scotland and England, 1285–1815* (Edinburgh).

Mason, S. (1975). *Montesquieu's Idea of Justice* (The Hague).

Mason, S. (1988). 'Ferguson and Montesquieu: Tacit Reproaches?', *BJECS*, 11:193–203.

Mason, S. (1990). 'Montesquieu on English Constitutionalism Revisited', *SVEC*, 278:105–46.

Mass, E., and Postigliola, A., eds. (1993). *Lectures de Montesquieu* (Naples).

Masson, P. M. (1916). *La Religion de Jean-Jacques Rousseau*, 3 vols. (Paris).

Masters, R. D. (1968). *The Political Philosophy of Rousseau* (Princeton).

Mastnak, T. (1998). 'Abbé de Saint-Pierre: European Union and the Turk', *HPT*, 19:570–98.

Maston, T. B. (1962). *Isaac Backus: Pioneer of Religious Liberty* (Rochester, NY).

Mather, F. C. (1992). *High Church Prophet: Bishop Samuel Horsley (1733–1806) and the Caroline Tradition in the Later Georgian Church* (New York).

Matoré, G. (1953). *La Méthode en lexicologie* (Paris).

Matoré, G. (1968). *Histoire des dictionnaires français* (Paris).

Matthews, R. K. (1984). *The Radical Politics of Thomas Jefferson* (Lawrence, KS).

Maus, I. (1992). *Zur Aufklärung der Demokratietheorie: Rechts- und demokratietheoretische Überlegungen im Anschluß an Kant* (Frankfurt).

Mautner, T. (1994). 'Moses Mendelssohn and the Right of Toleration', in Albrecht *et al.* 1994.

Mautner, T. (1996). 'Carmichael and Barbeyrac: The Lost Correspondence', in Palladini and Hartung 1996.

Maxwell, K. (1995). *Pombal, Paradox of the Enlightenment* (Cambridge).

May, G. (1964). *De Jean Jacques Rousseau a Madame Roland* (Geneva).

May, G. (1970). *Madame Roland and the Age of Revolution* (New York).

May, H. (1976). *The Enlightenment in America* (New York).

May, L. P. (1975–8). *Le Mercier de la Rivière (1719–1801), aux origines de la science économique*, 2 vols. (Paris).

Mayer, D. N. (1994). *The Constitutional Thought of Thomas Jefferson* (Charlottesville).

Méchoulan, H. (1990). *Amsterdam au temps de Spinoza* (Paris).

Méchoulan, H. (1991). *Être Juif à Amsterdam au temps de Spinoza* (Paris).

Mee, J. (1992). *Dangerous Enthusiasm: William Blake and the Culture of Radicalism in the 1790s* (New York).

Meek, R. L. (1954). 'The Scottish Contribution to Marxist Sociology', in Saville 1954.

Meek, R. L. (1967). *Economics and Ideology and Other Essays* (London).

Meek, R. L. (1970). 'Smith, Turgot and the "Four Stages" Theory', *History of Political Economy*, 3:9–27.

Meek, R. L. (1976). *Social Science and the Ignoble Savage* (Cambridge).

Meek, R. L., ed. (1962). *The Economics of Physiocracy: Essays and Translations* (London).

Meinecke, F. (1957). *Machiavellism* (London). 1st publ. in German in 1924.

Mejer, O. (1880). *Febronius: Weihbischof I. N. von Hontheim und sein Widerruf* (Tübingen).

Melching, W., and Velema, W., eds. (1994). *Main Trends in Cultural History* (Amsterdam).

Melton, J. H. (1988). *Absolutism and the Eighteenth-Century Origins of Compulsory Schooling in Prussia and Austria* (Cambridge).

Melton, J. H. (2001a). *The Rise of the Public in Enlightenment Europe* (Cambridge).

Melton, J. H. (2001b). 'Pietism, Politics, and the Public Sphere in Germany', in Bradley and Van Kley 2001.

Mendus, S. (1988). *Justifying Toleration* (Cambridge).

Menger, A. (1899). *The Right to the Whole Produce of Labour*, trans. M. E. Tanner (London).

Menzel, W. W. (1996). *Vernakuläre Wissenschaft: Christian Wolffs Bedeutung für die Herausbildung und Durchsetzung des Deutschen als Wissensschaftssprache* (Tübingen).

Merlan, P. (1951). 'From Hume to Hamann', *The Personalist*, 32:11–18.

Merlan, P. (1954). 'Hamann et les Dialogues de Hume', *Revue de métaphysique et de morale*, 59:285–9.

Merland, M. A., and Reyniers, J. (1979). 'La Fortune d'André François Le Breton', *Revue française d'histoire du livre*, 9:61–90.

Merrick, J. (1990). *The Desacralization of the French Monarchy in the Eighteenth Century* (Baton Rouge).

Merrick, J., and Medlin, D., eds. (1995). *André Morellet (1727–1819) in the Republic of Letters and the French Revolution* (New York).

Merry, H. J. (1970). *Montesquieu's System of Natural Government* (West Lafayette, IN).

Mervaud, C. (1985). *Voltaire et Frédéric II: une dramaturgie des lumières, 1736–1778*, SVEC, 234.

Mews, S., ed. (1992). *Religion and National Identity* (Oxford).

Meyer, D. H. (1976). *The Democratic Enlightenment* (New York).

Meyer, J. (1993). *Bossuet* (Paris).

Meylan, P. (1937). *Jean Barbeyrac (1674–1744) et les débuts de l'enseignement du droit dans l'ancienne Académie de Lausanne* (Lausanne).

Meysonnier, S. (1989). *La Balance et l'horloge: la genèse de la pensée libérale en France au XVIIIe siècle* (Montreu, IL).

Michaelis, L. (1999). 'The Deadly Goddess: Hölderlin on Politics and Fate', *HPT*, 20:225–49.

Middlekauff, R. (1996). *Benjamin Franklin and his Enemies* (Berkeley).

Mille, J. (1971). *G. F. Le Trosne (1728–1780), un physiocrate oublié* (New York). 1st publ. 1905 (Paris).

Miller, D. (1981). *Philosophy and Ideology in Hume's Political Thought* (New York).

Miller, D. (1984). *Anarchism* (London).

Miller, D., and Siedentop, L., eds. (1983). *The Nature of Political Theory* (New York).

Miller, J. (1982). 'The Glorious Revolution: "Contract" and "Abdication" Reconsidered', *HJ*, 25:541–55.

Miller, J. (1984). *Rousseau: Dreamer of Democracy* (New Haven).

Miller, J. C. (1959). *Alexander Hamilton* (New York).

Miller, P. N. (1994). *Defining the Common Good: Empire, Religion and Philosophy in Eighteenth-Century Britain* (Cambridge).

Miller, R. D. (1970). *Schiller and the Idea of Freedom* (Oxford). 1st publ. 1959 (Harrogate).

Miller, S. A. (1960). *Sam Adams: Pioneer in Propaganda* (Stanford).

Miller, S. J. (1978). *Portugal and Rome, c. 1748–1830: An Aspect of the Catholic Enlightenment* (Rome).

Miller, S. J. (1994). 'The Limits of Political Jansenism in Tuscany', *Catholic Historical Review*, 80:762–7.

Miller, T. P. (1995). 'Francis Hutcheson and the Civic Humanist Tradition', in Hook and Sher 1995.

Milsom, S. F. C. (1981). *The Nature of Blackstone's Achievement* (London).

Minerbi, M. (1973). 'Diderot, Galiani, e la polemica sulla fisiocrazia (1761–1771)', *Studi storici*, 14 (1973), pp. 147–84.

Minto, W. (1883). 'Mandeville', *Encyclopedia Britannica*, 9th edn, xv, pp. 472–3.

Mitchell, B. (1957–62). *Alexander Hamilton*, 2 vols. (New York).

Mitchison, R. (1983). *Lordship to Patronage: Scotland 1603–1745* (Baltimore).

Mitrofanov, P. (1910). *Joseph II*, 2 vols. (Vienna).

Mizuta, H., and Sugiyama, C., eds. (1993). *Adam Smith: International Perspectives* (New York).

Modéer, K., ed. (1986). *Samuel von Pufendorf, 1632–1982* (Stockholm).

Mohnhaupt, H., ed. (1988). *Revolution, Reform, Restauration* (Frankfurt).

Molivas, G. (1994). 'Natural Rights and Liberty: A Critical Examination of Some Late Eighteenth-Century Debates in English Political Thought' (doctoral thesis, University College London).

Molivas, G. (2000). 'From Religion to Politics: The Expression of Opinion as the Common Ground between Religious Liberty and Political Participation', *HPT*, 21:237–60.

Moloney, B. (1969). *Florence and England: Essays on Cultural Relations in the Second Half of the Eighteenth Century* (Florence).

Momigliano, A. (1966). *Studies in Historiography* (London).

Momigliano, A. (1990). *The Classical Foundations of Modern Historiography* (Berkeley).

Monod, P. K. (1989). *Jacobitism and the English People, 1688–1788* (Cambridge).

Monro, H. (1975). *The Ambivalence of Bernard Mandeville* (Oxford).

Moore, J. (1988). 'Natural Law and the Pyrrhonian Controversy', in P. Jones, ed., 1988.

Moore, J. (1990). 'The Two Systems of Francis Hutcheson: On the Origins of the Scottish Enlightenment', in Stewart 1990.

Moore, J. (1994). 'Hume and Hutcheson', in Stewart and Wright 1994.

Moore, J. (2000). 'Hutcheson's Theodicy: The Argument and the Contexts of *A System of Moral Philosophy*', in Wood 2000.

Moore, J. (2002). 'Utility and Humanity: The Quest for the *Honestum* in Cicero, Hutcheson, and Hume', *Utilitas*, 14:365–86.

Moore, J., and Silverthorne, M. (1983). 'Gershom Carmichael and the Natural Jurisprudence Tradition in Eighteenth-Century Scotland', in Hont and Ignatieff 1983a.

Moore, J., and Silverthorne, M. (1984). 'Natural Sociability and Natural Rights in the Moral Philosophy of Gershom Carmichael', in Hope 1984.

Moore, J., and Silverthorne, M. (1995). 'Protestant Theologies, Limited Sovereignties: Natural Law and Conditions of Union in the German Empire, the Netherlands and Great Britain', in Robertson 1995.

Moore, S. (1991). 'Rousseau on Alienation and the Rights of Man', *HPT*, 12:73–85.

Moran, M., and Parry, G., eds. (1993). *Democracy and Democratization* (Oxford).

Moravia, S. (1970). *La scienza dell'uomo nel settecento* (Bari).

Moravia, S. (1974). *Il pensiero degli idéologues: scienza e filosofia in Francia, 1780–1815* (Florence).

Morazé, C. (1948). 'Finance et despotisme: essai sur les despotes éclairés', *Annales*, 3:279–96.

Morgan, E. S. (1988). *Inventing the People: The Rise of Popular Sovereignty in England and America* (New York).

Morice, G. P., ed. (1977). *David Hume: Bicentenary Papers* (Austin and Edinburgh).

Morison, S. E., ed. (1956). 'William Manning's *The Key of Liberty*', *WMQ*, 13:202–54.

Morize, A. (1909). *L'Apologie du luxe au XVIIIe siècle et* Le Mondain *de Voltaire* (Paris). Repr. Geneva; 1970.

Morman, P. J. (1987). *Noël Aubert de Versé: A Study in the Concept of Toleration* (Lewiston, NY).

Mornet, D. (1933). *Les Origines intellectuelles de la Révolution française, 1715–1787* (Paris).

Morris, M. F. (1979). *Le Chevalier de Jaucourt: un ami de la terre, 1704–1780* (Geneva).

Morris, R. B. (1967). *John Jay, the Nation and the Court* (Boston, MA).

Morris, R. B. (1985). *Witnesses at the Creation: Hamilton, Madison, Jay, and the Constitution* (New York).

Morrow, J. (1990). *Coleridge's Political Thought* (Basingstoke).

Morrow, J. (1991). 'Republicanism and Public Virtue: William Godwin's *History of the Commonwealth of England*', *HJ*, 34:645–64.

Morton, A. L. (1952). *The English Utopia* (London).

Mosher, M. A. (2001). 'Monarchy's Paradox: Honor in the Face of Sovereign Power', in Carrithers *et al.* 2001.

Mossner, E. C. (1954). *The Life of David Hume* (Austin and London). 2nd edn 1980 (Oxford).

Mousnier, R. (1974–80). *Les Institutions de la France sous la monarchie absolue*, 2 vols. (Paris).

Mozzarelli, C., and Olmi, G., eds. (1985). *Il Trentino nel settecento fra sacro romano impero e antichi stati italiani* (Bologna).

Mulholland, L. A. (1990). *Kant's System of Rights* (New York).

Mulsow, M. (1997). 'Gundling vs Buddeus: Competing Models of the History of Philosophy', in Kelley 1997.

Multamäki, K. (1999). *Towards Great Britain: Commerce and Conquest in the Thought of Algernon Sidney and Charles Davenant* (Helsinki).

Munck, T. (2000). *The Enlightenment: A Comparative Social History, 1721–1794* (London).

Munz, P. (1952). *The Place of Hooker in the History of Thought* (London).

Murphy, A. E. (1986). *Richard Cantillon: Entrepreneur and Economist* (New York).

Murphy, A. E. (1997). *John Law: Economic Theorist and Policy-Maker* (New York).

Murphy, J. G. (1970). *Kant: The Philosophy of Right* (London).

Muthu, S. (2003). *Enlightenment against Empire* (Princeton).

Myers, A. R. (1975). *Parliaments and Estates in Europe to 1789* (London).

Myers, R. (1995). 'Montesquieu on the Causes of Roman Greatness', *HPT*, 16:37–47.

Naves, R. (1938). *Voltaire et l'*Encyclopédie (Paris).

Naville, P. (1967). *D'Holbach et la philosophie scientifique au XVIIIe siècle* (Paris). 1st publ. 1943.

Necheles, R. (1971). *The Abbé Grégoire, 1787–1831* (Westport, CT).

Nelson, J. R. (1987). *Liberty and Property: Political Economy and Policymaking in the New Nation, 1789–1812* (Baltimore).

Nelson, W. H. (1961). *The American Tory* (Boston, MA).

Nenner, H. (1977). *By Colour of Law: Legal Culture and Constitutional Politics in England, 1660–1689* (Chicago).

Nenner, H. (1995). *The Right to be King: The Succession to the Crown of England, 1603–1714* (Basingstoke and Chapel Hill).

Nicholls, D. (1995). *God and Government in an 'Age of Reason'* (London).

Nicholson, C. (1994). *Writing and the Rise of Finance* (Cambridge).

Nicholson, P. (1971–2). 'Kant on the Duty Never to Resist the Sovereign', *Ethics*, 86:214–30.

Nicholson, P. (1991). 'John Locke's Later Letters on Toleration', in Horton and Mendus 1991.

Nisbet, H. B. (1982). '"Was ist Aufklärung?': The Concept of Enlightenment in Eighteenth-Century Germany', *Journal of European Studies*, 12:77–95.

Nisbet, R. A. (1980). *History of the Idea of Progress* (London).

Noel, C. (1990). 'Charles III of Spain', in Scott 1990.

Nokes, D. (1985). *Jonathan Swift: A Hypocrite Reversed: A Critical Biography* (Oxford).

Northeast, C. M. (1991). *The Parisian Jesuits and the Enlightenment, 1700–1762*, *SVEC*, 288.

Norton, D. F., ed. (1993). *The Cambridge Companion to Hume* (Cambridge).

Norton, D. F., Capaldi, N., and Robison, W. L., eds. (1979). *McGill Hume Studies* (San Diego).

Noxon, J. H. (1973). *Hume's Philosophical Development* (New York).

Nuttall, A. D. (1984). *Pope's Essay on Man* (Boston, MA).

Nuttinck, M. (1969). *La Vie et l'oeuvre de Zeger-Bernard van Espen* (Louvain).

Oakeshott, M. (1962). *Rationalism in Politics* (London).

Oakeshott, M. (1975a). *Hobbes on Civil Association* (Berkeley).

Oakeshott, M. (1975b). *On Human Conduct* (Oxford).

Oakley, F. (2003). *The Conciliarist Tradition: Constitutionalism in the Catholic Church, 1300–1870* (New York).

O'Brien, C. C. (1992). *The Great Melody: A Thematic Biography and Commented Anthology of Edmund Burke* (Chicago).

O'Brien, C. H. (1969). 'Ideas of Religious Toleration at the Time of Joseph II', *Transactions of the American Philosophical Society*, 59: part 7.

O'Brien, K. (1997). *Narratives of Enlightenment: Cosmopolitan History from Voltaire to Gibbon* (Cambridge).

O'Connor, T. (1995). *An Irish Theologian in Enlightenment France: Luke Joseph Hook, 1714–1796* (Dublin).

Oestreich, G. (1982). *Neostoicism and the Early Modern State* (Cambridge).

Ogle, A. (1893). *The Marquis d'Argenson* (London).

O'Gorman, F. (1973). *Edmund Burke: His Political Philosophy* (Bloomington, IN).

O'Gorman, F. (1989). *Voters, Patrons and Parties: The Unreformed Electoral System of Hanoverian England, 1734–1832* (New York).

Ogris, W. (1988a). 'Aufklärung, Naturrecht under Rechtsreform in der Habsburgmonarchie', in P. Krause, ed., *Vernunftrecht und Rechtsreform* (Hamburg).

Ogris, W. (1988b). 'Joseph von Sonnenfels als Rechtsreformer', in Reinalter 1988.

O'Hagan, T. (1999). *Rousseau* (London).

O'Hagan, T., ed. (1991). *Revolution and Enlightenment in Europe* (Aberdeen).

O'Hagan, T., ed (1997). *Jean-Jacques Rousseau and the Sources of the Self* (Aldershot).

O'Halloran, C. (2004). *Golden Ages and Barbarous Nations: Antiquarian Debate and Cultural Politics in Ireland, c. 1750–1800* (Cork).

O'Higgins, J. (1970). *Anthony Collins: The Man and his Works* (The Hague).

Ohlmeyer, J., ed. (2000). *Political Thought in Seventeenth-Century Ireland* (Cambridge).

Oldham, J. (1992). *The Mansfield Manuscripts and the Growth of English Law in the Eighteenth Century*, 2 vols. (Chapel Hill).

Olscamp, P. J. (1970). *The Moral Philosophy of George Berkeley* (Oxford).

Omond, G. W. T. (1897). *Fletcher of Saltoun* (Edinburgh).

O'Neill, O. (1986). 'Kantian Politics: The Public Use of Reason', *PT*, 14:523–51.

O'Neill, O. (1989). *Constructions of Reason: Explorations of Kant's Practical Philosophy* (Cambridge).

Onuf, P. S. (1989). 'Reflections on the Founding: Constitutional Historiography in Bicentennial Perspective', *WMQ*, 46:341–75.

O'Regan, P. (2000). *Archbishop William King of Dublin (1650–1729) and the Constitution in Church and State* (Dublin).

Orcibal, J. (1997). *Etudes d'histoire et de littérature religieuses: XVIe–XVIIIe siècles* (Paris).

Oresko, R., Gibbs, G. C., Hatton, R. M., and Scott, H. M., eds. (1997). *Royal and Republican Sovereignty in Early-Modern Europe* (Cambridge).

Orieux, J. (1970). *Talleyrand, ou le sphinx incompris* (Paris).

Orwin, C., and Tarcov, N., eds. (1997). *The Legacy of Rousseau* (Chicago).

Osborne, J. W. (1972). *John Cartwright* (Cambridge).

Osen, J. L. (1995). *Royalist Political Thought during the French Revolution* (Westport, CT).

Osler, M. J., ed. (1991). *Atoms, Pneuma and Tranquillity: Epicurean and Stoic Themes in European Thought* (Cambridge).

Osterhorn, E. D. (1962). *Die Naturrechtslehre Valentin Albertis* (Freiburg).

Osterloh, K. H. (1970). *Joseph von Sonnenfels und die österreichische Reformbewegung im Zeitalter des aufgeklärten Absolutismus* (Hamburg and Lübeck).

Othmer, S. C. (1970). *Berlin und die Verbreitung des Naturrechts in Europa* (Berlin).

Outram, D. (1995). *The Enlightenment* (Cambridge).

Ozouf, M. (1988). *Festivals and the French Revolution*, trans. A. Sheridan (Cambridge, MA). 1st publ. in French in 1976.

Ozouf, M. (1989). *L'Homme régénéré: essais sur la Révolution française* (Paris).

Oz-Salzberger, F. (1995). *Translating the Enlightenment: Scottish Civic Discourse in Eighteenth-Century Germany* (New York).

Oz-Salzberger, F. (2003). 'The Political Theory of the Scottish Enlightenment', in Broadie 2003.

Pagden, A. (1995). *Lords of all the World: Ideologies of Empire in Spain, Britain and France, c. 1492–c. 1830* (New Haven).

Pagden, A., ed. (1987). *The Languages of Political Theory in Early Modern Europe* (Cambridge).

Pagden, A., ed. (2002). *The Idea of Europe: From Antiquity to the European Union* (Cambridge).

Page, A. (2003). *John Jebb and the Enlightenment: Origins of British Radicalism* (Westport, CT).

Painter, G. D. (1977). *Chateaubriand: A Biography*, 1 (London).

Palladini, F. (1990). *Samuel Pufendorf, discepolo di Hobbes* (Bologna).

Palladini, F., and Hartung, G., eds. (1996). *Samuel Pufendorf und die europäische Frühaufklärung* (Berlin).

Palmer, R. R. (1939). *Catholics and Unbelievers in Eighteenth-Century France* (Princeton).

Palmer, R. R. (1941). *Twelve Who Ruled: The Year of the Terror in the French Revolution* (Princeton).

Palmer, R. R. (1959–64). *The Age of Democratic Revolution*, 2 vols. (Princeton).

Pangle, T. L. (1973). *Montesquieu's Philosophy of Liberalism* (Chicago).

Pangle, T. L. (1988). *The Spirit of Modern Republicanism: The Moral Vision of the American Founders and the Philosophy of Locke* (Chicago).

Pappas, J. (1962). *Voltaire and d'Alembert* (Bloomington, IN).

Pappas, J. (1979). 'Le Roi philosophique d'après Voltaire et Rousseau', *Annales*, 51:535–46.

Pappas, G. S. (2000). *Berkeley's Thought* (Ithaca, NY).

Parekh, B., ed. (1973). *Jeremy Bentham: Critical Assessments* (London).

Parekh, B., ed. (1974). *Jeremy Bentham: Ten Critical Essays* (London).

Parel, A., and Flanagan, T., eds. (1979). *Theories of Property: Aristotle to the Present* (Waterloo, ON).

Paret, P., ed. (1968). *Frederick the Great: A Historical Profile* (Berkeley).

Parkin, C. H. (1956). *The Moral Basis of Burke's Political Thought* (Cambridge).

Parkin, J. (1999). *Science, Religion and Politics in Restoration England: Richard Cumberland's De Legibus Naturae* (Woodbridge, Suffolk).

Parry, G. (1963). 'Enlightened Government and its Critics in Eighteenth-Century Germany', *HJ*, 6:178–92.

Parry, G. (1982). 'Locke on Representation in Politics', *HEI*, 3.403–14.

Parssinen, T. M. (1973). 'Association, Convention, and Anti-Parliament in British Radical Politics, 1771–1848', *English Historical Review*, 88:504–33.

Pascal, R. (1938). 'Property and Society: The Scottish Historical School of the Eighteenth Century', *Modern Quarterly*, 1:167–79.

Passmore, J. A. (1951). *Ralph Cudworth: An Interpretation* (Cambridge).

Passmore, J. A. (1965). 'The Malleability of Man in Eighteenth-Century Thought', in Wasserman 1965.

Passmore, J. A. (1970). *The Perfectibility of Man* (London).

Pateman, C. (1988). *The Sexual Contract* (Cambridge).

Paty, M. (1977). *D'Alembert et son temps* (Strasbourg).

Paul, A. (2001). 'Forms of Government: Structure, Principle, Object, and Aim', in Carrithers et al. 2001.

Paulson, R. (1983). *Representations of Revolution, 1789–1820* (New Haven).

Payne, H. C. (1976). *The Philosophes and the People* (New Haven).

Peach, W. B. (1979). *Richard Price and the Ethical Foundations of the American Revolution* (Durham, NC).

Pearce, R. H. (1965). *Savagism and Civilization* (Baltimore).

Pedersen, S. (1986). 'Hannah More Meets Simple Simon: Tracts, Chapbooks, and Popular Culture in Late Eighteenth-Century England', *JBS*, 25:84–113.

Pencak, W. (1982). *America's Burke: The Mind of Thomas Hutchinson* (Washington, DC).

Pendleton, G. T. (1982). 'Towards a Bibliography of the *Reflections* and *Rights of Man* Controversy', *Bulletin of Research in the Humanities*, 85:65–103.

Penovich, K. R. (1995). 'From "Revolution principles" to Union: Daniel Defoe's Intervention in the Scottish Debate', in Robertson 1995.

Perkins, M. (1959). *The Moral and Political Philosophy of the Abbé de Saint-Pierre* (Geneva).

Perkins, M. (1965). *Voltaire's Concept of International Order*, SVEC, 36.

Perkins, M. (1989). 'Six French *Philosophes* on Human Rights, International Rivalry and War', *SVEC*, 260:1–158.

Perrot, J. C. (1984). 'L'Economie politique et ses livres', in Chartier and Martin 1984.

Perrot, J. C. (1992). *Une histoire intellectuelle de l'économie politique: XVII–XVIII siècle* (Paris).

Perry, R. (1986). *The Celebrated Mary Astell: An Early English Feminist* (Chicago).

Perry, R. (1990). 'Mary Astell and the Feminist Critique of Possessive Individualism', *ECS*, 23:444–57 (1990).

Peters, M. (1980). *Pitt and Popularity: The Patriot Minister and London Opinion during the Seven Years War* (New York).

Peterson, C. (1988). 'Das schwedische Gesetzbuch von 1734', in Mohnhaupt 1988.

Pettit, A. (1997). *Bolingbroke and the Polemical Response to Walpole, 1730–1737* (London).

Pezzl, Johann (1783). *Faustin* (Vienna).

Philips, D. (1985). 'The 'Revisionist' Social History of Crime and the Law in Britain, 1780–1850', in Cohen and Scull 1985.

Phillipson, N. (1973). 'Towards a Definition of the Scottish Enlightenment', in Fritz and Williams 1973.

Phillipson, N. (1981). 'The Scottish Enlightenment', in Porter and Teich 1981.

Phillipson, N. (1983). 'Adam Smith as Civic Moralist', in Hont and Ignatieff 1983a.

Phillipson, N. (1989). *Hume* (London).

Phillipson, N. (1993a). 'Politeness and Politics in the Reigns of Anne and the Early Hanoverians', in Pocock 1993a.

Phillipson, N. (1993b). 'Propriety, Property and Prudence: David Hume and the Defence of the Revolution', in Phillipson and Skinner 1993.

Phillipson, N. (2000). 'Language, Sociability and History: Some Reflections on the Foundations of Adam Smith's Science of Man', in Collini *et al.* 2000a.

Phillipson, N., and Mitchison, R., eds. (1970). *Scotland in the Age of Improvement* (Edinburgh).

Phillipson, N., and Skinner, Q., eds. (1993). *Political Discourse in Early Modern Europe* (Cambridge).

Philp, M. (1986). *Godwin's Political Justice* (Ithaca, NY).

Philp, M. (1989). *Paine* (New York).

Philp, M. (1995). 'Vulgar Conservatism, 1792–1793', *English Historical Review*, 110:42–69.

Philp, M., ed. (1991). *The French Revolution and British Popular Politics* (Cambridge).

Picavet, F. (1891). *Les Idéologues* (Paris). Repr. New York, 1971.

Pignatelli, G. (1974). *Aspetti della propaganda cattolica a Roma da Pio VI a Leone XII* (Rome).

Piguet, M. F. (1996). *Classe: histoire du mot et genèse du concept des physiocrates aux historiens de la Restauration* (Lyon).

Pinson, K. S. (1968). *Pietism as a Factor in the Rise of German Nationalism* (New York). 1st publ. 1934.

Pittock, M. G. H. (1991). *The Invention of Scotland* (London).

Pittock, M. G. H. (1994). *Poetry and Jacobite Politics in Eighteenth-Century Britain and Ireland* (Cambridge).

Pittock, M. G. H. (1997). *Inventing and Resisting Britain: Cultural Identities in Britain and Ireland, 1685–1789* (Basingstoke).

Pitts, J. (2005). *A Turn to Empire: The Rise of Imperial Liberalism in Britain and France* (Princeton).

Plamenatz, J. (1958). *The English Utilitarians,* 2nd edn (Oxford). 1st publ. 1949.

Plamenatz, J. (1965). '"Ce qui ne signifie autre chose, sinon qu'on le forçera d'être libre"', in *Rousseau et la philosophie politique, Annales de philosophie politique,* v (Paris).

Plaschka, R. G., *et al.*, eds. (1985). *Österreich im Europa der Aufklärung* (Vienna).

Plohmann, M. (1992). *Ludwig Julius Friedrich Höpfner (1743–1797): Naturrecht und positives Privatrecht am Ende des 18. Jahrhunderts* (Berlin).

Plongeron, B. (1969). 'Recherches sur l'"Aufklärung" catholique en Europe occidentale, 1770–1830', *Revue d'histoire moderne et contemporaine*, 16:555–606.

Plongeron, B. (1973). *Théologie et politique au siècle des lumières, 1770–1820* (Geneva).

Plongeron, B. (1989). *L'Abbé Grégoire (1750–1831), ou, l'arche de la fraternité* (Paris).

Pluche, Noël Antoine (1732–50). *Spectack de la nature,* 8 vols. (Paris).

Plumb, J. H. (1967). *The Growth of Political Stability in England, 1675–1725* (London).

Pocock, J. G. A. (1960). 'Burke and the Ancient Constitution', *HJ*, 3:125–43.

Pocock, J. G. A. (1975). *The Machiavellian Moment: Florentine Political Thought and the Atlantic Republican Tradition* (Princeton).

Pocock, J. G. A. (1979). 'The Mobility of Property and the Rise of Eighteenth-Century Sociology', in Parel and Flanagan 1979.

Pocock, J. G. A. (1981). 'Virtues, Rights and Manners', *PT*, 9:353–68.

Pocock, J. G. A. (1982). 'The Political Economy of Burke's Analysis of the French Revolution', *HJ*, 25:331–49.

Pocock, J. G. A. (1984). 'Radical Criticism of the Whig Order in the Age between Revolutions', in Jacob and Jacob 1984.

Pocock, J. G. A. (1985). *Virtue, Commerce and History: Essays on Political Thought and History, Chiefly in the Eighteenth Century* (Cambridge).

Pocock, J. G. A. (1987). *The Ancient Constitution and the Feudal Law* (Cambridge). 1st publ. 1957.

Pocock, J. G. A. (1989). 'Edmund Burke and the Redefinition of Enthusiasm', in Furet and Ozouf 1989a.

Pocock, J. G. A. (1993b). 'Political Thought in the English-speaking Atlantic, 1760–1790', in Pocock, ed., 1993a.

Pocock, J. G. A. (1998). 'Catharine Macaulay, Patriot Historian', in Smith 1998.

Pocock, J. G. A. (1999–2003). *Barbarism and Religion*, 3 vols. (Cambridge).

Pocock, J. G. A., ed. (1980). *Three British Revolutions, 1641, 1689, 1776* (Princeton).

Pocock, J. G. A., ed. (1993a). *The Varieties of British Political Thought, 1500–1800* (Cambridge).

Poland, B. C. (1957). *French Protestantism and the French Revolution* (Princeton).

Pole, J. R. (1966). *Political Representation in England and the Origins of the American Republic* (London).

Pole, J. R. (1978). *The Pursuit of Equality in American History* (Berkeley).

Pole, J. R. (1987). *The American Constitution – For and Against* (New York).

Polin, R. (1971). *La Politique de la solitude: essai sur la philosophie politique de Rousseau* (Paris).

Pomeau, R. (1967). 'Voyage et lumières dans la littérature française du XVIIIe siècle', *SVEC*, 57:1269–89.

Pomeau, R. (1995). *Voltaire en son temps*, 2 vols. (Oxford).

Pompa, L. (1990a). *Vico: A Study of the* New Science, 2nd edn (Cambridge). 1st publ. 1975.

Pompa, L. (1990b). *Human Nature and Historical Knowledge: Hume, Hegel, and Vico* (Cambridge).

Popkin, J. D. (1989). *News and Politics in the Age of the Revolution: Jean Luzac's 'Gazette de Leyde'* (Ithaca, NY).

Popkin, J. D. (1995). 'Dutch Patriots, French Journalists and Declarations of Rights: The *Leidse Ontwerp* of 1785 and its Diffusion in France', *HJ*, 38:553–65.

Popkin, J. D., and Popkin, R. H., eds. (2000). *The Abbé Grégoire and his World* (Boston, MA).

Popkin, R. H. (1971). 'The Philosophy of Bishop Stillingfleet', *Journal of the History of Philosophy*, 9:303–19.

Popkin, R. H. (1979). *The History of Scepticism from Erasmus to Spinoza* (Berkeley).

Popkin, R. H. (1987a). *Isaac la Peyrère (1596–1676)* (Leiden).

Popkin, R. H. (1987b). 'Condorcet, Hume and Turgot', in Williams, ed., 1987.

Popkin, R. H. (1988). 'The Dispersion of Bodin's Dialogues in England, Holland, and Germany', *JHI*, 49:157–60.

Popkin, R. H. (1989). 'Condorcet's Epistemology and his Politics', in Dascal and Gruengard 1989.

Popkin, R. H. (1991). 'The Deist Challenge', in Grell *et al.* 1991.

Popkin, R. H. (1992). 'Jewish Anti-Christian Arguments as a Source of Irreligion from the Seventeenth to the Early Nineteenth Century', in Hunter and Wootton 1992.

Popkin, R. H. (1993). 'Sources of Knowledge of Sextus Empiricus in Hume's Time', *JHI*, 54:137–41.

Popkin, R. H. (1994). 'Hartlib, Dury and the Jews', in Greengrass *et al.* 1994.

Popkin, R. H. (1996). 'Prophecy and Scepticism in the Sixteenth and Seventeenth Centuries', *British Journal of the History of Philosophy*, 4:1–20.

Popkin, R. H., and Weiner, G. M., eds. (1993). *Jewish Christians and Christian Jews from the Renaissance to the Enlightenment* (Dordrecht).

Porter, R. (1988). *Edward Gibbon: Making History* (London).

Porter, R. (2000). *Enlightenment: Britain and the Making of the Modern World* (London).

Porter, R., ed. (1996). *Rewriting the Self: Histories from the Renaissance to the Present* (London).

Porter, R., and Teich, M., eds. (1981). *The Enlightenment in National Context* (Cambridge).

Postema, G. J. (1986). *Bentham and the Common Law Tradition* (New York).

Poster, M. (1971). *The Utopian Thought of Restif de la Bretonne* (New York).

Postigliolia, A., *et al.*, eds. (1995). *L'Europe de Montesquieu* (Naples).

Potter, J. (1983). *The Liberty We Seek: Loyalist Ideology in Colonial New York and Massachusetts* (Cambridge, MA).

Potts, R. W. (1981). *Arthur Lee: A Virtuous Revolutionary* (Baton Rouge, LA).

Préclin, E. (1929). *Les Jansénistes du dix-huitième siècle et la Constitution civile du clergé* (Paris).

Press, V. (1988). 'Kaiser Joseph II – Reformer oder despot?', in Vogler 1988.

Prestwich, M., ed. (1985). *International Calvinism, 1541–1715* (New York).

Price, K. B. (1957). 'Ernst Cassirer and the Enlightenment', *JHI*, 18:101–12.

Primer, I. (1975). 'Mandeville and Shaftesbury', in Primer 1975.

Primer, I., ed. (1975). *Mandeville Studies* (The Hague).

Prior, C. W. A. (2000). *Mandeville and Augustan Ideas: New Essays* (Victoria, BC).

Proctor, C. E. (1990). *Women, Equality, and the French Revolution* (New York).

Pross, W. (1987a). 'Herder und die Anthropologie der Aufklärung', in J. G. Herder, *Werke*, II, ed. W. Pross (Munich).

Pross, W. (1987b). 'Herder und Vico', in Sauder 1987.

Pross, W. (1999). 'Die Begründung der Geschichte aus der Natur: Herders Konzept von "Gesetzen" in der Geschichte', in Bödeker *et al.* 1999.

Pross, W. (2002). '"Natur" und "Geschichte" in Herders Ideen zur Philosophie der Geschichte der Menschheit', in J. G. Herder, *Werke*, III/1, ed. W. Pross (Munich).

Pross, W. (2003). 'Diversité des faits et unité de vue: Herder et la construction de la philosophie de l'histoire au siècle des Lumières', in P. Pénisson and N. Waszek, eds., *Herder et les lumières*, in *Revue Germanique Internationale*, XX (Paris).

Prothero, I. (1997). *Radical Artisans in England and France, 1830–1870* (Cambridge).

Proust, J. (1962). *Diderot et l'Encyclopédie* (Paris). Revised edn Geneva, 1982. 1st publ. 1962.

Proust, J. (1965). *L'Encyclopédie* (Paris).

Proust, J. (1968). *L'Encyclopédisme dans le Bas-Languedoc au XVIIIe siècle* (Paris).

Proust, J. (1972). 'Questions sur l'*Encyclopédie*', *RHLF*, 72:36–52.

Puisais, E., ed. (2001). *Léger-Marie Deschamps, un philosophe entre lumières et oubli* (Paris).

Putterman, E. (1999). 'The Role of Public Opinion in Rousseau's Conception of Property', *HPT*, 20:417–37.

Quinton, A. (1973). *Utilitarian Ethics* (London).

Radcliffe, E. (1993). 'Revolutionary Writing, Moral Philosophy and Universal Benevolence in the Eighteenth Century', *JHI*, 54:221–40.

Radzinowicz, L. (1948–86). *A History of English Criminal Law and its Administration*, 5 vols. (London).

Raeff, M. (1966). *Origins of the Russian Intelligentsia* (New York).

Raeff, M. (1974). 'The Empress and the Vinerian Professor: Catherine II's Projects of Government Reforms and Blackstone's Commentaries', *Oxford Slavonic Papers*, 7:18–41.

Raeff, M. (1975). 'The Well-Ordered Police State and the Development of Modernity in Seventeenth- and Eighteenth-Century Europe', *AHR*, 80:1221–43.

Raeff, M. (1983). *The Well-Ordered Police State* (New Haven).

Rahe, P. A. (1992). *Republics Ancient and Modern*, 2 vols. (Chapel Hill).

Rahe, P. A. (2001). 'Forms of Government: Structure, Principle, Object and Aim', in Carrithers *et al.* 2001.

Rakove, J. W. (1990). *James Madison and the Creation of the American Republic* (London).

Ranum, O. (1976). 'Introduction' to Bossuet, *Discourse on Universal History* (Chicago).

Raphael, D. D. (1985). *Adam Smith* (New York).

Raphael, D. D., ed. (1967). *Political Theory and the Rights of Man* (Bloomington, IN).

Rapp, S. M. (1965). *Das Werk des Enzyklopädisten Louis de Jaucourt* (Tübingen).

Raskolnikoff, M. (1992). *Histoire romaine et critique historique dans l'Europe des lumières* (Rome: Collection de l'Ecole française de Rome, 163).

Ratschow, C. H. (1964–71). *Lutherische Dogmatik zwischen Reformation und Aufklärung*, 2 vols. (Gütersloh).

Rawls, J. (1972). *A Theory of Justice* (Cambridge, MA).

Rawson, J. (1989). *The Spartan Tradition in European Thought* (Oxford).

Razavi, M. A., and Ambuel, D., eds. (1997). *Philosophy, Religion and the Question of Intolerance* (Albany, NY).

Read, J. H. (2000). *Power versus Liberty: Madison, Hamilton, Wilson, and Jefferson* (Charlottesville).

Rébelliau, A. (1900). *Bossuet* (Paris).

Redekop, B. W. (2000). *Enlightenment and Community: Lessing, Abbt, Herder and the Quest for a German Public* (Montreal).

Redwood, J. (1976). *Reason, Ridicule and Religion: The Age of Enlightenment in England, 1660–1750* (Cambridge, MA).

Reed, T. J. (1990). 'Talking to Tyrants: Dialogues with Power in Eighteenth-Century Germany', *HJ*, 33:63–79.

Reed, T. J. (1991). *Schiller* (Oxford).

Reibstein, E. (1962). 'Allgemeine Staatsrecht und Völkerrecht bei C. G. Svarez', *Zeitschrift für ausländisches öffentliches Recht und Völkerrecht*, 22:509–39.

Reid, J. P. (1981). *In Defiance of the Law: The Standing-Army Controversy, the Two Constitutions and the Coming of the American Revolution* (Chapel Hill).

Reid, J. P. (1988). *The Concept of Liberty in the Age of the American Revolution* (Chicago).

Reid, J. P. (1989). *The Concept of Representation in the Age of the American Revolution* (Chicago).

Reill, P. H. (1975). *The German Enlightenment and the Rise of Historicism* (Berkeley).

Reinalter, H., ed. (1988). *Joseph von Sonnenfels* (Vienna).

Reinalter, H., and Klueting, H., eds. (2002). *Der aufgeklärte Absolutismus im europäischen Vergleich* (Vienna).

Reiss, H. S. (1956). 'Kant and the Right of Rebellion', *JHI*, 17:179–92.

Remec, P. P. (1960). *The Position of the Individual in International Law According to Grotius and Vattel* (The Hague).

Rendall, J. (1978). *The Origins of the Scottish Enlightenment* (London).

Renouvin, P. (1921). *Les Assemblées provinciales de 1787* (Paris).

Renwick, J. (1974). *Marmontel, Voltaire and the Bélisaire Affair, SVEC*, 121.

Rescher, N. (1967). *The Philosophy of Leibniz* (Englewood Cliffs, NJ).

Rétat, P. (1971). *Le Dictionnaire de Bayle et la lutte philosophique au XVIIIe siècle* (Paris).

Reventlow, H. G. (1984). *The Authority of the Bible and the Rise of the Modern World* (London).

Rex, W. E. (1965). *Essays on Pierre Bayle and Religious Controversy* (The Hague).

Rials, S. (1988). *La Déclaration des droits de l'homme et du citoyen* (Paris).

Richard, C. J. (1994). *The Founders and the Classics: Greece, Rome and the American Enlightenment* (Cambridge, MA).

Richter, M. (1969). 'Comparative Analysis in Montesquieu and Tocqueville', *Comparative Politics*, 1:129–60.

Richter, M. (1977). 'Introduction' to *The Political Theory of Montesquieu* (Cambridge).

Richter, M. (1989). 'Montesquieu, the Politics of Language and the Language of Politics', *HPT*, 10:71–88.

Richter, M. (1995). 'Montesquieu's Comparative Analysis of Europe and Asia', in Postigliola *et al.* 1995.

Richter, M. (1998). 'Montesquieu and the Concept of Civil Society', *European Legacy*, 3:33–41.

Richter, M. (2000). 'Two Eighteenth-Century Senses of "Comparison" in Locke and Montesquieu', *Jarhbuch für Recht und Ethik*, 8:385–406.

Richter, M. (2002). 'That Vast Tribe of Ideas: Competing Concepts and Practices of Comparison in Eighteenth-Century Europe', *Archiv für Begriffsgeschichte*, 44:199–219.

Ricuperati, G. (1970). *L'esperienza civile e religiosa di Pietro Giannone* (Milan).

Ricuperati, G. (1987). 'The "Veteres" against the "Moderni": Paolo Mattia Doria and Giambattista Vico', in Carpanetto and Ricuperati 1987.

Riedel, M. (1975). 'Gesellschaft, bürgerliche', in Brunner *et al.* 1972–97, II.

Riff, M. A., ed. (1987). *Dictionary of Modern Political Ideologies* (Manchester).

Riley, P. (1973). 'An Unpublished MS of Leibniz on the Allegiance Due to Sovereign Powers', *Journal of the History of Philosophy*, 11:319–36.

Riley, P. (1978). 'The General Will before Rousseau', *PT*, 6:485–516.

Riley, P. (1980). 'Introduction to the Reading of Alexandre Kojève', in Freeman and Robertson 1980.

Riley, P. (1982). *Will and Political Legitimacy: A Critical Exposition of Social Contract Theory in Hobbes, Locke, Rousseau, Kant and Hegel* (Cambridge, MA).

Riley, P. (1983). *Kant's Political Philosophy* (Totowa, NJ).

Riley, P. (1986). *The General Will before Rousseau* (Princeton).

Riley, P. (1990). 'Introduction' to Jacques-Bénigne Bossuet, *Politics Drawn from the Very Words of Holy Scripture* (Cambridge).

Riley, P. (1991). 'Rousseau's General Will: Freedom of a Particular Kind', *Political Studies*, 39:55–74.

Riley, P. (1992). *Essays on Political Philosophy* (Rochester, NY).

Riley, P. (1994). 'Introduction' to François de Fénelon, *Telemachus* (Cambridge).

Riley, P. (1996). *Leibniz' Universal Jurisprudence: Justice as the Charity of the Wise* (Cambridge, MA).

Riley, P. (2001a). 'Rousseau, Fénelon and the Quarrel between the Ancients and Moderns', in Riley 2001b.

Riley, P., ed. (2001b). *The Cambridge Companion to Rousseau* (Cambridge).

Ritchie, D. (1893). *Darwin and Hegel* (London).

Ritchie, R., and Timms, E., eds. (1991). *The Austrian Enlightenment and its Aftermath* (Edinburgh).

Ritschl, A. (1880–6). *Geschichte des Pietismus*, 3 vols. (Bonn).

Ritter, C. (1971). *Der Rechtsgedanke Kants nach den frühen Quellen* (Frankfurt)

Rivers, I. (1973). *The Poetry of Conservatism, 1600–1745* (Cambridge).

Rivers, I. (1991–2000). *Reason, Grace and Sentiment: A Study of the Language of Religion and Ethics in England, 1660–1780*, 2 vols. (Cambridge).

Robbins, C. (1950). 'The Strenuous Whig: Thomas Hollis of Lincoln's Inn', *WMQ*, 7:406–53.

Robbins, C. (1959). *The Eighteenth-Century Commonwealthman* (Cambridge, MA).

Roberts, F. (1973). 'Gottfried Arnold as a Historian of Christianity' (doctoral thesis, Vanderbilt).

Roberts, H. van D. (1935). *Boisguilbert: Economist of the Reign of Louis XIV* (New York).

Roberts, M. (1986). *The Age of Liberty: Sweden, 1719–1772* (Cambridge).

Roberts, W. (1996). *A Dawn of Imaginative Feeling: The Contribution of John Brown (1715–66) to Eighteenth-Century Thought and Literature* (Carlisle).

Robertson, J. (1983a). 'Scottish Political Economy beyond the Civic Tradition: Government and Economic Development in the Wealth of Nations', *HPT*, 4:451–82.

Robertson, J. (1983b). 'The Scottish Enlightenment at the Limits of the Civic Tradition', in Hont and Ignatieff 1983a.

Robertson, J. (1985). *The Scottish Enlightenment and the Militia Issue* (Edinburgh).

Robertson, J. (1987a). 'Antonio Genovesi: The Neapolitan Enlightenment and Political Economy', *HPT*, 8:335–44.

Robertson, J. (1987b). 'Andrew Fletcher's Vision of Union', in Mason 1987.

Roberston, J. (1993). 'Universal Monarchy and the Liberties of Europe: David Hume's Critique of an English Whig Doctrine', in Phillipson and Skinner 1993.

Robertson, J. (1994). 'Union, State and Empire: The Britain of 1707 in its European Setting', in Stone 1994.

Robertson, J. (1997). 'The Enlightenment above National Context: Political Economy in Eighteenth-Century Scotland and Naples', *HJ*, 40:667–97.

Robertson, J., ed. (1995). *A Union for Empire: Political Thought and the British Union of 1707* (Cambridge).

Robson, R. J. (1949). *The Oxfordshire Election of 1754* (London).

Roche, D. (1965–70). *Livre et société dans la France du XVIIIe siècle*, 2 vols. (Paris).

Roche, D. (1978). *Le Siècle des lumières en province: académies et académiciens provinciaux, 1680–1789* (Paris).

Roche, D. (1981). *Le Peuple de Paris: essais sur la culture populaire au XVIIIe siècle* (Paris).

Roche, D. (1987). 'Académie et politique au siècle des lumières', in Baker 1987.

Roche, D. (1988). *Les Républicains des lettres: gens de culture et lumières au XVIIIe siècle* (Paris).

Roche, D. (1993). *La France des lumières* (Paris).

Roche, D. (1998). *France in the Enlightenment*, trans. A. Goldhammer (Cambridge, MA).

Rodolico, N. (1920). *Gli amici e i tempi di Scipione dei Ricci* (Florence).

Roessler, S. E. (1996). *Out of the Shadows: Women and Politics in the French Revolution, 1789–1795* (New York).

Roger, J. (1963). *Les Sciences de la vie dans la pensée française du XVIIIe siècle* (Paris).

Rogers, G. A. J., and Tomaselli, S., eds. (1996). *The Philosophical Canon in the Seventeenth and Eighteenth Centuries* (Rochester, NY).

Rogers, K. (1982). *Feminism in Eighteenth-Century England* (Brighton).

Rogers, P. (1970). 'Swift and Bolingbroke on Faction', *JBS*, 9:71–101.

Rogers, P. (1979). *Henry Fielding: A Biography* (London).

Roosevelt, G. G. (1990). *Reading Rousseau in the Nuclear Age* (Philadelphia).

Rosa, M. (1972). 'Encyclopédie, "Lumières" et traditions au XVIIIe siècle en Italie', *DHS*, 4:109–68.

Rosa, M. (1992). *Di fronte alla rivoluzione: politica et religione in Italia dal 1789 at 1796* (Florence).

Roscher, W. (1847). 'Umrisse zur Naturlehre der drei Staatsformen', *Allgemeine Zeitschrift für Geschichte*, 7:79–88, 322–65, 436–73.

Roscher, W. (1874). *Geschichte der National-Ökonomik in Deutschland* (Munich).

Roscher, W. (1892). *Politik: Geschichtliche Naturlehre der Monarchie, Aristokratie, und Demokratie* (Stuttgart).

Rose, R. B. (1978). *Gracchus Babeuf: The First Revolutionary Communist* (London).

Rosen, A. D. (1993). *Kant's Theory of Justice* (Ithaca, NY).

Rosen, F. (1983). *Jeremy Bentham and Representative Democracy: A Study of the Constitutional Code* (Oxford).

Rosen, F. (1992). *Bentham, Byron and Greece: Constitutionalism, Nationalism and Early Liberal Political Thought* (Oxford).

Rosen, F. (1999). 'Crime, Punishment and Liberty', *HPT*, 20:173–85.

Rosen, F. (2000). 'The Idea of Utility in Adam Smith's *Theory of Moral Sentiments*', *HEI*, 26:79–103.

Rosen, F. (2003). *Classical Utilitarianism from Hume to Mill* (London).

Rosen, G. (1999). *American Compact: James Madison and the Problem of Founding* (Lawrence, KA).

Rosenberg, N. (1960). 'Some Institutional Aspects of the Wealth of Nations', *Journal of Political Economy*, 68:557–70.

Rosenblatt, H. (1997). *Rousseau and Geneva: From the First Discourse to the Social Contract, 1749–1762* (Cambridge).

Rosenblum, N. L. (1978). *Bentham's Theory of the Modern State* (Cambridge, MA).

Ross, I. S. (1972). *Lord Kames and the Scotland of his Day* (Oxford).

Ross, I. S. (1995). *The Life of Adam Smith* (Oxford).

Rossi, P. (1979). *I segni del tempo: storia della terra e storia delle nazioni da Hooke a Vico* (Milan).

Rossi, P. (1984). *The Dark Abyss of Time*, trans. L. G. Cochrane (Chicago).

Rossiter, C. (1953). 'Richard Bland: The Whig in America', *WMQ*, 10:33–79.

Rossiter, C. (1964). *Alexander Hamilton and the Constitution* (New York).

Rota, E. (1923). *Giuseppi Poggi e la formazione psicoligica del patriota moderno, 1761–1843* (Piacenza).

Rothkrug, L. (1965). *Opposition to Louis XIV: The Political and Social Origins of the French Enlightenment* (Princeton).

Rothschild, E. (1992). 'Adam Smith and Conservative Economics', *Economic History Review*, 45:74–96.

Rothschild, E. (1996). 'Condorcet and the Conflict of Values', *HJ*, 39:677–701.

Rothschild, E. (2001). *Economic Sentiments: Adam Smith, Condorcet and the Enlightenment* (Cambridge, MA).

Rotta, S. (1993). 'Montesquieu et le paganisme ancien', in Mass and Postigliola 1993.

Rouché, M. (1940). *La Philosophie de l'histoire de Herder* (Paris).

Roussel, J., ed. (1988). *L'Héritage des lumières: Volney et les idéologues* (Angers).

Rowen, H. H. (1994). 'The Dutch Republic and the Idea of Freedom', in Wootton 1994a.

Rozbicki, M. J. (2001). 'Proposals to Enslave the British Poor, 1698–1755', *Slavery and Abolition*, 22:29–50.

Rubini, D. (1967). *Court and Country, 1688–1702* (London).

Rublack, H. C., ed., (1992). *Die lutherische Konfessionalisierung in Deutschland* (Gütersloh).

Ruddy, F. S. (1975). *International Law in the Enlightenment: The Background of Emmerich de Vattel's Le droit des gens* (New York).

Rudé, G. (1962). *Wilkes and Liberty* (Oxford).

Rudolph, J. (2002). *Revolution by Degrees: James Tyrrell and Whig Political Thought in the Late Seventeenth Century* (Basingstoke).

Ruello, F. (1963). 'Christian Wolff et la scolastique', *Traditio*, 19:411–26.

Rüping, H. (1968). *Die Naturrechtslehre des Christian Thomasius* (Bonn).

Rüping, H. (1979). 'Thomasius und seine Schüler im brandenburgischen Staat', in Thieme et al. 1979.

Ryder, M. (1982). 'The Bank of Ireland, 1721: Land, Credit and Dependency', *HJ*, 25:557–82.

Saastamoinen, K. (1995). *The Morality of the Fallen Man: Samuel Pufendorf on Natural Law* (Helsinki).

Sack, J. J. (1993). *From Jacobite to Conservative: Reaction and Orthodoxy, c. 1760–1832* (Cambridge).

Sacke, G. (1931). 'Zur Charakteristik der gesetzgebenden Kommission Katharina II', *Archiv für Kulturgeschichte*, 21:166–91.

Sagave, P. P. (1987). 'Friedrich der Große und die französische Kultur', in Hauser 1987.

Sahmland, I. (1990). *Christoph Martin Wieland und die deutsche Nation* (Tübingen).

Said, E. (1978). *Orientalism* (New York).

Sakamoto, T., and Tanaka, H., eds. (2003). *The Rise of Political Economy in the Scottish Enlightenment* (London).

Salmon, J. H. M. (1995). 'Constitutions Old and New: Henrion de Pansey before and after the French Revolution', *HJ*, 38:907–31.

Salmon, J. H. M. (1999). 'Liberty by Degrees: Raynal and Diderot on the British Constitution', *HPT*, 20:87–106.

Salter, J. (1992). 'Adam Smith on Feudalism, Commerce and Slavery', *HPT*, 13:219–41.

Sampson, R. V. (1956). *Progress in the Age of Reason* (Cambridge, MA).

Sánchez Agesta, L. (1979). *El pensamiento político del despotismo ilustrado* (Seville).

Sandoz, E. (1990). *A Government of Laws: Political Theory, Religion and the American Founding* (Baton Rouge).

Sandoz, E. (1993). *The Roots of Liberty: Magna Carta, Ancient Constitution and the Anglo-American Tradition of Rule of Law* (London).

Saner, H. (1973). *Kant's Political Thought* (Chicago).

Santato, G. (1988). *Alfieri e Voltaire: dall'imitazione alla contestazione* (Florence).

Sapiro, V. (1992). *A Vindication of Political Virtue: The Political Theory of Mary Wollstonecraft* (Chicago).

Sarrailh, J. (1951). *La Crise religieuse en Espagne à la fin du XVIIIe siècle* (Oxford).

Sashegyi, O. (1958). *Zensur und Geistesfreiheit unter Joseph II* (Budapest).

Sauder, G., ed. (1987). *Johann Gottfried Herder* (Hamburg).

Saunders, D. (2003). 'The Natural Jurisprudence of Jean Barbeyrac', *ECS*, 36:473–90.

Saunders, D., and Hunter, I. (2003). 'Bringing the State to England: Andrew Tooke's Translation of Samuel Pufendorf's *De officio hominis et civis*', *HPT*, 24:218–34.

Saville, J., ed. (1954). *Democracy and the Labour Movement* (London).

Savonius, S. J. (2004). 'Locke in French: The *Du gouvernement civil* of 1691 and its Readers', *HJ*, 47:47–79.

Schama, S. (1977). *Patriots and Liberators: Revolution in the Netherlands, 1780–1813* (London).

Schama, S. (1989). *Citizens: A Chronicle of the French Revolution* (London).

Schandeler, J. P. (2000). *Les Interprétations de Condorcet*, *SVEC*, 2000:3.

Schapiro, J. S. (1934). *Condorcet and the Rise of Liberalism* (New York).

Schelle, G. (1888). *Du Pont de Nemours et l'école physiocratique* (Paris).

Schelle, G. (1897). *Vincent de Gournay* (Paris).

Schieder, T. (1983). *Friedrich der Große: Ein Königtum der Widersprüche* (Frankfurt).

Schiera, P. (1968). *Dall'Arte di Governo alle Scienze dello Stato* (Milan).

Schilling, B. N. (1950). *Conservative England and the Case against Voltaire* (New York).

Schlereth, T. (1977). *The Cosmopolitan Ideal in Enlightenment Thought* (Notre Dame, IN).

Schlesinger, A. M. (1958). *Prelude to Independence: The Newspaper War on Britain 1764–1776* (New York).

Schlobach, J. (1990). 'Französische Aufklärung und deutsche Fürsten', *Zeitschrift für Historische Forschung*, 17:327–49.

Schlumbohm, J. (1975). *Freiheit: Die Anfänge der Bürgerlichen Emanzipationsbewegung in Deutschland im Spiegel ihres Leitwortes, c. 1760–c. 1800* (Düsseldorf).

Schmidt, J. (1989). 'The Question of Enlightenment: Kant, Mendelssohn and the Mittwochgesellschaft', *JHI*, 50:269–91.

Schmidt, J., ed. (1996). *What is Enlightenment?: Eighteenth-Century Answers and Twentieth-Century Questions* (Berkeley).

Schmidt, W. (1995). *Ein vergessener Rebell: Leben und Wirken des Christian Thomasius* (Munich).

Schmidt-Biggemann, W., and Stammen, T., eds. (1998). *Jacob Brucker (1696–1770): Philosoph und Historiken der europäischen Aufklärung* (Berlin).

Schneewind, J. B. (1993). 'Kant and Natural Law Ethics', *Ethics*, 104:53–74.

Schneewind, J. B. (1995). 'Voluntarism and the Origins of Utilitarianism', *Utilitas*, 7:87–96.

Schneewind, J. B. (1997). 'Bayle, Locke and the Concept of Toleration', in Razavi and Ambuel, eds., 1997.

Schneewind, J. B. (1998). *The Invention of Autonomy: A History of Modern Moral Philosophy* (Cambridge).

Schneewind, J. B., ed. (2004). *Teaching New Histories of Philosophy* (Princeton).

Schneider, H. P. (1967). *Justitia Universalis: Quellenstudien zur Geschichte des 'christlichen Naturrechts' bei Gottfried Wilhelm Leibniz* (Frankfurt).

Schneiders, W. (1971). *Naturrecht und Liebesethik* (Hildesheim).

Schneiders, W. (1974). *Die wahre Aufklärung: Zum Selbstverständnis der deutschen Aufklärung* (Freiburg).

Schneiders, W., ed. (1983). *Christian Wolff, 1679–1754: Interpretationen zu seiner Philosophie und deren Wirkung* (Hamburg).

Schneiders, W., ed. (1989). *Christian Thomasius, 1655–1728: Interpretationen zu Werk und Wirkung* (Hamburg).

Schneiders, W., ed. (1993). *Aufklärung als Mission* (Marburg).

Schnorrenberg, B. B. (1992). 'Liberty or Luxury: Catharine Macaulay Graham and the Socio-Economic Foundation of the State', *Enlightenment and Dissent*, 11:58–69.

Schochet, G. J. (1975). *Patriarchalism in Political Thought* (Oxford).

Schoeps, H. J. (1952). *Philosemitismus im Barock* (Tubingen).

Schofield, T. P. (1986). 'Conservative Political Thought in Britain in Response to the French Revolution', *HJ*, 29:601–22.

Schofield, T. P. (1987). 'A Comparison of the Moral Theories of William Paley and Jeremy Bentham', *The Bentham Newsletter*, 11:4–22.

Schofield, T. P. (1999). 'Political and Religious Radicalism in the Thought of Jeremy Bentham', *HPT*, 20:272–91.

Scholem, G. (1973). *Sabbatai Sevi: The Mystical Messiah, 1626–1676* (Princeton).

Schonhorn, M. (1991). *Defoe's Politics: Parliament, Power, Kingship and Robinson Crusoe* (Cambridge).

Schröder, J., and Pielemeier, I. (1995). 'Naturrecht als Lehrfach an den deutschen Universitäten des 18. und 19. Jahrhunderts', in Dann and Klippel 1995.

Schröder, P. (2001). *Naturrecht und absolutisches Staatsrecht: Eine vergleichende Studie zu Thomas Hobbes und Christian Thomasius* (Berlin).

Schröer, C. (1988). *Naturbegriff und Moralbegründung: Die Grundlegung der Ethik bei Christian Wolff und deren Kritik durch Immanuel Kant* (Stuttgart).

Schwab, R. N., Rex, W. E., and Lough, J. (1971–3). *Inventory of Diderot's Encyclopédie*, 6 vols., *SVEC*, 80, 83, 85, 91, 92, 93.

Schwaiger, C. (1995). *Das Problem des Glücks im Denken Christian Wolffs* (Stuttgart).

Schwoerer, L. G. (1974). *No Standing Armies!: The Antiarmy Ideology in Seventeenth-Century England* (Baltimore).

Schwoerer, L. G. (1993). 'The Right to Resist: Whig Resistance Theory, 1688 to 1694', in Phillipson and Skinner 1993.

Schwoerer, L. G., ed. (1992). *The Revolution of 1688–1689: Changing Perspectives* (Cambridge).

Scott, H. M. (1983). 'Whatever Happened to the Enlightened Despots?', *History*, 68:245–57.

Scott, H. M. (1996). 'The Rise of the First Minister in Eighteenth-Century Europe', in Blanning and Cannadine 1996.

Scott, H. M., ed. (1990). *Enlightened Absolutism: Reform and Reformers in Later Eighteenth-Century Europe* (Ann Arbor).

Scott, J. W. (1996). *Only Paradoxes to Offer: French Feminists and the Rights of Man* (Cambridge, MA).

Scott, P. H. (1979). *1707: The Union of England and Scotland* (Edinburgh).

Scott, P. H. (1992). *Andrew Fletcher and the Treaty of Union* (Edinburgh).

Scott, S. F., and Rothaus, B., eds. (1985). *Historical Dictionary of the French Revolution, 1789–1799*, 2 vols. (Westport, CT).

Scruton, R. (1982). *Kant* (Oxford).

Scurr, R. (2000). 'Social Equality in Pierre-Louis Roederer's Interpretation of the Modern Republic, 1793', *HEI*, 26:105–26.

Seed, J. (1985). 'Gentlemen Dissenters: The Social and Political Meanings of Rational Dissent in the 1770s and 1780s', *HJ*, 28:299–325.

Sekora, J. (1977). *Luxury: The Concept in Western Thought, Eden to Smollett* (Baltimore).

Seligman, A. (1992). *The Idea of Civil Society* (New York).

Sella, D., and Capra, C., eds. (1984). *Il ducato di Milano dal 1535 al 1796* (Turin).

Sellers, M. N. S. (1994). *American Republicanism: Roman Ideology in the United States Constitution* (Basingstoke).

Sellés, M. A., *et al.*, eds. (1988). *Carlos III y la ciencia de la ilustración*, 3 vols. (Madrid).

Semmel, B. (1973). *The Methodist Revolution* (New York).

Semple, J. (1993). *Bentham's Prison: A Study of the Panopticon Penitentiary* (Oxford).

Sen, S. R. (1957). *The Economics of Sir James Steuart* (London).

Senn, P. R. (1958). 'The Earliest Use of the Term "Social Science"', *JHI*, 19:568–70.

Sève, R. (1989). *Leibniz et l'école moderne du droit naturel* (Paris).

Sewell, W. H. (1980). *Work and Revolution in France: The Language of Labor from the Old Regime to 1848* (Cambridge).

Sewell, W. H. (1994). *A Rhetoric of Bourgeois Revolution: The Abbé Sieyès and 'What is the Third Estate?'* (Durham, NC).

Shackleton, R. (1949). 'Montesquieu, Bolingbroke and the Separation of Powers', *French Studies*, 3:25–38.

Shackleton, R. (1961). *Montesquieu: A Critical Biography* (Oxford).

Shackleton, R. (1972). 'The Greatest Happiness of the Greatest Number: The History of Bentham's Phrase', *SVEC*, 90:1461–82.

Shackleton, R. (1978). 'When did the French *Philosophes* Become a Party?', *Bulletin of the John Rylands Library*, 60:181–99.

Shackleton, R. (1971). 'Les Mots "despote" et "despotisme"', in Bene 1971.

Shackleton, R. (1988). *Essays on Montesquieu and on the Enlightenment*, ed. D. Gilson and M. Smith (Oxford).

Shalhope, R. E. (1972). 'Toward a Republican Synthesis: The Emergence of an Understanding of Republicanism in American Historiography', *WMQ*, 29:49–80.

Shalhope, R. E. (1982). 'Republicanism and Early American Historiography', *WMQ*, 39:334–56.

Shanley, M. L. (1998). 'Mary Wollstonecraft on Sensibility, Women's Rights and Patriarchal Power', in Smith 1998.

Shapiro, B. J. (2003). 'Empiricism and English Political Thought, 1550–1720', *Eighteenth-Century Thought*, 1:3–35.

Sheldon, G. W. (1991). *The Political Philosophy of Thomas Jefferson* (Baltimore).

Sheldon, W. F. (1970). *The Intellectual Development of Justus Möser* (Osnabrück).

Shell, S. M. (1980). *The Rights of Reason: A Study of Kant's Philosophy and Politics* (Toronto).

Shelton, G. (1981). *Dean Tucker and Eighteenth-Century Economic and Political Thought* (London).

Shennan, J. H. (1986). *Liberty and Order in Early Modern Europe: The Subject and the State, 1650–1800* (London).

Shennan, J. H. (1998). *The Parlement of Paris* (Stroud, Gloucestershire). 1st publ. 1968.

Sher, R. B. (1985). *Church and Society in the Scottish Enlightenment: The Moderate Literati of Edinburgh* (Princeton).

Sher, R. B. (1990). 'Professors of Virtue: The Social History of the Edinburgh Philosophy Chair in the Eighteenth Century', in Stewart 1990.

Sher, R. B. (1994). 'From Troglodytes to Americans: Montesquieu and the Scottish Enlightenment on Liberty, Virtue, and Commerce', in Wootton 1994a.

Shklar, J. N. (1969). *Men and Citizens: A Study of Rousseau's Social Theory* (Cambridge).

Shklar, J. N. (1984). *Ordinary Vices* (Cambridge, MA).

Shklar, J. N. (1987). *Montesquieu* (Oxford).

Sidgwick, H. (1906). *Outlines of the History of Ethics for English Readers*, 5th edn (London).

Sigmund, P. (1963). *Nicholas of Cusa and Medieval Political Thought* (Cambridge, MA).

Silberstein, L. (1928). *Lemercier de la Rivière und seine politischen Ideen* (Berlin).

Silvestri, G. (1954). *Un europeo del settecento: Scipione Maffei* (Treviso).

Simms, J. G. (1982). *William Molyneux of Dublin, 1656–1698* (Dublin).

Simms, J. G. (1986). 'The Case of Ireland Stated', in his *War and Politics in Ireland, 1649–1730* (London).

Simon, J. (1995). 'Natural Freedom and Moral Autonomy: Emile as Parent, Teacher and Citizen', *HPT*, 16:21–36.

Simon, J. L. (1885). *Une académie sous le Directoire* (Paris).

Simonutti, L. (1996). 'Between Political Loyalty and Religious Liberty: Political Theory and Toleration in Huguenot Thought in the Epoch of Bayle', *HPT*, 17:522–54.

Singer, B. C. J. (1986). *Society, Theory and the French Revolution* (New York).

Singerman, A. J. (1987). *L'Abbé Prévoste: l'amour et la morale* (Geneva).

Sinopoli, R. C. (1992). *The Foundations of American Citizenship: Liberalism, the Constitution and Civic Virtue* (Oxford).

Skalweit, S. (1952). *Frankreich und Friedrich der Grosse. Der Aufstieg Preußens in der öffentlichen Meinung des 'ancien régime'* (Bonn).

Skinner, A. S. (1966). 'Introduction' to Sir James Steuart, *An Inquiry into the Principles of Political Oeconomy* (Edinburgh).

Skinner, A. S. (1993). 'The Shaping of Political Economy in the Enlightenment', in Mizuta and Sugiyama 1993.

Skinner, A. S. (1996). *A System of Social Science: Papers relating to Adam Smith*, 2nd edn (Oxford).

Skinner, A. S., and Wilson, T., eds. (1975). *Essays on Adam Smith* (Oxford).

Skinner, Q. R. D. (1974). 'The Principles and Practice of Opposition: The Case of Bolingbroke versus Walpole', in McKendrick 1974. Repr. in Skinner 2002.

Skinner, Q. R. D. (1978). *The Foundations of Modern Political Thought*, 2 vols. (Cambridge).

Skinner, Q. R. D. (1989). 'The State', in T. Ball *et al.*, 1989.

Skinner, Q. R. D. (1998). *Liberty before Liberalism* (Cambridge).

Skinner, Q. R. D. (2002). *Visions of Politics*, III: *Renaissance Virtues* (Cambridge).

Skuncke, M. C. (1992). 'Un prince suédois auteur français: l'éducation de Gustave III, 1756–1762', *SVEC*, 296:123–63.

Slaughter, T. P. (1981). '"Abdicate" and "Contract" in the Glorious Revolution', *HJ*, 24:323–37.

Sloan, H. E. (1995). *Principle and Interest: Thomas Jefferson and the Problem of Debt* (New York).

Small, A. W. (1909). *The Cameralists* (Chicago).

Small, J. (1864). *Biographical Sketch of Adam Ferguson* (Edinburgh).

Small, S. (2002). *Political Thought in Ireland, 1776–1798* (Oxford).

Smith, B. (1960). *European Vision and the South Pacific, 1768–1850* (London).

Smith, D. (1965). *Helvétius: A Study in Persecution* (Oxford).

Smith, H., ed. (1998). *Women Writers and the Early-Modern British Political Tradition* (Cambridge).

Smith, H. (2001). 'English "Feminist" Writings and Judith Drake's *Essay in Defence of the Female Sex* (1696)', *HJ*, 44:727–47.

Smith, H. (2002). 'Georgian Monarchical Culture in England, 1714–1760' (doctoral thesis, Cambridge).

Smith, O. (1984). *The Politics of Language, 1791–1819* (Oxford).

Smith, R. (1995). *Handel's Oratorios and Eighteenth-Century Thought* (Cambridge).

Smith, R. J. (1987). *The Gothic Bequest: Medieval Institutions in British Thought, 1688–1863* (Cambridge).

Smyth, J. (2001). 'Republicanism before the United Irishmen: The Case of Dr Charles Lucas', in Boyce *et al.* 2001.

Soboul, A. (1962). *Précis d'histoire de la Revolution française* (Paris).

Soboul, A. (1972). *The Sans-Culottes*, trans. R. I. Hall (Garden City, NY).

Soboul, A. (1979). 'Sur la fonction historique de l'absolutisme éclairé', *Annales*, 51:519–34.

Soboul, A. (1989). *Dictionnaire historique de la Révolution francaise* (Paris).

Soboul, A., ed. (1968). *Colloque Saint-Just, 1967* (Paris).

Solf, H. H. (1938). 'Gottfried Achenwall: Sein Leben und sein Werk, ein Beitrag zur Göttinger Gelehrtengeschichte' (doctoral thesis, Göttingen).

Soloway, R. A. (1969). *Prelates and People: Ecclesiastical Social Thought in England, 1783–1852* (Toronto).

Sommer, L. (1920–25). *Die österreichischen Kameralisten in dogmengeschichtlicher Darstellung*, 2 vols. (Vienna).

Sonenscher, M. (1984). 'The sans-culottes of the Year II: Rethinking the Language of Labour in Revolutionary France', *Social History*, 9:301–28.

Sonenscher, M. (1989). *Work and Wages: Natural Law, Politics and the Eighteenth-Century French Trades* (Cambridge).

Sonenscher, M. (1997). 'The Nation's Debt and the Birth of the Modern Republic: The French Fiscal Deficit and the Politics of the Revolution of 1789', *HPT*, 18:64–103, 267–325.

Sonenscher, M. (1998a). 'Enlightenment and Revolution', *JMH*, 70:371–83.

Sonenscher, M. (1998b). 'Fashion's Empire: Trade and Power in Early Eighteenth-Century France', in Fox and Turner 1998.

Sonenscher, M. (2002). 'Physiocracy as a Theodicy', *HPT*, 23:326–39.

Sonenscher, M. (2003). 'Introduction' to Sieyès, *Political Writings* (Indianapolis).

Sorenson, L. R. (1990). 'Rousseau's Liberalism', *HPT*, 11:443–66.

Spadafora, D. (1990). *The Idea of Progress in Eighteenth-Century Britain* (New Haven).

Spaemann, R. (1959). *Der Ursprung der Soziologie aus dem Geist der Restauration* (Munich).

Spaeting, R. (1971). 'On Christian Thomasius and his Alleged Offspring, the German Enlightenment', *Lessing Yearbook*, 3:194–213.

Sparn, W. (1976). *Wiederkehr der Metaphysik: Die ontologische Frage in der lutherischen Theologie des frühen 17. Jahrhunderts* (Stuttgart).

Spink, J. S. (1960). *French Freethought from Gassendi to Voltaire* (London).

Spranger, E. (1942). *Der Philosoph von Sanssouci* (Berlin).

Springborg, P. (1995). 'Mary Astell, Critic of Locke', *American Political Science Review*, 89:621–31.

Springborg, P. (1998). 'Astell, Masham and Locke: Religion and Politics', in Smith 1998.

Spurlick, J. (1986). 'What Price Economic Prosperity? Public Attitudes to Physiocracy in the Reign of Louis XIV', *BJECS*, 9:183–96.

Stafford, W. (1980). 'Dissenting Religion Translated into Politics: Godwin's *Political Justice*', *HPT*, 1:279–99.

Stafford, W. (1987). *Socialism, Radicalism, and Nostalgia: Social Criticism in Britain, 1775–1830* (Cambridge).

Stafford, W. (1992). 'Religion and the Doctrine of Nationalism in England at the Time of the French Revolution and Napoleonic Wars', in Mews 1992.

Stafford, W. (2002). *English Feminists and their Opponents in the 1790s* (Manchester).

Stanlis, P. J. (1958). *Edmund Burke and the Natural Law* (Ann Arbor, MI). 2nd edn 1965.

Starobinski, J. (1957). *Jean-Jacques Rousseau: la transparence et l'obstacle* (Paris). 2nd edn 1971.

Starobinski, J. (1988). *Jean-Jacques Rousseau: Transparency and Obstruction*, trans. A. Goldhammer (Chicago).

Starobinski, J. (1989). *Le Remède dans le mal: critique et légitimation de l'artifice à l'âge des lumières* (Paris).

Staum, M. (1980a). *Cabanis: Enlightenment and Medical Philosophy in the French Revolution* (Princeton).

Staum, M. (1980b). 'The Class of Moral and Political Sciences, 1795–1803', *French Historical Studies*, 11:371–97.

Staum, M. (1982). 'Images of Paternal Power: Intellectuals and Social Change in the French National Institute', *Canadian Journal of History*, 17:425–44.

Staum, M. (1985). 'Human, not Secular Sciences: Ideology in the Central Schools', *Historical Reflections / Réflexions historiques*, 12:49–76.

Staum, M. (1985–6). 'The Enlightenment Transformed: The Institute Prize Contests', *ECS*, 19:153–79.

Staum, M. (1986). 'The Institute Historians: Enlightenment and Conservatism', *Proceedings of the Western Society for French Historians*, 13:122–30.

Staum, M. (1987a). 'Individual Rights and Social Control: Political Science in the French Institute', *JHI*, 48:411–30.

Staum, M. (1987b). 'Human Geography in the French Institute', *Journal of the History of the Behavioral Sciences*, 23:332–40.

Staum, M. (1989). 'The Public Relations of the Second Class of the Institute in the Revolutionary Era, 1795–1803', *Proceedings of the Western Society for French History*, 16:212–22.

Staum, M. (1991a). 'The Legacy of Condillac in the Revolutionary Era', *Proceedings of the Western Society for French History*, 18:207–17.

Staum, M. (1991b). '"Analysis of Sensations and Ideas" in the French National Institute, 1795–1803', *Canadian Journal of History*, 26:393–413.

Staum, M. (1996). *Minerva's Message: Stabilizing the French Revolution* (Montreal).

Stein, P. (1963). 'The Influence of Roman Law on the Law of Scotland', *Juridical Review*, 8:205–45.

Stein, P. (1970). 'Law and Society in Eighteenth-Century Scottish Thought', in Phillipson and Mitchison 1970.

Stein, P. (1979). 'Adam Smith's Jurisprudence: Between Morality and Economics', *Cornell Law Review*, 64:621–38.

Stein, P. (1980). *Legal Evolution: The Story of an Idea* (Cambridge).

Stein, P. (1988). 'The Four Stage Theory of the Development of Society', in *The Character and Influence of the Roman Civil Law: Historical Essays* (London).

Steiner, B. E. (1971). *Samuel Seabury, 1729–1796: A Study in the High Church Tradition* (Athens, OH).

Steiner, P. (1998). *La 'Science nouvelle' de l'économie politique* (Paris).

Steintrager, J. (1977). *Bentham* (London).

Stella, P. (1966). *Il giansenismo in Italia* (Zurich).

Stephen, L. (1876). *History of English Thought in the Eighteenth Century,* 2 vols. (London). Many later editions.

Stephen, L. (1900). *The English Utilitarians,* 3 vols. (London). Repr. 1968 (New York).

Stewart, J. B. (1963). *The Moral and Political Philosophy of David Hume* (New York).

Stewart, M. A. (1991). 'The Stoic Legacy in the Early Scottish Enlightenment', in Osler 1991.

Stewart, M. A. (1994). 'The Kirk and the Infidel', Inaugural Lecture (Lancaster).

Stewart, M. A., ed. (1990). *Studies in the Philosophy of the Scottish Enlightenment* (Oxford).

Stewart, M. A., ed. (2000). *English Philosophy in the Age of Locke* (Oxford).

Stewart, M. A, and Wright, J. P., eds. (1994). *Hume and Hume's Connexions* (Edinburgh).

Stieda, W. (1906). *Die Nationalökonomie als Universitätswissenschaft* (Leipzig).

Stievermann, D. (1991). 'Politik und Konfession im 18. Jahrhundert', *Zeitschrift für historische Forschung,* 18:177–99.

Stipperger, E. (1984). *Freiheit und Institution bei Christian Wolff (1679–1754)* (Frankfurt).

Stoeffler, F. E. (1965). *The Rise of Evangelical Pietism* (Leiden).

Stoeffler, F. E. (1973). *German Pietism during the Eighteenth Century* (Leiden).

Stolleis, M. (1988). *Geschichte des öffentlichen Rechts in Deutschland,* 1 (Munich).

Stolleis, M., ed. (1977). *Staatsdenker im 17. und 18. Jahrhundert: Reichspublizistik, Politik, Naturrecht* (Frankfurt).

Stolleis, M., ed. (1983). *Hermann Conring (1606–1681): Beiträge zu Leben und Werk* (Berlin).

Stone, H. S. (1997). *Vico's Cultural History: The Production and Transmission of Ideas in Naples, 1685–1750* (Leiden).

Stone, L., ed. (1994). *An Imperial State at War: Britain from 1689 to 1815* (London).

Storez, I. (1981). 'La Philosophie politique du chancelier D'Aguesseau', *Revue historique,* 266:381–400.

Stourzh, G. (1970). *Alexander Hamilton and the Idea of Republican Government* (Stanford).

Straka, G. M. (1962). *Anglican Reaction to the Revolution of 1688* (Madison, WI).

Strakosch, H. E. (1967). *State Absolutism and the Rule of Law: The Struggle for the Codification of Civil Law in Austria, 1753–1811* (Sydney).

Strauss, L. (1953). *Natural Right and History* (Chicago).

Strauss, L. (1963). *The Political Philosophy of Hobbes* (Chicago).

Stroup, J. (1984). *The Struggle for Identity in the Clerical Estate: Northwest German Protestant Opposition to Absolutist Policy in the Eighteenth Century* (Leiden).

Strugnell, A. (1973). *Diderot's Politics* (The Hague).

Strugnell, A. (1983). 'Diderot on Luxury, Commerce and the Merchant', *SVEC,* 217:83–93.

Sugarman, D., ed. (1983). *Legality, Ideology and the State* (London).

Sullivan, R. E. (1982). *John Toland and the Deist Controversy* (Cambridge, MA).

Sullivan, R. J. (1989). *Immanuel Kant's Moral Theory* (Cambridge).

Sweet, P. R. (1978–80). *Wilhelm von Humboldt: A Biography* (2 vols., Columbus, OH).

Szabo, F. A. J. (1994). *Kaunitz and Enlightened Absolutism, 1753–1780* (Cambridge).

Szechi, D. (1997). 'Constructing a Jacobite: The Social and Intellectual Origins of George Lockhart of Carnwath', *HJ,* 40:977–96.

Szechi, D. (2002). *George Lockhart of Carnwath: A Study in Jacobitism* (East Linton).

Szymkowiak, A. (2002). 'Kant and the Question of the State: Freedom, Permission, and Republicanism' (doctoral thesis, Boston, MA).

Tackett, T. (1986). *Religion, Revolution and Regional Culture in Eighteenth-Century France* (Princeton).

Tagliacozzo, G., ed. (1981). *Vico: Past and Present* (Atlantic Highlands, NJ).

Tagliacozzo, G., and Verene, D. P., eds. (1976). *Giambattista Vico's Science of Humanity* (Baltimore).

Tagliacozzo, G., and White, H. V., eds. (1969). *Giambattista Vico* (Baltimore).

Talmon, J. L. (1952). *The Origins of Totalitarian Democracy* (London). Later editions.

Tamm, D. (1976). *Fra 'Lovkyndighed' til 'Restvidenskab': Studier over betydningen af fremmed ret for Anders Sandøe Ørsteds privatretlige forfatterskab* (Copenhagen).

Tamm, D. (1986). 'Pufendorf und Dänemark', in Modéer 1986.

Tarello, G. (1976). *Storia della cultura giuridica moderna*, 1: *Assolutismo e codificazione del diritto* (Bologna).

Targett, S. (1991). 'Sir Robert Walpole's Newspapers, 1722–1742' (doctoral thesis, Cambridge).

Targett, S. (1994). 'Government and Ideology during the Age of the Whig Supremacy: The Political Argument of Sir Robert Walpole's Newspaper Propagandists', *HJ*, 37:289–317.

Taveneaux, R. (1965). *Jansénisme et politique* (Paris).

Taylor, A. E. (1965). 'The Ethical Doctrine of Hobbes', in Brown 1965.

Taylor, B. (2003). *Mary Wollstonecraft and the Feminist Imagination* (Cambridge).

Taylor, C. (1984). 'Kant's Theory of Freedom', in Gray and Pelczynski 1984.

Taylor, C. (1989). *Sources of the Self: The Making of the Modern Identity* (Cambridge).

Taylor, S. (1992). 'William Warburton and the Alliance of Church and State', *Journal of Ecclesiastical History*, 43:271–86.

Teichgraeber, R. F. (1986). *'Free Trade' and Moral Philosophy: Rethinking the Sources of Adam Smith's 'Wealth of Nations'* (Durham, NC).

Teichgraeber, R. F. (1987). '"Less Abused than I had Reason to Expect": The Reception of *The Wealth of Nations* in Britain, 1776–1790', *HJ*, 30:337–66.

Teichgraeber, R. F. (2000). 'Adam Smith and Tradition: *The Wealth of Nations* before Malthus', in Collini *et al.* 2000a.

Terrasse, J. (1970). *Jean-Jacques Rousseau et la quête de l'âge d'or* (Brussels).

Thale, M. (1989). 'London Debating Societies in the 1790s', *HJ*, 32:57–86.

Thamer, H. U. (1973). *Revolution und Reaktion in der französischen Sozialkritik des 18. Jahrhunderts: Linguet, Mably, Babeuf* (Frankfurt).

Thieme, H. (1954). *Das Naturrecht und die europäische Privatrechtsgeschichte* (Basle).

Thieme, H., *et al.*, eds. (1979). *Humanismus und Naturrecht in Berlin-Brandenburg-Preussen* (Berlin).

Thomann, M. (1964). 'Christian Wolff et le droit subjectif', *Archives de philosophie du droit*, 9:153–74.

Thomann, M. (1968). 'Influence du philosophe allemand Christian Wolff (1679–1754) sur l'*Encyclopédie* et la pensée politique et juridique du XVIIIe siècle français', *Archives de philosophie du droit*, 13:233–48.

Thomann, M. (1969). *La Pensée politique de l'absolutisme éclairé* (Strasbourg).

Thomann, M. (1970). 'Une source peu connue de l'*Encyclopédie*: l'Influence de Christian Wolff', *Congrès national des sociétés savantes*, 3:95–110.

Thomann, M. (1974). 'Histoire de l'idéologie juridique au XVIIIe siècle', *Archives de philosophie du droit*, 19:127–49.

Thomann, M. (1977). 'Christian Wolff', in Stolleis 1977.

Thomas, D. O. (1977). *The Honest Mind: The Thought and Work of Richard Price* (Oxford).

Thomas, D. O., Stephens, J., and Jones, P. A. L. (1993). *A Bibliography of the Works of Richard Price* (Aldershot).

Thomas, P. D. G. (1971). *The House of Commons in the Eighteenth Century* (Oxford).

Thomas, P. D. G. (1996). *John Wilkes, A Friend to Liberty* (Oxford).

Thompson, E. P. (1963). *The Making of the English Working Class* (London).

Thompson, M. P. (1976). 'The Reception of Locke's *Two Treatises of Government*', *Political Studies*, 24:184–91.

Thompson, M. P. (1977). 'Hume's Critique of Locke and the Original Contract', *Il pensiero politico*, 10:189–201.

Thompson, M. P. (1986). 'The History of Fundamental Law in Political Thought from the French Wars of Religion to the American Revolution', *AHR*, 91:1103–28.

Thompson, N. (1998). *The Real Rights of Man: Political Economies for the Working Class, 1775–1850* (London).

Thomson, M. A. (1938). *A Constitutional History of England, 1642–1801* (London).

Thrasher, P. A. (1970). *Pasquale Pauli: An Enlightenment Hero, 1725–1807* (London).

Tillet, E. (2001). *La Constitution anglaise: un modèle politique et institutionnel dans la France des lumières* (Aix-en-Provence).

Todd, J. (2000). *Mary Wollstonecraft: A Revolutionary Life* (London).

Todorov, T. (1993). *On Human Diversity, Nationalism, Racism and Exoticism in French Thought* (Cambridge, MA). 1st publ. in French in 1989.

Tomalin, C. (1974). *The Life and Death of Mary Wollstonecraft* (London).

Tomaselli, S. (1985). 'The Enlightenment Debate on Women', *History Workshop*, 20: 101–24.

Tomaselli, S. (1992). 'Remembering Mary Wollstonecraft on the Bicentenary of the Publication of *A Vindication of the Rights of Woman*', *BJECS*, 15:125–33.

Tomaselli, S. (1995). 'Political Economy: The Desire and Needs of Present and Future Generations', in Fox *et al.* 1995.

Tomaselli, S. (1996). 'The Death and Rebirth of Character in the Eighteenth Century', in Porter 1996.

Tomaselli, S. (2000). 'Intolerance, the Virtue of Princes and Radicals', in Grell and Porter 2000.

Tomaselli, S. (2001a). 'The Most Public Sphere of All: The Family', in Eger *et al.* 2001.

Tomaselli, S. (2001b). 'The Role of Women in Enlightenment Conjectural Histories', in Bödeker and Steinbrugge 2001.

Tomaselli, S. (2005). 'Civilization, Patriotism, and the Quest for Origins', in Knott and Taylor 2005.

Tønnessen, K. D. (1979). 'L'Absolutisme éclairé: le cas danois', *Annales historiques de la Révolution française*, 51:611–26.

Topazio, V. W. (1956). *D'Holbach's Moral Philosophy* (Geneva).

Torrey, N. L. (1930). *Voltaire and the English Deists* (New Haven).

Tortajada, R., ed. (1999). *The Economics of James Steuart* (London).

Touchefeu, Y. (1999). *L'Antiquité et le christianisme dans la pensée de Jean-Jacques Rousseau*, *SVEC*, 372.

Trachtenberg, Z. M. (1993). *Making Citizens: Rousseau's Political Theory of Culture* (London).

Trevor Roper, H. (1963). 'The Historical Philosophy of the Enlightenment', *SVEC*, 27.

Trevor Roper, H. (1996). 'Pietro Giannone and Great Britain', *HJ*, 39:657–75.

Tribe, K. (1978). *Land, Labour and Economic Discourse* (London).

Tribe, K. (1984). 'Cameralism and the Science of Government', *JMH*, 56:263–84.

Tribe, K. (1988). *Governing Economy: The Reformation of German Economic Discourse, 1750–1840* (Cambridge).

Tribe, K. (1995). *Strategies of Economic Order: German Economic Discourse, 1750–1950* (Cambridge).

Trouille, M. S. (1997). *Sexual Politics in the Enlightenment: Women Writers Read Rousseau* (Albany, NY).

Trousson, R. (1964). *Le Thème de Prométhée dans la littérature européenne*, 2 vols. (Geneva).

Trousson, R. (1967). *Socrate devant Voltaire, Diderot et Rousseau* (Paris).

Trousson, R. (1969–70). 'J.-J. Rousseau et son oeuvre dans la presse périodique allemande de 1750 à 1800', *DHS*, 1:289–310, and 2:227–64.

Trousson, R. (1971). *Rousseau et sa fortune littéraire* (Paris).

Trousson, R. (1975). *Voyages aux pays de nulle part* (Brussels).

Trousson, R. (1988–9). *Jean-Jacques Rousseau*, 2 vols. (Paris).

Trousson, R. (1994). *Isabelle de Charrière* (Paris).

Trousson, R. (2000). *Jean-Jacques Rousseau jugé par ses contemporains* (Paris).

Trousson, R. (2001). *Visages de Voltaire: XVIIIe–XIXe siècles* (Paris).

Trousson, R., and Eigeldinger, F. S., eds. (1996). *Dictionnaire de Jean-Jacques Rousseau* (Paris).

Tuck, R. (1979). *Natural Rights Theories* (Cambridge).

Tuck, R. (1993). *Philosophy and Government, 1572–1651* (Cambridge).

Tuck, R. (1999). *The Rights of War and Peace: Political Thought and the International Order from Grotius to Kant* (New York).

Tucker, S. I. (1972). *Enthusiasm: A Study in Semantic Change* (Cambridge).

Tucoo-Chala, S. (1977) *C. J. Panckoucke et la librairie française, 1736–1798* (Pau).

Turner, F. (1986). 'British Politics and the Demise of the Roman Republic, 1700–1939', *HJ*, 29:577–99.

Tuveson, E. L. (1964). *Millennium and Utopia: A Study in the Background of the Idea of Progress* (New York).

Umbach, M. (2000). *Federalism and Enlightenment in Germany, 1740–1806* (London).

Urstad, T. S. (1999). *Sir Robert Walpole's Poets: The Use of Literature as Pro-Government Propaganda, 1721–1742* (Newark, DE).

Vaggi, G. (1987). *The Economics of François Quesnay* (Basingstoke).

Valjavec, F. (1945). *Der Josephinismus* (Munich).

Valsecchi, F. (1931–34). *L'assolutismo illuminato in Austria e in Lombardia*, 2 vols. (Bologna).

Valsecchi, F. (1974). 'Der Aufgeklärte Absolutismus (Italien)', in Aretin 1974.

Van den Dungen, P. (2000). 'The Abbé de Saint-Pierre and the English "Irenists" of the Eighteenth Century (Penn, Bellers and Bentham)', *International Journal on World Peace*, 17:395–414.

Van Deusen, G. G. (1932). *Sieyès: His Life and His Nationalism* (New York). Repr. 1968.

Van Dusen, R. (1970). *Christian Garve and English Belles-Lettres* (Berne).

Van Gelderen, M., and Skinner, Q. R. D., eds. (2002). *Republicanism: A Shared European Heritage*, 2 vols. (Cambridge).

Van Kley, D. (1975). *The Jansenists and the Expulsion of the Jesuits from France, 1757–1765* (New Haven).

Van Kley, D. (1979). 'The Church, State, and the Ideological Origins of the French Revolution: The Debate over the General Assembly of the Gallican Clergy in 1765', *JMH*, 51:629–66.

Van Kley, D. (1984). *The Damiens Affair and the Unravelling of the Ancien Règime, 1750–1770* (Princeton).

Van Kley, D. (1987). 'The Jansenist Constitutional Legacy in the French Pre-Revolution', in Baker 1987.

Van Kley, D. (1992). 'The Religious Origins of the Patriot and Ministerial Parties in Pre-Revolutionary France', *Historical Reflections / Réflexions historiques*, 18:17–63.

Van Kley, D. (1994a). 'From the Lessons of French History to Truths for All Times and All People', in Van Kley 1994b.

Van Kley, D., ed. (1994b). *The French Idea of Freedom: The Old Regime and the Declaration of Rights of 1789* (Stanford).

Van Kley, D. (1996). *The Religious Origins of the French Revolution: From Calvin to the Civil Constitution, 1560–1791* (New Haven).

Van Kley, D. (2001a). 'Introduction', in Bradley and Van Kley 2001.

Van Kley, D. (2001b). 'Catholic Conciliar Reform in an Age of Anti-Catholic Revolution: France, Italy, and the Netherlands, 1758–1801', in Bradley and Van Kley 2001.

Van Kley, D. (2002). 'Law Religion et les mouvements "patriotiques" à la fin du dix-huitième siècle', in Cottret 2002.

Vann, J. A. (1984). *The Making of a State: Württemberg, 1593–1793* (Ithaca, NY).

Van Treese, G. J. (1974). *D'Alembert and Frederick the Great* (New York).

Varella, J. (1988). *Jovellanos* (Madrid).

Vartanian, A. (1960). *La Mettrie's L'homme machine* (Princeton)

Vaughan, C. E. (1925). *Studies in the History of Political Philosophy before and after Rousseau*, 2 vols. (Manchester). Revised edn New York, 1960.

Vaussard, M. (1959). *Jansénisme et gallicanisme aux origines religieuses du risorgimento* (Paris).

Velema, W. R. E. (1993). *Enlightenment and Conservatism in the Dutch Republic: The Political Thought of Elie Luzac, 1721–1796* (Assen).

Velema, W. R. E. (1997). 'Republican Readings of Montesquieu: *The Spirit of the Laws* in the Dutch Republic', *HPT*, 18:43–63.

Venturi, F. (1946). *Le origini dell'Enciclopedia* (Rome).

Venturi, F. (1969–90). *Settecento riformatore: l'Italia dei lumi (1764–1790)*, 5 vols. in 7 (Turin).

Venturi, F. (1971). *Utopia and Reform in the Enlightenment* (Cambridge) 1st publ. in Italian in 1970.

Venturi, F. (1972). *Italy and the Enlightenment* (London).

Venturi, F. (1988). *Giovinezza di Diderot* (Palermo).

Vereker, C. (1967). *Eighteenth-Century Optimism* (Liverpool).

Vernière, P. (1954). *Spinoza et la pensée française avant la Révolution*, 2 vols. (Paris).

Vernon, J. (1997). *The Career of Toleration: John Locke, Jonas Proast and After* (Montreal).

Verona, L. (1975). *Jean Meslier, prêtre athée socialiste révolutionnaire, 1664–1729* (Milan).

Vignery, J. R. (1965). *The French Revolution and the Schools: Educational Policies of the Mountain, 1792–1794* (Madison).

Vilar, P. (1979). 'L'Espagne de Charles III', *Annales historique de la Révolution française*, 51:594–610.

Vile, M. J. C. (1967). *Constitutionalism and the Separation of Powers* (Oxford).

Viner, J. (1978). *Religious Thought and Economic Society* (Durham, NC).

Viroli, M. (1988). *Jean-Jacques Rousseau and the 'Well-ordered Society'* (Cambridge).

Vivenza, G. (2001). *Adam Smith and the Classics* (Oxford).

Vogel, U. (1982). 'Liberty is Beautiful: Von Humboldt's Gift to Liberalism', *HPT*, 3:77–101.

Vogel, U. (1988). 'When the Earth Belonged to All: The Land Question in Eighteenth-Century Justifications of Property', *Political Studies*, 36:102–22.

Vogler, G., ed. (1988). *Europäische Herrscher: Ihre Rolle bei der Gestaltung von Politik und Gesellschaft vom 16. bis zum 18. Jahrhundert* (Weimar).

Voitle, R. (1984). *The Third Earl of Shaftesbury, 1671–1713* (Baton Rouge).

Vollhardt, F., ed. (1997). *Christian Thomasius (1655–1728)* (Tübingen).

Vollhardt, F., ed. (2001). *Selbsliebe und Geselligkeit: Untersuchungen zum Verhältnis von naturrechtlichem Denken und moraldidaktischer Literatur im 17. und 18. Jahrhundert* (Tübingen).

Voltelini, H. von (1910). 'Die naturrechtlichen Lehren und die Reformen des 18. Jahrhunderts', *Historische Zeitschrift*, 105:65–104.

Vossler, O. (1963). *Rousseaus Freiheitslehre* (Göttingen).

Vyverberg, H. (1958). *Historical Pessimism in the French Enlightenment* (Cambridge, MA).

Vyverberg, H. (1989). *Human Nature, Cultural Diversity and the French Enlightenment* (Oxford).

Waddicor, M. H. (1970). *Montesquieu and the Philosophy of Natural Law* (The Hague).

Wade, I. O. (1938). *Clandestine Organization and Diffusion of Philosophic Ideas in France from 1700 to 1750* (Princeton). Repr. New York, 1967.

Wade, I. O. (1947). *Studies on Voltaire with Some Unpublished Papers by Mme du Châtelet* (Princeton).

Wade, I. O. (1959). *Voltaire and Candide* (Princeton).

Wade, I. O. (1969). *The Intellectual Development of Voltaire* (Princeton).

Wade, I. O. (1971). *The Intellectual Origins of the French Enlightenment* (Princeton).

Wade, I. O. (1977). *The Structure and Form of the French Enlightenment*, 2 vols. (Princeton).

Wagner, W. (1986a). 'Einführung', in Wagner 1986c.

Wagner, W. (1986b). 'Zur Vorgeschichte der Kodifikation von 1734', in Wagner 1986.

Wagner, W., ed. (1986c). *Das schwedische Reichsgesetzbuch (Sveriges Rikes Lag) von 1734* (Frankfurt).

Wagstaff, P. (1996). *Memory and Desire: Rétif de la Bretonne, Autobiography and Utopia* (Amsterdam).

Wahnbaeck, T. (2004). *Luxury and Public Happiness: Political Economy in the Italian Enlightenment* (Oxford).

Waldron, J. (1991). 'Locke: Toleration and the Rationality of Persecution', in Horton and Mendus 1991.

Waldron, J. (2002). *God, Locke and Equality* (Cambridge).

Walicki, A. (1989). *The Enlightenment and the Birth of Modern Nationhood: Polish Political Thought from Noble Republicanism to Tadeusz Kosciuszko* (Notre Dame, IN).

Walker, A. K. (1973). *William Law: His Life and Thought* (London).

Walker, D. (1985). *The Scottish Jurists* (Edinburgh).

Walker, D. (2003). 'Addison's *Cato* and the Transformation of Republican Discourse in the Early Eighteenth Century', *BJECS*, 26:91–108.

Walker, D. P. (1975). *The Decline of Hell* (London).

Walker, M. (1981). *Johann Jakob Moser and the Holy Roman Empire of the German Nation* (Chapel Hill).

Wallman, J. (1990). *Der Pietismus* (Göttingen).

Walsh, J., Haydon, C., and Taylor, S., eds. (1993). *The Church of England, c. 1689–c. 1833: From Toleration to Tractarianism* (Cambridge).

Walter, E. (1973). 'Sur l'intelligentsia des lumières', *DHS*, 5:173–201.

Wandruszka, A. (1963–5). *Leopold II*, 2 vols. (Vienna).

Wangermann, E. (1969). *From Joseph II to the Jacobin Trials*, 2nd edn (Oxford).

Wangermann, E. (1973). *The Austrian Achievement, 1700–1800* (London).

Ward, A. (1964). 'The Tory View of Roman History', *Studies in English Literature*, 4: 412–56.

Ward, W. R. (1992). *The Protestant Evangelical Awakening* (Cambridge).

Ward, W. R. (1999). *Christianity under the Ancien Régime, 1648–1789* (Cambridge).

Wardle, R. (1952). *Mary Wollstonecraft: A Critical Biography* (Lincoln, KS).

Warner, C. K., ed. (1969). *From the Ancien Régime to the Popular Front* (New York).

Warnock, G. J. (1953). *Berkeley* (London).

Warnock, G. J. (1986). 'On Passive Obedience', *HEI*, 7:555–62.

Wasserman, E., ed., (1965). *Aspects of the Eighteenth Century* (Baltimore).

Waszek, N. (1986). *Man's Social Nature: A Topic of the Scottish Enlightenment in its Historical Setting* (Frankfurt).

Waszek, N. (1988). *The Scottish Enlightenment and Hegel's Account of Civil Society* (Dordrecht).

Waterman, A. M. C. (1996). 'The Nexus between Theology and Political Doctrine in Church and Dissent', in Haakonssen 1996b.

Watts, M. (1978). *The Dissenters: From the Reformation to the French Revolution* (Oxford).

Webster, A. (1993). 'J. Barnave: Philosopher of a Revolution', *HEI*, 17:53–71.

Weil, R. (1999). *Political Passions: Gender, the Family and Political Argument in England, 1680–1714* (Manchester).

Weill, H. N. (1961). *Frederick the Great and Samuel von Cocceji* (Madison).

Weinbrot, H. O. (1978). *Augustus Caesar in Augustan England* (Princeton).

Weis, E. (1986). 'Enlightenment and Absolutism in the Holy Roman Empire: Thoughts on Enlightened Absolutism in Germany', *JMH*, 58, Supplement.

Welch, C. B. (1984). *Liberty and Utility: The French Idéologues and the Transformation of Liberalism* (New York).

Wellman, K. (1992). *La Mettrie: Medicine, Philosophy and Enlightenment* (Durham, NC).

Wells, R. A. E. (1983). *Insurrection: The British Experience, 1795–1803* (Gloucester).

Westerman, P. (1994). 'Hume and the Natural Lawyers', in Stewart and Wright 1994.

Weston, C. C. (1965). *English Constitutional Theory and the House of Lords, 1556–1832* (London).

Weston, C. C. (1991). 'England: Ancient Constitution and Common Law', in Burns and Goldie 1991.

Weston, C. C., and Greenberg, J. R. (1981). *Subjects and Sovereigns: The Grand Controversy over Legal Sovereignty in Stuart England* (Cambridge).

Weulersse, G. (1910). *Le Mouvement physiocratique en France, de 1756 à 1770*, 2 vols. (Paris).

Weulersse, G. (1950). *La Physiocratie sous les ministères de Turgot et de Necker (1774–1781)* (Paris).

Whale, J., ed. (2000). *Edmund Burke's Reflections on the Revolution in France* (Manchester).

Whaley, J. (1985). *Religious Toleration and Social Change in Hamburg, 1529–1819* (Cambridge).

Whaley, J. (2000). 'A Tolerant Society?: Religious Toleration in the Holy Roman Empire, 1648–1806', in Grell and Porter 2000.

Whatmore, R. (1996). 'Commerce, Constitutions and the Manners of a Nation: Etienne Clavière's Revolutionary Political Economy, 1788–93', *HEI*, 22:351–68.

Whatmore, R. (1998). 'The Political Economy of Jean-Baptiste Say's Republicanism', *HPT*, 19:439–56.

Whatmore, R. (2000a). *Republicanism and the French Revolution: An Intellectual History of Jean-Baptiste Say's Political Economy* (Oxford).

Whatmore, R. (2000b). '"A Gigantic Manliness": Paine's Republicanism in the 1790s', in Collini *et al.* 2000a.

Whelan, F. G. (1985). *Order and Artifice in Hume's Political Philosophy* (Princeton).

Whelan, F. G. (1988). 'Vattel's Doctrine of the State', *HPT*, 9:59–90.

Whelan, F. G. (1991). 'Population and Ideology in the Enlightenment', *HPT*, 12:35–72.

Whelan, F. G. (1996). *Edmund Burke and India: Political Morality and Empire* (Pittsburgh).

Whelan, F. G. (2001). 'Oriental Despotism: Anquetil-Duperon's Response to Montesquieu', *HPT*, 22:619–47.

White, M. (1978). *The Philosophy of the American Revolution* (New York).

White, R. J. (1970). *The Anti-Philosophers* (London).

White, S. K. (1994). *Edmund Burke: Modernity, Politics and Aesthetics* (London).

Whitman, J. O. (1990). *The Legacy of Roman Law in the German Romantic Era* (Princeton).

Wickwar, W. H. (1935). *Baron d'Holbach* (London).

Wieacker, F. (1952). *Privatrechtsgeschichte der Neuzeit* (Göttingen).

Wilhelm, U. (1995). *Der deutsche Frühliberalismus: Von den Anfängen bis 1789* (Frankfurt).

Wilkins, B. T. (1967). *The Problem of Burke's Political Philosophy* (Oxford).

Willey, B. (1965). *The Eighteenth-Century Background* (London).

Williams, D., ed. (1987). *Condorcet Studies II* (New York).

Williams, H. (1983). *Kant's Political Philosophy* (Oxford).

Willman, R. (1983). 'Blackstone and the "Theoretical Perfection" of the English Law in the Reign of Charles II', *HJ*, 26:39–70.

Wills, G. (1978). *Inventing America: Jefferson's Declaration of Independence* (Garden City, NY).

Wills, G. (1984). *Cincinnatus: George Washington and the Enlightenment* (Garden City, NY).

Wilson, A. M. (1972). *Diderot* (Oxford).

Wilson, E., and Reill, P. H. (1996). *Encyclopedia of the Enlightenment* (London). Revised edn 2004.

Winch, D. (1978). *Adam Smith's Politics* (Cambridge).

Winch, D. (1983). 'Adam Smith's "Enduring Particular Result"', in Hont and Ignatieff 1983a.

Winch, D. (1985). 'The Burke–Smith Problem and Late Eighteenth-Century Political and Economic Thought', *HJ*, 28:231–47.

Winch, D. (1987). *Malthus* (Oxford).

Winch, D. (1992). 'Adam Smith: Scottish Moral Philosopher as Political Economist', *HJ*, 35:91–113.

Winch, D. (1993). 'The Science of the Legislator', in Lacey and Furner 1993.

Winch, D. (1996). *Riches and Poverty: An Intellectual History of Political Economy in Britain, 1750–1834* (Cambridge).

Winch, D. (1997). 'A Great Deal of Ruin in a Nation', in Clarke and Trebilcock 1997.

Winch, D. (2002). 'Commercial Realities, Republican Principles', in Van Gelderen and Skinner 2002, II.

Winiger, B. (1992). *Das rationale Pflichtenrecht Christian Wolffs* (Berlin).

Winter, E. (1962). *Der Josephinismus: Die Geschichte des österreichischen Reformkatholizismus, 1740–1848*, 2nd edn (Berlin).

Wisner, D. A. (1997). *The Cult of the Legislator in France, 1750–1830*, *SVEC*, 352.

Wokler, R. (1975). 'The Influence of Diderot on the Political Theory of Rousseau', *SVEC*, 132:55–111.

Wokler, R. (1979). 'Rousseau on Rameau and Revolution', *Studies in the Eighteenth Century*, 4:251-83.

Wokler, R. (1980). 'The *Discours sur les sciences et les arts* and its Offspring: Rousseau in Reply to his Critics', in Harvey and Hobson 1980.

Wokler, R. (1983). 'Rousseau and Marx', in Miller and Siedentop 1983.

Wokler, R. (1987a). *Rousseau on Society, Politics, Music, and Language: An Historical Interpretation of his Early Writings* (New York).

Wokler, R., (1987b). 'Rousseau's Two Concepts of Liberty', in Feaver and Rosen 1987.

Wokler, R. (1987c). 'The Enlightenment', in Riff 1987.

Wokler, R. (1987d). 'Saint-Simon and the Passage from Political to Social Science', in Pagden 1987.

Wokler, R. (1988a). 'Natural Law and the Meaning of Rousseau's Political Thought', in Barber and Courtney 1988.

Wokler, R. (1988b). 'From Apes to Races in the Scottish Enlightenment: Monboddo and Kames on the Nature of Man', in P. Jones 1988.

Wokler, R. (1993). 'Democracy's Mythical Ordeals: The Promethean and Procrustean Paths to Popular Self-Rule', in Moran and Parry 1993.

Wokler, R. (1994a). 'Rousseau's Pufendorf', *HPT*, 15:373–402.

Wokler, R. (1994b). 'Projecting the Enlightenment', in Horton and Mendus 1994.

Wokler, R. (1995b). 'The Enlightenment Science of Politics', in Fox *et al.* 1995.

Wokler, R. (1997). 'Rousseau et la liberté', *Annales de la Société Jean-Jacques Rousseau*, 41:205–29.

Wokler, R. (1998a). 'The Enlightenment and the French Revolutionary Birthpangs of Modernity', in Magnusson *et al.* 1998.

Wokler, R. (1998b). 'Contextualizing Hegel's Phenomenology of the French Revolution and the Terror', *Political Theory*, 26:33–55.

Wokler, R. (2000a). 'The Enlightenment, the Nation-State and the Primal Patricide of Modernity', in Geras and Wokler 2000.

Wokler, R. (2000b). 'Multiculturalism and Ethnic Cleansing in the Enlightenment', in Grell and Porter 2000.

Wokler, R. (2000c). 'From the Moral and Political Sciences to the Sciences of Society by Way of the French Revolution', *Jahrbuch für Recht und Ethik*, 8:33–45.

Wokler, R. (2001a). *Rousseau*, 2nd edn (Oxford). 1st publ. 1995.

Wokler, R. (2001b). 'Ancient Postmodernism in the Philosophy of Rousseau', in Riley 2001b.

Wokler, R. (2002). 'Repatriating Modernity's Alleged Debts to the Enlightenment: French Revolutionary Social Science and the Genesis of the Nation State', in Joyce 2002.

Wokler, R. (2003). 'Isaiah Berlin's Counter-Enlightenment', in Mali and Wokler 2003.

Wokler, R. (2004). 'Rouseau' and 'Social Contract', in A. Kuper and J. Kuper, eds., *The Social Science Encyclopedia*, 3rd edn, II (London).

Wokler, R., ed. (1995a). *Rousseau and Liberty* (Manchester).

Wolf, E. (1963). *Große Rechtsdenker der deutschen Geistesgeschichte*, 4th edn (Tübingen).

Wolff, R. P., ed. (1967). *Kant: A Collection of Critical Essays* (Notre Dame, IN).

Wolin, S. (1960). *Politics and Vision* (Boston, MA).

Wolpe, H. (1957). *Raynal et sa Machine de Guerre* (Stanford).

Womersley, D., ed. (1997). *Edward Gibbon: Bicentennial Essays*, SVEC, 355.

Wood, G. S. (1969). *The Creation of the American Republic* (Chapel Hill).

Wood, G. S. (1992). *The Radicalism of the American Revolution* (New York).

Wood, G. S. (2002). *The American Revolution: A History* (New York).

Wood, G. S. (2004). *The Americanization of Benjamin Franklin* (New York).

Wood, P. B. (1993). *The Aberdeen Enlightenment: The Arts Curriculum in the Eighteenth Century* (Aberdeen).

Wood, P. B., ed. (2000). *The Scottish Enlightenment* (Rochester, NY).

Woodcock, G. (1963). *Anarchism* (Harmondsworth).

Woodress, J. (1958). *A Yankee's Odyssey: The Life of Joel Barlow* (New York).

Woolf, S. J., ed. (1972). *Italy and the Enlightenment* (London).

Wootton, D. (1994b). 'Introduction', in Wootton 1994a.

Wootton, D. (1994c). 'Ulysses Bound? Venice and the Idea of Liberty from Howell to Hume', in Wootton, ed., 1994a.

Wootton, D. (2000). 'Helvétius: from Radical Enlightenment to Revolution', *Political Theory*, 28:307–36.

Wootton, D., ed. (1994a). *Republicanism, Liberty and Commercial Society, 1649–1776* (Stanford).

Worden, B. (1978). 'Introduction' to Edmund Ludlow, *A Voyce from the Watch Tower* (London).

Worden, B. (1991). 'The Revolution of 1688–9 and the English Republican Tradition', in Israel 1991.

Worden, B. (2001). *Roundhead Reputations: The English Civil Wars and the Passions of Posterity* (London).

Wright, E. (1986). *Franklin of Philadelphia* (Cambridge, MA).

Wright, J. K. (1997). *A Classical Republican in Eighteenth-Century France: The Political Thought of Mably* (Stanford).

Yardeni, M. (1985). 'French Calvinist Political Thought, 1574–1715', in Prestwich 1985.

Yeo, R. (2001). *Encyclopedic Visions: Scientific Dictionaries and Enlightenment Culture* (Cambridge).

Yolton, J. W., ed. (1969). *John Locke: Problems and Perspectives* (Cambridge).

York, N. L. (1994). *Neither Kingdom nor Nation: The Irish Quest for Constitutional Rights, 1698–1800* (Washington, DC).

Young, B. W. (1994). 'William Law and the Christian Economy of Salvation', *English Historical Review*, 109:308–22.

Young, B. W. (1996). 'Christianity, Commerce and the Canon: Josiah Tucker and Richard Woodward on Political Economy', *HEI*, 22:384–400.

Young, B. W. (1998). *Religion and Enlightenment in Eighteenth-Century England* (Oxford).

Yovel, Y. (1980). *Kant and the Philosophy of History* (Princeton).

Zagorin, P., ed. (1980). *Culture and Politics from Puritanism to the Enlightenment* (Berkeley).

Zammito, J. H. (2002). *Kant, Herder and the Birth of Anthropology* (Chicago).

Zande, J. van der (1992). 'Popular Philosophy and the History of Mankind in Eighteenth-Century Germany', *Storia della storiografia*, 22:37–56.

Zande, J. van der (1995). 'In the Image of Cicero: German Philosophy between Wolff and Kant', *JHI*, 56:419–42.

Zande, J. van der (1998). 'The Microscope of Experience: Christian Garve's Translation of Cicero's *De officiis* (1783)', *JHI*, 59:75–94.

Zande, J. van der, and Popkin, R. H., eds. (1998). *The Skeptical Tradition Around 1800* (Dordrecht).

Zebrowski, M. K. (1991). 'The Corruption of Politics and the Dignity of Human Nature: The Critical and Constructive Radicalism of James Burgh', *Enlightenment and Dissent*, 10:78–103.

Zeller, E. (1886). *Friedrich der Große als Philosoph* (Berlin).

Zimmer, A. Y. (1978). *Jonathan Boucher, Loyalist in Exile* (Detroit).

Zinsser, J. P. (1998). 'Emilie du Châtelet: Genius, Gender and Intellectual Authority', in Smith 1998.

Zinsser, J. P. (2002). 'Emilie de Breteuil, Marquise du Châtelet and Bernard Mandeville's *Fable of the Bees*', French Historical Studies, 25:595–624.

Zuckert, M. P. (1994). *Natural Rights and the New Republicanism* (Princeton).

Zurbuchen, S. (1991). *Naturrecht und natürliche Religion: Zur Geschichte des Toleranzproblems von Samuel Pufendorf bis Jean-Jacques Rousseau* (Würzburg).

Zurbuchen, S. (1995). 'Politics and Ethics in the Huguenot Diaspora: Isaac de Beausobre in Berlin', in Laursen 1995.

Zurbuchen, S. (1998). 'Die schweizerische Debatte über die Leibniz–Wolffsche Philosophie und ihre Bedeutung für Emer von Vattels philosophischen Werdegang', in Coleman et al. 1998.

Zurbuchen, S. (2005). 'Religion and Society', in Haakonssen 2005a.

Zurbuchen, S. (forthcoming). 'Emer de Vattel: His Swiss Background and his Influence in America'.

Zvesper, J. (1977). *Political Philosophy and Rhetoric: A Study of the Origins of American Party Politics* (Cambridge).

Index

The note '(biog)' in an entry refers to inclusion in the biographical appendix; the pages in bold indicate extended passages.

Abbadie, Jacques, 711 (biog.)

Abraham, 355

absolutism, 41, 45, 62, 115, 116, 117, 126, 140, 153–4, 155, 163, 164, 169, 176, 246, 384, 386, 433, 436, 437, 482, 513–14, 523–4; *see also* despotism; monarchy

Achenwall, Gottfried, 267, 276, 536, 711 (biog.)

Acherley, Roger, 317, 335, 711 (biog.)

Act of Settlement (1701), 320, 613

Act of Toleration (1689), 94, 95, 320

Act of Union (1707), 55, 444

Act of Union (1800), 55

Adams, Abigail, 712 (biog.)

Adams, John, 343, 346, 603, 635, 712 (biog.)

Adams, Samuel, 613, 712 (biog.)

Addison, Joseph, 66, 68, 69, 70, 106, 405, 712 (biog.)

agrarian policy, 385, 480, 486, 488–92, 575, 684

agriculture, 384, 385, 419, 420, 421, 422, 423–4, 425, 426, 427–8, 429–30, 431, 432, 435, 436, 437, 439, 440, 441, 442, 448, 455–6, 467, 468, 474, 544, 604

Aguesseau, Henri François d', 180

Alberti, Valentin, 261

Alembert, Jean Baptiste le Rond d', 11, 15, 89, 109, 173, 174, 175, 176, 178, 179, 186, 189–90, 243, 500, 503, 507, 586–7, 693, 701, 712–13 (biog.)

Alfieri, Vittorio, 713 (biog.)

Alfred, king of England, 71, 73, 209

Allegiance controversy of 1689–91, 43–5

Almain, Jacques, 113

Almond, John, 664

American colonies, 107, 141, 255, 459

American Declaration of Independence, 348, 613

American Revolution, 60, 61, 140, 271, 330, 487, 522, 580, 587, 592, **601–25**, 632, 660, 664, 688, 690

Amo, Anton Wilhelm, 713 (biog.)

Amthor, C. H. (Sincerus), 531

anatomy/physiology, 233–4, 235, 237, 244, 708

Anne of Austria, 23

Anquetil-Duperron, Abraham Hyacinthe, 148, 152

anthropology, **232–8**

Antraigues, Comte Emmanuel d', 119

Aotourou, 168

Appolis, Emile, 121, 124

Aquinas, Thomas/Thomism, 126, 252, 253, 261, 269, 296, 349

Arbuthnot, John, 238, 713 (biog.)

Archinto, Alberico, 122

Arendt, Hannah, 690

Argenson, René Louis de Voyer, Marquis d', 416, 713 (biog.)

Argis, Boucher d', 193

aristocracy, 31, 32, 68, 154, 155, 275, 318, 319, 331, 337, 338, 576, 578, 584, 586, 603

Aristotle, 28, 51, 68, 69, 117, 120, 223, 253, 255, 275, 276, 292, 295, 296, 297, 349, 369, 512, 530, 531, 534, 576, 584

Arminianism, 92, 141

Arnall, William, 75, 77

Arnauld, Antoine, 112

Arnold, Gottfried, 101, 134

Arnoux, Abbé, 487

arts, 164, 165, 176, 203, 207, 209, 211, 212, 243, 384, 392, 415, **475–80**, 579

Ascham, Anthony, 44

Astell, Mary, 62–4, 68, 713–14 (biog.)

Astley, Thomas, 149

Atkyns, Robert, 321, 335

Atterbury, Francis, 51, 714 (biog.)

Atwood, William, 48, 56, 59, 714 (biog.)

Aubert de Versé, Noël, 92

Augustine, St, 71, 77, 95, 102, 105, 111, 120, 133, 134, 349, 368, 374

Augustus, Emperor, 69, 203, 415, 483

Austin, John, 42
Austria, 94, 107, 119, 129–31, 256

Babeuf, François Noël (Gracchus), 465–71, 489, 491, 714 (biog.)
Backus, Isaac, 714–15 (biog.)
Bacon, Sir Francis, 20, 174, 176, 189, 203, 222, 230, 231, 501
Badaloni, Nicola, 219
Bagehot, Walter, 78
Baker, Keith Michael, 429, 699
Balfour, James, 291
Baltimore, Lord, 612
Baluze, Etienne, 12
Banbury, Charles, 567
Bandini, Sallustio, 439
Bangorian controversy, 52
Barbeyrac, Jean de, 93, 140, 219, 220, 254–5, 258, 267, 278, 361–2, 715 (biog.)
Barclay, John, 159, 161
Barère de Vieuzac, Bertrand, 654
Barker, Jane, 715 (biog.)
Barlow, Joel, 681, 715 (biog.)
Barnard, F. M., 220, 246
Barnave, Antoine Pierre Joseph Marie, 640–1, 715 (biog.)
Baron, Richard, 54
Barrington, John Shute, First Viscount, 48, 53, 716 (biog.)
Barruel, Abbé Augustin, 119, 126, 480
Barthez, Paul Joseph, 705
Basnage, Henri, 92
Basnage (de Beauval), Jacques, 81, 92, 716 (biog.)
Batoni, Pompeo, 515
Baudeau, Abbé Nicolas, 426, 429, 434, 436, 716 (biog.)
Bayle, Pierre, 170, 175, 206, 399, 500, 716 (biog.); and church-state relations, 105; and Condillac, 88; and Descartes, 206; dictionary of, 174; and Diderot, 190; and *Encyclopédie*, 181; and Leibniz, 196; and Mandeville, 391; on religion, 80, 85, 86, 87, 88, 92, 93, 95, 98, 103, 104, 254; and scepticism, 79, 88, 254; and science, 206; as subversive, 181; and theodicy, 195; and Voltaire, 108, 206
Beattie, James, 294
Beaumarchais, Pierre Augustin Caron de, 504, 716–17 (biog.)
Beausobre, Isaac de, 101
Beccaria, Cesare Bonesana, Marchese de, 219, 439, 503, 508, 516–17, 520, 522, **551–7**, 557, 561, 562, 563, 564, 565, 566, 567, 569, 571, 717 (biog.)
Becher, Johann Joachim, 527–8, 531, 537, 717 (biog.)

Beckford, William, 74
Beckmann, Johann, 536
Bell, Andrew, 183
Bembo, Pietro, 120
Benedict XIV, Pope, 97, 120, 122, 124
Bengel, Johann Albrecht, 133
Bentham, Jeremy, 279, 357–8, 374, 375, 522, 551, **557–63**, 565–6, 567, 568, 569–70, 571–2, 702, 703, 717 (biog.)
Berch, Anders, 535
Berington, Joseph, 717–18 (biog.)
Berkeley, George, 46, 401–3, 718 (biog.)
Berlin, Isaiah, 243, 588
Bernard, Jacques, 92
Bernardin de Saint-Pierre, Jacques Henri, 479, 516, 718 (biog.)
Berruyer, Issac, 117
Bertieri, Giuseppi, 129
Bertin, Henri Léonard Jean Baptiste, 420
Bible, 80, 82, 84, 85, 95, 109, 112, 120, 133, 141, 208, 223–4, 225, 226, 296, 354, 355, 367, 414
Bichat, Marie François Xavier, 705, 708
Bielfeld, Jakob Friedrich vom, 508
Bignon, Louis-Claude du, 177
Billaud-Varenne, Jacques Nicolas, 652–3, 654, 718 (biog.)
Bill of Rights (1689), 320, 612, 613
Bizon, Abbé Augustin Clément de, 122, 123, 124, 128, 130
Blackburne, Francis, 718–19 (biog.)
Blackhall, Offspring, 62
Blackstone, Sir William, 53, 318, 319–20, 321–3, 334, 335–7, 341, 342, 343, 345–6, 357, 564, 567, 570, 572, 612, 620, 719 (biog.)
Blake, William, 662, 687
Bland, Richard, 719 (biog.)
Blount, Charles, 85
Bodin, Jean, 10, 42, 45, 81, 159, 161, 689, 690
Boehme, Jakob, 134
Boëthius, Daniel, 279
Bohun, Edmund, 45
Boisguilbert, Pierre Le Pesant, Sieur de, 415, 422, 439, 719 (biog.)
Bolgeni, Gianvincenzo, 126
Bolingbroke, Henry St John, Viscount, 41, 49, 64, 72–4, 75, 77, 196, 197, 198, 319, 320, 323, 326–7, 611, 612, 719–20 (biog.)
Bonald, Louis Gabriel Ambroise, vicomte de, 119, 700, 702 (biog.)
Bonnet, Charles, 222, 234, 235
Bonneville, Nicolas, 474
Bonola, Rocco, 126, 128
books/publication, 174, 176, 180, 181, 185, 187; *see also Encyclopédie*
Bordeu, Théophile de, 705

Bossuet, Jacques Bénigne, 10, 17, 93, 117, 148, 204, 207, 223, 228, 354–5, 358, 513, 720 (biog.)
Bottari, Giovanni Gaetano, 122
Boucher, Jonathan, 720 (biog.)
Bougainville, Louis Antoine de, 149, 168
Boulainvilliers, Henri, comte de, 13, 34, 35, 115, 578, 721 (biog.)
Bourgogne, duc de, 10
Bowring, John, 570
Brenellerie, Paul Philippe Gudin de la, 697
Briasson, Claude, 182
Brienne, Loménie de, 118, 438
Brissot (de Warville), Jacques Pierre, 79, 89, 90, 91–2, 490, 645, 721 (biog.)
Brizard, Gabriel François, 479
Brooke, Henry, 71, 721 (biog.)
Brosse, Charles du, 243
Brothers, Richard, 662
Brown, John, 66, 721 (biog.)
Brucker, Johann Jakob, 101, 175, 192, 194, 370, 721–2 (biog.)
Brunner, Otto, 530
Bryson, Gladys, 706
Buchanan, David, 443
Buchanan, George, 43
Buckingham, duke of, 71
Budde, Johann Franz, 268
Buffier, Claude, 190
Buffon, Georges Louis Leclerc, comte de, 182, 187, 220, 222, 225–6, **235**, 244, 698, 722 (biog.)
Bulkley, John, 48
Bunyan, John, 663
Burdin, Jean, 705
Burgh, James, 49, 73, 324, 330, 663, 664, 666, 667, 722 (biog.)
Burke, Edmund, 61, 108, 126, 142, 217, 326, 463, 592, 608, 662, 663, 666, 669, 722 (biog.); on common law, 344–5; on constitution, 330, 675–6; on contract, 348, 374, 674; on family, 676, 679; on French Revolution, 217, **673–83**; and Gibbon, 217; and Godwin, 682; and Hobbes, 675, 678; and Hume, 675, 677; on institutions, 675; and Locke, 374; and Montesquieu, 18; and Paine, 676, 679; and Priestley, 671; on reason, 675, 678, 681; on rights, 672, 674, 675, 678; and Wollstonecraft, 679
Burlamaqui, Jean Jacques, 220, 254, 255, 258, 278, 359, 360–1, 723 (biog.)
Burnet, Gilbert, 57, 723 (biog.)
Burnet, Thomas, 225
Butel-Dumont, Georges Marie, 379

Caballero, José Antonio, 127, 129
Cabanis, Pierre Jean, 694, 699, 708, 723 (biog.)
Calamy, Edmund, 53, 723 (biog.)
Calas, Jean, 93, 96
Calonne, Charles Alexandre de, 438
Calvin, John, 132
Calvinism, 43, 54, 92, 96, 98, 112, 137, 140, 141, 253, 255, 400, 668
Cambacérès, Jean Jacques Régis de, 694
cameralism, 119, 138, 513, **525–46**
Campanella, Tommaso, 222
Campbell, John, 149
Camper, Pieter, 235, 244
Campomanes, Pedro Rodríguez, conde de, 127, 440, 723–4 (biog.)
Cantillon, Richard, 423, 426, 724 (biog.)
Capua, Lionardo da, 219
Carlos III, 119, 123, 127, 507
Carlos IV, 127, 128
Carmichael, Gershom, 48, 254, 291, 292, 297–9, 300, 301, 302, 308, 724 (biog.)
Caroline, queen of England, 504
Carte, Thomas, 73, 305
Cartwright, 'Major' John, 330, 341, 666, 724 (biog.)
Carvalho e Melho, Sebastian, 122
Cary, John, 56
Casaux, Charles, Marquis de (Alexandre Cazaud), 490, 724–5 (biog.)
Cassander, Georg, 101
Cassirer, Ernst, 2, 189
Catherine II ('The Great'), Empress of Russia, 107, 426, 504, **507–9**, 515, 517, 518, 520, 580, 581, 725 (biog.)
Catholic Enlightenment, 120–2, 125, 127
Cato, 69, 482
Cavour, Camillo di, 126
Chalut, Abbé, 487
Chamberlayne, Edward, 60
Chambers, Ephraim, 175, 180, 183
Chapelier, Isaac René Guy le, 644–5, 648
Charlemagne, 38–9, 486, 708
Charlemont, Lord, 665
Charles I, king of England, 44, 661
Charles Stuart, the Young Pretender, 46, 73
Charrière, Isabelle de (Belle Van Zuylen), 725 (biog.)
Chastellux, François Jean, marquis de, 725 (biog.)
Chateaubriand, François René, vicomte de, 700, 725 (biog.)
Châtelet, Madame du, 196
Chaumette, Nicolas, 465, 654
Chaupy, Abbé Bertrand Capmartin de, 117
Choiseul, duc de, 123

Chomel, Noël, 176
Christian VII, king of Denmark, 507
Christianity, 16, 49, 64, 82–5, 98, 99, 100, 108,
   110–43, 159, 177, 195, 204, 215–17, 223–4,
   234, 245, 251, 307, 348, 387, 588, 678; and
   French revolutionary discourse, 654, 655;
   Gibbon on, 210, 213, 214, 215–17; and
   scepticism, 82–5, 86–7, 108–9; and toleration,
   100–2, 103, 108; in Voltaire, 159, 208
church, 49, 52, 54, 105, 677
Churchill, Awnsham, 149
Churchill, John, 149
Church of England/Anglicanism, 50–4, 63,
   141–2, 253, 661–2, 668
Cicero, 69, 72, 234, 349, 405, 472
citizen/citizenship, 67–9, 97, 190, 273, 287, 288,
   372, 574, 591, 638–9, 640, 648, 690
Civil Constitution of the Clergy, 114, 119, 125,
   128, 130, 639
civilisation, 109, 164, 167, 190, 202, 205, 207,
   209, 215, 217, 227, 229, 231, 234, 236, 238,
   245
civil society, 29, 156, 193, 229, 236, 240, 274,
   280, 281, 304
Clarke, Samuel, 252, 277
Clavière, Etienne, 490, 725–6 (biog.)
Cleghorn, William, 294
Clement XI, Pope, 111
Clement XIII, Pope, 122, 123
Clement XIV, Pope, 124
Clerc, Jean Le, 195
Clerk, Sir John, 59
Clodius, 71
Cloots, Jean Baptiste Du Val-de-Grace
   (Anacharsis), Baron, 726 (biog.)
Cocceji, Heinrich von, 257, 308, 726 (biog.)
Cocceji, Samuel von, 308, 726 (biog.)
Cocks, Sir Richard, 69
Codignola, Ernesto, 126
Coke, Sir Edward, 45, 675
Colbert, Jean Baptiste, 159, 382, 384, 404, 414,
   415, 418, 422, 436, 455
Coler, Johannes, 530
Coleridge, Samuel Taylor, 686
Collins, Anthony, 81, 726 (biog.)
commerce, 14, 55, 106, 172, 430, **457–64**, 660,
   665; in Burke, 677; in Diderot, 201; and
   Encyclopédie, 176, 194; in Fénelon, 384, 385;
   Fletcher on, 58; and French Revolution, 639,
   640, 641; in Gibbon, 211; in Godwin, 683;
   and grain trade, 420, 421, 425, 426, 427, 435,
   436; in Herder, 169; in Hume, 164, 165; in
   Kames, 305; in Melon, 410, 411; in
   Montesquieu, 13, 31–2, 155, 158, 407, 408; in

Paine, 685; and physiocracy, 427, 429, 441; and
   publication, 172–5, 180, 181, 182, 185, 187;
   after Revolution of 1688, 66; in Smith, 148,
   170, 308, 313, 447, 455; in Voltaire, 21, 159;
   see also economy; international system;
   mercantile system
Committee of Public Safety, 652, 653–4, 709
comparative method, **147–51**, 238
Comte, Auguste, 203, 709
Condillac, Etienne Bonnot de, 88, 141, 220, 221,
   236, 237, 241, 243, 693, 696, 701, 705, 726
   (biog.)
Condorcet, Marie Jean Antoine Nicolas de
   Caritat, marquis de, 79, 90–2, 109, 202, 429,
   436, 437, 456, 466, 468, 641, 648–9, 688, 691,
   692, 693, 694, 699, 703, 708, 727 (biog.)
Congress of Vienna, 247
Conring, Hermann, 256
consent, 190, 347, 348, 349, 350–3, 356, 357,
   362, 364, 365, 367, 368, 372, 373, 374, 591,
   602, 607, 608, 617, 671, 672, 673
Constant, Benjamin, 30, 579
Constantine, Emperor, 213–14, 216
constitution, 115–16, 129, **151–9**, 271, 514, 515,
   584, 589, 590, 594, 626–7, 630, 631–2, 637,
   675–6, 688; *see also* government(s)
constitution, English, 19–21, 40, 41, 70, 73, 74,
   76, 77, 78, 156, **317–46**, 577, 580, 601–7,
   610–11, 612, 623, 635, 662, 664; ancient, 47,
   49, 70, 75, 661, 667; as balanced, 76, **324–31**,
   332, 336, 337–9, 515, 603, 665; checks in, 318,
   332, 333, 336; and common law, 341, 342,
   346; as mixed, **318–20**, 324, 331, 336, 603, 665
constitution, United States, 74, 105, 602, **610–20**,
   624
contract, 47, 49, 53, 56, 190, 229, 255, 270, 272,
   273, 274, 275, 276, 278, 286, 287, 288, 298,
   301, 308, 319, **347–75**, 478, 554, 574, 593, 594,
   595, 597, 602, 603, 627, 639, 672–3, 674, 688,
   698
Cooper, Anthony Ashley, *see* Shaftesbury,
   Anthony Ashley Cooper, third earl of
Copernicus, Nicolaus, 223
Corneille, Thomas, 176
Cornwallis, Lord, 440
Corsini, Neri Maria, Cardinal, 122
Costa, Uriel da, 86
Coste, Pierre, 88
Council of Constance, 111
Counter-Enlightenment, **218–22**, 243
Counter-Reformation, 80
Country platform, 64–70, 71, 72, 74, 327, 330,
   605, 664
Court, Antoine, 96

Coxe, Tench, 727 (biog.)
Craig, John, 686
Crèvecoeur, Michel Guillaume Jean de, 727 (biog.)
Croce, Benedetto, 219
Cromartie, earl of, 59
Cromwell, Oliver, 99, 163, 617
Crusades, 213, 217
Cuccagni, Luigi, 125
Cudworth, Ralph, 15, 85, 86, 101, 669
Culloden, battle of, 45, 54
culture/custom, 152, 160, 162, 170, 205, 218, 221, 222, 227, 229, 232, 234–5, 236, **238–47**, 698–9; *see also* society
Culverwell, Nathaniel, 253
Cumberland, Richard, 233, 234, 238, 241, 252, 727–8 (biog.)
Cuvier, Baron Georges, 694

Dalrymple, Sir John, 311–12, 313, 728 (biog.)
Damilaville, Etienne, 194
Dann, Jakob Heinrich, 137
Daries, Joachim Georg, 277, 728 (biog.)
Daubenton, Louis Jean Marie, 186, 235, 244
Daubenton, Pierre, 186
Davenant, Charles, 65, 488, 728 (biog.)
David, Antoine, 182
David, Israelite king, 85, 354, 355
Davie, George, 706
debt, public, 66, 326, 458–9, 468, 482, 488, 489, 490, 493, 604, 605
Declaration of the Liberties of the Gallican Church, 110, 111, 116, 117
Declaration of the Rights of Man and of the Citizen, 194, 492, 632, **633–9**, 656, 690
Declaratory Act of 1720, 56
Defoe, Daniel, 40, 59, 61, 66, 73, 728 (biog.)
Degola, Eustachio, 126
deism, 63, 83, 85, 86–7, 195, 203, 681; *see also* God; religion
Delolme, Jean Louis, 317, 336–9, 342–3, 635, 728–9 (biog.)
De Luca, I., 545
democracy, 154, 164, 274, 275, 318, 319, 330, 331, 337, 338, 576, 578, 584, 585, 586, 587, 590, 603, 604, 611, 617, 635, 640, 642, 648, 689, 690, 704; *see also* representation; republic/republicanism
Democritus, 706
Denina, Carlo, 221
Denne, Samuel, 568
Derathé, Robert, 219
Desaguliers, John, 41

Desbrulous, Jacques Savary, 176
Descartes, René/Cartesianism, 20, 173, 174, 189, 195, 200, 206, 219, 225, 226, 230, 235, 501, 506, 701, 706
Deschamps, Léger Marie, 480, 729 (biog.)
Desmoulins, Lucie Camille Simplice, 656, 729 (biog.)
despotism, 24, 25, 26, 28, 31, 36–7, 38, 41, 115, 151, 153–4, 155, 160, 163, 288, 334, 432, 433, 434, 436, 442, 503, **511–21**, 522, 523, 582, 590, 591, 596, 633, 635, 656, 657; *see also* absolutism; monarchy
Destutt de Tracy, Antoine Louis Claude, Comte, 692, 694, 695, 696, 700, 729 (biog.)
Devonshire, duke of, 389
Dicey, Albert, 42
Dickinson, John, 43, 440, 729–30 (biog.)
Diderot, Denis, 88, 148, 179, 201, 379, 427, 434–5, 479, 579–83, 693, 705, 730 (biog.); and Babeuf, 470; and Brucker, 175, 192, 194; and Catherine II, 507, 515, 580, 581; and Christianity, 168; on citizen, 190; on colonialism, 167; on commerce, 201; comparison in, 167–9; on corruption, 201; on despotism, 518–20, 582; and *Encyclopédie*, 173, 175, 176, 177, 179–80, 184, 186, 187, 189, 190–3, 194, 579; and Herder, 170, 221, 222; and Hobbes, 191, 192; on human nature, 168, 191, 192, 201; and Hume, 165; on justice, 190, 191; on laws, 168, 190, 191, 192, 582; on mind, 201; and Montesquieu, 167; on morality, 168–9, 189, 192; and Pufendorf, 190–1, 192, 193; and Ramsay, 179–80; and religion, 109, 168–9, 579; on representation, 581, 582; on resistance, 190; on rights, 190; and Rousseau, 189, 192, 193, 581; on social compact, 190; and Voltaire, 161, 207; and Wolff, 277
Diodati, Lorenzo, 185
Diodorus Siculus, 224
Dissent/Dissenters, 51, 53, 62, 94, 107, 140, 141, 142, 237, 660, **668–73**, 682
Dithmar, Justus Christoph, 532, 533, 534–5, 730 (biog.)
Dobbs, Francis, 730 (biog.)
Dobruška, Moses (Franz Thomas von Schönfeld; Junius Frey), 479
Dodwell, Henry, 51
Domat, Jean, 471
Doria, Paolo Mattia, 730 (biog.)
Drayton, William, 731 (biog.)
Dreitzel, H., 538
Drennan, William, 731 (biog.)
Dubos, Abbé Jean-Baptiste, 12–13, 26, 34–5, 36, 238, 731 (biog.)

Ducange, Charles, 12
Duchesne, André, 12
Duhamel de Monceau, Henri Louis, 423
Dulaney, Daniel, 731 (biog.)
Dumarsais, César Chesneau, 731–2 (biog.)
Dumont, Etienne, 691
Duni, Emanuele, 229
Dupac de Bellegarde, 124, 130
Dupont de Nemours, Pierre Samuel, 426, 429,
    436, 437, 440, 732 (biog.)
Durand, Laurent, 182
Durkheim, Emile, 152
Du Tillot, Guglielmo, 511
Dyche, Thomas, 175

Earberry, Matthias, 51
Eaton, Daniel Isaac, 686, 732 (biog.)
Eberhard Ludwig, duke of Württemberg, 135,
    137
economy, 58, 59, 60, 68, 106, 107, 155, 157, 177,
    236, 379, 386, 393–4, 397, 398, 401, 402, 403,
    404, 410–12, 414, 415, 417, 431, 540, 543, 558,
    561, 583, 639, 660, 677, 678, 683, 684–7, 702,
    703; and cameralism, **530–7**, 544; in Fénelon,
    383, 385, 386; and luxury, 380, 381, 382;
    Mandeville on, 387, 389, 393–4; Montesquieu
    on, 406, 407; in physiocracy, 419–20, 421, 422,
    423, 424, 431; see also cameralism; commerce
Edelman, Johann, 84
Eden, Sir Frederick Morton, 732 (biog.)
Eden, William, Lord Auckland, 567, 571–2, 732
    (biog.)
Edict of Nantes, Revocation of, 92, 93, 107, 140,
    254, 354, 501, 701
Edict of Toleration (France), 94
education, 200–1, 212, 368, 369, 460, 461, 462,
    575, 582, 597, 641–3, 692, 693–4, 696, 705; see
    also knowledge
Edward I, king of England, 612
Edward II, king of England, 43
Eglantine, Fabre d', 655
Eidous, Antoine, 186
Eilschov, Friedrich Christian, 278
Elizabeth I, queen of England, 71
Elliot, Gilbert, 567
empire/colonialism, 47, 108, 147, 159, 160,
    166–7, 169, 170, 459, 468, 484, 638, 660, 664,
    665
empiricism, 81, 88, 90, 91, 141, 162, 173, 174,
    280, 281, 282, 283, 675; see also reason;
    science
Encyclopedia Britannica, 150, 183–4
Encyclopédie, 93, 149, 150, 166, 172–5, 221,
    359–60, 379, 499–500, 502, 579, 694
Engels, Friedrich, 709

England, 13, 14, 18, 22, 31–2, 54–7, 107–8, 142,
    157, 160, 164, 165, 423–4, 456, 488, 501; see
    also constitution, English; parliament, English
English, George Bethune, 82
Epicurus, 195
equality, 28, 56, 63, 229, 272, 278, 287, 288, 323,
    366–7, 381, 406, 426, 485, 573, 575, 579, 590,
    592, 603, 627, 641, 642, 643, 650, 683, 695
Erasmianism, 100, 101
Erastianism, 52
Esprit, Jacques, 399
Establishments of St Louis, 34
Estates General, 22, 115, 116, 626–7, 628–9, 631,
    636, 690; Third Estate, 628, 629, 631
Eugen, Duke Karl, 135, 137, 138
Europe, 147–8, 165, 166, 167, 168, 170, 209, 212,
    409
Evans, Caleb, 140, 141
executive/executive power, 42, 64, 65, 74, 77,
    288, 325, 326, 329, 331, 332–3, 335, 337–8,
    575, 606, 617, 634, 635, 637, 665; see also
    monarchy
Eybel, Joseph Valéntin, 732–3 (biog.)

Fabricius, J. A., 79
Fare, Etienne de la, 117
Fauchet, François Claude, 733 (biog.)
Faucher, François Xavier de, 131
Febronius, see Hontheim, Johann Nikolaus von
    (Justinius Febronius)/Febronianism
Feder, J. G. H., 267
Feijóo y Montenegro, Benito Jerónimo, 127, 733
    (biog.)
Feller, François Xavier de, 131
Fénelon, François de Salignac de la Mothe,
    10–12, 20, 38, 46, 73, 93, 134, 382, 388, 389,
    391, 392, 403, 404, 405, 406, 407, 413, 414,
    417, 474–5, 733 (biog.)
Ferdinand, duke of Parma, 123
Ferguson, Adam, 148, 165, 219, 221, 236,
    239–40, 241, 243, 246, 314, 445, 446, 447, 457,
    459, 460, 461, 462, 463, 706, 733–4 (biog.)
Fernando VII, king of Spain, 128
feudalism, 28, 58, 158, 245, 274, 275, 305, 311,
    313, 468, 591, 632–3, 641, 677, 707
Fichte, Johann Gottlieb, 247, 279, 282, 592–6,
    734 (biog.)
Fielding, Henry, 41, 71, 734 (biog.)
Filangieri, Gaetano, 439, 734 (biog.)
Filleau, Jean, 112, 128, 131
Filmer, Sir Robert, 42, 45, 46, 72, 359, 661, 670
Finetti, Germano Federigo, 224–5, 230
Firmian, Count Leopold, 511
Fischer, Christoph, 530
Fletcher, Andrew, 57–9, 734 (biog.)
Fleury, Abbé Claude, 385, 474

Fleury, Cardinal André Hercule de, 112, 117
Flood, Henry, 665, 735 (biog.)
Follini, Abbate Bartolomeo, 124
Fonseca Pimental, Eleanora, 735 (biog.)
Fontenelle, Bernard le Bovier de, 178, 190, 202, 205, 735 (biog.)
Forbes, Duncan, 706
Forbonnais, François Véron Duverger de, 379, 425, 439, 542, 544, 735 (biog.)
Fordyce, David, 294, 735–6 (biog.)
Formey, Jean Henri Samuel, 277, 736 (biog.)
Forster, J. R., 148
Foucault, Michel, 2, 692, 693, 703, 706
Fourier, Charles, 203
France, 32, 41, 54, 98, **110–19**, 123, 156, 160, 161, 163, 164, 165, 170, 334, 424, 430, 486–7, 488, 603
Francis, Philip, 441
Francis I, 11
Franke, August Hermann, 101, 132, 137, 138, 268, 736 (biog.)
Franklin, Benjamin, 91, 440, 736 (biog.)
Frederick, prince of Wales, 71
Frederick I, king of Prussia, 137, 504
Frederick II, king of Prussia, 138, 170, 246, 257, 415–16, 503, 504–7, 509, 513–14, 519, 522, 538, 591, 736–7 (biog.)
Frederick II, landgrave of Hesse-Cassel, 258
Frederick William I, 137, 504, 506, 507, 526, 533
Frederick William II, 246
freedom, 38, 41, 46, 49, 50, 51, 55, 56, 57, 62–4, 67, 68, 69, 75–6, 190, 194, 228, 254, 255, 281, 305, 353, 374, 386, 430, 475–6, 565, 569–70, 594, 597, 606, 612, 617, 663, 669, 670, 671–2, 681, 705; in Beccaria, 552, 555, 556; Blackstone on, 318, 321, 322, 324; Bolingbroke on, 327; and common law, 341, 342, 344; Delolme on, 339–40; and English constitution, 317–18, 324, 327, 602, 603; Fichte on, 247, 592–3; and French revolutionary discourse, 639–40, 641, 645, 654; Herder on, 245, 246; Hume on, 163–4; in Kant, 247, 282–3, 285, 286, 287, 288, 289, 371, 591; Montesquieu on, 18–19, 25, 26, 28–9, 31, 36, 38, 156, 157, 158, 331, 333, 334, 548–9, 550, 551, 569; in Rousseau, 255, 364–5, 368–9, 576; Smith on, 449; Voltaire on, 21; Wolff on, 269, 270, 272, 276; *see also* right(s)
French Constituent Assembly, 637, 638, 639, 640
French Constitution of 1791, 640, 643, 646
French Constitution of 1795, 695
French Directory, 693, 696
French Legislative Assembly, 646–7, 648, 694
French National Assembly, 119, 125, 468, 631–3, 636, 637, 643, 648, 690, 691, 696, 702

French National Convention, 647, 648, 649, 650, 652, 654, 657, 693, 694, 701
French political clubs, 644, 645, 646
French Revolution, 60, 105, 114, 125, 126, 128, 138, 142, 155, 188, 194, 217, 246, 271, 466, 522, 587, 589, 591, 592, 593, 596, 615, **626–47**, 660, 667, **673–83**, 688, 690, 702, 704–5, 708
Frey, Junius, *see* Dobruška, Moses (Franz Thomas von Schönfeld; Junius Frey)
Furetière, Antoine, 176
Furneaux, Philip, 737 (biog.)
Fürstenau, C. G., 535

Galiani, Ferdinando, 229, 379, 419, 426–7, 428, 435–6, 439, 441, 442, 737 (biog.)
Galileo, 223, 226
Gallicanism, 110, 111, 113, 114, 116, 118, 119, 120, 121, 125, 126, 129, 130, 131, 142
Garat, Dominique-Joseph Gassendi, 691, 692, 693
Garve, Christian, 737 (biog.)
Gassendi, Pierre, 222, 360
Gasser, Simon Peter, 531, 532–3
Gatterer, Johann Christoph, 148, 149
Gaveston, Piers, 71
Gay, John, 71
Gazzaniga, Pietro Maria, 129
Gébelin, Antoine Court de, 232–3, 243
Geneva, 583, 584–7
Genovesi, Antonio, 229, 439, 737 (biog.)
Gentile, Giovanni, 219
George II, king of England, 73, 504
George III, king of England, 73, 140, 142
Gerdil, Giacinto Sigismondi, 737–8 (biog.)
Gergy, Languet de, 117
German Enlightenment, 525, 545
Germanus, Moses, 84
Germany/Germanic nations, 35–6, 94–5, **132–9**, 220, **251–90**, 502
Gerson, Jean, 113
Gessner, Salomon, 480
Giannone, Pietro, 101, 221, 738 (biog.)
Giarrizzo, Giuseppe, 218
Gibbon, Edward, 148, **210–17**, 221, 738 (biog.)
Gibson, Edmund, 53
Girard, Gabriel, 175, 190
Girondins, 643, 647, 648–9, 650
Gobel, Jean Baptiste, 655
God, 45, 142, 195, 197, 203, 204, 228, 234, 251, 252, 261, 263, 264, 265, 270, 273, 296, 297–8, 299, 301, 306, 307, 310, 471
Godwin, William, 467, 566, 670, 676, 681–3, 702, 738 (biog.)
Goethe, Johann Wolfgang von, 139, 198, 220, 244

Goeze, Johann Melchior, 96
Goguet, Antoine Yves, 221, 225, 240, 241, 738
  (biog.)
Goldsmith, Oliver, 198
Gorani, Giuseppe, 520, 739 (biog.)
Gordon, Thomas, 604, 739 (biog.); *Cato's Letters*,
  49, 66, 69, 326
Gordon Riots of 1780, 108
Gouges, Marie Olympe de, 638, 739 (biog.)
Gournay, Vincent de, 422, 739 (biog.)
Goussier, Louis, 186
government(s), 40, 47, 76–7, 163–4, 191, 207,
  212, 219, 274–6, 287, 289, 298–9, 301, 303,
  305–6, 308, 310, 340, 429, 431, 433, 437, 457,
  458–9, 472–3, 474, 670, 671, 673; as agency of
  the people, 622, 623, 624; balanced powers of,
  606, 623–4; checks and balances in, 332, 623,
  635, 648; and constitution, 610–11; and
  English constitution, 317; and French
  revolutionary discourse, 631, 634, 635, 648;
  mixed, **318–20**, 324, 331, 336, 578, 584, 603,
  611, 623, 624; Montesquieu on, 13, 26, 35–6,
  37, 151, 152, 153–7, 202, 204, **331–7**;
  Rousseau on, 575–7; separate powers of, 74,
  290, 515, 548, 549, 590, 591, 623, 631, 633,
  634, 692; and United States Constitution
  (1787), **616–20**; *see also* constitution; *specific
  forms of government*
Gracchus, Tiberius and Caius, 482–4
Grattan, Henry, 665, 740 (biog.)
Gravina, Gian Vincenzo, 219, 231, 740 (biog.)
Gray, Thomas, 198
Grayson, William, 621
Greece, ancient, 49, 57, 58, 67, 76, 154, 209, 227,
  241, 245, 362–3, 366, 367, 415, 481, 575, 577,
  578, 585, 595, 603, 640, 643, 697
Green, T. H., 351, 352
Grégoire, Abbé Henri Baptiste, 99, 105, 125,
  740 (biog.)
Grimaldi, Francesco Antonio, 740 (biog.)
Grimm, Friedrich Melchior Baron von, 518,
  519, 520, 740 (biog.)
Grolman, Ludwig von, 138
Grotius, Hugo, 45, 101, 140, 220, 225, 227, 257,
  258, 270, 271, 277, 291, 292, 296, 297, 300,
  302, 304, 308, 315, 351, 480, 492
Grove, Henry, 405
Gundling, Nicolaus Hieronymus, 267,
  741 (biog.)
Gusdorf, Georges, 237
Gustav III, king of Sweden, 258, 507, 741 (biog.)
Guyon, Madame, 134

habeas corpus, 602, 612
Habermas, Jürgen, 179

Haën, Anton de, 130
Hakluyt, Richard, 149
Hale, Sir Matthew, 341, 675
Haller, Albrecht von, 705
Hamann, Johann Georg, 87, 139, 169, 220, 741
  (biog.)
Hamburg, decree of 1785, 94
Hamilton, Alexander, 688, 741 (biog.)
Hampden, John, 647
Handel, George Frederick, 71, 73
Hanover, House of, 65, 72, 319–20, 330, 605
Hanway, Jonas, 568
Hardouin, Jean, 207
Harley, Robert, 40
Harrington, James, 47, 50, 67, 73, 76, 473, 489,
  490, 684
Harris, James, 243
Harris, John, 175
Hartley, David, 660
Hausväterliteratur, 530, 534
Haydn, Joseph, 130
Hays, Mary, 741 (biog.)
Hazard, Paul, 2
Hazlitt, William, 686
Hedinger, Johann Reinhard, 135
Hegel, G. W. F., 9, 13, 103, 219, 348, 360, 361,
  372, 374, 375, 690, 703
Heiberg, Peter Andreas, 741–2 (biog.)
Heineccius, Johann Gottlieb, 267, 742 (biog.)
Helvétius, Claude Adrien, 109, 179, 200–1, 202,
  470, 479, 491–2, 503, 588, 701, 702, 705,
  742 (biog.)
Henry III, king of England, 612
Henry IV, king of France, 22, 207, 209, 414,
  482
Henry VII, king of England, 75
Henry VIII, king of England, 75
Herder, Johann Gottfried von, 148, 152, 169–70,
  218, 219, 220–2, 226–7, 232, 233, 234, 235,
  237–8, **240–6**, 503, 523, 690, 742 (biog.)
Hering, Christoph, 530
Herrenschwand, Jean Frédéric, 490, 742
  (biog.)
Hersche, Peter, 130
Hervey, Lord, 75
Heumann, C. A., 267
Heydenreich, Karl Heinrich, 279
Hickes, George, 51
Hippel, Theodor Gottlieb von, 743 (biog.)
Hippocrates, 238
history, **9–18**, 25, 28, 30, 32, 34–9, 69, 84, 152,
  159, 164, 201, 203–6, **206–10**, 217, **221–2**,
  228–9, 230, **231–8**, **240–6**, 267, 280, 304, 305,
  310, 681
Hoadley, Benjamin, 47, 48, 52, 75, 743 (biog.)

Hobbes, Thomas, 23, 24, 29, 42, 45, 52, 77, 80, 83, 87, 109, 191, 192, 193, 220, 224, 233, 234, 251, 252, 253, 263, 265, 271, 292, 302, 308, 347, 350, 354, 355, 359, 360, 361, 365, 370, 374, 390, 399, 405, 478, 479, 480, 491, 497–8, 513, 523, 524, 576, 675, 678, 689

Hoffman, Leopold, 131

Hogarth, William, 71

Hohberg, Wolf Helmhard von, 530

Holbach, Paul Henri Dietrich, baron d', 42, 81, 109, 175, 184, 186, 194, 202, 222, 506, 705, 743 (biog.)

Holberg, Ludwig, 267

Hollis, Thomas, 664, 743–4 (biog.)

Holy Roman Empire, 256–7, 258

Home, Henry, Lord Kames, *see* Kames, Henry Home, Lord

Homer, 238, 383, 474

Hontheim, Johann Nikolaus von (Justinius Febronius)/Febronianism, 128, 131, 142, 744 (biog.)

Hooke, Nathaniel, 483–4, 744 (biog.)

Hooker, Richard, 253, 665

Höpfner, L. J. F., 276

Hopkins, Stephen, 744 (biog.)

Horace, 72

Horne, George, 142, 744 (biog.)

Horsley, Samuel, 142, 744–5 (biog.)

Hotman, François, 12, 13

Hourwitz, Zalkind, 82

Howard, John, 567–8, 745 (biog.)

Huet, Pierre Daniel, 79, 80, 88

Huguenots, 92, 94, 96, 98–9, 137, 140, 254, 354, 701

human nature, 77, 109, 160, 177, 211, 218, 227, 231–2, **232**, 235–6, **238**, 239, 264, 270, 280, 281, 292, 358, 363, 371, 393–5, 471, 476, 477, 478, 479, 480, 492, 657, 658, 673, 700, 705; in Bayle, 206; in Berkeley, 401–2; in Bonnet, **235**; in Bossuet, 354; in Buffon, **235**; in Diderot, 168, 192, 201; in Fénelon, 387; in Ferguson, **239–40**, 243; in Gibbon, 211; in Helvétius, 200, 201; in Herder, 169, 234, **240**; in Hobbes, 191, 192; in Hume, 156, 161–2; in Hutcheson, 301, 399–401; in Kames, 306; in Kant, 371; in La Mettrie, 235–6; in Leibniz, 260; in Mandeville, 391, 392, 393–5; in Montesquieu, 156, 211, **238**, 405; in Morelly, 472; in physiocracy, 430; in Pufendorf, 191, 260; in Quesnay, 430; in Rousseau, 192, 193, 363, 477, 480, 574, 588; in Shaftesbury, 395–9; in Smith, 193; in Vico, 229, **240**; in Volney, 698; in Voltaire, 159, 209, 211, 417; in Wolff, 270; *see also* civilisation; culture/custom

Humboldt, Karl Wilhelm von, 198, 596–7, 745 (biog.)

Hume, David, 41, 49, 77, 78, 88, 89, 90, 148, 150, 205, 236, 238–9, 253, 282, 328–30, 361, 375, 457, 490, 504, 619, 660, 666, 675, 677, 686, 706, 745 (biog.); comparison in, 161–5; on constitution, 319, 320, 330; on contract, 355–6, 357, 358, 374; on freedom, 163–4; on government, 162, 163–4, 303, 356–7; and Grotius, 302, 304; and Herder, 170, 221, 241; on history, 164; on human nature, 161–2, 302; on justice, 164, 302, 304; and Kames, 306, 307; and Kant, 587, 588; and Locke, 303, 355–6, 358; on monarchy, 163; and Montesquieu, 152, 155, 156, 157, 161, 164, 165, 205; on natural rights, 292, 293, 294, 302–4; on property, 163, 164, 302, 303; on religion, 84, 87, 152, 155; on scepticism, 79, 91, 205, 302–4; and Smith, 308, 309, 445, 449, 457, 458, 459, 460, 462, 463; on utility, 304, 357, 358; and Voltaire, 152, 161, 162, 180

Hunton, Philip, 43

Hus, Jan, 97

Hutcheson, Francis, 141, 253, 256, 291, 292, 293, 299–302, 304, 306, 308, 309, 399–401, 445, 446, 706, 745–6 (biog.)

Hutchinson, John, 661

Hutchinson, Thomas, 746 (biog.)

Ickstatt, Johann Adam von, 136, 746 (biog.)

Ickstatt, Peter Josef, 136

idéologues, 692, 694, **695–701**, 705–6, 707, 708

individual, 38, 201, 281, 321, 364, 367, 574, 668, 669, 672, 675

Inglis, Charles, 746 (biog.)

Innocent X, Pope, 110

Institut national des sciences et des arts, 693, 694, 695, 697; *Classe des sciences morales et politiques*, 694, 695, 696–7, 698, 699

international system, 489, 490; *see also* commerce

Iredell, James, 615–16, 746 (biog.)

Ireland, 50, 54–7, 95, 108, 664–5

Irish parliament, 55, 56

Iselin, Isaak, 241, 747 (biog.)

Italy, 119, 120–2, 123, 124, 129, 438, 439

Jacobins, 126, 202, 645, 649–50, 692

Jacobites, 42, 45–7, 54, 59, 70, 72, 73, 488; *see also* Stuart, House of

Jacquelot, Isaac, 195

Jäger, Johann Wolfgang, 134

James I, king of England, 46

James II, king of England, 40, 43, 44, 45, 46, 57, 320

Jansen, Cornelius, 111

Jansenism, **111–16**, 117, 118, 119, 120, 121, 122, 123, **124–31**, 133–4, 136, 138, 140, 141, 142, 143, 471, 476, 477
Jaucourt, Louis, chevalier de, 93, 184, 186, 187, 193, 359–60, 579, 584, 747 (biog.)
Jay, John, 688, 747 (biog.)
Jebb, John, 568, 667, 747 (biog.)
Jefferson, Thomas, 56, 91, 105, 440, 487, 492, 614, 620, 695, 747–8 (biog.)
Jennens, Charles, 73
Jenyns, Soame, 666, 748 (biog.)
Jews/Judaism, 16, 80, 81–5, 86, 99, 161, 204, 207, 208, 216, 228, 594, 638
John, king of England, 612
Johnson, Samuel, 198, 748 (biog.)
Jones, Sir William, 748 (biog.)
Jones, William, 142
José I, king of Portugal, 122
Joseph II, emperor of Austria, 94, 95, 100, 120, 126, 130, 131, 137, 246, 257, 433, 503, 504, 507, 509–10, 515, 516, 517, 521, 556, 748–9 (biog.)
Jovellanos, Gaspar Melchior de, 127, 128, 129, 749 (biog.)
judicial power/judiciary, 74, 325, **332–6**, 342, 606, 615–16, 617, 634, 647
Julian the Apostate, 212–13
Julius Caesar, 69, 483
Jurieu, Pierre, 87, 92–3, 140, 254, 354, 749 (biog.)
jury, system of, 334, 340, 342, 343, 602, 667
Justi, Johann Heinrich Gottlob von, 131, 152, 508, 526, 536, **537–41**, 543, 545, 749 (biog.)
justice, 36, 164, 190, 191, 192, 209, 302, 304, 306–7, 308, 312, 315, 371, 448, 457, 461, 464, 467, 493, 497, 550, 552, 556, 575, 626–7, 628, 631, 634
Justinian, 16, 103

Kaiser, Gerhard, 139
Kames, Henry Home, Lord, 236, 244, 292, 293, 294, 304–7, 310, 311–12, 313, 315, 445, 446, 750 (biog.)
Kant, Immanuel, 84, 95, 103, 132, 198, 199, 220, 226, 233, 237, 244, 246, 247, 253, 257, 266, **279–90**, 347, 352, 364, 369–73, 503, 553, 556–7, 587–92, 594, 595, 750 (biog.)
Karl Alexander, duke of Württemberg, 135
Karl Eugen, duke of Württemberg, 135, 137, 138
Kaunitz, Prince, 107
Kentish petition, 61–2
Killiecrankie, battle of, 54
King, William, 45, 750 (biog.)
Klein, Ernst Ferdinand, 258

knowledge, 174, 175, 176, 177, 178, 184, 185, 188, 189, 200, 202, 203, 231, 262, 266, 269, 642; *see also* education; mind
Knox, William, 750 (biog.)

labour, 48, 288, 385–6, 401, 430, 451–2, 460, 461, 468, 478, 555, 556, 566, 568, 570, 591, 595, 639, 643, 683
La Bruyere, Jean de, 159
Lacratelle, Pierre Louis, 691, 692, 693
Lafayette, marquis de, 93, 99, 690
Lafitau, Joseph François, 150, 238, 698
Lambert, Johann Heinrich, 227
Lamennais, Hughes Félicité de, 119
La Mettrie, Julien Offray de, 235–6, 705, 751 (biog.)
Lami, Giovanni, 122, 124, 125
landowners, 421, 422, 423, 429, 431, 432, 433, 437–8, 462–3, 466; *see also* agrarian policy; property
Lange, Joachim, 133, 268
language, 174, 176, 177, 200, 231–2, 236, 242, 243, 244, 262
Lanjuinais, Joseph, 503, 504, 751 (biog.)
La Rochefoucauld, François de, 20, 77, 380, 399
Lauderdale, Lord, 685, 686
Launay, Abbé Le Corgne de, 117
Laverdy, Clément Charles François de, 420
Law, John, 32, 33, 177, 403, 404, 406, 409, 422, 488, 489, 751 (biog.)
Law, William, 51, 291, 296, 297, 751–2 (biog.)
law(s), 56, 160, 163, 164, 168, 192, 200, 201, 211, 220, 229, 256–7, 259, 269, 271, 273, 293, 311–12, 366, 386, 387, 432, 582, 594, 615, 616, 633, 634, 674, 675; and Catherine II, 508; common, 31, 335, **340–6**; and constitutionalism, 612–16; criminal, **547**; Diderot on, 581, 582; and Holy Roman Empire, 256–7; Kames on, 305–6; Kant on, 283, 370–1, 372, 373; Montesquieu on, 9–10, 13, 17–18, **26–31**, 32, 34–8, 151, 156–7, 158, 204, 331, 557, 560, 561, 562, 563, 565, 566, 571; Roman, 17–18, 25, 34, 256, 258, 259, 304, 315, 341; Rousseau on, 192, 193, 219, 577; Thomasius on, 263–4, 265, 266, 267; *see also* legislation/legislator; natural law
learned societies, 176, 177–9, 186
Le Breton, André François, 175, 180, 182, 183, 184
Le Clerc, Jean (Joannes Clericus), 752 (biog.)
Lee, Arthur, 752 (biog.)
Lee, Richard Henry, 752 (biog.)
legislation/legislator, 9, 28, 29, 74, 289, 322, 323, 325, 326, 332–3, 335, 339, 367, 368, 447, 448, 449–50, 455, 456, **457–63**, 484, 485, 515, 575,

606–7, 613–14, 616, 617, 634, 635, 636, 649, 653, 664–5; *see also parlement(s)*; parliament, English; representation
Leibniz, Gottfried Wilhelm von, 12, 23–4, 101, 189, 195, 196, 197–8, 222, 252, 253, 255, 259, 260, 263, 269, 280, 281, 283, 360, 361, 369–70, 498, 506, 587, 752 (biog.)
Le Mercier de la Rivière, Pierre Paul, 426, 429, 434, 435, 436, 517, 753 (biog.)
Le Monnier, Louis, 186
Lenglet-Dufresnoy, Nicolas, 151, 161
Leopold II, Emperor, 119, 125, 126, 127, 129, 137, 246, 257, 439, 507, 510, 515, 520, 521, 522, 556, 753 (biog.)
Le Paige, Louis Adrien, 93, 123, 136, 753 (biog.)
Lepelletier, Michel, 643
Leslie, Charles, 46, 47, 48, 51, 61–2, 753 (biog.)
Lessing, Gotthold Ephraim, 132, 753–4 (biog.)
Le Trosne, Guillaume François, 432, 434, 436, 754 (biog.)
Lévesque, Pierre Charles, 697
Lévesque de Pouilly, Louis Jean, 207
Levi, David, 83
Lichtenburg, Georg Christoph, 222
Lilburne, John, 663
Limborch, Philip van, 86
Lindsay, Theophilus, 668
Linguet, Simon Nicolas Henri, 117, 152, 467, 520–1
Lisbon earthquake, 197, 198, 199
Livy, 69, 213
Locke, John, 20, 43, 45, 47–50, 52, 54, 68, 75, 88, 93, 142, 191, 203, 236, 266, 298, 315, 324, 347, 350–3, 356, 359–60, 361, 385–6, 391, 593, 660, 664, 705, 754 (biog.); and *Encyclopédie*, 173–4, 189, 359; and Hume, 358; influences/relations, 46, 52, 56, 57, 61, 73, 81, 105–6, 141, 201, 203, 220, 221, 228, 255, 284, 297, 298, 303, 315, 323, 351, 352, 355–6, 358, 359–60, 361, 362, 369, 374, 382, 385, 493, 501, 591, 702; on mind, 228; on natural law, 355–6; on natural rights, 291, 292; on religion, 92, 93, 97, 100, 102, 104, 105–6; on senses, 174, 200, 203
Louis, St, king of France, 11
Louis XIV, king of France, 10, 95, 96, 110, 111, 112, 116, 135, 153–4, 159, 209, 354, 382, 403, 415, 701
Louis XV, king of France, 181, 207, 519
Louis XVI, king of France, 87, 92, 118, 246, 494, 503, 626, 631, 637, 643, 645, 646–7
Lower, Richard, 233
Lowth, Robert, 662
Luc, Jean André de, 226
Lucas, Charles, 754–5 (biog.)
Lucas, Jean Maximilien, 85

Lucretius, 224, 226, 228, 242, 706
Ludewig, Johann Peter von, 267, 533
Ludlow, John, 67
Luther, Martin, 132, 209
Lutheran Church, 137, 138, 258
Lutheranism, 103, 132, 134, 135, 137, 138, 253, 261, 262, 268, 273
luxury, 11, 37, 76, 77, **379–418**, 422, 453–4, 478, 574
Luzac, Elie, 278, 755 (biog.)
Lycurgus, 49, 68, 369

Mably, Abbé Gabriel Bonnot de, 433, 470, 479, **481–7**, 491, 492, 577–9, 627, 628, 755 (biog.)
Macaulay (Graham), Catherine, 73, 755 (biog.)
McCulloch, John Ramsay, 443
Macfarquhar, Colin, 183
Machiavelli, Niccolò, 33, 67, 68, 73, 77, 221, 416, 481, 505, 529, 656
Mackenzie, Sir George, 381
Mackintosh, Sir James, 494, 661, 680, 755 (biog.)
Mackworth, Sir Humphrey, 62, 325, 756 (biog.)
Madan, Michael, 563, 564, 565, 571
Madison, James, 56, 333, 440, 492, 614, 617, 618–20, 623, 624, 688, 756 (biog.)
Maffei, Francesco Scipione, 756 (biog.)
Magna Carta, 75, 602, 612
Maimbourg, Louis, 214
Maimonides, Moses, 83
Mair (Major), John, 113
Maistre, Joseph Marie, comte de, 87, 119, 700, 756 (biog.)
Malcolm III, king of Scotland, 311
Malebranche, Nicolas, 20, 189, 192, 359, 360, 361, 471
Malesherbes, Guillaume Chrétien de Lamoignon de, 93, 106, 179, 180–1, 757 (biog.)
Mallet, David, 71
Malthus, Thomas, 757 (biog.)
Malves, Abbé Gua de, 180
Mamachi, Tommaso Maria, 124, 125
Mandeville, Bernard (de), 32, 109, 382, 383, **387–95**, 396, 398, 399, 400, 401–2, 403, 416–17, 757 (biog.)
Manley, Mary Delariviere, 73, 757–8 (biog.)
Mansfield, William Murray, earl of, 758 (biog.)
manufacture, 165, 384, 385, 429, 431, 436, 437, 447, 455, 544
Marat, Jean Paul, 643, 645, 646, 758 (biog.)
Marcus Aurelius, 499, 505
Mare, Paolo Marcello del, 125
Maria Theresa, empress of Austria, 119, 129, 130, 503, 506, 511, 516, 517
Marius, 483
Markham, William, 662

Marmontel, Jean François, 102, 509, 758 (biog.)
Marsilius of Padua, 52, 113
Martini, Karl Anton von, 131, 257
Martini, Martin, 223
Marx, Karl, 60, 240, 444
Mary II, queen of England, 44, 320
Mas, Enrico de, 219
materialism, 63, 109, 201, 202, 235, 588, 671, 701, 706
Matsen, Nicolaus, 107
Maultrot, Gabriel Nicolas, 114, 115, 136, 140, 758 (biog.)
Maupeou, chancellor, 112, 115, 136, 582, 627
Maupertuis, Pierre-Louis Moreau de, 88, 705
Maxwell, Henry, 55
Mayhew, Jonathan, 759 (biog.)
Mazarin, Jules, Cardinal, 514
Mazzini, Giuseppi, 126
Meiners, Christoph, 235, 267
Melon, Jean François, **409–12**, 413, 414, 415, 423, 759 (biog.)
Mendelssohn, Moses, 276, 759 (biog.)
mercantile system, 446–7, 449–52, 453, 455, *see also* commerce
Mercier, Louis Sébastien, 102, 480, 510, 759 (biog.)
Mercier de la Rivière, Pierre Paul, *see* Le Mercier de la Rivière, Pierre Paul
Meslier, Jean, 579, 759 (biog.)
metaphysics, 204, 205, 237, 253, 280, 281, 283, 701
Methodism, 142
Mey, Abbé Claude, 114, 115, 136, 140, 760 (biog.)
Michels, Robert, 576
Middleton, Conyers, 69
Migazzi, Cardinal Christoph Anton, 131
military, 67, 71, 73, 76, 77, 212, 327, 330, 384, 385, 408, 415–16, 459–60, 482, 493, 602, 660
Mill, James, 184, 201, 443
Mill, John Stuart, 597, 703
Millar, John, 236, 311, 314, 445, 446, 685–6, 706, 760 (biog.)
Milton, John, 43, 47, 64, 67
mind, 200, 201, 203, 227–32, 233, 235, 236, 237–8, 270, 398; *see also* knowledge
Mirabeau, Victor Riqueti, Marquis de, 426, 432, 434, 435, 439, 468, 693, 760 (biog.)
Mirandola, Pico della, 230, 243
Molanus, Gerhard, 101
Molesworth, Robert, 56, 66, 69, 70, 299, 760 (biog.)
Molyneux, William, 55–6, 59, 664, 760–1 (biog.)

Monarchiens, 634, 635, 636
monarchy, 13, 40–1, 44, 70, 73, 76, 141, 163, 164, 254, 275, 329–30, 331, 335, 336, 337, 338, 354, 381, 383, 384, 386, 429, 431, 432–4, 437, 498, 502, 513–14, 515, 522, 523, 576, 578, 581, 582, 584, 586, 590, 594, 617, 619, 628, 676, 690; and American Revolution, 603, 605, 606, 611–12; and constitution, 318, 319, 325–6, 333, 345, 346; corruption of, 327, 605, 606; and crown-in-parliament, 41–2, 50, 62, 64, 319, 321, 323, 664; and divine right of kings, 47, 48, 141, 191, 254, 320, 354; and English constitution, 602–3; executive power of, 325, 326, 329–30, 337–8; Fénelon on, 10–12; French, 110, 111, 112, 113, 114, 115, 116, 117, 118, 176, 177, 178, 181, 627, 633, 635–7; Montesquieu on, 12, 26, 31, 33, 35, 37, 151, 153–5, 169, 405, 407, 408, 522, 523; Pufendorf on, 191; and Revolution of 1688, 40–2, 320; Spanish, 127–9; Voltaire on, 19; *see also* absolutism; despotism; executive/executive power; sovereign/ruler; tyranny
Monboddo, James Burnett, Lord, 221, 243, 244, 761 (biog.)
Montagnards, 649–50
Montagu, Mary Wortley, 20
Montaigne, Michel de, 20, 153, 159, 161, 399
Montesquieu, Charles Louis de Secondat, Baron de la Brède et de, 17, 74, 148, 167, 202, 238, 358–9, 404, 414, 417, 523, 617, 618, 689, 690, 706, 761 (biog.); and Anquetil-Duperron, 152; and Aristotle, 28; and Beccaria, 551–2, 553, 554; and Bentham, 557, 560, 561, 562; and Bolingbroke, 74; and Bossuet, 17, 204; and Boulainvilliers, 34, 35; and Burke, 18; and Catherine II, 508, 515; comparison in, **151–9**; and Constant, 30; and constitution, 151, 155, 156, **331–7**, 515, 602; and d'Alembert, 15; on despotism, 24, 26, 28, 31, 36–7, 38, 151, 153–4, 155, 160, 334; and Diderot, 167; and Dubos, 26, 34–5, 36; on England, 13, 18, 31–2, 40, 157; on freedom, 18–19, 25, 26, 28–9, 31, 36, 38, 156, 157, 158, 331, 333, 334, 548–9, 550, 551, 569; and Gibbon, 211, 214; and Herder, 152, 169–70, 221, 222, 241, 242, 245; history in, **9–12**, 15–18, 19, 25, 28, 30, 32, 34–9, 152, 204; and Hobbes, 29, 359, 405; and Hume, 152, 155, 156, 157, 161, 164, 165, 205; on judiciary/power of judging, 332, 333–6, 337, 342; and Justi, 152, 538; and Law, 33; on laws, 9–10, 13, 17–18, **26–31**, 32, 34–8, 151, 156–7, 158, 204, 331, 515, 548–51, 557, 560, 561, 562, 563, 565, 566, 571; and Linguet, 152; and Machiavelli, 33; and Malebranche,

359; and Mandeville, 32; and Melon, 409; monarchy in, 12, 26, 31, 33, 35, 37, 151, 153–5, 169, 405, 407, 408, 522, 523; and Morelly, 470; religion in, 16, 31, 152, 153, 155–6, 157, 159, 204; and Robertson, 205; and Romilly, 565; and Rousseau, 29, 37, 220; and Saint-Simon, 708; and Scottish theorists, 158; on separation of powers, 74, 548, 549, 576, 692; on state, 27; and Tacitus, 70; and Tocqueville, 30; and Voltaire, 9, 19, 20, 22, 25, 31, 38, 152, 155, 160, 161, 211, 515; and Williams, 490; and women, 26, 33, 37
Montijo, Condesa de, 128
morality, 68, 84, 85, 86, 98, 189, 255, 256, 295, 365, 367, 657, 677, 680, 696, 698, 699; Berkeley on, 401, 402; in Burke, 675, 677; in Diderot, 168–9, 192; and empiricism, 280, 281; in Fénelon, 384; in Fichte, 281; in Hegel, 374; in Helvétius, 200, 201; in Hobbes, 689, 690; in Holbach, 202; in Hume, 302, 303, 304; in Hutcheson, 299–302; in Kant, 282–3, 285, 286, 289, 290, 370–3, 588, 589, 590; in Leibniz, 280; in Mably, 578; and Mandeville, 390–1; in Montesquieu, 15, 158; and natural law, 251, 252; in Price, 669–70; in Rousseau, 261, 265; in Shaftesbury, 396; in Smith, 148, 308, 309, 461, 463, 464; in Thomasius, 265–6, 267; in Voltaire, 209, 417; in Wolff, 270, 271, 272, 273, 276, 280; in Wollstonecraft, 679
More, Hannah, 683, 761 (biog.)
More, Henry, 256
More, Sir Thomas, 76, 385
Morellet, Abbé André, 93, 762 (biog.)
Morelly, Etienne Gabriel, 470, 471–3, 475–6, 477–8, 479, 579, 762 (biog.)
Mornay, Philippe du Plessis, 43
Moscati, Pietro, 233, 244
Moser, Friedrich Carl von, 139, 762 (biog.)
Moser, Johann Jakob, 135–7, 138, 139, 762 (biog.)
Möser, Justus, 246, 762–3 (biog.)
Moses, 83, 225, 354, 364, 367, 368
Moshammer, F. X., 545
Mosheim, J. L. von, 101
Mothe le Vayer, François de la, 80
Mounier, Jean Joseph, 631–2, 634, 635, 763 (biog.)
Moyle, Walter, 49, 66, 67, 763 (biog.)
Mozart, Wolfgang Amadeus, 130
Münchhausen, G. A. von, 267
Muratori, Lodovico Antonio, 121–2, 125, 127, 129, 221
Murray, James, 140, 141

Napoleon Bonaparte, 129, 246, 522, 694, 696, 700, 709
Napoleonic wars, 257
nation, 152, 240, 629–30, 633, 635, 673
Native Americans, 48, 167
natural law, 48, 49, 103, 190, 192, 219, 220, 227, 246, **251–90**, 296, 297–8, 301, 303, 305–6, 307, 312, 315, 350–3, 355–6, 361–2, 480, 523, 627, 639, 684; *see also* law(s)
natural man, 168, 251, 363, 364, 366, 574, 698
natural rights, 47, 49, 73, 190, 280, 281, **291–316**, 321, 323, 365, 614, 660, 661, 671, 674, 675, 678, 684, 695; *see also* right(s)
nature, 16, 160, 177, 196, 203, 222, 226, 228, 234, 239, 371, 655, 656; state of, 28, 29, 220, 229, 236, 280, 286, 287, 304, 355, 359, 360, 361, 365, 385, 579, 678
Naudé, Gabriel, 80
necessity, 228, 369, 384
Necker, Jacques, 420, 429, 438, 629
Nedham, Marchamont, 47
Netherlands, 129, 131
Nettelbladt, Daniel, 277, 763 (biog.)
Newton, Sir Isaac, 20, 45, 88, 89, 91, 162, 174, 189, 226, 501
Nicholas of Cusa, 349
Nicolai, Friedrich, 132
Nicole, Pierre, 380, 471
Noinville, Durey de, 176
Nonconformity, 51, 63, 140, 142
Nonjurors, 45, 51
Noodt, Gerard, 140, 763 (biog.)
Nordenskjöld, August, 764 (biog.)
Nordenskjöld, Carl Fredrik, 764 (biog.)
North, Lord, 140
Novalis, 139, 247
Numa, 364, 368, 369, 575

Oakeshott, Michael, 347
obedience, 44, 45, 46, 62, 64, 141, 661, 662; *see also* resistance
obligation/duty, 259, 265, 266, 269, 270, 271, 272, 273, 276, 277, 281, 282, 285, 300, 302, 306, 315, 321, 364, 365, 367, 368
O'Connor, Arthur, 764 (biog.)
O'Connor, Charles, 55, 108, 764 (biog.)
Ogilvie, William, 493–4, 684, 764 (biog.)
O'Leary, Arthur, 764–5 (biog.)
optimism, **195–9**
Orobio de Castro, Isaac, 82, 86
Ørsted, Anders Sandøe, 279
Otis, James, 40, 608, 664, 765 (biog.)
Owen, Robert, 702

Pagano, Francesco Mario, 765 (biog.)
Pagano, Mario, 229
Paige, Louis-Adrien Le, 115
Paine, Thomas, 69, 83, 94, 148, 322, 463, 473,
    592, 601, 611, 661, 662, 666, 670, 676, 678,
    679, 680, 681, 684–5, 688, 690, 765 (biog.)
Paley, William, 42, 53, 323, 335, 563–5, 569, 570,
    571, 612, 765 (biog.)
Panckoucke, Charles Joseph, 182–3, 184, 185,
    766 (biog.)
Panduro, Lorenzo Hervas y, 128
Pani, Tomasso Vincenzo, 96
Pâris, Deacon, 112
parlement(s), 21, 112, 115, 116, 117, 118, 124,
    136, 154, 180, 183
parlement of Paris, 22, 23, 113, 114, 115, 123, 181,
    183, 628, 629
parliament, English, 20, 41–2, 56, 60–2, 64, 68,
    69, 70, 73, 74, 76, 77, 321–4, 327, 328, 329,
    330, 337, 338–9, 340, 345, 346, 577, 591, 602,
    603, 605, 607–8, 609, 612, 620, 663, 664, 665,
    666; *see also* legislation/legislator
parti dévot, 116, 117, 118
Pascal, Blaise, 159, 360, 380, 471
Passionei, Cardinal Domenico, 122
Patouillet, Louis, 131
Patullo, Henry, 423, 441
Pauw, Cornelius de, 698
Peace of Ryswick, 67
Peace of Westphalia, 256
Penn, William, 46, 612
people, 47, 50, 60–2, 190, 288, 622, 623, 636,
    644, 646, 647, 648, 650–1, 652, 653, 654, 666,
    673, 689; sovereignty of, 324, 574, 577, 578,
    581, 586, 591, 592, 594, 596, 615, 620–5, 627,
    634–5, 637, 643, 647, 649, 650–1, 689, 692,
    772 (biog.)
perfection, 73, 89, 91, 203, 211, 243, 260, 270,
    272, 273, 274, 276, 278, 280, 285
Pericles, 209
Perrault, Claude, 235
Petition of Right, 612
Petty, William, 423
Peyrère, Isaac la, 80, 83, 223
Philip the Fair, 124
philosopher king, 73, **497–504**, 510, 522, 524
philosophes, 73, 89, 109, 166, 180, 500, 501, 502,
    503, 505, 506, 700, 701, 702, 704, 707, 708
physiocracy, **419–38**, 455, 466–7, 468, 469, 470,
    517–18, 523, 545, 579, 641
Pidansat de Mairobert, 113
Pietism, 101, 103, **132–9**, 141, 143, 268
Pinson, Koppel, 139
Pitcairn, Archibald, 59

Pitt, James, 75, 76, 77
Pitt, William, 97, 683
Pius VI, Pope, 127
placemen, 65, 66, 70, 73, 74, 77, 605, 643
Plato, 192, 253, 255, 256, 349, 357, 369, 384,
    385, 396, 403, 418, 497–8, 499, 501, 505
Plongeron, Bernard, 120
Plowden, Francis, 766 (biog.)
Pluche, Abbé Noël Antoine, 177, 471
Pluquet, François, 481
Poggi, Giuseppi, 126
Pombal, Sebastião José de Carvalho e Melho,
    marques de, 101, 511, 766 (biog.)
Pompa, Leon, 219
Pompignan, Lefranc de, 118, 142
Pope, Alexander, 71, 72, 74, 196–8, 413, 604,
    700, 766 (biog.)
Portecarrero, Maria Francisco de Sales de, 128
Pownall, Thomas, 767 (biog.)
Prades, Jean Martin de, 180
Presbyterian Church in Scotland, 51, 60, 253, 295
Presbyterianism, 53, 57
Prévost, Abbé Antoine François, 107, 149, 767
    (biog.)
Price, Richard, 140, 324, 339, 668, 669, 671,
    673, 676, 767 (biog.)
Priestley, Joseph, 140, 661, 662, 668, 669, 671–2,
    767 (biog.)
priests/priestcraft, 54, 85, 86, 87, 101, 108, 681,
    707
Pringle, John, 291
Proast, Jonas, 105, 768 (biog.)
progress, 89, 173, 177, 199–203, 209, 211–12,
    397, 588–9, 642
property, 237, 272, 492, 650; and arts and
    sciences, **475–80**; in Babeuf, 469; in Bentham,
    562; and Bolingbroke, 73; and British
    radicalism, 683; in Burke, 677; and
    Carmichael, 298; in Dalrymple, 311–12; and
    English constitution, 602; in Fénelon, 474; in
    Fichte, 594, 595; and French Revolution, 632,
    633, 640, 645, 650; in Godwin, 467, 683; in
    Helvétius, 491; in Humboldt, 596; in Hume,
    163, 164, 302, 303, 304; in Hutcheson, 300,
    301; in Kames, 305, 311–12; in Kant, 285–6,
    287, 288, 591; in Linguet, 467; in Locke, 48,
    303, 353; and luxury debates, 381; Mably on,
    481, 482, 484–5, 486, 579; in Mandeville, 393;
    in Molyneux, 56; in Montesquieu, 405, 406;
    in Morelly, 470, 471–3, 475; in Ogilvie, 493;
    in Paine, 685; in physiocracy, 419, 426, 431,
    432, 467, 468; in Robespierre, 467–8, 494; in
    Romilly, 564; in Rousseau, 478, 573, 575, 579;
    in Smith, 308, 312–14, 457; in Spence, 684; in

Wolff, 272, 275; in Wollstonecraft, 679; *see also* landowners

Protestantism, 18, 19, 41, 53, 68, 80, 100, 251, 348

Prussia, 129, 257, 260, 277, 487, 590

Pufendorf, Samuel, 24, 48, 102, 136, 140, 175, 190–1, 192, 193, 219, 220, 224, 228, 233, 251, 252, 253–4, 257, 258, 259, 260, 261–2, 263, 264, 265, 266, 267, 273, 277, 280, 281, 283, 291, 292, 296, 297, 298, 300, 302, 304, 308, 315, 360, 385, 480, 513, 523

Purchas, Samuel, 149

Pyrrhonism, 79, 80, 89, 98

Quebec Act, 108

Quesnay, François, 201, 420, 423, 424, 425–6, 427, 429–32, 433, 434, 435, 441, 448, 456, 768 (biog.)

Quesnel, Pasquier, 111, 117, 125

Radicati di Passerano, Alberto, 768 (biog.)

Raeff, Marc, 138

Raleigh, Sir Walter, 71

Ramsay, Andrew Michael, 46, 179, 475, 768 (biog.)

Rapin (Rapin-Thoyras), Paul de, 41, 768–9 (biog.)

Rational Dissent, **668–73**

Rautenstrauch, Stephen, 130

Rawls, John, 347, 375

Raynal, Abbé Guillaume Thomas François, 149, 161, 165–7, 221, 518, 519, 579, 584, 769 (biog.)

Réamur, René Antoine de, 177

reason, 16, 30, 84, 89, 120, 139, 141, 160, 162, 165, 175, 191, 195, 196, 199, 202, 205, 210, 211, 221, 228, 229, 230, 236, 237, 252, 263–4, 265, 268, 281, 283, 284, 289, 558, 579, 588, 589, 596, 628, 629, 630, 632, 633, 637, 639–40, 641, 642, 649, 655, 668, 675, 678, 680, 681, 682; *see also* empiricism

Rees, Abraham, 184

Rees, David, 140

Reeves, John, 683

Rehberg, August Wilhelm, 593

Reid, Thomas, 314, 769 (biog.)

Reimarus, Hermann Samuel, 84, 234, 769 (biog.)

religion, 16, 21, 31, 52, **79–87**, 88, **91–109**, 152, 153, 155–6, 157, 159, 168–9, 188, 197, 201, 202, 204, 207, 208, 210, 243, 251, 252, 254, 261, 268, 310, 501, 569, 579, 620, 668, 671, 708; *see also* Christianity; deism; God; toleration, religious; *specific sects*

representation, 60, 339, 581; and American Revolution, 603, 604, **606**, 613–14, 615, 617, 624, 664, 665; and English parliament, 665; and French revolutionary discourse, 630–1, 633, 634, 635, 636, 637, 640, 641, 643, 644, 648, 649, 653; and Hobbes, 689; in Kant, 591; and Price, 670; and Priestley, 672; in Rousseau, 577, 586; *see also* democracy; legislation/legislator; vote/voting

republic/republicanism, 13, 26, 37, 151, 154, 164, 289, 290, 334, 373, 407, 408, 437, 467–8, 472–3, 478, 481–3, 486, 491, 492, 514, 574, 575, 577, 581, 583, 584, 585, 586, 590–2, 595, 603, 605, 617–20, 627, 639, 643, 645, 652, 656, 657, 658, 662, 681, 682, 684, 685, 688, 690, 696, 697, 701; *see also* democracy; representation

resistance, 190, 191, 254, 255, 278, 289, 320, 323, 662, 673; *see also* obedience; revolution

Restif de la Bretonne, Nicolas Edme, 769 (biog.)

Retz, Cardinal de, 10, 240

revolution, 43, 44, 116, 205, 384, 480, 580–1, 592, 594, 605, 638, 649, 658–9; *see also* resistance

Revolution of 1688, 40–3, 44, 47, 52, 65, 75, 319–20, 326, 328, 602, 604, 673

Revolution Settlement of 1689, 660

Ricardo, David, 443

Ricci, Scipione de, 124, 125, 769–70 (biog.)

Richard II, king of England, 43

Richelet, Pierre, 176

Richelieu, Armand Jean du Plessis, Cardinal, 10, 415, 514

Richer, Edmond, 113

Richerism, 113, 134

Ridpath, George, 59

right(s), 45, 50, 68, 190, 193, 255, 259, 269, 271–2, 274, 275, 276, 278, 281, 282, 283, 284, 285, 286, 287, 289, 309, 345, 352, 355, 356, 372, 593, 594, 595, 602, 628, 632, 633, 634, 638–9, 640, 662, 663, 669, 670, 672, 673, 674, 690, 698; *see also* freedom; natural rights

Robertson, William, 148, 149, 171, 205, 214, 221, 241, 698, 770 (biog.)

Robespierre, Maximilien François Isidore, 465, 466, 467–8, 494, 592, 593, 643, 645, 647, 649, 650, 654, 656–8, 709, 770 (biog.)

Robinet, Jean Baptiste René, 222

Roda y Arrieta, Manuel de, 128

Roederer, Pierre Louis, comte de, 480–1, 698, 770 (biog.)

Rohr, Julius Bernhard von, 531, 534, 770 (biog.)

Roland de La Platière, Marie Jeanne (Manon Philpon), Madame, 770 (biog.)

Romagnosi, Gian Domenico, 771 (biog.)
Roman Catholic Church, 14, 17, 18, 22, 51, 52,
80, 88, 94, 95, 96, 97, 100, 108, 111, 116, 119,
125, 128, 180, 183, 258, 468, 639; Augustinian
Order, 124, 126, 127, 128; Dominican Order,
124, 127, 128; Franciscan Order, 121, 124,
128; Jesuit Order, 101, 116, 117, 118, 120, 121,
122–4, 127, 128, 129, 141, 180, 200, 476;
Unam sanctam (papal bull), 123; *Unigenitus*
(papal bull), 111, 112, 113, 114, 115, 116, 117,
120, 121, 123, 127, 130, 134
Romanticism, 257, 707
Rome, ancient, 14, 15–20, 25, 34, 49, 57, 69, 70,
75, 154, **212–17**, 227, 245, 256, 257, 334,
362–3, 384, 407–8, 413, 415, 481–4, 486, 575,
578, 595, 603
Romilly, Jean, 93, 571
Romilly, Sir Samuel, 564–5, 567, 570, 771 (biog.)
Romme, Charles Gilbert, 655
Roscher, Wilhelm, 523–4
Rossi, Paolo, 219
Rouché, Max, 220
Rousseau, Jean Jacques, 103, 104, 142, 148, 185,
186, 203, 218, 219, 281, 360, 417, 468, 470,
477–81, 504, 522, 523, 553, 554, 573–7,
583–4, 595, 627, 692, 697, 771 (biog.); on
ancient polity, 362–3, 364, 366, 367–8; on
consent, 362, 364, 365, 367, 368; on contract,
347, 359, **362–9**; on freedom, 255, 364–5,
368–9, 576; and French Revolution, 627, 630,
634, 635–6, 637, 640, 657, 658, 689, 704–5;
and Geneva, 584; on human nature, 192, 193,
363, 477, 480, 574, 588; influences and
relations, 53, 58, 29, 37, 87, 165, 178, 180,
189, 192, 193, 201, 207, 210, 220, 224–5, 233,
243, 244, 246, 287, 362, 364, 365, 369, 370,
374, 390, 464, 470, 475, 478, 479, 480–1, 576,
578, 579, 581, 583, 586–9, 590, 591–2, 593,
594, 595, 596, 597, 698, 702; on sovereignty,
577, 581, 586, 591, 592, 689; and Venice, 584;
on will, 192, 287, 362, 364–5, 367, 368–9
Ruddiman, Thomas, 59
Rush, Benjamin, 440
Rutherforth, Thomas, 334, 771 (biog.)
Rutledge, James, 489–90, 772 (biog.)

Sacy, Lemaistre de, 112
Sade, Donatien Alphonse François, marquis de,
772 (biog.)
Saige, Guillaume-Joseph, 627
St Bartholomew's Day Massacre, 102
Saint-Cyran, Abbé de, 111, 112
St Evremond, 399
Saint-Just, Louis Antoine Léon, 467–8, 480, 592,
647, 649, 653, 658, 772 (biog.)

Saint-Lambert, Jean François, marquis de, 184,
193, 379–81, 382
Saint-Martin, Louis Claude de, 480
Saint-Pierre, Charles Irénée Castel, Abbé de,
404, 416, 772 (biog.)
Saint-Simon, Claude Henri de Rouvroy, comte
de, 203, 705, 707–9, 772–3 (biog.)
Sales, Jean Baptiste Delisle de, 697
Sanctis, Francesco de, 219
Sanderson, Robert, 45
sans-culottes, 650, 651, 654, 656, 697
Sarpi, Paolo, 221
Sarraih, Jean, 128
Sartorius, Georg, 536
Savigny, Freidrich Carl von, 246
Say, Jean-Baptiste, 419, 420, 546
scepticism, **79–92**, 96, 98, 108–9, 153, 195, 196,
202, 205, 254, 302–4
Schiller, Johann Christoph Friedrich, 773 (biog.)
Schleiermacher, Friedrich, 139
Schlözer, August Ludwig von, 148, 149, 536, 773
(biog.)
Schmauss, J. J., 267
Schmid, L. B. M., 545
Schreber, D. G., 535
Schröder, William von, 528–9, 530, 537,
773 (biog.)
science, 79, 88–9, 90, 91, 174, 175, 176, 177, 189,
202, 203, 204, 205, 206, 207, 211, 218, 222,
226, 227, 230, 231, 239, 292, 296, 360, 392,
415, **475–80**, 502, 579, 642, 671, 692, 697, 698;
see also empiricism
Scotland, 50, 54, 57–60
Scott, William, 296
Scottish Country Party, 57
Scottish Parliament, 57, 58, 60
Scottish theorists, 9, 60, 148, 158, 221, 236, 240,
253, 255, 267, 280, **291–316**, 443–62, **464**, 640,
660, 685, 706
Seabury, Samuel, 773 (biog.)
Seckendorff, Veit Ludwig von, 528, 773–4
(biog.)
secularism, 174, 204, 206, 208, 210
self-preservation, 228, 234, 240, 245, 589, 698
Seller, Abednigo, 45
Seneca, 69, 349
Septennial Act, 70, 667
Servetus, 96
Seton, William, 59
Seven Years War, 117, 198, 199, 278, 421, 424,
439, 466, 601
Sextus Empiricus, 79, 80
Shaftesbury, Anthony Ashley Cooper, third earl
of, 66, 68, 197, 198, 253, 299, 380, 395–9, 405,
416, 774 (biog.)

Sharp, Granville, 664
Shebbeare, John, 774 (biog.)
Sheridan, Thomas, 774 (biog.)
Sherlock, William, 45, 774–5 (biog.)
Shute, John, *see* Barrington, John Shute, First
    Viscount
Sibbald, Sir Robert, 59
Sidney, Algernon, 47, 57, 67, 75, 370, 647, 702
Sieyès, Abbé Emmanuel Joseph, 358, 468, 591,
    592, 629–31, 632, 636, 639–40, 641, 648, 651,
    688, 690–1, 693, 694–5, 698, 699, 700, 705,
    775 (biog.)
Simioli, Giuseppe, 122
Simon, Richard, 80, 83
Sirven, Pierre Paul, 568
slavery, 26, 159, 160, 164, 166, 167, 274, 275,
    298, 364, 365, 639, 640, 669
Smellie, William, 183–4
Smith, Adam, 77, 148, 149, 170, 183, 193, 236,
    253, 291, 292, 293, 294, 304, 307–10, 312–14,
    315, 379, 396, 417, 419, 420, **443–62**, **464**,
    508, 540, 546, 589, 685, 686, 706, 775 (biog.)
Smith, Sir Thomas, 665
Smollett, Tobias, 149
sociability, 47, 68, 173, 179, 188, 191, 233, 252,
    262, 264, 270, 397, 579, 588, 673
social science, **690–5**, 696, 699–700, 701–4,
    705–9
Société de 1789, 691, 692, 695
society, 147–51, 152, 156, 157–9, 160, 161–2,
    167, 169, 170, 173, 200, 203, 204, 207, 209,
    211, 218, 235, 261, 264, 281, 287, 304,
    310–12, 396–9, 401, 431, 477, 479, 480, 574,
    575, 588, 633, 639–40, 654, 675, 676, 679; *see
    also* civilisation; culture/custom
Socinianism, 93
Socrates, 349, 357
Solomon, King, 414
Somers, John, Baron, 47, 61
Sonenscher, Michael, 442
Sonnenfels, Baron Joseph von, 131, 503, 526,
    535, 538, 541–5, 775 (biog.)
Sorbonnists, 115
sovereign/ruler, 308, 431, 433, 527–9, 534,
    539–41, 546, 554, 555, 574–5, 689; *see also*
    monarchy
sovereignty, 41–2, 46, 60–2, 255, 256, 259, 260,
    275, 278, 287, 288, 321–4, 355, 361, 576, 581,
    627, 630, 631, 633, 635, 637, 644, 648, 663,
    666, 689, 690; popular, 324, 574, 577, 578,
    581, 586, 591, 592, 594, 596, 615, 620–5,
    627, 634–5, 637, 643, 647, 649, 650–1, 689,
    692
Spain, 119, 123, 127–9, 438, 439
Spedalieri, Nicola, 126

Spence, Thomas, 684, 776 (biog.)
Spencer, Herbert, 597
Spener, Philipp Jakob, 132, 133, 134, 137, 138,
    776 (biog.)
Spinelli, Cardinal, 122
Spinola, Cristobal de, 101
Spinoza, Baruch, 80, 83–4, 85–6, 88, 98, 189,
    195, 222, 225, 227–8, 231, 246, 359
Staël, Anne Louise Germaine Necker, madame
    de, 704, 776 (biog.)
Stamford, earl of, 40
Stamp Act, 607, 613
Stanislas Augustus, king of Poland, 507
Stanislas I Leszczynski, 776 (biog.)
Stark, Johann August, 138
Staszic, Stanislaw, 521
state, 27, 52, 53, 98–100, 103–4, 105–7, 113, 135,
    190, 219, 246–7, 251, 272–3, 275, 277, 283,
    285, 286, 287, 288, 348, 361, 364, 374, 431,
    432, 447, 485, 493, 574, 593, 595–6, 597,
    688–90, 705
Steele, Sir Richard, 776 (biog.)
Steida, William, 535
Stephens, William, 41
Steuart (also Denham), Sir James, 445, 447,
    449–50, 490, 546, 777 (biog.)
Stewart, Dugald, 314–16, 443, 456, 685, 706,
    777 (biog.)
Stiebritz, Johann Friedrich, 533
Stieda, William, 535
Stillingfleet, Edward, 81, 85
Stock, Simon, 129
Stoicism, 63, 64, 68, 253, 299, 500, 501, 506,
    578
Stone, Harold, 219
Stuart, House of, 320, 488, 605; *see also* Jacobites
Sturm, Johann Jakob, 135
Sturm und Drang, 139, 220
Súarez, Francisco, 350
Sully, Maximilien de Béthune, duc de, 22, 23,
    190
Svarez, Carl Gottlieb, 257
Swieten, Gerhard van, 129, 130
Swift, Jonathan, 56, 61, 71, 102, 604, 777 (biog.)
Synge, Edward, 95
Synod of Pistoia, 125, 126, 128

Tacitus, 12, 35, 70, 210, 656
Tagliacozzo, Giorgio, 219
Talleyrand-Périgord, Charles Maurice de, 693,
    694, 698, 777 (biog.)
Tamburini, Pietro, 100, 124, 125, 128,
    778 (biog.)
Tarbat, Viscount, 59
Tavira y Almazan, Antonio, 128

taxation, 21, 55, 56, 66, 71, 141, 424, 426, 429, 431, 432, 458, 607, 633, 664, 665
Tennis Court Oath, 631
Terme, Jean de, 130
Terror, the, 649, 650, 652, 653, 654, 656, 690, 692, 706
Tertullian, 216
Test Acts, 53
Thelwall, John, 681, 683, 685, 778 (biog.)
Theophrastus, 151
Thirty Years War, 95, 256
Thomas, Reid, 291
Thomasius, Christian, 101, 132, 252, 253, **259–67**, 268, 273, 276, 277, 280, 281, 283, 370, 778 (biog.)
Thompson, James, 71, 703
Thompson, William, 702
Thomson, James, 74
Tindal, Matthew, 49, 52, 86, 778 (biog.)
Tocqueville, Alexis de, 30, 421–2, 435
Toland, John, 48, 52, 54, 66, 67, 81, 86, 778–9 (biog.)
toleration, religious, 16, 20, 21, 22, 31, 46, 52, 54, **91–109**, 132, 137, 207, 216, 254, 354, 388, 501, 502, 504, 505, 508, 509, 668; *see also* Edict of Nantes, Revocation of; religion
Toleration Act of 1689, 51
Tone, Theobald Wolfe, 56, 74, 97, 108, 662, 665, 779 (biog.)
Tooke, John Horne, 779 (biog.)
Tories, 42, 45, 47, 56, 62, 63, 65, 70, 72, 73–4, 141, 329, 604, 660, 661
Torregiani, Ludovico Maria, 122
Toussaint, François, 186
Toussaint L'Ouverture (François Dominique Toussaint), 779 (biog.)
Towers, Joseph, 661, 779–80 (biog.)
Tracy, Antoine Louis Claude, *see* Destutt de Tracy, Antoine Louis Claude, Comte
trade, free, 59, 60, 427, 430
Tran, John, 295
Transylvania, 94
Treaty of Augsburg, 256
Treaty of Westphalia, 95, 256
Trenchard, John, 67, 604, 780 (biog.); *Cato's Letters*, 49, 66, 69, 326
Treschow, Nils, 279
Triennial Act, 320
Tronchin, Jean-Robert, 586
Tucker, Josiah, 330, 661, 672–3, 780 (biog.)
Turgot, Anne Robert Jacques, baron de l'Aulne, 89, 90, 93, 109, 184, 186, 203, 420, 424, 426, 427, 428, 429, 433, 437, 440, 455, 456, 503, 579, 780 (biog.)

Turnbull, George, 291, 780–1 (biog.)
Turretini, J. A., 101
tyranny, 31, 77, 155, 513, 606; *see also* absolutism; despotism; monarchy
Tyrrell, James, 47, 49, 781 (biog.)
Tyson, Edward, 235

Ulloa, Bernardo de, 781 (biog.)
Union of 1707, 59
United States, 67, 105, 440, 453, 566, 670; *see also* American Revolution
United States Articles of Confederation, 616, 617
Urquijo, Mariano Luis de, 128, 129
Ussher, James, 208, 223, 224, 225
utilitarianism, 173, 201, 374, 375, 523, 547, 553, 554, 555, 569, 572, 682
utility, 159, 209, 304, 309, 357, 358, 369, 386, 390, 393, 394, 671
Uztáriz (Ustariz), Gerónimo de, 781 (biog.)

Valla, Lorenzo, 120, 122
Valletta, Giuseppe, 219
Van Espen, Zeger Bernhard, 114, 128, 781 (biog.)
Vasquez, Francisco Saverio, 127
Vattel, Emerich de, 136, 277, 278, 781–2 (biog.)
Velestinlis, Rigas, 782 (biog.)
Velez, Rafael de, 129
Venice, 583–4
Verner, David, 291
Verri, Pietro, 439, 503, 520, 782 (biog.)
Versé, Noel Aubert de, 782 (biog.)
Vertot, Abbé, 411
Vico, Giambattista, 203, 218, 219–20, 222, 224, 225, 227, 228–30, 231–2, 233, 240, 476, 782–3 (biog.)
Vicq-d'Azyr, Félix, 708
Villanueva, Joachín Lorenzo, 129
Virgil, 72, 213
Volney, Constantin François de Chasseboeuf, comte de, 697–9, 783 (biog.)
Voltaire (François Marie Arouet), 79, 148, 150, 162, 174, 181, 185, 187, 197, 198–9, 211, 427, 503, 523, 556, 568, 587, 697, 783 (biog.); and Barclay, 159; and Bayle, 108, 206; and Bodin, 159; and Bossuet, 148, 207, 228; and Catherine II, 507; and Colbert, 23; on comparison, 159–61; and Diderot, 161, 207; and *Encyclopédie*, 500–1; and Frederick II, 138, 504–5, 506, 507; on freedom, 19, 20–1, 24; and Gibbon, 210, 211, 214; on government, 19–23, 24–5, 155–60, 207, 322; and Henri IV, 22; and Herder, 170, 221, 241, 245; on history, 9, 25, 159, **206–10**, 217; and Hume, 152, 161,

162, 180; and Joseph II, 509; and La Bruyere, 159; on laws, 24–5; and Leibniz, 196; and Locke, 200; and Louis XV, 207; on luxury, **412–17**; and Montaigne, 159, 161; and Montesquieu, 9, 19, 20, 22, 25, 31, 38, 152, 155, 160, 161, 211, 515; and Panckoucke, 182; and Pascal, 159; and Plato, 499; and Pope, 197; and Raynal, 161; on religion, 21, 22, 81, 82, 93, 96–7, 100, 102, 104, 106, 109, 152, 155, 207, 208, 210; and Rousseau, 207, 210; and Shaftesbury, 197; and Sully, 22, 23; and Tacitus, 210

vote/voting, 68, 69, 74, 591, 606, 607, 648–9, 665–6, 672; *see also* representation

Wake, William, 52, 101
Wallace, Robert, 454
Walpole, Sir Robert, 69, 70–2, 73, 75, 326, 328, 605
War of the Austrian Succession, 466, 482, 578
Warburton, William, 52–3, 783 (biog.)
Warren, Mercy Otis, 784 (biog.)
Washington, George, 99
Watson, Richard, 661, 662, 784 (biog.)
wealth, 429, 430, 431, 447
Weber, Max, 157
Wesley, John, 141, 142, 670–1
West, Gilbert, 71
Whigs, 42, 43, 45, 46, 47, 48, 49, 52, 53, 54, 56, 62, 63, 64, 65, 66, 70, 72, 75–8, 140, 328, 329, 604, 660, 670, 672, 686
Whiston, William, 225
Whitacker, John, 142
White, R. J., 500
Wieland, Christoph Martin, 784 (biog.)
Wilde, John, 267
Wildman, John, 43
Wilkes, John, 141, 344, 580, 660, 663–4, 680, 784 (biog.)
Wilkesites, 74, 330, 663

will, 195, 228, 252, 266, 287, 356, 360, 361, 362, 364–5, 367, 368–9, 374, 627, 629, 630, 639, 643, 647, 649, 653, 657; general, 192, 287, 362, 370, 574, 575, 597, 627, 630, 634, 635, 636, 637, 641, 644, 648, 649, 657, 697; and voluntarism, 251, 252–3, 254, 256, 263, 266, 269, 347, 348–50, 356, 359, 362
Willebrandt, Johann Peter, 107
William, Scott, 291
William III, king of England, 40, 44, 45, 92, 320
William of Ockham, 113, 349
Williams, David, 490–1, 785 (biog.)
Williams, Elisha, 785 (biog.)
Williams, Samuel, 624
Willis, Thomas, 233
Wilson, James, 611, 621–2, 785 (biog.)
Winckelman, Johann Joachim, 241
Wittola, Marc Anton, 130
Wolff, Christian, Freiherr von, 132, 196, 198, 252, 253, 257, 259–60, 268–78, 280, 281, 283, 370, 498, 505, 506, 587–9, 785 (biog.)
Wollaston, William, 786 (biog.)
Wollstonecraft, Mary, 63, 678, 679, 680–1, 786 (biog.)
Wolsey, Cardinal Thomas, 71
women, 26, 33, 37, 62–4, 591, 638, 641, 672, 679, 680–1
Wythe, George, 615
Wyvill, Christopher, 666

Young, Arthur, 611

Zedler, Johann, 150
Zeiller, Franz von, 257
Zevi, Sabbatai, 80, 82
Zincke, Georg Heinrich, 533, 535, 543, 786 (biog.)
Zinzendorf, Karl von, 521
Zinzendorf, Nicolaus Ludwig Graf von, 132, 134, 139
Zubly, John Joachim, 786 (biog.)